AMERICAN PHILOSOPHY

An Encyclopedia

AMERICAN PHILOSOPHY

An Encyclopedia

John Lachs
Robert Talisse
Editors

NEW YORK AND LONDON

First published 2008 by Routledge
Taylor & Francis Group
270 Madison Avenue
New York, NY 10016
USA

Simultaneously published in the UK by Routledge
Taylor & Francis Group
2 Park Square
Milton Park, Abingdon
Oxon OX14 4RN
UK

Routledge is an imprint of Taylor & Francis Group, an informa business

Printed in the United States of America on acid-free paper
10 9 8 7 6 5 4 3 2 1

International Standard Book Number-10: 0-415-93926-7 (Hardcover)
International Standard Book Number-13: 978-0-415-93926-3 (Hardcover)

Library of Congress Cataloging-in-Publication Data
American philosophy : an encyclopedia / John Lachs, Robert Talisse, Editors.
p. cm.
Includes index.
ISBN 978-0-415-93926-3
1. Philosophy, American–Encyclopedias. I. Lachs, John. II. Talisse, Robert B.
B850.A43 2007
191.03–dc22
2007019148

Visit the Taylor & Francis Web site at http://www.taylorandfrancis.com
and the Routledge Web site at http://www.routledge-ny.com

Contents

Contributors

Mitchell Aboulifia
Pennsylvania State University

Scott Forrest Aikin
Vanderbilt University

Thomas M. Alexander
Southern Illinois University, Carbondale

George Allan
Dickinson College

Douglas Allen
University of Maine, Orono

Holly Andersen
University of Pittsburgh

Douglas R. Anderson
Southern Illinois University

John P. Anton
University of South Florida

Bruce Aune
University of Massachusetts at Amherst

Guy Axtell
University of Nevada

Jason Barrett-Fox
University of Kansas

Saba Bazargan
Rutgers University

Endre Begby
University of Pittsburgh

Jason Bell
Vanderbilt University

Lisa Bellantoni
Albright College

Arnold Berleant
Long Island University, C.W. Post

Joseph Betz
Villanova University

David Boersema
Pacific University

James Bohman
St. Louis University

Raymond Boisvert
Siena College, NY

Patrick L. Bourgeois
Loyola University, New Orleans

Michael Bradie
Bowling Green State University

Eric Bredo
University of Virginia

Joseph Brent
University of the District of Columbia

Evelyn Brister
Rochester Institute of Technology

Michael Brodrick
Vanderbilt University

Rogene A. Buchholz
Loyola University, New Orleans

Thomas O. Buford
Furman University

Tom Burke
University of South Carolina, Columbia

Lawrence Cahoone
College of the Holy Cross

CONTRIBUTORS

James Campbell
University of Toledo

John Capps
Rochester Institute of Technology

John Catalano
University of South Carolina, Lancaster

Gary L. Cesarz
Southeast Missouri State University

J. Caleb Clanton
Vanderbilt University

Justin Clarke-Doane
New York University

Andrew D. Cling
University of Alabama in Huntsville

John M. Cogan
Southern Illinois University, Carbondale

Vincent Colapietro
Pennsylvania State University

Wesley Cooper
University of Alberta

John Corcoran
State University of New York at Buffalo

Harvey Cormier
State University of New York at Stony Brook

Robert S. Corrington
Drew University

Shane D. Courtland
Tulane University

Tommy J. Curry
Southern Illinois University, Carbondale

Donald Davidson
University of California, Berkeley

Cornelis de Waal
Indiana University

S. Kate Devitt
Rutgers University

Kim Díaz
Texas A&M University

Paul R. Dokecki
Vanderbilt University

Patrick K. Dooley
St. Bonaventure University

Kathleen Eamon
Vanderbilt University

Abraham Edel
University of Pennsylvania

Rem B. Edwards
University of Tennessee, Knoxville

Michael Eldridge
University of North Carolina at Charlotte

Catherine Z. Elgin
Harvard University

Steven Fesmire
Green Mountain College

Matthew Festenstein
University of Sheffield

James Fieser
University of Tennessee at Martin

J.A. Fisher
University of North Florida

Matthew J. Fitzsimmons
Grand Valley State University

Matthew Caleb Flamm
Rockford College

Ken Foldes
St. John's University

Paul J. Ford
Cleveland Clinic Lerner College of Medicine

Mathew A. Foust
University of Oregon

Sergio Franzese
University of Lecce

Richard M. Gale
University of Tennessee

James Garrison
Virginia Tech

William J. Gavin
University of Southern Maine

Cynthia Gayman
Murray State University

Martin P. Golding
Duke University

Michael F. Goodman
Humboldt State University

Russell B. Goodman
University of New Mexico

Dwight Goodyear
Westchester Community College

James Gouinlock
Emory University

Joseph Grange
University of Southern Maine, Portland

John Scott Gray
Ferris State University

Anthony J. Graybosch
California State University, Chico

Judith M. Green
Fordham University

Pete A.Y. Gunter
University of North Texas

Susan Haack
University of Miami

Hans V. Hansen
University of Windsor

Karen Hanson
Indiana University

Gary L. Hardcastle
Bloomsburg University

Peter H. Hare
State University of New York at Buffalo

Richard E. Hart
Bloomfield College,

Casey Haskins
Purchase College, State University of New York

William J. Hawk
James Madison University

D. Micah Hester
UAMS College of Medicine

H. Scott Hestevold
University of Alabama

Larry A. Hickman
Southern Illinois University, Carbondale

Risto Hilpinen
University of Miami

Max Hocutt
University of Alabama

Brendan Hogan
Pacific Lutheran University

Seth Holtzman
Catawba College

Christopher Hookway
University of Sheffield

Andrew W. Howat
University of Sheffield

Franz Huber
California Institute of Technology

Robert E. Innis
University of Massachusetts, Lowell

Henry Jackman
York University

Dale Jacquette
Penn State University

Mark Johnson
University of Oregon

CONTRIBUTORS

Angelo Juffras
William Paterson University

John J. Kaag
University of Oregon

Jacquelyn Ann Kegley
California State University, Bakersfield

Heather E. Keith
Green Mountain College

Angus Kerr-Lawson
University of Waterloo

Victor Kestenbaum
Boston University

Elias J. Khalil
Monash University

Marcin Kilanowski
Nicolaus Copernicus University

Joel W. Krueger
Southern Illinois University, Carbondale

Felicia E. Kruse
Xavier University

Christopher Kulp
Santa Clara University

Robert Lane
State University of West Georgia

John W. Lango
Hunter College, City University of New York

Lenore Langsdorf
Southern Illionis University, Carbondale

David LaRocca
Harvard University

James Jakób Liszka
University of Alaska, Anchorage

John A. Loughney
Westfield State College

John Lysaker
University of Oregon

Noëlle McAfee
American University

Lee A. McBride III
College of Wooster

William L. McBride
Purdue University

Robert McDermott
California Institute of Integral Studies

Dana Noelle McDonald
Southern Illinois University at Carbondale

Douglas M. MacDonald
Furman University

Fritz J. McDonald
State University of New York at New Paltz

Hugh P. McDonald
New York City College of Technology

Jennifer McErlean
Siena College

Tibor Machan
Chapman University

Leemon B. McHenry
California State University, Northridge

Terrance MacMullan
Eastern Washington University

Phillip McReynolds
Pennsylvania State University

Edward H. Madden
State University of New York at Buffalo

Mary Magada-Ward
Middle Tennessee State University

Mary B. Mahowald
University of Chicago

Joseph Margolis
Temple University

Armen T. Marsoobian
Southern Connecticut State University

Richard K. Matthews
Lehigh University

Rosa Maria Mayorga
Virginia Polytechnic Institute and State University

José Medina
Vanderbilt University

Mark Migotti
University of Calgary

Marjorie C. Miller
Purchase College, State University of New York

Cheryl Misak
University of Toronto

Jeff Mitchell
Arkansas Tech University

James A. Montmarquet
Tennessee State University

Eric C. Mullis
Queens University of Charlotte

L. Ryan Musgrave
Rollins College

William T. Myers
Birmingham Southern College

Robert Cummings Neville
Boston University

David L. O'Hara
Augustana College

Philip Oliver
Vanderbilt University

Frank M. Oppenheim, SJ
Xavier Univeristy

Helmut Pape
Bamberg University

Gregory Fernando Pappas
Texas A&M University

James O. Pawelski
Vanderbilt University

Charls Pearson
American Semiotics Research Institute

David Perley
University of Toronto

Christopher Perricone
Iona College

Michael L. Peterson
Asbury College

Jessica Pfeifer
University of Maryland

Sami Pihlström
University of Helsinki

Andrew Piker
Texas A&M University Corpus Christi

Janusz Polanowski
Nashville Tech University

Scott L. Pratt
University of Oregon

Bjørn T. Ramberg
University of Oslo

Allyson L. Robichaud
Cleveland Clinic

Yvonne Raley
Felician College

Michael L. Raposa
Lehigh University

Michael J. Raven
New York University

Nicholas Rescher
University of Pittsburgh

Tom Rockmore
Duquesne University

Sandra B. Rosenthal
Loyola University, New Orleans

Stephen David Ross
State University of New York at Binghamton

CONTRIBUTORS

David L. Rouse
University of Virginia's College at Wise

Tadd Ruetenik
Pennsylvania State University, Altoona

Richard Rumana
William Paterson University

Cheyney Ryan
University of Oregon

Frank X. Ryan
Kent State University

Nick C. Sagos
University of Montreal

Patricia A. Sayre
St. Mary's College

Dennis J. Schmidt
Penn State University

Jeff Sebo
New York University

Patrick Shade
Rhodes College

Don Sherburne
Vanderbilt University

Linda Simon
Skidmore College

Robert Sinclair
Simon Fraser University

Beth J. Singer
Brooklyn College, CUNY

Marcus G. Singer
University of Wisconsin, Madison

Peter Skagestad
University of Massachusetts, Lowell

Ignas K. Skrupskelis
University of South Carolina

Andrew F. Smith
State University of New York at Stony Brook

Richard Smyth
University of North Carolina, Chapel Hill

Robert C. Solomon
University of Texas at Austin

Eric Charles Steinhart
William Paterson University

James P. Sterba
University of Notre Dame

Arthur Stewart
Lamar University

James A. Stieb
Drexel University

John J. Stuhr
Vanderbilt University

Alfred I. Tauber
Boston University

Eugene Taylor
Harvard University

John Teehan
Hofstra University

Nicholas J. Teh
University of Pittsburgh

James E. Tiles
University of Hawaii at Manoa

Glenn Tiller
Texas A&M Corpus Christi

Rosemarie Tong
University of North Carolina, Charlotte

Griffin Trotter
St. Louis University

Nancy Tuana
Pennsylvania State University

Dwayne A.Tunstall
Southern Illinois University, Carbondale

David Vessey
University of Chicago

Jessica Wahman
Dickinson College

Kathleen Wallace
Hofstra University

Douglas Walton
University of Winnipeg

Roger A. Ward
Georgetown College, Kentucky

Eric Thomas Weber
Southern Illinois University, Carbondale

Paul Weiss
Yale University

David Weissman
City College of New York, City University of New York

Jennifer Welchman
University of Alberta

Henny Wenkart
Reconstructionist Rabbinical College

Judy D. Whipps
Grand Valley State University

Norman Whitman
Vanderbilt University

Wesley J. Wildman
Boston University

Bruce Wilshire
Rutgers University

Takashi Yagisawa
California State University, Northridge

George Yancy
Duquesne University

Alphabetical List of Entries

Introduction

American Philosophy: An Encyclopedia is the first complete encyclopedia of American philosophy ever published. Emerson's call to Americans to enjoy an "original relation" to the universe and to take pride in our native abilities has evidently still not been answered. We take inspiration from French, German, and English sources, not from American masters and our own experience. There is relatively little public awareness and appreciation of American philosophy. Germans and Russians seem to know more about the intellectual accomplishments of our nation than graduate students in our universities.

In this volume, we call attention to the fact that the classics of American thought rival the best philosophy anywhere. Emerson invites comparison with Nietzsche; Peirce is a more versatile and more solidly grounded genius than Leibniz; Dewey has Hegel's scope and subtlety without the cheap dialectic and nasty statism. Admittedly, few philosophers can match Kant in technical sophistication, but both James and Santayana easily outdo him in the insights they provide into the intricacies of human nature. Even American idealism, in such thinkers as Royce, Hocking, and Blanshard, compares favorably with its European counterparts.

In conceiving *American Philosophy: An Encyclopedia*, we interpreted "American" in an expansive but, in another respect, also in a restrictive sense. We have taken a generous view of who count as American philosophers. Although clearly not everyone does or should, we have included thinkers with traceable connections to the main styles, positions, and concerns of classical American philosophy, as these are displayed in the likes of Peirce, James, Royce, Santayana, and Dewey. Phenomenologists and logical empiricists working on this continent are not, in this sense, American philosophers; Wilfrid Sellars, Quine, and Marvin Farber are. This is a judgment call, and readers may feel unhappy that their favorite topic was excluded or that the thinker they love to hate is honored by having found a place within these covers. In such matters, the lines are always blurry: who and what belongs is a matter of decision, and we have not been hesitant to exercise the privilege of choice.

In another way, this encyclopedia is restrictive. In a broadly used and perfectly intelligible sense, "American" means "of or from the United States." That is the usage we followed, not because we wanted to deny Canadians, Mexicans, and others whatever benefit being called "American" confers, but on account of the task we undertook. We set out to provide a useful guide to the sort of philosophy that flourished in the works of such thinkers as Royce and Dewey (and continues to flourish today), and the accepted name of such thought is "American philosophy." We chose this name for the encyclopedia to communicate what it is about rather than for imperialistic purposes.

It is simply impossible to cover every topic and thinker in one volume even within the limited area of American philosophy. Readers will no doubt find that some entries they expected to see have not been included, and they may judge some of those that appear here as unworthy or inappropriate. The urgent time constraints imposed by the publisher made it impossible to include a few entries we had commissioned. Beyond this, however, we assume responsibility for whatever peculiarities of selection the book displays. We trust that no major topic, thinker, or movement has been overlooked. To assure completeness in that sense, we sent lists of proposed entries to several dozen leading experts in American thought and asked for their suggestions. We owe a debt of gratitude to all who responded. The encyclopedia would have been far less adequate without their help.

We attempted to recruit the best-qualified person to write each entry. In some cases, overcommitment and valid personal reasons made it necessary for invitees to decline our offer. Nevertheless, we made certain that all entries were penned by qualified experts, and we have read and approved everything that appears here. We take responsibility, therefore, for any factual errors that may have found their way into the book. On the other hand, we allowed contributors considerable leeway in approach and judgment, so the evaluative element in each entry is the sole responsibility of the author.

A unique feature of *American Philosophy: An Encyclopedia* is the self-assessments it contains of significant living American philosophers. We thought that such self-assessments would be useful and informative, and invited everyone with current standing in the field to contribute one. Not everyone accepted; some appeared reluctant to write about themselves. In the case of philosophers where we are able to present both an assessment and a self-assessment of their work, the picture that emerges is richer and more complete than a critical summary by another author could ever be.

For ease of use, the **516 entries** in this volume are arranged alphabetically, as represented in the **Alphabetical List of Entries.** A **Further Reading** section follows each essay, leading readers to additional relevant literature. Many of the thinkers, movements, influences and concepts discussed are covered in several essays, and so a thorough, analytical **Index** is provided at the end of the book.

This volume has been in preparation for a very long time. It started as a collaboration between John Lachs and Michael Sullivan over ten years ago as a project of Garland Publishers. The consolidation of the publishing industry landed the book with Routledge in the Taylor & Francis Group. In the meantime, Michael Sullivan needed to finish his JD and PhD, and to prepare himself for tenure. His place as Associate Editor was taken by Robert Talisse. The editors take pleasure in seeing the book at last completed and ready to assume its place as an indispensable reference tool.

We hope that this volume will provide interested inquirers with the information they need and aid the vibrant renaissance of American philosophy. We thank all those colleagues who contributed to this enterprise, Mark Georgiev, Kristin Holt-Browning, and Kate Aker of Routledge for effective help in bringing the book through the difficult process from conception to birth, and each other for an agreeable and productive collaboration. Above all else, we thank the generations of American philosophers who thought and wrote from their deepest experience and contributed to the self-understanding of our nation.

John Lachs
Robert Talisse
Vanderbilt University

A PRIORI/A POSTERIORI: KNOWLEDGE

Apriori (or *a priori*) knowledge is often taken to be exemplified by logic and arithmetic, where sense experience is thought to be irrelevant. *Aposteriori* (or *a posteriori*) knowledge is often taken to be exemplified by physics and chemistry, where it is thought that self-evidence and intuition must be supplemented with experimental data based on sense experience. However, usage varies. For some philosophers, apriori beliefs are known with absolute certainty and aposteriori beliefs are relatively suspect. For others, apriori beliefs are mere prejudices that have not been subjected to unbiased investigation and aposteriori beliefs are relatively reliable. Moreover, some philosophers seem to assume that epistemic processes leading to apriori beliefs are infallible and thus that all apriori beliefs are knowledge, known to be true. Other philosophers readily grant that the mistakes occurring in the history of logic and mathematics provide ample proof to the contrary.

The English word "apriori" is derived from the Latin phrase *a priori*, which has been translated "from the prior" or "from what precedes." Aristotle has warned us of the many senses of "prior." In earlier times, "apriori" was said to indicate conclusions of inferential reasoning from cause to effect. Even today, some dictionaries continue to list that meaning as primary – although reference to causal relations or, more generally to inference, is rare in modern philosophical definitions of the word. Today, it is primarily used to distinguish the epistemic sources of beliefs that serve as *premises* rather than conclusions. It is true that the expression "apriori reasoning" does occur, but nearly always as elliptical for "reasoning from apriori premises."

Described negatively, an apriori belief is one arrived at by a process not involving sense experience in any essential way. It is usually assumed without explanation that logical deduction does not involve sense experience and thus that all deductions from apriori premises are apriori. The traditional view that logical deduction is independent of sense experience has been disputed by prominent philosophers – explicitly by John Stuart Mill, and implicitly both by Willard Van Orman Quine and, in public statements recently published, by Alfred Tarski. Thus, in certain contexts, caution would dictate that we explicitly define particular acts of deduction to be apriori if they did not involve sense experience. Described positively, an apriori belief is one that is obtained by "intuition" (or other processes through which "self-evident truths" are known) or that is the conclusion of an apriori deduction whose premises are all so obtained. Of course, all of the words used in these descriptions are understood differently by different writers and different readers. Philosophers do not feel bound to respect prior usage, even their own, and thus the usage of "apriori" in each philosophical work must be interpreted separately.

The English word "aposteriori" is derived from the Latin phrase *a posteriori*, which has been translated "from the posterior" or "from what follows." In earlier times, it was said to indicate inferential reasoning from effects to causes. Some dictionaries continue to list that meaning as primary. Today, again as with "apriori," it is more often used to distinguish the epistemic sources of beliefs that serve as *premises* rather than inferences. It is true that the expression "aposteriori reasoning" does occur, but nearly always as elliptical for "reasoning from aposteriori premises."

Aposteriori belief can be described positively as follows: a belief is aposteriori if it is arrived at by a process based essentially on sense experience; this automatically includes beliefs that are conclusions of deductions whose premises are all so obtained. However, if this is accepted, then we must accept the possibility that one person's aposteriori belief has the same propositional content as another person's apriori belief. To take a simple example, imagine that one person believes "If Abe is brave and calm, then Abe is calm" by deducing it from logical truths and another believes it by deducing it from the aposteriori belief that Abe is calm. The possibility that the same result could have been arrived at by different process does not change the nature of the process actually used.

Although the above is a very simple consideration, it points to a widespread confusion. There are two senses of "belief" that are frequently not distinguished. In the *temporal* sense used above, each belief comes into existence at a particular time during the life of a person who believes it and perishes no later than the death of the believer. Each belief depends for its existence on its believer. No two persons have the same belief, although in many cases two persons have beliefs with the same propositional content. However, there is also a *non-temporal* sense of "belief" in which two persons living at different times can have the same belief. The word "belief" is frequently used elliptically for "the content of a belief," the proposition believed. In this sense, there are beliefs that no one still believes: there are beliefs in the *non-temporal* sense that are not *the contents of* any belief in the *temporal* sense. No belief in the *non-temporal* sense is a belief in the *temporal* sense.

Thus, the adjectives "apriori" and "aposteriori" that above signified properties coherently applicable only to temporal beliefs are ambiguous; they also signify properties coherently applicable only to non-temporal beliefs. Clearly, new definitions are needed. Should a non-temporal belief be defined to be apriori if none of the temporal beliefs having it as content is aposteriori? It is in no way essential to the nature of a proposition how it happened to be adopted as a belief, especially if it were believed by a very small number of people of dubious mental capacity. Much of the literature implicitly presupposes that we all have the same mental capacities.

Not only have the adjectives "apriori" and "aposteriori" signified properties coherently applicable only to non-temporal beliefs but they have even come to signify also properties coherently applicable only to propositions – many of which have never been thought of and which, therefore, have never been believed or disbelieved. In a sense, every belief is a proposition, but not every proposition is a belief. Another pair of definitions is needed – one that does not assume that a process of belief formation has been performed.

This problem has been attacked by assuming that there are distinctive domains of investigation whose propositions are either all apriori or all aposteriori. However, not all philosophers adopting this strategy have agreed on which subjects contain apriori propositions. Some have been interpreted as taking logic, arithmetic, and geometry to be apriori, whereas others have been seen as agreeing on the first two but not the third. Moreover, as hinted above, Mill has been interpreted as denying that logic is composed exclusively of apriori propositions.

Roles similar to that played by the adjective pair "apriori/aposteriori" are played by other pairs used instead or in addition: "analytic/synthetic," "logical/factual," "tautological/informative," "necessary/contingent" and others. In many cases, however, the other pairs are used for properties that cut across those signified by "apriori/aposteriori," thus giving rise to questions such as whether every (some, or no) analytic (or synthetic) proposition is apriori (or aposteriori). For reasons given above, such questions must be interpreted separately in each philosophical work. In the 1950s, Quine and others seriously challenged many sharp either/or approaches to these distinctions proposing instead a kind of gradualism admitting twilight zones and blurry borders. A number of contemporary philosophers have been so discouraged by the contentious confusion surrounding the words "apriori" and "aposteriori" that they studiously avoid using them as technical terms.

The most prominent of early usages of "a priori" in American philosophy is probably in the 1877 article "The Fixation of Belief" by Charles Sanders Peirce (1839–1914), America's greatest logician. This classic has been reprinted often; it appears in a critical edition on pages 109–23 of the 1992 Houser-Kloesel volume. Here Peirce does not explain how "a priori" is to be understood. He merely used it to name "the a priori method" which he then denigrated by saying that it "does not differ essentially from" the method of authority (1992: 119). Peirce was clearly no fan of the pair "a priori/a posteriori." The word "apriori" occurs nowhere else in the 1992 volume and the word "a posteriori" does not occur at all. In the longer 1998 Houser-Kloesel volume, "a posteriori" occurs only once and "apriori" occurs on only four pages, always causally without definition – as some authors use "intuitively" today. Houser and Kloesel did not even see fit to index either "a priori" or "a posteriori." The pair "a priori/a posteriori" was never part of Peirce's technical vocabulary. The same avoidance is found in the much later classic logic text by Morris Cohen (1880–1947) and Ernest Nagel (1901–85), where neither word is used.

Further reading

Cohen, M. and Nagel, E. *Introduction to Logic and Scientific Method*. New York: Harcourt, Brace, 1934.

—— *Introduction to Logic*, second edition with new exercises, indexes, bibliography, and editor's introduction by John Corcoran. Indianapolis, IN: Hackett, 1993 [1934/1962].

Peirce, C.S. *The Essential Peirce: Selected Philosophical Writings Vol. I (1867–1893)*, ed. N. Houser and C. Kloesel. Bloomington, IN: Indiana University Press, 1992.

—— *The Essential Peirce: Selected Philosophical Writings Vol. II (1893–1913)*, ed. N. Houser and C. Kloesel. Bloomington, IN: Indiana University Press, 1998.

JOHN CORCORAN

A PRIORI/A POSTERIORI: METHOD

The Latin terms *a priori* ("from what is prior") and *a posteriori* ("from what is posterior") were introduced by the scholastic philosophers of the medieval period to distinguish between two ways of knowing, or two methods of coming to truth. *A posteriori* is taken to designate claims or truths that we come to know through our senses, after having had particular experiences; while *a priori* claims or truths are ones that we could know independently of or prior to any particular experience. Examples of *a priori* judgments have included not only mathematical or logical theorems (2+2 = 4, "A implies B if and only if the negation of B implies the negation of A"), but the existence of God according to Anselm's ontological argument, "truths of reason" for Leibniz and Hume, and perhaps certain moral truths such as "we have a duty to keep promises."

This distinction is closely related to two others, that between analytic and synthetic judgments, as well as between necessary and contingent truths. The analytic/synthetic distinction is a semantic one that is framed in terms of language and meaning. In the analytic judgment "All bachelors are unmarried," the meaning of the predicate (being unmarried) is already contained in the meaning of the subject (being a bachelor). Such judgments are true in virtue of their form alone: one need not survey all bachelors, asking them to check the box as to whether or not they are unmarried. Thus the *a priori* method for arriving at truth is consistent with analytic judgments. Synthetic judgments, however, do require us to go out into the world to verify. For example, "All bachelors are happy" cannot be known in virtue of its form alone as the concept of happiness is not part of the definition of bachelorhood. Knowledge, in this case, could only be arrived at by *a posteriori* methods which, unlike *a priori* methods, bring us claims that extend or amplify our knowledge since the predicate goes beyond what is contained in the mere concept of the subject.

The distinction between necessary and contingent claims is conceived of as either an ontological assertion (about what necessarily exists) or a modal assertion (about a claim's logical status). Necessary truths are ones that could not have been otherwise, while contingent truths happen to be the case, but could have been otherwise and are thus merely possible.

In the history of thought, these triumvirates were believed to be inseparable. All *a priori* claims were thought to be analytic and necessary, and all *a posteriori* claims were thought to be synthetic and contingent. This position was challenged by Immanuel Kant. For Kant, there can be synthetic *a priori* knowledge as well as analytic *a priori* knowledge. For example, that "events have a cause" or that "objects persist over time" are *a priori* truths about all of our experience, even though they cannot be learned from experience. Such universal, necessary truths are not the result of inductive generalization based on empirical observation of particular events and objects, since inductive generalizations can never have either certainty or universality whereas these claims have both. Kant's understanding of, or perhaps development of, the *a priori* is fairly unique since it occurs against the background of his complex view of the mind as contributing certain *a priori* forms or categories to all sense experience. Such forms will "show up" in our experience but they do not reflect features of the external world: they reflect the subjective filter through which all experience comes and are, in that sense, "independent" of any particular experience.

Pragmatist views

When it comes to American philosophy, pragmatist epistemology mostly discounts *a priori* methods.

Much influenced by the sciences, the pragmatists embraced the experimental method, which they assumed to be generally an *a posteriori* approach. For Charles Peirce, truth can only arise via public methods as pursued by a community of inquiry. The meaning of a term or statement is not discovered by an *a priori* method, but is indicated by the particular actions one who affirms or denies the statement would be prepared to undertake. William James elaborates on this "radical empiricism," arguing for example that while we can neither prove nor disprove a metaphysical claim about God's existence, the statement "God exists" has meaning because belief in God makes a difference in how people live and act. Undertaking a pragmatic study of the word "true," James finds its meaning to be a matter of anticipation and success: if one acts on a true statement, one will not likely be disappointed in his expectations; while if one acts on a false statement, one will likely be disappointed. He emphasizes the necessary presence of "belief" or "choice" in coming to decisions precisely because there are no deductions, *a priori*, of absolute truths. Humans have to choose on the basis of imperfect evidence.

John Dewey's "instrumentalism" also highlights the experimental method of inquiry. Inquiry is brought into action by "problematic situations" in which some equilibrium is disturbed. The function of inquiry is to find those methods that will arrive at a new kind of equilibrium. Because Dewey envisions a continuity between methods in the social sphere and in the scientific one, eternal truths deduced via some *a priori* method have no place in this scheme. For Dewey, we need to persistently test the meaning and worth of ideas, practices, and institutions, by examination of their social consequences, i.e., has there been an increase or decrease in ignorance, oppression, disorder?

In one sense, then, an *a priori* meaning or truth would be impossible on the pragmatist view: all knowledge must be anchored by experimentation, and there can be no "sense" outside of possible experience. However, pragmatists do recognize and explain what previous thinkers have taken as *a priori* truths. Dewey, for example, sees the assertion of "eternal verities" as motivated by insecurity and the attempt to flee the uncertainty of practical activity. Such an escape is misguided, but this does indicate to Dewey that purely conceptual systems may be understood as regulative ideals expressing hope that nature will be intelligible. More generally, in this pragmatic shift from eternalism to temporalism, the *a priori* is collapsed into the analytic, where analytic truth is a matter of linguistic convention and language is an inherently social phenomenon.

It is in the work of W.V.O. Quine that we see the final "dethroning" of the *a priori*. In his famous essay on the dogmas of empiricism, Quine denies that there is a sharp or even clear distinction between analytic and synthetic truths. He argues that Kant's notion of "containment" (where the meaning of the predicate is contained in the subject) is a vague metaphor which cannot function as a basis for the distinction. Further, Quine urges us to abandon the verificationist ideal as the results of some particular experiment cannot be said to either verify or to disconfirm some hypothesis. Extending Pierre Duhem's holistic model of experimentation, Quine points out that all testing occurs against a full background of assumptions or "auxiliary hypotheses." Some of these assumptions will be about the equipment used, some will concern scientific claims made on the basis of previously "proven" theory, some will be metaphysical (every event has a cause, the world is constructed of physical particles), and some will be logical or mathematical. Thus when some result predicted by a hypothesis fails to occur, it might mean the hypothesis is incorrect, but it could also be that one or more of the auxiliary assumptions are incorrect. If I heat water to 100 degrees Centigrade yet it fails to boil, I am not likely to conclude that "water heated to 100 degrees will boil" is untrue. Rather, the more likely conclusion is that an auxiliary assumption is false: perhaps my heating element malfunctioned, or the altitude was significantly above sea level, or the water contained some impurities or nitrates. Quine's way of expressing this is to say that the test situation or experiment "underdetermines" my conclusion or interpretation. There are any number of ways that the experimenter might account for the results or make revisions, including to call into question the supposedly analytic statements of math and logic that were implicitly assumed when undertaking the experiment. Given Quine's holism, "no statement is immune to revision," not even the law of excluded middle or of contradiction – although these are so centrally located in our total system that their revision would severely disturb our body of knowledge, and accordingly we are loath to give them up. But our preference to maintain these truths is not a sign of either an *a priori* or analytic status; it is a sign merely of our preference, in accordance with the work of the scientist, to revise as little as possible and follow the parsimonious "maxim of minimal mutilation."

Further reading

Dewey, John. *Logic: The Theory of Inquiry.* New York: Henry Holt, 1938, especially Chapter XXV on the philosophies of knowledge.

James, William. *Pragmatism: A New Name for Some Old Ways of Thinking*. New York: Longmans, Green, 1907, especially Lecture I on rationalism and empiricism and Lecture VI on truth.

Peirce, Charles. "The Fixation of Belief," *Popular Science Monthly* 12 (November 1877), 1–15.

—— "How to Make Our Ideas Clear," *Popular Science Monthly* 12 (January 1878), 286–302.

Quine, Willard Van Orman. "Two Dogmas of Empiricism" in *From a Logical Point of View: Nine Logico-Philosophical Essays.* Cambridge, MA: Harvard University Press, 1953.

JENNIFER MCERLEAN

A PRIORI/A POSTERIORI: PRAGMATIC

"Empiricism" has been given such a broad range of meanings throughout the history of philosophy that it retains virtually no defining characteristics that can be applied to all supposedly empirical philosophies. The distinction between the a priori, analytic, non-factual statement on the one hand, and the a posteriori, synthetic, factual statement on the other, has been considered an inclusive characteristic of empiricism. However, there has been much controversy within the empiricist camp regarding the adequacy of this distinction. Cases have been made for the existence of a synthetic a priori by several philosophers who fit into the empiricist category on other grounds. This so-called principle of empiricism has also been questioned from another direction, in controversies concerning the denial of the long-held absolute distinction between the analytic and the synthetic.

In the midst of this controversy, the a priori running through pragmatism can be said to occupy a unique position. This pragmatic a priori was explicitly developed in the early twentieth century by C.I. Lewis. However, it can be found implicitly operative in the thought of the other great American pragmatists – C.S. Peirce, William James, John Dewey and G.H. Mead – although they made little effort to develop it or bring it into explicit focus.

Drawn from a fundamentally Kantian approach adapted to fit the needs of contemporary logic and science, the pragmatic a priori is coextensive with the analytic, yet cannot be said to be empirically vacuous. Pragmatism carries the a priori–a posteriori, analytic–synthetic distinction beyond the conventionalism of language, beyond the functionalism of decisions of usage, and beyond the distinction between logic and knowledge about the world. The analyticity of the a priori is an absolute one founded on meaning relations, an all-pervasive one which underlies empirical knowledge as well as propositions of logic and mathematics, and an experimental one which arises through a creative organization past experience and is tested by its fruitfulness in organizing future experience.

According to pragmatism, meanings emerge from and are embodied in our behavioral or dispositional responses to that which presents itself in experience. These meanings underlie all perceptual experience, and in fact make it possible. A priori truth as legislation for the way we interpret experience emerges within the context of purposive attitudes of interpretation. Lewis points out that our purposes are not set by what is given in experience; rather, they are established by us. But, our purposes are formulated in light of, and have their realization in, experience. In a similar way, he further notes, the a priori is prior to present experience, but not completely independent of experience in general. Dewey compares the rule-like or regulative aspect of the a priori, as well as its emergence within experience, to the law of contracts which regulates in advance the making of certain kinds of business engagements. The law of contracts develops out of what has worked in the past, and it imposes conditions to be met in future.

The origin of our analytic structures is empirical, pragmatic, or functional. Genetically, meanings arise through the cumulative effect of past experience and the creative relational organization of experience, as embodied in our modes of response or dispositions to act in certain types of ways when presented with certain types of data. But, at any point in the process, a meaning or dispositional rule contains, logically, all that it has creatively organized, or conversely, all that it now has the power or potential to generate within the ongoing course of experience. Thus Peirce claimed that the habit, disposition or "living meaning" as generative rule "virtually contains" the features it generates, and the conclusion is compelled to be true by the conditions of the construction.

Before one can make empirical generalizations about facts, one must have delineated facts through meanings which are prescriptive as to what experiences will constitute the experience of particular kinds of facts. Before one can make the empirical claim that a particular kind of fact is "there," one must have the structure of the experiences which are to count as exemplifications of the presence of a particular kind of fact. Thus, the analytic a priori structure of meanings provides the tools without which synthetic a posteriori statements or empirical generalizations about the nature of experience cannot be made. Facts, at their very core, emerge neither from mind alone nor from the universe alone, but rather from the interaction of the two; this interaction constitutes experience.

There is an interrelation of the absoluteness of relationships of meanings, and the functionalism of attitudes of response as the determining factor in the fixation of meanings. The purpose of the creation of meanings is the establishment of beliefs which allow for successful interaction with a surrounding universe. And while the absoluteness of the analyticity of an a priori coerces the mind within any system, it can nonetheless be replaced or exchanged for another system.

While the meanings embodied in our conceptual schemes are drawn from the empirical situation, the relation between the meanings can be stated apart from any particular instances of fact. Meaning, *qua* created structure, contains no truth claim as to applicability in experience. As James points out, what we can know is only that if these things are anywhere to be found, then eternal truths will obtain of them. This if–then is what Lewis calls the hypothetical certitude of a priori claims about experience. One can know in advance of any experience, as an "eternal truth," that if a particular a priori meaning structure is applied in experience, then certain features must obtain in experience. For, if these features are not present, one will refuse to interpret the experience as the experience of that particular kind of thing, as these features are analytically contained in the meaning. On the other hand, in the case of a synthetic a posteriori proposition – an empirical generalization – if the expected features do not occur, one will see the thing as a counter-instance and modify one's empirical generalization. However, if the application of the concept or a priori structure is not generally useful in organizing experience, then it will be replaced by another legislative meaning, another logically distinct generative rule, although the same words may be used. Pragmatic meaning is not a relational system among words, but rather among possibilities of experience contained in our dispositional tendencies as ways of acting toward a situation.

Decisions to replace one a priori structure with another may be fairly simple, limited, or unreflectively implicit in our modes of response, or may be complex, encompassing, or highly theoretical and explicit. The change in a simple definition is a replacement of an a priori structure. The deepest and most complex type of replacement of an a priori structure is illustrated in the switch from Newtonian mechanics to Einstein's theory of relativity, which is a priori legislative shifts as to what facts are "there" for empirical investigation. Moreover, the physical referents of Newtonian concepts are not identical to Einsteinian concepts that have the same name. "Mass" as used by Newton cannot be translated into "mass" as used by Einstein. The paradigm change from Newton to Einstein requires a replacement of the entire meaning interrelated conceptual network. The pragmatic a priori provides a philosophical grounding for these kinds of radical shifts in conceptual sets that are captured in Kuhn's examination of the structure of scientific revolutions.

Although there is a theoretically sharp distinction between analytic a-priori knowledge and synthetic a-posteriori knowledge, all knowledge is fallible and contextual. Just as all empirical generalizations are subject to error, so the empirical claim of the applicability of a meaning to a segment of experience is always fallible. Moreover, we can never be certain if, and when, a highly confirmed empirical generalization about an object becomes incorporated into the very meaning of the object, related necessarily to the dispositional rule which now has the power to generate it. The cumulative effects of experience can lead to new empirical generalizations about the same meaningful contents of experience, or it can lead to the perception of different contents by the replacement of the meanings in terms of which contents of a particular type can emerge within experience.

Further, we do not, at any level of experience, test beliefs in isolation, but rather as parts of a whole set of claims. Something similar to auxiliary hypotheses in science is operative in our common sense awareness of the world around us. No part of a relevant corpus of knowledge is immune from change in the face of repeated disconfirming instances, and any part of a belief structure can be held in the face of disconfirming evidence by changing other parts of the structure. Experience reveals that an improvement is necessary, but clearly not which improvement is needed. Whether we change empirical generalizations in the face of disconfirming evidence or restructure a set of meanings that do not adequately capture experience is not itself dictated by the evidence or by strict rules of rationality or procedure, but is rather a pragmatic decision rooted in such human capacities as creative intelligence or educated imagination.

The uniquely pragmatic distinction between the a priori and the a posteriori, which is always operative within the structure of knowledge, though always elusive for our recognition because of its fallibilistic, holistic, contextualistic features, is inextricably woven into the complex fabric of the pragmatic understanding of a noetic creativity which is rooted in purposive biological activity and constitutive of the nature of experience as experimental.

Further reading

Dewey, John. *Logic: The Theory of Inquiry, The Later Works, Vol. 12: 1938*, ed. Jo Ann Boydston. Carbondale and Edwardsville, IL: Southern Illinois University Press, 1981–9.

James, William. "Necessary Truths and the Effects of Experience" in *Principles of Psychology, Vol. II, The Works of William James*, ed. Frederick Burkhardt. Cambridge, MA: Harvard University Press, 1981.

Lewis, C.I. *Mind and the World Order.* New York: Dover, 1929.

—— "A Pragmatic Conception of the A Priori" in *Collected Papers of Clarence Irving Lewis*, ed. John Goheen and John Mothershead, Jr. Stanford, CA: Stanford University Press, 1970.

Rosenthal, Sandra B. *Speculative Pragmatism*. Amherst, MA: University of Massachusetts Press, 1986. Paperback edition: Peru, IL: Open Court, 1990. Chapters 2 and 3.

SANDRA B. ROSENTHAL

ABDUCTION

Abduction is reasoning from effect to possible cause; the logic of the adoption of an hypothesis. The term originates in Charles S. Peirce, whose later writings often use the term "retroduction" as a synonym. Peirce claimed he was the first to name this type of reasoning in English, adding that his term was a translation of Aristotle's *apagoge*.

Abduction suggests some general rule as an explanatory hypothesis for a given fact. Peirce gives the following example: when we know that all the beans in this bag are white and we also have before us some white beans, we guess or reason abductively that these beans are from this bag. Because of the suggestive and hypothetical nature of abductive reasoning, it does not lead to necessary or even probable conclusions, but only to possible conclusions which may then be tested.

Peirce asserted that all logic consisted in the colligation of certain facts and then the observation of what arises out of that colligation. In abduction this means bringing together a general principle or law with some particular fact and observing tentatively that the fact could in fact be subsumed under that principle. Given a class, we observe some fact and then hypothesize that the fact is a member of that class, all the while recognizing that it could very well not be so. This tentative conclusion is thus put in the form of a question or of an hypothesis to be investigated.

In abduction, the facts of the premise are taken to be an *icon* or likeness of the hypothesis. Peirce gave the example of Kepler's observation that the measured locations of Mars could be taken to resemble points on an ellipse, leading to the hypothesis that Mars' orbit was in fact elliptical, a premise that could then be tested by further observation. Although abduction proves nothing, it is essential to all reasoning because it is only by means of abductive inference that any new knowledge arises. Therein, Peirce asserted, lies the only justification of abduction.

Abduction is possible because, as Peirce hypothesized, there is a continuity between mind and nature, such that no problem can be understood to be utterly insoluble, given sufficient time and research. Because of this, minds are able to study facts closely and then "devise a theory to explain them" causally or relationally.

Peirce argued that as ideas spread they become more general and less precise. This has certainly been the case with his term "abduction." Peirce's term has been adopted by researchers in the social sciences, artificial intelligence and computing, theology, and other disciplines. In the philosophy of science it is often used simply to refer to the reasoning by which theories are discovered or proposed (as distinct from the processes by which they are justified).

Abduction is sometimes defined as "inference to the best explanation." However for Peirce this is erroneous since abduction is neither inferential nor conclusive but conjectural, and so the explanation it yields can only appear to be best. Its actual value must be determined by means of inductive and deductive inference.

Further reading

Peirce, Charles S. *Collected Papers of Charles Sanders Peirce*, ed. C. Hartshorne, P. Weiss, and A. Burks. Cambridge, MA: Harvard University Press, 1958 [1935], especially 2.96; 2.623–5; 5.144.

DAVID L. O'HARA

ABSOLUTE

The St Louis Hegelians imported and distributed Hegel's idea of *Geist* (Spirit or Absolute) into mid nineteenth-century America. Unlike Aristotle's distant Absolute, Hegel's Absolute lives within the world's process and somehow develops within it. What followed in classic American philosophy?

C.S. Peirce recognized that the concept of reality implies *community* – a reality that lacks definite limits but can grow indefinitely in knowledge. Peirce's Absolute functioned as a community of persons and signs, led by the human scientific community.

The father of William James insisted that God, the Absolute, is all and William was nothing. Reacting, William made this Absolute his *bête noire*. He felt that an Absolute Reality established a "block-universe." Hence, it ruled out freedom and novelty. James saw that W.K. Clifford's kind of scientific materialism was an Absolute because it reduced all reality to deterministic matter. James also confronted F.H. Bradley's spiritual Absolute. It lay beneath this world's mere Appearances, all those finite relationships, both internal and external. These differed from the One Reality, the Absolute Truth, which determines all else. James recoiled from these views since he felt reality was an on-going stream, pluralistically open to future novelty.

Josiah Royce's vision differed from James's. Although it led him to oppose Bradley's kind of Absolute, Royce used not feelings but the ideas of infinity and infinitesimals to show that finite relations were far more than mere appearances and pointed to an infinitely more real Absolute. Earlier Royce had found that the appeal-function in erroneous judgments implied a unique, all-knowing Absolute. Royce experienced that "truth is true!" and that his Method of Reflection uncovered some self-reinstating truths which could not, with personal integrity, be contradicted. This sensitized him to the presence of the Absolute in human knowing and reflecting. Eventually, Royce heeded Charles Peirce's caution that he avoid using the philosophical term "Absolute" interchangeably with the religious term "God." Unlike his frequent usage of the term "Absolute" in his middle period writings, Royce used it only three times in his late classic, *The Problem of Christianity*. There he spoke instead of "the Universe of Interpretation," the "Interpreter-Spirit" or "Logos-Spirit" to emphasize the fluent, novelty-prone character of the Real World of Royce's final years. Yet his Logos-Spirit knew all absolutely and directed the Universal Community to its absolute goal, the Beloved Community.

John Dewey countered by viewing all classical philosophies as *non*-reconstructed because they claim that humans possess a higher mode of knowing than the inquiry mode required by positive science. Reputedly, this higher mode can reveal the Absolute, the nature and features of Ultimate Reality. Dewey detected how Absolute Idealisms of all types fallaciously generalize from the quality of unity felt at the successful close of a particular inquiry up to some all-inclusive experience – that of trans-finite or Absolute Experience – where no distinction of mediate and immediate any longer obtains. Dewey rejected this mode of failing to accept the unavoidable human mode of thinking by inquiry where judgments must involve differences as well as unities.

For Alfred N. Whitehead, Creativity is the Absolute, the Category of all categories. For him God is the creature of Creativity, even though God can somewhat limit Creativity's initiatives. God's primordial nature is a vision wherein every possibility is seen as a potential for realization. These potentials are "eternal objects" which become actualized only when grasped by actual entities. How these objects' eternity arises remains a puzzle. These objects have to be eternally and absolutely fixed yet they can be such objects only insofar as they refer essentially to temporal process.

Further reading

Royce, Josiah. *Metaphysics: His Philosophy 9 Course of 1915–1916*, ed. W.E. Hocking, Richard Hocking, and F.M. Oppenheim. Albany, NY: State University of New York Press, 1998.

Whitehead, Alfred North. *Process and Reality: An Essay in Cosmology*, corrected edition, ed. David Ray Griffin and Donald W. Sherbourne. New York: Free Press, 1978.

FRANK M. OPPENHEIM, SJ

ACTION

"By their fruits ye shall know them," Jesus instructed in the Sermon on the Mount, and William James added, in his *The Varieties of Religious Experience*, "not by their roots." The American philosopher adapted this lesson from the Gospel of Matthew to serve as a banner for a new philosophy, pragmatism, which would judge beliefs by their "good consequential fruits for life." This consequentialism has had mixed consequences. As the "pragmatic theory of truth" it "has given pragmatism such a bad name," as a sympathetic critic, David Wiggins, has recently lamented. Critics are put in mind of Peter Pan urging everyone to believe in fairies so that Tinkerbell won't die. In a formulation that recommends the power of positive thinking, as in the children's story *The Little Engine That Could* ("I – think – I – can"), it lacks philosophical depth. If the Standard Model of *justified true belief* distorts pragmatist insights and the power of positive thinking is anodyne, there is much room in between once American pragmatism is understood as offering revisionary rather than descriptive accounts of knowledge and truth. When James relates in *Pragmatism* that the term "pragmatism" is derived from the same Greek word *pragma*, meaning action, from which our words "practice" and "practical" come, he is signaling that the theoretically oriented Standard Model is to be replaced by knowledge and truth as guides for "dealing with" or "handing" the environment "better than" if we lacked them: "The essential thing," as he remarks the sixth chapter of *Pragmatism*, "is the process of being guided." Peirce's recommendations for making our ideas clear, his unique operationalism and verificationism, signal a similar revisionist turn in American philosophy, as does Dewey's assimilation of knowledge and truth to warranted assertibility. The notions of truth and knowledge can be discarded in order to emphasize the revisionary character of this moment in philosophy. James straddled the fence here, by expansively developing the revisionary view in *Pragmatism* as an account of "half truth," while leaving a theoretical space for "objective truth," similar to Peirce's conception of an ideal future consensus. It is better to follow Dewey's recommendation here, discarding the Standard Model's concepts of knowledge and truth, and focusing on what can be pragmatically salvaged from its concept of belief.

The pragmatic banner is best defended precisely as a theory of belief, and specifically as a theory that assimilates belief to the category of *action*, as opposed to a passive register whether construed as a behavioral disposition or internal state, the only function of which is to correspond to reality. Thinking about belief in action-oriented terms leads to pragmatic *voluntarism* about belief, classically defended by James in his essay "The Will to Believe," which counsels each individual's right within evidential parameters to adopt those beliefs that guide him or her to a more meaningful life. The primary challenge for voluntarism's defense is to bring into proper focus belief's relationship to *evidence*. It will hardly do to ignore this relationship in favor of judging belief exclusively by its promoting expected utility. Assuming that Tinkerbellism about truth is ruled out, pragmatism about belief must show how belief provides "the better guide" without necessarily guaranteeing it by maximizing expected utility, Tinkerbell fashion. It could do so by finding a balance between the claims of evidence and good consequences, in which evidence provides a necessary condition for belief and, when the evidence itself is not sufficient, good consequences provide a sufficient condition. Belief typically does have good consequences. Evolution has selected us for being believers. That process has put the responsible believer in a special relationship to evidence, but it's not a relationship that excludes good consequences of the sort that account for the evolution of believers in the first place. W.K. Clifford was surely correct in "The Ethics of Belief" to urge that "it is wrong always, everywhere, and for anyone, to believe anything upon insufficient evidence," but standards of sufficiency not only are different from context to context, they must also be blended appropriately with whatever weight further consequences may have, when measuring the belief's "good consequential fruits for life."

A combined evidence-and-consequences view fits the religious contexts that James was concerned about in *Varieties* as well as other contexts in which evidence for hypotheses tends to be insufficient and yet good consequences may attend belief. James's general idea can be taken one step further by considering the good "fruits" of believing the hypothesis itself, apart from the hypothesis's evidential value and apart from further good consequences. For instance, a subject might find it good in this sense to believe that certain character traits have objective value, value that is independent of what people merely happen to value. The goodness of the believed hypothesis in this respect is what Robert Nozick calls *symbolic utility* and F.P. Ramsey before him called *ethically non-neutral propositions*; both philosophers can be viewed as continuing the pragmatist tradition on this topic. Dewey is associated with an account of the etiology of symbolic utility/ethical non-neutrality, viewing it as arising from an action's instrumental value, which then becomes intertwined by psychological and social associations with the action's having intrinsic value as an end in itself. Symbolic utility or ethical non-neutrality normally exhibits Deweyan intertwining, but causal instrumentality and symbolic/deontological upshot are conceptually distinct.

This intrinsic utility may be had because of the hypothesis's capacity for meaning, expressiveness, or representation. For instance, James remarked in the essay "The Will to Believe" that "all of us in this room" (he was addressing the Philosophical Clubs of Yale and Brown Universities in the 1890s, just before the turn of the century) believe in fighting for "the doctrine of the immortal Monroe," though he added "for no reasons deserving of the name." The people in that room did not have evidence that compelled belief; nor did they have knowledge of the good consequences of so believing that tipped the scales; rather, the belief itself had a meaning for Americans at that time which was a weighty factor in their sharing it – the belief had what Nozick calls symbolic utility. They had no *further* reasons for their belief about the Monroe doctrine beyond the symbolic utility of believing that European powers should no longer colonize the Americas. (In Ramsey's terms: *That European powers colonize the Americas* is an ethically non-neutral proposition, describing a world they prefer not to exist.)

So pragmatic voluntarism at this stage includes a hypothesis's evidential value but also its expected and symbolic utility. In virtue of the latter it has a deontological element, as Ramsey recognized. There are certain actions one must or must not do, because of their ethical non-neutrality. Although pragmatism is commonly understood as a consequentialist doctrine as regards its implications for ethics, pragmatic voluntarism with reference to symbolic utility/ethical non-neutrality reveals the non-consequentialist aspect that makes it distinctive as a version of ethical consequentialism.

The next step is to understand evidential value under the rubric of action, as something *done*. This is a program that can be traced back to James's emphasis on ideas as guides and Peirce's operationalism and verificationism, and it continues to be pursued. When subjective-probability theorists like Richard Jeffrey talk about "doing Bayesianism," for instance, they are taking this step towards pragmatic voluntarism. Bayes' theorem and related techniques for exploring relationships between hypotheses and evidence are being recommended as tools for doing good work, not discoveries about the mind/brain's interior. "Judgmental probabilities are not generally in the mind or brain, awaiting elicitation when needed," Jeffrey writes, "the important question about us is not whether we have probabilities in mind, but whether we can fabricate useful probabilistic proxies for whatever it is that we have in mind." Jeffrey adds the important qualification that "The fabricators are not generally the ultimate users, but innovators like Bruno de Finetti, who showed us how to use exchangeability ... Intelligent users mostly choose such probabilistic constructs ready-to-wear, from catalogs."

These points about "doing evidence" extend to "doing expected utility" and "doing symbolic utility": The "catalog" of a subject's culture's common meanings makes "constructs" available for beliefs that either intrinsically or because of their further consequences make life more meaningful and valuable, as perceived by participants in that culture. Ideally these constructs are harmonious marriages of means and ends, Deweyan intertwinings given cultural stability. Those who adopt a moral leader's beliefs "ready to wear" are not simply responding to evidence but also buying into a vision of the world's unfolding, which is being factored here into elements of expected and symbolic utility. Pragmatic voluntarism is not individualism, if that means abstraction from a cultural context. On the contrary, the role of leaders is an exception to the rule that individuals take symbolic utility from the culture's common meanings, what *we* believe that invest our lives with meaning. Even pathological cases like compulsive hand-washing draw upon a culture's association of such activity with cleanliness and purity. Creators of cultural artifacts that add to these meanings show how the process can go in the opposite direction, from individual to cultural stock of common meanings. But the preponderant direction is top-down, from culture to individual. What dominates in pragmatic individualism is neither the individual, nor the individual's private inner states, nor the world external to the individual described in culturally neutral terms (e.g. by a natural-scientific description). What dominates is the encultured agent.

Having expanded pragmatic voluntarism to include evidential, expected-utility, and symbolic-utility elements, one further step can be taken: to sketch a theory of mind in the spirit of this voluntarism. Consider the qualifier "not by their roots" that James mentions in his addendum to the aphorism "By their fruits ye shall know them." An action-oriented theory of mind that includes pragmatic voluntarism would view the brain's information-processing, the mind's qualia or subjective appearances, and equally the pencil and paper and the laptop computer as roots of mentation rather than the fruits by which the mind shall be known. The mind is minding, intelligent action enabled by its internal and external roots. This is not behaviorism. It does not make problems about the privacy of qualia disappear. It affirms rather that voluntarism, not privacy, is the mark of the mental. Nor is it an "externalism" that spreads out the mind into the environment of pencil and paper, laptop, etc. It affirms rather that the content of belief and other mental states is a construct we make, neither internal nor external. The dependencies of the mind on the inner and outer are dramatic, but the problem of understanding these dependencies is different from the problem of understanding the mind. That problem is solved by understanding the mind's characteristic activity, which includes pragmatic voluntarism. This separation is worth emphasizing, because conflation has led to preoccupation with the inner, on one hand, and an obscure idea of the mind's being spread out in the environment, on the other hand. This is to conflate roots and fruits. Consider the following remark from Peirce's *Collected Papers*:

> A psychologist cuts out a lobe of my brain (*nihil animale a me alienum puto*) and then, when I find I cannot express myself, he says, "You see, your faculty of language was localized in that lobe." No doubt it was, and so, if he had filched my inkstand, I should not have been able to continue my discussion until I had got another. Yea, the very thoughts would not come to me. So my faculty of discussion is equally localized in my inkstand.

This passage can be read as implying that the mind is localized in *both* places, the lobe and the inkstand. But it can also be read as chiding that urge to localize, and pragmatic voluntarism's fruits/roots distinction illuminates this alternative. Beginnings of support for this interpretation: Peirce analyzed dispositions, e.g. a sugar cube's disposition to dissolve in water, by reference to what it actually does or would do; he does not "localize" the disposition both in internal micro-structure and water.

"Doing mind" in the sense of the previous paragraph revisits *epiphobia*, the fear that one's theory of mind is leaning towards epiphenomenalism, eliminating the causal efficacy of the mind. If belief is not an internal state with causal powers apt to cause behavior characteristic of the belief, still the behavior that expresses pragmatic voluntarism – willing oneself to "do evidence," "do expected utility," and "do symbolic utility"; choosing from the "catalog" of one's culture's store of knowledge about doing these things; perhaps contributing to that store; etc. – will still be the cause of the further behavior that is characteristic of a given belief. The behavior that expresses pragmatic voluntarism, on the other hand, is not characteristic of particular given beliefs but rather of adopting a certain general strategy for believing. "But won't *that adoption* be caused by an inner state, a belief that the adoption is advisable?" Let this inner state be something passive, not a voluntary action in any sense. It is appropriate for the doing-mind theory to draw the line between fruits and roots at just this point. One's beliefs are rooted in such phenomena, though equally they are rooted in external objects such as persuasive books and inkstands. Your beliefs properly so called, to the extent that you have adopted the pragmatic strategy, are expressions of will. Furthermore everyone's beliefs reflect this strategy to some extent, since everyone's beliefs are colored by the catalog of belief-shaping constructs. When William James spoke to people about the will to believe, he did not suppose them ignorant of the pragmatic strategy, but rather he wanted to defend their use of it against charges of epistemic irresponsibility such as those leveled by Clifford, and to enhance their use of the strategy.

The doing-mind theory has been discussed with reference to belief, but it represents an approach that should fit other mental states as well, such as desire, attention, will, and the rest. The path has already been started: Doing evidence (doing Bayesian subjective probability) measures degree of belief by bets one is *willing* to place on lotteries and the like; desire will be articulated by adopting Bayesian strategies for determining the desire's place in a continuum of degrees of desire. Good further consequences are consequences one wants. Symbolic utility is about what one prefers for its own sake. Such "conative" mental states, just as the cognitive ones like belief, should be understood by their characteristic activity rather than their inner or outer roots. Pragmatic voluntarism means that one should *do* desire as well as *do* belief. By their fruits – in action and action's consequences, upshots, and Deweyan means/end intertwinings – ye shall know them.

Further reading

Clifford, W.K. "The Ethics of Belief," *Contemporary Review*, 1877.

James, William. *The Varieties of Religious Experience*. Cambridge, MA: Harvard University Press, 1985.

Jeffrey, Richard. *Probability and the Art of Judgment*. Cambridge: Cambridge University Press, 1992.

Nozick, Robert. *The Nature of Rationality*. Princeton, NJ: Princeton University Press, 1993.

Peirce, Charles. *Collected Papers of Charles Sanders Peirce*. Cambridge, MA: Harvard University Press, 1931–58.

Ramsey, Frank P. "Truth and Probability" in R.B. Braithwaite (ed.) *The Foundations of Mathematics and other Logical Essays*. New York: Harcourt, Brace, 1926.

Skagested, Peter. "Peirce's Semiotic Model of the Mind" in Cheryl Misak (ed.) *The Cambridge Companion to Peirce*. Cambridge: Cambridge University Press, 2004.

Wiggins, David "Reflections on Inquiry and Truth Arising from Peirce's Method for the Fixation of Belief" in Cheryl Misak (ed.) *The Cambridge Companion to Peirce*. Cambridge: Cambridge University Press, 2004.

WESLEY COOPER

ACTUAL OCCASION

Alfred North Whitehead (1861–1947) describes his *Process and Reality* as an essay on Speculative

Philosophy, with eight Categories of Existence. Among these are "'actual entities' – also termed 'actual occasions'": "the final real things of which the world is made up . . . drops of experience, complex and interdependent" (Whitehead, *Process and Reality*: 18). The terms *actual entity* and *actual occasion* are synonymous except for God, who is the only actual entity that is not an actual occasion, the only complex and relational drop of experience that is not an event. Such a view owes a debt to Gottfried Leibniz, whose monads are self-determining entelechies, to contemporary physics for atoms of becoming, and to Baruch Spinoza and later empiricists for centers of feeling and experience.

The world we know is made up of societies of actual occasions, where a society is a kind of nexus, an aggregate of actual occasions, constituted by the feelings of the members. Most of the things we encounter in our experience are societies, where a society is defined by a common form (Whitehead calls it an *eternal object*), and where the common form is felt or prehended by the members of the society that reproduce that form through their feelings. An actual occasion is a event of feeling, a moment of experience.

Prehension is the term Whitehead uses to analyze and describe actual entities in relation and in experience. "A prehension reproduces in itself the general characteristics of an actual entity: it is referent to an external world, and in this sense will be said to have a 'vector character'; it involves emotion, and purpose, and valuation, and causation" (19). An actual occasion feels or prehends the past, feels or prehends past occasions that have become and perished, feels or prehends their feelings or prehensions. In this way, actual occasions feel other actual occasions and feel their feelings, prehend their prehensions. Through such feelings, actual occasions are perspectives on the universe. "[E]ach actual entity includes the universe, by reason of its determinate attitude towards every element in the universe" (45).

Actual entities are subjects that feel, subjects of feeling. The actual occasions they prehend are objects that have felt, past actual occasions that have perished and no longer feel but whose feelings remain for subsequent prehension. In this way, actual occasions prehend the past. Whitehead calls these *physical prehensions*. Actual entities are moments of experience as both subjects that prehend and objects that are prehended, and as both physical and mental.

An actual occasion is a drop of experience and takes place indivisibly, yet it can be analyzed into components and prehensions. It can be understood to originate in prehensions of the past (physical prehensions), it abstracts from these prehensions into the qualities or eternal objects prehended in the past, it supplements these qualities in its own experiences (conceptual prehensions), and it coordinates these prehensions into an act of becoming in which it creates itself as an entity different from any past entity. In other words, it creates something novel according to its feelings of the past and of the aggregate of eternal objects or forms – the primordial nature of God – synthesizing them in feeling into its subjective aim and into its final feeling of satisfaction. This aim and satisfaction fulfill the occasion as an aesthetic experience of contrasting feelings. "The subjective aim, whereby there is origination of conceptual feeling, is at intensity of feeling" (27). In *Adventures of Ideas*, Whitehead speaks of this as *beauty*.

Further reading

Whitehead, Alfred North. *Adventures of Ideas*. New York: Macmillan, 1933.

—— *Modes of Thought*. New York: Capricorn, 1938.

—— *Process and Reality*, corrected edition, ed. D.R. Griffin and D.W. Sherburne. New York: Free Press, 1978.

STEPHEN DAVID ROSS

ACTUALITY

Actuality (Greek *energeia*; Latin *actualitas*; German *Aktualität* and also *Wirklicheit*; French *actualité*) is a conception that functions at two levels, that of ontology, where the concept is object-oriented and amounts to existence or reality, and that of semantics, where the concept is state-of-affairs oriented and amounts to truth or factuality. The contrast-range in which the idea mainly figures in technical philosophy is that of necessary/actual/possible, where that possibility contrast itself has two principal aspects, namely the Aristotelian potentiality of what something can do, and the mere conceivability of supposition and hypothesis of what might be. In general discourse, however, actuality has a wider range, and has the actual contrast with falsification (fake, pretended, inauthentic, merely seeming), supposition (putative, estimated), and simulation (initiation, virtual, simulated, modeled, ersatz).

In philosophy it is the first of these senses – where actual contrasts what is with what is not – that is at the forefront. Accordingly, actuality stands in contrast with fictionality, representing what is real over what is simply made up in imaginative fancy. To lose one's "robust grip on reality" by comprising one's grip on what is actually so is to enter the realm of psychopathology.

Secondarily, actual also has the meaning of now-existent: more in the Romance languages and German than in English it characterizes the current, contemporary, and up-to-date.

Throughout the otherwise much controverted domain of occidental philosophizing, one basic idea seems to have gained virtually universal acceptance. This is the idea already inherent in the etymology of the term (for actuality is derived from Latin *actus* or again from German *Wirklichkeit*, from *wirken*, both of which mean action) that to be is to act (Latin *actuosus* = active, energetic). What is paramount for actuality is thus action. After all, only what is actual can operate in the world's causal commerce. Nonexistent possibilities and unrealized potentialities can play no role here. What is not actual has no place in "the real world" apart from its role in the thought of intelligent beings.

Aristotle accordingly associated actuality with entelechy or energeia, and St Thomas saw the actual being of things as making itself manifest through self-presentation on the world's stage. Throughout the Aristotelian tradition actuality was seen as prior to potentiality: something must be in order to act. The fulfillment of actuality is accordingly seen as a full realization of inherent potential, and its complete realization stands coordinate with a thought's final course of telos. And so, in this Aristotelian sense actuality is the full realization of something's inherent capacity for the full realization of its potential as the kind of thing it is (e.g. a thriving hen in the case of the egg or the flourishing oak in the case of an acorn).

A cognate use of the term is represented by the distinction between an actual and a potential infinite in mathematics. The set of positive integers is demonstrably infinite and thus accordingly constitutes an actually infinite manifest. But the contrary then is a merely potentially infinite process. We can never reach the end of it; however far we actually go we remain in the domain of the finite and do not reach infinity. Counting is only potentially infinite: counting proceeds ad indefinitum but not ad infinitum.

So much for what actuality is. In turning to the different question of what is actual one is thrust into the arena of metaphysics, where actuality is a matter of reality at large, of being *qua* being. Here materialism and idealism, monism and pluralism, and all the big issues of traditional metaphysical theorizing come upon the stage as competing themes regarding the matter of what is actual.

No philosopher has denied actuality to existing concrete things and processes and to realized states of affairs. But abstracta in contrast to concrete are something else again. Some theoreticians (generally dubbed "Platonist") ascribe actual existence to abstracta, while others (generally dubbed "Nomilists") accept only concrete existents as actual, relegating the generic features and relation of such existents to a secondary and subordinate status.

In the theory of modality there is an ongoing dispute about whether various merely logical possibilities such as nonexistent individuals or worlds are, with Meinong, to be seen as in some way actual or real. Those who are prepared to concede some sort of diluted actuality to that which is merely (albeit actually) possible have come to be called actualists. By contrast those who see the nonexistent as functioning only in the realm of thought as matters of supposition or hypothesis – "things of the mind" (*entia rationis*) as the medievals put it – have come to be called conceptualists.

Crucial to any adequate account of actuality is the issue of how it contrasts with mere possibility. There are two fundamental approaches here, and as such they go back to the Presocratics. One account is that of the ancient atomists. Mooting the question of why cows have horns when dogs do not, the atomists replied that this is merely an artifact of our local environment. Elsewhere in the infinite cosmos there are worlds whose cows lack horns but whose dogs do not. The cosmos-as-a-whole contains innumerable worlds and in this vast range all theoretical possibilities are realized. The contrast between the actual and the merely possible is a matter of local parochialism that loses its grip in the big picture. There just are no unactualized possibilities – all of them are realized somewhere or other. The Pythagorean Heracleitus by contrast took the line that there is just one universe in which just one set of possibilities is realized. The world has to make up its mind, so to speak, regarding what is actual, and all alternatives to this reality are flat-out unrealized and nonexistent. (In the present day this conflict between a many-worlds view of actuality and a one-world approach has sprung back to life in speculative cosmology in physics.)

There remains the epistemic issue of our cognitive access to actuality, of how we are to gain knowledge of what is really and actually so. And it is just here that the conception of actuality has come to play its leading role on the stage of American philosophy. In tune with the optimistic can-do spirit of America's ethos, its philosophers have generally rejected scepticism, relativism, nihilism. And from Benjamin Franklin to Ayn Rand they have generally evidenced a robust respect for actual reality.

This is particularly manifest in the school of realistic pragmatism that runs from C.S. Peirce to John Dewey, and C.I. Lewis, whose shared conviction is that the actuality of things lies at the end of the road of rational inquiry. The upshot of this general standpoint is that pragmatic efficacy as manifested in successful applications is the ultimate arbiter of actual truth regarding the actual nature of things.

In all, the concept of actuality has been called upon to render a considerable variety of philosophical services. The theorist who makes use of the concept is thus under an obligation to specify just exactly what he has in mind here if misunderstanding and confusion is to be averted. The term is decidedly not among those that are self-explanatory.

NICHOLAS RESCHER

ADAMS, ELIE MAYNARD

E.M. Adams (1919–2003) – metaphysician, epistemologist, and philosopher of culture – developed a humanistic realism defending the reality of both value and meaning and challenging philosophical naturalism. He was born in Clarkton, Virginia, and was educated at the University of Richmond (AB, 1941; MA, 1944), Colgate-Rochester Divinity School (BD, 1944), and Harvard University (MA, 1947; PhD, 1948). He taught at the University of North Carolina at Chapel Hill from 1948 until a few years before his death.

As department Chair from 1960 to 1965, Adams created a major research department. He proposed and directed the Curriculum on Peace, War, and Defense from 1970 to 1972 (bringing academic scrutiny to issues fueling Vietnam War protests), served as Faculty Chairman, proposed and organized the Program in the Humanities and Human Values (a continuing liberal education program for out-of-school adults), authored almost a hundred scholarly articles, devoted countless hours to students, and supervised many theses and dissertations. Beyond UNC-CH, he helped lead the American Philosophical Association and other philosophical organizations, and served on journal editorial boards. His last book, *A Society Fit for Human Beings* (1997), was written to reach the broader public and articulates a vision of a humanistic civilization in which knowledge of value and meaning is as important as scientific knowledge.

Early philosophical development

Though Adams's dissertation was on scientific explanation and anticipated developments in the philosophy of science, he turned to the work of his Harvard teachers. He concluded that both C.I. Lewis's sense datum theory of sense experience and Ralph Barton Perry's interest theory of value failed to escape phenomenalism, the view that we are aware only of private phenomenal states. Adams became convinced that the "of" in "sensory experience of x" indicates an intentional or semantic content that constitutes and individuates the experience. This semantic content is internally related to the experience; it identifies the experience. Not only can physical object discourse be of or about sensory experience, sensory experience can be of or about an objective physical realm. The content of the experience can be expressed in language having the same semantic content, leading Adams to characterize an experience as a "structure of meaning." In sense experience, some object is "taken up semantically" and taken to obtain in the world existentially. A veridical experience is one in which the object that is the semantic content of the experience also has an existential status in the world. Adams contended that the semantic could neither be explained nor explained away; semantic intentionality is categorial, a basic way reality can be structured, how we must understand the world.

Adams conceived of philosophy as an a priori discipline (fundamentally metaphysics and epistemology) in which we discover the basic structures of reality – the categories. Influenced by his colleague Everett W. Hall, Adams came to a fuller account of philosophy as the program of categorial analysis. Categorial analysis of ordinary discourse about some subject examines not only what it does and does not make sense to say about it, but also if categorial conclusions in that area fit within a comprehensive categorial system, if that categorial system accounts for the entire culture, and if dialectical ad hominem arguments establish that denial of that system ultimately leads to insoluble logical perplexities that reveal inconsistency with the necessary presuppositions of experience, thought, knowledge, and action. Philosophy is systematic and objective, though there is no theory-neutral methodology. This conception of philosophy as a kind of linguistic analysis (with a nod to phenomenology) placed Adams broadly within the analytic movement.

Adams discovered that his account of sensory experience applied to emotive experience too, opening up an epistemology of value: value discourse is of or about emotive experience, and emotive experience is of and about a value reality, a position developed in *Ethical Naturalism and the Modern World-View* (1960). Influenced by Hall's metaphysics of value, and building on C.I. Lewis's analysis of contrary-to-fact conditionals, Adams proposed that the basic structure of a value sentence is "If *X* is *F*, then *X* (or *Y*) ought to be *G*." That is, given some context or situation, some normative requirement obtains in the world. The "ought" is part of the connective; the entire "If ... then ... ought ..." is the semantic content of an emotive experience and indicates a value structure in reality. Something is good if it is as it ought to be and bad if not. A normative requirement arises in a context; if that context changes, the value might change. Values are objectively real but contextual. Normativity is categorial, a form of intentionality that stands in an internal relation to a context. Something can be real through being constituted by an inherent normative requirement.

Adams explored implications of value realism: Anything real must be causally efficacious, implying real teleological causation; there is logical room for objective essences, how a kind of thing ought to be by nature; the functions of biological organisms and their parts cannot be explained away by Darwinian evolutionary theory; and the mind functions teleologically and has a value structure both through its constitutive governing principles and the ethics of thought.

Adams started off in the dominant movement in modern Western thought called "scientific naturalism," a world view based on the metaphysical categories of modern science. Developing his ideas dialectically against contemporaries and the broad history of philosophy, he concluded naturalism is indefensible. Naturalism's categories and its empiricism are too narrow, distorting philosophy and other disciplines and even generating destructive misconceptions of philosophy. False naturalistic metaphysical and epistemological assumptions deep in modern Western civilization put it partly out of touch with reality, deranging it. In such a culture, lived experience reveals a growing inability to live life with inner strength, wisdom, and happiness. Many philosophers work uncritically within their culture's basic metaphysical and epistemological assumptions. But Adams came to believe that meaning and value are categorial. These are the central categories of the humanities, since the humanities study the structures of meaning and value in humanity, society, and culture. Adams argued we need a systematic philosophy of the humanities, a realistic humanism; he set out to develop one. So began his break with the main direction of contemporary philosophy and modern Western thought.

A new humanistic world view

Philosophy and the Modern Mind (1975) and *The Metaphysics of Self and World* (1991) further develop his systematic philosophy. Dispositional knowledge requires taking *P* to be real, having good reasons for so taking *P*, being correct, and having those reasons be responsible for being correct. Two more conditions are needed for episodic acts of knowing, encounters with objective reality. In an "epistemic encounter," one's taking *P* to be real is "partially self-warranting"; the occurrence of the experience is some evidence for its veridicality. Also, *P*'s being real must help explain why the experience occurred; what makes the experience veridical must cause the experience to occur. The mode of experience is then a source of original ideas about the world.

For Kant, categorial truths reveal the world only as it is present to the mind and not the world in itself. Adams argued for categorial realism over Kant's categorial idealism. If we cannot discover the categorial structure of experience and thought as they are in themselves (not merely as they are present to the mind), then how they yield knowledge and how we can act in and on the world would be unintelligible. Also, within categorial realism and value realism it makes sense that the mind evolved with the function of giving us knowledge of the world in itself. Categorial truths, then, formulate the transcendentally necessary structure of the world; they are true of any world in which knowledge and experience and action are possible. Adams was a foundationalist about epistemic encounters and categorial truths. Philosophy appeals to them to critically assess, and if necessary to correct, the culture's world view; philosophy is our most fundamental level of cultural criticism and reconstruction.

Adams held that the mind is a dynamic system of semantic states and acts organized under a value structure (all embodied biologically) so that as a system it functions to produce further states and acts. But he rejected mind/body dualism. Expressions of the mind in language and action also are constituted by a semantic dimension. Along with semantic realism, this semantic theory of the mind and the entire subjective realm places the mind, action, and language in the world as real structures of meaning. We grasp the meaning of others' actions and expressions by "perceptual understanding." We are conscious of the contents of our own mind and actions and expressions not by reflection but by our mental states and acts being the focus of the mind so that we can recall, avow, reflect on, critically assess, and correct them. The entire mind, though, is not consciously present. The contents of the mind – beliefs, values, intentions, and the like – and its expressions are constituted both by a semantic content and logical form. Logical form, logical properties, and logical relationships are the particular forms, properties, and relationships of structures of meaning. In emotive reasoning, we feel the normative requirements grounded in the logical structure of the mind. Given some belief, we feel required to form some other belief, even if unaware of the reasons why. Reflective reasoning directly grasps the logical form of our mental states and acts, their logical properties, and the logical relationships. Given some belief, we reflectively grasp that it functions as a reason for some conclusion.

Regarding any epistemic power of the mind, a knowledge-yielding experience is identified and unified by a semantic content with a logical form. This experience is expressible in language having the same content and logical form as the experience, stands in logical relationships with other experiences, makes a truth-claim, and can be epistemically assessed as veridical or non-veridical. Adams concludes that our epistemic powers include sensory perception (internal and external), emotive experience, perceptual understanding, and reflection (reflective awareness). Our epistemic powers are broader than what naturalism acknowledges.

Adams defends moral realism. Our moral feelings embody moral judgments telling us what is fitting or unfitting for any person in a given context. Moral discourse presupposes a conception of personhood. A person is the kind of being who ought to have a normative self-concept under the imperative to "define and live a life of one's own"; that life must be justifiable under rational and moral criticism. Personhood is a natural social kind; in a social kind, the concept of the thing is internal to and shapes the inner dynamics of the thing. The imperative to define and live a life has the status of a responsibility; it must be known in order to be fulfilled. Adams characterizes personhood as a natural social office, constituted by that inherent natural responsibility and by natural human rights, the freedoms and means needed to carry out that responsibility. A society with sufficient resources has an inherent normative requirement to help people function well as persons. A person first develops a culturally generated identity but should come to critically examine oneself and thus the internalized culture to reach a rationally defensible identity and culture. Liberal education crucially aims for such cultural freedom. In *A Society Fit for Human Beings*, Adams critically examines various sectors of the culture under a humanistic world view.

Persons, society, and the organic realm, must be conceived humanistically, using concepts indigenous to the humanities. But a naturalistic world view cannot account for humanistic subject matters, even by the theory that real structures of meaning and value emerged from a naturalistic universe. Adams concluded that humanistic realities require a humanistic world view. We explain structures of meaning and value by appealing not atomistically to their parts but wholistically to their larger contexts of meaning or value. This wholism pushes outward toward an Ultimate context, which must be real but that is beyond our literal conceptual grasp. In a humanistic world view, with meaning and value as categorial, Ultimate Reality must be ultimate in meaning and value; this is what belief in a Divine Reality amounts to. So, a humanistic world view provides rational grounds for faith in a creative power or dynamic (not a Being) in the universe working towards what ought to be and thus manifesting a "wisdom." In *Religion and Cultural Freedom* (1993), Adams argues that we can understand religion in a way consistent with cultural freedom; one can have religious faith and a commitment to a culture free under reason.

Further reading

Adams, Elie Maynard (ed.) *Categorial Analysis: Selected Essays of Everett W. Hall on Philosophy, Value, Knowledge and the Mind*. Chapel Hill, NC: UNC Press, 1964.

—— *Philosophy and the Modern Mind: A Philosophical Critique of Modern Western Civilization*. Chapel Hill, NC: UNC Press, 1975; reprinted Lanham, MD: University Press of America, 1985.

—— *The Metaphysics of Self and World: Toward a Humanistic Philosophy*. Philadelphia, PA: Temple University Press, 1991.

—— *Religion and Cultural Freedom*. Philadelphia, PA: Temple University Press, 1993.

—— *A Society Fit for Human Beings*. Albany, NY: SUNY Press, 1997.

Holtzman, Seth. "Science and Religion: The Categorial Conflict." *International Journal for Philosophy of Religion* 54, 2 (2003), pp. 77–99.

Weissbord, David (ed.) *Mind, Value and Culture: Essays in Honor of E. M. Adams*. Atascadero, CA: Ridgeview, 1989.

Seth Holtzman

ADAMS, HENRY BROOKS

Henry Brooks Adams (1838–1918) was born in Boston into the most prominent American family of his time. His great grandfather was President John Adams, his grandfather was President John Quincy Adams, and his father, Charles Francis Adams, was Congressman and Minister to Great Britain. Their eminence was not merely political, but intellectual, literary, and moral as well. Henry's ambition was to become, like them, a great man, preferably a statesman. On graduating from Harvard in 1858, after the expected Grand Tour of Europe, he plunged innocently into politics, believing he was destined for the White House. As his father's secretary, he considered a career in diplomacy. He hoped to become a successful literary journalist and took up residence in Washington with the expectation that he was a statesman in the making, but, as a major consequence of the Civil War, the nature of national politics had become a chaotic and unprincipled competition for power which Henry found degrading, disgusting and incomprehensible, far from the ideal of national democracy he had intended to bring into being on the sober, scientific principles advocated by his grandfather. He quickly became profoundly disillusioned with "this wilderness of men and women as monotonous as the brown stone houses they lived in" whose lives seemed to him more and more to be in the grip of forces beyond human control and to represent a formless dissipation of the energy required for social progress. Barred by principle and his inability to understand the world around him from active involvement in the world of national politics, Henry took to traveling widely and to writing stinging, embittered, and cynical commentaries on that world as an outsider. He also began writing histories, biographies, collections of letters, and, indeed, a remarkably varied, numerous and often brilliant literary production. Three of these – *The History of the United States during the Administrations of Thomas Jefferson and James Madison* (1890–91), *Mont-Saint Michel and Chartres* (1913), and *The Education of Henry Adams* (1961) – remain important works of American literature. The *Education* is considered one of the most brilliant autobiographies ever written by an American author.

In 1870, Henry was called to the bedside of his sister, who was dying in agony from tetanus. The effect on him was immediate and profound. When his wife committed suicide without explanation in 1884, Henry began slowly to construct a philosophy of force to account for the nature of the world he perceived. In doing so, he set two forces up against each other, "The Dynamo and the Virgin," to represent physical and spiritual power. From his studies of the medieval world, he knew that belief in Mary as Queen of Heaven had generated the equivalent of a billion dollars to build the great churches of Europe in the thirteenth century, an expression of power he could not imagine in the modern world. On the other hand, the dynamo as symbol of the actual physical force which built the industrial world was undeniable. Henry turned to physics, specifically to the physicist Josiah Willard Gibbs's analysis of entropy in his "Rule of Phase." This, he believed, would provide him with a genuine, physical science of history, which would integrate the theory of the dissipation of energy into a more general theory of force to account for human history. In this reduction of history to physics, he proposed two "laws," which appeared in his 1909 article, "The Rule of Phase Applied to History," first, that human history moved in "phases," and second, that it accelerated, so that each "phase" became more intense. The forces occurred in order of intensity; first came the era of the forces of animal nature, mainly reproduction, then religion, the power of faith, then mechanical invention, then the electrical period, initiated by the dynamo. These phases would be followed by a brief "ethereal phase" characterized by the force of thought reaching its limits, itself followed by an indefinite phase of space or pure mathematics, "an ocean of potential thought," but:

> if, in the prodigiously rapid vibrations of its last phases, Thought should continue to act as the universal solvent which it is, and should reduce the forces of the molecule, the atom, and the electron to that costless servitude to which it has reduced the old elements of earth and air, fire and water; if man should continue to set free the infinite forces of nature, and attain the control of forces on a cosmic scale, the consequences may be as surprising as the change of water to vapor, of the worm to the butterfly, of radium to electrons.
>
> ("The Rule of Phase Applied to History," in Henry Adams, *The Degradation of the Democratic Dogma*, New York: Macmillan, 1920, p. 109)

While this philosophy of force is obviously a metaphor for the nature of human history, it is remarkably prescient. When Henry Adams died in 1918, he thought his prediction for the human future might be literally verified.

Further reading

Adams, Henry. *The History of the United States during the Administrations of Thomas Jefferson and James Madison*. New York: Charles Scribner's Sons, 1890–1.

—— *Mont-Saint Michel and Chartres*, with an introduction by Ralph Adams Cram. Boston, MA: Houghton Mifflin, 1913.

—— "The Rule of Phase Applied to History" in *The Degradation of the Democratic Dogma*, with an introduction by Brooks Adams. New York: Macmillan, 1920.

The Education of Henry Adams, An Autobiography, with a new introduction by D.W. Brogan. Boston, MA: Houghton Mifflin, 1961.

Contosta, David R. and Muccigrosso, Robert (eds) *Henry Adams and his World*. Philadelphia, PA: American Philosophical Society, 1993.

JOSEPH BRENT

ADAPTATION

Adaptation is a process by which characteristics of an evolving agent change in order to accommodate and exploit regular features of its ongoing activities. Adaptation processes are instantiated in a broad range of so-called *complex adaptive systems* (Gell-Mann 1994; Holland 1995). Time scales for such changes depend on the nature of the activities of the evolving agent. The activities of an animal's nervous system adapt within seconds, minutes, or hours to changing environmental conditions. The animal's immune system will adapt in a matter of hours or days to relevant conditions as well. An individual organism as a whole may adapt its habits and behaviors to seasonal changes, or to new social circumstances, on various time scales. A community or business firm or industry may adapt, within weeks, months, or years, to changing economic conditions. A biological species may adapt to widespread environmental changes, typically over long time spans where changes in characteristics of individual organisms eventually become characteristic features of the species as a result of various natural selection pressures. Entire ecosystems may adapt quickly or over the course of millennia to larger global changes.

An "adaptation" may refer to any stable result of an adaptation process. If a process of adaptation led to the reduction of body hair in *Homo sapiens*, e.g. in response to widespread long-term ambient temperature and humidity changes or as a way of combating insect infestation, then reduced body hair is the adaptation that resulted from that adaptation process.

Adaptation is often contrasted with exaptation, where a feature or characteristic has naturally evolved for certain uses and is then co-opted for other uses. Examples include three bones in the jaws of the ancestors of mammals that were exapted into the bones of the middle ear, or the classic theory that birds' feathers were first adapted for the purpose of insulation and later exapted for gliding.

The concept of adaptation had substantial impact on American philosophy (and the whole English-speaking world) in the late nineteenth century following the appearance of Darwin's theory of the evolution of biological species by means of natural selection (1859). In Darwinian biology, adaptation is a process by which a species maintains and perhaps improves its fit with an environment in order to remain viable in that environment. Adaptation may be driven by changes in the environment, requiring correlative structural and behavioral alterations or adjustments in the organism. It may also be driven by spontaneous structural and behavioral changes in individual organisms, particularly as such changes affect their viability in relationship to their environment.

This biological conception of adaptation played a formative role in Dewey's conception of experience as an adaptive process (1934), as it did in Mead's notion of "the act," social or otherwise (1938). The notion of adaptation is a crucial component of a pragmatist emphasis on the formation and reformation of habits, from Peirce's evolutionary cosmology (1893) to Mead's evolutionary social psychology. As a central element of a Darwinian theory of evolution, where natural selection is presented as a possible alternative to intelligent design, the concept of adaptation has been conceived naturalistically in many strains of Anglo-American philosophy since the latter half of the nineteenth century. The concept of adaptation has also been given theologically friendly treatments by A.N. Whitehead (1929), Charles Hartshorne (1967), and others.

Further reading

Darwin, Charles. *On the Origin of Species by Means of Natural Selection*. London: John Murray, 1859.

Dewey, John. *Art as Experience*. New York: Minton, Balch, 1934. Critical edition reissued as Volume 10 of *The Later Works of John Dewey* with an introduction by Abraham Kaplan. Carbondale, IL: Southern Illinois University Press, 1987.

Gell-Mann, Murray. *The Quark and the Jaguar: Adventures in the Simple and the Complex*. New York: W.H. Freeman, 1994.

Hartshorne, C. *A Natural Theology for our Time*. La Salle, IL: Open Court, 1967.

Holland, John H. *Hidden Order: How Adaptation Builds Complexity*. New York: Basic Books, 1995.

Mead, George Herbert. *The Philosophy of the Act*, edited with an introduction by Charles W. Morris. Chicago, IL: University of Chicago Press, 1938.

Peirce, Charles S. "Evolutionary Love," *Monist* 3 (1893): 176–200. Reprinted in *The Essential Peirce Vol. 1*, ed.

Nathan Houser and Christian Kloesel. Bloomington, IN: Indiana University Press, 1992, Ch. 25.
Whitehead, A.N. *Process and Reality.* New York: Macmillan, 1929.

TOM BURKE

ADDAMS AND HULL-HOUSE, JANE

During her lifetime (1860–1935), Jane Addams was the model of an engaged intellectual: a local and international scholar, sociologist, and activist for social justice. That she was the first woman to win the Nobel Peace Prize (1931) indicates the degree to which she was truly a "world citizen" – before the term came into vogue, and before women were considered capable of contributing much to either American politics or scholarship. Though pragmatism and American philosophy encourage interdisciplinary approaches, Addams's work spans an unusually broad range and grounds theoretical and applied projects in ethics, social/political philosophy, epistemology, philosophy of education, and aesthetics. She has had a sizeable interdisciplinary impact in sociology and education departments, and in academic programs such as American studies, multicultural and ethnic studies, peace studies, urban studies, women's studies, and labor studies. Coupled with her prolific range of publishing and extensive speaking, these contributions cement her place as a founder of classical American philosophy alongside Emerson, Peirce, James, Royce, Santayana, Locke, Dewey, and Mead – and as a co-founder specifically of the Chicago School of pragmatism. James, Dewey, and Mead studied, responded to, or drew on her work; William Isaac Thomas and social scientists engaged with the budding discipline of sociology at the University of Chicago studied Addams's Hull-House theories and practices with keen interest.

Addams's contributions are deeply linked to the context in which she lived and worked. In 1889, she co-founded (with Ellen Gates Starr) Chicago's Hull-House settlement house in an impoverished community of recent immigrants. Hull-House faced slum conditions of rapid industrialization, health and child labor issues with no social aid. The mission of Hull-House was to co-operatively transform the impoverished physical surroundings and social experiences of the immigrant population, and to enable residents to actively participate in local civic life and national democracy. Responding to such demanding needs, Addams furthered pragmatist thought and practice in ways unlikely to be explored by her academic colleagues, who were engaged primarily in scholarly debates and publishing. Addams's work at Hull House is often credited with shaping the then-developing discipline of sociology itself, especially at the University of Chicago. Some academicians, especially in sociology and philosophy, realized Hull-House was a real-time laboratory for ideas being hotly debated in academia. Addams and her academic colleagues all benefited from Hull-House–academia connections, but the different focus of Addams's work enabled her to enrich pragmatism with original contributions.

One significant difference lay in who was doing the activist and theoretical work of Hull-House. In turn-of-the-century patriarchal America, some of the first mid-to upper-class American college-educated women like Addams and Starr found in the settlement movement a rare chance to work in the public arena (even if in a still-feminized and devalued domestic, nurturing capacity). As such, these women brought both women's voices and concerns of those in urban slum settings into their practices and theory. It quickly became clear at Hull-House that a methodology of its leaders "solving" a community problem by applying some pre-formatted theory from top down was simply unproductive; the very definition of what constituted a problem, and what might constitute workable solutions, needed to arise from the context and community itself. Herein lies one of Addams's overarching contributions to pragmatism: she and her colleagues developed *in practice* the model of transactional experimentation mostly theorized by other pragmatists.

Some of the main pragmatist insights guiding Addams's projects were these: the epistemological insight that knowledge arises from experience, needs repeated testing in practice, and subsequently transforms experience; the ethical insight that values combine both personal and social dimensions; the political view that a democracy weds individual with collective empowerment, and that a robust one includes a plurality of viewpoints with which to improve itself; a view of business and labor that focused on the whole person (rather than a mechanical laborer) in a time of dehumanizing industrialism; and the aesthetic view that creative engagement was a human necessity for civic, cultural, and humanitarian engagement.

In the Hull-House laboratory, these blossomed into new pragmatist insights. The pragmatist focus on developing theory from practice, and not the other way around, led to a bottom-up approach that incorporated new voices: Addams interwove the experiences of ethnic minorities, women, and the working classes into Hull-House practices and into pragmatism itself. Once experiences of these groups were taken seriously, Addams was able to build and show a real-world pragmatist critique of laissez-faire capitalism that other pragmatists had treated more abstractly. Pragmatists had likewise written much about personhood – a relational self with a social and civic dimension, especially Dewey's work on education as a birthright: in the Hull-House setting, Addams developed her view that full selfhood also requires the ability for democratic participation. The traditional pragmatist focus on experimentation, fallibilism, and viewing mistakes as productive led Addams in the Hull-House setting to develop a richer account of the collective dimensions of knowing – her concepts of "social intelligence" and "habits of social sympathy" were developed based on Hull-House evidence. She developed a pragmatist ethical analysis of charity and argued for reciprocity in charitable relations, critiquing the way that what often passes for "charity" is in fact a relation between unequally situated parties that often denies full personhood to the recipients.

The Hull-House setting allowed Addams and her colleagues to develop these ideas in a real-time setting, thereby invigorating pragmatism in new and substantial ways. Though her work is still occasionally framed as a sideline of philosophy and as an add-on to the main lineage of pragmatism, interest in her work has been blossoming steadily for the last quarter-century. One hopes the trend continues: at the turn of this century, many now find her work on citizenship, social justice, multiculturalism, and pluralism within a democracy to be particularly insightful and resonate anew.

Further reading

Addams, Jane. *The Second Twenty Years at Hull House.* New York: Macmillan, 1930.

—— *Twenty Years at Hull-House.* New York: Penguin Group, 1981 [1910].

—— *Democracy and Social Ethics.* Urbana, IL: University of Illinois Press, 2002 [1902].

—— *The Long Road of Woman's Memory.* Urbana, IL: University of Illinois Press, 2002 [1916].

Brown, Victoria Bissell. *The Education of Jane Addams.* Philadelphia, PA: University of Pennsylvania Press, 2003.

Elshtain, Jean Bethke. *The Jane Addams Reader.* New York: Basic Books, 2002.

Knight, Louise. *Citizen: Jane Addams and the Struggle for Democracy.* Chicago, IL: University of Chicago Press, 2006.

Stebner, Eleanor J. *The Women of Hull House: A Study in Spirituality, Vocation, and Friendship.* Albany, NY: SUNY Press, 1997.

L. RYAN MUSGRAVE

ADJUSTMENT

One of the most conspicuous features of the European settlement of North America was the need to adjust tools and methods to novel environmental conditions. In practice, the distinction between what worked and what did not was often vital. For the Puritans, what worked was thought to do so because of divine ordination. For the Transcendentalists of a later generation, "self-reliance" meant adjustment to what is experienced as personal instead of what is demanded by religious dogma or tradition.

With the publication of Darwin's *Origin of Species* in 1859 and developments in experimental psychology during the last decades of the nineteenth century, the term "adjustment," and its cognate "adaptation," took on added significance. Charles Peirce, for example, constructed statistically based proofs of adaptation through natural selection and compared human inventions to the way that nature "proceeds by similar experimentation to adapt a stock of animals or plants precisely to its environment." He related adjustment or adaptation to what he termed the logic of abduction, or hypothesis.

For his part, Josiah Royce wrote of adjustment in several senses: a technological sense in which tools (and ideas as tools) must be adjusted to their ends; a biological sense in which organisms, including the human organism, adjust to the stimuli of their environment; and a more strictly psychological sense in which consciousness is the result of interrupted adjustment to an environment.

For William James, adjustment or adaptation was central to the pragmatic method. He wrote of adaptation in terms of the experimental procedures required to ascertain the truth of a statement, such procedures "adapting" the knower to the situation just in case they "work."

In George Herbert Mead's highly complex account of adjustment, self-consciousness and personality are results of the ability to adjust to one's own behavior as if it were viewed from the perspective of another.

While acknowledging that the terms "accommodation," "adaptation," and "adjustment" are frequently treated as synonyms, John Dewey nevertheless argued that the attitudes they represent are quite different. Some occasions call for *accommodation* to an environment, while others call for *alteration* of aspects of an environment. But when accommodation and alteration are in harmony, Dewey wrote, then *adjustment* has taken place. For Dewey, adjustment is thus treated as the successful outcome of experimental inquiry.

Further reading

Dewey, John. *A Common Faith: The Collected Works of John Dewey: The Later Works, Vol. 9: 1925–1953*, ed. Jo Ann Boydston. Carbondale, IL: Southern Illinois University Press, 1986.

James, William. *Meaning of Truth*, in *The Works of William James: The Meaning of Truth*, ed. Frederick Burkhardt and Fredson Bowers. Cambridge, MA: Harvard University Press, 1975.

Mead, George Herbert. *Selected Writings*, ed. Andrew J. Reck. New York: Bobbs-Merrill, 1964.

Royce, Josiah. *Studies of Good and Evil*. New York: Kessinger, 2003.

LARRY A. HICKMAN

ADLER, FELIX

Felix Adler (1851–1933) was a philosophical idealist, social reformer, and institution builder. Born in Germany, Adler emigrated to the United States with his family when he was five. His father eventually became a prominent Reform rabbi in New York City. Adler was educated at Columbia College, graduating in 1870, and the University of Heidelberg, where he was attracted to "neo-Kantian idealism and … its critique of religion" (Radest 1969: 16).

After teaching for three years at Cornell University, Adler and some prominent New York citizens organized the Society for Ethical Culture in 1876. The organization's work included a weekly platform address, social reform efforts, and the establishment of well-regarded schools.

Adler, as noted above, was a philosophical idealist, albeit a pluralistic one. From 1902 until his death in 1933, he was Professor of Social and Political Ethics in the Department of Philosophy at Columbia University. "For a generation of Columbia students," wrote John Herman Randall, Jr. Adler "emphasized the inadequacies and superficialities of an uncritical and complacent 'liberal' religion, teaching the essence" of the neo-orthodoxy that was to develop in the 1930s but without the "Christian or Reformation limitations." He also, continued Randall, "socialized the Kantian ethic, reconstructing the moral ideal into a democratic and social form not too alien to that of Dewey, with whom he cooperated in many a matter of practical policy" (1957: 121). Indeed, many of the second generation of Ethical Culture leaders aligned themselves with Dewey's philosophy and approach to religion.

Further reading

Radest, Howard B. *Toward Common Ground: The Story of the Ethical Cultural Societies in the United States*. New York: Frederick Ungar, 1969.

Randall, John Herman, Jr. "The Department of Philosophy" in *A History of the Faculty of Philosophy: Columbia University*, ed. Jacques Barzun. New York: Columbia University Press, 1957, pp. 102–67.

MICHAEL ELDRIDGE

AESTHETICS

A noteworthy quality of American thought from shortly after the Revolution to the present is a commitment to the pervasiveness and importance of aesthetic qualities and experience. It is a trait shared with writings in European continental thought after Romanticism influenced by Friedrich Nietzsche and Martin Heidegger, especially phenomenology, French poststructuralism, and postmodernism. This emphasis on aesthetic experience emerges from a critical perspective toward the abstraction of scientific knowledge and the destructive influences of technological rationality, emphasizing lived experience. John Dewey (1859–1952) describes the aesthetic, qualitative side of experience by saying that art is the culmination of nature, because it is charged with meanings capable of immediately enjoyed possession; science is its handmaiden (Dewey, *Experience and Nature* 358).

Though he says this of art, Dewey's emphasis is on immediately enjoyed meanings and qualities. We live in a qualitative world. We experience things in their qualitative determinations (Dewey, *Qualitative Thought* 176). With many of his contemporaries, he understands these to be aesthetic. The qualitative side of felt experience is aesthetic, and is inseparable from ethics and truth. Indeed, the continuous relation between knowledge and feeling in experience characterizes the pervasiveness of aesthetic qualities far beyond the culminating achievements of art.

A common view of the American tradition, closely linked with pragmatism as a term, emphasizes the relation between belief and practice. William James's definition of pragmatism has become iconic: to attain clearness in thought of an object we need only consider its practical effects (James, *Pragmatism* 43), our sensations and reactions. Perfect clearness and practical effects appear to be as far from aesthetic qualities and experience as possible. Yet when we recall James's emphasis on feelings and effects both in the will to believe – faith, optimism, commitment – and on the sensible and corporeal side of experience, it is credible to understand the terms of this definition in ways that are as aesthetic as they are logical and practical. Knowledge, practice, and value (ethical, aesthetic, spiritual) compose the continuity and interrelational field of experience. Such a view is opposed in principle to the modern academic view of the separation of faculties and of disciplines. American thought historically is fundamentally interdisciplinary, in this way aesthetic. Aesthetic experience cannot be separated from logic, epistemology, and practice; moreover, this relationality is much closer to aesthetic qualitativeness than to logical structure.

Many factors contributed to this aesthetic side of American thought. One is the historical relationship of colonial experience to nature, largely an aesthetic experience in Ralph Waldo Emerson (1803–82) and Henry David Thoreau (1817–62). Another is the related importance of Romanticism, which in Emerson and Thoreau presented humanity and nature in a relationship known best to poets and other artists. In "The Poet," Emerson describes the three children of the universe as the love of truth, the love of good, and the love of beauty. As sayer and namer, the poet represents beauty, where beauty is the creator of the universe. A third factor, also visible here, is the sense of continuity between humanity and nature, mind and body, truth and beauty. Nature and experience were understood as richly continuous and interpenetrating fields, filled with aesthetic qualities of unity, wholeness, and relationality, reflecting the inadequacy of separating aesthetics from knowledge, truth, and science as well as other spheres of value.

A fourth among many other factors was the emphasis upon affect and feeling, linking mind and body, subjectivity and objectivity, expressing the importance of felt qualities in the rich tapestry of human experience, individual and collective. Art and aesthetics responded to these felt qualities far more directly than did logic and science, though it was central to most American thought of this period that science and logic be themselves understood in terms of felt qualities, thereby aesthetic as well as practical. The practical side of American pragmatism rests on the qualitativeness of experience.

A striking example of this can be found in Charles Sanders Peirce (1839–1914), whose importance for American philosophy for many years lay in logic and the founding of pragmatism (or pragmaticism). Internationally, Peirce became famous for his theory of signs, and again among the three functions of signs are those that express the qualitativeness of felt experience. Peirce's semiotics repeated the structure of his phenomenology, where firstness is qualitativeness, secondness is immediacy or facticity, and thirdness is mediation or relationality. Quality, fact, and relation are the universal characteristics of thought, experience, and the world, and of all signs and meanings as well.

In an epistemological context, these express conditions of knowledge and truth, and play a role in inquiry. Yet they are far more recognizable as aesthetic categories – and again, in Peirce, it is impossible to separate the aesthetic from the logical. Experience is qualitative, whether epistemological, practical, or aesthetic, as it is factical and relational. Perhaps more important, the term that brings these together in Peirce – habit – is no more logical than it is aesthetic, and indeed, relation, connection, linkage are all aesthetic activities.

Peirce is explicit about the pervasiveness and also the primacy of aesthetics, both in the ways in which firstness as presence is given before secondness and thirdness, and in the way in which aesthetic value is in some way final. Normative science in general considers the conformity of things to ends, aesthetics considers ends that embody qualities of feeling, ethics ends that lie in action, and logic ends of representation (Peirce, *Essential Peirce* 2.200). Because aesthetics concerns what is admirable without any ulterior reason, ethics must appeal to aesthetics, and logic must appeal to ethics (Peirce, *Collected Papers* 1.191). Particularly striking in this view is that in a world of relations, laws, and signs, the final goodness, value, or quality of a meaning or truth, of anything whatever, lies in its immediacy and presentness. Aesthetic value is qualitatively final.

A second point worth noting is that the meaning of "aesthetic" here has relatively little to do with art (though art has relatively more to do with it) and more to do with the structure of experience. Aesthetic quality pertains to experience without ulterior conditions: causes, outcomes, structural expectations.

Such a view of aesthetic experience as qualitative, affective, corporeal, and relational, to which logic and science, ethics and practice, and even art answer, was a shared theme across almost two centuries of American thought, from the beginning of the nineteenth till the end of the twentieth century. Even William James, who wrote little explicitly on aesthetics and art, shared this powerful image of the richness and complexity of qualitative experience. In his hands, such experiences embodied the force of beliefs he classified largely as practical, where truth and knowledge carry practical force. His understanding of the will to believe was expressed primarily in spiritual terms. Even so, he does not neglect art and aesthetics when he speaks of affects and feelings, praising their ambiguities (James, *Essays in Radical Empiricism* 142–3).

And in speaking of living in the midst of certain moral and spiritual beliefs, he describes the relation of feelings to the world as a key that fits – an aesthetic as well as a moral image.

In the same period of American philosophy, Dewey and George Santayana (1863–1952) were the most explicitly attentive to aesthetics and art. Santayana was perhaps most aligned with aesthetics, and wrote about it repeatedly, in *The Sense of Beauty* (1953) and *Reason in Art* (1905), but also in *The Realm of Essence* (1927). Throughout these works, quality and feeling were interrelated in such a way that the lines of demarcation that divided categories of understanding and reflection no longer held.

Santayana was a figure like Emerson, widely respected as a philosopher while known and admired as a poet and essayist as well as a literary critic. Many of his writings were directly on art and aesthetics, some more oblique though no less penetrating. He begins *The Sense of Beauty* with an insight that characterizes the sweep of aesthetics in experience far beyond the realm of art and in philosophy: the sense of beauty has a more important place in life than aesthetic theory has ever taken in philosophy, and the fine arts are not the only spheres in which human beings show their susceptibility to beauty (Santayana, *Sense of Beauty* 5).

In these few words, Santayana emphasizes the pervasiveness of aesthetics and beauty, their importance in art and far beyond art, their experiential links with other realms of life and experience, the importance of feeling, and his own distinctive emphasis on aesthetic contemplation. In all these qualities save the last, Santayana shared many perspectives toward art and beauty with his American contemporaries, especially the reach of beauty throughout life and experience, practical and intensely felt. In this way, feelings and experiences were neither separated from reflection and understanding nor subordinated to them in the flow of lived experience. Like Peirce, if more strongly, Santayana can say that "all values are in one sense aesthetic" (32); they "make us happy only in contemplation" (33), they are "the only pure and positive values in life" (33).

For Santayana, beauty is pleasure objectified, a quality of things (51). It belongs to the beautiful object and the world, though it is given in felt experience. Qualities are not relegated to private or subjective experience, but belong as much to things as to us. This is an ongoing theme in American thought, expressed by Dewey as that "*Things* are beautiful and ugly, lovely and hateful, dull and illuminated, attractive and repulsive. Stir and thrill in us is as much theirs as is length, breadth, and thickness" (Dewey, *Experience and Nature* 108). Aesthetic qualities belong to things because experience does not divide subject from object, mind from body, humanity from world. Things are treated, used, acted upon and with, enjoyed and endured. They are things *had* before they are known (21).

Santayana's distinctive perspective lay in the purity of a contemplation that has always played a role in aesthetic experience, from Plato through Kant and later, but that did not match the practical and experiential side of American pragmatism – a side not absent from Santayana. Even so, his sense of the immediacy and purity of aesthetic quality was present not only in relation to beauty and art, but in his metaphysical account of the realms of being: essence, matter, truth, spirit. The first, the realm of essence, is that of quality, akin to Peirce's firstness and to Whitehead's eternal objects. First of all the world and experience is composed of qualities, entirely complete in themselves and immediately intuitable as such (Santayana, *Realm of Essence* 4.18).

Such an emphasis on immediately intuited qualities always turns toward the aesthetic. In Santayana's lovely language, he reveals a consummate sensitivity to beauty that is often lacking in his contemporaries. It is an indefinable quality in virtue of a special emotion, half wonder, half love, which is felt in its presence. The most material thing, in so far as it is felt to be beautiful, is instantly immaterialized, raised above external personal relations, concentrated and deepened (8). The material world is filled with beauty, with essence, beauty is the poetry of the world as essences are concentrated, deepened, a world of revelation. Such a view is frequently associated with NeoPlatonism, the world in its essential beauties, spread throughout our experiences in feelings, immediate and complete in themselves.

This extraordinary affinity with felt immediacy and contemplative quality allowed Santayana to speak of reason in art in a way that has always been regarded as anomalous in a philosophical tradition that begins with the exile of the poets in Plato's *Republic*. In most of the American tradition, but more explicitly in Santayana, reason is as aesthetic as it is scientific (also moral and religious) and art is a culmination of reason as well as of experience. It is so through building works that transcend both instrumentality and contemplation, the humanization and rationalization of objects and experiences (Santayana, *Life of Reason*, "Reason in Art" 301–3).

In this way Santayana expresses a remarkable sense of the sweep of art throughout human social life, far beyond the sense of beauty common in a world that has separated function from beauty, practicality from fine art. The sweep of art is personal, linking body and soul, person to world, but also individual to others and humanity to nature. Moreover, it does so intensely and concretely, tangibly embodying its relations in individuals and works. The role of reason is to embody these relations, the specific role of art to do so materially and sensibly. Art transcends the body beyond the reach of thought, but it does so through the body, its senses and feelings.

Santayana's view bears affinities with Alfred North Whitehead's (1861–1947) both in relation to certain central themes, such as intensity of feeling and essences, and in the cultural sweep and pervasiveness of beauty. Although Whitehead is frequently known for his work in logic and science, aesthetic values permeate his systematic vision. Eternal objects are Whitehead's essences, and he shares Santayana's sense of intuition in both a mathematical and aesthetic sense. He develops a sense of beauty in *Adventures of Ideas* (1933) that begins from a sense of an immediate quality and intuitive value but proceeds to treat it as a higher value than truth, perhaps the highest value in a sensible world even in relation to God. It is the mutual adaptation of the several factors in an occasion of experience, with levels and gradations; there are different gradations and types of beauty (Whitehead, *Adventures of Ideas* 324).

This notion of gradations in beauty is linked with the notion of mutual adaptation to provide a sense of complexity to beauty that Whitehead maintains throughout his work. Actual occasions are drops of experience: individual becomings in the complexity of relations. These relations – to other actual occasions, to the past, social and cosmic, including feelings and qualities – are felt in a unity of becoming that is otherwise inexhaustibly complex. Beauty here rests on a becoming of endless complexity. In relation to feelings – and actual occasions are subjects of feeling, feel or prehend in order to become – beauty is intensity of feeling, and each occasion strives to maximize the intensity of its feelings, the unity in a single act of becoming of an inexhaustible multitude of contrasting feelings, where contrasts are a synthesis of many feelings in one.

This allows Whitehead to speak of the relation between truth and beauty as another contrast, so that where truth is conformation, "Beauty is a wider, and more fundamental, notion than Truth" (341), because it brings into intensely felt unity the multiplicity inherent in becoming. Indeed, a world of multiplicities felt in unified moments of becoming produces both gradations of beauty and a beauty, an aesthetic value, that grows richer as it becomes more complex, building on tensions and diversities within itself. Finite realizations give rise to an infinitude of perfections beyond perfections. These include diverse types and discordances, contributing their richnesses to beauty.

Adventure, the search for new perfections, the becoming of the world, is aesthetic for Whitehead. Individual actual entities or occasions aim at and are fulfilled in intensity of feeling (Whitehead, *Process and Reality* 27). Becoming pervades the universe, and each act of becoming is an aesthetic striving for intensity of feeling, intensity of contrast, toward beauty. This view of intensity of contrast and feeling is developed by Stephen David Ross in *A Theory of Art: Intensity by Contrast* (1983) into a general theory of aesthetics and art.

The major figure in American aesthetics of the period stretching from the early nineteenth century to the mid-twentieth century is Dewey, who not only wrote extensively on art in *Art as Experience* (1934) and the penultimate chapter of *Experience and Nature* (1958 [second edition]), but whose work throughout bears an overarching emphasis on qualities. In *Experience and Nature*, Dewey characterizes two dimensions of experience as means and ends, relations and qualities, where "experience" is a double-barreled word as William James describes it. It includes and joins subject and object together, *what* human beings do and suffer and *how* they act and are acted upon, processes of *experiencing* (Dewey, *Experience and Nature* 8). Such a totality is both reflective and aesthetic.

Reflection is vital for life yet subservient to aesthetic qualities. Means serve qualitative ends. In reflection immediate qualities are dimmed, subordinated to evidence and meaning. Philosophy, like other forms of reflection, takes us away from things in primary experience as they directly act and are enjoyed (19). The question for reflection and practice is whether they render experience more luminous, whether they unify and intensify qualities and feelings, or dull and disrupt them.

Art, then, is both means and ends, charged with immediate meanings and qualities. Dewey describes it as the culmination of nature, with science its handmaiden (358). Where instrumentalities and enjoyments, means and ends, come together experience is fulfilled. This is preeminently true in art.

In *Art as Experience*, Dewey describes experience in general as ongoing and interactive, between a creature and its environing conditions. He compares this with an aesthetic experience, felt as a whole, with its own unifying quality (35), where every successive part flows freely (36). Aesthetic experience is qualitative, unified, complete. This is a view of experience, of what is aesthetic in experience, and of art. It is perhaps worth noting that it is a partial view of art, that many major works throughout the twentieth century have been fragmentary, disruptive, oblique, intentionally disunified, that they were produced to present these and not unified qualities, that such qualities are given to us in experiences that are plural and partial, that there are knowledges they provide and meanings they embody that are very different from the ones Dewey emphasizes. Even so, one might argue that the values they encompass are pervasive, if not their execution, and that they enter into flows of experience in continuous and interactive ways.

The view of art as an experience is the dominating image of *Art and Experience.* Yet in that work Dewey also develops a rich and nuanced sense of art and of aesthetic experiences, closer to a sense of pregnancy with promise and of intensity of feeling, richer and more multiple. In particular, Dewey speaks insightfully and concretely of the medium of a work of art, something neglected in many aesthetic theories. In art, materials are joined with expression deeply and inseparably, constituting a medium of expression (64). Through their medium, works of art compose a language, indeed many languages, for each art has its own medium and its own kinds of expression and communication. "Each medium says something that cannot be uttered as well or as completely in any other tongue" (106).

Dewey understands art to express the highest values, to be more moral than moralities, by keeping alive purposes that transcend familiar habits. He offers little on the ways in which art becomes a consecration of the status quo, fixed in museums, works for the elite, little on the ways in which aesthetics outstrips art in meanings that transcend habit. Yet *Art as Experience* begins and is centered on the principle that art can be empty when it is institutionalized. The actual work of art is what it produces in experience; when it is isolated from ongoing experience it loses its aesthetic qualities.

In speaking of the expressiveness of works of art as language, Dewey foreshadows the linguistic turn, which in many ways marks the transformations brought to aesthetics in American thought after the middle of the twentieth century. From mid-century onward, language and expression became central formative as well as expressive conditions of aesthetics and art. On the one side, art was understood as language. On the other side, the fluidity of language and its continuities with experience and the world maintained and extended the sense of inseparability among them, contributing to the conviction that the expressiveness of art permeates human experience and the natural world.

Among the American authors whose later work contributed to a pervasive and enduring sense of the vitality and significance of art and aesthetic experience was Justus Buchler (1914–91), whose metaphysics of natural complexes included a theory of poetry as query, extending the notion of inquiry into a plurality of modes of judgment, rooted in ontological parity – the sense that no form of existence is primary. Poetry can build complexes that evoke questioning with a freedom unmatched by any other spheres of language (Buchler, *Main of Light* 126–7). Art, especially poetry, explores the world by inventing and building new orders of complexes, new ways of experiencing and judging.

Other authors were Kenneth Burke (1897–1995), known for his performative, rhetorical, and social theory of literature and action; Stanley Cavell (1926–), whose readings of aesthetics and film influence his understanding and practice of philosophy; Arthur Danto (1924–), art critic of *The Nation* for many years and known for a deep understanding of how profoundly twentieth-century artists have transformed the meaning of art, so that ideas of art and aesthetic experience are now always fully in question; Nelson Goodman (1906–98), whose *Languages of Art* and *Ways of Worldmaking* offered an influential view of art as language; Albert Hofstadter (1911–89), who contributed to aesthetic theory in the United States especially in translating Heidegger and bringing his work on art and poetry into prominence; Susanne Langer (1895–1985), whose *Philosophy in a New Key* (1957) and *Feeling and Form* (1953) were influential in aesthetics for a generation, offering a systematic theory of the arts as symbolic forms of sentience; Joseph Margolis (1924–), who sees himself as engaged with pragmatism's future in his many writings on psychology and art; Craig Owens (1951–90), art critic and contemporary culture theorist; Stephen Pepper (1891–1972), whose notion of a consummatory field of aesthetic experience built on Dewey's theory of an experience; Richard Rorty (1931–), famous for his rejection of epistemological philosophy and defense of pragmatism, who suggests that art and literature may replace the authoritarian claims of philosophy in a liberal democracy; Stephen David Ross (1935–), whose earlier writings extend the scope of pragmatism in education, science, literature, ethics, and art from Dewey through Buchler to Whitehead (*Literature and Philosophy* and especially *A Theory of Art: Inexhaustibility by Contrast*), and whose later writings link the American tradition with European continental philosophy, with an emphasis on twentieth-century art and aesthetics as political resistances and intellectual interventions (*The Gift of Beauty* and *The World as Aesthetic Phenomenon*); Paul Weiss (1901–2002), whose systematic writings on metaphysics and religion included works on art; Richard Wollheim (1923–83), who wrote extensively on Freud and psychoanalysis and perceptively on art from a psychoanalytic point of view; and many others.

One of the ways in which American aesthetics can be characterized over the past two centuries to the present is that in the midst of forceful criticisms of industrialization and academicization, it sustained the conviction that experience is filled with radiant fulfillments and enchanted qualities.

Further reading

Buchler, Justus. *The Main of Light: On the Concept of Poetry.* New York: Oxford University Press, 1974.

Cavell, Stanley. *The World Viewed: Reflections on the Ontology of Film*, enlarged edition. Cambridge, MA: Harvard University Press, 1979.

Danto, Arthur. *The Philosophical Disenfranchisement of Art*. New York: Columbia University Press, 1986.

Dewey, John. *Art and Experience*. New York: Putnam, 1934.

Emerson, Ralph Waldo. "The Poet" in *The Essays of Ralph Waldo Emerson (Collected Works of Ralph Waldo Emerson)*, reprint edition. Cambridge, MA: Belknap Press, 1979.

Goodman, Nelson. *Languages of Art: An Approach to a Theory of Symbols*, second edition. Indianapolis, IN: Hackett, 1976.

Hofstadter, Albert. *Agony and Epitaph; Man, his Art, and his Poetry.* New York: George Braziller, 1970.

Langer, Susanne Katherina Knauth. *Philosophy in a New Key: A Study in the Symbolism of Reason, Rite, and Art.* Cambridge, MA: Harvard University Press, 1957.

Margolis, Joseph. *Art and Philosophy.* Atlantic Highlands, NJ: Humanities Press; Hassocks: Harvester Press, 1980.

Pepper, Stephen Coburn. *The Work of Art*. Bloomington, IN: Indiana University Press, 1955.

Rorty, Richard. *Consequences of Pragmatism*. Minneapolis, MN: University of Minnesota Press, 1982.

Ross, Stephen David. *The Gift of Beauty: The Good as Art.* Albany, NY: State University of New York Press, 1996.

Santayana, George. *The Sense of Beauty: Being the Outlines of Aesthetic Theory.* New York: Modern Library, 1953.

Weiss, Paul. *The World of Art*. Carbondale, IL: Southern Illinois University Press, 1961.

Wollheim, Richard. *Art and its Objects: with Six Supplementary Essays.* New York: Cambridge University Press, 1980.

STEPHEN DAVID ROSS

AFRICAN AMERICAN PHILOSOPHY

When scholars speak of African American philosophy it is not exactly clear to what they are referring. With so few African American philosophers, and even fewer courses offered at American universities in the history of African American philosophy, it is almost impossible to isolate a specific figure or time period that uniquely spawned African American thought. The overall marginalization of African American thought has all but erased its discussion from mainstream philosophical discourse; at best it is given the title of "applied philosophy" to denote its lack of philosophical rigor (Shelby 2005: 13). Despite the contemporary academic climate, African American philosophy has shared an intellectual history that has been one facet of a larger diasporic reality for Africans displaced by the Atlantic slave trade. Historically, African American philosophy revolved around the role Africa played in the imagination, intellect, and identity of African people in the United States. However, most contemporary academic conversations often refer to African American philosophy as a tradition of philosophic thought in "Black" America. It is largely agreed upon by African Americans working on African American philosophy that African American philosophy deals with the experience, identity, and spirituality of African American people. In this regard African American philosophy has largely been defined on the basis of problems encountered by African Americans. In "Philosophy and the Afro-American Experience," Cornel West identifies

> The two basic challenges presently confronting Afro-Americans are those of self-image and self-determination. The former is the perennial human attempt to define who and what one is, the sempiternal issue of self-identity; the latter is the political struggle to gain significant control over the major institutions that regulate people's lives. These challenges are abstractly distinguishable, yet concretely inseparable. In other words, culture and politics must always be viewed in close relation to each other. The major function of Afro-American philosophy is to reshape the contours of Afro-American history and provide a new self-understanding of the Afro-American experience which suggests desirable guidelines for action in the present. Afro-American philosophy attempts to make theoretically explicit what is implicit in Afro-American history to describe and demystify the cultural and social practices in this history and offer certain solutions to urgent problems besetting Afro-Americans.
>
> (2006: 11)

The very question of "what is African American philosophy" burdens the inquirer not only with the various traditions of interpretation in African American thought and the recurrent problem of race, but also the historiography of the anti-Black context in which Black philosophers wrote. While it is certain that African American philosophy has its root in the diasporic realities of African peoples throughout the Caribbean and the African continent, most mainstream African American authors choose to deal with intellectual traditions accepted by continental or American philosophical traditions in the United States. This tendency aims at developing a canon of African American thought which seeks to converse with white intellectual traditions in the United States, but fails to read African American thought as an extension of the larger Africana experience that was historically rooted in a Pan-African identity.

Reading the history of African American philosophy

African American philosophy was the outgrowth of African culture meeting and actively resisting the anti-Black racism of American slavery. The harshness of slavery and the brute dehumanization of African people brought to America demanded strategies and spiritual insights to cope with the social climate of America.

> In the long history of human bondage, it was only the black slaves in the United States who created a genre of literature that at once testified against their captors and bore witness to the urge of every black slave to be free and literate.
>
> (Gates 1987: ix)

Slave narratives "not only provide an excellent account of the slave experience, they also show that the authors engaged in speculation about the moral implication of slavery" (McGary and Lawson 1992: xxi). These narratives exposed not only the contradiction of white Americans who enslaved them but "the metaphysical system drawn upon to justify their enslavement" (Gates 1987: ix). Slave narratives expressed the collective experience of those enslaved under the "peculiar institution" (Gates 1987), as "a reflection upon social history" (McGary and Lawson 1992: xxi). There is a traceable lineage of African American thought from 1760 to the present (Gates 1987) based not only on the desire for freedom, but the "discussion and speculation on such concepts of oppression, paternalism, resistance, political obligation, citizenship and forgiveness" (McGary and Lawson 1992).

In the early 1800s another form of African American thought took up the religious language of Christianity to argue against both slavery and the genocidal tendencies of people from Europe. The publication of both the *Ethiopian Manifesto* by Robert Alexander Young and David Walker's *Appeal to the Colored Citizens of the World* in 1829 signaled a historic development in African American philosophy. These authors sought to reclaim not only a cultural continuity with Africa, but established the valorization of African people through the historic African (Black) civilizations of Ethiopia and Egypt. The primary concern of this time period resided in the concern for a "general union" of the race and the defense of this union by violence if necessary. The articulation of an African cultural union, what has now been established as the African Diaspora, though criticized by Walker's close friend Maria W. Stewart, laid the intellectual foundations for the conceptual categorization of African American thought in the years to follow.

In the mid-1800s, a conceptual categorization emerged that would forever change the landscape of African American thought. Harold Cruse remarked in 1967 that "it can be seen that the present day conflict within the Negro ethnic group, between integrationist and separatists, has its origins in the historical arguments between personalities such as Fredrick Douglass and Martin R. Delaney." This division in ideology marks the divide between Africanists and Americanist (Carruthers 1999: 174). African American thought from this point on has concentrated not only on the union of African Americans but on whether or not African Americans belong in the United States or Africa. Martin Delaney argues in his *Principia of Ethnology: The Origin of Races and Color, with an Archeological Compendium of Ethiopian and Egyptian Civilization* (1879), "The Political Destiny of the Colored Race" (1854), and *The Condition, Elevation, Emigration, and Destiny of the Colored People of the United States, Politically Considered* (1852) for a divine origin of races created by God and divinely motivated to return to Africa – the birthplace of civilization. This view contrasts Fredrick Douglass' Americanist view which holds "the struggle for African American social equality amounts to a demand for full citizenship" (Lott 2002: 100). Douglass believed that America was the land of African Americans. From his charges laid at the feet of African people in America in 1848 in a speech called the "Address to the Colored People of the United States" to his reflects on "The Constitution of the United States: Is it

Pro-Slavery or Anti-Slavery?" in 1860, Douglass maintained his belief that African Americans improve themselves through social elevation. Douglass genuinely believed that African Americans were citizens of the United States included in the Constitution and able to achieve social equality through the mastering of trades.

At the end of the nineteenth century there was an explosion of African American intellectual thought that carried on throughout the mid-twentieth century. These intellectuals focused on the meaning of race and the role that meaning played in what came to be known as Pan-Africanism. In 1891, Alexander Crummell wrote an essay entitled "The Race-Problem in America" (1969) in *Africa and America* that says "races, like families, are the organisms and the ordinance of God" (46). Crummell thought that races held specific tendencies and traditions of civilization. W.E.B. DuBois would take up this tradition in his famous essay entitled "The Conservation of Races" (1897) in arguing that a race is "a vast family of human beings, generally of common blood and language, always of common history, traditions and impulses, who are both voluntarily and involuntarily striving together for the accomplishment of certain more or less vividly conceived ideals of life" (485). While the later DuBois was most certainly a Pan-Africanist, the earlier DuBois championed the idea of "The Talented Tenth" and supported more of an integrationist strategy. DuBois' integrationist strategy made him a target of criticism from both Booker T. Washington and Marcus Garvey. Booker T. Washington is considered an accommodationist by some (Lott 2002: 101) and a racial realist by others (Bell 1996). Washington advocated a political strategy of self-reliance, which demanded African Americans take up vocational labor over the liberal arts training advocated by DuBois. Washington did not believe that white Americans would actually give African Americans equality, so Blacks had to make whites dependent on their labor and skills. Garvey, a self-proclaimed follower of Washington, also believed that equality and freedom in the United States was not possible. Garvey became the leader of the largest Pan-African movement in African American history. He advocated a Pan-African nationalism that maintained that African Americans were a beautiful and civilized people whose home was in Africa.

> The time has come for the Negro to forget and cast behind him his hero worship and adoration of other races, and to start immediately to create and emulate heroes of his own. We must canonize our own saints, create our own martyrs and elevate to positions of fame and honor black men and women who have made their distinct contributions to our racial history.
>
> (Garvey 1986: 415–16)

Reading the history of African American philosophy achieves this end. It reveals the creation and reconstruction of diasporic traditions in service of the Black racial legacy.

The process of reconstructing Africans' stolen legacy is a point of contention among the various African American philosophical traditions. Ultimately, the understanding and definition of African American philosophy changes, based on the tradition of interpretation one follows; as do the answers to questions initially raised by Cornel West concerning self-image, self determination and the solutions to the problems of African Americans.

Traditions of interpretation

In recent years, African American scholars in philosophy have positioned themselves against essentialist or biological accounts of race in African American thought and culture. This position is called anti-essentialism. Many prominent scholars like Cornel West and Tommie Shelby champion a humanist rendering of African American philosophy that places African American thought and political theory under the rubric of a larger human goal. Largely influenced by the American pragmatist tradition, Cornel West aims for an understanding of African American philosophy as a philosophical tradition that takes part in the larger role of community building and a multicultural democratic vision. This view of African American philosophy is perhaps the most dominant version taught in American universities. African American philosophy is understood then to be not only "the interpretation of Afro-American history, highlighting the cultural heritage and political struggles, which provides desirable norms that should regulate responses to particular challenges presently confronting Afro-Americans" but also "the application of the philosophical techniques of interpretation and justification to the Afro-American experience" (West 2006). Shelby's definition is almost synonymous to West's. He (Shelby) defines African American philosophy as the application of "the traditional analytical and critical tools of philosophy to central problems within Black political thought" (2005: 13). In contrast to his own humanist tradition, West (2006) identifies three other viable traditions of African American philosophy: (1) the vitalist, (2) the rationalist and (3) the existential.

The vitalist tradition "lauds the uniqueness of Afro-American culture and personality" (West 2006: 12). West distinguishes between a strong vitalism which makes ontological claims about African American superiority and genetic superiority and weak vitalism which argues that African Americans stand above other groups because of the values and practices they hold. This description would be applicable to Black nationalists who believe "Blackness" speaks to a cultural superiority and Afrocentrists who maintain that African Americans are nothing more than Africans in America who share a common culture or worldview based on communal values and spirituality.

The rationalist tradition "considers African American culture and personality to be pathological; it assumes that African Americans have an inferiority specifically to white Americans" (18). The strong rationalist argument would hold that African Americans are genetically inferior to other racial groups, while the weak rationalist argument would say that "African Americans stand below other racial groups because of certain values, modes of behavior or defects acquired from their endurance of political oppression, social degradation and economic exploitation" (13). The early works of E. Franklin Frazier single-handedly defined weak rationalism for West (19), because Frazier concentrates on the cultural depravity of African American culture by labeling it superstitious, ignorant and full of self-hatred. The contemporary champion of the weak rationalist view is John McWhorter whose 2001 book entitled *Losing the Race: Self Sabotage in Black America* argues that African Americans' reliance on cultural myths, language (Ebonics) and their historic distrust of white society doom them to a culture of failure.

The existential tradition is seen by West to be "restrictive, constraining and confining (13). West argues that the "existential response to the challenge of self-image and self-determination is this: a candid acceptance of personal marginality to both Afro-American culture and American society plus moral sermonizing to all Americans" (2006: 23) which fails to contribute to political struggles outside the realm of individuality. The most noted figure in this tradition is Lewis Gordon. While Gordon holds that existential thought is the impetus behind the revolt and resistance in African American culture, he also maintains that an existential phenomenology of "Blackness" reveals tools to deal with the social context of anti-Black racism.

The most serious challenge to the humanist tradition is the Afro-centrist/nationalist tradition. African-centered thought criticizes West's conceptualization of African American philosophy because it "evades African nationalism in the United States by ignoring the Pan-African context of the tradition, which is at least two centuries old in this country [the United States]" (Carruthers 1999: 174). E. Franklin Frazier's "The Failure of the Negro Intellectual" (1962) marked the boundary of the eternal divide between Black thought in the academy. Frazier argued that

> the price of slow integration which the Negroes are experiencing must be bought at the price of abject conformity in thinking. We have no philosophers or thinkers who command the respect of the intellectual community at large. I am not talking about the few teachers of philosophy who have read Hegel or Kant or James and memorized their thoughts. I am talking about men who have reflected upon the fundamental problems which have always concerned philosophers such as the nature of human knowledge and the meaning of human experience. We have no philosophers who have dealt with these and other problems from the stand point of the Negro's unique experience in the world.
>
> (Frazier 1962: 60)

African-centered thought seeks to answer this challenge by reaching back to Africa, specifically Kemet, and drawing from the Maat and the Mdw Ntr, philosophical insights specific to Africa. This reconstructive project produced African Deep Thought in opposition to "philosophy" because "philosophy" is married to a European articulation of knowledge and epistemology (Carruthers 1995). These scholars usually maintain a bio-genetic determinism of race that corresponds to the spiritual conceptualization of African culture and the exclusive African ontology that follows from their essentialism. Their answer to the question of self-determination and self-image ultimately lie in the acknowledgement of ancient African civilization and the uplift of the African personality.

The problem of race in African American philosophy

Many African American philosophers see philosophy as a reflection upon the structures of white racism and the effect those structures have on Black bodies. In *Blackness Visible: Essays on Philosophy and Race* (1998), Charles Mills argues that "personhood, or the lack of it, captures the defining feature of the African-American experience under conditions of white supremacy (both slavery and its aftermath)". Just as in Leonard Harris' work *Philosophy Born of Struggle: Anthology of Afro-American philosophy from 1917*, African

American philosophy becomes the creative activity of resistance that frees African Americans from the shackles of race – "the unifying theme [of African-American philosophy] has to be something like the struggles of people of African descent in the Americas against the different manifestations of white racism" (Mills 1998: 6).

This resistance can occur either in the embracing of or rejection of race. Some authors advocate embracing the empowering and nationalist aspects of race. In *On Race and Philosophy* (1996), Lucius Outlaw defends the use of race as a tool of organization that helps those affected by racism and white supremacy. Outlaw's use of race focuses on social collectivities, or "populations identified as such on the basis of the degree to which persons share more or less particular sets of varied and varying physical and cultural characteristics" (11) to speak of experience, aspirations and the life world of the oppressed. This account is similar to the idea of "radical constructionism" presented by Paul Taylor in *Race: A Philosophical Introduction* (2004). Race, or speaking of race, is a way to convey the standpoint of an individual within a community affected by the specific racialized context; for the radical constructionist, our social practices create populations as well as breeding groups, by connecting certain bodies and bloodlines to certain social locations and modes of treatment. Lewis Gordon's work on existential phenomenology (2000) is important to this tradition because one's "existence in Black" determines the relationship one has with whiteness and society. For Gordon, the lived experience of the Black not only reveals the problem of racial subjectivity, but constructs a process of liberation and resistance in African American philosophy.

Other Black philosophers argue for the eliminativist position; contending that race has absolutely no use to people of African descent. Both Anthony Appiah, author of *In My Father's House* (1992), and Paul Gilroy hold this view. Anthony Appiah (1992) believes that race should be eliminated and we should speak only of culture. This notion is continued in his 2005 work, *The Ethics of Identity*, where Appiah continues to dispel the myth of race and creates and ethics of identity rooted in a new liberal humanism that reveals that all people are just human. Paul Gilroy also advances an eliminativist theory in *Against Race* (2000) contending that African Americans should relinquish the illusion of cultural continuity with African and abandon race loyalties in favor of "more powerful visions of a planetary humanity from the future into the present and to reconnect them with democratic and cosmopolitan traditions that have been all but expunged from today's black political imaginary" (356).

The most recent field to deal specifically with the issues of race as sociological jurisprudence in African American philosophy is Critical Race Theory. Critical Race Theory came about as a discipline in the late 1980s as the result of a series of writings by Derrick Bell responding to white Critical Legal scholars who questioned the usefulness of anti-discrimination law and civil rights. Bell, a racial realist, holds that racism is a permanent part of American society. Critical Race Theory is an "organizational concept, bringing together under a single rubric various race-based theories, values, and attitudes against the existing legal order" (Brown 2003: 2). While Critical Race Theorists' epistemology is race-based experience, not all believe in the essentialized notions of race we find in a Derrick Bell. Critical Race Theory has historically proclaimed that race is a social construct conditioned by the historical conditions of white privilege specifically in law and the institutions of American society. This proclamation, however, has led Critical Race Theorists to embrace the tension that arises from advocating the experiential knowledge of Black and other racial identities and the recognition that these identities themselves are merely historical products in the United States instead of reducing the issue of racial identity to an ethical dilemma.

Further reading

Appiah, Kwame Anthony. *In My Father's House.* New York: Oxford University Press, 1992.

Bell, Derrick. "Racial Realism" in Kimberlé Crenshaw, Neil Gotanda, Gary Peller and Kendell Thomas (eds) *Critical Race Theory: The Key Writings that Formed the Movement*. New York: W.W. Norton, 1996, pp. 302–14.

Brown, Dorothy A. *Critical Race Theory: Cases, Materials and Problems.* St Paul, MN: Thomson/West, 2003.

Carruthers, Jacob. "The Fragmented Prophesy and Hybrid Philosophy of Cornel West" in *Intellectual Warfare.* Chicago, IL: Third World Press, 1999, pp. 173–99.

Delaney, Martin R. *Principia of Ethnology: The Origin of Races and Color, with an Archeological Compendium of Ethiopian and Egyptian Civilization.* Baltimore, MD: Black Classic Press, 1879.

Douglass, Frederick. "Address to the Colored People of the United States" in Tommy L. Lott (ed.) *African American Philosophy: Selected Readings.* Upper Saddle River, NJ: Prentice Hall, 1848, pp. 104–7.

DuBois, W.E.B. "The Conservation of Races" in Tommy L. Lott (ed.) *African American Philosophy: Selected Readings.* Upper Saddle River, NJ: Prentice Hall, 1897, pp. 141–7.

Frazier, E. Franklin. "The Failure of the Negro Intellectual," *Negro Digest* 1 (February, 1962): 26–36.

Garvey, Marcus. "African Fundamentalism: A Racial Hierarchy and Empire for Negroes" in *The Philosophy and Opinions of Marcus Garvey*, ed. Amy Jacques Garvey. Dover: The Majority Press, 1986, pp. 415–16.
Gates, Henry Louis. *The Classic Slave Narratives*. New York: Penguin Press, 1987.
Gilroy, Paul. *Against Race: Imaging Political Culture Beyond the Color Line*. Cambridge, MA: Belknap Press, 2000.
Gordon, Lewis. *Existentia Africana: Understanding Africana Existential Thought*. New York: Routledge, 2000.
Lott, Tommy L. *African American Philosophy: Selected Readings*. Upper Saddle River, NJ: Prentice Hall, 2002.
McGary, Howard and Lawson, Bill. *Between Slavery and Freedom: Philosophy and American Slavery*. Indianapolis, IN: Indiana University Press, 1992.
Mills, Charles W. *Blackness Visible: Essays on Philosophy and Race*. New York: Cornell University Press, 1998.
Outlaw, Lucius. *On Race and Philosophy*. New York: Routledge, 1996.
Shelby, Tommie. *We Who Are Dark: The Philosophical Foundations of Black Solidarity*. Cambridge, MA: Belknap Press, 2005.
Taylor, Paul. *Race: A Philosophical Introduction*. Malden, MA: Polity Press, 2004.
West, Cornel. "Philosophy and the Afro-American Experience" in Tommy L. Lott (ed.) *The Companion to African American Philosophy*. Malden, MA: Blackwell, 2006, pp. 7–32.

TOMMY J. CURRY

AGAPASM

The term "agapasm" was coined by American pragmatist Charles S. Peirce (1839–1914) in his 1893 essay "Evolutionary Love." The essay was the fifth in a series of five that came to be known informally as Peirce's "cosmology or metaphysical series." Agapasm describes the cosmological outlook to which Peirce himself subscribed, and though the term itself is not often used outside Peirce studies, the ideas to which it refers have had an important impact on subsequent work in American philosophy.

According to Peirce, agapasm is the view that the central principle or motive force in the evolution of the universe is "agape," or cherishing love. Two related terms are "agapism," the claim that some evolution is effected by agape, and "agapasticism," which is simply the doctrine that argues for the truth of agapasm. The claim that love or agape is the motive force of evolution is regarded by many as one of Peirce's more unusual assertions. However, when one looks at what Peirce was trying to accomplish, one sees more clearly the force of his argument.

Peirce argued that there were three plausible ways in which evolution might have occurred. The first was by pure chance or fortuitous variation. This Peirce named "tychasm" – from the Greek word for chance, *tyche* – and he associated it with Darwinian theory as he understood it. The second way evolution might be understood is as the result of a fully deterministic process simply working out causally what was initially destined to be – that is, evolution by mechanical necessity. This Peirce called anancasm, after the Greek word for necessity, *ananke*. Peirce aligned this kind of evolution with the work of August Weismann, among others. Despite the power of these theories, Peirce believed the world too orderly to be completely explained by chance and too full of contingency to be a result of necessity; he therefore looked for a middle position that might better fit with human experience of evolutionary development. This third way was agapasm, which he associated roughly with Lamarckian evolution.

He understood agape to be a reasonable principle of change precisely because it allowed for some chance and for some necessity. Perhaps his most telling analogies were to the rearing of a child and the growing of a garden. In these situations, agape – the cherishing concern for what will evolve – places some general constraints on what can occur; the child must have some discipline and rules, and the garden must be tilled and cultivated. However, the parent or gardener, at the same time, must leave room for the child or plant to develop on its own – freely. The dimension of constraint represents the element of necessity in the growth process, and the dimension of freedom represents the element of chance. Thus, agapasm includes some chance or spontaneity, *tychism*, and it also involves some lawlike determination or necessity, *anancism*. As Peirce saw it, love or agape has no natural opposite and therefore fits well this mediating role.

Although some interpreters rightly link agapasm to Peirce's other attempts to effect what he called a "marriage" of science and religion, it is also reasonable to consider agapasm as a strictly speculative cosmological outlook. On this score, its power is that it accounts for our experiences of lawfulness and order in the general development of both the physical world and human cultures, while at the same time allowing for some chance or spontaneity that can make sense of our experiences of freedom and the world's occasional display of radically contingent events. It is especially powerful as a way of assessing development in human history, for example in the arts and sciences. It is also a useful way of looking at the growth process in education. In this capacity, the middle road of agapasm squares nicely with similar arguments in the work of both William James and John Dewey.

Further reading

Hausman, Carl. *Charles S. Peirce's Evolutionary Philosophy.* New York: Cambridge University Press, 1993.

Peirce, Charles S. *The Essential Peirce Vol. I*, ed. N. Houser and C. Kloesel. Bloomington, IN: Indiana University Press, 1992.

DOUGLAS R. ANDERSON

AGENT/AGENCY

"Agent" and "agency" are concepts that imply various types and levels of causality. What distinguishes these terms is the fact that both agent and agency imply distinctive degrees of intentionality. In order to discuss this kind of causal action it is necessary to recall both Hume's skeptical conclusions concerning causality and Kant's reconstruction of causality as an *a priori* structure of the human mind. Under the influence of William James' *Principles of Psychology* and John Dewey's analysis of the "Reflex Arc Concept in Psychology," American philosophy resisted reducing causality to a habit of mind or a mental structure shaping empirical experience. In so doing it opened up a new and influential way of dealing with the major questions of human existence. After the work of James and Dewey, American pragmatism began to examine the human person and its environment as an organic unit that coordinated its response to shifting environmental pressures through its holistic experiential resources.

Hume argued against the epistemological validity of causality and traced such ways of thinking to associative patterns influencing the human mind to organize sense data in ways that appeared to make causal efficacy a real part of the human world. This skeptical conclusion was inevitable given the sensationalist epistemology that grounded this style of empirical philosophy. Bereft of its key concept of causality, science threatened to disappear as a discipline worthy of academic pursuit. It was Immanuel Kant who rescued the scientific enterprise by arguing in his *Critique of Pure Reason* that humans are in possession of certain pure categories of reason that operate necessarily and universally whenever we think. Among these categories is the concept of causality by which we come to understand the connection between cause and effect. While this preserved the scientific enterprise, it also exacted a very heavy price. Henceforth the world would be split into noumena (things in themselves) and phenomena (things as they appear to us). Given the way in which our sense and our mind shape and clothe the world, we can never know things in themselves but only the world as structured by our knowing process.

This dichotomy between the real world and the known world became the official dogma until American philosophy began to explore other ways of viewing the knower/known relation. The upshot of the naturalism advocated by James and Dewey was the restoration of the direct connection between the human being and the world of experience. Instead of understanding thinking as that which blocks direct access to the world, American pragmatists and naturalists began to model knowing after an instrument we use to shape our relation to our environment. Thus knowledge (and by extension, science) were transformed into modes of inquiry that sought to see the various ways in which the balance between an organism and its environment could be understood, enriched, altered or restored. Hence agency and agent were born and baptized as essential elements in all questions bearing on the way we know things. Of course, Darwin was also a major influence in this transformation. This shift from the knower as contemplative theorist to active agent is caught in Dewey's description of his own philosophy as "instrumentalism."

One can see in this transformation of the understanding of knowing the real meaning of pragmatism as concerned with results, consequences and effects. This is not some crass form of materialism but rather an effort to detect the many ways in which meaning evolves from altered modes of dealing with the world. It liberates the knower to experiment with novel forms of inquiry so as to penetrate the depths of nature and let situations express their problematic structures. Agent and agency are the ways in which humans take account of the fact that they live in an unfinished universe and are therefore co-creators of its future. Agency in the most general sense refers to those factors that have causal influence. Agent, on the other hand, refers more specifically to those entities that can be said to have a personal effect on processes. An agent is therefore one on whom we can confer moral understanding. So understood, agency can be said to operate on at least four levels: the physical, the biological, the personal and the cultural. Each form of agency builds upon the other and the discoveries made at one level are transformed when a different level is experienced. The question of intelligence at work is at a minimum level when we come to examine the material world. Here the laws of nature operate with the regularity that allows the sciences to aim at great predictability. The biological level manifests the emergence of creativity and various forms of "mind" (in the sense of taking initiative to alter situations). Living entities are quasi-effective agents involved in their own destiny. The personal level involves the ways in which individual human beings use their intelligence to become effective agents in shaping their own satisfactions and solving their own problems. Finally, the cultural level is that domain within which humans share their goals, purposes, needs and desires in order to flourish as cooperative agents. In sum, agency and agents appear at every level of the realm of nature and manifest increasing forms of cooperative intelligence. These forms of problem solving are the results of the active presence of agents and agency in the exchange that takes place between growing entities inhabiting various ecological niches.

Finally, it can be said that American philosophy seeks to persuade human beings that they are much more than solitary knowers. American philosophers have struggled to convince human beings that the spectator theory of knowledge is simply wrong. We are not watchers of the clock but active participants in the ongoing drama of finding ourselves alive in an ever changing environment. This environment has been given to us and is a source of our well being. As agents we have also altered that environment and have constructed built environments of great complexity and beauty. Whatever the value of these environments, we must see that it is our responsibility to shape them so that the entire range of natural and built experience reflects what is best for all those creatures affected by our agency. To think is to appreciate, guard and transform our world. That is what American philosophy at its best has taught us.

JOSEPH GRANGE

ALLAN, GEORGE

George Allan (1935–) is Professor of Philosophy Emeritus at Dickinson College. He graduated from Grinnell College in 1957, completed a MDiv degree from Union Theological Seminary, and received a PhD in philosophy from Yale in 1963. Allan was on the Dickinson College faculty from 1963 to 1996, and was academic dean from 1974 to 1995.

Allan has published three books exploring the ontological foundations for social value: *The Importances of the Past: A Meditation on the Authority of Tradition* (1986), *The Realizations of the Future: An Inquiry into the Authority of Praxis* (1990), and *The Patterns of the Present: Interpreting the Authority of Form* (2001). Allan has published two books on philosophical and educational issues regarding the liberal arts: *Rethinking College Education* (1997) and *Higher Education in the Making: Pragmatism, Whitehead, and the Canon* (2004). He has also published *The Stars Above, The Stones Beneath: Sermons on Christian Humanism* (2003) and over sixty articles in metaphysics, social philosophy, philosophy of history, education, and philosophy of education, usually from a process or pragmatic perspective.

Central to Allan's philosophy is a deep concern about the sources and care of value. *The Importances of the Past* demonstrates through the King Arthur legend how social structures find resonance in the authority of traditions. His *Realizations of the Future* takes up the question of the formation through praxis of an adequate ethical stance. *Patterns of the Present* examines the interplay between form and the foundations of social value. It takes a fallibilist approach, arguing that the open-ended quality of systemic hierarchies prevents any single form of value from becoming an absolute foundation for personal and social values.

Further reading

Allan, George. *The Importances of the Past*. Albany, NY: SUNY Press, 1986.

—— *The Realizations of the Future*. Albany, NY: SUNY Press, 1990.

—— *Patterns of The Present*. Albany, NY: SUNY Press, 2001.

—— *Higher Education in the Making*. Albany, NY: SUNY Press, 2004.

JOSEPH GRANGE

AMBIGUITY

In *Word and Object* the pragmatic philosopher W.V. Quine distinguishes between "vagueness" and "ambiguity" by saying that an ambiguity can be resolved, whereas a vague term has borderline cases rather than two different possible meanings. An ambiguous term like "cold" remains so only insofar as it is not given further specification indicating whether the word refers to "the flu" or to "the temperature." Sentences can also be ambiguous. We can say "she caught the ball," or "she caught a cold." Or, we can say "I lost hope," or "I lost my wallet." Going further, a sentence which appears to be descriptive, such as "the door is closed," may, in different circumstances, function as a command (the door is to be closed), a complaint about the temperature, or a reassurance to someone who is afraid of burglars, etc. Not only words and sentences but also images may be ambiguous. Flowers, for example, may indicate either innocence or seduction. The equivocation involved in these ambiguities can be cleared up by specifying the context in more detail.

The term "ambiguity" is not found in the index to *The Collected Papers of Charles Sanders Peirce*, but it is employed 217 times in the index of *The Collected Works of John Dewey.* William James also uses it on several occasions. When Dewey uses the term, it is mostly in the sense of solving a problem, whereas for James, ambiguity is often synonymous with vagueness. Thus for example, Dewey studies the ambiguity of the word "significance," which can mean either "meaning" or "importance." He notes the ambiguity of the word "value," which can mean either to "enjoy" or to "evaluate." For Dewey, the term "natural" is among the most ambiguous of all words employed to justify courses of action. It can mean "innate" or "customary," or "normal." Through reflective thinking we transform confusion and ambiguity into illumination, definiteness and consistency. The intent here is to achieve resolution by putting the term into its proper context.

When James uses the term "ambiguous," however, it is usually as a synonym for the "vague" rather than as an alternative to it. Thus in *Pragmatism* he suggests that there are three different levels of reality – common sense, science, and philosophy – and no one of these is any "truer" than the alternatives. James ends the lecture by asking the reader if there may not after all be a possible ambiguity in truth. In *Essays in Radical Empiricism* he argues that the body itself is a primary instance of the ambiguous. Sometimes, it is treated purely as a natural object. Sometimes, again, we think of it as owned, i.e. as "my body." He uses "appreciations" or "affectional facts" as exemplars of "pure experience" because these form an ambiguous sphere of being. We can say "seductive visions" or "visions of seductive things."

These instances indicate that, while James was not opposed to making distinctions to attain clarity of meaning, he was at least equally eager to avoid explaining something "away" via logical analysis. James remained suspicious of language, and logic, throughout his life. In fairness to Dewey, it should be noted that he recognized and spoke positively of the ambiguity of qualities of appreciation used by James as models of pure experience.

Further reading

Dewey, John. *The Collected Works of John Dewey, 1882–1953*, ed. Jo Ann Boydston. Carbondale and Edwardsville, IL: Southern Illinois University Press, 1969–91; published as *The Early Works: 1882–98* (EW), *The Middle Works: 1899–1924* (MW), and *The Later Works: 1925–53* (LW).

James, William. *Pragmatism.* New York: Longmans, Green, 1907, Lecture 5.

—— *A Pluralistic Universe.* New York: Longmans, Green, 1909, Lecture 8.

—— *Essays in Radical Empiricism.* New York: Longmans, Green, 1912, Chapter 5.

Quine, W.V. *Word and Object*. Cambridge, MA: MIT Press, 1960.

William J. Gavin

ANABAPTISM

Anabaptism is a diverse religious movement with roots in the Protestant Reformation. The term, coined by enemies of the movement, comes from Greek words meaning "rebaptizer." It refers to the view (believer's baptism) shared by members of the movement – and condemned by Catholics and Protestants – that baptism should be a sign of a person's voluntary decision to follow Jesus. Since these persons had already been baptized as infants, they were accused of being "rebaptized."

Anabaptist groups arose in the sixteenth century in Switzerland, Germany, and Holland and spread very quickly. Catholic and Protestant authorities, alarmed by the popularity of these groups, tried to stamp them out through persecution – imprisoning and killing thousands of Anabaptists. The dedication of the Anabaptists to their faith and their willingness to endure torture and death rather than recant made the persecution largely ineffective. While thousands were killed, many thousands more were inspired by their example and took their places. Eventually, Anabaptists began to emigrate from areas of intense persecution, with a number ultimately moving to America.

There are four major groups of Anabaptist churches in the United States today: Hutterites, Mennonites, Amish, and Brethren. The Hutterites take their name from Jacob Hutter, an early Anabaptist pastor who led one of several groups that emigrated to Moravia, a more tolerant area in present-day Austria. The Hutterites developed a communal living style modeled after that of the early church as described in the book of Acts. The Hutterites continued to encounter persecution, and Jacob Hutter himself was arrested and burned at the stake in 1535. In spite of this persecution, the Hutterites survived, emigrating to the United States in the 1870s. There they faced renewed persecution for being conscientious objectors during World War I, and as a consequence, most moved to Canada where they continue to live in communal colonies today.

The Mennonites take their name from Menno Simons, a Dutch Catholic priest who converted to Anabaptism in 1536. A gifted leader, Menno managed to escape arrest and so was able to write, travel, and teach extensively. Today, Mennonites live in many different countries of the world, including the United States. Some Mennonites are quite conservative, living in rural areas and limiting their use of technology; others are very much assimilated, living in urban areas and making full use of technology. Ethnically, Mennonites are also quite diverse. While many come from European ancestry, an increasing number are African-American, Asian-American, and Hispanic.

The Amish are followers of Jakob Ammann, a leader of the Swiss Anabaptists who called for greater purity among members and stronger measures of church discipline. When most other leaders did not accept his views, the Amish broke away from the Mennonites in 1693. Most Amish to this day are quite conservative. Amish groups in the United States typically prohibit the ownership of cars, tractors, televisions, and computers. They use horse-drawn buggies for transportation and dress distinctively – a beard without a mustache being required for men and a prayer cap for women.

The first Brethren church was formed in Germany in 1708 and was led by Alexander Mack, Sr. While Brethren churches are not direct descendants of the original Anabaptists, they were essentially influenced by Anabaptist (as well as Pietist) beliefs and practices. Contemporary Brethren churches in the United States include Church of the Brethren, Grace Brethren Churches, Brethren in Christ, and the Brethren Church.

Anabaptist beliefs and practices have varied widely, and there is much on-going scholarly debate as to how they can best be characterized. For almost any specific doctrine or practice widely held by Anabaptists, it is possible to present an Anabaptist figure or group that did not hold it. There are, however, some common themes that emerge from Anabaptist history that continue to be of central importance for contemporary Anabaptist groups.

First is the emphasis on practice. Protestant Christianity has tended to emphasize the importance of correct belief. Martin Luther, for example, took the Pauline theology articulated in the book of Romans to be the hermeneutic key to the Bible. Theology is central and correct belief is essential for salvation. Anabaptists, by contrast, took Jesus' Sermon on the Mount to be the hermeneutic key to the Bible. Practice is central, and following Jesus' teachings in one's life is essential for salvation. For the Anabaptists, correct beliefs were important, not because they were sufficient in themselves, but because they were important for right practice.

Second is the emphasis on separation of church and state. Anabaptists held that the church should be composed of believers who voluntarily chose to separate themselves from the world and dedicate themselves to a life of purity. They rejected the notion of a state church, where infant baptism signaled both church membership and state citizenship. While they practiced church discipline in the attempt to retain church purity, they repudiated physical or legal coercion (which was defended by both Catholics and Protestants) in matters of religion. Believer's baptism was a powerful practice that embodied this separation between church and state.

Third, Anabaptists have been deeply committed to nonresistance and peace. As a rule, Anabaptists are committed to nonviolence in all aspects of life, taking seriously Jesus' commands to love our enemies and not to resist evildoers. While there is some variance in the ways in which Anabaptist groups have historically put these commands into practice, many Anabaptists have been willing to suffer and even be killed rather than use force or violence when faced with injustice. Anabaptists have traditionally refused to go to war, and many believe in the importance of actively promoting peace.

Anabaptist voices have rarely been heard in academic American philosophy. But there is much here to be explored, including a similarity of mphasis on practice, choice, freedom, community, and social justice. Conservative Anabaptist groups with religious convictions against voting present a special challenge to notions of democracy. At the same time, there is much to learn about community from groups that have survived such dangers as severe religious persecution, forced emigration, and the temptations of contemporary culture.

Further reading

Bender, Harold S. *The Anabaptist Vision*. Scottsdale, PA: Herald Press, 1944.

Kraybill, Donald B. *Who Are the Anabaptists? Amish, Brethren, Hutterites, and Mennonites*. Scottsdale, PA: Herald Press, 2003.

Kraybill, Donald B. and Hostetter, C. Nelson. *Anabaptist World USA*. Scottsdale, PA: Herald Press, 2001.

JAMES O. PAWELSKI

ANALYTIC: ANALYTIC/SYNTHETIC

Traditionally regarded as the analytic–synthetic *distinction,* an analytic statement is commonly viewed as a judgment wherein the meaning of the subject is contained in the predicate, and thus whose truth is knowable merely by understanding the meaning of the terms. Alternatively, the predicate of a synthetic statement has content not contained in the subject, and therefore asserts something whose truth is independent of the meaning of the terms alone. "Elm Street is a street" exemplifies an analytic judgment, whereas "Elm Street is a dead-end street" makes a synthetic claim.

Although Leibniz had previously separated "truths of reason" from "truths of fact," and Hume had distinguished "relations of ideas" from "matters of fact," in modern form the analytic–synthetic distinction dates from Kant. According to Kant, the content of the predicate in an analytic proposition is "contained" in its subject; and though such a judgment is factually "uninformative," the terms may "elucidate" one another. He further links analytic and synthetic to the notions of the a priori (before experience) and a posteriori (from experience). Kant's transcendental idealism arises from the innovative suggestion that in addition to widely accepted a priori analytic and a posteriori synthetic statements, there are also synthetic a priori judgments setting universal and necessary conditions for the possibility of empirical experience.

In the first half of the twentieth century, most analytically inclined philosophers continued to accept the analytic–synthetic distinction, but without Kant's murky allusions to "containment" or "elucidation." Frege tried to free logical properties of judgment from psychological traits of judging by focusing upon the *extensional* meaning of judgment. He argued that a statement is analytic if both terms have the same *referents* – if the truth conditions of one always concur with those of the other. Sufficiently sanitized, an analytic statement is merely a logical tautology, though, as Wittgenstein observed, tautologies are senseless but not nonsense: they have no factual content but reveal an essential function of language.

In America, philosophers riding the groundswell of pragmatism greeted the analytic–synthetic distinction more warily. The following sections trace the course of these criticisms from the progressively radical reinterpretations of Peirce, Lewis, and Dewey to the ultimate rejection of the distinction by Quine.

Peirce on perceptual judgment

Countering the alleged psychologism of James and Dewey, C.S. Peirce anticipated logical empiricism by insisting that the analytic–synthetic distinction is properly logical rather than psychological. But where traditional approaches exclude belief and doubt as subjective emotions, Peirce finds these integral to an objective logic of inference, since he regarded the *sole* purpose of thought as the restoration of belief interrupted by the "irritation of doubt." Rather than being content with formal relations, an authentic logic of reasoning explores the dynamic function of doubt–belief.

Peirce allows that some judgments are analytic in the sense of being necessary, undoubted, and prior to cognitive experience. But these are not logical axioms or supreme principles of reason. In fact, they are the reverse: "perceptual judgments" or noncognitive "habits of mind" that predispose us to respond to problems in certain ways. Based upon prior experiences in navigating a neighborhood, I have concluded that "Elm Street is a dead-end street," a judgment that tacitly influences my choice of routes in subsequent ventures. "Tacit" is the operative notion here, for, as Peirce notes, a perceptual judgment is usually articulated only in response to some doubt raised about it – justifying an avoidance of Elm Street to ourselves or others, or coming to realize we are no longer sure about a belief.

Perceptual judgments are a priori and necessary in the sense that they lie beneath, and are tools for achieving, the synthetic empirical claims we make about the world. Each of us believes an inestimable number of perceptual judgments, many of which may never be questioned in the course of a lifetime. But to say such judgments are undoubted is emphatically not to claim they are undoubt*able.* To the contrary, it is the imposition of doubt upon a previously undoubted belief that calls forth inquiry – the proper subject of inferential logic. Peirce finds it absurd to seek analyticity in rational tests of certitude such as identity or noncontradiction, for the very notion of a test means the analyticity of the proposition is in doubt.

The pragmatic a priori of C.I. Lewis

Trained at Harvard by Josiah Royce and William James, C.I. Lewis's eclectic epistemology triangulates Kant's idealism, Peirce's pragmatism and logical empiricism. Lewis accepted the analytic/synthetic distinction, and the need to dissociate logic from psychology. But where Peirce equated analytic statements with perceptual judgments, Lewis saw these as "leading ideas" atop a hierarchical pyramid descending from comprehensive logical principles to everyday judgments. Leading ideas resemble Kant's pure concepts of the understanding inasmuch as they express intellectual conditions of human experience. They are not self-evident, however, for they arise in the mind's reflection upon its own inherent *intentionality* – in thought's essential need to go beyond itself and make sense of an objective world. Affirming Peirce's dictum that we know the world only by productively *acting* upon it, Lewis's analytic judgments are not eternal verities but arbitrary postulates we "try out" then accept insofar as they help us predict and control external consequences. Such propositions are *pragmatically* a priori – non-falsifiable and too general to be directly tested themselves, yet subject to revision or abandonment should experience reveal them to be "inconvenient, fantastic, or useless."

Whereas analytic statements are nonempirical guides to inquiry, synthetic statements are generated inductively by ongoing empirical confirmation. Beginning with the minimal evidence afforded by what Lewis calls "the sensory given," such judgments gain credibility with accumulated confirming evidence.

Dewey's operational equivalence

In the wake of blistering attacks by Gilbert Ryle and Wilfred Sellars, the sensory "given" has fared poorly in latter-day epistemology, and Lewis's reliance upon it suggests an embarrassing gap between analytic and synthetic. For John Dewey these, like other alleged dualisms of subject/object, mind/matter, and value/fact, mark complimentary *functions* of inquiry rather than irreconcilable opposites. As such, it is not inappropriate to regard Dewey's discussion of the analytic and synthetic in *Logic: The Theory of Inquiry* (1938) as both elucidating and rectifying Lewis's pragmatic a priori.

For Dewey, logic cannot be divorced from other forms of human problem-solving activity that are richly biological and social. Peirce's "doubt-belief" thus becomes a full "circuit of inquiry" in which a disrupted state of habituated equilibrium initiates the search for a hypothetical solution. When successfully enacted in the encountered world, this rectifying plan is vested in a cognitively grasped objective (or object) that returns to and enriches a renewed dispositional matrix. Propositions are literally hypothetical *proposals*, distinguished from *judgments* about determinate outcomes: assertoric propositions (S is P) are really disguised hypotheticals (if S, then P).

Seeing propositions as dynamic plans for constructive activity helps clarify Dewey's motive for recasting the synthetic and the analytic, respectively, as *generic* and *universal* propositions. Generic propositions are either *particular* ("this is gray"), *singular* ("this gray thing is a cat"), or *relations of kinds* ("some cats are gray"). Universal propositions are "*ways of being x*" either applicable to existences ("an electric current is potential divided by resistance") or not necessarily applicable ("an electric current is not not an electric current"). Both propositional forms aim to achieve a "dynamic equivalence" of subject and predicate (or antecedent and consequent). In generic propositions, the content of the subject is constructed in the predicate by an aggregate of material properties, e.g. "this diamond is *x, y, z* . . ." Since the range of potential properties is unlimited, generic "equivalence" merely indicates the set of properties that satisfy whatever is troubling us about the diamond in the present context. It is "synthetic" inasmuch as there is no pretense that the predicate "exhausts" its subject. On the other hand, for a universal "way of being *x*" the predicate expression *does* indicate full logical equivalence with the subject, e.g. "an electric current is a 'way of being' potential divided by resistance." And if the predicate is complex, *all* the properties must cohere with one another in order to satisfy the subject.

One might object that "electric current" and "potential divided by resistance" are not even cognitively synonymous, let alone tautologous. Equally puzzling is the demand that such universal propositions be "applicable" to existences. Dewey replies that equivalence or tautology requires neither identical intensional content nor duplicate extensional reference. Instead, the relation between a predicate and subject is *operational.* A universal predicate lets us *do* something with its subject we could not otherwise do: connect it to other propositions. For example, "an electric current is equal to potential divided by resistance" may lead to "potential divided by resistance is equal to the voltage of a current," thus extending the applicability of the original subject. According to Dewey, series of such propositions extend upwards and downwards, like "rungs in a ladder," where "leading principles" ultimately terminate in concrete applications such as designing an electrical circuit.

Dewey acknowledges a second form of universal proposition, markedly closer to the standard sense of analyticity. He freely admits that purely formal logical and mathematical systems are governed by rules and theorems that have no concrete applications (though, of course, many do). But even these are sustained not by self-evidence or some standard of indubitably, but by their *usefulness* in promoting the inferential power and elegance of the system. Though formal systems and the empirical sciences pursue different goals, they share the underlying methodology of problem-solving activity.

Quine's "two dogmas"

The most famous pragmatic response to the analytic/synthetic distinction is W.V. Quine's signature essay, "Two Dogmas of Empiricism" (1951). For Quine, the boundary between the analytic and synthetic should not be relaxed or reconfigured, but obliterated "in order to espouse a more thorough pragmatism." Quine's argument is engagingly lucid, and involves a two-pronged strategy: (1) any defense of analyticity based upon either intensional concepts like synonymy or extensional notions such as semantic reference falls prey to circularity: one must already grasp analyticity in order to define or denote it in these ways; (2) the attempt to salvage analytic propositions by sensory verification fails to recognize the holistic function of language in justification.

The dogma of analyticity

Quine concedes two forms of statements whose analyticity is unproblematic: (a) logical truths such as "no unmarried man is married," and (b) propositions where equivalent meanings are simply stipulated. The difficulty arises with the notion of the predicate "containing" the meaning of the subject in so-called *synonymous* expressions, e.g. "a bachelor is a never married male." We can't simply appeal to synonymy as a ground of analyticity, since "having the same meaning" is just what we're calling "analytic." Nor does it help to shore up synonymy with some anterior notion such as *definition*, for definitions are either (a) lexical, which simply report usage whose origins are in question, (b) explicative, which cannot without circularity specify the common ground from which the explication arises, or (c) formal rules that simply reflect the tradeoff between the number of definitions accepted as "primitive" and the length of the inferences they entail.

If definition is a nonstarter, perhaps synonymy can be rescued by appeal to the *interchangeability* of the terms, here rooted not in fuzzy intensions but in the allegedly firmer soil of semantic reference. In this case two terms are declared interchangeable, and thus synonymous, if each can be substituted for the other without changing their truth values. Though easily rendered formally, Quine insists that such maneuvers do nothing to illuminate *cognitive* synonymy: e.g. although every "creature with a heart" is a "creature with kidneys," these phrases are not cognitively synonymous, and thus their extensional equivalency sheds no light on the analytic relation between "bachelor" and "never married man."

The dogma of reductionism

Perhaps the whole problem with analyticity is that empiricists – by dabbling with cognitive acuity and logical parlor tricks – have stopped being empirical about it. But what if analyticity could be aligned with the empiricists' own cornerstones of sensory evidence and verification? In this case a synthetic proposition would be one whose confirmation by evidence is likely, and an analytic proposition the limiting case of being confirmable "no matter what." This could also salvage the notion of synonymy as a legitimate criterion of analyticity, for synonymous statements would be recognized as those with identical methods of confirmation.

According to Quine, this approach is doomed because it invokes *reductionism* – the untenable notion that any given factual claim can be translated into reports of direct sense experience. And though the radical claim that a statement's meaning is reducible to a single sensory report is long abandoned, empiricists cling to a modest version in which each statement corresponds to a range of sensory events that cumulatively establish the likelihood of its truth. But Quine rejects even this modified version. Statements about the world face the tribunal of sense collectively, not individually – in defense of which he notes that the truth of *any* statement can be preserved despite discrediting evidence *if* we are willing to question other assumptions about it, including perhaps even the veracity of perception or our own sanity. Rather than being divided between contingent synthetic claims and indubitable analytic propositions, our beliefs constitute a continuous range from a periphery of sense-reports to interior concepts that are comparatively theory-laden and general. But even the principles of logic, mathematics, and theoretical science are *posits* – tools for helping us reweave the web of belief in the face of recalcitrant experiences.

Quine's pragmatic challenge to the analytic–synthetic distinction has won many sympathizers, including Nelson Goodman, Morton White, and Hilary Putnam. Critics, however, maintain that some notion of analyticity is indispensable to any coherent account of either formal systems or our everyday use of language. H.P. Grice and P.F. Strawson, for example, contend that analyticity, necessity, and cognitive synonymy constitute an internally coherent family of terms, which Quine takes out of context in appealing to extensional criteria such as semantic reference. Others follow Wittgenstein in restricting analyticity to pure logical tautology, noting that Quine himself does not contest logical truths or stipulations. Even such counterproposals, however, concede a severe curtailment of the distinction, and in the wake of challenges from pragmatism it is hard to envision the analytic and the synthetic ever again enthroned in resplendent isolation.

Further reading

Dewey, John. *Logic: The Theory of Inquiry. John Dewey: The Later Works, 1925–1953; Vol. 12: 1938*, ed. Jo Ann Boydston. Carbondale and Edwardsville, IL: Southern Illinois University Press, 1986.

Grice, H.P. and Strawson, P.F. "In Defense of a Dogma," *Philosophical Review* 65 (March, 1956): 141–58.

Lewis, C.I. *Mind and the World-Order: Outline of a Theory of Knowledge.* New York: Dover, 1929.

Peirce, C.S. "Memoir 21: On First Premises," in *Logic, Considered as Semeiotic*, MS L 75 (1902): 253–62, 315–26. Analytically reconstructed by Joseph Ransdell. Available at http://members.door.net/arisbe/menu/library/bycsp/175/verv-1–07.htm

Quine, W.V. "Two Dogmas of Empiricism," in *From a Logical Point of View*, second edition. Cambridge, MA: Harvard University Press, 1964, pp. 20–46.

FRANK X. RYAN

ANALYTIC: KNOWLEDGE

The analytic approach to the theory of knowledge (epistemology) became especially important in the English-speaking philosophical world in the middle decades of the twentieth century. It drew, however, on two earlier strains of Anglo-American philosophy, one distinctive to the American pragmatic tradition, the other less so.

Pragmatism, naturalism and analytic epistemology

In analytically oriented epistemology, the dominant "naturalism" of American pragmatism manifests itself in two main views: (1) the idea that knowledge itself must be investigated via the techniques of the natural and social sciences; (2) a companion opposition to "first-philosophy" as providing a necessary prior investigation of all knowledge-claims, including those of the sciences.

In its radical form, this position is most closely associated with W.V.O. Quine's advocacy of a "naturalized epistemology." Quine's position is "radical" in its implicit rejection of ancient philosophical debates concerning "What is knowledge?" Thus, a traditional starting point of such debates has been the view, suggested in Plato's dialogue, *Theaetetus*, that knowledge is "true, justified belief." If, however, epistemology is limited to scientific investigation of how knowledge is acquired, specifically philosophical arguments concerning what makes a belief "justified" become irrelevant.

A less radical position, most prominently associated with Alvin Goldman, accepts the analysis of "justification" as a distinctively philosophical (non-scientific enterprise), but advocates a substantive position on justification – that it consists in "reliably formed belief " – which makes the *remaining* project of epistemology mostly an empirical, scientific one. For this remaining project would be to investigate empirically such forms of belief acquisition – e.g. perception, memory – as may be reliable under a given set of circumstances.

Such positions draw not only on John Dewey's naturalist epistemology and metaphysics – in which science is both a paradigm of how to inquire; and the results of science, the determinant of what exists – but also Dewey's opposition to the "quest for certainty." A radically "naturalized epistemology" can achieve no more certainty than the temporary, limited assurance provided by the empirical sciences. Moreover, even if a philosophical analysis makes knowledge require something close to 100 percent reliability of one's relevant faculties (e.g. perception), the traditional philosophical project of determining, from examination of one's *own* beliefs, whether certainty has been attained – this becomes impossible. Ultimately, whether justification and knowledge have been attained, on Goldman's view, will depend on the never entirely certain investigations of science.

Traditional empiricism and analytic epistemology

A quite different strain in analytical epistemology concerns is "empiricist" – and "foundationalist" – in that it hearkens back to traditional positions concerning the foundation of all knowledge in sense perception and inner reflection. In earlier American philosophy, C.I. Lewis, the leading Harvard epistemologist in the period between William James and Quine, defended broadly this type of view, in which our "only probable knowledge" of physically reality was grounded in our "certain knowledge" of our own sense perceptions.

For some critics, a weakness of the "reliabilist" account is its dependence on "external" factors not accessible to the knower herself (but only to those who are scientifically investigating the reliability of her belief formation process). Traditionally, empiricists tried to show how all knowledge was strictly based on experiences immediately accessible to the knower – and logical inferences strictly based on these. This makes the grounds of knowledge *internal* to the belief process.

The internalist tradition, however, is not limited to those analysts who follow Lewis is construing knowledge as grounded in sensory foundations. Such "coherence theorists" as Wilfrid Sellars and Keith Lehrer understand knowledge and the role of perception more holistically. If we rely on perceptual evidence, they insist, we do so for *reasons.* As the process of asking for and supplying reasons has no distinctive end-point – in sense perception or in anything else – "coherentists" hold that beliefs can ultimately be evaluated in relation to all of the other beliefs of that subject. Beliefs can only be justified by other beliefs.

Another type of criticism of traditional foundationalism comes from "fallibilism." This position – which may be upheld by advocates of a coherence or a foundational view – disputes the claim that knowledge requires complete certainty. Fallibilism insists, with such American philosophers as William James, there is no special internal experience constituting knowing – thus, guaranteeing that (to one who has it) assurance that she does indeed have knowledge.

Chisholm, Gettier, virtue epistemology

Perhaps the most influential post-World War II American epistemologist (excepting Quine), Roderick Chisholm of Brown University, however, embraced a notion of "being evident" according to which justification, a main ingredient of knowledge, will have a distinctive internal mark. This is in the tradition of Plato, Descartes, and a kind of "rationalism" generally alien to the American tradition. Yet, Chisholm's methodology of exact definition and careful reformulation in the light of criticisms of his own position – characteristic of successive editions of his classic, *A Theory of Knowledge* – influenced an entire generation of analytic philosophers in America.

Analysts of knowledge in later twentieth-century American philosophy have particularly sought to address a problem dating from Edmund Gettier's 1963 paper "Is Justified, True Belief Knowledge?" Here Gettier showed fairly conclusively that a belief might be true and justified – *without* constituting knowledge. In a typical "Gettier Case": (a) I have excellent evident that you own a Ford (I see you driving one every day, etc.), believe on this basis that you do own one, yet (b) even though this belief is true (you do own a Ford), my evidence turns out to have been mistaken (the Ford I saw you driving was not the one you own, etc.). What must be "added" to true, justified belief – in order to ensure knowledge – theorists in the analytic tradition have asked, but, as yet, to no agreed upon solution.

A still later trend in "analytic" discussions of knowledge and belief has been an appeal to "epistemic virtues." These are qualities analogous to the moral virtues, but pertaining to truth rather than right action. Such theorists as Ernest Sosa and Linda Zagzebski have greatly stimulated interest in "virtue epistemology" and even the hope the "Gettier problem" might at last be solved.

Further reading

Audi, Robert. *Belief, Justification and Knowledge.* Belmont, CA: Wadsworth, 1988.

Chisholm, Roderick. *A Theory of Knowledge.* Englewood Cliffs, NJ: Prentice-Hall, 1966, 1977, 1989.

Lehrer, Keith. *Theory of Knowledge.* Boulder, CO: Westview, 1991.

Sosa, Ernest. *Knowledge in Perspective.* Cambridge: Cambridge University Press, 1991

Zagzebski, Linda. *Virtues of the Mind.* Cambridge: Cambridge University Press, 1996.

James A. Montmarquet

ANALYTIC: TRUTHS

It is a matter of controversy in philosophy as to whether there are any analytic truths, for many philosophers, influenced by Quine, are dubious of a distinction between analytic and synthetic truths. It is even a matter of controversy, if there is such a distinction, which truths would fall on the analytic side of this distinction, for philosophers have drawn the analytic/synthetic distinction in a number of different ways, not all of them equivalent.

Immanuel Kant drew the distinction between analytic truths and synthetic truths as follows. An analytic truth is a truth whose subject contains the content of the predicate, a synthetic truth is a truth whose subject does not contain the content of the predicate. This is a notion that applies to sentences containing a subject, predicate, and copula, such as

"Squares are rectangles," a (purported) analytic truth, and "Cockroaches are commonly found in New York City apartments," a (purported) synthetic truth.

Gottlob Frege found Kant's analytic/synthetic distinction lacking, and used the resources of his logic to draw a new distinction. On Frege's distinction, a truth is analytic if and only if it is either (a) a logical truth or (b) a sentence that can be converted into a logical truth by substitution of synonymous terms. "All vixens are vixens" is a logical truth, hence it is an analytic truth on Frege's definition. On the assumption that "female fox" is synonymous with "vixen," then "All vixens are female foxes" is also analytic, for it can be converted into "All vixens are vixens" by substitution of synonymous terms. Given that there is no way to convert "Cockroaches are commonly found in New York City apartments" into a logical truth by substitution of synonymous terms, this truth is a synthetic one.

The definitions of "analytic truth" given by Kant and Frege have been the most influential upon subsequent discussion of analyticity. However, these definitions do not exhaust the variety of definitions of analyticity that have been provided by philosophers. C.I. Lewis, for example, equated analytic truths with necessary truths, propositions that are true in all possible worlds. The variety of definitions of "analytic" in the philosophical literature has contributed to the confusion over these notions.

W.V. Quine argued that neither the Kantian nor the Fregean distinction between analytic and synthetic truths is an adequate distinction, for each rests on unexplained notions. Kant's distinction rests on an unexplained notion of conceptual containment. Frege's distinction is based on the unexplained notion of synonymity. Quine's arguments against the analytic/synthetic distinction have been very influential, and have had repercussions in a wide range of areas of philosophy. To cite one example, any attempt to draw the epistemological distinction between *a priori* and *a posteriori* knowledge in terms of the analytic/synthetic distinction would fail if there were no such distinction. These arguments of Quine against the distinction between the analytic and synthetic were anticipated by the pragmatists, especially John Dewey, who rejected the distinction between observation and theory underlying the logical positivist distinction between the analytic and synthetic.

An early reply to Quine by H.P. Grice and P.F. Strawson suggested that Quine overlooked the existence of an obvious distinction. If I were to claim that my four-year-old son has developed a novel proof of the Church–Turing thesis, what I have said is very likely false. The falsehood of this is a matter of fact, and the claim that it is unlikely that a four-year-old has developed such a proof is synthetic truth. On the other hand, if I claim that my four-year-old son is an adult, what I have uttered is a conceptual falsehood. The claim that "No child is an adult" is a clear and obvious instance, according to Grice and Strawson, of an analytic truth. This argument does not, however, address Quine's concern. Quine argued in his article "Two Dogmas of Empiricism" that there is no way to account for this purported distinction, to draw the line between analytic and synthetic. Grice and Strawson, by providing examples, did not present an adequate way of drawing such a distinction.

Recent defenses of analyticity by Jerrold Katz and Paul Boghossian argue that Quine has overlooked the proper way to draw the analytic/synthetic distinction. Katz defended the analytic/synthetic distinction by arguing that Quine unnecessarily looked for a clarification of a semantic distinction that can only be drawn within semantics. According to Katz, linguists can appeal to intuitions about semantic matters such as redundancy and synonymy to draw a distinction between the analytic and synthetic. Given that speakers recognize that "free gift" to be redundant, we can classify "Gifts are free" as an analytic truth. As Katz himself recognized and argued, such a conception of analyticity would play a vastly different role in philosophy from the more widely accepted Fregean conception.

In "Analyticity Reconsidered," Paul Boghossian argues that there is a conception of analyticity that is not susceptible to Quine's arguments. According to Boghossian, we can appeal to implicit definition for an account of analytic truth. When certain sentences are stipulated as true, we implicitly define the terms contained in that sentence. If I stipulate that "If, if p then q, and p, then 'q' is true" is true, I have implicitly defined "if . . . then." Looking at how terms are implicitly defined in theories, we can tell when a truth is analytic; in light of the definition of "if . . . then" given above, the logical truth "If p then p" is explained to be analytic. The trouble with using such an account to explain analytic truth is, as Paul Horwich points out, we often implicitly define terms in theories that turn out to be false. The term "phlogiston" was implicitly defined in a false theory. Sentences containing a term might suffice to define a term implicitly, but does not suffice to make the sentence true. Thus

Boghossian's account does not capture the basic notion of analyticity as truth in virtue of meaning.

Further reading

Boghossian, Paul. "Analyticity Reconsidered," *Noûs* 30, 3 (1996): 360–91.

Grice, H.P. and Strawson, P.F. "In Defense of a Dogma," *Philosophical Review* 56: 141–58.

Horwich, Paul. *Meaning*. Oxford: Oxford University Press, 1998.

Katz, Jerrold J. *Sense, Reference, and Philosophy*. New York: Oxford University Press, 2004.

Lewis, C.I. "A Pragmatic Conception of the A Priori," *Journal of Philosophy* 20 (1923): 167–77.

Quine, W.V. "Two Dogmas of Empiricism," *Philosophical Review*, 60, 1 (January, 1951): 20–43.

—— *From a Logical Point of View*, revised edition. Cambridge, MA: Harvard University Press, 1961.

Fritz J. McDonald

ANANCASM

Anancasm is one of three modes of evolution identified by Charles Peirce, who distinguished anancasm, or evolution by mechanical necessity, from evolution by fortuitous variation (*tychasm*) and evolution by creative love (*agapasm*). Peirce reserved *anancism* for the proposition that mechanical necessity is operative in the cosmos and *anancasticism* for the doctrine that evolution is anancastic. Peirce saw Clarence King's cataclysmic theory of evolution and Herbert Spencer's theory as prime models of anancasticism. For Peirce, anancasm, like tychasm, is a degenerate form of agapasm.

Peirce applied his three modes of evolution not only to the physical universe, but also to the development of thought, as in his 1893 Lowell Lectures on the History of Science. Mostly concentrating on the latter, Peirce distinguished two varieties of anancastic evolution: *genuine anancasm*, or development under the influence of something external, and *degenerate anancasm*, or development under a rule of logic or inward necessity (Peirce saw Hegelianism as an example of degenerate anancasm). What distinguishes both varieties of anancasm from agapasm is that they are inherently without purpose.

The word anancasm derives from the Greek *ananke*. Originally referring to physical constraints such as the chains of prisoners or slaves, the term became more abstract; it was used, for instance, to denote the irresistible element in sexual passion. Ananke was later personified by the Greek as the goddess of unalterable necessity, compulsion, or the force of destiny. Within philosophy, a theological or cosmological notion of ananke is found in Plato, Parmenides, and Empedocles as well as among atomists, stoics, and neo-Platonists.

Further reading

King, Clarence. "Catastrophism and Evolution," *The American Naturalist* 11, 8 (August, 1877): 449–70.

Peirce, Charles S. "Evolutionary Love" in *The Essential Peirce Vol. 1*, ed. Nathan Houser and Christian Kloesel. Bloomington, IN: Indiana University Press, 1992, pp. 352–72.

Schreckenberg, Hans. *Ananke: Untersuche zur Geschichte des Wortgebrauchs*. München: Verlag C.H. Beck, 1964.

Cornelis de Waal

ANOMALOUS MONISM

"Anomalous monism," a Davidsonian conception of mental events, has been one of the most influential views in contemporary American philosophy of mind. Donald Davidson's principle of "the Anomalism of the Mental" states that there are no strict laws relating mental and physical events. This principle relies on Davidson's general event ontology and his view of causation. In particular, it relies on the principle of "the Nomological Character of Causality" according to which events related as cause and effect fall under strict laws, that is, laws that are precise and exception-less (as opposed to vague generalizations and probabilistic regularities). According to Davidson, there are no strict psychophysical or psychological laws; all strict laws are physical. Davidson's peculiar combination of monism and anomalism has the virtue of preserving the central insights of both physicalism (the ontological view that the mental emerges from the physical and does not constitute an independent substance) and folk psychology (the common-sense view of mental phenomena). The Davidsonian view of the relation between the physical and the mental claims to integrate both scientific discourse and ordinary accounts of mental events. This integration is achieved by exploiting the *autonomy* of our ordinary discourse about the mental, which functions independently of any talk (whether scientific or not) of physical processes. In this respect, a crucial component of Davidson's anomalous monism is the thesis of the *irreducibility* of the mental: intentional mental predicates and concepts cannot be reduced to physical predicates or concepts because while the former are governed by *constitutive principles of rationality*, the latter are not so governed. This irreducibility thesis underscores Davidson's deep commitment to rationality as a constitutive mark of the mental. Given this commitment, it is difficult to see how mental states can be irrational without losing their mentality. In his writings Davidson repeatedly addresses the problem of apparently irrational belief and action. Although he emphasizes that irrationality is not simply a spurious phenomenon whose psychological reality can be dismissed or explained away, he argues that genuine instances of irrationality nonetheless presuppose and require the overall rationality of the mental system in which they occur. In this way his theory deals with the problem of irrationality in a way that always preserves the overall rationality of the mind. This treatment of irrationality is grounded in Davidson's semantic and epistemic *holism*. Anomalous monism may appear to entail *property dualism* or *dual-aspect theory*, that is, the view that events can have two kinds of autonomous properties or aspects, physical or mental. However, while Davidson argues that mental properties cannot be reduced to physical ones, he also holds that the mental properties of an event depend entirely on its physical properties. This claim is developed through Davidson's introduction of a *supervenience thesis* into his token physicalism for events. According to this thesis, mental properties supervene on physical properties and no two events can be exactly alike in every physical respect and yet differ in some mental respect. In short, Davidson's doctrine of anomalous monism is a contemporary version of non-reductive materialism that includes three central theses: a causal and nomological thesis, an irreducibility thesis, and a supervenience thesis.

Further reading

Davidson, Donald. "Mental Events" in *Essays on Actions and Events*. Oxford: Oxford University Press, 1980, pp. 207–28.

—— "Knowing One's Own Mind" in *Subjective, Intersubjective, Objective*. Oxford: Oxford University Press, 2001, pp. 15–38.

—— "Paradoxes of Irrationality" in *Problems of Rationality*. Oxford: Oxford University Press, 2004, pp. 169–88.

—— "Laws and Cause" in *Truth, Language, and History*. Oxford: Oxford University Press, 2005, pp. 201–19.

José Medina

ANTINOMIANISM

The components of the term "antinomianism" mean "against law"; it was first used by Martin Luther during a controversy with his student John Agricola. Luther argued that moral law served to prepare sinners for grace by making them aware of sin. Agricola rejected even this negative sense of law, claiming that repentance depends solely on preaching the gospel of salvation. Luther wrote *Against the Antinomians* (1539) which was codified in Lutheranism in the 1577 Formula of Concord that established the opinion that law was useful to (1) reveal sin, (2) establish general moral decency in society, and (3) provide a rule of holy life for the regenerate. A similar controversy emerged among the Puritans in New England. While the Puritans emigrated from England on the grounds that church law (Anglican) was hindering their ability to access divine grace, they faced a test of communal cohesion when Anne Hutchinson rejected demands that she observe the (Puritan) legal and moral law as a means of preparing for conversion. She held to a "covenant of grace" which was separate from the works of law. She was condemned as an antinomian, enthusiast, and heretic and banished from the colony in 1637. In the Lutheran and Puritan theological controversies the question is whether moral law has a role in revealing or discovering divine grace. Christian orthodoxy generally argues for a positive role of moral law, hence rejecting antinomianism, in order to sustain hermeneutic continuity between the Old Testament emphasis on law and the grace emphasized in the New Testament, as the primary means of revealing human sin and sinfulness, and as a sign that the Holy Spirit is guiding the lives of believers toward peace with God and communal harmony.

Philosophical uses of the term "antinomianism" refer to a general skepticism of the metaphysical status of moral law or the articulate rejection of moral or communal standards of behavior and inquiry. Nietzsche is frequently cited as an exemplar of the antinomian position, due to his challenge of Christian "slave" morality and his claim that human history carries us beyond good and evil to the will to power. Used in this way, antinomianism is less a pejorative term and more a description of a philosophical attitude adopted because (1) of the failure to construct undefeatable arguments for the reality of moral law, (2) the claim that human inquiry and communal life is more productive without dependence on transcendent standards or goals, or (3) the ultimate good of absolute human freedom requires that any ostensible "obligation" be deconstructed and dismissed. Philosophical uses of antinomianism retain a hint of the controversial theological origins of this doctrine, despite the fact that most philosophers do not accept the historical goal of distinguishing a more consistent biblical or theological understanding of the ways divine grace is discovered in human experience.

Further reading

Battis, E. *Saints and Sectaries: Anne Hutchinson and the Antinomian Controversy in the Massachusetts Bay Colony.* Chapel Hill, NC: University of North Carolina Press, 1962.

ROGER A. WARD

ANTINOMIES

The term "antinomy" is used in two different senses in the philosophical literature. In one sense, discussed below, the term "antinomy" is synonymous with "paradox." Antinomies, in this sense, are a specific kind of logical problem. The term "antinomy" is also associated with a purported epistemological problem noted by Immanuel Kant in the *Critique of Pure Reason* (1781, 1787).

In Kant's account, an antinomy is a philosophical problem in which we are led to contradictory conclusions regarding a metaphysical issue based on arguments that are *prima facie* equally good. For example, Kant claims that arguments could be presented for and against the claim that the universe has existed for an infinite amount of time. Kant argued that the apparent contradiction between the conclusions drawn from such arguments can be resolved through proper understanding of his distinction between "things as they appear to us" and the "thing in itself." Through proper application of this distinction, Kant contends that there are false premises in the arguments that generate these contradictory conclusions, and similar difficulties with the premises that generate the other antinomies discussed by Kant in the *Critique of Pure Reason*. These "antinomies" in the Kantian sense do not, if Kant is correct, lead us to genuine contradictions.

As mentioned above, in ordinary usage, the word "antinomy" is synonymous with "paradox." A paradox is any statement that is unacceptable yet results from an argument, the premises of which we accept. Let us say that a barber in Brooklyn shaves every man who lives in his neighborhood who does not shave himself, and only those men in the neighborhood who do not shave themselves. If the question is asked whether the barber shaves himself, a paradox results from these innocent-seeming premises. If he shaves himself, then it is not the case that he shaves only those men who do not shave themselves; and if he does not shave himself, then it is not the case that he shaves all the men who do not shave themselves. The contradictory conclusion of the line of reasoning shows us that we had accepted a claim that must now be rejected. This paradox, the paradox of the barber, has a quite easy solution: it is impossible for there to be a barber who fits this description.

In the definition of the term "antinomy" given by W.V. Quine in *The Ways of Paradox* (1966), an antinomy is a specific, important kind of paradox. In an antinomy, we are forced by a paradoxical argument to reject a line of argument that we previously considered to be trustworthy. I will discuss two of the important antinomies cited by Quine in his discussion: the antinomy of the liar, and Russell's antinomy. Each of these antinomies has had a vast influence in philosophy, logic, and mathematics.

The antinomy of the liar can be stated in a form that refers to lying, and one of the best-known formulations of the antinomy is as follows: Epimenides, a Cretan, said that all Cretans are liars. If what he said was true, and all Cretans have always lied, then Epimenides said truly that he was lying. If he is lying, then he must be uttering a falsehood, so we have derived a contradiction: the utterance of Epimenides is both true and false. An even more troubling formulation of the liar paradox, one that does not depend on external circumstances (such as whether all Cretans have always lied) can be stated as follows. I will call the following sentence *E*: *E* is false. If *E* is true, then *E* is false. If *E* is false, then *E* is not false, i.e. *E* is true. We must either accept that there are true falsehoods, or find some way of blocking the inference that led us to the antinomy.

John Dewey contended, in *Logic: The Theory of Inquiry* (1938), that the antinomy of the liar results from a confusion in different readings of the logical form of utterances such as "All Cretans are liars." One way of reading this utterance, what Dewey calls the "generic" proposition, is the claim that we can identify someone as a Cretan based on the fact that such a person has a tendency to lie. Reading the utterance as a "universal" proposition requires reading the statement as one according to which all Cretans are necessarily liars. Contradiction only occurs, according to Dewey, when we have confused the generic and universal propositions. This attempted resolution of the paradox overlooks formulations that are not cast in terms of claims about liars, such as the troubling formulation of the paradox noted in the last paragraph.

Bertrand Russell's antinomy concerns classes. We can talk about classes of things – the class of philosophy professors, the class of laptop computers, the class of baseballs. We can also talk about classes that contain classes. In addition to the class of philosophy professors and the class of mathematics professors, there is also the class of classes of professors, a class that contains both of the aforementioned classes.

On the assumption that all that is required to specify a class is to specify a condition for being a member of that class, Russell's antinomy results. Consider the following class: the class of all classes that do not belong to themselves. In order to be a member of this class, something has to not be a member of this class. In order not to be a member of this class, the object has to be a member of this class. So an object is a member of this class if and only if it is not a member of the class, a contradiction. In order to resolve this antinomy, restrictions on the conditions for class-membership are required.

The antinomy of the liar and Russell's antinomy thus reveal that our naïve, pretheoretical conceptions of truth and class stand in need of refinement.

Further reading

Kripke, Saul. "Outline of a Theory of Truth," *Journal of Philosophy* 72, (1975): 690–716.

Quine, W.V.O. *The Ways of Paradox and Other Essays*, revised and enlarged edition. Cambridge, MA: Harvard University Press, 1966.

FRITZ J. MCDONALD

ANTI-REALISM

Realism is the view that the world exists independently of our thoughts about it, and that the objects of our knowledge are things in the world. Anti-realism, as the name suggests, denies realism. According to anti-realists, the world depends on us in some way. Exactly which objects of our knowledge are denied independent reality, and why, depends on whether the anti-realism in question is global or local. Global anti-realists deny realism about everything. They argue that human beings are incapable of meaningfully thinking about the world independently of their conceptualizations of it, because whenever we think about the world, we employ the perspective of our own understanding. Local anti-realists, on the other hand, deny realism about some particular domain of things. They take issue with specific philosophical conceptions like properties or numbers, claiming that if we were not around to think about them then things like these wouldn't exist. Thus, whereas the global anti-realist doubts our ability to meaningfully access a world independent of our perspective, the local anti-realist holds that our perspective is all there is of the things in question.

Global anti-realism

Early anti-realist views were idealist. The philosopher Immanuel Kant thought that knowledge could only be obtained if experiences were ordered by human understanding. According to his transcendental idealism, knowledge is made when our sensory inputs are structured by our ways of experiencing and the categories of our understanding. Thus, the world independent of our understanding becomes an inaccessible and unknowable world as it is in itself. The philosopher G.W.F. Hegel rejected Kant's notion of a world as it is in itself, but embraced his theory that objects of knowledge depend essentially on us and our understanding. According to Hegel's idealism, the only world is the one constructed by systems of knowledge, since the world is just experience systematized by mind or spirit. Thus, for Hegel, no conception of a world independent of that conceptualization remains.

These early idealisms gave rise to several distinct strains of anti-realism. Constructivists agreed with idealists both that the world of our understanding somehow depends on us for its existence, and that trying to conceive of it independently of our organizational frameworks makes no sense. Unlike the idealists, however, constructivists argued that different conceptual schemes might be possible and/or useful. For example, Nelson Goodman argued that different worlds are created by our different ways of seeing the world (i.e. scientifically, ethically, aesthetically). According to Goodman, no one way of seeing the world should be seen as more objectively true than any other. Rather, different worlds might be useful for different purposes. A common variant of constructivism is in the philosophy of science. According to Thomas Kuhn, the history of science teaches us that scientific theories are merely elaborate frameworks that help us to order our experiences and predict and control the world. On this view, competing scientific theories describe different worlds, and there is no fact as to which theory is really the correct one.

Another strain of anti-realism comes from American Pragmatism. Early pragmatists William James and John Dewey based their anti-realism, in part, on an instrumentalist theory of truth. They argued that the truth is not a matter of a correspondence between our beliefs and some ready-made reality. What is true depends on us and our practical interests: the true ways of thinking about the world are the ones that are useful to us, and the false ones are not. Because of this, what is real, in a sense, depends on us and our interests and goals.

Other pragmatists disagreed with Dewey and James about the nature of truth, but came to similar anti-realist conclusions. George Santayana, for example, thought that our beliefs about the world were true just in case they corresponded with the world, but he argued that this correspondence is in principle unknowable, since it would require a completely neutral (i.e. value-free) perspective which humans are prevented from having. Humans can only discern what is pragmatically true, i.e. instrumentally useful. Another example is contemporary philosopher Hilary Putnam. Putnam advocates a view he calls "internal realism." According to Putnam, all thought about the world is constrained by language and there are no intrinsic connections between language and the world. Thus, trying to theorize about a world independently of ourselves and our conceptual organization is no longer possible, rather like trying to get a God's-eye point of view on the world.

Some non-pragmatist anti-realists also find a correspondence notion of truth problematic, though they eschew Dewey and James' instrumental notion of truth. According to Michael Dummett, considerations about meaning from the philosophy of language reveal that true sentences are simply those that we are warranted in asserting. Thus, our conception of the world is limited by what can be warranted in assertion. For example, we might never be warranted in asserting the sentence, "A city will never be built here." If this is so, then there is no fact as to whether or not a city will ever be built here.

One thing that all of these global anti-realisms have in common is their emphasis on considerations from the theory of knowledge (epistemology) or the theory of meaning (semantics). Consider the sentence "The sun is hot." Constructivists like Kuhn, for example, think in terms of how the sun is known. To even think about a thing like the sun takes conceptual organization. Thus, the idea of a sun independent of that organization loses its meaning. Our sun, the one that the earth revolves around, and that is one of billions upon billions of stars in the universe, is a very different sun than the one that Tycho Brahe saw, since his sun went around the earth and the earth was at the center of everything.

Realists argue that the anti-realist overemphasizes epistemology and/or semantics, at the price of metaphysics. Metaphysics is the part of philosophy that attempts to characterize reality or existence as a whole. Realists think that the reality of a thing like the sun has nothing to do with us and what we know about it because its existence and what it is made of do not depend on us and our conceptual schemes. According to realists, when we know true sentences about the sun we know things about that big thing up in the sky.

Local anti-realism

Local anti-realists are frequently motivated less by epistemic and semantic considerations than their global cousins, instead arguing that realism in many philosophical domains is unnecessary and/or metaphysically unattractive. These anti-realists tend to be very naturalistic, appealing to a principle called Occam's Razor, which counsels us to never multiply entities beyond necessity. They are critical of what they see as a willingness on the realist's part to invent entities to solve supposed philosophical problems.

Normative domains are those areas of thought that tell us what we ought to do (ethics, rationality) or how we ought to believe (epistemology, logic). Realists in these domains hold that there are facts about what we ought to do or believe just as surely as there are facts about cats and dogs. Anti-realists deny that there are any normative facts. According to J.L. Mackie's error theory, for example, sentences with evaluative terms are false because there don't happen to be any of the properties in question. Nevertheless, evaluative sentences can still be seen to play an important role in human interactions and behavior. Another kind of normative anti-realism has several variants and goes by many names (expressivism, non-factualism, non-cognitivism, emotivism). The unifying claim behind these views is that there are no genuine normative properties at all. A secondary claim endorsed by some but not all theorists in this camp is that sentences that contain normative terms, e.g. "Murder is wrong," are neither true nor false.

One form of local anti-realism with deep historical roots is nominalism. Nominalists deny the existence of universals and abstract Platonic forms, with a common variant in the philosophy of mathematics that denies that numbers are abstract objects. Realists about redness, for example, argue that there is some abstract object, or universal, which exists over and above individual red things. Furthermore, they argue that what makes a particular thing red is its participation in this abstract universal, redness. Nominalists, on the other hand, argue that redness is just the sum total of all the particular red things. What makes a thing red is its appearing in a red way, not its participating in the universal or form of redness.

A more recent variant of local anti-realism is fictionalism. Fictionalists argue that the sentences in some particular domains (e.g. mathematics, propositions, moral properties) are strictly false though they may be true in their respective fictions. Strictly speaking it is false that Sherlock Holmes lived at 221b Baker Street because there is no Sherlock Holmes. Nevertheless, that sentence is true in the fictional stories. Likewise, fictionalists about mathematical entities think that the sentence "Two is the only even prime" is really false, because there is no number two. Nevertheless, in the fiction of mathematics there is a two, and in that fiction, it has the property of being the only even prime. However, unlike Arthur Conan Doyle stories, which presumably fill some aesthetic need, philosophical fictionalists claim that their respective fictions serve some important philosophical and/or communicative function.

In addition to the global constructivists mentioned above, some anti-realists in the philosophy of science limit their worries to particular entities of science. These local anti-realists tend to be motivated by epistemic and/or semantic concerns about theoretically defined unobservables. Mature and successful scientific theories frequently involve reference to entities that cannot be directly observed, such as electrons or forces. Realists in the philosophy of science argue that the success of theories that appeal to unobservables is evidence for these unobservables' existence. Anti-realists respond that the history of science is filled with theories that were successful, but which were later found to be false. Given the indirectness of the evidence that we have for unobservables, anti-realists advise a localized skepticism, and argue that electron theory is neither true nor false, though it is, of course, very instrumentally useful.

A more recent variant of anti-realism about unobservables in science is the constructive empiricism of Bas Van Frassen, who argues that the acceptance of a theory only commits one to belief in the observable entities of that theory. This view differs from the scientific local anti-realists just discussed in holding that the sentences of a scientific theory are either true or false.

Further reading

Blackburn, Simon. *Truth*. New York: Oxford University Press, 2005.

Devitt, Michael. *Realism and Truth*. Princeton, NJ: Princeton University Press, 1997.

Goodman, Nelson. *Ways of Worldmaking*. Indianapolis, IN: Hackett, 1978.

James, William. "Pragmatism's Conception of Truth" in *The Writings of William James*, ed. John J. McDermott. Chicago, IL: University of Chicago Press, 1977.

Kuhn, Thomas. *The Structure of Scientific Revolutions*. Chicago, IL: University of Chicago Press, 1996.

Luntley, Michael. *Language, Logic and Experience*, LaSalle, IL: Open Court, 1988.

Okasha, Samir. *Philosophy of Science, A Very Short Introduction*. New York: Oxford University Press, 2002.

Putnam, Hilary. *Reason, Truth and History*. Cambridge: Cambridge University Press, 1981.

Van Frassen, Bas. *The Scientific Image*. Oxford: Clarendon Press, 1980.

Wright, Crispin. *Truth and Objectivity*, Cambridge, MA: Harvard University Press, 1992.

J.A. Fisher

APEL, KARL-OTTO

Karl-Otto Apel, (1922–), who is one of the most important post-war German philosophers, builds on sources drawn from both the analytic and continental philosophical traditions. Apel, who studied in Berlin, taught at Mainz, Kiel, and for many years at Frankfurt, before retiring in 1990. He has received numerous honors, including honorary doctorates. Apel was for many years closely associated with the German social theorist Jürgen Habermas, his colleague at Frankfurt, whom he strongly influenced.

Apel is the author of many books, a number of which are available in English. Apel's approach is best represented in *Towards a Transformation of Philosophy* (*Transformation der Philosophie*, 1973), a collection of essays combining a distinctive pragmatic and hermeneutic reinterpretation of Wittgenstein's thinking influenced by many others, including Kant, Heidegger, Peirce, and Morris. The result can be described as a semiotic transformation of a Kantian form of transcendental philosophy based upon the concept of *Kommunikationsgemeinschaft*, literally communicational society, which further inspires Habermas' theory of communicative action.

With the possible exception of Chisholm, arguably no one has done more recently to make the case for foundationalism. Kant can be read as suggesting that philosophy contributes to human emancipation through reason. In invoking ethical foundationalism, Apel similarly suggests a link between claims for truth and knowledge – a link he regards as intrinsic to discussion of any kind – and social utility. Apel transforms transcendental philosophy by substituting a plural subject for the supposedly traditional, monological subject. He is mainly concerned with a reflexive, transcendental–pragmatic foundationalism, which he regards as necessary for the rational justification of ethics;

and the difference between real and merely ideal conditions of communicative ethics, also called discourse ethics, and perhaps better known in the variation later developed by Habermas.

Like Kant, Apel maintains that individuals should act as if they belonged to an ideal speech community. Like Aristotle, Apel argues that to reject this claim is to become involved in a so-called performative contradiction. Apel calls this approach transcendental pragmatics to indicate that it combines transcendental reflection in the Kantian sense and a pragmatic relation to the real world. He uses the term "transcendental hermeneutics" to refer to the Heideggerian idea of reflection as grounding reason through a hermeneutic circle.

Apel links his position to a transcendental–pragmatic subject described in Charles Morris' three-dimensional semiotics. Yet if our norms depend on a given historical moment, he neither identifies nor shows there are universal presuppositions of real discussion. Apel specifically links his position to Cartesian foundationalism. He contends that Peirce shows an unbreakable link between the objective scientific–technological investigation of nature and the intersubjective possibility of consensus underlying everything we do. This link, which is presupposed by the modern interest in human self-emancipation, is useful in formulating regulative principles of practical and postulated scientific progress. It might be more accurate to say that Peirce, who does not focus on human self-emancipation, thinks we can go from doubt to belief through the process of scientific inquiry.

Further reading

Apel, Karl-Otto. *Analytic Philosophy of Language and the Geisteswissenschaften*, trans. Harald Holstelilie. Dordrecht: Reidel, 1967.

—— *Toward a Transformation of Philosophy*, trans. Glen Adey and David Fisby. Milwaukee, WI: Marquette University Press, 1980.

—— *Charles S. Peirce: From Pragmatism to Pragmaticism*, trans. John Michael Krois. Amherst, MA: University of Massachusetts Press, 1981.

—— *Understanding and Explanation: A Transcendental-Pragmatic Perspective*, trans. Georgia Warnke. Cambridge, MA: MIT Press, 1984.

—— *From a Transcendental-Semiotic Point of View*, ed. Marianna Papastephanou. Manchester: Manchester University Press, 1998.

—— *The Response of Discourse Ethics to the Moral Challenge of the Human Situation as such and Especially Today.* Leuven: Peeters, 1999.

Benhabib, Seyla. *The Communicative Ethics Controversy.* Cambridge, MA: MIT Press, 1990.

Mendieta, Eduardo. *Adventures of Transcendental Philosophy: Karl-Otto Apel's Semiotics and Discourse Ethics.* Lanham, MD: Rowman and Littlefield, 2002.

Tom Rockmore

ARCHITECTONIC

C.S. Peirce once complained to William James, who had praised Peirce for "teeming with ideas," that: "My philosophy ... is not an 'idea' with which I 'brim over'; it is a serious research to which there is no royal road ..." (*The Thought and Character of William James* II.419). He envisioned diverse fields of experimental research, including philosophy, standing in systematic relationship to one another. Serious research meant for him, at the very least careful attention to the bearing of one branch of inquiry on other branches (e.g. of phenomenology on psychology or logic on metaphysics).

Peirce explicitly advocated an architectonic approach to philosophical inquiry and, in so doing, formally acknowledged his debt to Immanuel Kant, in particular, to Chapter III ("The Architectonic of Pure Reason") of the last part of the *Critique of Pure Reason* ("Transcendental Doctrine of Method"). This chapter is in fact the penultimate one of the entire work, followed only by "The History of Pure Reason." Peirce in effect reverses this order, making the actual history of experimental reason prior to any doctrine of method. In the chapter in the *Critique* that so influenced Peirce, however, Kant defines architectonic as "the art of constructing systems," contending scientific knowledge exhibits a "systematic unity" and, thus, the art of unifying the diverse areas of human inquiry into a systematic whole provides "the doctrine of the scientific in our knowledge" (Kant 1965: 53; A832/B860). What is likely to be overlooked is that Peirce's opposition to Descartes is, in reference to the art of envisioning a systematic approach to human inquiry, as fundamental as was Peirce's indebtedness to Kant. In his *Discourse,* Descartes observed: "often there is less perfection in works made of several pieces and in works made by the hands of several masters than in those on which but one master has worked." Buildings designed and overseen by a single architect "are commonly more beautiful and better ordered than those that several architects have tried to patch up, using old walls that had been built for other purposes," just as towns laid out "on a vacant plain" by a single engineer are typically superior to those ancient cities which haphazardly have taken shape in the course of time. Peirce conceded: "Works of sculpture and painting can be executed for a single patron and must be by a single artist." But he immediately added:

> a great building, such as alone can call out the depths of the architect's soul, is meant for the whole people, and is erected by the exertions of an army representative of the whole people. It is the message with which an age is charged, and which it delivers to posterity.

Such a building is ineluctably a communal task; hence, "thought characteristic of an individual – the piquant, the nice, the clever – is too little to play any but the most subordinate rôle in architecture" (CP 1.176).

Thus, Peirce insisted, "philosophy ought to be deliberate and planned out." In "The Architecture of Theories," he explained this to mean:

> every person who wishes to form an opinion concerning fundamental problems should first of all make a complete survey of human knowledge, should take note of all the valuable ideas in each branch of science, should observe in just what respect each has been successful and where it has failed, in order that, in the light of the thorough acquaintance so attained of the available materials for a philosophical theory and of the nature and strength of each, he may proceed to the study of what the problem of philosophy consists in, and of the proper way of solving it. I must not be understood as endeavoring to state fully all that these preparatory studies should embrace; on the contrary, I purposely slur over many points, in order to give emphasis to one special recommendation, namely, to make a systematic study of the conceptions out of which a philosophical theory may be built, in order to ascertain what place each conception may fitly occupy in such a theory, and to what uses it is adapted.
>
> (CP 6.9)

We find, at the center of Peirce's architectonic approach to philosophical inquiry, his efforts to articulate a set of interrelated, universal categories (see, e.g., CP 6.32–3). Moreover, his conception of this approach stresses the communal nature of human investigation, also the need to conceive of the various branches of experimental investigation as hierarchically related to one another (ranging from the most abstract and general to the most concrete and specific), and finally the imperative need to undertake any particular investigation in a thoroughly deliberate manner. The scientific inquirer is, at bottom, a specific form of deliberative agent and, accordingly, scientific rationality is reconceived in terms far closer to the classical notions of *praxis* and *phronesis* than those of *theoria* and *episteme*.

For Peirce, however, scientific knowledge cannot be defined in terms of its systematic character. He not only explicitly rejects S.T. Coleridge's definition of scientific knowledge as "systematized knowledge" but also takes this definition to be an improvement upon the formulations of Kant (CP 7.54). Peirce takes it to be "the last development of that sort of philosophy that strives to draw knowledge out of the depths of the *Ich-heit*" or the self (in Kant's case, self-conscious and self-critical Reason). But knowledge is only to be drawn from experience and, for Peirce, the architectonic approach concerns not the final form into which knowledge must be cast in order to secure its scientific character but the thoroughly deliberate manner in which the ongoing, interminable pursuit of unknown truths is most effectively undertaken.

Due largely to the influence of such thinkers as Nietzsche and Kierkegaard, there is today a deep suspicion regarding the will to system and, due to James as much as Nietzsche, an equally deep skepticism concerning the value or even possibility of framing a comprehensive, integrated vision of the cosmos. For this reason, however, George Santayana's way of conceiving the matter deserves to be recalled:

> The spirit of system, though it so often renders the mind fanatical and obstinately blind to some facts, is essentially the effort to give all facts their due, not to forget things once discovered and understood, and not to have illusions and vices comfortably unchallenged.

That is, this spirit is that of consistency when, in turn, "consistency is but a form of honour and courage," making "singleness of purpose" (Santayana 1942: 521). This captures the spirit underlying of many philosophers, including Peirce and Santayana himself, who are committed to systematic philosophy. It is, however, imperative to distinguish between systematic philosophizing and a philosophical system because it is one thing to strive ceaselessly for maximal consistency and scope, quite another to aim at constructing a closed system allegedly achieving conceptual finality.

Further reading

Hookway, Christopher. *Peirce*. London: Routledge, 1985.

Kant, Immanuel. *Critique of Pure Reason*, trans. Norman Kemp Smith. New York: St Martin's Press, 1965.

Kent, Beverley. *Charles S. Peirce: Logic and the Classification of the Sciences.* Kingston: McGill-Queen's University Press, 1987.

Manchester, Paul. "Kant's Conception of Architectonic in Its Historical Context," *Journal of the History of Philosophy* 41, 2 (2003): 187–207.

Murray, Murray. G. *The Development of Peirce's Philosophy.* Indianapolis, IN: Hackett, 1993.

Peirce, Charles S. *Collected Papers of Charles Sanders Peirce.* Vols I–VI, ed. Charles Hartshorne and Paul Weiss. Cambridge, MA: Harvard University Press, 1931–5. Vols VII and VIII, second edition, ed. Arthur W. Burks. Cambridge, MA: Belknap Press, 1958. Cited in text as CP.

—— "A Brief Intellectual Autobiography by Charles Sanders Peirce," ed. K.L. Ketner, *American Journal of Semiotics* 2, 1–2 (1983): 61–82.

Santayana, George. *Realms of Being*, revised edition, ed. Irwin Edman. New York: Charles Scribner's Sons, 1953 [1942].

Whitehead, A.N. *Process and Reality*, corrected edition, ed. D.R. Griffin and D. Sherburne. New York: Free Press, 1978.

VINCENT COLAPIETRO

ARGUMENTATION

Suppose two people (A and B) disagree, and their disagreement is something that must be resolved. They have a variety of options to achieve this end: A can threaten B or actually inflict some violence on B and thereby gain his assent, A could offer B something B wants in exchange for his assent, or A could persuade B to change his mind by marshalling reasons that count against the truth of B's position and for the truth of A's. If A takes the latter route, and assuming that B cooperates by marshalling his own reasons, A and B resolve their disagreement by way of *argumentation*.

Given the description above, argumentation is the activity of reason-exchange between speakers with the dual goals of (i) gaining the truth about some matter of controversy between them, and thereby (ii) resolving their disagreement. As such, argumentation has both *epistemic,* or knowledge-directed, ends and *pragmatic,* or speaker-related, ends. With arguments, we not only strive to gain or impart knowledge of what is the case, we also promote understanding between people.

A setting wherein the speakers are committed to these goals and pursue them by the exchange of reasons is an *argumentative context*. These contexts function properly when the participant speakers cooperate in their pursuit of these ends, so argumentative contexts have a set of specialized rules that must be followed in order for the speakers to make joint progress.

Let us assume that A is a proponent of a certain proposition, p. If B has doubts about p, it is A's job to rationally convince B of p. A must shoulder the *burden of proof* to argue for p. This, again, is on the assumption that A is trying to convince B of p; if B wants to show A that not-p, B must also shoulder an equivalent argumentative burden. A's job, at this point, is to give an argument for p – this includes clarifying what p amounts to, marshaling evidence for p, explaining the relevance of this evidence for p, and providing some response to standard (if there are any) arguments for not-p. B's duties are to respond *helpfully* and *honestly* to A's argument. The requirement of helpfulness is that if B disagrees with A's case for p, B must couch his responses in terms of failings in A's argument. B can take issue with the veracity of A's premises, so A must give further arguments for them or revise them. Or B may take issue with the support A's premises provide for p, so A must explain further the relevance between them and his conclusion. Or B may introduce some additional feature that undermines A's initial argument (for example, that the argument is fine so long as we do not pay attention to some fact, but once we recognize this fact, the argument fails), so A must address this new issue. B's response is honest when B agrees to all the premises and support-relations between premises and conclusions that he antecedently endorses. That is, if A produces premises that B takes as true, then B would be dishonest were he to challenge A regarding them. The rule of honesty is that one does not feign doubt in order to make one's opponent's burden of proof heavier. If B cannot helpfully or honestly reject A's argument, then B is obliged to accept the argument, and thereby B is obliged to accept the conclusion. If B does not accept A's argument and has responded helpfully and honestly, it is incumbent on A to revise the argument accordingly. Ideally, after a few iterations of A giving arguments and B responding helpfully and honestly to them, B either accepts A's argument for p or A's case for p fails, and A is no longer warranted in holding it true. Either way, the disagreement should be resolved or at least A and B have taken steps toward its resolution, since at least one speaker has had to revise his view in a manner reflective of the other's reasons.

Charles Sanders Peirce's theory of the fixation of belief takes argumentation to be central to the successful resolution of doubt. The story of the fixation of belief is that of the four options for believers in the face of controversy (retreating to tenacity, appealing to authority, relying on what is agreeable to reason, and subjecting all views to scientific scrutiny), the scientific option is the most appealing on reflection. In subjecting a view to scrutiny, one must be open to challenges and be willing to revise or reject the view if it cannot withstand that scrutiny. Additionally, one must be willing to contribute to the scrutiny of others' views.

John Dewey's logical theory, developed in the 1938 *Logic*, concerns the general features of inquiry – the linguistic and experiential processes of resolving indeterminate or problematic situations. Inquiry and the arguments it yields transform indeterminate situations into determinate ones by distinguishing warranted solutions from unwarranted. Argumentation, from a Deweyan perspective, is the means by which inquirers demonstrate and evaluate the warrant for their respective solutions to shared problematic situations.

Nicholas Rescher formalized the norms for argumentative exchange in his 1977 *Dialectics*. There, Rescher renders the norms for argumentation as a syntax for a meta-language corresponding to various argumentative strategies and assertional moods. In a sense, the objective of Rescher's dialectical logic is to formalize the previously informal features of argument.

Recently, studies in argumentation have been heavily influenced by research in communication-theory and the pragmatics of language-use. Frans van Eemeren and Rob Grootendorst have made the case that argumentation's norms are clearest against a backdrop of the broader objectives of human communication, and Douglas Walton has suggested that argumentation's norms are understandable as extensions of the basic requirement of cooperation in communication.

Further reading

Burke, F. Thomas, Hester, D. Micah, and Talisse, Robert B. (eds) *Dewey's Logical Theory*. Nashville, TN: Vanderbilt University Press, 2002.

van Eemeren, Frans H. and Grootendorst, Rob. *A Systematic Theory of Argumentation: The Pragma-Dialectical Approach*. Cambridge: Cambridge University Press, 2004.

Rescher, Nicholas. *Dialectics: A Controversy-Oriented Approach to the Theory of Knowledge*. Albany, NY: SUNY Press, 1977.

Walton, Douglas. *Informal Logic*. Cambridge: Cambridge University Press, 1989.

Scott F. Aikin

ARGUMENTUM AD HOMINEM

Argumentum ad hominem is the term used in logic for a form of argument in which one party attacks the argument of a second party by attacking the ethical character of that second party. Essentially, the argument is, "He has a bad character, so his argument is worthless." A third party (an audience) is also often implied, as the argument is meant to discredit the character of the second party in the eyes of some audience to whom the argument was directed. *Argumentum ad hominem* has traditionally been treated as a fallacy, in the logic textbooks, typically because such an argument brings in irrelevant personal matters (Hamblin 1970). However, one philosopher, Henry W. Johnstone, Jr (1920–2000), advocated the radical view that *argumentum ad hominem* is characteristic of philosophical argumentation, even writing (1978: 134) that he regarded it as "the only valid argument in philosophy". By showing that *ad hominem* arguments could be reasonable in some cases, Johnstone revealed the depth of the problem of identifying criteria for judging when they are fallacious.

Recent research on argumentation has moved toward the position that this type of argument is not always fallacious (Walton 1998). For example in law, attacking the character of a witness or defendant in cross-examination is sometimes admissible, and regarded as an important and relevant kind of evidence. On the other hand, *ad hominem* arguments are sometimes such powerful devices of rhetorical persuasion, to cite negative campaign tactics in politics as an example, that they have a devastating effect as smear tactics even when based on little more than innuendo. The five basic types of *ad hominem* arguments are described below.

Direct *ad hominem*

In the direct type, the simplest and most basic type, a direct attack on the arguer's ethical character is used to discredit his argument. For example, it might be argued, "He is a liar, therefore his argument is not credible." Ethical character for honesty is often the focus of this attack. By suggesting that an arguer cannot be trusted to tell the truth, an opponent can attack not only his argument, but his capability for taking part in a collaborative discussion. The term "abusive," used by the textbooks for this type, suggests fallaciousness. To allow for the possibility of non-fallacious instances, the more neutral term "direct" is preferable. Alternatively, it might be called the ethotic type of *ad hominem*, following Aristotle's comment (*Rhetoric* 1356a) that persuasion is achieved by the speaker's personal character (*ethos*).

Circumstantial *ad hominem*

In the circumstantial type, the first party attacks the second party by claiming that she does not practice what she preaches, and then employs the alleged contradiction to imply that she has bad character as a credible arguer. For example, the argument of a rock star who claims to be an environmentalist might be attacked by saying, "This enviro-boy drives a gas-guzzling Hummer." The implied suggestion is that the inconsistency shows he is a hypocrite.

Bias *ad hominem*

In the bias type of *ad hominem*, the one party attacks the other by alleging that his argument is compromised by personal interest at stake, like financial gain. Such an allegation of bias works by casting doubt on the impartiality of a participant in a discussion.

Poisoning the well *ad hominem*

In the poisoning the well type, an arguer is claimed to be closed to any balanced consideration of the truth of a matter. The classic case is that of Cardinal Newman, who was attacked by arguing that, as a Catholic, he would always revert to the Catholic view, instead of considering the evidence as a basis for his decision. The British novelist and clergyman Charles Kingsley attacked Newman, arguing that Newman's claims could not be trusted because, as a Catholic priest, Newman's first loyalty was not to the truth. Newman wrote a whole book, *Apologia Pro Vita Sua* (1864), directed to refuting this *ad hominem* attack, pointing out that it threw such an aura of suspicion on anything he might write that the well would be poisoned.

Tu quoque ad hominem

In the *tu quoque* type, one *ad hominem* argument is rebutted by mounting another one against the original *ad hominem* arguer. The failure of ethical character cited in the first attack is countered by replying, "You're just as bad." This variant is sometimes called the two wrongs fallacy.

Other types, not mentioned here, have also been studied (Krabbe and Walton 1993; Walton 1998), and some work has been done on classifying various subtypes.

Further reading

Aristotle. *Rhetoric*. Cambridge, MA: Loeb Library, 1934.

Hamblin, Charles L. *Fallacies*. London: Methuen, 1970.

Johnstone, Henry W., Jr. *Philosophy and Argument*. University Park, PA: Pennsylvania State University Press, 1959.

—— *Validity and Rhetoric in Philosophical Argument*. University Park, PA: The Dialogue Press of Man and World, 1978.

Krabbe, Erik C.W. and Walton, Douglas. "It's All Very Well for You to Talk: Situationally Disqualifying *Ad Hominem* Attacks," *Informal Logic* 15 (1993): 79–91.

Newman, John H. *Apologia Pro Vita Sua*. London: Longman, Green, 1864.

Walton, Douglas. *Ad Hominem Arguments*. Tuscaloosa, AL: University of Alabama Press, 1998.

Douglas Walton

ARMINIANISM

Arminianism was a theological movement of the Reformed Church initiated by Dutch theologian Jacobus Arminius (1560–1609). Arminius, who studied with Calvin's successor Theodore Beza at Geneva in the 1580s, sought to maintain a Calvinist doctrine of predestination while offering a view of human faith and sin that would make God seem less arbitrary and more just. In doing so, he brought about a rift in the Reformed Church that was analogous to – though in theological detail distinct from – the rift between St Augustine and the Pelagians.

In outline, Arminius' controversial version of salvation holds the following: (1) God has foreknowledge of all that is destined to be; (2) only God's Grace, through Christ, has the power to provide true faith and thus salvation; (3) persons, nevertheless, have the ability or freedom to agree or cooperate with the Grace offered to them or to resist and reject the Grace; (4) only those who cooperate with God's Grace are saved, while those who remain incorrigible are condemned. This position was seen to directly challenge the Calvinist doctrine of "justification by faith alone." Thus, in effect, from a strict Calvinist outlook, God's sovereignty is challenged, and humans appear to be given one "work" by which they can choose their own salvation – the "work" of choosing to accept Grace. Most doctrinaire Calvinists argued that the Arminian position threatened their belief in predestination, and therefore posed a fundamental challenge to their religion.

In American thought, Arminianism appeared first as the foil in Jonathan Edwards's (1703–58) attempt to recover a sound Calvinism in New England. Arminianism was the chief opponent in his renowned Freedom of the Will. Edwards's own compatibilist version of free will maintained room for predestination and God's thoroughgoing sovereignty over against the Arminians' seemingly looser account of freedom. However, as Edwards argued against the Arminians in the colonies, John Wesley adopted Arminianism in England and emphasized its focus on personal responsibility and accountability in matters of faith, sin, and salvation. By the time of the second Great Awakening (1790–1840), Methodists and Presbyterians in the United States preached an Arminianism that appealed to the frontier spirit then developing among European-Americans.

Within Christian theology in the United States, Arminianism remains a popular outlook. In theological circles, it still serves as a technical interpretation of the relationship between God and persons, and is not simply a loose libertarianism. Its theoretical focus on human responsibility has sustained nineteenth- and twentieth-century Christian movements in social reform. Human works can be construed as the effects of one's acceptance of Grace; thus one can understand oneself to be carrying out God's work responsibly. Outside of theology proper, Arminianism has had a wider cultural effect. In the trajectory of American philosophy, the Arminian and Unitarian emphases on choice and will created an intellectual climate in which these ideas were seen to be more important than the ideas of submission to God and the dismissal of affairs in this world. Both the Transcendentalists and the pragmatists came to emphasize individual freedom together with individual responsibility. From Emerson's "Self-reliance" to James's "Will to Believe," one can see a groundwork laid by the ascendance of Arminian thought in American religions. John Dewey's early emphasis on engaging Christianity in social reform and his later emphasis on a faith in our human ability to transform the world can also be seen as rooted in the Arminian challenge to a sovereign God. Thus, in both its technical theological guise and in its practical import, Arminianism remains a live idea in American culture.

Further reading

Edwards, Jonathan. *Freedom of the Will*, ed. P. Ramsey. New Haven, CT: Yale University Press, 1957.

Pinnock, Clarke (ed.) *Grace of God, the Will of Man: A Case for Arminianism*. New York: Zondervan, 1989.

DOUGLAS R. ANDERSON

ART

The term "art," used as a freestanding noun without qualification, is ordinarily taken to designate, collectively, paintings and sculptures, visual art (or "artworks," as we now often say); whereas the expression "the arts" usually designates what in an older idiom, but also still today, is meant by "the fine arts" ("*les beaux arts*"): music, dance, theatre, the visual arts – and, less frequently, the literary arts, probably because literature is not taken to depend on the primacy of any sensory modality and perhaps also because the use of language is thought to have an ineliminable practical function that somehow threatens or compromises the "disinterested" interest in the beautiful (in the arts). All such qualifications are now generally waived, so that "art" or "the arts" is allowed to range, increasingly, over the literary arts as well and even over architecture and furniture and utensils and the like, so long as the primary considerations associated with the appreciation and criticism of "the fine arts" are congruently extended to such apparently more problematic "things." But then, the more inclusive use is accompanied by questioning the meaning of "fine" and "beautiful" or their ubiquity, or, for that matter, the meaning of "aesthetic," a term of art made canonical in Western philosophy by its remarkably influential (though not earliest) use in Immanuel Kant's *Critique of Judgement* (1790), along the lines (now well beyond Kant's intention) of the perception or experience of, or subjective feeling of pleasure in the perception of, purportedly intrinsic beauty somehow posited as a discernible objective property of artworks *or* natural things or (even) "things" conceived more loosely than as determinate objects.

The term "aesthetic" is now philosophically entrenched but distinctly puzzling, as if everyone could be counted on to know what it designates. Until, that is, we ask for a determinate definition intended to bring Kant's term of art into accord with ordinary usage. We realize then that the "aesthetic" has no reliable descriptive use, whether in Kant's specialized and now quite marginal sense or in our own looser derived practice.

Kant took the "aesthetic" to be rightly associated with a distinct kind of judgment (aesthetic judgment), primarily addressed to claims about a certain "feeling" of pleasure initially marked in our experience of nature and extended to the arts, which may then be systematically contrasted with the discrimination of the "moral" and the "factual," that is, with certain logically very different kinds of judgment answering to logically very different kinds of discrimination also said to be entitled to a measure of objective standing.

All this is very doubtful now, though the term "aesthetic" persists without the definition of any satisfactory evidential grounds. Kant believed the judgment of beauty to be grounded in a feeling of pleasure, hence entirely subjective: without implicating conceptual distinctions of any kind regarding the "objects" of such judgments, hence disinterested (that is, not inherently dependent on any practical interests); and yet universal in form (that is, justified in imputing a similar pleasure among all who may be similarly confronted). All such qualifications are now thoroughly contested; some are even thought preposterous when actually applied to the appreciation of artworks. For objective appreciation (as in art criticism) is thought to entail reference to the objectively describable features of particular artworks (or other suitable objects).

Works of art, artworks, or works of fine art tend, now, to be collected as a distinct kind of "thing" or object – meaning by that only to ensure the individuation and reidentifiability of the numerically distinct referents of critical and appreciative discourse, regardless of how such *denotata* are characterized or designated. Objects of these sorts are thought to be quite different from physical objects and interestingly complex "in nature," partly at least because of the remarkable ways in which we analyze them and speak about them critically and appreciatively, and partly because we seem to tolerate, for instance in interpreting poetry, a certain logical laxity about incompatible interpretations – famously, in reading Wordsworth's much-cited "Lucy" poem – consistent with objectivity, in a way that is not usually thought acceptable, conceptually, in speaking of the things of the physical world alone.

What kind of "thing" is an "artwork," then, we ask, if such claims are even admissible: that is, when (say) two incompatible interpretations of the same artwork are deemed to be objectively valid, or when the assignable meaning of a poem is determinately explicated in incompatible ways? There you have the central puzzle of the "logic" (or "metaphysics" or "epistemology") of art – or, more widely construed, the logic of "cultural" entities and phenomena in general, or (even more widely) of anything open to pertinently similar examination, itself (the pattern of examination in question) being regarded as a mode of culturally formed practice.

Artworks and physical objects

Artworks taken generically, then, are thought to possess and to exhibit properties of a kind not rightly attributed to physical things, except perhaps figuratively or by some courtesy of usage. This is how the question arises as to whether the real world harbors "objects" of fundamentally different kinds (say, physical things and cultural artifacts) or whether all that is real is uniform in nature (usually, then, nothing but physical or material objects) – a claim that would itself require some further account of how culturally generated attributes are (or can be) rightly ascribed to actual things. Such quarrels are dubbed metaphysical, though (following a usage that has sprung up since Kant) metaphysical and epistemological distinctions are now taken to be essentially the same, albeit viewed from different conceptual vantages.

The point is that comparisons regarding the "nature" of the physical and the cultural are admitted to be as public as any standard issues of scientific analysis, though metaphysical distinctions are decidedly more general than scientific distinctions, more abstract, more committed to isolating conceptual categories thought to bear on organizing a systematic account of what is real *qua* real. The idea is that we are free to "divide" the world in terms of perspicuously selected categories that help to spell out our rationales for distinguishing between different kinds of judgment, predication, argument, explanation, interpretation, mode of appreciation, and the like. That's all. The practice need not, then, harbor any deeper privilege regarding cognitive access or evidential grounds.

The simplest intuition supporting the systematic difference between artworks and physical objects derives from admitting that there is no known analysis of natural language that might show it to be adequately dissected or characterized in terms restricted to whatever is fairly taken to count as the corresponding analysis of physical objects and physical phenomena: in particular, regarding such fundamental contrasts as that between a physical sound and a spoken (or "uttered") word or sentence (or, say, a physical sound and a musical tone, or a physical movement and a dance step).

This elementary challenge to any attempted reduction of artworks and cultural entities to mere physical things would, if successful, lead directly to the defeat of any similar effort to reduce human persons or selves physically or biologically – that is, the seemingly transformed members of *Homo sapiens*, changed into linguistically apt speakers of a natural language, into agents of culturally formed competences not otherwise acquired.

Here, of course, we normally speak of speech as intrinsically meaningful and as having meaning and significance; as involving, conveying, implicating reference and predication and truth-claims and speakers' intentions and the like. Accordingly, we ask ourselves whether speech can be literally said to possess such properties or whether their attribution signifies no more than their being imposed on, or imputed to, "mere" physical things, somehow projected from epistemically independent sources (say, from the distinctive activity and mental life of human selves or persons acting as authors or creators or appreciative percipients).

It takes very little effort to see that the problem regarding language is, first of all, an analogue of the "metaphysical" problem regarding artworks; and, second, that the problem regarding both leads to a regress involving the analysis of what it is to be a human self relative to being a member of *Homo sapiens*, a person capable of being an artist or critic or appreciative percipient. The best conjecture seems to be that human selves (persons) are themselves culturally formed transforms of the members of *Homo sapiens* resulting from the normal ability of human infants to internalize the mastery of a natural language and thereupon to acquire the "second-natured" ability to speak, to engage in reflexive thought, to absorb the cultural habits of a home society, to act and behave in accord with such acquired abilities, to become the apt and fluent members of an appropriately apt society, and (among other things) to produce, create, understand, appreciate, and prize artworks that, as a result, are seen and judged to manifest attributes of meaning and signification and the like that pose the metaphysical question now being broached.

These distinctions also serve, conveniently, to classify the theories of many of the best-known, influential Anglo-American philosophers of art of our time if, for the sake of simplicity, we do not press too strenuously between explicitly disjunctive or reductionist views and the distinct tendency to favor such views. Among widely respected theorists, currently, we may count Arthur Danto, Richard Wollheim, and Kendall Walton as definitely tending toward the reductive pole; Monroe Beardsley, the dean of American aesthetics, less so, except for the strong exclusion of intentional ascriptions (read psychologically); Nelson Goodman, less pointedly, since he treats aesthetic properties semiotically but also as behaving extensionally (in the sense of according with the constraints of first-order predicate logic); and Joseph Margolis, not at all, since he opposes all such disjunctive tendencies, preferring instead to regard artworks as the culturally emergent utterances (speech, for instance) of human selves or agents, themselves the cultural transforms of the members of *Homo sapiens* as they master their home language and culture.

The cultural world

To see the matter in this way is to grasp the sense in which the metaphysics of artworks cannot be separated from the general metaphysics of what we mean to feature in speaking of human culture – the "cultural world" – in which language, human selves, history, social customs and practices and traditions and institutions and norms of conduct, and science itself first take form and are "found" among real things.

Philosophy has not resolved the metaphysical question satisfactorily, though its general lineaments are clear enough. Theory ranges between the extremes of reductionism and what may be called emergentism: that is, between the view that the analysis of artworks does not require anything beyond admitting their being mere physical things (for instance, paintings and sculptures and pieces of music) – though obviously not "mere" in the sense in which they are "ordered" or "configured" in some telling or instructive way – provided only that, in drawing the usual attributes of meaning, significance, intentionality, value, and the like *from* the (would-be) independent mental life and behavioral practice of suitably trained human agents, we acknowledge that our ascriptions to pertinent objects are also objectively valid and conceptually coherent.

The trouble with the latter strategy – reductionism, whether piecemeal or unrestricted – is that it inexorably implicates the prior accessibility of what we already suppose falls within the space of what we are calling the emergent cultural world, that is, the original appearance of culturally formed *sui generis* properties and things that (on the emergentist argument) cannot be satisfactorily analyzed or explicated in purely physicalist or materialist terms. So that, what seems to be the success of reductionism regarding artworks ultimately depends on reductionism's inability to provide a reductive analysis of the "second-natured" ability of persons themselves – on the unearned admission of which the trick is illicitly turned.

This is hardly a knockdown argument as it stands, but it serves to identify the essential contest and, rightly completed, leads to a *reductio*. For, if we may speak of "uttering" artworks in a sense akin to that in which we are said to utter speech, then, first of all, the metaphysical puzzle regarding artworks will be judged a perfect analogue of the metaphysical issue regarding speech and language; and, secondly, we will have to admit that the literary arts already implicate the metaphysical problem of language. Provisionally, then, artworks are culturally formed artifacts that intrinsically possess properties of meaning, signification, expression, representation, stylistic, emotional, and valuational features that we deny may be literally and objectively ascribed to physical objects as such. Here, we typically insist that properties rightly ascribed to things of different kinds must be "adequated" to the nature of such things (as in claiming that stones cannot, in any literal sense, be said to smile): what we validly predicate of a thing must be adequated to, must be congruent with, the attributes that form that thing's nature.

Artworks, selves, and the human sciences

All properties peculiar to artworks may be conveniently collected as "Intentional," where the Intentional is generously construed as equivalent to "culturally significant." An artwork, then, is a "thing" that is real in whatever sense the cultural world is real – in particular, the sense in which human selves, their societies, their language, history, practices, institutions, traditions, actions and activity, machines and technology, and norms and values are admitted to be real – to be culturally constituted or constructed. In short, human selves and what they characteristically "utter" – their speech, their art, their actions, their future progeny for that matter – are real, as real as physical things, distinguished entirely and adequately in terms of such Intentional attributes rightly ascribed to culturally emergent things but not to physical or material things as such. The argument is no more than a *faute de mieux* conjecture, since the matter continues to be contested and since there is no final way to defeat reductionism.

In this sense, the metaphysical analysis of artworks plays a particularly strategic role in fashioning an adequate account of what "there is" in the real world: for example, regarding the relationship between the natural and the human sciences, cognitive conditions for the natural sciences themselves (within the cultural world), and the very nature of what may be meant by the emergence and evolution of the cultural from the inanimate and subhuman biological world. Darwinian speculation makes a plausible case for the evolution of true language from prehuman communicative skills that begin to manifest the rudiments of reference and predication up to a certain critical complexity – on reaching which, the familiar reflexive powers of speech and thought may be taken to be fully and first manifested.

The empirical conditions are certainly not well understood. But the conceptual issues are clear enough. On present philosophical evidence, the cultural cannot be convincingly reduced to the physical; is emergent in some *sui generis* way along the lines suggested; and is causally effective if it is indeed real. But if that is so, then the doctrine of the causal closure of the physical (under exceptionless covering laws) must be false. This suggests what is so troubling about the admission of artworks and other culturally specified things. But there seems to be no logically compelling reason for disallowing speculations of these sorts; and, of course, metaphysical economy depends on how we are obliged to answer questions of the sorts already sampled.

There's another advantage that may be mentioned. If you take the model of "utterance" seriously, then the culturally "emergent" Intentional features of artworks (and language and action) may be said to be indissolubly "incarnate" in mere physical properties (that is, emergent relative to the physical); accordingly, artworks are indissolubly "embodied" (emergently) in material things. This complex state of affairs – the incarnation of what is Intentionally emergent, in the physical – is unique to cultural things, a fortiori to artworks. But, inasmuch as the analysis of artworks parallels the analysis of language and human selves, the exemplary analysis of the first shows the way to overcoming every form of dualism affecting the second that springs from the Cartesian tradition. Enlanguaged thought, for instance, is never disjoined from its neurophysiological embedding: thought is the entire incarnated property thus embedded (whatever it may entail), in spite of the fact that human reflection never penetrates experientially to the latter. There is, therefore, the prospect of an elegant, if somewhat heterodox, metaphysical simplification made possible by a careful analysis of artworks that promises to ramify through every sector of philosophical inquiry.

Further reading

Kant, Immanuel. *Critique of Judgement*, trans. J. Meredith. Oxford: Clarendon, 1964.

Margolis, Joseph. *What, After All, is a Work of Art?* University Park, PA: Pennsylvania State University Press, 1999.

JOSEPH MARGOLIS

ASIAN PHILOSOPHY, INFLUENCE OF

It is difficult to assess the influence of "Asian philosophy" on "American philosophy." If one uses these terms in broad nonacademic ways, there are numerous influences. However, when the terms are used in more narrow, academic, and scholarly ways, one may conclude that some scholars identified with American philosophy have used Asian philosophies, either uncritically or simply to support their philosophy, but that genuine influences have been rare.

There are considerable influences of Asian philosophy excluded from this article. Hundreds of philosophers in America have done significant work in Asian philosophy, but they do not do "American philosophy." Similarly, numerous American philosophers have done significant East–West comparative philosophy shaped by Asian philosophy, but, once again, they are not identified with "American philosophy." In addition, there are numerous religious, literary, and cultural movements, such as "the Beat Movement," "the Hippie Movement," "the Counterculture Movement," and "the New Age Movement," that are strongly American and have been influenced by Asian philosophies, but these cannot be classified under "philosophy" or "American philosophy."

Influences on Transcendentalism, Pragmatism, and other American philosophies

The first significant influence of Asian philosophy on American philosophy is usually identified with American or New England Transcendentalism. Some may question whether this was "American philosophy" in the scholarly sense, but transcendentalists were certainly engaged with philosophical ideas and their writings had considerable influence on later American philosophy.

Reacting against philosophical materialism, utilitarianism, and narrow Calvinistic Christianity and influenced by Platonism, mysticism, and European Romanticism, key American transcendentalists were also influenced by Asian philosophy. The main influences were from Hinduism, especially Vedanta, but there was also interest in Buddhism and Confucianism. Asian philosophy fit in nicely with the transcendentalist emphasis on the universal spiritual unity of humankind, metaphysical idealism, the spiritual nature of the cosmos, and a kind of intuitive, universal, religious experience.

Ralph Waldo Emerson (1803–82), founder and most influential proponent of American Transcendentalism, was also the transcendentalist most influenced by Asian philosophies, especially the Upanishads and other Hindu scriptures and certain Hindu philosophical ideas. Hindu ideas are not only key to such poems as "Brahma" and "Hamatreya," but they also influenced Emerson's formulations in such essays as "Plato," "Illusions," and "Immortality." Although Emerson developed his idea of the "Over-Soul" before studying Asian philosophy, his later writings were influenced by Hindu Vedic ideas and especially by the monistic system of Advaita Vedanta. Emerson appreciated the Vedanta focus on the all-encompassing spiritual Absolute or Brahman, identity of Brahman with the universal Soul or Self or Atman, and the analysis of the world of illusion. Emerson felt that this Hindu philosophical orientation was often close to his own philosophical approach, even if he was quite critical of Hindu and especially Buddhist philosophy for what he took to be their fatalistic resignation and inaction,

Transcendentalist Henry David Thoreau (1817–62) was not as influenced by Asian philosophy as was Emerson, but he was familiar with and moved by some of the Asian scriptures and philosophies. Not so interested in Asian metaphysical ideas, what Thoreau seemed to appreciate most in Buddhist and Hindu philosophies were various methods and meditative techniques for achieving detachment, discipline, contemplation, and spiritual fulfillment.

A major development occurred in the late nineteenth century when Harvard University, probably influenced by the tradition of New England Transcendentalism, introduced Indian philosophy as part of its philosophy curriculum. Josiah Royce (1855–1916) was probably the most significant American philosopher in the late nineteenth century influenced by Indian philosophy. He found that Indian philosophy and especially Vedanta provided support for his monistic idealism, his search for the Absolute in the universe. Later he became interested in the moral teachings of Buddhism.

George Santayana (1863–1952) was another significant Harvard philosopher influenced by Asian philosophy. Hindu Vedanta provided him with a resource for his metaphysics of essence going beyond traditional Western philosophy. Early Indian thinkers and Hindu Samkhya provided him with a naturalistic resource for his Critical Realism. Buddhism provided a major resource for his ethical thinking. While rejecting Buddhist, as well as Hindu, claims to universal validity and much of its applicability, Santayana was attracted to a Buddhist ethical approach in helping him to construct an alternative morality free from egoism and achieving inner equilibrium, peace, and sympathy for others.

Much of the appeal of Asian philosophies for transcendentalists, Royce, Santayana, and other American philosophies can be related to dissatisfaction with American philosophy and culture that they viewed as narrow, egoistic, utilitarian, materialistic, and overly rationalistic.

American Process Philosophy has remarkable similarities with Buddhist philosophy, especially with the Buddhist critique of traditional philosophies of permanent self and unchanging substances. Charles Hartshorne (1897–2000) studied Buddhist philosophy and submitted that Buddhism, especially in its critique of enduring substances, anticipated much of American process philosophy.

When thinking of distinctive "American philosophy," one usually thinks first of "American Pragmatism." Along with Transcendentalism, such Pragmatism is the major, American, philosophical development sometimes viewed as having been influenced by Asian philosophies. The reasons are clear. Many Asian philosophical approaches, especially Chinese philosophy and even more especially Confucian philosophy, emphasize characteristics key to pragmatism: humanism focusing on improving our human condition; emphasis on human experience and on contextualized relational situatedness of human beings; anti-metaphysical approach; focus on pragmatic criteria for truth claims and for proper living; a pragmatic aesthetic aimed at self-cultivation and improving human life.

It is important to note that most American pragmatists have had little interest in Asian philosophies. Several, including Peirce, offered scientific and other pragmatic criteria for attacking Eastern philosophy as spiritual, metaphysical, and mystical confusion.

The influential American pragmatist William James (1842–1910) was familiar with and appreciated Asian philosophies, although he had an ambivalent attitude toward them. He rejected Hindu monism that devalued his pluralism, Indian metaphysics, and Buddhist and other forms of detachment and quietism. The greatest influence of Asian thought was on James's open-minded and inclusivistic phenomenological formulations in *The Varieties of Religious Experience* of religious experience and especially of mysticism.

Probably the major American philosopher most often identified with Asian philosophy was American pragmatist John Dewey (1859–1952). Dewey, who expressed admiration for Japanese philosophy and especially for Chinese philosophy, lived in China (1919–21). Dewey had influential Chinese students and disciples, especially Hu Shih (1891–1962). Dewey's pragmatic philosophy had a strong influence on philosophy in China, even if this influence was short lived. What isn't so clear is whether Dewey himself was in any way influenced by Chinese philosophy even if he felt comfortable with some of the Chinese philosophical orientation. What is most significant is that during the last part of the twentieth century and continuing into the twenty-first century, many American philosophers deeply influenced by Dewey have been exploring how Confucian and other Asian philosophies can contribute to a more adequate philosophical pragmatism.

Growing influences and future prospects

Although one can conclude that the overall genuine influence of Asian philosophy on distinctive American philosophy, by American philosophers who really understood Asian philosophy, has been limited, the present situation reveals growing influence and the likelihood of exciting new philosophical developments. On the one hand, numerous philosophers throughout Asia are very familiar with Western philosophy in general and American philosophy in particular. On the other hand, numerous Western philosophers, including those primarily influenced by American philosophy, are very familiar with various Asian philosophical traditions. This East–West philosophical dialogue and encounter is already leading to new exciting results, including possibilities for the revitalization and development of American philosophy.

Remarkable in this regard are the numerous conferences in China and in the United States bringing together philosophers identified with American pragmatism and with Chinese philosophy. Starting in the late twentieth century, one finds many lectures and publications on such topics as Dewey and Confucian philosophy. David Hall, Roger Ames, and a long list of other significant American philosophers have been formulating major research projects focusing on remarkable convergences between American pragmatism and Chinese philosophy, their reciprocal reinforcements and creative interactions, and how each can be reformulated and developed in more adequate ways. Robert Cummings Neville of Boston University, who has done significant work in American, Christian, and Chinese philosophy, has popularized the term "Boston Confucianism," where one finds new creative attempts to apply Chinese philosophy to American philosophy.

Similarly, philosophers shaped by distinctive American philosophical traditions are now studying and using various Asian philosophers as a catalyst for rethinking their philosophical positions. Among the many illustrations are American environmental philosophers who find Daoism and other Asian philosophical approaches invaluable for formulating more adequate philosophies of nature and environmental ethics; feminist philosophers who find Buddhist and other Asian resources invaluable for critiquing dominant, male, philosophical orientations; philosophers of mind and others doing epistemology who are impressed by various Asian analyses of consciousness, mind, and mind–body interaction; political and social philosophers who are being influenced by Asian approaches to violence and nonviolence, war and peace; philosophers of art who are being influenced by exposure to Asian aesthetics; moral philosophers who find that they can learn much from Asian philosophies about ego construction and attachment, greed, violence, compassion, loving kindness, and other ethical concerns; and philosophers stimulated by challenges of contemporary contextualism, pluralism, multiculturalism, and global philosophical reflection.

The future is bright. Philosophers grounded in American philosophy are engaged with and being influenced by Asian philosophy. They are not simply using Asian philosophy in an opportunistic and uninformed way for their American philosophical projects. This is leading to proposals for dialogue, new ways of thinking in American philosophy, and new philosophical developments. What is not clear is the extent to which what emerges will be classified as "American philosophy" in the sense of something distinctively "American."

Further reading

Clarke, J.J. *Oriental Enlightenment: The Encounter Between Asian and Western Thought*. London and New York: Routledge, 1997.

Grange, Joseph. *John Dewey, Confucius, and Global Philosophy*. Albany, NY: SUNY Press, 2004.

Inada, Kenneth K. and Jacobson, Nolan P. (eds) *Buddhism and American Thinkers*. Albany, NY: SUNY Press, 1984.

Neville, Robert Cummings. *Boston Confucianism: Portable Tradition in Late-Modern World*. Albany, NY: SUNY Press, 2000.

Riepe, Dale. *The Philosophy of India and Its Impact on American Thought*. Springfield, IL: Charles C. Thomas, 1970.

Shusterman, Richard (ed.) *The Range of Pragmatism and the Limits of Philosophy*. Oxford: Blackwell, 2004.

Douglas Allen

ASSERTIBILITY

Assertibility became a systematic concept in philosophy of science when John Dewey in 1938 in his *Logic. The Theory of Inquiry* (Dewey 1986) introduced "warranted assertion" and the general term assertability to describe the end processes of research, inquiry and reflection are ending in such that assertability expresses a stable relation between the beliefs and the process of inquiry leading to it. For Dewey knowledge in general is equivalent to warranted assertability. But he rejects Bertrand Russell's claim (Russell 1940, 1996) that warranted assertability might be substituted for truth (Dewey 1998: 201). A belief resulting from a certain line of inquiry justifies the assertion of its truth relative to it. However, this does not mean that the warranted proposition is true unrestrictedly. The warranted assertion suggests that other lines of inquiry are feasible.

The classical pragmatists Peirce, James and Dewey rejected an unqualified correspondence account of truth. They introduced various conditions of assertability relating the truth of a proposition to its logical, psychological, semiotical, moral and social conditions. In his paper *The Fixation of Belief* from 1877 Peirce argues that the distinction between a belief and a true belief is redundant because we always hold that all our beliefs are true. This anticipates some contemporary minimalistic accounts of truth because it implies that to assert that *P* and to assert that *P* is true are epistemologically equivalent. In this way, for Peirce the settlement of opinion and the unrestricted assertability of an opinion become the end of inquiry (Peirce 1992: 115) and are connected with his account of truth. At other places Peirce stresses the social aspect of assertion and assertability: To assert a proposition is an act by which we take on a social or moral responsibility for its truth. That is, the person asserting a proposition stands in for its truth as consistent with all knowledge, experience and conduct available to her. If some of the assertability conditions are not met by the person uttering it, she will be "liable to the penalties of the social law (or, at any rate, those of the moral law) in case it should not be true, unless he has a definite and sufficient excuse" (Peirce CP 2.315). Asserting the truth of a proposition in our communicative practice means to claim a normative status for it. On the other hand, truth or assertability functions for Peirce also as a methodological ideal stressing the necessary goal-directness of all inquiry. Peirce transforms assertability into a normative requirement for the goals of inquiry which he describes as a "great hope" (Peirce CP 5.406) motivating people that inquires of all sorts. For when we undertake an empirical inquiry, we assume that we will be able to find what we are looking for. We hope that there is a belief to which our inquiry will finally, perhaps in the long run, lead us. The goal-directness of inquiry connects the assertability conditions of proposition with action. Peirce describes this connection realized in inquiry in terms of general semiotical and logical properties of order relations – transitivity, reflexivity and anti-symmetry – and therefore pragmatism entails that the relation between beliefs, actions and thoughts in our processes of knowledge acquisition achieves such a logical ordering. Therefore, Peirce's pragmatism is a methodological theory of assertability conditions for theoretical propositions based on a logical and relational account of knowledge.

Whereas James and Dewey both stress the continuity with the overall orientation of Peirce's pragmatic and logical account of the normative role of assertability in inquiry and everyday experience, both follow another agenda that does not include the formal properties of logical order relations Peirce was interested in. As we saw above, for Dewey the relation to a line of inquiry establishes a specific sort of assertability of a proposition. William James rather stresses the importance of the temporal, contextual, emotional and even performative conditions of assertability. Our changing perceptions and beliefs induce us to form just so many different kinds of assertions that bring out the truth or cash value these perceptions have for *us*, for the extent of our actually available experience, knowledge and interests. Consequently, in his lectures on pragmatism, published in 1907 as *Pragmatism: A New Name for Some Old Ways of Thinking*, James describes the assertability of a proposition as a relation an idea and a person actually stand in. For James, the assertability of a proposition will depend on the fact that relative to some perceptual experiences made, and relative to the knowledge, interest and ideals we entertain, we are able to assimilate, corroborate and verify some specific beliefs about the content of that very experience. For James, the assertability of a proposition, relative to some perceptual experiences and beliefs of a person, is a relative and time-dependent property: It may be said to "happen" to a proposition that it is validated and asserted by this person here and now. However, this does not turn the assertability of a proposition into a random feature: It has to obey requirements like its consistency with other propositions and its capability to lead the individual into fruitful action. Furthermore, James in *The Will to Believe* stresses another neglected feature of assertability: There are requirements of the cognitive economy that arise for the assertability of a proposition because of the finite time- and information-perspective of an individual person. For example, sometimes a person has to decide about whether she believes in a certain important proposition or not although she does not have the time to check all the assertability conditions. James stresses that if the issue is important, she is justified to make a decision and intuitively assert a proposition or not.

It is evident that the different ways of thinking of the three classical pragmatists about the issue of assertability highlight the difference between their philosophies. That is to say, their way of doing philosophy manifests itself in the psychological, moral, semiotic, or logical properties they take to be crucial for constituting the assertability of a proposition.

Further reading

Dewey, John. "Propositions, Warranted Assertibility and Truth " in *The Essential Dewey*, ed. Larry Hickman and Thomas M. Alexander. Bloomington, IN: Indiana University Press, 1998, pp. 201–12.

James, William. The Will to Believe. The Works of William James, Vol. 6, ed. J.H. Burkhardt, F. Bowers, and I.K. Skrupskelis. Cambridge, MA: Harvard University Press, 1979.

Pape, Helmut. "Pragmatism and the Normativity of Assertion," *Transactions of the C.S. Peirce Society* XXXVIII, 4 (2003): 521–42.

Peirce, Charles S. *Collected Papers of Charles Sanders Peirce* (CP). Vols I–VI, ed. Charles Hartshorne and Paul Weiss. Cambridge, MA: Harvard University Press, 1931–5. Vols VII and VIII, second edition, ed. Arthur W. Burks. Cambridge, MA: Belknap Press, 1958. CP 2.315 refers to the second volume and the 315th section.

—— *The Essential Peirce. Selected Philosophical Writings Vol. 1, 1867–93*, ed. N. Houser and C. Kloesel. Bloomington, IN: Indiana University Press, 1992.

Russell, Bertrand. *An Inquiry into Meaning and Truth*. London: Allen and Unwin, 1940; second edition London: Routledge, 1996.

Tenant, Neil. "On Negation, Truth, and Warranted Assertibility," *Analysis* 55, 2 (1995): 98–104.

HELMUT PAPE

ATHEISM

Atheism can refer to a single claim or to a group of claims. In the single claim case, the meaning of "atheism" is contained in its etymology. It is ancient Greek for "without god." Atheism is also a philosophical position. As such, it groups together several (seemingly) disparate claims. Taken together, these claims argue constructively against theism, the belief that godlike entities exist. Unlike agnosticism, atheism is not centrally concerned with the status of theistic beliefs. It is not typically concerned with the validation or invalidation of various theist positions. Instead, atheism presents a world-view that dispenses with many of theism's starting points altogether. Atheism does not oppose as much as occlude theist concerns, preferring to substitute its own explanations in the place of traditionally theistic descriptions. Some versions of agnosticism tread a similar line, choosing not to ask or answer theological questions, rather than asserting the uncertainty of their outcomes. Atheist doctrine can oppose monotheistic world-views or polytheistic world-views. I will use the two senses interchangeably, as what counts against god in the singular can often count against the existence of gods plural. Philosophically, atheism aims to show two things: (1) that arguments for god's existence fail; (2) that there are constructive reasons for thinking that belief in god is unnecessary. Most arguments against theism assume one of two general starting points. The first argues that some aspect of god's description is conceptually confused or logically incoherent. Second, the benevolent or agential nature of god is taken to task. Atheists routinely point to the horror of persistent evil as a determinant element of their disbelief. This "problem of evil" approach is usually reserved for the god of the Judeo-Christian tradition, but need not be limited to it. Other theistic traditions ascribe less benevolence to their gods and so evade part of this critique. Still, the gods of polytheistic religions are active agents in the lives of their believers and so bear some responsibility for the outcomes of their alleged actions. Most theistic traditions posit an omniscient, omnipotent, omnipresent being or set of beings, in their respective theology. Atheism asks what reasons there are for assuming that these genera of entity exist. In this sense, many questions of theology overlap with questions in science and philosophy. As with theism, there exist divisions within atheism. Some atheists take all talk of god to be without cognitive meaning. These atheists sometimes refer to themselves as "non-theists" rather than as "atheists." This is because they find any god-talk, pro or con, to be meaningless. To believe or disbelieve in a nonexistent entity comes to the same, logically speaking, for the "non-theist." Other atheists reject the existence of divine entities but do not consider theological questions inherently meaningless. This view is sometimes referred to as "positive atheism." Complicating matters further, certain theists believe in divine places or states of consciousness but do not believe in an agential god. Manifestations of nirvana assume this absent god form. Other theist sects believe in an afterlife while withholding belief in a governing god. Whether such beliefs should continue to be labeled "theist" despite their deep deferral of agency remains a matter for debate.

Historically, the debates between theists and atheists have closely mirrored the developments of modern science. Contemporary political debates over issues in bioethics would be impossible without the arrival and influence of modern science. Moreover, it is with the advent of scientific explanations for various natural phenomena that religion's traditional interpretative role comes under fire. Theistic descriptions of the natural world often take on an anthropomorphic form. Natural phenomena are cast as the consequences of divine action. Earthquakes, diseases, floods, famines, and other phenomena including death itself, are explained as the willing results of an intentional god. The structure of early theistic explanation remains the same whether dealing with a polytheistic tradition or a monotheistic one and it is this structure of explanation, with god as central agent, that philosophers criticize most. With the rise of modern science, mechanistic descriptions lacking intentionality come to replace anthropomorphic narratives and rationalizations. This substitution of anthropomorphism for mechanism leads to religion and science being at loggerheads. Actions require agents, and without manlike gods primitive cultures were at a loss to explain some of nature's more complex, and seemingly "intentional," workings. Science's ability to replicate, explicate, and occasionally entirely control, many of these multifaceted workings, firmly displaced the intentional/agential picture of explanation and prediction. Supernatural forces were no longer needed as links in an explanatory chain. Yet the displacement of anthropomorphism carries with it a price. Natural forces cannot in turn be influenced the way intentional divinities (such as gods or spirits) once were. The place left by science for prayer remains an open and vexed question.

In the American context, William James attempted to reconcile the experience of faith with philosophy. By casting nature in an evolutionary light, James sought to portray both faith and reason as evolving processes. Believers, for James, therefore construct faith on a participatory basis. The truth underpinning religious experience reveals itself through the activity of living one's faith. Faith and reason are understood pragmatically, as processes that humans, through their interpretations of religious experience, have a hand in shaping. As such, faith for James is an evolving compound, one guided by the sentiments and practices of its adherents. Yet despite James's sensitivity to religious experience, his is not an absolute god. As an evolving entity, the god that James describes is imperfect and thus stands outside many orthodox understandings of the nature of the divine. John Dewey, for his part, presents a more thoroughly secular and Darwinian understanding of theism. Taking religion to be a manifestation of cultural ideals, Dewey interprets faith communally.

Adopting a social perspective, he characterizes theism as a heritage of received values. These inherited values function as shared imaginings, prompting societies to abandon outdated values and to embrace novel solutions to the problems of communal living. For Dewey, this is the function of faith at its best. At its worst, theism and the faith that accompanies it serve further to entrench old ideals that may no longer serve the best interests of a community. The fact that all of the world's great religions discuss faith in some strongly communal sense serves only to underpin Dewey's viewpoint. As with James, the religious focus in Dewey is on the evolving nature of theistic practice.

An additional complication to the "god-as-prime-agent" view expressed above is the idea that the god of the monotheistic West is, by the tradition's lights, portrayed as a god demanding faith, not reasoned acceptance. What this means is that both believers and agnostics have made a case that one can only know of god's existence if they open themselves to the faith-experience. Therefore, for devout theists, the scientific approach gets things the wrong way around. Without faith, no signs of god's existence will be made available to atheists or agnostics, meaning that if one already believes then no further (cogent) proofs are required. Those seeking rational justifications for the existence of god have misunderstood the purpose of faith, or so this influential theistic argument maintains. Interestingly, common arguments of this type in no way limit the existence of god to the god of Western monotheism. Polytheists can also avail themselves of these sorts of arguments. Therefore, in using these types of arguments to block the encroachments of science upon faith, a tension is set up between polytheism and monotheism. While both views endorse a model of divinity, neither provides a reason to pick one over the other, therefore the "faith-first" argument alone merely secures some form of soft agnosticism or perhaps a weak polytheism. The freedom to believe or abstain from belief is central to many Christian church traditions. The import of choice cuts across other doctrinal divisions, for example those separating the Eastern Orthodox Church from the Roman Catholic Church. As such, it always appears odd to atheists that the god of some theists commands obedience. Why must obedience then be demanded? Is it not freely given? Would this failure to appreciate the wisdom of faith through respect for freely chosen belief not signal a failure of god's ethical perfection?

In the past, most cultures entertained several gods. Many theists take the preponderance of faith among primitive civilizations as an additional "proof" for theism. Nevertheless, anthropological models exist that well explain the popularity of theism. These anthropological models point us back in the direction of agential anthropomorphism. In fact, the agential characterization of god, whether monotheistic or polytheistic, returns at every turn. Therefore, the issue at bottom is one of agency and not of faith, as faith without agential consequence appears to have interested no past civilization. If the belief in god makes some qualitative difference to a community's life, then it is seemingly the belief itself that causes the beneficial beliefs or actions that believers ascribe to faith. Could it be that faith in positive outcomes is its own reward (*pace* god)? It bears noticing that the "universal" appearance of religion in all cultures does nothing to shore up the common description of god as omnipotent, omnipresent, and omniscient. The popularity of religion does not discharge the explanatory responsibility of establishing agential priority. For sense to be made of the three attributes of god (omniscience, omnipresence, and omnipotence) their contraries must also exist. Moreover, if the creator-god made all things then he made both the positive and the negative instances of all things, presumably in equal potential measures. Where there is great good, there can be great evil and vice versa. This equilateral creation of perfections and imperfections appears to count against the notion of god being omniscient, omnipresent, and omnipotent.

Viewed differently, if god created the universe but did not "design" the perfections and imperfections found in all existing persons, animals, and objects, then god has only a contingent stake in the workings of the world. If we take this contingency problem seriously, then it returns us to the agential problem above. This view is sometimes called "deism" and is different from "theism" in that the "deist" god does not take an active role in the workings of his creation. This further complication also counts against a straightforward understanding of the agential god examined above. It also renders most explanations of the workings and purposes of faith and prayer problematic. Are "deists" and "theists" believers in the same faith and god or not? What do considerations of "deism" contribute to our understanding of the nature of polytheist religions? Do they endorse or dissuade from polytheism? A survey of "polytheist," "deist," and "theist" literature uncovers little to no descriptive consensus regarding god's characteristics. God's immutable nature, as creator of all things, is in conceptual discord with his omniscience. The moral nature of god is problematic in that nothing about what type of universe an omnipotent being should to create follows from his ability to create a universe. The power to create, of itself, is ethically neutral. If god had chosen to create nothing, he would have remained morally perfect on most theist characterizations. In addition, the creation or non-creation of life seems to leave god's moral status unchanged. How can this be? Either creation itself is ethically neutral, or god's moral nature is internally contradictory, or both. Evil and its multiple manifestations prove the most challenging aspects to understand, as the uninterrupted evil that takes place daily seems to be constrained and guided by no being, let alone an omnibenevolent, omniscient, omnipotent god. Given the complexity with which god is described it is unsurprising that for some theists nonbelievers cannot divulge or understand god's plan. It is the overall plan that is good, they claim, and not individual acts. Yet without some rational access to the purposes and procedures guiding divine events, humans are left with faith alone. If god has agential purchase on events then he is responsible in part for the outcomes. If god does not have agential purchase then faith in god will yield little to no consequential change in the lives of theists. The finite nature of man and the infinite nature of god appear to render the two mutually incompatible.

Perhaps through the exercise of reason we can better understand both the nature of the divine and our yearning to understand beings with which we share no part of our nature. Perhaps man's quest for god will lead humanity to perfect man instead.

Further reading

Bernstein, Richard J. *The Abuse of Evil*. Malden, MA: Polity Press, 2005.

Dean, William. *American Religious Empiricism*. Albany, NY: SUNY Press 1986.

Dennett, Daniel C. *Breaking the Spell*. New York: Viking, 2006.

Nielsen, Kai. *Atheism and Philosophy*. Amherst, NY: Prometheus Books, 2005.

—— *Wittgensteinian Fideism*. London: SCM Press, 2006.

Stout, Jeffrey. *Ethics after Babel*. Princeton, NJ: Princeton University Press, 2001.

—— *Democracy and Tradition*. Princeton, NJ: Princeton University Press, 2005.

NICK C. SAGOS

ATTENTION

The role of attention span in consciousness was of especial concern to C.S. Peirce, William James, and Josiah Royce, following from theoretical and empirical trends in German psychology. For Peirce, proofs that attention affected thought were the positive correlation of increased attention with increased capacity to inscribe new memories and to recall lost ones, and increased accuracy of logical sequences of thought. Habits are a form of active attention to common details between sensations: "having had the sensation of performing a certain act, *m*, on several occasions *a*, *b*, *c*, we come to do it upon every occurrence of the general event, *l*, of which *a*, *b*, and *c* are special cases." Peirce's equation of attention to induction, the grouping of sensations by identical quality, had a major effect on subsequent American philosophy.

James's interest in attention was largely empirical; he frequently cited psychological studies of attention (especially Wundt's) that sought to establish the length of the "specious present" of human attention – the length of time in which the plurality of sensations are known in a "single pulse" so as to form one complex object of attention. James countered empiricist arguments that reduced thought to passive sensation, since subjective interest in success means we actively withdraw from some experiences in order to attend to others. The specious present is somewhat variable and somewhat fixed – variable, since by genius or by diligent work the complexity of the objects of attention may increase; fixed, because *some* specious present represents the limit beyond which we are unable to successfully conceive of plurality as unity. Attention also varies over a single lifetime, as youth are more spontaneously reactive to sensed objects, whereas habituated adults tend to group new stimuli by "permanent interests." James advocated increased attention through pedagogy, since: "The faculty of voluntarily bringing back a wandering attention, over and over again, is the very root of judgment, character and will ... An education which should improve this faculty would be *the* education *par excellence.*" To achieve it, James suggested connecting new material with students' extant interests.

For Royce, attention repeats in temporal part the eternal form, in which plurality is willfully comprehended as a single unity. But human attention is only somewhat godlike, as the power gained by attention – that is, the ability to repeat what is observed, so that observed external meanings become repeatable successes for the individual – is matched by the tragic error of being unable to see the whole picture, as human knowledge is more abstractly universal than particularly understanding of details. Indeed, for Royce, "finitude is inattention." For Royce as for James, the attention span is only "relatively fixed": it may comprehend lesser orders of serial inclusiveness, whether by tragic inattention or by the "sin" of willful limitation of attention; or greater orders, as by attentive participation in musical rhythm (in which we "at once" hear both single notes *and* whole movements); or by attention to august spans of geologic time, or by abstraction from the specious present so as to think of eternal moral, metaphysical or logical unities.

Further reading

James, W. "Attention" in *The Principles of Psychology.* New York: Dover, 1950 [1890], Vol. 1, pp. 402–58.

Peirce, C.S. "Some Consequences of Four Incapacities" in *Charles S. Peirce, Selected Writings (Values in a Universe of Chance)*, ed. P.P. Wiener. New York: Dover, 1966 [1958], pp. 39–72.

Royce, J. "The Temporal and the Eternal" in *Basic Writings*, ed. J.J. McDermott. Chicago, IL: University of Chicago Press, 1969, Vol. 1, pp. 611–37.

JASON BELL

AUTONOMY

The basic idea of autonomy is "to be self-directed in one's life," or, mainly in relationship to socio-political issues, "to be one's own master or law-maker." Another term for autonomy is "sovereignty," a term is arguably more closely associated with the self-governance of countries or states (although "autonomy," too, is used to refer to various political or legal regions being self-governing). There are many who view autonomy as a sort of mythical or invented notion – see, for example, J.B. Schneewind, *The Invention of Autonomy* (1998). This is akin to the view, also widely promulgated, that individuals do not really exist but are ideological constructs.

Whether this is all a matter of genuine debate or the deployment of conceptual sophistication for purposes of advancing a normative, even political, agenda, cannot be determined here. However, it is fair to say that figures such as Mill, Emerson, Dewey, and Royce all made contributions to the debate, some, like Mill and Emerson, defending the reality and value of individual autonomy, while others such as Royce and Dewey, disputing this and placing greater emphasis on the reality and value of what could be regarded as social wholes.

In any case, as far as the defenders of the reality and value of individual autonomy are concerned, when it comes to persons, autonomy is supposed to be a feature of someone's life under circumstances when he or she takes control of it and guides it by principles or rules he or she has freely accepted. Correspondingly, lack of autonomy characterizes the lives, especially, of slaves or those who are subjected by others to political subservience or even involuntary servitude, as well as of people who by their own volition give themselves over to ways of living that are influentially urged upon them by others (as, for example, in a cult or dogmatic religion or ideology). Sometimes lack of autonomy is also ascribed to people when their dire circumstances render it impossible for them to make informed or sensible decisions.

Some philosophers have even believed that the bulk of humanity lives in self-imposed lack of autonomy – for example, Aristotle thought many live in voluntary slavery, the lot of those who chose to live by the thoughts of others, and Ayn Rand believed that too many people are what she called "second-handers" because they abdicate their own critical reasoning and follow complacently what others expect of them. Others, such as Karl Marx, have argued that something like this is true of millions of workers at a certain – pre-socialist, pre-communist – stage of humanity's development, when they are in a state of what he called "false consciousness."

In the modern era autonomy has mostly been regarded as a desirable, healthy human state, both personally and politically, although some believe it has been overemphasized and made into a false ideal which for many has the tendency of alienating them from other people, including their families and communities. The promotion of the value of autonomy has been a result, some have argued, of the rise of various types of individualism. It is noted, for example, by communitarians such as the Canadian philosopher Charles Taylor, that when individuals become or are taken to be social "atoms," they are alienated from communities to which they literally and properly belong. Following the teachings of Hegel, and the "early" Marx in some important respects, Taylor and others of the communitarian school have lamented that human nature has been distorted by many thinkers, especially those with a classical liberal or bourgeois bent of mind, so that millions of modern human beings fail to see that their true humanity is best realized not as independent or autonomous individuals but as integral members of certain kinds of groups.

A vital aspect of the discussion of autonomy has focused on human free will. If human beings have free will – that is to say, if they are capable of determining their own significant thinking and conduct – that would lend support to the idea that autonomy is a vital aspect of the kind of being they are. And if such free will does exist, various important implications may well follow from it for purposes of understanding and developing human institutions – ethics, morality, law, politics, international covenants, and elements of global justice.

For those who deny free will, we do what we do out of desire or similar innate drives and reason, as David Hume put it, is but a slave of these – merely a calculative means of figuring out how to serve our desires. As such, genuine autonomy is problematic, although there are many who argue that free will isn't really necessary for it because the only freedom worth having is to be the intermediate cause of what we do. The source of autonomy, then, is that the person performs the action and is not made to perform it by someone else. This compatibilism is especially prominent among those who believe in both ethics and scientific determinism.

In the sphere of politics autonomy has been embraced by both libertarians and egalitarians – for example, by the late Robert Nozick and by Ronald Dworkin. The former argue that only if everyone's moral space – secured by respect for the right to life, liberty, and private property – is maintained, is a person free to act on his or her own initiative; the latter hold that without being provided with some basic goods by others who are well off, many people will not have the opportunity to act autonomously.

Communitarians, who are less concerned about individual liberty and rights than those in the (classical) liberal tradition of social and political thought, insist that only in properly constituted communities – nations, villages, towns, ethnically or religiously homogenous groups, professional associations, and so forth – can the sort of autonomy that is suitable for human life be fully secured. Defenders of multiculturalism, too, insist that human autonomy is much less individualistic than is assumed within the several varieties of liberalism that have emerged in the modern age.

Many of them also maintain that by defending the liberal idea of individualist autonomy as universal – by exporting it from Western Liberal societies to others in the Middle East, Asia, Africa and Latin America – what is promoted is a false humanism and, by some accounts (for example that of political theorist John N. Gray) an insidious, destructive, and corrosive hegemonic individualism.

Those who defend the liberal movement – such as Douglas B. Rasmussen and Douglas J. Den Uyl – insist, however, that crucial elements of modern liberalism rest on human nature itself and are thus properly introduced into cultures outside the West. The way for instance that women are treated in some societies – say, in parts of India, the Arab world, in sections of Ghana and even in Central Europe and Latin America – reflects a misunderstanding of human nature, a failure to appreciate that the world's population while highly diverse is also united by its membership in the human race.

Autonomy, then, is a highly controversial idea, what might be characterized, following W.B. Gallie and Alasdair MacIntyre, an essentially contestable concept. That is to say, the idea of autonomy is akin to those such as "liberty," "equality," "justice," "democracy," and so on in figuring prominently within a great variety of normative positions in ethics and politics, so it will continue to be debated without much of a chance of achieving some consensus in its use.

Suffice it to conclude here that autonomy is a concept related closely to the idea that healthy or well-integrated human beings need to be largely in charge of their own lives and actions rather than made subject to the will of others, especially political and economic rulers. But this idea is challenged considerably by the widespread modern belief that what people do is ultimately not – indeed, cannot be – really up to them because they are all subject to such impersonal forces as their DNA, genes, cultural influences, upbringing and, in the most general terms, to the ineluctable forces of an ever-developing, ever-evolving interconnected and deterministic macro-system of nature.

Not unless some understanding of this nature triumphs within which room is found for free and independent human agency – or it is superseded by the alternative of some type of supernaturalism or dualism – will autonomy gain the foundation it needs to be included as a genuine, bona fide vital element of human existence.

Further reading

Bellah, R., Madsen, R., Sullivan, W.M., Swidler, A. and Tipton, S. *Habits of the Heart: Individualism and Commitment in American Life*. New York: Harper and Row, 1984.

Bolton, J.D.P. *Glory, Jest and Riddle: A Study of the Growth of Individualism from Homer to Christianity*. New York: Barnes and Noble, 1973.

Dworkin, Ronald. *Sovereign Virtue*. Cambridge, MA: Harvard University Press, 2002.

Easton, L.D. and Guddat, K.H. (eds and trans.) *Writing of the Young Marx on Philosophy and Society*. Garden City, NY: Anchor Books, 1967.

Kant, Immanuel. *Critique of Practical Reason*, trans. Lewis White Beck. New York: Liberal Arts Press, 1956.

Machan, T.R. *Individuals and their Rights.* Chicago, IL: Open Court, 1989.
Mill, John Stuart. *Utilitarianism.* London: Longmans, Green, 1901.
Morris, C. *The Discovery of the Individual 1050–1200.* New York: Harper and Row, 1972.
Norton, David L. *Personal Destinies, A Philosophy of Ethical Individualism.* Princeton, NJ: Princeton University Press, 1976.
Nozick, Robert. *Anarchy State, and Utopia.* New York: Basic Books, 1974.
Rand, Ayn. *Capitalism: The Unknown Ideal.* New York: New American Library, 1967.
Rasmussen, Douglas B. and Den Uyl, Douglas J. *Liberty and Nature: An Aristotelian Defense of Liberal Order.* Chicago: Open Court, 1990.
Rawls, John. *A Theory of Justice.* Cambridge, MA: Harvard University Press, 1971.
Schneewind, J.B. *The Invention of Autonomy.* New York: Cambridge University Press, 1998.
Taylor, Charles. *Philosophy and the Human Sciences.* Cambridge: Cambridge University Press, 1985.

TIBOR MACHAN

AXIOLOGY

Axiology or value theory arose at the end of the nineteenth century as the study of non-moral sources of value, for example in economics, esthetics, knowledge, and politics. "Good" was confined to moral value, a connotation it did not have in the classics. The question is whether these different kinds of value have a common principle or element. The problematic of axiology arose because value was *not* conceived as an attribute of "being." Certain value contraries, such as good and bad, right and wrong, true and false, reality and appearance, beautiful and ugly, were interpreted as normative ideals: enduring standards.

"Values" in a wider sense are taken in the loose sense of any normative topic, including politics, rather than a concern with value theory proper. A more reductive view, where it is not a confusion of values with ethics, is that value theory is part of ethics, since moral values concern a special realm of what ought to be. In other words, morality is itself a wide topic that includes the study of values in all spheres of life.

Theory

The value theory that most of the pragmatists subscribed to was the vitalistic theory of value: that value for life is the chief deciding factor in values and what is useful to life has value. Life taken as a whole constitutes a norm for judging individual experiences of value. Indeed, the value of life and the problems of life are central issues for philosophy, a view they shared with Nietzsche, who is sometimes classified as a pragmatist. Since they thought that philosophy should be concerned with the problems of life, philosophy in general concerns value issues at the root. The practical working of truth, for example, reduces to "the question whether we can live by it." To some degree their life-centered theory may have reflected the influence of Darwinian evolution, which was very strong when the pragmatists began their careers. The more idealistic of the pragmatists also emphasized the value of the individual personality as the highest expression of life.

There was also the overarching approach or "temperament" of pragmatism to philosophical and certain other problems, that James called "meliorism." The pragmatists thought life could be improved by action. They were more positive about the prospects for life, by contrast with pessimistic views.

Scope

As Dewey noted, there is a great deal of controversy over the scope of values, from those that argue values pervade all of philosophy, and even the movement to make values a first philosophy, to more reductive views. Although there were differences among them, the pragmatists all argued for a wide scope for values.

If axiology were confined to moral values, then the first generation of pragmatists, Peirce and James, hardly discussed issues of value. James wrote a few essays on morals while Peirce left a few notes. However, in a broader sense, James and Peirce were concerned with axiological issues, since Peirce argued for a place for the normative sciences in philosophy, while James argued for an axiological element in truth: that truth is that which is good in the way of belief. The approach of these first-generation figures was the investigation of what Putnam has recently called "epistemological values."

Moreover, the pragmatists revalued the problem of value in accord with their critique of the relation of theory and practice. The pragmatists criticized the separation of theory and practice, particularly Dewey. Everything must yield to the test of practical results, so all studies are practical in some sense. Since practice is bound up with value, theory must also reflect value to some degree. The pragmatists were the first to emphasize the role of action in knowledge. Since practice was decisive for their epistemology, value considerations were central. Thus value was used differently than for other schools. It is particularly in this expansion of the notion of values that the pragmatists may claim originality. The emphasis on practical activity separates them decisively from subjective theories of value, as activity is public and in the world.

If they emphasized that knowledge is not value free, they also argued against any view of values as independent of knowledge. They all agreed that there could be genuine and strict propositions about value. Lewis was particularly concerned to show that values and morals were not irrational or relative, a stance which he took emotivism to foster.

Intrinsic value, evaluation, and other distinctions of value

The pragmatists accepted a number of distinctions in value inherited from the tradition. These include the notion of degrees of value, and of different kinds of value. They accepted the idealist view of ideals as standards and of a *summum bonum*, although Dewey modified the latter notion. All uphold the distinction of instrumental and intrinsic values, including, contrary to some early interpreters, Dewey. C.I. Lewis further distinguished inherent value from the intrinsic value of an experience, arguing that the former consists in potencies of an object to cause good experiences.

The pragmatists distinguished value and evaluation, although Dewey attenuated the distinction in a late work. Value is considered a quality, property or character of anything to which it is applied, for example a good tool. As a term with wide applicability, value can be applied to include things of value, and ideals, as well as activities. Evaluation is a more critical notion, connected with value judgments. Evaluation involves both a comparison of different lines of action and a critical appraisal of them. For example, warranted desires are those subjected to critical scrutiny or evaluation.

The relation of value and ethics

The pragmatists tended towards holism in the relation of values and ethics, especially the naturalistic school of Dewey and C.I. Lewis. While they argued for the consideration of values and consequences in moral deliberation, they avoided the individualism and axiological foundationalism of other forms of consequentialism, for example Utilitarianism, for which intrinsic value is the basis of moral obligation. For the pragmatists, values as kinds are evaluated as part of a larger whole, namely, value for life. The relation of parts to the whole may be more important than any one part, including the web of relations constituting the whole.

The pragmatists argued against the reductive view of the relation of values and ethics, since axiology is not confined to morals for any of the pragmatists. C.I. Lewis in particular separated values from morals on the epistemological ground that values could be confirmed empirically, whereas morals could not. Thus he upheld the distinction of is from ought, but included values in the former.

Although this was not a pressing issue, the pragmatists generally argued for the priority of moral values, which they identify with the practical, over aesthetic values. Peirce was an exception; he argued that the study of esthetics was basic to the normative sciences, since it examined what is good in itself.

Language, experience and culture

The pragmatists rejected what has been labeled “meta-ethics,” the study of the meaning of ethical terms. Dewey judged that “verbal usage gives us little help” and may be confusing, since many value terms are used in multiple ways, although it may be useful as a starting point.

Experience is the framework in which to explore the meaning of value terms. The pragmatists were highly critical of the distinction of subject and object, and thus of subjective and objective values. Values are part of the world of overall experience. They agreed on the actuality of value in the world. As the world is not devalued in the subject–object dichotomy for the pragmatists, the possibility of valuing the non-human is less difficult and more consistent with its theories of value.

Since collective conduct involves others, there is also a social aspect to values, which arise out of culture and are constitutive of individuals through habituation and education, a point emphasized by G.H. Mead and J. Tufts. Josiah Royce emphasized the inter-subjective influences on the formation of individual values.

Idealism and naturalism

There were two basic schools among the classical pragmatists, the idealist school, including Peirce, James, Royce and Schiller; and the naturalistic approach of Dewey, Mead and C.I. Lewis. For Peirce, the normative sciences of logic, ethics and esthetics are concerned with different values.

However, it is to Josiah Royce that we owe a more thoroughly worked out treatment of value from an idealist. Royce advanced an ethic based on the idea of loyalty to loyalty, and to the great community. However, each individual works out his or her own life plan, and thus the value of the individual personality is upheld. The emphasis on the value of the individual personality was even greater among the personalists, or personal idealists, such as R. Flewelling, who were critical of Royce's absolute form of idealism. Value is connected with self-realization or development of the individual personality.

F.C.S. Schiller made human values central, even a first philosophy. Ethics, which like the other pragmatists, he viewed as teleological or consequential, provides the goals by which reality is remade and thereby given meaning. Human goals alter reality with actions aiming at valued consequences. In this incorporation of human action and value into shaping reality, Schiller's humanism is the view that humans have largely risen above nature.

By contrast, Dewey and Lewis were naturalists. For Dewey, in the later works, the growth of the natural organism is conceived as the overall end. In turn, growth is tied to self-fulfillment, a natural process. Thus they rejected Moore's distinction of natural and non-natural properties.

Further reading

Altman, Andrew. "John Dewey and Contemporary Normative Ethics," *Metaphilosophy* 13, 2 (1982): 149–60, p. 158.

Dewey, John. *Human Nature and Conduct*. New York: Modern Library, 1957 [1922].

James, W. *Pragmatism and Other Essays*, New York: Washington Square Press, 1975 [1910].

Lewis, C.I. *Values and Imperatives*, ed. J. Lange. Stanford, CA: Stanford University Press, 1969.

Peirce, Charles S. *Charles S. Peirce, Selected Writings*, ed. P. Wiener. New York, Dover, 1968.

Schiller, F.C.S. *Our Human Truths*. New York: Columbia University Press, 1939.

HUGH P. MCDONALD

B

BARRETT, WILLIAM

William Barrett (1913–92), for many years Professor of Philosophy at New York University, was one of the most broadly based and learned philosophers of the twentieth century. He earned his doctorate at Columbia University with a dissertation on Aristotle's *Physics.* He is generally credited with introducing existentialism to the U.S. in his 1947 *Partisan Review* article, "What is Existentialism?" But he was far from thinking of existentialism as mainly an exotic French import. For example, in his famous *Irrational Man* (1958), he described William James as being as much an existentialist as a pragmatist. Barrett was greatly learned in the whole history of philosophy and enjoyed tracing existential themes throughout this history.

Barrett's first appointment after his doctorate was as Assistant Professor of Mathematics in Chicago. Mathematics plays a key role in major phenomenologists from Charles Peirce through Edmund Husserl to Aaron Gurwitsch. While not going all the way with Husserl's search for truths of eidetic necessity exemplified in structures of phenomena, Barrett nevertheless believed with Husserl that close description of phenomena is logically prior to scientific explanation of them. When this principle is violated, we get rampant reductionism and nihilism. Barrett never lost his love of mathematics and carried on lively discussions with the mathematicians at NYU.

Barrett tirelessly distinguished between phenomenology and the Descartes-inspired (and the British Empiricists') phenomenalism. In his last book, *Death of the Soul: From Descartes to the Computer* (1986), he asked: how did we get here – get to the late twentieth century? How did seventeenth-century rationalism's premature linkage of philosophy and natural science lead to the strangely detached, emotionally flattened, hyper-specialized life of today – this eclipse of the immediately experienced world that is actually all around us every minute? In what is perhaps his master-work, *The Illusion of Technique* (1978), he pounds home the fundamental point that while technology can create wonders within its sphere, it cannot illuminate the very assumptions that drive it (the book contains many allusions to the work of the later Ludwig Wittgenstein).

Barrett was well known and widely respected for his philosophical analyses of art. They far exceeded what has become known in many academic-philosophical circles today as aesthetics. Barrett believed that many of the great artists of the twentieth century were in much better touch with the immediate lived quality of our experienced world than are most academic philosophers mainly concerned with logic and science. His analyses are most forceful in his *Time of Need: Forms of the Imagination in the 20th Century* (1972) – see particularly "Backward Toward the Earth;" "Winner Take Nothing;" "The Atonal World." His probing analysis of Hemingway's work sensitizes us conceptually to what the art is revealing: the palpable presence of non-being circulating through our everyday experience. Barrett's analysis of Beckett's work articulates on a conceptual level emotional anesthesia and behavioral paralysis – themes at that work's heart.

Coinciding with the publication of *The Illusion of Technique*, William Barrett was sixty-five years old. At NYU at the time, this marked the mandatory retirement age. Accordingly, he was given the Great Teacher Award for that year and let go. Although, much to its credit, Pace University in Westchester County, New York, hired him, losing his position in Manhattan was a great loss for him, for the city and the nation, and for his colleagues and students. Soon the whole tenor of philosophy at NYU shifted radically to the modish "analytic style." Barrett was indeed a great teacher, and his broadly based learning was ever at his fingertips as he gripped students' attention. Along with his colleague and chairman, Sidney Hook, he knew the true meaning of "relevance." His teaching was integral to his power and eminence as a philosopher.

BRUCE WILSHIRE

BEAUTY

Beauty, the central concept of early modern aesthetics, today remains as indispensable to philosophical discussions in this area as it is controversial. The most important discussions of beauty in American philosophy are for the most part by twentieth-century professional philosophers who bring to the subject a knowledge of academic debates in aesthetics as well as an appreciation of the humanistic relevance of the sciences. But one seminal nineteenth-century figure deserving mention is Ralph Waldo Emerson, who in 1860 wrote that

> Beauty is the form under which the intellect prefers to study the world. All privilege is that of beauty; for there are many beauties; as, of general nature, of the human face and form, of manners, of brain, or method, moral beauty, or beauty of the soul

and

> Into every beautiful object, there enters somewhat immeasurable and divine, and just as much into form bounded by outlines, like mountains on the horizon, as into tones of music, or depths of space.

Emerson here brings the signature idealist theme of metaphysical transcendence together with an earthier romantic appreciation of the multiplicity of worldly, day-to-day experiences whose repleteness with meaning and feeling invites description as aesthetic.

From the turn of the twentieth century onwards, discussions of beauty exhibit a decided turn away from idealism and toward naturalism. We find this, for example, in George Santayana's *The Sense of Beauty* (1896), whose central thesis is that beauty is "pleasure objectified" or "pleasure regarded as the quality of a thing." Taking issue with a long tradition of aesthetic objectivizing and universalizing running from Plato through modern empiricism and idealism, Santayana characterizes aesthetic judgment as a process possessing a biological basis. At the phenomenological level, this process involves a kind of projection through which, in finding something beautiful, we routinely confuse a quality of our perception of x – which is actually produced by a relation between subject and object – with a quality we suppose to inhere completely in x itself. Santayana distinguishes three further aspects of the sense of beauty: the beauty of material (the pleasure we take in basic sensations like sound and color); the beauty of form (pleasure in symmetry and proportion), and the beauty of expression (pleasure in the remembered "reverberations" of feelings occasioned by percepts). He revisits these themes in his 1903 *Reason in Art*, with a stronger emphasis on how the beauties of fine art, in addition to arising from natural conditions, are also dependent upon contexts of practical purposiveness in ways not acknowledged by earlier efforts to establish the autonomy of art and aesthetic experience from nature and utility.

Santayana's argument in some ways anticipates the more thoroughgoing naturalism of John Dewey's 1934 *Art as Experience*, the most influential work in twentieth-century American philosophy of art. Beauty, however, only plays a marginal role in Dewey's argument. After centuries of subservience to doctrines of "form descending from without, as a transcendent essence, upon material," talk of beauty seems more likely now, in his view, to hinder than to advance an appropriately pragmatic and experimental inquiry into the continuities between art and ordinary experience. But Dewey does not deny that we experience beauty. Indeed, he characterizes it as one of many qualities of experience possessing a greater ontological footing in the public world than is acknowledged in a more relational and projective account like Santayana's. Beauty, so understood, emerges from intelligence's participation in real "situations" (a key Deweyan notion) whose organic complexity belies simple oppositions between subjective and objective poles of experience.

But even *Art as Experience*, for all its heterodox originality, did not quite capture how many modernist painters, sculptors, writers, musicians, and other artists were, by the early twentieth century, creating work that rejected both classical ideals of form and representation and the very idea of an artwork as the embodiment of a single, nontrivially definable aesthetic form of value, such as beauty. (Epitomizing this sensibility, the painter Barnett Newman remarked that "The impulse of modern art is the desire to destroy beauty," and quipped on another occasion that "Aesthetics is to artists what ornithology is to birds.") One encounters this philosophical innocence of artworld life also in such otherwise important contributions to American philosophical aesthetics as Stephen C. Pepper's *Aesthetic Quality: A Contextualistic Theory of Beauty* (1937) and *The Basis of Criticism of the Arts* (1945), D.W. Prall's *Aesthetic Analysis* (1936), and Suzanne Langer's *Philosophy in a New Key* (1942).

In the late 1950s, a more systematic argument for the rejection of beauty from the core concerns of the philosophy of art informs Monroe C. Beardsley's influential *Aesthetics: Problems in the Philosophy of Criticism*. Beardsley's account of the defining issues of aesthetics includes an analytically incisive critique of the "Beauty Theory." This idealized structure boils down to three propositions that, Beardsley suggests, have repeatedly informed unsuccessful efforts in the philosophy of art thus far: (1) beauty is a regional quality of perceptual objects; (2) beauty is intrinsically valuable; (3) "aesthetic value" means "value that an object has on account of its beauty." Beardsley is particularly critical of the second and third claims. He argues in the first case (drawing upon Dewey's general theory of valuation) from the non-self-evidence of the general proposition that there are intrinsic values anywhere and, in the second case, from an array of conceptual and empirical considerations which suggest that many experiences and objects that we prize aesthetically (such as modernist artworks) are in fact not beautiful in any traditional sense. This fact for Beardsley, as for many later writers, attests to the rich variety, and developmental autonomy, of what modern civilization has come to recognize as art.

By the end of the 1960s, skepticism about a necessary linkage between the concepts of art and of not only beauty but of the aesthetic generally attained a new threshold. Many philosophers were dropping the term "aesthetics," which they now saw as burdened with a moribund legacy of art-theoretical essentialism, as a description of their work in favor of the more neutral "philosophy of art." One benchmark of this anti-aesthetic and anti-essentialist turn is Nelson Goodman's *Languages of Art* (1968), whose uncompromising semiotic approach to its subject scarcely mentions beauty or aesthetic value. Instead, Goodman places fresh emphasis on how artworks of diverse kinds perform a variety of symbolic functions that appeal to what he maintains is the inextricable relationship of cognition and emotion in our experience of painting, literature, music, dance, architecture, and other arts. A yet more explicitly anti-aesthetic book is Arthur C. Danto's *The Transformation of the Commonplace*, which argues for the essentialist thesis that an artwork is an artifact that embodies a meaning that is grasped through interpretation and that is informed at a more basic level by the shared background theoretical beliefs about art which constitute a society's "artworld." Danto updates this argument in his more recent *The Abuse of Beauty: Aesthetics and the Concept of Art*, which advances the further idea that some artworks possess, in addition to the artistically conferred meaning or "thought" that is part of their artistic essence, an "internal" beauty which is entailed by (and hence internal to) that meaning. After approvingly narrating the story of artistic modernism's fateful severing of logical links between the concepts of art and beauty, Danto also affirms the indispensability of beauty, in art and in nature, as a fundamental human value.

Most of the discussions so far mentioned belong squarely to either or both of the analytic and pragmatic traditions of philosophy. Yet a more eclectic methodological sense pervades much of the more recent writing in this area. Stephen David Ross, for example, draws on the work of such European thinkers as Heidegger, Levinas, and Derrida to argue, in *The Gift of Beauty: The Good as Art*, that beauty is "abundance beyond opposition." Beauty, on this view, symbolizes and satisfies the human need for experiences that transcend fixed logical oppositions of thought, including those that pertain to our classifications of human identity and social practice. In this way, beauty's larger importance for our time is as much ethical and political as it is, more narrowly, aesthetic. Other writers have taken issue with the universalistic and noncontextual approach to beauty (among other aesthetic concepts) that characterizes most mainstream work in modern philosophical aesthetics. On this basis, such writers pursue reconstructive accounts of what beauty can still mean today. For example, feminist writers like Peg Zeglin Brand emphasize the ways in which modern Western discussions of beauty (and of its counterpart notion, the sublime) have often worked, consciously or otherwise, to legitimate cultural images of femininity and masculinity that are not always accurate or benign. This kind of argument underscores how, even if it is not literally true that "there is no disputing about taste," it remains a philosophically significant fact that taste (i.e. what people actually find beautiful) varies across human cultures. There is no guarantee that what pleases, say, a New York businesswoman in the way of art, nature, the physical and moral dimensions of human life will overlap – nor have philosophers to date produced arguments or principles that without begging the question show that they must overlap – with the preferences of a Japanese fisherman, a native American potter, or an Afghani farmer, and conversely.

Such considerations suggest, finally, that we may do well to abandon the traditional assumption that "beauty" possesses a single metaphysically or transcendentally fixed meaning and to picture its meaning instead as continually evolving in ways that, while remaining aware of the older traditions of usage, also reflect emerging local purposes and contexts of usage. A corollary of this point is that fresh efforts to explain beauty philosophically do well to attend to the term's myriad inflections as it translates through the variety of human languages. But if this is so, a further corollary pertains to "beauty's" resilience among our concepts. For one cannot coherently argue for the conclusion that beauty has become a useless category for global cultural conversation from the premise that the world's standards of beauty are so diverse as to be incommensurable (for a premise that asserts this still assumes that they are standards of *something*). Such considerations by themselves, of course, entail neither a specific theory of art or aesthetics nor, more generally – a relevant point for pragmatists – any specific account of how finished or complete our theories of such subjects can reasonably hope to be today. But they underscore how beauty remains very much alive as a subject that challenges American philosophers who would advance the above global conversation.

Further reading

Beardsley, Monroe C. *Aesthetics: Problems in the Philosophy of Criticism*. Indianapolis, IN: Hackett, 1981 [1958].

Brand, Peg Zeglin. *Beauty Matters*. Bloomington, IL; Indiana University Press, 2000

Danto, Arthur C. *The Abuse of Beauty: Aesthetics and the Concept of Art*. Peru, IL: Open Court, 2003.

Dewey, John. *Art as Experience*. Carbondale, IL: Southern Illinois University Press, 1989 [1934].

Emerson, Ralph Waldo. "Beauty," in Ralph Waldo Emerson, *The Conduct of Life*. Cambridge: Belknap Press, 2004 [1860].

Pepper, Stephen C. *Aesthetic Quality: A Contextualistic Theory of Beauty*. Westport, CT: Greenwood Press, 1970 [1965].

Ross, Steven David. *The Gift of Beauty: The Good as Art*. Albany, NY: SUNY Press, 1996.

Santayana, George. *The Sense of Beauty*. New York: Dover, 1955 [1896].

Sartwell, Crispin. *Six Names of Beauty*. London: Routledge, 2004.

Shusterman, Richard. *Pragmatist Aesthetics: Reliving Beauty, Rethinking Art*. Cambridge: Blackwell, 1992.

CASEY HASKINS

BEHAVIORISM

Developed by J.B. Watson in 1913, behaviorism was a movement in direct psychology away from the introspective examination of consciousness and speculation about its neurological basis, and toward the empirical study of behavior. Scientific studies of animal behavior had existed since the mid-to-late nineteenth century, but psychology during that period had been defined as the science of mind, which animals were thought to lack. Thus, studies of animal behavior took place only within the field of biology. Watson argued that psychologists should adopt the methods of experimental biology and confine their researches to behavior when studying human beings.

This thesis was an outgrowth of the functionalism that Watson had learned from the pragmatist philosopher John Dewey, the experimental psychologist James Angell, and others at the University of Chicago. As Dewey had stated it, functionalism was belief that "mind is not substantival but adjectival." In other words, "minds" do not exist; there are only animals, human and non-human, with capacities for sensation, emotion, thought and cognition. But what does not exist cannot be studied. So, functionalism implies that psychologists should not attempt to "introspect" the "contents" of otherwise inscrutable, because immaterial, "minds." Instead, they should study how human beings and other animals respond to and cope with changes in their environments. Psychology was no longer to be transcendental or analytical phenomenology. It was now to be a branch of natural science focused on the relation between stimulus and response.

Influenced by the Russian physiologist Ivan Pavlov, Watson believed that complex behavior could be broken down into chains of reflexive responses to conditioned and unconditioned stimuli. Having studied neurology with Jacques Loeb, he was aware of the theory that states of mind are just processes of the brain, but little was known about these processes. Besides, he believed, as had Loeb, that what had meaning was the organism's total response: neural, muscular, and glandular. Because it could be altered by identifiable changes in the organism's circumstances, behaviorists would look outward to the external causes of this response, not inward to its ghostly accompaniments. Watson boldly announced that, given control of a healthy infant's surroundings, he could mold it into any kind of adult, be it doctor, lawyer, or Native American chief. This hyperbole was never fulfilled, of course, but behaviorists would go on to influence education, psychotherapy, advertising, business management, and other practical pursuits, as well as sociology, political science, and anthropology.

A child of American pragmatism, behaviorism was eventually adopted by logical positivism, an influential philosophy of science that had come to America in the person of expatriate physicist Rudolf Carnap. Reinforcing Watson's animus against introspection, Carnap reiterated that unverifiable claims about what goes on in invisible and intangible "minds" cannot be the basis of objective science. If reports of thoughts and feelings were not to be disallowed altogether, their value had at least to be discounted. No longer were introspective reports to be taken as authoritative accounts of esoteric facts. Now they were to be treated as data requiring explanation, like other forms of behavior. Carnap allied these strictures on method with physicalism, belief that everything, including human behavior, can be described in the language of physics. A great many American psychologists accepted Carnap's ideas.

During World War II, the leadership of laboratory behaviorism fell to one of these psychologists, Professor B.F. Skinner of Harvard University. Studying pigeons and rats in the laboratories of the biology department, Skinner repudiated Watson's belief that all behavior could be reduced to mechanical reflexes. That was true of only what Skinner called respondent behavior. Operant (i.e. voluntary and purposive) behavior was, rather, to be explained by invoking E.L. Thorndike's law of effect – the principle that behavior is reinforced (i.e. made more likely) or weakened by its consequences. Skinner's extensive and rigorous experiments were designed to differentiate the effects on behavior of various "reinforcement schedules." Answering the charge that behaviorist emphasis on the environment leads to neglect of inner processes, Skinner replied that these too will eventually be revealed using the methods of natural science. Challenged to account for language, Skinner wrote a large book on that topic. Although Skinner agreed that behavior is physical, he did not think that physics could explain it; psychology was to be an autonomous science with its own distinctive laws and vocabulary. Like Watson before him, Skinner announced bold schemes of education and envisioned ambitious social experiments.

Behaviorism was the regnant philosophy of psychology in America from about 1920 to about 1970. It began to lose its dominance when MIT linguist Noam Chomsky wrote a critical review of Skinner's *Verbal Behavior*, arguing that behaviorism might explain the learning of vocabulary but could not account for syntax. Furthering the decline of behaviorism was the increasingly popular idea, fostered by Chomsky's students, that the newly developing digital computer was, or would eventually become, a thinking machine comparable to the human brain. This idea, and new means of observing the brain's workings, freed psychologists from the austere restraints that had for so long been imposed on them by behaviorism. The result in the last quarter of the twentieth century was the rise of cognitive psychology, marked features of which are revived preoccupation with consciousness and renewed speculation about the psychological meaning of brain processes. Cognitive psychology is now the leading paradigm of psychological science.

Although Skinner's younger colleague, Willard Quine, was the last great philosopher to endorse the main tenets of behaviorism, it should not be concluded that the movement is dead, or even moribund. Behavior analysts, as they refer to themselves in the twenty-first century, are far less common in departments of academic psychology than they once were; however, a very large number of them can be founds in such fields as pedagogy, criminology, speech therapy, emotional counseling, child rearing, animal training, advertising, psychological testing, and personnel management – occupations for which behaviorist methods are well suited. The science of biology also includes ethology, the study of animal behavior, and, despite continued opposition to behaviorist philosophy, there is still general agreement that psychology is of little use if it cannot explain behavior.

Further reading

Schwartz, Barry and Lacey, Hugh. *Behaviorism, Science, and Human Nature*. New York: W.W. Norton, 1982.

Smith, Laurence D. *Behaviorism and Logical Positivism: A Reassessment of the Alliance*. Stanford, CA: Stanford University Press, 1986.

Todd, James T. and Morris, Edward K. (eds) *Modern Perspectives on John B. Watson and Classical Behaviorism*. Westport, CT: Greenwood Press, 1994.

MAX HOCUTT

BEING

For most American philosophers, being's time has, well ... passed. Traditionally, beginning most notably with Aristotle, philosophers regarded metaphysics as the science of being *qua* being. This enquiry sought to discover the most abstract, universal, first principles of reality *in itself* apart from any essential reference to specific tangible things.

Yet one hallmark of American philosophy has been its sustained critique not only of the possibility and use of such enquiries, but of the very idea of being in itself.

Historically, this idea served several conceptual functions: (1) as a *substance* which (a) designates the generic *metaphysical stuff* from which all specific beings are made, or (b) contrasts states of being with non-being, as in specifying what things *actually* exist, (2) as a *substrate* that allows objects to remain *essentially* themselves amid contingent changes, and as a *modal conjunct* that affirms or negates statements of fact, as in assertions about past or future states *being* or *having been* or *potentially being* one way rather than another.

For Analytic philosophers, however, the term "being" lacks meaning precisely because it wholly abstracts from real things. Eminent logical positivist A.J. Ayer, for example, in his influential work *Language, Truth and Logic*, argues that such terms are meaningless unless they describe determinate objects or events that we can experience empirically and verify scientifically. Willard V.O. Quine alike maintains that meaningful linguistic terms must bear tangible, empirical referents. In *Ontological Relativity and Other Essays*, he identifies his verification theory of meaning as ontologically relativist because, he insists, it makes no *factual* difference what abstract being *is* in itself. Apart from our experience of specific realities, the term "being" is literally non-sensical.

While Analytic philosophers largely regard the term "being" and its investigation as nonsense, most Pragmatists have deemed it useless. In *The Quest for Certainty*, John Dewey opposes the search for abstract, immutable principles of being. The reality we experience, he argues, is contingent and probable, as is our knowledge of that reality, upon which we must act. It is useless to aspire to abstract knowledge independent of our experience, as we could neither test – nor use – such alleged knowledge.

Here, Dewey echoes William James' influential lecture "What Pragmatism Means."

Our beliefs, James holds, are guides for action which must work, i.e. which must admit practical applications, and which prove true only insofar as they allow us to respond effectively to our experience. On James' instrumental theory of truth, the operative query is what difference it would make – i.e. what practical consequences would follow – if one or another account of being proved true. If no such practical consequences follow upon our enquiries into being *qua* being, then such enquiries prove useless in enabling us to deal effectively with the realities before us.

C.S. Peirce made a similar point earlier and more bluntly, dismissing such queries as "more curious than useful." In "How to Make our Ideas Clear," he opposes our bent for lending abstract linguistic terms an ostensible reality they do not in fact exhibit. In this, his objections presage those of ordinary language analysts such as Gilbert Ryle, who decry our tendency to mistake an *abstract set* of specific things for a reality in addition to the realities that comprise that set. In *The Concept of Mind*, Ryle famously argues that we falsely infer from a set of activities collectively designated "the mind," that minds exist as abstract substances or beings irreducible to those activities. The mind, like being or substance, is a linguistic fabrication that we mistake for a real object. Such terms neither signify distinct realities, nor enhance our understanding of the activities or objects they ostensibly comprise.

While Analytic and Pragmatic philosophers resist such *speculative* metaphysics, even the few American philosophers who engage such enquiries depict being in anything but a traditional sense. Josiah Royce, for instance, may seem an apt representative of speculative metaphysics in its idealist guise. Yet he maintains, in the *World and the Individual*, that ideas embody meanings or purposes only as embodied in definite, actual individual beings, rather than in abstract possibilities of being. Any idea that aspires to truth, he holds, must be validated in actual beings in principle available to our experience.

For pragmatic naturalists like George Santayana, enquiries into being *qua* being could not even begin unless firmly rooted in an empirically accessible basis. Against any investigations that seek knowledge prior to and independent of our experience, he insists in *Skepticism and Animal Faith* that our investigations always commence "in the middle of things," with an instinctive belief in real objects that is in principle beyond our ability to prove. To study being *qua* being, he suggests, we would require an epistemic vantage point in principle isolated from the experience that defines reality as we know it.

Process philosophers, even more strikingly, see the problem with investigating being *qua* being as not simply methodological or linguistic but *itself* metaphysical. As pluralists, these philosophers reject reducing the ultimate constituents of reality to one substance, or even to one type of substance or being. In *Process and Reality*, Alfred North Whitehead argues that ultimate realities are not generic substances but specific individual beings. Such beings, moreover, neither remain the same thorough change, nor bear a wholly common metaphysical stuff, nor exemplify a determinate state of being or non-being – but are always in transition.

In reconceiving Aristotle's conception of being *qua* being, these latter metaphysical approaches may seem wholly contrary to the dominant – largely Analytic and Pragmatic – trajectory of American philosophy. Yet despite vast methodological differences among these three philosophical approaches, they share an experiential bent that ties truth claims – even those regarding being *qua* being – directly to human experience. In this, they all alike recast being in its traditional guise: Analytic and Pragmatic philosophers by tying any such idea irrevocably to empirical experience, and Process philosophers most notably by turning that traditional conception quite literally on its head.

Further reading

Dewey, John. *The Quest for Certainty*. Whitefish, MT: Kessinger, 2005 [1929].

Kim, Jaegwon and Sosa, Ernest (eds) *A Companion to Metaphysics*. Oxford: Blackwell, 1999

Loux, Michael (ed.) *Metaphysics* (Routledge Contemporary Introduction to Philosophy, 1). London: Routledge, 1997.

Peirce, C.S. "How to Make our Ideas Clear," in *The Essential Peirce: Selected Philosophical Writings Vol. 2 (1893–1913)*, ed. N. Houser and C. Kloesel. Bloomington, IN: Indiana University Press, 1998.

Ryle, Gilbert. *The Concept of Mind*. Chicago, IL: University of Chicago Press, 2000 [1949].

Santayana, George. *Skepticism and Animal Faith*. Whitefish, MT: Kessinger, 2005 [1923].

Lisa Bellantoni

BELIEF

Contemporary American philosophers are engaged in the full range of debates about belief, with no particular view being thought of as holding more in the United States than elsewhere. Those debates include the following. Can any of our beliefs carry certainty and if so, are those beliefs the foundation for all knowledge? Is justified true belief knowledge? Is it rational to believe anything at all, or should we be skeptics? Are there degrees of belief and if so, how should they be measured? If belief is a propositional attitude, what is the nature of such propositions? How should beliefs be revised? How are beliefs justified? Do beliefs represent reality?

There is another set of debates about what a belief *is* – is it an attitude we take to a proposition, distinguishable from doubting whether *p*, wondering whether *p*, or wishing that *p*? Is it a feeling associated with the idea that *p*? Is it a special kind of mental state? If there is anything special about how the concept of belief is treated in American philosophy, that distinctiveness is to be found in the originator of pragmatism, Charles S. Peirce (1839–1914), who, following the Scottish empiricist Alexander Bain, argued that a belief involves a habit or disposition to act in a particular way in appropriate circumstances. He linked this dispositional account of belief to his views about truth and inquiry, the result of which is an interesting, and some think compelling, view of belief which can be identified as being unique to classical American pragmatism. At its heart is the idea that there are two intertwined constitutive norms of belief. A belief is such, in virtue of being a belief, that it aims at truth and (thus) it is answerable to experience.

Peirce's account of inquiry sees inquiry as the struggle of rid ourselves of doubt and acquire, in its place, belief. Any item in our background corpus of settled belief is susceptible to doubt, if it is prompted by some positive reason, such as a surprising experience. When experience conflicts with an inquirer's settled belief, he is immediately thrown into doubt and doubt 'essentially involves a struggle to escape' (Peirce V. 372). Inquiry is that struggle to regain belief.

A belief, on Peirce's view, provides the inquirer with an expectation – if I believe that *p*, then I habitually expect the consequences or the predictions I derive from *p* to come about when the appropriate occasion arises. It is in this way that inquirers are thrown into doubt by recalcitrant experience – that experience upsets or disrupts a belief or expectation. As soon as the inquirer is thrown into doubt, inquiry is ignited and continues until a belief or habit of expectation is re-established. Peirce himself put the point in the following way. An inquirer who has some end in view finds that two different lines of action present themselves, bringing action to a halt: "he waits at the fork for an indication, and kicks his heels ... A true doubt is accordingly a doubt which really interferes with the smooth working of a belief-habit" (Peirce V.510).

One consequence of this account of inquiry is that beliefs must have consequences – if you believe that *p*, there must be something you expect to be the case, under certain circumstances. Then if what you expect fails to come about under the appropriate circumstance, your belief will be disrupted. Another way of putting this is to say that beliefs are such that they are responsive to or answerable to something.

There is most certainly a whiff of verificationism here. Only pragmatically legitimate beliefs – beliefs which are connected to experience – are genuine beliefs. Only they can be the subject of an inquiry, for only beliefs that manifest themselves in a set of expectations are such that we can inquire into whether our expectations are upheld or knocked down by experience. But it is only a whiff of verificationism, as Peirce had a view of expectations and answerability to experience that is far broader than any verificationist ever considered. He thought, for instance, that we could have expectations in diagrammatic contexts and thought experiments. And he thought, along with his fellow pragmatists John Dewey and William James, that ethical statements could be answerable to experience. And Peirce took the pragmatic maxim to be elucidating an aspect of meaning, not the whole of it.

There is a second route to the pragmatist view of beliefs as dispositional states which aimed at the truth and responsive to experience. That is to think about the commitments we undertake when we believe. Think of the difference between the phrases "I suspect that *p*" or "it seems to me that *p*", on the one hand, and "I believe that *p*" on the other. What I do when I use the first two phrases is distance myself from the commitments involved in using the last phrase. I distance myself from the commitments that come with belief or assertion. One sort of commitment I make is to defending *p* – to arguing that I am right to believe it or that the evidence and argument supports it. To believe commits one to engage, if called upon, in the project of justification. Failing to incur this commitment – failing to see that one is required to have reasons for one's belief – is to degrade belief into something like mere opinion, prejudice, or tenacity. A belief, that is, is something that is held for reasons.

Another commitment I make is to giving up the belief in the face of sustained, powerful evidence or argument against it. A "belief" which thinks so well of itself that it is in principle immune to recalcitrant reasons and experience is not a genuine belief at all. A "belief" which is such that nothing could speak against it is empty. Part of what it is to be a belief, as opposed to some other attitude towards a proposition, such as an idle entertaining of a thought, a lie about what one believes, is that there must be something that can speak for or against a belief and that belief must be responsive to what can speak for or against it. As Peirce insisted, there is a distinction between tenacity – holding on to an opinion come what may – and belief. Again, believing is, by its very nature, responsive to or sensitive to reasons for and against it.

The idea is that I cannot get myself to genuinely believe *p* by the flip of a coin – by saying that if the coin lands heads, I will believe *p* and if it lands tails I will not believe *p*. A believer thinks that her belief is what fits best with the reasons and argument. That is what a belief is – something which is aimed at the truth or at getting things right. The concept of belief, to use an expression of Wittgenstein's, is internally related to the concepts of experience, reasons, and truth. We cannot understand "I believe that *p*" without understanding that I take *p* to stand up to the reasons and experience and without understanding that I take *p* (although I may well be mistaken) to be true.

There are clearly many issues to be sorted out by this kind of fallibilist. Are beliefs about mathematics and logic such that we must be committed to some experience or reasons that can speak for or against them? Peirce argued that, indeed, we must keep these beliefs open to experience and argument, even if they may never fall to it. What about religious beliefs that are taken on faith and are not open to experience and argument? This kind of theorist must take Wittgenstein's line that, important as they might be, these are not beliefs, properly speaking. And there is an interesting set of questions about the psychological reality of various mental states to be explored: paranoia ("believing", against the evidence, that everyone is against you), the desire to not believe unpalatable truths, self-deception, etc. Those who want to defend the classical pragmatist view of belief have work such as this to look forward to.

Further reading

Adler, Jonathan. *Belief's Own Ethics.* Cambridge, MA: MIT Press, 2002.

Misak, Cheryl. *Truth and The End of Inquiry: A Peircean Account of Truth*, second edition. Oxford: Oxford University Press, 2004.

Peirce, Charles Sanders. *Collected Papers of Charles Sanders Peirce Vols I–IV*, Vols I–VI, ed. C. Hartshorne and P. Weiss. Cambridge, MA: Belknap Press, 1931–5. Vols VII and VIII, ed. A. Burks. Cambridge, MA: Belknap Press, 1958.

Wittgenstein, Ludwig. *Lectures and Conversations on Aesthetics, Psychology, and Religious Belief*, ed. Cyril Barrett. Berkeley, CA: University of California Press, 1938.

CHERYL MISAK

BERTOCCI, PETER ANTHONY

Peter Bertocci (1910–89) dedicated his academic career to elaborating the theistic Personalism of his predecessors at Boston University. As a Personalist, he viewed persons and their lived experience as both the fundamental metaphysical reality and the proper starting point for philosophy. He saw the lived experience, and, in particular, the experience of moral struggle, as pointing in broadly teleological fashion to the existence of a Divine Person. In articulating his conception of God, Bertocci drew on the work of his teacher, Edgar Sheffield Brightman, arguing that if God is truly a person and capable of activity, then God must be a temporal and hence limited being engaged with us in a process of moral striving. Much of Bertocci's work is an exploration of this moral striving, the freedom that is its precondition, and the orchestration of a "symphony of values" that is its end. Because as co-creators with God we engage in a variety of freely chosen activities that do not always intersect in harmonious ways, we should not expect personal reality to be free of suffering. Our task in the face of the inevitable presence of evil is to cultivate a willingness to live with the creative insecurity that comes from loving other persons with all their disconcerting capacity for growth, practicing the art of forgiveness as we work together to realize our various potentials. Bertocci's own commitment to this task is strikingly evident in the style in which he writes, always fully present as a person addressing other persons.

Further reading

Bertocci, Peter Anthony. *Free Will, Responsibility, and Grace*. New York: Abingdon Press, 1957.

—— *Religion as Creative Insecurity*. New York: Association Press, 1958.

—— *The Person God Is*. New York: Humanities Press, 1970.

PATRICIA A. SAYRE

BLANSHARD, BRAND

Brand Blanshard (1892–1987) championed "the rational temper" in some of the most trenchant, fair-minded, and lucid appraisals of the chief doctrines of twentieth-century philosophy ever published. Although usually and appropriately classified as a rationalist and idealist, what is most salient about him was that he was both fully informed about the technical detains of influential philosophical currents and able to articulate a standpoint independent of those currents.

Born in Fredericksburg, Ohio, Blanshard was educated at the University of Michigan, Oxford (as a Rhodes Scholar), Columbia and Harvard. He taught at Michigan, Swarthmore and, from 1945 until retirement, at Yale.

His reputation was first established by the publication of *The Nature of Thought*, a two-volume work that appeared in 1939. In this monumental treatise Blanshard made a lasting contribution to the tradition of idealism founded in Germany by G.W.F. Hegel more than a century earlier. But his was a neo-Hegelianism thoroughly revised in the light of contributions by other philosophical traditions, including recent developments in pragmatism, realism, positivism and logical theory; it was also an idealistic system expressed with a clarity and elegance seldom found in the writings of followers of Hegel.

In a trilogy, *Reason and Goodness* (1961), *Reason and Analysis* (1962), and *Reason and Belief* (1974), Blanshard constructed one of the most subtle and elaborate systems of thought produced in the twentieth century. Among the vast array of arguments advanced in these books, here are a few. He argued against the doctrine of Hume that causation is merely the constant conjunction of events and the view of logical positivism that a priori statements are merely consequences of linguistic conventions. There are, Blanshard said, genuine "necessary connections" in the world. A naturalist in ethics, he held that "to call an experience intrinsically good is to say that it is fulfilling and satisfying." Since he granted "that the word 'good' has [in addition] an aura of emotional and associative meaning," he could "keep emotive meaning and also keep it in its place." A naturalist in religion too, he took "the service of reason" as his religion. "That service calls for the use of one's reason to embrace as much as one can of the reason implicit in the universe, and its use at the same time to define and harmonize the ends of practical life."

Although in most of his publications Blanshard addressed the technical issues typically discussed in professional magazines, he wrote also for a general audience. *The Uses of a Liberal Education and Other Talks to Students* (1973) is a collection of lively essays on such topics as "Can Men be Reasonable?" "In Defense of the Humanities," "Limited Minds and Unlimited Knowledge" and "The Idea of a Gentleman." Few distinguished philosophers have been in such demand as lecturers. He took pride in his ability to present abstract ideas in a way that made them intelligible and interesting to people without formal training in philosophy. In personal manner, he was unfailingly kindly and courteous, traits also manifest in his many published exchanges with other scholars.

In his final book, *Four Reasonable Men: Marcus Aurelius, John Stuart Mill, Ernest Renan, and Henry Sidgwick,* published when he was ninety-two years old, Blanshard biographically presented exemplars of "a quiet habitual reasonableness", "the great grey virtue" that he had been promoting throughout his life.

Further reading

Idealistic Studies. "Truth and Reason," *Idealistic Studies* IV (January and May 1974). Critical essays by seven scholars and replies by Blanshard.

Idealistic Studies XX (May 1990). Appreciative essays by five scholars after Blanshard's death, and a bibliography of his publications, 1980–7.

Review of Metaphysics. "Internal Relations and their Importance in Philosophy," *Review of Metaphysics*, XXI (December 1967). Critical essays by four scholars and Blanshard's replies.

Schilpp, P.A. (ed.) *The Philosophy of Brand Blanshard.* Chicago, IL: Open Court, 1980. Contains a bibliography of Blanshard's publications, 1916–80.

Peter H. Hare

BLAU, JOSEPH L.

Joseph L. Blau (1909–86) was an important historian of American philosophy, including social and political philosophy and the philosophy of democracy. He was also a historian and philosopher of religion, writing on American philosophies of religion as well as the history and philosophy of Judaism. He received his undergraduate and graduate degrees from Columbia University (his PhD in philosophy was awarded in 1945), working while a graduate student as a New York City high school teacher, and he taught at Columbia from 1944 to 1977, first in the Philosophy Department and then in the Department of Religion, which he helped to found in 1961. In addition to his excellence as a scholar and writer, Professor Blau was a great teacher. His distinction in all these areas was recognized in 1980 by the publication of a Festschrift, a volume of fifteen articles by colleagues and former students entitled, *History, Religion, and Spiritual Democracy.* And shortly before his death, the Society for the Advancement of American Philosophy voted to bestow upon him its Herbert W. Schneider Award for Distinguished Contributions to the Understanding and Advancement of American Philosophy, an award that was presented posthumously.

Blau's work on American philosophy ranged over its entire history. In addition to treating such prominent thinkers as Ralph Waldo Emerson, John Dewey, William James, Josiah Royce, and George Herbert Mead, he showed the importance of lesser known figures such as Benjamin Rush, Francis Wayland, Henry James the Elder, Chauncy Wright (whom Blau was one of the first to fully appreciate), Francis Ellingwood Abbott, and John Fiske. His writings on American political life and thought include treatments of Thomas Paine, Thomas Jefferson, and Dewey's social thought and theory of democracy, as well as works on more general topics such as the relation between church and state, religion and politics, and religious freedom. He edited *Cornerstones of Religious Freedom in America*, and among his publications in the area of political thought is the widely read *Social Theories of Jacksonian Democracy: Representative Writings of the Period.* The most significant of the books that Blau edited is the comprehensive anthology *American Philosophic Addresses. 1700–1900*, prepared as a companion to Herbert W. Schneider's *A History of American Philosophy.* Blau worked closely with Schneider on the *History*, compiling a bibliography of primary and secondary sources for each section of this book. For years the foremost resource for scholars wishing to study the American philosophers, these materials remain valuable. Schneider and Blau should be credited with reviving interest in and revealing the vitality and diversity of earlier American philosophy which, as Blau noted in the introduction to the anthology, even Ralph Waldo Emerson had denigrated.

Blau's most notable work on American philosophy is *Men and Movements in American Philosophy*, which has been translated into many languages including Korean and Hindi. *Men and Movements* traces the various schools and developments in American philosophic thought through an interesting selection of representative figures, both major and minor. The book opens with a discussion of the Puritan background and concludes with a section on the emergence of naturalism, the school of thought with which Blau himself identified and whose main representatives he takes to be Santayana, Morris Raphael Cohen, and Dewey. That Blau was both a naturalist and a philosopher of religion is not strange in view of his acceptance of Dewey's views in *A Common Faith* and his long affiliation with the New York Society for Ethical Culture.

Further reading

Blau, Joseph. "Chauncey Wright: Radical Empiricist," *New England Quarterly* 19 (1946): 495–517.

—— "The Recovery of Thomas Paine," *The Critic and Guide* 5 (1951): 57–60.

—— "John Dewey and American Social Thought," *Teacher's College Record* 61 (1959): 121–7.

—— "John Dewey's Democratic Theory," *The Reconstructionist* 25 (30 October 1959): 7–14.

—— *Cornerstones of Religious Freedom in America*. Boston, HA: Beacon Press, 1949; revised and enlarged edition, with a new introduction, New York: Harper and Row, 1964.

—— *Social Theories of Jacksonian Democracy: Representative Writings of the Period*. New York: Hafner, 1947. Reprinted, New York: Liberal Arts Press, 1952; Indianapolis, IN: Bobbs-Merrill, 1961.

Wayland, Francis. *The Elements of Moral Science*, ed. J.L. Blau. Cambridge: Belknap Press, 1963.

Wohlgelernter, Maurice (ed.), Martin, James A., Jr, Blumenthal, David R., Hare, Peter H. and Radest, Howard B. (eds) *History, Religion, and Spiritual Democracy: Essays in Honor of Joseph L. Blau*. New York: Columbia University Press, 1980.

BETH J. SINGER

BOAS, GEORGE

George Boas (1891–1980) taught at Johns Hopkins University for thirty-five years, specializing in the history of philosophy, general intellectual history, aesthetics, and art history. A close associate of Arthur O. Lovejoy, Boas "conceived philosophy as intelligent response to all human experience," according to his colleagues at Hopkins, Victor Lowe, Maurice Mandelbaum and Kingsley Price, authors of his obituary in the APA *Proceedings and Addresses*. They claim, "No American philosopher of the twentieth century wrote on as many subjects as he did." Boas authored more than a dozen books, served as a Lieutenant Commander in the U.S. Navy during World War II, and was a long-time member of the Board of Trustees of the Baltimore Museum of Art. He also organized support for his Hopkins colleague, Owen Lattimore, who was falsely accused by Joseph McCarthy of spying for the Soviet Union in 1950. Boas, then Chair of the Hopkins Philosophy Department, led an effort that succeeded in raising $40,000 for Lattimore's defense. One can get an indication of Boas's philosophy by reflecting on the wide range of his interests, which included both science and aesthetics, and the constant attention to history. He readily identified himself as a relativist but one who took ideas seriously, as one would expect of Lovejoy's collaborator in the history of ideas approach. Not surprisingly he stood against the rising tide of ahistorical philosophy as manifested in the linguistic turn and philosophical analysis. In his 1957 book *Dominant Themes in Philosophy* he paid no attention to logical positivism and philosophical analysis. The only twentieth-century philosophers he discussed were either pragmatists or existentialists, praising the former for their "emphasis" on "novelty and the element of uncertainty in all life." Of the latter he noted, "If we close our historical study with Sartre's existentialism, it is because we believe it to be a beginning, not an end."

Further reading

Boas, George. *Dominant Themes in Philosophy: A History*. New York: Ronald Press, 1957.

Lowe, Victor, Mandelbaum, Maurice, and Price, Kingsley. "George Boas," *Proceedings and Addresses of the American Philosophical Association* 53, 5 (May 1980): 581–2.

Simpson, Joanne Cavanaugh. "Seeing Red," *Johns Hopkins Magazine* (September 2000). Available at http://www.jhu.edu/~jhumag/0900web/red.html (accessed 30 January, 2006).

MICHAEL ELDRIDGE

BODY

American philosophers have consistently criticized traditional notions of the human body and, more specifically, notions concerning the relationship between the body and mind. In *The Principles of Psychology* James construed the matter in terms of consciousness as he took up the traditional mind/body problem by discussing the relationship between consciousness and the brain. For methodological reasons he posited a dualism of subject and object but went on to add that every mental event must have a brain correlate, that is, consciousness is a property of minds with brains. In the Preface he writes that "I have kept close to the point of view of natural science throughout the book" and further "This book … contends that psychology when she has ascertained the empirical correlation of the various sorts of thought and feeling with definite conditions of the brain, can go no farther …, that is, as a natural science" (1890: I.v–vi). This stance makes him sound like a parallelist (and, indeed, Dewey took him to be one), who advocates a kind of pre-established harmony between subject and object; however, he criticized traditional parallelist accounts and went on to suggest that the world has evolved to the extent that the interaction of mind, brain, and external environment is possible. The psychological account of the *Principles* that strove to be scientific relied heavily on physiology, and flirted with determinism later created difficulties for the James who would, in un-naturalist fashion, advocate human immortality.

Naturalism and the notion of evolution were also central to Dewey's and Mead's (and to some extent, Santayana's) understanding of the body. That is, both saw that the specter of metaphysical dualism could be dismissed if it was understood that the body and mind evolved together and that their interaction was necessary for adaptation to a ceaselessly changing environment. This strategy entailed re-contextualizing the discussion so that the problem of a metaphysically isolated mind and mechanical body could be avoided altogether. Further, this was supplemented by the pragmatic assertion that the traditional rationalist and empiricist accounts were fatally flawed since they did not consider action in its entirety. In conduct, an action in the present is contextualized by the past and is directed toward the future and if such temporal connections are fully taken into account, then one will begin to see how the body influences the mind and vice versa. In any instance of action, the body registers and conserves operations continuous with the physical and social environment, while the mind considers the meaning, implications, and possible consequences of them. For action to be efficient, both processes must be called into play.

In *Experience and Nature* and elsewhere, Dewey contributed a cultural critique of the traditional accounts of the body that construe it as metaphysically inferior to the mind. More specifically, Plato, Paul, and Aquinas are criticized for conceiving the body in morally disparaging terms and for implicitly justifying the classical and medieval social divisions between those who worked primarily with their hands and those who worked primarily with their minds. This is because the former are inescapably tied to the needs and desires of their bodies, while the latter hold those needs and desires in check and are thereby imbued with the freedom necessary for abstract thought. Indeed, Dewey was concerned about the metaphysical dualism of body and mind not only because it was philosophically untenable but also because it has socially pernicious effects. The artificial division of mind and body tends to produce entrenched physical habits that inhibit the work of the mind, negatively affect health, and, in the worst case, allow and even encourage individuals to conceive themselves as automatons. For Dewey, if the practical integration of body and mind is not brought about "we shall continue to live in a society in which a soulless and heartless materialism is compensated for by soulful but futile and unnatural idealism and spiritualism" (1927–8: 30). This aspect of Dewey's thought sets a precedent for feminist philosophers who likewise criticize the manner in which cultural forces influence conceptions of the human body as well as the quality of somatic experience. Such work advances Dewey's critique by further exploring the conceptual separation of mind and body and by discussing the relationship between the division and the construction of gender.

Dewey's emphasis on embodied experience lead him to advocate the work of F. M. Alexander, whose "Alexander Technique" allows practitioners to become aware of ineffective somatic habits and to consciously change them so that the quality of embodied experience may be improved. Presumably, Dewey advocated and practiced this technique since it gives the practitioner the opportunity to integrate the body–mind and to offset the tendency to ignore the body. Richard Shusterman has developed this aspect of Dewey's thinking by proposing the discipline of "Somaesthetics" which advocates studying and practicing the somatic techniques that allow individuals to improve sensory acuity, movement, posture, and experiential awareness. These improvements are emphasized since they are necessary for fulfilling somatic experience.

Somaesthetics can be divided into three subdisciplines. Analytic somaesthetics explores the manner in which perception and somatic practices influence the construction of reality. This includes the phenomenological analyses of Maurice Merleau-Ponty as well as the work of those who draw from the neurosciences in order to demonstrate the manner in which the body shapes perceptual experience. It also includes the sociopolitical inquiries of Michel Foucault and Pierre Bourdieu that study the manner in which the body is "shaped" by social forces. Pragmatic somaesthetics proposes specific methods of somatic improvement such as the Alexander Technique, Feldenkrais method, martial arts, and yoga and goes on to assess the effectiveness of their respective techniques. Lastly, practical somaesthetics just is the practice of such disciplines.

Further reading

Alexander, F.M. *The Use of the Self.* London: Orion Books, 2002.

Bermudez, J.L., Eilan, N., and Marcel, A. (eds) *The Body and the Self.* Cambridge, MA: MIT Press, 1995.

Bourdieu, Pierre. *Distinction: A Social Critique of the Judgment of Taste*, trans. Richard Nice. Cambridge, MA: Harvard University Press, 2002.

Butler, Judith. *Bodies That Matter: On the Discursive Limits of Sex*. New York: Routledge, 1993.

Dewey, John. "Mind and Body" in *The Later Works: 1925–1953, Vol. 3, 1927–1928*, ed. Jo Ann Boydston. Carbondale, IL: Southern Illinois University Press, 1984, pp. 25–40.

Flanagan, Owen. "Consciousness as a Pragmatist Views It" in *The Cambridge Companion to William James*, ed. Ruth Anna Putnam. Cambridge: Cambridge University Press, 1997, pp. 25–48.

Gallagher, Shaun. *How the Body Shapes the Mind*. Oxford: Oxford University Press, 2005.

James, William. *The Principles of Psychology.* Cambridge, MA: Harvard University Press, 1983 [1890].

Mead, George Herbert. *George Herbert Mead on Social Psychology*, ed. Anselm Strauss. Chicago, IL: University of Chicago Press, 1977.

Merleau-Ponty, Maurice. *Phenomenology of Perception*, trans. Colin Smith. New York: Routledge, 2002.

Rabinow, Paul (ed.) *The Foucault Reader*. New York: Pantheon, 1984.

Santayana, George. *Skepticism and Animal Faith: Introduction to a System of Philosophy.* New York: Dover, 1955.

Shusterman, Richard. *Pragmatist Aesthetics: Living Beauty, Rethinking Art*. New York: Rowman and Littlefield, 2000.

ERIC C. MULLIS

BODY/MIND

The idea that a human being is a union of a "mind" and a "body" is one of the most profound and far-reaching philosophical assumptions of Western culture. Mind–body dualism is indelibly inscribed in much of our psychology, in most of our traditional philosophy, and in our ordinary and scientific language alike.

One of the greatest contributions of American Pragmatism has been to challenge this alleged mind–body dichotomy, to recognize the pervasive harm it has done throughout history, and to replace it with a non-dualistic account of the way our higher cognitive activities are intimately tied to developing processes of organism–environment interactions. William James' *Principles of Psychology* (1890) introduced this new view of mind, marshaling a massive body of empirical evidence from animal studies, biology, physiology, psychology, phenomenology, and neuroscience in support of a naturalistic view of mind as inextricably rooted in non-conscious and conscious bodily experiences. Although the amiably open-minded James refused to rule out mind–body dualism as a live hypothesis, in chapter after chapter he shows how bodily processes, feelings, emotions, and patterns of movement lie at the heart of both what and how humans conceptualize, think, and reason.

James famously argued that there is no mind-stuff that somehow comes down to visit our body-stuff. Rather, what we call "body" and "mind" are aspects of an ongoing, continuous flow of experience that is at once thought *and* feeling, and hence a process of bodily, organic interaction. James saw that every mental process must be realized in a functional neuronal assembly:

> We must find the minimal mental fact whose being reposes directly on a brain-fact; and we must similarly find the minimal brain-event which will have a mental counterpart at all. Between the mental and physical minima thus found there will be an immediate relation, the expression of which, if we had it, would be the elementary psycho-physic law.
>
> (James 1890: I.177)

The obvious problem with such a non-dualistic, naturalistic view is how to explain the emergence of "mental" processes (such as conceptualization and reasoning) from material, bodily interactions. John Dewey addressed this problem with a functional account of mind based on the idea that increasing complexity in lower-level organic processes can give rise to "higher" cognitive functions. The key to overcoming dualism is to show continuity among all levels of functioning. Dewey coined the term "body–mind" to emphasize the origins and structures of "mind" in the organic activities of embodied creatures in interaction with their changing environments (physical, social, and cultural). "Mind," for Dewey, is not a thing, but rather a functional process that emerges from psycho-physical activities whenever organisms develop to the stage where shared meanings and communication are possible: "Mind denotes the whole system of meanings as they are embodied in the workings of organic life; consciousness in a being with language denotes awareness or perception of meanings" (Dewey 1925/1981: 230).

Both James and Dewey, then, understood "mind" as inseparable from the embodied, multi-dimensional flow of experience that, in certain animals, gives rise to shared meanings. Their view is evolutionary, naturalistic, non-dualistic, process-oriented, and functionally defined.

Many decades later, we are now witnessing the explosion of empirical research in cognitive neuroscience that presupposes the fundamental tenets of the James–Dewey program. The cognitive sciences are asking how our higher cognitive operations work by recruiting structures of sensory-motor processes. Within this framework, mind is not an autonomous, metaphysically distinct entity, but rather an embodied capacity for meaning-making, experience, thinking, feeling, and communicating. Dewey's prescient pronouncement could serve as a motto for contemporary research on the body–mind:

> To see the organism *in* nature, the nervous system in the organism, the brain in the nervous system, the cortex in the brain is the answer to the problems which haunt philosophy.
>
> (Dewey 1925/1981: 224)

This naturalistic call-to-arms will strike many people as far too reductionistic, far too brain-oriented. However, the brain and the body are just a part of the complex system of organic transactions that make mind. To see how all aspects of the picture fit together will require a plurality of methods of inquiry drawn from biology, physiology, neuroscience, phenomenology, linguistics, psychology, economics, and sociology, to name a few of the relevant disciplines. The principal constraint is that there is no mind without body, so that all of the functional capacities we attribute to mind, from perception to feeling to imagining to reasoning to willing, must be tied to the ongoing flow of organic processes that we call our body.

Further reading

Dewey, John. *Experience and Nature, John Dewey: The Later Works, 1925–1953, Vol. 1*. Carbondale, IL: Southern Illinois University Press, 1981 [1925].

James, William. *The Principles of Psychology.* New York: Dover, 1950 [1890].

Lakoff, George and Johnson, Mark. *Philosophy in the Flesh: The Embodied Mind and Its Challenge to Western Thought*. New York: Basic Books, 1999.

MARK JOHNSON

BOWNE, BORDEN PARKER

Borden Parker Bowne (1847–1910) was born in Leonardville, New Jersey. He studied at New York University, graduating in 1871 as valedictorian. After spending a short time preaching in a New York church, Bowne traveled to Europe to continue his studies in Paris, Halle, and Göttingen. Though he studied with several thinkers, he primarily acknowledged his debt to Hermann Lotze, who sought to have Bowne write a doctoral thesis under his tutelage. Lotze's careful, systematic metaphysical outlook served as a model both in style and in content for Bowne's later metaphysical writings. On returning to New York in 1875, Bowne worked for the *Independent* as journalist and editor. In 1876 he accepted a teaching position in the philosophy department at Boston University, remaining there until his death in 1910.

Bowne is most remembered for founding and developing the tradition of theistic Personalism in the United States. Though the term "Personalism" had been used by both Charles Renouvier in France and George Homes Howison in the U.S., its popularity in American philosophical circles was instigated by Bowne's later writings, especially *Theism* (1902), *Personalism* (1908), and *Studies in Christianity* (1909). Bowne's work led to an eighty-year-long tradition of Personalist thought centered around the Boston University Philosophy program and carried out by such noted thinkers as Edgar Sheffield Brightman (1884–1953), Ralph Tyler Flewelling (1871–1960), and Peter A. Bertocci (1910–89). This tradition spawned numerous teachers of philosophy in American colleges, influenced the tenor of philosophy or religion on the American scene, and sustained a connection between philosophy and social action that was exemplified by its most celebrated student, Martin Luther King, Jr.

Bowne began his philosophical career as a critic. The speculative evolutionary philosophy of Herbert Spencer had an enormous impact on American intellectual culture in the later years of the nineteenth century. It was defended by numerous scholars, among whom the most influential was perhaps John Fiske. Finding Spencer's Fiske's work to be weak both in its attempt to handle new scientific concepts and in its technical, rational structure, Bowne wrote extensively to expose these weaknesses. The style of the young Bowne was excessively polemical and this brought his thought to the center of debates on the relations of science, religion, and philosophy.

Bowne's work developed in two directions. On the one hand, he constructed a metaphysical system of theism in which he argued that "person" was the ultimate category of being. On the other hand, he wrote extensively in ethics, both theoretically and practically. His aim was to allow his metaphysical and ethical views to work in concert.

For Bowne, Hegel seemed a better evolutionist than Spencer because his model was organic and not mechanical. Nonetheless, Hegel seemed to depersonalize God; this turned Bowne away from Hegel because for him the ground of being and becoming must be a personal force. That is, it must function teleologically, it must be creative, and it must operate with something like a moral conscience. This personalistic idealism, for Bowne, made good sense of his own Christian outlook, providing both for a caring creator and for the human freedom and responsibility requisite for the amelioration of our historical situation.

In his metaphysics, Bowne worked, in some respects, under the influence of Lotze. He remained, for example, adamantly opposed to any form of radical pluralism on the basis that things that are too radically discontinuous cannot, in any practical way, be brought into conversation or community. On the logical side, he suggested pluralism requires us to discourse about that which, in principle, we cannot discourse. However, his Personalism also led him away from the pantheistic developments of many versions of idealism, including Lotze's monism. Though the universe has a telos, Bowne argued, it is one that offers a variety of avenues for fulfillment. God, as a supreme person, allows room for human freedom and responsibility among created persons. Though finite persons are unable to create *ex nihilo*, they do have the power to effect transformations in their own lives and cultures.

The personalistic side of Bowne's metaphysics argued against all forms of materialism and mechanism on the grounds that such views left no room for moral responsibility and discourse. Thus, Bowne's Christian ethics developed against the backdrop of his metaphysics. Though he adhered to church doctrine, Bowne also believed that the meaning and interpretation of this doctrine was open to challenge and revision. God created persons as moral agents whose work was, in part, to find their own way in the world. In contemporary terms, Bowne might be considered more of a virtue ethicist than a deontologist, despite the extensive influence on his work of Kant's *Critique of Practical Reason*. There are procedural rules to follow, Bowne argued, but no hard and fast, final moral codes or recipes should determine our behavior. Rather, recognizing all persons to be ends-in-themselves and embracing our good wills, we must venture our own pragmatic assessments of the situations in which we find ourselves. Bowne's own conscience led him to defend women's suffrage in the 1890s and, on more than one occasion, led him to defend colleagues' rights to teach Methodist theology in their own way without external interference.

In his later years, Bowne shifted his metaphysical focus somewhat. Influenced perhaps by William James, he oriented himself to an experimental approach. He eased off the rigor and narrowness of Lotzean system building and gave more attention to the everyday experiences of persons in the world. This led him to identify himself on a few occasions as a "transcendental empiricist." Bowne's influence in American philosophy in the twentieth century is underestimated, and it reflects his own dual interest in metaphysics and ethics. In philosophy of religion, his Personalism kept idealism alive in many quarters well into the latter half of the century. In ethics, his personalist melding of Kantian procedure and Christian concern for transformation underwrote an ongoing emphasis on social reform in protestant thought in general and in Methodism in particular.

Further reading

Auxier, Randall E. "The Relevance of Bowne," *Personalist Forum* 13, 1 (1997): 1–2.

Bowne, Borden Parker. *Personalism*. New York: Houghton Mifflin, 1908.

—— *Studies in Christianity*. New York: Houghton Mifflin, 1909.

McConnell, Francis John. *Borden Parker Bowne*. New York: Abingdon Press, 1929.

Douglas R. Anderson

BRAIN-IN-A-VAT

Thought experiments involving brains in vats are used to present the skeptical problem raised by René Descartes in the *Meditations on First Philosophy* (1641). The main difference between the brain-in-a-vat thought experiment and Descartes' original example is the science fiction setting of the brain-in-a-vat thought experiment. It has been very common to present the skeptical argument in this fashion due to the influence of Hilary Putnam's discussion of skepticism in *Reason, Truth, and History* (1981).

The thought experiment is as follows: we take for granted that we know facts about the world around us. I may think that I am sitting in a chair, in front of a long wooden table, in the New York Public Library, writing encyclopedia entries on my iBook. I supposedly know these purported facts on the basis of my experience – I can see that there is a computer in front of me. However, it is possible that I could have the exact same experiences without any of these facts being true. For it is possible that an evil scientist could have kidnapped me in the crib, removed my brain from my body, placed it in a vat, and used neural stimulation to generate all of my life's experiences. So while it may seem to me that I am seeing a computer, a table, and a library, it is possible that none of these things actually exist. I have no way to rule out the possibility that I am a brain in a vat on the basis of any experience I have had, for all of my experiences are fully consistent either with contact with objects in the external world or with neural stimulation within the vat.

Given the possibility that I am being deceived by the evil scientist and his dreadful vat, how can I claim to know that I am in a library, or typing on a computer? I certainly cannot claim to know that I am not a brain in a vat. If this is granted, then it seems I cannot make any claim to knowledge of the external world. The skeptical argument proceeds as follows:

> S1: If I do not know that I am not a brain in a vat, then I do not know that I am in the New York Public Library writing encyclopedia entries.
>
> S2: I do not know that I am not a brain in a vat.
>
> Conclusion: I do not know that I am in the New York Public Library writing encyclopedia entries.

One can rule out any other claim to knowledge of the external world by substituting that claim for the consequent of the conditional in premise S1. Thus, if the skeptical argument is sound, I cannot claim to have any knowledge of the external world.

It is a complex and difficult matter to answer this skeptical argument and it will not be possible to address each of the attempts that have been made to answer the argument in an entry of this length. It will suffice to say that philosophers have challenged premises S1 and S2 of the skeptical argument in a variety of interesting and complex ways. These challenges have not satisfied the Cartesian skeptic.

Further reading

Putnam, Hilary. *Reason, Truth, and History.* New York: Cambridge University Press, 1981.

Williams, Michael. *Unnatural Doubts: Epistemological Realism and the Basis of Skepticism.* Oxford: Blackwell, 1991.

FRITZ J. MCDONALD

BRIGHTMAN, EDGAR SHEFFIELD

Edgar Sheffield Brightman (1884–1953) was the leading American personalist during the twentieth century. Born in Holbrook, Massachusetts, on 20 September 1884, he attended Brown University for his undergraduate studies, where he studied philosophy under a classically trained faculty (1902–6). Attracted by the thought of Borden Parker Bowne, he pursued graduate study at Boston University (1908–10), and at Berlin and Marburg (1910–12), where he produced a dissertation. Brightman received degrees from Boston University in both theology and philosophy in 1912. He taught at Nebraska Wesleyan University and Wesleyan University in Connecticut (1912–19). Accepting an invitation to teach at Boston University Graduate School in 1919, Brightman continued there until his death in 1953. He occupied the Borden Parker Bowne Chair of Philosophy from 1925 until 1953 and was President of the Eastern Division of the American Philosophical Association, 1936–7.

Inspired by Bowne's personalistic idealism and his unification of the ideas of Josiah Royce, Brightman was influenced by Bowne's view of the place of experience in philosophical understanding. All philosophical formulations must be reasonable interpretations of human experience that must never be entirely subordinated to logic or empiricism. Personal experience must be integrated into meaningful wholes by reason and logic. In this way Brightman's idealism was more thoroughgoing that Bowne's, more experiential and experimental.

Brightman viewed person as a concrete universal, indicating his indebt to Hegel, whom he read regularly throughout his career. Rejecting Bowne's static "self-identity" Brightman inserted the process "self-identifying." In "Why Personalistic Idealism?" Peter A. Bertocci succinctly states Brightman's view of person,

> a being for whom to be is to act and be acted upon. But I am an active being-becoming, a created unity-in-continuity who exists, as I sustain myself, in environments that enable me to change and grow and still identity my unified being-becoming, or myself, through change.
>
> (1980: 186)

Alfred North Whitehead and Charles Hartshorne influenced Brightman's temporalistic personalism.

The metaphysical implications of his process view of person impacted his view of God. As Person, God is omnitemporal rather than eternally unchanging. Facing the problem of evil, particularly the suffering experienced in both evolution and among persons, Brightman argued that one cannot consistently contend that God is both omnipotent and omnibenevolent. As a solution, within the nature of God is a recalcitrant, nonrational Given that limits God's full realization of will-to-good. God is infinite in goodness and limited in power. Nevertheless, God sustains the orderly world in which free persons can creatively find their individual and social fulfillment. Within this framework, Brightman works out in his *Moral Laws* (1933) ethical principles allowing responsible persons to realize their full personhood. Hegel's influence is again clear; the ethical life is a special instance of the concrete universal.

After 1970 Brightman's influence declined as scholarly interest in theism faded. Yet, his historical importance is assured through his influence on the moral and philosophical thought of Martin Luther King, Jr.

Further reading

Auxier, Randall E. *Hartshorne and Brightman on God, Process, and Persons: The Correspondence, 1922–1945*. Nashville, TN: Vanderbilt University Press, 2001.

Bertocci, Peter A. "Why Personalistic Idealism?" *Idealistic Studies* 10, 3 (1980): 181–98.

Brightman, Edgar Sheffield. *The Problem of God*. New York: Abingdon Press, 1930.

—— *Person and Reality* (posthumous), ed. Peter A. Bertocci with Janette E. Newhall and Robert S. Brightman. New York: Ronald Press, 1958.

Deats, Paul, and Robb, Carol (eds) *The Boston Personalist Tradition in Philosophy, Social Ethics, and Theology*. Macon, GA: Mercer University Press, 1986.

THOMAS O. BUFORD

BUCHLER, JUSTUS

Justus Buchler (1914–91) should be considered a major American philosopher. Broadly comprehensive as well as unique, his system of categories provides important insight into nature and man, judgment, meaning and method, art, science and philosophy. It is unusually fruitful, shedding new light on philosophic issues ranging from the ontological status of universals and possibilities to the nature and interrelation of conduct and discourse. It provides a new understanding of interaction and communication, revealing as no other philosophic system does, the diverse ways in which we communicate.

While Buchler's terminology is technical and requires careful interpretation, his writing is clear and precise and his reasoning is methodic and rigorous. The categories of his system were developed jointly and reciprocally, so to fully appreciate any of his books it is helpful to consider it in relation to the others. Doing so is worthwhile as it enriches as well as clarifies our understanding of all of them and of the system as a whole. But even considered independently, each of these works reveals the ingenuity and profundity of Buchler's philosophic thinking.

Justus Buchler received a bachelor's degree from City College of New York and a master's degree and doctorate from Columbia University. As a member of the Philosophy Department at Columbia from 1937 to 1971 he taught in a then famous undergraduate program, Contemporary Civilization, which he chaired from 1950 to 1956, and he was chairman of the Philosophy Department from 1964 until 1967. He also lectured at the William Alanson White Institute of Psychiatry and served on the Academic Freedom Committee of the American Civil Liberties Union, helping develop policies concerning academic due process and the civil liberties of students. In 1959 he was appointed Johnsonian Professor of Philosophy and in 1973, after he had left Columbia, he was awarded the Nicholas Murray Butler Medal. In 1971, he became Distinguished Professor of Philosophy at the new State University of New York at Stony Brook, where he taught until he retired in 1981.

Buchler developed an original philosophic system including a general metaphysics or ontology and a theory of human experience, activity, and productivity. The opening sentence of *Metaphysics of Natural Complexes* summarizes its central thesis: "Whatever is, in whatever way, is a natural complex." Every constituent of a complex is also a complex and every complex is a constituent of others. There is no single, all-inclusive complex and every complex is an order of indefinitely many constituents and located in indefinitely many other orders. Buchler also calls constituents traits. To be a trait or constituent of a complex is not necessarily to be contained in it. A relation is as much a trait as is a part or component; so are possibilities and potentialities. The traits of a complex in any given order comprise its integrity and the totality of its integrities comprise its contour. Insofar as any complex has the traits that it does rather than any others, Buchler says it is prevalent; insofar as it ceases to prevail, loses traits, acquires new traits or undergoes change, it is alescent.

Experience, activity, and productivity are dealt with in Buchler's books on the concepts of judgment, method, and poetry. Holding conventional concepts of experience to be too narrow he introduced a more inclusive concept, proception. Proception encompasses all dimensions of the human life process, including the physical, the psychological, and the social. Buchler describes it as a process of involvement. Any complex with which an individual is involved in any way is a procept.

Judgment, as Buchler defines it, is not limited to thoughts or propositions but may also take the form of action or of organizing or arranging materials. Thus it includes what he calls active and exhibitive as well as assertive judgments. A judgment of any of these kinds may have other dimensions: as something we do, judging assertively, making an assertion, is active judgment. Exhibitive judgment includes making, shaping or arranging materials of any kind and art is methodic and purposeful exhibitive judgment. Poetry is exhibitive judgment in the medium of language. When developing or articulating a judgment is methodic and exploratory or inventive Buchler calls it query. Science and philosophy are kinds of query; so is artistic creation, and writing poetry is exhibitive query.

Further reading

Buchler, Justus. *Charles Peirce's Empiricism*. New York: Dover, 1939.

—— *Toward a General Theory of Human Judgment*. New York: Dover, 1951; second, revised edition 1979.

—— *Nature and Judgment*. New York: Columbia University Press, 1955.

—— *The Concept of Method*. New York: Columbia University Press, 1961.

—— *Metaphysics of Natural Complexes*. New York: Columbia University Press, 1966.

—— *The Main of Light: On the Concept of Poetry*. New York: Oxford University Press, 1974.

BETH J. SINGER

BURKE, KENNETH

Kenneth Burke (1897–1993) was born in Pittsburgh and attended both Ohio State University and Columbia University briefly. He lived in New York City and rural Andover, New Jersey, while working throughout his life as a writer (of poems, fiction, and reviews), editor, and translator. He is generally known as a critic: initially, as a literary critic; increasingly, in contemporary terms, as a cultural critic. Although he often taught and lectured at various universities, he never held a tenured academic position. His first book of short stories was published in 1924 and his first distinctively philosophical work, *Counter-Statement*, in 1931. Collections of his poems (published over the years in magazines) were published in 1955 and 1968.

Timothy W. Crusius notes, in *Kenneth Burke and the Conversation after Philosophy* (1999), that Burke's "philosophical identity" has been associated with American Pragmatism, Critical Theory, Hermeneutics, and Postmodernism (4–5, 17–18). While honoring Burke's refusal to be labeled as within any particular school – but to be always "Other"; always offering a counterstatement to any ideology – Crusius argues that Burke "is a skeptic in a specifically postPhilosophical way" that "led away from theoretical philosophy in the classical sense – contemplation of the eternal – to practical philosophy"; "still more specifically, Burke is a praxis philosopher for the linguistic turn" who developed "a philosophical anthropology" (230–2).

The case for affiliation with American pragmatism is suggested in Burke's definition of reality, in *Permanence and Change* (1935), as "what things will do to us or for us" (22). Crusius reminds us that the working title of that book was *A Treatise on Communication* (35). Human beings are, in Burke's phrase, symbol-using (misusing) creatures. His persistent attention to the use of language – rather than to linguistic systems – justifies characterizing his work as a philosophy of communication (in contrast to language). Burke proposed that people are motivated by their biological and social differences to engage in symbolic action aimed at mediating those differences, rather than merely referring to things. He distinguishes between the "scientistic" function of language as semiotic systems that define what something is or is not, and the "dramatistic" function of language as acts that propose what shall or shall not be done; the latter is "necessarily suasive"; which is to say, rhetorical (*Language as Symbolic Action*, 1966: 44–5). By using symbols (understood as "patterns of experience," or "abstractions from situations") human agents develop terminologies (vocabularies), each of which may be "a reflection of reality," but also, "must be a selection of reality," and thus, "must function as a deflection of reality" (45). In communicative acts, agents accomplish agency within particular scenes and for particular purposes; to this "pentad" of terms he later added "attitude."

Burke's approach might be summarized in the title of his first nonfiction book, *Counter-Statement* (1931). His philosophy of communication proposed communicative interaction among persons as a counterstatement to all ideologies, and advocated symbolic action – an alternative available to human animals – as preferable to violent motion, which is available to all animals. Human beings/animals, as "bodies that learn language," develop overlapping attitudes, interests, and goals and thus achieve moments of identification (however fleeting and uncertain) that transcend their persisting differences.

Further reading

Burke, Kenneth. *Counter-Statement*. Berkeley, CA: University of California Press, 1931.

—— *Language as Symbolic Action: Essays on Life, Literature, and Method*. Berkeley, CA: University of California Press, 1966.

Crusius, Timothy W. *Kenneth Burke and the Conversation after Philosophy*. Carbondale, IL: Southern Illinois University Press, 1999.

Rueckert, William H. (ed.) *Critical Responses to Kenneth Burke, 1924–1966*. Minneapolis, MN: University of Minnesota Press, 1969.

Simons, Herbert W. and Melia, Trevor (eds) *The Legacy of Kenneth Burke*. Madison, WI: University of Wisconsin Press, 1989.

LENORE LANGSDORF

C

CALKINS, MARY WHITON

Mary Whiton Calkins (1863–1930), prominent self-psychologist and absolute personalist idealist, spent the duration of her career at Wellesley College, until her retirement from her position as Full Professor of Psychology and Philosophy in 1929. She began her career at Wellesley as Instructor of Greek after finishing her BA (1885) and MA (1887) from Smith College and publishing her first book *Sharing the Profits* (1888). At Harvard, she fulfilled all requirements for a PhD in psychology in 1895. Study under William James, Josiah Royce, and Hugo Münsterberg was influential in the development of her psychology and philosophy.

Calkins began the development of self-psychology and absolute personalist idealism in 1900. Self-psychology differed from other schools in its tenet that the conscious person is the basal concept of psychology. From 1901 to 1905, Calkins advocated "the double standpoint in psychology," which systematically treated experience from the schools of psychological atomism and self-psychology. By 1909, Calkins revised her recommendation in favor of a "single-tracked self-psychology." The chief influences on Calkins's metaphysics were G.W.F. Hegel, F.H. Bradley, and Royce. Absolute personalist idealism understood the universe to be ultimately mental and personal in nature, and held that one all-inclusive Absolute Person comprised the lesser mental selves of the universe within it.

Author of over 150 books and articles combined, Calkins received many honors throughout her life in the fields of psychology and philosophy, including her election as first woman president of both the American Psychological Association (1905) and the American Philosophical Association (1918), as well as the honorary degrees of LittD from Columbia (1909), and LLD from Smith College (1910).

Dana Noelle McDonald

CARNAP, RUDOLF

Rudolf Carnap (1891–1970) was born in Ronsdorf, Germany to Anna and Johannes Carnap in 1891. He attended the Gymnasium in Barmen before studying at the Universities of Jena and Freiburg/LB. Physics, mathematics, and philosophy were his principal interests, though politics, too, was an early and lifelong concern. His philosophy teachers included Bruno Bausch (for Kant), Hermann Nohl (for Hegel), and Gottlob Frege (for logic). Carnap began doing experimental research in physics in 1913, hoping to earn a doctorate in physics, but his studies were interrupted by the outbreak of World War I. After serving as an officer for more than four years, including two years at the front, he turned to philosophy. A Dr Phil Degree was granted to him by the University of Jena on 9 December 1921 for a dissertation titled "Der Raum. Ein Beitraq zur Wissenschaftslehre." It distinguished three kinds of space (i.e. formal, intuitive, and physical), and argued that contradictory claims are made about it because the same word – space – is used to signify these distinct domains. Carnap began teaching philosophy at the University of Vienna in 1926. There, with Moritz Schlick,

Frederick Waismann, and Otto Neurath, he was a principal contributor, from 1926 to 1935, to the work of the Vienna circle. Carnap was made Professor of Natural Philosophy at the University of Prague in 1931, but left Prague for the United States in 1935 because of Nazi influence in Czechoslovakia. Carnap taught at the University of Chicago from 1936 to 1952, and the University of California, Los Angeles, from 1952 until his death in 1970. He became an American citizen in 1941.

Carnap's self-described "secular humanism" is apparent in his summary of the concerns that motivated the Vienna Circle:

> I think that nearly all of us shared the following three views as a matter of course which hardly needed any discussion. The first is the view that man has no supernatural protectors or enemies and that therefore whatever can be done to improve life is the task of man himself. Second, we had the conviction that mankind is able to change the conditions of life and that the external and the internal situation of life for the individual, the community, and finally for humanity will be essentially improved. The third is the view that all deliberate action presupposes knowledge of the world, that the scientific method is the best method of acquiring knowledge and that therefore science must be regarded as one of the most valuable instruments for the improvement of life.
>
> (Schilpp 1991: 83).

One sees the evidence of these beliefs in the elaborations of Carnap's philosophic ideas. So, the impatience with "supernatural protectors or enemies" becomes the view that religious and metaphysical claims are "meaningless pseudo-statements ... [hence] declarative sentences which are devoid of cognitive meaning" (Schilpp 1991: 878). Cognitive meaning is empirical meaning: sentences lacking it cannot be meaningful or true, because no empirical difference would obtain if they were true.

Carnap's regard for humanity was focused and passionate:

> [N]either socialism nor world government are regarded as absolute ends; they are only the organizational means which, according to our present knowledge, seem to give the best promise of leading to a realization of the ultimate aim. This aim is a form of life in which well-being and the development of the individual is valued most highly, not the power of the state.
>
> (Schilpp 1991: 83)

Carnap's philosophic work did not much amplify this belief. His writings were devoted, almost exclusively, to his reflections on scientific knowledge. This was not usually a study of scientific results. It was never an inquiry into the history or logic of scientific discovery. Science supplies paradigms of knowledge. Philosophy should recast scientific theories in ways that satisfy the assumptions of Carnap's epistemic foundationalism. (Carnap reports that a physicist once rebuked him: "Physics is not like geometry; in physics there are no definitions and no axioms": Schilpp 1991: 37.)

Five questions dominated Carnap's thinking about scientific knowledge. What is the relation of scientific theory to experimental evidence? What form should theories have when they are reformulated so that their statements are unambiguously phrased and related? What is the character of the inductive procedures which measure the probability that particular theoretical claims are true, given the empirical evidence. What is the relation of philosophic thinking about science to scientific theory itself? How are the sciences related to one another, and to the humanities and social sciences? A sixth question – what values direct our theory-making? – is less prominent in Carnap's writings, but always implied (e.g. as in the remark quoted above that science is an instrument for improving life).

Consider these six points in turn.

1 The relation of theoretical concepts to observation reports

Carnap emphasized his empiricism. No theoretical statement is meaningful if we cannot specify what empirical difference would obtain if it were true. No theory is confirmed in the absence of reports that such empirical data do obtain. Still, there is uncertainty about the meaning of theoretical concepts. How do they receive cognitive content; how are they made to bear on the empirical world? Carnap considered three ways of supplying their empirical sense: theoretical terms are introduced by definitions that couple them to observation terms; they are introduced, contextually, within a theory's axioms when other terms in the axioms are empirically defined; or they are introduced by "reduction sentences," e.g. as dispositional terms are introduced, but not defined, by reference to the effects that occur when dispositions are exhibited. (See Carnap 1956.)

2 The form of reconstructed theories

Carnap's reconstructions integrate logical – deductive – form with empirical content. Statements having theoretical terms are coupled to observation reports within theories that are reconstructed as deductive systems. Such systems begin as uninterpreted calculi. They are interpreted when "correspondence rules" join theoretical terms to the observation terms that supply their sense. Moving from the top down – from a theory's highest-order laws to lower-order laws, and observation sentences – we explain lower-order sentences by deducing them from sentences that are higher-order. Moving from the bottom up, we confirm the higher-order sentences by affirming that such empirical differences as give them sense do obtain. (See Carnap 1967a: 78–88; and 1967b.)

3 Inductive logic

Carnap emphasized that observation reports never confirm a system's higher-order, theoretical sentences to the point of certainty. There is, at best, a high degree of probability that theoretical claims are true, given relevant observation reports. Carnap's inductive logic formulates rules that establish the degree of confirmation supplied to a theoretical claim by an observation report. Applying such rules after affirming that smoke is repeatedly observed, we determine the degree of confirmation for the claim that fire is the cause. The phenomena – smoke and fire – are related contingently, so that the sentence, "If smoke, then fire," is synthetic. The relation of the sentences reporting their relation (thereby confirming the lawful relation of smoke to fire) is, Carnap said, analytic. (Carnap 1950.)

4 Object and metalanguages

Reconstructed scientific theories are expressed as "object languages": we use them to make well-confirmed claims about actual states of affairs. Reconstruction is carried on within a "metalanguage" (Carnap 1967b: 277–314). This formulation, deriving from Alfred Tarksi's semantical definition of truth (Linsky 1952: 13–47), emphasizes the difference between talk about the world, and the philosopher's talk about scientific talk.

5 The unity of science

Carnap believed, under the influence of Otto Neurath, that the humanities and social sciences, as much as physics, chemistry and biology, are appropriate topics for scientific inquiry. If nature is unitary, then so must these inquiries and practices be susceptible to integration: all of them may be reformulated in the terms of aphysicalist language (Carnap 1934).

6 Value

Carnap distinguished the syntactic, semantical, and pragmatic aspects of theory formation. Usually, the values driving his theoretical concerns were narrowly focused by methodological issues within a science (e.g. operational definitions for mental functions). But sometimes the perspective was larger, as when he considered the utility of theories for promoting human health and welfare: Thus one of the main problems, perhaps the most important and the most difficult one after the terribly urgent problem of the avoidance of atomic war, is the task of finding ways of organizing society which will reconcile the personal and cultural freedom of the individual with the development of an efficient organization of state and economy (Schilpp 1991: 84).

Carnap was forty-five years old, accomplished, and fully formed when he joined the University of Chicago. He was recognizable in America – and vastly influential (see Quine 1967: 270–1) – because he, like home-grown pragmatists, was indebted to Kant. They emphasized the use of plans to direct behaviors that alter experience. He stressed reconstructed conceptual systems, and their value-driven application to experience. Carnap's a priorism and idealism – questions about the external world had no cognitive value for him (Carnap 1956: 213–15) – were harder to assimilate, for they imply that values direct our world-making, not our encounters with a world we alter but do not make.

Carnap's effects on American philosophy are principally these two: an a priorist emphasis on the "logical syntax" of reformulated conceptual systems (e.g. theories), and an idealist bent that reduces questions in the material mode – are there things of a specific sort? – to questions in the formal mode – does Assertability language have resources for affirming that a thing or things at issue do or may exist? The one effect is technical; the other is transcendental. Carnap, the philosopher of science, was not Locke's underlaborer, clearing the conceptual ground for empirical inquiry. Scientific theories were his preferred instruments for creating a thinkable experience. The critic of all metaphysics was a metaphysician in the style of Kant: we determine the existence and character of the world – we make it intelligible – by virtue of the language used to think it.

Further reading

Carnap, Rudolf. *The Unity of Science*, trans. Max Black. London: Kegan Paul, 1934.

—— *Meaning and Necessity*. Chicago, IL: University of Chicago, 1956.
—— *An Introduction to the Philosophy of Science*, ed. Martin Gardner. New York: Dover, 1995.
Linsky, Leonard. *Semantics and the Philosophy of Language*, ed. Leonard Linsky. Urbana, IL: University of Illinois Press, 1952.
Quine, W.V.O. *Word and Object*. Cambridge, MA: MIT Press, 1967.
Schilpp, Paul Arthur. *The Philosophy of Rudolf Carnap*. LaSalle, IL: Open Court, 1991.

DAVID WEISSMAN

CARUS, PAUL

Paul Carus (1852–1919) was a public philosopher, born and educated (Tübingen PhD) in Germany, but who became prominent in the United States as the editor of *The Open Court*, a fortnightly periodical, and the quarterly philosophical journal, *The Monist*. He published dozens of books on monism, the view that all of reality is a single system, his proposed Religion of Science, and his interest in Eastern philosophy and religion. In the latter part of the nineteenth century and the early years of the twentieth century he was much a part of the international intellectual scene, regarding the physicist Ernst Mach, who influenced the Logical Positivists (or Vienna Circle), as a close friend, providing D.T. Suzuki, who was to become prominent as an interpreter of Zen Buddhism, with employment early in his career, and publishing over a twenty-four-year period "more of [the pragmatist Charles Sanders] Peirce's philosophical articles during Peirce's lifetime than any other editor," according to J.F. Sheridan, as quoted in Henderson (1993: 127).

But Carus is not remembered for his own philosophical work. Those who have studied his thought argue that his many interests, including "his long-standing passion for reconciling opposites" (Henderson 1993: 166), or at least what are conventionally regarded as opposites, such as religion and science, theism and atheism, and nature and morality, do not ultimately cohere. Meyer writes:

> Paul Carus had attempted to apply science to human affairs, to treat experience on an objective and rational level, to establish a religion of science. He failed. The public to which he spoke was deaf to his voice: his ideas were too abstruse for the average man and too simple for the intellectual.
>
> (Meyer 1962: 606)

But his work lives on in the Open Court Publishing Company, which continues to publish philosophy books, *The Monist*, revived in 1962 (after a twenty-six-year gap) by Eugene Freeman, and the American Philosophical Association's biannual Carus Lectures, which are funded by the publishing company. He also serves as an example of the sort of public philosophy that was often practiced prior to the professionalization of philosophy in the twentieth century, which resulted in philosophy being almost exclusively found in academia. Carus, say his critics, attempted too much. But those who aspire for philosophy to have a public presence think that present-day academic philosophy attempts too little.

Further reading

Hay, William H. "Paul Carus: A Case-Study of Philosophy on the Frontier," *Journal of the History of Ideas* 17, 4 (October 1956): 498–510.
Henderson, Harold. *Catalyst for Controversy: Paul Carus of Open Court*. Carbondale, IL: Southern Illinois University, 1993.
Meyer, Donald Harvey. "Paul Carus and the Religion of Science," *American Quarterly* 14, 4 (Winter 1962): 597–607.

MICHAEL ELDRIDGE

CATEGORIES

Categories are basic schemes of classification. Some American philosophers, most notably William James, claim that appealing to or theorizing about categories is contrary to the spirit of pragmatism. Much of John Dewey's philosophy is also set against accepting traditional ontological categories, although he allowed for the legitimacy of an investigation into the irreducible traits found in every subject of scientific inquiry. In general, Dewey urged that we think of categories in terms of their function within experience, rather than as discrete kinds of being. In contrast to James and Dewey, C.S. Peirce and George Santayana are prominent examples of American philosophers who took categories as fundamental to their systems.

Peirce's categories are a complicated part of his intricate architectonic system. His first attempt at delineating a set of universal categories draws from his Kantian roots. He sought to arrive through a logical analysis of judgments at a set of categories necessary for bringing structure or unity to experience. He reduced Kant's twelve categories to five, namely, Being, Quality, Relation, Representation, and Substance. As his system developed, however, Peirce dropped Being and Substance from the list, set out two new methods of derivation and settled, albeit fallibly, on categories corresponding to the remaining three. He called these categories Firstness, Secondness, and Thirdness.

Peirce's first way of arriving at his triumvirate is through a mathematical proof intended to demonstrate that the categories are universal. His second (related) way is through phenomenological investigation intended to show that the categories are manifested in actual experience. Generalizing from these two approaches, he described the categories as follows. Firstness is a logically monadic category. Experientially, it is associated with quality or feeling. For example, the sweetness of honey is a First. Firsts are ineffable and must be identified without reference to anything else. Secondness is a logically dyadic category. Experientially, it is associated with "otherness." For example, receiving a surprising punch brings home the reality of Secondness. Seconds involve two things in brute contact with each other. Thirdness is a logically triadic category. Experientially, it is associated with mediation. For example, representation is triadic since it involves a sign, an object, and an act of interpretation. Referring to another of Peirce's examples, "a *gives* b to c" manifests Thirdness since the act of *giving* involves an irreducibly triadic relation. Peirce holds that these categories are not discreet kinds of being. Rather, they are three hierarchically ordered, omnipresent aspects of whatever is real. Thus every possible object of experience has an element of Thirdness and hence an element of Secondness and Firstness.

Santayana's categories were developed over a thirty-year period that culminated in the publication of his four-volume *Realms of Being*. In this work he sets out his ontology. This ontology is a detailed description of a basic classificatory scheme that frames our total vision of everything we encounter in experience. Santayana's original plan was for a three-realm ontology comprised of Essence, Matter, and Spirit, but he later added a fourth realm: Truth.

Santayana noted that whatever we encounter in experience has certain qualitative features. These distinguishable features are "essences." For Santayana the "realm of essence" is the infinite multitude of logically distinct terms of thought and the forms embodied by matter. Essences do not, however, depend for their reality on thought or matter; they have eternal being independent of any particular instantiation. The category of Matter, by contrast, comprises everything that exists in space and time. It is axiomatic for Santayana that whatever exists must embody some essence, but matter is distinguished from essence by being in flux. The "realm of matter" is his name for the dynamic world of physical stuff that we encounter in action. "Truth" is defined as that segment of the realm of essence that has been (contingently) embodied by matter. Contrary to most accounts of truth, Santayana's is logically independent of thought and language. Any essence that achieves material embodiment becomes part of the "realm of truth" or the ideal and eternal catalogue of past events. "Spirit" is consciousness. Santayana resisted all reductive accounts of consciousness and identified spirit with the act of being aware. In his terms, it is the difference between being asleep (and not dreaming) and being awake. Like essence and truth, spirit is also causally powerless. It is generated by physical processes of the brain but has no influence over the course of events.

Santayana did not offer anything like a "proof" for deriving his categories and allowed that other classificatory schemes are possible. He presented his ontology as a faithful, if subtle, expression of the common-sense categories used in everyday experience. The justification of his categories is derived principally from their organizing power and their providing a coherent conceptual framework for discussing a vast array of philosophical problems and rival systems.

Further reading

Dewey, John. "The Subject-Matter of Metaphysical Inquiry" in *John Dewey: The Middle Works, 1899–1924, Vol. 8, 1915*, ed. Jo Ann Boydston. Carbondale, IL: Southern Illinois University, 1976–88 [1915].

James, William. "What Pragmatism Means" in *The Works of William James – Pragmatism*, ed. Frederick Burkhardt. Cambridge, MA: Harvard University Press, 1975 [1907].

Peirce, C.S. "Harvard Lectures on Pragmatism" in *The Essential Peirce*, Vol. 2, ed. Peirce Edition Project. Bloomington, IN: Indiana University Press, 1998.

Santayana, George. *Realms of Being* (a one-volume edition which contains Santayana's four books: *The Realm of Essence* (1927); *The Realm of Matter* (1930); *The Realm of Truth* (1938); and *The Realm of Spirit* (1940)). New York: Charles Scribner's Sons, 1942.

Glenn Tiller

CAVELL, STANLEY

Walter M. Cabot Professor of Aesthetics and the General Theory of Value at Harvard since 1963 (now Emeritus), Stanley Cavell (1926–) has distinguished himself as a philosopher with a rare capacity to bring the rigor of the Analytic tradition, the imagination of the Continental tradition, and the experimentalism of the American tradition to bear on a diverse range of texts, from Platonic dialogues to Hollywood comedies. Unconstrained by disciplinary habits of hyper-localized specialization, Cavell's work on a wide range of intellectually engaging issues resists paraphrase and summary, but makes itself very available to quotation (often paraphrases contain so many of Cavell's words, they are nearly quotations). For this reason, attempts to reduce his work to a thesis or system drain the experiential quality of the writing, which is defined by his distinct voice and attention to the tone of philosophy. More than most, Cavell makes the *writing* of philosophy an issue of philosophical significance. The best way to account for Fred Astaire is to watch him dance; but there is no passive accounting for what goes on in Cavell's work. The distinctive authorship of his writing turns reading into something more like a live encounter with another person, an enabling space for one's own awkwardness and idiosyncratic interests.

From a musical family, Cavell trained first as a musician at Berkeley in the 1940s. Later at Juilliard, he began to ditch composition class for film screenings. Time in southern California led to more formal studies in "pragmatism and positivism" at UCLA. Through the recommendation of Morton White, Cavell committed to graduate study at Harvard in the mid-1950s, a time that coincided with the visit of J.L. Austin, who subsequently unseated Cavell's confidence in his proposed dissertation project. Austin's immense influence on Cavell's approach to Wittgenstein, in effect, revealed "elements of voice" in philosophy that convinced Cavell to go onward in it differently. Cavell's training as a musician feels particularly relevant to his claims and his unique voice, as he mentions: "in philosophy it is the sound which makes all the difference." Cavell has labored to discover the equivalent of "perfect pitch" in his philosophical compositions.

Cavell's first book, *Must We Mean What We Say?* (1969), reflects quintessential attributes of his career to follow: diverse intellectual and disciplinary interests brought together along definitive and innovative conceptual lines. Here, essays on Austin, Wittgenstein, Beckett, Kierkegaard, Shakespeare, music, and other topics, reveal a characteristic discernment of central and abiding philosophical concerns presented according to a fundamentally paradigm-shifting approach that self-consciously enacted the philosophy it was speaking of. Cavell's achievement was to write about skepticism, ordinary language philosophy, psychoanalysis, aesthetic judgment, and acknowledgement, while maintaining sensitivity to the implications of his claims from within the very text.

A life spent attuned to the philosophical significance of film yielded Cavell's first major work on the subject, *The World Viewed* (1971). A landmark work of theory, his exploration stood in opposition to the prevailing poststructuralist readings of film, offering instead a more personal, inhabited viewer-based understanding of moviegoing experience. Patient with film form, he analyzed the ontology of the medium, making it relevant to a cultural understanding of film history, criticism, and theory. A decade later, in *Pursuits of Happiness* (1981), Cavell illustrates how, as he claims, "film exists in a state of philosophy," by reflecting on a genre of movies – Hollywood comedies of remarriage – that are both constitutive and generative of philosophical reasoning. The films concern the nature of conversation in a marriage, and how, more broadly, we can bear witness to "a new creation of the human" by means of negotiations of speech and imagination. Cavell's sensitivity to the influence of feminism in film studies led to the development of another genre-cycle, the Hollywood melodrama of the unknown woman, which is explored in *Contesting Tears* (1996). Here the woman uses her voice to create an independent identity, which often means simply a reality as human in a world otherwise unable to hear her.

By the late 1970s, Cavell revised and expanded his dissertation into a 500-page excursus on Wittgenstein, skepticism, morality, and tragedy known as *The Claim of Reason*. This is arguably four books in one. The 187-word opening sentence signals the reader to the grandness and complexity of the project underway, namely, to understand the nature of human judgment, knowledge of other minds, the meaning of ethical claims, and the radical implications of acknowledgment. This work ends, memorably, with *Othello* as an illustration of the way skepticism – when manifested as a refusal to acknowledge others, and to know oneself – leads to disastrous, tragic consequences. Because philosophy has seemed prone to a similar sort of tragedy, Cavell develops a theory of what he calls "living our skepticism."

Just a few years after Cavell asked whether philosophy could become literature and still know itself as philosophy, he expanded his work on Shakespeare with a new set of readings entitled *Disowning Knowledge* (1987), a work credited with providing a wholly new approach to established literary critical readings of Shakespeare.

Cavell publicly founded his interest in the roots of American thinking with *The Senses of Walden* (1972), an intimate account of Thoreau's time at

Walden Pond, and the religious and philosophical significance of this event for our understanding of American identity, ideas, and myths. *Senses* is a uniquely pedagogical work, since it shows with great nuance how reading and listening are connected to our understanding of philosophical prose, especially of work such as Thoreau's *Walden* that may leave some philosophers believing they must be equipped with tin ears. The question of Thoreau's voice is complemented by Cavell's voice, and by listening to both a reader has a chance to glimpse how everyday life – common books, the woods, a pond – are sights of extraordinary philosophical lessons.

Almost a decade after its first appearance, Cavell updated *Senses* to acknowledge his overlooking of Emerson, the act of overlooking itself becoming central to Cavell's interpretation of Emerson's role in American life. How could an American philosopher not acknowledge Emerson, or feel his proximity to philosophy, especially when writing on Thoreau? Cavell makes Emerson's "repression" in the culture he helped found a phenomenon to dwell seriously on. In a series of seminal essays on this and related topics, Cavell pretty much single-handedly brought Emerson into the first ranks of contemporary philosophical discourse, thereby more than compensating for his initial oversight. At present, more than ever before, academic philosophers believe Emerson has bona fide philosophical credentials. More than twenty years of writing on Emerson culminated in the book *Emerson's Transcendental Etudes* (2003), which includes Cavell's understanding of Emersonian moral perfectionism, and other aspects of Emerson's philosophical contribution to American thinking.

Further reading

Cavell, Stanley. *The Claim of Reason: Wittgenstein, Skepticism, Morality, and Tragedy.* Oxford: Oxford University Press, 1979; new edition, 1999.

—— *A Pitch of Philosophy: Autobiographical Exercises.* Cambridge, MA: Harvard University Press, 1994.

—— *Philosophical Passages: Wittgenstein, Emerson, Austin, Derrida.* Oxford: Blackwell, 1995.

—— *Contesting Tears: The Hollywood Melodrama of the Unknown Woman.* Chicago, IL: University of Chicago Press, 1996.

—— *Cities of Words: Pedagogical Letters on a Register of the Moral Life.* Cambridge, MA: Harvard University Press, 2004.

—— *Philosophy the Day After Tomorrow.* Cambridge, MA: Harvard University Press, 2005.

DAVID LAROCCA

CERTAINTY

"Certainty" in philosophy most often refers to a mental state (*indubitability*) or a property of sentences or propositions (*truth* or *truth-value*). Belief *X* is said to be "certain" if it cannot be doubted or if the proposition expressing *X* is *true*. But American philosophy has always reacted skeptically when certainty is put in terms of Descartes' *rationalism* (innate ideas) or Bertrand Russell's *analysis* (deductive logic). The canonical list of American philosophers (John Dewey, William James, Charles S. Peirce, George Santayana, and Josiah Royce, among them) claims that *there is no certainty* and no *foundations* for knowledge. Hence, the *postmodern* paradox: To say with "certainty" or at least with knowledge that there is no certainty, but there is knowledge, is to resurrect knowledge on a *non-foundational* basis. This brief essay describes the historical attempts by *American philosophy* to resurrect knowledge if not "certainty."

And experience

Charles S. Peirce arguably founded American *pragmatism* and provided many of its essential claims. In the "The Fixation of Belief" (1877) he wrote that only experience can teach us anything. He created, in "Some Consequences of Four Incapacities Claimed For Man" (1868), an attitude towards *realism* (theories about what would exist if human beings ceased to) that allowed real things to be a manifestation of ourselves and yet something without us. In short, Peirce rejected Descartes' approach but not his *project* of shoring up our knowledge of the external world. For Peirce, we cannot begin in complete doubt, nor with a *thing in itself*; we begin with *experience*. Like Royce, Peirce reads experience in terms of *semiotics* (theories of *meaning* or *signs*). He writes that we can only think in signs, indeed that "man" is an external sign and that every word or thought he uses *is* "man" himself.

And absolute idealism and error

Josiah Royce is next historically. Royce thought that all reality is the thought of some unifying consciousness (*absolute idealism* or *Hegelianism*) and in *The Religious Aspect of Philosophy* (1885) proposed that some purposive agent thinks ideas independent of ours. With Royce came the question of *religious certainty*, and that of error. We can be wrong (have something to be wrong about) because the absolute has the idea right. Royce wrote in *The World and the Individual* (1899) that the world and the self are also composed of (absolute) aspects and temporal (changing, contingent) aspects. James battled with his Harvard colleague over the absolute, and Dewey ultimately rejected any form of non-*naturalism* (anything beyond the world's natural processes), but Peirce was largely given an academic hearing because of Royce.

In religious experience

Also partly because of Royce, William James wrote *The Varieties of Religious Experience* in 1902. Here he debated whether religious experience could be made secular or scientific or whether it was altogether supernatural. Regardless, he thought it has important consequences. Though *Varieties* is subtitled a mere "study of human nature," James proposes that we can distinguish between a healthy or sick soul tainted by "radical evil." Religious experience then becomes useful for evaluating character or internal state, though James shied away from calling it "true" or veridical. James continues in *Pragmatism* (1907) that the pragmatist is loyal to *both* scientific facts, and to such experiences. But religious experience is only one kind. Pragmatism's method interprets things in terms of practical concrete results: whether a man going around a squirrel, itself going around a tree, is a matter of whether one is north, south, east or west of it, or whether one alternatively faces its hind parts then its head. Again, in "Dilemma of Determinism," (1884 lecture) James argued that the idea that all is determined makes no difference to experience, and hence makes no difference. James argued that we thus make *truths* (interpret or construct them) but we do not simply make them because the world or the situation provide some essential resistance to any interpretation. He argues that we cannot weed out the human contribution in interpretation but that the trail of the "human serpent" is over all.

And naturalism

George Santayana, influenced by Royce and James at Harvard before he moved to Europe, wrote *Scepticism and Animal Faith* in 1923, thus providing a necessary link to Deweyan naturalism. Santayana rejected minds, wills, or even reason or reasoning, as anything beyond individual human minds of animals responding to natural and perilous circumstances. Like the positivists, he comes close to disdaining "unverifiable" ethical or religious language, but instead secures them in a sort of "animal faith." After subjecting common-sense beliefs to a skeptical crucible more rigorous than Descartes', he announces his intention to have an "honest" philosophy (one that can be thought *and* lived). His "honest" philosophy, however, proposes "essences" that are not unlike Plato's forms and subject to some of the same complaints. In addition, the reality of essences appears not to square with Santayana's belief that "objective truths" are rather humble facts about the world that might be achieved by any competent person.

The quest for certainty

Finally, John Dewey wrote the *Quest for Certainty* in 1929. In the tradition of the other pragmatists, Dewey tried to reconstruct philosophy based on a concept of experience sensitive to how it is actually lived and to the new Darwinian biology. Actual scientific practice shows that *Experience and Nature* (1925) are inseparable: a scientist appeals to experience to get at nature, and nature to ground experience. Meanwhile, Dewey's *Logic: The Theory of Inquiry* (1938) illustrates the manifold non-hierarchical paths to resolving a "problematic situation." Lying in between, *The Quest for Certainty* specifically rejects the rationalistic realism and romantic idealism of Descartes, Kant, and Hegel.

According to Dewey, the quest for certainty is the attempt to transcend and vouchsafe ordinary, "practical" knowledge claims by appealing to timeless and necessary truths that exist and can be known prior to experience. Dewey argued that such theorizing is useless without its practicality: knowing is a kind of doing and true objects of knowledge have practical consequences for action. So actually, we do not want to transcend belief, we want to satisfy it. Doing then provides "insurance but no assurance." Early on, such as in "The Reflex Arc Concept in Psychology" Dewey rails against thinkers who want to cut out items like "stimulus" and "response" from their proper context within experience and announce their independent existence. This multiplication of existents so exercised Dewey his whole life to the point that he devoted his last book, *Knowing and the Known* (1949), to explaining that experience is "transactional" not "interactional."

New directions

Philosophical descendents of Peirce, Royce, James, Santayana, and Dewey have explored these and many other themes involving the concept of certainty. C.I. Lewis reviewed Dewey's *Quest for Certainty* and wrote on Royce and Santayana, Isaac Levi wrote about evidence and fallibility, and F.C.S. Schiller wrote about logical necessity. Of special note are books that seek to extend the historical and ideological development of American Philosophy and pragmatism to a larger set than the canonical pragmatists like Scott Pratt's *Native Pragmatism* (2002).

Further reading

Bentley, Arthur and Dewey, John. *Knowing and the Known*. Westport, CT: Greenwood Press, 1976.

Dewey, John. *The Quest for Certainty*. Whitefish, MT: Kessinger Publishing, 2005.

James, William. *Pragmatism and Other Writings*. New York: Penguin, 2005.

Levi, Isaac. "Certainty, Probability and Correction of Evidence," *Noûs* 5 (1971): 372–5.

Lewis, C.I. "Review of John Dewey, *The Quest for Certainty*." *Journal of Philosophy* 27, 1 (January 1930): 14–25.

Peirce, C.S. "The Fixation of Belief," *Popular Science Monthly* 12 (November 1877): 1–15.

Pratt, Scott. *Native Pragmatism: Rethinking the Roots of Pragmatism*. Indiana, IN: Indiana University Press, 2002.

Royce, Josiah. *The World and the Individual*. New York: Dover, 1959.

Santayana, George. *Skepticism and Animal Faith; Introduction to a System of Philosophy*. Whitefish, MT: Kessinger Publishing, 2005.

Schiller, F.C.S. "Review of *The Quest for Certainty*," *Mind* 39, 3 (July 1930): 372–5.

Shook, John. *Pragmatic Naturalism and Realism*. Amherst, NY: Prometheus, 2003.

James A. Stieb

CHANGE

As a central concept of metaphysics, philosophers have traditionally divided on whether change is a genuine feature of reality or an illusion of sense perception. The dispute about the reality of change can be traced to the ancient Greek philosophers Parmenides and Heraclitus, and was very much alive in the classical American philosophers. The focus on change and the refusal to look to the eternal in the American thinkers is a general trend but not universal feature of their thought. Monists such as Josiah Royce, for example, following the tradition of absolute idealism in Germany and Britain, sided with Parmenides in arguing that change is always occurring in our experience but cannot be attributed to ultimate reality which must be conceived as permanent and static. But the pluralists such as William James, John Dewey, and Alfred North Whitehead sided with Heraclitus in proposing ontological schemes that view time and change as a fundamental feature of reality. Change is understood in terms of a dynamic process of events. George Santayana, while more eclectic in his approach, was equally preoccupied with the ancient debate and sought to understand change as the flux of momentary actualizations of essences that are themselves eternal.

The role of the specious present

A rich vein of philosophical activity about change begins with James' attempt to formulate a novel theory of experience against the British Empiricists. Instead of focusing on sense experience and its role in epistemology, James sought a wider interpretation of experience for metaphysics. The core of this philosophy grows out of two important innovations in James' earlier work, *Principles of Psychology*, namely, the concept of the specious present and the stream of consciousness. With regard to the former, James notes that no experience is an instantaneous present, but rather always involves a duration that includes bits of the immediate past and anticipations of the future. Each duration is an indivisible unity that realizes itself as the totality of its temporal parts. James now explains the stream of consciousness as comprised of the durations that flow one into another. While consciousness is sensibly continuous, change is understood as the difference between the durations, no one of which is repeatable even though characters or objects in the stream will repeat themselves.

Implications for metaphysics

The description of change in James' phenomenological description of consciousness is then generalized to all forms of existence in his philosophy of radical empiricism. Our own experience gives us some basis for understanding the rudimentary streams of experience that compose the whole of nature. The point is also developed by Whitehead in *Process and Reality*. Whitehead explains an event as a sequence of actual occasions or durations much in the same manner of James' stream of consciousness. The actual occasions do not change; rather they become in whole units as they emerge from their immediate predecessors. Once they complete their becoming, they contribute their data to their successors and perish. Whitehead explains change as the difference in character between one actual occasion and the next. He also explains how there is genuine novelty by the selective activity of the basic occasions, without which the world would simply sink into monotonous repetition. Through a process of selection and elimination, occasions take data from the past that is compatible with their aims to contribute new entities in the present. Dewey's *Experience and Nature* develops a similar view by his emphasis on events making up the temporal process.

While the idea that change originates internally was an important feature of Aristotle's teleological conception of nature, James, Dewey and Whitehead's view must be seen in contrast to the ontology of substance, according to which self-identical objects undergo change of properties. It is this latter view that has been a dominant feature of Anglo-American analytical philosophy.

Royce uses the concept of the specious present to grand effect in *The World and the Individual*. His main task is to explain how temporal succession and change can retain a genuine reality in a universe that is ultimately eternal and changeless. Royce hypothesizes a grand conscious organism, the Absolute, which experiences the universe as a simultaneous whole. Within the arteries of Being, Royce argues, there are different apperceptive time-spans. All is conscious life within but the experience of time is radically different in what is perceived by us as inanimate nature. So, for example, the process of time and change in the inorganic goes on with a vast slowness compared with human experience. For a consciousness having the same content as ours, but with a different apperceptive time-span, what seems to us to last a second is stretched out into a series lasting an entire era. In an extrapolation from human experience, Royce now invokes the idea of the specious present to explain how all of the apperceptive time-spans come together in the experience of the Absolute. Our natural interest in temporal succession binds us to a world of longing and restless pursuit of fulfillment, but if we were to understand the significance of our experience of the present as a simultaneous whole, we would understand the experience of eternity from the view of the Absolute. Just as we experience in any one duration of consciousness, a unity of elements – past, present and future – in any one specious present, the Absolute experiences the whole of cosmic history and the future as one grand specious present. The difference, however, is that where our specious present happens as a duration of a temporal series, the specious present of the Absolute is one unchanging eternal moment. *Sub specie temporis* (under the aspect of time) change is quite real in all the apperceptive time-spans, but *sub specie aeternitatis* (under the aspect of eternity) there is no change nor is there any such experience of a not yet, a no longer, a coming to be or a passing away. Julius Caesar's death on the Ides of March, the beginning of World War I and the event of our sun going supernova happen all at once and remain eternally present.

Pragmatism and social progress

From the practical standpoint, the emphasis on a reality of change plays out in an important way in Dewey's educational and social theory. The world as we experience it both individually and collectively is an admixture of the precarious and transitory aspect of things, and the stable, patterned regularity of natural processes that allows for prediction and human intervention. The human task is defined as rendering more of it stable and therefore less subject to misfortune. This is accomplished in education by an emphasis on values and practice that make for social continuity. Social habits and institutions that promote it provide this stability but the achievement of a satisfying life will involve social criticism as an agent of change against the tendency of stagnation in dogmatic principles. Dewey emphasized an open-ended, flexible and experimental approach to the problems of practice aimed at the attainment of democratic habits of cooperation and public participation. Change in this context is understood as the lifeblood of an organism's ability to adapt and the plasticity of mind to discover new truths and evaluate alternative possibilities.

Further reading

Campbell, Keith. *Metaphysics: An Introduction*. Encino, CA: Dickenson, 1976.

Dewey, John. *Democracy and Education: An Introduction to the Philosophy of Education*. New York: Macmillan, 1916.

James, William. *Essays in Radical Empiricism*. New York: Longmans, Green, 1912.

Loux, Michael J. *Metaphysics: A Contemporary Introduction*, second edition. London and New York: Routledge, 2002.

Santayana, George. *The Realms of Being*. New York: Charles Scribner's Sons, 1942.

Sprigge, Timothy. "The Distinctiveness of American Philosophy" in Peter Caws (ed.) *Two Centuries of Philosophy in America*. Oxford: Blackwell, 1980, pp. 199–214.

Whitehead, Alfred North. *Process and Reality*. Cambridge: Cambridge University Press, 1929.

LEEMON B. MCHENRY

CHARACTER

Ralph Waldo Emerson defined character as "a reserved force which acts directly by presence, and without means" (1926: 325). On this rather Romantic definition, character is "a certain undemonstrable force, a Familiar or Genius, by whose impulses the man is guided." More than the sum of one's actions and more than intellect or talent, character is a kind of self-sufficient moral strength that can be perceived, not by the eye, but by the intuition.

William James and John Dewey held a less Romantic and more Aristotelian view of character. They would have agreed with Aristotle that character comes from habit. It is important to understand that they held habit to be more than just routinizations of behaviors. James pointed out that, while natural laws describe certain unchanging habits of matter, human physiology is complex enough to be able to develop habits of various sorts. These habits (which can be somatic, perceptual, intellectual, and emotional, as well as behavioral) constitute the malleable part of human nature, while temperament constitutes the part that does not change. He gave several maxims for changing one's own habits (and thus shaping one's own character), including the importance of starting the process with as strong a determination as possible and of not allowing any exceptions until the habit is strongly entrenched.

Both James and Dewey held that character is crucial for education. In his *Talks to Teachers on Psychology*, James argued that a teacher's task is to build up a character in the students, with this character consisting in certain habitual tendencies of action or restraint. For Dewey, morality becomes moralism when learning tries to shape the intellect without also shaping character. Education must help the learner see the organic connection between the content of the material being studied and its moral value. That is, students must be taught not only the facts, but also how these facts can be used in the ongoing shaping and reshaping of individual and social habits.

In the mid-twentieth century, Harvard psychology professor Gordon Allport argued that character is not a precise enough concept to be studied scientifically. He proposed, instead, that psychologists bend their efforts toward studying "personality." As a result, personality psychology eclipsed the study of character in psychology.

In the 1990s, high-profile cases of student violence made character education a national priority. President Bill Clinton called for all American schools to teach character education, and upon assuming office President George W. Bush tripled the Department of Education's character education budget. Despite this high-profile support, however, character education has remained controversial, with some claiming that it is a political cover for religious indoctrination and others claiming that human nature is too labile to be accurately described in terms of reliable traits of character. These critiques notwithstanding, character education programs of various types have been introduced into many American schools. Much of the money the Department of Education has received for character education has gone toward the empirical testing of these programs to see which may be effective and what their specific results may be.

University of Pennsylvania psychologist Martin E.P. Seligman has recently argued that the study of character should be reintroduced into psychology. He and Christopher Peterson have published a classification of character strengths and virtues, with the aim of bringing together psychological knowledge about the nature, measurement, and cultivation of character strengths that are pervasively valued across time and across cultures. Seligman and Peterson hypothesize that there are individual differences in character, such that certain persons are naturally better at some of the character strengths than others. This work paves the way for an alternative to a one-size-fits-all approach to character education. By identifying their "signature strengths," students can cultivate their characters by focusing first on developing further the strengths they already have. This also points the way toward the social nature of character, with successful communities relying on the input of persons with a variety of natural character strengths.

While this may not be the most Romantic way of thinking about character, it certainly seems in keeping with the views of James and Dewey. A further way of thinking about the consonance among these views is by defining character as both a product and a process. If character is not only something that is instilled in us, but also something we choose, then character education should help students learn how to take more and more control of their own processes of habit formation and character development. Seen in this way, a democratic education should not just be about helping xstudents learn how to take part in collective governance, but it should also help them develop their own powers of individual self-governance, so that they can more effectively regulate their own somatic, perceptual, intellectual, emotional, behavioral, spiritual, and social habits as they work, in community with others, to develop their own character (Pawelski 2004).

Further reading

Dewey, John. *Human Nature and Conduct. The Middle Works of John Dewey: 1899–1924, Vol. 14, 1922*, ed. Jo Ann Boydston. Carbondale, IL: Southern Illinois University Press, 1978.

Emerson, Ralph Waldo. "Character" in *Emerson's Essays: First and Second Series Complete in One Volume*. New York: Harper and Row, 1926, pp. 324–44.

Pawelski, James O. "Character as Ethical Democracy: Definitions and Measures," *Journal of College and Character*, (October 2004); available at http://collegevalues.org/pdfs/James%20Pawelski.pdf (accessed 14 May 2007).

JAMES O. PAWELSKI

CHARITY, PRINCIPLE OF

The philosopher Donald Davidson argues that the principle of charity solves the double problem we are confronted with in *radical interpretation*, namely: how to assign meaning to an utterance without knowing the speaker's beliefs, and how to identify her beliefs without knowing the meaning of her utterances. In Davidson's view, interpretation involves the double task of reconstructing the beliefs and the meanings of a speaker simultaneously. In radical interpretation we are confronted with this task without being able to rely on any prior familiarity with either the beliefs or the meanings of the speaker. Given the holistic interdependence of belief and meaning, in order to reconstruct the meanings expressed in an utterance, the radical interpreter has no option but to assume that the speaker's beliefs are in agreement with those of the interpreter. So, the principle of charity is a methodological injunction underlying interpretation which tells us that we must maximize agreement in order to optimize understanding. This principle is more than a heuristic device to be employed in the initial stages of interpretative engagement: it is both a constraint and an enabling principle in all interpretation. Davidson insists that this principle is not an option, but something that forces itself on us. It is a transcendental condition of communication: in order to understand each other, we must assume that there is a massive overlap between our beliefs and those of our interlocutors, that their beliefs are – by our lights – largely true. The principle of charity thus offers the basis of a rudimentary theory of belief and a rudimentary theory of meaning. It is the foundation of a methodology of interpretation that authorizes us to use our own beliefs about the world as a guide to the speaker's beliefs and meanings. A corollary of the principle of charity is that meaningful disagreements can only be partial and localized, for a disagreement is intelligible only against the background of a massive agreement on true beliefs. It also follows from this principle that interpretation is relative to interpretative standpoints and that the same utterance can be adequately interpreted by a plurality of theories of interpretation that are equally correct on methodological and empirical grounds. According to Davidson, there can always be more than one theory of interpretation adequate to the linguistic evidence available, that is, there can always be theories that provide alternative attributions of belief and alternative assignment of meaning while offering an equally satisfactory account of the speaker's overall behavior. Davidson names this failure of uniqueness *the indeterminacy of interpretation* (a counterpart to Quine's *indeterminacy of translation*). But this indeterministic semantic view does not result in a skeptical perspective on human knowledge. On the contrary: Davidson derives a transcendental argument against radical skepticism from the principle of charity. Drawing on this principle, Davidson argues that when we push skeptical theses to their ultimate consequences, we should realize that they are nonsensical or self-undermining: since meaning requires a critical mass of true beliefs, it cannot be the case that none of our knowledge claims has ever expressed a justified true belief and has ever amounted to genuine knowledge. For our knowledge claims to make sense at all, there must be a network of true beliefs that support their intelligibility (independently of whether any particular one of our claims happens to be correct or incorrect). Insofar as we communicate, there is a massive background of shared true beliefs that supports the meanings that we convey to each other; and if communication is a fact, it follows that radical skepticism is wrong. On this view, the most basic form of skepticism is semantic skepticism since everything turns on whether there is (or there has ever been) genuine communication, i.e. genuine exchanges of meaning and mutual understanding, in our linguistic interactions. The principle of charity is thus the cornerstone of Davidson's holistic view of intelligibility, rationality, and knowledge: for a single belief to be intelligible and rational, it must cohere with an entire system of largely true beliefs. On this view, coherence yields correspondence and guarantees that our system of beliefs is, overall, in touch with reality. According to the holistic view that derives from the principle of charity, nonsensicality, irrationality, and lack of knowledge can only be the exception but not the rule.

Further reading

Davidson, Donald. "Truth and Meaning", in his *Inquiries into Truth and Interpretation*, Oxford: Oxford University Press, 1984, pp. 17–36.

—— "Three Varieties of Knowledge", in his *Subjective, Intersubjective, Objective*. Oxford: Oxford University Press, 2001, pp. 205–20.

—— "Expressing Evaluations", in his *Problems of Rationality*. Oxford: Oxford University Press, 2004, pp. 19–38.

José Medina

CHICAGO PRAGMATISTS

The University of Chicago was founded in 1890 under the leadership of William Rainey Harper, who had been chosen as its first president by John D. Rockefeller, the university's principal benefactor. Originally expected to be only an undergraduate institution, under the guidance of Harper and Rockefeller the university expanded into a full-fledged graduate institution, rivaling those few already established in the United States at the time. Harvard, Johns Hopkins, Michigan, and others set the precedent, long held in Europe, of the primacy of graduate teaching, research, and publication in professional fields and soon assumed an important place at the fore of America's burgeoning scientific push into modernity. Despite his proclivity for pushing his university forward, Harper was still a deeply devout person and sought scholars with whom he shared that inclination.

One of the first people Harper contacted was James Tufts, a professor of philosophy at Michigan and a proponent of the connection of German idealist dialecticism, Protestant Christian values, and the new psychology. Tufts originally sought a career in ministry but began the pursuit of philosophy during his second year at Yale Divinity School. Before Yale, Tufts had studied at Amherst under Charles E. Garman who, while supporting a fundamentally theistic idealism, was tolerant of developments in laboratory psychology, aided by the fact that he was close friends with William James, who by that time had set up the first psychology laboratory in the United States at Harvard. The invitation stimulated Tufts, still a relatively young scholar, to finish his doctorate in Germany before recommending his former colleague, John Dewey, from Michigan. Tufts recommendation of Dewey stressed both Dewey's ability as a philosopher and his religious disposition.

When Tufts accepted the original Chicago appointment, Dewey replaced him with a thinker with similar philosophical proclivities: George Herbert Mead. As colleagues, Mead and Dewey were close and soon developed a close friendship to complement their similar intellectual positions. As a younger scholar new to Michigan, Mead was trained similarly in the cross connections of Protestant ethics, German idealism, and the new psychology, and was interested in Dewey's projects. Mead had spent a large part of his graduate education at Harvard working with Josiah Royce, the most famous American advocate of German idealism, and William James. Though Mead never finished his doctorate, James took a great liking to Mead and even offered to support his stay at Harvard, supplementing him, as well, with money for tutoring the James children during the summers. Instead of staying at Harvard, though, Mead ventured to Germany to study and stayed in Leipzig for three years, eventually returning at Dewey's request. Mead eventually followed Dewey from Michigan to Chicago.

Just before leaving Michigan at the end of the 1894 spring semester, Dewey delivered a famous speech on reconstruction to Michigan's students explaining that the primary difficulty in seeing religion as a hopeful force is that it impedes action. Dewey was concerned that some new vehicle for change was necessary. In 1894, at the urging of Tufts, Dewey accepted a job at the University of Chicago and entered a vastly different social scene. Upon his arrival in Chicago, Dewey withdrew his family from the church and proceeded to investigate the ameliorative capacity of democracy. In 1894, Chicago was a bustling, overcrowded city in the midst of a huge influx of immigrants, a city in turmoil with population growth constantly threatening to overstretch resources. The Deweys were thrown into this turmoil upon their arrival in July of 1894 as the city had just entered into the Pullman strike and had seen, only days before, the burning – in protest of working conditions – of numerous buildings erected for the World's Fair, though no one was charged with the crimes. The conditions in Chicago forced Dewey and the later Chicago group to reconsider their language for solving social problems, moving more and more to secular language of industrial ethics opposed to more religiously tinged frameworks.

The middle years: Jane Addams and democracy

Dewey met Jane Addams, the famous activist and social theorist, before his arrival in Chicago and continued their friendship upon his settlement there. Addams, though not affiliated with the university, is a key member of the Chicago School largely because of the effect her ideas had on Dewey. Addams and her colleague Ellen Gates Starr set up the first of many settlement houses on Chicago's busy Halstead Street to educate and offer assistance to the city's vast and growing immigrant population. Addams and Starr, among others affiliated with Hull House, had successfully rallied, in 1893 – the year before Dewey's arrival – for what would become the Illinois Factory Inspection Act that limited child labor and improved working conditions in the factories of Chicago. Dewey was forthcoming about how much he learned from Addams, whose theories of democratic reform would underpin the Chicago Pragmatists' later programs of democratic and education reform. Dewey even named his daughter Jane, after Addams.

Dewey and his colleagues showed great support for Addams' work at Hull House and remained dedicated to her and it throughout the next twenty years, even after Dewey's departure to New York. Dewey was on Hull House's first board of trustees, and he, Tufts, Mead, James R. Angell, and A.W. Moore were also on the board of directors and attended and even gave some lectures at Hull House.

James R. Angell and A.W. Moore joined the faculty in the middle 1890s due to their conformity to the already established goals of the department: the desire to combine Hegelian dialectics with psychology. Dewey brought Angell to Chicago from a one-year stint at the University of Minnesota and hired Moore after he graduated with his doctorate from Chicago in 1895. Moore began as a teaching fellow and then became a professor.

The later years: Chicago functionalism

Dewey's argument in his 1896 essay "The Reflex Arc Concept in Psychology" marked an important personal and departmental transformation. It took issue with psychological structuralists' belief that mind consists of a series of individual reflexes. Dewey takes his alternative model from Charles S. Peirce's theory of inquiry and argues that certain stimuli interrupt the habitual repetition of mind. These disruptions stimulate inquiry due to the agitation that the disruption causes. Moore and Angell continued this line of inquiry with an article published that same year on habit and attention. They wanted to disprove the formalist notion that the mind consists of discrete mental elements, arguing that differences in reaction times under certain conditions were explicable by means of differing relations between habit and attention. Viewing mind in an evolutionary-historical perspective, the new Chicago functionalism saw the process of mind as being rooted in an organism's interactions with its environment. Consciousness arrives at those moments when physiological processes are not enough for the organism to prove adequate to the requirements of its conditions.

In the late 1890s, Dewey and his disciples were pursuing its fundamentally unique functionalist project, a project that reached into every aspect of history and philosophy for the thinkers involved, leading William James to exclaim, upon reading *Studies in Logical Theory*, the group's most mature rendition of its functionalist position, that Dewey and his cohort had indeed created a new school of philosophy. James's influential 1904 essay entitled "The Chicago School" articulated his vision of Chicago's program. He argued that Chicago had unified a body of thought and method into a cohesive system that was much in need of elaboration but nonetheless was full of potential and originality. James saw Dewey and his colleagues as cohesive in their unification of biology and psychology, of phenomenological individualism with the unification of fact and value. The Chicago School also exemplified in different ways the use of the genetic or historical method. This unity struck James as very different from pragmatism in Cambridge, where its major proponents, Charles Peirce, Josiah Royce, and himself, disagreed about the role and function of pragmatism.

Functionalism allowed the Chicago School to subsume all philosophical subdivisions under psychology because each dealt with different aspects of an organism's relation to its environment. Thinking becomes a purposive activity in problematic situations. The Chicago School approached the conditions of immigrants and workers as problematic situations but traced the roots of these problems to the very origins of the education system, where structuralist tendencies ruled. Dewey and his cohort believed that the separation of the means and ends of education left students detached from the conditions under which they would live in the real world of production. Education was the perfect *topos*, according to the Chicago School, the perfect laboratory for improving the relation between functionalist psychology and democratic change. In 1896, with blessings but minimal financial assistance of the university, Dewey started his famous laboratory school. This school began with three teachers and thirty-six students, and a building equipped with only tables and chairs. By 1904, when Dewey decided to leave Chicago because Harper decided to remove his wife, Alice Dewey, from the position of the school's principal, the laboratory school had grown to twenty-three teachers and 140 students. After Dewey's resignation and move to Columbia, Mead, Angell, and Tufts continued the department's interest in education with Mead becoming an outspoken advocate of industrial or "manual" education.

Further reading

Deegan, Mary Jo. *Jane Addams and the Men of the Chicago School*. New Brunswick, NJ: Transaction Books, 1986.

Feffer, Andrew. *The Chicago Pragmatists and American Progressivism*. Ithaca, NY: Cornell University Press, 1993.

James, William. "The Chicago School," *Psychological Bulletin* 1 (1904): 1–5.

Rucker, Darnell. *The Chicago Pragmatists*. Minneapolis, MN: University of Minnesota Press, 1969.

Westbrook, Robert. *John Dewey and American Democracy*. Ithaca, NY: Cornell University Press, 1991.

JASON BARRETT-FOX

CHISHOLM, RODERICK M.

Roderick M. Chisholm (1916–99) was one of the most important epistemologists and metaphysicians of the twentieth century. Born in North Attleboro, Massachusetts, Chisholm studied philosophy as an undergraduate with Curt John Ducasse at Brown University; he then pursued graduate work at Harvard where his teachers included Willard Quine (then a new instructor from whom Chisholm rented a room). After serving in the army as a clinical psychologist and then at the University of Pennsylvania as a philosophy professor, Chisholm returned to Brown in 1947 where he spent the rest of his career. Known for uncompromising intellectual integrity and his passion for seeking philosophical truth, Chisholm earned a reputation as a legendary teacher of philosophy; and for more than half a century he wrote with characteristic clarity and rigor on a remarkable range of philosophical subjects, including axiology, the foundations of ethics, and the philosophy of Brentano and Meinong. He is best known, however, for his work in epistemology and metaphysics.

Epistemology

Chisholm attempted to answer the Socratic question, "What can I know?" framing this philosophical challenge in terms of "the problem of the criterion": to know whether a belief is a good one, one must have a criterion for sorting justified beliefs from unjustified beliefs; but one cannot know whether one's criterion works unless one already knows that the beliefs that it picks out *are* justified beliefs. Chisholm rejected the skeptic's charge that this circle is vicious; and he also rejected *methodism* – the view that one should break the skeptic's circle by offering (as empiricists do) general principles of evidence that serve as a criterion or method for determining what in particular one does know. Instead, Chisholm embraced *particularism*: he claimed to know particular things about himself and the world and then used this knowledge to derive principles of evidence. Influenced by the commonsensism of Thomas Reid and George Edward Moore (whom Chisholm met while a student at Harvard), Chisholm claimed to know, in particular, that he had certain beliefs, feelings, desires, and attitudes, that he had certain experiences and perceptions, that he had a body, that he intentionally did certain things that he could have avoided doing; and Chisholm claimed to know similar facts about his past. He then formulated various principles of evidence that were themselves confirmed by the fact that they justified the particular things that Chisholm claimed to know. Reflected in Chisholm's principles is an "epistemic hierarchy" that implies that some truths known (e.g. that one is sad) are "epistemically preferable" to others (e.g. that one perceives a sheep in the field).

Chisholm's epistemology is *foundationalist* in the sense that known truths with a higher epistemic status (e.g. truths that are certain or evident) serve as the justification for propositions with a lesser epistemic status (e.g. propositions that are "epistemically in the clear" or "probable"). Ultimately, Chisholm claims (in the *internalist* tradition) that one has certain epistemic *duties* to believe things with the right kind of justification; and the nature of these duties and justification is to be understood in terms of our having certain *ethical* requirements regarding when we ought to believe and ought to withhold belief.

Metaphysics

Reflecting agreement with Brentano regarding "the primacy of the intentional" – that one's knowledge about the world can be defended only in terms of one's knowledge about one's self – the foundations of Chisholm's epistemology include *selfpresenting properties*. A selfpresenting property (e.g. *being sad*, *desiring chocolate*) is such that if one has it and believes that one has it, then one is certain that one has it. Chisholm took seriously the apparent implication for "the unity of consciousness": siding again with Brentano, he argued that the bearer of *self* presenting properties is a person (i.e. a self) who *is* (per Reid) an enduring subject of experience, not (per Hume) a mere bundle of successive experiences. The enduring self, Chisholm argued, cannot be identical with the gross brain (which undergoes a constant replacement of parts), but is instead a tiny thing – a tiny threedimensional physical entity that persists without loss of parts or an entity so tiny that it is partless (i.e. a *monad*).

Chisholm's conclusions about the nature of the persisting self were motivated by his commitment to *mereological essentialism* – the view that no whole can exist without exactly the parts it has. If a car loses a bolt, then the remaining object may be a car, but it cannot be the *same* car. Strictly, there are no persisting cars and brains; rather, talk about persisting cars and brains should be analyzed as talk about series of nonpersisting objects that have persisting parts in common.

Rejecting determinism, Chisholm defended *libertarianism* ("freewillism"), arguing that a person can *freely* undertake a certain activity when there is no sufficient causal condition for one's undertaking it *and* one's undertaking it or refraining from undertaking it is within one's power. In developing his views regarding possible worlds, numbers, intentionality, events, time, and space, Chisholm adopted a realist ontology, defending necessarily existing *properties* (e.g. *being human* and *being a unicorn*) that, like Plato's universals, exist regardless of whether they are exemplified. Not until late in his career did Chisholm address the existence of a deity. Consistent with his view that intentional (i.e. psychological) states cannot be reduced to physical states, Chisholm argued that talk of biological purpose cannot be reduced to talk of nature or evolution. Citing Aquinas's fifth way, he concluded that there likely exists at least one necessary substance that is an intelligent designer.

Further reading

Chisholm, Roderick M. *Perceiving: A Philosophical Study.* Ithaca, NY: Cornell University Press, 1957.

—— *Person and Object: A Metaphysical Study.* LaSalle, IL: Open Court, 1976.

—— *Brentano and Intrinsic Value.* Cambridge: Cambridge University Press, 1986.

—— *Theory of Knowledge*, third edition. Englewood Cliffs, NJ: PrenticeHall, 1989.

—— *A Realistic Theory of Categories: An Essay on Ontology.* Cambridge: Cambridge University Press, 1996.

Hahn, Lewis Edwin (ed.) *The Philosophy of Roderick M. Chisholm* (The Library of Living Philosophers, Vol. XXV). Chicago, IL: Open Court, 1997.

H. Scott Hestevold

CHRISTIAN SCIENCE

Christian Science is a religious movement begun by Mary Baker Eddy (1821–1910). The movement was one of several in the late nineteenth century that emphasized the ability of the mind to cure physical ailments, and was cited as an exemplary case of "mind cure" outlooks in William James's *The Varieties of Religious Experience* (1902). In 1875, Eddy published *Science and Health*, the text that served as the foundation for her founding of The First Church of Christian, Scientist, four years later. Eddy and the church opened sites for learning and disseminating Christian Science beliefs and practices, and in 1908 founded *The Christian Science Monitor.* Christian Science remains viable in the twenty-first century.

In *Science and Health*, Eddy described the metaphysical bases for Christian Science practice. Christian Science is essentially a Christian theological outlook; it is grounded in a faith in the revealed doctrines of the Christian Bible. However, philosophically it resembles many idealistic theories of the nineteenth century. The theoretical outlook centers on the belief that matter is not substantially real, but is a product or manifestation of Mind. Eddy resists the pantheistic tendencies of philosophical idealism, asserting that our finite minds are distinct from the Divine Mind or Spirit. Nevertheless, we have access to the Divine Mind and this access is the basis for our ability to heal ourselves through Mind. Ultimately, disharmony, disease, and physical discomfort are unreal. When we recognize this and turn to the Truth and Love that are identifiable with God, we will be able to heal ourselves through the power of the Divine Spirit. In this process, Eddy suggests, the finite person becomes divine-like.

Though Christian Science is one among many mind-cure movements of the late nineteenth and early twentieth centuries, it has withstood the test of time better than most. From a philosophical point of view, it might be considered as a pragmatic idealism, just insofar as the idea that everything is essentially Mind is taken literally and then employed in a very practical way.

Further reading

Eddy, Mary Baker. *Science and Health with a Key to the Scriptures.* Boston, MA: The Christian Science Board of Directors, 2000 [1875].

Gill, Gillian. *Mary Baker Eddy.* Reading, MA: Perseus Books, 1998.

DOUGLAS R. ANDERSON

CHRISTIANITY

The history of Christianity in American philosophy can be understood as a transaction between individual innovation and community solidarity. Among religious philosophers in the American tradition, especially those identified as pragmatists, there has generally been a suspicion of religious institutions, and at times an outright rejection of them. This suspicion regarding the traditional church does not preclude a commitment to attitudes and practices that bring communities together. On the contrary, American philosophy takes very seriously the corporate aspect of religion; it just does not believe the corpus of believers is headed by eternal doctrines or authoritative leaders.

Puritanism

There was a strong commitment to community in the sermons of the early American Puritans, who were cleaving from what they took to be an oppressive European tradition. A sense of isolation led to a profound sense that, if the American religious experiment were to be successful, it would require extraordinary solidarity within the community. Preacher John Winthrop, speaking during the difficult voyage across the Atlantic, exhorts his parishioners to meet the needs of one another. The community should not tempt God by assuming that its deficiencies will be taken care of by divine beneficence. "We must be willing to abridge ourselves of our superfluities for the supply of others' necessities," Winthrop instructs his anxious flock. We as individuals, he proclaims, must "make others' condition our own," avoiding the tendency to seek solitary betterment. The individual and the community should be thought of as inextricably bound.

These relatively pleasant words of communal comfort appear to clash with those of Jonathan Edwards, the most notorious figure in American Puritanism. The fame of Edwards's "Sinners in the Hands of an Angry God" sermon has contributed to some mistaken appraisals of Edwards and his message. Edwards was not a fire-and-brimstone showman, continually yelling about individual guilt and eternal misery. "Sinners" is indeed a bit of dreadful preaching. It continually refers to the individual as dangling above the fires of Hell, with only the whim of God to save him. Edwards tells his parishioners that "your wickedness makes you as it were heavy as lead, and to tend downward with great weight and pressure towards hell" with nothing you possess capable of stopping you any more "than a spider's web would have to stop a falling rock." This kind of dramatic and sinister preaching, however, is an anomaly for Edwards. What's more, one should not overlook in the sermon Edwards' call, similar to that of Winthrop, for an individual to identify with the unfortunate condition of others. Near the end of the sermon, Edwards shifts focus from the individual's wickedness to the community's sympathy: "If we knew there was one person, and but one, in the whole congregation, that was to be the subject of this misery, what an awful thing it would be to think of!" Edwards continues by referring to this tragedy on the communal scale: "How might all the rest of the congregation life up a lamentable and bitter cry over him!" One person's tragedy is to be shared by all. Edwards was taking to its limits the ideas of God's ultimate sovereignty and humanity's persistent individualism, and using it to promote a sense of solidarity in which individuals and the community are, once again, inextricably bound.

Iconoclasm and pragmatism

Ralph Waldo Emerson's goal was that of inspiring a new and confident American spirituality. Absent from his writing is the assumption of human fragility characteristic of Puritanism. For Emerson, the Christian message is that humanity possesses the power of ingenuity, one that allows each individual the ability to achieve a moral freedom that approaches divinity. The religious establishment, much more cautious regarding humanity's powers, bristled at such an optimistic suggestion; to Emerson, however, such a notion of personal divinity and infinite creativity seemed eminently Christian. "If man is at heart just," says Emerson in his "Divinity School Address" to Harvard seminarians, "then in so far is he God; the safety of God, the immortality of God, the majesty of God do enter into that man with justice." Emerson does not indicate that the following of external religious doctrine is necessary to attain piety. Following doctrines and believing in miracles, in fact, goes against one's personal sensibilities. "That which shows God in me, fortifies me," he proclaims. "That which shows God out of me, makes me a wart and a wen." Understandably, some members of the Harvard establishment were not pleased with his Address.

The anti-establishment spirit within American Christian philosophy shows up most polemically in the writings of Henry James, the father of philosopher William James. Henry James was critical of doctrinal religion, and believed that traditional teachings, such as those of the harsh-minded and individualistic Puritans, serve only to promote personal egotism. He maintained that individualism itself was the original sin of humanity. A seminary dropout, Henry James believed that bourgeois Protestant church life was the enemy of true Christianity. What is unique about Henry James is that he believed the church tradition, with all of its egotism, actually served a necessary purpose in the history of salvation. People must first be made acutely aware of their selfishness in order to reject it completely for the sake of a truly communal consciousness. "Our natural selfhood," he explains in *Christianity: The Logic of Creation*, "is the indispensable *matrix* or mould by which we attain to our true self-consciousness as a divine creation." In other words, heightened individualism is necessary as a stage toward developing the communal Body of Christ. James forcefully rejected the established theology of his day, referring to it as a putrid waste product that needs to be removed from sight. Yet he ends up with a philosophy much like that of Winthrop and Edwards: The individual is bound to the community, and the community depends on the individual.

This theme informs the work of his son. William James' most popular work on religion, *The Varieties of Religious Experience*, is a psychological treatise derived from his assessment of largely, though not exclusively, Christian religious experiences. James never fully identified himself with Christianity, but was influenced by the socialistic Christianity of his father. And like many sons, he chose to rebel against some of the values he inherited. William James displays an individualistic bias – and also a mildly antiestablishment attitude – when he defines religion as "the feelings, acts, and experiences of individual men in their solitude, so far as they stand in relation to whatever they may consider the divine." According to William James, religious traditions are derived from these individuals, and thus are of secondary concern to him. He never maintains, however, that individual experience is all there is to religion. If the ingenious feelings and acts provided by these exceptional individuals are not ultimately appreciated by the community, then the solitary insights have little more than the value of personal comfort. For William James, religion begins with the individual, but does not end there: Once again there is, within American religious philosophy, a transaction between individual innovation and community solidarity.

The Christ and the community

Among American philosophers, it is Josiah Royce who developed most extensively the idea of Christian community. Communities have psychologies of their own, says Royce in *The Problem of Christianity*, and "are no more a topic for mystical insight, or for fantastic speculation, than is the mental existence of an individual man." In other words, we can study the psychology of communities just as well – or just as poorly, as Royce implies – as we can study the psychology of individuals. The most important concept in Royce's social psychology is the concept of loyalty, since it distinguishes a religious community from a merely natural social group. A religious community – the Beloved Community in Royce's words – links "many highly self-conscious and mutually estranged social individuals in one," without excluding the importance of significant individuals. In fact, the bond between members of a community requires "some potent and loyal individual, acting as leader," who "first declares that for him it is real." So for Royce, the community depends on a individual savior, namely a Christ figure – the vine that accounts for the unity of the various branches.

Cornel West believes this idea of an individual uniting the community is well exemplified in African-American Christianity. In "Prophetic Christian as Organic Intellectual: Martin Luther King, Jr," West writes that "the Christocentric language of the black church exemplifies the intimate and dependent personal relationship between God and individual and between God and a world-forsaken people." This idea is particularly relevant to traditionally oppressed racial communities, who are hindered both by institutional barriers and by existential despair. The religious attitude that developed as a response to this oppression is neither escapist – focusing on heaven rather than acknowledging a troubled earthly situation – nor utopian – demanding perfection on earth. It is represented in the pragmatic Christianity of King, who, in the spirit of Royce's savior, was a loyal individual who loves the community when no one else does. The theme of American Christianity as a transaction of individual and community is thus present in the contemporary writings of West. It ranges from the emigrant Europeans living precariously on a boat to the New World, to people of color living day-to-day on the streets of inner-city America. Each requires an individual savior to bring the community together.

Further reading

Edwards, Jonathan. "Sinners in the Hands of an Angry God" in Stuart Rosenbaum (ed.) *Pragmatism and Religion: Classical Sources and Original Essays.* Urbana, IL: University of Illinois Press, 2003.

Emerson, Ralph Waldo. *Selected Writings.* New York: Random House, 1992.

James, Henry. *Christianity the Logic of Creation.* New York: Appleton, 1857.

James, William. *The Varieties of Religious Experience: A Study in Human Nature.* Cambridge, MA: Harvard University Press, 1985.

Royce, Josiah. *The Problem of Christianity,* Foreword by Frank M. Oppenheim. Washington, DC: The Catholic University of America Press, 2001.

West, Cornel. "Prophetic Christian as Organic Intellectual: Martin Luther King, Jr" in *A Cornel West Reader.* New York: Basic Books, 1999.

Winthrop, John. "A Model of Christian Charity" in Stuart Rosenbaum (ed.) *Pragmatism and Religion: Classical Sources and Original Essays.* Urbana, IL: University of Illinois Press, 2003.

TADD RUETENIK

CIVIL DISOBEDIENCE

Civil disobedience is the act of deliberately violating a government's law to protest injustice. It is often done to protest a specific law as unjust. For instance, Southern blacks deliberately sat at segregated lunch counters in Woolworth stores in the 1960s and ordered food, even though the local and state segregation laws prohibited it. Civil disobedience may also be carried out in protest of a law just in itself being used to protect policies considered unjust. In Birmingham, Alabama, in 1963, the Reverend Martin Luther King, Jr, led blacks in protest, violating court injunctions which barred public demonstrations protesting segregation laws. King argued that the First Amendment to the Constitution gives the people the rights to peacefully assemble and to petition the government for redress of grievances.

Standards for judging a law unjust

It is usually claimed that a positive law is unjust because it violates a higher law. King's very influential 1963 "Letter from Birmingham Jail" lists these six ways that one may know a law is unjust: (1) the man-made law opposes the moral law or the law of God; (2) the human law contradicts natural law or eternal law; this was taught by St Thomas Aquinas in his influential "Treatise on Law"; (3) the positive law degrades human personality instead of uplifting it; (4) the law made by a majority compels obedience from the minority but none from the majority; (5) the faulty law is inflicted on a minority that had no say in making the law; (6) the law is just on its face, but unjust in its application, like King's violation of the Birmingham injunction denying a parade permit to blacks.

American law grew out of English law. The legal positivist John Austin, in *The Province of Jurisprudence Determined* (1832), taught that none of these are adequate legal defenses for breaking a law. He taught that the only valid law in a polity is the command of a political superior to a subject, and the political superiors are those who have the power to punish disobedience.

It is sometimes asserted that one may disobey laws that violate one's conscience, but conscience is so subjective and can be so capriciously formed that this justification for civil disobedience is not widely accepted.

Civil vs criminal disobedience

There is the tendency to contrast the civil disobedience of good people with the criminal disobedience of bad people. As this contrast is often developed, the civil disobedient never breaks a law prohibiting what is evil in itself, seeks some public benefit, is not violent, breaks the law openly, does not try to evade arrest, and accepts trial and punishment. Often none of these are true of the criminal disobedient. The ordinary criminal violates the rights of persons or destroys property, seeks selfish gain, physically injures, acts on the sly, strives to escape arrest, denies guilt in court, and seeks to avoid punishment. However, most still would call an act an act of civil disobedience even if it lacked some of these ideal qualities. Thus, in 1968, Fr Daniel Berrigan, SJ, broke into a draft board and burned draft files to protest the Vietnamese war, yet this is considered civil disobedience.

Debated points

It is thus debated to what degree civil disobedience must be violent or non-violent, accepting or avoiding of arrest and punishment, and even whether it is legal or illegal. For instance, consider the way American law prohibiting the sale of artificial contraceptives was changed. A married couple were recruited to go to a doctor and get advice about, and a prescription for, artificial contraception, even though doing so violated the law. The police were notified in advance and were present to observe. The police arrested, and the local prosecutor took it to trial and obtained a conviction. The law-breakers appealed. The case went all the way to the US Supreme Court, as Griswold v. Connecticut, and, in 1965, the law prohibiting the sale of artificial contraceptives was found unconstitutional. Thus this deliberate act of civil disobedience turned out not to be illegal.

History of the phrase and tactic

The phrase "civil disobedience" seems to have been first used in 1866 as the title of Henry David Thoreau's famous essay. This was four years after his death and the essay was first presented as a lecture titled, "On the Relation of the Individual to the State." Thoreau's act of civil disobedience was his refusal to pay a tax as his act of protest of the Mexican War, a war he considered fought to extend slavery. For his disobedience, he spent a night in the village jail, until Ralph Waldo Emerson paid the tax for him and he was released. Mahatma Gandhi, inspired by Thoreau, led the movement for India's independence using civil disobedience as a method of non-violent revolution in winning India's independence from Britain. The movement succeeded in 1947. The success of this effort has had the contemporary result of making non-violent resistance an attractive pacifistic alternative to war.

Probably the third most important figure in the development of non-violent civil disobedience was Martin Luther King, Jr. His influence in restraining the black civil rights movement of the 1960s was responsible for its enormous success in rendering segregation unconstitutional. King's tactics were an important motive force in great gains for blacks in better and integrated public schooling, voting rights, access to public office, hotel and restaurant accommodations, opportunities in higher education, and employment. The murder of King in 1968 prevented his possible success in using the tactic to stop the Vietnamese war and achieve economic rights for blacks to relieve their poverty.

Developments in civil disobedience

Since the civil rights movement of the 1960s, there have been two developments in the use of civil disobedience. First, it was long associated with the political left, but the political right has learned to use it too, for instance in illegally praying in public schools. Second, police forces have learned to be very accommodating to many acts of civil disobedience, for instance as mothers block traffic at an intersection near their children's school in demanding the installation of a traffic light.

Further reading

Betz, Joseph. "Can Civil Disobedience Be Justified?" *Social Theory and Practice* I, 2 (1970): 13–30.

Fischer, Louis (ed.) *The Essential Gandhi*. New York: Vintage Books, 1962.

King, Martin Luther, Jr. "Letter from Birmingham Jail," 1963; available at http://www.thekingcenter.org/prog/non/Letter.pdf (accessed 14 May 2007).

Thoreau, Henry David. "Civil Disobedience," 1866; available at http://thoreau.eserver.org/civil.html (accessed 14 May 2007).

JOSEPH BETZ

CIVIL WAR

As a watershed event in American history, the Civil War likewise marked a turning point in American philosophy. The manner in which philosophy had been practiced in the antebellum United States, the structure of the discipline, and, indeed, its place within nineteenth-century intellectual culture were utterly transformed. What exactly was the nature of this transformation and why did it occur? Moreover, in what respects did the Civil War act as its catalyst? In order to gain insight into these questions, we must first get a sense of the character of American philosophy prior to the war.

Pre-war American philosophy

During the first half of the nineteenth century, Bruce Kuklick notes, "American colleges were small, sleepy institutions, peripheral to the life of the nation" (2001: 2). Philosophy courses often were taught by holders of chairs or college presidents at the behest of divinity-school theologians, mainly Unitarian in affiliation, and the most serious of (primarily New England) parish ministers. They centered on supporting natural theology, whereby a reconciliation of faith with science was sought to explain how nature, as the unfolding of a divine idea, could be understood through the acquisition of empirical knowledge. Also covered were questions of ethics, with Unitarianism stressing humanity's inherent goodness. Outside the academy, Emerson popularized Boston Transcendentalism, or the doctrine that truth transcends the physical world and is realizable only through intuition or an appeal to individual conscience rather than through the dogmas of established religion or empirical investigation.

Not only did the horrors of the Civil War lead to a rejection of the Unitarian ethic and the Transcendentalist appeal to conscience. They also made the intellectual ground of the time fertile for the reception of an entirely new way of conceiving of the relationship between religion and science. And the unleashing of industrialism and national expansion, held in check for decades by the debate over slavery, brought new difficulties and the need for a novel mode of thought to deal with them. It is hereby unsurprising that the structure of the academy was to undergo a drastic change.

Professionalization of the discipline

Union soldiers often went to war with every intention of upholding Northern values. Yet, among the most useful lessons they learned was that soldiers who understood the mechanics of battle fought more effectively and more bravely than those who were motivated chiefly by enthusiasm for the cause. The war, that is, brought about a newfound admiration for professionalism at the expense of purity of faith. The former saved lives and brought victories.

This push for professionalization deeply penetrated academia after the war. The primacy of divinity schools in the scholarly world ended, and the explicitly Protestant thought that governed American philosophy all but disappeared. Theologians lost control of education to academic administrators. The founding of a litany of private universities and public land-grant institutions, along with the rise of discipline-specific academic journals, played a significant role in this regard. Philosophy came into its own as a technical discipline in distinction from theology and the natural and social sciences, and the professional philosopher gained a level of esteem within intellectual circles once reserved for clerics. In the process, the first form of philosophy native to American academia – pragmatism – was born.

Pragmatism

Pragmatism emerged just after reconstruction. While it took several decades to coalesce into a discernible philosophical form, it was designed from the first, Louis Menand states, to "put Americans into a better relation with the conditions of modern life" (2001: xi). This included, notably, responding to the reception of Darwinism into the scientific landscape.

If the Civil War represented anything to the American mind, it represented a fundamental failure of prevailing ideas to cope with immediate events. This explains at least in part why, after the war, the intellectual community was highly receptive to an entirely new conception of the nature of ideas. This conception arose from Darwin's theory of natural selection, whereby species are to be understood not as immutable kinds. Most noteworthy about species are the processes of adaptation to environmental conditions that lead to their variation. Changes in nature occur in accordance with the reproductive success of the better adapted rather than with a supernatural plan.

Correspondingly, the central theme of pragmatism is that ideas themselves operate within processes of human adaptation. They are not "out there" waiting to be discovered but are instead "instruments," as William James declares. They are useful to us "*just insofar as they help us to get into satisfactory relation with other parts of our experience*" (1975: 34). Moreover, John Dewey remarks, the test of their validity "is found in the consequences of the acts to which the ideas lead, that is in the new arrangements of things which are brought into existence" (1984: 109). Ideas are hereby to be treated as modes of action geared toward coping with a changing and, at best, semi-hospitable world. The mind is not an entity but a function, not that which has being but a form of doing. And experience is nothing other than the ongoing test of the adaptability of our patterns of thought.

To regard ideas as fixed instead of malleable not only represents a failure to understand the place of humanity in the world. It threatens to allow ideas to crystallize into ideologies that can become the basis for causes defended by a call to arms. Ideologies all too easily breed violence and even lead to national suicide.

Conclusion

The Civil War taught Americans in the starkest of terms that ideas have consequences. Among the most significant consequences of the ideas cultivated by American intellectuals in its wake were that science rightly superseded religious authority as the dominant discourse inside the academy, universities could serve as the primary repositories of knowledge in an increasingly complex society and train persons to serve those seeking to cope with this complexity, and philosophy had an independent role to play in this regard. By the close of the nineteenth century, American philosophy in particular had achieved an identity of its own – one intended to prevent the nation from driving itself to the brink of extinction ever again.

Further reading

Dewey, John. *The Quest for Certainty, John Dewey: The Later Works, Vol. 4, 1929*. Carbondale, IL: Southern Illinois State University, 1984 [1929].

Hall, G. Stanley. "Philosophy in the United States," *Mind* 4 (1879): 89–105.

James, William. "The Moral Equivalent of War" in *Memories and Studies*, New York: Longmans, Green, 1911, pp. 267–96.

—— *Pragmatism* and *The Meaning of Truth*. Cambridge, MA: Harvard University Press, 1975 [1907].

Kuklick, Bruce. *A History of Philosophy in America: 1720–2000*. New York: Oxford University Press, 2001.

McPherson, James M. *What They Fought For: 1861–1865*. New York: Doubleday, 1994.

Menand, Louis. *The Metaphysical Club*. New York: Farrar, Strauss, and Giboux, 2001.

ANDREW F. SMITH

CLASSIFICATION

Classification is the process of grouping individuals into classes and then classes into higher classes. Aristotle is generally credited with first developing a theory of classification. Many, such as Whitehead in *Science and the Modern World*, view classification as typifying a science in its early development, but quantification typifying a science in its mature development.

Charles S. Peirce was interested in the classification of inferences and the sciences. He classified inferences as "Deduction or inference *a priori*, Induction or inference *a particularis*, and Hypothesis or inference *a posteriori*." He rejects natural classification in the sense of there being some one and only correct classificatory scheme for any given area of investigation. Rather, classification is always relative to some problem being addressed. Induction allows us to identify common characteristics on the basis of which we can establish useful classifications.

Classification of the sciences should follow from classification in logic. Thus Peirce is interested in organizing the sciences, not in terms of what they study, but how they study or make inferences. Under the deductive sciences or those whose objective is to trace out consequences he places mathematics, law, and political economy. Under the inductive, and thus classificatory, sciences he places natural history, descriptive astronomy, chemistry, logic, philosophy, physiognomy, and physical geography. Under the hypothetic sciences he places physics, mechanics, history, and geology.

While Peirce occasionally indicated that he thought mathematics might be an inductive and thus classificatory science, Josiah Royce views classification as the very heart of mathematics. If exactly defined classifications are at the heart of number theory and geometry, then the opposition between classification and quantification is false.

John Dewey, much like Peirce, viewed classification as always relative to some purpose or end. Different systems of classification serve different ends. Classifications that aid a woodworker are different from classifications that aid a botanist. Classifications are good if they promote convenience, economy and efficiency. Classifications also have heuristic value. They suggest what we should look for in particular cases and what gaps in a classificatory scheme might be filled in the future.

C.I. Lewis developed a technical concept of classification, distinguishing it from a class. Membership in a class is restricted to what exists, while a classification includes all things that a term might correctly apply to, whether it exists or not. Membership in a class includes everything a term denotes. A classification includes everything comprehended by a term. Lewis remains fully within the pragmatic tradition in that there are multiple classificatory systems, the choice among which is a matter of what is useful.

Further reading

Lewis, C.I. *Collected Papers of Clarence Irving Lewis*, ed. John D. Goheen and John L. Mothershead, Jr. Stanford, CA: Stanford University Press, 1970.

Whitehead, A.N. *Science and the Modern World*. New York: Free Press, 1997 [1925].

DAVID L. ROUSE

COBB, JOHN B., JR

John B. Cobb, Jr (1925–) has been one of the leading interpreters and developers of the philosophy of organism developed by Alfred North Whitehead. Cobb is primarily a theologian, but his commitment to the philosophical achievement of Whitehead as a foundation for theological understanding has not only involved him in interpreting and developing the Whiteheadian categories, it has also deeply influenced his theological orientation. His output has been prodigious; to date he has written twenty-one books, coauthored seven more, edited or coedited eight collections of articles, and produced literally hundreds of articles on his own. A few of his books most relevant for philosophers will be cited below in the bibliography.

Born in Japan 9 February 1925, the youngest of the three children of missionary parents, Cobb lived the first fourteen years of his life primarily in Hiroshima and Kobe. In 1939 he returned to the United States to complete high school and start college. At nineteen he joined the United States Army and served/studied in the Army's Japanese language program. In 1947 he was once again a civilian and entered the University of Chicago, where he selected an interdepartmental program of study. After one year, still well shy of a BA, he entered the University of Chicago Divinity School, receiving his MA degree in 1949 and the PhD in 1952.

When Cobb entered the Chicago Divinity School, Whitehead's philosophy had already arrived, carried there by two brilliant, forceful interpreters, Henry Nelson Wieman and Charles Hartshorne. Wieman's interpretation stressed the naturalistic side of Whitehead's thought, whereas Hartshorne emphasized the metaphysical elements there. Cobb threw in his lot with the Hartshorne orientation and, with Hartshorne as his dissertation advisor, argued in his thesis that faith and theology are not independent of philosophical speculation, a stance in opposition to thinkers like Wieman, Schleiermacher, and Tillich.

Cobb began his teaching career in a small junior college in Georgia. From 1953 to 1958 he was on the faculty at the Candler School of Theology at Emory University. In 1958 he went to the School of Theology at Claremont as the Ingraham Professor of Theology, where he served until his retirement in 1990. In 1971 he was instrumental in launching the journal *Process Studies*, and in 1973, with the support of the Claremont complex, he and David Ray Griffin founded the Center for Process Studies. The Center now houses what is undoubtedly the world's finest collection of books and articles dealing with process thought and also sponsors many national and international conferences; it also supports resident scholars who need to use the collection for their research.

Cobb's third book, *A Christian Natural Theology: Based on the Thought of Alfred North Whitehead*, is his most significant contribution to philosophy and philosophical theology. In it he argues his fundamental conviction that theology requires philosophical underpinning, defends his choice of process philosophy as the far-and-away most appropriate underpinning for Christianity, and does a marvelously clear-headed job of explicating, and modifying where necessary, the complex fabric of Whitehead's mature philosophical speculation.

In the 1970s, without abandoning his prior interests, Cobb became very involved with issues in the field of ecology. Whitehead's metaphysics emphasizes the notion of relatedness: building upon the prominence of this feature of his philosophical and theological understanding, Cobb wrote books and articles focusing upon the environment and, especially, the relationship between economic growth and ecological sustainability.

Further reading

Cobb, John B., Jr. *The Structure of Christian Existence.* Philadelphia, PA: Westminster, 1967.

—— *God and the World.* Philadelphia, PA: Westminster, 1969.

—— *Is It Too Late? A Theology of Ecology.* Denton, TX: Environmental Ethics Books, 1971; revised edition, 1995.

Cobb, John B., Jr, and Daly, Herman. *For the Common Good: Redirecting the Economy Toward Community, Environment and a Sustainable Future.* Boston, MA: Beacon Press, 1989; revised edition, 1994.

Don Sherburne

COHEN, MORRIS RAPHAEL

Morris Raphael Cohen (1880–1947) was born in Minsk, Russia, and emigrated to the United States in 1892. He graduating from the City College of New York in 1900, and earned a doctorate from Harvard in 1906. He was appointed an instructor in mathematics at City College in 1906 before transferring to the Department of Philosophy in 1912. He remained at City College until 1938, when he became a professor at the University of Chicago. Illness forced his retirement in 1941.

"My philosophic studies have been somewhat restricted to the logic of mathematical physics and applied ethics, and on epistemologic problems I can speak only with an innocence which I trust may not be regarded as too childish" ("The Distinction between the Mental and the Physical," *Studies in Philosophy and Science*, New York: Henry Holt, 1949: 90). This self-description understates Cohen's achievements. He was a systematic philosopher who moved easily through detailed analyses of science, philosophy, history, law, and social policy. He believed that nature has a decided form, and that scientific method – competing, testable hypotheses – is the only effective way to study it. No hypothesis is more than probable, but truth is our aim. Cohen's realism was usually emphatic: the existence and character of things are independent of our ways of knowing them. Logic and sufficient reason (hence causality) are intrinsic to nature, where they constrain everything that is or can be; nature is replete with possibilities, most unrealized. His principle of polarity affirms that there is "necessary opposition in all determinate effects ... [E]very static, but also every kinetic, system involves a balance or equilibrium which makes description in the form of equations applicable" (*Studies in Philosophy and Science* p. 12).

Cohen's ethics expressed his belief that humans flourish best in a rational order that mitigates conflict and maximizes opportunities for self-expression. Natural law is an immanent constraint and an ideal: it limits and promotes conditions for well-being. Positive laws appropriate to this constraint are formulated after empirical investigations that identify human wants and aspirations. But, "No doctrine of natural law can claim a greater degree of certainty and completeness than attaches to the basic ethical principles which it presupposes" (*Reason and Nature* p. 414). Cohen located these ethical principles in the ideal of justice. Yet, there is a mismatch between this ideal and the means for knowing and achieving it. Altruism turns pragmatic when the ideal evades us, for there is no accord about justice: is it local to a time and place, or universal? Law fills the breach:

> [L]aw must be, as it is, in large part a special technique for determining what would otherwise be uncertain and subject to conflict. It is socially necessary to have a rule of the road but it is morally indifferent whether it requires us to turn to the right or to the left.
>
> (*Reason and Nature* p. 420)

This willingness to accommodate one's circumstances – seek the principles of natural law, but accept practical solutions – was also apparent in his metaphysics. Writing of mind and body, wanting to affirm that mental activities may be bodily without being able to conceive how this might be, Cohen sabotaged his realism: "anything may be said to exist in a given universe of discourse if it can be shown that it occupies a position therein" (*Studies in Philosophy and Science* p. 97). This anticipation of Carnap and Quine, written in 1917, was anomalous, but not an aberration. For Cohen's realism was also compromised in this other way. A reader once questioned his exposition of special relativity: are things shortened in the direction of motion, or do they merely appear shortened? Cohen responded by taking cover in Einstein's operationalism (*Studies in Philosophy and Science* pp. 241–2).

Cohen expressed these competing emphases while frequently citing Aristotle's distinction between that which is first in knowledge and that which is first in being. This could have been entrée to a comprehensive metaphysics of nature, or, more modestly, a sharp distinction between the priorities of knowledge or expression, and the character of things themselves. But Cohen hesitated.

A famous critic – more than a hundred of his papers appraised other thinkers – Cohen had no taste for cleverness, paradox, or mere technical virtuosity. Peirce was his soulmate, Spinoza his inspiration. Cohen cited him when responding indirectly to the claim that Cohen, himself, said little that was new: "Spinoza never valued ideas for their novelty, and had no hankering to be the founder of a new system of philosophy" (*The Faith of a Liberal*, New York: Henry Holt, 1946: 13). Cohen was the belligerent opponent to all the truisms of his time: intuitionism, not hypothesis, was thought to be the style appropriate to all knowledge; the external world was said to have no thinkable properties; logic was thought to be a syntactic calculus; mind and body were said to be categorially different; justifications for morality were transcendental, theological, or emotivist, without foundation in the details of human character and struggle. Was it originality, or mere courage, to affirm that "logic is the simplest chapter in ontology" (*Studies in Science and Philosophy* p. 150), that sufficient reason and causality are intrinsic to natural processes, that truth is correspondence, that mind is very likely a function of matter, that humans are remarkable among animals for being perfectible though justice would require our perfection?

Further reading

Cohen, Morris. *American Thought: A Critical Sketch*. Glencoe, IL: The Free Press, 1954.

—— *Law and the Social Order: Essays in Legal Philosophy*. Hamden, CT: Archon Books, 1967 [1933].

—— *Reason and Nature: An Essay on the Meaning of Scientific Methods*, second edition. New York: Dover, 1978 [first edition 1931].

Cohen, Morris and Drabkin, I.E. *Source Book in Greek Science*. Cambridge, MA: Harvard University Press, 1948.

David Weissman

COLUMBIA NATURALISM

John Stuart Mill's conception of nature set the pattern for naturalism at Columbia. If nature is *all that is*, then there can be nothing outside it. To suggest that something is supernatural is an oxymoron. The supernatural – if there is that – can neither affect nor effect anything within nature, for if it did, it would be *connected* with nature, detected and known, and be *part of* all that is. Since what is truly supernatural can have no connection with anything in nature, it can be no different than if it did not exist. It is also to say that it *is unknowable.* Hence, how can one claim to be supernaturally inspired or have a revelation? Woodbridge and Dewey initiated naturalism at Columbia. Since the supernatural was sometimes taken to be concerned only with theistic views, they preferred an even broader distinction, that of the natural and the non-natural.

The natural and the non-natural were the supreme example of a chasm separating two areas that knowledge could not bridge. There were other such unbridgeable dualisms which naturalists abhorred – Descartes' mind–body dualism, and those of British empiricism. "The attempt to construct knowledge out of mental states, the relations between ideas, and the relation of ideas to things, has been . . . decidedly without profit," said Woodbridge (*Nature and Mind*). "Mental activity is part of the physical world. Ideas are a revelation of the world . . . in consequence of our contacts with the world, but in no sense likenesses of anything" (*Realm of Mind*). Woodbridge and his followers took the encountered world as primary. The subject-matter of inquiry cannot be called in question (*Nature and Mind*). "Reality," was *not* to be conceived as partly, or wholly, lying behind "appearances."

Naturalists also rejected a distinction about what is permissible and not permissible for us to know. There is a long tradition warning humans about trying to know too much, as exemplified in stories about Pandora's Box, of Adam and Eve, and, "Curiosity killed a cat." Naturalists were sympathetic to the *Nicomachean Ethics*, especially where Aristotle exhorted mankind not to listen to those who say, "O man, remember your mortality, think as a man should." Instead, he urged, "Leave nothing unattempted in the desire to know."

Naturalism has seemed to many to imply atheism, and although some naturalistic philosophers like Nagel have defended atheism, there have been other naturalists, like Randall, who have been religious. Naturalism can accommodate religion as long as it does not claim that its authority is supernatural and beyond our comprehension. Randall found no conflict between religion and science; the conflict is between older scientific beliefs that have become enshrined as religious beliefs and new science. Randall thought that religion is neither true nor false; it is adequate or inadequate in its functions, namely consecration, celebration, and moral clarification. In "Natural Teleology," Woodbridge denied that the universe tended toward some unitary outcome.

The early Santayana, who wrote the *Life of Reason*, was admired as a naturalist, and often quoted. Woodbridge was impressed by Santayana's estimate of Aristotle. In Aristotle, everything ideal had a natural basis and everything natural had an ideal fulfillment a mantra for subsequent Columbia naturalists such as Ernest Nagel and Justus Buchler, who often cited Santayana.

Dewey represented the pragmatist strain in Columbian naturalism (variously called experimentalism or instrumentalism). He found the notion of truth so emotionally beclouded that rather than talk about "truth," he preferred to talk about reliably warranted conclusions – the result of competent empirical inquiry. Part of naturalism was its admiration of the hypothetical–deductive–experimental method of science; it was not only fertile but also public (anyone could repeat its operations to see if one could come to the same conclusions); it was self-corrective and did not perpetuate error (as could occur with authoritarian methods). Dewey's *Logic: The Theory of Inquiry*, in 500 pages, saw inquiry (particularly scientific inquiry) as important, especially in the reinterpretation and reconstruction of human experience.

John Herman Randall, Jr, combined Aristotelian functionalism (learned from Woodbridge) and Deweyan pragmatism. Both were compatible, even though each was cast in a different conceptual vocabulary. Randall pointed out that in Aristotle, *to be* was to be an ousia, which was (1) to be something you could point to; (2) to be a subject of discourse; and (3) to be the outcome of a process of change, i.e. the characteristics of "substance." These characteristics were in contrast to Cartesian substance which "inhered" in things, but was (1) nothing you could point to; (2) nothing which could be described; and (3) that which endured unchanged during a process of change – each one non-natural and unknowable.

In *The Structure of Science* Nagel described science as an institutionalized art of inquiry, achieving generalized theoretical knowledge, and which has emancipated men's minds from ancient superstitions and the hard crust of unreasoned custom. Nagel, along with Randall, downplayed their underlying Deweyan pragmatism. Randall subsumed pragmatism under functionalism. As editors of the *Journal of Philosophy*, not wanting to seem wedded to a particular position, they avoided calling themselves pragmatists. Nevertheless, they adhered to certain pragmatist views. Instead of talking about truth in their writing, they preferred to speak of "reliably warranted conclusions."

In "Naturalism Reconsidered" Nagel stated that philosophy at its best is a critical commentary upon existence and upon our claims to have knowledge of it. Its mission is to illuminate what is obscure in experience and its objects. There is no one "big thing" which, if known, would make everything else coherent and unlock the mystery of creation. Nagel then offered two theses central to naturalism. The first is the existential and causal primacy of organized matter. It is one of the best-tested conclusions of experience. There is no place for disembodied forces directing the course of events, no place for the survival of personality after the corruption of the body. Second, naturalists give their allegiance to the method of modern empirical science because it appears to be the most assured way of achieving reliable knowledge.

Naturalism offers no cosmic consolation for the unmerited defeats and undeserved sufferings which all men experience. Human reason is potent only against evils that are remediable. The actual limitations of rational effort do not warrant a romantic despair, blind to possibilities implicit in the exercise of disciplined reason for realizing human excellence.

Justus Buchler thought that "being," "reality," and "existence," and other terms of generic identification, suffer from many disadvantages and perplexities. He introduced the notion: "whatever is, in whatever way, is a natural complex," which "permits satisfactory generic identification ... [and] encourages ... generalizing precisely and portraying uniquely." "The essential philosophical direction is from differentiation to generalization." He was pluralistic; a natural complex "does not suggest a finished collectivity or an absolutely determinate whole." The idea of nature "implies the perennial conceivability of complexes more inclusive than any that is dealt with." Nature is "providingness."

Most of the succeeding generation of philosophers educated at Columbia were perfunctory in their naturalism. Philosophy was no longer taught by former ministers; Naturalism did not need to be professed. Many were enamored with new fashions like analytic philosophy. However, in this century, when one considers the resurgence of religious fundamentalism, naturalism will probably resurface as a counterweight – initially as secularism.

Further reading

Dewey, John. *Logic: The Theory of Inquiry.* New York: Henry Holt, 1938.

—— *Experience and Nature.* New York: Dover, 1958.

Nagel, Ernest. *The Structure of Science: Problems in the Logic of Scientific Explanation.* New York: Harcourt, Brace, 1961.

Nagel, Ernest and Cohen, Morris Raphael. *Introduction to Logic and Scientific Method.* New York: Harcourt, Brace, 1934.

Randall, John Herman, Jr. *Nature and Historical Experience.* New York: Columbia University Press, 1958.

Randall, John Herman, Jr, and Buchler, Justus. *Philosophy: An Introduction.* New York: Barnes and Noble, 1971.

Singer, Beth. *Ordinal Naturalism: An Introduction to the Philosophy of Justus Buchler.* Lewisburg, PA: Bucknell, 1983.

Talisse, Robert. *On Dewey: The Reconstruction of Philosophy.* Belmont, CA: Wadsworth, 2000.

Woodbridge, Frederick. *The Realm of Mind.* New York: Columbia University Press, 1926.

—— *Nature and Mind.* New York: Columbia University Press, 1937.

Angelo Juffras

COMMUNICATION

Communication is widely known to be among the ideas that form the core conceptual battery of the pragmatic philosophical tradition. Of course the notorious plurality of "pragmatisms" – thirteen by Arthur O. Lovejoy's count in his famous article "The Thirteen Pragmatisms" – can only have increased with time, and the ensuing diversity of pragmatic thought makes it difficult to distill this concept into a singular formulation (Lovejoy 1908). That is to say, articulating the meaning of this concept from a pragmatic perspective in an encyclopedic fashion itself begs the kind of genealogical or genetic reconstruction that serves as a pillar of pragmatism, methodologically speaking. This article, therefore, will chronologically proceed through the classical pragmatists, Peirce, Mead, and Dewey, outlining the contributions to a pragmatic conception of communication interspersing this presentation with the extension of this concept by more recent pragmatic thinkers.

Communication as an activity must be located within the pragmatic version of the "primacy of practical reason" thesis. This thesis asserts that all human activity must be circumscribed within the wider constraints of a theory of action. Philosophy, mathematics, logic and reflection generally speaking, then, and the tools, rules, and methods of thought linked to the "problematic situation" are fundamentally practical in their origin and function. Likewise the tools, rules, and methods of thought are linked to a problematic situation and hypothetical in their status. Communication features the interaction of two or more individuals and their ability not only to cope with emergent problems in their action contexts, but to include the projected consequences of the proposed action in a meaningful way. Communication then, is fundamentally geared towards the sharing of ideas for the purposes of addressing a problem, whether it be understood in ways that are expressive of an individual's unique perspective, identity and interests; instrumental with regard to selecting the most efficient means to achieving an agreed-upon end; or regulative with regard to the legitimacy of ends and action ideals themselves. Communication is the means and end of reflective activity in its various guises.

C.S. Peirce

The *structure* of communication is a concern, as well, for the pragmatists. The sign theory of Peirce, the founder of semiotics, goes a long way to providing a schematic backdrop to communication that is rooted in a sign's behavior. Peirce's innovation loosens it from traditional understandings of sign-signified relations. Along with the sign and the signified, the name and the object of traditional referential semantics at the root of *most* metaphysics and theories of meaning, Peirce introduces the "interpretant," or the "third" as fundamentally constitutive of signification. The importance of this development can be traced through pragmatism in various ways. This notion of sign theory is important for tracing the concept of communication in at least two ways.

(1) In introducing the interpretant; that a sign-signified event is always for some interpreter, else how could the signifying function come about in the first place? That signs are *for* some interpreter wrenches the referential function of signification out of its static two-place relation and is transformed by the inclusion of an interpreter, a third, for whom the reference exists. Thus, communication is inscribed into the event of signification, a conclusion that Peirce, according to one interpreter, extended too far into what might be considered a re-enchantment of nature.

(2) The sign relation includes within its very structure the future directed and conditional character meaning of concepts dependent upon further communication. That there is a temporal component to the meaning of our concepts, whose basis is the sign function, is not only a pillar of the sign–object–interpretant relationship but also at the heart of the pragmatic theory of meaning. As Peirce wrote later in his life in "Issues of Pragmaticism" (1958) regarding the meaning of our concepts, "The entire intellectual purport of any symbol consists in the total of all general modes of rational conduct which, conditionally upon all the possible different circumstances and desires, would ensue upon the acceptance of the symbol."

Peirce is famous for noting that the progress of inquiry and the regulative ideal of truth serve to substantiate the idea that the community of inquirers will converge on the truth "in the long run." The scientific method, shot through with fallibilism due to, among other things, the necessarily limited, if objective, perspective of any individual inquirer, requires communication, for experimentation, verification, and justification of any claim.

Communication then has an effect on the meaning of words and the meaning of the world of which those signs are cognizant. A worry slips in here, however, that Jürgen Habermas has referred to as "semiotic idealism" in his essay "Peirce and Communication" (Habermas 1992). If indeed we have general theory of signs, and each sign is a sign for some other sign and for some interpretant, as Peirce writes in "Some Consequences of Four Incapacities," then the interpretant for which any sign exists, then the natural world, seems to be at base communicative; a conclusion that rings too closely to the medieval worldview of the book of nature for many contemporary pragmatists (Peirce 1958). For what do we construct our understanding of the "interpretant" above in term of our generalizing capabilities except a sufficiently universal theory of signs, a "semiosis of nature" that could interpret the scientific findings in terms of their relevance for the progress of inquiry until it converges in the long run (Habermas 1992)? There may have been excesses in Peirce's claims for the accomplishments of the regulative ideal of truth for an unlimited communication community in terms of defining and understanding ultimate reality. But at least the interdependence Peirce demonstrated between a communication community and reality shows that the necessarily perspectival character of all experience and the limitation upon our faculties requires the agent to engage in communication for the purposes of settling doubt. Else how would agents be able to organize their formulations and improve their scientific understanding? Peirce's communication community is thus aptly phrased as a "metaphysics of communication" that grounds the pragmatism he sets forth (Westbrook 2005).

G.H. Mead

Mead's contributions to the concept of communication are largely rooted in articulating the birth of the self through socialization processes that serve as the touchstone for an analysis and development of symbolic interaction that at once enshrines the ability to communicate in the ontogenetic structure of human selfhood, and at the same time offers foundations for extrapolating from this theory for wider purposes. Specifically, Mead argues that the emergence of the self from an undifferentiated collection of impulses and instincts is made possible by the internalization of the perspectives of another individual, whom they encounter in the aforementioned problematic situation. In this situation, it is crucial to emphasize the emergence of communication in a situation of social cooperation (Joas 1985). This perspective is not just an additional epistemological access point to the situation at hand. The crucial aspect of this perspective is that it includes a perspective on the agent themselves as they project how they would appear to the other person. Thus the interaction with the other is a necessary component of selfhood and this selfhood is in turn dependent upon a communicative act. Communication is that act that is made in lieu of this reflective consciousness of not only the possible actions of the other in a situation complex, but how their own actions will be perceived by the other. This internalization of another's view on one's action is constitutive of self-consciousness and the normative expectations that the agent carries with them in the action contexts that follow. In addition, Mead offers not only the internalization of a second-person perspective, but in addition generates an intersubjectively general perspective out of these two. The nature of this perspective encompasses the "you," the "I," and the "we," where "we" includes all potential participants in the communication at hand, and thus in the problem context.

While there are capacities-specific issues, in terms of the condition of the possibility of communication itself depending upon some type of *a priori* structures be they read in terms of imagination, the body in terms of factical meaning, or language, Mead does not want to offer such hypostases. The concrete issuance of individuality through this socialization and communication process is irreducible. It is clear that the later, though less remarked-upon, writings of Mead on such themes as temporality, metaphysics, and metaphilosophy bear out a much richer picture of the philosophical issues that accompany his theory of intersubjectivity than the "highlights" that are handed down à la slogans such as "individualization through socialization" denotes. Communication, again, finds its genesis in cooperative interaction that simultaneously generates individuals through the multiplication of perspectives on self, other, and a general perspective on both.

John Dewey

John Dewey's contribution to a pragmatic understanding of communication is, as is often noted, the most articulate with regard to aesthetic and political considerations. His understanding of the individual, which he notes relies so heavily on G.H. Mead's work, extends the insights of Peirce as well. While Peirce would emphasize the regulative ideal of truth and reality as the *telos* of inquiry, Dewey would emphasize the function of communication as the overcoming of conflicts and felt difficulties for the purposes of realizing our ends-in-view. The communication of these ends-in-view is essential. As the problem situation among individuals, rooted as it is in the overflowing impulses, clashing interests and implicit ideals guiding action, problematic situations, the very nexus and font of real inquiry, cannot be got at except through communication. Through the communicative exchange of the frustrated interests that create the situation, the elements of the problem come to light and suggest to community of inquiry, through the imaginative flashes of insight Peirce called abduction, hypotheses for action, or in Dewey's terms new ways of seeing old things.

One of the main concerns that inflects Dewey's concept of communication is the ability to abstract from action contexts for the purposes of situation-distant reflection: "There is a natural bridge that joins the gap between existence and essence; namely communication, language, discourse" (Dewey 1926). Communication is enabled by abstraction for the purposes of discussion and reference. This is all inscribed within the adopted pragmatic framework that Peirce sets for pragmatism in the doubt–belief matrix of inquiry set out in "The Fixation of Belief" (Peirce 1958). Peirce himself noted that abstractive observation is a necessary condition for the possibility of communication and Dewey no less emphasizes the pivotal role of abstraction in enabling communication:

Where communication exists, things in acquiring meaning thereby acquire representatives, surrogates, signs and implicates, which are infinitely more amenable to management, more permanent and more accommodating, than events in their first estate. By this fashion, qualitative immediacies cease to be dumbly rapturous, a possession that is obsessive and an incorporation. Likewise, in relation to the agent of communication, much like Mead, Dewey writes "communication is a condition of consciousness" (Dewey 1926). This abstraction, however, is hypothetical. To select out different features of a complex phenomenological problem situation is to hypothesize as to their meaning, in terms of their relevance with regard to the problem at hand and as they suggest or entail a variety of solutions in their isolation.

In addition, communication has a more pronounced politically normative role for Dewey from which, no doubt, Peirce would have recoiled. Communication, in Dewey's hands, becomes the event by which the alienation of contemporary society is overcome. His political and aesthetic theory depends upon an understanding of the fragmentation of experience due to a variety of social forces and draining of creative power of individuals. For Dewey, the separation of aesthetic concerns and lived, everyday experience was one of the great failures of the contemporary division of labor. Thus, the creativity that Mead argues is at the heart of communicative interaction, thereby separating it off from mere stimulus–response behaviorism, is essential for Dewey's understanding of democracy, and communication is the medium of democratic transformation of and is at the root of democracy itself. The work of art embodies this ideal of communication by being locus of both the universal and the particular in terms of the materials out of which it is constructed. "Art is a more universal mode of language than is the speech that exists in a multitude of mutually unintelligible forms" (Dewey 1926). The connection between universal character of aesthetic communication, the normative sense of "experience," and democracy Dewey is presenting is captured quite well when he claims that democracy is the very notion of community itself (Dewey 1927). Communication then at once offers grounds for the critique of the deficits of a given polity and the very medium for its realization:

> If one asks what is meant by experience in this connection my reply is that it is that free interaction of individual human beings with surrounding conditions, especially the human surroundings, which develops and satisfies need and desire by increasing knowledge of things as they are. Knowledge of conditions as they are is the only solid ground for communication and sharing; all other communication means the subjection of some persons to the personal opinion of other persons.
>
> (Dewey 1939)

Further reading

Aboulafia, Mitchell. "George Herbert Mead and The Many Voices of Universality" in Lenore Langsdorf and Andrew R. Smith (eds) *Recovering Pragmatism's Voice: The Classical Tradition, Rorty, and the Philosophy of Communication*. Albany, NY: SUNY Press, 1995, pp. 179–94.

Alexander, Thomas. "John Dewey and the Roots of Democratic Imagination" in Lenore Langsdorf and Andrew R. Smith (eds) *Recovering Pragmatism's Voice: The Classical Tradition, Rorty, and the Philosophy of Communication*. Albany, NY: SUNY Press, 1995, pp. 131–54,

Colapietro, Vincent. "Immediacy, Opposition, and Mediation" in Lenore Langsdorf and Andrew R. Smith (eds) *Recovering Pragmatism's Voice: The Classical Tradition, Rorty, and the Philosophy of Communication*. Albany, NY: SUNY Press, 1995, pp. 23–48.

Dewey, John. "Creative Democracy –The Task Before Us" in *The Later Works of John Dewey, 1925–1953*. Carbondale, IL: Illinois University Press, 1980–90 [1939].

Habermas, Jürgen. "Peirce and Communication" in *Postmetaphysical Thinking*, trans. William Mark Hohengarten. Cambridge, MA: MIT Press, 1992.

Joas, Hans. *G.H. Mead: A Contemporary Re-examination of his Thought*, trans. Hans Joas. Cambridge, MA: MIT Press, 1985.

Langsdorf, Lenore and Andrew R. Smith. *Recovering Pragmatism's Voice: The Classical Tradition, Rorty, and the Philosophy of Communication*. Albany, NY: SUNY Press, 1995.

Lovejoy, Arthur O. "The Thirteen Pragmatisms," *Journal of Philosophy, Psychology and Scientific Methods* V (1908).

Mead, George Herbert. *Mind Self, and Society*, ed. Charles Morris. Chicago, IL: University of Chicago Press, 1934.

Peirce, Charles S. "Some Consequences of Four Incapacities" in *Charles S. Peirce, Selected Writings: Values in a Universe of Chance*, ed. with an introduction and notes by Philip P. Weiner. New York: Dover, 1958, pp. 39–72.

Westbrook, Robert. *Democratic Hope: Pragmatism and the Politics of Truth*. Ithaca, NY: Cornell University Press, 2005.

Brendan Hogan

COMMUNITARIANISM

As a political and social philosophy, communitarianism is a relatively recent and controversial concept. All communitarians stress the value of community, in part as a response to and rejection of atomistic liberal individualism, but this valuing of community can be in support of conservative, progressive or leftist philosophies. Canadian philosopher Will Kymlicka describes two types of communitarians. There are "(t)hose that look backward" who "lament for the decline of community" and who seek to "retrieve a conception of the common good" which limits the role of diversity and which is more common in moral conservativism. There are also what he calls the "forward-looking" communitarians who "seeks new ways to build bonds of community that integrate and accommodate (rather than constrict) our diverse choices and lifestyles" (2002: 271–3). This second form of communitarianism generally embraces progressive reform and democratic dialogue. Kymlicka argues that there are elements of both nostalgic conservativism and forward-looking progressivism in the writings of most communitarian philosophers, as can be seen in American communitarian philosophy and activism.

All communitarian thinkers focus on social commitment and one's responsibility to the communal welfare, stressing the role that community plays in the development of a social "good." Amending the social contract conception of personal rights in continual conflict with social order, communitarian philosophies understand the individual as both the creator and the product of community, dependent on society for full humanity. Communitarians have also argued against the universalism inherent in the liberal ideal of citizenship, advocating instead for a consideration of the traditions and values of particular communities situated in particular historical times.

Although American society was founded in liberal political theory, what is now called "communitarian" experimentalism and philosophy also has a long and rich history in this country. Some place the beginnings of communitarianism in Amitai Etzioni's early 1990s works, while others mark the beginnings of communitarian philosophy with the philosophical critiques of John Rawls' (1971) *A Theory of Justice*, particularly in the work of Charles Taylor, Alasdair McIntyre, Michael Walzer, and Michel Sandel. However it can be argued that communitarian thinking has deep roots in American philosophy and traditions, developing alongside political liberalism in both theory and practice.

The communitarian ideal of cooperative living was tested out in a number of utopian communal societies that explicitly rejected competitive individualism. Many of these societies were religiously based, such as the Oneida or Amana communities, while others were based on economic principles, such as Owen's New Harmony, or in philosophic principles such as the transcendental communities of Fruitlands and Brook Farm. These nineteenth-century communities were laboratories which expressed the desire for communities that promoted unity and growth. In their rejection of atomistic individualism in favor of social unity, principles such as those of the New England transcendentalists established philosophic traditions that later communitarian thinkers built on.

Two conflicting social ideologies grew out of the post-civil war era, the competitive ideal of social Darwinism and cooperative model of society as an interdependent organism. Social Darwinism was an extension of individualistic liberalism which argued that the individual is positioned in a series of competitive relationships with others, in which success was necessary to preserve his or her survival. Along with the laissez-faire capitalism of that era, the competitive individualism of social Darwinism promoted the scramble for materialistic achievement at the expense of other classes and/or individuals. Yet, during this same time, the idea of society as a unified "organic community" had taken hold of the American imagination and was influencing the pragmatist thinkers and activists. American pragmatists from the Progressive era, influenced early and mid-twentieth century American communitarians such as Randolph Bourne, Waldo Frank and Lewis Mumford (Blake 1990).

Similarities with contemporary "forward-thinking" communitarian thought which advocates diversity and deliberative democracy can be seen in classical pragmatist thought (Green 1999: 5). Pragmatist philosophers like Josiah Royce (1855–1916), John Dewey (1859–1952), and Jane Addams (1860–1935) saw the self as inherently social, embedded in and ontologically connected to the larger community. Community for these pragmatists represented the physical locations as well as the human values, social networks and histories of a place. Because pragmatists understand the individual continually developing in interaction with his or her environment, a healthy community establishes the conditions necessary for full humanity. Even philosophical reflective living requires community, according to Dewey. "A man really living alone (alone mentally as well as physically) would have little or no occasion to reflect upon his past experience to extract its net meaning" (1980: 9). Democracy, as expanded and articulated by these pragmatists, describes an interactive and interdependent community, as a way of being in the world with others. As a political system, it ideally provides for egalitarian political representation. As a social system, it provides a basis for shared life. As Dewey said, "A democracy is more than a form of government; it is primarily a mode of associated living, of conjoint communicated experience" (1980: 93).

In 1916, the last year of his life, Josiah Royce said, "the detached individual is an essentially lost being" (1967: 46), and "we are saved by community" (1967: 131). Like other communitarian thinkers Royce rejected ethical individualism as "one great foe of the great community" (1967: 43), but he also rejected utilitarian collectivism which argues for the greatest good for the greatest number. His ideal community is composed of those possessing loyalty or "the devotion of the self to the interests of the community" (1967: 45). He describes the Great Community (which he sometime referred to as the Beloved Community) as a community committed to loyalty and unity, at times referred to in a religious sense, other times as a political and social community. At the beginning of World War I, he emphasized the necessity of an international community. Later thinkers such as Randolph Bourne and Martin Luther King were influenced by Royce's ideal of the Beloved Community.

Jane Addams, the founder of the Hull House settlement house, formulated a communitarian social ethic predicated on an assumption of equality and interaction between various classes and races. The settlement house movement put into practice theories of communitarian ideals; the goals of each house were particular to the communities that it served and the local community members took part in planning the functions of the organization. Like other progressive communitarians, Addams aspired to a community-based ethical democracy that protected pluralistic cultures and cooperative living. For Addams, the value of community required paying attention to diverse voices that compose and recreate public life. In her pragmatist communitarianism, the individual is seen as embedded in the community, not in an adversarial role. She believed that friendship and direct experience of the lives of many diverse others is an essential part of communitarian democracy.

Critics of communitarianism, particularly formulated by conservative thinkers, are concerned that the idea of community requires a sense of belonging based in identity similarities with the norms of a particular group, and isn't adequate to ensure the rights of those who occupy non-dominant positions. An example of this can be found in the feminist critique. Elizabeth Frazer and other feminist critics of communitarian thought are concerned that "preserving community" prioritizes relationships based on dominant norms rather than encouraging multiple voices and divergent opinions. Feminists and gay rights thinkers are skeptical of communitarian calls for the preservation of community values, rightly fearing that those values re-impose a traditional notion of family and/or gender that has isolated women from the political realm or discriminated against non-traditional family dynamics. Communitarian thinking could justify keeping in place the patriarchal and hierarchal structures of older cultural values, ruling out the possibilities of differences and change. Yet, feminists such as Frazer recognize that communitarian philosophy is also consistent with feminism in important ways, such as the emphasis on particulars rather than the distanced universals (1999: 2). Others have pointed out that many of the main ideas of communitarianism are similar to many non-Western philosophies, and point away from hierarchical power hegemonies. "Forward-looking" or progressive communitarianism, such as that proposed by Addams and Dewey, establishes a more inclusive definition of community. For Addams in particular, protecting and listening to diverse views in the community provides a method for creativity and change; she argues that a community's decision-making authority requires a multiplicity of voices for any decision to be authentic, representative and useful.

In the end, the communitarian–liberal debate between community and the individual is rarely an either–or dialogue. Most communitarians take for granted basic individual rights, and don't recommend overthrowing the gains of political liberalism. Yet, communitarian thinkers show us the darker side of Western liberalism, the insufficiency and isolation that can result from thinking of the individual as independent from community. This on-going fruitful dialogue between liberal and communitarian philosophers continues to illustrate tension between individual rights and community values.

Further reading

Addams, Jane. *Democracy and Social Ethics.* Urbana, IL: University of Illinois Press, 2002.

Bell, Daniel. *Communitarianism and Its Critics.* Oxford: Clarendon Press, 1993.

Blake, Casey Nelson. *Beloved Community.* Chapel Hill, NC: University of North Carolina Press, 1990.

Dewey, John. *Democracy and Education* in *The Collected Works of John Dewey: Middle Works, Vol. 9, 1916*, ed. Jo Ann Boydston. Carbondale and Edwardsville, IL: Southern Illinois University Press, 1980 [1916].

Frazer, Elizabeth. *The Problems of Communitarian Politics: Unity and Conflict*. Oxford: Oxford University Press, 1999.

Green, Judith. *Deep Democracy: Community, Diversity, Transformation.* Lanham and New York: Rowman and Littlefield, 1999.

Kamenka, Eugene. *Community as a Social Ideal.* New York: St Martin's Press, 1982.

Kymlicka, Will. *Contemporary Political Philosophy: An Introduction*. Oxford: Oxford University Press, 2002.

Royce, Josiah. *The Hope of the Great Community.* Freeport, NY: Books for Library Press 1967 [1916].

Walzer, Michael. *Spheres of Justice: A Defense of Pluralism and Equality.* Basic Books, 1983.

Judy D. Whipps

COMMUNITY

It is impossible to overestimate the importance of the role of community in American history.

While our rhetoric has been – and continues to be – strongly individualistic, our existence has been social. From our earliest settlements to our current neighborhoods, when American life has been successful it has been so because of communities. Although our political discussions have focused more upon the importance of individuals finding their own priorities and rejecting the well-worn path as they search for their personal truth, and upon the necessity that individuals be left free from the imposition of societal values, the reality of our communal existence has so far kept this rhetoric from being destructive. Further, although our analyses of the nature of democracy have often tilted toward liberty and away from equality, we recognize that without an egalitarian emphasis in democracy – without a communal focus – democracy, however free, becomes just a method of counting votes.

Community matters to us because we live as social beings. Our social existence connects us in essential ways with our fellows, ways far more intimate than the relationships of cars in a traffic jam or groceries on a shelf. A fulfilled human existence requires the creation of shared values through participation in cooperative actions to advance a common good; and an emphasis upon the importance of community could counteract its loss in contemporary American life.

The importance of community to the well-being of a society was clearly recognized in American philosophy, especially during its classical period. We find there, for example, an understanding of the self as an ongoing social process that is rooted in community. John Dewey writes that individuals, although born organically human and growing in close association with others, are not yet members of a community. Their selves, and their membership in a community, come through the same processes: "To learn to be human is to develop through the give-and-take of communication an effective sense of being as individually distinctive member of a community" (*The Public and Its Problems* 331–2). George Herbert Mead, in a similar fashion, notes that the self "is essentially a social structure, and it arises in social experience." The community thus gives rise to the self. He continues that the individual

> enters his own experience as a self or individual, not directly or immediately, not by becoming a subject to himself, but only in so far as he first becomes an object to himself just as other individuals are objects to him or in his experience; and he becomes an object to himself only by taking the attitudes of other individuals toward himself within a social environment or context of experience and behavior in which both he and they are involved.
>
> (*Mind, Self, and Society* 140, 138).

Developing individuals recognize the shared values that make community possible by the same processes that give rise to the self. The members of a community internalize as their own values the values of the group, and thereby commit themselves to the community's future existence. It is necessary for them to understand themselves as rooted, and to ground their attempts to better the lives of their fellows in improving the institutions of the community. For Josiah Royce, community is the focus of human loyalty. As he writes, "we are saved through the community"; and, for him, the isolated individual cannot prosper. "The detached individual is an essentially lost being" (*The Hope of the Great Community* 131, 46). Dewey further notes that community is possible only when there are functioning institutions of democracy. As he writes, democracy is "the idea of community life itself" (*The Public and Its Problems* 328). The members of such a community both benefit from its values and assume a responsible role in their maintenance.

While philosophers seek precision, "community" is a concept that offers little. Often the eulogistic emphasis that community is a social good seems to cloud over serious attempts to find a clear descriptive meaning for the term. So vague does the meaning of "community" appear to some, in fact, that James Mark Baldwin cautions us that "[n]o technical use of this term is recommended" ("Community" 201). Still, if we abandon attempts to hammer our diverse social possibilities into a single descriptive mold, we can explore the many forms of human association and formulate a pluralistic interpretation of "community." Very generally, the term refers to social groupings of some level of permanence, often in a specific geographical area, that gives rise to human association and shared activity. On top of these "objective" criteria, both Royce and Dewey see the necessity for some level of affective identification with the group and its ongoing well-being. Through the development of shared values, the community becomes a social place where the notion of "we" can function as powerfully as "I" (Dewey, *The Public and Its Problems* 330).

A community can be seen to be inimical to outside interests. A gang of criminals, for example, must be admitted to be a kind of community, offering as it does dedication to common goals, a sense of honor, affective identification, and so on. At a more extreme level, political parties or religions can undermine the stability of the world in the service of their private understanding of "truth." These are examples of parochial communities, however, groups with a focus only on their internal success. A worthwhile community, on the other hand, looks outward as well and emphasizes the importance of, in Dewey's words, "interaction and cooperative intercourse with other groups" (*Democracy and Education* 89) so that its members can grow in ways beyond those that the community makes possible. Royce's presentation of this point is a bit more abstract. For him, the goal is that of being not just loyal to one's particular group, but "loyal to loyalty" (*The Philosophy of Loyalty* 121). This sort of "loyalty to loyalty" would require that individuals strive to advance procedural values like respect and tolerance and cooperation that can integrate groups with each other. It would thus replace a simple loyalty to the inherited traditions of that particular group, be they monarchism or racism, spirituality or progress. By opening itself up to what is beyond the group, a community recognizes further possibilities for human flourishing.

Participation in the processes of community living requires for some a change in emphasis. Individuals should seek not what they can get out of cooperating, but rather how all of the members of the group can benefit through the process of cooperation. This shift ranges across the full sweep of society's interlocking institutions. In light of this emphasis, for example, political democracy is seen as only a small portion of the communal possibilities of democracy, often overpowered by a simple-minded focus upon winning elections. Far more might result from efforts at cooperative inquiry to solve society's problems. In addition to political democracy, a full communal life would require a heightened level of economic democracy, resulting in a situation in which society's productive processes would become more secure and meaningful. Further institutional changes to advance community would be necessary in the procedures of the institutions of family, religion, and education. Education is an especially important focus for increased communal life because of the need to counteract America's strong focus upon schooling for individual success. Emphasis upon a cooperative approach to education would help the young recognize possibilities for shared growth, and make them better at solving the problems of the community. This educational focus would also need to expand beyond the schools into the larger world of business, religion and politics. This broad understanding of community calls for fundamental reconstruction of society's institutions and practices and relies upon individuals having a high degree of faith in their fellows.

An emphasis upon community, like that found in classical American philosophy, presents us with an understanding of human existence as rooted within natural and social processes that find their meaning within experience. The ultimate value of participating in these processes is in the growth that community life makes possible: the richness of individuals' lives. In our communities, we educate the next generation to pass on our fundamental values; but, recognizing that all value systems involve internal conflicts and that situational adaptations will require further changes, part of this education is to foster a reconstructive stance. The community, in other words, cannot simply replicate itself. It must, rather, reconstruct itself – its values, its solutions to ongoing human problems, its hopes for the future – by means of cooperative intelligence that attempts to make use of the contributions of all. Fundamental to community is thus the belief that, by addressing our problems in a communal way, we will transmit our inherited virtues and overcome our inherited weaknesses. This faith in the advancing of social life that is present in classical American philosophy demonstrates an alternative to current doubts about the future, if we can recover the spirit of community.

Further reading

Baldwin, James Mark. "Community" in James Mark Baldwin (ed.) *Dictionary of Philosophy and Psychology*, 3 volumes. New York: Macmillan, 1901–5, Vol. 1, pp. 200–1.

Campbell, James *The Community Reconstructs: The Meaning of Pragmatic Social Thought*. Urbana, IL: University of Illinois Press, 1992.

Dewey, John. *Democracy and Education* in *The Middle Works of John Dewey, 1899–1924, Vol. 9, 1916*, ed. Jo Ann Boydston. Carbondale, IL: Southern Illinois University Press, 1976–83 [1916].

—— *The Public and its Problems* in *The Later Works of John Dewey, 1925–53, Vol. 2, 1925–1927*, ed. Jo Ann Boydston. Carbondale, IL: Southern Illinois University Press, 1976–83 [1927].

Mead, George Herbert. *Mind, Self, and Society from the Standpoint of a Social Behaviorist*, ed. Charles W. Morris. Chicago, IL: University of Chicago Press, 1934.

Royce, Josiah. *The Philosophy of Loyalty*. New York: Macmillan, 1908.

JAMES CAMPBELL

COMMUNITY PSYCHOLOGY

Community psychology is part academic social science discipline and part perspective on the person in the social world. As a discipline, community psychology is the applied study of the relationship between social systems and individual well-being in community settings. As a perspective, community psychology views the person in ecological context as part of interrelated social systems.

The discipline of community psychology

Community psychology developed in the United States after World War II during an era of political contention and social change. The field's initial disciplinary roots were in clinical psychology and social psychology, growing from rejection of the overly narrow and victim-blaming medical model of clinical practice and psychology's constricted view of the social world. Many of the founders of community psychology read fairly widely in philosophy, especially the American pragmatism of George Herbert Mead and John Dewey. Mead's emphasis on the origins of thought and the self in the social world contributed to the assumptive base of the discipline by challenging traditional psychology's emphasis on the individual person and intrapsychic dynamics, and his symbolic interactionism was a major influence on the methodology of the field. Dewey's transactional epistemology and his emphasis on knowledge being put to use in furtherance of democracy were also foundational aspects of the discipline.

With political roots in the community mental health and deinstitutionalization movements, the broader civil rights struggle, the Great Society and War on Poverty federal agendas, and a generally progressive social climate, the field became formalized in the mid-1960s as the twenty-seventh of the now fifty-six divisions of the American Psychological Association. It was originally called the Division of Community Psychology, Division 27, but members changed the name in the 1980s to the Society for Community Research and Action (SCRA), in recognition of both the field's dual mission of scholarly research and social action and its commitment to work beyond the disciplinary boundaries of psychology. The biannual SCRA meetings have come to attract community activists and academics from dozens of community psychology graduate programs in the United States and throughout the world. The field's major journals are the *American Journal of Community Psychology* and the *Journal of Community Psychology.* Several important textbooks have recently been published (e.g. Dalton *et al.* 2001; Nelson and Prilleltensky 2005; Levine *et al.* 2005), as well as a handbook for the field (Rappaport and Seidman 2000).

SCRA members have recently defined their group's mission to be that of "an international organization devoted to advancing theory, research, and social action . . . [and] committed to promoting health and empowerment and to preventing problems in communities, groups, and individuals" (Society for Community Research and Action 2006). Accordingly, SCRA has developed a research-based intervention/prevention agenda focused on (1) human and community flourishing; (2) the contextual understanding of human action; (3) the interchange between academia and applied community settings; and (4) the liberation of the oppressed, with due regard and respect for cultural differences. SCRA also places priority on the career development of researchers and practitioners.

The community psychology perspective

Community psychology entails a particular way of viewing the world of persons-in-community and a complementary methodology and style of action. To illustrate, in the late 1940s, toward the end of his life, Kurt Lewin, the founder of action research and an early influence on community psychology, had come to prefer Karl Marx's perspective on the social environment to that of Sigmund Freud. Lewin had earlier theorized that $B = f(P, E)$ – behavior is a function of the person (P) and the environment (E). Given his commitment to democracy and to his adopted United States, he was not claiming to be a Marxist. He was acknowledging, rather, that Freud's narrow, mostly nuclear family interpretation of the environment, used by Lewin himself in his own dynamic psychology, was seriously limited. In order to make social psychology truly social, Lewin called for the use of Marx's political, economic, and social view of the environment (Marrow 1969). Community psychology tends to combine Freud and Marx, opting for a depth view of persons and their psychosocial development and a broad multi-level, ecological-systems view of the environment. The ecological perspective spans the intersubjective environment of family and intimates; the realm of mediating structures, such as neighborhoods, social support groups, religious congregations, and voluntary associations; the realm of macro systems, such as bureaucratic organizations, governments, and cultures; and beyond.

Regarding community psychology's methodology, consider Abraham Kaplan's (1964) cautionary tale of "a drunkard searching under a street lamp for his house key, which he had dropped some distance away. Asked why he didn't look where he had dropped it, he replied, 'It's lighter here!'" (11). Preference for the methodological security of the light of the street lamp over the willingness and courage to search for the key where it "really is," even though it means venturing into the darkness, is what David Bakan (1966) called "methodolatry," social and behavioral science's version of idolatry. Community psychology tends to reject the need or desirability of choosing between *either* the light (quantitative, experimental inquiry, which sometimes takes the form of ideological scientism) *or* the darkness (qualitative, interpretive, more humanities-like inquiry). Preferred is a *both/and* position, a methodologically tolerant, charitable, open-minded, and multi-faceted human science. In that regard, Richard Bernstein (1986) has argued that "it is methodologically prudent to be open to different types of research strategy" (74). The fullness of the realm of persons-in-community requires a variety of methods, all of which should be applied at one time or another in understanding and acting on behalf of the well-being of persons-in-community. Moreover, in their action research approach, community psychologists see theory, research, and practice as equally important and inextricably interconnected.

The style of community psychology research and action is well captured in guiding principles recently articulated by SCRA:

> Community research and action requires explicit attention to and respect for diversity among peoples and settings;
>
> Human competencies and problems are best understood by viewing people within their social, cultural, economic, geographic, and historical contexts;
>
> Community research and action is an active collaboration among researchers, practitioners, and community members that uses multiple methodologies;
>
> Change strategies are needed at multiple levels in order to foster settings that promote competence and well-being.
>
> (Society for Community Research and Action 2006)

Finally, values are central to the community psychology perspective. Practitioners of community psychology are committed to creating and enhancing democratic social forms (à la John Dewey), characterized by human freedom, free and uncoerced communication (à la Jurgen Habermas), diversity, and social justice. The field readily admits that theory and research are value-laden and places ethics at the center of its identity.

Further reading

Bakan, David. *The Duality of Human Existence: An Essay on Psychology and Religion*. Chicago, IL: Rand McNally, 1966.

Bernstein, Richard. *Philosophical Profiles: Essays in a Pragmatic Mode*. Philadelphia, PA: University of Pennsylvania Press, 1986.

Dalton, James H., Elias, Maurice J., and Wandersman, Abraham. *Community Psychology: Linking Individuals and Communities*. Belmont, CA: Wadsworth, 2001.

Kaplan, Abraham. *The Conduct of Inquiry: Methodology for Behavioral Science*. San Francisco, CA: Chandler, 1964.

Levine, Murray, Perkins, Douglas D. and Perkins, David V. *Principles of Community Psychology: Perspectives and Applications*, third edition. New York: Oxford University Press, 2004.

Marrow, Alfred. *The Practical Theorist: The Life and Work of Kurt Lewin*. New York: Basic Books, 1969.

Nelson, Geoffrey and Prilleltensky, Isaac (eds) *Community Psychology: In Pursuit of Liberation and Well-being*. New York: Palgrave Macmillan, 2005.

Rappaport, Julian and Seidman, Edward. *Handbook of Community Psychology*. New York: Kluwer Academic/Plenum, 2000.

Society for Community Research and Action. "About SCRA." Available at http://www.scra27.org/about.html (accessed 16 May 2006).

PAUL R. DOKECKI

COMPATIBILISM

Compatibilism is a title given to a group of theories that maintain the compatibility of human freedom with causal determinism. Provided that all human actions are causally predetermined, that seems to imply, initially, that it is impossible for people to do otherwise when all antecedent causes for their actions are (or could be) known. Since the commonsense view of morality requires the "freedom to do otherwise" as a necessary condition for the attribution of moral responsibility, there has always been a *prima facie* tension between determinism and such attributions. Compatibilists seek to undermine the threatening nature of determinism. Given an appropriate understanding of the concepts of causal determinism, free will and moral responsibility, the typical compatibilist would claim that this tension will "dissolve" since it was merely illusory to begin with.

Though most compatibilists share this common core, there is still variation in their particular theories. One such variant, which I will refer to as "Classical Compatibilism," has been famously espoused by the likes of Thomas Hobbes, John Locke, David Hume, and John Stuart Mill. Contemporary proponents include A.J. Ayer, Moritz Schlick, and Donald Davidson. There are two key features associated with this variant of compatibilism. First, classical compatibilists maintain that a proper linguistic understanding of "freedom" shows that its negation is *not* merely "to be caused." Instead, to warrant an ascription of "unfree" it requires a particular type of causation – "compulsion." If an agent is acting under "compulsion" that agent is not able to do what she wants or desires to do. If that agent is able to do what she desires or wants, classical compatibilists claim that we can refer to her as "free" despite the fact that her actions may have been causally determined. Second, classical compatibilists provide a conditional analysis of the phrase "could have done otherwise." If we say that an agent was "free" to do A as opposed to B, we only mean that *had* the agent "desired" ("chosen," "willed," "wanted," etc.) to do A then the agent *would* have done A. This is a counterfactual understanding of "freedom" which does not require the rejection of determinism.

Another variant of compatibilism has been espoused by Harry Frankfurt, Daniel Dennett, and Gerald Dworkin. According to this form of compatibilism, which I will refer to as "Hierarchical Compatibilism," what makes an action an expression of "freewill" is that the action has the appropriate connection with an agent's second-order desiring. When we say that an agent (X) desires (D1) a particular action (A), the object of D1 is A. This would be an example of a first-order desire. A second-order desire, on the other hand, has an object which is a first-order desire. Thus, to say that agent (X) has a second-order desire (D2) is to say that – X desires (D2) that a particular desire (D1) will be the determining factor to move X to a particular action (A). According to hierarchal compatibilists, a paradigmatic example of a person without "freewill" is the kleptomaniac. Though the kleptomaniac acts upon the first-order desire to steal, this person has the second-order desire to refrain from acting on the first-order desire. Since the kleptomaniac's second-order desire is abnormally impotent in controlling her ultimate behavior, we have a commonsense intuition that she is acting without "freewill" and thus we absolve her of moral culpability. Hierarchical compatibilists build upon this intuition. All that is meant by "freedom," is that hierarchical control over behavior (which the kleptomaniac lacks) is exercised by an agent. These compatibilists view this relationship, in which the higher-order desires control the lower-order desires, as a necessary and sufficient condition for the attribution of "freewill" and "moral responsibility."

A third variant of compatibilism, introduced by P.F. Strawson, is commonly referred to as "Reactive Attitude Compatibilism." According to this form of compatibilism there are certain "attitudes" that are overtly moral. These attitudes include gratitude, resentment, approbation, shame, guilt, pride, and indignation. Most ethical theories seem to acknowledge some connection between these attitudes and holding one another morally responsible. What is peculiar about this form of compatibilism is that it seems to equate moral responsibility with the *mere expression* of such attitudes. Therefore, when humans experience such attitudes (in a nondeviant and appropriate manner), that is sufficient for the existence of moral responsibility. Once the role of reactive attitudes is understood, these compatibilists maintain, the threat of causal determinism evaporates. Humans seem to be simply unable to give up the thoughts and views that are a part of these attitudes. This "inability" is cashed out in different fashions depending upon which compatibilist one consults. To some theorists, this inability is an empirical fact about human psychology. We are incapable, due to the actual structure of our mind, of sincerely viewing other humans as inappropriate objects of our reactive attitudes. To other theorists, this inability is the result of practical reason. Regardless of psychological ability, some reactive attitude compatibilists would maintain that it would be irrational to sincerely give up the views associated with our moral attitudes. Since they play a large role in the way that we value life and the relationships we have with others, the costs of abandoning these attitudes would be too high.

A fourth type of compatibilism has been advanced by Susan Wolf, Gary Watson, John M. Fischer, and Mark Ravizza. According to this set of theories, which I will refer to as the "Reason View," there is a significant distinction between what an agent merely desires and what an agent values or has reason to pursue. If an agent always acts upon her strongest desire, that is not enough to qualify as a candidate for "freewill." In order to be considered a "free-agent," one must also have the ability to act *for* the appropriate reasons/values. Thus, there is a normative component to this form of compatibilism. Regardless if the agents are causally determined to act for the "right reasons," the fact that their motivations "track" these reasons is enough to qualify them as acceptable objects of moral responsibility.

Further reading

Ayer, Alfred J. "Freedom and Necessity" in his *Philosophical Essays*. New York: St Martin's Press, 1954, pp. 3–20.

Davidson, Donald. *Essays on Actions and Events.* Oxford: Clarendon Press, 1980.
Dworkin, Gerald. *The Theory and Practice of Autonomy.* Cambridge, MA: Cambridge University Press, 1988.
Fischer, John Martin and Ravizza, Mark. *Responsibility and Control: A Theory of Moral Responsibility.* Cambridge, MA: Cambridge University Press, 1998.
Kane, Robert (ed.) *Free Will.* Malden, MA: Blackwell, 2002.
Nagel, Thomas. "Moral Luck" in his *Mortal Questions,* Cambridge, MA: Cambridge University Press, 1979, pp. 24–38.
Nozick, Robert. *Philosophical Explanations.* Cambridge, MA: Harvard University Press, 1981.
Watson, Gary (ed.) *Free Will.* New York: Oxford University Press, 1982.
Wolf, Susan. *Freedom within Reason.* Oxford: Oxford University Press, 1990.

SHANE D. COURTLAND

CONCEPT/CONCEPTION

Suppose two subjects have a disagreement over whether some law is just. They agree as to what the law addresses, its consequences, and the way it was passed. However, the two still disagree as to the justice of the law. Their disagreement here is explained by their different conceptions of the concept of justice.

The concept/conception distinction is designed to reflect the *public* and *normative* character of concepts. For the two subjects above to disagree, they must have a disagreement about something shared. That is, they must have different opinions about the same thing. Without a shared but disputed concept here, the disagreement devolves into a mere verbal matter. Because the two subjects disagree, each takes the other to be wrong about justice. In turn, each is committed to the thought that there are correct and incorrect conceptions of it.

A subject has a conception of a concept (call it X) when the subject takes some property or set of properties (P) as constitutive of X. The constitutive property P must individuate X from other concepts, it must reflect the normative features of X (in that a different conception of X without P is wrong about X), and it must be recognizable by subjects in cases of X. If one of the subjects in the above disagreement about the justice of a law had a conception of justice where fairness was a constitutive component, then she would not only hold that laws treating people unfairly are unjust, she would also hold that conceptions of justice without fairness as constitutive are incorrect.

In the face of conflicting conceptions of X, there are a variety of possible responses: (1) the platonic response: strive to discover and persuade others of the correct conception of X; (2) the deflationary-linguistic response: assess the disagreement as merely verbal and stipulate a meaning for the term "X"; (3) the revisionary response: conclude that X is a confused concept and either propose new concepts in its place or outline a way of avoiding the problems altogether; or (4) the pluralist response: explain the necessity of the contestedness of the concept and outline a means for living together in the face of intractable disagreement.

The platonic response has the benefit of accommodating the publicity and normativity of our concepts, but it often renders real solutions inaccessible, since the concepts themselves are logically separate from conceptions. The deflationary-linguistic response makes resolutions accessible, but the question is whether they are ultimately satisfying, since, on the example above, conflicts about justice are verbal only when one does not have to live with the consequences. The revisionary response amounts to dissolving a problem instead of solving it, and it is appealing especially in the face of intractable disagreement. It amounts to changing the subject. The question is whether the subject remains changed or whether the same problems arise in the new context. The pluralist response comes to making do with the seeming impossibility of resolution, which is reasonable given that we often must act before all discussions have come to an end. However, in the face of deep differences between conceptions, it is often difficult to find even temporary ways to tolerate the disagreements. Moreover, the pluralist strategy seems inconsistent with the normativity of concepts, since it amounts to refraining from correcting errors.

Further reading

Dewey, John. *Experience and Nature*, ed. Jo Ann Boydston. Carbondale, IL: Southern Illinois University Press, 1988 [1925].
Ezcurdia, Maite. "The Concept–Conception Distinction," *Philosophical Issues* 9 (1998): 187–92.
Gallie, W.B. "Essentially Contested Concepts," *Proceedings of the Aristotelian Society* 56 (1956): 167–98.
Plato. *Euthyphro*, *Meno* in *The Dialogues of Plato, Vol. 1.* Cambridge, MA: Harvard University Press, 1989.
—— *Parmenides.* Indianapolis, IN: Hackett, 1996.
Rawls, John. *A Theory of Justice.* Cambridge, MA: Harvard University Press, 1971.
Rorty, Richard. *Consequences of Pragmatism.* Minneapolis, MN: University of Minnesota Press, 1982.

SCOTT FORREST AIKIN

CONDITIONALS

Conditionals are claims expressing that something will, can, may, might, would, or could be if something else is, was, does, or did happen, as in "Johnny will pass the exam if he studies hard" or "If we had not gone to the movies we would still have some money for ice cream." The conditioning part is called the *antecedent,* the part that depends upon the condition the *consequent.* With *indicative conditionals* both antecedent and consequent are in the indicative mood, meaning they are statements of fact as in "If Jenny calls we go skating." With *subjunctive conditionals* the antecedent or consequent expresses something that is doubtful or non-factual, as in "If Jenny calls we might go skating," or "If we were to inquire into this question long enough, then eventually we would find the answer." *Counterfactual conditionals*, or *counterfactuals*, are subjunctive conditionals for which the antecedent is known or assumed to be false, e.g. "If he hadn't fallen off that roof, his leg wouldn't be broken." One method for determining the truth conditions of a subjunctive or counterfactual conditional is by devising the nearest possible world in which the conditional would be an indicative conditional with a true antecedent.

Though we generally have little problem understanding conditionals, there is no generally accepted theory about them; in fact, there is little agreement even over fundamentals (including the above distinction). A theory of conditionals aims to explain which conditional judgments are acceptable and which inferences that include them are good, or it aims to develop a conditional that is suited for particular purposes. An example of the latter is the *material conditional* – or material implication – which is a conditional that is deliberately made truth-functional by stipulating that it is equivalent with denying the conjunction of a true antecedent and a false consequent. Though useful in some areas, like mathematical logic, the material conditional has significant counterintuitive results that severely restrict its applicability. One of these is that *any* conditional with a false antecedent is true no matter what the consequent is, so that the conditional "If Bill lives in Buffalo, he is two-headed" would be true if Bill weren't living in Buffalo.

To Peirce, who refused to restrict the real to the actual, what he termed *would-be*s, *can-be*s, *could-have-been*s, etc. can be real. Peirce even argued that, for the pragmatist, reality consists essentially in what *would be* or *would not be.* To know something is to know not merely how it behaves under actual circumstances, but how it *would* behave under any circumstances, although many of these would never actually occur. Like Peirce, Dewey's theory of inquiry hinges heavily on conditional propositions. What Dewey called "indeterminate situations" are being charted in terms of possible operations and envisioning their consequences, preferably through a process of "dramatic rehearsal." In his 1938 *Logic: The Theory of Inquiry*, Dewey further distinguished between *contingent if–then propositions*, where the connection between antecedent and consequent is an existential one, and *universal if–then propositions.*

Further reading

Bennett, Jonathan. *A Philosophical Guide to Conditionals.* Oxford: Oxford University Press, 2003.

Jackson, Frank. *Conditionals.* Oxford: Blackwell, 1991.

Kwart, Igal. *A Theory of Counterfactuals.* Indianapolis, IN: Hackett, 1981.

Lycan, William G. *Real Conditionals.* Oxford: Clarendon, 2001.

Sanford, David. *If P, then Q: Conditionals and the Foundations of Reasoning*. London: Routledge, 2003.

Cornelis de Waal

CONDITIONS AND CONSEQUENCES

In one of several senses, *conditions* are or resemble qualities, properties, features, characteristics, or attributes. Being equilateral and being equiangular are two *necessary* conditions for being a square. In order for a polygon to be a square, it is necessary for it to be equilateral – and it is necessary for it to be equiangular. Being a quadrangle that is both equilateral and equiangular is a *sufficient* condition for being a square. In order for a quadrangle to be a square, it is sufficient for it to be both equilateral and equiangular. Being equilateral and being equiangular are *separately necessary and jointly sufficient* conditions for a quadrangle to be a square. Every condition is both necessary and sufficient for itself. The relational phrases "is necessary for" and "is sufficient for" are often elliptical for "is a necessary condition for" and "is a sufficient condition for." These senses may be called *attributive*; other senses that may be called *instrumental* and *causal* are discussed below.

Every condition *applies to* everything that *satisfies* it. Every individual satisfies every condition that applies to it. The condition of being equilateral applies to every square, and every square satisfies the condition of being equilateral. The *satisfaction* relation relates individuals to conditions, and the *application* relation relates conditions to individuals. The *satisfaction* and *application* relations are converses of each other. *Necessity* and *sufficiency*, the relations expressed by "is a necessary condition for" and "is a sufficient condition for," relate conditions to conditions, and they are converses of each other. Every condition necessary for a given condition is one that the given condition is sufficient for, and conversely.

In consequence of a chain of developments tracing back to Boole and De Morgan, it has become somewhat standard to limit the individuals pertinent to a given discussion. The collection of pertinent individuals is usually called *the universe of discourse*, an expression coined by Boole in 1854. In discussions of ordinary Euclidean plane geometry, for example, the universe of discourse can be taken to be the class of plane figures. Thus, squares are pertinent, but conditions, propositions, proofs, and geometers are not. Moreover, the collection of pertinent conditions is automatically limited to those coherently applicable to individuals in the universe of discourse. Thus, triangularity and circularity are pertinent, but truth, validity, rationality, bravery, and sincerity are not.

Some philosophers posit *universal* and *null* conditions. A universal condition *applies to* or *is satisfied by* every *pertinent* individual. A null condition *applies to* or *is satisfied by* no pertinent individual. In ordinary Euclidean plane geometry, the condition of being planar is universal and the condition of being round and square is null. Every figure satisfies the condition of being planar. No figure satisfies the condition of being round and square.

Some philosophers posit for each given condition a *complementary* condition that applies to a pertinent individual if and only if the individual does not satisfy the given condition.

In some of several senses, *consequence* is a relation between conditions. Being equilateral and being equiangular are two consequences of being a square. In the sense used here, given any two conditions, the first is a consequence of the second if and only if the second is a sufficient condition for the first. Equivalently, being a consequence of a given condition is coextensive with being a necessary condition for it. The relational verb "implies" is frequently used for the converse of the relational verb phrase "is a consequence of." Given any two conditions, the first implies the second if and only if the second is a consequence of the first. In the attributive senses under discussion, a consequence of a condition cannot be said to be a result of the condition nor can the condition be said to be a cause of its consequences. It would be incoherent to say that being equilateral is caused by being square.

There are *reflexive* and non-reflexive senses of "consequence" applicable to conditions. Both are useful. In the reflexive senses, which are used in this article, every condition is a consequence of itself. In the non-reflexive senses, which are not used in this article, no condition is a consequence of itself.

There are material, intensional, and logical senses of "consequence" applicable to conditions. All are useful. Because of space limitations, in this article, only material consequence is used although the other two are also described.

Given any two conditions, the first is a *material consequence* of (is *materially implied by*) the second if and only if every individual that satisfies the second satisfies the first. Being equilateral is a material consequence of being an equiangular triangle, but not of being an equiangular quadrangle. As is evident, material consequence is entirely *extensional* in the sense that whether one given condition is a material consequence of another is determined by their two *extensions*, the collections of individuals that satisfy them. Given any two conditions, the first is an *intensional consequence* of (is *intensionally implied by*) the second if and only if the proposition that every individual that satisfies the second satisfies the first is analytic or intensionally true. Being equal-sided is an intensional consequence of being an equilateral triangle. Given any two conditions, the first is a *logical consequence* of (is *logically implied by*) the second if and only if the proposition that every individual that satisfies the second satisfies the first is tautological or logically true. Being equilateral is a logical consequence of being an equilateral triangle.

Besides the one-place conditions – such as being three-sided or being equilateral – that are satisfied or not by a given individual, there are two-place conditions – such as being equal-to or being part-of – that relate or do not relate one given individual to another. There are three-place conditions such as numerical betweenness as in "two is between one and three." Given any three numbers, in order for the first to satisfy the betweenness condition with respect to the second and third, it is necessary and sufficient for either the second to precede the first and the third the second or the second to precede the third and the first the second. There are four-place conditions such as numerical proportionality as in "one is to two as three is to six." Given any four numbers, in order for the first to satisfy the proportionality condition with respect to the second, third, and fourth, it is necessary and sufficient that the first be to the second as the third is to the fourth. C.S. Peirce (1992: 225–8) discussed polyadic or multi-place conditions as early as 1885.

There are many debated philosophical issues concerning conditions and consequences.
Traditional philosophers ask ontological and epistemological questions about conditions. What are conditions? Do they change? Do they exist apart from the entities satisfying them? How do we know of them? How are propositions about them known to be true or to be false? In view of modern focus on identity criteria, philosophers now want to ask the questions involving them. One such ontological question asks for an identity criterion for conditions: what is a necessary and sufficient condition for "two" conditions to be identical? The widely accepted identity criterion for extensions of conditions is that given any two conditions, in order for the extension of the first to be (identical to) that of the second, it is necessary and sufficient for the two conditions to be satisfied by the same entities.

There are questions concerning the ontological status of conditions. Are conditions mental, material, ideal, linguistic, or social, or do they have some other character? What is the relation of conditions to properties? A given individual satisfies (or fulfills) a given condition if and only if the condition applies to the individual. A given individual has (or possesses) a given property if and only if the property belongs to the individual. Are the last two sentences simply translations of each other?

Philosophical terminology is not uniform. Before any of the above questions can be fully meaningful, it is necessary to interpret them or to locate them in the context of the work of an individual philosopher. We should never ask an abstract question such as what it means to say that something satisfies a condition. Rather, we should ask a more specific question such as what Peirce meant by saying that accuracy of speech is an important condition of accurate thinking.

John Dewey's voluminous writings provide a rich source of different senses for the words "condition" and "consequence." Except where explicitly noted, all references to Dewey are by volume number and page in the Southern Illinois University Press critical edition. Thus, (12.454) is page 454 of Volume 12.

It would be useful to catalogue the various senses Dewey attaches to "condition" and "consequence" the way that A.O. Lovejoy famously catalogued senses of "pragmatism." In several passages, Dewey links a sense of "condition" with a corresponding sense of "consequence" just as senses of these words were linked above. Two corresponding usages occur repeatedly in his writings and, it should be said, in most writings concerned with human activity including government and technology. In one, condition/consequence is somewhat analogous to means/end. In fact, Dewey sometimes uses the words "condition" and "means" almost interchangeably as in his famous pronouncement (12.454): "Every intelligent act involves selection of certain things as means to other things as their consequences." A little later, he adds (12.455): "in all inquiries in which there is an end in view (consequences to be brought into existence) there is a selective ordering of existing conditions as means." In the other sense, condition/consequence is similar to cause/effect – although identification is probably not warranted in either case. Dewey studiously avoids sharp distinctions, dualisms, dichotomies, and other artificialities. There are passages where both contrasts are relevant, but as far as I know, Dewey never explicitly notes that "condition/consequence" was used for both.

The means/end sense occurs, for example, in his 1945 *Journal of Philosophy* article, "Ethical Subject-Matter and Language" (15.139), where he suggested that the inquiry into "conditions and consequences" should draw upon the whole knowledge of relevant fact. The cause/effect sense occurs on page 543 in his response to critics in the 1939 Library of Living Philosophers volume. Here he wrote: "Correlation between changes that form conditions of desires, etc., and changes that form their consequences when acted upon have the same standing and function ... that physical objects have." There are scattered passages suggesting that Dewey regarded the means/end relation as one kind of cause/effect relation. In fact he regards a causal proposition as one "whose content is a relation of conditions that are means to other conditions that are consequences" (12.455).

In some of the senses Dewey uses, *conditions* are or resemble qualities, properties, features, characteristics, or attributes. These senses were referred to above as *attributive*. However, in the two of senses in question, the *instrumental* sense and the *causal* sense, let us say, *conditions* are or resemble states or events more than qualities, properties, features, characteristics, or attributes. After all, the attributive condition of being equiangular, which is a consequence of the condition of being an equilateral triangle, could hardly be said to be brought about through use of the latter as means or said to be caused by the latter. Accordingly, an attributive condition is neither earlier nor later than its consequences, whereas an instrumental or causal condition necessarily precedes its consequences. As Dewey (12.454) himself puts it, "The import of the causal relation as one of means-consequences is thus prospective."

From a practical point of view, Dewey's causal and instrumental senses of "condition" and "consequence" are at least as important as the attributive senses. In the causal sense, fuel, oxygen, and ignition are conditions for combustion as a consequence. In the instrumental sense, understanding, evidence, and judgment are conditions for knowledge as a consequence.

This essay has benefited from the suggestions of several scholars including William Corcoran, Forest Hansen, Peter Hare, Larry Hickman, John Shook, and above all Nathan Houser.

Further reading

Dewey, John. *John Dewey: The Later Works, 1925–1953, Vol. 12, 1938*, ed. Jo Ann Boydston. Carbondale, IL: Southern Illinois University Press, 1986.

—— *John Dewey: The Later Works, 1925–1953, Vol. 15, 1942–53*, ed. Jo Ann Boydston. Carbondale, IL: Southern Illinois University Press, 1986.

Peirce, C.S. *The Essential Peirce: Selected Philosophical Writings (1867–1893)*, Vol. I, ed. N. Houser and C. Kloesel. Bloomington, IN: Indiana University Press, 1992.

Schilpp, Paul A. (ed.) *The Philosophy of John Dewey* (Library of Living Philosophers). LaSalle, IL: Open Court, 1939.

John Corcoran

CONSCIOUSNESS

After several decades of neglect, consciousness has found its way back to the center of philosophical and scientific analyses of mind. Much recent theoretical and empirical work on consciousness reinvigorates themes and concerns treated at length by some of the main figures of classical American philosophy. For instance, James and Dewey both developed rich embodied models of consciousness that are today recognized as important antecedents to contemporary accounts. Similarly, Mead's conception of mind as a socially constituted phenomenon can be seen as anticipating the spirit of contemporary distributed or extended accounts of mind, according to which consciousness is (at least partially) constituted by factors external to the subject. Reflecting a methodological orientation advocated by figures like James and Dewey, contemporary consciousness studies has become a highly pluralistic affair. Important contributions from disciplines such as philosophical and experimental psychology, neuroscience, cognitive linguistics, cultural anthropology, and comparative philosophical and religious studies, among others, are being woven together within the narratives and debates emerging from this energetic field of inquiry.

To suggest that there is a single unified view rightly termed *the* American Philosophical View of Consciousness is of course misleading. For instance, James's mature view of consciousness as developed in his *Essays in Radical Empiricism* (1912) bears little resemblance to Royce's idealistic conception of Absolute Mind. Like any substantive philosophical tradition, one finds a host of views admirably represented. However, a broad overview of the tradition can discern some shared points of emphasis. James and Dewey are the classical American thinkers who offer the most extensive analyses of the problem of consciousness. Generally speaking, they developed what might be termed *ecological* conceptions of consciousness. Ecological conceptions of consciousness grow out of a rejection of the sharp ontological distinction between organism and environment. Both James and Dewey insist on the mutuality and reciprocity of conscious subject and world. Simply put, their ecological conceptions of consciousness stress the integrated and interactive nature of the mind–world relation. Constitutively speaking, then, conscious phenomena are not realized solely within some sort of nonphysical substance, neural substrate or collection of intracranial representations. Rather, consciousness emerges within the situated dynamics of embodied activity and is thus an emergent property of the body's participatory interaction with the world. In this way, consciousness under an ecological rendering is seen as an irreducibly embodied, embedded, and distributed phenomenon. Consciousness is *embodied* within a neurobiological system, which is always *embedded* in continually shifting environments, and is thus *distributed* across the real-time interplay of brain, body, and world. Metaphysically, both James and Dewey dispute mind–body dualism: the claim that mental phenomena are distinct from physical phenomena. (Dewey formulates this view as artificially bifurcating "experience" and "nature.") Their respective ecological conceptions of consciousness reflect this rejection, and attempt to offer conceptual resources for overcoming the Cartesian privileging of the mental parasitic on this dualism. Methodologically, James and Dewey call for an analysis of consciousness concerned with its everyday concrete transactions with the world. Accordingly, the form of the biological body's embeddedness in changing environmental contexts – both natural and cultural – is seen as crucial for discerning the structure and content of consciousness. To understand consciousness, one must look to everyday examples of consciousness *in action*. Consciousness thus always arises in what James terms real world "activity-situations."

James on consciousness

James's most extended treatment of consciousness is found in his seminal *Principles of Psychology* (1890), still a treasure trove of observational insights into mind and experience. In it, James proposes a "double-barreled" methodology for investigating consciousness. Psychology, as James here defines it, is the study of "the Science of Mental Life." For James, psychological analysis of consciousness entails both a third-person empirical analysis of the neurobiological "conditions" of consciousness as well as a first-person phenomenological investigation of the "phenomenal facts" of consciousness, or its experiential content. Moreover, the body's central role in shaping consciousness must be conceded. This is because "Mental phenomena are not only conditioned *a parte ante* by bodily processes; but they lead to them *a parte post*." Consciousness for James is therefore not a static process or fixed substance but rather a world-directed activity of the whole creature. Embodied consciousness is not something that we simply *have* but rather something that we *do*. This strong emphasis on the embodied and agential basis of consciousness – also shared by Dewey – leads James to declare that consciousness is "at all times primarily a *selecting agency*." What this means for James is that embodied consciousness, as a world-directed activity, is structured in and through the various sensorimotor forms of our environmental engagements or activity-situations. Consciousness emerges through our attentive interaction with the world. And consciousness is thus not a fixed entity substantially distinct from worldly activities of which it is a part. Rather, consciousness is enacted *within* the various kinds of brain–body–world couplings that specify the form and content of each activity-situation. This strongly relational characterization of consciousness will lead James to famously deny that consciousness exists – insofar as consciousness is thought to be some autonomous "thing" localized in the head of the subject. Instead, for James consciousness is a function of the body's attentional, sensorimotor engagement with the world. And this coupled system of brain–body–world, taken together, *is* consciousness. James's experiential monism in his *Essays in Radical Empiricism* (1912) is in part an attempt to articulate this view.

Dewey on consciousness

The topic of consciousness proper is not as central to Dewey's work as it is James's. However, Dewey writes extensively on various aspects of the mind and its relation to the world and other people. His classic essay "The Reflex Arc Concept in Psychology" (1896) develops an early embodied approach to consciousness and experience refined in later works such as *Human Nature and Conduct* (1922) and, especially, *Experience and Nature* (1929). Dewey affirms a body-based relational view of consciousness. In *Experience and Nature* (1929), he uses the term "body–mind" to emphasize the extent to which the two are inextricably linked within our prereflective experience of and navigation throughout the world. However, if James's analysis of consciousness is most concerned with discerning the physiological and phenomenological significance of its bodily rootedness – consciousness as embodied sensorimotor activity – Dewey's analysis marks a subtle shift, in that it centers on the environmentally *embedded* and *distributed* nature of consciousness. Specifically, Dewey urges that consciousness is ultimately a function of social interactions. Broadly construed, social interactions encompass the entire range of possible ways of engaging with and experiencing a value-laden, meaningful world organized with respect to human interests and ends. In this sense, all conscious experience of the human world is a kind of social interaction for Dewey. Consciousness is precisely "that phase of a system of meanings which at a given time is undergoing re-direction, transitive transformation," a continual converting of stimuli into world-directed responses by a situated agent.

In *Experience and Nature* (1929), Dewey distinguishes between mind and consciousness. Mind is the broader category. It is always "contextual and persistent", situated within "the whole system of meanings as they are embodied in the workings of organic life": the complex nexus of linguistic, social, political and institutional structures that largely determine how and what we think. However, consciousness is more "focal and transitive." It is activated in a local "awareness or perception of meanings" of certain parts of these larger structures. Consciousness for Dewey therefore emerges within the organism's adaptive functioning as it navigates meaningful environments. More precisely, "consciousness" refers to the various practices that enable an organism to maintain "equilibrium" or "coordination", as Dewey terms it, between itself and its world – whether through perception, linguistic practices, observing cultural norms, etc. The conscious subject's transactional encounters with meaningful environments – its ways of establishing "equilibrium" – are phases of mental activity that transform both subject and environment. Like James, Dewey in this way develops a relational model of consciousness. Unlike James, who argues for the primacy of the body and its sensorimotor capacities in shaping consciousness, Dewey seems to think that environmental embeddedness is the most significant formative agent. Thus, the term "consciousness" for Dewey seems to refer to a slightly different level of description for Dewey than it does for James. While consciousness for Dewey is clearly underwritten by a neurobiological substrate, the term is more rightly understood to refer to the level of organization at which an organism is able to incorporate the shared meanings of its environment into a successfully coordinated navigation of a human world. Consciousness is thus not simply a neurobiological phenomenon. It is a socially embedded collection of practices and habits, both novel and inherited, that collectively enable the organism to interact with and transform its environment. Consciousness is therefore distributed *across* this organism–environment interaction, and arises equally from factors internal to the subject as well as features of the world that the subject creates.

Consciousness and other American thinkers

Though James and Dewey arguably remain most relevant to contemporary discussions of consciousness, other classical American thinkers have a place in the dialogue. As mentioned earlier, Mead's social conception of mind might be fruitfully engaged with ongoing discussions of the various ways that social "scaffoldings" like language and technology, for example, augment cognitive processes such that mind is externalized and thus most aptly characterized as a public, extended phenomenon. Peirce and Royce have something to say about this as well. In another vein, Royce's work has recently enjoyed a mini-renaissance and has been used within certain theological circles to explore aspects of religious consciousness. Santayana's work on aesthetic experience harbors insights into the under-explored relationship between art and consciousness.

Further reading

Dewey, J. "The Reflex Arc Concept in Psychology", *Psychological Review*, 3 (1896): 357–70.

—— *Human Nature and Conduct. The Middle Works of John Dewey: 1899–1924, Vol. 14, 1922*, ed. Jo Ann Boydston. Carbondale, IL: Southern Illinois University Press, 1978.

—— *Experience and Nature* in *John Dewey: The Later Works, 1925–1953, Vol. 1, 1925*, ed. Jo Ann Boydston. Carbondale, IL: Southern Illinois University Press, 1981.

James, W. *The Principles of Psychology*, 2 volumes. New York: Dover, 1890.

—— *Essays in Radical Empiricism*. New York: E.P. Dutton, 1912.

Mead, G. *Mind, Self and Society*. Chicago, IL: University of Chicago Press, 1934.

Royce, J. "The External World and the Social Consciousness," *Philosophical Review* 3, 5 (1894): 513–45.

Santayana, G. *The Life of Reason*, 5 volumes. New York: Charles Scribner's Sons, 1905.

JOEL W. KRUEGER

CONSEQUENTIALISM

The charge that "the end justifies the means" is sometimes offered as a severe moral criticism of a person or group. It suggests that the person will regard lying, cheating, stealing, killing, or anything else as justifiable as long as those things get that person what she or he wants. Curiously, however, consequentialism, one of the main moral theories of modern Western philosophy, can be summed up fairly with that five-word phrase. And American pragmatism is a somewhat rebellious offspring of this view.

The original consequentialism, utilitarianism, was the empiricist's moral theory. It tried to make morality scientifically respectable, holding that there was nothing religious or supernatural about goodness or badness. Good people, good societies, and the right actions were the ones that produced as consequences the most pleasures and the fewest pains. We human beings do in fact seek pleasure and avoid pain as a scientifically observable matter, and therefore the moral realm was not, as rationalistic philosophers from Plato to Kant had argued, a suprasensible realm of abstract forms or principles. The ideal could come from the observably real world of what human beings want.

This is not as vicious or selfish a view as it has seemed to many people. As a utilitarian, one acts not to secure one's own pleasure but the most pleasure for all people indifferently – or even for any non-human pleasure- or pain-perceivers there may be. Lying and killing do turn out to be justifiable under certain circumstances, but, of course, that's the way it is; we are morally justified in lying to the sheriff looking for the runaway slaves in the cellar, and we can kill the career criminal with a gun who is trying to kill us.

This is above all a kind of moral naturalism. Jeremy Bentham, the first utilitarian, even said that the consequences we seek are fundamentally *physical* pleasures and the consequences we avoid physical pains. Religious, moral, and political "sanctions" or penalties for immorality all depend on physical pleasures and pains as their "groundwork"; they are what we really want to get or avoid in those matters (1789: 24–7). However, beginning with Bentham's follower J.S. Mill, consequentialist thinkers have argued that moral agents are in fact observed seeking other things besides quantities of physical gratification. Today the term "consequentialism" labels a variety of views according to which people desire both physical and intellectual pleasures, fairness, equality, freedom, life, virtue, or any number of other things. Anything intrinsically valuable – i.e. anything that is not valued merely as a means to some higher end – may end up counting in a consequentialist theory as a thing that agents seek or maximize in morally good acts. The main idea is that morality is not a lot of purely abstract ideals, principles, or forms that somehow exist apart from the natural world of desires, causes, and effects. It is instead a thing that arises as particular observable beings try to satisfy their real-life desires.

Pragmatism can be understood as a consequentialist theory of meaning and truth rather than of morals, though Peirce's "pragmaticism" complicates matters by emphasizing the nonconsequentialist idea that the truth represents the real (James 1977: 99–100; Dewey 2004: 89–92; Peirce 1877: 247–8 and 253–4). For a pragmatist, beliefs are meaningful just in case they have real consequences in practical experience, and they are true just in case those consequences tend to be good. A difference in meaning that makes no practical difference *is* no difference, and the true belief is one that *works* or can be verified as it brings us good consequences in our active lives.

Though the idea of verificationism has become associated with logical positivism and its dismissal of moral and religious claims as cognitively meaningless, the pragmatic verificationist does not single out moral or religious claims for dismissal. Instead the pragmatist naturalizes all meaning and truth, including moral and religious truth if there is any. If moral and religious claims have observably good and bad consequences, then they can be as meaningful and true as any other claims. And clearly they do have those consequences, otherwise we would have no real-life interest in making or disputing them. Peirce, again something of an exception, holds that pragmatism, part of the logic of science or the "Logic of Things," cannot be used to understand moral and religious ideas, or "Topics of Vital Importance" (1992: 108). Learning to think clear scientific thoughts and learning to live well are, for Peirce, two different projects. But James is famous for holding that scientific, moral, and religious claims alike tell us what kind of results to expect if we accept them and live our lives by them. That is what makes all of them, even religious and moral beliefs, *meaningful*; and if we expect and receive *good* or satisfactory consequences from religious and moral beliefs, we will call those beliefs *true*. (See, e.g., James 1979: 29n.)

Still, there is a telling difference between pragmatism and other consequentialisms. Though James dedicated his *Pragmatism* lectures to the memory of John Stuart Mill, Mill's utilitarianism and moral views like it are foundationalist philosophical theories. They all send us out in pursuit of final goals the value of which is known and fixed in advance. Pragmatism, by contrast, promotes pursuit of particular consequences, but not any *particular* particular consequences. James wanted, above all, to *set us free to change things*. We have growing knowledge of a changing world, and James wanted to help us make sure that some of those changes are for the better. He therefore encouraged us to see ourselves as individual knowers devising particular truths or true beliefs, doing so as a part of our various struggles to achieve goals we may not yet know (1977: 109–11). Dewey agreed, and he used this story of truth to promote indefinitely continuing education, unceasing development of the capacities of individuals (2004: 104–7). However, Peirce, one last time, may not have been on board. He often seemed, in his philosophical remarks on meaning and truth, much less interested in freeing individuals to change their lives and the world than in limiting inquiry to what made scientific sense (see, e.g., 1992: 119–22).

Further reading

Bentham, J. *The Principles of Morals and Legislation*. New York: Hafner, 1948 [1789].

Dewey, J. *Reconstruction in Philosophy*. Mineola, NY: Dover, 2004 [1920].

James, W. *Pragmatism* and *The Meaning of Truth*. Cambridge, MA: Harvard University Press, 1977 [1907].

—— *The Will to Believe and Other Essays in Popular Philosophy*, Cambridge, MA: Harvard University Press, 1979 [1897].

Peirce, C.S. *Reasoning and the Logic of Things*, ed. Kenneth Laine Ketner. Cambridge, MA: Harvard University Press, 1992 [1898].

HARVEY CORMIER

CONSERVATISM

The term "conservatism" most generally refers to a belief, often implicit, that existing social arrangements have at least a *prima facie* claim to validity; that is, they probably evolved for a good reason. Its more specific referent in modern Western politics is a family of political ideas that emerged in opposition to the French Revolution, especially stemming from Edmund Burke's *Reflections on the Revolution in France* (1790). This "traditionalist" conservatism shares with economic conservatism or libertarianism a skepticism of government power and support for a market economy, but values above all the enduring institutions and traditions of particular societies and distrusts excessive liberty, egalitarian reforms, or any attempt to remake society to conform to intellectual principle.

There has always been a tradition of conservative thought in the United States, but professional philosophers have not been prominent contributors to it. To the extent that the indigenous American philosophical tradition has a characteristic politics, it is progressive; after all, the Progressive movement was represented by the most prominent of all American philosophers, John Dewey. Still, American philosophy can claim one genuine political conservative, George Santayana. More striking, it has promoted certain ideas that are characteristically conservative, although without drawing from them partisan political conclusions. We may cite four such ideas: communitarianism, spontaneous order, normative immanence, and meliorism.

Conservative themes in American philosophy

Classic American philosophy is communitarian, conceiving society and social communication as constitutive for individuals. This is characteristic not only of the Americans' social and political thought, but their ethics, philosophy of mind, and even their epistemology. Josiah Royce saw the ultimate achievement of history, and the justification of human action, as the development of world community. George Herbert Mead argued that mind itself is emergent from social interaction, that is, communication. Charles Peirce argued that inquiry and logical thought presuppose the individual's identification with an indefinitely large and long-lived community, literally claiming that "logic is rooted in the social principle."

The Americans took this to imply not that individuality and freedom should be subordinated to social goals, but that social processes create the individual. Freedom can be achieved only in the context of formative social institutions, communicative interaction, and education. Thus liberty must not be so extreme as to undermine the social constitution that makes it possible in the first place. In this vein Dewey supported individuality, but criticized individualism, the valuation of the human individual above all things. This joining of individuality with community, and rejection of both collectivism (as in Marxism) and atomic individualism (as in various forms of liberalism), is characteristic of the Americanist tradition.

"Spontaneous order" refers to the notion that order can emerge without design, human or divine, from systems of interacting elements. This idea, arguably carried by Galilean and Newtonian mechanics, was central to Darwinism. Its humanistic employment came from the Scottish Enlightenment, first in Adam Ferguson's concept of "civil society," then more famously in Adam Smith's theory of the market economy. Traditional conservatives since Burke have admired the free market, even if they refused to make it an ultimate good. But the broadest meaning of spontaneous order as evolved by the Scots went beyond economics: it was the belief, called by historian Karl Polanyi "the discovery of society," that social traits emerge from the social interactions among citizens rather than being imposed either by God or king.

Heavily influenced by the Scots and Darwin, the Americans, most notably Mead and Dewey, accepted that order and complex functions emerge out of the undesigned interaction of components of lower complexity. The Americans did not apply this lesson to economics, remaining at least rhetorically critical of capitalist individualism (although we should remember that they worked in an era of pre-Keynesian government disengagement). Nevertheless, their concern for the welfare of a free – that is, spontaneous – civil society would not allow them to endorse the imposition of order from above.

The Americans' characteristic rejection of dualism led to a belief in "normative immanence," the idea that the norms which govern a process – for example, moral rules governing society – are themselves a product of that process, rather than of some external, transcendent source. Politically, this implies the rejection of what the conservative Michael Oakeshott called "political rationalism," the reform of social life from the perspective of transcendent principles achieved by philosophical speculation. Santayana, Dewey, Mead, and James all regarded moral and aesthetic norms as emergent from life, experience, action, and communication. And while many of the Americans were supporters of social reform, they conceived those reforms as re-balancing and re-conceiving components of existing social life, rather than as foreign to social experience.

Lastly, the politics of Americanist philosophers have been meliorist rather than utopian. Although American political life has been marked by various brands of utopianism, especially religious, the American philosophers steered clear of endorsing sectarian ideals, hoping to improve, not reinvent, society. When asked whether he was or would consider endorsing Marxism, Dewey quipped that he had struggled for many years to divest himself of dogmatic religion, and had no desire to take on another. This dovetails with their basic communitarianism. For just as there can be no radical break with the social past, there is no individual who avoids socialization. The capitalist entrepreneur, the rebel, and the genius must satisfy a desire, speak a language or work in a symbolic medium shared with others; they can only "reconstruct" a part of culture by accepting other parts of it. Otherwise they would fail to communicate at all, and become not revolutionary but merely eccentric.

Santayana

Embodying these themes was the one genuine political conservative produced by the American philosophical tradition, the Spanish-born but American-educated Jorge Augustín Nicolás Ruiz (aka George) de Santayana (1863–1952). Santayana merited a place in Russell Kirk's classic *The Conservative Mind: From Burke to Eliot* (1986; the first edition was subtitled "From Burke to Santayana," but the second ended with Santayana's own student at Harvard, T.S. Eliot). Santayana wrote as a concerned observer of the political scene rather than political theorist *per se.* His observations are most fully expressed in *Character and Opinion in the United States* (1920), his novel *The Last Puritan* (1935), and *Dominations and Powers: Reflections on Liberty, Society and Government* (1951).

Santayana was opposed to Deweyan progressivism, doubting that the combination of universal suffrage, social equality, market economy, technological progress, and enlightened government would lead to the simultaneous achievement of international peace, individual liberty, and material prosperity for all. His conservatism was based in his naturalistic recognition of finitude; humans and human society are not endlessly malleable. His critique of the direction of American society under liberalism was reminiscent of Alexis de Tocqueville's; he regarded the combination of mass democracy and capitalism, or "industrial liberalism," as a drive toward collectivist utility. Like Tocqueville, Santayana thought that such liberalism would undermine liberty by enforcing uniformity, in contrast to traditional social hierarchies which, while unequal, had maintained a looseness and respect for differences that preserved the space for rational freedom. To the utopian hopes of liberals he objected,

> They do not see that the peace they demand was secured by the discipline and the sacrifices that they deplore, that the wealth they possess was amassed by appropriating lands and conducting enterprises in the high-handed manner which they denounce, and that the fine arts and refined luxuries they revel in arise in the service of superstitions that they deride and despotisms that they abhor.
>
> (Santayana 1951: 438)

His polemic against liberalism, however, never led Santayana to be an ideologue of the right, any more than of the left. It is that refusal to see life in simplistic terms, hence a caution regarding novel schemes of social analysis, that was conservatism for him.

Further reading

Kirk, Russell. *The Conservative Mind: From Burke to Eliot.* Washington, DC: Regenery, 1986.

Oakeshott, Michael. "Rationalism in Politics" in his *Rationalism in Politics and Other Essays.* Indianapolis, IN: Liberty Press, 1991.

Santayana, George. *Character and Opinion in the United States: With Reminiscences of William James and Josiah Royce and Academic Life in America.* New York: Charles Scribner's Sons, 1920.

—— *The Last Puritan: A Memoir in the Form of a Novel.* New York: Charles Scribner's Sons, 1936.

—— *Dominations and Powers: Reflections on Liberty, Society, and Government.* New York: Charles Scribner's Sons, 1951.

LAWRENCE CAHOONE

CONSTRUCTIVISM

Constructivism is a thesis about the nature of concepts. Constructivists argue that one best understands the meaning and reference of a concept through a consideration of that concept's social and practical consequences. In this constructivism offers both an ontological and a semantic account of concepts. For constructivists, agents construct principles through practical reasoning; beliefs and reasons therefore exist in a privileged relation to each other. Agents establish the truth or falsity of a judgment via argumentation. Thus, constructivist arguments are rendered valid or invalid through norms attached to relevant social conventions. Constructivism is not relativism, however. Unlike the relativist, the constructivist believes that certain judgments are true and that others are false. In constructivism, the procedures we use to determine the truth or falsity of a judgment also serve as grounding for that judgment, much as the prior decisions of judges construct a body of precedence in law. Originally advanced as a thesis within the sociology of science, constructivism is also widely influential inside and outside the social sciences. Constructivist arguments are commonly found in the philosophy of social science, the philosophy of natural science, the philosophy of mathematics, and within ethics and political theory. This entry concentrates on the normative aspects of constructivism. As applied to ethics, constructivism is a metaethical claim that argues for a view of moral judgments as complex composites. That is, that moral judgment is "constructed" out of a specific type of interaction: one that obtains between reasons, norms, and causes. So for the constructivist, our moral judgments draw their force from the relations we stand in with regard to others. Against moral realism, its principle competitor, constructivism argues that norms are social in nature and that this sociality is not reducible solely to causal explanations, as some realists argue.

Such a causal reduction, according to constructivism, would straightforwardly eliminate moral agency as it renders critical judgments inert. Moral realists, in contrast, view moral properties as causal representations; for them norms do not interfere with our apprehension of moral facts. The facts exist and do not need social conventions to guide them. Constructivism argues that social conventions, practices, and norms, are the ground of ethical principles and that without these only a brute causality remains, one devoid of normativity. We can identify facts because we have procedures for so doing, the constructivist argues. Procedures ground facts and not vice versa. Constructivists therefore reject the idea that full-fledged moral properties can emerge non-socially, as they are bound (in part) by convention. Moral realism proposes that just this is the case. Realism argues that moral properties exist as facts functioning entirely apart from human procedures, purposes, or concerns. Moderate positions of course exist between these two views, and are commonly held. Few constructivists think of causality as an illusion, just as few realists view rules and norms as nonexistent. Yet even between more restrained accounts, rifts remain. For most constructivists, the social features of inquiry and of moral judgment are inseparable from the moral properties they identify. This is different from stating that moral properties exist without moral agents, a position seemingly entailed by some very strong versions of moral realism.

In America, the moderate position has been the most influential. The writings of John Dewey (1859–1952) exemplify this moderated stance. For Dewey, the analysis of moral judgment requires three things. First, it requires a moral agent. This agent, like all moral agents, has been socialized according to the norms of her society. Second, for there to be a moral judgment there needs to be an ethically ambiguous circumstance, one requiring the agent to decide how to act – in short, a moral problem. This moment of uncertainty is what Dewey terms a "problematic situation." Third, there needs to be an ongoing interaction, between the norms that the moral agent already endorses, the causal demands of the situation that is causing the problem, and the intercession of the agent's intelligence. Without this form of triangulation, no moral judgment is formed and no reasonable resolution to the problem is formulated. This three-part relation schematically depicts the dynamics of early constructivist thinking. The causal circumstances that prod the moral agent to act are conceptually free of the agent's norms and beliefs. Yet the agent's deliberations are not reducible to causal factors alone. Norms intercede as well by limiting the range of available options. Without the explanatory presence of norms, all ethical judgments are reduced to reactions instead of being guided critical activities. Constructivists hold that the social nature of norms preconditions the causal relations experienced by the moral agent and they make moral judgment possible.

William James (1842–1910) also articulates a version of constructivism that he extends to objects. In *Pragmatism*, James conceives of an object as the sum of its potential effects. Looking to sensation, James asks what sensations different objects elicit when we encounter them. How do we react to them? The judgments we form about the objects we encounter, argues James, are all we can know about objects. In James, ideas have a functional status. An idea's meaning can only be uncovered by looking to its effects. As a consequence of this view, James states that ideas and objects without effects are to be thought of as meaningless. The linkage between James's conception and constructivism lies in his notion that objects, and the ideas they engender, are processes. To define the effects an object has (either potentially or actually) one needs to employ some standard. This standard is always hypothetical according to James. We must test our assumptions about an object's effects before we know what type of object it is.

Here James employs a verificationist standard. The meaning of an idea or of an object is to be found by looking at its method of verification. Absent such a process, one cannot know the truth value of the object or the ideas it generates. Our reasons for believing that a certain object or idea is a good one are "constructed" out of our experience. In James's phrase, our experiences and judgments are "funded."

George Santayana (1863–1952) is another philosopher who advocates a constructivist account of knowledge and knowing, although from a decidedly more institutional perspective. Taking the notions "object," "subject," and "symbol" as primary, Santayana developed a system of philosophy in which the interactions of these three elements cause both reason and knowledge. Less individualistic and empiricist than Dewey or James, Santayana believes, as they do, that ideas are to be judged by their longevity. The longer a particular iteration of objects, subjects, and symbols, can survive the tribunal of lived experience, the greater the likelihood of its truth. Yet truth for Santayana is explicated through institutions and remains wholly procedural, with better iterations eventually replacing poorer ones. Although in agreement with the procedural elements in James, Santayana's philosophy countenances realism in a way that James's does not. Truth is essentially correspondence with the facts, for Santayana. However, as limited beings, the only scientific metric available to us as humans is a pragmatic one. Verification must do. So for Santayana if our judgments lead to acceptable outcomes, given our purposes, then we are justified in our actions. If they are not, we are not. These purposes are, Santayana reminds us, always social conditioned and social structured and although it is experience that serves as final arbiter, our experiences are themselves infused with social norms and expectations. Santayana's institutional view of the way we form judgments adds another dimension to the constructivist tapestry.

Constructivism is regulative in another sense also. Metaethically, constructivism attempts to explain not only the emergence of moral judgments but the status of ethical properties as well. It does not, however, justify specific moral commitments or actions the way normative ethics does. In its epistemic mode, constructivism is in fact not primarily a first-order normative theory. Rather, constructivism attempts to justify the claims of normative theory by claiming that moral judgments operate like other social practices. Moral judgments have a distinct target but they do not have a different structure than any other social convention. By defining norms as social conventions (conventions we may have differing reasons for following) the constructivist explains the binding nature of norms without endorsing reductionism. This purely epistemic side of constructivism is often called "social constructivism." Social constructivism insists that facts and norms are man-made, again standing against realism by placing human interests and values at the center of epistemology. Recent attempts have, however, been made to derive a normative theory from the constructivist ideal. The work of John Rawls (1921–2002) provides an example of a normative form of constructivism. Rawls proposes that ethical principles can be constructed from specific features of human reason and action. The features Rawls has in mind are impartial and universal. Where Dewey is concerned with examining the means–ends relations of individual moral agents, Rawls follows Immanuel Kant (1724–1804) in concentrating on the most general features of moral reasoning. Because of this impartial and impersonal stance, Rawls's view is often differentiated from other constructivist views by the label "Kantian Constructivism." Adopting a procedural standpoint, Rawls attempts to devise decision-procedures for moral problems dealing with justice. Rawlsian constructivism attempts to remain metaethically uncontroversial. This means limiting what is claimed about features of moral reason and action to their most generalizable aspects.

One such limitation is the omission of an agent's desires or preferences from deliberation. As different agents have different sets of preferences and desires, including these in deliberation introduces partiality on Rawls's view. Other aspects of our moral reasoning are admissible but only if they are held in "reflective equilibrium" with our other "considered moral judgments." "Reflective equilibrium" obtains only if the situations of others factor into our deliberations about our own moral lives. An outcome that privileges only us cannot be said to be in Rawlsian equilibrium. Citizens of liberal democracies can base moral principles on the ideals of liberty and democracy but only if these ideals are held reflectively. This is because Rawls believes that the mutual adjustment of our "considered moral judgments" and moral ideals will, if balanced correctly, ensure fair terms of cooperation for all similarly situated citizens. If such terms of fair cooperation are reached, then justice can be said to obtain, at least as long as the reflective balance holds. Rawls is clear that "reflective equilibrium" is a heuristic method and should not be understood foundationally or immutably. Constructivism, old and new, is therefore a method for establishing problem-solving procedures that do justice to both our social mores and our epistemic responsibilities without giving in to brutal causality.

Further reading

Brandom, Robert B. *Articulating Reasons: An Introduction to Inferentialism*. Cambridge, MA: Harvard University Press, 2001.

Dewey, John. *The Later Works, Vol. 7*, ed. Jo Ann Boydston. Bloomington, IN: Indiana University Press, 1932.

Lachs, John and Hodges, Michael. *Thinking in the Ruins: Wittgenstein and Santayana on Contingency*. Nashville, TN: Vanderbilt University Press, 1999.

Nielsen, Kai. *Naturalism without Foundations*. Amherst, NY: Prometheus Press, 1996.

Rawls, John. *Collected Papers*. Cambridge, MA: Harvard University Press, 1999.

Rorty, Richard. *Philosophy as Cultural Politics*. Cambridge University Press, 2007.

NICK C. SAGOS

CONSUMMATORY EXPERIENCE

Consummatory experience is a key term in Dewey's general theory of experience denoting those events in which the depth and intensity of meaning is so heightened as to constitute a pervasive, qualitative and organizing whole. Consummatory experiences are those in which the awareness of value and significance is so great that they demarcate themselves as particularly distinct events. Each is "*an* experience," in Dewey's terms. They also indicate the potential for experience in general to take on and develop integrated meanings. Thus, consummatory experience should be a primary object for philosophical reflection, so much so that Dewey says the test of any philosophy of experience is how well it deals with the "aesthetic" (LW 10.278).

It is erroneous to confuse the consummatory with the "aesthetic" if the latter is taken to mean some sort of detached, contemplative enjoyment of fine art or scenes of natural beauty. Dewey criticizes most aesthetic theories because they begin with such a highly refined type of experience set apart from life and so miss how the aesthetic in fact pervades all aspects of life. Without ignoring art, Dewey begins considering those moments in which experience "comes alive" with vitality and significance. The aesthetic, he says, "is no intruder in experience from without ... but ... is the clarified and intensified development of traits that belong to every normally complete experience" (LW 10.52–3). We find the roots of the consummatory in all the various ways human beings discover and create meaning and value: gardening, cooking, making love, decorating a home, playing sports, taking a walk in the mountains, talking with a close friend, reading to a child and so on. Such experiences constitute the core meanings of one's life and fine art arises from them. Art reveals the possibilities of experience.

Dewey does not say that all experience is already consummatory: it is not. One of the major problems of human existence is that we fatalistically accept the absence of the consummatory in daily experience. The result is meaningless routine punctuated by superficial excitement or sublimated religiosity. In such conditions the aesthetic possibilities of experience disappear. Many experiences, if not all, could be consummatory if their aesthetic potential was recognized – if we practiced an "art of life." What Dewey desires to stress is the continuity between those significant moments and the ways in which the arts produce and develop such experiences further. A child, for example, may have a deeply meaningful experience being sung to at night; from this may come a love of music, learning to play an instrument or even being a composer, like Franz Schubert, whose *Lieder* draw on the folk songs of his youth. The lesson Dewey takes from such examples is that experience can grow in meaning. That is, the habits that are the ways we engage the world significantly are dynamic; they can be developed to further our ability to have consummatory experiences. The first "art" is the art of living, hence the importance of aesthetics for ethics, politics, and education.

Dewey's most extended analysis of the consummatory experience is found in Chapter 3 of *Art as Experience*, though the idea pervades his mature philosophy. Dewey reminds us that by "experience" he does not mean "feelings" or "consciousness," but the complete interaction of living human beings with the world, an interaction that is thoroughly mediated by culture. (For Dewey, "experience" is illustrated more in skilled activities like hunting, farming or building than in sense perceptions.) Consummatory experiences have wholeness, closure and temporality.

For the most part the events of life do not hang together particularly well – the day is broken up into little chores, a budding friendship never deepens, a planned "evening out" is carried through, but with a sense of exhaustion, not joy. But there are those times when they do. Such experiences stand out, each is "*an* experience," and each has its own "individuating quality" that emotionally binds all the elements together: it was *that* day I excelled at work, *that* evening when we realized we were in love, *that* time camping with the kids. In these experiences the various parts flow together, constituting a sense of wholeness; each moment carries forward and develops the meaningful possibilities of the situation. This does not mean that there cannot be pauses or "spaces," but they too support and become integral parts of the whole, like the "empty" parts of Chinese painting. Such experiences are not primarily "known," except in retrospect, but are lived through ("had" or "undergone" in Dewey's terminology). Even a consummatory intellectual experience is like this.

Consummatory experiences have "closure" or dynamic balance that emotionally articulates the situation as a whole. The relationship between the phases of doing and undergoing are perceived as to belong together rather than frustrate each other.

Finally, such experiences are inherently temporal in a "historical" sense because they develop dramatically. Each phase "sums up and carries forward" so that they are experienced *as* the phases *of* that situation. In this way the ending is not "the end," but the continuous integration of the whole. In listening to music, we do not just hear "sounds" at each moment; the sounds develop meaning with reference to previous notes and future musical possibilities. In good music, each moment "sums up and carries forward" the whole and closure occurs throughout the performance.

The term "consummatory" has two drawbacks. It has nothing to do with "consumerism." Many readers of Dewey also make the mistake that Dewey is only thinking of positive experiences. Nothing could be further from the truth, as Dewey's own examples indicate (a storm, a rupture of friendship, or a narrowly avoided disaster). Consummatory experiences raise our awareness of the possibilities of experience to be meaningful, but not all meanings are happy ones (LW 10.48). We experience terror or fear and perhaps in nightmares these become intensified and whole; artists like Kafka can take these sorts of possibilities and make great literature out of them. Samuel Beckett can elevate and masterfully sustain the aesthetic quality of the sense of existential alienation. Dewey's analysis of the consummatory applies to these examples as well as to Beethoven's *Ninth Symphony*.

In his account of consummatory experience, Dewey developed a far richer and more sophisticated view of experience than is to be found in traditional empiricism. The test of a philosophy of experience, he said, is its ability to account for the aesthetic. To understand this feature of his thought is to have the key to the rest.

Further reading

Alexander, Thomas. *John Dewey's Theory of Art, Experience and Nature: The Horizons of Feeling*. Albany, NY. SUNY Press, 1987.

Dewey, John. *Art as Experience. The Later Works: Volume 10, 1934*. Carbondale, IL: Southern Illinois University Press, 1987. Cited in the text as LW.

McDermott, John J. *The Culture of Experience*. New York: New York University Press, 1976.

THOMAS M. ALEXANDER

CONTEXT

The most general meaning of "context" – the Latin etymology of which suggests the action of weaving or joining together – is that something requires reference to factors outside of itself to be intelligible. In this sense, anything whatsoever – for example, physical objects, actions, sentences, or beliefs – belongs to indefinitely many possible contexts, expressible in a wide range of cultural idioms. But contextual understanding is by nature selective: when we seek to explain something we are typically more interested in some contexts than in others. And if we are thinking critically, that will in turn lead to a more reflexive investigation of the higher-order context or contexts of inquiry itself. How that self-investigation should proceed is a fundamental concern of modern philosophy, and American philosophers, especially in the pragmatist tradition, have made a number of seminal contributions to this discussion.

C.S. Peirce inaugurated what would become an increasingly explicit pragmatist interest in these themes with his doctrines that beliefs are not self-standing mental entities but dispositions to action, and that truths are just those beliefs which are fated to win the consensus of all inquirers. Peirce also maintained that the concepts of truth and reality are logically linked to that of an inquiring community. From this naturalistic emphasis on the interpenetration of thought and social action it is only a short step to the proposition that all inquiry occurs in a social context. But that proposition, so stated, is ambiguous between two further ideas which are not equivalent: (1) the truism that all inquiry arises in varying social and historical contexts; and (2) the more controversial idea that norms of inquiry themselves, such as the ideal of truth, can also vary in basic ways from context to context. Although only the first of these would have been acceptable to Peirce, a gesture towards the second informs the pragmatism of William James, who offers a more liberal interpretation of the conditions under which a wide spectrum of human beliefs can merit being described as "true." In domains of inquiry lacking settled methods of justification, such as religious belief, we are, for James, entitled to regard even scientifically untestable propositions as bearers of a kind of instrumental truth to the degree that they developmentally advance and, at least provisionally, unify an individual believer's experience. To this extent, the creative and indeterministic character of individual experience supplies an important context for human thought and inquiry.

A more explicit interest in contextuality, plus a greater emphasis on both senses of the above-mentioned idea of socially contextualized inquiry, marks John Dewey's pragmatism. A fundamental Deweyan theme is that all intelligent behavior involves an ongoing reinterpretation and reconstruction of environments that call for action on the part of an organism. For Dewey, intelligence is always "situated" (a key term also for George Herbert Mead's related theory of the social self). "Thinking," he wrote in his 1931 article "Context and Thought,"

> takes place in a scale of degrees of distance from the urgencies of an immediate situation in which something has to be done. The greater the degree of remoteness, the greater is the danger that a temporary and legitimate failure of express reference to context will be converted into a virtual denial of its place and import ... [P]hilosophic thinking is, upon the whole, at the extreme end of the scale of distance from the active urgency of concrete situations. It is because of this fact that neglect of context is the besetting fallacy of philosophical thought.

Dewey lists various more specific mistakes to which philosophers have been prone in this connection. These include the "analytic fallacy," occurring whenever aspects of a subject under analysis are treated as final terms, and the counterpart fallacy of "universalization," which occurs when a particular context for a problem, once identified, is then mistakenly generalized into a condition for all problems. Dewey further develops these themes in *Logic: The Theory of Inquiry* (1938). Inquiry in any intellectual field, including science and philosophy, reflects a fundamental dynamic of all intelligent activity: an organism's ongoing effort to achieve equilibrium with an environment on various levels that correspond to our different modern classifications of experience – survival-seeking, moral, aesthetic, and so on. Inquiry in Dewey's sense is a human being's (or, in an extended sense, community's) experimental response not just to a narrow, causally insulated, stream of stimuli but to a "whole situation." Inquiry's developmental stages include an initial experience of a problematic blockage of aims or desires; further clarification of the problem; and the development of a solution which will typically draw on skills of reasoning but may also employ a wider range of material and symbolic (e.g. artistic) resources.

More recent pragmatism, responding to the broader climate of post-Wittgensteinian Anglophone philosophy, has given increasing attention to language as an encompassing context of social practice that in one way or another grounds all thought and behavior. A centerpiece of W.V.O. Quine's seminal critique of empiricism, for example, is the view that the meaningfulness of a speaker's utterances is a function not of inner mental events ("meanings") but of the speaker's dispositions to act within a larger public behavioral setting. Our ontological commitments, or beliefs about what is real, are also contextual (or relative) for Quine, in the sense that what counts as ultimately real for a speech community – whether it be the Homeric gods or the particles of modern physics – presupposes that community's entrenchment of a larger theoretical or theory-like vocabulary whose interpretation of experience is justified not aprioristically but pragmatically.

Donald Davidson, drawing on Quine's work, further refines and interprets its naturalistic focus with a critique of modern philosophy's reliance on the dualism of "scheme and content." The latter's most familiar expression, Davidson notes, is the Kantian distinction between the a priori categories of reason (our conceptual scheme) and the empirical input of the senses (that scheme's experiential content). But this critique has yet another, perhaps less expected, target: conceptual relativism. While the latter appears in a variety of guises in cultural anthropology and postmodern philosophy, its general form – typically manifested in assertions about plural conceptual schemes, or incommensurable scientific paradigms and cultural belief-systems – still exhibits the basic dualistic Kantian structure of organizing abstract concepts-plus-organized-experiential-content. Such relativism more fully, and, Davidson insists, incoherently, embodies the idea, mentioned earlier, that the norms of rational thought itself vary according to historical and/or social context.

A yet more explicit invocation of the idea of contextuality figures in the work of another contemporary pragmatist, Richard Rorty, who offers an interpretation of recent philosophy's struggle to overcome its traditional impulses toward metaphysical essentialism and epistemological foundationalism. Rorty's work acknowledges a particular indebtedness to the work of Dewey and Davidson as well as to European figures such as Wittgenstein and Derrida. Rorty suggests that philosophers today would do well to reconceive their activity as "recontextualization," by which he means a process of reflectively "reweaving" old and new beliefs to the end of creating fresh and useful interpretations of experience. This argument represents perhaps the most radical departure by a recent American philosopher from a more orthodox philosophical tradition which pictures knowledge as a representational relationship between mind and world whose basic structure transcends any kind of contingent situatedness in culture and history. Drawing on Davidson's critique of traditional (e.g. Kantian and empiricist) distinctions between the subject and object of experience, Rorty suggests that there is no ultimate, intrinsically privileged, context that any of our beliefs or dispositions "really" belongs to; that we are best off dropping older distinctions between contexts and things contextualized; and that talk of "doing things to objects" is best recast as talk about weaving and reweaving beliefs (since there is no way of identifying an object except by citing beliefs that depend for their intelligibility upon some further web of beliefs whose pattern we are always more or less self-consciously creating).

Rorty's argument exemplifies itself, since it effectively proposes a further recontextualization (in his sense) of the trajectory of pragmatism while at the same time it returns the discussion of the idea of contextuality in a fresh way to that idea's above-mentioned etymological roots. Rorty's position is hardly without its critics today among other philosophers influenced by the themes sketched above. But his views, like all those discussed above, aptly illustrate the impulses toward self-criticism and self-reinterpretation which energize the pragmatist tradition's very active participation in philosophy's global conversation about its aims and methods.

Further reading

Davidson, Donald. "On the Very Idea of a Conceptual Scheme," in his *Inquiries Into Truth and Interpretation*. Oxford: Oxford University Press, 1984.

Dewey, John. "Context and Thought" in *John Dewey: The Later Works, Vol. 6, 1931–1932*, ed. Jo Ann Boydston. Carbondale, IL: University of Illinois Press, 1985 [1931].

James, William. *Pragmatism*. Indianapolis, NA: Hackett, 1981.

Mead, George Herbert. *Mind, Self, and Society From the Standpoint of a Social Behaviorist*. Chicago, IL: University of Chicago Press, 1934.

Peirce, Charles Sanders. "What Pragmatism Is" in *The Essential Peirce, Selected Philosophical Writings 1893–1913*. Bloomington, IN: Indiana University Press, 1998.

Quine, Willard Van Orman. *Ontological Relativity and Other Essays*. Washington, DC: Columbia University Press, 1977.

Rorty, Richard. "Inquiry as Recontextualization: An Anti-dualist Account of Interpretation" in his *Objectivity, Relativism, and Truth*. Cambridge: Cambridge University Press, 1990.

Casey Haskins

CONTINGENCY

Contingency – like related tropes such as possibility, indeterminacy, dependence, uncertainty, historicity, provisionality, fallibility, and incompleteness – is a central theme in the metaphysics, epistemology, and ethical theory of many American philosophers. While this notion appears in the work of many philosophers, it is belief in, and celebration of, the breadth and depth of contingency that is a characteristic mark of much American philosophy.

Initially this was not the case. Early American philosophical writers, transplanted from Europe but not from European traditions of thought, identified the divine with the necessary and completely actualized. They viewed humans and their world as this God's creations, argued for God's determinism of events in this world and predeterminism of fate in the next life, and strove to make compatible this theological view of a world without contingency and the demand for accountability of individuals for their lives. Nonetheless, strains of contingency were apparent. In his 1701 *A Christian at His Calling*, Cotton Mather declared that Christians have both a general calling to serve God and a personal calling to serve society through some useful occupation, and he concluded that anyone who fails in both of these callings is like a man rowing a boat with only one oar – unable, it turns out, to reach the shore of eternal blessedness.

This view that life is not the result of necessary, predetermined forces but, instead, contingencies and possibilities at least substantially within human power to direct pervades the almanac and autobiographical writings of Benjamin Franklin, the Deistic metaphysical and political concerns of later American Enlightenment figures such as Thomas Paine, Ethan Allen, Thomas Jefferson, and James Madison, and the transcendentalism of Emerson and Thoreau. Reinforced by the apparent wide possibilities of nature and contingencies of social life in America, these thinkers rejected necessity, determinism, resignation, and prayer. They embraced contingency, freedom, meliorism, and hard work without assurance of success – evident in Franklin's gospel of self-help, Jefferson's views on self-government, and Emerson's embrace of self-reliance.

This attitude is set forth most fully, self-consciously, and systematically in the pragmatism of Peirce, James, and Dewey. Against determinism (for which he claimed no scientific evidence), Charles Peirce argued for tychism, the theory that chance and spontaneity are objective realities in a world that is dynamic and evolutionary rather than static and fixed. This metaphysics of contingency paralleled Peirce's epistemology that stressed beliefs are fallible, incomplete, and contingent on perspective. Truth, understood by Peirce as the view that would result from an infinite amount of inquiry over an infinite amount of time, is an ideal or limit-condition on the actual beliefs of finite persons – beliefs that are simply more or less justified.

William James developed even more fully a philosophy of radical contingency and indeterminism. In "Necessary Truths and the Effects of Experience," the final chapter of *Principles of Psychology*, James argued that necessary truths and laws of logic have arisen from wholly "accidental" naturalistic causes that over time have formed our organic mental structures. Similarly, in "The Dilemma of Determinism," he set forth a powerful, novel defense of indeterminism, real possibilities, and an unfinished world. James argued that determinism and indeterminism cannot be refuted theoretically or empirically because neither view is self-contradictory and both agree on the facts, disagreeing only about whether they could have been different. From a practical standpoint, however, James showed that determinism entails untenable belief in pessimism (evils are unavoidable) or subjectivism (evil is not real but just relative to one's point of view). Rejecting both these options and insisting, like Emerson, that our world is malleable, James explained in "The Moral Philosopher and the Moral Life" that we must invent new ways of harmonizing interests at odds with one another.

This commitment to contingency is even more deeply embedded in the philosophy of John Dewey. For Dewey, traditional debates about necessity vs contingency or determinism vs free will are empty. Accordingly, Dewey didn't take the task of philosophers to be proof of contingency in general. Instead, the focus, through experimental inquiry, must be on particular, specific contingencies in order to more fully direct them. From his logic to his politics, Dewey considered not *whether* reality is contingent or precarious, but rather *how* it is contingent and how it can be made more secure and instrumental. Finally, invoking Dewey a generation later, Richard Rorty in *Contingency, Irony, and Solidarity* and other works has renewed attention to the notion of contingency by claiming that language, self, and community are historical contingencies rather than expressions of necessary or universal realities.

Further reading

Dewey, John. *The Quest for Certainty* in *John Dewey: The Later Works, 1925–1953, Vol. 4, 1929*, ed. Jo Ann Boydston. Carbondale, IL: Southern Illinois University Press, 1984 [1929].

Emerson, Ralph Waldo. "Self-Reliance" in *The Works of Emerson*. New York: Tudor Publishing, 1940 [1841], pp. 30–59.

James, William. "The Dilemma of Determinism" in *The Will to Believe and Other Essays in Popular Philosophy, The Works of William James*, ed. Frederick H. Burkhardt. Cambridge, MA: Harvard University Press, 1979 [1896], pp. 114–40.

Lewis, Clarence Irving. *Mind and the World Order*. New York: Kessenger Publishing, 2004 [1941].

Menand, Louis. *The Metaphysical Club: A Story of Ideas in America*. New York: Farrar, Straus and Giroux, 2001.

Peirce, Charles S. "The Doctrine of Chances," "Design and Chance," and "The Doctrine of Necessity Examined" in *The Essential Peirce, Selected Philosophical Writings*, Vol. 1, ed. Nathan Houser and Christian Kloesel. Bloomington, IN: Indiana University Press, 1992 [1878. 1883, 1892].

Rorty, Richard. *Contingency, Irony, and Solidarity*. Cambridge: Cambridge University Press, 1989.

JOHN J. STUHR

CORPORATE PERSONALITY

Corporate personality is an oft-debated question concerning whether or not collectives/corporations should be understood as persons. The issue is most often discussed within a juridical framework, usually as it relates to corporate rights and obligations. If a corporation can be deemed a person then several commercial benefits would follow: it would have similar legal rights and protections afforded to individual citizens, perpetual life (changes among officers and shareholders would not affect its status), and limited shareholder liability. While corporations have no physical existence, they do hold property and enter into contracts. Additionally, legal precedent has established that corporations are persons with rights and duties. But on what grounds does the legal system make such a claim? Traditionally, there are essentially four competing claims of justification: fiction theory, concession theory, contract theory, and realist theory. The first of these claims is the earliest known defense of corporate personality. Fiction theory, as John Dewey notes in his historical analysis of the subject matter, is traceable back to Pope Innocent IV's (1243–54) claim that the corporation has no body, soul, or will and thus cannot be considered a person. Hence, the designation of corporation as person must be considered nominalistic as it exists only as a creation of the mind. This idea, Dewey argues, is closely related to (and often conflated with) another popular theory during the Middle Ages, concession theory, which holds that no corporation or association can be deemed legitimate (i.e. legal) unless it is recognized by the state. State power, in the feudalistic age, was threatened by the consolidation of guilds; as a result, state power was eager to suppress its rivals. Hence, a corporate entity was not legitimate unless it was recognized by the state. According to Dewey, these theories, when conflated, comprise much of the justification of early American legal precedent: they are fictional entities that are nonetheless recognized by the state as subjects having the right to enter into contracts, hold and transfer property, and sue or be sued. However, as the nature of industry changed so too did the defense for corporate personality. With the growth of joint-stock companies in the nineteenth century, focus moved away from fiction and concession theories and became more concerned with individual stockholder rights and the aggregate/contractual dimension of corporations. Thus the contract theory holds that corporations consist of rights-bearing individuals contracting with one another for organizational purposes – the corporation becomes a legitimate entity/subject upon its contractual creation. This position moves the debate over corporate essence away from the state legitimation of concession theory to the associational character of right-bearing individuals who comprise the corporation. However, questions concerning liability prompted a new formulation in the twentieth century: realist theory. According to this theory (and in contrast to contract theory), corporations comprise an independent existence separate from that of its shareholders. The corporation has its own holdings and its own interests, similar to that of a physical person, irrespective of its shareholders. According to realist theory the corporation should be understood as an actually existing social entity with its own personality. However, in his treatment on the subject, Dewey criticizes these traditional approaches to corporate personality for being beholden to the wrong logical method. He argues that the issue of corporate subjectivity should not be defined by whether or not corporations share certain essential or intrinsic characteristics that define persons (i.e. the search for universals by finding analogous characteristics between persons and corporations). Instead, he suggests we should define corporations in terms of their social consequences and relations.

Further reading

Blumberg, Phillip I. "The Corporate Personality in American Law: A Summary Review," *The American Journal of Comparative Law* 38, Supplement, "US Law in an Era of Democratization" (1990): 49–69.

Dewey, John. "Corporate Personality" in *The Later Works, Vol. 2, 1925–1927, Essays, The Public and Its Problems*, ed. Jo Ann Boydston. Carbondale, IL: Southern Illinois University Press, 1984.

Machen, Arthur, Jr. "Corporate Personality," *Harvard Law Review* 24 (1911): 253–67, 347–65.

Maitland, F.W. "Translator's Introduction" in Otto Gierke, *Political Theories of the Middle Ages*. Cambridge: Cambridge University Press, 1900.

MATTHEW J. FITZSIMMONS

COSMOLOGY

Philosophical cosmology has a different set of interests from the type of cosmology currently being done in astrophysics. While the latter is concerned with the birth of matter, gravity, and space time from a singularity, the former is concerned with the structure and role of meaning in the vast expanses of nature, a nature that cannot be reduced to matter and energy. There are many orders that cannot be translated into physical energy, such as possibilities, and there are structures that pertain to a much larger conception of the "population" of the world. Put differently, while astrophysics talks of the "universe," philosophical cosmologists talk of the "world" and or of "nature." As we shall see, these are larger conceptions than those of scientific cosmology.

Further, many philosophers are less concerned with the conditions of origin for the innumerable orders of the world and more concerned with what could be called structural issues. Cosmogenesis often gets played down as the focus shifts to the generic features of existence, to use Dewey's apt phrase. The concept of "ground," especially in neoplatonic cosmologies, is rendered more problematic and no longer serves as a first principle that generates all others. Other cosmologies rethink ground in ways that are not necessarily incompatible with Big Bang cosmology, but which would locate the Big Bang in orders of lesser scope.

In a taxonomy of philosophical cosmologies within the classical American tradition, four stand out as having the greatest scope combined with interpretive precision. They are: (1) transcendentalism's neoplatonic cosmology; (2) pragmaticism's agapastic cosmology; (3) process cosmology; and (4) ordinal cosmology.

Starting in 1836 in his epoch-making essay *Nature*, Emerson creates a neoplatonic cosmology that challenges the then dominant patriarchal vertical cosmology of a divine agent creating the world out of nothingness. Emerson shifts his focus to the depths of nature rather that toward a supernatural realm of absolute meaning and value. Nature itself is constituted by a series of emanations that have no first emanation or governing primal source that somehow stands back from the nature that is allegedly created by an extranatural power.

The world of nature is one that has neither beginning nor ending; only a series of endless emanations that rise out of each other in a chaotic and tumbling fashion. To go against the realm of infinite emanations is to become insane. This insanity comes from the desire to find an *arche* or first principle from which to deduce all others in, for example, the tradition of Leibniz. In Emerson's perspective the Big Bang would be but one special and violent form of emanation, but would not exhaust the fecundity of nature's endless self-fissuring. Elsewhere Emerson uses Spinoza's distinction between *nature naturing* and *nature natured* to signal that the depths of nature are inexhaustible and not a once-and-for-all created event. His own rethinking of *natura naturans* could be translated as the power of nature creating itself out of itself alone (via endless emanations), while *natura naturata* would be the innumerable orders of the world as manifest from out of the bosom of *nature naturing*.

Within the heart of nature is the Over soul that represents the depth-structure of the human process. We are cosmic beings who have ridden on the back of endless nature and our essence is found in the light that pours out of the orders of the world. Emerson celebrates the infinitude of the self, although he modifies this commitment after 1844. The self, while limited by temperament, is the agent through which infinite nature comes to an awareness of its own depths and its own scope. In a striking parallel with the Western esoteric traditions, Emerson sees the cosmic self as a microcosm of the vast macrocosm. In his neoplatonic cosmology the human process edges out the former infinite god as the locus of truth and ceaseless self-transfiguration.

While Plotinus has but one emanating source (the One), Emerson pluralizes the emanational patterns so that there is no ground of all grounds. In the tradition of German Idealism, by which he was influenced, the ground is more like an abyss (*abgrund*) than a place upon which to stand in atemporal security. His neoplatonic cosmology is radically decentering and invokes the depth-powers of the torrents that we call nature.

Peirce, on the other hand, seeks a form of rational stability in his pragmaticist cosmology. He coined the term "pragmaticist" to distinguish his form of pragmatism from that of William James, who had popularized the term "pragmatism." In Peirce's pragmaticist cosmology the focus shifts to the future where the world of nature is seen to be evolving toward a state of ultimate convergence. While Emerson placed far more emphasis on nature than on history, Peirce made history a foundational category in his cosmology. The past is seen as the seed bed of a triumphant future in which what he called "concrete reasonableness" would shape the laws and habits of the universe of nature. Even the divine order is caught up in this process-style evolutionary cosmology.

What makes Peirce unique among the pragmatists, such as James and Dewey, is that he created foundational categories that were cosmic in scope. While James has an ontology of vital centers of power and Dewey has an event ontology, Peirce sought the absolute starting point for nature in its vast scope and fecundity. In this process of forging his cosmology he unfolded the three primal categories that he called "firstness," "secondness," and "thirdness." These three structures operate both in his cosmology and in his phenomenology (theory of human experience). Our concern is with the former use.

Firstness is the most difficult category to define, for the simple reason that it lies before language and any attempt at meaning-formation. Peirce likened firstness to the Garden of Eden before language emerged – a state in which all was primal perfection and there was no stain of existence/actuality. In other contexts Peirce envisions firstness as pure qualitative immediacy: that is, not a known and articulated quality *per se* but the realm of what could be called "pure quality." As pure it is not any order or structure that could be encountered by sign-using creatures like ourselves. Attempts have been made to link firstness to the unconscious in nature but these moves are still problematic (cf. Corrington 1993).

Secondness is much easier to define as it involves two forces in dyadic interaction. It is an emergent (emanation) from firstness and represents the class of finite powers. Peirce gives the example of the rough hand of the sheriff upon one's shoulder as an example of secondness. It is important to note that secondness is not yet intelligible as it is a bare causal relationship that has no admixture, at this point, with thirdness. It should further be noted that Peirce considers sequential talk of the three primal cosmological categories to be an abstraction, or what he calls a form of "prescinding" in which a category is ripped out of the total phenomenon which may represent a swirling admixture of all three categories.

The category of thirdness is the most important cosmologically. It represents the mediation of firstness and secondness around a law or general principle of reasonableness. Thirdness can also be defined as cosmic habit, that is, the realm of attained habits that the innumerable orders of the world have fallen into over the length of evolution. The entire universe of nature is growing both at its edges and at its center: namely, at the point where thirdness reweaves the fabric of dyadic secondness around a mediating third that is the upshot of secondness as it passes over to its teleological fulfillment in thirdness. Nature groans toward the full manifestation and display of thirdness in which all human sign systems will ideally converge with the reasonableness at the heart of nature and the divine (which will be fully revealed in both its secondness – sheer existence – and thirdness).

The culminating moment of his pragmaticist cosmology lies in his concept of agapasm. He believes that evolution is not solely Darwinian but also involves a principle of cosmic and evolutionary love in which the purity of firstness and the ravages of secondness get redeemed around crystalline thirdness that stands in a loving relationship to the "lower" orders of creation. Cosmic mind unites thirdness with all orders of creation: "In genuine agapasm, on the other hand, advance takes place by virtue of a positive sympathy among the created springing from continuity of mind." (Corrington 1993: 196). Like later process thinkers, Peirce was a panpsychist: namely, one who believed that so-called matter was actually a form of frozen mind and that mentality is the genus of which mere matter is a nonfoundational species.

Process cosmology carries Peirce's panpsychism forward and makes it a foundational category in its strongly evolutionary perspective. While Peirce talks about the feelings a primitive protoplasm has, process thought speaks of the ultimate constituents of the world as having highly complex feelings in their own right. The basic building block of process cosmology is the atomic structure termed the "actual occasion." These occasions are in space and time although they are akin to infinitesimals: namely, a reality that is infinitely small yet greater than zero. The actual occasion is a drop of experience that has what are called "prehensions" of all past occasions in the universe or world of nature. A prehension is a feeling of feelings that is open to the influence of other occasions. While it is impossible to have a present prehension, the past is almost immediately available for what is called "ingression," that is the internal presence that shapes what the new actual occasion is to be. An actual occasion, small and episodic, has both positive and negative prehensions of the past world of occasions. A negative prehension is one that rejects a possible ingression into the brief life of the given occasion while a positive prehension is one that lets a past event, now solidified, matter to it.

The actual occasion has a special form all of its own, termed the "subjective form," that determines the shape its world of ingressions will take. It also has a subjective aim which is its inner teleological purpose, its drive to become something unique and valuable to the universe. The aim and the form work in consort with each other to make the actual occasion a unique event in the world, one that cannot be repeated by any other occasion. The time between the birth of the actual occasion and its solidification into its unique status is very brief but during this period it scans the universe to find its relevant internal matter.

The second major constituent of the world of nature is the "eternal entity," which is akin to a Platonic form in that it is a nonchanging possibility that gives the universe its texture and permanent structures. The actual occasion also allows eternal entities to become relevant to it as it shapes its internal life and becomes immortal as just the structure that it is and no other. For both Whitehead and Hartshorne eternal entities reside in what is termed the "primordial mind of God," which is the eternal and always relevant repository of the forms that shape the world of nature and which collectively occupy the eternal mind of the absolute side of God. God entertains these eternal entities and further helps, via persuasion, to make appropriate ones relevant to the given actual occasion as it goes through its series of prehensions. God does not work by coercion or by the blind use of power but by persuasion, by providing a divine lure (the initial aim) that can appeal to the actual occasion as it struggles to pick its way among the formal possibilities of its being.

But God has a second nature that is truly processive and that represents a distinctive contribution of process cosmology to philosophical theology. The second divine nature is the "consequent nature" and represents God as growing with the universe of occasions. In this nature, God itself prehends all of the actual occasions that have become objectively immortal, that is, completed in their becoming. Hence, the process God is both eternal and temporal but in different respects. One implication drawn from this perspective is that the human society of occasions is not subjectively immortal but only objectively so as its occasions become remembered by the consequent nature of God – its internal subjectivity ceases to prevail in nature and its orders.

Ordinal cosmology is of more recent vintage and represents a refinement on pragmatism and naturalism. Created by Justus Buchler, ordinal metaphysics challenges the idea that there are ultimate simples in nature and argues instead that everything whatsoever is complex in its own traits and in its relational traits. Instead of the actual occasion, Buchler speaks of "natural complexes" that have no built in "what." This is an important point in that it refuses to assign any one trait to nature as a whole and allows the orders of the world to have nonreductive traits that are in each case unique. There is no order *of* nature or order *for* nature, only orders in relation. All container images are rejected in the ordinal perspective. Further, like Emerson, Buchler downplays any sense of the ultimate whence or whither of nature and works *in medias res.* Peirce's eschatology and process divine lures are denied in a universe that has fecundity but no telos. This is naturalism at its most refined and at its starkest. It is a cosmology that puts the sense of origin in the heart of nature. Again like Emerson, Buchler uses the twin terms *nature naturing* and *nature natured* as his ultimate cosmological realities with the former term referring to the sheer fecundity of a depth-less nature and the later term referring to the uncountable orders of the world. In place of religious grace Buchler uses the term "providingness."

Perhaps most important in the ordinal perspective is the commitment to ontological parity, which is contrasted to ontological priority. As the terms suggest, priority schemes privilege one reality over all others and makes the others less real – this is often done almost unconsciously and without systematic elaboration. Thus, for example, Schopenhauer can make will more real than phenomena and thus push the realm of finite experiences into the less real. The commitment to ontological parity is harder to realize in principle as it entails an ongoing effort to let all discriminanda be equally real. Hence, Hamlet is not less real than Shakespeare, only differently real. The sense of parity allows the world of nature to express all of its richness without condemning any orders to the dubious realm of the less real.

Further reading

Buchler, Justus. *Metaphysics of Natural Complexes*, second expanded edition, ed. Kathleen Wallace and Armen Marsoobian, with Robert S. Corrington. Albany, NY: SUNY Press, 1990.

Corrington, Robert S. *An Introduction to C.S. Peirce.* Lanham and New York: Rowman and Littlefield, 1993.

Emerson, Ralph Waldo. *Essays and Lectures.* New York: Library of America, 1983.

Marsoobian, Armen, Wallace, Kathleen, and Corrington, Robert S. *Nature's Perspectives: Prospects for Ordinal Metaphysics.* Albany, NY: SUNY Press, 1991.

Whitehead, Alfred North. *Process and Reality*, corrected edition, ed. David Ray Griffin and Donald W. Sherburne. New York: Free Press, 1978.

Robert S. Corrington

CREATIVITY

In ordinary usage, "creativity" usually denotes a psychological phenomenon, a state or a process within an individual human being. This is the primary sense of creativity that analytic philosophers seem to have in mind when investigating, for example, the creative processes of scientific discovery, such as the creation of novel hypotheses. The concept of creativity has, however, been thematized by American philosophers from broader perspectives. In both pragmatism and process philosophy, as well as in the traditions of idealism and personalism, creativity is viewed as a metaphysically significant, even cosmic, process of the emergence of something new. The novelties produced in such creative processes are, however, not chaotic or random but (humanly) significant.

Creativity in pragmatism

American pragmatism is a philosophy of creativity *par excellence.* The pragmatist insists that ideas must be put into action in order to find out their proper meaning. We should make creative use of our thoughts and concepts, experimentally employing them in the course of experience. Even the most theoretical ideas should be creatively tested in terms of human practices. Insofar as reality itself is inseparable from experience and practices, also creativity will receive a metaphysical articulation in pragmatism. Moreover, creativity and habituality are not opposites in pragmatism; just as habits can be intelligent and reflective, the tacit knowledge and skills our practices depend on can themselves be creative, yielding new applications in new situations. The pragmatists' celebration of human creativity as a natural process is entirely opposed to the kind of mystification of the Creative Genius one finds, for example, in romanticism (which is not to say that pragmatism would have nothing to do with romanticism).

Charles Peirce, the father of pragmatism, developed an abductive methodology of scientific inference. This is essentially an account of the creative process of inventing novel explanatory hypotheses. More metaphysically, attempting to reconcile Darwinism with a view of purposiveness in nature, Peirce ended up with a speculative cosmological system in which the development of the universe is itself a process of creative evolution, guided by evolutionary love.

William James, because of his more individualist and psychological focus, discussed creativity on a more human scale, though he was also influenced (in addition to Peirce) by Henri Bergson's doctrine of creative evolution. In James's pragmatism, the world is not ready-made or absolutely independent of our interests and practices; rather, we actively and creatively contribute to organizing experience into a meaningfully structured reality. Thus, pragmatic creativity turns into creative world-construction. This position has received new (indeed, creative) reinterpretations in neo-pragmatism, for example in Richard Rorty's and Hilary Putnam's campaign against metaphysical realism.

John Dewey developed both Peircean and Jamesian themes further. For him, creativity – as thinking and experience in general – is essentially social, as it was for Peirce; like Peirce, he was interested in the creative character of scientific inquiry. But like James, he found human creativity world-transforming. It is in and through our experimental practices that we in effect make and remake the world we experience. Through such creativity, experience grows and new possibilities emerge. When a problematic situation is transformed into a more satisfactory one by means of inquiry, intelligence is used creatively. The new pedagogy Dewey promoted, for instance through his experimental school, was supposed to enhance creativity, whereas traditional pedagogical ideas were seen by Dewey as obstacles to creativity.

The fourth major classical pragmatist, G.H. Mead, joined Dewey in defending an irreducibly social creative reconstruction of meanings and problematic situations. Yet in Mead, again, creativity ultimately applies not only to thought and inquiry but to natural metaphysics as well. Mead's ideas on creativity have been particularly well received in recent German social theory, for example in Hans Joas's work.

Creativity in other American traditions

The tradition of process philosophy, whose main representatives include A.N. Whitehead and Charles Hartshorne, also emphasized creativity as a cosmic process of natural evolution. According to process philosophers, God is the supreme or eminent creative power while remaining open to creative influence by His creatures. As in pragmatism, it is argued that we are not only created but creative. We help to determine reality; the development of the universe is not pre-determined independently of human creative possibilities.

If the universe itself is creatively "malleable" (as James put it), "unfinished," and open, then presumably some form of *idealism* (or perhaps panpsychism) must be true. Idealistic overtones are common to both pragmatist and process-metaphysical treatments of creativity. The world we live in is not a meaningless, machine-like "block universe" (to adopt another expression from James). Instead, it is a humanly meaningful process of purposive development, responsive to our needs and interests; it is a world we can creatively manipulate and reorganize into a more pragmatically relevant shape.

Among the subcurrents of twentieth-century idealism, American *personalism*, in particular, has celebrated the creative powers of the basic elements of reality. According to personalists (e.g. the "Boston personalists," namely Borden P. Bowne and his followers in the late nineteenth and early twentieth centuries), the world is at its most fundamental level constituted by personal beings – that is, by creative centers of activity and spirituality, the supreme among which is God. While personalism is not widely supported today, it is one of the now classical American articulations of the idealist perspective on creativity one may find in pragmatism and process philosophy, too. A very different form of idealism, the absolute idealism defended by Josiah Royce, among others, also attempted to make sense of creativity, though it is difficult to see how individual creativity can be maintained within absolute idealism. Genuine human creativity may seem to require the kind of conception of God – the supreme creator – as finite that (Jamesian) pragmatism, personalism, and process philosophy shared.

Creativity is a multifaceted idea central to, or at least implicitly present in, most of classical American philosophy; only crude forms of materialism and determinism have not paid much attention to this notion, as it seems to be an inherently indeterminist one. One of the open issues that future pragmatists and other American philosophers will face is the limits of human creativity. This question has a lot to do with pragmatist views on experience and learning. Is our learning of new things, our coming to possess new knowledge (in science or in ordinary experience), a creative process in which the object of knowledge is "constructed" (or even technologically "produced") rather than being discovered as it independently is, or are we in our epistemic activities answerable to an objective reality which we cannot fundamentally alter, however creative we are? As this problem indicates, the notion of creativity is at the center of the traditional dispute between idealism and realism, to which American philosophers have contributed voluminously.

Further reading

Anderson, Douglas R. *Creativity and the Philosophy of C.S. Peirce*. The Hague: Martinus Nijhoff, 1987.

Hartshorne, Charles. *Creativity in American Philosophy*. Albany, NY: SUNY Press, 1984.

Joas, Hans. *The Creativity of Action*. Chicago, IL: University of Chicago Press, 1997.

Rosenthal, Sandra B. *Speculative Pragmatism*. Amherst, MA: University of Massachusetts Press, 1986.

Rosenthal, Sandra B., Hausman, Carl R., and Anderson, Douglas R. (eds) *Classical American Pragmatism: Its Contemporary Vitality*. Urbana and Chicago, IL: University of Illinois Press, 1999.

Smith, John E. *America's Philosophical Vision*. Chicago, IL: University of Chicago Press, 1992.

Sami Pihlström

CRITICAL COMMONSENSISM

Charles S. Peirce introduced the concept of critical commonsensism around 1905 to describe the way in which his pragmatism ("pragmaticism") claims practical indubitability for beliefs based on everyday experience. Critial commonsensism amounts to the thesis that at no point in the development of human knowledge *all* propositions may be doubted at the *same time* because at all times we need a large number of indubitable beliefs providing the ground to decide about beliefs claims that may turn out to be true or false without undermining our entire web of knowledge about the world. Peirce calls critial commonsensism "critical" because, alluding to Kant, he holds that under some conditions, a critical evaluation and rejection of some instinctive beliefs is possible. But he acknowledges their instinctive and acritical nature as a starting point and basis for all other sorts of knowledge. Instinctive beliefs and inferences are acritical because they are brought about by our unconscious makeup. These indubitable beliefs are dispensed from doubt because (1) it is impossible because they are mainly unconscious processes that cannot be subjected to criticism and (2) they are internally related to those habits that constitute the practice of our human form of life. Critial commonsensism amounts to the claim that

> there are indubitable beliefs which vary a little and but a little under varying circumstances and in distant ages; that they partake of the nature of instincts, this word being taken in a broad sense; that they concern matters within the purview of the primitive man.
>
> (Peirce CP 5.498)

Critial commonsensism is developed as a variety of Reid's philosophy of common sense. Peirce underwrites explicitly Reid's claim that there are beliefs and inferences that are instinctive and indubitable. These are what Reid calls "natural beliefs." In contrast to Reid, Peirce holds that indubitable beliefs might lose their indubitability. This happens whenever the development of human society, culture or science changes the original form of human life which gives rise to natural beliefs. In this case old indubitable beliefs will be replaced by new ones because the new forms of human life constitute different habits and interally related beliefs. A crucial epistemological feature of critial commonsensism is that these beliefs will always be very vague: the "acritical indubitable is invariably vague" (Peirce 1998: 350). Peirce claims that the vagueness of indubitable beliefs has two kinds.

(1) A vague statement is "objectively general" when it leaves the determination of an individual object represented by a belief open to its interpreter. For example, my claim "All men are mortal" is vague because it leaves it to the interpreter to choose any man he likes to check its truth. To such a general belief "the principle of excluded middle does not apply" (Peirce CP 5.502). Only a few statements – and no general ones – can be determinate with respect to all their interpretations.

(2) An indubitable belief may not only be objectively *general*, but also objectively *vague*. When I call an apple yellow, I leave it open whether this is a lighter or a darker shade of yellow. In general, there is always some predicative aspect in which a belief is objectively vague and in this respect the law of contradiction is not applicable to it. In stressing the vagueness of indubitable beliefs, critial commonsensism makes room for the change (i.e. of specification and interpretation) that constitutes the development of knowledge in science and in everyday experience.

Critical commonsensism, because of the vagueness and indubitability of instinctive beliefs, seems to contradict fallibilism. But this appearance is misleading. Rather, this points towards a tension in human knowledge in general between the practical certainty and theoretical uncertainty of knowledge. In his fallibilism Peirce claims that in principle all beliefs may be wrong. Consequently, fallibilism entails only the thesis that there are no beliefs that are in principle indubitable. But then critial commonsensism and fallibilism are compatible because critial commonsensism only requires *practical* indubitability: *any one* of the practically indubitable beliefs at some time may be doubted at some later time. So the critial commonsensism claim that indubitability cannot be avoided is a claim about the practical status of beliefs: Propositions are indubitable only for a group of believers and a specific period of time.

The idea but not the concept of critial commonsensism was taken up by some pragmatists, e.g. by John Dewey. In contemporary philosophy of science Peirce's thesis that because of the vagueness of all sorts of knowledge there will always be a constitutive relation between everyday and scientific knowledge has been largely ignored. But a trace of it resurfaced recently in Arthur Fine's "Natural Ontological Argument" (Fine 1996: 126f) that stresses the ontological continuity between common sense and the sciences.

Further reading

Fine, Arthur. *The Shaky Game. Einstein Realism and the Quantum Theory.* Chicago, IL: University of Chicago Press, 1996.

Peirce, Charles S. *Collected Papers of Charles Sanders Peirce* (CP), ed. Charles Hartshorne and Paul Weiss (Vols I–VI), Arthur W. Burks (Vols VII and VIII). Cambridge, MA: Harvard University Press, 1931–5; second edition Cambridge, MA: Belknap Press, 1958. CP 5.498, refers to the fifth volume and the 498th section.

—— *The Essential Peirce. Selected Philosophical Writings Vol. 2, 1893–1913*, ed. the Peirce Edition Project. Bloomington, IN: Indiana University Press, 1998.

HELMUT PAPE

CRITICISM

The term "criticism" appears only infrequently in American philosophy, but the concept plays a key role in many of American philosophy's most distinctive traditions, texts, and self-understandings.

Philosophy as criticism

The fullest and most explicit account of criticism in American philosophy is set forth by John Dewey in the final chapter of his *Experience and Nature.* Dewey defined philosophy as criticism, and defined criticism as judgment about goods or values. There are many fields and types of criticism, but for Dewey it is philosophy's generality that makes it distinctive. Dewey called it "criticism of criticism." Because life teaches us that goods are difficult to identify, secure, and sustain, intelligent judgment and the inquiry on which it is based has immense practical significance. This is the pragmatic value of philosophy, understood as criticism.

There is both something old and something new in this view or reconstruction of philosophy as criticism. It recovers the ancient notion of philosophy as love of wisdom, as a way of life, and as practical. This conception stands in sharp contrast to more recent views of philosophy as a discipline or body of knowledge with its own special subject matter, as a profession within modern universities, and as formal technique or arcane system or compendium of the arcane systems of earlier thinkers. It is this commitment to understanding philosophy as critically intelligent life itself that animates, for example: Emerson's plea that his readers become "Man Thinking" rather than bookworms; James's attack on the "PhD Octopus" that substitutes institutional certification for originality and force of intellect; and, Santayana's analysis of how Emerson and James overturned "the genteel tradition" in American thought on behalf of a naturalistic, radically empirical view of the universe as wild, in-the-making, and measured by action. As Santayana recognized, this view of philosophy as criticism also sets forth something new. To understand philosophy as criticism is to reject the traditional image of philosophy as idle contemplation, the old idea of knowledge for knowledge's sake, or concern with supposedly universal and eternal matters. It is to embrace a view of philosophy as wholly experiential and experimental, as thoroughly instrumental in its efforts to establish more enduring and extensive values, and as fully local, temporal, and relative to particular interests and concerns, like all activities constituted by their times and places.

Consequences of criticism

While there have been many American philosophers who did not share this view – from Puritans and Calvinists to American Hegelians, personalists, and idealists to more recent professional logic choppers and learned caretakers of past systems – this view of philosophy as criticism underlies radically empirical, naturalistic, pragmatic, and humanistic strains across American philosophy. It also explains three characteristics within these traditions. First, to view philosophy as criticism is, in American philosophy, to make values the center of philosophy. It is to reject the notion that metaphysics is "First Philosophy" (and that facts are more real or separate from values). It is to reject the notion that epistemology is the rigorous core of philosophy (and that knowing and knowledge are independent of the values and interests from which they arose). It is from this perspective that Emerson and Thoreau simply brushed aside the puzzles of most modern European metaphysics and epistemology; that Peirce classified logic, with ethics and aesthetics, as one branch or sub-set of "normative science"; that Bowne and James demanded a philosophy of personal intimacy with the universe and rejected fact/value and nature/experience dichotomies; and that Dewey railed against the "epistemology industry" and announced the need to recover philosophy from artificial problems that arise when a realm of existence is posited apart from a realm of values.

Second, understood as criticism, philosophy in the hands of many American thinkers became interdisciplinary and continuous with other modes of criticism, including both the sciences and literature (and other arts). Philosophy, science, and the arts, Dewey argued, all distinguish immediate goods from those that result from critical inquiry. Accordingly, American philosophers typically have aligned themselves with science, though not with xdetermination of belief, stressed that the background to his thought was the laboratory. And, Mead, Dewey, and later philosophers such as C.I. Lewis and Quine demanded that philosophy account for the world as science warrants. At the same time, American philosophers also have aligned themselves with poetry, novels, painting, music and the arts: Emerson focused on originality, imagination, and self-creation; James, frequently employing metaphors from painting and music, stressed the central role of temperament, affect, and the ways in which experience outstrips thought; and, Santayana, author of acclaimed poetry and fiction, suggested in his best-selling novel *The Last Puritan* that drama and fiction may be more effective modes of philosophic expression than traditional treatises and essays – a theme echoed more recently by Richard Rorty.

Third, American philosophers who have viewed philosophy as criticism in turn have viewed philosophy as in principle unfinished, always incomplete, always to be adjusted and reconstructed for the future in light of new developments. Thus there is in much American philosophy a strong (though not complete) strain of hostility to philosophical system, architectonic, and announcements of the completion of philosophy. While Peirce and Royce, for example, sought to develop systems, thinkers such as Emerson, Whitman, James, DuBois, Addams, and Dewey challenged persons to live with originality, grasp the future as open, recognize that old habits of thought may not fit new realities, and move forward with the work of conceptual and cultural criticism and intelligent reconstruction. For the same reason, these philosophers did not claim to have a crystal ball and resisted the idea that they should or could determine the future's agenda. Unlike traditional philosophy that holds that the future will be like the past, these American philosophers asserted that in important ways the future will not be like the past, and so that, as Dewey put it, each age must determine its own ills. As a result, critics often have contended that these thinkers are vague and do not explain concretely just what should be done. This complaint, however, is at odds with a commitment to philosophy as fallible, piecemeal, in-process inquiry and discrimination of values in light of changing, actual life conditions.

Criticism of American thought and life

Dewey's writings on psychology, science, logic, education, politics, ethics, art, and religion issue from this commitment to philosophy as criticism. So too do his many essays on issues of his day. Throughout this work, Dewey sought to clear away outdated conceptions and transform social practices. Instead of the quest for certainty, he championed experimental inquiry and developed an account of logic as the theory of that inquiry. In place of a politics of "ready-made" individualism, freedom as absence of constraints, and rationality as self-evident intuition, Dewey set forth a renewed liberalism dedicated to social relations and community, the availability of actual means for self-realization, and inquiry. In place of supernaturalism, he advocated a naturalistic expansion of religious experience. In place of rote learning, he focused on growth and the progressive education that secured it. Instead of fine art quarantined in museums, Dewey advocated a view of art as experience and the aesthetic dimension of daily life. And along the way he wrote critically about America's foreign policies, war, and totalitarianism, poverty, immigration, political parties, communications media, and the moral meaning of democracy.

This same critical orientation is evident, of course, in the work of many other American philosophers, including: Royce's account of loyalty, wise provincialism, and Great Community; Hocking's theory of the state and his analysis of liberalism and its enemies; James's "The Moral Philosopher and the Moral Life"; and, Lewis's theory of valuation. But it is also evident, perhaps more evident, in the work of American thinkers who often have been assigned to the margins of philosophy by persons who have not viewed philosophy as criticism. Nineteenth-century writers from Emerson and Thoreau to Whitman often have been considered too literary to be philosophers. Nonetheless, it is obvious that their concerns – nature, self, soul, community, American culture – are straightforwardly philosophical. Similarly, public leaders and politicians such as Franklin, Jefferson, Madison, Hamilton, and Lincoln, concerned with the most central and basic issues of political theory, wrote philosophical criticism. Women writers and activists, from Susan B. Anthony and Charlotte Perkins Gilman to Jane Addams, judged by some to have dealt with issues insufficiently eternal or theoretically, appear as important philosophers when philosophy is understood as criticism. And African-American writers such as Frederick Douglass, Booker T. Washington, W.E.B. DuBois, Alain Locke, Martin Luther King, Jr, and Malcolm X also engaged in far-reaching social criticism that addressed identity, community, democracy, equality, violence, power, and legitimation – topics considered in a different context by canonical writers from Plato to Hobbes to Locke. By understanding philosophy as criticism, the philosophical as well as social importance of this work and these writers becomes clear.

Further reading

Dewey, John. *Experience and Nature* in *John Dewey: The Later Works, 1925–1953, Vol. 1, 1925*, ed. Jo Ann Boydston. Carbondale, IL: Southern Illinois University Press, 1981 [1925].

—— *Logic: The Theory of Inquiry* in *John Dewey: The Later Works, 1925–1953, Vol. 12, 1938*, ed. Jo Ann Boydston. Carbondale, IL: Southern Illinois University Press, 1986 [1938].

Peirce, Charles S. "The Fixation of Belief" in *The Essential Peirce, Selected Philosophical Writings*, Vol. 1, ed. Nathan Houser and Christian Kloesel. Bloomington, IN: Indiana University Press, 1992 [1877].

Santayana, G. *Scepticism and Animal Faith*. New York: Charles Scribner's Sons, 1923. See especially Chs 11, 15, 27.

Stuhr, John J. "Pragmatism as Criticism" in Elias L. Khalil (ed.) *Dewey, Pragmatism, and Economic Methodology*. New York and London: Routledge, 2004, pp. 231–9.

West, Cornel. "Prophetic Pragmatism: Cultural Criticism and Political Engagement" in his *The American Evasion of Philosophy: A Genealogy of Pragmatism*. Madison, WI: University of Wisconsin Press, 1988, pp. 211–42.

John J. Stuhr

CULTURE

For purposes of philosophy, "culture" consists of common ways of feeling, thinking, and acting. New knowledge, and the application of that knowledge, disturb both the pattern of living and the meaning of life supplied by culture. One of the functions of philosophy is to reorganize and reinterpret human experience in times when the fabric of culture has been rent. The industrial revolution, the theory of natural selection, and various natural disasters have caused social disturbances and the need to re-adjust one's thinking and activities.

Normally, the answer to cosmic mystery has usually been answered by one's culture. Cultures enable the feeling of normality (or as William James would say, the feeling of rationality). This is usually accomplished by myths of origins and endings – that is, nature, while never encountered whole, can be unified in vision. Myths help to unify the natural world despite its tempestuous and capricious character. According to John Herman Randall, Jr, myths function as connectives (not to be confused with logical connectives). Even empirically verified theories of geological beginnings, "big bang" cosmologies, evolution, are myths – not because they are in any way false, but because they function as connectives. The current struggle between creationists and natural selection theorists is a struggle between which myths Western culture should adopt. This is not to deny the truth of natural selection, nor is it to assert the truth of creationism. One wishes only to indicate that the nature of the struggle is one of organizing culture. One of the effects of culture is that it makes what is believed, felt or done seem normal (even though it might seem strange to outsiders).

Testing for cultural influence

One way to test whether a belief, a philosophical thesis, or an action is a product of culture is to ask in disbelief, "How otherwise could it be?" An obvious non-philosophical example of this is the habit of sleeping with a pillow under one's head. How otherwise could this be? But in traditional Japan, people slept with their heads on a wooden block.

In philosophy, culture channels the way we think. The most obvious way is to see how very different Western and Eastern philosophies are. They are so different that Westerners are reluctant to acknowledge that Eastern thought constitutes philosophy. Only politeness and the fear of seeming unduly chauvinistic are reasons why Eastern thought is accorded recognition as philosophy (when in fact, during the early part of the twentieth century, most Western philosophers would not acknowledge traditional Eastern thought to constitute philosophy). It is not a question of fact that Eastern philosophy was not "real philosophy." It was due to Western philosophical culture.

But, even within Western philosophy itself, culture makes itself felt. Because Western philosophers are always arguing, raising questions, and being skeptical, philosophy seems to be countercultural. It is difficult to believe that culture could rein in such free thinkers. But it does. Ask yourself, "Should philosophers be rational?" How otherwise could it be? Well, they could be irrational. Could they? Since it is inconceivable that philosophers should prize irrationality, it suggests that rationality is culturally prized. Culture determines what is acceptable in philosophy. And philosophical culture insists on philosophy being a rational enterprise. This does not mean that without the influence of culture we would not prize rationality in philosophy. Rather, it means that without the influence of culture we would not even have philosophy.

In most parts of the world, people have been guided by precepts found in religious scripture, which itself is based on the testimony of persons who claim to have been inspired by a deity. The reports of their inspiration were oral. It was not until many centuries later that we got written accounts; i.e. scriptures. There was no philosophy as we conceive of it today.

Although some have seen philosophy as having evolved from ancient Near-Eastern myths, the origins of philosophy should be attributed to Greek culture. Were this not so, philosophy would have sprung up all over, East, West, North and South. The Greeks consecrated themselves to the ideals of wisdom and worshiped Athena. They celebrated the Seven Wise Men (long before the Pre-Socratics), which says that Greek culture strove to be rational. Not all people strive to be rational, deferring to the guidance of inspired religious prophets. The story of Adam and Eve is a warning about trying to know too much. Even the Greeks had deferred to such warnings (as in the story about Pandora), but their history shows a struggle to free themselves from such prophetic guidance. In his *Nicomachean Ethics*, Aristotle urged men not to listen to poets like Simonides (who warns men against trying to know too much), whereupon Aristotle exhorted readers to leave nothing unattempted in the desire to know.

The point is that there was in Greek culture something which did not exist elsewhere in Europe or the Near East, which made people aspire to rationality. The diffusion of this cultural attitude to other peoples has brought us to philosophy as it is practiced today, where we say about being rational, "How else can thinkers be?"

Dewey, more importantly than anyone else, showed how philosophy and culture were intertwined. In *Philosophy and Civilization* (1934) Dewey wrote, "Philosophy ... is itself a phenomenon of human culture," and "The life of all thought is to effect a junction at some point of the new and the old ... Thus philosophy marks a change of culture." In *Individualism Old and New* (1930), Dewey was concerned with "The Crisis in Culture," worried about how a distinctive American culture could be marred by pecuniary values and he worried about the failure of education to provide direction.

Cultural critics that come to mind

There are many philosophers who have been engaged in a struggle against the philosophical culture of their time, but, only a few will be discussed.

In the latter part of the nineteenth century, William James and Friedrich Nietzsche struggled against culture and its effects on philosophical thinking. James was aware that philosophical culture was aligned against his thinking and was engaged in a struggle against it. Nietzsche was conscious that Western philosophy was formed by culture and sought to expose its influence (which he thought was pernicious).

James went outside the philosophical culture of his time, thinking that there was "something more" than the mechanistic universe which satisfied the prevailing parsimonious positivists who studied nothing but the facts.

James had a different view of what is philosophically permissible, about being rational, the function of philosophy and discussed areas regarded as intellectually unfashionable, even disreputable. His "Will to Believe," his theory of truth, and his denial of consciousness, all ran afoul of the prevailing culture. James did not altogether succeed, but he made others reconsider prevailing attitudes. The positivistic view softened. His notion of how things are known to be true paralleled how things are known to be true when scientists inquire. Nevertheless, much of the philosophical world was outraged at James' notion of truth.

Friedrich Nietzsche was quite conscious of Western culture and despised it, railed against the transvaluation of values, calling for a change. He thought that Western, Christian values – e.g. the inability to be an enemy – were, from a biological point of view, pernicious. His *On the Genealogy of Morals* (1887), *Beyond Good and Evil* (1885), and *The Antichrist* (1895) speak to problems in Western culture and contrast it unfavorably to pagan culture of the past.

Further reading

Buchler, Justus and Randall, John Herman, Jr. *Philosophy: An Introduction*. New York: Barnes and Noble, 1971, Ch. III, "The Cultural and Historical Function of Philosophy."

James, William. *The Will to Believe*. New York: Longmans, Green, 1897.

—— *Pragmatism*. New York: Longmans, Green, 1907.

—— *Essays in Radical Empiricism*. New York: Longmans, Green, 1971.

Nietzsche, Friedrich. *On the Genealogy of Morals* and *Ecce Homo* (in one vol.), ed. and trans. Walter Kaufmann. New York: Random House, 1969.

——*Beyond Good and Evil*, ed. and trans. Walter Kaufmann. New York: Random House, 1966.

Randall, John Herman, Jr. "Unifications of Knowledge" in *Nature and Historical Experience*. New York: Columbia University Press, 1957.

ANGELO JUFFRAS

D

DANTO, ARTHUR

Arthur Coleman Danto (1924–) is one of America's foremost analytic philosophers. His work has ranged across several of the major fields and figures of philosophy, although today he is probably best known for his contributions to the philosophy of art. Born 1 January 1924 in Ann Arbor, Michigan, Danto spent most of his childhood in Detroit, where he was a frequent visitor to the Detroit Institute of Arts. As a young man he wanted to become an artist, and after serving for two years in the Army, he studied art and worked briefly as a painter. Around the same time he took up the study of philosophy, entering Columbia University as a graduate student in the late 1940s.

Although the philosophy department at Columbia was pragmatically oriented during Danto's time there, he became committed to doing analytical philosophy when he began teaching. In the mid-1960s he started writing books that treated a wide variety of philosophical subjects from an analytic point of view. Danto's work during the 1960s and 1970s was especially notable for what he chose to place under the loupe of analysis. For instance, his *Nietzsche as Philosopher* (1965) dealt with a thinker who had largely been marginalized in the English-speaking world, and contributed to a serious reconsideration of Nietzsche's thought. In *Mysticism and Morality: Oriental Thought and Moral Philosophy* (1972), Danto provided a rare examination of Eastern philosophy by a "philosopher of analytical persuasion (Danto 1987). Over the course of these two decades he also authored books on the philosophy of history, epistemology, the philosophy of action, the nature of philosophy, and Jean-Paul Sartre.

During his student days Danto had eventually made a conscious decision to abandon his painting career in order to fully devote himself to philosophy. Years later, in 1964, a visit to an Andy Warhol exhibition at the Stable Gallery in New York City proved to be a pivotal experience for the philosopher, one which set him on the path to formulating a highly original and insightful philosophy of art. It is unusual that a thinker can directly trace a theoretical breakthrough to a specific incident in his or her life, and for this reason alone Danto's fateful visit to the Warhol exhibit would be noteworthy. However, as we shall see, Danto argues that his philosophical reflections about art were not the result of exposure to art in general, but were the fruit of his attempts to understand the art world of the mid-1960s.

What so impressed and electrified Danto at the Warhol show were mock-ups of Brillo soap pad boxes that would be mistaken for the actual product if they were relocated on to supermarket shelves. The artist-turned-philosopher saw himself placed before the following question: What made Warhol's boxes works of art and hence distinguished them from normal Brillo boxes? The answer, developed at length in *The Transfiguration of the Commonplace: A Philosophy of Art* (1981), is that art objects in one way or another all embody a statement about something else, whereas everyday objects do not. Another way of making the same point would be to say that artworks incorporate a metaphor-like quality: for instance, Warhol's Brillo boxes instantiate the relation Brillo-box-as-work-of-art (Danto 1981: 208).

After having developed his thesis about the nature of art, Danto took a sort of Hegelian turn and argued that art has reached its historical conclusion (*The Philosophical Disenfranchisement of Art*, 1986). He interprets the historical development of art as having culminated in the mid-1960s, because the artwork of this period became a kind of philosophical reflection about its own essence. In Danto's view, the existence of such philosophically loaded art objects was a precondition to his discovery of the defining feature of art. He construes the radical pluralism of the contemporary art scene as further evidence that art has entered a post-historical phase.

In addition to his work as a philosopher, Danto has been the in-house art critic at *The Nation* since 1984, and continues to publish prolifically in the fields of esthetics and art criticism.

Further reading

Danto, Arthur critial commonsensism *Nietzsche as Philosopher*. New York: Macmillan, 1965.

—— *Mysticism and Morality: Oriental Thought and Moral Philosophy*. New York: Basic Books, 1972.

—— *The Transfiguration of the Commonplace: A Philosophy of Art*. Cambridge, MA: Harvard University Press, 1981.

—— *The Philosophical Disenfranchisement of Art*. New York: Columbia University Press, 1986.

Halvorson, Jonathan. "A Conversation with Arthur Danto," *Conference: A Journal of Philosophy and Theory* 7, 1 (Autumn 1996); available at http://www.columbia.edu/cu/conference

JEFF MITCHELL
PETER H. HARE

DARWIN, INFLUENCE OF

Darwin's theory of evolution has had a significant influence on American philosophy. His book *The Origin of Species*, published in 1859, helped inspire the development of American pragmatism. In subsequent years evolutionary ideas have continued to influence American philosophy.

Although the influence of Darwinism is undeniable, philosophers have not always agreed on either its interpretation or its application. For example, there has been disagreement as to whether Darwinism can be applied to non-biological topics such as ethics, economics, and social policy. Thus, while there has been widespread agreement on the basic truth of Darwinism, there has been less agreement as to the nature and proper extent of its influence.

Darwinism's influence was most evident in the late nineteenth and early twentieth centuries, when many philosophers saw it as having revolutionary philosophical implications. These philosophers include the first American pragmatists, social Darwinists, and John Dewey, who perhaps best exemplifies the philosophical influence of Darwinism. Since then Darwinism has become part of the accepted scientific background of contemporary philosophy. Thus, most contemporary philosophy is, at least implicitly, Darwinian because it presumes a naturalistic, evolutionary account of human nature and origins. Although Darwinism's contemporary influence is largely implicit, in some areas its influence is more evident. For example, evolutionary ethicists, evolutionary epistemologists and philosophers of biology continue to use Darwinism to explain phenomena including sociability, scientific theory change, and the development of altruism.

Darwin's reception in America

Darwin's *The Origin of Species* found a receptive audience among American scientists and philosophers. In the field of biology, scientists were already familiar with the claim that species could undergo transformation. Similar theories had been proposed by Jean Baptiste de Lamarck (1744–1829) and Etienne Geoffroy St Hillaire (1772–1844) in France, and they were widely discussed in Britain and the United States. In addition, thanks to Charles Lyell's (1797–1875) work in geology, scientists were beginning to reconsider the age of the earth, rejecting the biblical chronology in favor of estimates ranging from tens of thousands to even millions of years. This meant that the transformation of species could be gradual and invisible during a human lifespan. To this fertile soil Darwin contributed both a meticulous empirical study of variations among animal species (the result of his five-year voyage aboard HMS *Beagle*) as well as a theoretical explanation of the origin and evolution of species. Darwin argued that different species were the result of, first, random variations among individuals and, second, the natural selection of favorable variations over time. His account of the origin and evolution of species was widely viewed as an improvement over earlier evolutionary accounts.

American scientists appear to have accepted Darwin's theory more easily than did British scientists. Their acceptance may have been due, in part, to the smaller, more flexible institutional structure of American science. Richard Hofstadter has suggested that the US Civil War also played a part by distracting public attention from Darwin's work. As a result, sympathetic American scientists were able to study Darwin relatively undisturbed and were well prepared, after the war, to defend Darwin against his American critics. By 1875 Darwinism was dominant among American biologists.

Most American philosophers, like American scientists, quickly embraced Darwin's theory of evolution, although here Darwinism also met with stiff resistance. Before 1859, when *The Origin of Species* appeared, American philosophy was dominated by transcendentalism and idealism. These theories treated the natural world as dependent on either God or mind: transcendentalists, such as Emerson, argued that the natural world served primarily as a revelation of God's nature; idealists argued that the nature of the universe depended on mental abilities and categories. According to many idealists, the reality of the physical world derived entirely from the mind, guaranteeing the world's intrinsic rationality. In contrast, Darwinism explained natural phenomena by appealing to the effects of random variation and a life-or-death competition for resources. As a result, Darwinism posed a challenge to those who wished to view nature as fundamentally divine or fundamentally rational. Instead, Darwinism suggested that natural phenomena, including the origin and diversity of species, could be explained without resorting either to divine will or to an underlying rational order. This, in turn, required that philosophers reconsider humanity's place in nature.

Like American scientists, American philosophers soon accepted the basic truth of Darwin's theory. Nonetheless, they disagreed over its philosophical implications. On the one hand, some proponents of idealism attempted to show how Darwinism could be accommodated within an idealistic framework. These idealists, such as John Fiske (1842–1901) and the young John Dewey, used evolutionary concepts to explain the rational progress of human history as well as the incremental development of political institutions. On the other hand, some American philosophers viewed Darwinism as an opportunity to purge philosophy of religious and idealistic speculation. These philosophers recognized that Darwinism undermined both the biblical creation story and the design argument for God's existence. Because Darwinism provided a compelling scientific account of how complex, well-ordered species developed, it was no longer possible to use the existence of these species as evidence for a divine creator. Likewise, some philosophers argued that Darwinism could explain the development of political institutions without indulging in unverifiable idealistic speculation. These philosophers hoped that, freed of its religious and idealistic associations, American philosophy would be better able to support scientific inquiry into the natural and social worlds.

Darwinism also contributed to changes that were already taking place in American philosophy. During the nineteenth century, American philosophy was becoming increasingly professionalized and, with the introduction of graduate programs in American universities, philosophers were more likely to have advanced philosophical training and were less likely to approach philosophy with a theological background. In addition, developments in other areas of science, combined with breathtaking changes in industry and technology, had expanded the range of topics and resources available to philosophers. In this environment Darwinism was one more reason for philosophers to avoid unnecessary metaphysical speculation and to propose theories that were consistent with the best science of the day. For many philosophers, the challenge was then to achieve scientific respectability without thereby dismissing the philosophical significance of moral and political values. The first American pragmatists took up this challenge.

Darwinism and the first pragmatists

Pragmatism, as a philosophical movement, can trace its origin to a group of young philosophers and intellectuals meeting in Cambridge, Massachusetts, during the early 1870s. This group, known as "The Metaphysical Club," included Chauncey Wright, William James, Charles Sanders Peirce, and Oliver Wendell Holmes, Jr. Darwinism was among the topics they discussed, and these conversations played a crucial role in the subsequent development of pragmatism.

Chauncey Wright (1830–75) was a staunch defender both of Darwinism and of what he called the neutrality of science. He is notable for being one of the first American defenders of Darwin as well as, later, one of Darwin's correspondents. Within the Metaphysical Club, Wright played the role of "boxing master" (as Peirce described him), reining in the speculative tendencies of other members and drawing a sharp distinction between science and ethics. Wright was especially impressed with Darwinism as a method for exploring biological questions; unlike some, he refused to treat Darwinism as a general metaphysical system with ethical or social implications. Thus, while he embraced Darwinism as an explanation of biological and even some psychological phenomena, he argued that it could not be applied to the development of either physical laws or political institutions (as some promoters of Darwinism claimed). Unfortunately, because Wright published little and died young, he did not have much influence except on those who knew him personally. But the influence he did have was significant. Most importantly, his defense of Darwinism convinced others to forego overarching metaphysical systems. Wright showed that Darwinism was fully capable of explaining biological phenomena despite not being, or requiring, a general metaphysical theory. Rather, Darwinism's success was due to its taking biological phenomena on their own terms and not attempting to impose a metaphysical system on them. From this Wright concluded that philosophers should likewise adopt a flexible methodology which takes into account the concrete differences between various topics. Many pragmatists took this lesson to heart.

Foremost among these was William James (1842–1910). Among his other contributions James popularized the claim that pragmatism is primarily a method and not a settled body of doctrine. Like Wright, he was also deeply influenced by Darwin, having had first-hand experience of the controversy surrounding Darwinism. This came from traveling, as a young man, with the naturalist Louis Agassiz (1807–73) on Agassiz's 1865 expedition to the Amazon. Agassiz was one of Darwin's most prominent critics and the purpose of the expedition was to collect evidence consistent with Agassiz's competing theory of divine creation. James disagreed with Agassiz's theory on methodological grounds, arguing that it had no uniquely testable implications. Because Agassiz's theory was untestable, it made no difference whether the theory was true or not and, for this reason, the theory had no influence on an understanding of the natural world. James's insight – that the worth of a theory depends on the concrete difference that it makes – is a central idea of pragmatism.

Darwinism influenced James in other ways as well. James's two-volume *The Principles of Psychology* (1890) contains many Darwinian themes. This is most clear in the final chapter, "Necessary Truths and the Effects of Experience." Here James considers the origin of what he calls "intuitively necessary truths" ranging from mathematical and logical truths to metaphysical axioms (such as "nothing can happen without a cause"). These truths, he argues, are intuitively necessary because of how the brain is structured. This makes intuitively necessary truths analogous to instincts and, as such, they can be explained in much the same way: namely, as having evolved through chance variation and natural selection. As James points out, this is an explicitly Darwinian account of the origin of instinctive, intuitively necessary truths. This means, first, that these beliefs arose randomly and, second, that these intuitively necessary beliefs are truths not because they necessarily correspond to the world but because, instead, they give an advantage to their holder. Individuals with these beliefs are more likely to survive than those without them.

This account of intuitively necessary truths leads to two additional points, both of which indicate Darwinism's influence. The first is the element of chance or "spontaneity." Throughout his career James argued that chance was a necessary ingredient of a meaningful life. Without chance, he argued, the world is entirely deterministic, real choice is an illusion, morality becomes a sham, and human life loses its meaning. It is the existence of chance that provides opportunities for exercising choice and control over the direction of human affairs. This is a recurring theme in many of James's works, including "The Will to Believe" (1896), *Great Men and Their Environment* (1880), and "The Dilemma of Determinism" (1884). The second point concerns James's pragmatic theory of truth. This also owes a debt to Darwinism since, as is evident in his discussion of intuitively necessary truths, true beliefs are ones that work or that have survival value. Thus, as James argued in both *Pragmatism* (1907) and *The Meaning of Truth* (1911), truth is primarily a practical relationship between our ideas and our actions, and not an abstract theoretical relationship between ideas and an already given reality. First and foremost, we use the concept of truth to identify dependable beliefs: beliefs that can be reliably acted on. True beliefs are therefore useful beliefs and they remain true so long as they are not replaced by yet more dependable beliefs. For this reason James' pragmatic theory of truth is Darwinian in two senses: first, in linking truth to survival value, and second, in describing the evolution of true beliefs as the result of selection.

Although James deserves credit for introducing pragmatism to a wider audience, he gave Charles Sanders Peirce (1839–1914) credit for launching the movement. Peirce, like the other members of the Metaphysical Club, was influenced by Darwinism. But Darwinism's influence on Peirce was complicated and idiosyncratic. Unlike other pragmatists,

Peirce used Darwinism as the basis of an elaborate metaphysics.

In a lecture entitled "Design and Chance" (1883–4) Peirce wrote that his position "is only Darwinism analyzed, generalized, and brought into the realm of Ontology." Although Peirce would later distance himself from Darwinism, he would continue to develop an evolutionary account of the physical universe in general. The central concepts of this account are "tychism," "synechism," and "agapism." Tychism, according to Peirce, means that the universe contains truly chance events. Like James, Peirce wished to preserve the possibility of spontaneity and human individuality, neither of which seem possible in a deterministic world. Synechism is the thesis that nature is continuous: that physics, chemistry, biology and psychology gradually shade into each other. This thesis justifies Peirce in proposing a single, unified account of how the universe evolved. Agapism, finally, refers to Peirce's claim that "love," as opposed to competition, guides evolution.

Tychism, synechism, and agapism are most prominent in Peirce's 1892 essay "Evolutionary Love." Here Peirce develops an evolutionary cosmology, or theory of the universe's development, that takes the following form. First, he argues that, just as biological species have evolved, physical laws have likewise evolved from a state of primordial chaos. Second, he argues that even though the universe is no longer entirely chaotic, random events still take place. As a result, physical laws are probabilistic, not deterministic. Third, he argues that there are three ways for evolution to occur: through random variation (as Darwin proposed), through a non-random, deterministic process, or through the "law of love." Peirce illustrates the "law of love" by comparing it to the sacrifice a parent makes for a child. Because such sacrificial acts are done for a reason, Peirce claims that evolution through love is goal-directed. Fourth, and finally, Peirce claims that determinism cannot be supported scientifically and that, while Darwinian evolution can be supported scientifically, it is actually a "degenerate" form of agapism. The result is a evolutionary cosmology guided by self-sacrificing love.

Peirce's theory deviates from Darwinism in at least three respects. First, it downplays the importance of random variations and the subsequent effects of natural selection. Instead, it substitutes the entirely different mechanism of self-sacrificing love. Second, this theory is goal-directed. Unlike Darwinism, which distinguishes between evolution and progress, Peirce's cosmology implies that the universe is becoming increasingly well ordered and "sympathetic." Third, Peirce expands evolution to explain a wide range of phenomena, not just the origin of species. He uses evolution to explain the origin of physical laws, the course of human history, and everything in between.

Peirce's evolutionary cosmology was also at odds with the mainstream of pragmatic thought. Because it tries to explain the entire universe in terms of a single unifying principle, Peirce's cosmology has more in common with Leibniz or Hegel than it does with Wright or James. For this reason, even though Darwinism had an undeniable influence on Peirce, this influence had little subsequent effect on the pragmatic movement.

Oliver Wendell Holmes, Jr (1841–1935) is best remembered as an Associate Justice of the US Supreme Court. But Holmes, like Wright, James, and Peirce, was also a member of the Metaphysical Club and, as a result, his judicial philosophy shows Darwin's clear influence. Most notably, Holmes claimed that laws are neither inherently rational nor based on universal norms of justice. Instead, he argued, laws evolve in response to social pressures.

In a series of lectures published as *The Common Law* (1881) Holmes writes that "the life of the law has not been logic; it has been experience." This means that legal decisions do not follow with logical necessity. For example, judges can, in many cases, use the same legal principle to decide in favor of either the plaintiff or the defendant. In addition, judges base their decisions on a range of factors including legal precedent, social norms, moral principles, and the particular facts of the case. In these cases their experience is more important than logic. Experience, according to Holmes, is the accumulated wisdom (or know-how) implicit in a reasonable person's behavior: for example, recognizing the general distinction between bad luck and criminal negligence, and being able to apply this distinction in particular cases. This wisdom, embodied in the legal system, is the product of centuries of human interaction with other humans and with the natural world. As a result, as human wisdom and experience evolve, the legal system evolves as well.

Holmes's judicial philosophy is both pragmatic and Darwinian. According to Holmes, laws, like biological species, evolve in response to external pressures. As with biological species, it is a mistake to assume that laws have a timeless, essential nature, that they are progressing toward a goal, or that their changes are always rational. On the contrary, laws are best viewed as tools and, like any tool, are human artifacts that can be modified to serve different functions. From this it follows that laws do not depend on a universally valid foundation such as a priori principles of justice or universal human rights. As Holmes argues in his essay "Natural Law" (1918), laws instead owe their authority to their pragmatic success in guiding human behavior in socially desirable directions. Anything more than this is historically unsupported and unnecessary.

Of all the members of the Metaphysical Club, Holmes may have had the greatest social influence. This may be surprising, since he is best known for his dissents while on the Supreme Court. However, after his retirement in 1932, Holmes's dissenting opinions provided the judicial basis for New Deal social programs and the expansion of free-speech rights.

Social Darwinism

Darwinism had influence on American life and thought outside pragmatism. Throughout much of the nineteenth and early twentieth centuries, Darwinism's greatest influence was most likely through the social scientists and policy makers known as social Darwinists. The social Darwinists applied the Darwinian concept of natural selection to social groups. This led the most prominent social Darwinists to defend a set of ideologies that included laissez-faire capitalism and imperialism. Other social Darwinists used this theory to defend racism and eugenics programs.

Social Darwinist ideas were first put forward by the Englishman Herbert Spencer (1820–1903). In works that cite Darwin's *The Origin of Species*, Spencer argued that "the survival of the fittest" (a phrase he coined) described both the natural and the social worlds. Claiming that competition is necessary for the human race to improve, Spencer concluded that governments should only protect the most basic rights of life and liberty. Otherwise, governments should let nature take its course. For this reason Spencer opposed publicly funded education and child labor laws.

William Graham Sumner (1840–1910) was the most prominent American social Darwinist. Like Spencer, Sumner argued that competition functioned as a natural law governing human life. In modern society, this competition was for financial capital and other economic resources. As a result, Sumner opposed government regulation of business since, he argued, it limited social progress. The choice was obvious: "if we do not like the survival of the fittest, we have only one possible alternative, and that is the survival of the unfittest. The former is the law of civilization; the latter is the law of anti-civilization." Sumner concluded that governments could (and should) ensure free markets where citizens could compete for resources. But governments were not entitled to take affirmative action to increase equality or political participation among their citizens. Doing so would interfere with the natural order by punishing those who had shown greater fitness. Thus, Sumner valued freedom over other social values such as equality or democracy.

Spencer's and Sumner's ideas resonated with many Americans in the late nineteenth century. To many, their version of social Darwinism exemplified the American ideal of rugged individualism. Thus, social Darwinism helped justify the economic status quo at a time when the United States was becoming increasingly industrialized and multiethnic. Laissez-faire capitalism became the mechanism for social selection. Those at the bottom of the socio-economic ladder were free, through individual initiative, to rise as far as they were able. Those who failed were considered either less fit or less ambitious than those who succeeded. Similarly, social Darwinism helped justify American imperialism abroad. According to some social Darwinists, the United States's victory in the Spanish–American war and its annexation of the Philippines, Puerto Rico, and Guam were evidence of America's natural superiority. As Theodore Roosevelt wrote, "it is the great expanding peoples which bequeath to future ages the great memories and material results of their achievements." Social Darwinism thus provided both a scientific and a moral sanction for American expansionism: not only was it America's natural and manifest destiny to exert power overseas, but it was America's moral duty as well. As might be expected, American imperialism also had a laissez-faire economic dimension.

Social Darwinism, despite its appeal, also faced numerous criticisms. It is worth mentioning five of these criticisms. First, critics argued that social Darwinism exaggerated the role of competition in social evolution. According to these critics, such as John Fiske, Darwinism also explained the origins of altruism and sympathy, both of which help guide further social evolution. As a result, these critics concluded that Darwinism actually encouraged a sense of solidarity, not competition, among human beings. Second, critics argued that social Darwinism ignored significant differences between biology and sociology. As Lester Ward (1841–1913), one of the foremost critics of social Darwinism, argued, it was simply bad science to use impersonal natural laws to explain highly complex, intentional, social behavior: there was little reason to think that the former could adequately explain the latter. Third, critics argued that social Darwinists committed the "naturalistic fallacy" of inferring how humans ought to act from descriptions of how they do act. Again, as Ward noted, there is a distinction between what is natural and what is moral: "if nature progresses through the destruction of the weak," he wrote, "man progresses through the protection of the weak." Fourth, critics identified a blind spot in social Darwinists' opposition to government regulation. As these critics pointed out, laissez-faire economic policies also require significant government regulation in order to ensure free markets. As a result, the question is not whether to have regulation or not, but rather what sort of regulation is best. Fifth, and finally, pragmatists and others attacked social Darwinism's philosophical assumptions. For example, James and Peirce both questioned social Darwinism's commitment to determinism: as we have seen, they argued for "spontaneity" and "tychism" in order to show how humans could freely take control of their surroundings. Likewise, John Dewey argued that social Darwinism failed to recognize the role of human intelligence in reshaping the natural environment. Thus, human beings are not, as social Darwinists suggested, merely instruments of unchanging natural laws. Even Holmes disagreed with social Darwinists' use of natural law and natural rights to justify a limited role for government. Both of these concepts, Holmes argued, were philosophically baseless and legally irrelevant.

As a result of these and other criticisms, social Darwinism became increasingly marginalized after 1900 and was essentially defunct as a school of thought by 1920. Despite this, many of its central themes continue to be influential. For example, twentieth-century sociobiology and evolutionary ethics may be viewed as an extension of social Darwinism. More generally, social Darwinist themes continue to be cited in support of laissez-faire economic policies and limited government.

Darwinism and John Dewey

John Dewey (1859–1952) was the foremost American pragmatist of the twentieth century. Like other pragmatists, he was strongly influenced by Darwinism. However, there are several reasons for discussing Dewey separately. For one, he explicitly recognized Darwinism's philosophical significance and, indeed, Darwinism plays an especially central role in his philosophy. In addition, Dewey's stature as a prominent philosopher and public intellectual helped ensure Darwinism's continuing influence.

In his essay "The Influence of Darwinism on Philosophy" (1909), Dewey gives an incisive account of Darwinism's philosophical significance. Darwinism, he writes, introduced a "new logic" into philosophy, one that "forswears inquiry after absolute origins and absolute finalities." Before Darwin, Dewey writes, philosophers focused on the timeless and unchanging: the purpose of philosophy, as well as of science, was to discover the large-scale unchanging structures, or the "natural kinds," which both underlie and transcend the small-scale changes that take place in nature. After Darwin, philosophers and scientists were free to focus on these changes without reducing them to a more basic, unchanging reality. They were then able to view the world in dynamic, not static, terms. Even though the physical sciences had been moving in this direction for some time, as Dewey points out, Darwin's *The Origin of Species* played a decisive role in making this dynamic worldview acceptable. Not only did it provide compelling empirical evidence in support of change and evolution, but it also extended these concepts into the biological sciences. From there it was a short step to the social sciences and to philosophy.

According to Dewey, Darwinism influenced philosophy in the following ways. First, it provided a new basis for understanding biological and social phenomena – what Dewey calls "mind and morals and life." Second, more specifically, it provided an alternative to idealism and the claim that nature was inherently rational. After Darwin, philosophers were unable to infer the existence of an "ideal or rational force" guiding natural events. Third, Darwinism encouraged philosophers to focus on the concrete and specific, as opposed to the abstract and general. Philosophers were now free to examine the specific factors behind particular events and thereby forgo the search for general metaphysical explanations of the same phenomena. Fourth, philosophy acquired new practical responsibilities. By focusing on the specific conditions behind particular events, philosophy was in a position to identify problems, propose solutions, and help bring these events under control. As Dewey writes, it became the case that "philosophy must in time become ... a method of moral and political diagnosis and prognosis."

Dewey's philosophy is Darwinian to the core. Just as Darwin shed light on human nature by showing how humans evolved from more primitive species, Dewey sheds light on specific human activities by showing how these evolved from more basic interactions with the environment. For example, Dewey traces the methods of modern science to the more basic problem-solving techniques that children and nonscientists use instinctively. In doing so, he highlights, first, the continuity of modern science with other activities and, second, science's fundamental connection to concrete problems and solutions. Dewey does the same for other disciplines including art, religion, and even philosophy itself. In each case he describes how these disciplines evolved from more basic attempts to control and understand the world. He shows that the specific concepts and methods used in these activities are fundamentally means of solving particular, concrete problems. When this is forgotten, Dewey argues, these activities lose their relevance and the result is inaccessible art for art's sake, religion that is deaf to real human suffering, and philosophy that is pointlessly abstract.

Dewey's philosophy, as a result of Darwinism's influence, is grounded in concrete interactions (or "transactions") between humans and the world. This means that Dewey's philosophy is "naturalistic" in the sense that, as he writes in his *Logic: The Theory of Inquiry* (1938), "there is no breach of continuity between operations of inquiry and biological operations and physical operations." The continuity of "inquiry" (of which science is a paradigm example) with more basic operations has several implications. One implication is educational: because inquiry is continuous with natural biological operations, schoolchildren can be encouraged to learn by doing things. Properly guided, a child's natural curiosity and abilities will lead to increasingly sophisticated knowledge. A second implication is epistemological: again, because inquiry is continuous with more basic ways of solving problems, inquiry is inherently hands-on and instrumental. Unlike what Dewey calls the "spectator theory of knowledge," actual inquiries should terminate in plans of action designed to solve real problems. As a result, inquiry both arises from, and terminates in, the interaction of humans with their environment. A final implication is political: Dewey's theory of inquiry is fundamentally democratic. Because inquiry requires interaction with one's environment, inquiry into social problems requires participation and coordination among inquirers. In fact, a well-functioning scientific community is, for Dewey, the model of democratic participation.

Dewey's progressive theory of education, his instrumentalism, and his commitment to participatory democracy were among his most influential ideas. Significantly, they each derive from his philosophical naturalism which is grounded in Darwinism. Dewey's ideas continue to be influential even when he is not explicitly cited (for example, Quine's doctrine of ontological relativity is profoundly Deweyan in its rejection of natural kinds). In many cases, especially regarding the philosophical significance of science, his views have become the accepted norm.

Darwin's contemporary influence

Darwinism (and evolutionary theory more generally) continues to influence philosophy in various ways. For example, Darwinism continues to play a central role in contemporary philosophy of biology and in ongoing debates about the meaning and application of basic evolutionary concepts. Philosophers of biology have also been called to defend evolution against a succession of creationist theories.

More generally, philosophers continue to apply evolutionary theory to a range of specific philosophical issues. Two prominent applications are evolutionary ethics and evolutionary epistemology.

Evolutionary ethics attempts to explain social behavior in terms of natural selection. In this respect it is descended from social Darwinism, although it attempts to avoid the problems of that theory. A more recent precursor of evolutionary ethics is sociobiology, as popularized by E.O. Wilson's 1975 book *Sociobiology: The New Synthesis.* According to evolutionary ethicists, it is possible to give an evolutionary account of sociable behavior, including altruism. This runs counter to the intuition that evolution cannot explain behavior that diminishes an individual's reproductive fitness. However, as evolutionary ethicists and others have shown, altruistic behavior may be selected for when this behavior benefits close relatives or other members of a social group. These explanations have had success in explaining behavior among animals, but their application to humans is less clear. Because human behavior is at least partly a product of human culture, it is difficult to distinguish the effect, if any, of evolution on morality. Furthermore, even if evolutionary ethics sheds light on the development of morality, it has difficulty explaining how ethics is able to make demands that go beyond what is biologically advantageous.

Evolutionary epistemology consists of two related projects. The first uses evolutionary theory to understand the development of human cognitive abilities. This project, which is a kind of naturalized epistemology, would ideally explain how the human brain and nervous system evolved to reliably process information. This would provide a scientific basis for why humans reason as they do, thus placing empirical limits on the range of epistemological speculation. That is, if human cognitive processes are the result of specific evolutionary pressures, then epistemological theories must respect these built-in constraints. The second project uses evolutionary theory to explain the growth of knowledge in general and the acceptance of scientific theories in particular. Much in the spirit of pragmatists such as James and Dewey, this project attempts to understand the growth of knowledge as a selection process. For example, David Hull has argued that conceptual change in science can be explained in the same evolutionary terms as biological change.

Finally, Darwinism is now part of the accepted scientific background of contemporary philosophy. Because of Darwinism's influence (in addition to other factors) contemporary philosophy has, in general, left essentialism and teleology behind. Instead, it regards the universe as changing and mutable, and attempts to understand phenomena in terms of causes, not purposes. In addition, contemporary philosophy is generally consistent with the Darwinian account of the origin of species, including humans. This means that humans are natural organisms whose abilities cannot be explained by invoking supernatural phenomena such as immortal souls. This has clear implications for metaphysics and philosophy of mind, among other areas. In conclusion, Darwinism today entails a modest naturalism that limits both metaphysical speculation and appeals to supernatural processes.

Further reading

Dennett, Daniel. *Darwin's Dangerous Idea*. New York: Simon and Schuster, 1995.

Dewey, John. *The Influence of Darwin on Philosophy and Other Essays*. Amherst, NY: Prometheus Books, 1997 [1910].

—— *Logic: The Theory of Inquiry*. New York: Henry Holt, 1938.

Grene, Marjorie. "Darwin and Philosophy" in her *The Understanding of Nature*. Dordrecht: Reidel, 1974, pp. 189–200,

Hofstadter, Richard. *Social Darwinism in American Thought*. Boston, MA: Beacon Press, 1955 [1944].

Hull, David. *Science and Selection*. New York: Cambridge University Press, 2001.

James, William. *The Principles of Psychology*. Cambridge, MA: Harvard University Press, 1981.

Menand, Louis. *The Metaphysical Club*. New York: Farrar, Straus and Giroux, 2001.

Peirce, Charles S. "Evolutionary Love" in *The Essential Peirce, Vol. 1 (1867–1893)*, ed. Nathan Houser and Christian Klousel. Bloomington, IN: Indiana University Press, 1992, pp. 352–71.

O'Hear, Anthony. *Beyond Evolution*. New York: Oxford University Press, 1997.

Ryan, Frank X. (ed.) *Darwin's Impact: Social Evolution in America, 1880–1920*, 3 volumes. Bristol: Thoemmes, 2001.

—— (ed.) *The Evolutionary Philosophy of Chauncey Wright*, 3 volumes. Bristol: Thoemmes, 2000.

Wiener, Philip. *Evolution and the Founders of Pragmatism*. New York: Harper and Row, 1965 [1949].

Wilson, E.O. *Sociobiology: The New Synthesis*. Cambridge, MA: Harvard University Press, 1975.

John Capps

DARWINISM

The theory of evolution proposed by Charles Darwin (1809–82) in *The Origin of Species* (1859) explains the natural process which created the great diversity of life forms on earth. Although Darwin did not originate the idea of evolution, he did introduce the concept of natural selection as the mechanism by which evolution takes place. Natural selection is a causal process which acts on variation in populations, such that individuals who are better adapted to their environment survive and reproduce at higher rates than other individuals, thereby passing their traits on to their offspring. Over long periods of time, this process drives the transformation of ancestral species into new species, which differ significantly from their ancestors and from each other.

Although Darwin's *The Origin of Species* initially met with intense criticism from his scientific peers, the wealth of evidence that he marshaled in support of the theory produced widespread scientific acceptance within twenty years. Later, the rediscovery in 1900 of Gregor Mendel's (1822–84) work in classical genetics became the basis of mechanistic explanations for the source of variation and for the inheritance of traits, explanations which classical Darwinism lacked. Since the 1950s, the resulting synthesis has been the dominant unifying concept of contemporary biology.

Origins of Darwinism

In 1831, as a young man, Charles Darwin joined a five-year charting expedition aboard HMS *Beagle*, during which he collected natural specimens and studied the animals, plants, and geology of South America and the Pacific Islands. The idea of evolution of species was already considered seriously by some naturalists, and Darwin's natural observations eventually led him, too, to doubt the then prevalent assumption that species are fixed and unchanging.

Back in England, Darwin became convinced that the extensive empirical evidence he had collected pointed toward the "mutability of species," although he did not understand the mechanism that drove evolution until the 1840s. There were several influences on Darwin's development of the idea of natural selection as this mechanism. The first was the work of geologist Charles Lyell (1797–1875). Lyell demonstrated that geological deposits are laid down little by little, accumulating over long periods of time. While some of Darwin's contemporaries believed that the earth was only tens of thousands of years old, Lyell's geological investigations supported a longer time frame for geological history, which made slow, gradual change in the generation of species more plausible.

An additional influence on Darwin's theory was his understanding that artificial selection, the intentional breeding of plants and animals to produce desired traits, could quickly yield new varieties. What natural process, though, could play the role of the breeder, who selects organisms with desirable traits to parent the next generation? In rereading T.R. Malthus' *Essay on the Principle of Population* (1798), Darwin considered how the "struggle for existence" could act as a form of selection analogous to breeders picking the best of a brood. Not all members of a population survive to reproduce. Assuming that there are differences among individuals, those that do have offspring are more likely to possess traits which have allowed them to survive and thrive in their environments – to find food, to sense and escape danger, and to mate successfully. These adaptive traits, then, will spread throughout the population in subsequent generations. Thus, the theory of natural selection explains how gradual changes in populations can, in time, cause the dramatic degree of change needed to transform one species into another.

Darwin delayed publication of his ideas about evolution and natural selection for fifteen years, in part because he was reticent to instigate controversy. He anticipated the fierce criticism and scrutiny that he would receive from fellow scientists, and he knew that the evolution of species posed a direct challenge to both the theological doctrine of special creation and the design argument for the existence of God. In this Darwin followed David Hume (1711–76), who had earlier criticized the argument from design for concluding that a designing God must exist based on the beauty and complexity of living beings. Darwin's theory supported Hume's criticism, in that evolution provided an alternative, naturalistic means by which the diversity of life had come to be. Instead of there having been one creation event, "special creation," and a "fixity of species," Darwin described life forms as ever-changing, a description supported empirically by the fossil record, by the similarity of form between particular species, and by the geographical distribution of structurally similar species. He had hoped to amass more empirical evidence by delaying publication, but in 1858 he received a copy of a paper by another English naturalist, Alfred Russel Wallace (1823–1913), which proposed ideas so similar to his own that Darwin rapidly condensed and completed his manuscript on *The Origin of Species.*

Following the publication of *The Origin of Species*, most of Darwin's contemporary scientists came to accept evolution within a decade; it took another decade for the mechanism of natural selection to be as widely accepted. What some found disturbing about the theory was that species change lacked purpose or direction and relied strongly on the appearance of chance variations in a population. This was a significant difference between Darwin's theory and Jean Baptiste de Lamarck's (1744–1829) earlier theory of evolution. Lamarck had proposed that organisms acquire adaptive characteristics during their life spans in response to environmental distress, and then pass these new characteristics on to offspring. Lamarck's theory provided a larger role for progress in nature than Darwin's did, since it posited that variation arose in response to organismal need. For a time, each of these theories seemed a partial explanation of evolution. However, later research in genetics has not supported the inheritance of such acquired characteristics, and Lamarckism has been largely abandoned by evolutionary biologists.

Evolutionary theory after Darwin

Darwinian evolution is based on three elements: first, the production of mutations or variation between individuals in a population; second, interaction with the environment that preferentially selects the variants more suited to the conditions they encounter; and third, inheritance of variation from one generation to the next. The weakness in Darwin's theory of evolution was that he could not describe mechanisms for the production of variation between individuals or for the inheritance of traits. Both of these gaps were filled after the rediscovery of Gregor Mendel's work on genetics. Between the 1920s and 1950s, biologists developed the theory of genetics and showed that new traits arise continually through chance mutations in genes and are passed on to the next generation by genetic inheritance. The combination of natural selection with Mendelian genetics is known as neo-Darwinism, or the modern synthesis. Since the 1950s, advances in molecular and cellular biology and the discovery of self-replicating DNA as the carrier of genetic information have provided further support for the synthetic theory.

Evolutionary biologists have continued to refine the Darwinian theory of evolution through the twentieth century, in some ways anticipated by Darwin and in other ways unimagined by him. Selection pressures other than the basic mechanism of natural selection include sexual selection, or changes produced by non-random mating choices; kin selection, which explains how the sexual sterility of social insects like ants can nonetheless be adaptive when it boosts the reproductive fitness of the kinship group or colony; and genetic drift, the tendency of a neutral allele to vary randomly in frequency and to become fixed as non-adaptive shifts in traits in small populations.

Although "Darwinism" refers most specifically to Darwin's own theory of natural selection and to the neo-Darwinian synthesis in evolutionary biology, it is sometimes used in a more general sense. "Darwinism" can refer to any selection process. For example, the contemporary area of evolutionary epistemology called memetics holds that memes, or units of information, mutate, interact in the environment of ideas, and replicate through human communication to produce cultural evolution. "Darwinism" can also refer to any gradual, step-wise change, whether driven by chance processes or directed toward an ideal. For example, an often debated question in evolutionary biology has been whether teleological or functional explanations, which explain phenomena in terms of the purposes they serve, have a place in naturalistic science. If they do, then evolution may connote not just change, but progress. Darwin, for instance, indicated that the evolutionary process permits the development of more and more complex organisms. Another type of progress seen in Darwinism is the idea that increasing adaptation to an unchanging environment leads to "biological perfection." As Darwinism influenced thought outside of biology, it became even more closely associated with the idea of progress towards an ideal. Darwinism has had its widest influence on social science, morals, and philosophy via developing a worldview that emphasizes naturalistic mechanisms of progressive improvement. For example, the social Darwinists applied metaphysical aspects of Darwinian thought to justify social and economic policies which they thought would lead to the betterment of civilization.

In the twenty-first century, Darwinian evolution of species is widely accepted in the intellectual community as the foundation for contemporary biological science. Darwinism continues to stimulate inquiry in evolutionary and developmental biology as well as in philosophy of biology, fields where unrecognized extensions and implications of Darwinism are still being explored. Current questions include whether group selection can occur in non-kinship groups, the limits of adaptationism, how selection processes function to develop the immune system, whether natural selection can explain human altruism, and the development of evolutionary explanations for ethical norms (evolutionary ethics) and human cognitive processes (evolutionary epistemology and psychology).

Further reading

Bowler, Peter J. *Evolution: The History of an Idea*, third edition. Berkeley, CA: University of California Press, 2003.

Darwin, Charles. *The Origin of Species*. New York: Penguin, 1968 [1859].

Dennett, Daniel. *Darwin's Dangerous Idea: Evolution and the Meanings of Life*. New York: Simon and Schuster, 1996.

Eldridge, Niles. *Darwin: Discovering the Tree of Life*. New York: Norton, 2005.

Keller, Evelyn Fox and Lloyd, Elisabeth A. *Keywords in Evolutionary Biology*. Cambridge, MA: Harvard University Press, 1992.

Larson, Edward J. *Evolution: The Remarkable History of a Scientific Theory*. New York: Modern Library, 2004.

EVELYN BRISTER

DAVIDSON, DONALD

Donald Davidson (1917–2003) was a Quinean philosopher who shaped the agenda of (analytically oriented) American philosophy in the last part of the twentieth century with his contributions to epistemology, philosophy of language, philosophy of mind, and philosophy of action. He debunked the dualism between scheme and content, which he termed "the third dogma of empiricism." Davidson argues that this dogma is ultimately nonsensical because we cannot make sense of linguistic or conceptual schemes as distinct things that are separate and independent from the contents that they are supposed to organize and fit. He develops his argument against the scheme–content dualism as a transcendental argument for the intertranslatability of all languages and against linguistic relativism. Davidson contends that the only criterion of languagehood we have is translatability into a familiar language (ultimately my language or idiolect). He argues that the notions of translation and linguistic understanding are intimately tied to the notion of truth. The link between linguistic interpretation and truth is the centerpiece of Davidson's *semantic holism*, which claims that we cannot identify the meanings expressed in the utterances of a speaker independently of the repertoire of beliefs in which those meanings figure as component parts. (In this way, Davidson's commitment to holism entails a commitment to the compositionality of meaning, which is in turn a necessary condition for the learnability of language.) Since the beliefs of a speaker are expressed in the sentences the speakers holds to be true, Davidson argues for the semantic centrality of asserting, contending that holding-true is the most primitive semantic attitude. Exploiting the holistic thesis of the interdependence of belief and meaning, Davidson proposed to use the Tarskian definition of truth-in-a-language ("'p' is true-in-L if and only if p") as a recursive disquotational device for the elucidation of meanings in that language (that is, as a device that is disquotational because it correlates a quoted or mentioned sentence with a sentence that is asserted, and recursive because it can be applied to any sentence). Thus the meaning of an assertion is captured in a disquotational specification of its truth conditions. On Davidson's version of truth-conditional semantics, a theory of interpretation for a language X as spoken by subject Y becomes a theory of truth à la Tarski that can systematically produce indefinitely many T-sentences, that is, sentences that correlate any given sentence uttered by Y with a sentence in the meta-language used by the interpreter through the disquotational schema formulated by Tarski (e.g. "'*Es regnet*' is true if and only if it rains"). Davidson argues that successful communication does not required antecedently shared rules or conventions ("prior theories of interpretation") but only the convergence of "passing theories of interpretation" that interlocutors construct ad hoc in their encounter to understand each other. Thus the Davidsonian semantic approach offers an account of communication as a mapping between idiolects that can be captured by converging "passing theories" and does not require sharing conventions, rules, or "prior theories of interpretation." A corollary of this account is Davidson's controversial claim that there is no such thing as language as traditionally conceived in philosophy and linguistics, that is, as a system or code containing semantic rules and conventions that determine the standard meaning of words. This new holistic view of linguistic understanding that doesn't presuppose the traditional notion of a language is developed in Davidson's account of radical interpretation, which involves the interpretation of the linguistic behavior of a speaker without reliance on any prior knowledge either of the meanings of the speaker's utterances or of the speaker's beliefs. Through his account of radical interpretation Davidson formulates a general methodology of interpretation that is supposed to have universal applicability, for it is supposed to be capable of producing systematic theories of truth for the interpretation of any language (or idiolect) whatsoever. The central focus of this methodology of interpretation is not on individual words or isolated sentences, but on entire clusters of sentences or belief systems; for, in this holistic view, the meanings of the individual words of a speaker are a function of all the sentences that the speaker in question holds true taken together. Davidson's semantic holism is the cornerstone both of the methodology of "radical interpretation" and of his account of "the rationality of the mental."

Further reading

Davidson, Donald. *Essays on Actions and Events.* Oxford: Oxford University Press, 1980.

—— *Inquiries into Truth and Interpretation.* Oxford: Oxford University Press, 1984.

—— *Subjective, Intersubjective, Objective.* Oxford: Oxford University Press, 2001.

—— *Problems of Rationality.* Oxford: Oxford University Press, 2004.

—— *Truth, Language, and History.* Oxford: Oxford University Press, 2005.

—— *Truth and Predication.* Cambridge, MA: Harvard University Press, 2005.

Hahn, Lewis (ed.) *The Philosophy of Donald Davidson.* Chicago, IL: Open Court, 1999.

Lepore, Ernie (ed.) *Truth and Interpretation: Perspectives on the Philosophy of Donald Davidson.* Cambridge, MA: Blackwell, 1986.

José Medina

DAVIDSON, DONALD: AUTOBIOGRAPHY

What I think now of as the major influences on my thought are (1) the pluralistic, tolerant, quasi-historical attitude toward philosophical methods and positions I picked up from Whitehead and my teachers in literature and the history of ideas at Harvard; (2) the mixture of pragmatism and empiricism I was exposed to by Quine and C.I. Lewis; and (3) the idea of how a theory could be applied in semantics, science, psychology or philosophy that was pressed on me by Alfred Tarski and Patrick Suppes. I think of these as the major influences, not because I have a clear sense of how my thinking actually developed, but because I notice the connections between the work and teachings of these people as I was exposed to them and my present views and philosophical predilections.

The philosopher whose views I have for many decades found most congenial, and with whom I find myself most in agreement, is Quine. I learned from him how abandoning the analytic–synthetic distinction dictated a third-person interpretive approach to the problems of meaning, reference, and truth, and how accepting this approach revolutionized one's conception of belief, knowledge, and the nature of the social sciences. I find, and am often told, that various of my views are much like views of Kant, Spinoza, or Wittgenstein. In each of these cases, I think the resemblances are obvious. Though I read Wittgenstein as thoughtfully as I could at various times, it seems to me that I arrived at views similar to Wittgenstein's by routes that owed little to my having read him. Probably this is a shallow impression. I am increasingly struck by Kantian elements in my thinking, but I ask myself whether it was studying Kant that made much different. I cannot say. In this case, though, I do discern a dim historical sequence: C.I. Lewis was my introduction to Kant, and Quine's epistemology is in certain basic ways like that of Lewis. Those ways include: the idea that there is a class of beliefs (sentences) whose content is directly tied to sense experience; that the empirical content of other sentences depends on their relation to the beliefs (sentences) of the first sort; that it is partly a pragmatic question as to what structure we should give beliefs (sentences) of the second sort. I am not inclined to accept any of these ideas as expressed by Quine or Lewis (I would not call myself either an empiricist or a pragmatist), but I nevertheless think of myself as belonging to this tradition. I recognized from the start that anomalous monism – my basic theory of the relation between the mental and the physical – was strikingly reminiscent of Spinoza's ontological monism combined with conceptual dualism. But again I wonder whether my graduate student exposure to Spinoza played much of a role in forming my thoughts in this area. Because I taught him in my courses both in ethics and epistemology, Hume was a more direct inspiration, mainly because he helped me see clearly what was wrong with many philosophical positions and arguments, including his.

I now think that the starting point of much of my philosophizing is Cartesian, in this sense: I begin by asking what is entailed by the fact that thought exists. Various arguments persuade me that to have a single thought it is necessary to have many. To have thoughts at all one must realize that the content of a thought may be true or false, and know what its truth conditions are. Grasp of the concept of truth, of the idea of objectivity, can come only in the context of the sort of interaction with others that is made possible by language. (I do not know whether this was Wittgenstein's view, but the idea certainly has a Wittgensteinian flavor, and my reasons for holding it owe something to Wittgenstein.) If this is right, understanding others is a condition for having thoughts. Understanding others depends on the fact that we share, and that we know we share, a common world. Thus I am led to the idea of a fundamental triangle: two if its apices are creatures gifted with speech, and the third apex is a world shared through communication. The sides consist of (often very complex) causal relations. Each thinking creature must, then, have three sorts of empirical knowledge: knowledge of its own mind, knowledge of other minds, and knowledge of the shared (objective) world. This is an anti-Cartesian conclusion, since it rejects the primacy of first-person knowledge, rules out global skepticism from the start, and makes action as essential to knowledge as theoretical reasoning.

Much of my work has been devoted to exploring the question of what it is about human speech and action that makes it possible for one person to understand another. What makes the question challenging is the fact that the interdependence of beliefs, the evaluative attitudes, and speech prevent us from coming to understand one of these features of a person before understanding the others. We must come to grasp much of the whole pattern in order to be sure we have any of it right. The pattern is intelligible because it is, to a sufficient degree, rational. In attempting to sketch the nature of this pattern, I have tried to appropriate, and knit into a single unified whole, features of Tarski's truth definitions and of Ramsey's decision theory. The result is highly schematic, and much idealized. I would like to see the fit between formal semantics and natural languages improved; I would like a better view of how decision theory is related to actual intentional behavior; and I am certain that a theory of how a rational creature should (and more or less does) change its mind in the face of new evidence and further reflection is required as an essential element in the unified theory I envision.

Donald Davidson

DEISM

American deism is associated with historical luminaries such as Ethan Allen, Benjamin Franklin, Thomas Jefferson, James Madison, Thomas Paine, Elihu Palmer, and George Washington. These bright political mavericks carved out a new American republic, not from the remnants of broken regimes, but from the realm of ideas passed to them by Enlightenment reasoning. The philosophical underpinnings of their politics set the direction and agenda for intellectual life in the United States for generations to come. One component of their philosophy was deism.

Allen, Paine, and Palmer were open and outspoken deists writing books and pamphlets outlining their views. Others were more cautious. Franklin, upon reading an early draft of *The Age of Reason*, for example, advised Thomas Paine to burn it because of the "odium," "mischief," and "mortification" Paine would suffer. The revolutionary French atheists denounced the naiveté of their deistic American friends (Franklin and Paine) while in predominantly Christian America the clergy, especially Jonathan Edwards, vilified the deists as infidels. In this crossfire the deists managed to simultaneously found a nation and ground an intellectual tradition characterized by distrust of all authority except that of reason.

In his essay comparing deism to the Christian religion Thomas Paine wrote,

> Every person, of whatever religious denomination he may be, is a DEIST in the first article of his Creed. Deism, from the Latin word Deus, God, is the belief of a God, and this belief is the first article of every man's creed.

Deism, first and foremost, affirms the existence of God. To this metaphysical/religious claim deism adds a second, namely, that reason is the sole reliable source for knowing God and living rightly.

Deist "free thinkers" rejected rationalist metaphysical speculation and a methodology characterized by deductive logic operating on a priori first principles. In their place deists endorsed Lockean empiricism, Bacon's inductive logic, and Newton's laws of nature. Deism's new Enlightenment world view saw nature as working regularly and predictably, like clockwork, and, more importantly, as transparent to human understanding. Empirically confirmed laws of nature established that nature is fully rational. Nature's rationality, in turn, was traced (or ascribed) to divine rationality. William Paley's watchmaker argument circulated broadly and was widely accepted. Human reason was viewed as God's gift to humanity.

Paine wrote, "The creation is the Bible of the Deist. He there reads, in the handwriting of the Creator himself, the certainty of His existence and the immutability of His power, and all other bibles and Testaments are to him forgeries." For his fellow citizens Paine's commitment to God's existence was unproblematic. However, early American Christianity, with its dependence upon special revelation and its miracles, rejected reason as the sole source of knowledge. When James Madison said, "We hold it for a fundamental and undeniable truth that religion, . . . can be directed only by reason and conviction" he tipped his hand as a deist. Madison's pious-sounding sentiment entailed that *only* reason and conviction and *not* the Christian clergy were to be followed. Madison's First Amendment rejection of religious establishment was not ecumenical hospitality, i.e. no one church to be established over another. Distrust of all religious authority grounded in revelation, superstition and tradition, motivated Madison's caution. John Adams eloquently articulated deism's distrust of religious authority: "When philosophical reason is clear and certain by intuition or necessary induction, no subsequent revelation supported by prophecies or miracles can supersede it."

Deism, guided by God-like and God-given gift of reason, challenged all authorities, political kings or religious clergy and popes. Neither divine right nor any revelation was necessary for political or religious legitimacy when the cosmos, its God, and its intelligent inhibitors all were equally possessors of reason. The same reason that permits the People, legitimated by "the Laws of Nature and Nature's God," to declare their independence by rational assertion alone, "We hold these Truths to be self-evident . . ." (The Declaration of Independence, 4 July 1776), also enabled deistic thinkers to stand up to threats and intimidations by otherwise revered religious authorities. Jonathan Edwards in his *History of the Work of Redemption* (1773) castigated deists as denying "the whole Christian religion . . . and any revealed religion, or any word of God at all; and [deists] say that God has given mankind no other light to walk by but their own reason."

For deists the light of reason showed the God of nature to be eminently worthy of respect and adoration. In the commonly sanctioned moralities of the churches, those based on fear of hell and an offer of heavenly reward, deism saw no merit. The free-thinkers viewed Christianity's God as morally unworthy. "The Bible represents God to be a changeable, passionate, vindictive being; making a world and then drowning it, afterwards repenting of what he had done, and promising not to do so again" (Paine). To such a whimsical God, deists contrasted their deity who demanded freedom, equality, justice, slavery's abolition, women's suffrage, public education, and the progressive perfection of social reality. Such a conception of a rational and predictable God buttressed the common deist sentiment that miraculous divine interventions are unthinkable, incompatible with a rational God who operates through laws of nature, not by capricious responses to human pleadings. A law-governed creation with a non-intervening deity were both morally and rationally superior to the personalist theology of the churches.

Early American deists drafted no official creeds or doctrinal confessions. There were, however, these common themes stemming from Enlightenment progenitors: (1) God exists as Creator (Designer, First Cause, Supreme Architect) sustainer of the universe; (2) God is discovered rationally only through observed orderliness and regularities of nature; (3) reason and experience are sufficient and the only reliable guides to understanding reality and guiding morality; (4) popular institutionalized religions, e.g. Judaism, Christianity, and Islam, are based on supernaturalism, miracles and specially revealed knowledge which are all offensive to reason; (5) the God found in religious scriptures is unworthy of moral emulation; and (6) while the revealed religions produced intolerance and conflict, rational morality generates human freedom, equality, and tolerance.

American deism lost its cogency as its leading theorists died and reasonable critics, notably David Hume (*Dialogues Concerning Natural Religion* published posthumously 1780), challenged the inference to a Designer. Contemporary intelligent design theorists are reviving deistic arguments by appealing to irreducible complexity or fine-tuning. The prospects are not bright for reason alone to get much further than did America's deists.

Further reading

Allen, Ethan. *Reason the Only Oracle of Man, or a Compendious System of Natural Religion.* Bennington, VT: Haswell and Russell, 1784.

Franklin, Benjamin. *On the Providence of God in the Government of the World* (1732), *The Works of Benjamin Franklin*, ed. Jared Sparks. Boston, MA: Charles Tappan, 1844.

Koch, G. Adolf. *Republication Religion: The American Revolution and the Cult of Reason.* New York: Henry Holt, 1933.

Morais, Herbert A. *Deism in Eighteenth-Century America.* New York: Russell and Russell, 1960.

Paine, Thomas. *The Age of Reason.* New York: D.M. Bennett, 1878.

Palmer, Elihu. *Principles of Nature: or, A Development of the Moral Causes of Happiness and Misery among the Human Species*, third edition. New York: unknown publisher, 1806.

Walters, Kerry S. *The American Deists: Voices of Reason and Dissent in the Early Republic.* Lawrence, KS: University of Kansas Press, 1992.

—— *Rational Infidels: The American Deists.* Durango, CO: Longwood Press, 1992.

William J. Hawk

DELEDALLE, GÉRARD

Gérard Deledalle (1921–2003) was born on 17 October 1921, in Marcq-en-Baroeul near Lille. He was educated at St Vincent de Paul, a private boarding school run by Lazarist Brothers, where he studied the classics and philosophy, as well as theology and ecclesiastical history. During World War II, Deledalle began his studies at the Sorbonne. After the liberation, while working as an interpreter for the US Third Army Division, Deledalle discovered Dewey in the army library. In 1947 he married Janice Rhodes, a specialist in nineteenth-century British literature; the next year they had a daughter, Myriame.

In 1949, with Jean Wahl as his advisor, Deledalle registered his two theses for the Doctorat d'Etat. His main thesis, *L'Idée d'expérience dans la philosophie de John Dewey* (The Idea of Experience in John Dewey's Philosophy), is a chronologic and synthetic study of Dewey's writings. His supplementary thesis, a requirement for the now abolished state doctorate, entitled *Logique: la théorie de l'enquête*, is a translation of Dewey's *Logic: The Theory of Inquiry* with extensive notes and commentary. It took Deledalle almost twenty years to complete his two dissertations, defending them with honors at the Sorbonne in 1967.

While working on his dissertation, Deledalle discovered that if he wanted Dewey to be properly understood by a French audience, he first had to write a book on the history of American thought. That book appeared in 1954 under the title *Histoire de la philosophie américaine.*

In 1957 Deledalle traveled as a Smith–Mundt Fulbright Fellow to the US, spending considerable time at Columbia University. This brought him in close contact with several key figures in American philosophy, including Herbert Schneider, Sidney Hook, Justus Buchler, Ernst Nagel, Horace Kallen, Philip Wiener, Sidney Ratner, and John Herman Randall, Jr.

In 1962, Deledalle became Professor of Philosophy at the newly established University of Tunis. While in Tunis, he also became an avid amateur archeologist. Deledalle left Tunis in 1972 to direct the Franco-Japanese Institute in Tokyo. In 1974 he was appointed Professor of Philosophy at the University of Perpignan, spending four years at the University of Libreville in Gabon (1977–81). Deledalle remained at Perpignan until his retirement in 1990, after which he continued as Professor Emeritus till 2001. He died in Montpellier on 12 June 2003.

Also after his dissertation Deledalle continued to bring American philosophy to France. In 1970, he published the anthology *Le Pragmatisme*, containing selections of Peirce, James, and Dewey. It is also around this time that, encouraged by Jean Wahl, Deledalle moved from Dewey to Peirce, especially his semiotics, and began translating several of Peirce's semiotic writings. These translations were published in 1978 as *Écrits sur le signe.* The book was published in part thanks to Jacques Lacan who discovered the manuscript at the publisher and insisted upon its publication.

Upon his arrival at Perpignan, in 1974, Deledalle founded l'Institut de Recherches en Sémiotique, Communication et Education (IRSCE), which is dedicated to the study and interdisciplinary application of Peircean semiotics while connecting it with mainstream French semiotics. In 1984, Deledalle founded, with Algirdas Greimas, the French Association for Semiotics. Notwithstanding its multidisciplinary character, Deledalle sought to retain a solid philosophical grounding for semiotics, proceeding from the idea that only a philosophically grounded semiotics could address the problems French linguistics-based semiotics ran into. Much of this philosophical grounding is found in *Théorie et practique du signe* (1979), which opens with an extensive comparison of Peirce with Saussure.

Introducing Peirce's semiotics in a Saussure-saturated France proved no easy task. To introduce Peirce to a French audience, Deledalle had little other option but to try to translate Peirce's thought into generally understood Saussurean concepts. However, as Deledalle quickly discovered, the Saussurean approach was too different from Peirce's to allow for a true comparison, let alone a translation. Most significantly, Peirce's triadic understanding of the sign could not be translated into the dualistic meanings of Saussure's semiological concepts. Through his study of the two paradigms, Deledalle discovered that Saussure is actually closer to Peirce than his theoretical system allows him to be, and that recasting Saussure's approach in Peircean terms brings out several aspects of Saussure's thought that suffered from the restrictions his system had imposed upon him. As Deledalle put it:

> If I take the Peircean system for my point of reference, it is because its triadic nature allows the introduction into sign-analysis of nuances about which Saussure was sometimes well aware, but which the dyadic nature of his system did not enable him to express.
>
> (2000: 107)

In short, whereas a Saussurean interpretation of Peirce is bound to be severely deficient, a Peircean interpretation of Saussure is bound to cause a conceptual tidal wave in post-Saussurean thought that leaves little unscathed. With Deledalle we see the beginnings of that tidal wave.

Further reading

Deledalle, Gérard. *Histoire de la philosophie américaine.* Paris: PUF, 1954.

—— *La Philosophie américaine.* Lausanne: L'Age d'homme, 1983; new and expanded edition, Brussels: Deboeck-Westmael, 1988.

—— *Démocratie et Education, de John Dewey, Présentation et traduction.* Lausanne: L'Age d'homme, 1983.

—— *Charles S. Peirce: An Intellectual Biography*, trans. from French and introduced by S. Petrilli. Amsterdam: John Benjamins, 1989.

—— *Charles Sanders Peirce's Philosophy of Signs: Essays in Comparative Semiotics.* Bloomington, IN: Indiana University Press, 2000.

CORNELIS DE WAAL

DEMOCRACY

Democracy is firmly embedded as a value within contemporary politics, and almost universally praised as the ideal form of political organization, happily actualized in so many states – in theory, at least, although in practice many regimes manage to suspend or manipulate their constitutions as they see fit. Yet the bland reassurances of public ideology hardly conceal deep disagreements about the meaning of democracy, about its value or justification, and about its relationship to the institutions that actually rule us.

While in some sense, democracy designates a system in which the people rule, it is difficult to give an uncontentious account of what that entails. For some authors such as John Dewey and C.B. Macpherson, democracy is more or less the good life in practice. For others, it is any social organization in which the majority rules. And there is a great variety of other conceptions between these and cutting across them. These disagreements about the *meaning* of democracy are often related to arguments about its *value* or *justification*.

Indeed, in one way the ideological hegemony of democracy is a source of disagreement about its character and value. The less we want to question the desirability of democracy, the more we will argue about what this term means, and why we value it.

"Democracy" is famously first used to describe the institutions of Athens in the wake of Kleisthenes's reforms of the Athenian constitution (507 BCE), themselves devised in part as a way of balancing the competing interests of the urban and rural populations. The sovereign body of democratic Athens was the *ekklesia* with a quorum of 6,000: this comprised native Athenian men over twenty who met for plenary sessions and on other occasions. Its members enjoyed *isegoria*, that is, not only voting equality but the equal right to contribute to the public debate. In addition, there was a smaller council of 500 and committee of fifty to guide and make proposals. The *ekklesia* directly participated in law-making and many judicial functions, and the scope of its power covered all the common affairs of the city, including raising taxes and going to war (important for a naval power in the period of war with the Persians). Methods of election to public office included election and lot, and in due course payment for public office was instituted (important for taking power out of the hands of the better-off, and made possible by booty from the Persian war). Finally and notoriously, slaves, metics (resident workers, who flooded in as Athens grew as an imperial maritime power) and women were excluded from citizenship.

The form of government collapsed, replaced by an oligarchy. It is remarkable that our knowledge of Athenian democracy, which has been so central to the modern democratic imagination, derives principally from hostile critics, including Plato, Aristotle and Thucydides; indeed, there is evidence that the term had derogatory origins, signifying rule by bumpkins. In the subsequent two millennia, until quite late in the nineteenth century, "democracy" is at best ambivalent, and often straightforwardly feared or despised. Democracy was viewed as a form of class rule, prone to instability and collapse. For James Madison, in *The Federalist Papers*, for instance, "democracies have ever been spectacles of turbulence and contention; have ever been found incompatible with personal security and the rights of property; and have in general been as short in their lives as they have been violent in their deaths."

Liberal democracy

It is arguable that the concept of democracy undergoes the radical transformation in its fortunes that it has enjoyed over the last two centuries only by being radically *qualified* in a liberal or representative fashion in response to specific different structural and social conditions. On the one hand, once we stop viewing rulers as entitled to rule by virtue of their natural excellence or divine gift, everyone is entitled to legal and civil equality and in some sense the sovereign represents us all. On the other hand, for critics of classical democracy such as Madison, the Abbé Sièyes and Benjamin Constant, important features of modern societies limit the form that this political equality can take. In particular, the size and complexity of the modern state, the need to support private property and commerce (Madison's "personal security and the rights of property"), and the lack of inclination of most of us toward public affairs rendered the Athenian conception massively ill suited for modern politics.

The solution to this dilemma is found in the notion of representation. Just as we have lawyers to represent us in court, so with elected representatives in a parliament. For a few eighteenth-century thinkers, this was a device that *updated* the Athenian ideal. Tom Paine in *The Rights of Man* lauded "representation ingrafted upon democracy ... what Athens was in miniature, America will be in magnitude". But for others such as Madison, as we have seen, the point was the reverse: that representation in a republic *replaced* democracy. Furthermore, this strand of thought stressed the need to constrain even this mediated expression of popular will through the separation of powers and a set of constitutionally embedded rights. For Madison, the "true distinction" of America's governments lay "in the total exclusion of the people, in their collective capacity, from any share" in government. In the political discourse of the day, *republicans*, governed through representatives, were at odds with *democrats*, who sought to rule themselves.

Prominent twentieth-century accounts emphasize and more or less tacitly endorse the chasm between these two conceptions. For so-called "elitists" such as Joseph Schumpeter, democracy is only a method of selecting leaders, through competitive struggle. The people do not rule, nor, given general popular incompetence, should it: its role is confined to electing professional politicians. The reality of democratic politics, they argue, is that political leadership is more important than representation, that government is a matter of technical expertise and capacity to manage and administer large and complex bureaucratic organizations, that parliaments are dominated by organized parties, and that voters are largely passive, emotional and ill informed. At most the bond between the representative and her or his constituent rests in the former's wary anticipation of the retrospective verdict of the latter, when making (or publicizing) decisions. Of course, this is not meaningless, but it is a far cry from popular rule.

Pluralists also aspired to offer an empirical account of democracy's actual workings. Drawing on Alexis de Tocqueville and the tradition of liberal and republican thought that attaches great importance to "intermediary associations" that lie between the state and the individual citizen, political scientists such as David Truman and Robert Dahl shared with the Schumpeterian perspective doubts about the possibility – and desirability – of high levels of political participation and the view of democracy as primarily a method for the selection of political leaders. They also emphasized importance for democracy of the freedom of groups to associate in order to promote political interests (in stark contrast to the constraints on such organizations in fascist and communist states). Offsetting this variety of associations was a presumed consensus on values. Sceptics (including Dahl himself in later work) argue that this apparent pluralism is usually skewed toward some powerful interests: while groups of all sorts may be free to associate, government is particularly sensitive to corporate power and private business, not least since its tax base depends on the health of those groups.

Dimensions of disagreement

For critical conceptions of democracy, liberal representation and intellectual descendants who purport to be yet more realistic express a dismally limited view of what is valuable and what is possible. In spite of their claims, it is argued, these theories are not empirical – just particular value theories, endorsing particular political arrangements by giving them the honorific stamp of value, "democracy". The earlier liberal project of grafting representation on to democracy needs to be approached in a different way.

Broadly, critical theories take two forms, although various combinations of their arguments can be found. The first develops from the thought that liberal and post-liberal conceptions misunderstand the value and meaning of political participation. In one version, taking its cue from Jean-Jacques Rousseau, this rests on the value of individual freedom. The highest moral requirement is that a person is free and this requires the self-rule only possible through democracy. The problem that such accounts then grapple with is how to square the importance of my making rules for myself with the need to abide by the decisions of (the majority of) the group. In a second version, it is less self-legislation that is the central value than the intrinsic superiority of a life committed to political participation. The difficulty that this version then confronts is that this is simply one "conception of the good life" among others which may appeal to political animals among us but not to those who for whom politics is a grubby distraction or an irrelevance. In addition, both these versions of participatory democracy attract the worry that the demands that they make on citizens outstrip most individuals' inclinations and capacities.

Finally, a third version of this claim, to which much attention has been paid recently, draws a distinction between deliberative and aggregative views of participation. Liberal and post-liberal approaches are seen as dominated by the latter perspective: they view voting as the naked expression of individual preference, and a democratic procedure as way of aggregating these preferences in order to arrive at a particular outcome. Proponents of deliberative democracy argue that it is the process of debate, discussion and persuasion prior to this aggregation that is crucial for the legitimacy of the outcome. The discipline of public discussion, it is argued, transforms our initial preferences in the light of what we find we can offer as acceptable reasons to everyone else taking part. In a society characterized by a variety of religions and beliefs about religion, for example, believers in one particular outlook cannot simply rest their policy proposals on a claim about the truth of this outlook. Rather, public discussion demands that they seek out a reason acceptable to all. Critics of deliberative democracy worry that this represents democracy as an immense seminar and is too hopeful about the extent to which conflicts of interest, identity and perspective will allow democratic polities to arrive at meaningful and genuinely shared reasons.

The other form of critical theory (which can be combined with the first but has distinct sources and implications) approaches the question of the character of political participation from a different direction. The liberal and post-liberal conceptions of democracy, this form argues, purport to represent all but in fact bolster relations of domination prevalent in the societies with these systems. It is often argued that we need to extend democracy to embrace power relations in society that the conventional conceptions of democracy fail to grasp.

For example, socialists argue for greater democratic control of economic power. Feminists alternatively argue for the politicization of family relations and reproductive rights. Proponents of this kind of criticism (who also may focus on race, culture or ethnicity as dimensions of exclusion) divide into those for whom democracy in anything like its liberal form is irredeemable – inevitably the expression of class power, patriarchy or racial domination – and those for whom a more genuinely inclusive form of it is conceivable.

Paradoxes and challenges

As we have seen, at least since Plato democracy has often thought to be an especially *irrational* mode of political rule. Much discussion in the theory of democracy has been concerned with various updated versions of this challenge, sometimes presented as "paradoxes of democracy".

One of these was set out by Richard Wollheim. In essence, the idea is this. As a voter on a particular measure, I believe in the side that I take; so, for example, I believe that smoking should be permitted in restaurants and vote accordingly. When this vote goes against me, however, and if I am also a believer in democracy, I am entangled in a paradox, the argument runs. For I must then believe contradictory things: both that the ban on smoking is unjustified and that it is justified (since the majority supports it).

An initial point to make about this paradox is that it does not uniquely apply to democracy but to any political procedure that claims legitimacy for itself. If I believe both in permitting smoking in restaurants and also in the legitimacy of the oligarchy (or of a coin toss) I can be caught in Wollheim's paradox. Defenders of democracy in any case argue that the paradox dissolves once we clarify the nature of the democrat's beliefs. As a voter, I can be of the opinion that smoking in restaurants should be allowed, and think that the majority is wrong to ban it. But I can also believe that the majority has the right to implement a mistaken policy, provided that this policy has been properly arrived at (and that it does not itself erode the conditions for democratic decision-making). There is a conceptual gap between the best policy and the legitimate one.

A second paradox in the theory of democracy was set out by Anthony Downs. The vote of any individual in a sizeable electorate can only have the most insignificant impact on the outcome, and the costs of voting are likely to outweigh the benefits to that voter of her vote. Yet if enough voters chose to "free ride" on the democratic system, it would collapse. So democracies seem to rely on the *irrationality* of voters: that is, on their inability to see how best to promote their own interests. The "paradox" of continued widespread voting has notoriously been used not as evidence of mass irrationality but of the defectiveness of the theory of rational action underlying the account of voter behaviour. On the one side, proponents of this theory load the satisfaction of voting as a perceived benefit on the part of the rational voter. On the other, sceptics about this utilitarian account of rational action argue that this sort of cost–benefit calculation only hazily, if at all, captures the character of practical reasoning. Voting and political participation should not be understood either as the pursuit of an esoteric sort of preference or as a symptom of irrationality, but as emanating from a sense of obligation that is distinct from the utilitarian pursuit of self-interest.

A third version of this worry about irrationality stems from social choice theory and Kenneth Arrow's demonstration that (given some relatively weak assumptions) majority rule can lead to outcomes opposed by the majority of the population. For instance, if Jim's preferences are A > B > C, Joan's are C > A > B, and Jane's are B > C > A, then there is a majority for A over B (based on Jim's and Joan's preferences), a majority for B over C (based on Jim's and Jane's preferences), and a majority for C over A (based on Joan's and Jane's preferences). Majority rule, then, seems to allow a self-contradictory ranking of this mini-society's preferences. This is grist to the mill of the deliberative democrat, for whom, as we have seen, this purely aggregative view of what constitutes democratic procedure is in any case not the basis for the legitimacy of democracy. However, independently of that line of response, we may note that these "voting cycles" may be a feature of any group that votes, not just of democratic electorates. So if we are tempted in response to this Arrovian paradox to vest power in the hands of a committee of the wise, we should recall that, when this committee disagrees, and when they resolve this disagreement through voting, then this problem reappears. Institutions for containing democracy's "irrationality", as the political theorist Ian Shapiro has put it, may be no less "irrational" themselves.

Yet there is another form of challenge, at once more conceptual and more concrete, and hinted at in the second form of critical theory discussed above, that is impossible to overlook at the outset of this century. Democracy prescribes that the people should rule, but not who the people *is*. And it is difficult to see how a decision about the identity of the demos can be made democratically; for to make a democratic decision requires a demos which can decide, and that is what is at issue. Then is democracy a form of decision-making to be imposed on a set of boundaries or a population delineated by means external to the democratic process? Or do distinctively democratic values point toward particular ways of drawing boundaries? On the one side, there are those who see democracy in *cosmopolitan* terms: if we value democracy, it is argued, we should see boundaries as contingent and functional. Where a problem (say, an environmental issue such as the conservation of fishing stocks) requires action across state boundaries, this is best achieved through a transnational demos. On the other side, there are those who view established national identities as essential for the health of democracy, providing a shared language and cultural frame of reference that allows meaningful participation for all within it. Questions of the character and control of boundaries remain an important and deepening challenge for democracy.

Further reading

Dryzek, John. *Deliberative Democracy and Beyond: Liberals, Critics, Contestations.* Oxford: Oxford University Press, 2000.

Dunn, John. *Setting the People Free.* London: Atlantic Books, 2005.

Held, David. *Democracy and Global Order.* Cambridge: Polity Press, 1995.

Lukes, Steven. *Power: A Radical View,* second edition. Basingstoke: Palgrave, 2005.

Shapiro, Ian. *The State of Democratic Theory.* Princeton, NJ: Princeton University Press, 2003.

Young, Iris Marion. *Democracy and Inclusion*. Oxford: Oxford University Press, 2000.

MATTHEW FESTENSTEIN

DEMOCRACY AS A WAY OF LIFE

Articulated most fully in the philosophy of John Dewey, the notion of democracy as a way of life, in contrast to the more familiar notion of democracy as a way or form of government, is an important, rich, and radical idea in the writings of many American political philosophers.

Democracy often is understood in narrowly political terms. Unlike other political forms such as monarchy, aristocracy, theocracy, and totalitarianism, democracy is defined as rule by the people and characterized by: broad, if not universal, adult suffrage; equality in voting and regular elections; majority rule and minority rights; and opportunities for citizen involvement in elective and legal processes. In contrast, democracy also can be understood in broader social terms (that include but aren't limited to political institutions). Understood as a way of life, democracy is defined as: the responsible involvement in, and direction of, social practices by all persons affected by those practices; the ongoing development of the capacities of all persons so as to make possible and to expand this involvement and direction; and the shared and conscious commitment to the value of this way of life by a society's or social group's members.

This distinction between two notions of democracy is not merely theoretical. It has immediate and far-reaching practical significance. John Dewey seized on this significance, developed it throughout his political writings (such as *Democracy and Education*, *The Public and Its Problems*, *Liberalism and Social Action*, *Individualism: Old and New*, and *Freedom and Culture*), and employed it as the basis for a thoroughgoing criticism of American life and as a basis for an alternative. Calling democracy as a way of life the very idea of democracy in its generic sense, Dewey stressed four main points. First, Dewey argued, no country at any time – the United States of America included – is fully or finally a democracy. To think otherwise is smugly, arrogantly, and dangerously erroneous. It is to infer wrongly that because America's form of government is democratic that its actual social life is also democratic. Much the opposite is true, Dewey claimed: Individuals often do not recognize, much less direct, the forces that affect their lives. The United States, Dewey wrote, is a great society but not yet a great community.

Second, Dewey advocated major changes in economic, legal, political, educational, technological, religious, moral, and other cultural practices, associations, and institutions for America to become more fully democratic. These changes involve both the transformation of persons – i.e. the transformation of values, attitudes, loyalties, and habits – and the transformation of social conditions – i.e. laws, workplaces, schools, and neighborhoods. This makes clear a third main point: Habitual attachment to practices, associations, and institutions formed under very different conditions in earlier times readily can work against democracy now and in the future. Dewey argued, for example, that commitments to outdated conceptions of freedom, individualism, and intelligence now undermine democracy. Freedom (particularly economic freedom) understood as the absence of constraint, Dewey explained, must be replaced by freedom understood as the capacity to secure those conditions necessary for well-being. Individualism understood as rugged self-sufficiency must be replaced by individualism understood as a product of stable social relations. Similarly, intelligence as private intuition or self-evident insight must be replaced by experimental inquiry and collaboration.

Finally, Dewey argued that the reconstruction of democracy requires democratic means. Exclusion, discrimination, oppression, violence, and war do not provide persons with direction over the forces that affect their lives, nor do they promote the value of such a shared community life. While war may sometimes be necessary, Dewey believed it was never sufficient. A democratic way of life cannot be produced by force.

Dewey himself argued that this notion of democracy as a way of life is the moral meaning of democracy as set forth by Thomas Jefferson. And, calling democracy a name for free and enriching communion, Dewey asserted that Walt Whitman was its seer. In Dewey's own day, his notion of the great community's democratic way of life shares much with the more idealistic political philosophies of Josiah Royce – particularly Royce's distinction between societies and genuine communities, his concept of a Beloved Community, and his defense of wise provincialism – and William Ernest Hocking. More recently, many American philosophers (including John E. Smith, Hilary Putnam, Richard Rorty, and Cornel West) have drawn explicitly on Dewey's understanding of democracy as a way of life, his democratic faith, and his meliorism. Moreover, Dewey's work is a key origin of much of the revival of interest in deliberative democracy and community participation.

Further reading

Dewey, John. "Creative Democracy: The Task Before Us" in *The Later Works, 1925–1953, Vol. 13, 1938–1939*, ed. Jo Ann Boydston. Carbondale, IL: Southern Illinois University Press, 1988 [1939].

Stuhr, John J. "Democracy as a Way of Life, Democracy in the Face of Terrorism" in his *Pragmatism, Postmodernism, and the Future of Philosophy*. New York: Routledge, 2003, pp. 45–74.

Westbrook, Robert B. *John Dewey and American Democracy*. Ithaca, NY: Cornell University Press, 1991.

JOHN J. STUHR

DENOTATIVE METHOD

The term "denotative method" (or "denotative-empirical method" and "empirical method") was used by John Dewey to describe the philosophical methodology of his major work in metaphysics, *Experience and Nature* (1925, second edition 1929). The aim of the denotative method is to locate philosophical thought within all aspects of human "experience" (by which Dewey primarily meant our physical and cultural modes of living rather than subjective feeling) in its engagement with nature (LW 1.372, 377; see 361–2). It is a method for doing philosophy in a comprehensive way that is sensitive to the range of human existence. Philosophy thereby avoids committing the "intellectualist fallacy" of treating all experience ultimately as knowledge and all reality as ultimately an object of knowledge (an insight Dewey developed from James's "psychologist's fallacy" in his *Principles of Psychology*, Ch. VII). Moreover, philosophy is asked to understand the origin and development of ideas in a historical, cultural context, i.e. to understand ideas in terms of their "natural history."

Before examining the denotative method itself, it is important to avoid confusing it with "instrumentalism," Dewey's preferred term for pragmatic thinking that intelligently integrates ends and means, with constant re-evaluation, toward fulfilling modes of conduct. Instrumentalism focuses on inquiry and deals with experience in terms of knowledge and is exemplified in works like *The Quest for Certainty* (1927). But one of Dewey's central points is that knowing is only one type of experience. Philosophy has been so concerned with the problem of knowledge that it has regarded all forms of experience as essentially instances of "knowledge." This confusion has led to another: the identification of reality with the object of knowledge. Dewey's philosophy explicitly rejects identifying experience with knowing and reality with the known. Thus, the denotative method is not the same as instrumentalism, but, in fact, grounds it.

This is not to say that Dewey's exposition of the denotative method is clear. The first chapter of *Experience and Nature*, which was devoted to the subject, generated such confusion that Dewey entirely rewrote it for the second edition, with no better results. (Indeed, the second version lent itself more to the confusion of the denotative method with instrumentalism, insofar as Dewey's examples there were drawn from the sciences; the original version is to be preferred; see LW 1. Appendix 2.) Given the disposition of philosophers to turn experience and reality into issues of knowledge, *Experience and Nature* attempts to develop a metaphysics that avoids this reduction. In this sense, the "denotative method" embraces a variety of strategies to get philosophers to remember *experience as it is experienced*, our acting in and responding to the world, when doing philosophy, the goal of which for Dewey, as for the ancients, is wisdom, living well, "which is not knowledge" (LW 1.305).

To avoid this fallacy, the primary distinction the method makes is between primary experience and experience that has been refined by reflection and inquiry (LW 1.15, 366). By "primary experience" Dewey means the "life-world": being born, hunger, eating, sleeping, dreaming, waking, fear, surprise, pain, joy, sickness, health, etc., even death. Cultural practices "point" to these aspects, e.g. how we experience death, and so are important objects of philosophical reflection. Anthropology especially has great importance for philosophy.

Nor is primary experience an atomic, immediate sensation, but "a thing of moods and tenses" which the artist understands better than the logician (LW 1.367). Neither is it inherently simple and clear: the lived world is "tangled and complex" where "twilight, the vague, dark and mysterious" abound (LW 1.367, 369). Philosophy must recognize that its refined objects, like a theory of love or tragedy as well as rational objects, originate in this existential world where love and tragedy and even reasoning are lived through and undergone *as* the events they are. The method is "denotative" in that it indicates this primary world out of which reflective inquiry arises and makes philosophy remember and acknowledge it. Philosophy can thereby recognize that its refined objects are developments of primary existential experiences and see the dynamic continuity between the primary events and refined meanings.

The method also "denotes" in pointing to the lived world as the proper goal of philosophical reflection. Philosophy exists for the sake of making life luminous with meaning and value. With this in mind, Dewey says, "*denotation* comes first and last, so that to settle any discussion, to still any doubt, to answer any question, we must go to some thing pointed to, denoted, and find out answer in that thing" (LW 1.372). The method uses "refined, secondary products as a path, pointing and leading back to something in primary experience" (LW 1.16–17).

> There is here supplied, I think, a first-rate test of the value of any philosophy which is offered to us: Does it ends in conclusions which, when they are referred back to ordinary life-experiences and their predicaments, render them more significant, more luminous to us, and make our dealings with them more fruitful?
>
> (LW 1.18)

The denotative method works by "showing" rather than by defining or proving (LW 1.372). In addition to indicating the situations in the life-world that are the basis of all refined arts and technologies (including philosophy), the method points to the temporal and historical nature of experience: the present is an outcome of a history and carries that history with it; it itself is a phase of temporal transformation and creative redirection; it points to a range of future possibilities that can determine the meaning of the present (LW 1.384–5).

Thus the denotative method is Dewey's prescription for philosophers to see the continuities between philosophy and life, to acknowledge the world from which thought arises and to which it should ultimately be directed for the enrichment of human experience. It asks that philosophers experience broadly and richly and not rely on abstract, formulaic methods. To do this, philosophy must see ideas in the context of civilization. It requires philosophy to have extensive grasp of history, art, and the sciences and to see the cultural origins and implications of contemporary ideas.

Further reading

Alexander, Thomas M. "Dewey's Denotative–Empirical Method," *Journal of Speculative Philosophy* NS 18, 3 (2004): 248–56.

Dewey, John. *Experience and Nature* in *Later Works* (LW), Vol. 1, ed. Jo Ann Boydston. Carbondale, IL: Southern Illinois University Press, 1981, Ch. 1, Appendix 2.

—— "Philosophy and Civilization" in *Later Works* (LW), Vol. 2, ed. Jo Ann Boydston. Carbondale, IL: Southern Illinois University Press, 1984, pp. 3–10.

—— "The Postulate of Immediate Empiricism" in *Middle Works* (MW), Vol. 3, ed. Jo Ann Boydston. Carbondale, IL: Southern Illinois University Press, 1977, pp. 158–67.

Gouinlock, James. *John Dewey's Philosophy of Value.* Atlantic Highlands, NJ: Humanities Press, 1972, Ch. 1.

THOMAS M. ALEXANDER

DESIGNATION

To designate is to name, refer to or denote something. As a topic of logic, semantic theory, philosophy of language, and semiotics, explaining the nature of designation is vital to understanding the mind and its linguistic and artistic expression. It is essential to an adequate theory of designation to know whether psychology needs to be involved or altogether excluded, and to have a clear sense of the ontology of designation, of the kinds of things that can or cannot be designated.

American philosophy has taken up the problem of explaining designation in distinctive ways. The pragmatic tradition and contemporary Anglo-American analytic philosophy have made important contributions to the foundations of semantic theory, and in particular to the account of how it is that reference relates thought and language to designated objects. In the pragmaticist semiotics of C.S. Peirce, the concept of designation is understood, not as an abstract mapping of terms onto objects, but as a real-time occurrence in which thinkers and language users engage in specific actions, including psychological acts, whereby a word or phrase is related to an object. Designating an object is an activity, and thought and speech acts need to be understood accordingly as practices whose existence and properties are to be explained insofar as they potentially enable a human agent to survive. Communication as a social instrument is a valuable instrument for exchanging information and enlisting the support of multiple individuals in social activities.

Peirce's semiotic explains a sign as something that to a given language user stands for something. Peirce says that the sign "addresses" a thinker, speaker or writer, by virtue of creating in the mind of the individual an equivalent sign, or, as he also says, "perhaps a more developed sign." The sign stands for its object, and the sign that it creates in the mind of the language user is the interpretant of the original sign (2.228). Designation for Peirce is thus a three-part relation. A sign designates its object by virtue of standing for the object, and in the process it produces a simulacrum of itself in the mind or minds of those who consider the sign and understand its meaning. What is unexamined in Peirce's account, however, is more precisely what it is supposed to mean for a sign to "stand for" an object, and this, unfortunately, is what reference, designation, or denotation is all about; it is that which we require a satisfactory theory of designation to explain. Elsewhere, Peirce defines a symbol as a sign whose "representative character" constitutes a rule that determines its interpretant (2.292). This formula makes it clear again that for Peirce designation takes place via the replication of signs in uses and in the minds of those between whom communication is established. The visual similarity of sign and interpretant are crucial for Peirce's account, and it is reasonable to suppose that the way a sign and its interpretant looks might help to explain designation. There are nevertheless many signs that do not in any obvious sense resemble their objects, so that the designative relation between sign or interpretant remains indeterminate.

The succeeding generation of American philosophers, still influenced by the earliest roots of pragmatism, also understand designation as a real, virtually biological activity of language users rather than an abstract mapping of terms onto things. The prime example in this most recent period is W.V.O. Quine, whose theory of stimulus-meanings in *Word and Object* (1960) attempts to explain the reference of names in behaviorist terms. We refer to that which causes us to utter the name, according to the schedule of behavioral conditioning in which we have been socialized. The causal connection in language use as a basis for understanding how a particular term refers to a particular object is further exploited by Saul A. Kripke in his "new picture" of how naming works, in his lectures on *Naming and Necessity* (1982). Kripke describes an historical network of usages in which the reference of a name is passed along from user to user like the links in a chain. Kripke's causal or historical account of designation does not substitute causation for intended meaning, but rather presupposes that at an initial baptism or naming ceremony and at all subsequent uses of the name a speaker must intend to refer to or designate the same individual in significant uses of a proper name. Kripke adds a new element to the theory of designation by introducing the concept of rigid designation, according to which a proper name as a rigid designator refers to the identical object in every logically possible world in which the name refers at all.

Further reading

Glock, Hans-Johann. *Quine and Davidson on Language, Thought and Reality.* Cambridge: Cambridge University Press, 2003.

Hahn, Lewis Edwin and Schilpp, Paul A. (ed.) *The Philosophy of W.V. Quine.* Chicago, IL: Open Court, 1998.

Hughes, Christopher. *Names, Necessity, and Identity.* Oxford: Clarendon, 2004.

Kripke, Saul A. *Naming and Necessity.* Cambridge, MA: Harvard University Press, 1982.

Murphey, Murray G. *The Development of Peirce's Philosophy.* Cambridge, MA: Harvard University Press, 1961.

Nelson, Lynn Hankinson and Nelson, Jack. *On Quine.* Belmont: Wadsworth, 2000.

Peirce, C.S. *The Collected Papers of C. S. Peirce*, ed. Charles Hartshorne and Paul Weiss (Vols 1–6), A.W. Burks (Vols 7–8). Cambridge, MA: Harvard University Press, 1931–58 (quotations indicated by volume number and paragraph; 2.228 references Vol. 2, paragraph 228).

Quine, W.V.O. *Word and Object*. Cambridge, MA: MIT Press, 1960.

Soames, Scott. *Beyond Rigidity: The Unfinished Semantic Agenda of Naming and Necessity.* Oxford: Oxford University Press, 2002.

DALE JACQUETTE

DETERMINISM

Pierre Simon Laplace (1749–1827) provides the paradigmatic conception of a deterministic universe.

According to this conception, the conjunction of natural laws and the universe's initial condition leads to a complete determination of all its future conditions. Thus we could, *in principle*, have a sufficiently knowledgeable demon who could predict everything that would happen in the future. In order to accomplish such a feat, the demon would require information regarding "initial conditions" and "natural law." With the former, the demon would have to know the initial positions, velocities and masses of all elementary particles. With the latter, the demon would have to completely understand all laws governing the forces that act upon such particles. By having both sets of information, the demon could *in principle* predict *all* future states of the universe.

William James best captures the feelings that one tends to experience when confronted with the possibility that she lives in a deterministic universe:

> It professes that those parts of the universe already laid down absolutely appoint and decree what the other parts shall be. The future has no ambiguous possibilities hidden in its womb; the part we call the present is compatible with only one totality. Any other future complement than the one fixed from eternity is impossible. The whole is in each and every part, and welds it with the rest into an absolute unity, an iron block, in which there can be no equivocation or shadow of turning.
> ("Dilemma of Determinism" 1956: 150)

Living in the iron-block universe of determinism seems to undermine any real choice that a human might experience. For example, a thousand years before the existence of humanity, Laplace's demon would be able to predict the very thing you are thinking and feeling as you read this sentence. This demon, because of its superior knowledge, would see the universe for what it is – an iron block. In addition, the demon would recognize humanity's status as mere puppets of natural law.

C.S. Peirce, in "The Doctrine of Necessity Examined," famously criticizes the Laplacean view. According to Peirce, real scientists when employing natural law do not deal with perfect mathematical entities. The real world is extraordinarily complicated, and thereby our applications of natural law are prone to vary. Although determinists may want to attribute these variations to our limited cognitive abilities and poor measurement tools, Peirce questions what evidence they could present for such claims. The more sophisticated our measurements and observations have become, the more variation we have found (i.e. apparent smooth surfaces, with more detailed observation, become jagged and irregular). Thus variation is not eliminated with better observation; it is maintained. At best, then, natural laws are mere statistical regularities prone to variation. A plausible explanation for these variations, according to Peirce, is that there is some degree of indeterminism in the universe.

With a more contemporary understanding of natural law, Peirce's view appears to be vindicated. In the 1920s, the research of Werner Heisenberg (1901–76), Erwin Schrödinger (1887–1961) and Paul Dirac (1902–84) conjoined to create a new form of mechanics – quantum mechanics – according to which, phenomena at the atomic level (or smaller) seemed to obey laws that were not deterministic in nature. For example, in order to predict the future velocity and position of a particle, one has to be able to measure its current position and velocity. This could be done by shining a light on the particle. The problem, however, is that the light will affect the particle that it is employed to measure. To determine a particle's position, one would need to employ a light with a short wavelength, yet use of this light would change the velocity of the particle. To determine the velocity of the particle, one would need to use a light with a longer wavelength, yet this light would not accurately measure the position of the particle. Thus, according to quantum mechanics, one could accurately determine the position or the velocity of a particle, but not both! Knowledge of one value would entail the uncertainty (to a probabilistic degree) of the other.

Notice how this conception of "natural law" undermines the predictive power of the Laplacean demon. Quantum mechanics seems to render the precise measurement of the "initial conditions" as an impossible flight of fancy. For example, the demon could not, due to the limitations of the universe, determine the precise position and velocity of any particular particle. Without the accurate measurement of the initial conditions, the demon is unable, *in principle*, to predict the future states of the universe.

Or can it? It is true that almost all philosophers and scientists agree with the empirical verifiability of the laws of quantum mechanics. Yet their interpretations of what cosmological views are entailed by such laws are quite varied. David Bohm, for example, articulated a different interpretation of quantum mechanics that seemed to preserve a deterministic interpretation of the universe. With Bohm's interpretation, all particles, at all times, have a definite position and velocity. The laws of quantum mechanics are, on this view, mere mathematical models that allow us to predict, as best we can, these values. Thus, Bohm separates a question of epistemology from a question of ontology. The physical laws of the universe might constrain what values we can *know* exactly. This, however, does not imply that these exact values fail to *exist* independent of our knowledge.

This leads to a significant tension in the discussion of determinism. Is determinism an epistemic doctrine or is it a metaphysical doctrine? With the paradigmatic example of the Laplacean demon it seems, at least *prima facie*, to have an epistemic character. It is tied to the predictive capabilities of the demon. But, these capabilities are idealized; it is what the wise demon – *in principle* – could predict. If the thesis of determinism is epistemic in this manner, then we would have to solve the central issues of epistemology before we could decide whether the universe is actually deterministic.

On the other hand, it seems entirely plausible that determinism could be fully separated from epistemology. Pretend that we have a universe in which there are initial conditions with exact values and these values are only subject to laws which entail future exact values. Unlike the Laplacean version, these laws and values are too complex for any entity to comprehend. With this version, there would be no Laplacean demon to view humanity as mere puppets lacking freewill. It is important to note, however, that humans would still be puppets subject to the laws of cause and effect. With this purely metaphysical conception of determinism, we no longer have to solve the problems associated with epistemology. This separation with epistemology, however, is not entirely without its own negative consequences. This purely metaphysical conception seems to place the determinism/indeterminism debate into the same quagmire as the idealism/realism debate. It is philosophically interesting; yet *in principle* beyond our knowledge.

Further reading

Bishop, R. "On Separating Predictability and Determinism," *Erkenntnis* 58 (2003): 69–188.

Bohm, D. and Hiley, B. *The Undivided Universe: An Ontological Interpretation of Quantum Theory.* London: Routledge and Kegan Paul, 1993.

James, William. *The Will to Believe and Other Essays.* New York: Dover, 1956 [1896].

Laplace, S.P. *A Philosophical Essay on Probabilities*, trans F.W. Truscott and F.L. Emory. New York: Dover, 1951 [1820].

Peirce, C.S. "The Doctrine of Necessity Examined," *The Monist* 2 (1892): 321–37.

Popper, K. "Indeterminism in Quantum Physics and in Classical Physics," *British Journal for the Philosophy of Science* 1 (1950): 117–33.

Stone, M. "Chaos, Prediction and Laplacean Determinism," *American Philosophical Quarterly* 26 (1989): 123–31.

SHANE D. COURTLAND

DEWEY, JOHN: A COMMON FAITH

In 1935, the year following publication of his Terry Lectures (delivered at Yale University in 1934) as *A Common Faith* (ACF), John Dewey wrote to his friend and fellow philosopher, Max Carl Otto:

> My book was written for the people who feel inarticulately they have the essence of the religious with them and yet are repelled by the religions and are confused – primarily for them, secondarily for the "liberals" to help them realize how inconsistent they are.
>
> (LW 9.455; that is, Vol. 9 of *The Later Works*, p. 455)

Religious liberals had retreated during the nineteenth and early twentieth centuries from the traditional understanding of religion, insisting that there was a distinct religious sphere of life, different in kind from ordinary experience. Dewey could not abide this separation. He proposed a naturalistic understanding, locating the religious in experience. He thought this proposal would appeal to many of his generation who, like him, had rejected the faith of their parents but wished to have a religious way of life.

The faith he sketched in this compact book put the emphasis on one's commitment to inclusive ideals that would shape the person in an integrative manner. One would become a cohesive person (or group) through loyalty to broad, unifying ends. This faith did not differ from the social psychology that he articulated in *Human Nature and Conduct* (1922; MW 14). But there he only briefly made reference to the religious, notably in this sentence: "The religious experience is a reality in so far as in the midst of effort to foresee and regulate future objects we are sustained and expanded in feebleness and failure by the sense of an enveloping whole" (MW 14.181). "Foreseeing and regulating future objects" is the work of intelligence. But the intelligent person is enabled by a particular kind of sense, one "of an enveloping whole." This whole is available to people of wide knowledge and suitable imagination; it is neither esoteric nor otherworldly. Significantly, this sentence occurs in Section VIII, "Desire and Intelligence," which is included within Part III, "The Place of Intelligence in Conduct." Dewey, in all of his work, wanted to integrate desire and intelligence, interest and the active reconstruction of experience. One should not be misled by the religious language to think that Dewey had betrayed his hard-won naturalistic orientation.

Yet many readers have been misled by Dewey's surprising move in the second chapter, "Faith and Its Object." There he decided, despite objections from some of his colleagues, to use the term "God" of the naturalistic process of idealizing imagination in which the actual becomes an ideal reality. According to his student and collaborator, Sidney Hook, Dewey replied to Hook's objection,

> There are so many people who would feel bewildered if not hurt were they denied the intellectual right to use the term "God." They are not in the churches, they believe what I believe, they would feel a loss if they could not speak of God. Why then shouldn't I use the term?
>
> (Hook 1952: 253)

The reply to Dewey by some is that not everyone had Dewey's deep commitment to and understanding of naturalism. Some readers missed Dewey's careful qualifications and took the term "God" in its more usual meaning of a supernatural power.

But for those who read Dewey carefully, *A Common Faith* serves as a powerful statement of Dewey's lifelong commitment to intelligent action. Toward the end of ACF he affirms,

> There is such a thing as passionate intelligence, as ardor in behalf of light shining into the murky places of social existence, and a zeal for its refreshing and purifying effect. The whole story of man shows that there are not objects that may not deeply stir engrossing emotion. One of the few experiments in the attachment of emotion to ends that mankind has not tried is that of devotion, so intense as to be religious, to intelligence as a force in social action.
>
> (LW 9.52–3)

Dewey's hope for humanity was that we should become passionately intelligent, so much so that it would be regarded as a religious activity.

Further reading

Dewey, John. *The Middle Works.* Carbondale, IL: Southern Illinois University Press. *Human Nature and Conduct* is reprinted in Vol. 14 and is cited as MW 14.

—— *The Later Works.* Carbondale, IL: Southern Illinois University Press, 1967–72. *A Common Faith* is reprinted in Vol. 9 and is cited as LW 9.

Eldridge, Michael. *Transforming Experience: John Dewey's Cultural Instrumentalism.* Nashville, TN: Vanderbilt University Press, 1998, especially Ch. 5, "Dewey's Religious Proposal," pp. 126–69.

Hook, Sidney. "Some Memories of John Dewey, 1859–1952," *Commentary* 14 (1952): 245–53.

MICHAEL ELDRIDGE

DEWEY, JOHN: AESTHETICS

The term "aesthetics" originates with Alexander Baumgarten's *Aesthetica* (1750). Influenced by Descartes' concepts of "clear and distinct ideas," Baumgarten wanted to explore ideas that were "clear" but not "distinct," and so turned to the Greek word *aesthēsis*, "sense perception." Of course, questions concerning the nature of the beautiful, of artistic production (especially poetry), and of "image-making" in the soul go at least as far back as Plato. And while the eighteenth century made major contributions, culminating in Kant's *Critique of Judgment* (1790), significant philosophical treatment of the dimension of experience dealing with creative imagination, expressive feeling, the sublime in nature, and the importance of art in human existence is one of the genuine contributions of Romanticism. To the extent that a philosopher accords centrality to these issues, he or she is in some fundamental sense a child of that revolution. John Dewey is such a philosopher, and aesthetics is a central aspect of his philosophy of experience: "the theory of esthetics put forth by a philosopher ... is a test of the capacity of the system he puts forth to grasp the nature of experience itself" (LW 10.278). Though the key ideas that Dewey uses to articulate his aesthetic theory are found throughout his mature work, it is only with *Experience and Nature* (1925, 1929) that he directly began to address the subject. His culminating thoughts are found in *Art as Experience* (1934), and this essay will follow the argument of that book.

Dewey believed that aesthetics was important because it exhibited more clearly than any other activity the capacity for human beings to create meaning and value so that experience became intense, profound, and significant. The potentiality for such experience lay all around. Dewey was highly critical of the attempt to separate fine art and aesthetic experience from the other dimensions of life precisely because it cut the nerve of this important lesson. By segregating "art" into museums, cultural elites and artworlds, it lost its prophetic character for the range of human existence. The "origin of art" is found in the origin of experience, the rhythmic interactions of the "live creature" with its environment. Aesthetics as a practice of theoretical reflection should begin with focusing on moments when life takes on intensity and meaning, when it becomes alive, rather than with the experience of artworks in a museum – though of course, and this is exactly Dewey's point, there is continuity between the two. But if we begin with the "museum experience" this connection between art and life will be attenuated or lost. It is the pervasive nature of aesthetic experience in life, which the arts cultivate, that Dewey wishes to emphasize.

In living, there are times when the creature is in harmony with its environment and others when it is not and must struggle to re-establish it. Because of this rhythm of loss and recovery, experience takes on hues of tension and fulfillment – fulfillment that is felt as such because it is the resolution of tension. This is the source of art. A world of utter chaos or one of monotonous regularity would not foster aesthetic experience. When the relationship of "doing and undergoing" is directly felt or perceived in experience, it takes on meaning. The expressiveness of works of art derives from their resolution of creative tensions in the medium. Unfortunately, according to Dewey, modern life is filled with such disorganization and neglect of aesthetic immediacy that for the most part the experience of "deeply realized meanings" is rare. Given this, "aesthetics" for Dewey involves more of a revolution in existence, in the way we should live and experience the world, than a "theory of art." To achieve this, a new body of habits and awareness of possibilities must be cultivated. The ultimate implications of Dewey's aesthetics point to a whole way of life at odds with the bifurcated, repressed psychology of modernism. "Aesthetic perception" is nothing less than the whole field of the living body brought to ecstatic focus, incarnated in sense.

The key concept in Dewey's aesthetics is his idea of "consummatory experience" (q.v.). While many experiences contain promise of realization of depth and intensity in meaning, for the most part these promises are unfulfilled. A consummatory experience is one that develops those possibilities so that the realized meaning is felt or "undergone" as a controlling and guiding force in the experience: it is "*an* experience." While art tries to cultivate such experiences, they may occur ubiquitously: a hike in the autumn woods, the discovery of a friendship in a time of need, achieving peace at long last with a parent. Such experiences are pervaded with or marked by a distinctive, unique quality that binds all the phases and makes them felt as belonging to one whole. This gives meaning to the various parts as they are undergone. The consummatory is present or recurrent throughout the work and is not to be confused with a culmination at the end. Nor do such experiences have to be "happy," a common misunderstanding of Dewey at this key point; they may be episodes of strife, tragedy, or lonely agonies of doubt and despair. The intensity of their aesthetic qualities fuses each experience as a whole together so it is a revelation of existence. That such experiences can reveal deep aesthetic meaning is evident in the way arts have appropriated them. The *Iliad* examines thoughtless strife and St John of the Cross writes of "the dark night of the soul" in his poetry. Tragedy is a whole genre of drama that deals with pain and suffering. Human beings hunger for experiencing the meanings of existence in a direct and embodied way so that the possibility of existence itself is revealed.

Dewey pays close attention to three aspects of the artistic–aesthetic or consummatory experience: expression, form and quality. Dewey's theory of expression is almost as frequently misunderstood as his theory of consummatory experience. He rejects the simple notion of expression as mere externalization. The artist does not merely "externalize" some artistic intuition that is then internalized by the audience's experience of the artwork. First, mere externalizing is not expressing. A child throwing a tantrum is not "expressing" anything, except in the way a storm might "express" power to an observer. Expression requires artful mastery of a medium so that the artwork can become expressive to an audience. An actor like James Earl Jones playing King Lear expresses kingly rage because there is a thorough command of the medium (in this case the actor's body) so that it can embody the meaning of the rash, noble king in the play. Second, expression not only requires a medium, but implies an audience. In rejecting the idea of pure art – an art made for no audience – Dewey is not saying one must create for a specific audience or pander to dominant fads. The artist, in the process of creation, takes on the role of the appreciator throughout the creative process, using it to evaluate and modify the art product until it is finished. The artist may have an actual audience in mind, as Sophocles knew the Athenians for whom he wrote his plays. But the artist may also create for an audience as yet nonexistent – especially if one is creating beyond the accepted limits of a given artform. Works of great art create new audiences – Van Gogh taught people a new way of seeing just as Beethoven taught new ways of hearing. Finally, creation and appreciation are intertwined in the experiences of both artist and audience: the creator takes on the role of an appreciator and any act of appreciating a work calls for a creative response in an audience.

Dewey has an equally radical theory of form. Form is the dynamic way a work of art achieves a consummatory experience through the expressiveness of the medium; it is, in Heidegger's words, the "working of the work." Not only does this mean that form is the individual way that experience is creatively transformed that makes each work of art distinctively just what it is, but that form is the living interaction of the artwork with each audience that encounters it. Thus "a" work has many incarnations, many enactments, no two of which are identical. The "unity" of a work designates an ongoing history. This is more easily seen in the case of music, perhaps, where a score must be performed anew. But each reading of a poem or encounter with a Frank Lloyd Wright house is equally a "performance." Great works are those that speak across great distances and in many dialects. Euripides wrote *The Trojan Women* in 415 BCE to protest the brutal conquest of a small, neutral island by Athens. "You wanted power and glory, Athenians," he said, "this is what it means." His work speaks to us still, asking us to feel what life is to the war widow, the bereaved mother, the dignified old woman who, at the end, loses all. Form, then, is the dynamic, interactive organization of our own powers of response in relation to an expressive object. In this way, our experience of the world itself may be the realization of deep, aesthetic habits of perception in existence.

Features of Dewey's treatment of quality have already become apparent in his treatment of consummatory experience, expression, and form. Although a work of art develops in experience with a variety of different elements and moments of focus, nevertheless all of these phases are experienced as belonging to one whole experience. Running throughout these different parts is what Dewey calls "the pervasive qualitative whole." This quality is not itself an object of reflection – as Dewey explains elsewhere, it is what makes reflection possible (see "Qualitative Thought") – nor is it any sort of nameable type of quality; it is the quality that makes that experience uniquely *that.* It is dimly sensed at the commencement of *an* experience as the "promise" of the consummatory. As the experience develops, the phases are undergone with the sense of their carrying forward the fulfillment of that promise. If a phase of the work fails to do this, the work begins to fall apart and disappoint. As the work continues to build up toward its ultimate integration, one part or phase connects with the others, enriching and deepening their significance and expressiveness. This is perhaps most easily understood in overtly temporal artforms like drama or music. The restatement of a theme in a musical composition either strengthens or weakens the piece; where the musical possibilities of the initial parts have explored interesting tensions and resolved them in surprising but genuine ways, a restatement is felt as a reaffirmation of the unity of the piece. Or, where a novel moment in the music is set forth, such as the sudden use of the human voice in the choral "Ode to Joy" in Beethoven's Ninth Symphony, it is not felt as a break or incoherency in the composition, but as a flowering into human speech of the mute struggle for freedom that has been in the music from the start. This qualitative dimension is present in all experience, but for the most part it is suppressed and not noticed. One of the primary functions of art, for Dewey, is to raise this pervasive qualitative and meaning-constituting aspect of experience to consciousness, so that we experience it intensely suffusing the objects at the focus of our attention. This also happens in religious experience.

The concluding chapters of *Art as Experience* set forth Dewey's challenging and strangely neglected views of the implications of his aesthetics for the practice of philosophy and his theory of civilization. All experience is imaginative and creative to some degree for Dewey. The ultimate human concern is to live with a fundamental sense of meaning and value as directly embodied in experience. Not only is philosophy itself an art that requires imagination and creativity as well as a sensitivity to experience in its noncognitive modes, but also philosophy should seek to frame those ideals that contribute toward a civilization that can consciously create the conditions for lives of fulfillment. Art is a powerful instance whereby human beings can achieve such fulfilling experiences. But if art itself is regarded as an isolated phenomenon, unrelated to ordinary life or any other human pursuit, the lesson will not be learned.

Further reading

Alexander, Thomas. *John Dewey's Theory of Art, Experience, and Nature: The Horizons of Feeling*. New York: SUNY Press, 1987.

Dewey, John. *Art as Experience* in *The Later Works*, Vol. 10. New York: Minton, Balch, 1934; Carbondale, IL: Southern Illinois University Press, 1987.

—— *Experience and Nature* in *The Later Works*, Vol. 1. LaSalle, IL: Open Court, 1925, 1929; Carbondale, IL: Southern Illinois University Press, 1981, Chapter IX.

McDermott, John J. *The Culture of Experience*. New York: New York University Press, 1976.

THOMAS M. ALEXANDER

DEWEY, JOHN: EDUCATION

Considered the foremost educator of his day, from the Lab School he founded at the University of

Chicago to his co-founding of the Lincoln School in Manhattan and the New School for Social Research in New York, Dewey's philosophy of education has had a tremendous national and international impact. A wide swatch of today's teaching styles, pedagogical techniques and educational approaches trace their roots to his work – though he himself suggested his ideas are frequently misinterpreted, and criticized some popular approaches as too mechanistic or insufficiently rigorous. His philosophy of education and practical applications have been used not only by educators from pre-school to college/university settings, but in some respects by Western cultures generally (and some non-Western) to conceptualize and structure educational systems and institutions. Referred to alternately as "experiential education," "transformative education" and "progressive education," Dewey's approach brought his pragmatist views to bear on education and promoted learning through doing. He meant his claim that "education is life itself" in the deepest sense possible: that learning is deeply social and intimately wedded to one's experiences, aims, and context, all of which evolve and constitute both the learning individual and the learning community. To speak of "completing one's education" would be, for Dewey, akin to saying one had completed the task of breathing. He argued that persons are not individual containers that abstractly collect facts or knowledge, but human organisms that proceed and grow by continuously integrating past experiences within present realities and future aims. On this model, education is a transactional affair between organism and environment, where theory and practice inform each other as one learns collectively with others.

The pragmatists took ideas not to be fixed facts, but instead to be "thinking" and "theorizing" – dynamic, active processes that play out in lived experience. Dewey extended this reasoning to the process of gaining an education: facts, theories, and ideas were only worth whatever they could yield, change, or ameliorate in lived experience, and the most productive education blends theory and practice in this holistic way. Dewey was convinced humans learn the best when actively doing a thing, engaging many dimensions of the person rather than just some pure intellect (which Dewey thought was a mirage). We learn as whole persons, Dewey reasoned, not simply to acquire facts but in order to live better, and be more productive with our lives: we are constantly re-testing, revising, and applying anew in different contexts what we have "learned" in the past. In his view, then, very little about education is wholly static or finished – not ideas/facts or scholarship, which require consistent re-testing, are fallible, and ongoingly incorporate new insights; not students, who are persons with differing learning styles, background experiences, and future aims; and not educators, who are scholars and teachers consistently learning anew in their field, and experimenting with new teaching techniques.

Dewey's ideas on education developed partly in response to his context at the turn of the century. In the 1920s and 1930s, American academic institutions of higher education were in the throes of slowly transforming from an inherited European model of education – a firmly hierarchical one in which scholar-professors imparted foundational objective principles to students via the canonical texts of a field. Students were expected to memorize them unquestioningly, thereby "learning" the substance of the discipline, be it mathematics or philosophy. As pragmatism begins with the methodological assumption that facts and knowledge are not timeless universals, but are influenced by – and, in turn, themselves influence – their social context, Dewey's insight was to recognize this inherited model not as a "natural" way to structure or conceptualize education, but as historical, artificial, and ultimately changeable. He argued that the modern educational approach of his day remained so authoritative and hierarchical that it ultimately constituted a mere fact-delivery system – and a poor one at that. Dewey envisioned instead an educational system concerned with students' actual experiences, where students engaged with the material in ways that connected to their lives.

Experimentation and imaginative freedom, specifically, were twin cornerstones of Dewey's approach to pedagogy. He held that meaningful education needs to be structured, but that it cannot be precisely scripted: if so, it risks becoming formulaic, dead dogma that students may memorize but fail to understand beyond a surface level. Freedom to explore subject matter in multiple ways became a hallmark of Deweyan pedagogy: this included integrating out-of-classroom components into the learning process, student discussion and engagement rather than one-sided lectures, and a range of assignments and exercises requiring student contributions and critical thinking. Quality educators provide not only subject matter, but also multi-dimensional environments for interaction and connection with it. Humans are organisms equipped with a mind that, for Dewey, develops communally and in response to the environment: reading him, one gets the sense that knowledge itself is a living, developing mode of the mind and of personhood, rather than a stash of information. As such, he frequently uses the term "laboratory" for educational settings, which are places of testing and re-testing received ideas and where one examines their supporting evidence.

Dewey's educational approach was also deeply intertwined with his faith in democracy – both as a political form of society, and as an ethical commitment to the worth of individuals who co-operatively create a community. Staunchly anti-authoritarian, he argued that top-down educational institutions poorly prepared students to eventually take part in a dynamic democratic society. To do this, schools should instead value students, engage their experiences, and treat them as responsible thinkers and citizens. Educational settings were not merely training technical "knowers" but whole persons and citizens. Dewey argued democracy in fact required progressive education so citizens could gain aptitude for political analysis and building solutions: ethically, democracy required taking into account a plurality of views on the good life and robust, ongoing discussions of both politics and value. Education was for him the oxygen of a vibrant democracy, and in a sense he treats democracy ultimately as his beloved experimentation/laboratory setting writ large in political form. Aspirational democracy, as the pragmatists and Dewey understood it, is an ongoing process and working-out of ideas – an outgrowth of one's social education into broader citizenship.

Stemming from these commitments, Dewey's educational ideas advanced an ethics of sort as well – though not of the religious sort more common to other pragmatists like William James. Dewey's anti-authoritarian conviction yielded not so much a relativism about values as a pragmatist pluralism, where multiple perspectives on what is right or good would be available and open for exploration and debate. The "lab" model of an educational setting committed him to a communal approach – no wholly private ethics-of-one could exist, he thought, any more than a wholly individual education could. And paired with his passion for democracy, core values like tolerance, diversity, fallibilism, social engagement, and attention to marginalized perspectives undergird his educational philosophy. As his famous 1897 "pedagogic creed" makes clear, learning is, for him, an ethical responsibility for each of us. Individuals are lucky enough to inherit the mass of contributions from past generations, and with vigorous education we might be able to live up to the responsibility, challenge, and opportunity to extend that story and become a reflective citizenry. For this reason, any democracy in which educational systems were given scant attention, funds, or respect would be a self-contradictory one, in his view.

With the onset of the Cold War in the US, discussion of Deweyan concerns (or of students as multidimensional communal learners) largely evaporated. The emphasis swung hard toward the utilitarian task of educating for military aims, with an extreme emphasis on science and technological aptitude. But Deweyan ideals and practice have since swung back into mainstream popularity, often as a rebuttal to ongoing utilitarian pressures urging a focus on the "what" of learning, often to the exclusion of "who" or "how" concerns. Two current examples: many today frame America's schoolchildren as locked in competition with cohort generations of developing powers like China, Japan, and India. The now-familiar call for an emphasis on science, technology, and quantification of education has been renewed, so the US might "get ahead" as a business participant or world power (both political and military). Deweyan thinkers counter with an appreciation for the importance of arts and humanities in education, urging attention to the educational process and participants as persons rather than workers. Another current trend in education focused on "outcomes assessment" would gear curricula to standardized test material, measuring educational success by students' test scores. Many draw on Dewey's ideas to critique this approach as well, arguing that optimal educational practices would use an organic, qualitative approach fit for human organisms rather than a mechanistic one, obsessed about quantitative assessment. Dewey's conviction that "the process and the goal of education are one and the same thing" continues to fuel more holistic and imaginative educational approaches today, as well as practices in adult education, liberal arts methodology, global context/travel abroad experiences, and multicultural issues in education.

Further reading

Alexander, Thomas M. *John Dewey's Theory of Art, Experience, and Nature: The Horizons of Feeling*. Albany, NY: SUNY Press, 1987.

Campbell, James. *Understanding John Dewey: Nature and Cooperative Intelligence*. Chicago, IL: Open Court, 1995.

Dewey, John. *The Early Works, 1882–1898*, 5 volumes, ed. Jo Ann Boydston. Carbondale, IL: Southern Illinois University Press, 1969–72.

—— *The Middle Works, 1899–1924*, 15 volumes, ed. Jo Ann Boydston. Carbondale, IL: Southern Illinois University Press, 1976–83.

—— *The Late Works, 1925–1953*, 17 volumes, ed. Jo Ann Boydston. Carbondale, IL: Southern Illinois University Press, 1981–90.
—— *The Collected Works, 1882–1953*, Index, ed. Jo Ann Boydston. Carbondale, IL: Southern Illinois University Press, 1991.
Fesmire, Steven. *John Dewey and Moral Imagination: Pragmatism in Ethics.* Bloomington, IN: Indiana University Press, 2003.
Fott, David. *John Dewey: America's Philosopher of Democracy.* New York: Rowman and Littlefield, 1998.
Hickman, Larry. *Reading Dewey.* Bloomington, IN: Indiana University Press, 1998.
Rockefeller, Steven C. *John Dewey: Religions Faith and Democratic Humanism.* New York: Columbia University Press, 1991.
Ryan, Alan. *John Dewey and the High Tide of American Liberalism.* New York: Norton, 1995.
Shook, John R. *Dewey's Empirical Theory of Knowledge and Reality.* Nashville, TN: Vanderbilt University Press, 2000.
Sleeper, Ralph W. *The Necessity of Pragmatism: John Dewey's Conception of Philosophy.* New Haven, CT: Yale University Press, 1986.
Stuhr, John. *Experience and Criticism: John Dewey's Reconstruction of Philosophy.* Nashville, TN: Vanderbilt University Press, 2000.
Westbrook, Robert. *John Dewey and American Democracy.* Ithaca, NY: Cornell University Press, 1991.

L. RYAN MUSGRAVE

DEWEY, JOHN: ETHICS

Dewey's ideas about ethics underwent gradual but continual reconstruction during his 71-year-long public career. There is gradual shift from an ethics of self-realization to a mature pluralistic ethics that describes morality as contextual, experimental, imaginative, aesthetic, and democratic. The works that best represent Dewey's mature treatment of ethics are *Democracy and Education* (1916), *Reconstruction in Philosophy* (1920), *Human Nature and Conduct* (1922), "Three Independent Factors in Morals" (1930), and *Ethics* (1932). Dewey's concern with ethics arose out of his perception that individuals and institutions had not been able to find a viable alternative to the moral absolutism offered by custom and authority.

For Dewey, moral experience is the proper starting point of a philosophical inquiry about morality. Although there is no area of our experience that is exclusively or essentially moral, Dewey designated those situations that we experience as predominantly moral as those that demand of the agent that she discover what she morally ought to do among conflicting moral forces or demands. Philosophers might "step back" (into another reflective situation) from the unique situations that are experienced as having a moral component and design theories about our moral life. But those unique moral situations remain the primitive contexts of moral experience, i.e. of our moral practices and activities. This is the experiential subject matter to be studied, described, and appealed to in order to test our theoretical accounts.

Dewey characterized the generic elements and phases of our moral life as a process. There are three predominant stages in Dewey's model of moral inquiry. First, the agent finds herself in a morally problematic situation. Second, the agent engages in a process of moral deliberation. Finally, she arrives at a judgment that results in a choice. Moral deliberation is an experimental, emotional, and imaginative process that results in a moral judgment – a decision to act in one way or another. But judgments are not static. They continue throughout the entire deliberative process, and they are transformed as deliberation proceeds. Within this process, Dewey distinguishes between the direct judgments of value ("valuing") and the reflective judgments ("valuations").

In "Three Independent Factors of Morals," Dewey argued that the history of moral philosophy is characterized by one-sidedness because philosophers have abstracted one factor or feature of situations which are experienced as morally problematic and then made that factor supreme or exclusive. Hence, moral theories have been classified according to whether they take good (teleological–consequentionalist), virtue (virtue ethics), or duty (deontological theories) as their central category or source of moral justification. As Dewey points out, however, good, virtue, and duty are all irreducible features found intertwined in moral situations, they have no common denominator nor is there a set hierarchy among them. Dewey's faith in the instrumentalities of experience was tempered by the honest realization that the most intense moments of our moral life are tragic, in the sense that there is an irreducible, and sometimes irresolvable, conflict between positive moral demands or values. Moral life is then more than the struggle between good and evil.

In order to recover morality from "otherworldly" views on the one hand and arbitrary subjectivist views on the other, Dewey had to engage in a critical re-description of moral experience. He thought that traditional ethics had become bankrupt because it begins with an isolated subject or self which has a purely cognitive apprehension of moral truths. But this abstraction ignores the social (transactional) and affective (qualitative) character of moral experience. Dewey's ethics thus points to dimensions of moral life that tend to be overlooked and undervalued in much of modern ethical thought. He rejects their intellectualist, passive, and possessive views of our moral life in favor of a conception of morality as a social, creative, imaginative–emotional, hypothetical, and experimental effort to ameliorate situations and to bring new goods into existence.

For Dewey moral life is experienced as an open-ended but continuous process in which the past and the future are integral to the present. Meaning and guidance can be found in the present journey. Novelty and uniqueness are aspects of every moral situation. Nevertheless there are always stable elements that we can rely on. The most stable elements are habits and not the rules or any of the discursive resources preferred by traditional ethics. Habits reside in the background of a situation, but even they are not fixed and can change in their application to concrete circumstances.

Dewey does not offer a criterion for right conduct and thus challenges the traditional expectations about an ethical theory. Traditional ethical theories usually assume that the normativity or reasonableness of our specific moral judgments is solely derivative from a general standard of right conduct. For Dewey this is backwards and puts the emphasis in the wrong place or starting point. The validity of generalizations and standards depends on particular moral judgments. The traditional approach also neglects the context that can ground and guide judgment: the qualitative situations in which moral problems are experienced.

Dewey advocated an approach to moral decision-making that may be termed situational. He denies that moral judgments that do not follow rules or a set criteria are therefore arbitrary. He affirms that reasonable moral judgments and decisions come from intelligently exploring and assessing the situation in its qualitative uniqueness. To evaluate an action or to adjudicate between conflicts among possible actions or obligations in concrete circumstances we need to rely on the qualitative context rather than on some meta-rule, criteria, or fixed procedure.

Instead of trying to come up with theories that provide answers or decision-making procedures for all moral problems, Dewey prescribed that we should attend to the particular, the qualitative, and the unique equipped with the best habits available. Dewey's ethics does not deny the importance of having, using, and carrying forward our inherited moral knowledge in the form of principles, ideals, and habits. But it holds that these will lose their vitality and instrumental capacity the more they are absolutized, that is, when intelligence does not continue to reexamine them in light of present conditions. What needs to be dethroned is not moral generalizations *per se* but a way of using them that discourages moral sensitivity and precludes the genuine exercise of moral judgment.

Principles (as empirical generalizations) and ideals (as comprehensive ends-in-view) are important resources at the foreground of moral inquiry. But habits are more important because they determine, to some extent, our basic moral sensitivities in morally problematic situations and our way of thinking through them. For Dewey the most important instrumentalities for morality, the "cardinal" virtues, are the traits of character that can improve moral habits and, more importantly, better assist us in determining what morality requires here and now (i.e. in a situation). Dewey's contextualism thus advances a view about which habits are better to confront moral situations even if it is precluded from prescribing beforehand what to do in them. Such virtues include sensitivity, conscientiousness, sympathy, and open-mindedness. These are the habits he identified as contributing to moral "intelligence." Moral anarchy and chaos are not avoided by fixing moral rules, but by the proper cultivation of character.

The broadest possible characterization of Dewey's normative vision is that he advocated a moral life that is "intelligent," "aesthetic," and "democratic." These three adjectives characterize mutually dependent aspects of a single moral vision. This is the kind of moral life that can maintain its own integrity without the support and guidance of fixed and external foundations. What Dewey called "experimental intelligence" involves those habits of inquiry by means of which hypotheses are tested and by means of which working connections are found between old habits, customs, institutions, and beliefs and new conditions. With respect to moral life, "intelligence" refers to a way of appropriating a moral tradition. Dewey contrasts intelligence with the practice of guiding our lives by authority, custom, coercive force, imitation, caprice, or drift.

To say that a moral life is "aesthetic" is to point to its qualitative and inherently meaningful mode of engagement. Dewey contrasts what is aesthetic with what is mechanical, fragmentary, non-integrated, and non-meaningful. He thus invites us to drop legalistic–absolutistic models of moral conduct and to look instead to art as the paradigm of an activity that can steer between living aimlessly and living rigidly or mechanically.

To say that a moral life is "democratic" is to emphasize that it involves a certain way of interacting with others in the world, a certain kind of community, and a certain kind of communication. Dewey understood democracy as a form of moral association in which a certain way of life is instituted in the relations and interactions of its citizens. Dewey never provided more than a vague notion of what this broad ideal means in terms of habits, kinds of relationships, and kinds of communication. It is nevertheless clear that his notion of democracy was an outgrowth of his ideas about moral experience.

Further reading

Dewey, John. *The Middle Works, 1899–1924*, 15 volumes, ed. Jo Ann Boydston. Carbondale, IL: Southern Illinois University Press, 1969–72.

—— *The Later Works, 1925–53*, 17 volumes, ed. Jo Ann Boydston. Carbondale, IL: Southern Illinois University Press, 1976–83.

Edel, Abraham. *Ethical Theory and Social Change: The Evolution of John Dewey's Ethics, 1908–1932*. New Brunswick, NJ: Transaction, 2003.

Fesmire, Steven. *John Dewey and the Moral Imagination: Pragmatism in Ethics*. Bloomington, IN: Indiana University Press, 2003.

Gouinlock, James. *John Dewey's Philosophy of Value*. Atlantic Highlands, NJ: Humanities Press, 1972.

—— "Dewey and Contemporary Moral Philosophy" in John J. Stuhr (ed.) *Philosophy and the Reconstruction of Culture*. Albany, NY: SUNY Press, 1993, pp. 79–96.

LaFollete, Hugh. "Pragmatic Ethics" in Hugh LaFollete (ed.) *Blackwell Guide to Ethical Theory*. Oxford and Malden, MA: Blackwell, 2000, pp. 400–19.

Lekan, Todd. *Making Morality: Pragmatist Reconstruction in Ethical Theory*. Nashville, TN: Vanderbilt University Press, 2003.

Pappas, Gregory Fernando. "Dewey's Moral Theory: Experience as Method," *Transactions of the Charles Peirce Society* 33 (Summer 1997): 520–56.

—— "To Be or To Do: Dewey and the Great Divide in Ethics," *History of Philosophy Quarterly* 14 (October 1997): 447–72.

—— "Dewey's Ethics: Morality as Experience" in Larry Hickman (ed.) *Reading Dewey: Interpretive Essays for a PostModern Generation*. Bloomington, IN: Indiana University Press, 1998, pp. 100–23.

Welchman, Jennifer. *Dewey's Ethical Thought*. Ithaca, NY: Cornell University Press, 1995.

GREGORY FERNANDO PAPPAS

DEWEY, JOHN: INFLUENCE

During John Dewey's lifetime (1859–1952), his work was influential in three academic fields: philosophy, psychology, and education. He was for more than four decades an indefatigable contributor to journals of opinion and widely regarded as one of America's foremost public intellectuals. On the occasion of his ninetieth birthday, the *New York Times* hailed him as "America's philosopher."

By the time of his death, however, Dewey's influence had already begun to be eclipsed by new movements in academic fields and by a new public mood during the Cold War. New movements in philosophy included phenomenology, existentialism, Marxism, and linguistic analysis. In psychology there were behaviorism, psychoanalysis, and existentialist-based "humanist" movements. In the field of education Dewey's name was often exploited to sanction ideas that were far removed from his concept of learning as an experimental transaction between teacher and student. In some quarters, emphasis on teacher professionalization, school surveys, and even IQ testing replaced Dewey's concept of learning as a tool of social reconstruction.

The 1980s saw the beginning of a major revival of interest in Dewey's life and work. In his presidential address to the Eastern Division of the American Philosophical Association in December 1979, Richard Rorty called for a reexamination of the work of William James and John Dewey. The 1980s also saw a sharp rise in so-called "applied" fields of philosophy, some of whose practitioners discovered that Dewey's version of Pragmatism contained useful conceptual tools. In addition to bioethics, environmental ethics, agricultural ethics, and military ethics, Dewey's influence has been increasingly evident in fields as diverse as public administration, economics, architecture, restoration ecology, and religious studies. By the beginning of the twenty-first century, his work had been translated into more than three dozen languages. Research centers in the United States, Italy, China, and Germany serve as focal points for the study of his life and work.

Influence in psychology

Dewey was already a rising star in the field of philosophy and psychology when in 1894, at the age of thirty-four, he accepted a position as head professor of the department of philosophy at the new University of Chicago. During his decade at Chicago, his "Laboratory School" became internationally known for its pedagogical innovations. He published major studies of curricular reform in elementary schools, and he and his colleagues published a volume of essays that presented highly innovative studies of logical theory. His most influential contribution during this period, however, was his watershed 1896 essay "The Reflex Arc Concept in Psychology," which some historians have characterized as the founding document of the first American school of psychology: functionalism. In that essay he rejected the notion that a stimulus is something identifiable as external to the organism, arguing instead that it is a function of organic sensory and motor actions, environing conditions, expectations, and interests.

In 1942, a panel of seventy prominent psychologists commissioned by the editors of *The Psychological Review* to select the most influential essay published during its forty-nine year history awarded Dewey's "Reflex Arc" article the top honor.

It is a mark of Dewey's influence within professional circles that he was elected to serve as president of the American Psychological Association in 1898, the American Philosophical Association in 1905, the National Kindergarten Association in 1913, and the American Association of University Professors in 1915. He was also elected Honorary Life President of the National Education Association in 1932 and the American Philosophical Association in 1939.

Influence in education and politics

Dewey's influence transcended national boundaries. From 1919 to 1921 he lectured in China on philosophy, education, and democracy. Many of his Chinese students worked to reform the Chinese educational system along Deweyan lines. When the Communist Party came to power in 1949, Dewey's ideas were banned. Since the 1990s, however, as part of China's trend toward liberalization, Dewey's influence has been increasingly apparent. His ideas about teacher training, his well-known affection for the Chinese people, and his reputation as one of America's leading philosophers of democracy have contributed to his popularity within Chinese universities. In 2004 Fudan University in Shanghai inaugurated its "Center for the Study of Dewey and American Philosophy."

In 1924 Dewey spent six weeks in Turkey, during which he traveled widely, surveyed the nation's system of elementary school education, and proposed curricular reforms that were enthusiastically accepted by the government. Dewey was credited by one writer with inspiring the radical change from Arabic script to Roman letters implemented by President Atatürk.

Dewey traveled to Mexico in 1926, lecturing at the national university and visiting rural schools. In 1928 he visited Russia in order to observe the Soviet educational system. As he had during and after his trips to China, Turkey, and Mexico, Dewey wrote articles for various journals, including *New Republic*, conveying his impressions and insights to the American public.

Dewey's influence in American political life was felt well beyond his reports on his trips abroad, his numerous book reviews, and the complex political analyses he published in works such as *The Public and its Problems* (1927). A few months before the stock market crash of 1929 he met with progressive colleagues to form the League for Independent Political Action, whose aim was to form a progressive third party. During the Great Depression that followed the stock market crash, Dewey continued to propose numerous solutions to the nation's ills, including old-age pensions and the abolition of child labor.

Influence in technical philosophy

In the field of technical philosophy, Dewey's influence is perhaps best understood as part of a larger reaction against several planks in the platform of modern philosophy, from Descartes through Kant. Along with fellow Pragmatists Charles S. Peirce and William James, Dewey rejected the claim of René Descartes that it is possible to construct a foundation of certain knowledge. He argued instead that the quest for certainty in existential affairs is futile and that such knowledge is contextual and fallible. He also rejected the received "spectator" theory of knowledge, according to which knowing is the result of forming a correct idea or image of a preexisting fact or state of affairs. In its place he advanced an experimental theory of inquiry according to which the activity of knowing reconstructs existing conditions through interest, selectivity, and effort. Along with William James, he rejected treatments of essences that had been popular from the time of Plato and Aristotle. He argued that essences are functional instead of ontological: they are selected, as William James put the matter, as "teleological weapons of the mind." Each of these positions is best understood as a radical departure from traditional philosophical views, and each of them is also intimately related to Dewey's "Reflex Arc" essay. Many of these views, radical at the time they were introduced, are now accepted within mainstream philosophy.

Further reading

Dewey, John. *The Public and its Problems, The Collected Works of John Dewey: The Later Works, 1925–1953, Vol. 2*, ed. Jo Ann Boydston. Carbondale, IL: Southern Illinois University Press, 1984.

—— "The Reflex Arc Concept in Psychology" in *The Collected Works of John Dewey: The Early Works, 1882–1898, Vol. 5, 1985–1898*, ed. Jo Ann Boydston. Carbondale, IL: Southern Illinois University Press, 1972.

Pronko, N.H. and Herman, D.T. "From Dewey's Reflex Arc Concept to Transactionalism and Beyond." *Behaviorism* 10 (Fall 1982): 229–54.
Rorty, Richard. *Consequences of Pragmatism*. Minneapolis, MN: University of Minnesota Press, 1982.
Westbrook, Robert B. *John Dewey and American Democracy*. Ithaca, NY: Cornell University Press, 1991.

LARRY A. HICKMAN

DEWEY, JOHN: LIFE

John Dewey (1859–1952) was born the second of three sons to Archibald and Lucina Dewey in Burlington, Vermont, on 20 October 1859. Both Dewey's parents came from farming families, but his mother's family was by far the more privileged, all her brothers having gone to college. Lucina, an extremely devout Calvinist, was a strong influence on the young Dewey, and he entered the church at her behest, also acquiring an early appreciation for her philanthropic activities in the poorer parts of the Burlington community. Dewey's father ran a thriving grocery business in Burlington, which he sold upon entering the Union Army. After the Civil War, Archibald returned and purchased a tobacco shop that also became successful. School, for Dewey, was not as pleasant or natural as work early on, but at his mother's urging he pushed on to its highest levels, eventually becoming America's best-known public philosopher.

Dewey completed his grade school work at age twelve and chose the newly established college preparatory track, entering the University of Vermont at the age of sixteen. As a senior in college, Dewey demonstrated a knack for and interest in philosophy, fixating on issues in political, social, and moral philosophy. Graduating from the University of Vermont in 1879, he taught high school for two years in Oil City, Pennsylvania. While teaching, Dewey wrote a manuscript called "The Metaphysical Assumptions of Materialism" and sent it to William Torrey Harris, the editor of *The Journal of Speculative Philosophy*, along with a note asking whether or not the manuscript demonstrated enough skill to warrant more effort to be expended on the subject. Harris replied in the affirmative and published the essay later that year.

After the publication of Dewey's first paper in the *JSP*, he matriculated at the newly established Johns Hopkins University in 1882. Though President Daniel Coit Gilman encouraged Dewey to study theology as well as philosophy in order to better prepare himself for the theologically oriented job market, Dewey refused, studying instead under three significant secular philosophers: Charles S. Peirce, G. Stanley Hall, and George Morris. Dewey studied logic under Peirce, though their relationship was not very close. The two would later spend time respectfully debating about the content of Dewey's 1903 book *Studies in Logical Theory*, a book he put out during his tenure at Chicago and with the help of many of his colleagues there. Dewey was most influenced by G. Stanley Hall's new psychology, which Hall had learned under William James at Harvard, and George Morris's neo-Hegelianism. These two themes would become the two foundational currents in the young philosopher's thought. Dewey was most attracted to the latter because of its organic quality, its ability to deal with contradiction, and its inherent piety and optimism. Finishing his dissertation, titled "The Psychology of Kant," in 1884, Dewey followed Morris to Michigan and accepted a junior faculty position there. Dewey's use of Hegel flourished at Michigan, as its department had strong neo-Hegelian proclivities. It was at Michigan that Dewey published his first book, *Psychology*, which aimed to connect the new psychology of James and Hall with a religious neo-Hegelianism. Dewey's arguments in the *Psychology* disappointed James and Hall with their lack of empirical evidence and their reliance on proving the theological as part of the scientific enterprise. Critiques from Hall and James provided some of the impetus for Dewey to begin looking in new secular and scientific directions.

Until Morris's death, Dewey would be pulled in two different directions by Hall and Morris, Morris advocating religious orthodoxy and Hall advocating a strict empiricism that left no room for structures of thought grounded on faith. Early on it was Morris who triumphed as Dewey's strongest influence, but Morris's death signaled the death of religious orthodoxy in Dewey as well. In 1888 Dewey was offered a job at the University of Minnesota as professor of moral and mental philosophy; he accepted and moved himself and his family there, to remain only one year. George Morris died the next year, and the Deweys returned to Michigan; here John assumed the chair of the philosophy department, where he stayed until 1894, the year of his recruitment to the University of Chicago.

Dewey's instrumental pragmatism did not come to full fruition until the president of the newly founded University of Chicago, William Rainey Harper, offered Dewey a job in 1894. Like Johns Hopkins, the University of Chicago was primarily a graduate institution that was geared toward research. Once at Chicago, Dewey became close friends with Jane Addams, the proprietor of Hull

House and the 1936 recipient of the Nobel Peace Prize, eventually becoming a board member of Hull House himself. Dewey was compelled to come to Chicago, also, by his friend and former Michigan colleague, James Tufts. Dewey eventually worked as well with George Herbert Mead, James Agnell, and A.W. Moore. This new group of thinkers, interested in democracy, Darwin, and the relationship between the social organism and its environment, the individual and society, came to be known as the "Chicago School" of pragmatists. These philosophical concerns also translated to social concerns, and, later, Dewey would contribute to the founding of both the American Association of University Presidents and the National Association for the Advancement of Colored People in addition to championing the causes of academic freedom and women's suffrage.

Also at Chicago, Dewey's interest in practical pedagogy increased and he established the laboratory school and presided for a time over Chicago's department of pedagogy. Eventually, Dewey and Harper's relationship strained over Dewey's concern about a lack of financial support from Harper for the laboratory school. Dewey and Harper vehemently disagreed about Dewey's decision to place his wife, Alice, at the head of the laboratory school. Eventually, Dewey resigned and finished his tenure as a professor at Columbia, spending time teaching in both the philosophy department and the teachers' college. In New York, Dewey's status as a public intellectual led his brilliant student Randolph Bourne to ask Dewey to take a stand on World War I. Initially, Dewey supported American involvement in World War I but changed his perspective after the war, going so far as to play a leading role in a movement to outlaw war altogether. Dewey retired from teaching in 1930 but remained as an emeritus professor until 1939, after which he traveled and lectured widely until his death in 1952 at age ninety-three.

Further reading

Coughlan, Neil. *Young John Dewey*. Chicago, IL: University of Chicago Press, 1975.

Dewey, John. *The Collected Works of John Dewey*, ed. Jo Ann Boydston. Carbondale, IL: Southern Illinois University Press, 1967–91.

Dykhuizen, George. *The Life and Mind of John Dewey*. Carbondale, IL: Southern Illinois University Press, 1973.

Hickman, Larry. *John Dewey's Pragmatic Technology*. Bloomington, IN: Indiana University Press, 1990.

Sleeper, Ralph. *The Necessity of Pragmatism: John Dewey's Conception of Philosophy*. New York: Yale University Press, 1987.

Westbrook, Robert. *John Dewey and American Democracy*. Ithaca, NY: Cornell University Press, 1991.

JASON BARRETT-FOX

DEWEY, JOHN: LOGIC

John Dewey (1859–1952) had a broader view of logic than is customary today. After the rise of a mathematical metatheory for symbolic deductive logic early in the twentieth century, logic became identified almost exclusively with a formal study of deductive argumentation and algorithmic computation. Historically, in the European philosophical tradition beginning with Plato and Aristotle, at least two kinds of inference – deductive and inductive – have been distinguished. There is scant acknowledgment that there may be a "logic" of induction insofar as induction employs statistics and probability theory but is not amenable to the kind of metatheoretic treatment to which deduction lends itself. The *de facto* identification of logic with deductive logic that emerged in the last hundred years thus persists to the present day.

Dewey, on the other hand, cast logic as a normative theory of inquiry, incorporating themes from the philosophy of science, epistemology, and the cognitive sciences into a study of better and worse methods of reflective thinking. This would certainly include a study of inference as utilized for problem-solving purposes. Dewey regarded it as the only kind of study that could provide a full accounting of what inference is. Namely, anything less would cast inference out of context and thus in a distorted manner. It is generally agreed today that logic includes a study of better and worse forms of inference, particularly if one presupposes that inference is just deductive inference and that better and worse forms of inference are identified with valid and invalid deductive argument forms. Dewey indeed characterized logic in such a way that it includes a normative study of inference forms, but without presuming that inference (and thus the subject matter of logic) is only deductive inference.

In pursuing this kind of study, Dewey adapted several ideas from Charles S. Peirce. These include Peirce's doubt–belief conception of inquiry, the related idea that inquiry has a general pattern that supports the formulation of normative principles distinguishing better and worse methods of inquiry, and third, that this pattern is such as to require the complementary utilization of three kinds of inference: abduction, deduction, and induction.

The latter three kinds of inference characterize three stages of inquiry on Peirce's view. Inquiry in this view is initiated by some unexpected phenomenon, in response to which some conjecture arises that offers a plausible explanation and thereby a means of resolving the given uncertainty. Inferring an initially plausible explanation from would-be evidence – abduction – is the characteristic form of reasoning in this first stage of inquiry. The second stage of inquiry proceeds with examination of the conjecture, specifically to muster any consequences that would follow necessarily from its truth. Deduction – inferring necessary consequences from assumed premises – is the characteristic form of reasoning in the second stage of inquiry. The third stage of inquiry focuses on ascertaining the degree to which these consequences actually accord with experience. On the basis of pertinent new evidence, the characteristic form of reasoning in the third stage – induction – eventuates in judging respectively whether the initially plausible hypothesis is acceptable or requires modification if not rejection. Acceptance of the hypothesis constitutes the establishment of a belief in response to the initial unexpected phenomenon.

Dewey's version of the pattern of inquiry is likewise built around a picture of the fixation of belief in response to doubt, though he described it more generally as a controlled, directed transformation of some indeterminate situation into one that is coherent, unified, and otherwise determinate. One motivation for this more abstract formulation of the doubt–belief picture of inquiry is its depiction of doubt not simply as a subjective state but as the upshot of a truly unsettled objective situation. Likewise the established belief that concludes an inquiry is not just a cognitive feat coincident with the removal of subjective doubt but accompanies the implementation of activities that result in the settling of an initially unsettled objective situation. This objectivity is present in Peirce's view of inquiry, but Dewey perhaps draws it out more explicitly.

Inquiry as the successive transformation of an objective situation has, on Dewey's view, a general pattern reflecting Peirce's three stages outlined above, though in Dewey's various accounts we find half a dozen or so stages or phases of inquiry (depending on how you count): namely, (1) an inquiry is evoked by an indeterminate situation, occurring as an interruption in otherwise routine activities; (2) suggestions may quickly arise as to a possible solution to the difficulty presented; (3) the difficulty or perplexity inherent in the given interruption is identified and formulated as a problem to be solved, as a question to be answered; (4) hypotheses (suggestions) for solving the problem are introduced to serve as leading ideas, i.e. suppositions to initiate and guide observation and other efforts to obtain further factual information; (5) these hypotheses are clarified and elaborated with a view to determining what consequences they imply that may have a bearing on the problem; (6) selected hypotheses are tested, overtly or imaginatively, by appropriate experiments that either verify or disconfirm their consequences; and (7) the inquiry is eventually terminated (if all proceeds well enough) by a judgment as to whether the implementation of proposed hypotheses resolve the problem that initiated the inquiry.

Clearly the essential features of the so-called "hypothetico-deductive method" of scientific inquiry are embedded in this pattern. This account also retains a coordinated orchestration of abductive, deductive, and inductive inference at its core. Both the specification of the problem and the suggestion of possible solutions in phases (2), (3), and (4) are abductive in character. The clarification and elaboration of implications in phase (5) are deductive operations. The testing of selected hypotheses and the determination of whether new evidence verifies or disconfirms their consequences in phase (6) are inductive.

Insofar as false starts are not unlikely, the seven phases taken together should be viewed as nodes of a flow chart allowing loops from later phases back to earlier ones. Ultimately the goal is to form a judgment whose structure and content is that of a diagnosis and remedy for the initial unsettled situation. Facts and ideas are combined into a single judgment whose assertion is warranted just to the extent that (a) the process of inquiry as a whole adheres to logical norms and (b) implementation of final judgment actually promises to solve the initial problem as well as can be expected.

In the context of this overall pattern of inquiry, Dewey developed an unusual taxonomy of propositional forms for formulating facts and ideas as contents of the diagnosis and remedy that together constitute a final judgment. This is one of the more original facets of Dewey's logical theory. Dewey's theory of propositions is not fully developed, and its further development is hampered by the fact that it is not easily susceptible to symbolic formulation in typical twentieth-century terms, e.g. with a first-order deductive calculus at its core. Nor does Dewey work within the confines of a Tarskian extensional semantics. Dewey instead distinguishes various kinds of propositions on the basis of how they are utilized to formulate facts of a given case (elements of the subject of judgment) or else to formulate suggestions regarding actions to be taken in that case (elements of the predicate of judgment). As instruments of inquiry, their "truth" (or not) lies in the status of their mutual correspondence as formulations of facts and ideas in a single judgment. That is, propositions that articulate the subject and predicate of judgment, respectively, are mutually "true" to the extent that the assertion of that judgment is objectively warranted. This is Dewey's version of a classical pragmatist theory of truth.

Further reading

Burke, Tom. *Dewey's New Logic: A Reply to Russell.* Chicago, IL: University of Chicago Press, 1994.

Burke, F. Thomas, Hester, D. Micah, and Talisse, Robert B. (eds) *Dewey's Logical Theory: New Studies and Interpretations.* Nashville, TN: Vanderbilt University Press, 2002.

Dewey, John. *How We Think.* Boston: D.C. Heath, 1910/1933. Critical editions reissued as volume 6 of *The Middle Works of John Dewey* and volume 8 of *The Later Works of John Dewey.* Carbondale, IL: Southern Illinois University Press, 1978/1986.

—— *Essays in Experimental Logic.* Chicago, IL: University of Chicago Press, 1916; new critical edition Carbondale, IL: Southern Illinois University Press, 2006.

—— *Logic: The Theory of Inquiry.* New York: Henry Holt, 1938; critical edition reissued as volume 12 of *The Later Works of John Dewey* with an introduction by Ernest Nagel. Carbondale, IL: Southern Illinois University Press, 1986.

Kennedy, Gail. "Dewey's Logic and Theory of Knowledge" in Jo Ann Boydston (ed.) *Guide to the Works of John Dewey.* Carbondale, IL: Southern Illinois University Press, 1970, pp. 61–98.

Peirce, Charles S. *The Essential Peirce*, 2 volumes, ed. Peirce Edition Project. Bloomington, IN: Indiana University Press, 1992/1998.

Tom Burke

DEWEY, JOHN: METAPHYSICS AND EPISTEMOLOGY

Epistemology and metaphysics have struggled throughout history for the heart of philosophy. They began their separation and antipathy after the invention of the word "metaphysics" around 70 BCE. This was originally a term indicating a particular order of books written by Aristotle. The prefix "meta" subsequently took on a life of its own, the field becoming identified with investigation of what is "beyond" the physical. For Aristotle, the study had been "primary philosophy," the study of "being *qua* being," an attempt to articulate the general contours of whatever is.

With the overwhelming influence of Aristotle in the high Middle Ages, metaphysics became *the* main concern of philosophers. It was important to get one's metaphysics straight, i.e. have a general sense of the way things are, before indicating how that general sense spilled over into more limited fields such as those dealing with knowledge, morality, politics, or beauty. Metaphysics continued to reign supreme through the eighteenth century. The great academic systematizer Christian Wolff (1679–1754) made metaphysics (he called it "ontology") *the* foundational discipline in his masterful outline of philosophy. It was the keystone from which could be deduced key truths about the world. "Metaphysics" was seen as anchoring the "theoretical" side of philosophy, a side sharply distinguished from the "practical."

Wolff influenced one of the most important of all philosophers, Immanuel Kant. In his *Critique of Pure Reason* Kant preserved Wolffian assumptions about the sharp separation of practical from theoretical philosophy. Kant's *Critique*, at the same time, served as an important turning point. It demolished Wolff's foundation of a kind of knowledge having access to a realm beyond the physical. After Kant, metaphysics of the Wolffian sort was mortally wounded.

Meanwhile, although the word "epistemology" had not yet been coined (this would come in 1856), Kant had continued a trajectory begun by Descartes (1596–1650) which moved questions about knowing, not being, to the center. Philosophy continued to be identified with theory, but metaphysics, after Kant, was deposed from its foundational position, replaced by epistemology. Primary philosophy was now concerned with epistemological questions: Can we know at all? How can we be sure ideas in the mind match up with objects in the world? What are the conditions for the possibility of valid knowledge claims?

Dewey's early orientation

Such was the situation confronted by John Dewey as he embarked on his career in the late nineteenth century. The older position had insisted on getting one's theory of being straight before elucidating its implications for ethics, politics, aesthetics. The newer position insisted on carefully selecting, sharpening and justifying one's epistemological tools before going forward with any knowledge claims at all. Both retained a sharp theory/practice bifurcation.

Dewey's graduate training at Johns Hopkins was fortunate in that his teacher George S. Morris had studied with Friedrich Trendelenburg (1802–72), who developed a synthesis of Aristotle and Hegel (1770–1831). Aristotle provided a perspective older than the sharp bifurcations that had subsequently arisen. Hegel offered a grand synthesis in which the dichotomies would be overcome.

For both Aristotle and Hegel, biology, especially the notion of organism, offered an important model.

Dewey's original orientation was that of an "absolute idealist" in the Hegelian vein. "Mind" provided the safest general descriptive label for things. This was not a subjectivism which claimed that human minds construct external reality. Rather, it was the position that all existents were manifestations of Mind, i.e. were intelligible. Even "matter" was not just indiscriminate, unintelligible stuff. Metaphysics and epistemology were thus brought back together in one stroke. If we begin with the metaphysical assumption that all is Mind, then there is really no need to wonder how it is possible for human intelligence (one manifestation of Mind) to gain access to the world (another manifestation of Mind). Dewey was to change the language in which he articulated his positions, but one commitment was to remain intact: an emphasis on continuities rather than bifurcations.

Dewey and epistemology

During Dewey's years at the University of Chicago (1894–1904) he developed a position called "instrumentalism." This development supplanted the overly cerebral language of absolute idealism. Much influenced by science, Dewey began to think of human understanding on the model of experimental method. Although questions of knowing occupied him during the years of transition from the nineteenth to the twentieth centuries, he did not approach them from the stock position of epistemology, i.e. asking whether knowledge was possible at all. Once the pre-scientific assumptions had been set aside, it would be possible to "emancipate philosophy from all the epistemological puzzles which now perplex it" (*Reconstruction* 150).

In books like *Essays in Experimental Logic* and *Studies in Logical Theory*, Dewey articulated his instrumentalism. The key notion here was that ideas were not simply items collecting themselves in an internal mirror called "mind." This "mind-as-mirror" view, so favored by some philosophers, was actually an artificial construction, especially in its assumption that humans were essentially outside "spectators" of the world, not active participants in it. Mind as mirror was assumed to be primarily a passive receptacle. Once this step was taken, there was no possibility of getting beyond what became the central question of epistemology: whether ideas in the mind actually corresponded with things outside.

For Dewey, staying with the Pragmatist emphasis on engagement with things, mind functions "*in* an activity which controls the environment" (*Democracy and Education* 333). Ideas, rather than simple reflections in a mental mirror, are part of the human arsenal for successful engagement in the world. They are more like tools. They function as hypotheses, as initial "anticipations" (*Reconstruction* 162). They serve the purpose of reconstructing experience.

The favorite question of epistemologists and, subsequently, of too many introductions to philosophy textbooks, "How can we know at all?" only arises when we make the faulty initial assumption of conceiving ourselves as spectators rather than participants. When we think of ourselves as working with things, the epistemological, i.e. skeptical, question "Are they really there?" makes little sense. Tools implicate us in dealings with our surroundings. Since we are ultimately creatures of participation, our activities are aimed at securing and extending goods. To this end, reflection and thinking are crucial, but epistemology as traditionally practiced is not. Indeed, it is an impediment.

Dewey and metaphysics

When it comes to metaphysics, it, like epistemology, receives a sort of "pox on both their houses" approach. Identifying "metaphysics" with the attempt to access some transcendental realm beyond the physical, Dewey was mostly dismissive during his Chicago years. Non-empirical foundations for thought were both illusory and dangerous: illusory because they pretended a reach for human knowing which was beyond it, dangerous because such claims could easily lead to absolutisms, anchored in a spurious realm beyond the ambiguous, changing, world of the here and now.

After moving to Columbia (1905) his position evolved. A recessive tendency, the Aristotelian strain, began to regain prominence. This was occasioned by conversations with a colleague who defended a "naturalistic metaphysics." Frederick J.E. Woodbridge argued that metaphysics, as a well-articulated general description of how things are, was not an option. People could not avoid assuming one perspective or another, so it might as well be made explicit. Dewey's response culminated in 1925 with his own articulation of a naturalistic metaphysics, *Experience and Nature*.

Experience and Nature is important not only in the trajectory of Dewey's thought, but as an important moment in rehabilitating metaphysics itself. Dewey characterized metaphysics as the "ground-map of the province of criticism" (*Experience and Nature* 309). As creatures involved in practices (all good Pragmatists start here rather than with detached minds observing reality from outside), humans are constantly involved in evaluation. Theory, rather than being opposed to practice, is now seen as an important dimension of practice. What Dewey came to realize was the necessary link between evaluation and some generic notion of reality. To identify the "constituent structure of nature" is not, Dewey asserts, "an affair neutral to the office of criticism. It is a preliminary outline of the field of criticism, whose chief import is to afford understanding of the necessity and nature of the office of intelligence" (*Experience and Nature* 315).

Dewey, returning to the metaphor of organism, given new life by Darwin, provided content for his metaphysics. He formulated a metaphysics consistent with contemporary developments in science. It rejects the ultimate atomism of an earlier epoch. The basic unit of existence is not any kind of ultimate simple. It is an "event." The event, unlike the isolated atom, (1) must incorporate temporality as part of its growth; (2) has to take account of relations as inherent to what it is; and (3) cannot be understood by isolating some inner essence, but only by taking account of its interactions, activities, properties as it undertakes its trajectory.

Such a metaphysics gives new emphasis to continuity. For too much of its life, philosophy assumed a sharp separation between an "objective" value-neutral realm, and a "subjective" dimension which constructed values and projected them onto neutral subject matter. If a metaphysics is to be truly naturalistic, it will recognize the importance of relations rather than compartmentalizations. Dewey's favorite word for emphasizing relations was "experience," which meant both *what* was experienced and the *ways* of experiencing. Understood in this way, the grounding for the old dualisms of theory versus practice, as well as neutral fact versus subjective value, were challenged. It was now possible to recognize how the traits associated with human life, a life now deemed to be fully part of nature, must somehow have their analogues in other dimensions of existence.

> If experience actually presents esthetic and moral traits, then these traits may also be supposed to reach down into nature, and to testify to something that belongs to nature as truly as does the mechanical structure attributed to it in physical science.
>
> (*Experience and Nature* 13)

Further reading

Boisvert, Raymond D. *Dewey's Metaphysics.* New York: Fordham University Press, 1988.

—— *John Dewey: Rethinking Our Time.* Albany, NY: SUNY Press, 1998

Campbell, James. *Understanding John Dewey: Nature and Cooperative Intelligence.* Chicago, IL: Open Court, 1995.

Dewey, John. *Experience and Nature* in *The Later Works*, Vol. 1. Carbondale, IL: Southern Illinois University Press, 1981.

—— *Democracy and Education* in *The Middle Works*, Vol. 9. Carbondale, IL: Southern Illinois University Press, 1985.

—— *Experience and Education* in *The Later Works*, Vol. 13. Carbondale, IL: Southern Illinois University Press, 1988.

—— *Logic: The Theory of Inquiry* in *The Later Works*, Vol. 12. Carbondale, IL: Southern Illinois University Press, 1986.

—— *The Quest for Certainty* in *The Later Works*, Vol. 4. Carbondale, IL: Southern Illinois University Press, 1984.

—— *Reconstruction in Philosophy* in *The Middle Works*, Vol. 12. Carbondale, IL: Southern Illinois University Press, 1982.

Eldridge, Michael. *Transforming Experience: Dewey's Cultural Instrumentalism.* Nashville, TN: Vanderbilt University Press, 1998.

Tiles, J.E. *Dewey.* New York: Routledge, 1988.

RAYMOND BOISVERT

DEWEY, JOHN: PSYCHOLOGY

John Dewey affected the development of American psychology through his contributions to functional psychology, the first distinctively American school. As Gordon Allport wrote, "John Dewey stands second only to William James in giving American psychological science its characteristic stamp of activism, functionalism, and problem solving" (Allport 1968: 326).

Dewey sought to develop a naturalistic approach that avoided difficulties associated with both a reductive, deterministic account of human behavior, and an idealistic, voluntaristic account. In seeking to unite mind and nature in a unified view, he addressed an important turn of the twentieth-century topic that had also been tackled by William James.

James's *Principles of Psychology* (James 1890/1950) greatly affected Dewey, helping direct his thought in a more naturalistic direction, in contrast to his earlier idealism (Dewey 1887) (although aspects of his earlier thinking persisted). Dewey nevertheless thought James's work still contained elements of the traditional mind/body or voluntarism/determinism dualism (Dewey 1946). James adopted the concept of the stimulus–response reflex as his central organizing principle, making his work in this sense quite mechanistic or deterministic. On the other hand, he also posited inner mechanisms, such as emotionally driven attentional interests and a reflexive self, that gave his psychology a more voluntaristic emphasis. In fact, the resulting theory often seemed to oscillate between the two positions (Allport 1968).

Dewey criticized James's account while suggesting a better approach that built on it in many ways in a very influential paper, "The Reflex Arc Concept in Psychology" (1896). This paper was long regarded as the position statement of the functional school of psychology. The functionalists argued that psychological concepts, such as "mind," "consciousness" and "self," as well as more basic concepts like "stimulus" and "response," are often treated as reified entities, resulting in false metaphysical explanations. This could be corrected by reconceiving them as adaptive functions. Rather than talking about "the mind," for example, as though it were a thing, one would do better by focusing on "minding" as an activity, seeing how it is done and what it is good for.

The key insight in Dewey's critique was that behavior is usually constructed by cycles of organism/environment interaction, rather than sensory-motor reactions. This notion of a cycle of activity was quite different from the linear input–output model of the reflex theorists. It was also central to the interactional or "transactional" approach that Dewey used as the basis of all of his work. In essence, it gave a way of thinking about behavior that was neither externally determined by the environment nor internally constructed out of whole cloth by the self, but was rather a kind of joint product of sequences of organism and environment interaction taking place over time.

In his reflex arc paper Dewey argued that a model based on the sensory-motor reflex had to be wrong because it made it impossible to understand well-coordinated acts. Sensory-motor reflexes could only produce a "series of jerks" rather than the smoothly coordinated behavior one sees in an established habit. Rather than sensory input causing a motor response, Dewey argued that habitual activity was the product of "sensory-motor coordinations" or cycles in which motor behavior alters sensory input and is regulated by it in turn. One should think of a "response" not as a mere reaction to sensory stimulation, but as an implicit effort to bring about certain desired or preferred sensory stimulations. Viewed in this way, "stimulus" and "response" are acts, not sensory and motor events. A stimulus, like noting that the traffic light has turned green, is a product of motor behavior, like looking at and focusing on the light. By the same token, a response, like accelerating ahead into the intersection, is also regulated by sensory feedback. Since a given "response" may be a "stimulus" to a later act, whose preconditions it creates, the distinction is a matter of interpretation that depends on the unit of activity being considered. As Dewey put it,

> The fact is that stimulus and response are not distinctions of existence, but teleological distinctions, that is, distinctions of function, or part played, with reference to reaching or maintaining an end . . . [I]t is only the assumed common reference to an inclusive end which marks each member off as stimulus and response.
>
> (Dewey 1896: 365)

This part of Dewey's analysis undercut the mechanistic and deterministic reflex model, suggesting that it focused on an artificially isolated "arc," or fragment, of the whole sensory-motor cycle involved in activity. By failing to attend to the way people create their own preferred sensory input in interaction with the environment the reflex model failed as a scientific theory, despite its tough-minded pretensions.

The later part of Dewey's analysis also served to undercut the notion that behavior is willed by an inner self or ego, which might also be treated as a kind of metaphysical entity. Like the other pragmatists, Dewey believed that genuine thought only occurs when there is doubt about a matter that matters to one. The feeling of doubt or uncertainty, which stimulates conscious attention, arises when competing habits are elicited in novel, ambiguous or conflictual situations. Under these conditions sensory events are without meaning and motor responses are without objects. There is a split between what is real to the senses and what is ideal in terms of emotional response or impulse. The function of cognitive activity, thinking, is to reduce this gap by identifying a new goal object that allows activity to proceed. In general the "problem" and the "solution" help to define one another, since the character of the problem is not known until a solution is found that resolves it. This analysis, only briefly suggested in the reflex arc paper, suggested that conscious thought is an adaptive function, not a thing. It also suggested that conscious thought is situated activity driven by emotional interest in particular objects, rather than disinterested or universalized. Viewed in this way the test of the value of cognition is its assistance in directing action, beginning in the present unique situation, in as broadly harmonious and stably developing a way possible.

This view of cognition was amplified in later work in which Dewey distinguished between roughly delineated phases of a "complete act of thought" (Dewey 1910). An act of thought begins with (1) a "felt difficulty" followed by (2) a phase that involves locating or defining the difficulty. This is followed, in turn, by (3) a phase in which suggestions of possible solutions occur, which is followed by (4) reasoning regarding the implications of these hypothetical solutions. Finally, (5) possible solutions are tested via further observation and experiment, leading to their acceptance or rejection. Much of this is conventional, but Dewey's practical = interactional approach resulted in important differences from the symbolic view of problem solving. In Dewey's account thinking emerges from practical activity in which there is a "felt difficulty." It generally does not begin with a clearly defined "problem." It concludes when the initial practical difficulty has been resolved, and not merely when a symbolic "solution" has been found. The final characterization of both "problem" and "solution" ideally emerge from the inquiry, rather than being imposed from the outset. Furthermore, an act of thought that results in a hypothetical "solution" that is not tested in practice is not a "complete" act of thought. To be truly tested ideas generally need to be tried out.

Dewey's notion that reflective thinking always occurs in a particular situation also led him to place great emphasis on judgment which interrelates general ideas about the relation between actions and consequences gained from past experience and inquiry and the particularities of the present unique situation:

> Thinking is not like a sausage machine which reduces all materials indifferently to one marketable commodity, but is a power of following up and linking together the specific suggestions that things arouse.
>
> (Dewey 1910: 39)

So conceived, thinking is an art, not a science. On the other hand, all of the implements of science can be brought to bear in improving thinking. Each of the phases of thought can be improved by learning to use various tools, such as tools of observation, systematic analysis and experimental testing. Once again people act to alter their own environments in a desired direction, but in the case of conscious reflective thought artificially constructed cultural tools and artifacts can be used to refine the process. In this view thinking is an activity, like any other, although one with a specialized role in reknitting disrupted behavior. As such, it is not sequestered in the cranium, but in fair part in the externally observable world.

Dewey's psychology provided a *via media* between the deterministic reflex theory and voluntaristic theories based on the soul or ego. It can be seen as suggesting a similar synthesis between behavioristic and cognitive theories today, the former focusing on behavior without thought, and the latter on thought without behavior. The fact that Dewey's psychology was interactional or transactional in character also made it easy to bring social interaction into the analysis, allowing for the explanation of language learning and the development of reflective processes using linguistic symbols in thinking and selfhood (see, e.g., Mead 1934). While very helpful in suggesting how to develop a scientific yet humane psychology, it also had normative implications that Dewey used to great effect in his educational writings. The principal implications derived from its interactional and developmental orientation. To have a educative experience, students need to have a genuine felt problem to begin with, they need to work out a solution with care, carefully testing the way that one idea is related to another, and they need to act upon their idea, experiencing its practical consequences. Such authentic inquiry, especially when engaged in collaboratively, with public observation, experiment and discussion of the merits of different solutions, was the way to educate people for a democratic way of life

Further reading

Allport, G.W. *The Person in Psychology*. Boston, MA: Beacon Press, 1968.

Dewey, J. *Psychology*. New York: Harper, 1887.

James, W. *The Principles of Psychology*. New York: Dover, 1950 [1890].

Mead, G.H. *Mind, Self, and Society: From the Standpoint of a Social Behaviorist*. Chicago, IL: University of Chicago Press, 1934.

ERIC BREDO

DEWEY, JOHN: RELIGION

Following William James, Dewey relocates the religious from a concern with otherworldly powers to the attitudes and commitments of people, both individually and collectively. His understanding is most clearly set forth in the first chapter of *A Common Faith*, originally presented as the Terry Lectures at Yale University (1934). Dewey argues that both conventionally religious people and their atheistic opponents make the same error: they identify being religious with belief in a supernatural entity, such as the divinity of Judaism, Christianity and Islam. The one group thinks that such a being exists and the other thinks that he does not. Dewey thinks that what they assume – being religious is solely about God – is incorrect. One can be religious without thinking there is any such being at all. His argument for this way of being religious proceeds both negatively and positively: he shows that religion as such does not exist and that it is appropriate to regard a this-worldly commitment to an inclusive ideal as a religious one.

Against religion

Citing the Oxford Dictionary's definition of religion as representative of the conventional understanding, "Recognition on the part of man of some unseen higher power as having control of his destiny and as being entitled to obedience, reverence and worship" (LW 9.4; that is, Vol. 9 of *The Later Works*, p. 4), Dewey argues that there is no common referent for "unseen higher power," worship or obedience. The variety in objects of worship and the ways in which religious adherents have thought they should live is so great that the term "religion" is but "a strictly collective term" for a "miscellaneous aggregate" (9.7).

This does mean, however, that one cannot be religious. There is no separate sphere of religion but it is still possible to be religious. Dewey, despite his opposition to religion and even his aversion to traditional religions, takes his cue from these same religions, for they claim to produce a certain effect that can be specified and developed: "It is the claim of religions that they effect" a "generic and enduring change in attitude," one that can be called an "adjustment" in how a person or group lives. Sometimes we "accommodate" ourselves to existing conditions, conforming to them. We fit in to what is. Sometimes we are more active, "adapting" or reshaping the existing conditions, as when we build houses or air-condition them. When we act intelligently, doing both of these as the occasion requires, we achieve a flexible way of interacting in and with the world. We become a certain sort of person or group. The "inclusive and deep seated" changes that are a part of this adjustment

> relate not to this and that want in relation to this and that condition of our surroundings, but pertain to our being in its entirety. Because of its scope, this modification of ourselves is enduring. It lasts through any amount of vicissitude of circumstances, internal and external. There is a composing and harmonizing of the various elements of our being such that, in spite of changes in the special conditions that surround us, these conditions are also arranged, settled, in relation to us.

Whenever such a "change takes place there is a definitely religious attitude" (9.12–13).

No religion, no extra-worldly divinity, no sacred rituals, but there is a way to live that can be characterized as religious. It is a way of life that is fully a part of this world, thoroughly naturalistic. Not surprisingly, this attitudinal approach is unsatisfactory to those who value the traditional ways of being religious. It is too tame, too mundane – not robust enough. There is no appeal to sacred mysteries, divine drama, or to a great struggle between personified good and evil. Nor does it appeal to thorough-going secularists who have no need of religious language. They see no need to speak of intelligence in religious terms, as Dewey does. But neither of these groups, despite the title of his Terry Lectures, is Dewey's target audience. He is attempting to formulate a way of life that appeals to those who fully accept science yet wish to be religious. *A Common Faith* is not for everyone.

Further reading

Dewey, John. *The Later Works*. Carbondale, IL: Southern Illinois University Press, 1967–72. *A Common Faith* is reprinted in Volume 9 and is cited as LW 9.

Eldridge, Michael. *Transforming Experience: John Dewey's Cultural Instrumentalism*. Nashville, TN: Vanderbilt University Press, 1998, especially Ch. 5, "Dewey's Religious Proposal," pp. 126–69.

MICHAEL ELDRIDGE

DEWEY, JOHN: SOCIAL/POLITICAL

John Dewey claimed that the social is the *most inclusive* philosophical category, and so it is not surprising that he devoted many books and scores of articles to social philosophy and social problems. His writings ranged over many of the major issues in political philosophy – the nature of democracy, economic production and distributive justice, the meanings of freedom, equality and opportunity, the relations between individuality and community, the nature of social intelligence and the public role of education, the relation between government and both public and private life, the nature of political justification and the significance of scientific method for politics, revolution, violence, and war, and ancient and modern political philosophy – and also many of the largest American and international problems during his long lifetime – including industrialization, urbanization, labor unions, evolution, world wars, communism, totalitarianism, economic depression, private ownership of the press, political parties, immigration, national character, religion, international cooperation, and public education (but only a little about the advancement of women and even less about race and the consequences for America of racial slavery). Indeed, Dewey not only wrote social and political theory, but also was an active participant in social movements and political practice. For example, he founded the famous laboratory elementary school (the "Dewey school") in Chicago, worked with (and learned much from) Jane Addams at Hull House, founded the American Association of University Professors, chaired the international Commission of Inquiry into the Charges Against Leon Trotsky in the Moscow Trials, and spread a vision of liberal and progressive social change through extensive travel and lecturing in Japan, China, Turkey, Mexico, and Russia.

To all this work, Dewey brought a single, central focus: the demand to reconstruct and renew both social life and social theory in order to realize more fully America's proclaimed commitment to democracy. This reconstruction is necessary, Dewey thought, because rapid and far-reaching changes have created new problems and new possibilities, and have rendered ineffective earlier forms of social organization, thought, and value that remain democratic in name but now are counter-democratic in reality. This was Dewey's focus: the deliberate creation of a fuller and richer democratic culture in an age in which the frontier, as he characterized it, is moral rather than physical.

Democracy and democratic faith

Dewey did not identify democracy as a form of government but, instead, as a way of life. What way of life? Democracy, he claimed, is present when personal and community life are marked by faith in the capacity of human beings to exercise intelligent judgment and action when the proper conditions are provided, along with a shared commitment to provide these conditions as fully and broadly as possible and a dedication to the value of this commitment. Understood in this way, Dewey declared, the idea of democracy is the idea of genuine community.

Dewey viewed totalitarianism, in its many forms, as the enemy of democracy. Totalitarianism, he held, claims that faith in the capacities of the intelligence of persons is utopian. Democracy, in contrast, views the intelligence of common men and women as imperfect and fallible but, as experimental, also largely self-corrective. A democratic society, then, is a society in which persons participate in, and make decisions about, those activities and conditions that affect their lives. Dewey saw, of course, that totalitarian states on both the right and the left might make this sort of self-government and harmonious community life impossible, and he strongly criticizes them for this. At the same time, Dewey saw also that states with democratic governments might fail to nurture and sustain a democratic way of life. Concentrations of wealth (in "free" markets) and power (in "free" elections, a "free" press, and "free" assemblies), for example, may leave many persons formally free but without genuine opportunity or resources to impact intelligently the conditions in which they live. In the language that Dewey developed in *The Public and Its Problems*, these persons constitute *publics* – groups of people who are affected indirectly by the private agreements and activities of others. Often, Dewey argued, members of such publics are bewildered and lost, failing even to recognize themselves as a group undergoing the indirect consequences of the actions of others. Even more often, Dewey realized, such publics are powerless. Accordingly, to create a genuinely democratic culture, in America or elsewhere, persons must come to understand themselves as members of various multiple publics and then must deliberate and act (which, in turn, requires the creation of conditions necessary for such deliberation and action).

The reconstruction of liberalism

Dewey viewed this commitment to democracy as the core of liberalism. Liberalism, he argued, has three central values: individuality, liberty, and intelligence. Its alternatives, he wrote, are political drift and violence. Nonetheless, Dewey claimed that liberalism faced a crisis because it continued to interpret these three values in the same way they had been understood in earlier times – even though actual social life and its conditions now are radically different. As a result, liberalism must reconstruct its central values, and Dewey took up this task in books such as *Liberalism and Social Action*, *Individualism: Old and New*, and *Freedom and Culture*.

Early liberals like John Locke, Thomas Jefferson, and Adam Smith were committed to the innate or "ready-made" individuality of all persons and to their self-evident individual rights to life, liberty, and the pursuit of property and happiness. The effective exercise of these individual rights requires freedom from interference by others. So, these liberals believed governments that infringe on these rights are illegitimate and should be overthrown. This view of government was not shared by later liberals such as David Hume, Jeremy Bentham, and John Stuart Mill. They rejected the idea of self-evident truths claimed that actions and institutions must be judged by their consequences (rather than their origins), and often found that government must use its powers to create (rather than infringe on) liberties. This division within liberalism, Dewey argued, paralyzes it today. But both sides in this split, he observed, suffer from a kind of historical blindness which led them all to mistake their particular interpretations of individuality, liberty, and intelligence as immutable truths good at all times and places. Accordingly, Dewey stressed that any effective renascent liberalism must develop historical perspective and must note the actual social conditions that have rendered traditional liberal theories obsolete. Next, liberalism must reconstruct traditional liberal values of individualism, freedom, and intelligence in light of current social realities. And, finally, it must use this conceptual reconstruction to inform and guide the active reconstruction of social institutions, practices, and relations. That is, it must involve new practice as well as new theory.

Toward these ends, Dewey argued that individuality is (as George Herbert Mead, Dewey's colleague at Chicago, pointed out in his account of the social self) a social product and a social achievement, that genuine individuality depends upon stable social allegiances and relations, and that a society marked by economic, political, religious, and other forms of insecurity fails to provide them. Individuals, Dewey asserted, are confused and "lost." Individuality, thus, is fragile, and occurs only when persons are provided conditions necessary for continuing growth. Any renascent liberalism, Dewey concluded, must be committed to the development and attainment of those social conditions upon which real individuality depends.

Freedom, for Dewey, is the presence of, and participation in, these conditions necessary for the self-realization of individuals. Thus the traditional liberal value of freedom as freedom from interference must be reconstructed. It is purely absurd, Dewey argued, to think everyone equally free when some are in command of education, monetary capital, and social environment. Whether they did so in the past or not, so-called "free" markets no longer advance self-determination, self-government, or self-realization for many. It is only by keeping the motives for this "scandal of private appropriation" below consciousness, Dewey concluded, that its anti-democratic consequences are maintained.

Finally, in like manner Dewey argued that earlier conceptions of intelligence now are bankrupt. Dewey identified intelligence not with an innate faculty for perceiving supposedly static, self-evident, antecedent truths, but rather with inquiry, experimental action, and its results. This makes clear one of Dewey's most strongly held beliefs: the link between democracy and education (understood not narrowly as schooling but as the broad and regular use of intelligence). Democracy is opposed, Dewey claimed, by the authority of custom, superstition, and old beliefs, but also by propaganda, institutionalized violence, and new forms of control that threaten individualism and freedom. Force is built into the procedures of our existing society. As a result, Dewey judged that would-be revolutionaries who advocate violence propose nothing revolutionary at all. It is for this reason, Dewey thought, that democratic ends require democratic means. And it is for this reason that Dewey argued that America must make good on its promise of democracy by executing democratic ideals directly in all aspects of its cultural life. Dewey recognized that this is a large, ongoing task. He did not believe success was guaranteed. Instead, the justification for this democratic faith can be provided only after the fact in the results of taking up this challenge.

Further reading

Dewey, John. *Democracy and Education* in *John Dewey: The Middle Works, 1899–1924, Vol. 9*, ed. Jo Ann Boydston. Carbondale, IL: Southern Illinois University Press, 1980 [1916].

—— *Liberalism and Social Action* in *John Dewey: The Later Works, 1925–1953, Vol. 11*, ed. Jo Ann Boydston. Carbondale, IL: Southern Illinois University Press, 1987 [1935].

—— *Freedom and Culture* in *John Dewey: The Later Works, 1925–1953, Vol. 13*, ed. Jo Ann Boydston. Carbondale, IL: Southern Illinois University Press, 1988 [1939].

—— *Individualism: Old and New* in *John Dewey: The Later Works, 1925–1953, Vol. 5*, ed. Jo Ann Boydston. Carbondale, IL: Southern Illinois University Press, 1988 [1929].

—— *The Public and Its Problems* in *John Dewey: The Later Works, 1925–1953, Vol. 2*, ed. Jo Ann Boydston. Carbondale, IL: Southern Illinois University Press, 1988 [1927].

Kloppenberg, James T. *Uncertain Victory: Democracy and Progressivism in European and American Thought, 1870–1920*. New York: Oxford University Press, 1988.

Ryan, Alan. *John Dewey and the High Tide of American Liberalism*. New York: W.W. Norton, 1995.

Stuhr, John J. "Dewey's Social and Political Philosophy" in Larry A. Hickman (ed.) *Reading Dewey*. Bloomington, IN: University of Indiana Press, 1998, pp. 82–99.

West, Cornel. "*The Coming-of-Age of American Pragmatism: John Dewey in The American Evasion of Philosophy*. Madison, WI: University of Wisconsin Press, 1989.

Westbrook, Robert B. *John Dewey and American Democracy*. Ithaca, NY: Cornell University Press, 1991.

JOHN J. STUHR

DIALECTIC

Dialectic needs to be understood as a technical term of philosophy; however, as its roots in the Greek word διαλέγω (discourse, conversation, argument) indicate, it originally was understood to be closely bound to the nature of language, above all to the language of conversation. The give and take of a conversation is the proto-form of what eventually becomes the technical philosophical notion of dialectic.

Plato is the first to formulate dialectic as a technical term. While his initial inspiration and model for dialectic remains the give and take of conversation, he refines the sense of a conversation by making the logic of question and answer its heart. Several of Plato's dialogues self-consciously speak about the philosophical nature and significance of dialectic (*Symposium* and *Republic* are two of the most celebrated to do this), but even those that do not explicitly discuss dialectic do nonetheless perform and illustrate it in the character of the dialogue form itself. The so-called "Socratic Method" on display in the dialogues is thus really a dialectical procedure: Socrates poses questions and then examines the answers of his interlocutor by posing further questions until a contradiction founded in the assumptions of his interlocutor's views emerges. The Socratic practice of dialectic – the movement of questions and answers which aim at the discovery of assumptions hidden within a position – is what will later be called a "negative dialectic," that is, it leads to an aporia, a "not-knowing," rather than to any positive conclusion. The main achievement of Socratic dialectic is its exposure of the ignorance of unexamined positions. Socrates' well-known contention that his only real knowledge is of his own ignorance is a result of this dialectical process. Dialectic in this case serves the discovery of truth by virtue of its capacity to expose falsehood.

After Plato, and especially in the medieval period, dialectic comes to be associated more closely with formal logic. With this development dialectic comes to be regarded as the logic of debate: the assertion of a proposition and a contradictory proposition which in confronting one another leads to the transformation and new understanding of both propositions and thus to a "higher" truth. During this phase of its history, dialectic becomes, along with rhetoric, associated with the idea of persuasion. Here the dialectic becomes a method understood to have three stages: the assertion of a thesis, a counter-thesis, with the result being a synthesis of the two. This technical formalization of the notion of dialectic marks its most sterile moment, one in which it is taken simply to be a "tool" of philosophy.

The most significant revitalization of the notion of dialectic is found in Hegel, who understands dialectic not simply as a method but as the logic of the real itself. Hegel argues that contradiction and negation lie at the heart of being and, as such, dialectic, which is the logic of negation itself (the negation of a negation), describes the movement of being itself. Hegel's conception of dialectic is thus not at all mechanistic. Though he is often said to have described dialectic as the movement of "thesis, antithesis, synthesis" he did not do that; indeed, his sense of the dialectic is of a movement that subtly and fluidly unfolds the inner nature of all things.

After Hegel, Marx develops the concept of the dialectic in new ways by criticizing the idealism in Hegel's sense of it. In Marx we find a dialectical materialism wherein the contradiction driving dialectic is not found in some essential nature of things, but in the conflict of material situations.

Dialectic, especially in its Hegelian heritage, plays a central if largely unnoticed role in American philosophy. Though his initiation into philosophy was principally by way of Kant, Peirce came to realize that his "philosophy resuscitates Hegel, though in strange costume." In particular, his categories of firstness, secondness, and thirdness were seen by him as akin to Hegel's dialectical conception of the elemental stages of thought. Likewise, in *A Pluralistic Universe,* James acknowledged that Hegel's "'dialectic' picture is a fair account of a good deal of the world," even if Hegel's "all-inclusive reason" turns out to be nothing more than an unwarranted dogma of rationalistically inclined thinkers. Other figures such as Royce, Hocking, and Miller were also, in different ways, defenders of a philosophical idealism that made use of dialectical arguments to defend their respective positions.

The concept of the dialectic remains a vital notion today, in large measure as a result of the Hegelian/Marxist rehabilitation and expansion of it. Critical Theorists of the Frankfurt School are its chief representatives today. But however it is conceived, it still retains much of its original, Greek sense of being a process of uncovering otherwise hidden truths by pursuing the contradictions lurking in unexamined presumptions and in unreconciled situations.

Further reading

Hegel, G.W.F. *Phenomenology of Spirit* with "Preface" and "Introduction" in *Texts and Commentary*, trans. Walter

Kaufmann. South Bend, IN: University of Notre Dame Press, 1977.
Marx, Karl. *Economic and Philosophical Manuscripts of 1844*. Amherst, NY: Prometheus, 1988.
Plato, *The Republic*. New York: Penguin, Book 7.

DENNIS J. SCHMIDT

DIALOGUE

A philosophical dialogue is an exchange between two or more persons in order to resolve a disagreement, clarify an idea, test an assertion, or explore an issue. It presupposes the participants' relative ignorance (whether or not recognized) and the usefulness or necessity of their combined effort in overcoming it. The exchanges between Socrates and various interlocutors are paradigms of this approach to philosophizing.

A dialogical approach to philosophizing suits the Pragmatists, who argue that knowledge is contextual and fallible, that truth is justified by its consequences and so constantly needs to be refashioned. Charles Sanders Peirce defines the truth about something as the opinion on which all who investigate it will ultimately agree. Given sufficient opportunity for investigators with differing opinions to clarify their ideas through continuing experimental inquiry and mutual criticism, they will come eventually and "unavoidably" to a consensus, to a general opinion independent of whatever is merely individual or arbitrary. Reality is whatever in the indefinite long run the scientific community would agree is real.

John Dewey echoes Peirce's emphasis on experimental inquiry as the method in science for determining if an assertion is "warranted," i.e. true. He then applies this dialogical method to how decisions should be made in a democracy. Only as citizens learn to think and act "intelligently," to formulate their opinions in terms of publicly testable and revisable hypotheses, and to frame their values in terms of shared objective needs rather than private selfish desires, will they come to a genuinely democratic consensus on what constitutes their common good. Their lives will be improved and the communities in which they live will be more just only if they are able to interact creatively with others in choosing and then achieving their ends.

Recent versions of pragmatism retain this Deweyan focus on the moral and political implications of dialogue. Richard Bernstein, for example, advocates as an ideal of "practical discourse" the fashioning of "dialogical communities" that value solidarity, reciprocal judgment, and mutual recognition. Feminist philosophers such as Erin McKenna affirm the notion of inquiry as an open-ended public practice. By thinking through networks of conflicting experiences and interactions, the value of difference is appreciated and utilized in creating collaborative avenues for remedying societal injustices.

Some formal logicians have extended the constructivist theory of logic into an examination, with the help of game theory, of the link between dialogue and the rules of sound reasoning. The "second-person perspective" is a notion developed by Robert Brandom as an alternative in textual and cultural interpretation to the traditionally presumed special authority of the authorial or indigenous perspective, dialogue among equally respected voices functioning to adjudicate clashing viewpoints.

Despite the importance their philosophies give to dialogical matters, and although dialogue remains a widely practiced way to teach students how to think philosophically, it is not a mode by which American philosophers address one another or their fellow citizens. The monologic essay reigns supreme, with only one notable exception: George Santayana's puckishly inventive *Dialogues in Limbo*.

Further reading

Bernstein, Richard. *Beyond Objectivism and Relativism: Science, Hermeneutics, and Praxis*. Philadelphia, PA: University of Pennsylvania Press, 1983.
Brandom, Robert B. *Making it Explicit: Reasoning, Representing, and Discursive Commitment*. Cambridge, MA: Harvard University Press, 1998.
Dewey, John. *Reconstruction in Philosophy*. Boston, MA: Beacon Press, 1957.
Hamblin, Charles L. "Mathematical Models of Dialogue," *Theoria* 37 (1971): 130–55.
McKenna, Erin. *The Task of Utopia: A Pragmatist and Feminist Perspective*. Lanham, MD: Rowman and Littlefield, 2002.
Peirce, Charles Sanders. "How to Make Our Ideas Clear" in *The Essential Peirce: Collected Philosophical Writings, Volume 1 (1867–1893)*, ed. Nathan Houser and Christian Kloesel. Bloomington, IN: Indiana University Press, 1992, pp. 124–41.
Santayana, George. *Dialogues in Limbo*. Ann Arbor, MA: University of Michigan Press, 1957.

GEORGE ALLAN

DICHOTOMY

"Dichotomy" means a split so severe and so final that it cannot be repaired under any circumstances. The emergence of dichotomy in Western philosophy can be traced back to Plato and his theory of two levels of the real: the realm of forms that exhibits eternal, unchanging and permanent qualities and the realm of becoming which is always in the process of becoming something else. True knowledge can only be had within the realm of forms while guesswork and opinion is all that one can hope for in the realm of becoming. A more modern version of this dichotomy emerges with the work of Descartes. In splitting the world between the regions of mind and matter he established the mind/body bifurcation that continues to bedevil philosophy even to the present day. Dichotomies have been the bane of American philosophy since its very beginning. Whether it was the St Louis Hegelians trying to bring culture and spirit and body and mind together under the dialectical view developed by Hegel or Dewey's struggle to show that neither body nor mind were ultimate but rather abstractions derived from something far more basic – in each case unbridgeable gulfs appeared. These dichotomies even now continue to sap the cultural strength of philosophy as an academic discipline. When lines of thought are broken, dichotomies weaken philosophy's force as an instrument for further advancement of the human spirit.

Some of the more persistent dichotomies presently affecting philosophical thinking include:

1 The split between matter and mind. Is the brain the mind? Or is there a real distinction between an invisible organ (the mind) and a physical entity (the human brain)?
2 Is the world a deterministic manifold where every entity, event and action is the outcome of a causal law? Or is there a realm of freedom within which creativity and choice operate such that no absolute necessity guides human action?
3 Is there a transcendent creator existing outside the universe and causing the actions of its creatures? Or is there an immanent creator dwelling and acting within this cosmos and affecting the actions of its creatures?
4 Or is there no God but only a series of quite beautiful but ultimately finite events?

American philosophy has an approach to these questions and other sorts of dichotomies. It asks if these dichotomies are not really the outcome of mistaking abstractions for the rhythm and continuity of concrete experience. Is not the really interesting question the thinking body and the acting mind? Thus it would agree with Whitehead's assessment of the dualism separating mind and body, namely that it is the result of the fallacy of misplaced concreteness. In other words, we take the abstraction (mind and/or body) as being the concrete reality and therefore are forever trapped in futile attempts to either eliminate one (materialism or idealism) or bring them together through a series of acrobatic logical moves (supervenience or interactionism). The reality of the mind and body are to be understood through their action in the world. Thus pragmatism with its emphasis on the difference that experience makes is in the very best position to help dissolve the dichotomies that now hold philosophy captive. Or to address the other dichotomies listed above, recall James's solution to the debate between the atheist and the theist. If there is no real difference between the behaviors of both human beings, then the meaning of God in the debate between them is moot. Dichotomies dissolve under the pressure of experience.

JOSEPH GRANGE

DOUBT

Charles Sanders Peirce's paper on "The Fixation of Belief" (1877) is one of the classic documents of pragmatism, and the ideas which it contains echo through the writings of most of the pragmatists, both classic and contemporary. One of the most important of these ideas is a way of thinking about doubt that marks a major break between pragmatist logic and epistemology, on the one hand, and the Cartesian tradition in epistemology, on the other.

Doubt, reasons, and the heart

Peirce's most often cited remarks about doubt form part of attacks on Cartesianism in two well-known papers: "Consequences of Four Incapacities" (1868) and "The Fixation of Belief". On each occasion he draws attention to features of "real doubt" that are missing from the "doubts" that result from the sceptical thought experiments of the *Meditations.* Descartes proposes that philosophy should begin with universal doubt, and Peirce responds that my doubts about whether I am awake and not dreaming are "self-deception", they are "pretend" doubts. That we are experiencing an external world, for example, is something which "it does not occur to us *can* be questioned" (EP 1.28–9). In "The Fixation of Belief", he complains that some philosophers suppose we can start an inquiry merely by uttering a question, and responds that without "a real and living doubt . . . all discussion is idle" (EP 1.115). Comparing himself to Descartes, he suggested that they interpreted "absence of doubt" differently: for Descartes, this required "a conviction so firm that it is quite incapable of being destroyed", while he was happy with beliefs that are "perfectly free from all actual doubt" (EP 1.115). To support these claims, he needs an explanation of "real and living doubt" that shows both that philosophers' doubts are unreal, "paper" doubts, and also that rationality requires us to pay heed only to the "real" ones.

The earlier discussion emphasizes two points. The first is that doubt requires a positive reason: we cannot just doubt things at will on the basis of the Cartesian "maxim". This may be surprising since Descartes always offers reasons in support on the doubts he advocates: there are possibilities, albeit rather outlandish ones, that we need to rule out if we are to obtain secure knowledge of the world. A better way to understand Peirce's point may be that, for Descartes, we should always ask what reasons we have for holding any of our beliefs. And if the reasons we propose are insufficient, if we don't have conclusive reason for believing a proposition, this itself constitutes reason to doubt it. Peirce denies that. Unless we have identified a real possibility that a belief is false, then we have no reason to doubt it. The vast mass of beliefs of which we envisage no real doubt are to be trusted, even if we can offer no positive reason to accept them. The Cartesian strategy does not conform to our ordinary common-sense practice of seeking reasons for beliefs and doubts.

The second point is reflected in the slogan that Peirce proposes at the end of this discussion: "Let us not pretend to doubt in philosophy what we do not doubt in our hearts" (EP 1.29). The reference to the doubts that we recognize in our hearts suggests that emotional responses have a role in our evaluations of reasons for doubt. He holds that evaluations might take the form of emotional responses: "if a man is angry, he is saying to himself that this or that is vile or outrageous" (EP 1.43). Similarly, perhaps, when the heart tells me that some belief is doubtful, I employ an emotional way of saying that it is bad, or irrational, or risky. When we turn to the characterization of doubt in "The Fixation of Belief", this is confirmed. Whereas beliefs are "calm and satisfactory" states that we do not wish to avoid, doubt is "an uneasy and dissatisfied state from which we struggle to free ourselves and pass into the state of belief". Indeed, "The irritation of doubt is the only real motive for the struggle to attain belief." Once this irritation has vanished, no motivation for inquiry or reflection remains. Thus the fundamental characteristics of states of doubt are: such states do not guide action; they are an irritation; and they motivate us to carry out inquiries. Doubts present us with problems, which we endeavour to solve. They signal the problematic character of our situation through providing a kind of epistemic anxiety.

Doubt and inquiry

Peirce's position seems to be that we should take challenges to our beliefs seriously only if they provide genuine reasons for doubting them. And this will occur only if they produce genuine discomfort about the credentials of the belief in question, discomfort that motivates us to inquire into how far the belief should remain in place. If something that looks like a reason for doubt produces no discomfort, then it is not a real reason for belief. The flaw in Cartesian doubts is that their grounds are insufficient to produce real, emotional doubt. This suggests that our emotional evaluation of the grounds for doubt is at least as trustworthy as our more intellectual evaluations of it. Why should this be? Two factors may be involved.

The first reflects the inference of the Scottish philosophy of common sense upon thinkers such as Peirce. The evaluations we make of beliefs and inquiries reflect a range of instinctive beliefs, together with habits of inference and action. Our reflections on the specific reasons that can be offered in support of our beliefs may not be able to take account of all of the experience, all of the considerations, which sustain the belief and hold it in place. Indeed, a belief may be well founded and responsibly held, even if we cannot produce "sufficient" conscious reasons for accepting it. And, perhaps, the considerations that do hold it in place will be manifested in our affective responses. Descartes urged that if we cannot provide sufficient reasons for accepting a proposition, we have a reason to doubt it; Peirce's strategy allows that our beliefs may be well founded, even if we can provide no conscious reason for accepting them.

The second factor is that real doubt is a response to a position where our beliefs genuinely do not enable us to act and react to phenomena as we wish to. In later work, Peirce tells us that real doubt occurs when the attempt to act on our beliefs leads to surprise: expectations are disappointed. Belief is a stable habits: "it is (until it meets with some surprise that begins its dissolution) perfectly self-satisfied" (EP 2.336–7). Doubt, by contrast is "a privation of a habit" This must be more than the lack of a habit – it involves the absence of habit in an area where a habit is required for the guidance of action. The unreal doubts are, then, ones which do not interfere with the smooth operation of behaviour and action.

This development heralds the more sophisticated account of doubt defended by John Dewey in works such as *Logic: The Theory of Inquiry* (1982: 106–7). For Dewey, inquiry is prompted by our finding ourselves in an "indeterminate situation". Inquiry is the disciplined ("controlled or directed") attempt to make an indeterminate situation determinate. An indeterminate situation is "questionable": it is "uncertain, unsettled, disturbed". Moreover it is the situation itself that is questionable: "*We* are doubtful because the situation is inherently doubtful." Dewey emphatically rejects the idea that doubtfulness should be explained in terms the states of we inquirers rather than as a feature of "the existential situation in which we are caught and implicated". Peirce's claims may suggest the view that Dewey rejects: even if doubts need objective reasons, they are states of individual inquirers. But, especially in the remarks noted in the previous paragraph, he is making a decisive move in the direction that Dewey was to take further.

Further reading

Dewey, John. *Logic: The Theory of Inquiry.* New York: Irvington, 1982 [1938].

Peirce, Charles Sanders. *The Essential Peirce*, 2 vols. Indianapolis, IN: Indiana University Press, 1992, 1998. References given to EP, indicating volume and page number.

CHRISTOPHER HOOKWAY

DRAMATISM

In the American philosophical tradition, concepts relating to drama are most closely associated with John Dewey's theory of *dramatic rehearsal* in moral deliberation. Dramatism also refers more generally to Dewey's theory of the structure of any meaningful experience, widely discussed in contemporary philosophy as *narrative structure*.

According to Dewey, deliberation (moral, scientific, artistic) begins when incompatible factors in a situation engage us emotionally by disrupting stable habits. We hunt in imagination for ways to settle a perplexity by envisioning ourselves acting on the alternatives and undergoing the imagined consequences. This hunt continues until we hit upon a meaningful action felt to answer and offer closure to the difficulty. When a course of action appears to harmonize pressing interests, desires, ends, and other vying factors, a tone of relative equilibrium is restored. For Dewey, dramatic rehearsal was not a prescriptive procedure for how we should make moral choices. He did not aim to purify our normal cognitive processes and cultural milieu; instead, he aimed to more fully realize the potential of everyday reflection by giving a psychological description of the imaginative phase of prototypically normal deliberation.

Conceiving deliberation as dramatic highlights that it is story-structured. A dramatist composes with a refined awareness of possible meanings within a growing, multidimensional scene. Analogously, in our wisest deliberations we perceive relevant possibilities for mediating conflicts in a dynamic situation. Dramatic characters act "in character," and those acts are unintelligible if taken in isolation from their narrative contexts. Analogously, moral deliberation is dramatic because we must perceive and respond to interacting personalities, and the options before us are intelligible only in the setting of a life-narrative developing alongside other life-narratives.

One challenge to interpreting Dewey on dramatic rehearsal is that a stage drama or film calls up misleading associations. A dress-rehearsal for a scripted play is not sufficiently experimental. Dewey's moral stage is atypical, with co-authored scenes, improvisational acting, open-ended performances.

Taken in the context of Dewey's theory of experience, prefigured in the works of William James and Charles Sanders Peirce, deliberation follows the dramatic form of any experience transformed toward consummation. Any meaningful experience has a beginning, middle, and conclusion just as journeys have starting points, paths, and ends. When experience becomes sufficiently distinct and qualitatively unified to be called, in Dewey's idiom, *an* experience, a coherent story may be told about a perplexing situation.

Dewey argues that art exemplifies and celebrates such development toward consummation, so we can investigate the generic traits of artistic production and appreciation to learn how meaningful experiences develop in any walk of life. Dewey's use of dramatic form to metaphorically conceive the structure of moral deliberation is more, then, than illustrative rhetoric. The same generic developmental structure characterizes all significant experiences. This structure is simply clearer and more intensified in the arts.

Further reading

Alexander, Thomas. *John Dewey's Theory of Art, Experience, and Nature: The Horizons of Feeling*. Albany, NY: SUNY Press, 1987.

Dewey, John. *Human Nature and Conduct* in *The Middle Works, Vol. 15, 1922*, ed. Jo Ann Boydston. Carbondale, IL: Southern Illinois University Press, 1983.

STEVEN FESMIRE

DUBOIS, WILLIAM EDWARD BURGHART (W.E.B.)

William Edward Burghart DuBois (1868–1963) was an African American sociologist, historian and political philosopher. He was born 23 February 1868 in Great Barrington, Massachusetts, the only child of Alfred DuBois and Mary Silvina Burghart. He died on 27 August 1963 in Accra, Ghana, on the eve of the civil rights march on Washington. DuBois attended Fisk University after graduating as the only black student in his high school. He completed baccalaureate studies in philosophy at Harvard with William James and George Santayana and later received graduate degrees in history, becoming in 1895 the first black person to receive a PhD from Harvard. Over the course of his long life, W.E.B. DuBois helped found the NAACP, edited its monthly magazine *The Crisis*, edited the *Encyclopedia Africana*, and wrote over a dozen books and hundreds of articles. The US government branded him a subversive for his peace and racial justice activism and briefly detained him as an illegal foreign agent. Embittered by his experiences, he left the United States in 1961, never to return.

Much of DuBois's importance stems from his rejection of the accommodationist strategy advocated by Booker T. Washington, then the most powerful representative of African Americans. DuBois argued, first in his 1897 essay "The Conservation of Races" and again in his groundbreaking 1903 collection of essays *The Souls of Black Folk*, that American blacks should conserve their cultural distinctiveness and relate to whites as equals. DuBois dramatically redefined discussions of race in America from patronizing talk about the "Negro problem" to the more apt focus on "the problem of the color line." He dismissed the assumption on the part of whites that the inter-racial strife had to do primarily with the inferiority of black people and instead argued that the problem was the artificial boundaries that whites had erected to protect their political and economic privileges. DuBois advanced a theory that defined race less as a purely biological category in the older Lamarkian sense and more as a cultural and historical family that played a significant and meaningful role in individual lives. Behind his early arguments for the conservation of race is the hope that racialism, the recognition of racial and ethnic difference, need not lead to racism, the invidious discrimination against groups or individuals based on racial difference. DuBois's most novel articulation of this idea is the metaphor of the race gift, which suggests that each race carries a gift of unique experience that must be shared in an egalitarian manner with other races for the cultural and moral betterment of all. While his writings engaged throughout his life the problem of racism and encouraged race pride among people of African descent, the writings of his later years focused more on the need to resist capitalist and white supremacist imperialism around the world. His later works also move away from the Hegelianism and Pragmatism of his early career towards a more conventionally Marxist analysis.

Other important works not mentioned above include *The Suppression of the African Slave Trade to the United States of America* (1896), the first comprehensive historical treatment of the African slave trade in the US, *The Philadelphia Negro* (1899), the first sociological study of an African American community, and *Black Reconstruction* (1935), a seminal history of African Americans from 1860 to 1880.

Further reading

DuBois, W.E.B. *The Suppression of the African Slave Trade to the United States of America*. Mineola, NY: Dover, 1999 [1897].

—— *The Philadelphia Negro.* Philadelphia, PA: University of Pennsylvania Press, 1996 [1899].

—— *Souls of Black Folks. W.E.B. DuBois: Writings.* New York: Library of America, 1986 [1903].

Washington, Booker T. *The Future of the American Negro.* Boston, MA: Egg, 1899.

West, Cornel. *The American Evasion of Philosophy: A Genealogy of Pragmatism.* Madison, WI: University of Wisconsin, 1989.

Zack, Naomi. *Race and Mixed Race.* Philadelphia, PA: Temple, 1993.

TERRANCE MACMULLAN

DUCASSE, CURT JOHN

Born in France and educated through high school in France and England, for ten years Curt John Ducasse (1881–1968) was employed in business in Mexico, France and the US before enrolling in the University of Washington where he received an AB in 1908 and an MA in 1909. His Harvard dissertation, "The Fallacy of Counteraction and Its Metaphysical Significance" (1912) was directed by Josiah Royce. After teaching at the University of Washington between 1912 and 1926, he moved to Brown University where he taught until retirement in 1958.

One of the first practitioners of analytic philosophy in America, from as early as 1924 Ducasse held that language-facts constitute the basic data of philosophy. This method he employed self-consciously, criticizing the forms of analysis practiced by others. Most importantly, Ducasse's analysis was distinctive in being used to construct a philosophical system of exceptional scope that encompassed philosophy of science, epistemology, metaphysics, philosophy of mind, philosophy of religion, psychical research, philosophy of art, ethics, and philosophy of education. In philosophy of science he rejected Humean theories of causation in favor of the view that causal relations are observable. In epistemology he articulated an adverbial theory of perception later developed by his student Roderick Chisholm as well as by Wilfrid Sellars and his students. In metaphysics and philosophy of mind he defended mind–body dualism. In philosophy of religion and psychical research, he supported a version of William James's ethics of belief and the possibility of survival of death. In philosophy of art he argued for an emotionalist theory and a relativistic account of the standards of artistic criticism. His ethical theory he called "progressive and universal hedonism." Most noteworthy in his philosophy of education were his painstaking definitions of such terms as "education" and "wisdom."

Further reading

Dommeyer, F.C. (ed.) *Current Philosophical Issues: Essays in Honor of Curt John Ducasse.* Springfield, IL: Charles C. Thomas, 1966.

Ducasse, Curt John. *Causation and the Types of Necessity.* Seattle, WA: University of Washington Press, 1924.

—— *Philosophy as a Science: Its Matter and Its Method.* New York: Oscar Piest, 1941.

—— *Nature, Mind, and Death.* La Salle, IL: Open Court, 1951.

—— *Truth, Knowledge and Causation.* London: Routledge and Kegan Paul, 1968.

—— *Paranormal Phenomena, Science, and Life after Death.* New York: Parapsychology Foundation, 1969.

Hare, Peter H. and Madden, Edward H. *Causing, Perceiving and Believing: An Examination of the Philosophy of C. J. Ducasse.* Dordrecht and Boston, MA: Reidel, 1975.

Peter H. Hare

E

ECONOMICS

What can American philosophers and economists learn from each other? This entry focuses on one strand of American philosophy, namely, pragmatism as expressed in the thought of John Dewey (e.g. 1958). It also focuses on one strand of economics, namely, the theory of choice. In particular, the entry limits its scope to what economists can learn from pragmatism.

For pragmatism, agents make choices according to their experience with the environment rather than according to some ingrained, fixed essence. Likewise, for neoclassical economics, the dominant school in economics, agents behave according to incentives from the environment rather than according to fixed norms, rules, customs. If a university increases its rewards for research, academics would produce more research output.

Thus, pragmatism and neoclassical economics share a common platform. Both reject essentialism, which is known as normative and functionalist theories that characterize much of traditional sociology and anthropology (Joas 1993, 1996). For normative–functionalist theories, agents behave according to social norms and cultural customs that make their choices basically inelastic with regard to the changes of the environment or incentives. That is, agents are basically socialized and culturalized into particular roles or functions, which are insensitive to changes in market prices, budgets, and other environmental fluctuations.

On the other hand, pragmatism and neoclassical economics are far apart on how to model incentives. For pragmatism, incentives are not external data that confront the agent. Rather, incentives are constitutive of the agent where the agent's experience makes sense of the incentives. In this regard, the term "experience" denotes a theoretical meaning that is beyond its usual connotation. It highlights that the agent's goals are formed in the particular manner in which the agent is enmeshed with his environment. In contrast, for neoclassical economics, the agent's goals (so-called "preferences" or "tastes") are pre-given or considered as data that can be defined prior to "experience" – where "experience" is merely seen as the set of incentives that can be defined independently of the particular agent at hand. As such, the agent reacts to incentives by calculating the cheapest allocation that satisfies the given goals. So, agents are ultimately modeled as automata that react to the change of prices or incomes by choosing new bundles of goods that minimize the cost.

Of course, economic models have become more sophisticated, especially at the hands of Gary Becker (1996). Becker recognizes that goals change as a result of action, as when one starts to appreciate wine or music as one consumes more wine or music – what Becker calls the formation of habits. In Becker's model, goals evolve as a result of a loop reaction that entails path-dependency. Becker also recognizes that goals change according to the tastes of one's peer group. But still, the recognition of history (path-dependency) and society (socialization) is insufficient to capture the notion of experience as understood by John Dewey. In these sophisticated economic models, goals or tastes (deposited by history, society, culture, or whatever) are modeled as given in the face of current incentives.

How, then, would economic theory look if one considers goals as enmeshed with the environment – i.e. as captured by the notion of experience in pragmatism? The pragmatic statement that the agent cannot stand outside experience, or that he is molded by experience, is more than a statement about the social and cultural *origins* of goals. That is, the statement is basically not about embeddedness (a new buzzword in sociology; Granovetter 1985) of goals in history, society, and culture – which neoclassical economics can handle with great ease. Rather, the statement concerning the importance of experience is about the *present*. Irrespective of the origin or history of goals, do goals stand external to environmental incentives? For a pragmatic theory of rationality, the goal of the agent directs the agent's perception in a particular manner and, hence, makes the agent view the incentive in a particular way. Likewise, the incentive may influence the set of goals, i.e. the set of goals cannot be specified independent of the set of incentives. In this manner, there is neither goal-free incentive nor incentive-free goal. This undermines the sacred cow in neoclassical economics: The end/means dichotomy is, at first approximation, untenable.

While the goal is formed by the perceived incentive, the incentive is never goal-free. The same incentive can be interpreted differently depending on the perceiving/acting subject. That is, as Mousavi and Garrison (2003) maintain, the incentive has a meaning depending on the context of choice. So, rational choice is not as simple as assumed in neoclassical economics. The agent is not an automaton. He rather interprets the environment and, accordingly, ascribes meaning to the incentive at hand.

The role of context- or reference-dependent choice has been highlighted by experimental methods undertaken by practitioners in the emerging field known as "behavioral economics" (e.g. Camerer *et al.* 2004), which is known in psychology as "behavioral decision theory" (e.g. Tversky and Kahneman 1974, 1981; Kahneman and Tversky 1979). Agents have been found to reverse their choices once the incentive is worded differently – as if a half-empty glass differs substantially from a half-full one (Khalil 2003). Also, the idea that agents ascribe meaning and do not stand outside their experience has been highlighted by one strand of the budding field of "institutional economics" led by North (2005; Denzau and North 1994). This strand argues that institutions are not limited to customs, laws, property rights, and rules. They also include mental models, which Choi (1993) calls "paradigms and theories." Such models orient agents to view and act in the world in particular ways (Khalil 2006).

The fields of behavioral economics and institutional economics are expanding rapidly. Pragmatism, with its emphasis on the relevance of context and meaning, can provide a needed conceptual backbone to the findings of these exciting fields. A better understanding of decision-making should, eventually, improve our theories of innovative activity, investment, and economic development.

Further reading

Becker, Gary S. *Accounting for Tastes.* Cambridge, MA: Harvard University Press, 1996.

Choi, Young Back. *Paradigms and Theories: Uncertainty, Decision Making, and Entrepreneurship.* Ann Arbor, MI: University of Michigan Press, 1993.

Granovetter, Mark. "Economic Action, Social Structure and Embeddedness," *American Journal of Sociology* 91, 3 (1985): 481–510.

Joas, Hans. *The Creativity of Action.* Chicago, IL: University of Chicago Press, 1996.

Khalil, Elias L. "The Context Problematic, Behavioral Economics and the Transactional View: An Introduction to 'John Dewey and Economic Theory'," *Journal of Economic Methodology* 10, 2 (2003): 107–30. (An earlier version appeared in *Transactional Viewpoint* 2, 1 (2003).)

Mousavi, Shabnam and Garrison, Jim. "Toward a Transactional Theory of Decision Making: Creative Rationality as Functional Coordination in Context." *Journal of Economic Methodology* 10, 2 (2003): 131–56.

North, Douglass C. *Understanding the Process of Economic Change.* Princeton, NJ: Princeton University Press, 2005.

Tversky, Amos and Kahneman, Daniel. "The Framing of Decisions and the Psychology of Choice." *Science* 211 (30 January 1981): 453–8.

Elias L. Khalil

EDEL, ABRAHAM: AUTOBIOGRAPHY

In the 1920s I did Classics and Philosophy at McGill, and then, at the end of the decade, Litterae Humaniores at Oxford. Oxford at that time was a lively intellectual milieu. W.D. Ross and H.A. Prichard were lecturing on ethics, H.W.B. Joseph on Plato, and the influence of G.E. Moore and Bertrand Russell extended from Cambridge. Controversy on moral theory was high. The same was true of epistemology, where Prichard posed a realistic epistemology against Harold Joachim, who was defending Bradley and Bosanquet against the metaphysical realism of Cook Wilson. All this was much more stimulating than the uniform positivism and linguistic philosophy that took over in the 1930s.

I came to New York in 1930. The atmosphere at Columbia was quite different. Although my doctoral thesis was on Aristotle, there were a variety of other influences from the academic milieu – particularly from the psychologists, the economists, and the anthropologists (Otto Klineberg, Joseph Dorfman, Franz Boas, Ruth Benedict, Margaret Mead). At the same time (1931), I began teaching philosophy at City College, beginning as an assistant to Morris Raphael Cohen. This work broadened my view of the role of philosophy in its connection with the social sciences and the role of science generally. Instead of a purely theoretical exposition of philosophical positions, Cohen showed how philosophical issues lay at the root of the disciplines of psychology, social science, and history, as well as of the physical and biological sciences.

Much of my subsequent work has been to develop this approach for morality, to clear up the difficulties that have been commonly raised about the separation of fact and value, and to show how factual (scientific) views involve values and how values involve factual (scientific) materials. In the 1950s, May Edel and I published *Anthropology and Ethics*, attempting to develop the cooperative relations of the two disciplines.

My writings on morality since that time have emphasized the importance of the psychological and social sciences in understanding the morality of practical problems. *Critique of Applied Ethics: Reflections and Recommendations* (1994, written with Elizabeth Flower and Finbarr W. O'Connor) is devoted to this.

ABRAHAM EDEL

EDMAN, IRWIN

Irwin Edman (1896–1954) grew up along Morningside Avenue on the upper west side of Manhattan, the second child of Jewish parents. He was educated at Columbia College in the tuition of John Erskine, a novelist and a gifted interpreter of Shakespeare, and Frederick J.E. Woodbridge, the eloquent Aristotelian whose course in the history of philosophy was especially popular. As a graduate student, Edman suffered a little from ennui in John Dewey's courses. Dewey lectured ploddingly in soft, uneven tones, thinking out loud and fussing incessantly with crumpled pages of notes. But it was the age of a burgeoning faith in the power of intelligence to improve the world, and Dewey was its high priest. With repeated exposure, Edman began to detect a glimmer of promise in Dewey's chief insights, and in the method of their application to contemporary social and political problems. They seemed imbued with the spirit of progress. Edman would eventually edit as well as introduce a volume of essays on Dewey's influence titled *John Dewey: His Contribution to the American Tradition*, and a similar volume, *The Philosophy of Santayana.*

Edman was not a metaphysician in the style of Kant or Hegel. He would have been old-fashioned had he shared their taste for grand systems when all zeal for those had gone out with the nineteenth century. Conceptual sophistication did not appeal to him. But if metaphysics can be understood more generously to mean a temperamental fondness for deliberately setting the mundane events of daily experience against the background of a wider perspective, or simply a sense of wonderment concerning ultimate questions, then it ran swiftly in his blood, and found expression in nearly every word he wrote. The crux of his metaphysics is articulated in a beautifully written short volume by the title of *The Contemporary and His Soul*, but the essay, not the book, was his favorite literary form. Edman's essays are Emersonian in their themes and sensitivities. He traveled widely in the United States and abroad, and loved to reflect in writing about the meaning of a journey, the delights and the absurdities of transportation by train, by ship, and by air, or the effects of a new climate, or a new acquaintance. He was a devoted teacher, beloved by many students, and wrote incisively about pedagogy. Some of his most perceptive essays were originally published in *The American Scholar* and are collected in a volume called *Under Whatever Sky.* Others are collected in *Philosopher's Holiday.*

For some philosophers, the urge to sound the depths of ultimate reality is primarily epistemological or scientific. In them, intellectual curiosity has ignited a desire to know the truth about the nature of the universe. For others, and Edman belongs with these, the metaphysical urge is really a desire to see the complex tensions of experience resolved into something simple and harmonious, and hence beautiful and satisfying. Although his main contribution to aesthetics, *Arts and the Man,* is no more than a brief introduction to the subject, the entire body of his writing is in a way an effort to give novel and creative expression to philosophical insight. Edman was as much an artist with words as he was a philosopher.

Further reading

Edman, Irwin. *Philosopher's Holiday.* New York: Viking Press, 1938.

—— *The Philosophy of Santayana.* New York: Modern Library, 1942.

—— *Under Whatever Sky*. New York: Viking Press, 1951.
—— *The Contemporary and His Soul*. Port Washington, NY: Kennikat Press, 1967.
—— *John Dewey: His Contribution to the American Tradition*. New York: Greenwood Press, 1968.

MICHAEL BRODRICK

EDUCATION, AMERICAN PHILOSOPHERS ON

The most influential American philosopher of education was John Dewey. He believed that education is a definitive aspect of living things. Most broadly, it is the process by which creatures absorb and respond to stimuli, and thereby grow. It is a social process continuous with biological ones, needed for societal survival and reproduction of culture. Education, then, is that social process of forming and transmitting the aims and interests of society to its new members, and of refining the abilities of members to engage, refine, and pursue common goals.

Many American philosophers contributed to the philosophy of education. While their views are diverse, there are tendencies and important ideas common to them. Four main threads connect most American philosophers on the issue of education. The first has to do with the relation between tradition and scientific progress. American thinkers share the notion of social experimentation as a central theme for education. A second central theme is an attention to psychology, especially in the role of habits and intelligence in guiding conduct. Third, freedom is another important feature of education for American philosophers, insofar as the furthering of democracy through suffrage movements demanded an educated populace. Dewey was among the most passionate advocates for public education for this reason. Fourth, with this movement to greater freedom in education came an emphasis on democracy.

I will focus on Dewey's approach to the philosophy of education. But first, it is important to recognize the context in which Dewey's work arose. Other influential figures are also worth noting regarding the historical controversies that pertain to the education of women and African Americans.

Tradition and evolution

The early days of education in America were on the whole religiously motivated. It was against this backdrop that scientific advances inspired change. In a brief study of the history of *The Origins of American Philosophy of Education*, J.J. Chambliss claims that the philosophy of education as a field of study burgeoned in America between the years of 1808 and 1913. He refers us to Joseph Neef's *Sketch of a Plan and Method of Education* (1808), and to Paul Monroe's *Cyclopedia of Education* (1911–13).

In that time, debates in the philosophy of education rested on traditional ones between rationalism and empiricism. Historically, rationalism denotes the prioritization of principles of reason along with skepticism about the world of sensation. Empiricism, by contrast, generally understands all knowledge as founded essentially on our senses, holding to skepticism of the realm of intangible ideas. As philosophy in America came to have its own voice, thinkers such as William James and John Dewey described their views as Radical Empiricism and Naturalistic Empiricism, respectively, though theirs were not traditional notions of empiricism. What was "radical" about their versions of empiricism was that they took the world of experience to be the fundamental locus of inquiry while understanding experience as not limited to the senses. Given the scientific revolution that Darwin brought to the world, American philosophers commonly came to see continuities in the world of experience where previous generations saw breaks. And, these continuities were not only to be found between kinds of animals, but also between mind and body.

Chauncey Wright was among the first American philosophers to be greatly influenced by Darwin's work. Chambliss explains that Wright did not focus much on education, but his views were influential. Wright's views of science were continuous with his perspective on human conduct. He believed that like hypotheses, the meaning and weight of conduct must be measured by the consequences it brings in experience, not by its origins (Chambliss 1968: 77). Here we see seeds of American views on education and Pragmatism. For Wright, as for Pragmatists generally, conduct is a central notion in the study of any organism. In the context of education, this contrasts with the idea that education is concerned with knowledge of facts. American philosophers conceive of education as concerned with behavior and habits for living well. Wright was among the thinkers to move other philosophers in this direction.

Darwin was not alone in influencing American philosophers towards this intermediary position between rationalism and empiricism, however. Ralph Waldo Emerson called for a break from the traditions of thought that kept America so caught up in its European past. In his famous essay that predates Darwin's findings, "The American Scholar"

(1837), Emerson finds unity in nature, continuity between thought and matter. He also explains that each generation must write its own books, and prepare for its own future. He believed that we must not let ourselves get stuck in the traditional problems of our European past. We have an opportunity to set our own path.

In Emerson and later in the writings of Wright, James, and Dewey, we see a willingness to challenge long-standing dogmas. In their work we find an emphasis on hypothesis in both science and social endeavors. The traditions maintained from European heritage were brought into question both by thinkers seeking greater American independence, like Emerson, and by those struck by the insights of new scientific theories. Education could no longer be simply the study of classic texts. What was needed was an openness to explore the world afresh. For more on the subject of Darwin's influence, see Dewey's essay, "The Influence of Darwinism on Philosophy" (1977).

Psychology

Following the insights on evolution from the sciences, human beings, considered to be continuous with other animals, could be examined in a new light. And the field of psychology was still very young. It was in this setting that William James established himself as a preeminent scholar. His influential book, *The Principles of Psychology*, built upon early findings in psychology, aiming to make a textbook for the field. It quickly became much more. James's highest degree was medical, yet his work in psychology made significant contributions to the fields of psychology, philosophy, and education.

Given his work in psychology, James addressed teachers and students in his lectures, *Talks to Teachers on Psychology*, and *Talks to Students on Some of Life's Ideals* (James 1983). He began by stressing a key insight of the study of psychology, guided by the developments of evolutionary theory, that "man, whatever else he may be, is primarily a practical being, whose mind is given him to aid in adapting him to this world's life" (James 1983: 24). And, given the central place of habit in psychological functioning for James, he claimed that "Education, in short, cannot be better described than by calling it *the organization of acquired habits of conduct and tendencies to behavior*" (James 1983: 27).

Dewey also wrote a book on psychology, one that preceded James's. There is no doubt, however, that he was markedly impressed by James's work. In fact, a central feature of Dewey's views on education was drawn especially from his response to James's book. In a seminal essay, "The Reflex Arc Concept in Psychology," Dewey challenged the notion that James recounts regarding the reflex arc. The concept has to do with the ways in which minds come to have memory and to learn. In the basic picture that James retells, something stimulates a child, who then responds. Thus, if a child were excited by a flickering candle and responded by touching it, a second stimulus, a burning feeling, would lead the child to recoil. But what accounts for the fact that the first stimulus does not keep affecting the child in the same way? Why does he or she not go for the candle again?

The answer has to do with memory and habituation. While this basic picture of reflexes is helpful for certain purposes, Dewey noted that it was problematic for others. For, on Dewey's account, we cannot isolate singular stimuli as the evident ones in any given scenario, for stimuli are always many, and are always found in complex environments. This is to say that the child selects the stimulus. And we know part of Dewey's lesson well. Some things attract some children and not others. So, two elements in Dewey's philosophy of education can be seen to arise from this response to James. First, we must rethink the relation between stimulus and response, such that we understand the important role of selectivity. Second, we must recognize the multiplicity of possibilities for stimulation, situated in rich environments, ready to be attended to given the interests and selection of the pupil or inquirer.

Freedom

As education evolved in America for some, others still sought access to it in the first place. Women and African Americans were historically denied education. What follows is a brief account of some key figures in the efforts of these groups to obtain formal education, and to decide about what education for them should be.

In her essay, "Women, Education and History," Barbara Matthews discusses the history of women and education in America. Although many of the figures in her account are not commonly referred to as American philosophers, the roles of these women in American history were important in the development of both freedom and democracy in the context of education. The first advocate of women's education in her account (1878), Benjamin Rush, while appearing conservative by twenty-first-century standards, was radical in his day. Rush believed that women should be educated, since, among other reasons, mothers more than fathers raised the leaders of our country. As such, women's education, also important for the better management of household affairs on Rush's account, should consist in the study of liberty and government.

The advocates for women's education included Catherine Beecher (1823), Susan B. Anthony (1848), and Eleanor Flexner (1959). Concern for women in education did not only pertain to access for female students. While in the days of the colonies men were teachers, by the late 1880s women made up 63 percent of American teachers (Matthews 1976: 51). And, although women were the majority of teachers at the time, they earned on average between a third and a half of what men earned in the same position.

African Americans also overcame great odds at procuring access to formal education. In terms of the African American philosophers of education, three main positions are of great importance. In his essay, "The Educational Philosophies of Washington, DuBois, and Houston: Laying the Foundations for Afrocentrism and Multiculturalism," Frederick Dunn characterizes the three positions in question as follows.

In the effort to advocate education for African Americans, Booker T. Washington (1856–1915) held an accommodationist position (Dunn 1993: 26). This educational approach took the development of technical skills to be of central importance. Washington was taken to be a spokesperson for his race (ibid.: 27). His accommodationist philosophy of education was hailed by whites from the North and South. By contrast to Washington's advocacy of only technical education for African Americans, W.E.B. DuBois (1868–1963) held a liberationist view that sought an independent flourishing for African Americans (ibid.: 25). He was a segregationist, but he took Washington's approach to be oppressive (ibid.: 28). DuBois's segregationism sought independence in which African Americans could prosper in their own culture. Distinct from Washington and DuBois, Charles Hamilton Houston (1895–1950) was a desegregationist and a reformist (ibid.: 25). Houston believed that segregation was an obstacle to freedom and democracy (ibid.: 29). This brings us to a fourth central theme in American philosophy of education.

Democracy

Given the histories of conflict in American education, we can understand why American philosophers take education to be "the fundamental method of social progress and reform" (Dewey 1972: 93). It is in this setting that Dewey's democratic philosophy of education emerged.

Dewey's most famous work on education is his book, *Democracy and Education*. Later in his life, he wrote a much briefer account of his views in *Experience and Education*. The theory Dewey develops in these and other works has been of great influence on the philosophy of education ever since. Perhaps the most succinct presentation of his beliefs he published early on in his career in "My Pedagogic Creed." In it, he pronounced his view that "all education proceeds by the participation of the individual in the social consciousness of the [human] race" (Dewey 1972: 84).

Education, according to Dewey, is an end in itself (Dewey 1980: 55). It is that process from which ends come to be and are reformulated. Education must therefore be broad and general, and must emphasize the creative process of inquiry into the solutions to complex social problems. It must be remembered that the social aspects of education, for Dewey, are continuous with the physical and organic. In *Democracy and Education*, Dewey emphasized the continuity of organic processes of development with social ones in education (Dewey 1980: 79). Education is the method by which we help each other to overcome the difficulties of the past, to create new habits, and to learn to engage in and to reform collective inquiry and experimentation.

Dewey describes education as growth, guidance, development, and reconstruction. His "technical definition" of education calls it "that reconstruction or reorganization of experience which adds to the meaning of experience, and which increases ability to direct the course of subsequent experience" (Dewey 1980: 82). For Dewey, education is both a process and an end. This is to say that the very process of education continually improves on itself and adds powers of control and of meaning to previously indeterminate or problematic situations. Although we commonly justify an activity in terms of its external aims, Dewey argues that education has no more fundamental goal beyond itself (ibid.: 107). This is what it means for education to be an end in itself. Problems, goals, and solutions, according to Dewey, are products and refinements of education. Through education, we come to create, clarify, and test the meanings and purposes of our experience. In this way we can see education as a natural process that can be attended to carefully as a tool for cultural experimentation and progress.

Education is fundamentally social for Dewey. Its character is democratic inasmuch as it remains free and flexible to readjustment "through interaction of the different forms of associated life." Democracy, he continued, "must have a type of education which gives individuals a personal interest in social relationships and control, and the habits of mind which secure social changes without introducing disorder" (Dewey 1980: 105).

Further reading

Chambliss, J.J. *The Origins of American Philosophy of Education: Its Development as a Distinct Discipline (1808–1913)*. The Hague: Martinus Nijhoff, 1968.

Dewey, John. "The Reflex Arc Concept in Psychology" and "My Pedagogic Creed" in *The Early Works of John Dewey, Vol. 5, 1895–1898*, ed. Jo Ann Boydston. Carbondale, IL: Southern Illinois University Press, 1972, pp. 96–109 and 84–95.

—— *Democracy and Education* in *The Middle Works of John Dewey, Vol. 9, 1916*, ed. Jo Ann Boydston. Carbondale, IL: Southern Illinois University Press, 1980.

Dunn, Frederick. "The Educational Philosophies of Washing, DuBois, and Houston: Laying the Foundations for Afrocentrism and Multiculturalism," *The Journal of Negro Education* 62, 1 (Winter 1993): 24–34.

James, William. *Talks to Teachers on Psychology* and *Talks to Students on Some of Life's Ideals* in *The Works of William James*, ed. Frederick Burkhardt. Cambridge, MA: Harvard University Press, 1983.

Matthews, Barbara. "Women, Education and History," *Theory into Practice* 15, 1, special edition "Democracy in Education" (February 1976): 47–53.

Eric Thomas Weber

EDUCATION, CONCEPTIONS OF

Since the colonial period, conceptions of education in America have changed in response to shifting religious, political, and economic circumstances. To understand the central conceptions, we shall begin with the colonial period and describe their development and change into the early twenty-first century.

Colonial period

Puritan educators were deeply influenced by a Calvinist view of God and a humanist view of persons. Calvin's theology was influenced by the Great Chain of Being to which Plato, Aristotle, Plotinus, and Augustine made significant contributions. That vision manifested itself in Calvin's view that the Sovereign God created a hierarchically ordered world in which everyone has an appointed place, a place to which each is called. Obedience to God's call and hard, disciplined, well-planned work manifest God's way through us. The life of persons becomes highly organized, efficient, effective. Humanists believed that the young must find their calling, one that suits their talents and contributes to society. Influenced by Vives (1492–1540) and Erasmus (1466–1536) and classical writers such as Cicero and Quintillian, Puritan educators urged parents and teachers to carefully consider the talents, inborn tendencies, and interests of the young before embarking on an education.

These Calvinist and Humanist conceptions came together in the thought of William "Painful" Perkins, a Cambridge theologian who died in 1602. He thought that Calvin and the humanist were both correct. Educators must teach students their general calling to worship and obey God and their particular calling to live that life in the light of the specific talents God gave them. With this conception of education Perkins deeply influenced Puritan education before the Revolution. In the Southern colonies schools were influenced by the beliefs of the Church of England and sought to maintain the social order through passing on to the young the intellectual and social heritage of their forbears.

Late eighteenth to mid-nineteen century

By the American Revolution, the metaphysical–social axis of the colonial period shifted. The Enlightenment entered the colonies as the major works of Locke, Descartes, Newton, Gassendi and the Cambridge Platonists became available. The philosophical orientation turned from a hierarchical, metaphysical structure of eternal principles and a created order to the natural world and a naturalistic/materialistic scientific metaphysics. Though education was under the control of Christian churches, practical education took root in the form of technical academies that offered courses in subjects such as surveying and accounting. Capstone courses in the college curriculum, at Princeton for example, became less theological and more moral.

In addition, as the influence of the Great Chain of Being and Calvinism waned the new political order and the influence of the industrial revolution grew. Slowly politics and science filtered into education. By the 1830s the demand to educate the young for the new political and industrial order materialized in the common school movement led by Horace Mann and later in the Morrill Act establishing agricultural and mechanical colleges and universities in the 1860s. Government increased its influence on education, elementary through higher education.

Mid-nineteenth through early twentieth century

The publication of the *Origin of the Species* in 1859 challenged the fixed species of the Great Chain of Being lodged in the Christian doctrine of creation. A naturalistic conception of education began to claim ground once occupied only by the classical hierarchy of Calvinism and humanism. Biological evolution became a key element in the new conception of education advocated by John Dewey. But it was the social, political, economic problems of the late nineteenth century that provided the impetus for Dewey's ideas to germinate and flower.

Dewey argued that education should free students from the rigid structures of religious institutions and focus their learning on solving concrete problems of society. Both skepticism regarding the authority of traditional institutions and the strength of the scientific method opened new and dependable ways of learning leading to desirable changes in society. Learning must focus on mastering the methods of science to find solutions that will result in the good life of persons in a democratic society. Education should teach students to be curious, flexible, tolerant, and open-minded.

Educators with liberal Protestant leanings formulated a conception of education in direct contrast to the Comptean and Deweyan naturalism. They turned to Hegel's belief that the mind can grasp reality and understand how all things relate to it. Think of learning as a growing plant. As the buds emerge to flowers and later become fruit, our minds, in learning, emerge into the fruit of fuller self-consciousness. Not private and isolated, persons grow into fuller self-consciousness as they grasp their nature and their integral place in the total scheme of things.

The other facet of the Liberal Protestant Consensus is the biblical tradition. Deeply influenced by German biblical scholarship, they believed that God is progressively revealing himself to his people and guiding them to the brotherhood of man under the Fatherhood of God. The effect of the higher criticism of German biblical scholarship, such as Wellhausen's, undermined the conservatives' confidence that the Bible being divinely inspired is infallible. Yet, along with these achievements, Higher Criticism held firmly to the core of the biblical teaching, that Christianity is monotheistic, moral, and messianic.

The essential tenets of the Liberal Protestant conception of education are that the universe is deeply moral, the structure of which we can know through the revelation of God in the Judeo-Christian tradition. We can also know God through reason. Nature is God's creation; by our own devices, notably science, we can learn what God placed there. The sciences can be practiced and taught without pressure from religion; the truth the scientist finds and teaches is what God placed there. However, scientific standards and procedures are not enough to build a life on. Only on the basis of their purposive, aiming, valuing activity can persons find meaning. But values are not private or limited to society. Written in the heart of reality are moral patterns that are universal and available to all persons. By grasping these moral values, a person can integrate them into her life, thereby finding the meaning that is otherwise so elusive. Given this two-tiered universe, science can be taught and practiced and young people can develop lives good to live guided by the moral commandments of God.

In the meantime, under the impact of the failing economic institutions in the late 1920s and early 1930s, Theodore Brameld modified Dewey's educational philosophy. Dewey emphasized method almost to the exclusion of ends, but Brameld emphasized both method and ends toward which society should move. Brameld believed that the social sciences ought to be employed in the attempt to understand the culture, what its problems are, and the ends society desires.

Mid-twentieth to early twenty-first century

Fissures in the liberal protestant consensus began to appear during World War II, and manifested themselves in the central institutions of American society. Women, needed in the factories to produce the war machine, sought equal opportunity in the workplace alongside men. Afrikan Americans, historically subjugated to an inferior role in America and lacking educational opportunity and political enfranchisement, challenged the establishment in the 1954 case of Brown vs Board of Education. As the Johnson administration led the American people into an unpopular war in Southeast Asia, many lost confidence in the American political, governmental system. In 1969 Woodstock and its rejection of family, sexual, hierarchical, political institutions represented to many educators the failures of American education. All traditional metaphysical views from Platonic Idealism, to Deweyan naturalism, to the Idealism of Spirit, to the liberal protestant consensus were exhausted in their failure to provide orientation for American education.

In response to the exhaustion of traditional conceptions of education, several others arose. They are existentialism, analytic philosophy, and postmodernism. Existentialist philosophers are concerned with the social impact of technology during the twentieth century, the breakdown of values on which Western society tends to construct itself, and the loss of meaning that persons experience in their attempt to cope with their social and physical environment. Contemporary American culture is permeated with the belief that, by using the scientific method or some refinement of it, everything about persons can be understood. Persons are reasoners and need only to think correctly about their experiences to understand their meaning. With an understanding of technology and know-how, persons can find ways to make, build, and create a better world. Unfortunately, in the process of creating this technological utopia, persons are often viewed as things to be manipulated, gadgets to be used both individually and collectively. In reaction existentialists raised a group of significant questions and employ diverse methods in dealing with those questions. What does it mean to exist in society? What is truth? Is truth exhausted by the rational, objective kind of truth that the scientist knows, or is there also a personal, subjective kind which those in love know? If persons are always persons-in-relation, what is the nature of interpersonal relationships? Where and how, if at all, is meaning to be found and achieved? In the learning process, what are the conditions for the possibility of acquiring knowledge and behaving appropriately? Thinkers who contributed to this orientation are Scheler, Sartre, Heidegger, Merleau-Ponty, Marcel, and Buber.

Also during the twentieth century Analytic Philosophy was formulated and deeply influenced educators. Though it rested deep in British empiricism, this movement began with the work of Bertrand Russell (1872–1969), and developed under G.E. Moore and Ludwig Wittgenstein. In his early philosophy, the *Tractatus*, Wittgenstein believed that philosophy shows how the elements of the mind and the elements of matter can be analyzed into terms and mathematical relations.

However, in his *Philosophical Investigations*, Wittgenstein rejected the formal, logical approach of the *Tractatus* and adopted the ordinary-language approach. Language is a social phenomenon, a tool that persons have in common and that is used in every area of their cultural experience. There are no universal rules of language, no universal characteristic that all language has in common. The role of the philosopher of education, for example, is to seek clarity through analysis of language; they do not propose solutions to educational questions.

Some philosophers influenced by ordinary-language philosophy contend that persons not only use language but also through the educational processes set up by society persons learn to work toward goals. As decisions are made regarding the ends toward which students ought to be educated, those decisions are susceptible to being made on grounds that are indefensible. Therefore, philosophers must articulate goals toward which men and society ought to be educated and the grounds on which those goals can be justified. Clarification of language, of meaning, is important in this process, but more is required. Philosophers must be willing to propose and support how persons ought to be educated.

Influenced by positivism, existentialism, language analysis, and multiculturalism, educators turned to psychology, technology, to postmodernism. After *Sputnik* in 1959, psychologists sought ways to accelerate learning in the sciences and mathematics. Utilizing the learning theory of B.F. Skinner, they manipulated the environments of students to aid their learning. The expansion of technology into education was prompted by student uprisings in early 1970s; educators were asked to justify the money spent on education during the cold war. They did so by appealing to measurable, quantifiable outcomes. Learning must be evaluated on its outcomes using technological means. In addition, postmodernism developed along with the failure of the grand philosophical systems. Truth is in trouble. Whatever view of truth one holds is filtered through the spectrum of one's own historical, institutional, cultural, gender lens. Truth, reality, knowledge are all constructions, and no construction can claim superiority over any other.

Though some claim that postmodernism dominates American culture, it can equally be claimed that techno-managerial thinking has supplanted metaphysical thinking as the dominant, controlling "world view." For the curriculum of any school, those subjects that benefit business, government, and society should be taught. Furthermore, teaching outcomes can be tested and verified objectively, that is "scientifically."

Facing deep cultural changes in America, two different educational strategies developed early in the twentieth century remain viable. The first is essentialism, developed by William C. Bagley in the 1930s, best known now as the Back to Basics Movement. These studies are encouraged because of their centrality to Western understanding of the world, of society, and human flourishing. The essentialist contends that students must incorporate into their lives stabilizers provided by the culture itself, its past and present traditions and institutions. Only the time-tested content, the orderly sequence, the inherited principles, the guided discipline essential to one's culture will give one a stable way of life from which to confront the problems of a crisis culture. Reading, writing, mathematics, and the sciences are crucial for any person in any age. The philosophers who significantly contributed to the formation of the essentialist position are Plato, Edmund Burke, Bagley, Michael Polanyi, and Michael Oakshott.

A second strategy was an appeal to the return to the eternal truths and spiritual life of classical civilization. Espoused and encouraged by some religious educators, this was a rebirth of Platonism, Aristotle, and Christian theology. With this revival some educators such as Mortimer Adler and Robert M. Hutchins answer postmodernism, deflating the conflict between modernity and post-modernity. A general education is best achieved through a return to the Great Books of Western Civilization.

Thus the central conceptions guiding education range from the metaphysics of Idealism, Naturalism, and Process. As the twenty-first century begins, postmodernism and techno-managerial thinking dominate educational life in America. Will a new conception of education arise? It may, and it if does it will emphasizes the flourishing of persons in community. Both differences in perspective and in technology will be subordinated to and find their place within this new emphasis on personal categories.

Further reading

Adler, Mortimer J. *The Paideia Proposal*. New York: Macmillan, 1982.

Archambault, Reginald D. (ed.) *Philosophical Analysis and Education*. New York: Humanities Press, 1965.

Bagley, William C. *Education and Emergent Man*. New York: T. Nelson and Sons, 1934.

Brameld, Theodore T.B.H. *Toward a Reconstructed Philosophy of Education*. New York: Holt, Rinehart, and Winston, 1956.

Dewey, John. *Democracy and Education*. New York: Macmillan, 1926.

Hutchins, Robert M. *The Higher Learning in America*. New Haven, CT: Yale University Press, 1936.

Lovejoy, A.O. *The Great Chain of Being*. Cambridge, MA: Harvard University Press, 1936.

Marsden, George, and Longfield, Bradley J. (eds) *The Secularization of the Academy*. New York: Oxford University, 1992.

Piaget, Jean. *Genetic Epistemology*. New York: Columbia University Press, 1970.

Skinner, B.F. *Science and Human Behavior*. New York: Free Press, 1965.

Vygotsky, L. *Mind in Society*. Cambridge, MA: Harvard University Press, 1978.

Whitehead, A.N. *The Aims of Education*. New York: New American Library of World Literature, 1961.

Thomas O. Buford

EDUCATION, INFLUENCE OF PRAGMATISM ON

Societies reproduce themselves in two ways, biologically and culturally. Education is the name we give the activity of cultural reproduction. It is ubiquitous and inevitable, while formal schooling is not. Pragmatism is a very contextualized philosophy; to evaluate its influence on education requires locating its reproductive social context. Pragmatism is an "American" philosophy, so America is its proper context. We must, however, distinguish at least three kinds of America. The first is associated with Western modernity, which is perhaps most completely realized in the United States, while the second rejects modernity altogether. The last is largely an ideal whose time may never come in the United States of America. Pragmatism more or less opposes the first two and supports the third.

Modern liberal America assumes an atomistic individual born with innate rationality and free will existing apart from the body or material context. It assumes rationality is the fixed essence of "Man." It is utilitarian (hence calculative) when exercised in the capitalistic market place. Freedom demands we follow the dictates of reason, which provides privileged access to the ultimate foundations of infallible laws. Public institutions only arise from social contracts among otherwise isolated individuals. Religious modernity in America assumes an immortal soul and a heavenly source for certainty, but emphasizes rational knowledge of God's design. In such a society, the aim of education is to instruct reason to make wise choices according to immutably true laws.

Evangelical America follows religious traditions that precede the Age of Enlightenment that is the source of liberal America as we find it in the nation's constituting documents. It emphasizes the immortality of the soul and heavenly foundations for intuitively indubitable knowledge. It stresses community along with individuality and obedience to God's laws for the sake of salvation. Liberal evangelicals have played a prominent role in the quest for social justice as they seek the kingdom of heaven on earth, while conservative evangelicals often emphasize resignation to worldly suffering for heavenly reward. The aim of education in such a society is salvation through right direction of free will.

The third America not only endorses the nation's revolution, but also thinks the age of revolution, or revelation, will never pass. This is the America envisioned by Ralph Waldo Emerson when he gave the young nation its educational declaration of independence in his essay "The American Scholar." For such Americans, existence is congenial to the moral, aesthetic, and cognitive hopes of revolutionary minds. The universe is still incomplete and in flux, and, hence, cooperates with our creative efforts to redirect its course. This America calls on all peoples of every nation at any time to boldly continue the endless task of moral amelioration through intelligent inquiry. In such a society, the aim of education is to cultivate poetic meaning-makers in science, arts, and ethics.

Pragmatism is liberal in its commitment to intelligent inquiry as the key to freedom and is evangelical in its devotion to social justice and democratic community. The ideas forming pragmatism do not require strict adherence, but most pragmatists agree we live in a contingent, pluralistic universe without fixed foundations or absolute beginnings or endings. Pragmatists tend to think all essences, including the essence of rationality, human "nature," and will, are evolving and risk extinction. They are committed to the idea of a social created self that requires nurturance in caring and critical democratic community. Pragmatists are usually fallibilist; for them all knowledge claims are interpretative and subject to change. Above all, the preponderance of pragmatists are committed to working out meaning, truth, and value through their emergent consequences over time in a community of inquiry. In a pragmatist society, the aim of education is more education. Pragmatism is compatible with Emerson's America. The influence of pragmatism on American education, like the influence of pragmatism on America philosophy, remains outside the mainstream.

Pragmatism's founder, Charles Sanders Peirce (1887–8/1992) said little about education. For him learning was the mark of reason. His belief that the physiological basis of learning is embodied habits has been immensely influential (264). William James and John Dewey emphasize the importance of habits in education. Dewey identifies the mind and self with individual dispositions to act. For such pragmatists, to have a mind is to participate in the social practices of a culture; multicultural education, for example, implies participating in the practices of more than one culture. Pragmatism's emphasis on the importance of bodily habits and activity in learning contravenes modern liberalism and evangelicalism.

Jane Addams is often overlooked in the pragmatist pantheon, yet she is one of its most original thinkers and inspiring educators. Her work at Hull House (founded 1889) gives her philosophy a practical and problem-centered quality other pragmatists only talk about. "Within Addams's philosophy," Ellen Condliffe Lagemann writes, "three convictions were central." The first is the "importance of 'community' for life in a democratic society" (Addams 1994: ix). Second, Addams thought settlement work not only ameliorated the conditions of the oppressed, but also, reciprocally, benefited the privileged by offering opportunities to learn from those they sought to help in a pluralistic community of inquiry. Finally, being located in a diverse immigrant neighborhood, Hull House was "something of an open university where a constant flow of talk about politics, ideas, public events, art, philosophy, and the immediate problems of a destitute family or a gang of neighborhood boys provided constantly evolving and lived meaning to such abstract concepts as citizenship, culture, assimilation, and education" (ibid.: x). It was a place of active social experimentation that nurtured the diverse personalities' democratic participation demands. It is a model of an educational institution, perhaps unmatched in American history.

In *Talks To Teachers*, James (1899/1958) discusses his functionalism so dominant in American psychology, including educational psychology. He also emphasizes "democratic respect for the sacredness of individuality" in a "pluralistic" universe. Some of the chapter titles are: "The Child as a Behaving Organism," "The Laws of Habit," and "Interest." An essay included in the book pursues the theme of tolerance with an Emerson-inspired argument for the cultivation of creative individual differences in thought, feeling, and action as a democratic educational ideal. Another essay insists: "To recognize ideal novelty is the task of what we call intelligence" (ibid.: 187). For the liberal modernist, everyone is born with the same rational faculty, so if they exercise it correctly, everyone must act the same. James's version of intelligent functioning yields unique individuals compelled to acts of novel creativity as they make their contribution to the larger community in an unfinished and unfinishable creation.

Dewey is the leading American philosopher of education and the most influential educator in the history of the United States after Horace Mann who is the founder of the common school movement that defined America's public schools, which remain a bastion of liberal modernism. Many regard Dewey as inspiring the social justice strand of progressive education that emphasizes reflective, critical, and creative democratic citizenship; the importance of individual development, students' needs, interests and desires; the social construction of learning and knowing; and the school as a site of social reconstruction. Dewey gives the Emersonian answer to the perennial educational question: what is the aim of education? "Since growth is the characteristic of life, education is all one with growing; it has no end beyond itself" (1916/1980: 58). The capacity to cultivate growth is, for Dewey, the criterion for evaluating the quality of any educational program.

We have discussed education in American society, but we must address schooling in American society. Historians of education David Tyack and Larry Cuban remark that the common school movement relied on "a pervasive Protestant-republican ideology that held that proper education could . . . make the United States . . . God's country" (1995: 16). Further, "In the Progressive era . . . this evangelical enthusiasm became merged with a second faith . . . that a newly discovered 'science' of education provided the precise tools needed to guide the course of social evolution" (ibid.). It is important to distinguish social efficiency progressivism from social justice progressivism. Social efficiency progressives have an evangelical faith in scientism as capable of discerning the eternal laws of teaching and learning dictated by nature or the God of nature. Meanwhile pragmatists emphasize creative intelligence as a response to a Darwinian world. They seek a planning not a planned society. Social efficiency progressivism remains the prevailing force in the shaping of American public schools, though social justice alternatives play throughout the system.

In education, pragmatism's influence fluctuates with the fortunes of social justice progressivism. Today, pragmatist ideals serve as an alternative democratic voice to market-oriented education emphasizing the refinement of human resources as capital for the global production function. "Cooperate America" has become a global idea having little to do with national borders. We may say the same for "American" pragmatism. The context for evaluating the influence of pragmatism is expanding; what that means for the future influence of pragmatism on education involves consequences without borders.

Further reading

Addams, Jane. *On Education: Jane Addams*, ed. Ellen Condliffe Lagemann. New Brunswick, NJ: Transaction, 1994.

Dewey, John. *The School and Society* in *John Dewey: The Middle Works*, Vol. 1, ed. Jo Ann Boydston. Carbondale, IL: Southern Illinois University Press, 1976 [1899], pp. 1–109.

—— "The Child and the Curriculum" in *John Dewey: The Middle Works*, Vol. 2, ed. Jo Ann Boydston. Carbondale, IL: Southern Illinois University Press, 1976 [1902], pp. 271–91.

—— *Democracy and Education* in *John Dewey: The Middle Works*, Vol. 9, ed. Jo Ann Boydston. Carbondale, IL: Southern Illinois University Press, 1980 [1916].

—— "Experience and Education" in *John Dewey: The Later Works*, Vol. 13, ed. Jo Ann Boydston. Carbondale, IL: Southern Illinois University Press, 1988 [1938], pp. 1–62.

Emerson, Ralph Waldo. " The American Scholar" in *Ralph Waldo Emerson: Selected Essays*. New York: Penguin, 1985 [1837], pp. 83–105.

James, William. *Talks To Teachers*. New York: W.W. Norton, 1958 [1899].

Peirce, Charles S. "A Guess at the Riddle" in *The Essential Peirce*, Vol. 1, ed. N. Houser and C. Kloesel. Bloomington, IN: Indiana University Press, 1992 [1887], pp. 245–79.

Tyack, David and Cuban, Larry (1995). *Tinkering Toward Utopia: A Century of Public School Reform*. Cambridge, MA: Harvard University Press.

JAMES GARRISON

EDWARDS, JONATHAN

Born in East Windsor, Connecticut, to Timothy and Esther Edwards, Jonathan Edwards (1703–58) was the only son of eleven children. He was educated by his father in classics and theology and entered college in 1716 (later Yale). Valedictorian of his class in 1720, he remained at college to read for an MA in theology. A spiritual breakthrough at this time resolved his disquiet with the doctrine of God's sovereignty in relation to the eternal judgment of some souls and led him to formulate his most characteristic and profound insights into God's character and relationship to the universe. From 1722 he pastored briefly in New York and at Bolton before accepting a position as Senior Tutor at Yale in 1724. He began his long tenure in Northampton as the assistant to his maternal grandfather Solomon Stoddard in 1727, the same year he married Sarah Pierpont. Following Stoddard's death in 1729, Edwards began a distinguished preaching career including "A History of the Work of Redemption" and "Charity and its Fruits." A significant communal revival occurred in 1734–5 in Northampton and the Connecticut Valley, popularized internationally by Edwards's "A Faithful Narrative." Evangelist George Whitefield's visit in 1740 sparked the Great Awakening. Edwards reflected on this spiritual event in *Distinguishing Marks of the Work of the Spirit of God* (1741) and *Some Thoughts Concerning the Present Revival* (1742), precipitating his most widely recognized work, *Religious Affections*, published in 1746. In 1748 David Brainerd returned to Edwards's home deathly ill from his missionary travels and died, along with Edwards' daughter Jerusha who nursed him. Edwards edited and published Brainerd's diary which deeply influenced the modern missionary movement. Edwards was dismissed by his congregation in 1750 over disagreements concerning church membership and communion, and he removed his family to the Indian outpost Stockbridge in 1751. Between 1754 and 1758 he wrote and published *Freedom of the Will*, *The End for Which God Created the World*, *The Nature of True Virtue*, and *Original Sin*. Edwards was installed as President of the College of New Jersey (later Princeton) and died that same year, along with his eldest daughter, from a corrupted smallpox inoculation.

Edwards is characterized by his wide-ranging intellect, penetrating analysis, and philosophical power. He considered himself a biblical exegete, and all of his writings save *The Nature of True Virtue* are explicitly connected to correctly applying scripture to theological, philosophical, and experiential questions. His constructive criticism of Calvinist orthodoxy incorporated his idealism (sometimes associated with Berkeley) and dispositional ontology (Lee) to Locke's psychology. Edwards's ambitious plan to produce a comprehensive apology for the Christian religion by encountering the primary religious–intellectual challenges (McDermott) was somewhat limited by his premature death. His influence in the development of American Christianity, theology and philosophy is witnessed by the influence on his contemporaries Samuel Hopkins and Nathaniel Emmons, and controversies between luminaries such as Edwards A. Park and Charles Hodge. Perry Miller's study of the Puritans and Edwards helped ignite the massive volume and high caliber of devotional and scholarly work related to his life and writings, which continue to be debated and published.

Further reading

Cherry, Conrad. *The Theology of Jonathan Edwards: A Reappraisal*. Bloomington, IN: Indiana University Press, 1990.

Edwards, Jonathan. *The Works of Jonathan Edwards*, 23 vols. New Haven, CT: Yale University Press, 1957–2003.

Lee, Sang-Hyung. *The Philosophical Theology of Jonathan Edwards*. Princeton, NJ: Princeton University Press, 1988.

McDermott, Gerald, R. *Jonathan Edwards Confronts the Gods*. Oxford: Oxford University Press, 2000.

Marsden, George M. *Jonathan Edwards: A Life*. New Haven, CT: Yale University Press, 2003.

Roger A. Ward

EGO

The *ego* (Latin for "I," the first-person, singular pronoun) is ordinarily a term associated with the psychoanalytic analysis of the structure of the human psyche, though it is a misleading translation into English of Sigmund Freud's use of the informal, everyday *das Ich* (Bettelheim). In this sense, the term derives its meaning largely through its contrast to the id (or *das Id*) and the superego (*das Über-Ich,* i.e. the over-I or above-I). As its name suggests, the "it" is the vast, impersonal, and irrational region of the psyche completely under the sway of the pleasure principle (a region roughly comparable to what Plato identifies as the appetitive or desiring part of the soul). The "I" is in contrast allied with rationality and, moreover, the "agency" by which the reality principle influences human conduct.

More generally, however, the term *ego* is often used simply as a synonym for the "I" or self, with the emphasis on the active and even creative dimensions of the self (the individual self as an active being capably of truly innovative responses to both familiar and unusual situations). Specifically in reference to American philosophy, the ego (especially when identified with the "I") figures most prominently in the writings of William James and George Herbert Mead. Here it is conceived in an empirical and naturalistic manner. In intimate association with both Immanuel Kant's transcendental idealism and post-Kantian forms of the idealism approach, however, Josiah Royce defends the transcendental ego against such champions of the empirical ego as James, who is committed to eradicating the last vestiges of a supra-empirical self. Chapter X ("The Consciousness of Self") of James's *Principles of Psychology* is the *locus classicus* of the ego or "I" in its distinctively America register. Whereas the Freudian meaning of "I" derives principally from its contrast to the *it* and the *over-I,* also from the functions assigned by psychoanalysts to this part of the psyche (above all, the functions of mediating between the it and reality, also between the inchoate but tyrannical drives of the it and the internalized yet often punitive demands of the over-I), the Jamesian use of this word acquires its meaning mainly from the implicit contrast between "I" and "you" and the explicit one between "I" and "me." One of the defining characteristics of the stream of thought or consciousness (indeed, the first one James notes) is the feature of every psychic state or activity being "part of a personal consciousness." Though he will come to modify, if not abandon, this position in such later works as *A Pluralistic Universe* and *Essays on Radical Empiricism*, James in the *Principles* asserts: "It seems as if the elementary psychic fact were not *thought* or *this thought* or *that thought,* but *my thought,* every thought being owned" (226).

These American thinkers offered their accounts of the ego or "I" mainly against the background of Western thought, though James, Royce, Santayana and others were attentive to central doctrines in Eastern thought. Each one is either reacting to or drawing upon several of the most prominent traditions or figures in Western culture: the divergent perspectives on the human psyche articulated by Plato and Aristotle; the medieval attempt, following the definition of the person crafted by Boethius, to explain the human self as an individual *substance* of a rational nature; Descartes's appeal to the cognitive activity of the self as the indubitable foundation of all knowledge; Hume's dissolution of the self into a bundle of perceptions; Kant's insistence upon the ego as a transcendental condition of all possible experience; Hegel's elevation of the principle of subjectivity to the level of the Absolute; and Darwin's evolutionary explanation of the origin and nature of human life.

One trajectory is that of a thoroughgoing naturalism in which the "I" is, in one sense, an emergent function (the capacity of the embodied, active self to identify itself vis-à-vis others, to position itself as an "I" in relation to other selves) and, in another sense, the human organism itself. With his characteristic eloquence, Santayana represents this trajectory: "I, if I exist, am not an idea, nor am I the fact that several ideas many exist, one which remembers the other. *If I exist, I am a living creature* to whom ideas are incidents" (emphasis added). The self "slumbers and breathes below [the ideas so captivating to consciousness], a mysterious natural organism, full of dark yet definite potentialities; so that different events will awake it to quite disproportionate activities" (*Scepticism and Animal Faith* 149). Dewey also represents this trajectory:

> from the standpoint of a biological–cultural psychology the term "subject" (and related adjectival forms) has only the signification of a certain kind of actual existence; namely, a living creature [or organism] which under the influence of language and other cultural agencies has become a person interacting with other persons (concrete human beings).
>
> (LW 14.39)

If we take the human organism insofar as it has acquired a more or less integrated array of distinctive functions (including markedly reflexive functions such as self-criticism, self-reproach, and self-affirmation) to be the "proper *designatum*" of the term "I," *ego, self, subject*, or a number of rough equivalents, then we must take these words to refer "to an *agency of doing,* not to a knower, mind, consciousness or whatever" (LW 14.27).

Another trajectory is, however, a deep dissatisfaction with the apparent reductivism entailed by thoroughgoing naturalism. This can be seen in such critics of Dewey as John E. Smith and a number of authors ordinarily identified with personalism. For such thinkers, the self is an irreducible category and this means that all attempts to reduce the "I" to the organism explain away, rather than explain, the relevant phenomena.

The dependence of the ego (or "I") on the community or distinctive forms of human association (the "we") inclined such philosophers as Peirce, Royce, Dewey, and Mead to stress the social character of the individual self, so much so that their critics suppose that the private self is reduced to its social functions (e.g. Santayana, Hanson). But, the capacity of individual agents to dissociate themselves from virtually any actual community, moreover their ability to carry on an "internal conversation" (see, e.g., Colapietro, also Archer), themselves need to be seen as ones having their roots in the enculturation and socialization of individuals.

The treatment of the ego or "I" by James, Royce, Santayana, Dewey, Mead and other American authors invites comparison with central developments within Continental European philosophy, most notably Martin Heidegger's conception of *Dasein*, Jean-Paul Sartre's transcendence of the ego, Maurice Merleau-Ponty's phenomenological reclamation of the lived body, and (more recently) the decentering of the subject associated with such thinkers as Jacques Lacan, Michel Foucault, and Jacques Derrida. In addition, this treatment invites comparison with a variety of feminist approaches to subjectivity, e.g. Simone de Beauvoir, Julia Kristeva, and Judith Butler. Finally, the conception of the self that is implicit in the writings of the later Wittgenstein and developed by such analytic philosophers as Gilbert Ryle, Anthony Kenny, and numerous others in this philosophical tradition exhibits striking affinities as well as critical differences to conceptions defended by the American authors discussed here.

VINCENT COLAPIETRO

EITHER/OR FALLACY

The Either/Or Fallacy (aka False Dilemma) rides on a dubious premise rather than ambiguous language, irrelevant factors, or a formally invalid inference, and often exploits formally valid argument forms. It generally uses an argument, one premise of which is a disjunction of two options illegitimately set forth as the only two pertinent to an issue. For example, opponents characterized the 1982 US federal budget as a "choice between weapons and crippled children," and sought to persuade voters that the President favored weapons at the expense of sympathetic innocents. For this argument to be sound, the two options must be the only two available, and the disjunction exclusive rather than inclusive. However, federal budgets typically include both items and more.

The force of the fallacy derives from its use of valid argument forms; e.g. either constructive or destructive dilemmas, or disjunctive syllogism. Those who deliberately use the fallacy count on its formal validity to conceal the fact that it is unsound, for it misrepresents its disjunctive premise as exhausting the available options when there may be more. In some cases, the fallacy is used maliciously to suppress evidence, while in others it is a mistake based on ignorance of the alternatives or an oversimplification of an issue. In formal terms, the fallacy confuses contrary for contradictory propositions. This, of course, is not to say that only disjunctions of contradictories are legitimate; for the disjunction of contradictories is a tautology, and little of empirical significance usually follows from tautologies. It also is useful to note that since disjunctions and conditional propositions are logically equivalent, the questionable premise might appear as a conditional proposition. Thus, one should not assume from the absence of an explicitly disjunctive premise that a suspicious argument is not an instance of this fallacy. Finally, we should note that the fallacy rests on a misuse of the law of excluded middle. It would be mistaken, therefore, to suppose that we must reject that law to avoid the Either/Or Fallacy. Rather, what is required is a closer observance of the law of excluded middle.

American philosophy lays no special claim to the discovery of this fallacy, but it has been particularly keen on detecting and avoiding it. The writings of William James and John Dewey give ample evidence of this; e.g. James's neutral monism is an attempt to circumvent mind/body dualism and thus avoid the dilemma of choosing between materialism and idealism. The most important argument by an American philosopher against an allegedly false dichotomy is Quine's argument that the assumption that all propositions are either analytic or synthetic is an "ill-founded" dogma. If Quine is right, then the analytic/synthetic distinction, reductionism and the bifurcation between science and philosophy are instances of the Either/Or Fallacy.

Other common labels for this fallacy and its relatives are All or Nothing Fallacy (Fearnside and Holter), False Opposition, False Disjunction (Cohen and Nagel), False Dichotomous Questions (Fischer), and Bifurcation (Engel).

Further reading

Cohen, Morris R. and Nagel, Ernest. *An Introduction to Logic and Scientific Method*. New York: Harcourt, Brace and World, 1936, pp. 384–8.

Dewey, John. *Logic: The Theory of Inquiry*. New York: Irvington, reprint 1982, Ch. 10.

Engel, S. Morris. *With Good Reason*. New York: Bedford/St Martin's Press, 1999.

Fearnside, W. Ward and Holter, William B. *Fallacy: The Counterfeit Argument*. Englewood Cliffs, NJ: Prentice Hall, 1959, pp. 30–3.

Fischer, David Hackett. *Historians' Fallacies: Toward a Logic of Historical Thought*. New York: Harper and Row, 1970. pp. 9–12.

Hamblin, C.L. *Fallacies*. London: Methuen, 1970, pp. 45–6.

James, William. "The Notion of Consciousness" in *Essays in Radical Empiricism*. Cambridge, MA: Harvard University Press, 1976, pp. 268–71.

Kirby, Gary R. and Goodpaster, Jeffery R. *Thinking*, second edition. Upper Saddle River, NJ: Prentice Hall, 1999, pp. 172–3.

Quine, W.V.O. "Two Dogmas of Empiricism" in *From a Logical Point of View*. New York: Harper and Row, 1963, pp. 20–46.

GARY L. CESARZ

ELIOT, T.S.

Among the twentieth-century American poets and critics, Thomas Stearns Eliot (1888–1965) is the most self-consciously philosophical. Eliot studied under Royce at Harvard, who introduced him to idealism and the idea of community. Although he never completed his doctoral studies, he read deeply and wrote a dissertation on F.H. Bradley, who taught him that reality is an Absolute unified whole, composed of Appearance, which is dissected and interpreted by the mind; hence the world as we experience it. Bradley's, however, was not a dogmatic metaphysics; rather it was skeptical in the sense that it emphasized that the world was constructed by the mind, an essentially practical construction, which suggested an indefinite number of points of view. Eliot also found support for his own developing ideas in the works of Bergson and Russell.

Much of what drives Eliot's poetry from "The Hollow Men" to "The Wasteland" to the later *Four Quartets* is the desire to achieve a sense of unity, a sense of the immediacy of experience, that mystical sense by which through feeling one understands, that mystical moment in which the many and the one are one and the same. It is the poet's job to find an "objective correlative," the emotional equivalence of thought; that is what Dante and Shakespeare insisted upon. The function of poetry is both to give sensuous and emotional body to ideas and to make us see the world in new ways, in a sense to marry the present and the eternal. In order for the poet to express the full quality of the moment as it actually feels, he must seek rhythms implicit in human physiology, the rituals to which human beings have danced, the myths which inspired the primitive mind and still nourish modern consciousness. Hence Eliot is drawn to the works of Cornford, Frazer, Durkheim, and Levy-Bruhl, and, of course, more and more to the teachings of Christianity. Although it is questionable as to whether Eliot literally believed in Christian dogma, it is clear that he believed in the underlying structure of dogma, which expressed truths about human nature and perhaps the universe as well.

Poetry for Eliot is philosophical work, metaphysical and epistemological inquiry. The poet, although he occupies a specific place in history, acts, due to his knowledge and sensitivity to history, as an impersonal agent of literary and cultural tradition, much in the same way as the Homeric poet acted as a vehicle for the muses. In a related sense, the same is true of the critic. For Eliot, poetry and criticism were mutually illuminating. One might also argue that while Eliot's criticism clearly helped to support the movement of modern poetry, it was blatantly self-serving, as well. Early in Eliot's career tradition inspired and fed his poetic and critical endeavor. Later in his career, however, what was once the basis of experimentation turned into the fixed and immovable ground of a sterile morality.

Throughout his life, Eliot thought of poetry as both philosophical and dramatic. Plays such as *Murder in the Cathedral* and *The Cocktail Party* attempt to create a ritualistic drama that embodies all the elements of poetry, philosophy, and drama. Some critics have argued that Eliot never fully attained this lofty ideal.

Further reading

Eliot, T.S. *The Complete Poems and Plays*, New York: Harcourt, Brace, and World, 1952.

Gardner, Helen. *The Art of T.S. Eliot*. New York: E.P. Dutton, 1959.

Matthiessen, F.O. *The Achievement of T.S. Eliot: An Essay on the Nature of Poetry*. New York: Oxford University Press, 1959.

Moody, A. David (ed.) *The Cambridge Companion to T.S. Eliot*. Cambridge: Cambridge University Press, 1994.

CHRISTOPHER PERRICONE

EMERSON, RALPH WALDO

Ralph Waldo Emerson (1803–82) was born in Boston to a respectable but impoverished family. Having trained for the Unitarian ministry, he resigned his pulpit amidst a spiritual crisis in 1832. He toured Europe, where he met British literati – most importantly Samuel Taylor Coleridge and Thomas Carlyle – and upon his return to Boston, Emerson began a highly successful career as a public intellectual. The most prominent lecturer and essayist of his era, he presided over what has been aptly termed the American Renaissance (Matthiessen 1941).

Emerson is widely regarded as the chief expositor of New England Transcendentalism, but his influence extended well beyond that small circle of intellectuals to occupy a unique position in nineteenth-century American letters. Beyond his influence on Henry David Thoreau, Margaret Fuller, Nathaniel Hawthorn, Walt Whitman, Herman Melville and other literary figures (Packer 1982), not to speak of his profound impact on the course of American philosophy in the voice of pragmatism (Goodman 1990), Emerson finds a place in wider Western philosophy as he inspired Friedrich Nietzsche (Stack 1992) and later environmentalists.

Despite renewed attention to his philosophy (Buell 2003; Cavell 2003), Emerson worked during a "pre-philosophical" moment in American history, and he is rarely placed within the philosophical tradition. His thought was hardly systematic and lacks any singular conceptual schema, as he drew variously from neo-Platonism (especially Plotinus), Vedanticism, German–Coleridgean idealism, and Unitarianism. The resulting philosophy was then combined with selective elements of political heterodoxy in the guise of radical individualism. (Richardson 1995; Versluis 1993). In short, Emerson's philosophy cannot be neatly summarized.

Emerson's most important essays were published between 1836 and 1844. Beginning with *Nature* (1836), the Transcendentalist manifesto, he soon followed with "The American Scholar" (1837) – what Oliver Wendell Holmes called "our Intellectual Declaration of Independence." During this intense period, Emerson inaugurated the Transcendental journal, *The Dial*, with Fuller, and published two collections of essays – the *Essays, First Series* in 1841 and the *Essays, Second Series* in 1844. Less well-appreciated works include *Poems* (1846), *Representative Men* (1850), *English Traits* (1856), and *Conduct of Life* (1860).

While active in the abolitionist movement of the 1850s, Emerson resided most comfortably in the role of seer and mentor as he lectured widely on social and moral issues. Reformists, ranging from utopian farmers to abolitionist activists, sought to enlist him, but his proclivity for privacy left him largely peripheral to the political actions of his volatile period. Instead, he sought to establish a unique American philosophy, one centered on the freedom of the individual and the potential of self-perfection.

Dominated by an eclipsing religiosity, Emerson was preoccupied with establishing new criteria for moral conduct and outlining the precepts for citizenship in an evolving democracy that had no precedence and no European guidance. Espousing idealism, he still advocated personal action and commitment; championing the individual, he steadfastly remained committed to communal responsibility. He encouraged the full play of the creative energies of an emerging nation, whose manifest destiny was hardly obvious to him, or his radical Concord coterie.

In many respects, acknowledging important differences, Thoreau enacted, under the guise of natural history, Emerson's philosophy more clearly than his mentor's writings, which revolve around the central problem of defining the character of the individual and her placement in a bewildering universe (Steele 1987; Tauber 2001). Emerson's transcendentalism unifies the themes, which structure his thought, first as a foundation for his spirituality and then as a framework for his selfhood. We begin with his renewed search for the divine.

In pursuit of the divine

Emerson's *Nature*, originally published anonymously, represents his emergence as a mature thinker. This long essay outlines the key transcendental precepts of man's relation to nature, and herein lies a metaphysical statement from which virtually all of his later work may be traced (Duncan 1973). The questions that informed his early development as a preacher reappeared in only somewhat different form in his avatar as a secular essayist. Simply, he wrote in the throes of a religious crisis, and his philosophy is permeated with religious questions.

For Emerson, like so many of his romantic contemporaries, Nature was, in effect, the necessary expression of the divine. He conceived the universe as composed of soul, or spirit, and nature. Profoundly influenced by Coleridge's pantheism and romantic notions of the sublime, Spirit is life itself, a projection of God, that is *natura naturans.* This creative life force in nature sustains and reproduces life, indeed, spirit is transformed according to physical laws, and projected into matter, as *natura naturata.* Both the activity of natural forms and the laws of their activity perfectly express the supreme mind, and thus Emerson rejects materialism and seeks a form of idealism. Although Emerson distrusted sense impressions, he could not accept his own suggestion that perhaps nature is simply an "apocalypse of the mind." In fact, in adopting a Kantian perspective, Emerson held that nature is a phenomenon, an object of experience.

For Emerson, experience has a spiritual bias, and the divine presence reveals itself by the order and sublimity discerned by human's appreciation of the natural world. Emerson essentially asserts a teleological natural religion, where nature exists not for its own sake but as a means to an end: "It is the organ through which the universal spirit speaks to the individual, and strives to lead back the individual to it." This entire enterprise is designed to "emancipate us." At root, Emerson is still preaching, to free his brethren not from sin but from spiritual isolation. Nature, if properly engaged, becomes the means to personal salvation, the encounter by which meaning and significance emerges.

Accordingly, he claimed that spirit fulfills an existential function: The role of humans, as knowing creatures, is in effect to articulate Nature's divinity by simply witnessing it. So, by granting primacy to the spirit and at the same time acknowledging the objective reality of the world, Emerson sought to reinstate his displacement with a personal integration, both religious and profane. The spiritual thus seamlessly connects his self-consciousness to a world now rendered whole. This became his central project.

Like Johann Fichte's radical assertion of the knowing I, Emerson places individual consciousness at the center of the universe. Emerson's vision is bifocal: On the one hand he asserts that nature by itself cannot constitute reality, for reality must include – indeed, it may be a function of – consciousness. On the other hand, man equally depends on nature, for without the "not me," he could not become conscious. Emersonian idealism is, broadly speaking, Kantian, where both the world and idea depend upon each other, and indeed, reality is a synthesis of the two, held together by the coherence of the spirit (e.g. "The Over-Soul"). Beyond the reciprocity of nature's dependence on consciousness and Man's dependence on nature to articulate his own consciousness, nature is also the vehicle that permits the universal spirit to address humans. Thus God speaks through Nature to Man.

And how does Nature speak? Through correspondence. Natural phenomena are the symbols of the spirit, for in itself, nature is "deaf and dumb." But as symbol, nature provides a language by which humans might gain, through correspondence, insight, meaning, and signification. The distinctly romantic construction appears in the sublimity of individualized experience, the acute sensitivity of the beholder, and the creative sophistication of his or her "reading" of nature. The attained insight thus depends on human imagination and effort. When Emerson ended *Nature* with the proclamation that each person must create his own world, he meant precisely that. Nature was not redeemed so much as transformed in an ongoing creation of imagination. This vision of the natural world, specifically answering the Emersonian challenge that each must create a unique and profound relationship with nature, serves as the foundation of later environmentalism.

In pursuit of the self

Emerson created a metaphysics which would mend the divide of the self peering *at* the world, and from that foundation he built his moral philosophy. Like other romantic philosophers, he struggled to answer two of Immanuel Kant's basic challenges, namely (1) how to synthesize experience fractured by different rationalities (e.g. positivist, moral, aesthetic, or spiritual subjectivity), and (2) how to formulate moral choice (freedom). In response to the first question, Emerson replaced defining "a self" with the wider effort of mending the fracture of experience. In recognizing the limits of a self-consciousness that ultimately separated the self from the world, he would self-consciously place the self *in* the world by active search for correspondence, relentless introspective analysis, and pursuit of mystical revelry.

The second question led to a focus on individualism, where autonomy and freedom centered on individual responsibility and potential. For Emerson, the "Age of the I" (or as he wrote in his journal, "It is said to be the age of the first person singular") was marked by a keen self-reflection on consciousness, moral agency, and the demands of a newly evolving positivism, which championed a view of the world purged of subjectivity. Such an objective stance would reconfigure the understanding of personal experience, an epistemological issue (van Leer 1986), and the place of individual choice and independence, a moral concern (Taylor 1989). The parameters by which such self-governance might be achieved, and the strictures placed upon achieving that goal, led Emerson to a renewed interest in defining selfhood – its characteristics, its boundaries, its potentials. In that inquiry, self-consciousness itself became an object of his inquiry as it served as one means of capturing the self whether in its social, psychological, moral, or historical modes of discourse. The problem of true knowledge was thereby transformed from the concerns of epistemological skepticism to asking how to configure the moral universe, namely defining the relation of the self with its world – natural and spiritual.

Emerson turned self-consciousness outward to engage the Other in a way quite different from his predecessors, by formulating the self as radically dependent, in one sense, and radically free in another. The dependency on the Other is God (not the social contra Hegel); freedom is exercised by the recognition of that dependency and the acceptance or denial of faith is based on that relationship (and thus individually determined). (This recurrent theme is found in various essays, e.g. "Circles," "Self-Reliance," "Aristocracy," and "Fugitive Slave Law.") Emerson's construction of the self was thus a response to an existential insecurity of self-identity framed by an ethos of individuality (e.g. "Whoso would be a man, must be a non-conformist" ["Self-Reliance"]). What began as a search for the self's inner core, which spurred the reflexive inquiry in the first place, became an attempt to existentially "save" the self. That task became the focus of his ethics, an undertaking further elaborated by twentieth-century existentialists.

Conclusion

Emerson's celebration of a naturalized religion and a philosophical idealism centered on the self, defined himself in relation to nature, where he sought not only evidence of a divine presence but a vehicle of discerning value and meaning for lives secularized and seemingly isolated from, or perhaps deaf to, the spiritual. He is America's leading exponent of the idea that our relationship with nature is deeply personal and meaningful; that nature is intimate to our very being; that in opposition to a materialist conception of nature, we embrace nature as an expression of the spiritual and the aesthetic; and finally, because the sublime is constitutive to nature, an essentially religious sensibility serves as our basic link to Her. Emerson was not the originator of these ideas, but he was their chief American expositor, and his influence remains a potent force in American culture.

Emerson would not remain in the grips of an idealism divorced from the ordinary and the world that demanded action. His admonition to engage the world – one in constant flux and thus requiring unrelieved response – pushes the intellectual to political engagement for social reform. Indeed, the buoyancy of his optimism for freedom of choice and creativity – premised on responsibility, dynamic imagination, and self-perfection – makes him a critical political philosopher. Emerson promoted a unique American republicanism. Resolute in the protection of individual choice, he recognized the powerful demands of the collective, and in following that larger commitment to his community, he offered a political philosophy perched between the protection of individual prerogatives and obligations to others. And that understanding rests on his moral philosophy, one steeped in a Protestant sensibility and a romantic ethos, which asserts the autonomy of the individual and the freedom of choice. Emerson's elaboration of the tremulous balance between individual and state enunciates one of the most nuanced and deepest statements of the American predicament and remains his abiding legacy. Various versions of Emerson's opus are readily available in print and online at http://www.rwe.org/comm/ and http://emersoncentral.com/.

Further reading

Buell, L. *Emerson*. Cambridge, MA: Harvard University Press, 2003.

Burkholder, R.E. and Myerson, J. *Ralph Waldo Emerson: An Annotated Bibliography of Criticism*. Westport, CT: Greenwood Press, 1994.

Cavell, S. *Emerson's Transcendental Etudes*. Palo Alto, CA: Stanford University Press, 2003.

Emerson, Ralph Waldo. *The Collected Works of Ralph Waldo Emerson*, 5 volumes. Cambridge, MA: Harvard University Press, 1971.

—— *The Journals and Miscellaneous Notebooks of Ralph Waldo Emerson*, 16 volumes. Cambridge, MA: Harvard University Press, 1960–82.

—— *The Letters of Ralph Waldo Emerson*, 9 volumes. New York: Columbia University Press, 1939–94.

—— *Emerson's Prose and Poetry*, ed. J. Porte and S. Morris. New York: W.W. Norton, 2001.

Goodman, R. *American Philosophy and the Romantic Tradition*. Cambridge: Cambridge University Press, 1990.

Kateb, G. *Emerson and Self-Reliance*. Thousand Oaks, CA: Sage, 1995.

Porte, J. and Morris, S. *The Cambridge Companion to Ralph Waldo Emerson*. Cambridge: Cambridge University Press, 1999.

Richardson, R.D., Jr. *Emerson. The Mind on Fire*. Berkeley and Los Angeles, CA: University of California Press, 1995.

Stack, G.J. *Nietzsche and Emerson: An Elective Affinity*. Athens, OH: Ohio University Press, 1992.

Tauber, A.I. *Henry David Thoreau and the Moral Agency of Knowing*. Berkeley, CA: University of California Press, 2001.

Versluis, A. *American Transcendentalism and Asian Religions*. New York: Oxford University Press, 1993.

ALFRED I. TAUBER

EMOTION

"What is an emotion?" asked William James (1842–1910) in 1884, in the title of one of his most famous and widely read essays. His answer, briefly, was that an emotion is a feeling (a set of sensations) caused by a physiological disturbance in the body. But James was not the first American philosopher to ask this question, nor, to be sure, would he be the last. Before him, still in colonial times, the Puritan evangelical theologian Jonathan Edwards (1703–58) had raised a similar question about the "religious affections" (in a treatise that has often been compared with James's own *Varieties of Religious Experience*). But Edwards' conception of the religious affections had everything to do with spirituality, the origin of certain select emotions in God and their expression in good (godly) works. In other words, it was precisely the opposite of James's conscientiously secular conception of emotions as physiologically based feeling and his still somewhat limited notion of religious experience. Thus Edwards represented a long-standing tradition in which passions and affects (affections) remained the focus of an essentially theologically and ethically oriented psychology while James became the seminal American figure of a new secular psychology in the late nineteenth century. (Sigmund Freud, who would also become a major influence on American thought, represented the same transformation in Europe.) It would be James who would set the stage for an ambitious examination of the emotions in American philosophy, which would reach a fever pitch at the beginning of the twenty-first century. (It is also worth noting that, to this day, James set the example – in his own person – of the mutual benefits of philosophy and psychology, and at least with respect to the study of emotions, the two disciplines would develop together, though to be sure with some discomfort and mutual suspicion.)

In the United States, James's theory soon attracted some illustrious critics. One was Walter B. Cannon (1871–1945), a famous neurologist and physiologist who also researched the emotions via physiology, made major discoveries about the endocrine system, and developed the concept of homeostasis and coined the term "fight or flight" response. But Cannon challenged the James–Lange theory that the feelings of an emotion came about as the *result* of physiological changes. (The Jamesian theory is often called the James–Lange theory because a similar thesis was contemporaneously authored by Carl Lange in Denmark.) On the one hand, Cannon thus turned the Jamesian theory on its head (correcting James's own inversion of the commonsense theory of emotions as primary causes). On the other hand, James and Cannon together firmly grounded the concept of emotion in biology and physiology, whereas the passions and affects discussed for so many centuries before were essentially the province of ethics and theology (in Aristotle and St Thomas Aquinas, for example). Indeed, in the background of virtually all of the work on emotions in the twentieth century was the English evolutionary biologist Charles Darwin, who had published his own remarkable book, *Emotion and Expression in Animals and Men* in 1862. But another devotee of Darwin, James's fellow Pragmatist John Dewey (1859–1952), attempted to extend and synthesize both Darwin's and James's theories of emotion and integrate emotions with rationality. Thus while the more straightforwardly biological accounts of emotion were virtually silent on questions of meaning, the meaning of emotion became Dewey's central concern. Emotions were essential ingredients in the means–ends ("teleological") courses of action that defined human life.

The lively debates about the nature and role of emotions in human life were a central feature of American Pragmatism. They were paralleled in Europe by equally energetic explorations by phenomenologists and existentialists in the first half of the twentieth century. This included such illustrious thinkers as Martin Heidegger, Max Scheler, and Jean-Paul Sartre, not to mention Freud. But by mid-century, American psychology had been overwhelmed by behaviorism, most vigorously promulgated by John Watson and B.F. Skinner in psychology. At the same time there was a move in Britain, following Ludwig Wittgenstein (who at least suggested a behaviorist perspective) and Gilbert Ryle, who sarcastically dismissed "the ghost in the machine" of traditional philosophy, which was immediately echoed in American philosophy in the rigors of "logical positivism," which dominated American philosophy for several decades. (W.V.O. Quine, an heir to the logical positivists – though he called himself a pragmatist and occupied William James's old Chair at Harvard – was a close friend and ally of B.F. Skinner.) Consequently, the study of emotions was marginalized both in psychology and in philosophy. The European emphasis on phenomenology – the *experience* of emotion – was no longer of interest to philosophers (as it arguably had been for James and Dewey, not to mention Edwards the century before).

But in the early 1970s, the topic of emotions came back into American philosophy with a vengeance, and with a difference. A few years earlier, two British philosophers named Errol Bedford and Anthony Kenny published pieces in the Wittgenstinian tradition that avoided talking about emotions as experience as such but placed the emphasis on the *social context* and the *intentionality* of emotions, respectively. Bedford, following Wittgenstein, argued that whether an emotion is embarrassment or shame, for example, depends not so much on the internal states or feelings of the subject but rather on the social context. In other words, it is what *other* people would ascribe as the relevant emotion, depending on the circumstances and the putative responsibility of the subject, that determines the difference between emotions. Kenny, by contrast, focused on the medieval notion of intentionality, which points to the fact that emotions, unlike feelings, are necessarily directed to objects in the world, for instance toward a person at whom one is angry, or at oneself, caught in an awkward situation. In the 1960s, American philosophy remained very much in the thrall of the British, and Wittgenstein and his various followers largely determined the fashions in American philosophy. The place of emotions in philosophy remained rather marginal, but by the 1970s this had all begun to change.

The rebirth of emotion theory in American philosophy

Part of the reason for the renewed interest in emotion was a new sense of *détente* between American philosophy and European philosophy. This encouraged a new generation of philosophers to learn what they could from "Continental" philosophy as well as from the now-reigning "analytic" philosophy that dominated the major universities in the United States. (This *détente* lasted almost two decades, to the benefit of both sides of the divide, until post-modernism appeared to turn both sides hostile once again.) But because of the continuing interest and celebration of the emotions in European philosophy, American philosophical interest was once again energized as such exotic figures as Nietzsche, Kierkegaard, and Jean-Paul Sartre became major figures in the American curriculum. And with the interest in their philosophy came a newfound appreciation for emotion and emotional experience. Both Nietzsche and Kierkegaard celebrated a passionate immersion in life, and Jean-Paul Sartre famously defended the idea that we are responsible for our emotions and to a certain extent *choose* them for our own (often covert) purposes. American philosophy took note, and the long-standing antipathy to all matters "of the heart" started to give way to a new appreciation of the emotions and their role in human life.

At the same time, psychology too had taken a significant turn away from behaviorism and towards an appreciation of the "cognitive" complexity of the emotions. In the United States, Magda Arnold and Richard Lazarus were among the first of a new breed of emotions theorists who stressed the importance of what they called "appraisals" in the understanding of emotions. In other words, emotions weren't just dumb feelings but more or less intelligent responses to what Lazarus called "core themes" in human life, such as being threatened, being humiliated, being honored, being offended or frustrated. The cognitive aspect of emotions, which had been either ignored or treated as secondary by James (depending on how his work is interpreted), was elaborated by two New York psychologists named Stanley Schachter and Jerome Singer in 1962. They argued, against James, that an emotion is not just a state of "arousal" (the physiological disturbance that James had emphasized) but also the cognitive "labeling" of that emotion, the recognition of what sort of emotion it is. Between the notions of cognition and appraisal, the stage was set for a very different kind of analysis of emotion, one that put much less emphasis on the biological causes of emotion and the feelings that typically accompany emotion and much more emphasis on the ways in which our emotions help us to relate to the world and its problems.

In this new and encouraging environment, the interest and inspiration of European philosophy joined the new sophistication of American psychology and met up again with the renewed interest in emotions in American philosophy and inspired a revolution in thinking about emotions that continues to this day. In place of the old feeling and physiology theories, cognition and the acknowledgement of "emotional intelligence" became the watchwords of emotions studies. (The phrase "emotional intelligence" did not hit the popular media until it was announced in a best-selling book in the 1990s, but it had been kicking around academic research on emotions for many years.) Books started pouring out of distinguished academic presses by the dozens, journals and associations were formed, major conferences were organized, and "the philosophy of emotions" became a recognized field of philosophy. Interdisciplinary groups and organizations were formed, drawing from philosophy, the various branches of psychology and the other social sciences, from biology and medicine and, especially, from neurology, a science that had been in its infancy at the time of William James but was exploding with new knowledge by the beginning of the twenty-first century. And this is especially true with regard to the emotions.

If the rebirth of enthusiasm about emotions research began in the last half of the last century with a reaction against the bodily disturbance theory of William James, the end of that century saw the emergence of a vibrant counter-movement, a neo-Jamesian reaction, in which the identity of emotions once again shifted to the physiological. But whereas James had focused in on the importance of the peripheral symptoms of central nervous system activity, the activity of the endocrine system, for instance, the new Jamesians home in on the central nervous system itself, especially the brain. New brain imaging techniques that allow more or less direct observation of the brain at work have allowed neurologists to map primitive brain circuits for certain basic emotions – fear, for example – and this has spurred a not unfamiliar philosophical enthusiasm for the eventuality that "some day" neurological research will replace the "folk psychology" of our current-day understanding. Whereas the last century's studies of social context, core themes, and intentionality presupposed the qualified adequacy of our ordinary understanding and language of emotions, the new enthusiasm for the findings of neurology once again suggests to many philosophers the idea that "what emotions really are" are biological processes to be understood in terms of evolution and the study of the brain.

Thus today the philosophy of emotions is divided within by its approaches and favorite theories. It is a sign of the good health of the field that these differences have not resulted in the splitting off of schools or camps but rather a vigorous and on-going debate. Another good sign is that this is going on not just within the confines of philosophy but in a rich multi-disciplinary (and international) mix of scholars and researchers across a wide range of fields, prominently including psychology and neurology but also including such subjects as history and literature. What is emerging is something like a consensus (though with virtually all participants facing and pulling in the direction of their favored discipline) in which some emotions ("basic emotions") can be characterized to a significant extent (though this is precisely what is at issue) by their evolutionary, neurological structure. Foremost among these emotions is fear, the most thoroughly studied in brain research, and then there is anger, sadness, surprise, disgust, and affection. (The list varies with different theorists, but fear and anger are mentioned in virtually every inventory.) But then there are other "higher cognitive" emotions that seem to require reference to social learning and context in order to be intelligible, for example guilt, shame, embarrassment, and pride. Making the analysis more subtle and complex in recent years has been the realization among many theorists that many emotions that fall into that category "emotion" are not a homogeneous bunch but may have to be analyzed in quite different ways. But it was William James, again, who once argued that philosophy itself is defined by two contrary passions, a passion for making distinctions and a passion for seeing commonalities. Thus the question, "is *emotion* a uniform category?" is itself the on-going subject of considerable debate.

"What is an emotion?" Cognition and the brain

James's question, "what is an emotion?" still guides a good deal of the philosophy of emotion, but while nearly everyone now agrees that virtually all emotions involve both physiological and more highly cognitive elements, the balance of those ingredients is in question both in general and with regard to each particular emotion. In fear and anger, for instance, it may be agreed that there are certain physiological processes that are more or less essential to those emotions, but many philosophers would argue that those processes only constitute *emotions* insofar as they also involve a modicum of intentionality, a response to something fearful or dangerous in the case of fear, a reaction to something frustrating or offensive in the case of anger. To be sure, in their most primitive occurrences (as panic and rage, for instance) the intentionality may be diffuse, confused, and markedly unintelligent, but nevertheless a certain engagement with the world is essential to the emotion. In more sophisticated occurrences of those same emotions, such as fear of an internal revenue audit or anger at the latest government policy, the amount of cognition (that is, knowledge about the world) may be quite considerable, whatever physiological processes may be going on as well. But the intensity of the emotion, it is still widely believed, is to be found in the level of Jamesian arousal, whatever the nature of the beliefs in question.

In the case of such emotions as shame and pride, however, the importance of the social dimension tends to overwhelm any significance of the physiology. Nevertheless, shame does exhibit certain familiar range of physiological and bodily symptoms, from blushing or blanching to gestures of withdrawal and diminishment. So, too, pride has its postures (sometimes compared, unfairly, to the behavior of certain birds, notably peacocks). But theorists have been quick to talk about the "social construction" of such emotions, suggesting that not only do they depend on social norms and social language for their existence but that even their bodily manifestations are both expressions of and interpretable only by the social structures that sustain them. One suggestion, now almost universally rejected, is captured in the metaphor of a fruit with an inner pit or core and an outer flesh, where the core is a "hard-wired" biological structure and the flesh is the cultural overlay. But it has become evident to even the most ardent biologists and social construction theorists that such simple bifurcation simply will not do. Whatever the relation of the physiological components of emotions to their intentionality and social context, or of biology to culture more generally, it is much more developmentally and philosophically complex than this core and flesh metaphor would suggest.

Thus the "dialectic" of the philosophy of emotions returns to the juncture where we first took it up, when William James insisted that an emotion should be understood primarily in terms of its bodily manifestations and others, Dewey, for instance, insisted that it was the *meaning* of emotions that had to be accounted for as well. But now the discussion is much better informed and consequently more lively than it was a hundred years ago, but with the re-entry of appraisal theory and the concern with social context we also see the reappearance of a robust interest in emotions and ethics, and even emotions and religion. But this is what the interest in emotions has always been in American philosophy, a curious struggle between science and social significance, a tension between what is most personal about us and what is most obviously part of our biological heritage.

Further reading

Darwin, Charles. *The Expression of Emotions in Animals and Men*. New York: Oxford University Press, 1998 [1862].

De Sousa, Ronald. *The Rationality of Emotion*. Cambridge, MA: MIT Press, 1987.

Griffiths, Paul E. *What Emotions Really Are*. Chicago, IL: University of Chicago Press, 1997.

James, William. "What is an Emotion?" in Robert C. Solomon (ed.) *What is an Emotion?* New York: Oxford University Press, 2004 [1884].

Nussbaum, Martha. *Upheavals of Thought*. Cambridge: Cambridge University Press, 2001.

Prinz, Jesse. *Gut Reactions*. New York: Oxford University Press, 2004.

Robinson, Jenefer. *Deeper than Reason*. New York: Oxford University Press, 2005.

Salovey, Peter, Brackett, M. and Mayer, John (eds) *Emotional Intelligence*. Port Chester, NY: Dude Publishing, 2004.

Solomon, Robert C. (ed.) *What is an Emotion?* New York: Oxford University Press, 2004.

Robert C. Solomon

EMOTION, JAMES/LANGE THEORY OF

The James/Lange theory is a psycho-physiological theory on the bodily origin of emotions. The theory takes its names from William James and the Danish physiologist Carl Lange who both formulated it autonomously, and almost at the same time, in two independent publications: James in the article "What is an Emotion?" (*Mind* 9, 1884) and Lange in a booklet entitled *Über Gemüthsbewegungen* (Leipzig, 1885).

James's account of the theory, republished in chapter 25 of the *Principles of Psychology* (PP), reverses the traditional view according to which bodily movements and reactions follow from emotions triggered by an exciting perceived object. The theory is intended to undermine a traditional psychological theory of emotions (from Descartes to Bain) and to criticize its "essentialistic" account of emotions as individual and existing in between perceived objects and bodily reactions.

James's view follows as a necessary corollary of his assumptions about ideo-motor actions, instincts and reasoning, and claims that objects have the power to directly cause bodily changes which are subtle, infinite in number, and more or less obscurely felt. The awareness of such bodily changes is exactly what is called an "emotion," so that there is no need for a third psychic entity between object and bodily movement.

James substitutes the traditional three-stage schema (PO → E → BR) with a two-stage one in which emotion and bodily reactions are unified as the psychological and neural concurrent faces of the same nervous event (PO → BR/E): "My theory is that the bodily changes follow directly the perception of the exciting fact, and that our feeling of the same changes as they occur is the emotion" (PP II.449). The main tenet of the theory is the symptomatic equivalence between emotions and their bodily expression, so that if we try to abstract "from our consciousness of an emotion all the feelings of its bodily symptoms, we find we have nothing left behind." Bodily changes are "symptoms," namely, are all that emotions are "known as," unless they are to be taken as metaphysical entities; consequently from a psychological point of view a purely disembodied emotion is but a non-entity.

A major consequence and aim of James's theory is the dismissal of a descriptive and classificatory psychology of emotions. James criticizes the traditional view of emotions as a product of the language of psychology which, on behalf of its own cognitive purposes, oversimplifies the complexity of the phenomena and creates "typical" fictitious object that have no existence in actual human experience. In fact, none of the emotions depicted in the psychological literature correspond to real emotions felt by real individuals. In this sense, James is very careful in pointing out the difference between his own and Lange's twin theory. Although as for the physiological nature of the emotions the two accounts can be deemed almost equivalent, Lange's theory is still in the fashion of the old descriptive psychology, which regarded emotions as individual entities susceptible to be singled out and classified. Accordingly, Lange's attempt to assign a specific set of corresponding physiological events to each emotion appears as an inconclusive and inaccurate generalization about individual phenomena. In fact, since an "emotion" is but the felling of bodily changes and such changes are indefinite in number and present themselves in manifold combinations according to the nature of the individual, there is no limit to the number and forms of emotions which human beings can experience. Because of this complexity, it is impossible to state which bodily movements are supposed to correspond to a specific emotion, and a complete description of the physiological phenomena that correspond to an emotion is materially impossible, since such phenomena can change not only from individual to individual, but appear differently also in different occurrences in the life of the same individual. Accordingly, James claims that as far as its purpose goes, any classification of emotions is as true and "natural" as any other, whereas none of them can provide a conclusive objective account of the origin and nature of any real emotion. Thus such classifications are merely descriptive, and of little or no scientific relevance at all.

James's theory of emotions has been the target of much criticism, the most popular of which stressed the odd conclusions that such a theory would lead to, such as the claim that sadness is consequence of crying. James was the first to admit that an experimental evidence to support his theory was hard to provide and never really engaged in a full defense; he merely postulated that such extreme and nonsensical conclusions were not the meaning of his theory. Such criticisms were rather unfair and generally missed the point, however, since they were based on a conception which assumed an associative connection between emotions and bodily expressions, and the existence of a fixed relation between a particular bodily expression and certain feelings. In fact, James's theory rejects just such an associationist and causal standpoint and denies that emotions *qua* emotions and bodily movements *qua* bodily movements can be "associated" and move each other in whatever order.

James denied that an emotion could be aroused through mere simulation of its bodily expressions, as actors do, in the essay "The Gospel of Relaxation." James suggests an educational application of his theory, which accounts for the ability to control emotional states through the control of bodily attitude; to the extent emotion is a feeling of bodily changes, a change of bodily attitudes should translate itself into a change of emotional state. Thus, in virtue of their equivalence with bodily movements and behavior, emotions can be controlled through the control of behavior granting lesser waste of nervous energy and greater effectiveness to action.

By denying the existence of emotions as psychological entities and rejecting any causal – namely, mechanical – interaction between an emotion and its bodily expression, the theory of emotions appears as one of James's most effective attempts to overcome body–mind dualism in a physiological direction. James, however, has always rejected the charge of materialism, claiming that his theory is no more materialist than any other view which assumes a relation between emotions and the nervous system.

Further reading

Ayer, A.J. *The Origins of Pragmatism.* San Francisco, CA: Freeman Cooper, 1968, Bk II, Ch. 2.

Bird, G. *William James.* London: Routledge, 1986, Ch. 9.

Gale, R.M. *The Divided Self of William James.* Cambridge: Cambridge University Press, 1999, Ch. I, §§ 2, 3, 4.

James, W. *"The Will to Believe" and Other Essays in Popular Philosophy.* New York: Dover, 1956.

Kauber, R.M. and Hare, P. "The Right and Duty to Will to Believe", *Canadian Journal of Philosophy* (1974): 327–43.

Perry, R.B. *The Thought and Character of William James.* Boston, MA: Little, Brown, 1936, Ch. LXIII.

Seigfried, C. Haddock. *William James's Radical Reconstruction of Philosophy.* New York: SUNY Press, 1990, passim.

Wernham, J.C.S. *James's Will to Believe Doctrine.* Toronto: McGill-Queen's University Press, 1987.

SERGIO FRANZESE

EMPATHY

Empathy is experiencing, or at least emotionally resonating with, another sentient being's emotional state. It is synergistically sharing in another's suffering without the impingement of the same sources of suffering. In a general sense, empathy becomes connected with the foundation of moral actions because it explains an experiential relationship with other people. Although fallible as a tool of knowing or relating to one another, it can provide a shared foundation of experience.

Classical American philosophers largely address empathy indirectly and often use "sympathy" in place of, or to point toward, our current use of empathy. For instance in "On a Certain Blindness in Human Beings," William James describes the failure of individuals to relate to others' experiences and internal states as a common shortcoming. Although this essay concerns finding joy, the underlying message is about the importance of understanding another's situation through relating one's own desires with others' desires. Interestingly, James cites Josiah Royce within this essay as founding duty within the ability to appreciate fully (fully beholding) that others' life-experiences are as rich and equally painful as one's own. It is through resonating with and so experiencing another's suffering, that one can fully appreciate other people as important entities to whom there are obligations.

From Peirce's understanding of experience and meaning, empathy would be a type of quality of experience that would be meaningful as a "thirdness" that brings the experience of one individual ("firstness") into a special relationship with another individual ("secondness"). Again, there is a strong emphasis on the relationship and connectedness possible between individuals and that empathy is only meaningful in the effect it can bring about.

John Dewey's early writing in "A Common Faith," roots a shared experience and ability to relate to others' suffering as a foundation on which to build a commonality of religious experience. Similarly, Dewey's understanding of art relates to empathy as an internal emotional response that is a relationship with objects or other subjects. Although an internal response, it arises from engagement.

Given George Herbert Mead's phenomenological tendencies, empathy should be understood in relationship to the experiences of the social self. It is a sympathy that is taken to the point of relating to and trying to know the experience of others through the ability of putting oneself in another's place. For Mead, this experienced relatedness is a higher function that distinguishes humans from animals.

Jane Addams calls on empathetic experiences to move individuals toward an ethic of action, perhaps even to build a moral society based partly upon empathetic responses. This thread of empathy and action can be particularly found in the contemporary feminist philosophical tradition of an ethics of care. Philosophers such as Virginia Held hold the view that caring and empathy may be better guides to moral action than abstract rules. Addressing current practices in medicine, Jodi Halpern focuses on empathy as an important faculty that physicians should develop rather than repress in order to provide the best care possible for their patients. On these views, a lack of empathy leaves one vulnerable to missing the salient features necessary to achieving best outcomes.

Finally, Native American traditions can challenge underlying assumptions about individual experience at the very center of traditional American Pragmatism. By placing the emphasis on a unity of experiences in the whole group, one could understand empathy as unremarkable for a single individual. Rather, any lack of resonance with others in sorrow or suffering would demarcate a special separateness from the whole. Because "empathy" is thought to be unusual in Classical American Pragmatism we give it a special name. Based on a Native American view, the state of lacking empathy could warrant a special name. On the other hand, like many Native American philosophies, American Pragmatism shows a remarkable plasticity and interest in taking into account the varieties of differences in emotional experiences. Although empathy allows one to experience together an emotion and provides a basis for understanding similarities, it also allows individuals with different experiences to find a way of relating. Although empathy allows strong connections with the emotional states of others and so provides a basis for understanding similarities, it also allows for the possibility of relation through a celebration of and respect for difference.

Further reading

Addams, Jane. *Democracy and Social Ethics*. Champaign, IL: University of Illinois Press, 2001.

Halpern, Jodi. *From Detached Concern to Empathy: Humanizing Medical Practice*. New York: Oxford University Press, 2001.

Held, Virginia. *Feminist Morality: Transforming Culture, Society, and Politics*. Chicago, IL: University of Chicago Press, 1995.

James, William. "On a Certain Blindness in Human Beings" in his *Talks to Teachers on Psychology: and to Students on Some of Life's Ideals*, Cambridge, MA: Harvard University Press, 1983.

Mead, George H. *Mind, Self, and Society From the Standpoint of a Social Behaviorist*. Chicago, IL: University of Chicago Press, 1967.

Peirce, Charles S. *Philosophical Writings of Peirce*, ed. J. Buchler. New York: Dover, 1955.

Pratt, Scott. *Native Pragmatism: Rethinking the Roots of American Philosophy*. Bloomington, IN: Indiana University Press, 2002.

PAUL J. FORD
ALLYSON L. ROBICHAUD

ENGLISH PHILOSOPHY, INFLUENCE OF

John Locke and Isaac Newton were the major intellectual influences on American colonists and, later, on citizens generally. Locke's political philosophy and empirical epistemology influenced so many people that only to list them would be a task; we shall consider only those of greatest importance. Also, we must be prepared to find different authors giving different interpretations to the works of Locke and Newton. Locke held a social contract theory of the state where people should be equal and independent. Because people have to relinquish certain primal rights to achieve this goal, any government that contravenes the social contract deserves to be overthrown by rebellion. Indeed, citizens have not only the right but the obligation to rebel under such circumstances. Moreover, to maintain the social contract adequately, the ideal government must have checks and balances to prevent the legislative, judicial, or executive sections of the government to achieve dominance. This right and obligation to rebel under such circumstances is the groundwork of the Declaration of Independence and the checks and balances of the Constitution.

Jonathan Mayhew, an unorthodox minister, quite early defended Locke's doctrine of the right to rebel, a view accepted by Samuel Adams, John Adams, Alexander Hamilton, Thomas Jefferson, and Thomas Paine. Paine's pamphlets on commonsense were the strongest statement of this view and were written to encourage the Revolutionary soldiers whose spirits had begun to fail. However, after the Revolutionary War, the US Constitution did not establish the type of democracy envisioned by Sam Adams and Paine. Liberty, they discovered, did not entail political equality.

Locke's epistemology was also influential during the colonial and enlightenment years. Even before the Revolutionary War, Jonathan Edwards read Locke's Essay "Concerning Human Understanding" when it was first introduced as a textbook at Yale. Edwards agreed with Locke's rejection of secondary qualities as a part of objective reality but then realized that similar arguments could be directed against primary properties. He concluded that all substance is an infinitely exact and completely stable Idea in God's mind. Edwards also read Newton and accepted the notion of the universality of causation, a fundamental assumption of his Calvinistic view of agency theory. Dr Sam Johnson of Yale and subsequently president of King's College (Columbia) also read Newton and saw that his concept of the universality of causality inevitably led to a denial of free will since the implication of Newton's view was that motives are causes and not reasons in the decision-making of human beings.

Ethan Allen used Locke's epistemology and Newton's physics in his long, hard-hitting critique of historical Christianity in his *Reason, the Only Oracle of Man*. He thought that modem science and empirical philosophy were incompatible with the concepts of revelation, miracle, and prophesy. Allen never suffered public banishment the way Paine did after the publication of his *Age of Reason*. Ministers, of course, denounced Allen, especially in other states, since in Vermont few people wanted to antagonize the Green Mountain Boys, of whom Allen was the leader. Allen and his Boys captured the British Fort at Ticonderoga; Allen, and some of his Boys were captured in Montreal, and Allen spent three years in British prisons suffering every kind of abuse. He wrote a long narrative of his captivity and it, like Paine's *Common Sense*, roused the Revolutionary soldiers to the extent that their energy was renewed.

One of the most important devotees of Locke and Newton was Benjamin Rush. His research in chemistry and physiology was in many ways up to the standards of modem science at that time while his publications on political and ethical questions still have significance for contemporary life. He began with the Lockean premise that all knowledge comes from sensations and not from apriori elements. He strongly believed that the physical environment of a person determined the kind of person he would be. The criminal comes from one kind of environment and the law-abiding citizen from another, so, in a real sense, both types of citizens were determined by events outside of their control. However, he was neither a hard nor a soft determinist but believed that reason and understanding are able to modify environments to produce a significantly different result. His discussions of penology have a very modem ring. Prisons should not be considered as well-deserved punishment but as controlled environments in which the criminal character may be changed. In addition, Rush had been an ardent supporter of Locke's political philosophy which he thought justified the Revolutionary War.

The influence of English authors on the transcendentalists varies a great deal depending on which members of the Club are being considered. Ralph Waldo Emerson, Henry Thoreau, and Bronson Alcott were greatly influenced by Samuel Coleridge's distinction between reason and understanding, the former referring to apriori intuitive acquaintance with ultimate reality and the latter to the empirical practical truths of science and ordinary life. Coleridge had imported this distinction from the German philosopher Schelling. Wordsworth's poetry was an added influence, especially on Emerson and Alcott who interpreted metaphors as moral messages. However, there was no English influence on the thought of Theodore Parker; the apriori of his philosophy were entirely those of Thomas Reid and had nothing in common with Emerson's metaphysics. Both Emerson and Parker were influenced by Thomas Carlyle, though Parker apparently took Carlyle's emphasis on work more seriously than Emerson. Margaret Fuller was too much influenced by Goethe to be an Emersonian transcendentalist. She was influenced by Emerson's great integrity, but even here she felt depressed, as did Parker, by Emerson's inactivity. Fuller wrote Emerson to the effect that he often edited the menu while the cook did the work. Thoreau, one might say, was influenced most strongly by himself. He never took to heart the wise insight of Emerson that man is worthy only by the multitude of his affinities. The sage of Concord finally broke with Thoreau, writing that he would rather take the arm of an elm tree in preference to Thoreau's.

George Ripley was influenced by French and English writers who were interested in social reforms, and put their ideas into action by constructing his Brook Farm experiment in community living. Finally Ripley accepted the socialistic views of F.C.M. Fourier. He criticized Emerson's view that the only lasting reform was the regeneration of the souls of mankind. According to Ripley, the very structures of society stifled the realization of man's self-reliance and therefore the fundamental reform is with society itself. Frederick Henry Hedge was completely influenced by Coleridge and numerous German philosophers. He eventually taught German literature at Harvard. James Marsh, president of the University of Vermont, managed to publish an American edition of Coleridge's *Aids to Reflection* in 1829, a major event in spreading the influence of Coleridge in America. Later in Alcott's life, the English influence of Coleridge began to wane and he became influenced, surprisingly, by William Torrey Harris and his St Louis Hegelians.

The first appearance of original philosophical thought in America, developed by scientifically sophisticated thinkers, appeared in the Metaphysical Club which met in Cambridge in the early 1870s. The membership included Chauncey Wright, C.S. Peirce, William James, Wendell Holmes, and numerous others, but the originality arose in the thought of these four men. Together, yet in different ways, they rejected the British empiricist tradition; this based induction on past experience while these four men formulated a forward-looking empiricism which was inspired by the Galilean view that the hypothetical–deductive method of modem astronomy was the correct method for the whole of physics.

Wright sought to reinstate Galileo's views, which had been eclipsed by the British empiricists' emphasis on enumeration of past experiences and also to a certain extent by Newton's warning "hypotheses *non fingo*," which was often misunderstood because of its ambiguous status. Wright was critical of the "experimental methods" of agreement, difference, and co-variations introduced by Francis Bacon and extended and refined by J.F.W. Herschel and J.S. Mill. He argued that such methods might be relevant in discovering causes in low-order science but had no relevance for theoretical sciences like mechanics. He wrote that the only real use in the latter case was for verification, not discovery – for empirically checking the predicted consequences of a hypothetical deductive system. Wright never extended his criticism of Bacon and Herschel to J.S. Mill, no doubt because he had great admiration for Mill's moral character. He did accept Mill's version of utilitarian ethics but never thought of it as having any relevance for scientific method. On the other hand, William Whewell was a positive influence on Wright. Whewell did recognize the importance of Galileo and claimed that inductive generalizations were only significant in the discovery of hypotheses. Wright, however, insisted on the open-ended nature of hypothesis formulation. Hypotheses may originate in simple induction but also come from intuition, natural biases of the mind, or even dreams.

Holmes also was a close student of Whewell; from his correspondence we learn that he frequently met Wright in his quarters to read and discuss Whewell's books together and to consider their value. It seems likely that these discussions were the inspiration for Holmes's predictive theory of law. Statutes, he wrote, are not laws until they have been interpreted by judicial decisions.

Peirce formulated his pragmatic maxim of meaning in a paper read at a meeting of the Metaphysical Club. The meaning of a proposition, he said, consists in the whole set of practical consequences that can be predicted from it. Hence, part of the meaning of "this diamond is hard" is "if I scratch the diamond against glass it will leave a scratch on the glass." And so on for an unlimited number of consequences.

The first thing to note about this maxim is that Peirce had generalized forward-looking empiricism to all experiential concepts, not just theoretical or abstract ones. William James and John Dewey accepted this extension while Wright did not – that is why the former are pragmatists, but not Wright, who accepted a self-contained sensory given as did the British empiricists. The second point to notice is that most concepts are sufficiently complex so that any list of predictions would be inadequate for disclosing the meaning. The diamond ring at the bottom of the ocean causes a problem: can it be said to be hard if it cannot be put to the test? Peirce answered this point, as he did other problems, by introducing the concept of counterfactual inference – if the diamond ring could be put to the test it would scratch glass. As we shall see later, counterfactual inference is difficult to account for within an empiricist epistemology. How can one establish what could have been the case from what has been the case?

Some commentators have claimed that Peirce's pragmatic maxim is inconsistent with his evolutionary metaphysics, but Peirce thought otherwise. The synechism in the world constantly increases and eventually, for example, natural gases will follow Boyle's laws exactly instead of only approximately, as they do now. Unfortunately no predictions can be made when this event is likely to occur.

The major influence on Peirce's pragmatic maxim, according to Max Fisch, was Alexander Bain, the English empiricist author of *The Emotions and the Will*. According to Bain, belief is a volitional matter dedicated to action; however, it seems odd that a criterion of meaning should be a matter of volition. But Bain never meant that the acts of the will are idiosyncratic. Though Bain put his discussion of belief in the part of his book devoted to the Will, at the same time he insisted that belief always had intellectual content. Peirce also insisted on an intellectual core of belief; since a belief has an intellectual core then it is already public and not idiosyncratic. We shall see how James differed from Peirce on this crucial issue. James does plunge belief into an idiosyncratic interpretation.

James accepted Peirce's maxim that the whole meaning of a proposition consists in its predictable consequences, but he significantly enlarged the concept – not only the consequences of a proposition give it meaning but belief in it also has consequential meaning. James asked the question "Is life worth living?" Conclusive evidence is lacking because the world is a complicated mixture of good and evil. However, the decision that life is or isn't worth living gives rise to significantly different consequences. To be pessimistic about the future state of world events may lead to withdrawal from it and hence result in thinking that life is not worth living. However, if the unproved belief that life is worth living leads to participation in it, the belief, so to speak, creates its own confirmation in later experience. James is not simply saying that over-belief causes over-achievement but rather the epistemic claim that prior belief in p may result in producing evidence for the truth of p. Here he comes close to the Pauline doctrine that one must believe in God before the evidence for the belief becomes available.

Charles Renouvier encouraged this voluntaristic fideism in James's thought; this French philosopher was a long-term friend and early mentor of James. In his early article on "Bain and Renouvier" in *The Nation* (1876) James contrasted Bain's constant insistence on adequate evidence for every belief with Renouvier's insistence on the importance of accepting "needed or useful" beliefs. Renouvier's voluntarism was useful to James both in his recovery from his first and worst bout with depression and in the early development of his philosophical thought. It was only the voluntarism that James accepted; he developed a dim view of Renouvier's overall philosophy.

James's "enlargement" of Peirce's maxim was somewhat mitigated rather quickly. One year after he wrote the "Bain and Renouvier" article, he reviewed Tait's *Unseen Universe* for *The Nation* in which he held that "an act of trust" is not only licit – indeed it is a duty – if it makes a practical difference in mental peace. A member of the Metaphysical Club convinced him that "duty" was too strong a word, and James henceforth formulated his will-to-believe as a person's right. It was this sense that he used in his famous article in his book *The Will to Believe*.

Some commentators stress the influence of J.S. Mill on James; the latter was attracted to Mill's utilitarian moral philosophy because of its forward-looking analysis of right and wrong. True, James was attracted by any kind of forward-looking empiricism, be it in ethics or in the methods of modem science. This view perhaps appears supported by James's statement that were Mill alive at that date he would certainly have been at one with the pragmatists. However, what is there in Mill's version of utility that would have suggested to James the essential pragmatic view that the basis sensory "given" is to be interpreted hypothetically just like the hypotheses of modem astronomy and physics? In fact, Mill firmly believed in a self-contained given, the very opposite of the pragmatic maxim. Mill was even committed to Bacon's experimental methods rather than the hypothetical–deductive method of Galileo.

We have not mentioned Dewey, since he was not a member of the Metaphysical Club even though he was later influenced by several of its members. We shall discuss Dewey later and we shall also mention Wright, Peirce, and James in different contexts than the Metaphysical Club.

The publication of Charles Darwin's *Origin of Species* in 1859 had an enormous impact on American thought. Scientists, philosophers, and theologians were taken aback by this dramatic development. Initially many scientists and philosophers of science gave it a cool reception, and the religious gave it a very negative response. But, through the years, many people in all the categories accepted the concept of natural selection. One of the breakthroughs in accepting Darwin came in Cambridge, Massachusetts, at a meeting of the American Academy of Arts and Sciences in 1869. The Academy sponsored a debate between Asa Gray, a botanist, and Louis Agassiz, both of Harvard. Gray defended the concept of the mutation of species against Agassiz's claim that the whole concept of species evaporated if one accepts the concept of natural selection. Wright was corresponding secretary of the Academy at the time of the debate and recorded the main points made. Wright became, among philosophers, the most articulate defender of Darwin; he wrote numerous philosophical articles for the *North American Review* explaining the logical structure of explanation in geophysical sciences. Wright warned that one should not expect the explanatory power of natural selection to be as great as physical concepts like acceleration, momentum, or force. The notion of natural selection explains a concrete series of events, the origin of species, which is not a highly controlled series of events in a laboratory. The breeding of plants and animals under laboratory conditions might be interpreted as a controlled study, but even if such a study discovered biological laws of a Galilean type their application to a concrete series of events would still be difficult and imprecise. One must distinguish between prediction and explanation. In physics, prediction is precise but the background theoretical concepts are necessary to explain these predictions. In geophysical sciences a concrete series of events may be scientifically explained even though prediction is not possible or even relevant. Darwin and Wallace had amassed a huge body of empirical evidence on which they based their theory of natural selection. Darwin was impressed with Wright's work in general and had reprinted in England Wright's essay "The Genesis of Species," which he distributed to all of his own collaborators. Wright was a house guest of the Darwins in 1873 and his discussions with Darwin remained the highlight of his life.

Darwin's impact on American religion and philosophy was enormous. How could a believer in a Christian God accept Darwin's concept of natural selection? How could one accept his and Lyell's estimate of the enormous time-span, including the present, required for the present state of our universe when the Bible said that God created the world in six days? There were various strategies, by Christians who were nevertheless scientists and philosophers, to resolve this problem. Alfred Russel Wallace, co-founder of the concept of natural selection, for example, restricted natural selection to the lower species but excluded human beings from natural selection. This strategy was attractive to American ministers and priests. By another strategy, Asa Gray claimed simply that God's design of the world was much more complicated than previously thought, from which it does not follow, however, that God had not done the planning. This strategy, however, was still based on the notion that the evolution of species was a progressive and teleological one which Darwin had rejected.

Another strategy was to give a metaphorical interpretation to any false factual claim made in the Bible such as the claim that the Earth is flat, that God created the world in six days, etc. These strategies worked fairly well until the fundamentalist movement grew steadily through the years and exploded on the religious scene in the 1920s. Darwin was always their main enemy. They had accepted the Restoration's view that philosophical and theological glosses on the Bible were pointless. Only what the Bible said was relevant. Since the Bible said the world was created in six days, it must be so. They swept away all the strategies as irrelevant philosophical and theological glosses. They departed from the traditional Restoration concept of the "inner light" which meant that people are responsible because they have an innate conscience which tells them what is right and wrong. This inner light the fundamentalists reinterpreted into Pentecostal powers given to the Disciples, and/or to direct personal communication with the deity itself. The rejection of Darwin is still very much a part of present-day life in America, where fundamentalists are rewriting high school textbooks so that they include the creationist viewpoint and ignore Darwin completely.

Herbert Spencer was extremely influential in America, both positively and negatively. According to Spencer's Law of Evolution, all natural, psychological and social events evolve "from homogeneity to heterogeneity through differentiation and integration." This so-called law was rejected by philosophers who were learned in modem science and mathematics and even by intelligent philosophers who lacked scientific depth. Wright, Gray, and James were scientifically trained authors. This generalization, Wright felt, was pointless: it simply summarizes the most general features common to the evolution of the solar system, the evolution of species from protozoa to man, and the social development of society from tribes to nations. This summary of various similarities is useless because it does not lead to any new inference or observations as the concept of gravity does. According to Wright, "nothing justifies the development of abstract principles but their utility in enlarging our concrete knowledge of nature" (2000: 56). Also, Spencer's view that the real world, the noumenal world, was the "Unknowable!" is the metaphysical view alien to the working of science. The Harvard botanist, Gray, held similar views.

As one might expect, James's rejection of Spencer, is more colorful and less detailed than Wright's. James wrote that Spencer's

> dry school master temperament, the hurdy-gurdy monotony of him, his preference for cheap makeshifts in argument, his lack of education even in mechanical principles, and in general the vagueness in all his fundamental ideas, his whole system wooden, as if knocked together out of cracked hemlock boards – and yet the half of England wants to bury him in Westminster Abbey.
>
> (Myers 1986: 43)

John Fiske, a misfit member of the Metaphysical Club, disagreed; he accepted many of Spencer's views, adding new points here and there, in popularizing them. The fullest statements of his views are to be found in his massive *Outlines of Cosmic Philosophy.*

The reason Spencer and Fiske became favorites of many general readers in America is that the concept of progress explicit in their evolutionary philosophy appealed to the progressive-minded builders of the new world. Railroads supplanted canals, fabric mills with mechanical looms supplanted the cottage industry of weaving, farming machines supplanted hand tools, and the machine increased profits and made distribution of products to the consumer more efficient. Unfortunately, as Thorstein Veblen, noted the industrial age also created a permanent affluent society on the one hand and workers deprived of a decent living on the other.

We are not yet ready for the advent of modem American philosophy since absolute idealism was dominant in both England and America. James and Dewey were particularly effective in helping to dethrone absolute idealism and make way for analytical philosophy which controlled philosophy in England and America, only itself to be replaced, in very recent years, by a general acceptance of pragmatism. James's *The Dilemma of Determinism* is one of the most effective criticisms of absolute idealism and is perhaps his finest contribution to philosophy. James characterized F.R. Bradley's view as a determinism which yields a block universe in which nothing new or unique can ever occur. There is no possibility for something in the future to be different than it might have been. But, in this case, whether determinism is hard or soft, people cannot exercise free will. If deciding to do something makes no difference to what appears in the universe then free-will thinking and all novelty is ruled out. My paraphrase of James's view is as follows: If P at *t*1 has a choice between A and B and A leads inexorably to *x* while B leads inexorably to *y* and *t*1 *x* is already blocked in as part of the future, then it is impossible that P has made a choice, that P has free will, that P can make any difference in the world; so, in order to have free will, a pluralistic universe is required. It would also follow that regretting what one did would now make sense while, on Bradley's view, the concept of regret makes no sense.

It needs to be pointed out that Bradley and others thought that James was arguing that James's use of the word "chance" undercut all agency theory, but of course what James meant by "chance" at this point was that in a pluralistic universe there was a chance of something new appearing. Moreover James, somewhat agitated, wrote Bradley that James didn't give a damn about agency theory in this article but rather he was presenting a metaphysical requirement that any agency theory must meet if it were going to capture the sense of free will and human agency making a difference in the world. Dewey, in his early years, was an absolute idealist but, under the influence of Peirce, James, and Wright, became a pluralist. Dewey emphasized the overwhelming influence of chance and contingency which makes no sense on Bradley's view. The trouble with idealists is that they don't live in a world of actual existence and take insufficient cognizance that the real world is problematic, contingent and conflicting.

Dewey helped James and others in various ways eventually to undermine British Absolute Idealism. He was highly critical of the British classical educational system which had very little relevance to the affairs of ordinary life. It was, in short, an ivory tower that was passed along to the upcoming philosophers. Bradley, Taylor, and Green were products of this educational system and no one expected their philosophical views to have any practical relevance.

There was a world of ideas immune to all the contingencies that everyone meets every day. No academics expected their philosophy to have any everyday relevance.

Dewey proposed a whole new educational system but would eventually help to underline the ivory school of education. His point was that we must learn by doing – the best way to study journalism is not only to read the history of it but to write articles for the school page of the local newspaper, and similar devices for all the liberal arts. He also emphasized the great importance of manual skills to release their latent motor capacities so necessary for all education. In the grade schools one mixed the various types of liberal arts with some manual labor courses. Unfortunately, some educators overstated views somewhat similar to Dewey's, as was the case with Summerhill in England. Educators in the United States managed to sidetrack Dewey's educational ideas, and they are now long in the past. At the present time the United States system of public education has seriously deteriorated because of political and religious input.

Bertrand Russell and Alfred North Whitehead were, so to speak, the trumpets announcing the advent of modem philosophy, though ultimately they led in different directions. Russell, co-author of *Principia Mathematica*, used his logical apparatus for philosophical purposes seen first in his development of logical atomism. His view of mathematical logic was a large influence on the members of the Vienna Circle. Unfortunately he changed his philosophical viewpoints occasionally so that no developing system was achieved that would find a large following. However, it is not the case that Russell's influence consisted solely in providing philosophers with logical tools which could be used for philosophical purposes. To be sure, that contribution was a major one, though we must not overlook Russell's thoroughgoing empiricism (propositions confirmed or disconfirmed by scientific method) that was a pervasive influence on the members of the Vienna Circle. Though Whitehead was an eminent co-author of *Principia Mathematica* he was not an influence with it because he never used it for philosophical purposes himself or showed how it could be used by other philosophers.

In 1944 Russell changed his views on the problem of induction "chiefly owing to the discovery that induction used without common sense leads more often to false conclusions than to true ones . . . The conclusion is that scientific inference demands certain extra-logical postulates of which induction is not one" (Madden 1960: 323). In 1944, then, Russell still believed that the extrapolation of empirical propositions still required the use of certain extra-postulates. Unfortunately, at this time Russell was running against the tide of neo-Wittgenstinian philosophy according to which philosophical problems are pseudo problems due to linguistic muddles.

> The critic of induction does the unremarkable thing of refuting the view that positive observation, or stratification, etc., is a good reason for accepting an inductive conclusion when "good reason" means "logically conclusive reason." But, of course, he certainly has not refuted the claim that positive observations do constitute a good reason for accepting an inductive conclusion where "good reason" is used in its ordinary sense.
>
> (Madden 1960: 313)

It is difficult to say whether Whitehead was an English or an American philosopher. While in England he cooperated in producing a logical tool that is widely used in analytical philosophy but which played no role in his massive speculative process philosophy. It was only after he left England and taught at Harvard that he carefully developed through the years his process philosophy, which was influential in the thinking of numerous American philosophers including Charles Hartshorne, Paul Weiss, and John Hick. So it would seem that Whitehead was an American philosopher by the time he developed the philosophy that influenced other American philosophers. In any case, his process metaphysics led to its counterpart of process theology, interestingly elaborated by Hick, who claimed that god is not a fully formed entity for all eternity but, like all things, is in the process of greater and greater growth; This presumably finite god (we cannot go into Whitehead's two complementary concepts of god) strives constantly to bring more good into the universe and can only do this by infinite patience in persuading human beings to act morally. He cannot coerce them to be better for this is a self-inconsistent concept. Some commentators have pointed out that, given the facts of life, god's persuasive power is not strong enough to overcome the perennial greedy ways of human beings – the signs are not promising that it ever will be.

The trumpet call was answered. America was not simply influenced by English analytic philosophy from the 1930s until late in the 1980s but was dominated by it. Ordinary language philosophy, influenced by the "Blue Book" Wittgenstein at Trinity College, Cambridge, and by the commonsense views of Moore, also at Trinity, spread rapidly to Oxford and to the United States. Many Americans studied directly with Moore and Wittgenstein. Other American philosophers later studied the doctrine which had spread to Oxford. The doctrine was discovered also by Americans who did not cross the ocean because the Oxford philosophers published quite widely.

The members of the Vienna Circle were influenced by the *Tractatus* Wittgenstein, especially by his distinction between what is sayable within a language and what it can only show non-linguistically. This distinction, as we shall see, played an important role in the Circle's efforts to avoid self-inconsistency in the statement of their positivistic meaning criterion. The influence of the logical positivists in America became widespread with the publication of A.J. Ayer's *Language, Truth, and Logic*.

The logical positivists immigrated to America before World War II and were not immediately influential since, as refugees, it was not easy for them to secure teaching positions. However, after members of the Circle received appointments at the University of Chicago, Yale, Princeton, Minnesota, Iowa *et al.*, their influence escalated to great heights. We shall not list members of the two groups since such a list would be incredibly long; names will be used only when we are discussing specific issues.

The neo-Wittgenstinians and the logical positivists disagreed about the best way of eliminating metaphysics, the former defending the use of ordinary language, the latter constructing an "ideal language." The former felt that philosophical problems arise in the first place by the misuse of ordinary language. After one explains this misuse some specific metaphysical problems disappear. The concept of an ideal language emerged from difficulties in stating the logical positivists' meaning criterion without undesirable self-reference. The criterion states that to be cognitively meaningful a proposition must be either analytically true or false or refer to some empirical experience. If a sentence meets none of these criteria then it is not cognitively meaningful, though it may well have emotional or aesthetic significance. The problem of self-reference is that the criterion is neither a tautology nor a self-contradiction, nor has any empirical content. The response made by some members of the Circle was to construct an ideal language, Humean in structure, and to say that to be cognitively meaningful a proposition must be translatable into the ideal language. Unfortunately the criterion cannot be translated into the ideal language because the self-referential difficulty would again arise. At this point Wittgenstein's distinction between what a language can say and what it can show came into the strategy. One must simply see that an ideal language does reflect the structure of the world. The types of ideal languages differed greatly, some systematically constructed to expunge many metaphysical concepts and others constructed for specific issues, for example how to formulate an ideal language that would account for the counterfactual inference implicit in scientific laws.

G.E. Moore's contribution to the neo-Wittgenstinian tradition was not insignificant by any means. According to Alice Ambrose, one of the prominent neo-Wittgenstinians, Moore held a view not unlike the commonsensical views of Thomas Reid. When a philosophical statement leads to absurdity by ordinary language usage it may be dismissed. He used this strategy in rejecting John Dewey's claim that all empirical propositions are dubitable which Dewey had discussed in detail in *Quest for Certainty* (1929). Dewey argued that there is not only no certainty in empirical statements but also none in the Rationalists' tradition. Moore responded by this type of argument: "I am absolutely certain that I have two hands and any view which believes that such beliefs are confirmed by experience leads to absurd results. According to Dewey, the evidence for having two hands mounts and hence to say the belief that I have two hands is warrantable." Moore thought that the logical positivists shared Dewey's view of dubitability and required one to say that with the mounting evidence it became possible to say that one's belief in having two hands is highly probable!

On the other hand, Moore held views that were opposed to all varieties of the analytic movement. He, along with C.D. Broad, defended the sense-data interpretation of physical objects. Empiricists dislike speculative philosophy because it rationally convinces you of what is directly opposed to the ordinary experiences of daily life. But the most subtle cases of speculative philosophy, surprisingly enough, occur within the precincts of empirical philosophy. By the use of arguments from illusion, hallucinations, and so on, Moore and Broad claimed that the only things we can be directly aware of are phenomena or sense data. The acceptance of this view has led to countless problems of ever connecting the sense data with the external world. This duality has come to be totally debilitating. A person tries to locate a phenomenon or sense data within his consciousness but only finds the physical objects of ordinary life. In the first decade of the twenty-first century it would be difficult to find a philosopher who would accept the speculative concepts of sense data. In large part this result was brought about by C.J. Ducasse, Roderick Chisholm, Wilfrid Sellars, Keith Lehrer, Timothy Duggan, and B. Brody, all of whom were responsible for the adverbial epistemology which removed sense data from the philosophical scene.

Ducasse argued against phenomenalism in general and especially the sense-data theories of Moore and Broad. Ducasse, and especially Chisholm, were much influenced by Reid's way of getting rid of phenomena and sense data. According to the adverbial view, sensations are not entities but ways of being appeared to. "Sensing" rather than "sensation" is the correct word to use. Sensory experience is adverbial in nature and in no sense nominative. This brief reference to the adverbial view is insufficient to do justice to a complex concept but we have seen enough to see how its basic premise gets rid of sense data. Dewey's natural realism also contributed a share to undermining the empiricist who had a speculative dimension.

What often goes unnoticed is that the neo-Wittgenstinians' view is also positivistic and avoids the problem of self-reference by not stating the maxim but by acting on its prescriptions. Their strategy is to show that since a proposition has no logical or empirical dimensions it must be a proposal to give new meanings to ordinary words which result in the traditional philosophical problems in the first place.

Since ordinary language and ideal language philosophers shared variations of a positivistic-meaning criterion it is not surprising that they reached similar conclusions, though this was not always the case. The two groups did agree that the traditional solution to the problem of induction, namely, the introduction of a premise to the effect that nature is uniform, was hopelessly question begging. However, P.F. Strawson and Herbert Feigl believed that, while there were no justifications of induction there were vindications of it that made its use a rational choice. Induction can be shown to be a necessary condition of knowing the future even though it is not a sufficient one. Since induction is the sole way that we can discover the regularities of the world, if such regularities do in fact exist, then the use of inductive methods for knowing the future is a rational procedure. They hold that if there are any other ways of knowing the future, such as, for example, by soothsaying or intuition, they would not be acceptable unless their successes or failures were noted by induction. To be sure, Feigl and Strawson admit that to know that induction is a necessary but not sufficient way of knowing the future is hardly cheerful news. Feigl's fatalistic reply is that we must learn to be grateful for small mercies.

Carnap, as expected, held a more elaborate form of vindication, but nevertheless it was still a vindication because it made the same qualification that it was rational to use the inductive method even though we don't know that there are any future regularities to know. The fundamental problem in Carnap's vindication is that it depends on his inductive theory of probability wherein it is difficult to choose an adequate c-function. Hans Reichenbach also had an extremely elaborate vindication of induction based wholly on the frequency theory of probability which Carnap felt was an inadequate base for the vindication of inductive inference.

We have not yet mentioned all the groups included in the general rubric "analytic." There were linguistically oriented philosophers in England who were critical of the positivism of the neo-Wittgenstinians; they warned that language cannot be put into a straitjacket; it has numerous subtly meaningful usages in addition to the literal statements allowed to be "cognitive" by the positivists. These non-positivistic ordinary language philosophers had a large following in America, but not as much as either branch of positivism. However, the three types of analysis covered many years and it is likely that their relative influence fluctuated through the years.

John Langshaw Austin pointed out that there are cases where a word, phrase, or sentence is not only a linguistic entity but is itself an act or performance: "I, John Doe, hereby bequeath my whole estate to my son Arnold ..." in an authenticated will. Other linguistic acts would be "I do" at one's wedding, and "I swear to tell the truth, the whole truth, and nothing but the truth" in a court of law. All such assertions do something in everyday life, just as the rules of a card game tell people how to play a game. According to Austin, ordinary language has more subtle meaning than positivists can account for, and performative utterances are certainly meaningful though not statements.

H.L.A. Hart, interested in the language of the law, wrote that laws are the crucial support of the infrastructure of any functioning social structure, a view which implies that it is out of place to pass laws that infringe on personal morality. He stressed different ways in which rules of law may be obeyed; one can follow the law to avoid punishment or one can follow the law because one feels that a system of law without too many defects should be accepted as the bulwark of society; thus it is possible entirely for citizens not always to act according to selfish motives. Thus laws are clearly meaningful even though they are not cognitive in the sense of being statements. There are other words that are keys to detect other expressions which are also meaningful though not statements – directions, commands, prescripts, and so on. It is difficult to know sometimes how these writers make the distinction between "meaningful," "cognitive," and "non-cognitive." My impression is that many of the writers in this area equate "meaningful" and "cognitive," though there are exceptions. R.M. Hare denied the cognitive status of moral rules but insisted that they are nevertheless meaningful as prescriptive utterances in contrast to Ayer's view that moral rules are non-cognitive emotional preferences. Moreover "command" is somewhat a protean term. When an ensign tells a seaman to clean the head, and he does, he has not acted but has been determined to do what he did. If he refused to do the job the seaman would have acted but a very costly act it would be.

The analytical philosophers whom we have been considering have sometimes been referred to as ordinary language linguists to distinguish them from both the neo-Wittgenstinians and the logical positivists. Noam Chomsky became a significant critic of the philosophical linguists.

Gilbert Ryle's *Concept of Mind* (1950) is difficult to place in our schema. The book concerns the mind–body problem and was extremely influential in the United States. His influence was increased through the many years he was the editor of *Mind*. Ryle realized that any dualistic position on the mind–body relationship led to disaster; and to get rid of what he called "the Ghost in the machine" he used dispositional concepts to replace purely mental terms. One philosopher remarked that he was cheered that behaviorism had finally penetrated Oxford! Nevertheless, Ryle thought that the mind–body problem, like other philosophical issues, arises by confusing grammatical with logical distinctions.

It must be kept in mind that positivists not only have to eliminate metaphysical statements but must also account for all everyday and scientific truths that are perfectly acceptable. This condition was not always met by either branch of positivism, though the most outstanding example of this deficiency is counterfactual inference. The race was on to distinguish summary statements from scientific laws.

It was acknowledged on all sides that scientific laws permit counterfactual inference. This stick of dynamite, not changed in any way, would have exploded had it been properly detonated. Both camps of positivists had to explain this counterfactual inference without any reference to modal terms, else they had abandoned their positivism. One logical positivist offered the criterion that laws contained no terms that refer to an individual entity, while non-lawful generalizations have such referents. This criterion didn't survive the fact, however, that Kepler's laws of planetary motion did refer to individual planets. A more promising criterion was offered and defended through the years by Carl Hempel. He distinguished between highly developed sciences and lower-order ones. In such a system of laws the higher-order laws which contain theoretical concepts imply the lower-order generalizations. A law statement then can be characterized as a deduction from higher-order hypotheses which have been established independently of its entailments. This criterion was rejected by the Brown University strategy of creating counter-examples. Chisholm constructed a higher-order deductive system which yields as lawful the statement "Every Canadian parent of quintuplets in the first half of the twentieth century is named Dionne." Stephen Barker also constructed another counter-example, as did others, until the Brown counter-instance strategy became widely used in numerous contexts different from the one being discussed. The positivists never succeeded in finding a criterion of lawfulness (or lawlikeness, as Hempel preferred to say) that did not make a concession to modality, though numerous other criteria were suggested.

English writers on probability theory in the nineteenth and early twentieth century were a large influence on Carnap's highly technical inductive probability. Carnap pointed out that the first technically proficient formulation of the frequency theory of probability was made by R.A. Fisher and the mathematician Von Mises in the 1920s. John Maynard Keynes, a great English economist, strove to revive the old inductive concept of probability. In 1939 Harold Jeffreys, a geophysicist, in his *Theory of Probability* formulated a more involved theory of inductive probability. Carnap considered all these people and concluded, "utilizing results of Keynes and Jeffreys and employing the exact tools of modem symbolic logic, I have constructed the fundamental parts of a mathematical theory of inductive probability or inductive logic" (Madden 1960: 274).

In the 1920s Hans Reichenbach had constructed a frequency theory of probability that he felt applied to both statistical and inductive probability. Carnap, however, rejected this view and insisted that there were two separate types of probability statements, those that referred to statistical data and those that referred to the evidence for the probability of scientific theories. Carnap had a number of different ways of showing the difference between the two senses of probability, but one of the most telling ones perhaps is that in inductive probability statements evidence increases or decreases the probability, while in frequency statements evidence either confirms or changes the probability. Carnap was fond of Peirce's rejection of the frequency theory as applied to scientific hypotheses. One cannot, after all, pick universes out of a grab-bag and find in what proportion of them a law of physics holds good!

Karl Popper, an Austrian, was a long-time resident of England and influenced a number of philosophers, economists, and politicians in America. He characterized knowledge as resulting from individual genius and not from induction or any other source, hence providing a contrast to the British empiricist tradition. As we have seen, Wright had abandoned the same tradition years before but, unlike Popper, he was more generous and allowed the formation of theoretical hypotheses from any source whatsoever. Popper took seriously the fact that a confirmation instance of a scientific hypothesis committed the fallacy of affirming the consequent and used the valid form of denying the consequent in his methodological strategy. One commentator has been struck by the contrast between Popper and Galileo. Galileo was punished by the Catholic Church for holding a realistic view of astronomy when its predictions were based on the logical fallacy of affirming the consequent. Galileo, in fact, undercut Popper centuries before Popper ever wrote. Galileo was the first astronomer and physicist to argue persuasively that logic and science had significantly different forms of explanation and that the incredible accuracy of astronomical predictions was not vitiated by an irrelevant logical complaint.

Popper was a conservative economist who, with Milton Friedman, provided the unrestricted laissez-faire views which dominated the conservative reign of Margaret Thatcher. The views of Friedman and Popper have also provided the extreme laissez-faire views of American presidents beginning with Ronald Regan and continuing more or less constantly to the present day. The best-known critic of this tradition is the Keynsian-influenced economist John Kenneth Galbraith. Though in the minority of academic economists at the present time, his *Journey Through Economic Time* constitutes a history of the conservative–progressive economic disputes. Popper was knighted in 1965.

There was a small but nevertheless continuous resurgence of interest in Locke among nineteenth- and twentieth-century philosophers, though the influence was quite different from the eighteenth-century influence. In fact it is a dimension of Locke that is rarely examined. According to Locke, we are not only aware of making the gate open when we push against it but are also aware that the candle makes the wax melt, has the power to melt the wax. A fire possesses the power to melt a piece of wax, but what we need is an explanation of why fire has this power. For Locke the explanation of the power of an object to produce changes consists in specifying, if known, or discovering if not known, the real internal constitution of the object. These views seem to reflect his interest and training in science; nevertheless he sometimes writes as if power has some sort of independent existence from objects, and in other places says the notion of power refers to something ontologically irreducible.

Francis Wayland of Brown and James McCosh of Princeton, while accepting much of Reid's philosophy, rejected Reid's analysis of causality under the influence of reading Locke. Wayland is the first philosopher to reject the Humean material equivalence of "*p* is apriori" and "*p* is necessary," on the one hand, and "*p* is aposteriori" and "*p* is contingent," on the other. With this insight Wayland could have constructed a concept of scientific necessity which had empirical confirmation. And, to a certain extent, he considered this possibility but unfortunately in the end he interpreted the concept of power as a metaphysical tie between causes and effects. Finally Wayland failed to show why the assumed material equivalencies break down, though recent commentators have filled this vacuum.

McCosh was greatly influenced on the causal issue by Locke, though unlike Locke he was extremely careful not to reify the concept of power. Power is no ontological tie that binds but belongs to a powerful particular which is able to make something happen. No one ever said it more clearly than he: the exercise of causal power is not a force or power that has some existence of its own but refers to forceful objects at work. In the twentieth century Sterling Lamprecht, who was sympathetic to the point McCosh was making, wrote,

> Causality is a name for a certain quality of events, it is not a name for the agency behind the events. The agency is there, to be sure: it is the lava flow, the medicine, the light rays, the mechanic's muscles, the towing waves. There is no other force, there is no other cause than just these specific things. But these things are forceful: they operate: they produce. And they are forceful, operate, and produce in that specific way we call necessary. Causality names that kind of necessary operation.
>
> (McCosh 1867: 144)

Under the influence of these people and scientific studies, R. Harré and E.H. Madden constructed a causal model that included Wayland and

McCosh but also develops Locke's idea of the internal structure of a powerful particular which explains why it necessarily produces its effects. In order to know why a stick of dynamite must explode if properly detonated, we need to know the atomic structure of the dynamite *et al.*

The utilitarian views of William Paley, Jeremy Bentham, and J.S. Mill were extremely influential in moral philosophy both in the nineteenth century and in the middle of the twentieth century. Paley influenced Charles Grandison Finney, second president of Oberlin College, both positively and negatively. It is clear from Finney's own writing that he had studied his Paley carefully. Strangely enough Jonathan Edwards and Paley had certain elements in common and others not. Let us examine the interconnections among these philosophers. Paley and Bentham agreed in believing that right and wrong referred to outward acts rather than to intentions. Edwards and Finney believed that right and wrong referred primarily to intentions and only derivatively to acts insofar as they reflect intentions. Paley and Finney agreed in holding that rules and not specific cases should be the subject matter of utilitarian judgments, while Bentham held that specific acts should be the subject matter of such judgments. Hence it would be correct to call Finney an intention-rule-utilitarian. Correspondingly Paley would be a non-intention-rule-utilitarian and Bentham a non-intention-act-utilitarian. Finney disliked to be labeled a utilitarian because he thoroughly disliked Paley's concept of seeking personally advantageous consequences. Finney, like Edwards and his many followers, believed intentions crucial since an act motivated by good intentions might well go astray outside the control of the agent. Finney criticized utilitarians because they almost gave the impression that they referred right and wrong to outward acts rather than to intentions. Of course, that is precisely what Paley and Bentham meant to do! How can this be possible when we know he was a close student of Paley? Apparently it seemed so clear to Finney that intentions are involved fully in judgments of right and wrong that he found it difficult to believe that anyone held an opposite view.

Bentham and J.S. Mill influenced Wright and Norton in the nineteenth century, though both of them chose Mill's version whenever it differed from Bentham's. William James constructed a biologized version of utility in his "The Moral Philosopher and the Moral Life." Bentham and Mill continued to be strong influences in America in the twentieth century. In the mid-1950s Lucius Garvin and Charles Baylis strongly defended the classic utilitarian viewpoint against all systems that relied on moral intuitions. Later in the twentieth century, rule utilitarianism became quite fashionable though it is doubtful if any of the rule utilitarians realized that they had been anticipated by Paley or Finney a century or more earlier. J.J.C. Smart and R.M. Hare formulated "versions" of utilitarianism in later years which received a good deal of discussion in the 1970s and 1980s. However, Hare deviated a good deal from classical utility theory since he viewed moral rules as noncognitive prescriptions. Even Benjamin Rush in the eighteenth century held an early version of utilitarianism, the main object of which was to be the basis for his reformed penology, according to which prisoners should be rehabilitated if possible and not punished except by incarceration.

While the English utilitarians strongly influenced ethical theory, this view also had strong opposition from the nineteenth-century followers of Reid. What follows is a medley of their criticisms: we are usually ignorant of what will happen in the future; hence any moral judgment based on the consideration of likely future consequences is doomed to fail; acts have infinite consequences; if all virtues are justified by desirable consequences then each virtue loses its unique character; a child is perfectly aware of the differences between right and wrong without being capable of comprehending the greatest amount of happiness; the utilitarian has no way of choosing or deciding between different obligations when two of them come into conflict. Wayland was always anti-utilitarian but nevertheless was politically conservative and fearful of any violent actions. He argued against the approaching Civil War as disastrous and he rebuked the abolitionists for causing trouble. He finally realized that he was himself skating pretty close to the "half-frozen ice" of utilitarianism and decided that in order to have a legacy of liberty to transmit to upcoming Americans there must come a civil war. Should one give up high hopes for liberty for all in order to avoid terrible consequences? Wayland sadly concluded that "it ... is best to meet a difficulty just where God puts it. If we dodge it, it will come in a worse place" (Meddon 1963: 43).

Further reading

Blake, R.M., Ducasse, C.I., and Madden, E.H. *Theories of Scientific Method: The Renaissance through the Nineteenth Century.* Seattle, WA: University of Washington Press, 1960.

Blau, J.L. *Men and Movements in American Philosophy.* New York: Prentice-Hall, 1952.

Carnap, Rudolf. *Logical Foundations of Probability.* Chicago, IL: University of Chicago Press, 1950.

Chisholm, Roderick. “Law Statements and Counterfactual Inference,” *Analysis* 15, 5 (1955): 97–105.

—— *Theory of Knowledge.* Englewood Cliffs, NJ: Prentice-Hall, 1966.

Dewey, John. *Reconstruction in Philosophy.* New York: Henry Holt, 1920.

—— *The Quest for Certainty.* New York: Minton, Balch, 1929.

Ducasse, C.J. *Nature, Mind, and Death.* La Salle, IL: Open Court, 1951, Chs 12–16.

Feigl, Herbert. “Scientific Method without Presuppositions,” *Philosophical Studies* 5 (1954).

Fisch, Max. “Justice Holmes, The Prediction Theory of Law, and Pragmatism,” *Journal of Philosophy* 39 (1942), especially note pp. 86–7, 91.

Hare, P.H. and Madden, E.H. *Causing, Perceiving, and Believing.* Dordrecht and Boston, MA: Reidel, 1975, Ch. 4.

Hempel, Carl “Problems and Changes in the Empiricist Criterion of Meaning,” *Revue Intemationale de Philosophie* 4 (1950).

James, William. “The Dilemma of Determinism” in *The Will to Believe, The Works of William James.* Cambridge, MA: Harvard University Press, 1979.

Lamprecht, Sterling. *The Metaphysics of Naturalism.* New York: Appleton Century-Crofts, 1967.

McCosh, James. *The Intuitions of the Mind*, revised edition. New York: Robert Carter, 1867, pp. 227, 229, 230, 232, 233ff, etc.

Madden, Dennis and Madden, E.H. “John Dewey: A Commentary,” *Transactions of the C.S. Peirce Society* 39 (2002): 95–116.

Madden, E.H. (ed.) *The Structure of Scientific Thought: Readings in the Philosophy of Science.* Boston, MA: Houghton Mifflin, 1960.

—— *Chauncey Wright and the Foundations of Pragmatism.* Seattle, WA: University of Washington Press, 1963.

Madden, Marian C. and Madden, E.H. “Emerson, Goethe, and Fuller,” *Transactions of the C.S. Peirce Society* 34 (1998): 571–604.

Myers, Gerald E. *William James: His Life and Thought.* New Haven, CT: Yale University Press, 1986.

Peirce, C.S. “Induction as Experimental and Self-Corrective” in Collected Papers of C.S. Peirce, Vol. 6, ed. C. Hartshorne and P. Weiss. Cambridge, MA: Harvard University Press, 1935.

Schneider, Herbert W. *A History of American Philosophy*, second edition. New York: Columbia University Press, 1963.

Strawson, P.F. *Introduction to Logical Theory.* London, Methuen, 1952, Ch. 9.

Wright, Chauncey. *Philosophical Discussions* in *The Evolutionary Philosophy of Chauncey Wright*, Vol. 1, ed. F.X. Ryan. Bristol: Thoemmes Press, 2000.

Edward H. Madden

EPISTEMOLOGY

Epistemology, the study of knowledge, addresses questions about the nature of knowledge, the source(s) of knowledge, the justification for claims to knowledge, forms of knowledge, and even whether we have any knowledge at all. We claim to know many things: what a toothache feels like, that 2 + 2 = 4, that the Sun is larger than the Earth, how to drive a car, etc. These examples illustrate different kinds of knowledge. Sometimes by “knowledge” we mean knowledge by acquaintance, or knowledge of something with which we are immediately connected to (or acquainted with), such as having a toothache. There is also propositional knowledge, or knowledge that something is the case (i.e. knowledge that some proposition is true), such as knowing that the Sun is larger than the Earth. In addition, there is practical knowledge, which in this case means knowing how to do something, such as knowing how to drive a car. One issue within epistemology is the examination of how these various kinds of knowledge are related to each other. For example, is all propositional knowledge based on or even equivalent to knowledge by acquaintance?

A traditional answer to the question, “What is knowledge?” (at least for propositional knowledge) is that knowledge is Justified True Belief. Philosophers usually state this in the following way: *S knows that p* (meaning that some person S knows that some proposition p is the case) involves three necessary conditions. Those conditions are: (1) *S* believes that *p*; (2) *p* is true; and (3) *S* is justified in believing *p*. The first condition, the belief condition, simply states that for us to know something, we have to at least believe it. It would be strange to claim that one knows that Seattle is in Washington but one does not believe it. So, believing that p is a necessary condition for knowing that p. But it is not sufficient, since we can believe things without knowing them. A second condition for knowledge is the truth condition. This states that p, the proposition we know, is true. This means that we can not know something that is false. Now, we can know that something is false. For instance, one knows that it is false that one's cat is a dog. One can know that a proposition is false, but one cannot know a false proposition. Another way of saying this is that, while there can be false beliefs, there cannot be false knowledge. Again, one cannot know that 2 + 2 = 3 or that the Sun is smaller than the Earth, no matter how strongly one believes it. The third traditional condition for knowledge is the justification condition. The first two conditions, i.e. having a true belief, by themselves are not enough for knowledge. I must also have justification for the belief. Knowledge cannot just be true belief, otherwise, it is said, any lucky guess that turned out correct would be a case of knowledge.

This traditional notion of knowledge as justified true belief has been examined and criticized by philosophers for a long time. First, with respect to belief, it is not the same as just having an opinion. We can have opinions about anything without having any sort of evidence or warrant for those opinions. This is not the same as having a belief. As Charles Peirce noted, a belief involves not only something we are aware of, but a genuine belief (as opposed to a mere opinion) appeases the irritation of a real doubt and involves the establishment in our nature of a rule of action (or a habit). So, a belief involves the acceptance of some fact or process, with a readiness to act on that acceptance. If I really believe something, rather than just say that I do, then I take it as given that certain facts are the case and my future behavior is affected as a result.

As for truth, there are a number of philosophical views about what truth is. Philosophers often refer to one view, deemed a common-sense view, as the correspondence conception of truth. This view of truth states that what makes a particular proposition or belief true is that it corresponds to facts in the world. If my belief that the Sun is larger than the Earth is true, it is because in fact the Sun is larger than the Earth. It is that simple; if my belief corresponds to the facts, it is true (indeed, that is what makes it true), and if it does not correspond, it is not true. Another philosophical view of truth is called the coherence conception of truth. This view of truth states that what makes a particular proposition or belief true is that it coheres with other accepted propositions or beliefs. That is, no proposition or belief exists in isolation and when we say some belief is true (or false, for that matter) what we mean is that it is consistent with other beliefs (or, in the case of a false belief, that it is inconsistent with other beliefs). Many, probably most, of those other beliefs are ones concerning facts about the world, so truth is not merely some coherent fairy tale, according to the supporters of this view. A third view of truth is called the *pragmatist* conception of truth (thought not all pragmatist philosophers accept this conception). This view of truth, it is said, states that what makes a particular proposition or belief true is how it affects us in the future, that is, what consequences follow from taking it as true. The point here is that "true" is not simply a descriptive property of propositions or beliefs, but, rather, that "true" is also a prescriptive notion, directing our future beliefs and actions. As William James put it, truth happens to an idea; it is made true by events; its verity is itself an event or process.

One more word about truth here: It is quite common to have someone say that truth is relative or that something is "true for me." There are several things to say about this. First, there is a difference between *relativity* and *subjectivism*. When people say something is "true for me," that really is a claim that truth is subjective, that there are no objective standards for assessing whether some belief is true or not. To say that truth is relative is not the same thing. We can speak of beliefs being judged true or false relative to certain standards (for example, legal standards of evidence or proof vs scientific standards of evidence or mathematical standards of proof), but that is not the same as saying that it is subjective. So, one point is that the notion of truth as relative is not the same as the notion of truth as subjective. Beyond that, when someone says that something is "true for me," that really comes down to just saying that "I believe it" (and perhaps believe it so strongly that I will act in certain ways on that belief). But there must be some reason why something is "true for me" as opposed to being "false for me." In saying it is "true for me," the "for me" part doesn't really add anything. It just says that I believe it. That does not clarify or distinguish true beliefs from false beliefs or what makes some beliefs true and others false.

Finally, there is the third condition of knowledge discussed above, namely, the justification condition. When asked what kinds of support or evidence or warrant justify propositions or beliefs, philosophers traditionally spoke of *empiricist* justification or *rationalist* justification. An empiricist view of justification is the view that the source of all knowledge, and, so, the final justification of all knowledge, comes down to immediate sensory experience. Quite simply, we bump into the world. If we claim to know something and that claim cannot finally be shown to be based in sensory experience, then, under an empiricist view, that claim is not a case of knowledge. Obviously, matters get more complex than this; for example, we often, especially within science, have to base claims on probabilities and statistical analyses, but the point remains the same: for some belief to be knowledge, it ultimately must be based on sensory experience, however complex that experience is.

A rationalist view of justification rejects the view that the source, and justification, of all knowledge is sensory experience. The rationalist view says this empiricist view is false, since there are things we know that are not based on sensory experience, such as mathematical or logical knowledge. While, as children, we might come to learn that $2 + 2 = 4$, numbers and addition and equality are not things in the world that we bump into. We can demonstrate our knowledge of, in this case, simple arithmetic by showing two apples and two more apples give us four apples, but, say the rationalists, that is just a demonstration of knowledge, not the knowledge itself. (In addition, we know that $\sqrt{3} < 29$, but not because we have ever bumped into $\sqrt{3}$ apples in the world.) So, according to the rationalist view, not all knowledge is based on sensory experience and, in fact, there are "truths of reason" (which is why this view is called rationalism) that we know and are not a matter of sensory experience of things in the world. Besides the example of mathematical knowledge, rationalists claim that other basic concepts that we use, basic categories such as causality or unity or possibility, are not known by sensory experience. That is, we see objects in the world, but we do not "see" cause or unity. Today philosophers tend to address the issue of the justification of beliefs not so much in terms of empiricism and rationalism as in terms of *externalism* and *internalism*. Simply put, externalism is the view that what justifies a person's beliefs must be something external to the person, while internalism is the view that something internal to the believer can (at least in part) be relevant to justifying that person's beliefs.

The debate between empiricism and rationalism has a long history in American philosophy. Jonathan Edwards (1703–58) defended a version of rationalism, as did Ralph Waldo Emerson (1803–82) and George Holmes Howison (1834–1916). Even the contemporary linguist/philosopher Noam Chomsky (1928–) has defended a version of rationalism. In addition, empiricism has had strong advocates, including John Fiske (1842–1901), George Santayana (1863–1952), C.I. Lewis (1883–1964), and W.V.O. Quine (1908–2000).

In addition to stands regarding specific views of justification or warrant, such as empiricism or rationalism, many American philosophers have critiqued epistemology more broadly. Pragmatists, in particular, have questioned and rejected a commitment to *foundationalism*, i.e. the position that all knowledge rests on some indubitable, certain foundation. For the empiricists, this foundation is immediate sensory awareness; for the rationalists, this foundation is self-evident truths. Across the board, pragmatist philosophers have rejected this position in favor of *fallibilism*, the view that absolute certainty is not possible for any knowledge claim or any criterion of knowledge, or even as a desirable standard for knowledge. John Dewey (1859–1952) frequently challenged this "quest for certainty," insisting that knowledge could only be understood as the interaction between organisms and their environments. Further, both C.I. Lewis and Wilfrid Sellars (1912–89) argued against "the myth of the given," that is, that certain elements of our experience are simply indubitable and unanalyzable. Quine famously argued for "naturalized epistemology," claiming that justification for knowledge claims is not a matter of "first philosophy," independent of the standards and criteria of the natural sciences. Richard Rorty (1931–), more than most contemporary American philosophers, has identified epistemology, particularly foundationalist epistemology, as being antithetical to truly important philosophical concerns.

Besides the issues of belief and truth and justification, there are numerous other epistemological topics. For example, there is the broad question of whether we are *ever* justified in claiming to actually know something or if we might always be mistaken about our beliefs. This is the issue of *skepticism*, and it has to do with the kinds and levels of justification that are required for a belief to be justified to such an extent or in such a way as fully to be knowledge. A global, sustained skepticism has not been championed by American philosophers, though, as noted above, fallibalism has. There are also more specific epistemological topics, such as the nature of perception, which Hilary Putnam (1926–) has tied closely with pragmatism. Additionally, there is the topic of contents of knowledge, *what* can be known, particularly in contexts that involve evaluation. For example, can there be moral knowledge or aesthetic knowledge as opposed to moral and aesthetic belief?

One issue that has generated much attention in American philosophy is the issue of other modes of belief or knowledge (e.g. intuition, revelation). This issue points to even broader questions and concerns regarding epistemology. One concern is the place of value(s) and action as being constitutive of knowledge. A long-standing view held in common by many American philosophers is a rejection of the notion of disinterested inquiry. That is, knowledge is the result of inquiry, of a process of investigating and understanding phenomena. But all inquiry, it is held, is purposive. Values, as part of such processes, are not separable from the product of knowledge that results from such inquiry. So, at a fundamental, constitutive level, epistemology is axiological, both at the point of genesis of inquiry and at the point of consequence, i.e. subsequent action. This is at the heart of the *pragmatic maxim*: Consider what effects, which might conceivably have practical bearings, we conceive the object of our conception to have. Then, our conception of these effects is the whole of our conception of the object. Indeed, "knowledge" is not merely a descriptive term but it is a normative term as well, as was even implicitly indicated by philosophers who wanted to distinguish knowledge from true belief.

This acknowledgement, even emphasis, on the axiological nature of epistemology underlies and informs much contemporary feminist and "standpoint" epistemology. Rejecting the notion that there is knowledge in some ideal, non-contextual sense, philosophers such as Lynn Hankinson Nelson (1948–) and Sandra Harding (1935–) have stressed the point that traditional epistemology has overlooked *knowers* in its pursuit of standards and criteria of knowledge. There are multiple and varied "standpoints" from which inquirers seek to investigate and understand phenomena. Those standpoints are inextricably connected with relevant features of who or what those inquirers are: for example, gender, race, and other factors that constitute knowers. Cornel West (1953–) and others have made similar arguments with respect to race as being relevant to the constitutive elements of knowledge.

Further reading

Dewey, John. *The Quest for Certainty*. New York: Minton and Balch, 1929.

James, William. *Pragmatism*. Indianapolis, IN: Hackett, 1981.

Nelson, Lynn Hankinson. *Who Knows? From Quine to a Feminist's Empiricism*. Philadelphia, PA: Temple University Press, 1990.

Peirce, Charles S. "How to Make Our Ideas Clear" in *The Essential Peirce*, ed. Nathan Hauser and Christian Kloesel. Bloomington, IN: Indiana University Press, 1998, pp. 124–41.

Pratt, Scott. "Knowledge and Action: American Epistemology" in Armen T. Marsoobian and John Ryder (eds) *The Blackwell Guide to American Philosophy*. New York: Blackwell, 2004, pp. 306–24.

Putnam, Hilary. *The Collapse of the Fact/Value Dichotomy and Other Essays*. Cambridge, MA: Harvard University Press, 2004.

Quine, W.V.O. *Ontological Relativity and Other Essays*. New York: Columbia University Press, 1969.

Rorty, Richard. *Philosophy and the Mirror of Nature*. Princeton, NJ: Princeton University Press, 1979.

West, Cornel. *The American Evasion of Philosophy*. Madison, WI: University of Wisconsin Press, 1989.

DAVID BOERSEMA

EQUALITY

Equality has been a concept of central importance in American philosophy from its earliest days, though its meaning, character, implications, domain of operation, and relationships with other centrally important concepts have been hotly contested. Some of this controversy arises from a common fallacy of conflating two very different concepts of equality, one being a mathematical concept meaning identity, sameness, and interchangeability, and the other being a social and metaphysical concept meaning commensurability in value of importantly differing, non-interchangeable persons. Thomas Jefferson's use of the concept of social equality in the American Declaration of Independence of 1776 helped to fix its importance in the common sense of most Americans and to give it a high priority within democratic theory. When Jefferson wrote, "We hold these truths to be self-evident: that all men are created equal," he succinctly expressed three interrelated ideas: (1) rejection of hierarchal natural orders or levels of human being; (2) commensurability in primordial value of all human persons; and (3) entitlement of each human person to the most basic and far-reaching kinds of esteem and regard from their fellows as reflecting this overriding valuation of their worth already implicit within nature.

When Frederick Douglass denounced chattel slavery in the 1850s, calling for America to become America, and when Martin Luther King, Jr, declared in the 1960s that the time had come to fulfill the promise of America's founders to all of its citizens, it was this sense of primordial social equality as a touchstone for all other humanity-related thinking to which they appealed, attributing to it a profound significance that would require the remaking of American law, politics, economics, moral and religious thought, and habits of daily living, away from acceptance of group-based social hierarchy, and toward respect for the natural entitlements of every individual person. When Walt Whitman appealed in his late nineteenth-century poetry and prose to primordial human equality, he saw it as a stimulus toward revaluing the unique, diverse individualities of whole human beings, with special attention to their distinctive creative imaginations, their opportunities for coming to voice, their freedom from social constraints that could unwarrantably limit their becoming, and their freedom to engage in mutually enlivening transactions with other human persons and with the larger whole of nature. When Jane Addams expressed the meaning of social equality in her early twentieth-century philosophical writings and in her practical efforts to empower labor activists, peacemakers, and new immigrants to American cities, her watchword was working "with" others, rather than benevolently doing things "to" them from a position of hierarchical advantage, virtue, and wisdom.

John Dewey pointed out that the concept of equality is characteristically linked within American thought with the concepts of liberty and fraternity (or community) as a partial definition and formula for achieving democracy. Each of these concepts is vague in William James's sense, i.e. its meaning is highly important but imprecise, serving to indicate or point to a set of values and other considerations to be taken into account in fruitful thinking. Taken together as mutually conditioning one another, the concepts of liberty, equality, and community frame what Dewey called "a democratic angle of vision" that implies an approach to philosophy and a way of life, including a set of institutions for citizen self-governance. Dewey understood this democratic angle of vision as challenging two rivals: (1) a older hierarchical and authoritarian mainstream in Western philosophy and in many world cultures; and (2) a modern, socially atomistic angle of vision within which equality functions adjectivally to limit the scope of the central concept, primordial individual liberty.

From a democratic angle of vision, Dewey suggested, the meanings of "equality" are critical and reconstructive at both historical and metaphysical levels. Historically, the concept of equality indicated a critical rejection of inherited social hierarchies that Jefferson and others perceived as unjust, and of associated cultural patterns of received authority they perceived as intolerable. Reconstructively, "equality" suggested a more ideal future direction for an emerging multicultural American society, which they hoped would be characterized by living without fixed hierarchies, but with shared powers to direct a common life and shared commitment to the mutual flourishing of all. The deeper, not yet fully appreciated meaning of the concept of equality is metaphysical, Dewey argued: it indicates a rejection of all fixed kinds and categories as definitive of any aspect of reality, including humanity, in favor of a vision of the processive emergence of unique individuals within increasingly complex and well-integrated transactional networks that are necessary to their becoming and to which they contribute.

To treat human persons as equals from this democratic angle of vision that Jefferson, Dewey, and others have regarded as the definitive philosophical gift of the American experience means to treat them with a communally engaged sense of concern and regard for their uniqueness and their ultimate value, recognizing that as embodied, intelligent, growth-oriented social beings, they have basic needs that must be comparably well addressed if they and their communities are to flourish, and also that they have potential capabilities and unique gifts that must be awakened, informed, appreciated by others, and effectively contributed to the social whole in order for those individuals to live healthy, personally meaningful, and mutually beneficial lives. Instead of requiring that we treat all human individuals alike in some uniform, mechanical fashion, the moral meaning of equality is that we must treat others in ways that communicate respect for their unique "innerness," that respond in both personal and organized ways to their bio-organic and social-psychological needs, that contribute to the growth of their human capabilities and particular gifts, and that help them find opportunities to contribute to the overall growth and welfare of their communities. The political meaning of equality requires avoiding fixed hierarchies in institutional structures and practices, including all individuals and their significant groups in democratic dialogue and decision making about their common future, opening all offices to all community members on the sole basis of qualification to serve, and according significant weight in distributions of social benefits and burdens to the uniqueness of individuals and the particular shared needs of diverse groups, rather than the assumption that "one size fits all" or that the values and tastes of a majority should rule in all matters. In economics, the concept of democratic social equality requires a guiding recognition that it is social individuals who transact within systems of communication, organization, valuation, production, and exchange; that the efficiency and justice of these systems must be judged in terms of their wider consequences for the communities and individuals members it is their purpose to serve; that all such communities and individuals require certain basic goods and services, meaningful experiences of social recognition and effective contribution, and opportunities for developing their human capabilities and unique gifts; that such opportunities must be comparable in potential effectiveness though appropriately diverse in kind in order to be just; and that great differences in distributive outcomes cannot be justified in terms of distinguishable individual merit and tend to undermine the ability of whole social systems to treat human individuals as equals. In matters of law, these metaphysical, moral, political, and economic considerations must be taken seriously if a democratic principle of social equality is to prevail, rather than a misguided principle of mathematical sameness, a majoritarian principle of largest group dominance, or a power-based principle of reinforcing and transmitting hierarchical control. In the sciences and the arts, social equality is a principle of open access based upon gifts and emerging capabilities, uniqueness in contributions, appreciation of differences, and community-orientation of individual efforts. As a religious principle, equality is a call to agapic love and service to all members of the human family. As a principle of daily living, social equality is expressed in neighborliness, sharing to assure that everyone's needs are met, attending to and learning from others amidst commonalities and differences, listening, speaking up, respecting one another's innerness, and habitually pursuing mutual benefit.

Further reading

Addams, Jane. *Democracy and Social Ethics.* Urbana, IL: University of Illinois Press, 2002 [1902].

Bunge, Robert. *An American Ur-Philosophie: Philosophy Before Pragmatism (B.P.).* Lanham, MD: University Press of America, 1984.

Dewey, John. "Philosophy and Democracy" in *The Essential Dewey: Vol. 1 – Pragmatism, Education, Democracy,* ed. Larry A. Hickman and Thomas M. Alexander. Carbondale, IL: Southern Illinois University Press, 1998 [1919].

King, Martin Luther, Jr. *Where Do We Go From Here: Chaos or Community?* New York: Random House, 1967.

Seigfried, Charlene Haddock. *Pragmatism and Feminism: Reweaving the Social Fabric.* Chicago, IL: University of Chicago Press, 1996.

JUDITH M. GREEN

ESSENTIALISM

Essentialism is closely related to necessity. There are two kinds of necessity: necessity of the truth of a proposition (e.g. the truth of "All bachelors are unmarried"), and necessity of the possession of a property by an individual (e.g. the possession of personhood by you). The former is known as necessity *de dicto*, and the latter necessity *de re.* Debates on essentialism in the United States closely parallel those on necessities *de dicto* and *de re.* For any individual or kind of individual x and any property P, P is an essential property of x just if x necessarily has P, i.e. x has P in every possible world in which x exists.

Haecceity, world-indexing, materiality, origin, and composition

Alvin Plantinga offers four kinds of essential properties of individuals. First, being unmarried if a bachelor is an essential property of Socrates; so is having some property. Such properties are uninteresting essential properties of individuals, for they are based on necessities *de dicto* of the analytic kind ("It is necessarily the case that all bachelors are unmarried") or possessed by all individuals (every individual has some property). Second, being Socrates is an essential property of Socrates. In general, for any individual, being that very individual is called the individual's *haecceity*, and any individual's haecceity is an essential property of that individual. Socrates also has any property logically entailed by his haecceity as his essential property: e.g. the property of being either Socrates or Plato. Third, given that Socrates is snub-nosed in the actual world, being snub-nosed in the actual world is his essential property, even though the property of being snub-nosed is not; for in any possible world w in which he exists, Socrates is such that he is snub-nosed in the actual world, even though he may not be snub-nosed in w. In general, for any individual x, any property P, and any world w, if x has P in w, then having P in w is a world-indexed property essential to x. Fourth, assuming that Socrates is a material object, being material is his essential property. It is an essential property of any material object. Correspondingly, being non-material is an essential property of any non-material object.

Saul Kripke proposes different types of essential properties of individuals. One is origin. Assume that you originated in a particular egg e and a particular sperm s. Then having originated in e and s is your essential property. Nobody who did not originate in e and s, however similar s/he might be to you, could possibly be you. Another is composition. Assume that the shirt you are wearing is composed of cotton fibers. Then being made of cotton is an essential property of the shirt. No shirt that was not made of cotton, however similar it might be to the shirt, could possibly be that very shirt.

Natural kinds

Kripke also proposes essential properties of natural kinds, which are analogous to compositional properties of individuals. Given that the chemical structure of water is H_2O, having the chemical structure H_2O is an essential property of water. No natural kind that did not have the chemical structure H_2O, however similar it might be to water (colorless, tasteless, odorless, thirst-quenching, etc.), could possibly be water. The essentiality of this property to water is tied to the corresponding necessity *de dicto*, viz., the necessity of "The chemical structure of water is H_2O." Unlike "All bachelors are unmarried," this proposition is not analytic, hence its necessity does not stem from conceptual connections. Kripke calls such a proposition *metaphysically necessary.* Propositions ascribing the origin or composition of an individual are also metaphysically necessary.

Kripke pursues a similar line of reasoning to a surprising conclusion. Unicorns are an animal species that does not actually exist. So, there are no actual genetic traits, other micro features, or evolutionary characteristics that would mark unicornhood. Given this, unicorns lack essential properties which would distinguish them from other animal species. But no possible species could lack such essential properties. Therefore, unicorns are impossible.

Individual essence

According to Plantinga, *P* is an individual essence of *x* just if *P* is *x*'s essential property and no individual distinct from *x* has *P* in any possible world. Socrates's haecceity and his origin are his individual essences, but the properties of being unmarried if a bachelor, having some property, being snub-nosed in the actual world, and being material are not; neither is being made of cotton an individual essence of your cotton shirt. Note that Socrates's haecceity involves a particular person (himself) and his origin involves particular cells (*e* and *s*). It is unclear whether there is an individual essence that is a purely qualitative property involving no individual at all. If haecceities are independent of all purely qualitative properties, no purely qualitative property is an individual essence. Max Black discusses a world in which two qualitatively identical but numerically distinct spheres, and nothing else, exist. If, for every purely qualitative property, there is an analog of Black's world and it is a possible world, then no purely qualitative property is an individual essence.

Resistance to essentialism

According to W.V. Quine, a man who is both a mathematician and a cyclist may at best be said to be necessarily rational under the label "mathematician" and necessarily bipedal under the label "cyclist," but he is neither necessarily one way or another independently of a label, and to claim that he is is to accept Aristotelian essentialism. Aristotelian essentialism affirms claims of necessity *de re*, and Quine rejects all such claims as conceptually muddled. He also rejects all claims of necessity *de dicto* not reducible to logical truth, so he rejects Kripke's metaphysical necessities.

Further reading

Black, Max. "The Identity of Indiscernibles," *Mind* 51 (1952): 153–64.

Kripke, Saul. *Naming and Necessity.* Cambridge, MA: Harvard University Press, 1980.

Plantinga, Alvin. *The Nature of Necessity.* Oxford: Clarendon Press, 1974.

Quine, W.V. "Two Dogmas of Empiricism." *Philosophical Review* 60 (1951): 20–43.

TAKASHI YAGISAWA

ETHICS

In ethics, the theory of the evaluation of conduct and character, American thought is often said to be distinguished by its tendency to naturalism. Naturalism is the view that the world and its contents are essentially as empirical natural science takes them to be. Ethical naturalism is the view that values and value judgments must be continuous with empirical facts and scientific judgments. Values cannot be independent properties of things, events, or persons that operate outside of natural scientific laws. They must instead be reducible to or emergent from natural properties of things, events, and persons, taken individually or collectively. Pragmatism, America's most distinctive philosophical school, undoubtedly contributed to the rise of naturalism in American ethics in the late nineteenth and early twentieth centuries. But however ingrained naturalism may subsequently have become, American ethics have not historically been naturalistic.

In the seventeenth century, ethics was generally treated as a form of applied theology. This was not because the Puritan Calvinist communities did not value philosophic study generally. On the contrary, because these communities were theocratic, their leadership needed a broad education to fulfill their duties of political as well as religious leadership. To ensure that their communities were respectful of God's purposes, they looked not only to the Bible but also to natural events for revelation of divine will. Miraculous departures from the natural order signaled God's favor or displeasure, thus the leadership had to be able to distinguish these from merely unusual natural events. To this end, Puritan institutions offered solid if conservative grounding in the scholastic treatments of science, mathematics, and logic of the day and gradually incorporated newer approaches forged by continental rationalism and British empiricism as these made their way across the Atlantic. But philosophic ethics, which in contemporary European universities was more or less Christianized versions of Aristotle, Plato or Stoicism, were eschewed in favor of scriptural teachings. According to Puritan theology, the only way to become good was through God's grace. To know who was fit to live in or lead a Puritan community, its members needed to be able to discern the workings of grace in one another's characters empirically. Because classical ethical theories lacked any conception of divine grace, they were considered useless for this purpose.

However, in the eighteenth century, Puritan leaders and educators were not unreceptive to the new theories of virtue and morals proposed by British writers of the Moral Sense school (e.g. Anthony Ashley Cooper, 3rd Earl of Shaftesbury, Francis Hutcheson, David Hume). Puritan communities had been experiencing increasing difficulties in agreeing upon the marks of true "conversion experiences" of God's grace. Moral theories that provided resources for analyzing and explaining the workings of human moral psychology in terms of affective states or other empirically discernable qualities were thus of increasing interest.

Jonathan Edwards, the last and greatest philosophical exponent of Puritanism in America, developed a novel sentiment-based theory of virtue in his posthumously published *The Nature of True Virtue* (1765). Edwards, following British Moral Sense theorists Francis Hutcheson and David Hume, generally accepts John Locke's account of human knowledge as empirical in origin. All our ideas come to us via our senses, external and internal; the external senses providing ideas of objects external to our minds and the internal ones providing ideas from reflection upon either the operations of our own minds or our external ideas. Pleasure is such an inner, reflective sense, Locke argued, love of which is our primary motive to action. Hutcheson had argued that we also possessed inner aesthetic and moral senses, defined as mental *determinations* to feel distinct forms of pleasure and pain in reflection upon our ideas of things (aesthetic) or of persons (moral). It is because we possess a moral sense, Hutcheson argued, that we feel immediate and uncalculated approval or disapproval whenever we contemplate benevolent or malicious acts from a disinterested standpoint. That we have these feelings even when occupying a disinterested standpoint shows, moreover, that the moral sense is not simply an inclination to be pleased by whatever tends to our material advantage, or as Hutcheson puts it, our "natural" good. We approve benevolence in itself, as *good* in a distinct, moral, sense.

Edwards agrees that benevolence is the essence of true virtue, but argues that human nature unassisted by grace is incapable of having or approving benevolence itself. What we approve by nature is not benevolence per se, which he defines as "benevolence to [intelligent] being in general." It is instead benevolence to those in whom we take an interest either from self-love or from partial affections. The benevolence Hutcheson describes is thus not true virtue but rather a secondary, inferior kind. We do feel genuine approval for benevolence we observe but what we feel is not, as Hutcheson supposed, a pure disinterested affection. Edwards calls it a "love of complacency," i.e. an approval felt for those who act in ways agreeable to our own self-love or partial affections. Those who possess true virtue, by contrast, love all intelligent being uniformly, which entails that they primarily love God, who comprehends all intelligent being. Although we can conceive of such a wide benevolence intellectually, we neither possess it by nature nor immediately approve it when we do observe it. Edwards agrees with Hume that we can not create dispositions at will. Thus without God's intervention, we are incapable of true virtue.

The lesser sort is open to us, however. And for ordinary life, our limited benevolence coupled with our aesthetic taste for order and proportion are sufficient. Partial benevolence and self-love move us to care for others. And while the degree of our benevolence towards others is a function of our partiality to them, Edwards holds that the variability of our benevolence is offset by our aesthetic delight in order. For our sense of order is disagreeably affected whenever communities adopt policies that assign their members disproportionate benefits or burdens. Thus our inner senses, moral and aesthetic, together with our self-interest in leading pleasant lives, properly cultivated can both explain and sustain morally decent behavior in public and private life.

Edward's openness to new developments in British moral philosophy was not unusual in late eighteenth-century academic philosophy, but his unconcern about the skeptical implications of British empiricism was not widely shared. To many, Humean skepticism seemed the unavoidable consequence of so thoroughgoing an empiricism. Thus the majority looked instead to later Scottish Enlightenment figures such as Thomas Reid, Dugald Stewart, and Sir William Hamilton, whose empiricist epistemology, grounded in John Locke, was supplemented by rational a priori intuition. The Scottish Common Sense Realists rejected Locke's "copy" theory of ideas, because representational ideas afforded our minds no direct knowledge of the world outside us. They opted instead for a theory of ideas as signs, which we interpret with the help of intuitive a priori principles. These principles, implanted by our creator, are reliable a priori truths we can use to determine that the external world and other minds exist; what their general character must be; and further, what kinds of actions are good or right for beings like ourselves. Through our faculty of rational intuition we grasp the real character of things, events, and personal conduct. Regarding the latter, we do not merely "feel" that benevolent, justice, and charitable acts are right and good. We know them to have these qualities.

Scottish Common Sense Realism officially "arrived" on American shores in 1765, in the person of John Witherspoon, an Edinburgh graduate, called to the presidency of Princeton University. It soon became the philosophical orthodoxy in academic institutions around the country, especially the North East. In the nineteenth century, the approach had many able exponents, e.g. James McCosh (Princeton), Francis Bowen (Harvard), Noah Porter (Yale). None was as innovative in ethics as in other areas of philosophy, but their insistence both that ethics was as a proper a subject for rational, scientific investigation as any other and that study of human psychology was the key had an enduring influence.

Outside academia the philosophical landscape was more varied, as study of the leading social and political figures in the American Enlightenment reveals. Cambridge Platonism, the Natural Law Theories of Hugo Grotius and Samuel Pufendorf, among others, had wide and important influence. But the first serious challenges to the reigning academic orthodoxy came with the rise of Transcendentalism and Neo-Hegelianism, movements inspired in diverse ways by Kantian and post-Kantian philosophies.

Transcendentalism developed in the first half of the nineteenth century in response to the critical doubts about the historical veracity of the founding of Christianity. Hume's posthumously published "On Miracles" made painfully clear the difficulties of reconciling empiricism with belief in the miracles supposed to justify the Christian faith. German "higher criticism" exacerbated the problem by its insistence that the Christian Bible be studied as any comparable historical text would be, critically and in light of the best available philological, archeological, and sociological evidence. Puritan Calvinism's successor, Unitarianism, struggled with the question of whether faith could be justified if the miraculous events the Bible recorded were henceforth open to question. So too did the founders of Transcendentalism, Ralph Waldo Emerson, Henry David Thoreau, Bronson Alcott, and Theodore Parker. The Transcendentalists decided that the revelation which justified faith must be inward, personal, and immediate.

Following a suggestion of Samuel Coleridge, they held that we have two sources of enlightenment about the world, understanding and reason. The former constructs the phenomenal world of appearances from perception, while the latter provides, a priori, a grasp of the underlying principles that unify the real. Reason's insights guide the understanding's construction of the phenomenal world so that it approximates the real. Emerson, the leading figure of the group, took the term "transcendentalism" from Immanuel Kant, but unlike Kant held that the a priori truths of reason are true of reality, not merely the phenomenal world, for while these insights are mind-dependent, the mind ultimately responsible for them is God's. Reason's revelations are thus inner revelations of divine truth. No other justification of faith is required. While others in the movement did not share Emerson's metaphysical idealism, they shared his concern that the artificial forms of contemporary social life emphasized ephemeral appearances over the enduring truths of reason. And many endorsed his solution: withdrawal (at least periodically) from social activities for personal reflection and the contemplation of nature. By these means, we can better attend to our sources of inner truth.

So individualistic and personal a conception of knowledge – physical, moral, and spiritual – was not conducive to normative ethical theory-building. But it did suggest that character was the key to the improvement of human life and conduct. The cultivation of reason required the cultivation of classical moral virtues. Thus the Transcendentalists promoted virtue ethics of a broadly Aristotelian type, both in their writings and also in their social activism (including abolitionism, women's suffrage, educational reform, and experiments in communal living).

Hegelianism in St Louis was even less coherent a movement than Transcendentalism. It began with the 1858 meeting of William Tory Harris, who later founded the *Journal of Speculative Philosophy*, and Hans Conrad Brokmeyer. Both were interested in Transcendentalism and intrigued by the philosophy of Kant. With like-minded friends they began a Kant Club for the discussion of German philosophy. Interrupted by the Civil War, the members of this group later reformed and actively promoted the translation and dissemination of German philosophical classics, including Hegel. Although amateurs in the eyes of academic philosophers, they pushed their academic counterparts and the Transcendentalists to give closer and more critical attention to post-Kantian German thought. Harris not only provided an venue for publishing their commentaries and translations of German work, he also published articles by British neo-Hegelians, Transcendentalists, as well as early works by founding figures of American Pragmatism, such as Charles S. Peirce, William James, and John Dewey.

The result was no one form of idealism but a plethora, often united only by a common conception of the absolute mind or reality as an organic whole. Absolute reality, though itself inherently timeless, reveals itself to our temporally ordered human minds in progressive stages, just as biological entities progress through a series of incomplete stages towards their ultimate self-realization. Finite human minds participate in this universal process, thus human reason, insight, and character also progressively develop, both over the lifetime of an individual and through the collective lifetime of the species. This entails that while reason gives deeper insight into reality than mere sense perception, human reason is also developing through stages. Our insights into the nature of virtue, and the practices that can help us to realize it, grow progressively more comprehensive over time. They are not timeless truths as earlier intuitionisms, such as Scottish Realism and Transcendentalism, had supposed.

This gave Hegelian-inspired absolute idealisms and their reworkings of classical self-perfectionist virtue ethics an extraordinary appeal for philosophers struggling to come to terms with Darwin's theory of evolution. If, as Darwinism proposed, human nature is in continual, if gradual, evolution, then so too are our faculties of reason and moral insight. Thus what seemed self-evidently good or right at one stage of human evolution might seem equally self-evidently bad or wrong at another. There would be no way to know which of two conflicting intuitions was correct. Hegelian and other post-Kantian organic idealisms faced no such problem because they viewed the real as progressively unfolding. Progressive development is not random change. It is development towards better, fuller self-realization. Thus we may be assured our concepts of virtue and right action do not simply contradict those of earlier eras, but improve upon them.

In the period between the American Civil War and the First World War, absolute idealisms of various types became the new orthodoxy in American academic institutions. But idealist self-perfectionism was not the only normative ethical theory to rise to the challenges posed by evolutionary theory. British Hedonistic Utilitarianism gained acceptance among empiricists who rejected realism (and idealism). Utilitarianism coped easily with evolutionary theory by adopting a thoroughly naturalistic conception of moral value and judgment. Intrinsic value was reduced to pleasure and pain. And since everyone wants more pleasure and less pain at any given time, the best act, rationally speaking, is simply the one that maximizes the former and minimizes the latter.

Pragmatic ethics grew out of dissatisfaction with these approaches. Pragmatism was originally the centerpiece of an epistemological and metaphysical program of reform first developed in 1870s by members of the Cambridge, Massachusetts, based "Metaphysical Club," whose members included Chauncey Wright, Charles Sanders Peirce, William James, and Oliver Wendell Homes. The publications of Peirce and James influenced other philosophers who became important contributors to the movement's development, such as John Dewey, Josiah Royce, G.H. Mead, and C.I. Lewis.

Following Peirce's lead, they adopted an experimental approach to the question of human knowledge. An idea is not an imperfect sensory image of some external reality but rather a tool for organizing our experience. As such it is right for us when it helps us to organize experiences effectively and wrong for us when it does not. Beliefs are another kind of intellectual tool, tools for predicting, pursuing, or avoiding certain kinds of experiences. As such they are confirmed when they allow us to successfully predict, pursue, or avoid those experiences reliably, and disconfirmed when they do not. Our theories become progressively better as humans refine and develop them into more powerful instruments of inquiry. The pragmatist conception of knowledge and truth was experimental and naturalistic but interestingly entailed nothing about what the underlying fabric of reality must be: matter, matter and minds, or minds alone. Leading figures in the movement held different metaphysical positions, with importantly different implications for their ethical views.

Pragmatists applied the same experimental approach to moral ideas and beliefs that they applied to ideas and beliefs about the world. Ideas about what is valuable or virtuous were interpreted as tools for managing human lives, whose justification depended upon their success or failure in helping to achieve our practical goals. Because Pragmatism interpreted success or failure in experiential terms, pragmatic ethical theories were, like their utilitarian counterparts, generally speaking naturalistic. But the pragmatists rejected hedonism as an inadequate account of human psychology. The ingredients of human welfare and flourishing were held to be irreducibly plural. Thus the utilitarian strategy of promoting happiness by maximizing pleasure and minimizing pain cannot succeed.

So, for example, in a seminal article, "The Moral Philosopher and the Moral Life," William James argued that the possibility of moral value and judgment in the world emerge with the emergence of sentience. Once sentient beings exist, there begin to be wants and needs that create demands or claims that they should be fulfilled. Increase the number and nature of sentient beings and the number and nature of claims increases, as well as the occasions for conflict between those beings and their claims. James holds that the claims sentience gives rise to differ in kind and not merely intensity. Consequently, maximizing satisfaction of any one kind will not necessarily compensate for disappointing others. Some must inevitably be sacrificed that others may be fulfilled. But no one sort of want or need, James thinks, is demonstrably more entitled to fulfillment than any other. Thus it follows that when formulating plans of action, inclusiveness ought rationally to be our guiding principle. If we cannot avoid disappointing some claims, we can at least try to minimize the range and number we must disappoint, say by beginning with those claims whose pursuit is least compatible with the pursuit of others. James' consequentialism may be described as "ameliorating" rather than "maximizing," as it focuses upon lessening the number and severity of the inevitable disappointment of claims rather than increasing happiness through maximizing satisfaction of desires for pleasure.

James set the tone for later pragmatists in arguing that the amelioration of practical human life will proceed best if it follows the same principles of cooperative inquiry utilized in the natural and social sciences. No human being, however sympathetic and imaginative, can fully appreciate all the claims of others. Every human being will be blind to important implications of particular policies for those affected by them. Aiming at inclusiveness means we ought, ideally, to try to include in deliberative processes all those whose interests will be affected as participant-observers of ongoing social experimentation into social and personal conduct and character formation.

James' colleague, Josiah Royce, incorporated the pragmatic approach to the selection of moral concepts, beliefs, and principles into his own, original version of absolute idealism. Royce argued that even pragmatists require a conception of absolute understanding in order to make sense of the goals of inquiry. Since we want to avoid error – disappointed expectations – our goal is truth: an understanding that cannot fail our expectations. Absolute truth is an understanding that can be possessed only by an absolute mind or an absolute community of inquirers. Thus our inquiries are incoherent, except upon the assumption that there is or can be an absolute mind or community capable of absolute truth to whose realization our own inquiries contribute. Turning to practical life, Royce argues that moral life does not emerge with sentience per se but with reflection on how best to cope with our conflicting inclinations. As James notes, sacrifices are inevitable, but our sacrifices are essentially arbitrary unless guided by a conception of what it is for a life to have overall worth. It is these guiding conceptions (Royce sometimes uses the word "projects") that give meaning to our choices.

Meaning is a function of interpretation. According to idealists, interpretation, like language, is a social practice. It cannot be a "private," sui generis creation of isolated individuals. Royce holds that we are initiated into interpretative practices by our communities. Our communities also exhibit to us a range of guiding conceptions or life plans, together with their results, which we may adopt (and adapt) in order to give meaning and coherence to our choices. In *The Philosophy of Loyalty*, Royce argues loyalty to our guiding ideals is the disposition most essential to success in realizing a meaningful life. But life projects often clash with one another, sometimes so violently as to destabilize cooperative communal life. To knowingly adopt such a life project is self-defeating and so irrational. This leads Royce to a pragmatic reconstruction of Immanuel Kant's categorical imperative of morality. We are to be loyal to loyalty. That is, we should adopt and be loyal only to those life-defining projects that permit others to be loyal to theirs. And since life projects are the less likely to undermine loyalty the more inclusive of others they are, our first loyalties should be to the most inclusive projects open to us, projects such as the pursuit of truth.

Dewey began his career as a neo-Hegelian absolute idealist, but under the influence of James, and later Peirce, he abandoned metaphysical idealism in favor of empirical realism: the real is what we experience and not something that lies behind or beyond it. Reality is a transaction between ourselves and our world. Because Dewey also accepted

Darwinian evolutionary theory as substantially correct, he was led to the conclusion that both we and the social and natural world with which we interact are not static but changing. And the empirically real must change accordingly. Of course the empirical natural world changes very slowly in comparison with ourselves and our social environments over our lifetimes. But the fact of this change entails that truth – success in managing experience – is a more relativist concept for Dewey than for other pragmatists, since we cannot presuppose that a belief that succeeds for us now will continue to succeed for future generations whose empirical reality will be different than our own. Dewey abandoned the idea that there could ever be a final absolute truth, as Royce suggests, or even a final opinion, as Peirce puts it, to which all men are fated to agree.

In texts such as *Human Nature and Conduct*, Dewey, like Royce, argues our personal identities, including our moral characters, are largely socially constructed. We are born with physiological and psychological traits that are the basic stuff of our development as persons. Development of a functional and well-integrated personality out of the multiple competing drives that constitute raw human nature is an achievement, not a given, that would be quite impossible without the assistance of our social communities. Like James, Dewey was a radical pluralist, for whom the objects of our desires and interests differ in the kind and not merely in the degrees of satisfaction offered. Thus inclusiveness is for Dewey, as for James and Royce, one important criterion for the selection of individual and communal ends. But Dewey goes beyond James or Royce in the significance he assigns the transformations that occur in the course of a typical lifetime both in our social environments and in our own skills, interests, and capacities. The desires and interests we had a decade ago are not necessarily the ones we have now or that we shall have a decade hence. The mental and physical abilities and the resources in our possession a decade ago are not necessarily those we possess now or shall possess a decade hence. Life is a process of continual adjustment to new challenges and changing resources through which we pursue not a single set of ends but a series of emergent "ends-in-view." For us, success is a matter of achieving an ongoing equilibrium between our ends-in-view, our physical and mental capacities, and our natural and social environments that is both satisfying and meaningful to us.

Given the similarities between Dewey's and James' accounts of moral evaluation, Dewey's ethics might be considered a form of ameliorating consequentialism. But it may be more helpful to think of him as a "satisfycing" consequentialist, given his insistence that our best strategy, rationally speaking, is to focus upon *satisfying* the demands of and capitalizing upon the opportunities in our current situations. While these situations overlap significantly with the life-situations of our predecessors, and the principles of value and virtue they developed are in many respects still applicable, Dewey holds, we must bear in mind that new situations have genuinely novel features. We cannot unreflectively rely upon values or virtues customary in our communities if we hope to fare well. We must be prepared reflect, to adjust our principles for the selection of ends-in-view so that the projects they direct us towards will make for meaningful, internally harmonious, stable, individually and socially fulfilling lives. Our chances of success in coping with the novel challenges of our situations will be undesirably limited if we cannot readily cooperate with others. Communities of inquiry are as vital in moral and social matters as in theoretical and physical sciences. In *Democracy and Education*, Dewey made this the basis of his distinctive argument for democracy in social life – democratic institutions are best because they best promote the sort of open communication essential to cooperative inquiry.

By the beginning of the First World War, the pragmatic approaches to ethics pioneered by James, Royce, and Dewey, and developed in new directions by G.H. Mead and C.I. Lewis, among others, helped to displace but did not replace idealist ethics as the reigning orthodoxy in academia. This was because the pragmatists focused their attention on developing criteria for the evaluation of theoretical principles. Convinced that these principles would change over time, they did not presume to dictate what their content should be. Thus most did not produce distinct normative theories of right conduct or good character to compete with those produced by rival approaches. But Pragmatism's enduring influence can nevertheless be seen in later American ethics, even when these depart substantially from the main line of classic Pragmatism.

For example, in the 1930 and 1940s, attempts to utilize naturalistic inquiry to justify normative ethical principles of conduct or character were called into question by Emotivism, a theory of moral language first expounded by members of the "Vienna Circle" (Logical Positivism). On the Logical Positivist understanding of meaning, propositions are only meaningful to the extent the terms involved are reducible to verifiable descriptions of the physical world. Other non-descriptive utterances are "emotive," that is, expressions of feelings or emotions, which can neither be true nor false. On this view, the idea that we engage in rational moral "deliberation" and "argument" turns out to be mistaken. This initially made the theory seem implausible. American philosopher Charles L. Stevenson defended Emotivism by arguing that moral language operates on two distinct planes. It expresses belief about matters of fact and also attitudes which we want others to adopt. Thus moral deliberation and argument do involve genuine reasoning about matters of fact. And facts are not irrelevant to the process of establishing agreement in attitudes. However, attitudes are not determined by facts. So to the extent our ethical views are determined by our attitudes, then these views cannot be considered true or false or empirically verifiable. Likewise the normative ethical "principles" of right action or virtue we invoke to support our views are simply expressions of general attitudes which we would like others to share. Thus we cannot look to natural scientific methods to help us determine which we should adopt. It is in the end a matter more of taste than judgment.

Naturalistic inquiry into normative or practical ethical questions is thus a pointless procedure. However, Emotivists granted that other sorts of questions about ethical language and behavior were open to both logical and naturalistic inquiry. That is, we can study (1) the language employed in ethical debates and its underlying logic; (2) ethical concepts, such as good, right, and obligation, their patterns of use and how they are specified; and (3) the psychological mechanisms involved, such as desire and practical reason. These "meta-ethical" questions (from the Greek word *meta* meaning what lies beyond or behind normative principles telling us which acts are right or dispositions good) can be treated within the parameters of logical and/or scientific inquiry. Thus if ethical theorists are to be naturalists, they must limit themselves to meta-ethical inquiries and make no claims about the content of our normative principles. Stevenson's defense of Emotivism helped to make this type of meta-ethical inquiry the focus of academic ethics in America for the next several decades.

During this period, philosophers influenced by the British Prescriptivist R.M. Hare concentrated efforts to develop new ways to justify choices between normative ethical principles consistent with Emotivist conceptions of ethical language, by focusing on the purely logical features of ethical concepts. In 1971, John Rawls' *A Theory of Justice* challenged this trend with a defense of a more holistic approach that was in effect, if not name, a revival of pragmatic theorizing.

Rawls proposed that practical principles, such as his principle of "justice as fairness," could be justified by use of the method Nelson Goodman had named "reflective equilibrium." In reflective equilibrium, particular principles are justified by bringing them into coherence with our beliefs and our ethical convictions, by a process of gradual mutual adjustment. Neither the principles we choose among nor the beliefs or convictions we aim to bring into equilibrium are treated as self-evident or epistemically "privileged." All are open to revision. Of any competing set of principles, the most reasonable one to adopt is the one that achieves for us the widest equilibrium with the least distortion to our principles, convictions, and beliefs. Rawls called his approach "Kantian Constructivism," but it may also be considered an offshoot of classical American pragmatism. Rawls' work helped to stimulate a "practical ethics" movement which has since called upon philosophers to give as much attention to normative ethical issues arising in civil, professional and personal life as to meta-ethical problems. This movement continues to play a vital role in shaping the increasingly heterogeneous character of American ethical thought.

Further reading

Dewey, John. *The Moral Writings of John Dewey*, revised edition, ed. James Gouinlock. Amherst, NY: Prometheus Books, 1994.

Edwards, Jonathan. *The Nature of True Virtue*, Foreword by William K. Frankenna. Ann Arbor, MI: University of Michigan Press, 1960.

Emerson, Ralph Waldo. *The Collected Works of Ralph Waldo Emerson*, ed. Robert E. Spiller and Alfred Fergusson. Cambridge, MA: Harvard University Press, 1971.

Flower, Elizabeth and Murphey, Murray G. *A History of Philosophy in America*, 2 volumes. New York: G.P. Putnam's Sons, 1977.

James, William. *The Will to Believe and Other Essays in Popular Philosophy*, Cambridge, MA: Harvard University Press, 1979 [1897].

Rawls, John. *A Theory of Justice*, revised edition. Cambridge, MA: Harvard University Press, 1999 [1971].

Royce, Josiah. *The Philosophy of Loyalty*, Introduction by John J. McDermott. Nashville, TN: Vanderbilt University Press, 1995.

Stevenson, Charles L. *Facts and Values: Studies in Ethical Analysis*. New Haven, CT: Yale University Press, 1963.

Stroh, Guy W. *American Ethical Thought*. Chicago, IL: Nelson-Hall, 1979.

JENNIFER WELCHMAN

ETHICS OF CARE

The ethics of care has its roots in a feminist moral perspective characterized by relationality, empathetic imagination, and social context, rather than rationality, calculation, and rules. With its early expression in late twentieth-century American psychology, the ethics of care is widely studied today by philosophers.

Psychology

In her pivotal work in psychology, *In a Different Voice* (1982), Carol Gilligan presented evidence of a moral perspective that she suggested had been largely ignored by philosophy and psychology. Gilligan primarily criticized Lawrence Kohlberg's stages of moral development, claiming that they were developed androcentrically. Assuming a progressive hierarchy of Kantian-like universal rationality, Kohlberg's moral stages detail what he believed was healthy growth from entirely heteronomous moral beliefs in individuals, driven by individualistic desires, obedience to authority, and fear of punishment; to a more relational sense of others, in which subjects wished to fit in with others and to abide by the law; to, finally, autonomous utilization of ethical principles such as a social contract and universalizable moral rules that transcend the law.

Using dilemmas such as the case of "Heinz" (in which an impoverished man must decide whether to steal medicine to save the life of his wife), Kohlberg interviewed subjects to determine their level of autonomous moral judgment. Individuals scoring highest did so because of their stated adherence to moral laws and principles, and not because of any concern about punishment, social norms, or emotional attachment.

Upon the discovery that often girls and women seemed to score consistently lower on Kohlberg's scale (at stages three and four, emphasizing "conventional" morality), Gilligan sought to explain these trends not by assuming that female moral development was somehow lacking, but by considering whether Kohlberg's scale was gender-biased. *In a Different Voice* details the possibility that there may be a distinctly feminine moral perspective – one that prioritizes a "web of relationships" rather than rationality and principles.

In one of Gilligan's adaptations of Kohlberg's studies, "Jake," an eleven-year-old boy, represents what Kohlberg thought to be a relatively high stage of moral development. Using logic to work through Heinz's dilemma, Jake resoundingly affirms Heinz's stealing as the best option because humanity outweighs the law, and stealing to save a human life is the best possible choice. Like Kant's assumption of universal human rationality, Jake's view of human rights and moral capabilities assumes a certain universality and mathematical-style calculation. Representing the way Gilligan suggests many girls and women perceived morality, the eleven-year-old "Amy," however, is not so sure about Heinz's actions. She views the problem more contextually, and is suspicious about the strict nature of the question and the universal response it seems to require. Instead of answering based on the dilemma of stealing or a person dying, Amy wonders if there is a better way to resolve Heinz's problem. Rather than "advancing" up the hierarchy to a more detached, logically calculated, and universal (post-conventional) understanding of morality, Amy stays at what Kohlberg viewed as a conventional, socially constrained, level, wondering whether Heinz might be able to borrow the money for the medicine from friends or family, rather than doing something illegal. Amy is determined to find a more creative course of action for Heinz so that he does not end up in jail – an event she is sure would further plague his already sick wife. Instead of calculating the weight of human life and the wrongness of stealing, Amy seeks a solution that will sustain relationships. She refuses to answer what she considers to be an unrealistic question and presses the idea that there must be some other way for Heinz to act. As Jake asserts that Heinz must act above the law, Amy concludes that moral responsibility depends on the situation. Perhaps, according to Gilligan, Amy is not socially constrained on a conventional level, but socially informed and desirous of maintaining healthy relationships.

From this and other studies, Gilligan concludes that women tend to reason differently than men about moral issues. Even if the apparent discrepancy which Gilligan points to in her work with men and women is not necessarily always evident, her work asserts that the experience of many women expresses a social view of ethics as empathetic, relational, and based on caring rather than a rationally calculated version of justice. Annette Baier further adds that what Gilligan's female subjects valued were ties to others and the preservation of the caring relationships that affirm life.

Philosophy

The ethics of care becomes normative as well as descriptive (or dissolves this distinction altogether) in the philosophical work of Nel Noddings. Like Gilligan's claim of a different voice, Noddings, in *Caring: A Feminine Approach to Ethics and Moral Education* (1984), suggests that women experience an alternative moral domain. Basing her philosophy on the assumption that women, as mothers and caretakers, offer the world an ethic that casts moral decisions on traditionally feminine qualities, such as mothering, Noddings expands Gilligan's descriptive claims by creating an ethical theory based on the web of relationships rather than rules or principles.

Noddings notes that with moral theory's traditional emphasis on principles, justice, and justification instead, perhaps, of practice, ethical theory has been largely discussed in paternal, rather than maternal, language. This is not to say, Noddings states, that all men will disagree with her view or that all women should accept it. Noddings's ethics of care is merely grounded in the social experience of caregivers, who, at least in family life in many cultures, have primarily been women. Noddings writes that this theory is feminine in the sense of reciprocity, responsiveness, and empathy.

Noddings's moral theory begins with the felt experience of being cared for. From this, an individual cultivates morality by imagining, developing, and maintaining other caring relationships – by becoming the "one-caring." Ethical caring is cultivated via natural experience (the feeling of being cared for) and learned experience (developing the habit of extending care to others). One bases her ability to care for others in the natural responses she feels in close relationships. Thus, caring both originates in and is oriented toward the web of relationships, as natural caring motivates ethical caring. The extension outward from already existing caring contexts to potential relationships is the result of our ability to imagine such relationships based on our own past experiences.

In this ethic, what Noddings suggests as the "ethical ideal" has its source only within the web. To learn to care is to imply a specific kind of response to another – one that acknowledges, from experience, that the desire to feel cared for is reciprocal and shared. From this, the "best self," the moral agent within the relational context, is cultivated. Noddings describes this emergence as a feeling of "I must" in response to others whose interests press us to action.

Consider the difference between an ethic based on caring and one more traditionally construed. Noddings writes that the only universals in the ethics of care are the remembered feelings and attitudes of caring that are available to all human beings. The theory, however, produces no universalizable principles or rules. On the other hand, Kant's moral theory represents the more traditional Western view in espousing universalizable principles and a moral law that has no room for emotion of any kind. In fact, Kant famously viewed acts of caring based on the inner pleasure of relational thinking to have no moral worth.

The ethics of care has been expanded to account for what many philosophers perceive as gender bias. For example, Joan Tronto favors a feminist, rather than a feminine, theory of caring to avoid traditional gender distinctions. While a feminine perspective implies traditional gender roles, a feminist theory is by definition reconstructive, and so examines the usefulness of our existing and potential relationships. And Noddings suggests that the feminine as a foundation for ethics is merely a useful metaphor based on the alternative experience of women, one that denotes reciprocity and can be practiced by both men and women. As gender roles change, "parenting" might become a better metaphor than "mothering."

The contextual nature of the ethics of care has made it an amenable partner to other philosophical traditions, such as pragmatism, race theory, phenomenology, and some Asian philosophies that eschew rational calculation as the primary keystone of ethics, preferring instead a situational, relational approach. Though critics abound concerning issues such as empirical rigor, the maintenance of rigid gender roles (such as mothering), and a potentially problematic sense of justice and fairness, the ethics of care has had a wide impact on twentieth- and twenty-first-century ethics.

Further reading

Baier, Annette. "What do Women Want in Moral Theory?" in Mary Jeanne Larrabee (ed.) *An Ethic of Care: Feminist and Interdisciplinary Perspectives.* New York: Routledge, 1993, pp. 19–32.

Gilligan, Carol. *In a Different Voice: Psychological Theory and Women's Development*. Cambridge, MA: Harvard University Press, 1982.

Held, Virginia. *Justice and Care: Essential Readings in Feminist Ethics*, Boulder, CO: Westview Press, 1995.

Power, F. Clark, Higgins, Ann, and Kohlberg, Lawrence. *Lawrence Kohlberg's Approach to Moral Education*. New York: Columbia University Press, 1991.

Larrabee, Mary Jeanne. *An Ethic of Care: Feminist and Interdisciplinary Perspectives.* New York: Routledge, 1993.

Noddings, Nel. *Caring: A Feminine Approach to Ethics and Moral Education*. Berkeley, CA: University of California Press, 1984.

Tronto, Joan C. "Women and Caring: What Can Feminists Learn about Morality from Caring?" in Virginia Held

(ed.) *Justice and Care: Essential Readings in Feminist Ethics*. Boulder, CO: Westview Press, 1995, pp. 101–15.
Ward, Janie Victoria, Gilligan, Carol, and McLean Taylor, Jill, with Bardige, Betty. *Mapping the Moral Domain*, Cambridge, MA: Harvard University Press, 1988.

HEATHER E. KEITH

ETHICS, BUSINESS

The application of ethics to the business context usually takes one of two traditional approaches: the turn to the "top down" use of abstract ethical theories embodying universal principles, or the inculcation of accepted virtues. There have been many problems with the use of these approaches that have made the search for alternative approaches all the more important. The application of a moral rule to a specific case can be used by ill-intentioned individuals to justify behavior which common sense judges to be immoral. Moreover, actions done with the best of intentions by virtuous people may nonetheless be misguided and can only be so judged by something other than intentions. Rules seem to judge intentions, yet bad intentions can misuse rules. Part of the problem of making ethical decision-making relevant for the business community may be an implicit, unexpressed, but nonetheless pervasive and "common-sense" perception by practitioners that the above problems are in fact the case.

Classical American Pragmatism, that movement incorporating the philosophies of Charles Peirce, William James, John Dewey, G.H. Mead, and C.I. Lewis, offers a unique conceptual framework that provides a unifying ground for how and why we evaluate rules and traditions and choose among various principles in an ongoing process of dealing with change and novelty. It focuses on the return to situations in their concrete fullness and richness as the very foundation for the development of moral decision-making as inherently contextual and situational, and for the emergence of moral "rules" as tentative working hypotheses abstracted from the fullness of concrete decision-making.

It is not that traditional moral theories do not get hold of something operative in our concrete moral decisions, but that in lifting out one aspect, they ignore others, reducing moral action to some fixed scheme. And the relative weight given to any of these rules, each supposed to be absolute, as well as to a host of other considerations in coming to a decision as to what ought to be done, will depend on the novel and complexly rich features of the situation in which the need for the decision arises.

Value situations, like all situations as understood within the pragmatic context, are open to inquiry and require the general method of experimentalism by which a progressive movement from a problematic situation to a meaningfully resolved or secure situation takes place. In the case of value inquiry as the embodiment of experimental method, this involves moving from a situation filled with problematic or conflicting valuings to a resolved or meaningfully organized experience of the valuable through an expansive reconstruction or reintegration of the situation.

In this process, we are often reconstructing moral rules. Principles are not directives to action but are rather suggestive of actions. Just as hypotheses in the technical experimental sciences are modified through ongoing testing, moral principles are hypotheses which require ongoing testing and allow for qualification and reconstruction. The most important habits we can develop are habits of intelligence and sensitivity, for neither following rules nor meaning well can suffice. But bringing about good consequences in the contextual richness of different situations through moral decision-making helps develop, as by-products, both good character traits ("virtues") as habits of acting and good rules as working hypotheses needing ongoing testing and revision.

Moral reasoning as concrete rather than abstract and discursive incorporates in its very dynamics moral sensitivity and moral imagination. The operation of reason cannot be isolated from the human being in its entirety. Moral reasoning involves sensitivity to the rich, complex value-ladenness of a situation and to its interwoven and conflicting dimensions, the ability to utilize creative intelligence or moral imagination geared to the concrete situation, and an ongoing evaluation of the resolution. The goal is not to make the most unequivocal decision, but to provide the richest existence for those involved. This requires an enrichment of the capacity to perceive the complex moral aspects of situations rather than a way of simplifying how to deal with what one does perceive. Moral maturity in fact thus increases rather than decreases moral problems to be mediated, for it brings to awareness the pervasiveness of the moral dimension involved in concrete decision-making. When we slide over the complexities of a problem, we can easily be convinced that absolute moral principles are at stake. And the complexities of a problem are always context-dependent and must be dealt with in the context of a concrete situation.

Moral reasoning as concrete, then, is not working downward from rules to their application, but working upward from the full richness of moral experience and decision-making toward guiding moral hypotheses. The resolution of conflicting moral perceptions which provide the context for new ideals cannot be resolved by a turn to abstractions but through a deepening sensitivity to the demands of human valuings in their commonness and diversity. Such a deepening does not negate the use of intelligent inquiry, but rather opens it up, frees it from the products of its past in terms of rigidities and abstractions. In the area of ethics, this deepening focuses intelligent inquiry on the experience of value as it emerges within human existence, allowing us to grasp different contexts, to take the perspective of "the other," to participate in dialogue with "the other" to determine what is valuable.

And, this "other" is not some separate entity of any sort. Pragmatism focuses on a relational understanding of humans, communities, and corporations alike, thereby negating the ingrained tradition of atomic individualism which ultimately places the individual and the group in an irreconcilable conflict, with all the moral pitfalls this involves. There is an ongoing process of adjustment between the unique creativity of the individual entity of whatever sort, and the conforming dimension of the "common other" within which it is embedded and with which it is inextricably intertwined as an organic whole. Value emerges within these relational contexts, and the adjustment between the two dimensions of the shared and the unique gives rise to the novel and creative dimensions of moral decision-making. This calls for an understanding of the internal dynamics of a corporation as a community in which the input of diverse, novel voices in interaction with corporate conformity leads to thriving business firms. It further calls for an understanding of the corporation itself as a novel voice that feeds into, is changed by, and is inseparably intertwined with, the larger "common other" of the society at large. In this way the nature of the corporation carries with it both corporate social and moral responsibilities and corporate answerability.

Though moral diversity, just as diversity in general, can flourish within a community, when such diversity becomes irreconcilable conflict, intelligence must offer growing, reconstructed contexts which can provide a workable solution. Workability cannot be taken in the sense of workable for oneself only, for individuals are inextricably tied to the community of which they are a part. Nor can workability be taken in terms of the short-range expedient, for actions and their consequences extend into a indefinite future and determine the possibilities available in that future. Finally, workability in the moral situation cannot be taken in terms of some abstract aspect of life such as economic workability, etc., for moral situations are concrete, and workability in the moral situation must concern the ongoing development of the concrete richness of human experience in its entirety. Workability and growth go hand in hand. Workability involves resolution of conflict through reconstructed expanded contexts, and the expanding understanding of varied and diverse interests through a widening of perspective is precisely concrete growth. Workability and growth, properly understood, are inherently moral, and the ethical dimension of business decisions involves consideration of both in their concrete fullness. In this way, pragmatism can hold that the ultimate goal in the nurturing of moral maturity is the development of the ability for ongoing self-directed growth.

What particular skills, then, must be cultivated if ethics is to thrive in the business context? What is needed is the development of the reorganizing and ordering capabilities of creative intelligence, the imaginative grasp of authentic possibilities, the vitality of motivation, and a deepened sensitivity to the sense of concrete human existence in its richness, diversity, and complexity. The importance of this latter cannot be over-stressed. It is this deepened, "felt" dimension that regulates the way one selects, weighs, and conceptually orders what one observes. The vital, growing sense of moral rightness comes not from the indoctrination of abstract principles or the inculcation of fixed virtues handed down by a particular socio/cultural context, but from attunement to the way in which moral beliefs and practices must be rooted naturally in the very conditions of human existence. It is this attunement which gives vitality to diverse and changing principles as working hypotheses embodied in concrete moral activity. And it provides the ongoing direction for well-intentioned individuals to continually evaluate and at times reconstruct ingrained habits and traditions.

The cultivation of the ethical skills highlighted by the pragmatic position will allow those engaged in business activity to utilize ongoing change in the concrete contexts of corporate life, with the increasing complexity, pluralism, and diversity these contexts manifest, to bring about ongoing enriching growth of the firm in its multiple relations.

Further reading

Donaldson, Thomas and Dunfee, Thomas W. *The Ties that Bind*. Cambridge, MA: Harvard Business School Press, 1999.

Freeman, Edward R. *Business Ethics: The State of the Art*. New York: Oxford University Press. 1992.

Rosenthal, Sandra B. and Buchholz, Rogene A. *Rethinking Business Ethics: A Pragmatic Perspective*. Oxford: Oxford University Press, 2000.

Werhane, Patricia H. *Moral Imagination and Management Decision Making*. Oxford: Oxford University Press, 1999.

ROGENE A. BUCHHOLZ
SANDRA B. ROSENTHAL

EUGENICS

"Eugenics" is a term derived from Greek words meaning "well-born." The practice of eugenics has been around at least since the time of Plato, who argued in Book V of the *Republic* for state-controlled reproduction and infanticide of "defective" newborns. In 1865, Sir Francis Galton proposed that the term be used for "the science of improving stock." By "stock," he meant "men, brutes, and plants." With regard to humans, Galton appropriated his cousin Charles Darwin's work to refute the religious doctrine of a fall from grace and to support his view of human progress. Eugenics, he thought, was a means by which to accelerate the progress. "What Nature does blindly, slowly, and ruthlessly," Galton wrote, "man may do providently, quickly, and kindly" (Kevles 1985: 12). The "may" in this statement is a significant caveat, since it allows also for the improvident and cruel ways eugenics has been practiced throughout history.

Positive eugenics, by which reproduction and survival of the "most fit" is promoted, is generally viewed as more acceptable (or less unacceptable) than negative eugenics, by which reproduction and survival of "the unfit" is discouraged or prevented. Although governmental imposition of both types of eugenics is broadly condemned, individuals have been permitted and sometimes encouraged to make choices consistent with them. The Nazi Holocaust is the best-known and most despicable example of governmentally sanctioned negative eugenics, but other horrendous instances of eugenics have occurred and continue to occur around the globe. American history yields its own shameful examples of eugenics in its treatment of Native Americans, African Americans, and people who are mentally impaired.

In the nineteenth century, various forms of philosophical idealism and theories of evolution influenced the writings of American philosophers while also lending support to the development of eugenic attitudes and practices. Darwin's theory was considerably more controversial than that of Louis Agassiz, who disagreed with Darwin about the randomness of mutations. William James, who accompanied Agassiz on his expedition to the Amazon in 1866, found the Darwinian view more acceptable. Although Agassiz was a passionate opponent of racial miscegenation, neither his view of evolution nor Darwin's necessarily involves advocacy of eugenics.

An important difference between evolution and eugenics is that eugenics requires deliberate human intervention whereas evolution, for Darwin, occurs naturally and inevitably, and, for Agassiz, through divine design. The distinction between evolution and eugenics is evident in American philosophy through its emphasis on democratic participation and individual liberty, both of which are at odds with governmentally sponsored eugenics. John Dewey is an apt example in this regard. While endorsing Darwinian evolution, he critiqued the eugenicist ideal of Plato and advocated a society that maximizes the possibility of full and equal participation of all its members in the benefits that government provides. For Dewey, facilitating such participation through education and rational persuasion is indispensable to promotion of social welfare and justice.

Unaddressed through support for democracy and individual liberty is the possibility of eugenic practices either prior to conception through sterilization or after conception through prenatal testing and abortion of "defective" fetuses. The latter option was not available until the latter part of the twentieth century. Earlier, prominent American eugenicists – including Charles Davenport (a biologist), Alexander Graham Bell, Margaret Sanger, and Oliver Wendell Holmes, Jr – wrote eugenics textbooks, led drives for sterilization laws that emerged in thirty-three states, and supported immigration restriction as a means through which the problem of the "unfit" might be resolved. On grounds that deafness was hereditary, Bell, the inventor of the telephone, recommended a legal prohibition against marriage between deaf persons. Sanger, a member of the American Eugenics Society and ardent promoter of birth control, argued that it was not only wrong to give birth to children with impairments but also wrong to provide governmental funds to provide for them after birth. Such funds, she claimed, should be used instead to improve the standard of civilization. In the Buck vs Bell decision of the US Supreme Court (1927), Justice Holmes proclaimed the legality and desirability of coercive sterilization of the "unfit" with the infamous statement: "Three generations of imbeciles are enough." Even President Woodrow Wilson (1913–21) supported the eugenics movement in the United States.

As the atrocities of the Nazi Holocaust became widely known, those who had previously hailed eugenics as a social good began to recognize its potential for evil. The term "eugenics" gradually became identified with practices that are totally and indefensibly inhumane. At the same time, medical technology developed various means by which pregnant women could undergo testing to determine various characteristics of their potential offspring. These technologies differ from contraception and sterilization because they involve termination of embryos or fetuses that have already begun to exist.

Today, women may legally terminate fetuses diagnosed in utero with anomalies that would lead to impairments in their potential children. Because these decisions are made by women themselves rather than imposed by law, and because they apply to fetuses rather than born human beings, they are widely supported as morally incommensurate with the "eugenics" that is considered despicable. Philip Kitcher, however, regards the abortion of fetuses diagnosed with severe anomalies as a commendable form of eugenics. In such circumstances, he believes that the practice of eugenics reflects the justifiable conviction that it is irresponsible not to do what can be done to prevent human suffering. Two groups regard this position as a condemnable form of negative eugenics: those who impute full moral status to severely impaired fetuses, and those who, while supporting abortion in general, believe that abortion of anomalous fetuses expresses a discriminatory attitude toward people born with disabilities.

In the twenty-first century, advances in genetics and reproductive technology have made it possible to practice positive eugenics through "genetic enhancement," i.e. prenatal interventions intended to increase the social advantages of offspring after birth. Although some philosophers defend this practice on grounds of reproductive liberty and responsible parenthood, Kitcher is concerned that maximizing reproductive liberty through the permissibility of "genetic enhancement" is a form of "laissez-faire eugenics" that threatens to increase social disparities and prejudice. As a corrective, he proposes a "utopian eugenics" that would insure equal access not only to reproductive options but also to social supports for parents of children with impairments. Kitcher's position is consistent with John Rawls' theory of justice: an effort to maximize individual liberty while preventing the exacerbation of inequities that occur naturally and through the choices of individuals.

Further reading

Black, Edwin. *War against the Weak: Eugenics and America's Campaign to Create a Master Race.* New York: Four Walls and Eight Windows, 2003.

Buck v. Bell. 274 US 200 (1927).

Dewey, John. *Democracy and Education.* New York: Macmillan, 1944.

Fleck, Leonard M. "Is 'Responsible Eugenics' Disingenuous Ethics?" *APA Newsletter on Philosophy and Medicine* 99 (Fall 1999): 92–7.

Kevles, Daniel J. *In the Name of Eugenics: Genetics and the Uses of Human Heredity.* New York: Alfred A. Knopf, 1985.

Kitcher, Philip. *The Lives to Come: The Genetic Revolution and Human Possibilities.* New York: Simon and Schuster, 1996.

O'Keefe, Katharine. "American Eugenics Society," available at http://all.org/abac/contents.txt

Parens, Erik and Asch, Adrienne (eds) *Prenatal Testing and Disability Rights.* Washington, DC: Georgetown University Press, 2000.

Perry, Ralph Barton. *The Thought and Character of William James.* New York: Harper and Row, 1964.

Plato. Republic, trans. G.M.A. Grube. Indianapolis, IN: Hackett, 1974.

Rawls, John. *A Theory of Justice.* Cambridge, MA: Harvard University Press, 1971.

Thayer, H.D. *Meaning and Action: A Critical History of Pragmatism.* New York: Bobbs-Merrill, 1968.

MARY B. MAHOWALD

EVIDENCE

The evidence for a belief (claim, statement, etc.) is something that indicates the truth of that belief (etc.): *E* is evidence that *p* when *E*'s being the case makes it more likely that it is true that *p*. Pragmatists have treated the topic in a number of different ways.

Charles Peirce described four methods of "fixing" belief, each with its own assumptions about evidence. The method of tenacity involves deliberate avoidance of evidence that one's belief is false; the method of authority takes the pronouncement of an institution such as a state or church as sufficient evidence for a belief; the a priori method considers only evidence accessible by reason alone; only the method of science takes seriously the evidence of both reason and the senses. Peirce was committed to fallibilism, according to which any belief might be shown false by future evidence. He maintained that the beliefs of a genuine inquirer, one motivated by the sincere desire to find the truth, must be sensitive to the evidence, otherwise he is not a genuine inquirer at all, but instead a "sham reasoner."

William James argued in "The Will to Believe" that we have a "right to adopt a believing attitude in religious matters, in spite of the fact that our merely logical intellect may not have been coerced." When the evidence alone is not sufficient to decide between two incompatible beliefs, and when one's choice between those beliefs is "living," "forced," and "momentous," she is justified in accepting that belief.

John Dewey understood evidence in terms of an inquirer's success in overcoming problematic situations. Facts observed by the inquirer can serve as evidence, and whether a fact counts as good evidence depends on whether it can be used by the inquirer to solve the problem at hand. Thus, in taking inquiry (traditionally conceived of as the search for truth) to be the same thing as problem-solving, Dewey blurred the traditional distinction between a fact's counting as evidence and its being useful in the solution of a problem.

Inspired by Dewey, Richard Rorty severed the traditional connection between evidence and truth. On Rorty's view, a true claim is simply one that can be defended against objections. This makes justification context-dependent, a matter of conversational success. It follows that justification cannot be grounded in an objective relationship between evidence and truth.

Susan Haack has argued that one's evidence for a belief has both a causal and a logical aspect. Haack distinguishes two aspects of the belief that *p*: *s*-belief (the state of believing that *p*) and *c*-belief (the content of the belief that *p*, i.e. the proposition that *p*). One's evidence that *p* involves more than having other beliefs that entail *p*; her *s*-belief that *p* must stand in causal relations with other mental states, including belief, states the contents of which stand in logical relations with her *c*-belief that *p*.

Further reading

Dewey, John. *Logic, The Theory of Inquiry.* New York: Henry Holt, 1938.

Haack, Susan. *Evidence and Inquiry.* Cambridge, MA: Blackwell, 1993.

James, William. "The Will to Believe" in *The Will to Believe and Other Essays in Popular Philosophy*, ed. Frederick H. Burkhardt, Fredson Bowers and Ignas K. Skrupskelis. Cambridge, MA: Harvard University Press, 1979 [1896], 13–33.

Peirce, Charles Sanders. "The Fixation of Belief" in *The Writings of Charles Sanders Peirce: A Chronological Edition*, ed. Christian Kloesel. Bloomington, IN: Indiana University Press, 1986 [1877], Vol. 3.242–57.

Rorty, Richard. *Consequences of Pragmatism: Essays, 1972–1980*. Minneapolis, MN: University of Minnesota Press, 1982.

Robert Lane

EVIL

Evils can be "mapped" as follows: physical evils (all natural disorders and human sufferings, pains, ignorance, errors, misunderstandings, and mis-communications); moral evils (ethically disordered free choices, attitudes, and habits); metaphysical evils (the mere lack of infinite perfection, simply being finite); and religious evils (sins as the free disobedience to God's known will, and the "mystery of iniquity" at work at the physical, human, and super-human or demonic levels).

Philosophers either decline to define evil or strive to do so. Some define it as the contrary of good, others as a lack of the perfect good, and still others as a privation of a good that *should* be at hand (for example, a lack of eyesight in a stone is not an evil, but in a dog which *should* see, it is a physical evil). This third, privative view of evil presupposes a dynamically ordered, goal-seeking universe.

With Calvin, the New England Puritans held that "In Adam's fall, we sinned all." For them human nature was totally depraved because it stemmed from Adam's seed. Infected by his sin, humans formed a "damned mass," from which only sinful deeds can arise, unless grace intervenes. Only a few persons are elected by grace to be reborn into friendship with God. These Puritans rejected the gentler doctrine of Dutch theologian Arminius, who taught that human nature is not totally depraved and can do some good deeds by itself.

About a century later, Jonathan Edwards wrote of "a sinful depravity of the heart." Meanwhile, he held that those elected and reborn by grace find the object of their affection changed from themselves to God. Yet the sinner loves his or her evil way and even those reborn by grace are not free from evil's fatal attraction.

In the eighteenth century, Benjamin Franklin leaned toward Arminius's view and adopted the Enlightenment's spirit of trusting human reason. Franklin accepted Newton's determinism for the physical order. Yet he recognized that people make some free choices, since he saw that otherwise there could be no responsibility in human affairs nor any reason for having religion.

By the late nineteenth century, however, the imported evolutionary system of Herbert Spencer led to a universal determinism. Spencer held that all evils in the world, natural and moral, necessarily stem from a failure to adapt to changing natural or moral conditions.

From William James's father, Charles Peirce early in his career adopted a view of evil he held throughout his life. Peirce saw that since "God is love," his "is a love which embraces hatred as an imperfect stage of it[self]; ... even love needs hatred and hatefulness as its object."

For Josiah Royce, evils of all kinds poured into his experience and philosophical musings. Through the decades his reflections and writings on the problem of evil exceeded those of Peirce, James, and Dewey, taken together. Royce's philosophy of evil seems to have matured through four stages. In his early years (1875–92), he met evil with courageous endurance. In a rather heroic spirit, he then taught people to "grasp evil by the throat" and thus triumph over it.

From 1893 to 1908, Royce grew more conscious of union with an immanent divine Absolute who strengthens suffering humans as their co-suffering Companion. Through their trials this delivering Captain leads them to embrace, detest, and thus subdue evil. Moreover, in this struggle, by exercising genuine loyalty to universal loyalty, they were attaining fully mature moral perfection for themselves as human persons and enhancing communities.

Next, from 1909 to 1913, Royce came to see what he called "the essence of atonement." He taught that sufferings needed to be appropriated and idealized into sorrows which would allow a person to detect life's higher values. Elevated to this level, a person could identify with those who suffer vicariously so that atoning energies might heal both the moral traitors and the communities they have wounded. He was convinced of the ultimate triumph of love. He insisted that into our human world no baseness or cruelty of treason could enter so deep or so tragic except that loyal love shall in due time be able to oppose to just that deed of treason its fitting deed of atonement. Such is the heroism of atoning souls in this sin-scarred world.

Finally, from 1914 to 1916, Royce identified philosophically with the hero of John Bunyan's *Pilgrim's Progress*. Pilgrim dialectically balanced a certain acquiescence with self-assertion, duty with truth-seeking, and fallibility with an unearthly confidence in God. So, the most mature Royce recommended that when the genuine loyalist is confronted by evils of any or all kinds, he or she, like Pilgrim, adopt the pragmatic attitude and movement of trudging ever forward and upward in one's advance toward making the Beloved Community more of a reality.

John Dewey recoiled from immorality, whether in families or in big business. Yet he emphasized not so much theories of evil as the instrumental riddance or lessening of as many of the world's evils as intelligent cooperation can achieve. He invited people to view values like honesty, justice, health, wealth, and learning, not as fixed ends, but as directions in changing experience's quality. Happiness needs to be viewed, not as something to be possessed, but as a process of growing, of "moving in advance." Dewey recognized optimism and pessimism as incubi that paralyze endeavors to track the causes of evil. Instead, he proposed a meliorism which holds that humans can improve presently existing conditions – an attitude that arouses confidence and a reasonable hopefulness.

For W.E. Hocking the greatest evil is the possible meaninglessness of the whole universe, and hence the meaninglessness of its every part. He thought everyone was responsible for a "righteous hatred of evil."

For John Dewey, persons construct good and evil either a priori or experientially. The a priorists often build their construction upon an eternal platonic value. The experientialists build theirs upon verified or verifiable consequences, using scientific advances for guidance. A key choice for Dewey, as for Nietzsche, is to move beyond ethical theories of good and evil and adopt ones that require the intelligent discernment of the better and the worse as revealed by scientific method.

Alfred North Whitehead regarded evil as standing halfway between perfection and triviality, often being the violence of strength against strength. Since the human soul, like every process, is a synthesizer, the evil of the soul lies in the clash of vivid feelings, in denying to each other their proper expansion.

For contemporary ethicists, like Joseph Fletcher, depersonalizing a human being is the greatest moral evil. For him the worst thing in life is not evil or suffering, but plain indifference to what happens. Hence, the one thing worse than evil itself is indifference to evil.

Further reading

Dewey, John. "The Construction of the Good" in *The Quest for Certainty*. New York: Capricorn Books, 1960, pp. 254–86.

Flower, Elizabeth and Murphey, Murray G. *A History of Philosophy in America*, 2 volumes. New York: G.P. Putnam's Sons, 1977.

Lachs, John and Hester, D. Micah (eds) *A William Ernest Hocking Reader*. Nashville, TN: Vanderbilt University Press, 2004.

Peirce, Charles S. *The Collected Papers of Charles Sanders Peirce*, ed. C. Hartshorne and P. Weiss (Vols 1–6), and A. Burks (Vols 7–8). Cambridge, MA: Harvard University Press, 1931–58, Vol. 6.287.

Royce, Josiah. *The Problem of Christianity*, 2 volumes. New York: Macmillan, 1913.

—— *The Hope of the Great Community.* New York: Macmillan, 1916, pp. 25–70.
Stroh, Guy W. *American Ethical Thought.* Chicago, IL: Nelson-Hall, 1979, p. 261.
Whitehead, Alfred N. *Adventures of Ideas.* New York: New American Library, 1955.

FRANK M. OPPENHEIM, SJ

EVOLUTION

The publication of Charles Darwin's *On the Origin of Species* in 1859 marked a pivotal moment in the intellectual life of the United States. On both sides of the Atlantic debates on the scientific, moral and religious significance of Darwin's ideas captivated the attention of the general public, as well as that of scholars. However, in the United States, Darwinian evolution arrived at such a moment that it would have a seminal impact on American thought. Ralph Waldo Emerson was urging American scholars to free themselves from a constraining homage to European intellectual traditions and to foster a home-grown philosophical take on the world. Renowned scientist Louis Agassiz had recently emigrated from Europe and assumed a professorship at Harvard, enhancing the status of the sciences in the nation. Also at Harvard about this time we have the formation of the famed Metaphysical Club, an informal gathering that included Charles Sanders Peirce, William James, Oliver Wendell Holmes, Jr, Chauncey Wright and John Fiske, among others. The concept of evolution provided a stimulus to intellectual growth perhaps unmatched in American history.

American thought had long been influenced by idealistic and theological concerns. Emerson's work helped to prepare the ground for a less static and dogmatic understanding of the natural world and humanity's relation to it. However, Emerson's romantic transcendental worldview clashed with the materialistic and mechanistic aspects of Darwinian evolution and the conflict between these elements was to assume a major place in American discussions of evolution. So, while evolutionary ideas were to find a welcoming environment in America there were deeply ingrained intellectual trends that mitigated against the Darwinian version of evolution. Perhaps most emblematic of this was the fierce resistance to Darwin by Agassiz, inspired at least partly by religious concerns. Given Agassiz's stature, and the fact that many of the foundational figures in American philosophy at that time were directly exposed to Agassiz's influence, Darwin's theory faced a significant roadblock to acceptance.

Fortunately for Darwin, there were skillful and talented minds at Harvard at this time who undertook the defense and propagation of his ideas. One of the most committed was Chauncey Wright. Wright, a regular member of the Metaphysical Club, was credited by Peirce and James as having one of the most astute minds of the day, one that attracted the attention and admiration of Darwin himself. A consideration of the philosophy of Chauncey Wright allows us entrance into one of the central questions concerning evolution – one which continues to roil the discussion of the topic – and that is the legitimacy of extending evolutionary ideas beyond biology. The basic ideas of evolutionary thinking, that of a dynamic, changing universe in which contingency and chance are integral aspects, were quickly and widely accepted by the intellectual community in the United States and only challenged seriously by more conservative religious thinkers. However, what these ideas meant for religion, morality and psychology was a topic provoking much disagreement.

The clash of evolutions

Charles Darwin was not the only evolutionary thinker to excite the imagination of America. Herbert Spencer's impact was, initially, perhaps even more widespread than Darwin's. Spencer conceived of the Law of Evolution as a universal process in which matter underwent change from a simple, undefined state to increasingly complex and differentiated states. Humans were part of this universal evolution of matter and as such were subject to this process of ongoing change. Implicit, and often explicit, in Spencer's conception of evolution was the notion of progress. The evolution of the universe is not a random, directionless process but is one of ongoing progress toward higher levels of existence – and such progress supports a moral interpretation of evolution as supplying not only the conditions but the values for moral life. Spencer's conception of evolution was one well suited to American intellectual culture. The universe is not a cold mechanistic place, even if ruled by mechanistic laws. It is a place where improvement is possible; where individual human strivings for success are supported at the deepest levels of existence.

A consequence of Spencer's influence was the development of a social and economic philosophy that has come to be known as Social Darwinism. This philosophy, in which "survival of the fittest" (Spencer's term, not Darwin's) was the engine behind human progress, accorded the individual the highest moral priority and advocated a laissez-faire economics that justified the unfettered accumulation of wealth as an expression of the natural law of the universe. It also rejected social welfare programs on the grounds that they perpetuated the survival of the unfit and thereby weakened the species and slowed evolutionary progress. This philosophy appealed to late nineteenth-century industrialists such as Andrew Carnegie and John D. Rockefeller, as well as scholars and academics such as William Graham Sumner. Spencer's social philosophy continued to exert influence on American thought, even after his evolutionary theory was rejected.

To the foundational figures of American philosophy, Spencer's ideas were as central to the evolution controversy as were Darwin's. They were embraced enthusiastically by another member of the Metaphysical Club, John Fiske. Fiske's multivolume work *Outlines of Cosmic Philosophy* is an example of an effort to extend evolutionary thinking to areas outside biology. While possessing a competent grasp of Darwin's theory (even garnering some supportive comments from Darwin) Fiske's approach developed along lines more in keeping with Spencer. He saw in evolution the possibility of a single system of law for physics, biology, psychology and the social sciences. This evolutionary law would not only unify the sciences but would provide support to the belief in moral progress as a natural component of the universe. Fiske's conception of this progress differed significantly from Spencer's egoistic individualism. For Fiske the goal of evolutionary progress was Cosmism – a move from egoism to altruism and, ultimately, to a worldwide federation for mutual cooperation and support. (Wiener 1949: 141–4).

In contrast to the use of evolution by thinkers such as Fiske stands Chauncey Wright. Wright's dogged defense of Darwinian evolution earned him the thanks and praise of Charles Darwin, who not only maintained an ongoing correspondence with Wright but included laudatory references to him in his 1871 *Descent of Man*. Darwin even asked for Wright's assistance in clarifying a conceptual problem in his own thinking on evolution, leading Wright to publish his most significant essay, "The Evolution of Self-Consciousness" (1873).

Wright defended Darwin against critics who took his theories to task for their supposed antireligious implications, and against ostensible supporters who improperly extended the application of evolution. Wright's conceptual basis was that of the neutrality of science, sometimes referred to by Wright as "nihilism." This was a methodological stance which held that science was solely concerned with accumulation of knowledge about the natural world, gained through observation and experimentation. Science espouses no moral or theological views, nor should it be constrained by such views. Evolution was concerned with articulating theories on biology and psychology that were empirically based and open to testing and verification. Wright saw in Darwin the tools for establishing a scientific basis for these disciplines, still struggling to free themselves from theological and metaphysical presuppositions. One of the more significant contributions of Darwinian evolution to this endeavor was its rejection of teleology. Wright recognized that there is no progress implied by the theory of natural selection and so no moral conclusions could be drawn from an understanding of evolutionary processes. In this he opposed all variants of Spencerism, including Fiske's, that succumbed to the "subtle poison" that is teleology (Wright 1958: 17) on the grounds that such speculations could not be justified by the evidence. In this vein he also took issue with C.S. Peirce's cosmological evolution and clashed with William James over the moral implications, or lack thereof, of evolution.

Wright's significance lies in his insistence on the autonomy of scientific investigations. He sought both to protect evolution and to limit its scope, not on religious or moral grounds, but because this was the way to establish an effective science of the natural world that could stand next to the achievements of the physical sciences. The issues raised by Wright continue to resonate throughout the history of evolution in American thought. The opposition to teaching evolution that continues into the twenty-first century represents the sort of unwarranted attack on the autonomy of science that motivated much of Wright's work. Also, the efforts to develop an evolutionary psychology, which owes much of its impetus to American thinkers in biology and psychology, may be seen as a continuation of Wright's proposed but unrealized aspirations to develop a psycho-zoology.

Despite the respect of his eminent colleagues, Chauncey Wright's take on evolution was not to win the day among his contemporaries – as may be seen by a consideration of the evolutionary thinking of Charles Sanders Peirce and William James. However, we can see the spirit of Wright's approach in the writings of John Dewey

Evolution and Pragmatism

Pragmatism, born at the dawn of the evolution controversy, developed, in large measure, as a philosophical movement responding to a world now defined in evolutionary terms. Contingency, change, organism/environment interaction, probabilism, are concepts shared in common by pragmatic and evolutionary theories. So too is the rejection of an absolutistic metaphysics and dogmatism of all stripes. And yet there is not a strict correspondence between Darwinian evolution and the evolutionism of various pragmatists. Indeed, looking at the originators of Pragmatism, Peirce and James, we can see an apprehension about just how much evolution could, or should, say about the human condition.

Peirce developed an evolutionary cosmology in which chance played an ineliminable role. Chance is an objective quality of the universe – a concept he labeled "tychism" and which roughly corresponds to the role that random variation plays in Darwin's theory. However, tychism is an aspect of the universe as a whole, and not merely of biology. This raised a difficulty. In Darwin's theory random variations supply the material that under the pressure of environmental conditions leads to evolution via natural selection. In Peirce's system there is no environment outside the universe to provide selection pressures to allow natural selection to function. Therefore natural selection is an inadequate theory of evolution (Flowers and Murphey 1977: 614–15).

Peirce instead suggested three models of evolution: tychasm, anancasm, and agapism. Tychasm is evolution that works simply through chance variations. It is random and without direction. Darwinism is an example of such evolution, although Peirce believed that tychastic evolution went beyond biology. Anancasm is a mechanistic form of evolution that works deterministically. Hegel's philosophy of the development of Spirit is an example of this type of evolution, in which one stage leads directly and necessarily to the next. It avoids the randomness of tychasm, but remains without purpose, and cannot account for the spontaneity and creativity Peirce saw in the universe, and so it too was incomplete.

The ultimate form of evolution was agapasm. Since there is no environment to provide selection pressures to drive evolution, as in the Darwinian theory, there must then be an internal principle that serves as the engine of cosmic evolution. This, Peirce says, is a principle of attraction that he identifies as love. This principle of "Evolutionary Love" provides a direction to the evolutionary process lacking in the other variants. If we keep in mind that the universe, in Peirce's thinking, is ideal then we can understand agapastic evolution as an evolution of thought, and the principle of attraction, the objective of thought, is truth. This is the purpose behind the unfolding of the universe.

In setting out truth, or "concrete reasonableness," as the goal of the universe Peirce does not mean that the universe is moving toward some pre-established Idea, whose truth is determined *a priori*. Truth, for Peirce, is the result of a process of investigation, conducted according to the standards of logic and the scientific method, carried out by the community of rational beings. This is an ongoing, evolving process that could only be said to be complete when there were no longer rational beings to ask questions. It signals the depths of Peirce's evolutionism that ideas, truth, even the laws of nature, were seen to be evolving.

Although Peirce's evolutionary system was left incomplete at his death, it speaks to the power evolutionary ideas exerted at the end of the nineteenth century, and it also bespeaks of the anxiety produced by the Darwinian model for evolution. Peirce's evolutionary theory incorporated many of the philosophical consequences of Darwinism but he could not accept its lack of direction. Peirce developed an evolutionary worldview that retained room not only for purpose and progress, but for ideals and for love, and even for God.

We can find these same concerns with Darwinism in the works of William James. James early on recognized the historic significance of Darwin's work: "A real science of man is now being built up out of the theory of evolution," James wrote in an 1875 letter. Darwin's theory was integrated into James' thinking on psychology and looms large throughout his *The Principles of Psychology* (1890). It is possible to see James as one of the first evolutionary psychologists, following only Darwin in appreciating the impact of evolution in shaping our mental faculties.

For James, Darwin's work argued for the continuity of human physiology with the rest of the biological world. This made it possible to take psychology out of the hands of the metaphysicians and establish it as a science. To understand the workings of the mind we need to grasp the physiological processes involved in various mental functions, and to understand those processes we need to understand how they function to mediate the needs of the organism against the demands of the environment. James's work on human instincts and emotions is a direct outcome of this evolutionary perspective. Also of particular importance for James was that Darwin presented a view of nature that was dynamic, full of change and spontaneous variations. This provided a powerful tool against all the philosophical absolutes that James believed cluttered the way to intellectual progress. The mind does not perceive static discrete entities that it then works into an experience but rather there is a stream of consciousness which experiences objects and entities already in relation; and this experiencing is not a passive reception but is a selective process guided by the needs and interests of the organism.

We can also see the influence of Darwinian evolution in James's philosophical thought. James's Radical Empiricism stems from a deep commitment to the notion of the continuity of human experience with the rest of the natural world. Even if an experience, such as a hallucination, cannot be verified by empirical scientific methods, that does not disqualify the reality or significance of that experience. As a lived experience it is just as much part of the world of experience as any other, and as with any experience we must ask how it stands in relation to other experiences and assess what the function of that experience may be. When James talks of the "cash value" of a belief we can hear echoes of the Darwinian notion of survival value.

Perhaps the most significant lesson taken from evolution by James is that the human perspective is inextricably intertwined with all our knowings and doings. Human physiology is a product of natural selection, and our physiology sets the conditions for our attempts to know the world. Therefore the mental equipment we necessarily use to come to knowledge bears the stamp of human needs and interests in its very constitution – "The trail of the human serpent is thus over everything" (James 1907). This does not mean we cannot come to reliable knowledge but that what knowledge we come to cannot be considered final but must continue to be assessed and verified by future experiences – in a sense, it must continue to fit the environment in order to survive.

Despite James's appreciation of Darwin's theory he was wary of some implications of this worldview. Specifically, James rejected the reductionistic materialism others saw entailed by evolution, and he recoiled at the consequences for morality that followed from this. In response to these concerns James presents an impassioned justification of faith in "The Will to Believe" (1896). In this work James continues to express commitment to the empirical method to determine matters of fact, but recognizes that there are some issues that cannot be settled by the facts. In opposition to those who argued that only a neutral agnosticism is warranted in such circumstances, James defended the right to believe that side of the issue that led to a richer life for the examiner. James has taken a great deal of criticism for this apparent failure of scientific nerve, a failure to follow the scientific worldview all the way, but he also has been hailed for opposing an arrogant scientism. In the context of a discussion of evolution we can find a thread of continuity even here. Evolution told James that the world is a scene of constant motion in which human actions and ideas have practical consequences. When science is unable to decide an issue the world does not wait passively. Events continue to transpire, with or without the consent of the rational intellect, so even the decision to not take a stance on an issue has practical consequences. At this point the only question is what set of consequences is to be chosen – that which follows a neutral stance or that which follows an act of willful believing? This choice can only be an individual's prerogative.

James set boundaries around evolutionary science in order to protect the moral and spiritual life of humans. We see here, as with Peirce, an ambivalence over the implications of Darwin's ideas. This ambivalence, however, is nowhere to be found as we turn to the next major figure, John Dewey.

In 1909, marking the fiftieth anniversary of the *Origin of the Species*, and also marking his own fiftieth birthday, John Dewey wrote "The Influence of Darwin on Philosophy," setting out just how significant an impact Darwin's ideas have had:

> prior to Darwin the impact of the new scientific method upon life, mind, and politics, had been arrested . . . the impact of Darwin upon philosophy resides in his having conquered the phenomena of life for the principle of transition, and thereby freed the new logic for application to mind and morals and life.

Dewey saw Darwin as the climax of a process of scientific thought that had torn down the divide between humans and the rest of the universe. After Darwin, a full-bodied naturalism was finally possible, and all aspects of life could be viewed as continuous with natural processes at work throughout the universe. Where Peirce and James had resisted the implications of Darwinism for the study of the mind and morality, Dewey enthusiastically welcomed the new method.

In his 1898 "Evolution and Ethics" Dewey even outdoes Darwin's Bulldog, T.H. Huxley, in his embrace of evolution. In this early essay, Dewey takes issue with Huxley's claim that ethical progress requires that we combat the evolutionary process. While Dewey opposed Spencer's position that there is moral progress inherent in evolution, he argues that the conditions for ethical life are byproducts of the evolutionary process. Our ability to deliberate, to anticipate the consequences of our actions and choices, our capacity for imagining the responses of others to our actions, are evolved components of a moral consciousness. The ability to value and to distinguish the good from the bad, right from wrong, are outgrowths of the same evolutionary processes that gave rise to all our mental abilities.

Evolution presents the human saga as one of a struggle to adjust to a dangerous and ever-changing environment. This struggle for physical survival shaped our cognitive strategy, which Dewey labels a "quest for certainty." Human thought is not a neutral evaluation of the world but is, as James recognized, a focused attempt to satisfy our needs and desires. Certainty in the mental realm is equivalent to security in the physical realm and so provides a powerful selection force in the history of ideas. The evolutionary perspective allows us a new insight by allowing us to see ideas as responses to changing, and hence uncertain, physical and cultural environments. It provides "the greatest dissolvent in contemporary though of old questions" but also "the greatest precipitant of new methods ... of new problems." (Dewey 1909)

Dewey's works represent one of the first attempts to develop a fully naturalistic understanding of human psychology and morality in light of Darwinian evolution. As such he stands, with Wright, as a precursor to contemporary efforts to develop evolutionary accounts of psychology, morality, and religion.

Evolution in contemporary American thought

With the linguistic turn in philosophy that followed Dewey's death in 1952, evolution assumed a less prominent role in philosophy, even as the evolution controversy continued in the classrooms and courtrooms of the United States. However, it did continue to exert an influence. As we saw with Dewey, Darwinism opened up the door to developing a more fully naturalistic philosophy. To the degree that naturalism remained a major element of American philosophy, evolution remained a factor in American thought. It may be detected, in more or less prominent roles, in the works of G.H. Mead, Charles Hartshorne, W.V.O. Quine, and Richard Rorty, among others.

Evolution became a more central concern again after the 1975 publication of E.O. Wilson's *Sociobiology*. This work laid the ground for the field known as Evolutionary Psychology – a field significantly staffed by American researchers – and initiated a move to develop evolutionary accounts of epistemology and ethics. Daniel Dennett has assumed the mantle of the early pragmatists in drawing out the philosophical implications of Darwinian evolution, and advocating an evolutionary perspective in addressing traditional philosophical topics. In his 1995 *Darwin's Dangerous Idea* he calls evolution a "universal acid" (echoing Dewey's "greatest dissolvent") because of its power to break down ideas to their more basic elements. Dennett argues for the need to apply this acid test to our accumulated wisdom in order to better assess that wisdom and to free it from historical distortions and errors.

This renewed interest in the philosophical implications of evolution takes place alongside renewed attempts to discredit evolution, or at least constrain its extension into the realms of morality and religion. The anxiety that evolutionary ideas provoked among members of the Metaphysical Club in the late nineteenth century continues to color the evolution debates in the early twenty-first, but also alive today is the sense of the new possibilities opened up by those same ideas.

Further reading

Dennett, Daniel. *Darwin's Dangerous Idea*. London: Allen Lane, 1995.

Dewey, John. "Ethics and Evolution" in *The Early Works, 1882–1898, Vol. 5. 1893–1898*, ed. Jo Ann Boydston. Carbondale, IL: Southern Illinois University Press, 1975 [1898].

Fiske, John. *Outlines of Cosmic Philosophy*. New York: Houghton Mifflin, 1916 [1874].

Flowers, Elizabeth and Murphey, Murray G. *A History of Philosophy in America*, 2 volumes. New York: Capricorn Books, 1977.

James, William. *The Principles of Psychology*. New York: Holt, 1890.

Menand, Louis. *The Metaphysical Club*. New York: Farrar, Straus and Giroux, 2001.

Peirce, Charles Sanders. "How to Make Our Ideas Clear" in *Charles S. Peirce: Collected Writings*, ed. Philip P. Wiener. New York: Dover, 1958 [1878].

Wiener, Philip P. *Evolution and the Founders of Pragmatism*. New York: Harper Torchbook, 1949.

Wright, Chauncey. "The Evolution of Self-Consciousness" in *The Philosophical Writings of Chauncey Wright*. New York: Liberal Arts Press, 1958.

John Teehan

EVOLUTIONARY EPISTEMOLOGY

Evolutionary epistemology is an approach to the theory of knowledge that emphasizes the evolutionary dynamics of knowledge acquisition and evaluation. As such, it has its roots in Charles Darwin's *Origin of Species* and *The Descent of Man*.

Chief among the early American supporters of Darwin's work were the American pragmatists Charles Peirce, William James, Chauncey Wright, and John Dewey, and the psychologist James Mark Baldwin. Much of the work on evolutionary epistemology in the late twentieth century derives from the work of the American psychologist Donald Campbell (for historical references, see Campbell 1974; Bradie 1986).

Two programs

Evolutionary epistemology comprises two interrelated yet arguably distinct projects. On the one hand, there are projects that aim to explain or understand the development of the physical and psychological mechanisms by means of which animals and humans come to acquire and process information about the world. These have been labeled EEM programs, where EEM is an acronym for "Evolution of Epistemic or Epistemological Mechanisms." On the other hand, there are projects that aim to understand the nature and development of the content, norms and methods of information systems, knowledge corpuses and scientific theories or traditions. These have been labeled EET programs, where EET is an acronym for "Evolution of Epistemic Theories." EEM programs involve the application of evolutionary biological methods to the study of the development of brains, sensory organs, nervous systems, motor systems and the like which are, as far as we know, the *sine qua non* for sentient and sapient creatures. EET programs, on the other hand, trade on analogies or metaphors drawn from evolutionary biology and may very well turn out to be false or unfruitful characterizations of the development of knowledge. Given the truth of a broadly Darwinian perspective, EEM programs are probably on the right track although filling in the details is fraught with all the problems and more that attend to phylogenetic reconstructions. Brains and their cultural products, unlike bones, do not fossilize easily. If one includes the problem of reconstructing the phylogeny of the evolution of mental capacities, the difficulties become formidable indeed. The verdict is still out with respect to the various attempts to reconstruct the development of human knowledge in terms of evolutionary models.

Phylogeny and ontogeny

Another distinction can be drawn between phylogenetic evolution and ontogenetic development. If we are trying to understand the structure of the human brain, for instance, we can ask two separate though related questions. Both can be couched as "Why do human beings have the kind of brains that they do?" Such questions, as Ernst Mayr pointed out, can be given either proximate or ultimate answers. The ultimate, or phylogenetic, answer will turn on the contingencies of the evolution of the brain in the human lineage. The proximate, or ontogenetic, answer will turn on the details of the interaction between the genetic makeup of particular human beings and the ambient environment in which they develop. Both questions are part of the EEM program. EET questions can be similarly partitioned. One can ask, for example about the development of human understanding of the nature of motion from Aristotle through Descartes, Newton, Einstein and the present. This question, in effect, is asking about the phylogeny of a particular strand of human understanding about the nature of the universe. On the other hand, one may inquire into the development of a given individual's knowledge and understanding of the nature of motion as he or she develops from child to adult. Such questions, in effect, are asking about the ontogeny of a particular strand of human understanding in particular individuals.

EEM phylogenetic projects

These include attempts to reconstruct the emergence of the biological substrate that serves as the basis for sentience, cognition, and knowledge. In the *Principles of Psychology*, William James argued that the organic basis of human mental capacities were the product of a Darwinian process of accidental variation and selective retention (James 1890). A philosophical example of this is Karl Popper's three world stages view. Popper pointed out that, according to the best modern theories, the early universe was composed of matter, energy, and radiation. Before life could emerge, suitable planets had to be formed. When life did finally emerge on the planet Earth, natural selection kicked into gear, and lineages began to proliferate and diversify. At some point, organismic brains evolved the capacity for sentience. At some later point, consciousness emerged. Another long period ensued until the emergence of sapient creatures capable of knowing. At this point, a World-3, what Popper called the world of objective knowledge, came into being (Popper 1972). Popper went on to argue that the evolutionary process in all three independent but mutually interacting worlds was the same. On the view argued for here, the evolution of life and minded creatures is a result of Darwinian evolution broadly construed. These are EEM processes. Once humans evolved to the point where they could codify and develop their knowledge of the physical world, the evolution of that understanding is no longer a matter of biological selection but involves other mechanisms that may or may not share relevant structural similarities to evolution by natural selection. This is EET territory.

EEM ontogenetic projects

EEM ontogenetic projects are concerned with the development, in the individual organism, of the physical structures that support cognitive and epistemic activities. One such is the theory of "neural Darwinism" as developed by G.M. Edelman, Jean-Pierre Changeaux and their colleagues.

EET phylogenetic projects

The phylogenetic models of the growth of knowledge have tended to focus on the growth of scientific knowledge. For Peirce, the method of science involves a continual testing of our beliefs against the data provided by experience. The net effect is the evolution of scientific knowledge toward an ever more complete scientific understanding of the world (Peirce 1877). More recently, models of so-called Universal Darwinism and the "science" of memetics have been postulated as models of conceptual development in general.

Thomas Kuhn's model portrays science as a series of periods of "normal science" punctuated by periods of scientific "revolutions." In the revolutionary stages, many of the specific methods, theories and norms associated with the previous stage of normal science are called into question. What happens during these revolutions is something Kuhn likened to a "gestalt shift" as sometimes radically new perspectives are tried out and adopted. Near the end of *The Structure of Scientific Revolutions*, Kuhn notes the similarity to the competition between varieties that characterizes the selective processes of biological evolution. The winning scientific perspective is analogous to the survivors of selection. He draws the obvious conclusion: just as we do not see biological evolution as progressing toward some global goal so perhaps we should rethink our view of scientific progress as a series of stages leading to a "permanent fixed scientific truth."

Stephen Toulmin's evolutionary model of science also rejects the unidirectionality of scientific change and the notion of "global" progress. Toulmin's 1972 book, *Human Understanding*, the first of a projected trilogy, lays out an ambitious project for interpreting the history of ideas as in terms of a form of epistemological Darwinism. The general Darwinian model of variation within populations as the material on which selection acts is, for Toulmin, just "one illustration of a more general form of historical explanation; and ... this same pattern is applicable also, on appropriate conditions, to historical entities and populations of other kinds" (Toulmin 1972). Science, on this view, develops in a two-step process with the same structure as evolution by natural selection. At each stage in the historical development of science, a pool of intellectual variants – theories, laws, techniques and procedures, and norms – exist along with a selection process that determines which variants survive and which die out.

Donald Campbell coined the term "evolutionary epistemology" in his influential review of the literature (Campbell 1974). In that paper, Campbell developed what he called the "blind variation and selective retention" model (BVSR) that was designed to cover both biological evolution and conceptual change. The heart of Campbell's view is to construe the evolution of organisms as the result of a nested hierarchy of levels of biological and conceptual development. The key to this process is the subsumption of organismic evolution and conceptual change under the rubric of "problem solving." So, the earliest forms of life and most basic organisms first must develop techniques for finding nourishment and sustenance. The organisms move about randomly in search of food. At the next stage various "vicarious" sensory modalities evolve that allow for exploration of the environment without the organisms having to move into potential danger. The more advanced modalities, overlapping to an extent, include the development of habits, instincts, visually supported thought, mnemonically supported thought, "socially vicarious exploration" including the development of observational learning and imitation, and the development of language.

David Hull takes a Darwinian approach to scientific change very seriously (Hull 1988). He proposes, in effect, to develop an empirical hypothesis about the development of knowledge along selectionist lines. Rather than interpreting scientific change as *merely* analogous to biological evolution, he argues that both biological evolution and conceptual development are examples of a common selectionist structure. For his analysis, Hull borrowed a useful distinction, first introduced by Richard Dawkins, between "replicators" and "vehicles." Replicators are what gets handed down from one generation to the next and vehicles are what serve as the packages containing the replicators in any given generation. Hull replaced the term "vehicle" with "interactor" to emphasize the fact that the selection forces that pick out the fittest variants work in virtue of the interaction between vehicles and their environments. For Hull, the interactors in science are the scientists themselves who compete with one another for success. Success is measured by inclusive conceptual fitness or the measure of how widespread one's views become. What get replicated are their ideas, theories, conjectures and methods. In contemporary science, most workers are members of a research group, or "deme," and these groups compete with one another as well.

The Darwinian models of science proposed by Campbell, Popper, Toulmin, and Hull all share a commitment to a selectionist model of scientific theory change. Not all those who invoke Darwin here, however, see a corresponding commitment to such a model. Nicholas Rescher argues for what he calls "methodological Darwinism" as opposed to "thesis Darwinism" (Rescher 1990). On his view, it is methods that compete with one another for acceptance, not theses or theories.

EET ontogenetic projects

Evolutionary models of the ontogenesis of knowledge in individual organisms have also been constructed. As Campbell has noted, these views have their roots in nineteenth-century philosophers and psychologists (Campbell 1974). William James, following Stanley Jevons, noted that creative genius is a function of the generation of random ideas that are discarded when they are contradicted by experience. For James, both the phylogenetic evolution of human knowledge and customs as well as the ontogenetic development of knowledge in individuals is marked by a process of random variation and selection (James 1880). In the twentieth century, B.F. Skinner's theory of operant conditioning has obvious affinities to the theory of natural selection, as he himself has noted (Skinner 1981).

Evolutionary epistemology and the tradition

The evolutionary approach to epistemology is most closely allied with naturalistic approaches to epistemology. There is no doubt that evolutionary approaches to epistemology entail a radical re-evaluation of what it means to do "proper epistemology." It is appropriate to note here that John Dewey argued that one of the consequences of taking Darwin seriously would be to restructure the kinds of questions that philosophers ask and the kinds of answers they deem appropriate (Dewey 1910). Not all are prepared to be so accommodating. On some views, if epistemologists abandon the task of providing justifications, they have abandoned epistemology. Campbell's approach was to argue that evolutionary epistemology was "descriptive" and hence complementary to the traditional normative approach. Hull concurs in part although he allows a role for contextually articulated epistemic norms that arise from the practice of science itself.

Students of the human epistemic condition stand at a fork in the road. In one direction lies the tradition that denies the relevance of any or most of the considerations discussed above to "real epistemology." In the other lie research projects that seek to integrate the latest work on evolutionary biology, psychology, and computer modeling into a philosophically sophisticated understanding of the nature of knowledge, how it is acquired, and how it is transmitted.

Further reading

Bradie, Michael. "Assessing Evolutionary Epistemology," *Biology and Philosophy* 4 (1986): 401–59.

Campbell, Don. "Evolutionary Epistemology" in P.A. Schilpp (ed.) *The Philosophy of Karl R. Popper*. LaSalle, IL: Open Court, 1974, pp. 412–63.

Dewey, John. *The Influence of Darwin on Philosophy and Other Essays in Contemporary Thought*. New York: Henry Holt, 1910.

Hull, David. *Science as a Process: An Evolutionary Account of the Social and Conceptual Development of Science*. Chicago, IL: University of Chicago Press, 1988.

James, William. "Great Men, Great Thoughts, and the Environment," *Atlantic Monthly* 46, 276 (1892): 441–59.

Peirce, C.S. "The Fixation of Belief," *Popular Science Monthly* 12 (1877): 1–15.

Popper, Karl. "Evolutionary Epistemology" in J.W. Pollard (ed.) *Evolutionary Theory: Paths into the Future*. London: John Wiley, 1984.

Rescher, Nicholas. *A Useful Inheritance: Evolutionary Aspects of the Theory of Knowledge*. Savage, MD: Rowman and Littlefield, 1990.

Skinner, B.F. "Selection by Consequences," *Science* 213 (1981): 501–4.

MICHAEL BRADIE

EVOLUTIONARY LOVE

"Evolutionary Love" is the title of an article that the American philosopher Charles S. Peirce published in *The Monist* in 1893, the last in a series of five essays appearing in that journal. There Peirce referred to the doctrine of evolution by creative love as *agapasticism*, and to the philosophical principle that this doctrine embodies and articulates as *agapism*. In the article, he contrasted agapism with two other principles that have been employed historically to account for the process of evolution: chance or fortuitous variation (*tychism*) and mechanical necessity (*anancism*). Peirce associated Charles Darwin with the former and regarded philosophers like G.W.F. Hegel and Herbert Spencer as proponents of the latter.

Tychism was not entirely rejected by Peirce. The idea that "chance begets order" is one that he affirmed, citing its importance as a component of the kinetic theory of gases developed by British physicists in the decades leading up to the publication of Darwin's *Origin of Species* in 1859. Nevertheless, while Peirce recognized the limited significance of the Darwinian principle of fortuitous variation in evolutionary theory, he supplied a vigorous attack on natural selection ("survival of the fittest") as an explanation of how the changes that do occur by chance are formed into patterns that endure. In Peirce's view, Darwin borrowed this idea from nineteenth-century discussions of political economy and merely extended it to the biological realm. Peirce juxtaposed to this modern "Gospel of Greed" the idea of love as a creative, harmonizing force. The form for evolutionary progress is not generated by competition among selfish individuals, he contended, but rather it "comes from every individual merging his individuality in sympathy with his neighbors."

Peirce's conviction that "growth comes only from love" is one that he felt was empirically justified. A person's ideas will grow and develop, just like the flowers in a garden, only to the extent that they are cherished and nurtured. The universe as a whole continues to evolve because it is a divine creation, the work of a God of love and one in which humans are able to participate in some small fashion when they respond to it lovingly. This philosophy is one that Peirce claimed to have borrowed from John's Gospel in the Christian New Testament, but he saw it as having direct application to nineteenth-century evolutionary theory. In particular, he regarded it as being consistent with views espoused by the French scientist J.B. Lamarck, who argued that evolution involves a gradual process of habit-formation, so that it is neither purely mechanical nor entirely fortuitous.

It should be noted that Peirce was less concerned about the biological problem concerning the origin of species than he was with the cosmological question of how the entire universe evolves. Organisms adapt to particular environments but the cosmos as a whole has no environment; consequently, natural selection had little value for explaining how the latter changes. Peirce conceived of divine love as a force that has projected the cosmos into independence and now is gently drawing it back into harmony with the Deity's purposes. These purposes are neither rigidly determined in advance nor do they come about by pure chance, so that Peirce saw his doctrine of evolutionary love (like Lamarck's theory) as mediating between the competing principles of mechanical necessity and of fortuitous variation.

Further reading

Colapietro, Vincent. "C.S. Peirce's Reclamation of Teleology," in Jean De Groot (ed.) *Nature in American Philosophy*. Washington, DC: The Catholic University of America Press, (2004), pp. 88–108.

Hausman, Carl R. *Charles S. Peirce's Evolutionary Philosophy*. Cambridge: Cambridge University Press, 1993.

Hookway, Christopher. "Design and Chance: the Evolution of Peirce's Evolutionary Cosmology" in *Truth, Rationality, and Pragmatism: Themes from Peirce*. Oxford: Oxford University Press, 2000, Ch. 6.

Peirce, Charles S. "Evolutionary Love" in *The Essential Peirce: Selected Philosophical Writings*, Vol. 1, ed. Nathan Houser and Christian Kloesel. Bloomington, IN: Indiana University Press, 1992, pp. 352–71.

MICHAEL L. RAPOSA

EXISTENTIALISM, AMERICAN

It is difficult to define existentialism, but the difficulty is more or less understandable. That is, if existentialism means anything, it means an insistence on radical creativity. So there is a need to keep the definition of existentialism itself somewhat open and continually creating itself.

One handle on the difficulty is gained by locating existentialism relative to the old debate between intellectualism and voluntarism. Crudely put, as it often is, do we first articulate an idea of the desirable and then will the means to obtain it; or is the will already inclined in a certain direction, and only then do the ideas of the desirable take shape within the focus of acknowledgeable consciousness? William James finds that this framing of the issue needs further clarification. Nevertheless, to insist on the distinction requires that existentialists be placed on the voluntarist side.

Another handle on the difficulty of defining existentialism is found by locating this attitude of thought within the nineteenth century. The importance of forerunners in that century is commonly conceded, long before the word "existentialism" was coined: at least Kierkegaard, Nietzsche, and probably Dostoevsky. Not nearly so often do we hear the names of Americans: Thoreau, Emerson, Charles Peirce, William James, for example. Recent tradition places them within different pigeon-holes. It was not until William Barrett in *Irrational Man* asserted that William James could more profitably be classified as an existentialist than a pragmatist that some people began thinking of him and his colleagues in a different light.

Moreover, focusing on these nineteenth-century American thinkers throws existentialism itself into fresh light. What was it about that century that evoked the existential habit of thought? To name only a few of the century's most obvious and salient features: It can be called the century of disruption and uprootage. Life trembles in the repercussions of revolutions from all sides: industrial, politico-economic, scientific and technological. Great masses of people moved abruptly from rural and agricultural lives to urban and industrial ones. The speed of change accelerated convulsively, so that frameworks for evaluating what is happening to us and what we are doing totter, flag, and cannot keep pace. All that is solid melts into air, as Karl Marx put it. But if we cannot evaluate what is happening, we are dumbfounded and lost, terrified and perhaps numbed, disoriented badly. Radical creativity is demanded for survival.

The so-called return to Nature that we find in Emerson and Thoreau is completely understandable. For, traditionally, frameworks for evaluation were tied to rituals that celebrated cusps in the regenerative yearly cycle of Nature: winter solstice, spring equinox, summer solstice, etc. The frameworks encompassed as well the cycles in the development and maturation of each individual member of a culture: most notably the rite that celebrated the passage of children into young adulthood, or the rites that honored the passage from a life into the death of that life. The human species was formed over many millennia of evolution within Nature, and to rediscover and re-locate ourselves in Nature is to rediscover and re-locate our very identity.

Nature abounds both in life-regenerating regularities and in spontaneities. Thoreau and Emerson declared that if radical creativity is not to go badly astray, it must be re-rooted in Nature. But this phrase "creativity re-rooted in Nature" easily remains a mere airy abstraction, and, ironically, all the more misleadingly if taken to be true with respect to our deepest needs because if we remain on the level of mere abstract ideas we will fail to grasp the implications of this truth for our concrete experience. Above all, we will fail to grasp the difficult *means by which* this re-rootage might be achieved.

The most insidious occasion for failure is inherited Cartesian psycho/physical dualism (by now so deeply habitual that it might also be called common-sensical dualism). To regard mind as a non-physical "substance" of some kind prompts the inference that what we immediately perceive are "contents of our private minds or consciousnesses." This in turn masks from sight how we are caught up ecstatically and immediately in Nature's energic regularities and spontaneities; or, to use A.N. Whitehead's term, how we are *irradiated* by Nature. Worse to come: how can we be existential and radically creative in this age of disruption, disorientation, and peril when the supposed psycho/physical dualism distracts us with the pseudo problem of how non-extended and non-physical mind could possibly interface with, interact with, our physical bodies and the rest of physical Nature? How could we be radically creative when we doubt how we can, on a primal level, think about, and act upon, the actual world itself? Many of the difficulties experienced by ecologists in bringing home to the public the glaring urgency of ecological crises is that people tacitly believe that they are sealed-off in their minds or souls from Nature "out there."

In the most eloquent and perceptive ways, Thoreau and Emerson free us from the distractions of psycho/physical dualism. Take a passage from Thoreau's *Journals*:

> I hear the sound of Heywood's Brook falling into Fair Haven Pond – inexpressibly refreshing to my senses – it seems to flow through my very bones – I hear with insatiable thirst – it allays some sandy heat in me – it affects my circulations – methinks my arteries have sympathy with it. What is it I hear but the pure water falls within me, in the circulation of my blood – the streams that fall into my heart.

Thoreau's sensibility is so attuned that he is buoyed, energized, empowered by this experience to take radically creative action on many fronts. A "sandy heat" in him is allayed, a desiccation – what William James will later regard as his own "bogey."

Consult now a key passage from Emerson's "Circles":

> The one thing we seek with insatiable desire is to forget ourselves, to be surprised out of our propriety . . . to do something without knowing how or why . . . Nothing was ever achieved without enthusiasm. The way of life is wonderful; it is by abandonment. . . . Dreams and drunkenness, the use of opium and alcohol are the

> semblance and counterfeit of this oracular genius, and hence their dangerous attraction for men. For the like reason they ask the aid of wild passions, as in gaming and war, to ape in some manner these flames and generosities of the heart.

The utterly refreshing and re-orienting *spontaneities* of Nature are exhibited here. We long to do something "without knowing how or why." *Abandonment* is the secret. Our clinging only to the calculative and/or inferential intellect is what's to be abandoned. There are springs of initiative that this intellect knows nothing of. They pertain to the ecstatic and oracular bases of our bodily beings. They are what drugs and intoxicants counterfeit. Retaining some confidence in the intellectualist/voluntarist distinction, we should say that Emerson falls on the latter side.

We expect that the idea of freedom will loom large in any existentialism. But what distinguishes the American variety is emphasis placed on our grounding in Nature as bodily beings (that this existentialism emerged in the New World in contact with indigenous peoples is no accident). Great emphasis is placed on the spontaneities of Nature before attention is turned to the traditional distinction to be drawn between negative freedom – freedom from restraint – and positive freedom: that is, the ability and willingness to do the good and right thing. Without getting our grounding and rooting straight, we risk floating away in mere intellectualist abstractions. Just as the polar opposition and simplistic dualism mind/body – if one then not the other – is abandoned by our thinkers, so is spontaneous/instinctual, and for similar reasons. We are bodily beings. An intellect conceived to be free-roaming, exclusively mental, and deliberative cannot reasonably be set over against a "merely instinctual" body – not if we want to intelligently approach what actually happens, and can happen, in the actual world. Yes, as William James puts it, there is a fifth level of human will, what he well calls "the dead heave of the will," that sometimes flatly opposes our appetites and sensuous desires. But this should be seen within the total context of our lives, not supposed to be the paradigm of all willings, decisions, choices, all freedom.

It is unwise to precipitously equate the spontaneous and the uncaused. The most humanly significant sense of spontaneity is of unpredictable events which excite growth and renewal. When will the next bird sing, the next leaf fall, the next fish jump, the next breeze swing the boughs of the pines? When we feel ourselves belonging in this unpredictable much at once, we are most alive, vital, ecstatic. Though more than merely random, we act without knowing how or why. The act is probably caused somehow, but why should we care much about what or whether it is? Emerson says, he has "eaten angels' food":

> He believes in miracle, in the perpetual openness of the human mind to new influx of life and power . . . he who working for universal aims found himself fed, he knew not how, clothed, sheltered and weaponed, he knew not how . . . Only in the instinct of the lower animals we find the suggestion of the methods of it, and something higher than our understanding. The squirrel hoards nuts, and the bee gathers honey, without knowing what they do.
> ("The Transcendentalist")

Emerson finds the "suggestion of the methods" of "the miracle" in the instinct of "the lower animals." Though all animals and birds use signs, only we perhaps are aware that we do. So in continuity with our kin, we can participate in miracle through our distinctively aware use of signs.

A master of radically creative development as well as of continuity is the American scientist, philosopher, logician, mathematician, Charles Peirce. He claimed that his first memory was of being four years old, listening to Emerson discoursing on Nature. Of his many gifts, being poetic would not be numbered among them. Yet his great differences from Emerson only underline how basic are the themes that bind them in continuity.

Radical human creativity and spontaneity are rooted for Peirce in instincts we share with other animals. Animals survive only because they can, on average, guess fairly reliably about what probably lies around the bend or over the crest of the hill. As scientists, and thinkers generally, we are at our most creative when we have developed this instinct of guessing into radically creative hypothesis formation. This is a non-mechanical matter: it is fed from innumerable, far-flung sources and roots in the much at once that irradiates us from every side and quarter – no infallible rules for creative hypothesis formation can be formulated. Peirce – a great contributor to the development of formal logic – distinguished this "argumentation" from much looser "argument." The latter flowers from "musing," a recollection of the Greeks' idea of being possessed by the muses, inspired to ecstasy, loud or quiet.

For Peirce, thinking in the wake of Darwin, we are organisms adapting in environments, stumbling, groping, imagining. Philosophy's first order of business is to jettison Descartes, once and for all, and break through the illusion that we are pure minds or consciousnesses that reflect their "mental contents" within themselves. We can stay gripped in the illusion that we can doubt everything but our own thinking and can found rationalistically a philosophy of necessary truths. But this is to stay entranced and self-deluded within reified abstractions and verbalisms. In fact, as functioning organisms, we cannot gain the false summit of an originating universal doubt: we cannot in fact doubt everything except our own private activity of thinking.

Though it is not customary to do so, I suggest that a fruitful hypothesis for grasping the thorny and many-faceted Peirce is to suppose that, among other things, he is an existential thinker. Along with Emerson, he believed that empathy and sympathy are essential for creativity on every front: the heart is a perceptive organ, and it must be kept open if mind is to be. This is anything but mere sentimentality. A master of reason in its many forms, nevertheless Peirce believed that in none of its forms can it be completely enclosing and self-grounding. Astutely he observed that no reason can be given for being reasonable, for to give a reason is already to be reasonable. There is a primal choice involved, a primal nisus or inclination that is allowed to be realized. It is not far-fetched to call this an existential choice.

In William James, American existentialism comes to full flower. He builds on the whole tradition so far outlined. There is no world "out there," but we are organisms prompted by instincts, impelled by needs, irradiated by environments, and interfusing with them. Needs, guesses, purposes, beliefs are not mere "contents of minds" (no mere psychological impertinence, as Sidney Hook put it later). Take what we call beliefs. The concrete reality is an organism's believing in something believed-in. When the believing and the believed-in occur within one being, it is self-deluding to sunder them or insulate them from one another. That is, if the believed-in is one's capacities, they have outer limits, of course. But there is no determinate, fixed quantity of these capacities. In certain pressing and crucial situations, the intensity with which one is *believing positively in* one's capacities may make the difference in one's ability to perform a task or not, may make the difference in one's capacities themselves, the difference in what's *believed-in*. For committed intellectualists to believe that it's some kind of sin to believe before the evidence comes in is for them to willfully overlook the fact that the evidence that does come in may depend decisively on one's prior belief. It is, says James, rationalistically motivated irrationality.

Understandably, one can call this voluntarism. Even so, there is a danger here. For calling it this may suggest a naive version of the voluntarism/intellectualism issue, even a faculty psychology that holds to distinct, insulated capacities. This would mask from sight James's whole approach which is organicist, coherentist, and, if you will, continuityist (though not the through and through continuity of the rationalist or absolute idealist). For James, the secret of the control of will is the secret of the control of attention. And over and over in his last work he inveighs against what he calls vicious intellectualism: which is to believe that what's not explicitly included in the definition of something is excluded from that thing. No, actual things and events tend to ooze into what intellectualistic logic declares they are *not*.

James's explicit work on the freedom of the will brings the whole question of existentialism into startling focus. In the section on the will in *Talks to Teachers on Psychology*, James underlines the futility of the two commonplace opposing positions on this freedom. The determinist believes that if we knew all the forces impinging on us from within and without at any moment we would see that one and only one resultant action could ensue. But this is verbalistic mystification, for we can in fact never know what all these putative forces are or might be. The free-willist, on the other hand, believes that at any moment we can experience a whole range of possible actions lying before us. Yes, we can only do one of them at any moment, yet we might have done another. Of course, the objection to this is plain. We can in fact not turn time back, and the determinist will argue that it only seemed before we acted that we might do something else.

Can we allow ourselves to be reduced to futility on a matter of such pressing importance for our lives as is the issue of our own freedom? Allowing this would be inherently self-defeating. It would be to be duped by intellectual fiddle-faddle. James takes a radically creative approach to the issue. Employing an intriguing variant of scientific caution, he writes that *if* freedom of the will were to be true, it would be absurd to *wait* for evidence of *this* to appear! So, logically speaking, if freedom of the will were to be true, the very first act of freedom would be to freely believe in this freedom. So he does so believe, and with the most liberated of consciousnesses, and with the most impressive generation of evidences, he believes. He can cite the evidence of his own life: his recovery from incapacitating depression in his advanced youth – his leap of faith, one can say, in believing in his own freedom, and in then living a productive life against the odds. Who is in a position to say him nay, and why should he care if anyone tries?

It is a commonplace that existentialism emphasizes the individual and the limits of reason. But this is misleading if we forget that (1) for all versions of existentialism the individual is constituted only in the most intimate reciprocity with others in situations, and indeed is constituted in reciprocity with the cosmos, about which existentialists certainly do wonder, and that (2) reason itself is no fixed set of rules and principles, but is constituted in diverse and pluralistic ways, given the situations in which it is to be applied. Peirce and James, in their different ways, insist on these points.

What of American existentialism in the twentieth and twenty-first centuries? John Dewey left a huge and complex body of work: a special study would be needed to single out particular features that belong in the tradition, such as his theories of education. Looking beyond Dewey, what we mainly see in American academic philosophy is a tacit denial of the tradition. It's as if it never happened. So-called analytic philosophy connects itself to the rationalists of the Enlightenment and to the seventeenth-century physicist–philosophers, especially Descartes. Left unquestioned are those figures' primal detachment from the world presented in immediate experiencing, the much at once. That is, left unquestioned is how it is possible to objectify a world "out there," and also – if one is a Cartesian – a world "in here." In accepting unquestioningly these abstractions, any idea of an immanent divinity is blocked, and also, of course, any inkling of a super-natural domain. What we get is what Eugene Halton has called the sub-natural.

But the tradition of American existentialism is too broad and powerful to be simply blocked by analytic philosophy. The human need to make sense of experiencing in its immediacy is too profound and abiding. Some noted American academic philosophers, such as John Lachs and John McDermott, do continue to develop the tradition in singular ways. But revealingly enough, other academic thinkers who find their seat in departments other than philosophy also valuably continue the tradition. To name but four: James Livingston, who grasps the wide-ranging significance for the culture of the tradition's radical reconfiguring of subjectivity; Cornel West, who retains a great respect for Emerson and who speaks of a prophetic pragmatism; Eugene Halton, just mentioned, who outlines well the impoverishing effects of the analytic constriction of philosophical vision; Richard Poirier, who insists on re-rooting us in the tradition, especially as exemplified in Emerson and William James. Many others outside academia altogether are nourished and sustained by the tradition and contribute to our lives.

Further reading

Barrett, William. *Irrational Man: A Study in Existential Philosophy.* New York: Doubleday-Anchor, 1959.

Halton, Eugene. *Bereft of Reason: On the Decline of Social Thought and Prospects for its Renewal.* Chicago, IL: University of Chicago Press, 1995.

James, William. *The Will to Believe, and Other Essays in Popular Philosophy*, New York: Longmans, Green, 1897.

Lachs, John. *The Relevance of Philosophy to Life*, Nashville, TN: Vanderbilt University Press, 1995.

Livingson, James. *Pragmatism and the Political Economy of Cultural Revolution, 1850–1940.* Chapel Hill, NC: University of North Carolina Press, 1997.

Poirier, Richard. *The Renewal of Literature: Emersonian Reflections.* New Haven, CT: Yale University Press, 1988.

Schrag, Calvin. *Existence and Freedom.* Evanston, IL: Northwestern University Press, 1961.

West, Cornel. *The American Evasion of Philosophy: A Genealogy of Pragmatism.* Madison, WI: University of Wisconsin Press, 1989.

Wild, John. *The Challenge of Existentialism.* Bloomington, IN: Indiana University Press, 1955.

Wilshire, Bruce. *Wild Hunger: The Primal Roots of Modern Addiction.* Lanham, MD: Rowman and Littlefield, 1998.

BRUCE WILSHIRE

EXPERIMENTALISM

Classical Pragmatism exhibited from its earliest days a strong experimental component in terms of both stated methodology and actual practice. Charles S. Peirce expressed the spirit of the movement's experimental method as early as the 1870s in essays that tied the meaning of a concept to its conceivable practical consequences. He argued that the only alternatives to self-correcting methods of the experimental sciences were the methods of tenacity, a priori thinking, and authority. His theory of truth was also experimentally based: it involved convergence toward an ideal limit within a community of experimental scientists. In addition to his role as a founding Pragmatist, Peirce had a career as a scientist employed by the US Coast and Geodetic Survey.

Experimentalism also played an important role in the work of William James. His *Principles of Psychology* (1890) included discussions of the methods of the new German experimental psychology. In *The Varieties of Religious Experience* (1902) he suggested that the "healthy-minded" religionist might utilize the methods of the experimental sciences to undercut what he regarded as the excessive positivism that he thought had blocked legitimate inquiry by defining the subject of experimental science too narrowly. James thought that one of the chief benefits of experimentalism was its ability to demonstrate the bankruptcy of the older rationalistic philosophies, especially absolute idealism. James thus greatly extended the notion of experimentally derived truth beyond Peirce's community of scientists to a wider community of inquirers. In addition to his contributions as a founding Pragmatist, James operated an experimental laboratory at Harvard University and on occasion served as his own experimental subject.

It was John Dewey, however, who explicitly identified his own philosophical position as experimentalism. His appellation is appropriate in both broad and narrow senses. In the broad sense, Dewey recognized the importance of experimentation as an indispensable component of scientific method, characterizing it as "the art of conducting a sequence of observations in which natural conditions are intentionally altered and controlled in ways which will disclose, discover, natural subject-matters which would not otherwise have been noted."

When taken with Dewey's statement of what he called "the philosophic fallacy," that is, treating the results of inquiry as if they had existed prior to inquiry, this statement illuminates Dewey's position with respect to traditional epistemology and metaphysics. It reveals Dewey's commitment to a form of realism – in this case the view that there are naturally occurring conditions that do not depend on cognitive activity in order to be experienced as real. But it also reveals his commitment to a form of idealism – in this case the view that it is only through the inferential activities of mind that what is experienced noncognitively becomes an affair of knowledge. In other words, knowing involves a minimal level of experimental control. Dewey utilized this distinction between what is experienced and what is known to undercut the traditional split between facts and values. He argued that what is experienced as valued, when it proves problematic, can be proven to be *valuable* only by means of experimental tests.

Dewey distinguished experimentalism from empiricism. He contrasted the empiricism of Aristotle, whose primary tools were observation and classification, with contemporary experimental science, which systematically invents and adapts a wide variety of tools and instruments with a view to the manipulation of variables within sequences of inquiry. Dewey thus stressed the instrumental nature of modern science.

In a narrower and more technical sense of experimentalism, Dewey employed the term "experimental logic" to designate one aspect of his theory of inquiry. He identified his logic as functionalism in the sense that it treated ideas as functions of mind; as geneticism in the sense that it analyzed the ways in which standards of inquiry have developed over time; as instrumentalism in the sense that it treated ideas as tools of inquiry constructed within the processes of inquiry; and as experimentalism in the sense that it was a theory of how the value of ideas may be tested.

Dewey rejected scientism. He thought that there were vast areas of human experience where knowing has no business. He also thought that the sciences, especially the human sciences, were still in an immature state; experimentalism as a method of inquiry would develop only as it was applied to wider fields of human concern, including those that are social and moral.

Dewey thought experimentalism was deeply ingrained in the American experience, with its distrust of dogma, absolutism, and authority, and was thus an indispensable component of democratic life. He regarded democracy not so much as a form of government as an experiment in the manner in which various publics are able to interact for the common good.

Further reading

Dewey, John. *Experience and Nature* in *The Collected Works of John Dewey: The Later Works, 1925–1953, Vol. 1, 1925*, ed. Jo Ann Boydston. Carbondale, IL: Southern Illinois University Press, 1981.

—— "Introduction to *Essays in Experimental Logic*" in *The Collected Works of John Dewey: The Middle Works, 1899–1924, Vol. 10, 1916–1917*, ed. Jo Ann Boydston. Carbondale, IL: Southern Illinois University Press, 1980.

James, William. *The Principles of Psychology* in *The Works of William James: The Principles of Psychology*, ed. Frederick Burkhardt and Fredson Bowers. Cambridge, MA: Harvard University Press, 1981.

—— *Varieties of Religious Experience* in *The Works of William James: The Varieties of Religious Experience*, ed. Frederick Burkhardt and Fredson Bowers. Cambridge, MA: Harvard University Press, 1985.

Peirce, Charles S. "The Fixation of Belief" in *The Writings of Charles S. Peirce: A Chronological Edition*, Vol. 3, *1872–1878*, ed. Christian J.W. Kloesel. Bloomington, IN: Indiana University Press, 1986.

Larry A. Hickman

EXTERNAL/INTERNAL RELATIONS

Imagine that someone asks her local supermarket clerk, "Would your cash register still be the *same* register if you had never operated it?" Unless the clerk had already taken at least an undergraduate course in metaphysics, she would answer, "Yes, of course." If the same clerk is asked the question, "Would a wife still be a wife if she divorces her husband or if her husband dies?" the clerk would most likely answer, "No." The clerk's answers to the above questions are representative of the commonsensical view of external and internal relations (CVR).

CVR is the philosophical position which states that every individual has both internal and external relations to its relata, namely, the other individuals and universals that it is related to (that is, if universals are conceived of as general terms, and not as abstract individuals). CVR's distinction between external and internal relations is very similar to the Aristotelian distinction between the accidental properties and essential properties of an individual. Like Aristotelian accidental properties, external relations are those relational properties that are not essential to an individual's identity. In other words, an individual's external relations are those relations that could be taken away from an individual and that individual would still remain what it is. On the other hand, internal relations are similar to Aristotelian essential properties; they are those relational properties that are essential to an individual's identity. Accordingly, internal relations constitute what it is to be that individual. Stated in more technical terms, for an individual *X* to be internally related to an individual *Y* means that *X* would not be what it is unless it is related to *Y*, whereas for *X* to be externally related to *Y* means that *X* would be what it is even if it was not related to *Y*.

CVR is one of the three major views on external and internal relations. The second major view is the doctrine of internal relations (DIR). DIR states that all of an individual's relations are internal ones. Traditionally, the doctrine of essentialism (DOE) presupposes DIR. DOE states that an entity necessarily is constituted by its relations to its relata and that if even one of its necessary relations no longer obtains, then that entity would cease to be what it is. Stated differently, according to DOE, when an entity's relations are altered, it either (a) becomes an entirely different entity or (b) ceases to exist altogether. For the purposes of this entry, the above description of DOE will suffice. DIR had several well-known proponents in the United States during the late nineteenth and early twentieth centuries. Among them were Josiah Royce, Mary Whiton Calkins, and Brand Branshard.

The third view on external and internal relations is the doctrine of external relations (DER). DER states that all of an individual's relations are external ones. Traditionally, DER has not had nearly as many proponents in the United States as either CVR or DIR. Consequently, DER, as a separate doctrine, will not be discussed here.

External and internal relations in early twentieth-century America

The issue of external and internal relations did not become a significant one among philosophers in the United States until 1899 with the publication of the first volume of Josiah Royce's *The World and the Individual* (WI). In the third lecture of WI, Royce launched a full-frontal assault on philosophical realism. His argument against realism goes along these lines:

1 To know something is to be in a cognitive relation with the thing known.
2 Realism is a philosophical position that attempts to know things in the world as they are in themselves.
3 A significant corollary of realism is DER.
4 As a corollary of realism, DER supports realism's contention that for anything to exist, it has to exist independently of everything else.
5 Accordingly, for something to exist independently means that it is self-sufficient, and thus not related to anything else. This includes a thing's relations to its relata (e.g. greater than, lesser than, heavier than, lower than).
6 Yet, if everything that exists is an independent thing, including even a thing's relations, then one would have to posit additional relations to relate a thing to its "independent" relations *ad infinitum*.
7 This means that one cannot have knowledge of anything in the world, because one cannot enter into a cognitive relation with anything.
8 Thus, realism is an absurd philosophical position.

In short, Royce argued that realism leads to a radical metaphysical atomism and insurmountable epistemic ignorance, which would have been unacceptable to the then-dominant idealistic sensibilities of Anglo-American philosophy.

The nascent realists in the United States, represented by such philosophers as Ralph Barton Perry and William Montague, attempted to refute Royce's critique of realism in the years immediately following the publication of WI. In critical reviews of Royce's WI, Perry and Montague both argued that realism does not entail DER. Indeed, in these critical reviews, Perry and Montague contended that Royce's critique of realism depends on the false presupposition that realism necessarily entails both DER and the metaphysical position that existence entails complete independence.

While criticizing Royce for his mischaracterization of realism, Perry and Montague both argue that realism taken to its logical conclusion entails some variant of CVR. Over the next decade, Perry and Montague, along with Edwin B. Holt, Walter T. Marvin, Walter B. Pitkin, and Edward G. Spaulding, founded a philosophical movement called new realism. The new realists were among the first philosophers in the United States to revive CVR.

Another notable philosopher who revived CVR in America was William James. In *Essays in Radical Empiricism*, especially in the third chapter, "The Thing and Its Relations" (1905), James defended the existence of both external and internal relations against F.H. Bradley's critique of them. Bradley's critique of relations is a simple yet devastating one: He thought that metaphysical relations are unintelligible, since, once one postulates their existence, one is led into numerous irresolvable contradictions. In his rebuttal of Bradley's critique, James argued for a version of CVR. James argued that relational properties are not just logical concepts which one projects onto discreet individuals to join them together in one's mind; one actually experiences the relational properties (e.g. betweenness, similarity, with-ness, conjunction, and disjunction) connecting individuals with universals. Hence James thought that no amount of dialectical maneuvering could negate the reality of relations.

External and internal relations revisited: Blanshard and Nagel

The last notable debate about external and internal relations in the United States was between Brand Blanshard and Ernest Nagel. Blanshard, a Bradleyan absolute idealist, was perhaps the last major American proponent of DIR. For internal relations, he defined them in terms of logical necessity – that is to say, if an individual *X* has a relational property *R* to an individual *Y*, where *X* necessarily has *R*, then *R* is considered to be an internal relation of *X*. However, he thought that if external relations existed at all, then they would have to be contingent relations. More specifically, if an individual *X* has a relational property *R* to an individual *Y*, where *X* has *R* only contingently, then *R* is considered to be an external relation of *X*.

Blanshard thought that internality of all an individual's relations could be proven once one examines the three general classes of relations. The first general class of relations is those relational properties between concrete individuals and other concrete individuals. The second general class of relations is those relational properties between concrete individuals and universals, regardless of whether universals are concretely exemplified in particular individuals (e.g. Jeff's red hair) or are not instantiated in any particular individual (e.g. redness). The second class also includes the relational properties between two or more universals. The third general class of relations is those relational properties between particular individuals which are causally related to one another.

Nagel thought that Blanshard's DIR led to at least two untenable conclusions: Either (1) there is only one genuine individual, since to know any particular "individual" one would have to know all of its actual and possible relations to everything else in the universe, or (2) every statement mentioning an individual would be an analytic one. Accepting (1) leads one to consider what has traditionally been called an "individual" to be merely a nexus of universals. Accepting (2) would force one to regard all of an individual's relational properties to be essential ones. In addition, Nagel thought that the major weaknesses of Blanshard's position were that it could neither sufficiently substantiate its conflation of casual relatedness with logical relatedness nor adequately explain what makes an individual more than a nexus of universals.

Hartshorne's relational metaphysics

An alternative to the above debates about external and internal relations is Charles Hartshorne's idiosyncratic metaphysics of relations. Hartshorne's metaphysics of relations can be understood as a peculiar variant of CVR. What Hartshorne's CVR did differently than the vast majority of theories about relations of his day was that it conceived of external and internal relations in terms of temporal modalities. For example, in Hartshorne's metaphysics of relation, the present is internally related to the past events because past events constitute the present, whereas the present is externally related to future events because future events do not affect the present *qua* present. Additionally, past events are externally related to the present because past events are what they are independently of how they are appropriated by individuals in the present.

One can better understand how internal and external relations are temporal in nature by examining how a presently existing person is related to her past and future selves. A person is internally related to her past self, because she would not be who she is unless she is affected by what has occurred to her in the past. On the other hand, a person is externally related to her future self because the future is technically nonexistent, and therefore does not alter her present identity. Something similar can be said of God in Hartshorne's metaphysics. God is internally related to all previously existing and presently existing entities, because God would not be God unless God was related to everything that previously existed and everything that presently exists, whereas God is externally related to all subsequently existing entities because nonexistent entities cannot affect God's present Self.

The metaphysics of relations after Hartshorne

Since the advent of modal analytic metaphysics in the 1960s, the terms "internal relations" and "external relations" appear to be outdated. Yet, the Aristotelian distinction that these concepts represent is still alive in such distinctions as the one between intrinsic properties and extrinsic properties. In any case the philosophical difficulties associated with the Aristotelian distinction between accidental properties and essential properties remain with philosophers today, especially those philosophers who still value metaphysics as a legitimate field of philosophical inquiry.

Further reading

Branshard, Brand. *The Nature of Thought*, 2 volumes. London: G. Allen and Unwin, 1939.

Hartshorne, Charles. *Divine Relativity: A Social Conception of God*. New Haven, CT: Yale University Press, 1948.

Holt, E.B., Marvin, W.T., and Pitkin, W.B. "Introduction" in *The New Realism*. New York: Macmillan, 1912. Reprinted in Roderick M. Chisholm (ed.) *Realism and the Background of Phenomenology*. Atascadero, CA: Ridgeview Publishing, 1960, pp. 151–85.

James, William. *Works of William James, Essays in Radical Empiricism*. Cambridge, MA: Harvard University Press, 1976 [1912].

Mellor, D.H. and Oliver, Alex (eds) *Properties*. New York: Oxford University Press, 1997.

Montague, William. "Professor Royce's Refutation of Realism," *Philosophical Review* 11, 1 (January 1902): 43–55.

Nagel, Ernest. "Sovereign Reason" in Sidney Hook and Milton R. Konvitz (eds) *Freedom and Experience*. Ithaca, NY: Cornell University Press, 1947.

Perry, Ralph B. "Professor Royce's Refutation of Realism and Pluralism," *Monist* 12 (1901–2): 446–58.

Rorty, Richard. "Relations, Internal and External" in Paul Edwards (ed.) *Encyclopedia of Philosophy*. New York: Macmillan, 1967, Vol. 7, pp. 125–33.

Royce, Josiah. *The World and the Individual, First Series: The Four Historical Conception of Being*. New York: Macmillan, 1899.

Dwayne A. Tunstall

F

FACTS

Philosophers are divided on the concept of "facts." Some philosophers find the concept straightforward and necessary. Others find it deeply problematic and potentially misleading. The concept of "facts" remains controversial even though, in everyday situations, its use is mostly innocuous.

At first glance, "facts" are crucial in understanding the concept of truth. Thus, it seems plausible that, first, a true proposition is one that refers to facts and, second, that facts are what make a proposition true. If this is correct, then our understanding of truth depends on a prior understanding of facts. Some correspondence theories of truth make this explicit, by defining truth in terms of correspondence to the facts. This would make facts an important and fundamental philosophical concept.

The concept of facts is most plausible when speaking of a particular state of affairs (e.g. the fact that Chicago is west of New York). In these contexts, facts can be understood as combinations of particular objects and their properties and relations. Because these objects, properties, and relations are part of the physical world, it is therefore tempting to view facts as likewise having physical reality. This is all the more plausible if facts are the referents or truthmakers of true propositions.

However, it is not clear that facts are actually so necessary or so plausible. Many references to facts can be easily eliminated: "It is a fact that grass is green" is equivalent to both "It is true that grass is green" and "Grass is green." In this case, speaking of facts adds nothing to the content of the proposition. Similarly, it is not necessary to invoke facts to explain what makes a proposition true. "Grass is green" is made true by green grass, by the chemical properties of chlorophyll, and by our semantic norms, among other factors. Beyond this nothing is added by claiming that "Grass is green" is made true by the fact that grass is green.

In addition, if facts are the referents or truthmakers of true propositions, it is difficult to make sense of the wide range of facts that would then exist. In addition to particular facts there would also be general facts (e.g. the fact that all humans are mortal), negative facts (e.g. that New York is not west of Chicago), and modal facts (e.g. the fact that human cloning is possible). These facts are less clearly real than particular facts which, in turn, undermines their ability to serve as either referents or truthmakers.

Difficulties such as these have led W.V.O. Quine, among others, to conclude that "facts" should be "fobbed off" and that philosophers would be justified in "absorbing or paraphrasing away the word." But facts also have their defenders, such as David Armstrong, who has argued that general facts (or "states of affairs") exist objectively.

Despite these philosophical difficulties, the concept of "facts" can be useful in everyday contexts where it is not expected to carry a heavy ontological burden. In these contexts, facts simply stand for the idea, as Bertrand Russell put it, that there is an objective world which does not depend on how humans think about it. William James makes a similar point when he praises pragmatism for being "uncomfortable away from facts," unlike more speculative philosophies. In this sense facts are simply the opposite of fictions and fantasies.

However, problems can arise when facts are sharply marked off from values. This, the so-called fact/value distinction, maintains that facts and values refer to entirely separate and non-overlapping categories. This has led some philosophers to conclude that moral propositions (e.g. "Stealing is wrong") do not state facts but are instead merely expressions of preference or encouragement. Other philosophers have argued that the fact/value distinction fails to stand up to scrutiny. For example, Catherine Elgin has argued that facts are relative to conceptual schemes which are constructed with certain values in mind. Thus, whether it is a fact that the endangered red wolf is the same species as the common gray wolf depends on the relative ranking of genetic, morphological, and behavioral evidence. Different values will result in different rankings and in different verdicts: here, as a result, there is no straightforward fact of the matter.

Likewise, Hilary Putnam has argued that facts and values are "entangled." Drawing on John Dewey, Putnam claims that both facts and values, conventionally understood, are necessary ingredients of any inquiry. These facts and values determine which inquiries are worth pursuing, provide guidance along the way, and help assess the end result. Significantly, inquiry may lead to the acceptance of either new facts or new values. Thus, while there may be an analytic distinction between facts and values, this distinction should not be viewed as a metaphysical dichotomy.

Challenges to the fact/value distinction do not affect the useful and innocuous distinction between fact and fiction. However, once again, these challenges would suggest that the concept of "facts" is not as fundamental as it may first appear.

Further reading

Armstrong, D.M. *Truth and Truthmakers.* New York: Cambridge University Press, 2004.

Elgin, Catherine. "The Relativity of Fact and the Objectivity of Value" in Michael Krausz (ed.) *Relativism: Interpretation and Confrontation.* Notre Dame, IN: University of Notre Dame Press, 1989, pp. 86–98.

Putnam, Hilary. *The Collapse of the Fact/Value Dichotomy.* Cambridge, MA: Harvard University Press, 2002.

Quine, W.V.O. *Word and Object.* Cambridge, MA: MIT Press, 1960.

Russell, Bertrand. *The Philosophy of Logical Atomism.* La Salle, IL: Open Court, 1985 [1918].

JOHN CAPPS

FAITH

"Faith" can be understood in general and in the American tradition in two fundamental ways. In its nominal form, "faith" is a doctrine of belief as when one talks of "a Christian faith." "Faith" can also be construed as an act, method, or attitude of believing as when one says "she believed by faith," "he took it on faith," or "her faith outweighed her reasoning." This second meaning has had a greater role in the development of American philosophy and therefore deserves more consideration here.

The first usage was commonplace in New England Calvinist thought and remains current today. In New England, "faith" meant "Christian faith." In the nineteenth and twentieth centuries, when the pluralism of American religious belief became both more apparent and more accepted, the idea of "faiths" and "inter-faith" activity became more prevalent. Finally, when his Terry Lectures were published in 1934 in *A Common Faith*, pragmatist John Dewey took the nominal version of faith outside the constraints of traditional religions. For Dewey, faith could be applied to any belief scheme, religious or otherwise, to which one was fundamentally committed.

Concerning the agentive version of "faith," the idea that faith could be an alternative to reason in establishing a world view was certainly not new even in 1492. The distinction was proposed in early Christian thought and became a central theme of scholastic philosophy. What one finds in early New England thought is a return to early Christianity's emphasis on belief *by* faith. Jonathan Edwards' emphasis in the primacy of faith for religious belief is evidenced in works such as his "Justification by Faith Alone."

Edwards' Calvinist version of belief by way of faith, however, comes with a particular epistemological constraint: faith is an act of a believer, but it is *not* an act fully controlled by the believer. That is, faith is an act one engages in or an attitude one achieves only through the grace of the sovereign God. In effect, then, one cannot choose Christian faith according to this neo-Augustinian outlook; one can only await the effects of a saving grace.

What is clear, however, is that this Christian faith – as act of believing – was both non-rational and epistemologically superior to the results of human reasoning. Thus, just as European philosophy was turning to embrace the power of individual human reason, New England Calvinism was running in the other direction, making faith the primary and sole authentic mode of achieving truth. This is not to say that Calvinists in America rejected the achievements of reason. As Edwards's fascination with Newton and Locke shows, reason was both efficacious and important in its place. However, where the most fundamental and eternal issues were to be considered, faith in a doctrine revealed by the sovereign God was the only sound route for believing.

In the later years of the colonies and the early years of the United States, the outlines of "faith" as a method began to shift. America's own enlightenment thinkers roundly rejected the primacy of faith and embraced reason as nature's instrument for human knowing. This is clearly reflected in the writings of Franklin and Jefferson but also in the thought of numerous clergy throughout the country. Indeed, this shift was in part underwritten by the growing support for Arminianism in American religious communities. Under the Arminians' defense of a limited freedom, faith-believing became a mode of action controllable by the individual believer. That is, one need not wait for grace, but could choose to believe by faith – or not. In both academic and grassroots settings this notion of free faith fit well with the developing American "frontier" temperament.

Thus, in the Transcendentalist movement, for example, one could follow faith *and* reason in a variety of mixtures. Emerson's self-reliance, notably, was described as "self-trust" – a kind of faith believing – that could set free one's other human powers. The Arminian element was key here. In the Calvinist conception, this sort of primordial, personal faith or self-trust was not a choice but was something one fearfully hoped for. In the Transcendentalist turn, such faith was an option for the individual to seize. Consequently, faith belief opened doors to claims of mystical experiences, to accepting revealed beliefs, to the powers of imagination as an epistemic faculty, and to what William James later called "the varieties of religious experience."

Faith, as a mode of believing, thus shifted from the "blindness" of an external cause to the immediacy of individual choice. Such a choice might be blind or not, but it was existentially "up to" the individual. Kierkegaard's powerful existentialist conception of faith marked one extreme to which an American believer might move in the nineteenth century. This extreme employed faith as a catalyst of religious belief to the exclusion of reason. Nevertheless, on the American scene, faith-believing often chose to incorporate the findings of reason and empirical experimentation. This American tendency to mix faith and reason was given its fullest articulation in the pragmatic movement. Charles Peirce, for example, argued that something like common-sense "faith" should govern our practical beliefs and actions and that reason had theoretical inquiry as its proper domain; over time, he suggested, the two would and should gradually have effects on each other. William James, on the other hand, took a more existentialist line. For James, all reasoning had a "faith" element at its root. That is, our most basic beliefs are always on trial and in the midst of experiment. They are not proved a priori but are taken on faith until experiential evidence should interfere and make us change our minds. This is what led James to talk about the "sentiment of reason." James came at the issue a bit differently in his notion of the "will to believe." Here his point was that in our daily conduct faith must govern our beliefs whenever reason fails to provide a clear decision – James routinely called these faith acts "passional" believing. Thus, for James, faith, as an instrument for establishing belief, was coupled with the idea of risk. To believe by way of faith is equivalent to risking oneself in the direction of a particular belief about the world and all the consequences that such a belief might entail.

In the twentieth century, faith, as an epistemic method, was used in all the forms already mentioned. The 1915 publication of *The Fundamentals* reinforced a desire by many to return to the Calvinist doctrine of salvation by way of God's grace. On the scientistic side of the ledger, positivists tried to eliminate faith and religion from intellectual discourse altogether. The pragmatists, most notably John Dewey, continued to look for ways to synthesize faith and reason in their experimental approach to inquiry and belief. And in liberal Christian theology, the Arminian emphasis on faith as freely chosen religious belief continued to develop in a variety of ways.

Perhaps the most significant appeal to the middle-ground efficacy of individual faith came from immigrant theologian Paul Tillich. Tillich took up James's affiliation of faith and risk and argued that faith-belief, especially in a world dominated by technological and scientific reason, required an inherent "courage" on the part of the believer. Faith was the outward experience of the "courage to be." Thus, faith acts were, under certain conditions, self-empowered acts of moral and religious courage. Tillich's James-like, existentialist approach, however, retained an element of the "Calvinist" sense of dependence insofar as faith's efficacy required that one be grasped by a transcendent power of being. This linking of faith, courage, and power arose amidst the developing social issues of the late twentieth century. Given the apparent radical failure of "reason" evidenced by the atrocities of Nazi Germany and the materialism of post-war technological society, a return to faith as an important way of believing – especially in the moral realm – seemed not only feasible but necessary.

Faith on the American scene thus reveals an historical trajectory in which it moves back and forth from center to periphery. However, it is important to point out that at almost any time in history, including the present, all versions of faith as a mode of knowing are still at work. The so-called religious fundamentalists of all religions still maintain faith's primacy and many still make faith dependent on God's agency. At the other extreme, those who continue to operate with overt or unstated positivistic tendencies argue that there is no room for faith in any epistemology. Presently, the majority seem to continue to take up the middle ground where faith (religious or practical) still lives in a working relationship with reason as co-contributors to our various world views.

Further reading

Ahlstrom, Sydney (ed.) *Theology in America*. New York: Bobbs Merrill, 1967.

Dewey, John. *John Dewey: The Later Works, Vol. 9, 1933–1934*, ed. Jo Ann Boydston. Carbondale, IL: Southern Illinois University Press, 1989.

James, William. *The Will to Believe*. New York: Longmans, Green, 1937.

Tillich, Paul. *Dynamics of Faith*. New York: Harper, 1957.

DOUGLAS R. ANDERSON

FALLACY

A fallacy is a type or instance of erroneous reasoning. Attempts to establish systematic accounts of reasoning errors have not progressed beyond presenting rough taxonomies of fallacy types. Fallacies are often classified as either formal or informal, with respective sub-classifications. Alternatively, errors in reasoning may be classified as principled or non-principled. Insofar as reasoning incorporates deductive, inductive, and abductive inferences, reasoning can be erroneous in any of these three ways, separately or collectively. None of these classification schemes is wholly adequate, but each is instructive.

The traditional distinction between formal and informal fallacies is exhaustive but not particularly explanatory. A formal fallacy is often characterized as an error in deductive reasoning where the conclusion is purported to be a deductive consequence of the premises when in fact it is not. Examples include arguments that "affirm the consequent" or first-order quantifier-shift arguments. An informal fallacy is any kind of error in reasoning other than a formal fallacy, such as equivocation, begging the question, or the gambler's fallacy. The list of common types of informal fallacy is quite long with no apparent systematic structure other than further loose classifications into various sub-categories (and there are many ways of doing the latter).

The distinction between principled and non-principled fallacies is also exhaustive but not explanatory. A principled fallacy is one that is based on a rule of inference that seems to be a good rule of inference but which is not in fact a good rule of inference. A nonprincipled fallacy is any other kind of fallacy besides those that are principled; and the distinction as a whole is somewhat fuzzy. This is as much a cognitive and pragmatic distinction as it is a logical one, and it distinguishes fallacy types differently than does the formal/informal distinction. A given instance of a formal fallacy may be non-principled in that one may make a formal error out of ignorance or by mistake, with no regard for the correctness or incorrectness of the given reasoning. Likewise, arguments that may seem to be good arguments are (unwittingly) informal fallacies due, e.g., to lack of evidential support or to lack of relevance or to ambiguity or vagueness or circularity. On the other hand, principled fallacies are not restricted to errors in deductive reasoning. For instance, the gambler's fallacy (not a formal deductive fallacy) is a principled fallacy in that it can seem like a good inference but in fact misidentifies the events and probabilities about which one is drawing conclusions. A number of non-principled fallacies rest on semantic or practical or rhetorical considerations other than mere ignorance or oversight. This may involve appeals to prejudices, biases, fears, allegiances, guilt, loyalties, and so forth, so as to persuade, confuse, or threaten in order to gain assent to the conclusion of an argument.

Another account of fallacies might begin by classifying those that abuse various principles of deductive, inductive, or abductive inference, respectively. This provides a broader conception of what is meant by a formal fallacy. C.S. Peirce argued that each of these kinds of inference has distinctive forms and principles by which good and bad inferences of that type are distinguished. Obviously, any kind of fallacy that is not specifically formal in this broader sense (e.g. an argument *ad hominem*, an argument that misses the point, an appeal to pity, etc.) would be an informal fallacy. An argument would be a formal fallacy in this broader sense solely because of its form or structure. Besides formal deductive fallacies, this would include statistical fallacies (e.g. the gambler's fallacy, or Simpson's paradox) and failures to meet standards of acceptable inductive argumentation, (such as in drawing conclusions about a population based on an inappropriately obtained sample). Likewise, abductive arguments (viz. hypothesis formation) often have a structure similar in form to the deductive fallacy of affirming the consequent. Such arguments will *not* be fallacious for that reason alone. An example of an abductive fallacy rather would be to assert the conclusion of an abductive argument as if it were true on the strength of the abduction alone rather than regard it as a possibly true hypothesis or supposition in need of deductive elaboration and inductive verification (a fallacy of "ignoring the question mark").

Further reading

Best, Joel. *Damned Lies and Statistics*. Berkeley, CA: University of California Press, 2001.

Capaldi, Nicolas. *The Art of Deception*. Amherst, NY: Prometheus Books, 1987.

Engel, Morris S. *With Good Reason: An Introduction to Informal Fallacies*, sixth edition. New York: St Martin's Press, 1999.

Gula, Robert J. *Nonsense: A Handbook of Logical Fallacies*. Mount Jackson, VA: Axios Press, 2002.

Huff, Darrel. *How to Lie with Statistics*. New York, W.W. Norton, 1993.

Peirce, Charles S. *The Essential Peirce*, two volumes. Bloomington, IL: Indiana University Press, 1992/1998.

TOM BURKE

FALLACY OF MISPLACED CONCRETENESS

Alfred North Whitehead coined the term "Fallacy of Misplaced Concreteness" in *Science and the Modern World* in 1926. It is the error of mistaking the abstract for the concrete, and more specifically the error of attempting to build systems of thought based on abstractions rather than the truly real or concrete things. Whitehead introduced this idea within his discussion of space, time and matter in the seventeenth-century cosmology. The Newtonian mechanistic materialism is his prime example of a theory that mistakes the abstract for the concrete because it represents the world in terms of instantaneous configurations of matter. The problem, Whitehead contends, is that we have no such experience of the world. Instants of time and points in space are pure abstractions of thought.

American philosophers influenced by a Hegelian concept of experience developed ontological schemes based on the idea of true concreteness. William James attempts to generalize from the specious present in the stream of consciousness to develop the ontology of experience in his radical empiricism. Whitehead makes a similar methodological move in proposing his actual occasions as the most basic, concrete units of his metaphysics.

Richard Rorty has criticized the very idea of establishing an ontological foundation of reality by claiming to identify units of experience as concrete. Rorty thus contends that it is abstraction all the way down since the attempt to establish concreteness is another version of privileged access to reality, which he denies is possible.

Further reading

James, William. *Essays in Radical Empiricism*. New York: Longmans, Green, 1912.

Rorty, Richard. *Philosophy and the Mirror of Nature*. Princeton, NJ: Princeton University Press, 1979.

Whitehead, Alfred North. *Science and the Modern World*. Cambridge: Cambridge University Press, 1926.

—— *Process and Reality*. Cambridge: Cambridge University Press, 1929.

LEEMON B. MCHENRY

FARBER, MARVIN

Marvin Farber (1901–80) graduated summa cum laude from Harvard University, and received his PhD there in 1925. Two years later he joined the faculty of the University of Buffalo and, with the exception of a three-year term as chairman of philosophy at the University of Pennsylvania, remained there throughout his career. While a professor he served as department chairman and also as acting dean of the graduate school, and held the titles of distinguished professor and distinguished service professor. In 1940 he became editor of *Philosophy and Phenomenological Research* and later served as editor of the series "American Lectures in Philosophy."

Although Farber studied under Edmund Husserl, he rejected Husserl's phenomenological idealism in favor of a naturalistic materialism. However, he remained interested in Husserl's thought throughout his career and frequently focused on contrasting the naturalist viewpoint with the phenomenological attitude or what he called the subjectivist framework. Moreover, he thought a plurality of methodological procedures to be important in dealing with fundamental questions of philosophy and was particularly interested in combining what he saw as the method of naturalistic materialism with phenomenological method, which together yielded his own "naturalist phenomenology."

He considered the phenomenological standpoint when isolated from naturalism to be an inadequate position, holding that while phenomenological method is useful in describing mental activity such as intentionality and symbolic usage, such inquiry cannot by itself provide knowledge about reality. He thus saw phenomenology as a significant method whose usefulness was limited to the study of mental activity.

Farber recognized the importance of the special sciences in approaching philosophic issues and considered evolution a powerful explanatory tool. He was highly critical of Husserl's failure to recognize the usefulness to philosophy of the special sciences, especially of his failure to incorporate either developmental psychology or scientific evolution not only in establishing his methodology but even in his constitution of the ontological realms of the natural and the social. He characterized Husserl as out of step with the evolutionary movement and an enemy of scientific naturalism.

Evolution is a fundamental and pervasive theme within Farber's own writings, which set his evolutionary, naturalist process philosophy over against the various idealist interpretations of cosmic process, and understood the natural and socio/cultural situatedness of humans within a historical context. Humankind emerges within nature and is part and parcel of it, and its thought processes are a crucial adaptive means for successful ongoing evolution. He was particularly influenced by the writings of Herbert Spencer, but while he embraced Spencer's cosmic evolutionary framework and thought Spencer's "survival of the fittest" a useful descriptive generalization for understanding biological evolution, he argued that its transfer from the biological to the socio/cultural realms was wrong both logically and ethically.

He considered his unique "naturalist phenomenology" capable of understanding the full richness of concrete human existence within a scientific evolutionary framework, incorporating all the rich findings of subjectivism without embracing its idealist ontology or cosmology. He understood a major role of philosophy as that of providing the critical evaluation and synthesis of the natural and social sciences, and stressed that the special sciences should be utilized "cautiously" within the framework of a humanistic naturalism to promote human freedom and happiness.

Further reading

Farber, Marvin. *The Aims of Phenomenology: The Motives, Methods, and Impact of Husserl's Thought*. New York. Harper Torchbooks, 1966.

—— *Phenomenology and Existence: Toward a Philosophy within Nature*. New York. Harper Torchbooks, 1967.

——. *Basic Issues of Philosophy: Experience, Reality, and Human Values*. New York. Harper Torchbooks, 1968.

——. *Naturalism and Subjectivism*. Albany, NY: SUNY Press, 1968.

SANDRA B. ROSENTHAL

FEIBLEMAN, JAMES KERN

James Feibleman (1904–87) was a singular case. Although he worked in a field dominated by the PhD, he was himself without a college degree. Honorary doctorates would eventually be conferred on him for nearly fifty books and over 200 essays, but the man who supervised the philosophical training of scores of graduate students and hundreds of undergraduates at Tulane University had himself attended college, at the University of Virginia, for only one year.

This autodidact genius was also unique in another respect. While other twentieth-century Anglophonic philosophers specialized in logic or the analysis of ordinary language, he wrote on virtually every field of humanistic learning, from anthropology and art to education and science. In this respect, he emulated nineteenth-century European intellectuals, though he never subscribed either to the tenets of Kant and Hegel, or to the phenomenology and existentialism that grew out of them. In his view, philosophers in America and England had all but abandoned their duty, which was to provide a comprehensive account of human knowledge; and philosophers in France and Germany had given up trying to understand the external world in favor of narcissistic navel gazing.

Feibleman's first books, written in the 1930s with Julius Friend, were attempts to understand society in other than Marxist terms. Wanting a grounding in scientific reasoning, Feibleman turned in the 1940s to the neglected work of Charles Peirce, founded the Peirce Society, and wrote an elegant book arguing that Peirce had a world-class *weltanschauung* based on his logic.

An admirer of the systems of Alfred North Whitehead and Samuel Alexander, Feibleman undertook to construct a comprehensive system of his own, which to him meant a book on every major field of inquiry. He began with a massive tome titled *Ontology* (Johns Hopkins, 1951) that, after a brief survey of the history of the subject, set forth the categories (essence, existence, and destiny) that seemed to him necessary to make sense of the world. By "essence" Feibleman meant the realm of Platonic forms, by "existence" the realm of concrete actuality, and by "destiny" the cosmic forces that unite them. It was metaphysics in the grand style, formulated in terms learned from George Santayana.

Like Santayana, Feibleman was a resolute realist and a determined opponent of subjectivism. Arguing that modern philosophers got the horse the wrong way around when they followed Descartes in putting epistemology before ontology, he maintained that we must start with the external world, then try to figure out how we come to delineate its features. In books of social philosophy, Feibleman argued that societies are best understood and evaluated by grasping their "implicit dominant ontologies," meaning the values and beliefs implicit in their cultures, or ways of coping with the world. In books on aesthetics he hewed to the venerable but unfashionable view that the aim of art is to produce beauty, which he defined as harmony of form.

Further reading

Feibleman, James K. *The Two-Story World: Selected Writings of James K. Feibleman*, ed. and with an introduction by Huntington Cairns. New York: Holt, Rinehart and Winston, 1966.

MAX HOCUTT

FEMINISM

Early feminism in America as well as in Europe was philosophically based in Lockean natural rights theory and Enlightenment liberal philosophy which posits the equality of persons as reasoning beings as its fundamental premise. Given that rationality is a core human trait, and that individual reason could achieve truth (and therefore virtue), the ability of rationality supposedly establishes the condition of equality. Unfortunately, the male natural rights theorists' definition of rational beings did not usually include women, who were instead seen as ruled by emotions and meant to occupy the private sphere of life, as Aristotle had advocated. Influenced by the political claims of liberal equality and individual autonomy in the founding documents of American democracy which inferred a need for critical participation in such a democracy, feminists rightly claimed rationality and therefore equality and the right of political participation. In this, early American feminists were also influenced by British writer Mary Wollstonecraft, who in 1792 first developed the argument for women's rights based on the equality of all rational beings, arguing in particular in support of women's education.

Beginnings of American feminism

American feminism as an organized movement began in the early to mid-1800s, although there were women thinkers and activists who could be called feminists prior to that time (notably Judith Sargent Murray, Abigail Adams, and Anne Hutchinson). The experimental utopian movements of this time, such as the Oneida Community and Owen's cooperative New Harmony movement, found fertile soil in the American experimentalist sentiment. For example, Fanny Wright, the founder of the short-lived 1926 Nashoba experimental community, went on to be one of the first women to give public lectures on women's equality. Many of these utopian movements were liberal experiments in equality and socialism, often joined with radical interpretations of Christianity. These communities often altered conventional gender roles, allowing women equal leadership roles in the communities and following alternative marriage and/or family relationships. Typical of these communities was a belief in the possibility of social progression, which created an environment conducive to critically examining social norms. Their experimentation provided evidence that women could successfully participate in leadership in public life, at least in a local community.

The Quakers, while not strictly a communal society, were one of the religious movements of that time that created space for women's leadership. They allowed women to occupy a leadership role in ministry, which ultimately led to women's activism in the abolitionist movement and fostered many of the important feminist thinkers of their time. Sarah and Angelina Grimké were two such women; they began a public speaking tour for abolition and for women's rights, and influenced the women at Seneca Falls.

The Grimké sisters were raised in an influential Southern slave-holding family; their father was a South Carolina Supreme Court judge and through his work Sarah in particular was exposed to liberal political and legal theory. After their conversion to Quakerism and their move to the North, both sisters eventually became involved in the abolitionist movement, becoming the first women to go on a multi-state speaking tour that included addressing audiences in churches, and even publicly speaking to the state legislature. In defense of their right to give public addresses, they had to argue against the dominant philosophy of "separate spheres" which held that men and women were destined by nature and by God to occupy different spheres of existence. Men were supposed to be made for the public sphere, and women designed for the private sphere – an idea that dates back to Aristotle and was articulated in Rousseau's *Emile*.

Angelina Grimké dismantled the separate spheres argument in her *Letters to Catherine Beecher*, claiming that as moral and rational beings the spheres of woman and man are the same. In these essays, she makes the connection between the abolitionist and the women's rights movements, pointing out that the Kantian argument that "human beings have rights because they are moral beings" also applies to women, who logically also have human rights that are not dependent on their sex. As she says, "whatever is morally right for a man to do, it is morally right for a woman to do" (Ceplair 1989: 194–5). Sarah Grimke's *Letters on Equality* (1838) reinterpreted the biblical passages that were used to support keeping women in inferior positions, pointing out that the cultural interpretation, not the actual text, is the cause of sexism. Sarah Grimké was also among the first to analyze women as in a particular economic and social class.

Elizabeth Cady Stanton, a friend of the Grimké sisters, was one of the women who took up the cause of women's rights and further developed the argument for women's suffrage. She was a primary author of the "Declaration of Sentiments" issued at the 1848 Seneca Falls convention of women. Her "Declaration" claims the natural rights of women in the language of the Declaration of Independence, starting with "We hold these truths to be self-evident, that all men and women are created equal." While many later feminists found enlightenment liberal feminism inadequate, it continues to be a major force in the feminist legal philosophy related to issues of equality.

One of the first American women to be recognized both as a philosopher and as a feminist was Margaret Fuller (1810–50). Fuller was a transcendentalist, and a colleague of Emerson, Thoreau, and the Alcotts. Fuller was the editor of the transcendentalist journal *The Dial* for its first two years, a position taken over by Emerson when she resigned to work as a journalist for the *New York Tribune*. Her major feminist text was her 1845 *Woman in the Nineteenth Century*. Instead of a liberal feminist claim that stressed the equality of women as rational beings, Fuller pointed to women's differences, and idealized the complementary nature of male and female. She believed that women's special qualities of intuition and emotional connectiveness needed a supportive environment for personal growth. Like the romantics and other transcendentalists Fuller understood the individual as in a state of continual growth and personal responsibility, which defined ethical behavior. According to her thinking, the social inequality of women interfered with their growth and kept women in a state of being unable to be individually responsible for their own lives.

Progressive Era feminism

The late 1800s were marked by a dramatic increase in the number of women attending college and graduate school. Many of these college-educated women became leaders in Progressive Era (1890–1915) social reform movements. Feminists of this time, such as Jane Addams and Charlotte Perkins Gilman, contributed to the development of American pragmatism. Their pragmatist feminism was based in an ideal of inclusive social democracy, developing a progressive model of change that occurred through education, social experimentation and dialogue with and among diverse populations. Addams's social ethics critiqued the ideal of liberal individualism which positions individuals as autonomous beings who are often in competition with each other for their freedoms. Instead, like her colleague John Dewey, she understood the individual as a social being, always effecting and being effected by her social environment. As such, she argued that women needed the education and the freedom to act socially and politically. Conversely, she also argued that our goal of democracy requires women's participation as part of the diverse and pluralistic voices needed in public life.

The social justice feminism of the pragmatist era included a comprehensive social movement for peace that went beyond the abolition of war, requiring social justice as its starting point. This early twentieth-century peace movement was an important national political arena for both activism and political philosophy, as women developed feminist critiques of militarism as a way of life that embraces hierarchical and competitive social structures. Yet the militaristic sentiment arising from the First World War effectively squelched many of the social reforms that progressive women had initiated. Ironically it was at this time (1920) that women finally gained the right to vote, mainly through the efforts of the more aggressively radical feminists led by Alice Paul.

"Second-wave" feminism

Coinciding with the civil rights era, the 1960s and 1970s saw an explosion of feminist theory and activism. Feminist activists and scholars developed a sustained feminist critique of social and political structures, including systems of education and the academic canon. Many feminists of this era were deeply critical of liberal feminism, believing that equality in terms of wages and civil rights would be inadequate in addressing the hegemonies of patriarchy, racism, classism, and heterosexism. The radical feminists of the 1960s adopted the rhetoric of revolution that spurred both grassroots political activism and experimental communities. Kate Millet in the influential *Sexual Politics* identified and critiqued systems of patriarchy, also pointing out the embedded gendered roles that supported patriarchy were systematically conditioned by the nuclear family. Many radical feminists proposed alternative family/household arrangements, and some proposed women-only communities as way to counter the gendered nature of social structures such as family, religion and politics.

The feminist critique developed in this era extended to all traditions within philosophy as well as transcending disciplinary boundaries. As feminist philosophers worked within and transformed many traditions, it also became increasingly difficult to isolate a particularly American feminist philosophy. Significant examples of feminist philosophy in what has been called the "second wave" of American feminist activism include radical philosopher Mary Daly's examination of both religion and the structure of language, Susan Moller Okin's critique of Western political thought, Sandra Harding and Evelyn Fox Keller's feminist philosophies of science, and Deweyan scholar Elizabeth Minnich's examination of the gendered content of the curriculum that perpetuates hierarchical and patriarchal ways of thinking. Other feminists developed Marxist, psychoanalytic, socialist, postmodern and phenomenological feminist theory, and within these traditions feminists developed a wide range of feminist epistemologies. Feminist epistemologies in general consider the concrete and specific conditions of embodied life and its effect on the knowing process and the ways that power, social hierarchies and social context affect knowledge. Some feminist epistemologists, such as Susan Bordo, critique Cartesian dualisms, pointing instead to the role of the situated body in the knowing process. Carol Gilligan's groundbreaking 1982 book, *In a Different Voice*, argued that girls are socialized to approach knowing and ethics through relational experience rather than distanced epistemological rationality.

Developing as it did with the civil rights movement, this "second wave" of feminism was largely influenced by women of color who faced the "double jeopardy" of gender and race discrimination. Pointing to the racist history of American slavery and Jim Crow segregation and continuing racial prejudices, black feminist activists responded with anger to white middle-class feminist assumptions that they were speaking for all women. Critical race feminism grew out this movement, alongside critical race legal theory, as a critique of liberalism and of "colorblind" laws which claim equality. bell hook's 1984 *Feminist Theory: From Margin to Center* points to the falseness of the ideas of "common oppression" and sisterhood claimed by many feminists who ignored the oppressions of racism, classism and heterosexism. Some of the work of critical race feminists established the basic theoretical framework that grew into the larger focus of postcolonial feminism (see below).

In the later twentieth century feminist philosophers began a recovery of the work of women philosophers in many traditions, re-discovering the presence of female thinkers whose names and voices disappeared from the historical record, and whose work was systematically eliminated from the philosophical canon. (See for example Mary Ellen Waithe's multi-volume *History of Women Philosophers.*) This work in the history of philosophy was complemented by feminist analysis of the gender bias in many of the works of historic philosophers, examining not just the claims they made about women's unequal position in relation to men, but also the effect that this bias had in shaping their philosophic positions as well as the discipline itself.

Pragmatist and postcolonial feminism

Feminist philosophers working in the American pragmatist tradition are recovering women's contributions to the creation of American pragmatism, as well as developing a particularly pragmatist form of feminist philosophy. Charlene Haddock Seigfried's 1996 book *Pragmatism and Feminism* demonstrated that pragmatist thought is a rich resource for contemporary feminists, and it demonstrated as well the wealth of women's contributions to the development of pragmatism. Although most of the male thinkers of the classical pragmatist era did not seriously consider the effects of gender, race or class oppression, their insistence that philosophy should address contemporary social problems and their articulation of the value of pluralistic community provides theoretical framing for feminist work. Both pragmatists and feminists advocate for the practical use of philosophy in the realm of personal and public experience, bringing the concrete and particular into the philosophic discussion. For pragmatists as well as feminists, the process of discovering truth is grounded in a social context and requires the points of view of many diverse others; pragmatist epistemology by necessity requires that one include the voices of marginalized others. The pragmatist feminist insistence on both social and political equality, empathy and dialogue also gives us resources to think about democracy and global issues.

The 11 September 2001 bombings and the Bush administration wars in the Middle East have increased American feminist philosophy's global focus. The long-standing feminist emphasis on women's rights has joined with a larger concern of human rights, which involves a consideration of the effect that American economic and political actions have on women's conditions world-wide. Feminists have joined with postcolonial theorists and activists in a fight against imperialistic and gendered oppression, while also being critical of Western forms of feminism that unreflectively claimed a universalized female experience. Chandra Talpade Mohanty's influential *Feminism without Borders: Decolonizing Theory, Practicing Solidarity* (2003) is an example of postcolonial feminism which joins a critique of global capitalism and racism with the feminist struggle against patriarchy.

All of these areas of feminist philosophy, from liberal feminism to postcolonial feminism, continue to be developed in a rich conversation within and among the various traditions of American philosophy.

Further reading

Addams, Jane. *Democracy and Social Ethics.* Urbana, IL: University of Illinois Press, 2002.

Alcoff, Linda, and Potter, Elizabeth (eds) *Feminist Epistemologies.* New York: Routledge, 1993.

Ceplair, Larry (ed.) *The Public Years of Sara and Angelina Grimké: Selected Writings, 1835–1836.* New York: Columbia University Press, 1989.

Collins, Patricia Hill. *Black Feminist Thought*, Boston, MA: Unwin Hyman, 1990.

Donovan, Josephine. *Feminist Theory: The Intellectual Traditions of American Feminism.* New York: Continuum, 1992.

Jaggar, Alison and Young, Iris Marion (eds) *A Companion to Feminist Philosophy.* Maiden, MA: Blackwell, 1998.

Kauffman, Linda S. (ed.) *American Feminist Thought at Century's End.* Cambridge, MA: Blackwell, 1993.

Lerner, Gerda. *The Grimké Sisters of South Carolina.* New York: Oxford University Press, 1998.

Millet, Kate. *Sexual Politics.* Urbana, IL: University of Illinois Press, 2000.

Minnich, Elizabeth Kamarck. *Transforming Knowledge*, second edition. Philadelphia, PA: Temple University Press, 2004.

Mohanty, Chandra Talpade. *Feminism without Borders: Decolonizing Theory, Practicing Solidarity.* Durham, NC: Duke University Press, 2003.

Naravan, Uma and Harding, Sandra (eds) *Decentering the Center: Philosophy for a Multicultural, Postcolonial, and Feminist World.* Bloomington, IN: Indiana University Press, 2000.

Seigfried, Charlene Haddock. *Pragmatism and Feminism: Reweaving the Social Fabric.* Chicago, IL: University of Chicago Press, 1996.

Tuana, Nancy and Tong, Rosemarie. *Feminism and Philosophy: Essential Readings in Theory, Reinterpretation, and Application.* Boulder, CO: Westview Press, 1995.

Wing, Adrien Katherine (ed.) *Critical Race Feminism: A Reader.* New York: New York University Press, 1997.

Judy D. Whipps

FEMINIST EPISTEMOLOGY

Feminist approaches to epistemology encompass a rich and varied exploration of a range of traditional epistemological issues including theories of objectivity, the role of subjectivity in the development of knowledge, foundationalism, the division between the context of discovery and the context of justification, the nature of evidence, the issue of value-neutrality, and the nature of truth. Feminist research in the area of epistemology is strongly linked to work in feminist philosophy of science in that many of the debates about theories of objectivity, the nature of evidence, etc., were developed in the context of the study of science.

Feminist epistemologies evolved both from and in reaction to mainstream philosophical theories. What makes these writings feminist is a robust attention to the role of gender in the framing of epistemological questions and concepts. However, feminist epistemologists are also influenced by and often write out of a particular tradition within philosophy, namely American pragmatist philosophy, analytic philosophy, and continental philosophy. Indeed, feminist research in all three traditions has developed to the point that it has begun to bring new perspectives and concerns to mainstream philosophy.

Analytic philosophy and feminist epistemologies

Key features of analytic philosophy are conceptual analysis and attention to the nature and limits of knowledge. Because of the strong interest in analytic philosophy on issues of knowledge, many feminist epistemologists have turned to theorists and approaches from the analytic tradition as a resource for their work.

The work of feminist epistemologists like Louise Anthony (1993), Jane Duran (1991), Helen Longino (1990), Lynn Hankinson Nelson (1990), Elizabeth Potter (2001), and Nancy Tuana (1996) are examples of the interaction of feminist and analytic approaches to epistemological concerns. These theorists build on the work of various analytic philosophers to address questions concerning objectivity, the nature of evidence, the relationship between scientific knowledge and commonsense beliefs, and the like. Feminist epistemologists influenced by analytic approaches, particularly those influenced by W.V.O. Quine, frequently embrace the importance of the naturalist move in epistemology in which epistemology is no longer seen as an *a priori* investigation, but must be anchored in scientific theorizing, e.g. the cognitive sciences.

While influenced by approaches within analytic philosophy, the work of these feminist epistemologists also diverges from them in significant ways. For example, those who have built upon Quine's version of naturalizing epistemology and his assertion that you cannot separate science from commonsense beliefs or even from ontology (i.e. you cannot distinguish the objects we talk about from the ways we talk about them) have also shown that attention to gender, particularly the role of gender biases in the development of scientific theories, requires an enriched approach to naturalizing epistemology that "rubs out one last boundary" left in place by Quine, namely that between values and science. Indeed, rather than attempt to expunge value from science, feminist epistemologists have undertaken the project of illuminating the role of such values in all their complexity and developed accounts of the ways in which such values can be empirically evaluated. In addition, these feminist epistemologists have examined the saliency of categories such as gender and race in the design of research programs and the construction of theories. In the hands of such feminist epistemologists naturalized epistemology includes attention to the social processes through which we become knowers and knowledge is generated, in addition to the mainstream emphasis on psychological, biological, and cognitive science explanations.

Pragmatist philosophy and feminist epistemologies

Pragmatist philosophy places great emphasis on the relation of theory to practice and experience. While pragmatist feminist contributions to feminist epistemology are at a relatively early stage of development, they build on both the resources of the tradition of pragmatism *and* the rich resources of over a decade of work in feminist epistemology. Pragmatist feminists such as Ann Clark (1993), Eugenie Gatens-Robinson (1991), Lisa Heldke (1987), Felicia Kruse (1991), Erin McKenna (2001), Marjorie Miller (1992), Marsha Moen (1991), Charlene Haddock Seigfried (1996), and Shannon Sullivan (2001) have used pragmatism's rich epistemological and metaphysical resources to examine the relevance of gender, race, and sexuality to people's knowledge, communities, practices, and other areas of lived experience.

Many pragmatist feminists have drawn on John Dewey and William James to criticize traditional epistemology from a pragmatist feminist perspective. They have argued that knowledge should not be conceived as accurate representations of a static world that stands apart from a passive, disembodied spectator who attempts to know it. Knowledge, rather, is a dynamic construction of active, embodied beings seeking knowledge that supports more effective practices. Linked to this perspective is a model of objectivity that links good knowing to responsible inquiry. This latter understanding of knowledge allows pragmatist feminists to then ask: which groups of embodied beings are involved in and which are excluded from the construction of a society's knowledge, and whose lives are or are not being improved by it? In this way, pragmatist feminists have argued that issues of gender, race, sexuality, and other particularities of lived experience are epistemically significant. Following Dewey, feminists like Heldke and Haddock Seigfried (1996) have developed a version of pragmatic naturalism that embraces both the pluralism inherent in Dewey's approach to naturalism and the normative emphasis of his theory of inquiry.

Pragmatist feminist epistemologists share with other feminist epistemologists the belief in the epistemic significance of a variety of subjective factors such as our specific cultural and social locations including gender, race, ethnicity, class, etc., and our personal commitments, desires, and interests. They have also questioned the individualistic conception of epistemic agency contained within traditional accounts. In this they are influenced by a pragmatist conception of a community of inquirers. Pragmatist feminist epistemologists share the belief with other feminist epistemologists that relationality is key to the development of knowledge and thus emphasize the importance of critical interchange among different communities to identify and evaluate assumptions and values.

While there is value in making a distinction between analytic and pragmatist feminist epistemologies, the distinction should not be seen as clear-cut. While there are feminist epistemologists who draw resources from only one of these traditions, many feminist epistemologists are influenced by resources from both traditions. Furthermore, in recognizing the role of values in knowledge practices and the ways in which knowledge is richly situated, these two approaches are converging in the work of many feminist epistemologists. Phyllis Rooney, for example, notes "the emphasis by many pragmatists and feminists on grounding our epistemological concepts in an understanding of ourselves as engaged inquiring actors in the world" (1993: 15). The turn toward social epistemology in many analytic and pragmatist inspired epistemologists is another reflection of this convergence. As argued for by Elizabeth Anderson, feminist epistemology is a "branch of social epistemology that investigates the influence of *socially constructed conceptions and norms of gender and gender-specific interests and experiences* on the production of knowledge"(1995: 54).

Continental philosophy and feminist epistemologies

The first influential intersection between continental theorists and approaches and feminist epistemology can be traced to the development of feminist standpoint epistemology. Feminist standpoint epistemologists trace their roots to a philosophical tradition that includes Hegel and Marx, and that recognizes divisions in power as being of epistemological significance. Building from the Marxist tenet that those in dominant social and political positions, because of the nature of their situation, lack certain types of knowledge, feminist standpoint epistemologists argue that the dominant position of white, middle- and upper-class males limits and distorts their perspective. Seeing knowledge as grounded in experience, standpoint theorists like Hilary Rose (1983, 1988) and Nancy Hartsock (1983, 1987) argue that the activities of caring assigned primarily to women provide them with different concerns and experiences that provide a starting point for developing knowledge claims that are potentially more comprehensive and less distorted. Sandra Harding (1991, 1993) has developed a robust standpoint epistemology, one that includes the tenet that the inclusion of such overlooked standpoints will contribute to a "strengthened" objectivity.

In addition to standpoint epistemology, continental philosophy has richly influenced other feminist approaches to epistemological issues. Some feminist epistemologists have been influenced by the rejection of the mainstream quest for indubitable foundations for knowledge found within the work of continental philosophers such as Jacques Derrida, Michel Foucault, and Hans Gadamer. Lorraine Code (1991), for example, supports Foucault's rejection of any attempt to find an absolute grounding for knowledge and adopts Gadamer's position that the "grounding" for knowledge comes not from any fixed basis but from a common history, tradition, and culture. Code, however, transforms their approach by arguing that attention to gender is essential to the development of a notion of rationality that fully includes women.

Another key feature of continental feminist epistemology is attention to embodiment, arguing for attention to the role of the body in the formation of knowledge about the world. Feminist philosophers, for example Carol Bigwood (1993), Judith Butler (1993), Elizabeth Grosz (1994), Shannon Sullivan (2001), Nancy Tuana (2001), and Iris Young (1990), have been influenced by the phenomenology of Maurice Merleau-Ponty, but have augmented it by arguing that embodiment is richly situated and not generic. Bodies have different genders, races, sexualities, class status, and levels of (dis)ability, among other things. For that reason, feminist epistemologists have explored the impact on knowledge of the intersection of gender with other bodily characteristics, especially that of race. As Linda Martín Alcoff demonstrates (1996), race uses perceptual practices and bodily appearances to mark itself on the body. In a racist world, for example, epistemic credibility and authority are not distributed equally across knowers.

One of the important contributions made by feminists working on embodiment is the argument that bodies are not precultural lumps of matter that only secondarily and passively come to be imprinted by social and political values. As Butler (1993) has shown, such an alleged asocial, "natural" body is itself the product of cultural and political ways of knowing bodies that tend to prescribe rigid sexual norms onto women's bodies in particular. Instead of thinking of bodies as sealed off from culture in this way, feminists have argued that bodies as formed in and through their active engagement with the world, such that rigid boundaries between self and world are rendered permeable. This allows feminists to understand how bodies are both shaped by sexist practices and, in turn, can contribute to the (re)shaping of the world.

Feminist epistemological writings have often crossed between mainstream philosophical traditions, but whether written in the vein of or in opposition to mainstream epistemological approaches, the "difference" of feminist epistemology proceeds not from a unique method but from the premise that gender is an important lens for analysis. Feminist epistemologists have shown that taking gender seriously provides new insights in all the areas of epistemological scholarship.

Further reading

Antony, Louise M. and Witt, Charlotte (eds) *A Mind of One's Own: Feminist Essays on Reason and Objectivity.* Boulder, CO: Westview, 1993.

Bigwood, Carol. *Earthmuse: Feminism, Nature, and Art*. Philadelphia, PA: Temple University Press, 1993.

Butler, Judith. *Bodies that Matter: On the Discursive Limits of "Sex."* New York, Routledge, 1993.

Code, Lorraine. *What Can She Know? Feminist Theory and the Construction of Knowledge.* Ithaca, NY: Cornell University Press, 1991.

Duran, Jane. *Toward a Feminist Epistemology.* Savage, MD: Rowman and Littlefield, 1991.

Grosz, Elizabeth. *Volatile Bodies.* Bloomington, IN: Indiana University Press, 1994.

Harding, Sandra. *Whose Science? Whose Knowledge?* Ithaca, NY: Cornell University Press, 1991.

Longino, Helen. *Science as Social Knowledge.* Princeton, NJ: Princeton University Press, 1990.

McKenna, Erin. *The Task of Utopia: Pragmatist and Feminist Perspectives.* Lanham, MD: Rowman and Littlefield, 2001.

Nelson, Lynn Hankinson. *Who Knows: From Quine to a Feminist Empiricism.* Philadelphia, PA: Temple University Press, 1990.

Potter, Elizabeth. *Gender and Boyle's Law of Gases.* Bloomington, IN: Indiana University Press, 2001.

Seigfried, Charlene Haddock. *Pragmatism and Feminism: Reweaving the Social Fabric*. Chicago, IL: University of Chicago Press, 1996.

Sullivan, Shannon. *Living Across and Through Skins: Transactional Bodies, Pragmatism, and Feminism*. Bloomington, IN: Indiana University Press, 2001.

Tuana, Nancy. "Material Locations: An Interactionist Alternative to Realism/Social Constructivism" in Nancy Tuana and Sandra Morgen (eds) *Engendering Rationalities.* Albany, NY: SUNY Press, 2001, pp. 221–44.

Young, Iris. *Throwing Like a Girl and Other Essays on Feminist Philosophy and Social Theory.* Bloomington, IN: Indiana University Press, 1990.

NANCY TUANA

FICHTE, INFLUENCE OF

J.G. Fichte (1762–1814) is a highly original and very influential German idealist philosopher. He belongs chronologically and conceptually to the movement known as German idealism, which is routinely held to include as well Kant, Schelling and Hegel. He was younger than Kant, but older than Schelling and Hegel.

Fichte's influence, as befits a philosopher of the first rank, is wide and enduring. Fichte influenced Kant negatively. The author of the critical philosophy rejected Fichte's Kantian claim to understand the critical philosophy better than its author in famously charging the younger man with mistakenly trying to deduce objects from concepts. Fichte, who welcomed Kant's influence on his own position, thought Kant's theory was correct but needed to be restated. Though he describes his position as only the correct form of Kant's, Fichte's position is original and cannot be reduced to a variant of the critical philosophy.

In different ways, Fichte influenced all the main and minor figures in this movement. After the publication of the *Critique of Pure Reason*, it was widely believed that Kant's position needed to be restated in systematic form. Though many writers claimed to be the only one to understand the critical philosophy correctly, Fichte's claim was widely accepted, including by the young Schelling and the young Hegel.

K.L. Reinhold and Schelling were Fichte's disciples. The effort to restate Kant's critical philosophy was begun by Reinhold in his "Letters on the Kantian Philosophy" (1787). He later recanted in becoming Fichte's disciple. The young Schelling was Fichte's disciple until a disagreement about the philosophy of nature in 1800. Fichte's influence on Hegel is not well known. Hegel's initial philosophical essay, devoted to ascertaining the *Difference* (1801) between the views of Fichte and Schelling, was influenced by both contemporaries. Fichte was important for Hegel's reading of Kant, his conception of the subject as finite human being, and his emphasis on scientific system as necessarily circular.

Not surprisingly since, as recent scholarship emphasizes links between German idealism and German romanticism, Fichte was influential on the rise of German romanticism, a complex philosophical and literary movement. Early German romanticism was in general inspired by, but also critical, of Fichte. German romanticism is described in different ways, for instance as Kantianism or again as absolute idealism, ways which need not detain us here. A number of prominent German romantics, including Hölderlin, Novalis, and Schlegel, reacted against Fichte. It is sometimes argued that Schelling's and Hegel's later criticism of Fichte's subjective idealism stems from Hölderlin. The latter insists on a re-enchantment of nature as beyond mere human powers in the course of rejecting both Fichte and Spinoza while arguing for a median path between them.

Novalis's so-called magical realism was considered to be a poetic form of Fichte's *Wissenschaftslehre.* Novalis' *Fichte-Studien*, his studies of Fichte from autumn 1795 to late summer 1796, represent his effort to synthesize insights drawn from Fichte and Spinoza. Like Fichte and Kant, he subscribes to the Copernican thesis that we know only what we make.

Friedrich Schlegel early on regarded Fichte as having completed Kant's Copernican revolution and provided the foundation for the new German literature. Schlegel later broke with Fichte over the supposed lack of realism and history in the latter's position. He further objected to what he regarded as Ficht's foundationalism as well as Fichte's supposed mysticism in the course of developing his own antifoundationalist epistemology. And his critique of Fichte's idealism led him to reject classicism.

It is not widely known that Fichte was also influential on Marx. The latter is best understood, not as Marxism claims as a non-philosophical materialist and anti-idealist, but rather as a German idealist philosopher. In the *Paris Manuscripts* and in other writings, Marx's concept of the subject as basically active is apparently directly appropriated from Fichte. This same view was later developed by Lukács, the important Marxist philosopher, who favors a Fichtean brand of Marxism.

During his lifetime, Fichte was influential on the formulation of German idealist and German romantic positions. His influence on later philosophy was impeded by his description by Schelling and Hegel as, like Kant, favoring subjective idealism, to which they opposed objective idealism. Later thinkers influenced by Fichte include among American pragmatists Royce and Peirce, and among European thinkers Sartre and Heidegger. Unlike Peirce, who hardly refers to Fichte, Royce knew Fichte well. In *The Spirit of Modern Philosophy*, he devoted Lecture Five to a presentation and critique of Fichte, depicted as the founder of post-Kantian German idealism. In his logical essays, Royce mentions Fichte as someone interested in the concept of truth. In the world and the individual, he came closer to what he thought of as Fichte's voluntarism. In his theory of representation Peirce, who classes Fichte with Hegel among the noologists, mentions Fichte as professing idealistic nominalism. Sartre's view that self-consciousness founds consciousness at the beginning of *Being and Nothingness* is borrowed from Fichte. Heidegger, who taught a course in Fichte, is said to have based his rectoral address on Fichte's *Addresses to the German Nation.*

Further reading

Beiser, Frederick. *German Idealism: The Struggle against Subjectivism, 1781–1801.* Cambridge, MA: Harvard University Press, 2002.

Pinkard, Terry. *German Philosophy 1760–1860: The Legacy of Idealism.* Cambridge: Cambridge University Press, 2002.

Tom Rockmore

FIRSTNESS

In the thought of Charles Sanders Peirce (1839–1914), Firstness is one of the three categories, along with Secondness and Thirdness, that constitute the underpinning of his philosophical system. Firstness is the category of qualitative "suchness," feeling, spontaneity, and immediacy.

Peirce intends his categories to delineate exhaustively all actual and possible modes of being. They are designed to articulate all relationships between and among things, regardless of the ontological status of those things. In making them intrinsically relational, Peirce attempts to overcome the limitations he finds in Aristotle's categories, which rely upon only one relation as their organizing principle (namely, predication), and in Kant's categories, which limit their analysis to the phenomenal realm. His aim is to achieve an indisputably universal explanatory framework with the power to analyze and integrate all dimensions of experience and knowledge, regardless of whether the objects of experience under consideration are mind-independent or mind-dependent, actual or possible, predicable or not.

The categories can be defined several ways. Ontologically considered, Firstness is that whose mode of being does not depend upon any relation to anything other than itself, or "that which is such as it is regardless of anything else" (CP 5.66; EP 2:160). Any instance or example of Firstness is called a "First." A First is a pure possibility, not an actual event or individual existent. For a thing or event to be actual requires a relation of Secondness: it becomes actual by exercising effort against something else (a Second) which resists it and delimits it (CP 1.23).

Peirce also treats his categories phenomenologically, as pertaining to "all that is in any way or in any sense present to the mind, quite regardless of whether it corresponds to any real thing or not" (CP 1.284). As such, a First is a mere quality, or "suchness," of feeling. A feeling in its pure state as a First is an immediate instance of consciousness that involves no reflection, analysis, distinction, or any cognitive process whatsoever. Each feeling is *sui generis*. It is "present and immediate" because it is not a representation of something previous to it; it is "fresh and new" because it cannot be second to a former state; and it is "initiative, original, spontaneous, and free" because it is not second to a determining cause (W 6.170). If we imagine "the first idea in the consciousness of Adam at the moment of his creation, when he found a lively feeling which had not become defined" (W 5.238–9), we come close to understanding the nature of a First. Peirce also suggests imagining one's consciousness as consisting of nothing but a "feeling of red" (CP 1.310) or of a single musical tone extended indefinitely (W 3.262–3). Each case would exemplify immediate consciousness of a First.

Firstness, however, is evanescent. "Stop to think of it, and it has flown!" (W 6.170). In experience, feelings never arise in a pure state because they are always filtered through previous experiences. When a feeling generates a further feeling, or when we become aware of it or act upon it, we are interpreting that feeling. The feeling is thus brought into a relation of Thirdness, in which it functions as a sign (a First) that represents something beyond itself (its object, the Second in the relationship) by generating an interpretation (an interpretant, the Third in the relationship). The qualities that constitute pure Firsts underlie all experience, but we never have direct experiential or cognitive access to them.

This is why Peirce insists that a First as such, independent of relationships of Secondness or Thirdness, can only be a possibility. A "mere *quality*, or suchness, is not in itself an occurrence, as seeing a red object is; it is a mere may-be" (CP 1.304). An actual occurrence of a quality is a relation of Secondness because the quality is delimited by its relations to time, to space, to any subject it may inhere in, and so forth. As an actual occurrence, the quality becomes interpretable and thus integrated into a semiotic relationship of Thirdness.

Every branch of Peirce's philosophical system is grounded in his theory of the categories. Because Secondness presupposes and depends upon Firstness, and Thirdness presupposes and depends upon the first two categories, the principle of Firstness underlies all aspects of his thought. In his metaphysics, for instance, Firstness appears as the principle of chance and spontaneity in the evolution of the universe. According to his theory of inquiry, the spontaneous, instinctive guesses of abductive reasoning are the means by which hypotheses are formed. In his classification of the three normative sciences, esthetics is the science of ideals, or that which is admirable in itself; and these ideals ground both ethics, which studies the application of ideals to self-controlled conduct, and logic or semiotic, the science of the general laws of self-controlled thought, or of sign interpretation (EP 2.260). Hence, for Peirce, the examination of qualitative possibilities through the category of Firstness is a necessary condition for philosophical inquiry.

Further reading

Hausman, Carl R. *Charles S. Peirce's Evolutionary Philosophy*. Cambridge: Cambridge University Press, 1993.

Peirce, Charles Sanders. *Collected Papers of Charles Sanders Peirce*, 8 volumes, ed. Charles Hartshorne, Paul Weiss, and Arthur Burks. Cambridge, MA: Harvard University Press, 1931–58. References cite volume and paragraph numbers (e.g. CP 5.66).

—— *The Essential Peirce: Selected Philosophical Writings*, 2 volumes, ed. the Peirce Edition Project. Bloomington, IN: Indiana University Press, 1992/1998. Cited as EP.

—— *The Chronological Writings of Charles S. Peirce*, 6 vols. to date, ed. the Peirce Edition Project. Bloomington, IN: Indiana University Press, 1982–. Cited as W.

Sheriff, John K. *Charles Peirce's Guess at the Riddle: Grounds for Human Significance*. Bloomington, IN: Indiana University Press, 1994.

Felicia E. Kruse

FISCH, MAX

Scholars in American philosophy tend to associate Max Fisch wholly with his Peirce studies. This identification, however understandable in recent years, misses the profound breadth of his contributions to scholarship. He has written definitive pieces in classical literature, law, philosophy, the history of science and medicine, education, intellectual history, philosophy of history, and of course the history of philosophy with special emphasis on Vico, Croce, and the "Golden Age" figures in American philosophy, especially Peirce.

A pervasive theme throughout Fisch's published work is that of organic units – institutions and communities that are irreducible to individual parts. He argued for the priority of social philosophy over ethics in Aristotle's *Sumuum Bonum*, emphasized the institutional cooperative character of science, stressed the international nature of science as manifested in the scientific academies around the world, including the one at Naples, the history of which he traced in fascinating detail. This emphasis on community was more than sustained in his later thoroughly researched study of the philosophy of Charles Peirce, wherein Peirce underlined what Fisch had always believed: "The very origin of the conception of reality shows that this conception essentially involves the notion of a COMMUNITY, without definite limits, and capable of an indefinite increase of knowledge." "If you really want to learn the truth, you will, by however devious a path, be led into the way of truth at last." As is well known, Thomas Kuhn has thrown doubt on all developmental views of science including Peirce's by claiming that the concepts of successive theories are incommensurable and hence must be construed as substituting a better calculator for a previous one but not approximating any final truth. Max Fisch was clearly aware that Kuhn stood Peirce's view on its head and turned the evolution of theories into the revolution of theories, though Fisch did not find any resource in Peirce's philosophy to meet the charge of incommensurability. He nevertheless excused Peirce on the grounds that he could scarcely be blamed for not answering a criticism that had not yet been made.

Through the years Fisch diligently studied the various influences on Peirce and what aspect of his philosophy is the most appropriate for understanding the whole of his philosophy. He emphasized the importance of the Greek philosophers in Peirce's later metaphysics, the thorough mathematical and scientific career of Peirce for understanding his pragmatism and philosophy of science, *et al.*, concluding with the claim that the best way to understand the whole of Peirce's philosophy is through his theory of signs or the science of semiotics. Would there be a semiotic resurgence without Peirceans? An observer can only wonder.

According to Fisch, the range of Peirce's present relevance is well-nigh universal. His work has been essential in reviving the current interest in semiotics or the science of signs, and linguists such as Noam Chomsky and Michael Shapiro have also shown interest in Peirce's work, though not strictly in its semiotic dimension. He has been influential in sociology and social psychology because his views reinforce the popular concept of symbolic interactionism as formulated by George Herbert Mead. He has influenced psychiatrists such as Harry Stack Sullivan, as well as research in physiological and psychological problems of perception (though Fisch doesn't tell us how). In philosophy of science he influenced Reichenbach's formulation of a pragmatic vindication of induction and Popper's view of scientific progress through hypothesis elimination. However, I have claimed that Peirce's self-corrective view is significantly different from Reichenbach's since the latter's vindication purported only to show that the repeated use of the straight rule will lead to success if success is possible. Peirce had no doubt about such success. While Peirce did stress hypothesis elimination and the economy of research, his view that the human mind is so constructed to form successful hypotheses scarcely squares with Popper's overall view. According to Fisch, Peirce influenced N.R. Hanson in developing his concepts in the logic of discovery, though numerous philosophers of science still reject the validity of any logic of discovery. In logic, Fisch claimed that Peirce managed to revive interest in Schroder's line of logic after it had been eclipsed by the Russell–Whitehead line. Is it possible that a partial eclipse still exists? Fisch effectively points out the richness of Peirce's philosophy and its relevance in one way or another to most fields and areas of philosophy.

Fisch was the chief editor of the Peirce Project, which was to include a two-volume biography of Peirce by Fisch and a chronological edition of Peirce's published and unpublished work. Fisch believed strongly that only such an edition would show the development and growth of Peirce's thought. There were to be twenty volumes of Peirce's work. Unfortunately Peirce dated less than a fourth of the writings he left unpublished, so the task of making a chronological edition was extraordinarily difficult, and only a handful of volumes have appeared though the project has been in operation twenty years.

Any subsequent volumes, however, will bear Fisch's imprint since the Project headquarters is full of his research notes, including details of editing and details of Peirce's life. Fisch never produced the two-volume biography, though his articles, mainly on Peirce, were published as a book – *Peirce, Semiotic, and Pragmatism* – in 1986. The biography was never finished because of Fisch's exceedingly high standards of research. His thoroughness of archival research and his striving after accuracy in every detail are legendary in our profession, and we may be grateful that he has produced a great many pearls for the necklace he was unable to complete.

Further reading

Fisch, Max H. "Alexander and the Stoics," *American Journal of Philology* 58 (1937): 59–82.

—— (ed.) *Classic American Philosophers.* New York: Appleton-Century-Crofts, 1966, especially Fisch's General Introduction.

—— "Evolution in American Philosophy," *Philosophical Revue* 56 (1947): 357–73.
—— "The Poliscraft" in J.P. Anton and C. Walton (eds) *Philosophy and the Civilizing Arts* (Festschrift for Herbert W. Schneider). Athens, OH: Ohio University Press, 1974, pp. 24–48.
—— "The 'Proof' of Pragmatism" in L.W. Sumner, J.G. Slater, and F. Wilson (eds) *Pragmatism and Purpose* (Festschrift for Thomas A. Goudge). Toronto: University of Toronto Press, 1981, pp. 28–40, 295–97.
—— Introductions to first three volumes of *Writings of Charles S. Peirce: Chronological Edition*. Bloomington, IN: Indiana University Press, 1982.
—— "Vico and Pragmatism" in G. Tagliacozzo and H.V. White (eds) *Giambattista Vico: An International Symposium*. Baltimore, MD: Johns Hopkins Press, 1969, pp. 401–24.
Madden, E.H. "Max H. Fisch: Rigorous Humanist," *Transactions of the C.S. Peirce Society* XXII (1986): 375–96.
Roberts, D.D. "The Well-Tempered Critic of Institutions," *Transactions of the C.S. Peirce Society* XXII (1986): 397–415.

EDWARD H. MADDEN

FIXATION OF BELIEF

In the philosophy of Charles Sanders Peirce (1839–1914), the process by which opinion on any given subject is settled through inquiry motivated by the psychological discomfort caused by doubt and uncertainty, originally set out in the 1877 article "The Fixation of Belief". The strategy of that article is to adopt a naturalistic point of departure, suspend the assumption of any intrinsic connection between inquiry and truth, and stipulate that since, to the believer, his/her own belief is indistinguishable from true belief, therefore *belief* is the sole object of inquiry (CP 5.375). The ensuing argument seeks to show how the search for belief, in the sense of *settled* opinion, naturally (if not inevitably) leads to the adoption of the scientific method as the one method that offers the best chance of success.

Three other methods are reviewed and dismissed as unfit to succeed in the long run. The method of *tenacity* is the simplest one: it consists in stubbornly clinging to whatever beliefs one already happens to have. Peirce stresses that it cannot be objected that this method is irrational, as we may not simply assume that a rational method will necessarily work better than an irrational one. What can be objected is that the method will be *ineffective*: unless I make myself a hermit I cannot help noticing that other people have different opinions from mine, and my recognition that their beliefs are as good and well-founded as mine is bound to shake my confidence in my own beliefs (CP 5.378).

One solution is to ensure uniformity of belief throughout the community by the method of *authority*: by letting the state decide what everyone is to believe and enforce those beliefs through education, propaganda, censorship, intimidation, and, if need be, massacres. This method, Peirce stresses, has in many places been remarkably successful over long periods of time (CP 5.379–80). Also, as with tenacity, Peirce does not accept the irrationality of the method as a valid objection. In 1871, Peirce had written:

> What [the inquirer] wants . . . is to see questions put to rest. And if a general belief, which is perfectly stable and immovable, can in any way be produced, though it be by the fagot and the rack, to talk of any error in such belief is utterly absurd.
>
> (CP 2.471)

But the if-clause is the operative clause here: in real life the fagot and the rack will ultimately prove inadequate. It is part of Peirce's argument that no community can have *all* beliefs settled by an authority: on most questions that arise people must figure out their own answers and they must devise their own methods for so doing; it is only a matter of time before it occurs to the more enlightened members of the community to direct their workaday epistemic methods towards questions whose answers have been legislated upon by the authorities. The two methods will in a number of cases yield different conclusions, and the resulting conflict will generate doubt (CP 5.381). George Orwell's novel *Nineteen Eighty-Four* has later emerged as an iconic reflection of this argument (Skagestad 1986).

The failure of the method of authority to ensure lasting consensus stems, then, as in the case of tenacity, from the failure of the method to specify the *content* of our belief; the same method can, with equal plausibility, be put in the service of contradictory beliefs. This deficiency may be remedied by the *a priori* method, the method of believing that which is agreeable to reason. This method, which Peirce credits with the construction of the major metaphysical systems, is intellectually far superior to the other two. It does, however, suffer from the defect that the agreeableness or disagreeableness of a belief to reason has no necessary connection with whatever that belief is about:

> Now, there are some people, among whom I must suppose that my reader is to be found, who, when they see that any belief of theirs is determined by any circumstance extraneous to the facts, will from that moment not merely admit in words that that belief is doubtful, but will experience a real doubt of it, so that it ceases in some degree at least to be a belief.
>
> (CP 5.383)

The solution is to turn to the method of science, in Peirce's words a method "by which our beliefs may be determined by nothing human, but by some external permanency – by something upon which our thinking has no effect" (CP 5.384). So, it is not sufficient to have a method that determines the content of our belief; that content must in turn be determined by the *object* of belief. The method of science, of course, acknowledges truth as the aim of inquiry and subjects the inquirer to the very canons of rationality which Peirce refused to presuppose at the outset of the discussion. These are now derived as the *results* of the discussion. Let us finally retrace the steps of the derivation.

The doubt which gives rise to inquiry exists in the first place, according to Peirce, because of a prior recognition that two contradictory beliefs cannot both be accepted: "The feeling which gives rise to any method of fixing belief is a dissatisfaction at two repugnant propositions. But here already is a vague concession that there is some *one* thing which a proposition should represent" (CP 5.384). Belief, in Peirce's view, is inherently *intentional*; it is inherently belief *about* something, and what "The Fixation of Belief" seeks to show is how stability of belief depends on reaching beliefs by a method which allows belief to be constrained, not by experience in general, but by *that something* which the belief is about. Peirce's discussion of the pre-rational methods of settling opinion thus does not tacitly presuppose any standards of rationality not already inherent in the concept of belief itself. For instance, Peirce no doubt did not believe that the method of the fagot and the rack could produce truth, but the reason why it cannot is not that this method clashes with our concept of rationality. On the other hand, it is not simply a contingent fact that it will not succeed: the method is doomed to be unsuccessful because it does not take the intentionality of belief sufficiently into account, and it is the recognition of this foreordained failure that prompts a demand for standards of *rational* belief. On this reading Peirce remains a thoroughgoing naturalist: no transcendental concept of truth or reality is presupposed here; the concept of an object of belief – as well as any normativity derived from this concept – is immanent in the belief-attitude.

Further reading

Misak, C.J. *Truth and the End of Inquiry: A Peircean Account of Truth.* Oxford: Clarendon Press, 1991.

Peirce, Charles. *The Collected Papers of Charles Sanders Peirce* (CP), ed. C. Hartshorne and P. Weiss (Vols. 1–6) and A. Burks (Vols. 7–8). Cambridge, MA: Harvard University Press, 1931–58.

Skagestad, P. *The Road of Inquiry: Charles Peirce's Pragmatic Realism.* New York: Columbia University Press, 1981.

—— "Pragmatism and the Closed Society: A Juxtaposition of Charles Peirce and George Orwell," *Philosophy and Social Criticism* 11, 4 (1986): 307–29.

—— "Review of C.J. Misak, *Truth and the End of Inquiry*," *Transactions of the Charles S. Peirce Society*, 28, 2 (1992): 311–21.

PETER SKAGESTAD

FLOWER, ELIZABETH

Elizabeth Flower (1915–95) was a member of the Philosophy Department at the University of Pennsylvania where she had received her doctorate in 1939. Her dissertation was in the field of ethics. She became full professor in 1974 and retired in 1985. She also lectured at Columbia University and Hamilton College and at universities in Mexico, Chile, Colombia, Guatemala, and Peru.

Flower's first graduate seminar in ethics at Pennsylvania was audited by Martin Luther King, Jr. She continued to be interested in ethics and the history of ethics. She was also influenced by her study of American Pragmatism, especially the writings of John Dewey. In addition to Dewey, she wrote about William James, C.I. Lewis, and other American philosophers and about legal and social philosophy as well as the philosophy of education, all subjects with which Dewey was concerned. The publication for which she is probably best known is *A History of Philosophy in America*, a two-volume work, published in 1977, which she co-authored with Murray G. Murphey who was Professor of American Civilization at the University of Pennsylvania.

In 1988 Murphey and Ivar Berg published *Values and Value Theory in Twentieth-Century America: Essays in Honor of Elizabeth Flower.* In 1995 at the 22nd annual meeting of the Society for the Advancement of American Philosophy, Flower and her husband Abraham Edel, with whom she collaborated on several publications, were each presented with the Herbert W. Schneider Award for Distinguished Contributions to the Understanding and Development of American Philosophy.

Further reading

Flower, Elizabeth. "Norms and Induction" in Roland Houde and Joseph P. Mullaly (eds) *Philosophy of Knowledge.* Philadelphia, PA: Lippincott, 1960.

—— "Mill and some Present Concerns about Ethical Judgments" in Carl J. Friedrich (ed.) *Liberty (Nomos IV)*. New York: Atherton Press, 1962.

—— "Rights, Strategies, and Strategic Rights" in Irvin Pollock (ed.) *Human Rights (Amintaphil I)*. Buffalo, NY: Jay Stewart Publications, 1971.

—— "A Moral Agenda for Ethical Theory" in Irving Louis Horowitz and H. S. Thayer (eds) *Value, Science and Democracy: The Philosophy of Abraham Edel*. New Brunswick, NJ: Transaction Books, 1987.

Flower, Elizabeth and Murphey, Murray G. *A History of Philosophy in America*. New York: G.P. Putnam's Sons, 1977; New York, Hackett, 1979.

BETH J. SINGER

FOUNDATIONALISM

Foundationalism is a well-known, very influential, but infrequently studied epistemological strategy, with roots in ancient Greek philosophy, and which is still widely popular. Foundationalism and realism are obviously related. Foundationalism is an epistemological strategy for knowledge of the mind-independent real, in short the world as it is, which is often known as metaphysical realism. At least since Plato, metaphysical realism continues to serve as the normative standard of what it means to know. Historically, epistemological foundationalism is a philosophical alternative both to skepticism, or the claim that we know only that we cannot know, and intuitionism, or the view that knowledge consists in a direct grasp of what is as it is.

It is at least interesting to note that epistemological foundationalism is not accorded attention in cognitive disciplines other than philosophy. For instance, it plays no visible role in modern science, where everything happens as if foundationalism were an irrelevant consideration. Neither Galileo, nor Newton, nor Einstein, nor indeed any reputable scientist has ever tried, or even voiced the concern, to put science on a foundationalist epistemological basis. Yet philosophers deeply acquainted with modern science, such as Descartes, Kant and Carnap, have routinely made this effort, as if science without an epistemological foundation were somehow incomplete.

Foundationalism is widely identified with Descartes but by no means limited to his position or to those influenced by him. "Foundationalism" is widely but imprecisely employed to refer to a large number of related doctrines, including reasoning on the basis of one or more indefeasible principles, a claim for certainty, an insistence on the subject (or subjectivity) as an indispensable clue to objectivity (or claims for objective cognition), or even the supposed capacity to specify the conditions of the possibility of knowledge.

"Foundationalism" is often conflated with "foundation." The latter is a common English word with multiple meanings, including "the act of founding," "the basis upon which something is founded," "funds given for the permanent support of an institution or cause," "an underlying natural or prepared base or support," and "a body or ground upon which something is built up or overlaid." One speaks by analogy of the foundations of knowledge. Aristotle is often said to be interested in the foundations of knowledge, understood as first philosophy, by virtue of his concern to enumerate the primary factors of being.

"Foundationalism" is typically understood on a Cartesian model as referring to some or more of the following: concern with certain knowledge, apodicticity, cognition beyond doubt of any kind, as defeating even the most radical form of skepticism, and so on. Descartes is often mistakenly regarded as the most important or even the first foundationalist; mistakenly so, since this strategy is already present in ancient philosophy. In his wake, foundationalism takes many forms, typically including an initial principle (or principles) known (beyond doubt) to be true that provide(s) the requisite foundation from which the remainder of the theory can be rigorously deduced. Beyond this minimal description, there seems to be little agreement about what "foundationalism" means or even who counts as a foundationalist. Thus Quine is seen by different observers to be a critic of foundationalism, a coherentist but not a foundationalist, and a foundationalist.

Foundationalism comes in many forms or flavors. All known types of foundationalism include a foundation, or basis, on which to construct a theory of knowledge: what Descartes, in a famous reference to Archimedes, describes as a fixed and immoveable point. Foundationalist theories of knowledge frequently appeal to the notion of a building or other structure that rests directly on its foundations or, in the case of a philosophical theory, on indefeasible philosophical underpinnings. For both a building and a theory of knowledge, if the underpinnings are secure then nothing can shake the edifice erected on them.

Modern foundationalists typically contend that all knowledge claims rest on, hence can only be justified by, a strategy that guarantees certainty. Understood in this manner, we can distinguish three ideal-typical forms of foundationalism relevant to ontology, perception, and principles. Ontological foundationalism typically appeals to a direct, intuitive grasp of the real, as in the Platonic theory of ideas in which thought surpasses appearance to grasp reality. Husserlian phenomenology, which is essentialist, describes a series of efforts to recover a similar claim for the direct grasp of phenomenal essences.

A second form of foundationalism, linked to perception in general, appeals to indefeasible perceptual statements, which, since they cannot be false, are necessarily true. Perceptual foundationalism, which originates in ancient stoicism, is widely exemplified in modern philosophy: in Descartes' rationalist emphasis on clear and distinct perceptions, in the persistent empiricist concern with perceptions resistant to problems of illusion and delusion in F. Bacon and Locke, and in analytic foundationalism running from Moore's commonsensism, the basis of his refutation of idealism, to Putnam's recent turn to what he calls natural realism.

A third type of foundationalism is based on principles regarded as necessary and as necessarily true. Examples include the Aristotelian claim for the law of noncontradiction as a necessary basis of all discussion, the Cartesian view of the cogito as indubitable, or even, in some interpretations, the Hegelian idea of Being.

Forms of foundationalism are widely disseminated throughout the history of Western philosophy, especially the modern tradition. Foundationalism is arguably the main modern strategy for knowledge. It is sometimes mistakenly thought that interest in foundationalism has waned, or at least recently waned, and that it is no longer a live option. On the contrary, foundationalism, which was widely popular throughout the modern period, remains popular, although not always under that name, even today. Moore and Russell, the founders of Anglo-American analytic philosophy, defend forms of foundationalism. Distantly following Thomas Reid, Moore's commonsensism consists of the conviction that there is direct intuition of empirical reality. This is the basis of his refutation of the supposed idealist denial of the existence of the external world. Russell's distinction between knowledge by description and knowledge by acquaintance presupposes direct acquaintance with what is as it is.

A number of thinkers – including Thomas Nagel, Robert Brandom, Michael Devitt, John McDowell and Robert Nozick – make claims that could only be justified through some kind of foundationalism. Recent foundationalists of various stripes, who increasingly diverge from the classical model, include the early Ludwig Wittgenstein, the early Rudolf Carnap, Roderick Chisholm, Karl-Otto Apel, Jürgen Habermas sometimes, Susan Haack and Richard Swinburne. In the *Tractatus* (1961), Wittgenstein features a picture theory of meaning. Following his reading of Wittgenstein's *Tractatus*, Carnap was initially committed to matching up protocol propositions to the empirical world. Chisholm proposes a foundationalist theory based on self-justifying, unfalsifiable beliefs. Apel features a transcendental ethics with Kantian (and Peircean) overtones. Habermas transformed Apel's approach into a consensus theory of truth with foundational intent, which he later abandoned. Haack has worked out a theory of foundherentism combining foundationalism and coherentism. Swinburne favors doxastic foundationalism for epistemic justification.

Descartes, who is routinely understood as the initiator and main example of foundationalism, combines foundational and antifoundational impulses in his complex position. His antifoundationalism, which is rarely mentioned, is evident in the sixth part of the *Discourse*, where in examining the idea of a logical circle, he claims that, with respect to experience, effects are explained by causes and causes by effects.

The antifoundationalist impulse in his writings is far outweighed by his better-known, more developed, very influential foundationalist impulse. Cartesian foundationalism requires the rigorous deduction of a complete theory, adequate to explain anything and everything, from an initial principle known to be true. Descartes holds that the truth of the initial principle is not directly grasped (Plato), nor assumed without proof (Aristotle), but, since it cannot be denied, it is necessarily true. According to Descartes, who silently presupposes the Aristotelian law of the excluded middle, since the cogito cannot be doubted without being affirmed, hence cannot be false, it must, therefore, be true. As an indubitable truth, the cogito functions within the Cartesian theory as a first principle, on whose basis, through rigorously deductive reasoning, a theory can be constructed that is necessarily true.

There is an obvious analogy between this argument and the indirect form of mathematical proof that is widely used in geometry. In the proof of the cogito in the *Discourse on Method*, Descartes doubts all things that could possibly be false with the aim of determining whether anything is absolutely certain before concluding that he cannot doubt his own existence. In the *Meditations*, he develops a similar train of reasoning to thwart a fictitious evil genius bent on deceiving him. He maintains that if he is deceived he must also exist before concluding that he exists each time he claims to do so.

Kant's epistemological foundationalism, which is not often mentioned and sometimes denied, rests on the twelve concepts of the understanding, or categories, he obscurely claims to deduce. Kant's approach to foundationalism is undermined by a triple unclarity concerning his understanding of principles, categories, and their deduction. In Aristotle, a principle is a beginning or starting point that, by the time of Wolff, becomes a fundamental, or highest, principle. In Kant, the ambiguous term "principle" refers to concepts of the understanding through which experience and knowledge of objects becomes possible. In the critical philosophy, the conditions of the possibility of objects of experience and knowledge are given in objectively valid, synthetic a priori judgments.

Though often criticized, foundationalism has never been entirely abandoned. Efforts to refute it in whole or in part or to refute different forms of the overall foundationalist strategy are routinely met by opposing efforts to formulate a viable form of the doctrine. Foundationalism is arguably as widespread as an epistemological strategy to know the mind-independent real as it has been in recent times, even in modern times, and perhaps is as widespread as it has ever been. Recent epistemological foundationalists include (in no particular order) the early Rudolf Carnap (and some other members of the Vienna Circle), Edmund Husserl, Roderick Chisholm, Karl-Otto Apel (and Jürgen Habermas), Susan Haack, Lawrence BonJour, Richard Swinburne, Robert Nozick, Thomas Nagel, Michael Dummett and many others.

Further reading

BonJour, Laurence. *The Structure of Empirical Knowledge*, Cambridge, MA: Harvard University Press, 1985.

Neurath, Otto. "Protocol Sentences" in A.J. Ayer (ed.) *Logical Positivism*. New York: Free Press, 1959, pp. 199–208.

Rockmore, Tom. *On Foundationalism: A Strategy for Metaphysical Realism*. Lanham, MD: Rowman and Littlefield, 2004.

TOM ROCKMORE

FOUNDHERENTISM

As the name indicates, foundherentism combines the strong points of the rival theories foundationalism and coherentism, while avoiding their weaknesses. Both the name and the theory originate with Susan Haack, who develops it in her 1993 *Evidence and Inquiry* while comparing it favorably with its competitors. According to foundationalism, an empirical belief is justified if and only if it is a basic belief – i.e. a belief that is wholly justified by direct experience – or it is a derived belief that is supported by basic beliefs. On this view, justification is a one-directional affair; no combination of derived beliefs can ever increase or decrease the justification of a basic belief. Coherentism denies that there are indubitable truths or basic beliefs that can act as a foundation and holds instead that an empirical belief is justified if and only if it is part of a coherent belief set. Foundationalists and coherentists have tried to save their positions by weakening them. The problem with these weaker versions, however, is the ad hoc character of the criteria they added. Because such weaker forms of foundationalism and coherentism lack a worked-out rationale for why the added criteria contribute to the justification of beliefs, they, far from saving their position, actually undermine their original rationale for justifying beliefs.

Foundherentism, however, is not a weakened version of foundationalism or coherentism, but is a genuine third alternative. Its fundamental tenets are captured in the following two theses (Haack 1993: 19):

(FH1) A subject's experience is relevant to the justification of his empirical beliefs, but there need be no privileged class of empirical beliefs justified exclusively by the support of experience, independently of the support of other beliefs.

(FH2) Justification is not exclusively one-directional, but involves pervasive relations of mutual support.

According to foundherentism, justification is a gradual affair that involves not only the belief content (C-belief), but also the reasons for holding the belief, that is, what causes the believe state (S-belief). For instance, one would be more justified in believing that a certain accused is innocent upon hearing well-corroborated evidence showing that he has a watertight alibi, than one would be simply on the ground that he looks innocent. Hence, whereas foundationalism and coherentism concentrate solely on belief content, foundherentism takes into account also belief states, thus allowing that empirical justification is in part logical and in part causal. Foundherentism is a double-aspect theory.

Rejecting the traditional analogy of a mathematical proof, Haack uses a crossword puzzle to show the structure of evidential support. Whereas a mathematical proof is one-directional, a crossword puzzle shows how a pervasive mutual support of beliefs is possible in a way that avoids vicious circularity. The crossword analogy also shows the interplay of foundherentism's two theses: FH1 is represented by the entry's relation to its clue; FH2 is represented by its relation to other entries, some of which are already filled in while others are not. The crossword analogy gives us three criteria for judging the quality of evidence: supportiveness (by both its clue and the intersecting entries), comprehensiveness (how much of the puzzle is completed), and independent security (because how the entry connects to its clue is independent of any of its intersecting entries).

Haack presents foundherentism as an illuminating account of our actual epistemic activities. To the question whether foundherentism is also truth indicative, she argues that *if* truth indication is possible for us, the foundherentist criteria are truth-indicative.

Further reading

De Waal, Cornelis (ed.) *Susan Haack: A Lady of Distinctions. The Philosopher Replies to Critics.* Amherst, NY: Prometheus Books, 2006.

Haack, Susan. *Evidence and Inquiry.* Oxford: Blackwell, 1993.

—— *Manifesto of a Passionate Moderate.* Chicago, IL: University of Chicago Press, 1998.

—— *Defending Science: Within Reason.* Amherst, NY: Prometheus Books, 2003.

Ryan, James. "The Foundherentist View of Justification by Experience," *Principia: Revista Internacional de Epistemologia* 4, 1 (2000): 79–88.

Cornelis de Waal

FRANKEL, CHARLES

A philosopher and Columbia University instructor beginning in 1939, Charles Frankel (13 December 1917 – 10 May 1979) held the Old Dominion professorship in philosophy and public affairs from 1970 until his death. Born in New York City, a 1937 graduate of Columbia, from which he also received his PhD in 1946, he died in Bedford Hills, NY. His schooling was interrupted by service as a lieutenant in the Navy during 1942–6.

Frankel had the distinction of serving as Assistant Secretary of State for education and culture from 1965 to 1967. While often considered a pragmatist in his scholarly writings, Frankel additionally played many public and professional roles of distinction: he was variously chair of the Committee on Professional Ethics of the American Association of University Professors, the US delegation to the 1966 UNESCO General Conference, and the board of trustees of the National Humanities Center in 1976–7. Beginning in 1977, he became president of the Center. In 1959, Frankel hosted a CBS-TV series, *The World of Ideas.*

Frankel's disaffection with the Johnson administration's Viet Nam policies led to his resignation from government service in 1967. Coming quickly thereafter, a 1969 book about his State Department tenure, *High on Foggy Bottom: An Outsider's Inside View of the Government*, was widely commented on during the late Viet Nam period. Some commentators felt Frankel's book and resignation contributed to the then accelerating disenchantment by Democratic Party intellectuals with their leaders.

His extensive scholarly writings explored in part the history of what has become known as "classical American thought," as well as political philosophy, philosophy of history, religion, and public and personal morality. In ways reminiscent of John Dewey, Frankel over a long life of writing focused on practical philosophy and education for civil, democratic life. When exploring the modern tradition of American philosophy, besides James, Dewey, Peirce, Santayana, and Royce, Frankel also complimented lesser figures whom he considered insightful and unfairly underappreciated: Chauncey Wright, Ralph Barton Perry, Clarence Irving Lewis, and Morris Raphael Cohen. Frankel had great strengths as a commentator on the state and role of academic philosophy in the late nineteenth and early twentieth centuries.

Further reading

Frankel, Charles. *The Case for Modern Man.* New York: Harper, 1956; second edition, with new preface. Boston, MA: Beacon Press, 1959.

—— *High on Foggy Bottom: An Outsider's Inside View of the Government.* New York: Harper, 1969.

—— *The Pleasures of Philosophy.* Chicago, IL: Norton, 1972.

Lachs, John and Hester, D. Micah (eds) *A William Ernest Hocking Reader: With Commentary.* Nashville, TN: Vanderbilt University Press, 2004.

Menand, Louis. *The Metaphysical Club.* New York: Farrar, Strauss and Giroux, 2001.

John A. Loughney

FRANKLIN, BENJAMIN

Benjamin Franklin (1706–90) was an American author and printer, scientist and inventor, patriot and public servant. His place within the philosophical tradition has been uncertain. Like many other eighteenth-century figures of philosophical interest, he was the author of letters and essays rather than interconnected systematic treatises. (His youthful *Dissertation on Liberty and Necessity, Pleasure and Pain* (1725) was brief and later repudiated as an *erratum*.) Moreover, in his time, the meaning of the term "philosophy" was not as narrowly circumscribed as it is at present. If we limit ourselves to the contemporary academic meaning of the term, Franklin would not qualify for consideration. If we consider his own situation, however, where philosophy's inclusion of the moral and the natural sciences fostered the broad application of reason to advance human well-being, Franklin offered a broad philosophical vision. We can explore this vision through his understanding of science, religion, ethics, and politics.

Franklin's scientific work was guided by a desire to use rationality to advance the common good. He was the inventor of such devices as bifocals and the lightning rod. He was also a broad experimentalist, with interests, for example, in medicine, the physics of heat, geology, climate, and navigation. Franklin's work in electricity, detailed in his *Experiments and Observations on Electricity* (1751, fifth edition 1774) established electricity as a central field of physics and led to him being made a Fellow of the Royal Society in 1756. Throughout his scientific work, Franklin suggested that we should forego theorizing as much as possible and study nature. Mistakes are uncovered by the sharing of results; and science advances by admitting the possibility of error and continuing experimentation "till we are instructed by Experience" (*Papers*: 18.180).

His adult religious thought demonstrated little of his childhood in Puritan Boston. He was a Deist, a follower of that loose perspective that offered a caring but distant God who is to be known indirectly through the workings of creation and who expects us to devote our rational skills to improving earthly existence. Franklin's other Deist tenets included a belief in human immortality and the acceptance of death as release into another realm, and a general disdain for the sectarianism of traditional religions. Doctrinal disputes and worship should be replaced with service to our fellow humans. As he writes, one of the religious beliefs that he never doubted was "that the most acceptable Service of God was the doing Good to Man" (*Autobiography*: 146). Franklin also believed that religion played a vital role in the social training of youth to help them develop into more community-oriented adults.

Franklin's ideas on morality go well beyond the aphorisms of his famous *Poor Richard's Almanack* (1733–58). The heart of Franklin's ethics was his "bold and arduous Project of arriving at moral Perfection" by evaluating his daily performance with regard to thirteen central virtues including temperance, industry and justice, and recording his performance in a little book that was erasable so that he might reuse it in future evaluations (*Autobiography*: 148–57). Another central element in his moral thinking was the deliberate and ongoing challenge to custom. His general desire to see beyond the inherited and the usual to discover what might be better appears here as a call to increase moral imagination. The final component of his moral thought was the desire to foster public service:

> when I am employed in serving others, I do not look upon my self as conferring Favours, but as paying Debts . . . I have received much Kindness from Men, to whom I shall never have any Opportunity of making the least direct Return . . . These Kindnesses from Men, I can therefore only return to their Fellow-Men.
>
> (*Papers*: 4.504–5)

Thus, for Franklin, the purpose of attaining economic security was the possibility of undertaking a higher level of service, as he himself demonstrated in his efforts to foster social institutions like libraries, academies, fire departments, and insurance companies in Philadelphia in his nearly quarter-century of service.

Franklin's political thinking contains a number of assumptions about the common good and its attainment. One is that humans have a social nature and can flourish only in society. A second assumption is the democratic and common-sense one that "Happiness consists more in small Conveniences or Pleasures that occur every day, than in great Pieces of good Fortune that happen but seldom to a Man in the Course of his Life" (*Papers*: 15.60–1). A third is that abstract and general thinking in political affairs is likely to be of less value than adaptive experimentalism. A fourth assumption is that our shared life leads to problems that can be ameliorated only by cooperatively constructed institutions that advance such group interests as education and information, health and security. A fifth assumption is that individuals, living in frontier America and connected with the daily realities of making their own living, would demonstrate priorities proper to a simple life and avoid the temptation to pursue material luxuries. Working within these assumptions, Franklin believed that it would be possible to develop a self-directing democracy.

While he was a powerful democratic thinker, especially with regard to the freedom of the common person, Franklin's actions and ideas with regard to equality were mixed in the way that most of the Founders' actions and ideas were. He was for the most part unable to see beyond his society's fundamental commitment to advancing its model of progress and could therefore make no compromise with what he saw as the seductiveness of the Native Americans' primitive ways. With regard to the related issue of the enslavement of Africans, Franklin repeated the standard prejudices; but, on the question of slavery itself, Franklin moved during the course of his life from accomplice with the institution to strong opponent.

Franklin's philosophical vision presents a broadly pragmatic understanding of the meaning and value of life. As he wrote in one of his many relevant formulations: "Opinions should be judg'd of by their Influences and Effects" (*Papers*: 2.203). His broad sense of pragmatism envisioned advancing the common good through attempts to improve science, religion, morality and politics. Whether contemporary philosophers can afford to reject such a broad philosophical vision is an important issue. Franklin himself poses the question this way: "What signifies Philosophy that does not apply to some Use?" (*Papers*: 9.251).

Further reading

Campbell, James. *Recovering Benjamin Franklin: An Exploration of a Life of Science and Service.* Chicago, IL: Open Court, 1999.

Cohen, I. Bernard. *Benjamin Franklin's Science.* Cambridge, MA: Harvard University Press, 1990.

Franklin, Benjamin. *The Autobiography of Benjamin Franklin*, ed. Leonard W. Labaree, Helen C. Boatfield, and Ralph L. Ketcham, second edition. New Haven, CT: Yale University Press, 2003.

—— *The Papers of Benjamin Franklin*, thirty-seven volumes so far (through August 1782), ed. Leonard W. Labaree and others. New Haven, CT: Yale University Press, 1959.

—— *The Writings of Benjamin Franklin*, ten volumes, ed. Albert Henry Smyth. New York: Macmillan, 1907.

Morgan, Edmund S. *Benjamin Franklin.* New Haven, CT: Yale University Press, 2002.

Van Doren, Carl. *Benjamin Franklin.* New York: Viking, 1938.

Walters, Kerry S. *Benjamin Franklin and his Gods.* Urbana, IL: University of Illinois Press, 1999.

JAMES CAMPBELL

FREEDOM

Freedom is a state of one's independence from factors that could have an impact on one's choice; it is the lack of constraints, whether physical, psychological, moral, legal, or cultural. Freedom can be also understood as the possibility of achieving reasonable goals, as the basis for self-determination. By some it is treated as something to which the human being is entitled by nature (Thomas Hobbes, Jean-Jacques Rousseau, Robert Nozick) and by others as a product of cultural, legal and institutional evolution (Charles Louis de Montesquieu, Edmund Burke, Alexis de Tocqueville, Fridrich A. von Hayek). Yet in spite of the variety of concepts concerning the character and the origin of freedom, the key question is whether we are free at all or there is no freedom because human choices and actions are causally determined. This question leads to the debate on determinism, which is intertwined with the issue of free will and responsibility of an individual.

The idea of free will rests on the presumption that a person has unrestrained ability to chose between actions and restrain from an action or the way in which he acts. It is a necessary precondition for the human being to be a responsible moral subject. It is realized in free choice of a certain way of behaving. An opposite opinion is presented by determinism. Determinists deny existence of free will, because according to them every event has its cause. Our choice of action is entirely governed by past states and laws. In consequence no action is voluntary, or a result of inner desire. All our states of mind, decisions and actions are results shaped unavoidably by previous causes. Our future is predestined, fixed just like our past.

Speaking about determinism, we can mention its hard version, denying the existence of our freedom and responsibility, and also a soft one, which claims that there is no conflict between freedom and determinism. In the case of the latter, it is understood that even if the action was a result of previous causes, there is a possibility to hold the doer responsible if the act was wrong, considering that he could have acted otherwise. For some, this soft determinism still excludes responsibility as the extreme version does, and they are ready to call it after Kant "a wretched subterfuge" or after William James "quagmire of evasion."

For William James and Charles Sanders Peirce, the existence of chance and change in the world is an argument against determinism. They are both admirers of tychism. According to Peirce, everywhere we can find free and spontaneous actions. Regularity is never without flaws and exceptions. James also agrees with that, juxtaposing determinism and mechanicism with a world of life and chance, ever-changing and unregulated. The universe given is open and continuous, where nothing is permanently established or regulated. In Peirce's and James's philosophy it is freedom and free will that are ascribed the greatest importance, together with an individual who is free and responsible for undertaken actions.

Josiah Royce also claims that we are free. Freedom and communication are for him crucial elements of a healthy society. What is necessary is the consciousness of such freedom. If given to an unprepared society, freedom is useless. Freedom involves real understanding of oneself and one's existence and comprehension of relations between ourselves and the others. Freedom formed in individuals starts to embrace the outside world and other people; it becomes a freedom expanding and exceeding individual freedom. As a result, there appears solidarity, which is an effect of expanding the sphere of personal freedom onto the environment. Yet this process is not without pitfalls. Royce mentions two sins which we can commit: the sin of narrowing our field of vision, of shutting the others off, and the sin of pride, connected with the conviction that we have grasped reality and absolute truth, thus closing the possibility of dialog with another human being. The opponents of such absolute truth are also John Dewey and his continuator Richard Rorty, who has a negative attitude to visions of all-encompassing, universal order or hopes for finding the ultimate truth, which would once and for all prescribe the patterns of our behavior. Such truths present in our culture are, as Nietzsche says, a mobile army of metaphors, or, as Rorty would say, dead metaphors, expired from being taken literally. We have to be conscious of all that so as not to be trapped in the stiffening shell of convention. It is important that our language, thinking, and behavior should suit the reality in which we exist, so that we could successfully deal with problems appearing within its frame. Rorty claims that what should be preserved from Dewey's work is the concept of man gradually changing his self-image; which leads him to liberation from what was previously given, and opens the possibilities for self-realization and growth, which enables him to exceed his limitations thanks to his creative abilities. This is so because for Dewey freedom consists not merely in the absence of constraint but in the power of being individualized self. His concept of freedom as individuality has three dimensions. Freedom consists in intelligent self-control, in the power of flexible and varied growth, and in participation in shaping the social conditions of individuality. The first dimension is concerned with the capacity for choice of an individual to reflect on his or her own goals, and to revise them as a result of that reflection. In the light of the second dimension, a moral one, we can say that one is in the possession of liberty only if one pursues the social goals that serve to realize his or her growth or individuality. Finally, liberty is concerned with the power to be an individualized self – making a contribution to the community by forming values and institutions regulating social relations. Dewey calls this new conception an "effective liberty." He agrees with past liberal thinkers that liberalism must be built around the defense of individual liberty, but he also attaches social conceptions of individuality to it, presenting "new" individualism, which is opposed to old-fashioned, traditional laissez-faire individualism. He believes that there is no such thing as the liberty or effective power of an individual, group, or class, except in relation to the liberties and effective powers, of other individuals, groups and classes. Dewey's intention is freedom of mind, freedom of action and experience, which are necessary to produce freedom of intelligence. Defense of his concept he bases the on free inquiry, free discussion and the moral development of public welfare, and not upon anything inherent in the individual as such or elsewhere. He considers the a priori search for truth within social reality as ending in the recognition of the pre-eminent influence of society over the individual or the individual on society. This is why Rorty says that we should take care of freedom, and the truth will take care of itself. But how should we be free and responsible if there are no absolute truth or laws, which could be our guidelines? As a response Rorty refers to the Protagorean/Emersonian tradition based on the thesis that human beings are on their own, and that their imagination will have to fill the role previously assigned to gods or scientific knowledge of the nature of reality in itself. What can constitute for us a reference point are just the values and beliefs of our culture and not some truth about the world and the human being.

On the limits of freedom and on free society

In these circumstances a question appears of whether we can exercise our freedom without any limits. We can find an answer in Rorty's as well as in Habermas's philosophy, or in other words in American and in continental pragmatism. Their commitment to freedom does not equal the acceptance of lack of bounds. In reference to this problem, it is worth recalling the distinction between *negative* and *positive* freedom, introduced by Isaiah Berlin in his essay *Two Concepts of Liberty*. The first one, according to Berlin, stems from the question: "What is the area within which a subject is or should be free and act according to their will without other people interfering?" In the negative understanding of freedom, being free means that no one else interferes with one's business. Freedom thus conceived is synonymous with freedom *from* – from intrusions into our activities. The second meaning, which Berlin refers to as *positive*, is related to the answer to the question "Who is to say what I am, and what I am not, to be or do?" or "By whom am I ruled?" In attempting to answer these questions and not the question "What am I free to do or be?" the *positive* sense of freedom manifests itself.

One may, however, entertain a certain doubt at this juncture, but Berlin says there is a difference between them, resulting from the fact that the *negative* and *positive* conceptions of freedom have evolved in historically diverging directions. This can be explained by the fact that the metaphor of being one's own master started to live its own life. As a result, a transition occurred, from considerations of being the master of one's fate to considerations in the categories of the *higher* and *lower* human nature, and to forming a conviction that one must live up to the former, *true* nature. Such understanding leads to legitimizing coercion of some over others, in the name of the good of the latter that they themselves fail to notice.

So understood, the *positive* conception of freedom – the freedom *to* – to act in the one proper way, appears to the advocates of the *negative* conception of freedom as a deceptive mask of brutal tyranny. This is also how Berlin as well as Rorty and Habermas see it, as they oppose submitting our culture to some absolute truths. Similarly to Berlin, Rorty realizes the threat coming from seeking and then imposing the only correct manner of thinking and acting. He is against anyone claiming the right to determine the best course of action by referring to some truth about the human being. What we have at our disposal are common moral convictions characteristic only of our community, in which moral rules depend on the moral identity of its members. These convictions influence our sense of obligation to others, by shaping solely the public side of our life, the side that competes with our private feelings and our private auto-creative efforts. What is important, in the light of the above, is that Rorty cares about building our communities upon successful interactions leading to agreements. This is supposed to take place not in the context of the one correct truth but in the light of variety. Rorty believes that what is left in the world devoid of absolute certainties is mutual communication. The objective of this communication is a safer life. For both Rorty and Habermas, the worst thing that we perpetrate is infliction of suffering. Rorty says that we should sensitize societies to human suffering. It is human sensitivity and imagination that gives hope for improving human relations. They make moral progress possible. Habermas would no doubt agree with this; he additionally believes that out of compassion, care, devotion, and openness emerge the forms of humanity thanks to which it becomes possible to endure conflicts.

Preventing suffering sets up the limits for our negative freedom. We can act freely as far as we do not harm the other. Rorty and Habermas agree with John Stuart Mill on that, in which they follow Dewey. All of them also say that what we need is freedom of speech and freedom of action. They are necessary for undisturbed communication to occur, so that full self-realization of an individual may take place, so that better views may come into being, and so that better actions may be taken. It will be possible if we take pains to uphold the formal conditions of undisturbed communication and if we create responsible members of our community, who will strive to achieve ever wider consensus by means of new, better descriptions and better arguments. For Dewey, Rorty as well as Habermas, this freedom can be succinctly referred to as "freedom as responsibility" – responsibility for the existence of proper relations between all those who create our societies, our communities, for our joint cooperative effort. It is connected with the responsibility for our action, for the consequences they may have on others, when we act within the social sphere, so that they do not bring about the humiliation or suffering of others. Such freedom – freedom as responsibility – is necessary in order to fully attain a successful society.

Important is that in the above mention successful society as envisioned by pragmatic philosophy there is acceptance of claims put forward by three traditions of thought concerning the issue of freedom: the republican claim that we need social institutions which more effectively will grant individuals their freedom; the liberal claim that human beings should be liberated from superstitions, coercion and pressures; and the idealist claim that an individual should be autonomous. Pragmatism highlights the need for abiding laws, constitutional government and division of powers, attaching great importance to the institutions which control political power and protect freedom of the individual; it also acknowledges the importance of individual self-realization. In this way pragmatism seems to meet the criterion highlighted by David Miller. According to him, in order to realize what human freedom requires, we must draw on the three abovementioned traditions of thought. Participation in shaping the society and the political system in which one lives; a range of unrestricted activities of one's choice; a way of life that is a result of conscious choices, not just a mechanical copy of others' patterns – these three factors are the foundation stones of freedom for any individual. As it refers to the elements from all three approaches to the issue of freedom, pragmatic philosophy definitely has a valuable perspective on how to understand the notion of freedom in its full scope.

Further reading

Berlin, Isaiah. *Four Essays on Liberty.* Oxford: Oxford University Press, 1969.

Dewey, John. "The Public and its Problems" in *The Collected Works of John Dewey 1882–1953*, Vol. 2. Carbondale, IL: Southern Illinois Press, 1991, pp. 235–373.

James, William. *The Dilemma of Determinism* in *The Will to Believe and Other Essays.* New York: Dover, 1956.

Mill, John Stuart. *On Liberty.* London: Dent, 1964.

Miller, David (ed.) *Liberty.* Oxford: Oxford University Press, 1991.

Rorty, Richard. *Contingency, Irony and Solidarity.* Cambridge: Cambridge University Press, 1988.

Royce, Josiah. *The World and the Individual.* New York: Dover, 1959.

Marcin Kilanowski

FRIENDSHIP

Four interrelated kinds of friendship have been philosophically conceptualized and practiced over the history of American philosophy, sometimes in combination and sometimes in tension with one another: (1) civic friendship or "fraternity"; (2) dyadic personal friendship between equals who encourage the development and contribution of one another's unique gifts; (3) communal friendship among a circles of thinkers or activists who share a common project or cause; and (4) intimate friendship within marriage and similar sexuality-inclusive relationships. The first of these kinds, civic friendship or "fraternity," involves a sense of common fate and mutual commitment that motivates active contribution to the general welfare among self-defined members of a people or a nation. At times, such civic friendships have been hierarchically organized and intolerant of differences, as was the case in the Massachusetts Bay Colony that expelled Roger Williams, Anne Hutcheson, and others; a similar intolerance within American conceptions of civic friendship also has been expressed as with-us-or-against-us patriotism in times of war. However, Roger Williams learned a new, still-contested, free and equal sense of civic friendship or "fraternity" from the Narragansett people of what is now Rhode Island, who took him in during the winter of his expulsion from Massachusetts and shared their land, resources, and stories with him. His description of the Narragansetts' fraternal lifeways in his dictionary of their language and in his letters to correspondents in England helped to shape John Locke's influential analyses of liberty and tolerance. These, in turn, influenced future generations of American thinkers, including Thomas Jefferson and Benjamin Franklin, as did their own observations of Native American lifeways and their intellectual interchanges with Haudenosaunee ("Iroquois") thinkers. In turn, Jefferson's framing of the American Declaration of Independence in terms of interlinked concepts of equality and liberty that could ground a distinctive kind of civic fraternity among those who joined him in mutually pledging "their lives, their fortunes, and their sacred honor" to the revolutionary struggle has come down to their descendants as part of a shared national common sense, reinforced at annual celebrations of its first announcement on the Fourth of July. Though its meaning is vague and widely contested, this Jeffersonian conceptual trinity of liberty, equality, and fraternity has had world-wide influence, marking out what John Dewey called "a distinctive angle of democratic vision." Its expression in American local practices of various kinds of civic service was ubiquitous and remarkable to Alexis de Tocqueville when he visited the United States in the 1830s.

During this same time period, however, as new technologies made possible mechanized factory labor, mass communications, increasingly devastating wars, and expansion of efforts to gain social control of opinion, Ralph Waldo Emerson and other New England Transcendentalist philosophers rejected inherited traditions of civic friendship as dangerous to the emergence of unique individual selves who would value above all a distinctive inner voice and a self-chosen path in living; as a counterweight, Emerson advocated the rare personal friendships of equals. Above all, Emerson emphasized "self-reliance" in the belief that each individual potentially manifests an eternal, divine "Oversoul" as a source of guidance in living and an indicator of one's particular gift to the world, *if* one learns to listen only to that inner voice and to speak and act accordingly. The friendship of an equal is a cosmic gift, in his view, because such a "not-me" can be a trustworthy witness and midwife to one's truth who offers rare opportunities to privately speak it sincerely, and thereby to hear it and to know it; such a friend recognizes and treats one's truth with tenderness, thereby offering encouragement to keep on in one's own right path in life.

The third kind of friendship, that of a group of individuals who share an intellectual project or an activist cause, combines elements of the first two kinds. Sometimes such groups have formed utopian communities. Sometimes they have formed discussion circles in which each of the members encourages the thinking and writing of the others. In spite of the dyadic emphasis of his writings on friendship, Ralph Waldo Emerson was a central figure in such a circle of intellectuals during and after his years of teaching at Harvard University, at various times including Henry David Thoreau, Margaret Fuller, Bronson Alcott, Henry James, Sr, and others. The originary group of classical American philosophical pragmatists, including Charles Sanders Peirce, William James, and others who became acquainted through their studies at Harvard, valued Emerson's views, and knew of the elevated discussions within his circle of friends; they formed their own all-male circle of friends (jokingly named "The Metaphysical Club") and began a long-lasting practice of engaging in critical discussions of philosophical ideas that reflected their distinctive standpoints and helped them to write in their own differing voices on a set of overlapping topics, thereby launching the world-wide pragmatist movement. Simultaneously, James enjoyed important dyadic friendships with Peirce and with Josiah Royce, his California-born American idealist colleague at Harvard, who eventually described himself as an "absolute pragmatist." All three deeply influenced the next generation of American pragmatists, including John Dewey and George Herbert Mead, who continued their Emersonian emphasis on the unique value of individuals and their habits of intellectual collaboration in fostering one another's thinking, but tended to place far greater emphasis on valuable social contributions in the on-going development of the self than had Emerson, Peirce, and James. In this, they echoed Royce's emphasis on the life-enriching value of loyalty one experiences through participation with others in a cause that frames their shared activities. Royce's ideal concept of "loyalty to loyalty" – an overriding commitment to framing one's own causes in ways that aim to assure that others will have the opportunity to experience similar loyalty, though theirs is a different cause – is both a condition on any particular cause-linked friendship and a call to a kind of universal attitude of friendship toward others' cause-linked friendships that can give rise to a world-wide "Beloved Community." Dewey and Mead also greatly appreciated and were influenced by the activistic examples of several circles of American intellectual women.

At the same period when Emerson was writing, small circles of women thinkers, some of whom who came to know one another through shared activism in the movement to abolish chattel slavery, began to exemplify this third kind of friendship and eventually a fourth. One such circle included Elizabeth Cady Stanton, Lucretia Mott, and other women who had read the works of Mary Wollstonecraft as well as those of Jefferson and Emerson, and had become convinced that the liberation of women from legal and customary social constraints was necessary to their effectiveness in opposing the great evils of their day. These constraints included not only laws that excluded women from most institutions of higher education, most of the professions, publishing in their own names, voting and holding public office, and managing their own financial affairs, as well as customary social practices that subordinated women to men within marriage, reinforcing through daily experience unequal gender norms and familial roles that led to silencing women's voices and suppressing the development and contribution of their particular gifts to meet the wider needs of the world. To challenge these legal and customary constraints, this circle of friends organized the historic Seneca Falls Convention on Women's Rights in 1848, at which they and over 140 others signed a Declaration of Sentiments modeled on Jefferson's American Declaration of Independence, in which they published their grievances and demanded changes in the existing gendered pattern of social relations to recognize women's natural equality with men. One of the social changes they called for and sought to exemplify in practice was reinterpretation of marriage as an intimate friendship of equals, a fourth kind of American friendship. Both Dewey and Mead tried to follow their example in marrying women who were their intellectual and social equals, fostering their careers and life satisfactions mutually while raising families together. At the same time, they admired, learned from, and supported the efforts of Jane Addams and her circle of women friends who founded and ran Chicago's Hull House, America's first settlement house to empower new immigrants in the ways of their new society from a stance of mutually beneficial civic friendship. A combination of all four kinds of friendship made possible the vast scope and the sustained, world-changing effectiveness of the American Civil

Rights Movement, guided by Martin Luther King, Jr, and a circle of mutually committed friends that incorporated several of King's key dyadic friends, including his marriage partner, Coretta Scott King, all of them together appealing to America's long tradition of civic friendship in encouraging others to join them in efforts to actualize a world-wide Beloved Community of mutual loyalty, provision for one another's needs, and creative pursuit of nonviolent solutions to problems that had in the past led nations to war.

Further reading

Addams, Jane. *Democracy and Social Ethics.* Urbana, IL: University of Illinois Press, 2002 [1902].

Akwesasne. Notes, "Basic Call to Consciousness," available at Six Nations website: www.ratical.org/many_worlds/6Nations

Dewey, John. "Philosophy and Democracy," in *The Essential Dewey, Vol. 1: Pragmatism, Education, Democracy,* ed. Larry A. Hickman and Thomas M. Alexander. Carbondale, IL: Southern Illinois University, 1998 [1919].

Emerson, Ralph Waldo. "Self-Reliance," "Friendship," and "The Over-Soul" in *Self-Reliance and Other Essays.* New York: Dover, 1993 [1841].

King, Martin Luther, Jr. *Where Do We Go From Here: Chaos or Community?* New York: Random House, 1967.

Lyons, Oren. "The American Indian in the Past" in Oren Lyons and John Mohawk (eds) *Exiled in the Land of the Free: Democracy, Indian Nations, and the US Constitution*. Santa Fe, CA: Clear Light, 1992.

Royce, Josiah. *The Philosophy of Loyalty.* Whitefish, MT: Kessinger, 2004 [1908].

Seigfried, Charlene Haddock. *Pragmatism and Feminism: Reweaving the Social Fabric*. Chicago, IL: University of Chicago Press, 1996.

Tocqueville, Alexis de. *Democracy in America*. Middlesex: Echo Library, 2007 [1835].

JUDITH M. GREEN

FRONTIER HYPOTHESIS

The Frontier Hypothesis was an explanation of the widely felt belief in American exceptionalism: the idea that America was a place different from the Old World, a place where the common person was hero and where the immigrant faced limitless opportunities. Living on the "free land" at the Western boundary of "civilization" was believed to transform life, as customs were modified to fit the new experience and a new form of democratic society grew. There is no doubt that there was a Frontier experience in America. The Census Bureau had carefully documented the settlement of the West; the only question was its meaning. The most powerful interpretation of its significance was offered by Frederick Jackson Turner.

Turner (1861–1932) was born in the semi-Frontier town of Portage, Wisconsin, where he developed an evolutionary understanding of social existence that emphasized the role of common folk in small groups facing the challenges of a primitive world. Turner thus rejected the "germ" theory that American democracy had been transmitted from Europe. He opposed the claims that democratic institutions "were propagated in New England by old English and Germanic ideas, brought over by Pilgrims and Puritans" and that "[i]t is just as improbable that free local institutions should spring up without a germ along American shores as that English wheat should have grown here without planting" (Herbert Baxter Adams, *The Germanic Origin of New England Towns*: 8). For Turner, on the contrary, the challenges and opportunities of Frontier life made America democratic.

Turner wrote:

> Up to our own day American history has been in a large degree the history of the colonization of the Great West. The existence of an area of free land, its continuous recession, and the advance of American settlement westward, explain American development.
>
> (*The Frontier in American History*: 1)

As the settlers went West, their inherited culture was either abandoned (like pianos and books) or simplified (like laws and religions); and what emerged from years of Frontier struggle was a new American culture. Initially, Turner writes,

> [t]he wilderness masters the colonist; but, with time and increasing numbers, the settlers re-set the balance: Little by little he transforms the wilderness, but the outcome is not the old Europe, not simply the development of Germanic germs ... The fact is, that here is a new product that is American.
>
> (*Frontier*: 4)

The central theme in Turner's position was that the West promoted democracy. On the Frontier, equality was a standing condition: no one was better than anyone else, high culture offered no advantages, and all had the same opportunities to improve. Turner also anticipated the problem of the closing of the Frontier. After the 1890 Census, he writes, "the frontier has gone, and with its going has closed the first period of American history" (*Frontier*: 38). The simpler situation that could be satisfied with individual solutions was now gone; and future Americans would have to deliberately create a more egalitarian democracy.

Turner's "Frontier Hypothesis" was immensely influential up through World War II, and Turner was, in the words of Merle Curti, "the scholar who in greater measure than any other in the past half century [1900–50] has forced the rewriting of the national history" (*Probing Our Past*: 32). His American story was that of the common person making a happy life through personal achievements in the expanse of the West. Turner's concern about the closing of the Frontier was echoed by such individuals as John Dewey, who writes in 1936 that, without a Frontier, "new social and political means must be set up to give the ideal of equality of opportunity any reality . . . we must take measures to provide an effective substitute for the opportunities that free land held out" (*Later Works*: 11.168).

We must, however, ask: Was the land really "free" Were the costs of settlement never higher than the rewards? Was there really an equal opportunity for all? In the face of such questions, the Frontier Hypothesis was oblivious to the destruction of Native American culture, optimistic in overlooking the many settlers who were destroyed by the Frontier, and blind to continued inequalities. Still, while this hypothesis missed many aspects of Frontier reality, it captured in simple and clear form the meaning which the Frontier and "free land" had for many people. The Frontier Hypothesis – or, better, the Frontier Myth – captured for a time the minds of Americans who were attempting to decide who they were.

Further reading

Adams, Herbert Baxter. *The Germanic Origin of New England Towns.* Baltimore, MD: Johns Hopkins University Press, 1882.

Bogue, Allan G. *Frederick Jackson Turner: Strange Roads Going Down.* Norman, OK: Oklahoma University Press, 1998.

Burnette, O. Lawrence, Jr (ed.) *Wisconsin Witness to Frederick Jackson Turner: Essays on the Historian and the Thesis.* Madison, WI: State Historical Society of Wisconsin, 1961.

Curti, Merle Eugene. "Frederick Jackson Turner, 1861–1932" in *Probing Our Past*. New York: Harper, 1955 [1949], pp. 32–55.

Dewey, John. "Education and New Social Ideals" in *The Later Works, Vol. 11, 1935–1937*, ed. Jo Ann Boydston. Carbondale, IL: Southern Illinois University Press, 1987 [1936], pp. 167–70.

Turner, Frederick Jackson. *The Frontier in American History.* New York: Henry Holt, 1920.

Wrobel, David M. *The End of American Exceptionalism: Frontier Anxiety from the Old West to the New Deal.* Lawrence, KS: University of Kansas Press, 1993.

James Campbell

FUNCTIONALISM

Functionalism was a loosely defined but highly influential movement in psychology and philosophy developed by William James, John Dewey, Addison Webster Moore, James Rowland Angell, and George Herbert Mead, among others, beginning in the 1890s.

Influenced by the evolutionary theory of Charles Darwin and American traditions that emphasized individuality and the practical requirements of frontier conditions, its proponents treated mind as a function of the biological organism rather than as a physiological entity with potentially identifiable parts; they stressed the processes by which individuals and communities adjust to altered circumstances; and they emphasized the practicality of psychological research and philosophical inquiry. As late as 1933 Edna Heidbreder could claim that functionalism was still alive and well in the sense that psychologists trained at the University of Chicago were distinctly aware of their heritage. But she also pointed out that functionalism had ceased to be identifiable as a school because it had more or less been absorbed into mainstream psychology and philosophy. Its methods and points of view had been generally accepted.

From one vantage point, functionalism may be viewed as a reaction against structuralism, which was perhaps best represented by E.B. Titchener's attempt to map, primarily by introspection, what he took to be the structure of the mind. Titchener had, to be sure, attempted to treat mental elements as processes. Because of his commitment to associationism, however, he regarded the analysis of such processes as a search for the most basic elements or components of mind. He attempted to determine the manner in which such building blocks fit together or combined to form more complex structures. The result was what the functionalists criticized as a static approach to mind depicted as assembled of individual elements. Dewey and James responded that they had nothing against introspection as one tool among many, but that mind as function is accessible in a number of ways – including introspection, controlled laboratory experiments, and attention to the behavior of animals, children, and the mentally ill in their natural settings.

Functionalists rejected associationism as insufficiently radical. They turned instead to the "radical empiricism" of William James, which accepted undifferentiated experience itself as primitive datum or phenomenon and maintained that it is only in retrospect that mental content and object become differentiated. In 1895 James argued that associationism provided no basis for explaining how the union of putative elements of consciousness could be achieved. In his view, context and interest provide the basis on which immediate experience could be broken up into parts, and those parts subsequently "remodeled" or reconstructed in accordance with the requirements of the organism attempting to adjust to its environment. James and the other functionalists thus turned traditional empiricism on its head.

Functionalists also rejected key elements of James Mark Baldwin's "genetic psychology." They argued that he had overemphasized the place of imitation and authority in the development of socialization and underestimated the role that interests and activities of individuals and communities play in that regard.

The founding documents of functionalism

The first edition of John Dewey's textbook *Psychology* (1887) contained elements of functionalism. They were somewhat obscured, however, by his use of the language of Hegelian idealism. As he revised subsequent editions Dewey moved away from idealism and toward an expanded statement of functionalism. In the second (1889) edition, for example, he wrote that an idea is only a function of mind. Even more pointedly, he argued that the effects of ideas on mind constitute a functional arrangement (or rearrangement) that corresponds to a change in the structure of the nervous system. The force of this argument was to accuse the structuralists of attempting to provide a static map of a moving target. It is possible to see the seeds of Dewey's essay "The Reflex Arc Concept in Psychology," published seven years later, in this argument. William James's *Principles of Psychology* (1890), which some historians consider the first major presentation of functionalism, depicted thought as a stream, emphasized interest and selectivity as key aspects of personal consciousness, and presented a behavioral account of habits.

Other historians (and some of Dewey's fellow functionalists) have viewed Dewey's 1896 "Reflex Arc" essay as the movement's founding document. Even though James had argued that consciousness is best understood as a stream, he had nevertheless maintained an account of behavior in which stimulus and response were treated as separate. Dewey argued that stimulus and response are not distinguishable *during* a process in which an organism adjusts itself to altered circumstances. They are instead functional phases of the completed act *after* it has been subject to analysis. Rejecting the notion that a stimulus is external to the organism, he characterized stimulus as a function of a complex of organic sensory and motor actions, environing conditions, and background of interest and expectations. In the classic case of the child reaching for the flame, for example, reaching involves a complex of motor reactions that must be understood as a part of the seeing. Hand is both stimulus and response for eye, and eye is both stimulus and response for hand. In Dewey's view, it is *the total act of coordination* that is the subject of psychology. It is a mistake for psychology to concern itself exclusively with individual elements of coordination that are isolated only in retrospect. In stressing the total act of coordination, Dewey laid the groundwork not only for functionalism, but also for behaviorism as well.

The relation of functionalism to behaviorism and instrumentalism

An important claim of functionalism was that organisms continually adjust to novel conditions during phases of equilibrium and phases of disequilibrium. James compared these phases to the perches and flights of birds. The breaks in our thinking – exemplified by the analysis of consciousness into percept and concept – are constructions: they should not be taken as mind-independent reality. Functional distinctions are tools that we use as a part of the process of adjustment. James even functionalized essences: essences, he argued, function as teleological weapons of the mind. It is in this sense that functionalism is closely related to instrumentalism.

William James's essay "Does Consciousness Exist?" (1904) is another key document in the development of functionalism. In it he reminded his readers that he had been arguing against the existence of consciousness as an entity for some twenty years, and that during that time he had attempted to give his students "its pragmatic equivalent in realities of experience." He identified consciousness as "the fundamental fact of psychology" and claimed that it "can neither be defined nor deduced from anything but itself." From his functionalist viewpoint, consciousness is entirely impersonal, but a self and its activities are a part of its content. Moreover, the pairs "subjective and objective," "representing and represented," and "the-thought-of-an-object and object-thought-of" are characterized not as distinctions of being, but as functional distinctions made by continually renewed retrospective experience for which the previous situation constitutes fresh content.

George Herbert Mead and James Rowland Angell acknowledged that the roots of functionalism lay in Dewey's "Reflex Arc" essay and rejected the idea that functionalism constituted an attempt to restrict the scope of psychology. Consciousness might have contents, but those contents must be understood in the context of function. The philosophical point was to undercut mind–body dualism and psychophysical parallelism.

Some commentators have suggested that Mead eventually rejected functionalism for behaviorism. Others have argued that his version of behaviorism was less a rejection of functionalism than it was an attempt to distance himself from fellow functionalists such as Angell who he thought had conceded too much to psychophysical parallelism.

In 1905 Dewey presented a very precise formulation of the relation between functionalism, geneticism, instrumentalism, and experimentalism. He wrote that functionalism deals with functions of experience, and not facts, states, or ideas. Genetic philosophy is a way of analyzing and organizing those functions. Instrumentalism is a theory of the significance of the knowledge-function. And experimentalism is a theory of the ways in which the worth of functions can be tested.

In contemporary analytic philosophy of mind, functionalism has taken on a different meaning: initially a response to behaviorism, it is a family of views that hold that mental states are to be explained in terms of causal roles.

Further reading

Cook, Gary A. *George Herbert Mead: The Making of a Social Pragmatist.* Urbana, IL: University of Illinois Press, 1993.

Dewey, John. *Psychology in The Collected Works of John Dewey: The Early Works, 1882–1898, Vol. 2, 1887*, ed. Jo Ann Boydston. Carbondale, IL: Southern Illinois University Press, 1967.

—— "The Reflex Arc Concept in Psychology" in *The Collected Works of John Dewey: The Early Works, 1882–1898, Vol. 5, 1895–1898*, ed. Jo Ann Boydston. Carbondale, IL: Southern Illinois University Press, 1972.

Heidbreder, Edna. *Seven Psychologies.* New York: Century, 1933.

James, William. "Does 'Consciousness' Exist?" in *The Works of William James: Essays in Radical Empiricism*, ed. Frederick Burkhardt and Fredson Bowers. Cambridge, MA: Harvard University Press, 1976.

—— "The Knowing of Things Together" in *The Works of William James: Essays in Philosophy*, ed. Frederick Burkhardt and Fredson Bowers. Cambridge, MA: Harvard University Press, 1978.

—— *The Principles of Psychology* in *The Works of William James: The Principles of Psychology*, ed. Frederick Burkhardt and Fredson Bowers. Cambridge, MA: Harvard University Press, 1981.

Mead, George Herbert. *Selected Writings*, ed. Andrew J. Reck. New York: Bobbs-Merrill, 1964.

Rucker, Darnell. *The Chicago Pragmatists.* Minneapolis, MN: University of Minnesota Press, 1969.

Shook, John R. "Introduction" in *Functionalist Psychology.* Virginia: Thoemmes Press, 2001.

Larry A. Hickman

FUNDAMENTALISM

A religious movement that began in early twentieth-century Protestantism to protect the "fundamentals" of the Christian faith against "modernist" tendencies, including Darwinism, secularism, and liberal theology. Since then, this term has also been applied to separatist persons and groups in other religions who seek to preserve what they see as the purity of their religion.

Developments in evolutionary theory and higher biblical criticism in the nineteenth century sparked much debate among Protestant Christians. By the turn of the twentieth century, many traditional Christian beliefs were being challenged and rejected or reinterpreted. In 1909, two wealthy Christian laymen, Lyman and Milton Stewart, donated money for the publication and distribution of a series of articles intended to defend the traditional beliefs. Written by conservative Christians from various denominations, some ninety articles were bound in twelve volumes and distributed free of charge to over 300,000 Christian workers in the United States and abroad. Called *The Fundamentals*, these volumes identified and defended fundamentals of the Christian faith such as the virgin birth, the physical resurrection of Jesus, the infallibility of the Scriptures, the substitutional atonement, and the physical second coming of Christ. Those who defended these traditional views eventually became known as fundamentalists.

Fundamentalists worked to try to eradicate modernist beliefs from the major Protestant denominations, with the most intense struggles occurring in Presbyterian and Baptist churches. Although the prominent fundamentalist William Jennings Bryan won the "Monkey Trial" in 1925, in which J.T. Scopes was found guilty of teaching evolution in a Tennessee school, this and other attempts to eradicate modernist influences from churches and schools ultimately failed. As a consequence, in the 1930s, fundamentalists felt the need to separate themselves from modernist Christians and to create their own independent churches and denominations. At this point, fundamentalism became associated not only with a desire to defend certain traditional Christian beliefs, but also with the practice of separation from those who did not hold them. For many, it came to be associated, as well, with anti-intellectualism and extremism.

By the late 1940s, many fundamentalists began to repudiate separatism and tried to present their views in more scholarly and popular ways. Calling themselves evangelicals (or neoevangelicals), they rallied around Billy Graham, *Christianity Today*, Wheaton College, and Fuller Theological Seminary. Those opposed to this new approach continued to call themselves fundamentalists and to follow a separatist path.

Beginning in the late 1970s, fundamentalists have turned to political activism to fight against issues such as legalized abortion, homosexuality, and the ban on school prayer. Under the leadership of men such as Jerry Falwell (Moral Majority) and Pat Robertson (Christian Coalition), they have become a powerful political force in the United States.

Although the term "fundamentalism" was originally coined to describe a movement in Protestant Christianity, it has since been applied to movements in other religions, such as Buddhism, Hinduism, Islam, Judaism, and Mormonism. In general, such movements tend to be characterized by literalism, separatism, and the defense of traditional beliefs and practices. While a few fundamentalists in some of these religious traditions have become radicalized and embraced violence, it is important to note that there is no essential link between fundamentalism and violence and that the vast majority of fundamentalists repudiate violence.

Further reading

Marsden, George M. *Fundamentalism and American Culture*, second edition. New York: Oxford University Press, 2006.

Sandeen, E.R. *The Roots of Fundamentalism*. Grand Rapids: Baker Book House, 1978.

Torrey, R.A. *The Fundamentals: A Testimony to the Truth*, 2 volumes. Grand Rapids: Baker Book House, 1994.

JAMES O. PAWELSKI

FUTURE

For philosophers who stress the eternality, determinism, and independence from human interests of existence, truth, and value, the concept of the future had little philosophic significance. They understand the future simply as one site, the next site, of fundamentally timeless Reality, Truth, and Goodness. By contrast, in the metaphysics, epistemology, and value theory of many American philosophers who take time seriously, the notion of the future has philosophic centrality. For them, the future is marked the open, contingent, in-the-making character of the universe, the fact that truths and values await action that will make and re-make them, and the finitude or limited future of human life. This second broad orientation to the future (rather than the past), combined with a celebration of the temporal and the finite (rather than the eternal and infinite), are identifying characteristics of American philosophy – particularly much American philosophy since the middle of the nineteenth century.

The future and American metaphysical traditions

Just as immense changes have occurred in American life since the time of the Puritans, there has been an immense change in the way American philosophers have conceived of the future. Thinkers such as John Winthrop, William Bradford, John Cotton, Increase and Cotton Mather, and Jonathan Edwards viewed the future, including one's fate in the next world, as determined by God. Human knowledge of that future, however, was understood to be limited, imperfect, and uncertain. As Increase Mather, the first President of Harvard College, sermonized in his 1697 "Man Knows Not His Time," humans, unlike God, have no advance knowledge of life or time of death or next life in heaven or hell. This combination of belief in divine predeterminism and human ignorance logically might be expected to lead to resignation or a carefree life (since one's fate is beyond one's control and already settled). The Puritans, however, turned it into a social gospel of hard work and perpetual self-interrogation by treating community standing and material success as outward signs of selection by God for grace and eternal life. Accordingly, while Increase Mather advised seizing the day (because one might not have tomorrow) to live a Christian life, a generation later his son, Cotton Mather, proclaimed that Christians must realize both this general calling and a second specific calling to succeed and be socially useful in one's chosen occupation or employment.

Time is money, Benjamin Franklin observed, and by his 1790 death, the Puritan work ethic had been substantially detached from Puritan theology in American thought. Franklin and the Deist political leaders and theorists of the American Revolution and Enlightenment believed in a Creator whose works were accessible by reason (rather than revelation) and a Creator who has not predetermined our world and does not intervene in it (thus rendering human action rather than prayer efficacious). Later Unitarian Christians (such as William Ellery Channing), transcendentalists (such as Ralph Waldo Emerson and Henry David Thoreau), writers (such as Walt Whitman), and some pragmatists (such as William James) took a more pantheist or pandeist approach by rejecting views of God as separate from the world. In all these thinkers, however, a revolution in conception of the future is evident: While the Puritans viewed the future as determined (and only our knowledge of it as uncertain), later American philosophers increasingly viewed the future itself as undetermined, contingent, in-process, and marked by real possibilities. As George Herbert Mead pointed out in *The Philosophy of the Present*, even the past is not determined or irrevocable, but instead continually is remade through the ongoing emergence of its new relations with its future in our present.

This view of the future as real possibility has two major dimensions. The first is most evident in the writings of Emerson and James that celebrate the future and its plasticity, counsel action and reconstruction, characterize America itself as the nation of the future to become aware of its own possibilities, and criticize all closed and backward-looking philosophical systems. Locating life in the transitions, as James put it, the spirit of this philosophy is thoroughly melioristic and ameliorative: The future warrants neither pessimism nor optimism, and though there is no guarantee of success, action and work may make it better than it otherwise would be. A second dimension of this view is developed most thoroughly by John Dewey. Like Emerson and James, Dewey declared that connection with a future, projection and reaching forward, and efforts to change the present are the salient features of human experience. Dewey, however, did not so much celebrate this fact as soberly recognize it and the challenge and responsibility it creates. This is the challenge to recognize intelligently and secure effectively possibilities that enlarge and enrich our lives rather than other possibilities. Dewey recognized that habits of thought and institutions formed in the past can become fixed and ineffective in the future. Realization of new possibilities demands intelligent reconstruction of our thoughts and lives, and the will to take up this reconstruction demands faith in intelligence and experimental inquiry – in effect, faith in the possibilities of the future.

The future and American epistemologies

Calling pragmatism a Copernican revolution, William James predicted that his philosophy would have impact equal to the Protestant Reformation. Predictions aside, James's pragmatism was a revolution in epistemology, and it took place through a radical change in conception and significance of the future for understanding truth, justification, and philosophical method. James defined pragmatism as a method for settling otherwise interminable philosophical disputes, as a theory of truth, and as an attitude or temperament. In each case, he stressed the role of the future. A belief's meaning, he held, is determined by tracing its practical consequences, its cash-value in future action. As a result, philosophy must adopt an experimental method and its conclusions must await the results of their being tested in, and by, future experience. And because there always are other experiences still to come, conclusions are always partial, incomplete, and fallible. This future-oriented method of philosophy made clear the inadequacy of traditional views of truth as agreement with reality. The practical meaning of a belief's "agreement with reality," James argued, can only be explained by its working in practice, its instrumentality, or its capacity to carry us satisfactorily from some experience to another. Accordingly, James argued that truth is made rather than ready-made; beliefs become true through future verification; truth – verity – is simply the result of processes of verification in the future; truth is an event. This pragmatic theory of truth is one outcome of what James called a broader pragmatic attitude. Pragmatism, he declared, looks away from the past, supposed necessities, and artificial first principles. Instead, it looks toward the future, possibilities, and consequences and results. Theories, James concluded, are instruments for the future, not answers to theoretical enigmas.

John Dewey developed further James's pragmatic theory of knowledge and his future-looking, experimental attitude. Like James, Dewey rejected philosophical commitments held in advance of, or independent of, actual inquiry. Like James, Dewey identified his philosophy with method focused squarely on the future rather than with any special results of that method. And, like James, Dewey sought to overturn and abandon philosophical traditions – from realism to idealism – based on assumptions not borne out in experience. In this vein, he was willing to give up the concept of truth and its philosophical baggage for the notion of warrant, evidence, justification, and results. And, because experience and its results are always perspectival and always informed by some interests rather than others, Dewey's instrumentalism shared much with the emphasis in relativity theory and quantum mechanics on the relativity of observations to observers – a parallel explored by Dewey's Chicago colleague George Herbert Mead in his writings on realism, pragmatism, and science.

If the future-oriented and future-defined epistemology of pragmatists like James, Dewey, and Mead is often taken as clearly American, it is at least as clear that this view was rejected both by earlier American philosophers and by many, if not most, of the American contemporaries of James, Dewey, and Mead. It is obvious that the pragmatic method, view of truth, and attitude are at odds with the past-oriented predeterminism, absolutism, and anti-experimentalism of the Puritans – for whom the idea that truths are made through human actions and its results would appear absurd. But so too this future-oriented theory of knowledge is at odds with the deep commitments of American Enlightenment thinkers to certainty, universal Reason able to grasp first principles, and principles themselves as self-evident and foundational. Dewey's titling his brief autobiographical essay "From Absolutism to Experimentalism" and his analysis in books like *Liberalism and Social Action* and *A Common Faith* of the cultural revolution in the seat of intellectual authority effected by a thoroughgoing experimentalism are indications of the depth of this difference. But this difference is evident in the work of many of the American colleagues of James and Dewey, as well as many of their successors. Charles Peirce, for example, described by James as the father of pragmatism, complained that James had "kidnapped" pragmatism only to identify it with a flawed account of meaning and truth, accounts overly psychological and insufficiently realist and uncommitted to a notion of truth independent of human interest and action. He renamed his own philosophy "pragmaticism" to make it too ugly for kidnappers. James's Harvard colleagues George Santayana and Josiah Royce, like European critics from G.E. Moore and Bertrand Russell to Theodor Adorno, also rejected pragmatism's focus on the future and temporality. Santayana, from the standpoint of his self-professed materialism, and Royce, from the standpoint of idealism, both argued that James confused truth (which is independent of experience and its results) for justification (which is dependent on and relative to experience). In response, Dewey later argued in *Experience and Naure* that Santayana's embrace of matter and Royce's embrace of the Absolute are just different ways of committing the fallacy of selective emphasis – breaking up the objective and subjective aspects of experience and then mistakenly inferring that the distinguished aspects existed separately from one another prior to the act of distinguishing them – that has thwarted the adoption of empirical method in philosophy.

The future and American theories of value and life

James held that the true is simply a subset of the good – that the true is the good with respect to belief. In this light, it is not surprising that James and Dewey held theories of value that were as future-oriented as their theories of knowledge. And it is not surprising that other American philosophers who rejected those theories of knowledge also rejected pragmatic theories of value. Just as James and Dewey denied the existence of predetermined, eternal, ready-made truths, so too they denied the existence of any such values. When interests and demands conflict, James advised, the best we can do in the present is to satisfy the most demand possible, but the larger demand of the moral life is that we invent some way in the future to satisfy and harmonize more demands and interests. This moral life, Dewey explained, requires rejection of the separation of means and ends – foolishly affirming values without appraising the conditions necessary for their realization or myopically prizing goals without considering the consequences of such action. Insisting that means and ends are temporal moments in an integrated means/ends continuum and that ends really are "ends-in-view," Dewey called for the application of experimental methods and inquiry to ethics and politics as much as to nature. And while Josiah Royce rejected much of pragmatism's world view, his ethics of loyalty to loyalty and the progressive fashioning of a Great Community reflect the same commitment to ideals of harmony and inclusion realized in the future. It is this same orientation to an open future, often expressed less technically and more powerfully, that motivates the writings of many American philosophical activists and critics – including the Declaration of Independence, the Seneca Falls Declaration, the Gettysburg Address, Chief Joseph's oratory, the Niagara Declaration of Principle, Randolph Bourne's "Trans-National America" essay, and Martin Luther King, Jr's "I Have A Dream" speech.

Further reading

Dewey, John. *Experience and Nature* in *John Dewey: The Later Works, 1925–1953, Vol. 1, 1925*, ed. Jo Ann Boydston. Carbondale, IL: Southern Illinois University Press, 1981 [1925].

—— *The Quest for Certainty* in *John Dewey: The Later Works, 1925–1953, Vol. 4, 1929*, ed. Jo Ann Boydston.

Carbondale, IL: Southern Illinois University Press, 1984 [1929].
—— "Time and Individuality" in *John Dewey: The Later Works, 1925–1953, Vol. 14, 1939–1941*, ed. Jo Ann Boydston. Carbondale, IL: Southern Illinois University Press, 1988 [1940], pp. 98–114.
Emerson, Ralph Waldo. "History" in *The Works of Emerson*. New York: Tudor Publishing, 1940, pp. 3–29.
James, William. "The Moral Philosopher and the Moral Life" in *The Will to Believe and Other Essays in Popular Philosophy, The Works of William James*, ed. Frederick H. Burkhardt. Cambridge, MA: Harvard University Press, 1979 [1891].
—— *A Pluralistic Universe, The Works of William James*, ed. Frederick H. Burkhardt. Cambridge, MA: Harvard University Press, 1977 [1909].
—— *Pragmatism, The Works of William James*, ed. Frederick H. Burkhardt. Cambridge, MA: Harvard University Press, 1975 [1907].
Mather, Increase, "Predestination and Human Exertions" and "Man Knows Not His Time" in Perry Miller and Thomas H. Johnson (eds) *The Puritans: A Sourcebook of their Writings, Vol. 1*. New York: Harper Torchbooks, 1963, pp. 335–48.
Mead, George Herbert. *The Philosophy of the Present*. La Salle, IL: Open Court, 1932.
Stuhr, John J. "Pragmatism, Pluralism, and the Future of Philosophy: Farewell to an Idea" in his *Pragmatism, Postmodernism, and the Future of Philosophy*. London and New York: Routledge, 2003, pp. 167–88.

John J. Stuhr

G

GENDER

Gender has been the object of intense theorizing in American philosophy in recent decades. Initially developed by feminist theorists, the evolution of gender theory has been closely tied to the evolution of feminism. Feminist theory has faulted the philosophical tradition for failing to bring under critical scrutiny the gender binarism and the subordination of women that have dominated Western culture. Feminist theorists have argued that the tacit identification of human experience with male experience that has pervaded the philosophical tradition makes highly questionable its most central notions (rationality, objectivity, truth, virtue, and justice). Against a traditional metaphysics that separates mind from body and self from society, feminist theorists have tried to show the crucial significance of embodiment for our mental life, the constitutive dialectic between self and other, and the existence of a collective disciplining of actions and embodied identities according to gender norms. Against a traditional epistemology that tacitly identifies rationality with masculinity and emotionality with femininity, some feminist theorists have argued that reason and emotion are symbiotically related; and some standpoint theorists have argued that differently gendered perspectives can make distinct contributions to the acquisition of knowledge, its justification, and the achievement of objectivity. In the first two generations of Feminist Theory gender was conceptualized first as an essence grounded in biology and later as a construction grounded in social practices. In so-called third-wave feminism many authors have contributed to the development of accounts of gender that try to dissolve the dichotomy between the biological and the social and to overcome the traditional debate between nature and nurture. In recent years Gender Theory has also broadened its scope and diversified its focus, producing abundant studies on masculinity as well as on femininity. The space in between gender dichotomies that challenges the male/female divide has also been investigated by Queer Theory. Gender and Queer Theory have been dominated by performative approaches which argue that gender is not only something we are, but also something we do. Gender and queer theorists have investigated the performative mechanisms of doing gender and have critically examined the norms that discipline and domesticate gender performance. The central focus of these investigations has been queering or transgressive gender performance, that is, performances of masculinity and femininity that problematize and destabilize gender dichotomies. Queer Theory constitutes an attempt to establish a strong link between academic research on gender and political activism. In this body of literature the performative insight that gender is something that we do leads to the critical insight that gender is also something we can undo and redo; and it is in this sense that Queer Studies claim to be critical interventions in gender politics that open up new possibilities for gender performance and call for the reconfiguration of gender boundaries. Especially influential here was the pioneer work of Judith Butler in *Gender Trouble* (1990). Butler developed studies that show how our gender identities are constantly being negotiated in our performance and how gender lines are being performatively drawn and redrawn in these negotiations. She argued that our performance has the power of resignifying gender, that is, the critical and subversive potential of contesting gender norms, queering the gender line, and rearticulating gender categories. But on Butler's view, although gender is something that we do, undo, and redo, it is not something that we simply make up, for our bodies (the agents of our gender performance) do matter. Butler and her followers have analyzed how our embodied performances signify gender and sexual orientation, articulating an account of how our gender and our sexuality are simultaneously disciplined by overlapping gender and sexual norms (a complex and heterogeneous normative framework called heteronormativity). The recent research on the intersection between gender and sexuality that has enriched Gender Theory should be put in the context of a more general interest in the intersectionality of identity. The recent literature in Gender Studies offers a wide range of explorations of how gender interacts with other identity categories such as race, ethnicity, class, and sexuality. This research on the intersections of identity categories has resulted in fruitful collaborations between Gender Theory and theories that focus on other aspects of identity: especially, race theory, philosophy of ethnicity, oppression/liberation theory, and gay/lesbian theory or sexuality studies. In recent years special attention has also been given to global issues concerning gender inequality and sexual oppression. Gender has been theorized at the global level by third-world feminism, which gives voice to the problems, concerns, and demands of women in non-Western contexts. This is a new, global stage of Feminism and Gender Theory which studies gender dynamics in global contexts and examines the problems afflicting women and gender/sexual minorities (GLBT people) around the world.

Further reading

Addams, Jane. *Democracy and Social Ethics*. New York: Macmillan, 1902.

Alcoff, Linda. *Visible Identities: Race, Gender, and the Self*. New York: Oxford University Press, 2005.

Butler, Judith. *Bodies that Matter: On the Discursive Limits of "Sex"*. New York and London: Routledge, 1993.

Davis, Angela. *Women, Race, and Class*. New York: Vintage Books, 1983.

Moraga, Cherrie and Anzaldúa, Gloria (eds) *This Bridge Called My Back: Writings by Radical Women of Color*. New York: Kitchen Table/Women of Color Press, 1984.

Narayan, Uma. *Dislocating Cultures: Identities, Traditions, and Third-World Feminism*. New York and London: Routledge, 1997.

Seigfried, Charlene H. *Pragmatism and Feminism: Reweaving the Social Fabric*. Chicago, IL: University of Chicago Press, 1996.

Sullivan, Shannon. *Living Across and Through Skins: Transactional Bodies, Pragmatism and Feminism*. Bloomington, IN: Indiana University Press, 2001.

José Medina

GENEALOGICAL PRAGMATISM

Genealogical pragmatism is the term that the American philosopher and scholar John Stuhr uses to characterize his reconstruction of classical American pragmatism. Moreover, it is a reconstruction of pragmatism that is carried out in light of recent postmodern thought and with particular attention to the genealogical strain in postmodern thought. Stuhr develops his notion of genealogical pragmatism in detail in two books: his *Genealogical Pragmatism* and his *Pragmatism, Postmodernism, and the Future of Philosophy*.

Genealogical pragmatism has its roots, then, in two philosophical traditions. Out of the American philosophical tradition, it draws on a wide range of thinkers, including Emerson, Royce, and Santayana, but is especially focused on the classical pragmatism of Peirce, James, and Dewey, with particular emphasis on the latter two thinkers. Out of the postmodern and Continental traditions, genealogical pragmatism also draws on a number of thinkers, including Derrida, Foucault, Deleuze, and Adorno, with a particular emphasis on Foucault's understanding and practice of genealogy.

As a pragmatic philosophy, Stuhr maintains that genealogical pragmatism is inherently reconstructive (Stuhr 1997: ix–xii). This means that it is at once instrumental and situated. As instrumental, it is focused on the amelioration of present ills and the realization of future possibilities for enriched individual and communal experience. As situated, it is focused on particular and plural practices, experiences, and purposes. Thus, in characterizing genealogical pragmatism, Stuhr notes the pragmatic and especially Jamesian focus on practice, purpose, and pluralism (Stuhr 1997: 63–77). Genuine philosophical problems, according to this pragmatic orientation, are those that arise out of concrete experiences and practices, and the meaning and truth of philosophical theories are tied to their practical and experiential consequences.

Furthermore, a genuinely genealogical pragmatism, according to Stuhr, is one that recognizes that the identification of philosophical problems, the proposal of solutions, and the judgment of the practical adequacy of these solutions is relative to and conditioned by particular, localized interests and purposes. Given the differences and oppositions inherent in social and political life, a philosophy that is committed to pluralism in both theory and practice must be conscious of its own interests and purposes and the ways in which these lead to exclusions of other interests and purposes. Thus, Stuhr maintains, a philosophy that is both pragmatic and genealogical must submit its own theories and practices to genealogical inquiry and criticism – that is, criticism that calls into question and destabilizes its own practical and theoretical commitments.

Stuhr finds inspiration for this genealogical view of pragmatism in Dewey's understanding of philosophy as "inherently criticism" (Stuhr 1997: 113; Dewey 1981: 298) and his "genetic method" of philosophical criticism (Stuhr 1997: 111; Dewey 1982: 93–4; 1976: 3–20). Stuhr cites Dewey's remark in *Experience and Nature* (1981: 40) that philosophy conceived of as criticism is "a kind of intellectual disrobing" that inquiries into its own interests and purposes (Stuhr 1997: 111–12). Moreover, Stuhr finds the potential to radicalize and extend this genealogical strain in pragmatism through the genealogical work of Foucault (see, especially, Stuhr 2003: 135–52).

Although genealogical pragmatism has distinct roots in both American pragmatism and postmodernism it is not simply a combination of elements from these two philosophical approaches. Instead, it seeks to incorporate the disparate temperaments and insights of these two traditions, while also moving beyond them through mutual interrogation, critical reconstruction, and an envisioning of future possibilities for philosophy and individual and communal experience. Stuhr argues that the relationship between pragmatism and postmodernism has generally been undertheorized and oversimplified in terms of identity or difference, and he seeks, through his genealogical pragmatism, to achieve a more nuanced view of the relationship of these traditions that will make possible a more complex and constructive interrelation between them (Stuhr 1997: 87–114).

Stuhr contends that the most significant differences between pragmatism and postmodernism are not primarily doctrinal, but rather are differences of temperament and will (Stuhr 1997: 103). Pragmatism and postmodernism share deep suspicions and criticisms concerning the methods, categories, and problems of traditional philosophy. The temperament of pragmatism, however, is focused on reconstruction, recovery, meliorism, and a "will to intimacy" that involves the commitment to ideals such as community and democracy (Stuhr 1997: 103–9). The temperament of postmodernism, on the other hand, stresses practices such as deconstruction and interrogation rather than reconstruction and recovery. Furthermore, postmodernism expresses a "will to oppositionality" that emphasizes difference instead of the pragmatic "will to intimacy" (Stuhr 1997: 103–9). Accordingly, postmodernism tends to be distrustful of ideals such as community and democracy for fear that the pursuit of such ideals may involve the suppression of differences and oppositions.

In the context of genealogical pragmatism these temperamental differences are viewed instrumentally in terms of their potentiality for deepening and extending the insights of these traditions. Thus, pragmatism and postmodernism are seen as challenges to each other that call forth critical reconstruction and deeper self-consciousness criticism. Stuhr contends that the primary challenge of postmodernism to pragmatism is a genealogical challenge; it is the challenge for pragmatism to confront the role that differences, oppositions, exclusions, violence, and particular and local interests and purposes play in its "will to intimacy" and the ideals of community and democracy bound up with this will (Stuhr 1997: 110). Furthermore, it is the challenge to recognize the contingency of this will and these ideals even as it works toward their realization.

Conversely, Stuhr maintains that the challenge of pragmatism to postmodernism is to avoid the temptation to give the values of oppositionality and difference a final or absolute status (Stuhr 1997: 108). According to Stuhr, this pragmatic challenge to postmodernism is itself genealogical; it is the challenge for postmodernism to recognize that it has its own interests, purposes, and "intimate values" bound up with its "will to oppositionality" (Stuhr 1997: 108). It is, moreover, the challenge for postmodernism to become instrumental and political through an increased focus on practice (Stuhr 1997: 108–9).

Finally, Stuhr emphasizes the strenuous, melioristic, and future-oriented qualities of his genealogical pragmatism. By turning toward concrete practices, purposes, and pluralism it turns away from the traditional philosophical preoccupation with a theoretical transcendence that would exempt philosophy from the contingencies of concrete experiences and practices and the hard work of continual criticism, inquiry, and reconstruction. Thus, genealogical pragmatism can be seen as a complex and multifaceted criticism and reconstruction of individual and communal experience and of the discipline of philosophy.

Further reading

Dewey, John. *John Dewey: The Middle Works, Vol. 12, 1920*, ed. Jo Ann Boydston. Carbondale, IL: Southern Illinois University Press, 1982 [1920].

—— *John Dewey: The Late Works*, Vol. 1, *1925*, ed. Jo Ann Boydston. Carbondale, IL: Southern Illinois University Press, 1981 [1925].

Foucault, Michel. "Nietzsche, Genealogy, History" in *The Foucault Reader*, ed. Paul Rabinow. New York: Pantheon, 1984.

Stuhr, John. *Genealogical Pragmatism: Philosophy, Experience, and Community*. Albany, NY: SUNY Press, 1997.

—— *Pragmatism, Postmodernism, and the Future of Philosophy*. New York: Routledge, 2003.

BRIAN D. RABINOVITZ

GENERALITY/GENERALS

In Charles Peirce's philosophy these terms, along with "continuity," are the preeminent types of *Thirdness*, the category responsible for the element of intelligibility in the universe of brute individuals (*Secondness*). "Generals" (aka "universals") and "generality" (aka "universality") have traditionally to do with words or terms such as "mineral" or "red" that are *predicable* of a plurality of objects and are contrasted with "singulars" such as "Hurricane Katrina" or "John Lennon" which refer only to one individual or object. A "general" (in thought) is also contraposed to an "individual" object (in nature) which is *non-predicable*. Most importantly in Peirce's system generality is a major type of "Thirdness" whose essence is *mediation*, the principle of intelligibility and science. That is, a "third" is that which mediates, relates or *links* together two or more things which otherwise would remain im-mediate and unrelated. As Peirce avers in "On a New List of Categories" (1867) generality involves "*reducing a manifold to unity*" (as Kant and Hegel concur), thereby making the manifold "intelligible" *qua* correspondent with a concept, i.e. a "one."

Generality in logic

According to Peirce anything is a general or has generality which is (a) *non-individual* as applying to more than one or an indefinite number of individual(s) and thus able to exist in more than one place at a time such as a linguistic term, law or property, e.g. "horse," "gravity," "blue"; or (b) *indeterminate* with respect to a property and respecting which the law of excluded middle does not apply, e.g. "triangle" – indeterminate as to whether it is acute or obtuse (Peirce notes a term's "generality" can be diminished or increased by the addition or subtraction of properties), and "human being" – indeterminate when defined as "rational animal" as to properties of e.g. race and ethnicity. The issue of how an "individual" can be both fully determinate (as non-general) and fully indeterminate (as a brute second, devoid of generality and determinacy) *and yet also "general"* (as saturated with generality *qua* essence, law, habit) is another form of the question, How do thirds and seconds, generals and individuals in Peirce's philosophy "get together"? Many agree with J. Boler (1963) that Peirce fell short of the "*concrete* universal" (à la Hegel) he needed to unify the two; see on this R. Winfield's excellent essay, "On Individuality" (1991). Peirce further holds that (c) all "predicates" of a proposition are general (the subject being singular) and exhibit both "subjective generality," *qua* able to exist in several subjects or minds at the same time, and "objective generality," *qua* able to exist in several objects concurrently; and (d) Peircean generals are also not *actual* but most significantly *potential* (as predic*able* habits, tendencies or dispositions) having an "*esse in futuro*" (CP 5.48). Peirce writes,

> When an experimentalist speaks of a *phenomenon* such as ... "Michelson's phenomenon" ... he does not mean any particular event that did happen to somebody in the dead past, but what *surely will* happen to everybody in the living *future* who shall fulfill certain conditions.
>
> (CP 5.425)

This real potential and futural nature of the generals of science Peirce believes is underwritten by his *Logic of Relatives* which (in brief) allows categorical/indicative propositions to be translated into sets of subjunctive conditionals.

Generality in semiotics

For Peirce all *signs*, whether internal/mental or external/physical, involve generality because as a type of thirdness they have to do with a "mediation" of two or more things. That is, a sign (or representation) points beyond itself to an "other" by connecting a meaning ("interpretant") *to* an object *for* a subject. Signs or symbols and the generality they involve pertain not only to linguistic items such as words, concepts and laws, but to individual physical objects as well, e.g. a flag, statue, red light, badge, gesture. A "flag," for example, points not to itself, as *this* individual piece of cloth, but (a) *to* a country (the USA) containing a multitude of elements, hence *to* an infinite multiplicity or collection, and thus *linking* this entire multitude of individuals together, (b) *for* a plurality of citizens or subjects (c) *in* whose minds the *same* flag-meaning or interpretant exists; thus exhibiting both *subjective* and *objective* generality, as well as generality as such (i.e. *qua* mediation, continuity and unity).

Generality in scholastic realism

The "realist–nominalist controversy" is crucially important to Peirce for unless there are "real generals" (i.e. general terms to which something "independent" of thought corresponds) *science*, that is, explanation, induction, prediction and law, *would be impossible* in that all statements of science involve general terms. In brief, *nominalism* holds that generals exist only in the mind and what alone exist are isolated individuals having nothing in common. *Realism*, by contrast, holds that mediation and generality are truly actively involved in the individuals of the universe, being both "in" them (as natural kinds) and "governing" them (as laws). Moreover the "something" in nature the real generals in our mind correspond to and cognize is always "general" and never *the individual as such* (e.g. "Seabiscuit"). For as Peirce would say, what the scientist is interested in and *is actually knowing* in the particular sample(s) of gold or beryllium before her is the *molecular structure* which is one and the *same* (hence a general, a continuity) in all possible samples. This "general" is the true object of knowledge and the "really real," *qua* constant, enduring element, in all the changing and ephemeral particulars that instance it – what perhaps can be called the "Platonic strand" of Peirce's thought. Two questions Peirce must answer to carry his position however are: (1) "How can we be certain that there really are generals in the world or 'operative in nature'?" And (2) "Given there are such generals, how can we be certain that the generals *in us* (Thinking) correspond to the generals *in the world* (Being)?" Hence, that we really *know* the world – that "Science" is not just a pipe-dream?

Generality in objective idealism and evolutionary cosmology

Peirce's answer to (2) is found in his "Monism" of Mind which he takes over from Schelling and Hegel and calls *Objective Idealism*, "the one intelligible theory of the universe." In essence his answer, as J. Margolis points out, is that there are not *two* separate domains of reality (in us/outside us, mind/matter) but only *one*, namely Mind, i.e. the "general" (*qua* embodied molecular structure, law, kind), which however can be viewed from two sides: as something *subjective* (a law as thought by "us") and as something *objective* (the same law as existent in nature). Peirce will insist in his *Berkeley Review* (1871) that, "To make a distinction between the *true conception of a thing* and *the thing itself* is, [the realist] will say, only to regard *one and the same thing* from two different points of view." As Hegel similarly says, the truth or absolute Concept is that "knowledge and the object of knowledge are the *same*" (1807) – and in Margolis's words, "being (considered apart from thought) and being (considered as the object of a true judgment) are one and the same" (1993). See also e.g. Peirce's remarks in his *Apology for Pragmatism*: "Thought is not necessarily connected with a brain. It appears in the work of bees, of crystals, and throughout the purely physical world" (CP 4.551). Peirce however does not offer any rigorous *proof* of his doctrine – a weakness attaching to his answer to (1) as well. See e.g. his Harvard "stone-experiment" (CP 5.100) in which Peirce before a class of Harvard philosophy students contends that the mere fact he can successfully "predict" the subsequent behavior of a stone upon its release from his hand is demonstrative proof for the existence of general principles (in this case "gravity") in nature. That is, as Kant and others have shown, prediction, as based on *induction*, can never yield the strict generality and necessity that a "law" requires.

Generality also figures prominently in Peirce's *Evolutionary Cosmology* according to which the universe is a vast Mind perfecting itself through cosmic time. Peirce postulates that the universe (or Mind) has a built-in *generalizing tendency* for matter (or mind-stuff) to take on habits or laws, for chance regularities to repeat. The goal of the process is total Generality or the *Reasonableness* for which "the Heavens and the Earth have been created" (CP 2.122), where generality is embodied in all individuals, thirdness in secondness. Finally, generality for Peirce is clearly privileged over individuality – indeed in his system even individual persons are conceived merely as parts of a Communal Personality. As Boler writes: "the actuality of discrete individuals is … *only a scar of battles fought at a higher plane*, and is unintelligible when considered apart from the general process … of thirdness" (1963). We would say for Peirce the universe and all the infinite individuals comprising it is indeed totally saturated with generality and intelligibility, hence, from a "theoretical" vantage point, generality is "all in all" – *but nevertheless,* and from a "practical" perspective, the reality, strength and stubbornness of individuals *qua indeterminate, unintelligible secondness* will ever maintain itself as an ineliminable, irreducible element of experience.

Further reading

Boler, John F. *Charles Peirce and Scholastic Realism*. Seattle, WA: University of Washington Press, 1963.

Hegel, G.W.F. *Phenomenology of Spirit*, trans. A.V. Miller. New York: Oxford University Press, 1977 [1807].

Margolis, Joseph. "The Passing of Peirce's Realism," *Transactions of the Charles S. Peirce Society* XXIX, 3 (Summer 1993): 293–330.

Peirce, C.S. *Collected Papers of Charles Sanders Peirce* (CP), 8 volumes, ed. C. Hartshorne and P. Weiss (Vols 1–6) and A. Burks (Vols 7–8). Cambridge, MA: Harvard University Press, 1931–58.

Winfield, Richard Dien. *Freedom and Modernity*. Albany, NY: SUNY Press, 1991.

KEN FOLDES

GENERALIZED OTHER

The Generalized Other is a concept that the American pragmatist George Herbert Mead employs in order to help explain the social development of the self. For Mead, the genesis of the self involves language, social roles, and generalized others. To understand the latter, an account must first be provided of the former.

Mead is not interested in the grammatical structure of language, syntax; rather, he is interested in semantics and pragmatics. For Mead, animals gesture, that is, they act in a fashion that calls out responses in other members of their species. For example, when a dog growls, it can serve to "frighten" another dog, which must fight or flee. Human beings also gesture to one another, but they have a very special form of gesture at their command, namely, the vocal gesture. What makes the vocal gesture special, assuming a suitably developed nervous system, is that different individuals can respond in a similar fashion to a functionally identical gesture. For example, when I say "Boo" loudly to you, I may become startled, that is, I can become scared by my own gesture. The word has the same functional meaning for both of us, although a response is typically suppressed in the speaker – that is, remains implicit – while it becomes explicit for the listener. However, when a dog growls, he does not respond to his own gesture, even implicitly. He only frightens other dogs. When I use vocal gestures, what Mead calls significant symbols, I can anticipate how you will respond to them because I hear them as you do. And when someone else is not present, I can talk to myself by anticipating the internalized responses of others to specific significant symbols. Gestures become significant symbols for human beings, and as such they allow us to respond to our gestures as others respond to them.

For Mead the development of language is the first step in the development of the self. It allows us to engage in reflexive behavior, for example by talking to ourselves. The ability to turn the experience of the individual back on him or herself is crucial to the process of taking of social roles, which is the next step in the development of the self. We know that children learn to take various roles by playing: for example, one child plays doctor and another patient. In order to take these roles one must be able to anticipate the responses of others, which involves responding to oneself as if one were the other: that is, reflexively responding to one's own behaviors. This capacity allows children to imaginatively play various roles even when others are not present, in an analogous fashion to the manner in which they can talk to themselves when others are not present. Role playing, for Mead, becomes more complex as children grow older and is an important feature of our social life as adults.

However, Mead does not wish to leave the impression that selves are simply social roles. Selves are more complex than specific social roles. In order to understand how this is so, Mead discusses the difference between play and the game. Play involves interactions between individuals in which one role follows another in succession: for instance, one says something in the role of a doctor and the patient replies. But games are more complex. In baseball, for example, one must be able to respond to all of the roles in the game: that is, one must grasp how each of the players on the field can react at any given instant. In role taking we engage a specific other, but in the game we have multiple roles to consider. When one has internalized all of the various roles and relationships that are entailed in a game, they form a system or organized community, and this organized community can be spoken of as the generalized other. In Mead's words:

> The organized community or social group which gives to the individual his unity of self may be called "the generalized other." The attitude of the generalized other is the attitude of the whole community. Thus, for example, in the case of such a social group as a ball team, the team is the generalized other in so far as it enters – as an organized process or social activity – into the experience of any one of the individual members of it.
>
> (Mead 1934: 154)

Mead claims that the self arises when one views one's behaviors from the perspective of the generalized other. Different social groups or organizations, such as "political parities, clubs, corporations," can be said to give rise to generalized others, as can "abstract social classes or subgroups, such as the class of debtors and the class of creditors" (Mead 1934: 157). Multiple selves in an individual are commonplace. And these selves operate at different levels of abstraction. Whether there is a self that unifies all of these selves is an open question for Mead. It is possible that there may be a moral self that performs this function.

Further reading

Mead, George Herbert. *Mind, Self and Society: From the Perspective of a Social Behaviorist*. Chicago, IL: University of Chicago Press, 1934.

MITCHELL ABOULAFIA

GENETIC METHOD

The expression "the genetic method" has multiple uses in the literature of American philosophy. One important use is associated with the theory of inquiry championed by John Dewey (1859–1952) and based on what has been called the *genetic thesis*, the view that "the way to get insight into any complex product is to trace the process of its making – to follow it through the successive stages of its growth". The quoted sentence is from Dewey 1916. The genetic thesis was taken to imply that ideas cannot be fully understood if their historical and social contexts are not taken into account. Thanks largely to Darwinism, the genetic method in some form had a powerful vogue in many fields of inquiry at the end of the nineteenth century and the beginning of the twentieth. The genetic thesis has been traced through Charles S. Peirce (1839–1914), Charles Darwin (1809–82), and Friedrich Nietzsche (1844–1900) to Aristotle. Another important use is associated with the mathematical philosophy developed by E.V. Huntington (1874–1952). This article focuses on these two usages.

The genetic method and the genetic thesis are to be sharply distinguished from various errors known as *genetic fallacies*. These include the beliefs that justice requires descendants to be held responsible for the crimes of their ancestors and that the validity of an idea is to be measured by moral worth of the person who originated it.

The genetic method in Dewey's theory of inquiry contrasts with other methods according to the subject field of the inquiry. In history, Dewey contrasted it with the biographical method that approaches history through the lives and adventures of important individuals. In section 3 of Chapter 16 of his influential 1916 classic *Democracy and Education*, which is still in print, he wrote the following.

> Genetic method was perhaps the chief scientific achievement of the latter half of the nineteenth century. Its principle is that the way to get insight into any complex product is to trace the process of its making – to follow it through the successive stages of its growth. To apply this method to history, as if it meant only the truism that the present social state cannot be separated from its past, is one-sided. It means equally that past events cannot be separated from the living present and retain meaning. The true starting point of history is always some present situation with its problems.

Interestingly, although he is known for having advocated the genetic method, this is one of the few times Dewey used the expression "genetic method." In fact, it is the only time he used it in this work.

The genetic method in mathematical philosophy is one of two traditional approaches for establishing foundations of mathematics, the other being the apparently much older *postulational method*. The expression "genetic method" dates from the end of the 1800s, but the method itself is much older; forms of it, or at least foreshadowings of it, are found in Plato's dialogues. The genetic method, also known as the constructive method, focuses epistemically on objectual knowledge in mathematics and ontically on the objects of mathematics. The postulational method, also known as the axiomatic method, focuses epistemically on propositional knowledge in mathematics and ontically on the propositions of mathematics.

In standard cases such as classical number theory (arithmetic) and geometry, the genetic and postulational approaches are complementary. No mathematical object is a mathematical proposition. The objects of arithmetic are odd or even, not true or false. The propositions of arithmetic are true or false, not odd or even. For example, concerning the numbers 5, 7, and 12 that are referred to in the proposition that 5 + 7 = 12, the genetic method might construct 5, 7, and 12 from 1 alone, while saying nothing about the proposition. In contrast, the postulational method might deduce the proposition that 5 + 7 = 12, while saying nothing about how 5, 7, and 12 depend constructively on 1. Other than these basics, little can be taken for granted in discussing these methods, and even these trivialities have been disputed by reputable mathematicians and philosophers.

People do not seek foundations for a field unless they are confronted with some sort of difficulty that reveals to them their lack of certainty about it and engenders in them the discomfort of incertitude. As has been said by others, mathematics does not need foundations; people need foundations for ideas with which they are uncomfortable.

The usual motivation of the postulational method is the belief that incertitude concerning a given proposition can be removed by deriving it from propositions concerning which there is certitude. Analogously, the usual motivation of the genetic method is the belief that incertitude concerning a given entity can be removed by deriving it from entities concerning which there is certitude. The senses attached to the word "deriving" may vary. Nevertheless, it should be clear that propositional deriving is not the same as objectual deriving. For some authors, the former is deducing or inferring and the latter is constructing or defining – distinct processes not always distinguished.

Forms of Euclidean geometry are often cited as paradigm cases of successful applications of the postulational method. Often cited as successful applications of the genetic method are various stages in the so-called arithmetization of *analysis* – the branch of mathematics that studies such problematic entities as negative, algebraic, transcendental, and complex numbers. Construction of the integers including negative integers and zero from natural numbers, or positive whole numbers, was thought to put the problematic negative numbers and zero on an equal footing with the natural numbers. Likewise, and perhaps even more impressively, complex numbers, which include all real and all imaginary numbers, were derived from the integers. Confidence in the genetic method prompted the mathematician Leopold Kronecker (1823–91) to say, "God created the integers, all else is the work of man."

Proponents of the genetic method criticize the postulational method for presupposing the existence of its basic entities – for postulating what should be constructed. Sometimes they paraphrase Bertrand Russell's famous quip, that postulation has all of the advantages that theft has over honest toil. Proponents of the postulational method criticize the genetic method for not realizing that it makes tacit assumptions that need to be treated by the postulational method – for tacitly presupposing what should be explicitly postulated. Ignoring the postulational foundations of the genetic method leaves the latter in a kind of limbo. The result is reminiscent of the kind of chicken–egg standoff so familiar in philosophy.

Incidentally, there are many scholars, perhaps most, who see advantages of both methods and who have no inclination to choose between them or to regard them as in conflict. Moreover, structures implicit in the two methods have become subjects of intense mathematical study by mathematicians for whom incertitude was never a motivation. Constructions and formal postulate systems have been found to be intrinsically interesting mathematical objects.

The topic is further enriched by the existence of a kind of combination of the two in a *constructional postulate system*. Here the presuppositions and constructions of an application of the genetic method are treated postulationally as in the Whitehead–Russell *Principia Mathematica*. There are foreshadowings of this in Euclid. His first two propositions are about constructions. His proofs include demonstrations that the constructed entities are indeed those whose constructions were to be effected.

As mentioned, not everyone in foundations of mathematics is either a *postulationalist* or a *constructionalist*, as proponents of the genetic method are sometimes called. These *neutralists*, let us say, have a critical distance from both methods. They point out a curious asymmetry in each method. They ask, for example in the case of the postulational method, why certitude should be assumed more "objective" than incertitude. Why should certainty in the postulates be used to *certify* conclusions, to overcome incertitude in the propositions derived from them? Perhaps the process of deriving a problematic proposition from given propositions should *decertify* premises, render the given propositions problematic. Likewise, perhaps the process of deriving problematic entities from unproblematic ones should lead us to view the latter with suspicion. After all, *modus tollens* is no less cogent than *modus ponens*.

Many of the issues mentioned above continue to be studied and debated by mathematicians and philosophers. For whatever reason, the postulational method seems largely to have won out over the genetic method, which survives today almost exclusively in postulational guise, as motivating background for *constructional postulate systems*. The genetic method was pursued vigorously in America by mathematicians influenced by E.V. Huntington, who might have been the first American mathematician to use the expression "genetic method" in print. The postulational method was developed intensely and extensively in the first half of the 1900s by a group of American philosophers and mathematicians who came to be known as the

American Postulate Theorists. Perhaps the *locus classicus* for the postulational method in the United States is Huntington's accessible 1917 exposition *The Continuum*, which is still in print. Interestingly, although this book is focused on the postulational method, it contains several fascinating applications of the genetic method. Since the mid-1970s, recognition has begun to be accorded to the enormous contribution of the American Postulate Theorist group, which included such well-known figures as Alonzo Church, E.V. Huntington, C.H. Langford, C.I. Lewis, H.M. Sheffer, and Oswald Veblen, the first Professor at the Institute for Advanced Study and a friend of John Dewey.

Further reading

Dewey, J. *Democracy and Education*. New York: Macmillan, 1916.

Hilbert, D. *Foundations of Geometry*. LaSalle, IL: Open Court, 1899.

Huntington, E. *The Continuum*. Cambridge, MA: Harvard University Press, 1917; reprinted New York: Dover, 1955.

Kramer, E. *The Nature and Growth of Modern Mathematics*. New York: Hawthorn, 1970.

Scanlan, M. "Who were the American postulate theorists?" *The Journal of Symbolic Logic* 56 (1991): 981–1002.

Toeplitz, O. *The Calculus: A Genetic Approach*. Chicago, IL: University of Chicago Press, 1963.

JOHN CORCORAN

GENTEEL TRADITION

The term "genteel tradition," which has become common parlance in American cultural criticism, was originally coined by George Santayana (1862–1952) to refer to an American intellectual mentality inherited from Europe, specifically from Calvinism and German transcendental philosophy. The phrase originally appeared in "The Genteel Tradition in American Philosophy," which was delivered as an address to the Philosophical Union of the University of California at Berkeley on 25 August 1911. The essay was first published in the *University of California Chronicle* and was subsequently reprinted in a collection of Santayana's essays, *Winds of Doctrine: Studies in Contemporary Opinion* (1926). Santayana continued to comment on this strain in American culture in several of his critical essays.

Before departing permanently to live and travel in Europe, Santayana visited the west coast of the United States for the first and only time, spending the summer of 1911 teaching at the University of California at Berkeley. Here, Santayana took the opportunity to comment on the New England culture of his upbringing (where he had lived as a Spanish expatriate) and to contrast it with a new and developing uniquely American attitude. "The Genteel Tradition in American Philosophy" set about to critique the staleness of the inherited Calvinist philosophy, to herald the emergence of a new American one, and to offer its own perspective – removed from each of the previous two – on the relationship between the human spirit and the natural world.

The genteel tradition, as Santayana saw it, found its Calvinist roots in an "agonized conscience" that believes, "that sin exists, that sin is punished, and that it is beautiful that sin should exist to be punished," and so expressed the tension between a debased physical embodiment and a spiritual exaltation in the purity of the Absolute. This then combined with a transcendental focus on the mind as both the source and the object of all knowledge and produced an intellectual moralism suited to survival in physical hardship. However, this puritan outlook, initially beneficial, became ill adapted to the inhabitants of a spacious and bounteous new land, where a pioneer spirit – rugged, individualistic, and entrepreneurial – was consistently better rewarded. The spartan moralism of the genteel intellect and its alienation from physical life was at odds with a young, expanding country with a democratic and adventurous attitude. To contrast the traditional but outmoded way of life and the new one not yet fully articulated, Santayana offered a particularly memorable architectural metaphor: he identified the genteel tradition with a reproduction of a colonial mansion and the new mentality with a skyscraper. One housed the American intellect, the other epitomized the élan vital of the American will. The genteel tradition is further feminized as an idle backwater peculiar to the world of the American woman and contrasted with the teeming rapids of aggressiveness embodied in the American male.

Throughout the essay, Santayana discusses the legacy of these competing cultural strains to such noteworthy American writers as Ralph Waldo Emerson, Walt Whitman, and William James. In Emerson's transcendentalism, Santayana saw a genteel intellect adapting to the new individualism. The Calvinist tendency to shun the flesh and glorify the spirit became an invocation to view one's own singular consciousness as a conduit of divinity itself. Whitman, by contrast, represented a complete rejection of the genteel tradition in his radically democratic valorization of all experience. The problem with Whitman, according to Santayana, was that a rejection of the previous philosophy did not amount to the positive production of a new one. It was in William James that Santayana located the beginnings of an actual transformation of genteel thought into something uniquely American. Without simply rejecting the traditional attitudes, James's pragmatic philosophy reformed them by pluralizing religious experience and making truth a tool of doing business with the world.

At the close of his address to the Philosophical Union, Santayana articulated his own naturalistic position. Taking advantage of the majestic splendor of northern California's natural wonders, he offered his vision of a human spirit dwarfed by nature, which challenged the anthropocentrism of both the genteel mentality and the enterprising American sensibility. Santayana claimed that spirit, despite its material origins, was not at home in the physical world, but he disagreed that this gave reason to despise bodily instincts or to deify ideas, thus counteracting the genteel belief in a universe suited to one's rational and moral expectations. Furthermore, despite the promises of business, industry, and westward expansion, in the end nature would prevail over the ambitions of the human will. In short, Santayana argued that the spirit is transcended, not by the supernatural, but by nature itself, and it is to this transcendent power that we owe our piety.

After publishing "The Genteel Tradition in American Philosophy," Santayana continued to speak and write critical works on American culture and its genteel legacy, nine of which were compiled by Douglas L. Wilson and span twenty years of Santayana's writing. The final essay in this collection, "The Genteel Tradition at Bay" was first published in *The Saturday Review of Literature* as a critical review of an anti-modernist symposium, *Humanism and America*, and later found publication under the same title as a self-contained volume. In the three-part essay, Santayana fired his by then famous epithet at what he believed to be the self-described Humanists' reactionary and self-righteous intellectualism. The critique develops into a broad and incisive account of the transformations of European culture since the Middle Ages and ends once again by placing the issue in a natural context. Santayana's critique of the genteel tradition is, ultimately, a rejection of moral and intellectual absolutism through discovery of one's limited place in the natural world.

Further reading

Santayana, George. *Winds of Doctrine: Studies in Contemporary Opinion*. New York: Charles Scribner's Sons, 1926.

Wilson, Douglas L. (ed.) *The Genteel Tradition: Nine Essays by George Santayana*. Cambridge, MA: Harvard University Press, 1967.

JESSICA WAHMAN

GERMAN PHILOSOPHY, INFLUENCE OF

Although there are scattered references (as often as not unflattering by virtue of the alleged threat posed to religious orthodoxy) to Hegel (1770–1831) in American publications at least as early as the 1820s and to some others (e.g. David Strauss, 1806–74) soon thereafter, and although Ralph Waldo Emerson (1803–82) invoked the authority of Kant (1724–1804) for his appropriation of the term "Transcendental" as the name for his version of Idealism in an essay of 1842, it is above all with the publication of John B. Stallo's *General Principles of the Philosophy of Nature* in 1848 that historians identify the beginnings of a serious influence of German philosophy in the United States. Stallo (1823–1900) was one of a number of residents of Ohio, mostly Cincinnatians, who have come to be labeled "the Ohio Hegelians," their intellectual activities having predated those of the so-called "St Louis Hegelians" by nearly two decades.

Hegel loomed very large among mid-nineteenth-century American philosophers. A reading of Stallo's *General Principles*, best characterized as an expression of "evolutionary idealism," introduced Emerson to Hegel's thought and contributed to Emerson's later characterizations of the Absolute as the union of the Ideal and the Real and of liberty as the self-realization of spirit. (Many of Emerson's key ideas, especially those concerning fate, history, nature, the search after power, and the exceptional individual, were to be reciprocally formative influences on the thought of the German philosopher, Friedrich Nietzsche (1844–1900), who regarded Emerson as his "soul-brother" and only regretted that his incomparably rich thought had been somewhat "clouded" by other German philosophy.) Within the so-called "Kant Club," a subsection of the St Louis Philosophical Society that was founded during the immediate post-Civil War years, Henry Conrad Brokmeyer (1826–1906), a refugee from the 1848 revolution in Germany, worked with his colleagues, William Torrey Harris (1835–1909) and Denton J. Snider (1841–1925), to translate Hegel's *Phenomenology*. They also established a revue, *The Journal of Speculative Philosophy*, as an outlet for their own work and that of like-minded thinkers; it endured for twenty-six years, with Harris serving as editor throughout this time, and published essays by Emerson, William James, John Dewey, and C.S. Peirce, among others. Hegel as filtered through his early American interpreters often came to be seen not only as the master synthesizer of all of reality through the power of the dialectic, but also as implicitly justifying "New World democracy in the creative realms of time and space," as Walt Whitman (1819–92) once put it in an extraordinarily eulogistic essay – while expressing wonder that this intellectual gift should have come from Germany, or indeed from anywhere in the old world.

But other, quite different strands of German thought soon began to exert influence in the New World as well. Stallo's own later evolution was in the direction of an anti-mechanistic philosophy of science (even if this term itself was not in use at the time), expounded in his book *The Concepts and Theories of Modern Physics*, published in 1881, that found favor with Ernst Mach (1838–1916) back in the "old world." Later in the same decade another German immigrant, Paul Carus (1852–1919), who had received a PhD from Tübingen and taught in Dresden before leaving Germany because of censure of his religious views, came to the United States and became editor of a new professional journal, *The Monist*, that was to serve as a vehicle for the generation of philosophers – Dewey, Peirce, the Englishman Bertrand Russell, and others – who were then just beginning to make their marks. Carus' metaphysical realism, equally opposed to the neo-Kantians' insistence on the mental basis of scientific laws and to materialism, ran afoul of V.I. Lenin, in the latter's notorious, primarily anti-Machian diatribe, *Materialism and Empiriocritism*, where he called Carus "a leader of a gang of American literary fakers who are engaged in doping the people with religious opium." This is one small but clear piece of evidence that German-influenced American philosophy was beginning to achieve international recognition, including recognition back in Germany, by the early years of the twentieth century.

First pragmatists

One of the first American philosophers to achieve a truly international reputation was William James (1842–1910). His father, Henry James, Sr, had studied in Germany and had become a devotee of the mystical eighteenth-century Swedish scientist/theologian/philosopher Emanuel Swedenborg. William James went to Germany in 1867, in part for health reasons, and spent some months there. James's own attitude toward the philosophy of Hegel was most famously expressed in his article "On Some Hegelisms," first published in the British journal *Mind* in 1882. It begins with the observation that, at the very time at which Hegel's thought is attracting enormous attention in Great Britain and the United States, there may be only a single member of the younger generation of German philosophers who is interested in it, and it ends with a long footnote in which James wittily compares some notes that he made while having deliberately put himself under the influence of nitrous oxide to Hegel's alleged obsession with reconciliation and togetherness, which James accuses him of having pursued unscrupulously in the interest of his own self-gratification. Nevertheless, Hegel's influence on James was not quite so thoroughly negative as this might lead one to believe, and indeed the main text itself shows James taking both Hegel and his American followers quite seriously.

On the other hand, while James was himself far less obsessed with Kant than with Hegel, it is a commonplace that a text attributed to the French neo-Kantian Charles Renouvier (1815–1903), *Essais de Critique Générale*, had a crucial impact on James's life, leading to his overcoming an emotional crisis (in 1870) and to getting on with his eventually highly productive career. ("Attributed" is the appropriate word because the book's chapter on free will, which had the greatest impact on James, had in fact been composed by Jules Lequier (1814–62), Renouvier's deceased former classmate – as Renouvier was honest enough to inform James.) Renouvier's move in the direction of relativizing the Kantian categories, very influential in the France of his day, can be seen, at least schematically and in retrospect, as pointing in the direction of pragmatism.

The evolution of the thought of another American philosopher of the same era who has been identified with pragmatism (even if the term itself was popularized by James and eventually repudiated by his contemporary), Charles Sanders Peirce (1839–1914), resembles in some general respects Renouvier's philosophical development. Peirce began his philosophical career as a sort of neo-Kantian who wished to combine Kant's Transcendental Analytic with an idealism derived from Plato rather than from Hegel. Peirce's important paper of 1867, "On a New List of Categories," took as its starting-point Kant's view that there is knowledge when the manifold has been reduced to a unity in a proposition, and proceeded to argue that the mind can recognize a proposition as standing for, or representing, given objects only through the medium of signs, or the sign relationship. This new emphasis gradually led

Peirce in directions, particularly in the areas of logic and the philosophy of mathematics, for which Kant no longer served as much of a guide – although the Kantian insight that synthesis involves triadicity continued to have important resonances in the various stages of Peirce's later, highly original systematic thinking. At the same time the work of another German thinker, Georg Cantor, in set theory strongly influenced Peirce's own research and writing on the foundations of mathematics.

Other Harvard connections

Yet another contemporary of James and Peirce whose philosophical directions were strongly conditioned by German thought was Josiah Royce (1855–1916). Although he received his doctorate in 1878 from Johns Hopkins University, where Peirce was to hold his only (relatively) long-term teaching appointment for five years beginning the following year, Royce had also studied in Leipzig and Göttingen. As the American standard-bearer of a philosophy of absolute idealism (he himself favored the terms "absolute voluntarism" or "absolute pragmatism"), Royce self-consciously developed a sympathetic but critical stance toward Kant, according a far more central place than Kant did to God, considered as Absolute Knower, on the side of metaphysics and epistemology, and a priority to "loyalty" over Kant's categorical imperative on the side of ethics. Not surprisingly, he also found much in common with Hegel, while stressing a more Kantian view of the will against the latter. Royce occupied a position in the Harvard Philosophy Department for more than three decades, until his death, sharing its limelight with James until the latter's decease in 1910.

One of Royce's early doctoral students at Harvard was George Santayana (1863–1952), who was born in Spain but grew up in the Boston area. Between college and graduate school Santayana studied for two years in Germany, and his subsequent PhD thesis dealt with the German philosopher of feeling, Rudolf Hermann Lotze (1817–81), whose lectures Santayana's *Doktorvater* had attended in Göttingen. Both Lotze and Santayana were, each in his own way, rather idiosyncratic thinkers to whom it is not easy to assign standard labels such as "idealism" or "pragmatism," and Santayana tended to polemicize against the entire mainstream tradition of modern Western philosophy. Nevertheless, Santayana himself acknowledged that his most important early work, *The Life of Reason; or, the Phases of Human Progress*, was influenced by Hegel's *Phenomenology*, and it is not difficult to detect the Lotzean influence in, to take just one salient example, Santayana's treatment of religious piety.

Santayana stayed on at Harvard as a Philosophy Department faculty member until his early retirement in 1912. Among his early graduate students, one who was to become especially illustrious, although eventually more for his work in history and psychology than in philosophy, was W.E.B. DuBois (1868–1963), the author of *The Souls of Black Folk*. DuBois also worked with James and Royce before spending two years (1892–4) in Berlin, where economic history became his principal focus. In a preface written for an edition of this work that was published more than fifty years after the original, DuBois acknowledges these three Harvard professors in the context of their having helped him to anticipate the Freudian revolution in psychology, but regrets not having been sufficiently aware, in 1903, of the importance of Marx, even though, as he puts it, Marx "was mentioned at Harvard and taken into account in Berlin." Thus we can observe the beginnings of the influence of yet another strand of German philosophy on a nascent strand of American philosophy, African-American thought.

Certainly the best-known African-American philosopher of the first half of the twentieth century who continued to work as a professional philosopher was Alain Locke (1886–1954), whose name is also closely associated with the movement known as the Harlem Renaissance. After distinguishing himself as an undergraduate at Harvard, he was awarded a Rhodes Scholarship for three years at Oxford, and then spent a year studying in Berlin shortly before the outbreak of the First World War. The studies in value theory that he undertook there with Hugo Münsterberg (1863–1916), whom he had already encountered at Harvard – Münsterberg was a frequent transatlantic shuttler – and in theories of culture with the well-known sociologist Georg Simmel (1858–1918) were to prove especially significant for his future career development. Soon after beginning his teaching career at Howard University, an appointment that would continue for most of the remainder of his life, he returned to Harvard for a two-year period (1916–18) to complete his Doctoral thesis, developing a highly original open-ended theory of values that owes much to his training in German thought.

Dewey and Hook

Among the few well-known American philosophers who were, loosely speaking, contemporaries of DuBois, Locke, and others previously mentioned but who never had a close connection with Harvard was John Dewey (1859–1952). He was also one of the few who did not spend any portion of his youth studying philosophy in Germany. But it would be quite incorrect to conclude from these facts that Dewey was immune to the influence of German philosophy; quite the contrary. His early infatuation with Hegel's thought, which continued throughout his life to affect his evolving pragmatist style of thinking about the fluid nature of truth and reality, began during his undergraduate years at the University of Vermont. Later, his Johns Hopkins PhD dissertation, completed in 1884, dealt with the psychology of Kant. Still later, he was to find himself critically engaged, at numerous points in his exceptionally long career, with that other German philosopher with whom DuBois, like so many other American thinkers, found it necessary increasingly to reckon as the twentieth century wore on, Karl Marx (1818–83).

Dewey refers to Marx at least as early as his 1898 *Lectures on Psychological and Political Ethics*, in the context of his perception that economic theorists are feeling an ever-increasing need to find a standard of value. Dewey characterizes Marx's "quasi-mathematical" solution as inadequate, while not conveying Marx's terminology with complete accuracy. This tendency to inaccuracy was to persist through much of Dewey's decades-long polemicizing with Marx, some of the most extensive examples of which occur in *Freedom and Culture* (1939). It is also clear, however, that Dewey saw Marx as an antidote, albeit a partly wrongheaded one, to the excessive individualism against which he himself also inveighed. And he famously became involved with the practical outcome of one of the policies of the Soviet regime, which presented itself as the heir of Marx, when he chaired the international commission that met in Mexico in 1937 to investigate that regime's charges against Leon Trotsky. (The charges were adjudged baseless; Trotsky was assassinated three years later by Soviet agents.)

But if Dewey himself never quite came fully to terms with Marx on the basis of a clear understanding of his thought, the same can certainly not be said of one of his most famous Doctoral students, Sidney Hook (1902–89), who also became a lifetime friend of Dewey's. Hook in his early years was a political activist, at first collaborating with the American Communist Party and then aligning himself, politically if not philosophically, with the Trotskyite left opposition to it. Continuing the tradition of travel to Germany that has been traced in this article, Hook spent a year in Munich (1928–9) on a Guggenheim grant and also became one of the first Americans to visit the Marx–Engels Institute in Moscow. His ensuing work, *From Hegel to Marx*, did much to acquaint American readers both with the story of that intellectual voyage through the time of the so-called "Young Hegelians" and with the core ideas of Marx's philosophy mostly undistorted through Soviet lenses. At the same time, in much of his early work Hook tended to emphasize common points between Marxism and pragmatism. (His thesis, as published, had the intentionally ironic title, *The Metaphysics of Pragmatism*.) Although he had been quite aware of the dangerous tendencies in German politics that were to lead to the triumph of Nazism, he found that political scene highly stimulating during his grant year.

In an important sense, political events have certainly had a major impact on the history of the influence of German thought on American philosophy, and Sidney Hook's own later conversion into a fierce mid-twentieth-century "Cold Warrior" and rabid anti-Communist is an outstanding example of this. As was noted earlier, some of the nineteenth-century figures who disseminated German, especially Hegelian and neo-Hegelian, ideas in the United States were refugees from the religious wars and class wars and wars *tout court* that had taken place in their original homeland. (One of those not previously mentioned, August Willich (1810–78), who was the foster-son of the German philosopher/theologian Friedrich Schleiermacher, had actually sparred with Marx over tactics – Marx being more the intellectual, Willich more the activist – while both were members of the Communist League in London in the early 1850s.) The wave of intense anti-German feeling that was generated by President Wilson's decision to enter World War I on the side of the British and French undoubtedly caused a lessening of German, particularly Hegelian, influence in philosophy at the time and during the immediate post-war period. (Anecdotes abound of the removal of German books and courses from schools and of widespread intimidation of individuals who attempted to converse in German in public. Royce evinced extreme hostility toward Germany in a book published just before his death, *The Hope of the Great Community*. The title of Santayana's monograph of the time, *Egotism in German Philosophy*, speaks for itself, although he was later to maintain that similar tendencies exist in other philosophical cultures as well. And Dewey, though more restrained in his short book, *German Philosophy and Politics*, and in his essay "On Understanding the Mind of Germany," than either Royce or Santayana, nevertheless wrote a very positive review of the latter's diatribe.) But remarkably enough, as we have already begun to see, this diminution of influence was far from total or permanent. The same must be said concerning the half-century just completed, the next post-war period, despite Hitler and all the horrors that his name evokes.

Twentieth-century refugee intellectuals

A huge new wave of refugee intellectuals from Germany and Austria, most but not all of them Jewish, came to the United States beginning in the mid-1930s and exerted influence along a number of quite diverse philosophical lines. A small and far from exhaustive sample includes such names as Hans Kelsen (1881–1973), Paul Tillich (1886–1965), Rudolf Carnap (1891–1970), Hannah Arendt (1906–75), Alfred Schutz (1899–1959), and Herbert Marcuse (1898–1979). Of these, probably the least influential – to the extent to which such matters can be quantified – was Kelsen, whose legal positivist theory combined with his concern for international law had made him a giant in the relevant European intellectual milieux, but who later lived and taught (in the Political Science Department and Law Faculty of the University of California at Berkeley) somewhat in isolation from the American philosophical community, even from many specialists in the philosophy of law. Tillich's impact was greater on theology than on philosophy in America, but his thought, heavily influenced by Kierkegaard (and some later existentialists) while endorsing a conception of faith as that which deals with what is of Ultimate Concern that necessarily downplays the priority accorded to Christianity by the Dane, cut across disciplinary lines and attracted many philosophical admirers as well as strong detractors.

Like Kelsen and more than Tillich, Carnap had already established a major reputation in Europe before migrating to the New World (in 1935). A member of the so-called "Vienna Circle" of philosophers, with whom Kelsen also had connections, Carnap in his writings epitomized the philosophical stance of hostility toward metaphysics and of corresponding friendliness toward natural science that characterized most members of that Circle (eventually organized under the name Verein Ernst Mach) and that came to be known by the name of logical positivism or logical empiricism. The impression made on this group by the early work of the Viennese-born Ludwig Wittgenstein (1889–1951), his *Tractatus Logico-philosophicus*, was enormous, although he himself met with some of its members only occasionally, and never held a university teaching position on the Continent or in America, but only in England. Carnap was a professor first at the University of Chicago and later at the University of California at Los Angeles, where he replaced his prematurely deceased former co-editor of the journal *Erkenntnis* and fellow refugee (from Berlin), Hans Reichenbach (1891–1953). In addition to this role as a professor in America, Carnap's early influence on one of the best-known American philosophers of the mid-to late twentieth century, Willard Van Orman Quine (1908–2000), whom he first met when Quine was visiting Prague, was considerable, and they carried on an extensive and amicable correspondence. A number of other former Vienna Circle participants eventually also made considerable contributions to American academic philosophy – among them Herbert Feigl (1902–88), Gustav Bergmann (1906–87), and Carl Gustav Hempel (1905–98). Nevertheless, it seems fair to say that it is Wittgenstein, more than any single one of the others, whose name and philosophical ideas – both his early logical atomism and his later, radically different insistence on the dominant role of language in shaping and often "bewitching" our intelligence – have exerted the greater influence on American philosophy and philosophers. Indeed, his may well have been the greatest such influence of all twentieth-century German and Austrian thinkers. (I am assuming that the idea, attractive to some but very difficult to defend in detail, of a deep German/Austrian philosophical divide is ultimately untenable.) At the same time, however, the significance of this assertion is somewhat mitigated by the fact that Wittgenstein's New World influence was in large measure filtered through Great Britain.

It would be inappropriate to consign Hannah Arendt to any easily identifiable philosophical "school" or "movement." True, she was an early student of Martin Heidegger (1889–1976) and continued to refer to his philosophical work, as well as to the thought – more congenial to her – of Karl Jaspers (1883–1969), in many of her own writings, thus implying some affinity with "existentialism," broadly understood, as well as with phenomenology. But Arendt as a philosopher was truly *sui generis*, and her influence as a political philosopher and moralist with an admiration for the life of the ancient Greeks and a very jaundiced view of contemporary society, as well as both a product and a portrayer (the latter especially in her biography of Rahel Varnhagen) of German Jewish culture and a witness to its destruction by the Nazi movement to which Heidegger himself had been drawn, is widespread and has been steadily rising since the time of her death. Although she was also affiliated with the University of Chicago, much of her life after her arrival in the United States in 1941 was spent in New York City, where she eventually joined the New School for Social Research's Graduate Faculty, an institution that from its outset in the early 1930s included a number of German Jewish refugee professors.

Schutz, who was unique in also holding another full-time, non-academic position (with a bank), became associated with the New School shortly after he reached New York and from there did much, through his students and his writings, to propagate the ideas of Edmund Husserl's phenomenology in the United States, while extending them especially to the social world, about which Husserl himself (1859–1938) had written little until near the end of his life. In the process of introducing phenomenology to America, Schutz was abetted by an American professor who had studied with Husserl in Freiburg in the early 1920s and had written a Harvard dissertation on "Phenomenology as a Method and as a Philosophical Discipline" in 1928, Marvin Farber (1901–80). The two collaborated with others in establishing the journal *Philosophy and Phenomenological Research*, which Farber edited for many years, maintaining a strong personal loyalty toward his former master, Husserl, while in fact nudging the journal in very different philosophical directions and himself harboring a deep commitment, not fully revealed until a posthumous publication, to Marxism–Leninism.

Some reciprocal influences in the past half-century

But perhaps the most strenuous individual effort to promote, not so much the phenomenology of Husserl, but rather existential phenomenology, or in general "Continental [meaning Continental European] Philosophy" as this broad set of philosophical approaches and their successors have come to be called, was that of John Wild (1902–72). Wild, who spent more than half of his adult life at Harvard, initially professing a traditional metaphysical realism with strong roots in Aristotle, had studied with Heidegger at Freiburg in the early 1930s and was inspired by an extended visit to Europe in 1958 to initiate a sort of "crusade" on behalf of the then-dominant European philosophies as a counterbalance to the "analytic" thinking which had by that time achieved hegemony within his own department. He left Harvard in 1960 and, during the two years that he spent at Northwestern University before moving on to Yale – considered at the time to be more congenial to widely diverse philosophical interests than Harvard – was the driving force behind the establishment of the Society for Phenomenology and Existential Philosophy, the membership of which had by the end of the century become the largest of any professional philosophical organization in the United States besides the American Philosophical Association itself. It is interesting to note that the last book of his to be published during his lifetime was a work on William James.

Through an apparently strange chronological inversion that is explainable in part, once again, by the convergence of certain philosophical trends with political events, the time of greatest influence of the last of the German émigré philosophers listed earlier, Herbert Marcuse, occurred after his retirement from Brandeis University in the mid-1960s. (He went on to teach post-retirement at the University of California at San Diego.) Marcuse had been a prominent member of the so-called "Frankfurt School" (now known more commonly as the "First Frankfurt School") of "Western Marxist" philosophers, disaffected from and unaffiliated with the international Communist Party, before the Second World War. The Institute of Social Research, as it was officially known, re-established its offices at Columbia University during the wartime period. Among other well-known Frankfurt *Schülers* who settled at least for a time in America were the social theorists Theodor Adorno (1903–69), lead author of the ground-breaking cross-cultural sociological study *The Authoritarian Personality*, and Max Horkheimer (1895–1973), who both eventually returned to Germany, and Wilhelm Reich (1897–1957), whose eccentric psychiatric and sexual ideas led to his persecution first by journalists and then by the Federal Government, and who died in prison. Reich's was in fact only the most extreme example of government persecution of immigrant German philosophers – and a somewhat unusual one, since he did not share the left-wing political views that, for example, provoked FBI investigations of Carnap and of a number of other German-born philosophers of science during the McCarthy Era, led to warnings by Sidney Hook against "suspicious activities" that might evoke charges of disloyalty, and apparently caused Marcuse to refrain from any reference to Marx (despite his obvious Marxian orientation) in his radical critique of

Freud, *Eros and Civilization*, which was published in the mid-1950s. By an irony of history, it was above all the anti-Establishment hostility to the war against Vietnam that led to the later apotheosis of Marcuse, by then best known for his work of social criticism, *One-Dimensional Man*, when he came, somewhat serendipitously, to be regarded as the guiding spirit behind the French "Student Revolt" of 1968. This event had reverberations in many other countries as well, including the United States and Germany.

Among philosophers, the type of politically engaged theorizing epitomized by Marcuse's work has come to be known as "Critical Theory." By far the best-known member of the "Second Frankfurt School" of Critical Theorists is Jürgen Habermas (1929–). Habermas has made frequent visits to the United States and taught in this country and has dealt in his writings with numerous contemporary American social and political philosophers, most notably John Rawls (1921–2002). Meanwhile, a well-known colleague of Habermas', Karl-Otto Apel (1922–), has done much to heighten awareness of and interest in American philosophy, in particular the thought of C.S. Peirce, in Germany. At the same time Rawls himself, beginning with his *magnum opus*, *A Theory of Justice*, and even more fully in some of his later work, came increasingly to identify his own project, on the side of ethics, with the Kantian tradition. Thus, as the twentieth century ended and the new one began to take shape, the long-standing tradition of influence, not just one-sided but truly reciprocal and mutual, between German and American philosophy continued.

Further reading

Easton, Loyd D. *Hegel's First American Followers*. Athens, OH: Ohio University Press, 1966.

Flower, Elizabeth and Murphey, Murray G. *A History of Philosophy in America*. New York: Capricorn Books, 1977.

Hardcastle, Gary L. and Richardson, Alan W. (eds) *Logical Empiricism in North America*. Minneapolis/London: University of Minnesota Press, 2003.

Phelps, Christopher. *Young Sidney Hook: Marxist and Pragmatist*. Ithaca, NY: Cornell University Press, 1977.

Reisch, George A. *How the Cold War Transformed Philosophy of Science: To the Icy Slopes of Logic*. Cambridge: Cambridge University Press, 2005.

Schneider, Herbert W. *A History of American Philosophy*. New York: Columbia University Press, 1946.

Young-Bruehl, Elisabeth. *Hannah Arendt: For Love of the World*. New Haven, CT and London: Yale University Press, 1982.

WILLIAM L. MCBRIDE

GESTURE

The role of gesture is central to the philosophy of pragmatism, especially for George Herbert Mead and John Dewey. Mead developed his famous "conversation of gestures," with influence from Dewey; and Dewey's "The Theory of Emotion. (I). Emotional Attitudes" was done in collaboration with Mead. In addition, Mead's 1895 paper, "A Theory of Emotion from the Physiological Standpoint" is an extension of Dewey's ideas on physiological psychology, and the arguments presented in Dewey's "The Theory of Emotion (I) Attitudes" form a very large part of Mead's analysis of the conversation of gesture.

For Mead, the connection between gesture and act is paramount. Gestures are the beginnings of acts and as such reveal the probable future phases of the act. Gestures anticipate what is to follow and thus serve as means of eliciting response even before there is awareness of meaning. A gesture represents a tendency or attitude of an organism, and a "conversation of gestures" consists in the continued readjustment of one individual to another. Non-significant gestures have meanings and are signs in that they mean the later stages of the act, but their function does not include an awareness or consciousness of their meanings. In the process of becoming aware of meanings, the biological organism is transformed into the minded organism and the self; non-significant gestures become significant symbols, meanings "in mind," ingredients in conscious communications; the conversation of gestures becomes conversation of meanings. Through meaning, gesture opens upon a community. Language is a gesture that is conscious and significant. The logical structure of meaning is found in the triadic relationship of gesture to adjustment response and to the resultant of the social act which the gesture initiates. While the conversation of gesture does not necessarily involve consciousness of meaning, language emerges out of gesture when consciousness of meaning attaches to the gesture. Language, as a social process that grows out of gesture and includes awareness of meaning, is broader than speech, for it includes sign language, as, for instance, the gestures made by little children before they can utilize articulate speech. These are significant gestures. For Mead, language, thought, and action are inseparably intertwined in the ongoing social act constituted by the "conversation of gestures." A treatment of speech as a type of gesture reveals the implications of speech in relation to body and to world. Within this context of meaningful human behavior, including the relation between speech and gesture, the nature of the connection between gesture and its meaning is revealed. The gesture, as a bodily and behavioral expression, manifests its meanings immediately so that, for example a gesture of anger does not make one think of anger, but, rather, is anger itself. This understanding is made possible by the commonly shared and intersubjective world. Humans fail to comprehend well the gestures of animals or even of primitive people because there must be some coincidence "with the inner possibilities" and some meaningful communal background or world for a gesture to be experienced as meaningful. It is against this commonness of background that an originary gesture fits and can be understood and interpreted.

Further reading

Dewey, John. "The Theory of Emotion. (I) Emotional Attitudes," *Psychological Review* 1 (1894): 553–69.

Mead, George Herbert. "A Theory of Emotions from the Physiological Standpoint," *Psychological Review* (1895): 162–4.

—— *Mind, Self, and Society*, ed. C.W. Morris. Chicago, IL: University of Chicago, 1934.

Rosenthal, Sandra B. and Bourgeois, Patrick L. *Mead and Merleau-Ponty: Toward a Common Vision*. Albany, NY: SUNY Press, 1991.

PATRICK L. BOURGEOIS

GIVEN

A proposition (p) is given for a subject (S) at a time (t) when S does not have to have or give reasons at t for holding that p is true. Propositions can have this status on the basis of their pragmatic or epistemic status.

A proposition p may be *pragmatically given* for S at t when p is either a reasonable assumption or is something not under scrutiny in S's current deliberations and reasoning regarding some other proposition (q). S, in introducing p as a premise or relevant detail in her case for or against q, may utter something along the lines, "Given that p," or "If we can assume that p," or "We don't have any objections to p, here, do we?" The crucial feature of pragmatically given propositions is that they do not have any *positive* evidence on their side, but that they occupy the default attitude in the deliberations at t. Propositions may occupy this position if they are either shared commitments between two discussants or dominant options in the circumstances. Commitments are shared between two discussants if the commitments are ones the discussants would assent to in the circumstances. As a consequence, such overlappings of assent is a source of premises for arguments which may resolve disagreements. A proposition is a dominant option in a situation if it is the safest bet or the most lucrative choice given the values and risks at stake with the options available. For example, in mountain climbing, the costs of failing to tie in one's rope are high enough to justify checking one's rope again – one must always assume that one is not tied in. Importantly, circumstances may change so that S's interlocutor may change her mind and no longer assent to p (and so it is no longer a shared commitment) or the circumstances change so that some danger passes (and so p may no longer be a dominant option). As a consequence, at this later time, p may not be a given, and S must have or give reasons then for holding that p.

A proposition p may be *epistemically given* for S at t when S has epistemic justification for holding that p is true, but S does not require further reasons for p's truth. One version of the view is that one's experiences furnish unique and independent reasons for believing. For example, if S were to look at a stop sign in good light at t, S would see something red. That S is experiencing a red sensation at t (or perhaps, experiencing redly) is not something our subject would have to give further reasons for believing. S would only need to direct her attention to her experiences, and if she is aware of such a sensation, she is justified in believing that she is experiencing it. Experiences are *given* to subjects, in that they are immediate constituents of consciousness, and propositions about these states are justified when subjects are directly aware of their being the case.

Both conditions for givenness have been criticized within American philosophy. Pragmatic givens, it is regularly noted, are often confused with truths of a different kind, such that their status is taken to be revelatory of basic (or necessary) structures of reality, instead of revelatory of the current dialectical situation. The correctives to taking pragmatic givens as more than dialectical are those of contextualism, historicism, and pluralism, as found in the works of John Dewey, Nicholas Rescher, and Joseph Margolis respectively. Epistemic givens have been rejected on the basis of a suspicion of direct epistemic support. In light of this suspicion, Wilfrid Sellars terms the view, "the myth of the given." Philosophical programs corrective of the commitment to epistemic givens are those of anti-foundationalism, constructivism, and inferentialism, as found in the works of Richard Rorty, Thomas Rockmore, and Robert Brandom respectively.

Further reading

Brandom, Robert. *Making It Explicit*. Cambridge, MA: Harvard University Press, 1994.

Margolis, Joseph. *Reinventing Pragmatism: American Philosophy at the End of the Twentieth Century*. Ithaca, NY: Cornell University Press, 2002.

Rescher, Nicholas. *A System of Pragmatic Idealism*. Princeton, NJ: Princeton University Press, 1994.

Rockmore, Tom. *On Constructivist Epistemology*. Lanham, MD: Rowman and Littlefield, 2005.

SCOTT FORREST AIKINZ

GOD

The focus of this entry will be how the most influential American philosophers, especially those whose philosophy has been considered, rightly or wrongly, to be expressive of the America of its day (which doesn't entail that it was unique to America) employed the concept of God. These philosophers are primarily William James and John Dewey. An unfortunate consequence of this limitation is that the brilliant work that was done in the last forty years by American analytical theists, primarily William Alston and Alvin Plantinga, will be left out because they were concerned with the God of traditional Western theism, and there is nothing especially "American" about this. They could have been writing in the Middle Ages. The most important distinction between philosophies is whether or not they take the really real to be temporal. The philosophies of James and Dewey are through and through temporalistic, even their God being temporal, which helped to prepare the way for the process theology of Alfred North Whitehead and Charles Hartshorne. In stark contrast to these temporalists was Josiah Royce's conception of God as an all-knowing, timeless Absolute.

William James

William James's philosophy is a mixture of pragmatism and mysticism and thus presents us with two Gods, one being the melioristic God of pragmatism and the other a supernatural God of mysticism. Each will be discussed in turn and then a suggestion will be made as to how they can be unified.

The melioristic God of pragmatism is a blue-collar God who is our co-worker in the struggle to make good win out over evil in the long run. In the 1897 "The Will to Believe," James claims that one of the common denominators of religions is the belief "that the best things are ... the things in the universe that throw the last stone." But good will not win out over evil in the long run unless we collectively lead the morally strenuous life. Thus, this common denominator really is the conditional prediction that if we collectively exert our best moral effort, then good will win out over evil in the long run. This sets up a will to believe option, since by believing this conditional we psych ourselves up to make its antecedent true, thereby *helping* to make its desirable consequent true. But it isn't completely up to us whether it becomes true. We need the cooperative support of active forces in the world that are making for good. These forces are God and thus God is finite and processual. As James puts it, God is "but one helper ... in the midst of all the shapers of the great world's fate."

In the 1907 *Pragmatism*, it is James's purpose to show that his pragmatic theory of meaning, according to which the meaning of an idea or belief is a set of conditionalized predictions describing what will happen if we do certain things, can enable us to actualize our many different selves, in particular, our tough-minded self that wants to pursue science as well as our tender-minded self that wants to be religious and lead the morally strenuous life. The religion that he advocates as satisfying this pragmatic theory of meaning is the melioristic one from the earlier "The Will to Believe." When James is promoting his melioristic religion, he does not speculate about the nature of these friendly forces. This is accomplished in 1902 *The Varieties of Religious Experience*, whose message is that the essence, the life-blood of religion is found in religious experience, mainly of a mystical sort in which the subject becomes unified, wholly or partially, with an enveloping spiritual reality.

A metaphysical theory about the nature of this reality is called an "over belief." According to James's over belief the object of a veridical mystical experience is an enveloping supersensible mother-sea of consciousness, of which there might be and probably are many, thereby opening the door for polytheism. The enveloping individual is not the eternal one of monistic mysticism or Royce's Absolute since it has goals and uses the enveloped individual in realizing them. The monistic over belief fails to allow for free will and the reality of evil. The mother-sea of consciousness also is pressed into service in explaining a wide range of paranormal phenomena, such as automatic writing and mediumistic trances. While pursuing the mystical way, our active self, the one that meliorism is concerned with, must be overcome, as mystics have always claimed. But there is no clash here, for our active selves should not be denied some mystical R and R if it enables them to return to the war zone better equipped to do battle with the forces of evil.

Like James, Charles Sanders Peirce, also grounded our belief in God in experience, but not in the sort of mystical experiences that were central to James's account. He believed that religious belief was a sentiment-based common-sense certainty. This formed the basis of his "Neglected Argument" for God's existence. The argument begins by inviting us to the "refreshing" intellectual activity of "pure play" or "musement," in which we reflect on the order, design, and beauty of the world. This musing "will inevitably suggest the hypothesis of God's reality." This argument reeks with parochialism, since how one responds to such musement is based on how they have been acculturated, thereby qualifying this "Neglected Argument" as eminently worthy of neglect.

John Dewey

Dewey's conception of God evolved over a long career but only his most mature view, which is presented in the 1934 *A Common Faith*, will be considered. Like James, Dewey gives an account of God that undercuts the importance of traditional religious institutions, with their creedal beliefs in a supernatural being in whom are already realized all of the things that we prize and cherish. Each had his own special beef with such religions, James because of their "spirit of corporate dominion and dogmatic dominion" that have led to all sorts of horrible evils, Dewey because they were a block to the effective application of scientific-type inquiry to the problems of men in society. James and Dewey accomplished this undercutting by giving pride of place, respectively, to mystical experience and to "religious attitude," which is "'morality touched by emotion' only when the ends of moral conviction arouse emotions that are not only intense but are actuated and supported by ends so inclusive that they unify the self." Each individual must imaginatively project such an all inclusive, self-integrating project for herself. Dewey emphasizes that this ideal of a fully integrated self is crucially different from the absolute idealist's sense in that, unlike the latter, it is not an already established actuality but only a mere possibility. James makes a similar point in his insistence that the projected ideal state in which good has triumphed over evil is a mere possibility and needs our collective active efforts to become actualized.

To deepen our understanding of Dewey's God a number of objections will be considered along with possible responses. John Herman Randall has objected that there is an uncharacteristic reliance in *A Common Faith* on the personal, on achieving full integration of one's self that goes too far in the direction of the absolute idealist's Ideal Self, as espoused by T.H. Green. Randall suggests that it would better if Dewey had taken the religious not as adjectival upon experience but as an adverbial modification of acting overtly and publicly in communication with others. Dewey's response would be that one can achieve self-unification only by achieving unification with her fellow creatures and nature. Our ideal ends "assume concrete form in our understanding of our relations to one another." The self, furthermore, achieves unification only in and through its achieving unification with that "mysterious totality of being the imagination calls the 'universe'," because the self's project requires a cooperative natural environment.

There are a number of objections based on the highly revisionary nature of Dewey's account of God as a projected set of self-unifying ends. That an analysis is revisionary is not alone sufficient grounds for rejecting it, since it can be a well-motivated and justified revision, Dewey's justification being a broadly moral one. It could be objected that Dewey's "God" is radically polytheistic, since each person has her own projected ideal self that continually gets replaced with a new ideal self as she grows in self-integration. Furthermore, Dewey's God is only an imaginative projection of our minds and thus enjoys, or should we rather say, suffers from a second-class sort of existence, being a mere intentional object, not a subject in its own right.

If Dewey's account of God was confined to the imaginative projective one, this objection would be devastating. But Dewey says other things about God that make him into something more than a mere imaginative projection. Dewey also defines "God" as the ongoing active process of "uniting . . . the ideal and actual." This imputes some sort of objective existence to God, for nonexistent beings are notoriously powerless. God turns out to be those "natural force and conditions – including man and human association – that promote the growth of the ideal and that further its realization." These cooperative forces can be identified with the "stable," as contracted with "precarious," aspects of the world that are articulated in Dewey's *Experience and Nature.* This brings him quite close to James but with one exception. The Jamesian God who is working for the realization of good is a supernatural spiritual being whereas Dewey's God is just those forces within nature that are supportive of growth. James felt justified in introducing such a God, since he took mystical experiences, understood as apparent nonsensory perceptions of God, as constituting evidence, at least for mystics, for his existence. Dewey, on the other hand, although extolling the emotional benefits of mystical experiences, denied that they were cognitive because there are no objective tests for their veridicality and mystics disagree among themselves about the nature of the object of these experiences.

Process theology

The processual God of James and Dewey finds an elaborate development in the writings of Whitehead and Hartshorne. Since Hartshorne has worked out this idea in a deeper and more satisfying way only his views will be considered. Everything that is actual, including God, is a spiritual process, though not necessarily a conscious one, in which one's past is carried over into the present. The future, however, in virtue of being undetermined, is not yet real. This form of panpsychism is combined with the doctrine of "panentheism" in which everything is in God in the sense that God is aware of the past and present inner lives of everything, thereby allowing them to achieve a second-class kind of immortality through being remembered throughout an infinite future by God. In spite of being in God, they do not lose their own identity as centers of free, creative activity.

Hartshorne gives an agglomerative argument for the existence of God that combines the premises of the cosmological, teleological, and ontological arguments. He develops a modal version of the latter, similar to the versions subsequently given by Plantinga and Malcolm, that requires of a being than which a greater cannot be conceived that it have necessary existence rather than just plain old existence; otherwise, it would not qualify as a greatest conceivable being. Although God has necessary existence, he still endures in time, though without beginning or end. This omnitemporality of a necessarily existent God flies in the face of Anselm's claim that whatever exists in time has at least the possibility of failing to exist.

Hartshorne's conception of such an absolutely perfect being departs radically in yet another way from that of the great medieval theists. Whereas they thought for many contrastive terms – permance–change, one–many, activity–passivity, actuality–potentiality, for example – God has only the former property in the contrastive pair, Hartshorne's doctrine of the "dipolar" nature of God has him have each property in the pair, although in different ways. God, for example, is permanent in that his goodness is steadfast but changes in the way in which he responds to the suffering and free acts of creatures. God is all-powerful but nevertheless limited in his power so as to allow for creaturely free will. If his power were to be without limits, these creatures would not have any power of their own. He is the all-knower of whatever can be known but lacks knowledge of the future, including the free acts that he will subsequently perform in reaction to the free acts of creature. Making God finite in these ways not only allows for creaturely free will but also enables us explain how God and evil can co-exist.

Further reading

Dewey, John. *A Common Faith: John Dewey, The Later Works, Vol. 9, 1933–34*, ed. Jo Ann Boydston. Carbondale, IL: Southern Illinois University Press, 1989.

Fontinell, Eugene. *Self, God, and Immortality: A Jamesian Investigation*. Philadelphia, PA: Temple University Press, 1986.

Hartshorne, Charles. *A Natural Theology for Our Time*. LaSalle, IL: Open Court, 1969.

James, William. *The Varieties of Religious Experience*. Cambridge, MA: Harvard University Press, 1985.

Randall, John Herman, Jr. "The Religion of Shared Experience" in J. Ratner (ed.) *The Philosopher of the Common Man*. New York: Putnam, 1940.

Rockefeller, Steven C. *John Dewey: Religious Faith and Democratic Humanism*. New York: Columbia University Press, 1991.

Suckiel, Ellen Kappy. *Heaven's Champion: William James's Philosophy of Religion*. Notre Dame, IN: University of Notre Dame Press, 1996.

Richard M. Gale

GOOD

Good is an evaluative term indicating that a thing, act, person, or state of affairs is commendable or choiceworthy. As such, it has long been a subject of philosophical interest both in its own right and as a part of broader inquiries into value and valuation. Inquiry into the meaning and nature of good has revolved around several questions. What kinds of good are there? What kinds of things are good? Can assertions about goodness be true or false? And what is the *summum bonum*, or highest good, for humankind?

What kinds of good are there?

Historically good has been held to be divisible into two broad categories: *intrinsic* and *non-intrinsic*.

Intrinsic good is said to be a property or quality that makes what possesses it commendable or choiceworthy either "in itself" or "for itself." Although both characterizations agree in treating "intrinsic" good as non-derivative in some respect, they differ in important ways.

For example, if the intrinsic goodness of some thing *X* is understood in the former sense, then it is non-derivatively good as an object of choice. That is, it is not merely worthy of choice as a means or instrument to some other thing *Z*. Thus on a classical hedonistic account of value, the only thing intrinsically good is pleasure, all other things being good or choiceworthy solely as means or instruments for the production of pleasure. Similarly, for Aristotle, *eudaimonia* or "flourishing" is intrinsically good or choiceworthy, while wealth is only instrumentally valuable as a resource for creating conditions conducive to flourishing. Thus intrinsic good in this sense is typically opposed to "instrumental" good. The distinction is not absolute however. There is no bar in principle to a thing's being intrinsically good or choiceworthy for its own sake while also being instrumentally valuable for the promotion of other or higher intrinsic goods.

However, if intrinsic goodness is viewed as a property or quality that *X* possesses "in itself," then goodness is attributed in virtue of *X*'s inherent qualities or properties, independent of any particular conditions obtaining. G.E. Moore's method of isolation might be considered a test of intrinsic value in this sense: the method of "considering what value we should attach [to some thing], if it existed in absolute isolation, stripped of all its usual accompaniments." Alternately, Kant's suggestion that a good will is the only thing good in all circumstances or possible worlds might be taken to offer a related understanding of intrinsic good. When intrinsic good is understood in this second sense, intrinsic good is opposed to *extrinsic* good, meaning the extrinsically good thing's goodness is not independent of or non-derivative from conditions or relations external to it.

These two ways of understanding intrinsic and non-intrinsic good are not equivalent. Things said to be intrinsically good in the first sense – as objects of choice – may be only extrinsically good in the second sense – good only when certain conditions obtain.

What kinds of things are good?

The interpretation of intrinsic and non-intrinsic good a philosopher favors typically depends upon his or her conception of the properties or qualities that makes a thing or person good.

For example, on some *non-naturalist* accounts of good (e.g. Plato, G.E. Moore) good is an ideal quality or property of things or persons distinct from (and/or supervening upon) any natural, scientifically observable, properties or qualities they may possess. Things or persons may thus be intrinsically good, independent of whether they satisfy wants, needs, or interests of any valuer. Alternately, some have held that things or persons are good (or are *morally* good), when they conform to rational and/or self-evident principles of value. On this sort of view, things or persons are (or are not) intrinsically good independent of their appeal to anyone's wants, needs or interests. Thus on either sort of view, non-derivative, intrinsic goodness will usually be understood in the second sense, as a value things or persons possess in themselves, independent of any special conditions.

On *naturalistic* accounts, however, goodness is usually held to be a relational property or quality things or persons come to possess when they stand in certain relations to wants, needs, or interests of valuers. Pragmatic naturalists, e.g. John Dewey and C.I. Lewis, and naturalist realists, such as R.B. Perry, understand non-derivative goodness as a quality or feature things or persons possess when or if their natural qualities are such as to satisfy some valuer's (actual or rationally considered) wants, needs, or interests. On this sort of approach, valuing is inherently teleological, thus intrinsic goodness is typically understood in the first sense. That is, a thing is intrinsically good when or if it is choiceworthy in itself.

Naturalists differ among themselves about the status of the wants, needs, or interests that a thing must satisfy in order to be good, and thus differ in their views of the range of things or persons that can possess goodness intrinsically. Some hold that the needs, wants, or interests involved must be conscious subjective ones, whose satisfaction or frustration can be subjectively appreciated by their possessor (e.g. William James, John Dewey, C.I. Lewis, Brand Blanshard, and R.B. Perry). For these theorists, nothing can be good except in relation to conscious, sentient valuers. It will be conscious experiences – or states of affairs including conscious experiences – that are intrinsically good. Any thing causally productive of such experiences or states of affairs would to that extent be instrumentally good.

Others, following Aristotle's lead, including contemporary Biocentrists such as Paul Taylor, hold that consciousness or subjectivity is only necessary for a thing to be *subjectively good* to some valuer. Things can also be *objectively good* in virtue of a valuer's objective needs, whether or not these needs are subjectively appreciated. For Aristotle, any natural entity, animate or inanimate, has a natural *telos* it strives to realize, for which it needs certain resources or states of affairs to obtain. These constitute its objective needs. Whatever satisfies these needs are thus objectively good for it. Biocentrists make a similar sort of claim for living entities, holding that all living entities have a natural *telos* or end (e.g. survival) which is the basis for the ascription of objective needs. On either sort of view, the realization of a thing's *telos* or end is an objective intrinsic good while conscious states of satisfaction are only subjectively intrinsically good. Any thing causally productive of objective or subjective intrinsic good is thus instrumentally good.

But although the distinction between intrinsic and non-intrinsic good is both venerable and continues to be widely employed, some have criticized the usefulness. For example, C.I. Lewis argued that it is of little use for naturalistic evaluation of things or events in the world, since none of these can possess intrinsic value. Thus if a naturalist wants to differentiate between the goodness of a painting and the goodness of wealth, the intrinsic/instrumental distinction is useless. He or she must employ a different distinction, one that focuses on the good-making properties things possess, either in themselves or in reflation to other external things. Lewis proposes we speak of things like paintings, as "*inherently good*" (good-making) in virtue of their own internal properties, to distinguish them from things like wealth that are good (good-making) only in virtue of external relations to other things.

Another pragmatist, John Dewey, offers a more direct attack. Dewey argues the intrinsic/non-intrinsic distinction is not only useless but actually vacuous. Dewey argues that the requirement that a thing be choiceworthy for itself is a requirement no object or state of affairs can truly meet. Experiences or states of affairs only appear to meet this requirement so long as we hold the point of view from which the thing in question is being evaluated constant. In actual life, the point of view from which we evaluate is never held constant. Experiences or states of affairs intrinsically choiceworthy given the needs and interests that pertain at one time will not be intrinsically choiceworthy given those pertaining at another. Ascriptions of intrinsic value are thus relative to points of view which vary from person to person and time to time. Thus, nothing can properly be said to be intrinsically good or instrumentally good *per se*. Dewey argued the distinction should be dropped entirely in favor of a distinction between temporarily fixed ends (*ends in view*) and means.

Can assertions about goodness be true or false?

Views on the epistemic status of assertions that "*X* is good" are also largely determined by the views held about what makes any thing or person good. These epistemic views fall into two broad categories, sometimes referred to as "objective" and "subjective" views. However, since the terms "objective" and "subjective" are also used to distinguish between different types of interests that good things may realize (see above), for clarity's sake it is probably better to follow the lead of contemporary moral philosophers and label the two kinds of views as *cognitivist* and *non-cognitivist*.

Cognitivists hold that claims about goodness have cognitive content: i.e. they involve beliefs about the value of things or persons that may be true or false. Assertions about good are thus analogous to assertions about matters of fact. They are not mere verbal expressions of irrational tastes, feelings, or attitudes. Non-cognitivists hold the opposite view. According to non-cognitivists, to say that "*X* is good" is just to express one's tastes, attitudes, or feelings about that *X*. One might just as well say, "Hurrah for *X*." "Hurrah for *X*" clearly isn't an assertion that can be true or false – expressions of emotional states don't make assertions about the world at all. They simply don't involve the right sort of cognitive content. Thus on non-cognitivist views, assertions of value are utterly unlike assertions about matters of fact.

Cognitivist accounts of assertions of or about good may further be categorized as *intuitionist*, *rationalist*, and/or *empiricist*. If "*X* is good" is understood as asserting that *X* possesses an ideal, non-natural property, then the claim cannot be empirically confirmed or disconfirmed by the methods of the natural sciences. Intuition is required. Or if a theorist holds the view that things are good if or when they conform to a necessary or self-evident truth or true principle of value, again claims about good cannot be confirmed or disconfirmed by empirical means alone. If we can know such claims to be true or false, we must know it either by intuition or rational insight. Moorean non-naturalists could be considered intuitionists, as could most Scottish Common Sense realists and more recent critics of pragmatic naturalisms, such as Roderick Chisholm. Neo-Kant positions might be considered examples of rationalism.

However, if "*X* is good" is taken to be an assertion about the empirically detectable properties of *X*, e.g. that *X* is satisfactory or contributes to human flourishing, then we do not need to appeal to rational insight or intuition to confirm or disconfirm such assertions. Empirical inquiry into the natural, scientifically detectable properties of X will be sufficient for us to know if a particular thing is or is not good. Pragmatic naturalists like James, Dewey, and Lewis hold such views.

Non-cognitivist accounts cannot be distinguished by means of these epistemic categories since they deny that claims about the goodness can be confirmed or disconfirmed. Historically, such accounts have been labeled by reference to the methods adopted for investigating the activity of forming, expressing, and acting on attitudes, pro and con. For example, the British Moral Sense school of the eighteenth century, which influenced American intellectuals such as Jonathan Edwards, and Thomas Jefferson, chose to focus on human sensibility, the source of our affective attitudes, with a view to explaining the convergence in attitudes towards certain kinds of acts or persons in terms of the common characteristics of human sensibility.

Twentieth-century American non-cognitivists followed English language philosophy's "linguistic turn" in viewing our *talk* about values, rather than the psychological states they express, as the proper province of philosophical inquiry. Emotivists, including Charles L. Stevenson, were so-called because of their interest in the "emotive" or expressive function of value language and its role in discourse. A related view proposed by the influential British philosopher R.M. Hare, Prescriptivism, focuses instead upon the "prescriptive" function of talk about goodness, both the ways such talk is used to prescribe actions and the logical issues that arise for us as we try to act upon our own or others' prescriptive utterances. More recently, Allan Gibbard has proposed a new variant, "norm-expressivism," that shows the influence of both Emotivism and Prescriptivism.

What is the *summum bonum*, or highest good, for humankind?

Historically, inquiry into good has often been motivated by a desire to determine humankind's *summum bonum*, the best kind of life for humans to live. Here the focus is upon ranking different kinds of lives for their respective capacity to be or to realize good. The nature of the problem for any particular theorist will depend first upon whether he or she is a *monist* or *pluralist* about non-derivative goodness.

If one is a monist, like Epicurus or the hedonistic utilitarian Jeremy Bentham, then lives have only to be evaluated and ranked instrumentally: the best life is the one most instrumentally valuable for the production of the intrinsic good of pleasure. Some forms of Biocentrism are similarly monistic, ranking human lives in terms of their instrumental value for helping or hindering life generally. If, however, one is a pluralist, like Aristotle or James, then determining which is the best sort of life involves two distinct sorts of problems: first, the qualitative ranking of the intrinsic, non-derivative goods open to us and, second, the instrumental evaluation of the ways of life that give rise to them.

For pluralists, then, the first and most fundamental question is which of the non-derivative values open to us is the "highest" or most complete. According to Aristotle, the highest good for human beings is *eudaimonia* or flourishing because it is the one intrinsic good valued solely for its own sake, all other intrinsic goods being choiceworthy partly for their own sakes and partly for their contribution to our realization of *eudaimonia*. For pragmatic naturalists like James, however, there is no one highest or most complete good, thus the best life would be a life that allows or permits us to realize the most comprehensive array of the intrinsic goods open to pursuit. But as the opportunities and resources open to people vary substantially, so too will the kind of lives that are "best" for people to live. Dewey takes the same line of reasoning a step farther and argues that as we and our environments change significantly over the course of our lifetimes, we cannot even speak meaningfully of a best life for any one individual *per se*. We ought to drop talk of "final ends" or "best lives" and speak instead of ways of life as more or less satisfactory given the situations in which individuals find themselves and the resources, inner and outer, with which they have to work.

Further reading

Aristotle. *Nicomachean Ethics*, revised edition, trans. Terence Irwin. Indianapolis, IN: Hackett, 1999.

Dewey, John. *Theory of Valuation: The Later Works of John Dewey, 1925–1953, Vol. 13, 1938–1939*, ed. Jo Ann Boydston. Chicago, IL: University of Chicago Press, 1986.

Hare, R.M. *The Language of Morals*. Oxford: Clarendon Press, 1952.

James, William. *Essays in Religion and Morality*. Cambridge, MA: Harvard University Press, 1982.

Lewis, C.I. *An Analysis of Knowledge and Valuation*. LaSalle, IL: Open Court, 1946.

Moore, G.E. *Principia Ethica*, revised edition. Cambridge: Cambridge University Press, 1993.
Perry, R.B. *General Theory of Value*. Cambridge, MA: Harvard University Press, 1954.
Stevenson, Charles L. *Facts and Values: Studies in Ethical Analysis*. New Haven, CT: Yale University Press, 1963.

JENNIFER WELCHMAN

GOUINLOCK, JAMES S.

Born in Buffalo, New York, in 1933, James Gouinlock received his doctorate from Columbia University in 1969 after receiving a BA from Cornell where he majored in government. An assistant professor at the State University of New York, Buffalo, until 1971, he then joined the faculty at Emory University. At Columbia he was introduced to the thought of John Dewey as well as the Aristotelian naturalism of his mentor, John Herman Randall, Jr.

Gouinlock's first book, *John Dewey's Philosophy of Value* (1972), was a landmark in the recovery of Dewey's thought as well as the revival of American pragmatism. The reigning modes of Anglo-American philosophy had long dismissed classical American philosophy. Thus Gouinlock not only produced the first major critical study of Dewey's moral philosophy, but used Dewey to engage issues in emotivism, prescriptivism, the is/ought problem, and the utilitarian–deontological debate. Gouinlock's reliance on the empirical naturalism of Dewey and Randall directly challenged the approaches to ethics then popular. The book's undistorted presentation of Dewey's basic metaphysics as well as his ethics laid a basis for the renaissance in Dewey scholarship in history and political theory as well as philosophy.

Gouinlock's seminars in the history of moral and political philosophy at Emory also sharpened his criticisms of such contemporary figures as Rawls, Gewirth, Dworkin, Habermas, and Rorty, as seen in "Dewey and Contemporary Moral Philosophy" (1993) and "What is the Legacy of Instrumentalism: Rorty's Interpretation of Dewey" (1990, 1995). His anthology, *The Moral Writings of John Dewey* (1976, 1994), made available numerous writings that were out of print or gradually reappearing in the massive collected works of Dewey then underway. Gouinlock's broader concern with the retrieval of a public philosophy of liberal democracy became manifest with *Excellence in Public Discourse* (1986), a study in the political thought of John Stuart Mill as well as Dewey. There Gouinlock insisted that democracy requires more than merely having a well-informed electorate. There must also be a genuine "morale" or climate in society that respects pluralism and basic differences and is committed to accommodation and growth in a shared social end. It must be embodied in our daily political speech. He also expressed concern that the deterioration of content and civility in our public discourse was leading to a political culture of cynicism and short-sighted selfishness. "Dewey, Virtue and Moral Pluralism" (1987) began to explore the desirable virtues for a democratic morale.

Gouinlock's *Rediscovering the Moral Life* (1993) is an original, constructive, and forceful expansion upon all these preceding issues. Contemporary philosophy is sharply criticized for its self-imposed isolation from the world of daily living that is the true source for our moral dilemmas and philosophical questions. Moral philosophy must begin with understanding that world, with all its contingency, ambiguity and diversity, rather than with a conceptually purified alternative. Because our moral world is "polyglot," or filled with different intrinsic values, Gouinlock defends moral pluralism as a viable alternative to the extremes of absolutism and relativism. Pluralism "is the doctrine that there can be a range of defensible positions regarding a given moral issue" (Gouinlock 1993: 289). It also recognizes that the moral condition requires the cultivation of several core virtues such as rationality, courage, and respect for persons, because these secure conditions whereby the process of shared moral life may continue.

While Gouinlock distinguishes knowing and valuing and sees them as irreducible to each other, he is unwilling to let valuing be interpreted along emotivist lines. Moral claims may not be grounded on absolute cognitive truths, but there is a process of communication and intelligent evaluation that is essential to the moral life. Genuine disagreement is possible without discourse coming to an end. For Gouinlock, "Moral discourse is the organ of the moral life"(1993: 105). This process involves mutual clarification and evaluation of the facts, possibilities, and prospects of our morally problematic situations. Thus the pragmatic method is crucial in making our moral ideas clear.

Ultimately, this method sets forth the "conditions and potentialities of human endeavor" so that "the meanings of life experience" are made clearer in our practical situations. No philosophy can free us from genuine existential ambiguities or the possibilities of conflict or tragic error. But philosophy can make us comprehend the features of the moral condition and set forth comprehensive vision of life vital for democratic political welfare.

Further reading

Gouinlock, James S. *John Dewey's Philosophy of Value.* New York: Humanities Press, 1972.
—— *The Moral Writings of John Dewey.* New York: Macmillan, 1976; second revised and augmented edition, Buffalo, NY: Prometheus Books, 1994.
—— *Excellence in Public Discourse: John Stuart Mill. John Dewey. and Social Intelligence.* New York: Teachers' College Press, 1986.
—— "Dewey and Contemporary Moral Philosophy." in John Stuhr (ed.) *Philosophy and the Reconstruction of Culture.* Albany, NY: SUNY Press, 1993.
—— *Rediscovering the Moral Life.* Buffalo, NY: Prometheus Books, 1994.
—— "What Is the Legacy of Instrumentalism: Rorty's Interpretation of Dewey" in Herman Saatkamp (ed.) *Rorty and Pragmatism.* Nashville, TN: Vanderbilt University Press, 1995.

THOMAS M. ALEXANDER

GOUINLOCK, JAMES: AUTOBIOGRAPHY

I did my graduate work at Columbia, where the dominant influence was John Herman Randall, Jr, a man of learning and wisdom. He imparted a deep appreciation for the tradition of philosophy as search for the good through knowledge of the human condition. Randall breathed especially the spirit of Dewey, and he also conveyed great sympathy for the work of Santayana. At that time and for many years thereafter, the greatest influence on my reflections was the philosophy of Dewey. My affection for Santayana has grown with time. Nietzsche, with his unremitting demand for courage and independence, has also made a deep imprint on me. I recognize today that one of the greatest effects such thinkers have had on me is to enable me to achieve a grasp of the wisdom of Plato and Aristotle. I have never had any patience with the many philosophies that treat the moral life in sterile and impertinent terms. Dewey's demand that we use philosophy to study "problems of men" rather than academic twaddle has resonated with me.

A major scholarly purpose has been to understand and transmit the ideas of Dewey. I attempted to do so in both teaching and writing, especially *John Dewey's Philosophy of Value* (1972) and *Excellence in Public Discourse: John Stuart Mill, John Dewey, and Social Intelligence* (1986). These attempts appear to have been moderately successful. I think I achieved a good grasp of Dewey, and a number of students and scholars have in varying degrees relied on these texts in their own research. I have found, however, that simply to articulate, even critically, the thinking of someone else is confining. My own ideas cannot find sufficient room for themselves in analyzing the works of others. Accordingly, I initiated the statement of my own moral philosophy in *Rediscovering the Moral Life* (1993). This book expressed my impatience with contemporary theory, stated what I take to be the right way to undertake moral philosophy, and actually made and defended a number of moral claims. Although a few individuals have made generous comments about this book, I can say that it has not taken the world by storm. Undaunted, I am completing a sequel to it. Persuaded that there is much to be gained from knowledge of the conditions of human life, and persuaded that recent philosophy has grossly neglected this prime resource, I am engaged in an inquiry that seeks wisdom according to nature. Whatever its eventual fate with the profession or with the reading public, it will be a consummation of my own inquiry into the good, and in that regard I will be satisfied.

I like to think that my most significant thinking has not yet been published. In terms of the existing public record, I suppose *John Dewey's Philosophy of Value* has had more positive impact on the community of scholars than anything else I have written.

From another standpoint, I'm tempted to say that this book is also my least satisfactory. As I see it now, Dewey deserves a study that is more discerning of the significance of his philosophy in regard to fundamental human values, with less emphasis on its status in respect to transient scholastic debates.

JAMES GOUINLOCK

GRAMMAR

Grammar for a language is a system which provides linguistic characterizations of all and only sentences of the language. Philosophically, among such characterizations, the syntactic and the semantic are central, while the phonological and the orthographical are peripheral. Two grammatical theories in the study of natural language in the United States stand out: Noam Chomsky's and Richard Montague's.

According to Chomsky's "transformational-generative grammar," the characterization of the sentences of any natural language *L* is carried out in stages. First, a finite number of basic phrase structures, called "deep structures," are specified, along with a finite vocabulary. Second, a finite number of rules according to which the deep structures may be transformed are given. Third, it is declared that an item is a sentence of *L* just if it results from applying one or more transformation rules to a deep structure. Fourth, the deep structure of each sentence *S* of *L* is subjected to semantic interpretation, which specifies the linguistic meaning of *S*. Chomsky considers his theory to be a theory of human cognitive capacity, and as such a branch of psychology. He also believes in "universal grammar," a theory of the innate mechanism of the linguistic module of the mind common to all human beings. Chomsky's argument for the existence of such a mechanism is known as the "argument from the poverty of stimulus": almost all human beings acquire their first language by being exposed to low-grade linguistic data, and the most plausible explanation of this phenomenon postulates an innate cognitive system endowed with a linguistic module that is highly structured to impose significant constraints on humanly learnable languages. This rejection of the mind as *tabula rasa* puts Chomsky squarely within the rationalist tradition.

Three main features distinguish "Montague grammar." First, it aims to respect the "surface" structures of sentences, rejecting a sharp distinction between them and the deep structures. The role of transformation rules is thus drastically curtailed, and the logical form of a sentence is more or less transparent in its surface structure. Second, while Chomsky's main focus is on syntax, Montague's primary interest lies in semantics. The framework he uses is that of intensional (modal and tense) logic, which is obtained by adding indices as alethic relativizers to classic logic. For example, where classic logic characterizes a sentence as true or false, intensional logic characterizes it as true or false relative to a possible world or a time. Semantic values are thus subject to more parameters in intensional logic, and this gives it more flexibility. Third, unlike Chomsky, Montague does not consider grammar to be part of psychology, so the question of psychological reality is not deemed central to the evaluation of grammar. Instead, grammar is regarded as a branch of mathematical logic and to be evaluated accordingly.

Further reading

Chomsky, Noam. *Aspects of the Theory of Syntax*. Cambridge, MA: MIT Press, 1965.

—— *Rules and Representations*. New York: Columbia University Press, 1980.

Montague, Richard. *Formal Philosophy*. New Haven, CT: Yale University Press, 1974.

TAKASHI YAGISAWA

GRAY, ASA

Born in Oneida County, New York, Asa Gray (1810–88) practiced medicine before turning to biology, under the tutorage of the famous botanist John Torrey. After an appointment at Michigan, Gray became professor of natural history at Harvard, a position he held for more than thirty years. Gray figured prominently in Harvard's emergence as a legitimate research facility, building both a botanical library and a herbarium. Most significantly, however, he was one of the few influential scholars to both fully understand and endorse Darwin's theory of evolution in an era when most American colleges were still controlled by clergy who either denounced it as atheistic or insisted that natural selection must be guided by providence. Despite a personal affinity for the latter view, Gray believed Darwin was wholly justified in separating matters of empirical science from theological speculation, where human reason is notoriously feeble.

Further reading

Dupree, A. Hunter. *Asa Gray: American Botanist, Friend of Darwin*. Cambridge, MA: Harvard University Press, 1959.

Gray, Asa. *Darwiniana*. New York: Appleton, 1877.

Hodge, Charles. *What is Darwinism?* New York: Scribner, Armstrong, 1874.

Loewenburg, Bert J. "The Reaction of American Scientists to Darwinism," *American Historical Review* 38 (1933): 687–701.

—— "Darwinism Comes to America," *Mississippi Valley Historical Review* 29 (1941): 339–69.

FRANK X. RYAN

GREAT CHAIN OF BEING

The great chain of being is an idea about how the universe is structured, and a metaphorical description of its fundamentally hierarchical nature. Arthur O. Lovejoy argues that this idea is "one of the half dozen most potent and persistent presuppositions in Western thought." He finds the roots of the idea in aspects of Plato's and Aristotle's philosophies, which were systematized by the neo-Platonists, and became the general presupposition of most Western thinkers from the Middle Ages through the Enlightenment.

Lovejoy characterizes the idea of a chain of being as resting on three principles. He calls the first the "principle of plenitude": the universe is a ordered system that includes every conceivable kind of thing. The Source of all things, whether a theistic God who creates the hierarchy or a pantheistic God whose reality encompasses it, has the power to make actual every possibility of existence, and has done so. No kind of thing that could be is not. The "principle of continuity" follows deductively: there are no gaps in the hierarchy. If there is between any two natural species of being a theoretically possible intermediate type, it must exist.

The "principle of gradation" defines the hierarchy as marked by degrees of perfection, running from the least perfect kinds of things at the bottom to the most perfect as the top, and applying both to their existence and their worth. The more perfect a being, the more good it possesses and the more unvarying its existence. Base things are of minimum value and fleeting duration, whereas the greatest beings are invaluable and unperishing. To be is to be an instance of a kind, a result of God's timeless determination of all things in their kinds, an ordering which is both rational and right because divinely ordained.

Although Lovejoy says this idea fell into disrepute in the nineteenth century, it would be more accurate to say that it was naturalized. Modern science secularized the hierarchy by eliminating the intelligible beings that compose the levels higher than human beings – from angels and archangels up to and including God. Then under the influence of temporalistic philosophies and Darwinian biology, the hierarchy of natural kinds ceased to be timeless. Fixed essences were replaced by evolving structural conditions which were often interpreted as progressive, even as generating emergent kinds and levels of beings. What remains constant amid these changing beliefs is the conviction that the universe is intelligible, that it can be understood because its components comprise a single well-ordered rational system.

When the great chain is applied to human societies, it envisions a social order in which social roles and authority are based on inherent differences among individuals. At the bottom of the hierarchy is a large class of slaves or serfs or industrial proletarians or service workers, at the top a small controlling elite of landowners or nobles or owners or managers. Location on the hierarchy may be understood as a matter of property rights, birthright, or the proper recognition of natural talent, but all are understood as intrinsic natural qualities. Deference is due to those with a higher status than our own, in proper recognition of their superior worth. We would be doing violence to the natural order of things were we to disdain our betters or aspire to their status. Yet every station in life confers an honor appropriate to it, which others are obliged to acknowledge. The servant deserves respect as a servant, the master as a master. Our excellence is a function of the effectiveness with which we fulfill our appropriate social role, just as an acorn's excellence is constituted by its effectiveness in becoming a sturdy oak.

When applied to education, the chain of being is the presumption that subject matters should be organized with respect to each other in a manner that mirrors the gradations of the world. The medieval organization of learning into a *trivium* and *quadrivium* of sciences was explicitly hierarchical. Nowadays the hierarchy lingers in the presumption that physics is the most fundamental of the disciplines because complex things, from molecules to mammals to Mozart, are forms of matter/energy and can best be understood by analyzing them into their basic components. E.O. Wilson names this presumption "consilience," which he describes as the idea that any entity whatsoever is based on material processes that are ultimately reducible to the laws of physics.

Critics such as Jaakko Hintikka criticize Lovejoy for inaccuracies in his historical account and for illegitimately treating various similar but distinguishable ideas as though they were the same. His critics also complain that he neglected alternative ideas and their associated metaphors. For instance, Marion and Paul Kuntz show that the Jacob's Ladder image was at least as important during the Middle Ages as the chain image, and Francis Oakley argues that by the sixteenth century a "covenantal" notion of God's relation to the natural order was widely believed.

Lovejoy ends his book with a chapter in which he criticizes the great chain of being as "obviously" false. Its completeness leaves no room for additions or alterations. The structure of things is timeless and deterministic: what is or has been or will be is both logically necessary and maximally good. Both the good and the evil in the world, both the joy and the suffering, are features of the best of all possible worlds. However, says Lovejoy, the world is not that way. It is full of change, of surprising novelties and unredeemable loss, a welter of "impossible contradictions."

The "anti-rationalism" Lovejoy advocated is alive and well in current forms of pragmatism and postmodernism, but a hierarchical universe of ontological and moral plenitude is still advocated by many contemporary philosophers. Norris Clarke, for instance, defends a Thomistic sense of metaphysical plenitude and hierarchy, and William Desmond develops a metaphysics in which the contingent finitude of beings is evidence of the overflowing plenitude of the goodness of Being, its agapeic generosity. James Feibleman and Huston

Smith hold strongly hierarchical theories, the one naturalistic, the other theological.

Further reading

Clarke, Norris, SJ. *The One and the Many: A Contemporary Thomistic Metaphysics*. South Bend, IN: University of Notre Dame Press, 2001.

Desmond, William. *Being and the Between*. Albany, NY: SUNY Press, 1995.

Feibleman, James I. *Ontology*. Baltimore, MD: Johns Hopkins University Press, 1951.

Hintikka, Jaakko. "Gaps in the Great Chain of Being: An Exercise in the Methodology of the History of Ideas," *Proceedings and Addresses of the American Philosophical Association* 49 (November 1976): 22–38.

Kuntz, Marion Leathers and Kuntz, Paul Grimley (eds). *Jacob's Ladder and the Tree of Life: Concepts of Hierarchy and the Great Chain of Being*. New York: Peter Lang, 1988.

Lovejoy, Arthur O. *The Great Chain of Being: A Study of the History of an Idea*. New York: Harper and Row, 1960.

Oakley, Francis. "Lovejoy's Unexplored Option," *Journal of the History of Ideas* 48, 2 (1987): 231–45.

Smith, Huston. "Hierarchy Essential to Religion: The Great Chain of Being Reaffirmed Against Scientistic, Modernist, and Postmodernist Attacks," *Contemporary Philosophy* 13, 8 (1991): 3–9.

Wilson, Daniel J. "Lovejoy's *The Great Chain of Being* after Fifty Years," *Journal of the History of Ideas* 48, 2 (1987): 187–206.

Wilson, Edward O. *Consilence: The Unity of Knowledge*. New York: Knopf, 1998.

George Allan

GREEK PHILOSOPHY, INFLUENCE OF

The case of the influence of Greek philosophy in America is somewhat similar to that of the European Enlightenment in selecting strands of classical thought relevant to current cultural interests. In general, the classical tradition in America, less conspicuous during the Colonial period, grew more appreciative and useful in the decades preceding and during the revolutionary years. After the mid-point of the nineteenth century, when philosophy became an independent academic discipline, Greek philosophy gradually gained recognition with the rise in the universities of different philosophical trends and especially with the development of American Pragmatism. However, the question of influence has to be treated with a note of reservation. Gradual assimilation of select ideas borrowed from classical philosophy had a slow start, almost hardly noticeable during the first three centuries of the new nation. The more positive – "creative" might be a better word – phase became manifest at the end of the nineteenth century and continued through the first half of the twentieth and later under a different guise. More precisely, the question of influence in the sense of being a factor in the way that philosophy was taught and written in America remains a controversial, if not debatable theme.

Colonial period

The place of Greek philosophy in the communities of faith in the early life of the Colonies was restricted to the education of the seminarians and mainly as preparation to biblical studies and learning New Testament Greek. Before proceeding with issues of influence, a distinction is needed between usefulness of the classics in the Colonies and the limited interest in philosophical ideas. On the whole, philosophy as a systematic discipline was not cultivated in colonial America although the classics were taught in the established schools. The early interest in Greek subjects was limited mainly to the language and to a lesser extent to rhetoric and poetry, usually imported by scholars educated in England. Smatterings of philosophical ideas, when considered acceptable to the religious culture in the Colonies, only occasionally found a serious place in the mainstream of the values the Puritans held. Whatever presence such ideas enjoyed is better understood as limited extensions of the English response to the European renaissance movement. Classical political philosophy, for instance, became an object of interest in the pre-Revolutionary period, mainly in the modern form it took through the writings of Cicero and Seneca.

A distinction can be made between the modes of responding to the classical tradition that mark the earlier period on the one hand and the transition to the responses, on the other, that characterize the second half of the eighteenth century and after. The intellectuals in both periods proved quite eclectic in what they found in the classics as useful to their cultural, religious and political needs. The dominant religious interests in the Colonies exercised considerable restraints over what could be beneficial to the believers and contribute to stabilizing their faith. Whatever of the classical tradition was successfully absorbed after the middle of the eighteenth century was actually limited to the features of the European Enlightenment that helped promote new political ideas. Aristotle's social thought, for instance, was read only in the way it was accepted in the writings of Locke. Platonism, on the other hand, found its place in Puritanism through the seventeenth-century Christian Platonists of Cambridge University, Benjamin Whichcote, Ralph Cudworth, Henry More and others. In sharp contrast, the Americans while using the doctrines of the Cambridge Platonists to accommodate religious interests, made no scholarly attempt to study Plato himself apart from their Puritan credo.

A note of caution is perhaps needed at this point. Whatever was absorbed from the classical tradition during that period and later had already undergone serious changes during the late Hellenistic and Roman periods of intellectual history, and the end result was that the classical tradition in general became available to modern times primarily in Roman dress. This historical change is particularly important to understanding the limited presence of Greek philosophy in America during the colonial and post-colonial periods. The same reservation holds true for the reception of other features of the classics, from language and rhetoric to poetry and architecture. With regard to philosophy, the Greek thinkers that eventually held the interest of American intellectuals were Socrates, Plato, and Aristotle, and to a lesser degree the Stoics and the Epicureans. Again the preference for special classical philosophers differs from one period of American thought to another. For instance, the works of Aristotle during the colonial period were virtually ignored and not solely because of lack of texts and translations, in contrast to the influence that Greek philosophy was exerting in England.

Viewed in retrospect, the cultivation of the classics in the Colonies played a significant albeit inadvertent role in the intellectual preparation of the political outlook of the Revolution, although initially such a role was not intended. Once the Colonies passed the initial phase of settlement and communities were made adequately secure, the educational needs led to gradual enrichment for the cultural advancement beyond the outlook of the frontier fighter. The nine pre-Revolutionary colleges, mainly educational institutions for men, required all entering students to be trained in Greek and Latin. In New England the Boston Latin School, founded in 1635, contributed largely to this preparation, and Harvard College, founded in the next year, added in 1723 to its curriculum, besides Greek, Latin and Hebrew, courses in logic, ethics and metaphysics. Princeton, closer to a classical curriculum than Harvard, taught philosophy in the second year and moral philosophy in the third; added to these were lectures on Aristotle's theory of the mixed form of government. In various combinations of courses the same pattern was followed in the curricula of other sprouting colleges, from William and Mary to Cornell and Yale. Adding to the quality of teaching was the continuous exchange of students between the Colonies and England in addition to the influx of teachers from the standard institutions of Cambridge and Oxford and ones in Scotland. Stated in another way, philosophy in the Colonies was not a special preoccupation of teaching in the colleges. In the popular use of the term, "philosophizing" as an activity was also pursued in the other walks of life, from the farmers and the clergy to the holders of office in the governing of the land. Whatever the agent, the wisdom sought after was not an original system but a personal account of lively affairs meant to throw light on events of the affairs of public life in an environment of constant expansion and novel opportunities.

The importation of ideas from Europe, especially from England, played a significant role in the area of practical thinking, especially as these ideas had an impact on the already highly organized religious communities. While it may be incorrect to speak of a "philosophy" of the Puritans or of other religious groups, it would be correct to speak of the use of philosophical ideas for the elucidation of their religious commitment. Basically, in all religious congregations, the faithful members exhibited unquestionable confidence in the unshakable truth of their beliefs and their ultimate dependence on the providence God had granted to humanity.

Philosophy as a subject matter, however, was mainly taught in the courses of colleges but in a somewhat different way than as ideas in support of the beliefs held by the religious communities. A special feature of Protestant thought related to the classical tradition was the religious individualism whereby the salvation took the form of personal attainment. This was an important feature as it entered the set of beliefs that proved influential for the political developments in the next century. It was a type of individualism that gained further support when it was combined with the doctrines of John Locke. The Puritans, through their adherence to Calvinism, expected the lessening of the impact of individualism to prevent heresies. But it was not a philosophy of individualism as it was an extension of their theology of revelation in the sacred confirmation of faith. What might have been an unacknowledged indebtedness to Greek philosophy, namely the place of reason in community life, was accepted only as a principle to confirm the truths of faith, as in the case of God's covenant with human beings. The religious employment of reason asserted the acceptance of human knowledge primarily as knowledge of nature to show its harmonious connectedness with the Will of God and the divine rule. This blending of faith and reason, non-Hellenic is essence, once again brought reason under the dictates of religion, reasserting the medieval priorities, which was another way of accepting not philosophy but the faculty of reason within the frame of religious faith. To be sure, the individualism that sprouted under the cover of Protestantism was quickly tempered by the religious community to prevent misinterpretations of the biblical truth.

Interest in science was accepted as the study of God's work. However, no significant contribution was made to science. Locke's theory of knowledge made inroads in the outlook of the Puritans just as did Newton's work as "natural philosophy," not physics. Both thinkers were contemporaries: John Locke (1632–1704), Isaak Newton (1642–1727). Locke's *Essay concerning Human Understanding* published in 1690 soon found its way to New England. Jonathan Edwards read it at the age of fourteen in 1717. In 1695 Locke published his *The Reasonableness of Christianity* in which he claimed that Christianity deriving as it does its teachings from biblical sources contains nothing contrary to reason, thus making it the most reasonable institution for the benefit of humanity. Equally appealing was Locke's theory of *tabula rasa*, a doctrine he nowhere admitted as having its original source in Aristotle. Jonathan Edwards absorbed in his own way Locke's views and formed his theological outlook by bringing it in line with his Neoplatonism as a Trinitarian theology while leaning on a reconstruction of Ramus.

Greek philosophy began to make its presence felt in the decades before the Revolution. It made its appearance within the set of the political ideas of the Enlightenment. Classical models of freedom and constitutional rights were made stronger through the study of antiquity. However, no systematic study of either Plato or Aristotle was done in preparation for the impending social change. American leaders, when they referred to the ancients, did so by way of prudence and common sense rather than a carefully phrased new political philosophy. When the American Philosophical Society was founded in 1742, with Benjamin Franklin being one of its founders, its purpose was to promote "Useful Knowledge." Besides exchanging information by "physicians, botanists, mathematicians, chemists," the clause stating the inclusion of "a natural philosopher" had nothing to do with Greek philosophy. The same was true of a similar society founded in 1748 in Charleston, SC. During this phase an emigrant Presbyterian minister, James Wilson, with a love for Aristotle, and James March, a professor at the University of Vermont, who taught Plato, Aristotle and Kant, did much to keep Greek philosophy alive.

American Revolution

Locke's theory of natural rights was far more influential in America than any aspect of Greek political thought, Platonic or Aristotelian. The classical conception of political government exerted only a mild appeal. Actually it was Cicero's conception of government that influenced the Americans. This conception had already been influential in Locke's thought. Francis Bacon and John Locke were the two thinkers who instructed the Americans what to value in Greek political philosophers. Bacon and Locke were convinced that everything of value in classicism had already been revived, a view the Americans readily accepted while articulating the "practical" wisdom of happiness including the "pursuit power" (Hamilton) and "the taming of power" (Madison). Jefferson thought about happiness as "a dynamic balance between power and morals" (Koch 1961: 22). The more certain the Americans became of their political success in forming a constitution of states, the more independent they felt from ties to historical traditions. They had not "suffered a blind veneration for antiquity" (Madison). Actually, the founding fathers reached back to Athens via Rome by adopting the political ideal of Cicero's *concordia*, not Aristotle's *homonoia*. Intentionally left out of the revival of classical ideas were the ethical doctrines of Plato and Aristotle, which explains the vagueness that was allowed to linger in the part of the Declaration of Independence that stated "the Pursuit of Happiness" as an unalienable Right, endowed by the Creator. In fact, no theoretical foundation was provided to specify the precise meaning of happiness. Jefferson appealed to "common sense" rather than consult what the Greek philosophers had to say about the theory of happiness as *eudaimonia* in its ethical and political context. Thus, the use of the idea of happiness in the literature of the period as a Right remained undefined while it continued to suit the pursuit of the new freedom and whatever fruits it could yield. John Adams came closest to the Greek view as he mixed his borrowing from Locke and Aristotle to conjoin his ideas of power and morals. In preferring monarchy to aristocracy he conveniently distorted his Aristotle to fit the Lockean–Hobbesian view of the common good. Briefly stated, the American leaders put definite limits to the wider use of the political wisdom of classical humanism. In their view, ancient democracy had certain merits but could not adequately serve the goals of the Revolution, as Jefferson admitted in a letter to Isaak Tiffany written in 1816 that representative democracy made every political structure, including Aristotle's *Politics*, "almost useless." The eclectic approach to Greek political philosophy should not be overlooked although Thomas Paine did not hesitate to declare that he saw no reason why Americans should go "two thousand years back for lessons and examples." In a comparable vein, John Taylor of Virginia insisted that the political perfection of the Greek government and thought was irrelevant to America. The distance between the "present" and the "tradition" increased after the early post-Revolution era only to be gradually modified after the middle of the nineteenth century.

Nineteenth century and the rise of academic philosophy

Two movements around the middle of the nineteenth century deserve mention for their efforts to relate to the study of Greek philosophy and its pertinence to the intellectual life of the new nation: the Hegelian movement of St Louis that led to the programs of the Concord Summer School of Philosophy, and the Transcendentalists of New England. Much in these new trends was due to an encounter with German philosophy and the advanced classical scholarship of the German universities as the latter continued during the last decades of the nineteenth century and the early ones of the twentieth.

The Transcendentalists' criticism of utilitarianism and their attack on commercialism bear no relation to the type of Platonism they espoused. As a movement, Transcendentalism is best understood as a different expansion of idealism vacillating between a reasonable theology and philosophical inspiration. As such, its post-revolutionary stance aimed at strengthening the confidence in the new freedom for the spiritual gains of the common citizens. It may be said that it was an offspring of the Romantic Movement, but with a twist of its own. What is of special interest about its role as an intellectual attitude is the way it understood a connection between the Kantian theory of pure reason and a special interpretation of Plato. Although Transcendentalism did not succeed nor did it try to become a technical philosophy, it attracted followers who thought that with its help they could discern the continuity from the rationalized faith of Jonathan Edwards' puritanism to Emerson's way of receiving in the soul's reason the flow of the divine. Emerson was confident in his effort to blend into a harmonious unity the Bhagavad-Gita and the Platonism of Plotinus in a vision of idealism that would provide the democratic individual with a solid basis for rational faith and a new universality. Once again, the movement, dominated as it was by the metaphysics of Kant, as siphoned through Coleridge, had only limited room for Greek philosophy beyond what Plotinus' Plato could render appealing. Emerson could hold Plato and Plutarch in high esteem, yet the ancients never occupied a respectable place in the foreground of his thinking or his goals any more than did the recent growth of the experimental science of nature. Still, Emerson set the tone for the transcendental understanding of progress as advancing humanity to a higher plateau of freedom, beyond nature, history and science. In the closing part of his famous "The American Scholar" address he confidently exclaimed: "in yourself slumbers the whole Reason; it is for you to know all; it is for you to dare all." The Greeks remained luminaries in the background, a view that had already become firmly established in the American intellectual outlook.

The other movement, the Hegelianism of the Philosophical Society of St Louis, established formally in 1866, worked out a different philosophical program. Its members launched the *Journal of Speculative Philosophy* and while advocating German Idealism, the group also promoted the serious study of Aristotle. Two of its members, Denton J. Snider and Hiram K. Jones, organized a "Plato Club." Another group created in 1879 the Concord School of Philosophy. It included W.T. Harris, A. Bronson Alcott and Thomas Davidson, who abandoned Hegel in favor of Aristotle. Among the younger teachers who lectured at the Concord School was John Dewey. It can be argued that it was the vigorous and open philosophizing of these thinkers that broke the rigid pattern of text-book teaching, mainly by ministers at the colleges. The activities of this group should be credited with alerting the younger generation of students to the outstanding work of the university professors at the leading universities of Germany, France and England that were doing advanced research in classical philology and philosophy. The influence of the Greek philosophy in America was in large measure due to the fresh interpretations of the Greek mind in Europe. While we cannot speak of a direct Greek influence in the case of the St Louis thinkers, their way of pursuing philosophy left its mark on the next generation.

The contributions of classical philology during the second half of the nineteenth century were due to American scholars who had studied in German Universities. Lane B.L. Gildersleeve and others received their doctorates from Göttingen, and so did M.W. Humphries, H.W. Smyth, and Paul Shorey during the 1880s. Their work was strictly methodical and scientific with no explicit concern for the development of a new cultural character. As such, ethical philosophy was left outside the scope of philological research. In his Presidential Address "The Province of the American Philologist" before the American Philological Association in 1878, Gildersleeve outlined its goals as dealing with the texts and aiming at understanding the wisdom of the ancients. The evaluation of the ancient wisdom was better left to those philosophers who were qualified to meet the demands of the task. The volumes of the *American Journal of Philology* from 1880 to 1919 provide a fair picture of the limited interest of the philologists in philosophy. In fact their interest deepened after the philosophers had made Greek thought a respected field of studies. The Platonic studies of Paul Shorey are an exception, as are those of Harold Cherniss in later years. Both had responded to the philosophy of humanistic values of the Greeks and were followed by the contributions of F. Solmsen and Philip Merlan, also in the twentieth century.

Parallel to the philological studies was another encounter with German philosophy during the second half of the nineteenth century, contributing to a trend that coincided with the establishing of graduate studies in American universities. A number of gifted American students went to Germany, among them Josiah Royce, who after receiving his BA in 1875 with a graduation thesis on "The Theology of Aeschylus' *Prometheus*," immediately went to Germany to study philosophy for two years. Upon returning, he went to Johns Hopkins and received his PhD in 1878. Greek philosophy, however, remained peripheral to his religious idealism. Others who went to Germany were G.S. Morris from Johns Hopkins, G. Santayana from Harvard, and F.J.K. Woodbridge from Columbia. They were deeply affected by the new interpretations of Plato and Aristotle. Upon his return, Morris brought back with him an Aristotle radically different from that of the scholastic version. Developed as a dynamic idealist, Morris following the model of his teacher F. Trendelenburg. It was Morris who later influenced John Dewey to modify his Hegelianism in favor of Aristotle, a move that was reinforced through Dewey's association with Woodbridge at Columbia.

Twentieth century

A preliminary note is needed on the extent and power of "influence." What happened in the twentieth century is not much different from what took place early in the intellectual history of America. For instance, the philosophical trends that reached America from Cambridge and Oxford, or Paris, Berlin and Heidelberg, were conveniently absorbed in revised form through critical reconstruction and adjustment to the American established needs. As importations, the currents of value theory, existentialism, phenomenology and other winds of doctrine were influential but not converting forces. In a similar way, though not as powerful as in the past century, the same mode of receiving the currents of English and European trends, continued. The influx of the classical tradition and especially Greek philosophy, rather than being a catalytic force, generated a creative response that at best may be called one of creative accommodation. In this respect, the power of influence bears the signs of a mild effect rather than a revolutionary beginning in a new direction. The Greek philosophers were available to whatever purposes the American intellectuals thought proper. The "living" past entered the scene mainly as a fertile reservoir of ideas than a relevant "present" doctrine. In this sense, the mild acceptance of Greek philosophy is better viewed in the fashion in which the trends of rationalism and empiricism were treated in the nineteenth century.

Of all the new philosophical currents in the late nineteenth century, it was the naturalistic side of Pragmatism that made extensive use of Greek philosophy, Aristotle in particular, and felt a strong attraction to it. The affinity can be explained as resulting from the naturalistic strand that soon was to become the dominant feature of Pragmatism. The early Santayana and the mature Woodbridge are the two American philosophers who came close to building their work in response to Aristotle. Dewey, although a leading pragmatist, was freely using the Aristotelian tradition together with the Socratic dialectic within the spirit of his naturalistic humanism. In all three cases we see an adjustment of Aristotle's most usable principles to the contemporary cultural and theoretical problems. If we can speak of "influence," we find it here in the most creative features of the school.

Santayana, who taught courses on Plato and Aristotle at Harvard, was the first to present a defense and espouse advocacy of Greek philosophy as a rational mode of life in the five volumes of his *The Life of Reason* (1905–6). The work was inspired by a blending of Hegelian phenomenology and Plato with Aristotelian ethics and aimed to project the full story of the progress of the human mind. Still, Santayana's intellectual position owed more to James' *Principles of Psychology* than to Aristotle's *De Anima.* It was the closest any American thinker had ever come to understanding the naturalism of the Greeks, especially at a time, as he stated, when "the philosophical and political departments at Harvard had not yet discovered Plato and Aristotle." Woodbridge, after studying with Paulsen in Germany, returned to America and used Aristotle's ontology to liberate his thinking from the last strains of idealism. Like Santayana but more persistently, he contributed largely to the study of Greek philosophy as the reliable model for the new naturalism. Still, Woodbridge's indebtedness was not only to the ancients but also to Spinoza, Locke and Santayana. Although neither he nor Santayana were members of the emerging Pragmatism, both helped build the bridge that made Greek thought understandable to students working on either side of Pragmatism. Their work was continued by the students who wrote dissertations at Columbia, among them Herbert W. Schneider, John Herman Randall, Jr, Sterling Lambrecht, Richard McKeon, Irwin Edman, and A. Edel.

John Dewey's affinity to Greek philosophy was a blend of critical reservations and fruitful engagement. He borrowed an expression from T. Veblen to characterize the Greek epistemology as being a case of the "spectator's theory of knowledge." At the same time he came closer to the Greek view of philosophy as a way of life, a thesis he was eventually to posit within the context of social life. Dewey brought philosophy under the banner of democracy. Actually, of all the pragmatists it was Dewey who succeeded in making use of the Greeks while trying to transform the educational norms through the rational understanding of the changing cultural conditions. Dewey's instrumentalism prevented him from appreciating the Greek view of reason in the full meaning of its humanistic value. But like the Greeks, he still sought to transform experience and raise it to a heightened understanding of the pressing problems of life. His response to Plato took the form of an urgent recommendation to adopt the Socratic command for relentless inquiry without the dualism of the Platonic theory of transcendent Forms. Dewey found it impossible to accept what he believed was the Greek confidence in ultimate values. As a result he dismissed this essential part of the philosophy of the Greeks at the critical turning point of his own thinking. It was this view he passed on to the next generation of naturalists, some of whom wrote sustained works on Greek philosophy. Dewey wrote none; Woodbridge wrote at least two, among them *The Son of Apollo* (1929), which delighted Dewey and irritated Paul Shorey.

By the middle of the twentieth century the scholarly interest in the ancient Greeks had reached a high plateau of productivity. A great number of books and articles had been published expounding on select themes and offering full treatments of the philosophies of the ancients. However, it is difficult to speak of Greek influence in the mode of philosophizing of the Americans comparable to the way Descartes, Locke, Hume, Kant, and Hegel had exerted. Critical studies of Greek philosophy abounded, but few tried to place the Greeks within the scope of their own intellectual loyalties, as did P.E. More, for instance in the case of Plato. Far more interesting proved the historical approach of Dewey's student, John Herman Randall, Jr, who as a leading historian of philosophy wrote books on Plato, Aristotle, also the Hellenistic thinkers by applying the principles of his naturalistic cultural relativism. What distinguishes Randall's reading of the ancient is an open and critical discussion on the role of the ancient philosophers in effecting changes in ideas, methods and objectives. The results, though not generally accepted, were nevertheless illuminating as, for instance, his seeing Plato's theory of Forms as imaginative perfections, or Aristotle's ethical excellences as special cultural responses to changing conditions. Randall himself remained confident that he understood both Dewey and Aristotle while deepening the historical evaluation of their contributions. Much different were the studies on ancient philosophers that R. Demos, R. McKeon, A. Edel, M. Greene, J. Owens, John Wild, R. Brumbaugh, Charles Kahn, Reginald Allen, and others worked out, always seeking to come close to the substance of the original.

A cross between philosophy, philology and analysis began by the mid-point of the twentieth century with the creation of the Society for Ancient Greek Philosophy in 1954 with G. Vlastos as its first president. Vlastos' publications on Plato and the Presocratics bear the marks of the application of the analytical tools to the evaluation of philosophical arguments in the philosophical texts of the Greeks. The analytical movement succeeded mainly as an interpretive undertaking rather than one seeking to reach beyond the perimeter of professional expertise. On the other hand, the cultural impact the pragmatic naturalists sought to bring gradually lessened during the latter part of the twentieth century. The only exception seems to be the approach of the existentialists deriving from their study of Nietzsche a different intensity to reach the mind of the ancient thinkers of Greece, poets as well as philosophers.

Understanding philosophy as a way of life was a Greek achievement and grew out of the conditions of that particular cultural setting. The primacy their philosophy assigned to reason survived in a variety of ways after the decline of the classical world. They viewed philosophy as the pursuit of wisdom, at once a personal affair and a political concern. Still, it was reason as the method the Greeks had developed for the pursuit of wisdom, including science, which proved adjustable. As a distinct "way of life," however, the original conception of philosophy remained non-transferable to alien conditions. Thus, recasting the methods of philosophy did not entail the incorporation of the original Greek "way of life" despite efforts to claim its applicability and relevance. The meaning of "influence" in the case of American philosophy calls for special evaluation when discussing the continuous interest in the study of ancient thought. The closest, it seems, the American thinkers came to being influenced by the Greek philosophers were initially certain members of the St Louis Hegelians and the naturalistic pragmatists in their attempts to see philosophy as a way of life. Both were cases of imitations of a model that did not aim at bringing about wider public acceptance. The Greeks have been studied, often very seriously, but more often than not without any explicit intent to grant their "way of life" a leading role of substantive influence in culture.

Postscript

A complete picture of the place of Greek philosophy and its role in the development of American thought is still a vast subject for investigation. Without such a close study it is difficult to specify with precision what may be called, even in a loose sense, "influence." Be that as it may, the academic interest has grown to the point where American scholarship in this field is now internationally recognized. As for the cultural role of Greek philosophy and its influence as "a way of life," that remains an open issue.

Further reading

Anderson, Paul R. *Platonism in the Midwest*. Philadelphia, PA: Temple University Publications, distributed by Columbia University Press, 1963.

Anton, John P. *American Naturalism and Greek Philosophy*. Amherst, NY: Humanity Books, 2005.

Eadie, John W. (ed.) *Classical Traditions in Early America*. Ann Arbor, MI: University of Michigan, 1976.

Koch, Adrienne. *Power, Morals, and the Founding Fathers: Essays in the Interpretation of the American Enlightenment*. Ithaca, NY: Cornell University Press, 1961.

Reinhold, Meyer. *Classical Americana. The Greek and Roman Heritage in the United States*. Detroit, MI: Wayne State University Press. 1984.

Schneider, Herbert W. *History of American Philosophy*. New York: Columbia University Press, 1946.

Sleeper, Ralph W. *The Necessity of Pragmatism*. New Haven, CT and London: Yale University Press, 1986.

JOHN P. ANTON

GROWTH

In the American philosophical tradition, growth is understood as a time process of change that is necessary to life, characterized by continuous selective integration of the contents of transactions of individuals and environments in ways that increase the richness and complexity of both. Growth may involve physical, psychic, mental, and spiritual levels in the most complex organisms (such as humans), including choices that implicate and may even actively consider the future. Growth involves loss of old formations and habits within often uneven, semi-autonomous processes of becoming that respond to the organism's needs and to reflective individuals' ideals, as well as to challenges and opportunities that arise in transactions with partners and environing contexts.

In American pragmatist philosophy, the concept of growth has a metaphysical depth that combines a Heraclitean principle of on-going cosmic change with a Darwinian principle of responsive, adaptive evolution that can lead to continuous, integrated complexity and richness, for individuals as well as for the larger communities of which they are parts. For Charles Sanders Peirce, such a principle of growth is involved in his concepts of tychism, synechism, and evolutionary love; knowledge also grows when a time-spanning community of scientific inquirers gradually comes to understand through reflectively studied, purposively controlled transactions with various sectors of the world how to adjust their thoughts and actions in ways that tend to bring about desirable consequences in terms of experiencing, furthering, and stabilizing this cosmic tendency toward increasing complexity and richness. For William James, the evolution of the universe is unfinished; the world is still "in the making," and thus, still plastic to some extent, which means that our actions can have real consequences, and our thinking can affect these to some extent. James emphasized the individuated pluralism that is characteristic of growth processes as we experience them, such that differing characteristic needs, differing ranges and rates of adaptive adjustment, and differing powers and capacities for initiating genuinely new responses and directions for development are features of the members of life communities within this always-unfinished world.

John Dewey regarded this biologically rooted metaphysical principle of growth as offering guidance for inquiry, morals, education, religion, the arts, and social living in all its dimensions. In Dewey's works, the concept of growth is closely connected with those of reconstruction, development, evolution, liberation, revitalization, continuity, and on-going adjustment. In Dewey's philosophy, as John Herman Randall, Jr, has pointed out, cultural growth through reconstruction in ways of thinking involves a reworking of earlier material inherited from a tradition, as problematized by new needs in a particular context. It involves processes of criticism, verification, testing, and free speculation within a search for better hypotheses and more fruitful principles (Randall 1939: 87–8). The kind of logic of inquiry that can guide this growth-oriented way of thinking, criticizing, and planning for the future emphasizes continuity of lower, less complex forms and activities with higher, more complex ones through on-going processes of partial disintegration and re-integration of organisms and environments that always involve some aspects of breakage and loss, which allows them to incorporate new contents gained from their transactions (Dewey 1938: 23, 34).

Dewey's adoption of a genetic method for understanding the meaning of an idea or a cultural practice highlights such a process of re-integrative growth as at work in its history, which in turn will suggest how to reconstruct it in ways that will make it more liberatory and fruitful in terms of future growth. Tracing alternative lines of development taken by those cultures from which our contemporary social life traces, including the various strands and levels of "moral background" that underlie and fix or liberate our imaginations, helps us understand our contemporary cultural situation and the possible paths of growth before us as individuals, as particular societies, and as a complex, cosmopolitan global civilization (Dewey 1932: 22ff). This helps us to re-envision the moral self in ways that lead to growth, which we may tend to resist (Dewey 1932: 307).

Reconstructing our inherited American ethical tradition in liberatory and fruitful ways requires replacing fixed ends and rules with the guiding aim of fostering on-going processes of growth, within which diverse ideal goods – e.g. honesty, industry, temperance justice, health, wealth and learning – vaguely express desirable directions for change within the lived experience of individuals and communities (Dewey 1920: 177). In turn, this reconstructed moral vision guides Dewey's reconstruction of the aim of education: the individual's on-going growth throughout the phases of life, marked by developing skills, increasingly secured knowledge, continuously more fruitful participation in various aspects of culture and civilization, and a semi-autonomous capability to continue a process of ever-richer and more complex re-integrations (Dewey 1920: 184–5).

At a social level, the moral criterion of growth focuses our attention on human capacities, directions for their development, and transactional approaches that tend to foster rather than to preclude these. Instead of treating individuals at any point in life as fully determined by in-born gifts, predilections, personal choices, and an environment, this approach directs our attention to what women and men, girls and boys have real potential to become and to do in the future, especially if assured supportive conditions for their fuller development and more effective integration within their natural–social environment. This is why the democratic ideal serves as both the most insightful basis of criticism and the best guide to future betterment (Dewey 1932: 349). In comparison to other actual ways of structuring and directing social life, the American experience as an experimental reconstruction of Western culture shows that a democratic way of living is most productive of the all-around growth of each and all the members of a society; this, Dewey argues, is democracy's test and moral warrant (Dewey 1920: 186).

The now-traditional American democratic values of freedom, equality, and friendship are important because they are necessary to individual growth, which in turn is necessary to social stability, security, and growth. Individual freedom *means* overcoming of obstacles and flexible, adaptive, ideal-directed growth, which in turn advances social welfare. High levels of social and individual functioning require an adequate range of freedom to experiment beyond the limits of custom, even though this may lead to confusion and some mistakes in the short term. Making experiments in living work for the growth of all concerned requires creates habits and conditions for intelligently appreciating their results, desirable and undesirable, and guiding future choices accordingly (Dewey 1920: 207–8). Balanced social growth through experimental adaptation to the always-changing conditions of the world requires that each of a society's diverse members be stimulated to continuous individual growth, which requires continuous social opportunities for active contribution of one's developing skills, knowledge, and imagination (Dewey 1920: 209).

Such a growth-centered reconstruction of culture will gradually be absorbed through a process of adjustment into a background of ideas, beliefs, habits of living, and ritual practices that take on a religious quality, leading thereby to the revitalization of religion and new growth in art (Dewey 1920: 210). The initiation of a process of cultural liberation that leads to individual and social growth requires the *replacement* of inherited religious and scientific visions, characterized by "a fixed revelation of unchanging Being and truth" (Dewey 1930: 24), and by "mechanical materialism," respectively, with a process metaphysics and a flexible, functional, evolutionary, radically empiricist logic of scientific inquiry (Dewey 1920: 210). That "democratic faith" that focused Dewey's life as a philosopher in the American stream ultimately rests on a belief in growth as a self-guiding potential capability to generate aims and methods that allow future experience to grow in its "ordered richness" (Dewey 1939: 343). Difficult as it may be to give up old self-conceptions, old ways of thinking, and the comforting security of fixed "truths," Dewey argued, a growth-oriented approach to thinking and living is the best way to engage realistically with the world, to address most effectively the problems before us, to increase our understanding, and to experience the joy in living that we may find possible, even in conditions of suffering and adversity (Dewey 1930: 25).

Further reading

Dewey, John. *Reconstruction in Philosophy.* Boston, MA: Beacon Press, 1920.

—— *Logic: the Theory of Inquiry.* New York: Holt, Rinehart and Winston, 1938.

—— *Ethics*, revised edition, in *John Dewey: The Later Works, Vol. 7, 1932*. Introduction by Abraham Edel and Elizabeth Flower, ed. Jo Ann Boydston. Carbondale, IL: Southern Illinois University Press, 1989 [1932].

—— "Nature, Life and Body-Mind" [1920], "The Development of American Pragmatism" [1920b], "What I Believe" [1930], "Creative Democracy – The Task Before Us" [1939], and "Time and Individuality" [1940] in *The Essential Dewey, Vol. 1: Pragmatism, Education, Democracy*, ed. Larry A. Hickman and Thomas M. Alexander. Bloomington, IN: Indiana University Press, 1998.

Randall, John Herman, Jr. "Dewey's Interpretation of the History of Philosophy" in Paul Arthur Schilpp and Lewis Edwin Hahn (eds). *The Philosophy of John Dewey* (Library of Living Philosophers, Vol. I). LaSalle, IL: Open Court, 1939.

JUDITH M. GREEN

H

HAACK, SUSAN

In the 1970s Susan Haack (1945–) was known principally as a philosopher of logic; in the 1980s she began to write extensively and originally on questions of epistemology; and most recently she has added to her published repertoire papers on questions of a political, an ethical, and an aesthetic nature.

Animating and unifying this wide-ranging body of work has been a persistent concern with what Peirce once called "the integrity of belief." Haack's interest in non-classical systems of logic, for example, was motivated chiefly by a desire to get clear on what might count as a good reason to accept one logical system rather than another. What, for that matter, might in general count as a good reason for believing one thing rather than another? Such is the guiding question of epistemology as Haack sees it, and so her earlier work on the epistemology of logic appears, retrospectively, as something of a case study for her later work on the theory of knowledge as a whole. Flying equally in the face of Michael Dummett's heady idea that Frege's insights into logic and language point to the conclusion that the theory of meaning ought to replace metaphysics and epistemology at the center of philosophy, and of Richard Rorty's yet bolder and more sweeping idea that the traditional center of philosophy should be abandoned and not reoccupied, Haack remains persuaded "that the central questions of philosophy are metaphysical and epistemological" (1982).

For Haack, as for the classical American Pragmatists, the central concerns of philosophy are genuine but not privileged, and its questions are difficult but not intractable. It is not the business of philosophy to resolve such issues as the scope and limits of human knowledge, or the ultimate constituents of reality, in splendid isolation, with the grandiose aim of providing a priori or transcendental moorings for the rest of inquiry. But it is the business of philosophy to grapple with real issues; it matters, for example, – and not only to professional philosophers – whether or not epistemic standards are merely conventional or in what ways, if any, the natural and social sciences are epistemically exemplary. In earlier work directed against those who sought to defend the autonomy of philosophy from the sciences or the priority of descriptive over revisionary metaphysics, the first of these themes is paramount (1975, 1979), while in later pieces directed against those who have become dubious about the very possibility of the non-partisan pursuit of truth, it is the second that dominates (1993, 1996, 1997).

Haack has a sharp eye for false dichotomies and a notable aptitude for patiently disassembling them. In *Evidence and Inquiry* (1993) she argues in detail against the adequacy of both foundationalist and coherentist styles of theory of epistemic justification, developing instead a demonstrably superior intermediate theory called – revealing a Peircean preference for accuracy over euphony – "foundherentism." Aware that she is not the only contemporary philosopher to have impugned the dichotomy between foundationalism and coherentism, Haack proceeds to scrutinize in turn: Popperian falsificationism, Quinean naturalism, reliabilism, the "neurophilosophical" dismissal of folk psychology, including the epistemologically central concept of belief, espoused by Paul and Patricia Churchland, and the "vulgar pragmatist" dismissal of epistemological questions as the regrettable products of bad philosophical assumptions. Since each of these fashionable views is found wanting, the upshot is another dichotomy transcended: this time the meta-dichotomy between assuming that foundationalism and coherentism exhaust the non-skeptical alternatives in the theory of knowledge on the one hand, and hastening to something much more subversive of traditional epistemological ambitions on the other. Finally, Haack responds to the specter of skepticism by arguing that foundherentist standards of epistemic justification are not only a faithful reconstruction of those actually used by most people most of the time; they also provide the best indication of truth that we can have. As Peirce had insisted that fallible knowledge was far better than no knowledge at all, so Haack maintains that a modest degree of justified confidence in the truth-indicativeness of foundherentist standards is "a good deal better than nothing." Here, as elsewhere, she shows herself to be a resolute opponent of "all-or nothingism," a staunch meliorist in the spirit of William James.

Further reading

Haack, Susan. *Deviant Logic*. Cambridge: Cambridge University Press, 1974; second expanded edition *Deviant Logic. Fuzzy Logic: Beyond the Formalism*. Chicago, IL: University of Chicago Press, 1996.

—— *Philosophy of Logics*. Cambridge: Cambridge University Press, 1978.

—— "Philosophy/philosophy, an Untenable Dualism," *Transactions of the Charles S. Peirce Society* 29, 3 (Summer 1993): 411–26.

—— "Dry Truth and Real Knowledge: Epistemologies of Metaphor and Metaphors of Epistemology" in J. Hintikka (ed.) *Aspects of Metaphor*. Dordrecht: Kluwer, 1994.

—— "Concern for Truth: What It Means, Why It Matters," *Annals of the New York Academy of Sciences*, ed. Paul R. Gross, Normal Levitt, and Martin W. Lewis, 775 (Summer 1996): 57–63.

—— "The First Rule of Reason" in Jacqueline Brunning and Paul Forster (eds) *The Rule of Reason: The Philosophy of Charles Sanders Peirce*. Toronto: University of Toronto Press, 1997.

MARK MIGOTTI

HAACK, SUSAN: AUTOBIOGRAPHY

Born in 1945 and the first in my family to go to college, I was educated at state primary and high schools in England; at Oxford; and then at Cambridge. At Oxford I studied Plato with Gilbert Ryle and logic with Michael Dummett, and wrote my BPhil dissertation, on ambiguity, with David Pears; in Cambridge, where my philosophical education continued in part through lunch-time philosophical workouts with Elizabeth Anscombe, I wrote the PhD dissertation that eventually became *Deviant Logic* (1974). After my first academic job, at a women's college in Cambridge, I moved to the University of Warwick; and then in 1990 to the US, where I have worked ever since. *Philosophy of Logics* appeared in 1978, and a new, expanded edition of my first book, *Deviant Logic, Fuzzy Logic: Beyond the Formalism*, in 1996. *Evidence and Inquiry* was published in 1993; *Manifesto of a Passionate Moderate: Unfashionable Essays* in 1998; *Defending Science – Within Reason: Between Scientism and Cynicism* in 2003; and an anthology, *Pragmatism, Old and New*, in 2006.

If I deserve to be classified as an American philosopher, it is not because of my "resident alien" immigration status but because, ever since I discovered first Peirce and then the other classical pragmatists in the early 1970s, my thinking has drawn on the rich tradition of classical pragmatism as well as on the analytical techniques of my early training.

The quotation that opens *Evidence and Inquiry* is from Thomas Reid: "Let us remember how common the folly is, of going from one faulty extreme into its opposite." But my subtitle, *Towards Reconstruction in Epistemology*, reveals that Dewey helped convince me of the need to transcend false dichotomies; and my word for the middle way between the faulty extremes of foundationalism and coherentism – "foundherentism" – reveals my Peircean penchant for neologisms. The old pragmatists taught me early on to set aside Descartes's preoccupations with certainty and the refutation of skepticism, and to look not only to the individual knowing subject but also to the community of inquirers.

In *Manifesto of a Passionate Moderate*, arguing against the fashionable cynicism of some contemporary philosophy (including some contemporary neo-"pragmatisms"), I built on Peirce's distinction between genuine and sham inquiry; articulating a conception of philosophy as neither subordinate to science nor "just a genre of literature," I built on his meta-philosophical reflections; and distinguishing true from false understandings of the social character of science, I built on his conception of the community of inquirers.

But *Defending Science – Within Reason* is perhaps the most pragmatist of my books, drawing on

Peirce's Critical Common-Sensism and his Synechism, on Dewey's reflections on science and values, and on Mead's conception of the self and society; and, most of all – as I explore the sharing of evidence, the plurality of scientific methods, the differences between science and literature, tensions between science and religion, the role of science in society, and the handling of scientific evidence in court – liberated from the uneasy reluctance of analytic philosophy to stray beyond strictly linguistic, logical, or conceptual questions.

Most recently, I continue to stray beyond these kinds of question in papers on the ideal of intellectual integrity as it is expressed in works of literature; on the scope and limits of formal methods in philosophy; on Oliver Wendell Holmes's legal philosophy; and on the role of logic in the law.

SUSAN HAACK

HABERMAS, JÜRGEN

One of the most important German philosophers of the second half of the twentieth century, and perhaps the premier philosophical theorist of "modernity," Jürgen Habermas (1929–) bears a special relation to American philosophy. It was from his work that many post-World War II Continental philosophers first became aware of the value of classical American philosophy. Indeed, in his philosophical interests as well as his politics, Habermas inspires a strong comparison to John Dewey, despite their different methodologies and fundamental assumptions.

Habermas is a late representative of the neo-Marxist Institut für Sozialforschung (Institute for Social Research) of Frankfurt, Germany, which between the world wars combined empirical research with social theory in service of a "critical" social science, a social analysis that is simultaneously scientific and committed to a moral–political position, in its case, a democratic or "Western" Marxism. The horrors of the Second World War convinced Theodor Adorno and Max Horkheimer that the Enlightenment commitment to Reason, while irreplaceable as a basis for freedom, is "dialectical" or self-defeating, leading paradoxically to tyranny and barbarism (i.e. Nazism and Fascism). It was the historical role of Adorno's research assistant, Habermas, to accept his mentor's notion of critical social science yet expand his philosophical resources to include British and American philosophy, arguing that there is a form of reason that avoids dialectical destruction. That is the "communicative rationality" we use in inter-subjective discussions seeking agreement. It is intrinsically normative, committed to truth, goodness, and sincere self-expression, but because it is neither subjective nor "transcendental" it does not succumb to the "dialectic of Enlightenment." Habermas has spent his career crafting a rational, ethical, but non-metaphysical basis for progressive social criticism.

Unlike most other European thinkers, Habermas found classical American philosophy conceptually and politically inspiring. In his early *Knowledge and Human Interests* (1968) he took Peirce as an important formulator of methodology for philosophy and the sciences. (Peirce had been recently introduced to contemporary Germans by the work of Karl-Otto Apel.) Later in his monumental *Theory of Communicative Action* (1981) he recognized Mead's unique account of mind and reason as emerging from social communication as a precursor of his own notion of discourse. In general, the Americans provided Habermas with an exemplary case of a non-Cartesian, non-idealist notion of inter-subjective rationality based in the context of social interaction.

In his historical investigation of the philosophical roots of modernism and postmodernism, *The Philosophical Discourse of Modernity* (1985) Habermas located the Americans in the school of "left-wing Hegelianism," connecting them to those nineteenth-century followers of Hegel who found the basis for radical social implications in a "naturalization" of Hegel's idealism (e.g. Ludwig Feuerbach and Karl Marx). While this interpretation does not fit well with Peirce (whose major influences were Kant and Scottish thinkers), it is a very plausible description of Mead and Dewey, especially given the latter's early Hegelianism. The connection with Marx is also instructive, for while Marx was a fellow philosopher of *praxis* or practice, the Americans developed this perspective into a theory of mind as communication among embodied agents, avoiding Marx's identification of practice with production or labor. In this sense Habermas' turn toward the Americans reflected his move away from "Western Marxism" toward a more moderate, social democratic politics.

Indeed, it would not be misleading to consider Habermas *the German Dewey*. True, despite his breadth he never covered the range of philosophical topics that Dewey did (e.g. logic, philosophy of education, aesthetics, etc.), and the foundations of his thought lie in Kant rather than a naturalized version of Hegel – we cannot call Habermas a naturalist. But like Dewey Habermas pursues fundamental philosophical questions in the service of social reconstruction; like Dewey he combines fundamental philosophical research with the role of public philosopher, engaging other disciplines and the reading public; and like Dewey he reasserts that the Enlightenment ideals of truth and freedom are when properly interpreted compatible, not antithetical, having found, like Peirce and Dewey, the free community to be the proper venue for inquiry into truth. In sum, like Dewey, he is his generation's unparalleled philosopher of democracy.

Further reading

Aboulafia, Mitchell, Bookman, Myra, and Kemp, Catherine (eds) *Habermas and Pragmatism*. New York: Routledge, 2002.

Habermas, Jürgen. *Knowledge and Human Interests*, trans. Jeremy J. Shapiro. Boston, MA: Beacon Press, 1971 (*Erkenntnis und Interesse*, 1968).

—— *The Theory of Communicative Action. Volume Two: Lifeworld and System: A Critique of Functionalist Reason*, trans. Thomas McCarthy. Boston, MA: Beacon Press, 1987 (*Theorie des kommunikativen Handelns. Band 2: Zur Kritik der funktionalistischen Vernunft*, 1981).

——"Discourse Ethics: Notes on a Program of Philosophical Justification" in *Moral Consciousness and Communicative Action*, trans. Christian Lenhardt and Shierry Weber Nicholsen. Cambridge, MA: MIT Press, 1995 ("*Diskursethik: Notizen zu einem Begrüdungsprogramm*," *Moralbewusstsein und kommunikatives Handeln*, 1983).

—— *The Philosophical Discourse of Modernity: Twelve Lectures*, trans. Frederick G. Lawrence. Cambridge, MA: MIT Press, 1987 (*Der Philosophische Diskurs der Moderne: Zwölf Vorlesungen*, 1985).

Shalin, Dmitri N. (ed.) "Habermas, Pragmatism, and Critical Theory," Special Issue of *Symbolic Interaction* 15, 3 (Fall 1992).

LAWRENCE CAHOONE

HABIT

The American pragmatic tradition places great emphasis upon organisms, human or otherwise, carrying on a series of transactions or interactions with the environment. Knowledge is acquired through such interaction, rather than being deemed innate or self-evident. This emphasis on growth through interaction makes the topic of "habit" an important one for American philosophy. The present discussion will confine itself to three figures: Charles Sanders Peirce, William James, and John Dewey.

Charles Sanders Peirce

Peirce's articulation of the theme of "habit" has both an ontological and an epistemological dimension.

Ontologically, Peirce believed that there were three categories of being, or modes of existence. These are: chance, law, and habit. These three are closely related to his phenomenological categories of firstness, secondness, and thirdness. Chance is possibility, law the facticity of individual force, and habit-taking refers to the tendency of individual existences to exhibit a pattern of meaning or design. Peirce uses the term "habit" in a broad sense, to describe the tendency of any person or thing to behave in similar ways in similarly describable situations. All actual things, inanimate and animate, exhibit habits. All things have a tendency to take on habits. Laws, then, are the results of long periods of the taking on of habits. The uniformity that exists in nature has evolved by individual entities taking on sets of habits. Peirce's conception of habit here is not just subjective and psychological, but rather objective and cosmological in nature. It describes an actual characteristic of the universe, and not merely a psychological phenomenon. Habit is not only a psychological category, but also an ontological one.

Habit was also very closely associated with belief for Peirce, and hence to his whole theory of inquiry, which proceeded from doubt to inquiry, then to belief and action. Doubt is an irritant that is replaced by belief after inquiry takes place. This is articulated quite clearly in two of Peirce's most famous articles, "The Fixation of Belief" and "How to Make Our Ideas Clear." Doubt is not a habit, but rather the privation of a habit. It is a "condition of erratic activity", an irritant, which we try to get rid of by establishing a habit. Thought or inquiry is prospective in nature. The purpose of thought is to produce habits of action. Belief consists in the establishment of a habit, i.e. a rule of action, a tendency to act in certain ways in certain situations of a similar nature. The whole goal of thought is to create habits of action. To see the meaning of a thought, we need simply to ascertain what habit it produces, for what a thing means is simply what habits it involves. Peirce sometimes says that belief is a habit; and at other times that belief produces a habit. Habits seem to be the way that beliefs are translated into action. The meaning of a belief is the habit or rule of action it prescribes. The core of belief is the creation of a habit; and different beliefs are distinguished by the different types of action which result. From here is but a short step to Peirce's development of his notion of pragmatism, or, later, pragmaticism. "Consider what effects that might conceivably have practical bearings, we conceive the object of our conception to have. Our conception of these effects is the whole of our conception of the object." (CP 5.402)

William James

James's most extensive treatment of habit occurs in Chapter 4 of *The Principles of Psychology.* Looked at from the outside, creatures are "bundles of habits." Any attempt to define what habit is leads one to consider matter and a specific characteristic it possesses, viz. "plasticity." Plasticity in the broad sense of the term describes the possession of a structure weak enough to yield to an influence, but strong enough not to yield all at once. This allows living creatures to adapt to changing circumstances. The nervous system is a sort of moving equilibrium. The human being is born with the capacity to do more things than he or she is equipped to actualize. Habit or practice economizes the discharge of nervous and muscular energy. Habit streamlines the movements required to attain a given result; it makes them more specific and alleviates fatigue. Habit also lessens the conscious focalization with which our deeds are enacted. A violin player must first laboriously learn the musical chords and the variations of bowing; but afterwards these become nearly automatic, and she can think about more complicated matters. A dancer dances almost but not quite unconsciously, after having attended the Martha Graham dance school for years. Mere perception of the beginning of an act will carry it through to conclusion, freeing up the mind to consider broader more creative options. While we are inattentive to actions carried out through habit, we become immediately attentive to them if something goes wrong. "Habit is thus the enormous fly-wheel of society, its precious conservative agent" (p. 121). Going further, there are good habits and bad habits, and you can interfere with current habits. You can consciously choose a habit – which means that there are ethical ramifications to the law of habit. Personal habits are formed before twenty years of age; intellectual and professional ones by thirty. This leads James to offer a series of suggestions concerning habit formation. The first is to make our nervous system our ally and not our enemy by performing as many good acts as possible habitually early on in life, thus setting the mind free to do more creative work later on. When adopting a new habit we should commit ourselves with as intense and focused an initiative as possible, seizing upon the very first chance to act upon a resolution made. Good intentions by themselves are insufficient. Action or praxis must actually take place. The feeling that does not translate into action loses any value. One can detect here a nascent form of pragmatism in the making. The tendency to act must be actualized if habits are to be formed. In order to do this we should preserve the faculty of effort alive in ourselves by exercising it a little every day. Perform some small act of asceticism or heroism daily, so as to be ready when the real challenge to your habit takes place.

Embodied habit and consciousness are inversely related, in a dynamic tension. Habit insures a form of stability, with a minimum consciousness of "felt suitability." When habits are unstable, consciousness is intense. In the higher levels of the animal kingdom, the nerve centers are numerous, offering many alternatives; consciousness itself is characterized by "instability" in the sense of having diverse options from which to choose. This very "vagueness," James says, is an advantage, allowing the conscious person to adapt her conduct to the slightest changes in the environment. It is the very vagueness involved in a conscious situation that enables James to view consciousness as efficacious. Consciousness is always primarily a selecting agency. Whether we take it on the lowest level of sense, or on the highest level of the intellect, we find it always doing one thing, selecting one out of several of the materials so presented to its notice, highlighting and foregrounding that and marginalizing as far as possible all the rest. The item highlighted is always in close connection with some interest felt by consciousness to be predominant at the time.

John Dewey

Dewey outlines his views on habit quite extensively in the chapter entitled "The Place of Habit in Conduct," in *Human Nature and Conduct*, published in 1922. He uses the term "habit" quite broadly. It is meant to indicate that type of human activity which is influenced by previous activity; which has within itself a certain ordering or systematization of minor elements of action; but which is also projective, dynamic in quality, ready for overt manifestation; and which is operative in some quiet subordinate form even when not obviously dominating activity. Habits are acquired functions; they demand the cooperation of organism and environment. They are "funded" meanings or "acquired" meanings, not inner forces. Habits are ways of utilizing the environment. In this transaction, the environment has its own role to play. Habits require support from environing conditions.

Going further, all virtues and vices are both habits; they are interactions of individual and outside world. Moral issues are projective; they are concerned with the future, not the past. We cannot immediately or directly change our habits. This is mere wishful thinking. But we can change them indirectly by modifying conditions under which they operate. The self for Dewey is constituted by the interpenetration of habits; this is how it develops its "character," through interacting with the world. Habits are "implicated" in one another. They are more than mere tools or static things, laying in wait for possible utilization. Habits are "means" only when they enter into active organization with things. In actuality, the means/end dichotomy is rejected because habits, as means, are partly constitutive of the ends-in-view. Habits are, in short, patterns of organization. The dichotomy between reason and habit is a false one. Reason separated from of all influence of prior habit is pure fiction. All our thoughts and perceptions come to us filtered through the medium of habit. In knowledge, there are no immaculate conceptions. Meaning is acquired, not given in advance. When habits are working smoothly, they do not produce acute consciousness, but rather a vague awareness of well-being.

Dewey's social psychology argued against the priority given to impulses in psycho-analysis. By themselves, impulses are merely blind bursts of energy; they must be organized, through habit, to take on meaning. Habits are forms of energy organized in certain channels. Habits do not exist in addition to impulses. Rather, habits are the patterns impulses exhibit once they are meaningfully organized.

At any given moment we take several habits for granted. This is how we get things done; and also how we move on to think or deal with greater or more complicated matters. Repetition, however, does not constitute the essence of habit. What we acquire through habit is a predisposition towards ways or modes of responding to situations deemed similar in certain respects, but not to specific acts. Said differently, there is a difference for Dewey between "habit" and "habituation." Habituation is a form of accommodation, of "getting used to" or assimilating specific conditions which one does not want to change. Active habits have to do with adaptation rather than accommodation; they involve a more active transaction with or making over of the environment. Habits are adjustments *of* the environment, not merely *to* it.

For Dewey, social customs or habits exist prior to individual self development of habits. The chicken comes before the egg. At a very early age, we interact with others in specific contextual situations, and in doing so we take on a character or develop a self. Our way of behaving, then, is not derived from inner psychological processes, but rather from social psychology, where physics, physiology and chemistry are involved as much as psychology itself. However, all is not predetermined, or a one-way street. Although the chicken precedes the egg, the latter, once born, can modify the chicken. Diversity of customs, conflicting with one another, as well as less encrustation among younger members of society, allows for impulsive activity, and so for a more spiral-like sense of development – one with both continuity and novelty. Both organism and environment are being constantly modified through interaction.

So, although habits cannot be avoided, for Dewey there are good habits and bad habits. Habit as mere enslavement to old ruts is indeed bad. But in actuality, there are two kinds of habit, intelligent and routine. By "mechanization" of some of our bodily and cognitive activities we are freed up to perform other, more creative tasks. The jazz musician who has memorized all the musical chords of a piece is thereby "freed up" to improvise. The routine is undesirable, but the habits developed and employed by the cook, the musician, the carpenter – these are intelligent or artistic habits; they are to be nurtured and allowed to grow. The real opposition, then, is not between reason and habit but between routine habit and intelligent habit or art. Finally one can cultivate the habit of adopting intelligent habits. One should cultivate habits that enable one to adapt to constantly changing circumstances and environments. It enables the individual to act in some situations without having to think the situation through over and over again.

In closing, for all three thinkers, habit plays an enormous role; it enables us to maintain some relative stability, a moving equilibrium, in a post-Darwinian universe. It enables the individual to act in some situations without having to think the situation through over and over again, and in so doing it frees us up for other more creative experiences.

Further reading

Dewey, John. *The Collected Works of John Dewey*, ed. Jo Ann Boydston. Carbondale, IL: Southern Illinois University Press, 1969–91; published as *The Early Works: 1882–98* (EW), *The Middle Works, 1899–1924* (MW), and *The Later Works, 1925–53* (LW). See especially "The Place of Habit in Conduct" in *Human Nature and Conduct*, in Vol. 14 of *The Middle Works.*

James, William. *The Principles of Psychology*, 2 volumes. New York: Henry Holt, 1890. Especially Chapter 4, "Habit."

Peirce, C.S. *The Collected Papers of Charles Sanders Peirce* (CP), 8 volumes, ed Charles Hartshorne and Paul Weiss (Vols 1–6), and Arthur W. Burks (Vols 7–8). Cambridge,

MA: Harvard University Press, 1931–58. See especially "The Fixation of Belief" and "How to Make Our Ideas Clear" in Vol. 5; and "The Law of Mind" and "The Architecture of Theories" in Vol. 6.

William J. Gavin

HALL, EVERETT WESLEY

Everett W. Hall (1901–60) was a systematic philosopher known most for his work in epistemology, value theory, and philosophical methodology. Born in Janesville, Wisconsin, he was educated at Lawrence College (AB 1923; MA 1925) and Cornell University (PhD 1929). He taught at the University of Chicago (1929–31), Ohio State University (1931–3), Stanford University (1933–41), University of Iowa (1941–52), where he was Chairman of the Philosophy Department, and the University of North Carolina at Chapel Hill (1952–60), where he was Kenan Professor of Philosophy and Chairman of the Philosophy Department. In 1958–9 he was Fulbright Lecturer in Philosophy at Kyoto University in Japan. He was active in a range of philosophical organizations and held offices in the American Philosophical Association. He also was deeply involved in the academic institutions in which he served and the communities in which he lived. He defended a value realism, an intentionalistic conception of empiricist epistemology, and a conception of philosophy as categorial analysis that reveals the basic structure of reality.

A variety of influences

Hall was influenced first by the Idealist movement then still strong at Cornell. He accepted that metaphysics is legitimate and that philosophical problems are real problems. He also believed in the reality of the mind, though he rejected the standard idealist options. Nevertheless, early on he was cognizant of and affected by the work of analysts such as Moore, Russell, and Wittgenstein. He always aimed at achieving clarity by analyzing what it does and does not make sense to say about an issue and by attempting to define his terms in ways that addressed his contemporaries in the Anglo-American tradition. And he was always concerned with questions about the nature of philosophy, its method, and conflict between philosophical positions.

He quickly came to identify with the analytic movement. He never gave up the belief that the structural features of analyzed language reveal something about the necessary structure of reality; and he saw this analysis as a way of reaching, defending, and adjudicating metaphysical conclusions. At first he conceived of analysis in the manner of the ideal language program. Over time, he came to favor the analysis of ordinary language instead of an ideal language, but it is fairer to say that he internalized both movements and worked out a different view of philosophy than either. He took from philosophical movements what he found defensible and went his own way.

Categories and philosophy

In *Philosophical Systems* (1960) Hall contended that philosophical work is always carried out from some philosophical perspective or approach or style, which he called a philosophical system or a categorial system. A system is organized by and governed by commitment to a set of categories, fundamental ways that reality is structured (such as existence as the way that an object is real and exemplification as the way that a property is real). Categorial concepts are irreducible within the philosophical system and function as its framework. They are revealed by what the system takes to be the philosophically clarified structure of empirical commitments. For a realist, empirical commitments are about objects; for one sort of phenomenalist, they are about sense data. They are also revealed by the explicit categorial statements found in or applicable to some philosophical system, such as the positivist's verifiability theory of meaning or the Kantian claim that space and time are the forms of intuition.

Hall denied that an *ad rem* approach applies to philosophy; we cannot directly experience the categorial dimensions or aspects of reality. Furthermore, he held that proof and refutation (in the ordinary sense) can function only within a philosophical system, since they are formulated within that system. So, there can be no straightforward proof or refutation of a system itself. Furthermore, philosophers cannot help but operate from within a categorial system, whether aware of it or not, leading to the conclusion that there is no neutral ground in philosophy. Indeed, since Hall contends that even ordinary experience and language are categorially committed, everyone is inextricably in the "categorio-centric predicament." Still, he insisted, a philosophical system can be tested by how consistent and comprehensive it is and, more importantly, by how well it squares with the natural categories found in the linguistic structure of ordinary language and ordinary experience. He noted that any attempt to deny this kind of testing must be formulated using the very linguistic structure one is rejecting. This testing occurs through a kind of linguistic analysis he called "categorial analysis"; this is the method of philosophy which employs a kind of ad hominem reasoning. The categorial knowledge gained is neither analytic nor synthetic, neither a priori nor empirical (in the standard senses of these terms).

Intentionalistic empiricism: fact and value

Our Knowledge of Fact and Value (1961) is the most developed account of Hall's intentional empiricism. He was an empiricist not only because of the strong empiricistic direction of modern philosophy from Locke to Carnap, but also because he contended that empiricism is consistent with the categorial commitments found in the grammatical structures of ordinary language.

As a result of the intense work Hall did on the topic of intentionality with Gustav Bergmann and Wilfrid Sellers at Iowa in the 1940s, he argued that the grammar of "cognitive verbs" such as "know," "perceive," and "experience" indicates categorially that knowledge, perception, and experience inherently and irreducibly have intentionality. Indeed, he concluded that mind and language are inherently intentional. He charged much modern empiricism with rejecting that intentionality and with giving intentional terms a non-intentional interpretation because of a concern with trying to be true to the non-intentional subject matter of modern science.

Counter to that tradition, he argued that experience is both intentional and active. A perception, such as "I see that the flower has started to bloom" has as its intentional content a claim, an "inner sentence", by which it refers to an external object. In perception we take the world to be a certain way, and the perception can be veridical or not. We cannot compare a perception with what the perception is about in any straightforward manner. But we can assess perceptions in light of other perceptions in order to get clear about objects. Perceptions cannot be incorrigible but can be true with some degree of probability. Hall's theory of perception avoided the problem of the external world that threatens not only idealism but also skepticism and much empiricism. Lastly, since cognitive verbs, unlike verbs of action, pick out "acts" that do not affect their objects, he held that knowing is not a form of doing, contrary to pragmatism.

He noted that the content of a sensory perception is a factual claim about the world. The logical grammar of an atomic fact is "x is F." In *What is Value?* (1952), Hall had contended that categorial analysis shows that value is a categorial aspect or dimension of reality. The logical grammar of an atomic value is "x ought to be F." This committed him to a non-naturalistic value realism. Values are objectively real, not reducible to or explainable by the category of factuality. He extended his intentional empiricism through an analysis of emotions that led him to conclude that emotions are intentional and are a kind of perception. The content of an emotion, he argued, is a value claim about the world. Emotions form the empirical basis for knowledge of values in reality. In *Modern Science and Human Values* (1956), he used his analysis of value to indicate how the modern West developed early on a value-free science, and he maintained that this modern path was incomplete and therefore distorted our worldview. Hall's death from a sudden heart attack prevented him from finishing a book on aesthetics, which would have been an application of his value theory to a particular area of value.

Further reading

Adams, E.M. (ed.) "Common Sense Realism: Critical Essays on the Philosophy of Everett W. Hall," *Southern Journal of Philosophy* 4, 3 (Fall 1966).

Clark, Romane. "The Linguistic Metaphysics of Everett W. Hall," *Southern Journal of Philosophy* 3 (Fall 1965): 147–56.

Hall, E.W. *Modern Science and Human Values: A Study in the History of Ideas.* Princeton, NJ: D. van Nostrand, 1956.

—— *Philosophical Systems: A Categorial Analysis.* Chicago, IL: University of Chicago Press, 1960.

—— *Categorial Analysis: Selected Essays of Everett W. Hall on Philosophy, Value, Knowledge and the Mind*, ed. E.M. Adams. Chapel Hill, NC: University of North Carolina Press, 1964.

Hartshorne, Charles. "Professor Hall on Perception," *Philosophy and Phenomenological Research* 21 (June 1961): 563–71.

McLelland, Reginald F. "The Relationship of the Two Conceptions of Categories in Everett Hall's Philosophy," *Transactions of the Charles S. Peirce Society* 11 (Winter 1975): 37–56.

Rohatyn, Dennis A. "Hall and Mill's Proof," *Southwestern Journal of Philosophy* 2 (Winter 1971): 113–18.

SETH HOLTZMAN

HAPPINESS

Thomas Jefferson famously wrote in the Declaration of Independence that every human being has the right to "life, liberty, and the pursuit of happiness." For Americans, this pursuit of happiness has been more than just an abstract right. It has also been the concrete inspiration for many millions – among them immigrants, pioneers, entrepreneurs, and industrialists – to follow the American dream.

In *The Varieties of Religious Experience*, William James wrote, "How to gain, how to keep, how to recover happiness, is in fact for most men at all times the secret motive of all they do, and of all they are willing to endure." What is this happiness that motivates so many? Is it a good thing to pursue? Is it something that can ever be caught?

A look at the evolution of the meaning of the term "happiness" in Western intellectual history puts these questions in a helpful, broader perspective. Happiness was originally understood as a product of chance. Etymologically, the English word derives from the Old Norse *happ*, which means "luck" or "fortune." This etymological connection between happiness and luck occurs in virtually every Indo-European language (McMahon 2006).

Socrates and subsequent ancient philosophers argued that happiness is at least partly a function of human choice. By volitionally cultivating virtue, we can develop a character that is more conducive to happiness. The cultivation of virtue requires the development of good habits of thought and action.

With the rise of Christianity, the emphasis remained on the cultivation of virtue, but the means for its cultivation and its expected results changed tremendously. For Christians, virtue was something that could be achieved only with divine help, and a virtuous life was no guarantee of earthly happiness, but rather a pathway to happiness in the afterlife.

It was in the modern period that happiness was seen, not as a function of chance or as a reward for the virtuous few, but as a birthright for all. With unprecedented advances in science, technology, and medicine, it seemed that the causes of human unhappiness could be eradicated and that each person would be able to pursue happiness in their own way.

The two most influential types of theories of happiness in philosophy and the social sciences today are hedonic theories and eudaimonic theories. For hedonic theorists, happiness is a function of the way we feel in each moment of our lives. The psychological researcher Edward Diener, for example, defines happiness as "subjective well-being," which he operationalizes in terms of high positive affect, low negative affect, and high life satisfaction. In other words, the more pleasant emotions you have, the fewer unpleasant emotions you have, and the more satisfied you are with life, the happier you are. On this definition of happiness, empirical research indicates that most people are, in fact, happy, and that it is possible to become sustainably happier.

For eudaimonic theorists, happiness is more than a function of subjective states. Following Aristotle (whose term *eudaimonia* means "happiness" or "human flourishing"), these theorists argue that happiness requires certain objective conditions. For Aristotle himself, these conditions included virtue, along with the external conditions of wealth, friendship, physical attractiveness, high social status, and good children. For the contemporary philosopher Martha Nussbaum, the list necessary for happiness includes, among other things, living a normal life span, enjoying good physical health, experiencing normal human emotions, and having control over one's environment.

While Thomas Jefferson and the signers of the Declaration of Independence may be correct that the pursuit of happiness is a fundamental human right, happiness itself seems very difficult to define, and even harder to achieve. Modern optimism about the achievement of happiness has been difficult to sustain, given the intractability of certain diseases, the frequency of natural catastrophes, and, perhaps most of all, the high degree of misery humans continue to visit on each other. John Dewey criticized hedonic theories of happiness on the grounds that growth sometimes requires unpleasant choices. He would argue that those who live their lives in the quest for good feelings actually stunt their own growth.

It is good for these and similar critiques to temper a naïve optimism about the achievability of happiness and to clear the ground for the hard work of realistic progress. Current scientific study of well-being and human flourishing may not be able to guarantee everyone immediate happiness, but it may help us learn how to become more effective in its pursuit.

Further reading

Dewey, John. *Ethics* in *The Middle Works of John Dewey, Vol. 5, 1908*, ed. Jo Ann Boydston. Carbondale, IL: Southern Illinois University Press, 1978.

McMahon, Darrin M. *Happiness: A History*. New York: Atlantic Monthly Press, 2006.

Seligman, Martin E.P. *Authentic Happiness*. New York: Free Press, 2002.

James O. Pawelski

HARE, PETER H.: AUTOBIOGRAPHY

Deep maternal and paternal roots in American intellectual history going back to the earliest settlers have influenced me since childhood. Most directly, my grandmother's work in American cultural history and my father's desire to combine philosophy, religion, physics, mathematics, and the arts have motivated my career. With a temperamental craving for inclusiveness and connectedness, I tried as a Yale undergraduate to integrate these influences by majoring in philosophy while slaving on the board of *The Yale Literary Magazine.* Arthur Pap's seminar in contemporary empiricism and John E. Smith's course in Kant engaged me as much as the teachings of Brand Blanshard and Paul Weiss. I wrote a thesis on Alfred North Whitehead, an exemplar of the multi-disciplinary integration I sought. It is no accident that in the mid-1950s I had many of the same Yale teachers as Richard Rorty, Richard Bernstein, John Lachs, Andrew Reck and Donald Sherburne.

As a graduate student at Columbia, where the philosophy department was still dominated by Deweyan and Woodbridgean thought, I struggled to graft Columbia naturalism and realism on to what I learned at Yale. My irenic impulse worked overtime, and I championed "polarity" and "sociality" as ways of coping with philosophical conflict. After contemplating a dissertation in philosophy of science under Ernest Nagel, I was drawn to Justus Buchler, especially to his work on Peirce and Santayana. I saw Buchler as another exemplar of the integration I had found earlier in Whitehead. After I wrote an MA thesis under Joseph Blau on Wilmon Sheldon's philosophy of polarity, it was Buchler's suggestion that I write a dissertation on G.H. Mead's metaphysics of sociality in order to integrate Columbian naturalism and realism with the process philosophy of my undergraduate thesis.

Receiving in 1962 an appointment at the State University of New York at Buffalo, I found myself in a rapidly expanding and congenial philosophy department. So much so that at the age of thirty-six I became a full professor and chair of a department of thirty-eight full-time faculty perhaps more pluralistic than any department before or since. Several members of the department shared my interest in the American philosophical tradition, but I was also attracted to the mathematical logicians, various Marxists, linguistic analysts, specialists in Continental philosophy, and assorted other sorts of philosophers including a distinguished Buddhist. Although sometimes frustrating, twelve years of leading such a heterogeneous group was also immensely satisfying.

Edward Madden became my closest collaborator in the Department. In addition to authoring jointly numerous books and articles, in the late 1960s I briefly assisted Madden in editing the *Transactions of the C.S. Peirce Society: A Quarterly Journal in American Philosophy.* From the early 1970s until 2000 I edited the *Transactions* with Richard Robin and since 2000 have done so with Randall Dipert. My aim in this editorial work has been to encourage historical scholarship that reflects and advances the rich diversity of the American tradition. Working with *Transactions* contributors from outside the US has been especially rewarding.

In my current work I am connecting philosophy to other disciplines (e.g. poetry, biology, cognitive science) and diverse subject matter (e.g. photography, TV drama). Long term, I hope to complete a book about the *Somers* Mutiny, a celebrated 1840s event in US naval history. Interwoven with a gripping sea story will be literary history (e.g. Herman Melville, James Fennimore Cooper), cultural history, political history, theories of criminal, civil and military law, pragmatist epistemology, theories of moral responsibility, history of naval architecture, and political figures today (e.g. Donald Rumsfeld).

Further reading

Hare, Peter. *Evil and the Concept of God* (with Edward H. Madden). Springfield, IL: Charles C. Thomas, 1968.

—— *Causing, Perceiving and Believing: An Examination of the Philosophy of C.J. Ducasse* (with Edward H. Madden). Dordrecht: D. Reidel, 1975.

—— *A Woman's Quest for Science: Portrait of Anthropologist Elsie Clews Parsons.* Amherst, NY: Prometheus Books, 1985.

—— (ed.) *Doing Philosophy Historically.* Amherst, NY: Prometheus Books, 1988.

—— "Classical Pragmatism, Recent Naturalistic Theories of Representation and Pragmatic Realism" in P. Weingartner, G. Schurz and G. Dorn (eds), *The Role of Pragmatics in Contemporary Philosophy.* Vienna: Holder-Pinchler-Tempsky, 1998.

—— "Problems and Prospects in the Ethics of Belief," in John R. Shook (ed.) *Pragmatic Naturalism and Realism.* Amherst, NY: Prometheus Books, 2003.

—— "Dewey, Analytic Epistemology and Biology," in Elias L. Khalil (ed.) *Dewey, Pragmatism, and Economic Methodology.* London and New York: Routledge, 2004.

PETER H. HARE

HARTSHORNE, CHARLES

One of the few philosophers, if not the only one, to live in three centuries, Charles Hartshorne (1897–2000) began his career as a young professor at Harvard with an intellectual accomplishment that by itself would have satisfied most philosophers as a life's work, namely, the editing, along with Paul Weiss, of the first six volumes of the *Collected Papers of Charles Sanders Peirce.* He claimed (in his Autobiography in Hahn (ed.) *The Philosophy of Charles Hartshorne*) that Peirce and Alfred North Whitehead were the great geniuses in philosophy who influenced him more than any of his Harvard teachers. Although deeply inspired by both, Hartshorne is known mainly as a student and creative extender of Whitehead's process philosophy. After a brief stint teaching at Harvard, he moved to the University of Chicago for a long career of twenty-seven years. Then he moved to Emory University where he taught from 1955 to 1962, and finally to the University of Texas where he remained until his death.

Hartshorne's early writings focused on issues of consciousness, feeling, and sensation, developing what he came to call a philosophy of "panpsychism," namely, the thesis that everything has feelings. His main ideas concerning this thesis were extensions of Whitehead's philosophical cosmology according to which every actual thing is an occasion of experience. In 1948, however, he published *The Divine Relativity: A Social Conception of God*, which established his reputation as the founder of a new branch of process philosophy and theology. Whitehead had maintained that God is a single everlasting actual entity possessed of infinite capacity to conceive ideas and obliged to feel ("prehend" is the technical term) every finite entity when its creative coming-to-be ("concrescence," meaning "becoming concrete," is the technical term) is completed; God must integrate each thing as it achieves completed actuality with all the other actualized things, and is able to do this because of the infinite capacity for conceptualizing possible modes of togetherness. For Whitehead also, God supplies patterns or "lures for feeling" to each actual entity as it begins its process of concrescence, thus influencing each thing to be harmonious (although concrescing things can misplace that lure); the actual entity prehends the divine lure among the many things it prehends as it begins its concrescence. The problem with Whitehead's conception of God, however, is that at no finite time is God ever finished or definitely actual. Therefore, God's lure can never be prehended by finite actual entities because it is never actual itself; moreover, God cannot prehend a finished actual entity because God's concrescence never has a beginning that could be made of external things that God feels.

Hartshorne responded to this difficulty in Whitehead's view with his social conception of God. Instead of being a single actual entity, Hartshorne proposed that God is a society of sequential actual entities, each of which prehends its predecessor. Each divine entity within the society has an abstract necessary nature that requires the entity in its concrescence to prehend not only its own past entities but also all other finite actual entities that have become actual since the previous divine entity in the society. Thus, every finite actual entity can be prehended (must be prehended according to God's necessary nature) by the next entity in the divine society, and every entity in the divine society can supply appropriate lures to the emerging finite entities that immediately succeed it. Hartshorne called this conception "dipolar" as well as "social." The "abstract pole" is the metaphysical necessity in each entity within the divine society to prehend fully and without loss each thing that happens in the world, and also to supply prehendable lures for subsequent finite occasions to feel. The "concrete pole" is the accumulating actuality of God that is acquired in each successive moment as the entities within the divine society prehend, that is, take into their own being, the actualities of the advancing temporal world. Thus, the whole reality of God, including both abstract and concrete poles, is always relative to the world that has happened up to any time in the divine life. Yet at any moment within the divine life, God's integrative powers create a divine entity that surpasses both the previous divine life and what has happened in the world. The divine relativity to the world is a virtue, according to Hartshorne, because it includes everything in the world without loss, and adds its own harmony.

One of the unique features of Hartshorne's social conception of God is its "panentheism." The rough meaning of panentheism is that God is all of nature plus something more. For Hartshorne, every finite actual entity has its coming-to-be or concrescence with its own independent privacy and freedom (only for higher animals, Hartshorne said, is freedom significant). Yet as soon as it has achieved actuality or definiteness, each thing is prehended into God. So there is nothing actual outside of God; God is the sum total of temporally advancing actuality. On the other hand, because of the freedom of each entity in its concrescence, God is not responsible for moral evil in the world – that results from bad choices of other actual entities, plus conflicts that cannot be mitigated in the finite world, only in God. Thus God can be said to be good – God always harmonizes prehended actualities that outside of God's dipolar nature cannot be harmonized.

This conception of God has inspired two generations of theologians, including Hartshorne's distinguished students John B. Cobb, Jr, and Schubert Ogden. Hartshorne also has written distinguished books about the ontological argument, *The Logic of Perfection* and *Anselm's Discovery*, and about process philosophy's relations to its alternatives in metaphysics and epistemology, *Creative Synthesis and Philosophic Method*. In his later years he wrote extensively about how his philosophy stands in critical relation to others, especially in *Insights and Oversights of Great Thinkers, Omnipotence and Other Theological Mistakes*, and *Creativity in American Philosophy*. Hartshorne was an avid and expert ornithologist, writing extensively on birdsongs.

Further reading

Hartshorne, Charles. *The Divine Relativity: A Social Conception of God* (The Terry Lectures, 1947). New Haven, CT: Yale University Press, 1948.
—— *The Logic of Perfection and Other Essays in Neoclassical Metaphysics*. LaSalle, IL: Open Court, 1962.
—— *Anselm's Discovery*. LaSalle, IL: Open Court, 1965.
—— *Creative Synthesis and Philosophic Method*. London: SCM Press, 1970.
—— *Insights and Oversights of Great Thinkers: An Evaluation of Western Philosophy*. Albany, NY: SUNY Press, 1983.
—— *Creativity in American Philosophy*. Albany, NY: SUNY Press, 1984.
—— *Omnipotence and Other Theological Mistakes*. Albany, NY: SUNY Press, 1984.
Hahn, Lewis Edwin (ed.) *The Philosophy of Charles Hartshorne*. LaSalle, IL: Open Court, 1991.

ROBERT CUMMINGS NEVILLE

HEALTHY-MINDEDNESS

William James, in Lectures IV–VII of *The Varieties of Religious Experience*, contrasts the healthy-minded and sick soul and the religions based upon them in a passionate and moving manner, no doubt because as a man he was deeply conflicted by a continuing warfare between them within himself. The distinction between the healthy-minded and sick soul is based upon their respective attitudes toward evil. Healthy-minded persons either completely deny the reality of evil, as do mystics, or don't make a big fuss about it, feeling empowered to cope with or even defeat it. James's pragmatic religion of meliorism, which holds that if we collectively exert our best moral effort, good will win out over evil in the long run, is an expression of the Promethean attitude of the healthy-minded. When he was in his healthy-minded moods, he was itching to engage in a Texas death match with evil without any assurance of succeeding. In contrast, sick-souled persons are overwhelmed by evil, feeling incapable of coping with it on their own. They favor religions that stress the fallen condition of mankind due to original sin. Only by undergoing a conversion, which can happen suddenly or gradually, can they acquire the healthy-minded Promethean stance toward evil. James's description of the paralytic fear that was produced in him by the sight of a hideous catatonic youth, which is quoted in the "Sick Soul" entry, expresses the morbid preoccupation of the sick soul with the thought that the worst sort of evils can strike any of us at any moment, and we are helpless to do anything about it.

James misleadingly identified the healthy-minded and sick souls, respectively, with once-born and twice-born persons. The once-born person is innately healthy-minded whereas the twice-born must undergo a conversion, be born again, to become healthy-minded. The distinction between the once- and twice-born is genetically based, having to do with how one acquires a healthy-minded outlook, whereas the distinction between the healthy- and sick-minded is based on one's stance toward evil. There are sick souls that never succeed in making the transition to healthy-mindedness and healthy-minded souls who eventually turn into sick souls, often due to their confrontation with apparent gratuitous evils in their personal life.

Religions based on healthy-mindedness "consist in a grateful admiration of the gift of so happy an existence." James finds in the poetry of Whitman and Emerson an expression of this cosmic emotion. The mind-cure movement, as well as the gospel of relaxation and Christian Science, has "an intuitive belief in the all-saving efficacy of courage, hope, and trust." That those who hold this belief often become happier and healthier constitutes some evidence for its truth.

James gives pride of place to the sick soul. At many places, James stresses the insufficiency of meliorism, condemning it as being "the very consecration of forgetfulness and superficiality." He even goes so far as to give an account of the common denominator of religions that precludes the once-born's religion from counting as a religion. There is "a certain uniform deliverance in which religions all appear to meet. It consists of two parts:

1 An uneasiness; and
2 Its solution."

The once-born person does not satisfy the "uneasiness" condition.

Further reading

James, William. *Pragmatism*. Cambridge, MA: Harvard University Press, 1975, Ch. VIII.
—— *The Varieties of Religious Experience*. Cambridge, MA: Harvard University Press, 1985.

RICHARD M. GALE

HEGEL, INFLUENCE OF

In the early years of the twenty-first century Hegel's influence, which has long been considerable, is in an ascending phase. In the last few years, books on Hegel have been appearing faster than anyone but the most assiduous Hegel fan can read them, and in general Hegel is now directly and indirectly influential in increasingly many ways.

This has not always been the case. Hegel's influence has waxed and waned since his death in 1831. After a slow start, Hegel's impact in his own time became considerable. When he died, he was the most important thinker in the German-speaking world. Since his death, overall his influence has continued to grow.

Hegel only slowly attracted attention during his lifetime. In the Protestant seminary in Tübingen, he was overshadowed by his roommates, Friedrich Hölderlin, who became a great lyric poet, and Schelling, the *Wunderkind* of German philosophy. When he was invited to Jena in 1799, then the center of German intellectual life, by Schelling, the latter was already established. Hegel quickly became known as his intellectually slower colleague. Hegel's initial philosophical publication, *The Difference between Fichte's and Schelling's System of Philosophy* (1801), confirmed the view that Hegel was no more than Schelling's disciple. Hegel was only later acknowledged as an important philosopher when he published the *Phenomenology of Spirit* (1807). In the book, his famous comparison of Schelling's conception of the absolute to the night in which all cows are black[1] initiated a break, never later overcome, with his former roommate. Hegel, who left the university when it was closed after Napoleon's victory at Jena, strengthened his reputation when he was appointed to the University of Heidelberg (1816–18). During his period in Berlin (1818–31), he was celebrated, despite the resentment of Schelling and Schopenhauer, as the most important living German philosopher. His reputation during his lifetime was based on four books he published: the *Phenomenology*, two versions of the *Encyclopedia of the Philosophical Sciences*, the *Science of Logic* and the *Philosophy of Right* (1821). When he died in 1831, Hegel was considered important enough for an edition of his collected writings in twenty volumes to be prepared by his friends. This initial edition included his published works as well as versions of his unpublished lectures on philosophy of history, philosophy of religion, aesthetics, and the history of philosophy. Other editions appeared later.

After his passing, Hegel's reputation rapidly waned for several reasons. One reason was philosophical criticism of his views. Hegel was criticized by a number of philosophers. In his Munich lectures (1833–4), Schelling, the great German idealist philosopher and former friend, simultaneously defended his own position against Hegel's criticisms and severely criticized the latter's thought as essentially negative. His main complaint seems to be that Hegel substitutes concepts for reality. Adolf Trendelenburg, a contemporary German philosopher and philologist, with special interests in ancient philosophy, objected to Hegel's alleged conflation between logical negation and material negation.

Hegel's reputation was also affected by the break-up of the Hegelian school after his death. After his passing, the Hegelians split into different factions. It is often said that Hegelianism moved from the theological concerns of the right-wing Hegelians in the 1830s to social and political issues interesting left-wing Hegelians in the 1840s. The designation stems from D.F. Strauss, the author of an influential contemporary study of religion (1835–6), who inferred from his reading of Hegel that the incarnation did not take place in a single man but in the entire human race. In the ensuing controversy, he designated the participants as members of the center, right and left wings of the Hegelian school.

The right-wing Hegelians, who taught in the German university system, offered conservative interpretations of his work and were politically orthodox. The left-wing Hegelians, also called the young Hegelians, were, with the prominent exception of Gans, a professor of law in Berlin, situated outside the German university. They often held left-wing political views.

The left-wing Hegelians, most of whom accepted but further objected to the right-wing interpretation of Hegel as a basically theological thinker, were often very interesting. Eduard Gans argued that private property required an ethical justification. August von Cieszkowksi emphasized the transition from a theological to a secular viewpoint. Moses Hess began as a utopian socialist, who foresaw saw a social revolution resulting from the growing contradiction between wealth and poverty. He coined the famous reference, used by Marx and Engels in the "Communist Manifesto," to "religion as the opium of the masses." Arnold Ruge, who edited the *Hallische Jahrbücher*, helped to consolidate Hegelianism as a political movement. Heinrich Heine, the German romantic poet, a former student of Hegel and a friend of

Marx, wrote an influential book to introduce German philosophy to the French.

The two most important young Hegelians were Ludwig Feuerbach and Karl Marx. Feuerbach, who was influenced by Strauss, published an important work on religion. In the *Essence of Christianity* (1841), he claimed that God did not make man, but man rather made God. His critique of Hegel, which he worked out in a number of texts, is credited by Marxism as a crucial influence in the origin of Marx's theories.

Marx, who was by far the most influential left-wing Hegelian, is with, Søren Kierkegaard and Friedrich Nietzsche, arguably one of the three most significant post-Hegelian nineteenth-century thinkers. When Hegel died, it was widely thought that he had brought philosophy to a peak and to an end. It is significant that none of these three highly important thinkers was willing to accept the designation "philosophy" for his position.

All of them react to Hegel, but in different ways. Marx's position literally arises out of a series of early articles criticizing Hegel, with a particular focus on selected passages from the *Philosophy of Right*. The permanent Hegelian dimension in his thought includes the stress on history, the emphasis on political economy as central to grasping social reality, the use of Hegelian concepts and categories throughout his writings, including *Capital*, and so on. The Marxist view of Marx claims the latter solves problems classical German philosophy is unable to solve on the level of science situated beyond philosophy. More recent discussion suggests Marx does not turn his back on philosophy, but remains a full-fledged member of German idealism. If Hegel is the proponent of universal reason, then Nietzsche counts as an important opponent of reason in all its forms. He reacts, not directly against Hegel, whom he may not have read, but against the consequences of Hegel's approach.

The important development of modern science in the second half of the nineteenth century is related to the rise of German neo-Kantianism, which can be briefly characterized as a return back behind Hegel to Kant. The neo-Kantian revival, which increasingly understood itself as anti-Hegelian, developed as a series of schools. The Marburg school, which included Hermann Cohen and Ernst Cassirer, emphasized an approach to Kant as a philosopher of science, and the Southwestern school (Baden), founded by Wilhelm Windelband, stressed a Kantian approach to values (axiology).

In academic philosophy, Hegelian idealism underwent a revival in both Great Britain and the United States in the last decades of the nineteenth century. Hegelian schools arose in Cincinnati and later in St Louis. The St Louis Hegelians interpreted the Civil War as a conflict between abstract right (the South) and abstract morality (the North). The interest in Hegel was further spread in academic circles by Josiah Royce, a fine student of German idealism, around the turn of the century at Harvard. Royce thought that pragmatism was only a new name for German idealism. Royce was specifically interested in Hegel, about whom he wrote in a number of places, including *Baldwin's Dictionary*. Under Hegel's influence, he argued for a version of the absolute in his own position. He further discerned a relation between Hegel and Peirce in controversially claiming that the former's *Logic* was a particular instance of the latter's more general logical position. Nevertheless, Royce developed his Hegelianism in characteristically American ways: he glorified the individual, substituted stress on the community for Hegel's emphasis on the state and rejected Hegel's embrace of the culture of war.

In Great Britain, the last half of the nineteenth century saw the rise of British idealism, or again British Hegelianism, which can be roughly dated from the publication of J.H. Stirling, *The Secret of Hegel* (1865). British idealism, which includes British Hegelianism, is a heterogeneous collection of thinkers, with little in common, interested in different German idealists, such as Schelling (e.g. S.T. Coleridge), Kant (e.g. T.H. Green) or Hegel (e.g. F.H. Bradley, B. Bosanquet, Eduard Caird, J.E. McTaggart).

The debate in twentieth-century philosophy was dominated by four tendencies, all of which arose roughly around 1900. Two of them, Marxism and Anglo-American analytic philosophy, at least initially understood themselves through their refutation of idealism. Marxism, which was invented by Friedrich Engels, turns on the supposed watershed difference between idealism, represented by Hegel, in whom philosophy supposedly comes to a peak and to an end, and Marx, who allegedly works out materialism. The antagonism toward idealism displayed by William James continues in Anglo-American analytic philosophy. Its English founders, Bertrand Russell and G.E. Moore, were briefly Hegelians. But they quickly turned against idealism, leading to an analytic hostility toward Hegel, which still persists. In "Refutation of Idealism" (1903), Moore famously accused idealism of denying the reality of the external world. Russell thought the revolutionary innovations in logic in the last decades of the nineteenth century destroyed Hegel's metaphysics by overturning the Aristotelian logic it presupposed.

In reaction against orthodox Marxism, Marxist Hegelianism acknowledged the permanent Hegelian legacy in Marx. Its main figures included the Hungarian Georg Lukács, the Austrian Karl Korsch, and the Russian émigré to France, Alexandre Kojève. This movement arose in 1923 in simultaneous publications by Lukács (*History and Class Consciousness*) and Korsch (*Marxism and Philosophy*). Lukács was especially influential on the founders of the Frankfurt School, a loosely related group of social thinkers, organized as the University of Frankfurt in the early 1930s. The members of the first generation included Max Horkheimer, Theodor Adorno and Herbert Marcuse. Jürgen Habermas was later for a time associated with this group.

Kojève gave a series of seminal lectures on Hegel in France in the 1930s. These lectures were later collected in a book, which strongly stimulated Hegel studies in France. Besides Kojève, significant French Hegel scholars include Jean Wahl, Jean Hyppolite, and Bernard Bourgeois. Vincent Descombes (*Modern French Philosophy*) has argued that French philosophy from the time of Kojève until at least the 1980s can be understood as a series of reactions to Kojève's Hegel. Other French figures strongly influenced by Hegel include Jean-Paul Sartre, the leading existentialist, and Jacques Lacan, the Freudian psychoanalyst.

In the United States, interest in Hegel during the twentieth century was sparked in several ways. Santayana's multi-volume *The Life of Reason* (1905–6) was conceived in his student days as a response to Hegel's *Phenomenology of Spirit*. Beginning with C.S. Peirce, the first generation of American pragmatists were all interested in Hegel in different ways.

Peirce was initially opposed to Hegel, whom he believed slighted secondness. He later changed his mind and came to understand his position as the same, or virtually the same, as Hegel's, though stated in different terminology. This ambivalence, which affected his view of his relation to other thinkers is often on display. In the first of the Harvard lectures, Peirce is critical of Hegel while affirming that his own theory is a variant form of Hegelianism,[2] but in the last lecture he identifies pragmatism with Kantianism (Kantism) curiously defined as also including Aristotle and Reid.[3] Yet Hegel left a strong impact on Peirce. Peirce's fallibilism can be understood as a restatement of certain key Hegelian doctrines, which is rendered more plausible by Peirce's own conviction that he stood very close to Hegel, with the difference lying mainly in terminology.

In criticizing Descartes, Peirce examines and rejects an earlier form of the Kantian architectonic model of knowledge as a series of apodictic assertions about experience not later revisable in the light of further developments. Descartes and Kant share the commitment to a single fixed method, in effect a pre-established, fixed, invariant royal road to science and knowledge of all kinds. In reaction to Descartes and Kant, Peirce, like Hegel, favors a version of the developmental model of science and knowledge. As he grew older, Peirce increasingly stressed his growing agreement with Hegel. Yet unlike Hegel, who emphasizes the historical character of knowledge, Peirce, who also stresses that knowing is a process, stops short of characterizing it in historical terms.

For James, philosophy often took the form of actively engaging with other views, many of which he rejected. Whereas Peirce, who originally despised Hegelianism, grew steadily closer to Hegel, James, who knew next to nothing about Hegelianism, was content to ridicule it. In "On Some Hegelisms," an article that is appropriately accompanied by apologies for its superficiality,[4] James begins by writing that "Hegel's philosophy mingles mountain-loads of corruption with its scanty merits."[5] He goes on to say about that: "His [i.e. Hegel's] system resembles a mouse-trap, in which if you once pass the door you may be lost forever."[6]

John Dewey was initially linked to the St Louis Hegelians. His link came about when he sent two essays to W.T. Harris, a Hegelian who was editor of the *Journal of Speculative Philosophy*. When Harris accepted the essays, Dewey was encouraged to apply to the graduate program in philosophy at John Hopkins University. The three young lecturers there were G. Stanley Hall, later an important child psychologist, C.S. Peirce, who was hired through James' intervention, and G.S. Morris, a Hegelian. Dewey wrote a dissertation on Kantian psychology under Morris' direction, which further strengthened his awareness of Hegel.

Dewey's later naturalism can be considered as a non-metaphysical version of Hegelianism. It has been argued that he remained closer to Hegel than he was himself aware and that his own position was influenced in many ways, such as in his criticism of Kant, his naturalism, his experimental view of logic, his resistance to dualisms and his contextualism, among others, by his early reading of Hegel.

Broadly speaking, Dewey sympathizes with Hegel's insistence on ethics (*Sittlichkeit*), or the idea that individual identity is constructed through the practices and norms of the community, over Kantian morality (*Moralität*), which is based on the internalization of abstract norms and principles. Dewey, who around 1900 knew Hegel well, can be said to have naturalized the latter's position. Though he was never attracted to Kant, Dewey remained sympathetic to Hegel's synthetic approach in binding together subject and object, matter and spirit, the divine and the human.

There are often unsuspected similarities with respect to knowledge. For both Hegel and Dewey, knowledge is the result of an experiential and experimental process. Also for both, there is no foundation to knowledge or to the knowing process. Hegel's little-known fallibilistic model based on a trial-and-error approach to experience is astonishingly close to what later became Dewey's much better-known theory of warranted assertability. The difference, which is not slight, is the failure of Dewey, and indeed all the American pragmatists, to preserve the historical turn initiated by post-Kantian German idealism, and most fully embraced by Hegel. Dewey's well-known Darwinism often seems to take the place of history, more precisely the historicity of the cognitive process.

American academic interest in Hegel has recently increased. The Hegel Society of America, founded in 1968, is a learned society that promotes the study of Hegel and Hegelianism through its journal, *The Owl of Minerva*, and scholarly conferences. Recent North American Hegel scholars include H.S. Harris, the most important Hegel scholar writing in English, as well as Robert Pippin, Terry Pinkard and Robert Williams. Since the 1990s, analytic Hegelianism, a kind of non-idealist effort to combine Hegel with traditional analytic themes, has been focusing attention on Hegel in the writings of Richard Rorty, Robert Brandom, John McDowell, Kenneth Westphal, and German philosophers such as Pirmin Stekeler-Weithofer, Michael Quante, and others.

Notes

1 See G.W.F. Hegel, *Phenomenology of Spirit*, trans. A.V. Miller. New York: Oxford, 1977, p. 9.
2 See "The Maxim of Pragmatism," in *The Essential Peirce*, ed. the Peirce Edition Project. Bloomington, IN: Indiana University Press, 1998, II, pp. 143–4.
3 See "The Seven Systems of Metaphysics," in *The Essential Peirce*, II, p. 180.
4 William James, *The Will to Believe and Other Essays on Popular Philosophy*, New York: Dover, 1956, p. xiii.
5 James, *The Will to Believe*, p. 263.
6 James, *The Will to Believe*, p. 275.

Further reading

Löwith, Karl. *From Hegel to Nietzsche: The Revolution in Nineteenth Century Thought*, trans. David E. Green. Garden City, NY: Anchor Books, 1967.
Royce, Josiah. *Lectures on Modern Idealism*. New Haven, CT: Yale University Press, 1964.
Toews, John. *The Path toward Dialectical Humanism, 1805–1843*. Cambridge: Cambridge University Press, 1980.

Tom Rockmore

HERMENEUTICS

Hermeneutics has two separate, but related meanings. In the most general sense it refers to questions of interpretations, particularly the interpretation of texts or works of art. In this sense it has a long history connected to philology, rhetoric, and art and literary criticism. What makes hermeneutics philosophically significant is the additional belief that interpreting is not just one of many activities humans engage in, but a central human activity essentially connected to judgment. Hermeneutics in its narrow sense refers to a branch of phenomenology inaugurated by Martin Heidegger and developed by Hans-Georg Gadamer. This tradition arises out of a critique of the phenomenological emphasis on pure descriptions of experience; instead hermeneuts argue that all experience is interpreted, and therefore questions about the nature of interpretation will inform questions about the nature of perception, cognition, and even human nature. We will refer to this movement as Philosophical Hermeneutics. Paralleling the two meaning of hermeneutics, we will distinguish those classical pragmatists who addressed and contributed philosophically to questions of the nature of interpretation from those contemporary American philosophers who attempt to draw connections between classical pragmatism and Philosophical Hermeneutics.

Charles Sanders Peirce, Josiah Royce, John Dewey, and William James all argue that interpretation is a central activity of the mind, and understanding the nature of interpretation is crucial for understanding the way an organism consciously interacts with its environment. Peirce puts interpretation front and center when he claims that all meaning requires an interpretation to connect the sign and its reference. He writes that a sign is "anything which determines something else (its *interpretant*) to refer to an object to which it itself refers (its *object*) in the same way, the interpretant becoming in turn a sign, and so on *ad infintum*" (CP 2.303). Although Peirce never developed a theory of textual interpretation, and although interpretants are not just thoughts, but any sign that establishes the meaning of another sign, he shares with the hermeneutic tradition the view that interpretation is a central philosophical concept.

Royce's late writings were strongly influenced by Peirce's logic, and in the *Problem of Christianity* he argued that interpretation was a distinctively human act, separate from perception and conception. While perception and conception are binary – they relate a person and an object or a concept – interpretation always involves three parties, the interpreter, the interpreted, and that person for whom the interpretation takes place. Royce expands on an example provided by Henri Bergson. Perceptions are like gold coins – they present their value directly. Conceptions are like bank notes – they are promissory of being exchangeable for cash; they contain the expectation that they will have perceptual value in practice. Royce extends the example by pointing out that exchanges of currency are always between two people, and just as one's coin may carry no value in another land, so too might one's perceptions not be shared by another person. In the currency example, there needs to be an exchange rate, a way of mediating the varying values of the coins, so that the currency can remain valuable; likewise there needs to be an interpretation that will show the conceptual significance of diverse perceptions, and this activity of interpretation is separate from simply validating conceptions with perceptions. Through recognizing the essential and distinctive place of interpretation in social life, Royce thinks we can arrive at a conception of a "community of interpreters," who unite around the goal of shared insight. This ideal state of communally shared insights can then function normatively as an account of truth irreducible to criteria of use, as is stereotypically found among pragmatists. In contrast to Royce, John Dewey thinks all judgment is interpretive and all perception and conception are judgments, so while he makes interpretation more ubiquitous than Royce, he also lessens the need for a specific theory of the nature of interpretation.

Finally, Charlene Haddock Seigfried has argued that although William James had no explicit theory of interpretation, his writings reflect interpretive principles consistent with his pluralistic, radical empiricism. What he does say, and what his writings confirm, is that he believed that in order to interpret a text one must imaginatively grasp the "center of vision" of the author, that which unifies the style and the content of the text. Often this requires understanding the historical and cultural context of the production of the text. Just as is the case with perception, the meaning of a text is not determined prior to the interactive interpretation, but arises through that interpretation. As James sees all interpretive activity as purely reflective, its results, however, are provisional upon concrete investigations into the relevant experiences.

More recently, some philosophers have drawn comparisons between views in American pragmatism and views in Philosophical Hermeneutics. Most Anglo-American philosophers became aware of hermeneutics only with Richard Rorty's *Philosophy and the Mirror of Nature.* There Rorty, having already established himself as a neo-pragmatist, argues that philosophers should abandon the philosophical questions that arise with a representational theory of mind and a correspondence theory of truth. Instead of epistemological questions, we need hermeneutics, which he takes as the attempt to seek new insights and understandings – "edification" – through the creative use of language. The aim of philosophy, according to Rorty, should be the successful continuation of "the conversation of mankind"; it should function in the service of creating greater solidarity among human beings and should abandon the impossible project of intellectually grasping essences. He eventually abandoned and regretted using the term "hermeneutics," but he did not stop seeing Dewey and James's approach to philosophy as sharing essential features with Heidegger and Gadamer's approach. Above all, both pragmatism and Philosophical Hermeneutics are antifoundational and holist. They reject the representational account of the mind, take the world to be symbolic through and through, and see theorizing as arising out of practice. Rorty's work has led a number of philosophers to look more closely at the intersections of pragmatism and Philosophical Hermeneutic; Richard Bernstein and Joseph Margolis are perhaps the two most prominent thinkers engaged in this project.

Further reading

Bernstein, Richard. *Beyond Objectivism and Relativism.* Philadelphia, PA: University of Pennsylvania Press, 1983.

Dewey, John. *How We Think* in *The Middle Works of John Dewey, Vol. 6, 1910–1911*, ed. Jo Ann Boydston. Carbondale, IL: Southern Illinois University Press, 1978.

Margolis, Joseph. *Pragmatism without Foundations.* New York: Blackwell, 1986.

Peirce, C.S. *Collected Papers* (CP), Vols 1–2. Cambridge, MA: Belknap Press, 1960.

Rorty, Richard. *Philosophy and the Mirror of Nature.* Princeton, NJ: Princeton University Press, 1979.

Royce, Josiah. *The Problem of Christianity.* Chicago, IL: University of Chicago Press, 1968.

Seigfried, Charlene Haddock. *William James's Radical Reconstruction of Philosophy*. Albany, NY: SUNYPress, 1990.

DAVID VESSEY

HOFSTADTER, ALBERT

Born in New York City on 28 March 1910, Albert Hofstadter received his BS from City College of the City University of New York at the age of nineteen. He received the MA in 1934 and the PhD in 1935. His professional career began at New York University. He stayed there until 1950 when he joined the faculty of Columbia University. Hofstadter's next move was in 1967 when he joined the faculty of the University of California at Santa Cruz. From 1976 until 1978 he was Chairman of the Department of Philosophy, Graduate Faculty, New School for Social Research. He died 26 January 1989.

Poetry, Language, Thought was translated by Hofstadter and was published in 1971. The essays by Martin Heidegger in this volume soon became central pieces in philosophical discussions in the United States, including those in classical American philosophy. Their influence extended far beyond their origin in the continental or phenomenological tradition. Further, their influence was not restricted to the arts. Particularly important were the essays, "The Origin of the Work of Art" and "What Are Poets For?" The availability in English of works such as this encouraged the sort of philosophical breadth and pluralism that was congenial to philosophers such as James and Dewey.

The primary influence on Hofstadter's philosophical orientation is Heidegger, but there are influences of Dewey and they are not unimportant. *Agony and Epitaph: Man, His Art, and His Poetry* contains essays which do not immediately have an "American" ring, at least not in the context of classical American philosophy. Yet, a careful analysis of the first chapter, "What Philosophy Is and Does," reveals a notably interesting congruence of Dewey and Heidegger. Hofstadter believes that they "attribute to philosophy the essential role of giving imaginative shape to the growing world." Philosophy cannot do this if it forgets its history or attempts to deny or neglect its cultural context. He is sympathetic to pragmatism's view of philosophy in its function of "contributing to the shaping of history." Hofstadter is an example of how approaches congenial to American philosophy can be inspired by sources that derive more centrally from other traditions.

Further reading

Heidegger, Martin. *Poetry, Language, Thought*, trans. and Introduction by Albert Hofstadter. New York: Harper and Row, 1971.

Hofstadter, Albert. *Agony and Epitaph: Man, His Art, and His Poetry*. New York: George Braziller, 1970.

VICTOR KESTENBAUM

HOLISM

Semantic holism can be roughly characterized as the doctrine that the meaning of each word in our language depends upon the meanings of all of the others. The view is usually motivated by the ideas that (1) what we mean by our words is somehow determined by how we use them, and (2) just how we use any particular word in our language is never completely independent of how we use all of the others. For instance, if we take the meanings of each word depend upon the inferences and applications that it occurs in, then since the content of these inferences and applications will, in turn, reflect the meanings of the terms in *them*, holism seems to entail that the content of *each* of one's words depends upon *all* of the inferences and applications one is disposed to make.

The view has been widely held within the pragmatist tradition (e.g. James 1907; Quine 1951), but many philosophers reject holism because of its apparent consequence that *any* differences in belief result in differences in meaning. Since no two people use any term in exactly the same way, holism seems to entail not only that no two people mean the same thing by any term, but also that the meanings of all of the terms in everyone's language are constantly in flux. The holist thus has a hard time providing for any substantive notion of communication and disagreement (since both seem to presuppose that the parties involved mean the same thing by their terms). In much the same way, a substantive notion of "changing of mind" about a particular topic disappears, since when a new belief is formed, the meanings of the words of the believer's language change and thus the believer has a "new" topic in mind rather than a new view about the original topic. In short, holism makes meaning too unstable and leaves us with no room for the intuitive idea that there can be changes of belief without a corresponding change of meaning (see Fodor and Lepore 1992).

Whether such objections stick depends largely on whether one is just a holist about how the terms in a language *get* their meanings, or also a holist about what the meanings of the terms of a language *are*. Being a holist of the first sort does not require being one of the second. One could have a non-holistic conception of what the meanings of our words are (say, the objects or properties they refer to), and a holistic conception of how they got those references (say, the references assigned to all of the terms in the language corresponded to the set of objects and properties that maximized the number of truths in the speaker's total belief set). Indeed, such a pairing is characteristic of the Davidsonian combination of truth-theoretic and interpretive semantics (e.g. Davidson 1973; Jackman 2006). However, if one is a holist of the second sort, one is also typically a holist of the first. Defenders of conceptual or inferential role semantics (e.g. Harman 1973; Block 1986) can be, for instance, understood as holists of both sorts.

Holism about what meanings are is the more radical of the two doctrines since it *identifies* the meaning of a term with the set of applications and inferences associated with it, and most of the instability of meaning that holism purportedly entails follow only from this view of the doctrine. The function from use to meaning is, on such a view, one-to-one, and so there can be no difference of use without a corresponding difference of meaning. By contrast, the holist about how words *get* their meanings requires only that the meaning of a term *be determined by* the set of applications and inferences associated with it. This sort of holist thus can treat the function from belief to meaning as many-to-one, and so allows for the possibility that people with different beliefs could still mean the same things by their terms. Because of this, substantive notions of communication, disagreement and change of mind can all be accommodated within a holist framework of this sort.

The initial idea that meaning is determined by use is captured by the more moderate version of holism, while most of the problems traditionally associated with the view attach only to the more radical one. Consequently, even though both varieties of holism can justly be viewed as instances of "holism about meaning" one should not let the problems with the more radical view obscure the intuitive plausibility of the moderate one.

Further reading

Block, N. "Advertisement for a Semantics for Psychology," *Midwest Studies in Philosophy* X, ed. P.A. French, T.E. Uehling, Jr, and H.K. Wettstein (1986): 615–78.

Davidson, D. "Radical Interpretation" in D. Davidson, *Inquiries into Truth and Interpretation*, Oxford: Oxford University Press, 1984 [1973], pp. 125–39.

Fodor, J. and Lepore, E. *Holism: A Shoppers' Guide.* Oxford: Blackwell, 1992.

Harman, G. *Thought*, Princeton, NJ: Princeton University Press, 1973.

Jackman, H. "Descriptive Atomism and Foundational Holism: Charity, Holism & Compositionality: Semantics between the Old Testament and the New," *Protosociology 21: Compositionality, Concepts and Representations*, ed. Gerhard Preyer (2006).

James, W. *Pragmatism*. Cambridge, MA: Harvard University Press, 1975 [1907].

Quine, W.V. "Two dogmas of empiricism," in W.V. Quine, *From a Logical Point of View.* Cambridge, MA: Harvard University Press, 1953 [1951], pp. 20–46.

HENRY JACKMAN

HOLT, EDWIN BISSELL

Edwin Bissell Holt (1873–1946) was born in Winchester, Massachusetts. He took an undergraduate degree from Harvard in 1896 and began a graduate career in psychology there in 1897–8. In 1898–9, he traveled and studied business at Columbia University. He returned to Harvard in 1899 to resume the study of psychology and philosophy, whereupon his teacher Hugo Munsterberg wrote: "his soul has been conquered for philosophy."

Holt graduated with a PhD in psychology in 1901, and in the same year replaced Robert MacDougall as professor of philosophy and psychology at Harvard. Holt remained at Harvard until 1918. He was visiting professor of psychology at Princeton University from 1926 to 1936, and there he earned a reputation as an inspiring lecturer. He died in Rockland, Maine.

Holt collaborated with W.P. Montague, R.B. Perry, and others to launch a movement in epistemology called new realism. Holt's essay "The Place of Illusory Experience in a Realistic World" appears in *The New Realism: Cooperative Studies in Philosophy.* New realists reasoned that we are in immediate contact with the objects of our perception, and that all these objects exist independently of being perceived. This left them hard-pressed to give an account of perceptual error. Critical realists avoid the problem by distinguishing between immediate and ultimate objects of perception. In *The Concept of Consciousness*, which is perhaps his best-known work, Holt attempts to give a consistent account of consciousness. In doing so, he adopts the new realist epistemology and defends it against objections.

Holt was much influenced by his famous teacher William James, who had this to say of him in a letter: "Holt ... is a most original philosopher as well as a charming human being." Like *The Concept of Consciousness*, Holt's last book, *Animal Drive and the Learning Process*, is written in the spirit of James's *Radical Empiricism*. It is meant to reinforce the claim that consciousness does not exist as a thing or substance, but is a function of a bodily organ, which can be adequately explained in mechanical terms.

In psychology, Holt was a kind of behaviorist and anti-metaphysician. He wanted to explain mental states in terms of the behaviors they seem to manifest. Holt was among the first American intellectuals to make substantial use of the work of Sigmund Freud.

Further reading

Holt, Edwin Bissell. *The New Realism: Cooperative Studies in Philosophy.* New York: Macmillan, 1912.

—— *The Concept of Consciousness.* New York: Arno Press, 1973.

—— *Animal Drive and the Learning Process.* New York: Octagon Books, 1976.

MICHAEL BRODRICK

HOPE

Thomas Aquinas's characterization of hope as a future good that is desirable but difficult to attain captures key ingredients common to most accounts of hope. Hope can be interpreted as an emotion, but it is more frequently understood as a complex activity with affective and cognitive dimensions. The American frontier offers an indeterminate but promising horizon that has functioned as a powerful symbol of hope in American thinking and living.

Accounts of hope tend to differ in their view of the ground of hope or the nature of its appropriate object. Working with a Calvinist position that contrasts the sinful nature of humans with God's ultimate sovereignty, Jonathan Edwards ties both hope's object and agency to God. While false hopes focus upon improper objects (earthly goods) and grounds (human power), true hopes arise from God's grace given to those who, having recognized the corruptibility of temporal goods, renounce sin and embrace Christ as the Savior. In contrast, Ralph Waldo Emerson appeals to hopes that celebrate human ability. Emerson makes frequent appeal to the language of hope, whether in discussing the American scholar who creates a new tradition, the self-reliant individual who trusts his abilities, or the reforming person who embraces the work of the world. While he links these themes to a vision of the over-soul that unites all individuals into a single whole, Emerson's treatment of hope places greater weight on human abilities than Edwards would deem appropriate.

Josiah Royce interprets hope as a dynamic ingredient in the Beloved Community, a real and universal community. Royce argues that only through their devotion to the common life of this community can individuals unite in genuine loyalty to overcome their detachment and alienation. While members of this community constitute a community of memory insofar as they share a common past, they form a community of hope in virtue of the cooperative ideals that bind them together. Hope, as Royce envisions it, defines the futural dimension of a living, temporal community.

Joseph J. Godfrey offers a philosophical analysis of hope that considers both theistic and atheistic variants. Working with ideas from Immanuel Kant, Ernst Bloch, and Gabriel Marcel, Godfrey distinguishes between ultimate hope and fundamental hope, the former of which is hope that has a specific aim while the latter is a basic disposition of openness. Godfrey argues that trust is vital to both forms of hope, and he draws out their implications by relating each to two ontological models. One model focuses on an agent's use of objects while the other stresses the self's appreciation of other persons.

Hope plays an important role in pragmatist thinking. William James's notion of the will to believe provides the scaffolding for pragmatic hoping, since it warrants belief in goods for which we have insufficient intellectual evidence but whose realization matters a great deal to us. Drawing on James's ideas as well as John Dewey's understanding of humans as interactive organisms whose habits structure their actions and reconstruct their environment, Patrick Shade develops a pragmatic theory of hope that emphasizes hope's concrete grounds in habits of persistence, resourcefulness, and courage. Shade argues that these habits can be developed into the sustaining character-trait of hopefulness, an orientation towards an open horizon of promising possibilities. Pragmatic hoping offers us a form of conditioned transcendence whereby we grow and transform the problematic situations that give birth to hopes.

Late twentieth-century discussions of hope frequently focus on social hopes such as the elimination of tyranny and injustice. Bernard P. Dauenhauer emphasizes hope's intersubjective nature and the accompanying awareness of our finitude. He argues that hope so understood provides the basis for a politics of hope that precludes totalizing communities that threaten the projects or initiatives of individuals. Having argued against the need for a foundation of knowledge or norms, Richard Rorty recommends that we embrace social hopes whose viability depends not on their grounding but on their capacity to promote solidarity. Cornel West likewise addresses hope's basis in and aim at solidarity, especially in the context of African American struggles. Viewing hope as an agent of social change, West emphasizes the importance of drawing on historical connections and stories from the past to inspire us as we continue the struggle for improvement.

Discussions in bioethics and business ethics highlight the potentially important role hope can play in diverse contexts. William Ruddick, for instance, argues that physicians should cultivate legitimate (versus false) hopes to assist patients facing and recovering from illness. Hope has also been cited as a formative force for increasing productivity in the business world.

Further reading

Dauenhauer, Bernard P. *The Politics of Hope.* New York: Routledge and Kegan Paul, 1986.

Edwards, Jonathan. *Hope and Comfort Usually Follow Genuine Humiliation and Repentance* (September, 1737 sermon). Available at http://www.biblebb.com/files/edwards/comfort.htm.

Emerson, Ralph Waldo. *Essays and Lectures.* New York: Library of America, 1983.

Godfrey, Joseph J. *The Philosophy of Human Hope.* Dordrecht: Martinus Nijhoff, 1987.

James, William. *The Will to Believe and Other Essays in Popular Philosophy.* New York: Dover, 1956.

Rorty, Richard. *Philosophy and Social Hope.* London: Penguin, 1999.

Royce, Josiah. *The Problem of Christianity.* Washington, DC: The Catholic University of America Press, 2001.

Ruddick, William. "Hope and Deception." *Bioethics* 13 (1999): 343–57.

Schwartz, Robert H. and Post, Frederick R. "The Unexplored Potential of Hope to Level the Playing Field: A Multilevel Perspective," *Journal of Business Ethics* 37 (2002): 153–43.

Shade, Patrick. *Habits of Hope.* Nashville, TN: Vanderbilt University Press, 2001.

West, Cornel. *Restoring Hope: Conversations on the Future of Black America*, ed. Kelvin Shawn Sealey. New York: Random House, 1999.

PATRICK SHADE

HYPOTHESIS

A hypothesis is a supposition or conjecture suggested by given phenomena. Usually formulated in systematic conjunction with other assumptions, the significance of a given hypothesis lies in its consequences and its capacity thereby to explain the phenomena that initially suggested it. For example, barking sounds may suggest the hypothesis that a dog is present somewhere in the direction from which the sounds emanate. That hypothesis would explain the barking as well as entail the possibility of other verifiable phenomena (sensory, behavioral, etc.) that are commonly associated with dogs.

Hypotheses are thus tentative or provisional explanations, often with some initial empirical substantiation. They are formulated to explain some given phenomenon; but to be other than provisional they are in need of subsequent deductive elaboration and inductive verification by means of new evidence. Ad hoc hypotheses fail in this regard insofar as they are able to predict only the phenomena that led to their initial formulation. Without further verification, hypotheses as such are posited as viable assumptions rather than asserted. (After further investigation, the purported dog may in fact turn out to be a seal. Only new information can determine whether that is not the case.)

Hypotheses play an essential role in scientific inquiry, arising as more or less educated guesses that may account for some unexpected phenomenon. Subsequent deductive elaboration of a scientific hypothesis should yield descriptions of what would further occur as results of specific actions under certain circumstances. Respective experiments are conducted and/or observations are made to determine if such predictions hold up. The hypothesis is confirmed to the extent that predicted results actually come about. When such predictions are not successful, that is grounds for rejecting the hypothesis, or at least for not accepting it without modification. Such confirmation or rejection is not always straightforward insofar as deductive elaborations of a given hypothesis are typically pursued in conjunction with other assumptions, any of which may be as much responsible for successful or failed predictions as the given hypothesis.

Given that they require empirical justification, hypotheses give direction to subsequent inquiry by suggesting new courses of experimentation and observation. Their predictive failure also serves to suggest possibilities for future research in a given science insofar as the nature and consequences of their rejection or modification may be followed out.

Beyond direct experimental or observational confirmation, hypotheses may gain greater acceptance to the extent that they are able to explain other facts besides those which suggested the hypotheses to begin with, either by determining the causes of those facts or by determining the manner by which the causes of those facts operate. Increased acceptability of a hypothesis often depends as well on its systematic compatibility with other well accepted hypotheses.

In C.S. Peirce's theory of inference, hypotheses are conclusions of abductive inferences where, as inferred conclusions, they occur as questions rather than as assertions. Abduction is a kind of inference, then, whose premises are a collection of phenomena that in some way lack adequate explanation and whose conclusion is a possible explanation of those phenomena. Such abductive conclusions in turn serve as premises (givens) in deductive inferences aimed at elaborating their consequences. As predictions, any of these consequences (including the abductive conclusion itself) may be tested experimentally, in a way possibly to refute the given hypothesis. This is reminiscent of the so called hypotheticodeductive method of science except for Peirce's careful distinction between abduction and induction. Many treatments of induction combine hypothesis formation and hypothesis verification as aspects of induction. Peirce clearly distinguishes the latter, characterizing abduction as an ampliative kind of inference resulting in the formation of hypotheses. Induction meanwhile aims to ascertain the extent to which a given hypothesis is in fact believable and thus assertible as true. A hypothesis is thus the question addressed by inductive inference, such that a decision about its assertibility is the ultimate aim of designing and implementing appropriate experimental and observational activities and respective analyses of their results.

The Socratic "method of hypothesis" as laid out in Plato's *Phaedo* also differs from the hypotheticodeductive method in that the justification of a hypothesis follows not only upon an analysis and confirmation of its consequences but depends on its being a consequence of more encompassing hypotheses. In other words, it should serve as an unexplained fact in its own right. In short, a hypothesis must explain, but it must also be explained.

Hypotheses are sometimes contrasted with theories and laws, such that a hypothesis with high predictive and/or explanatory power may come to be regarded as an accepted theory and perhaps eventually as a law. Thus opponents of a given theory may insist that it is "just a theory" as if that were to undermine its scientific validity insofar as it falls short of being a "law." This characterization involves at least two misconceptions. First, theories are deductively closed systems of propositions, including any number of hypotheses plus their consequences. A hypothesis cannot become a theory in this sense merely by virtue of a high degree of confirmation, nor by any other means, though a highly tentative theory may become less tentative as its constituent hypotheses gain (collectively) in predictive and/or explanatory power. Second, hypotheses may be specialized explanations of particular phenomena, in which they do not have the kind of generality usually associated with laws. The hypothesis that a dog is producing distant barking sounds will never become a law no matter how certain one becomes of the truth of that explanation. Conversely, Newton's laws of motion are thought to be false (ultimately). Nevertheless, each is a *law* of Newtonian mechanics because collectively they are essentially definitive of Newtonian mechanics, not because any one of them singularly has a high degree of confirmation.

Further reading

Bostock, David. "The Method of Hypothesis" in *Plato's Phaedo*. Oxford: Clarendon Press, 1986, pp. 157–77.

Hanson, Norwood Russell. *Patterns of Discovery: An Inquiry into the Conceptual Foundations of Science*. Cambridge: Cambridge University Press, 1965.

Kuhn, Thomas S. *The Essential Tension: Selected Studies in Scientific Tradition and Change*. Chicago, IL: University of Chicago Press, 1977.

Peirce, Charles S. *The Essential Peirce*, 2 volumes. Bloomington, IL: Indiana University Press, 1992/1998.

Popper, Karl. *Conjectures and Refutations: The Growth of Scientific Knowledge*. London: Routledge and Kegan Paul, 1963.

TOM BURKE

I

I/ME

I/me is a central aspect of George Herbert Mead's evolutionary social psychology which gives an account of how individual thought and self-consciousness naturally emerge as products of reflexive discourse. The nominative and objective personal pronouns "I" and "me" are used to distinguish interlocutors in this reflexive discourse, in later evolutionary stages, wherein *I* converses with *me*.

One could say that thinking on this account is a matter of talking to oneself except for the fact that this reflexive discourse is supposed to be part of an evolutionary account of thought and talking in their present form. Hence the account must introduce reflexive conversation in a way that initially involves neither language nor talking as such, in which case thinking may be cast as reflexive conversation even if it is not literally a matter (always) of talking to oneself. At the same time, this account should culminate with a robust characterization of the I/me distinction that comports well with how we regard ourselves as thinking beings.

Mead attempts this by noting to begin with that our remote ancestors were always social creatures, regardless of the status of their cognitive capabilities. His account starts then with primitive communication abilities in place, such as we might expect to find in early primates and other animal life-forms. Given this minimal and uncontentious foundation, Mead proceeds to identify a number of evolutionary stages that could ultimately lead to self-conscious, thinking creatures.

First, at an early evolutionary stage, the capacity to *take attitudes of others* would have emerged as a kind of social interaction involving behaviormatching, perspectivetaking, and perspectiveswitching. An *attitude* in this sense is a readiness to act in specific ways (cf. Royce 1898, 1903). Taking attitudes of others is not just mimicry or mimetic behavior. It is instead a matter of matching a readiness to activate certain abilities though they may be held in abeyance, inhibiting their actualization.

Second, a generalized or amalgamated version of the foregoing capability would emerge as a capability to *take attitudes of a group*, specifically in determining one's own behaviors. Even if it is not yet a conscious or deliberate process, this already provides conditions for *reflexive* social stimulation and response, namely, general conditions for "coming back" on oneself in ways that one's group would. This of course presumes that one's group behaves (as a group) in certain regular ways that may be anticipated.

This second stage is to be distinguished from a third stage where individuals will eventually be able to *draw on organized attitudes* of the whole group. This capability will emerge if and when the stable exercise of second-stage capabilities not only results in the formation of respective behavioral habits on the part of individuals but also in the establishment of organized social habits ("institutions") at a group level. The latter are group-level habits that emerge within a dynamic communicative arena, involving both competitive and cooperative interactions, over and above biologically determined group behaviors. At this third stage, then, we have an early version of memetic or proto-memetic evolution in the sense that drawing on organized attitudes of one's whole group is possible (a) only when activities of taking attitudes of the group has engendered regular, reliable abilities to take such attitudes, and (b) because this reliability is facilitated by the use of *significant symbols*, namely signs specifically associated as signs with group-level habits and thus potential attitudes of the group. In other words, group habits (institutions) are established, stabilized, and transmitted via symbolic (versus genetic) media.

In a fourth stage, reflexive discourse is introduced in its simplest form as a succession of attitudes aimed at anticipating possible responses of others, given an established generalized sense of how others would act and react. This latter sense of a "*generalized other*" is possible because of the stability of societal institutions. Its inculcation as a coherent whole into the individual's repertoire of possible attitudes in turn makes possible a reflexive symbol-mediated conversation of attitudes, alternating between attitudes of the individual self and projected attitudes of the whole group as embodied in one's generalized sense of the group. Correlative nominal and objective selves thus emerge as respective participants in this conversation. The particular kind of succession of attitudes that this allows is *thinking* in its simplest form: a refined, modified, enhanced, reflexive version of *gestural* if not *vocal* conversation.

Elaboration and refinement of a capacity for reflexivized discourse occurs as a valid activity in its own right. At the same time, it is notable that Mead's initial account of reflexive discourse is presented purely in terms of communicative practices, with little if any attention given to grammatical or computational features of formal symbol systems. In other words, the present story so far goes through one way or another even if we assume operability of only the simplest kinds of gestural or verbal proto-languages.

The foregoing ability to think sets the stage, finally, for *individual mind* and *selfconsciousness*, not just as a refinement and elaboration of fourth-stage reflexive discourse on its own terms, but as a further result of objectifying this thinking activity. This objectification should become possible as one becomes capable of taking the same attitudes *towards oneself* that the community takes. In this sense, attitudes of a generalized other as directed towards oneself in one's own thinking gives substance to an objectified "me." This inevitably feeds back into one's sense of a generalized other, such that one may objectify others as thinking individuals in their own right. One's sense of a generalized other would now incorporate a sense of a generalized thinker, in which case we have a benign regress that potentially allows at least an abstract objectification of thinking activity relative to a community that takes in all thinking individuals. Such objectification, wherever the regress stops, is what engenders individual character, enabling one to communicate and coordinate activities with oneself in the roles of "I" versus "me." This in turn engenders the development of personal individuality as something that can be freed from external cultural constraints, as the individual develops an identity as a "society-of-two."

John Dewey, Mead's colleague and long-time friend, incorporated this view of the social self virtually wholesale into his own views of language and thought. It should also be acknowledged that many of the key ideas were derived from the works of Josiah Royce and William James (both of whom Mead studied under at Harvard), with some influence as well from Charles Peirce's theory of signs (see Thayer 1980). Nevertheless, this conception of self and mind is uniquely attributable to Mead, at least in the way the key details were pieced together into a coherent evolutionary account of self-consciousness. One may also note similarities with contemporary metarepresentational theories of mind (e.g. Sperber 2000).

Further reading

James, William. *The Principles of Psychology*, 2 volumes. New York: Henry Holt, 1938. Reprinted in the *Works of William James* series, Cambridge, MA: Harvard University Press, 1981.

Mead, George Herbert. *The Philosophy of the Present*, ed. Arthur E. Murphy. La Salle, IL: Open Court, 1932.

—— *Movements of Thought in the Nineteenth Century*, ed. Merritt H. Moore. Chicago, IL: University of Chicago Press, 1936.

—— *The Philosophy of the Act*, ed. Charles W. Morris. Chicago, IL: University of Chicago Press, 1938.

—— *On Social Psychology*, ed. Anselm Strauss. Chicago, IL: University of Chicago Press, 1956.

—— *Selected Writings*, ed. Andrew J. Reck. Chicago, IL: University of Chicago Press, 1964.

Royce, Josiah. *Studies of Good and Evil: A Series of Essays upon Problems of Philosophy and of Life*. New York: D. Appleton, 1898.

—— *Outlines of Psychology: An Elementary Treatise with Some Practical Applications*. New York: Macmillan, 1903.

Sperber, Dan (ed.) *Metarepresentations: A Multidisciplinary Perspective*. New York: Oxford University Press, 2000.

Thayer, Horace Standish. *Meaning and Action: A Critical History of Pragmatism*, second edition. Indianapolis, IN: Hackett, 1980.

TOM BURKE

IDEALISM: ABSOLUTE

There are ancient intimations of absolute idealism in, among others, Plato's theory of Forms and Aristotle's notion of God as the eternal self-actualizing pure form of thought-thinking-thought. However, these are not uniformly monistic and idealistic, but one or the other though not both. Still, variations of these themes reappear in and are relevant sources for modern idealism. Today, absolute idealism designates a metaphysical system wherein reality is one universal Being, fully individuated as a comprehensive, coherent unity of and condition for all subordinate forms of being and appearance. As the unconditioned condition, it is Absolute, and being of the nature of thought, it is Spirit.

Absolute idealism flourished in nineteenth-century Germany in the works of J.G. Fichte, F.W.J. Schelling and G.W.F. Hegel. Later in England, F.H. Bradley, Bernard Bosanquet and J.M.E. McTaggart developed unique versions of absolute idealism. In America, hints of absolute idealism appeared in Emerson's essays on Nature and the Over-Soul. But it was openly embraced by the St Louis Hegelians, and given potent expression in the achievements of Josiah Royce. Ironically, the ideas that inspired absolute idealism came from Immanuel Kant whose transcendental (critical) idealism was meant to put metaphysics on hold.

Kant's three monumental *Critiques* revolutionized philosophy by addressing the modal issues of the possibility of scientific knowledge, free moral action, and aesthetic and teleological judgment. Kant's idealism restricted knowledge to objects of possible experience, sensory phenomena "constituted" in conformity with synthetic *a priori* conditions of their possibility such as "categories of the understanding" (e.g. Causality) and ultimately the "synthetic unity of apperception" (a self-same consciousness that accompanies all experiences). These conditions are imposed by the human mind upon, not derived from, experience. The mind is not passive, but actively constructs its epistemic objects. In this sense, objects as known are representations or phenomena, not the "thing-in-itself" or noumena, the latter of which Kant conceived to be an unknowable reality that exists independently of experience. Thus restricted, Kant argued that since the soul, freedom, world-as-a-whole, and God are never presented in experience, they cannot be objects of knowledge. To think otherwise would be to misapply the categories and invite only antinomies and illusion. Having deprived classical metaphysics of its traditional objects, Kant undermined its possibility as a science, but redeployed its ideas (soul, freedom, God) in the "metaphysics of morals" and as regulative principles of "judgments of reflection" of aesthetics and teleological thought. Kant restored free will, for example, by arguing that since the will is not an object of experience, it cannot be determined by the categories, hence is free. This result was anticipated in his first *Critique* when Kant argued for the "spontaneity of the synthetic unity of apperception" which, as the fundamental condition of the categories, is not conditioned by them. However, like most revolutions, Kant's had unintended consequences.

Kant's German successors, though inspired by his thought, found his doctrines of the thing-in-itself and the synthetic unity of apperception problematic and incomplete. The thing-in-itself, they objected, is contradictory, for to claim that an unknowable somewhat exists as a necessary condition of knowledge is to claim to know something about that which is absolutely unknowable. Indeed, Kant sometimes seemed to attribute causality to the thing-in-itself, a violation of the restriction of the category of causality to objects of experience. The thing-in-itself had to go.

Fichte found that denying the thing-in-itself not only removed the contradiction, it implied a more thoroughgoing idealism. Without a thing-in-itself, Kant's objects of experience became, for Fichte, objects as such and the synthetic unity of apperception became the "absolute Ego." This Ego, being unconditioned, actualizes itself in an original act of self-positing whereby it posits itself and the non-ego as the arena for its moral action. In other words, the Ego is self-determining, hence free; but it also posits a limit to overcome and thereby actualize its freedom. In a rather ad hoc move, Fichte argued that the Absolute comes to recognize itself as Ego, but only in and through a subsequently posited finite ego, and non-ego becomes the world-for-consciousness. Fichte's emphasis on the will, action, and the practical consequences of thought later influenced the voluntaristic elements in Royce's idealism and Peirce's pragmatism, but his criticism of transcendental idealism had an immediate impact on Schelling and Hegel.

Schelling combined Fichte's leads with Kant's aesthetic doctrine of the "free-play of the faculties," creative imagination, and the regulative function of teleological forms of thought, and attempted to deduce a speculative physics. Schelling undertook to demonstrate that the Absolute is the "pure identity" of Spirit as invisible nature and nature as visible Spirit. He attempted to deduce from the Absolute, as pure identity, increasingly circumspect domains of experience that correspond to the levels of conscious activity and organic organization in nature and work his way back from nature to the Absolute's pure identity. This, however, implied that Schelling's system was essentially tautological with ad hoc assumptions inserted to give it an appearance of content. Thus, Hegel described Schelling's notion of the Absolute as "the night in which all cows are black."

Like his predecessors, Hegel rejected the thing-in-itself and its accompanying consequences. But unlike them, Hegel realized that the Absolute cannot be grasped by abstracting to ever broader universalizations, for that involves omitting content until one is left, in the end, with an empty abstraction. Rather, Hegel's Absolute was a teleological process of infinite Being actualizing itself in the totality of its differentiations whereby it is fully individuated as the "concrete universal." Hegel saw that the Absolute must be understood as a process that systematically reconciles, contextualizes, and eventually completes the system of concepts and experiences by which the Absolute is discovered to be an identity-in-difference rather than an abstract identity. This progression Hegel charted in the different forms of consciousness by which the Absolute is aware of itself, beginning with lower-order forms such as "sense-certainty," progressing through increasingly comprehensive forms of conceptual consciousness, and ultimately attaining full self-consciousness in reason. This progression is necessitated by the limitations (negations) inherent in the lower-order forms, the meaning and purpose of which cannot be grasped until they are comprehended in the context of higher-order forms of consciousness, eventually reaching reason's reflection upon itself. Thus, for Hegel, the Absolute is reason; not human reason, but a supra-personal reason that Hegel sometimes characterized as God, an infinite Being that actualizes itself in the rational unfolding of nature and finite rational beings.

Absolute idealism came to America by way of German immigrants in the early nineteenth century and American scholars who had studied at one of the great universities of Germany and England. Some who studied in Germany attended the lectures of Fichte or Hegel. Those who studied in England early on were exposed to filtered versions of German idealism such as Coleridge's, but later found, in the writings of F.H. Bradley, an original and uniquely British version of absolute idealism. In mid-nineteenth century, the St Louis Hegelians did all they could to spread Hegelian idealism through William Torrey Harris's *Journal of Speculative Philosophy* and Henry Brokmeyer's rough translation of Hegel's *Science of Logic*. Nothing, however, accomplished as much as Royce's formulation of absolute idealism.

Royce's thought went through at least three phases. He was influenced by the German idealists but was scarcely a devout disciple of any of them. Rather, Royce's idealism was an original alternative to those that came before. The earliest phase addressed a problem for any representational theory of knowledge, namely, the possibility of error. Royce realized that if we know only our own representations, then it is impossible to ever be in error since we can never test the representation against reality to determine whether it is true or false. To circumvent this, Royce argued for an infinite Absolute knower, who comprehends both reality and our representations and thereby guarantees that they are either faithful or unfaithful representations of the reality we cannot directly know. Although this solution makes truth and error possible, knowledge of the truth or error remained inaccessible to the finite knower. Still, the basic insight that knowledge for finite minds presupposes an infinite knower who fulfills the meaning and truth conditions of our ideas remained with Royce, though in different formulations, throughout his philosophic career. In his middle phase, Royce analyzed human knowledge in terms of its fragmentary and incomplete form, which prevents us from being certain of truth, falsehood, or completeness of our ideas. To address this new form of the problem, Royce distinguished between the "internal" and "external" meaning of ideas. The internal meaning expresses not only a semantic content, but a purpose that seeks fulfillment, i.e. truth. The external meaning of an idea is, as commons sense might hold, the facts that allegedly exist independently of the idea. Royce argued, though, that the facts become such and are significant only in the context of the internal meaning. For example, unless I can specify the internal meaning of "taxi," any car, indeed, anything I point to, will do. Royce further observed that any particular internal meaning is limited in its function of fulfilling a purpose, hence cannot do so except insofar as it is part of an absolute system of ideas thought by the Absolute. Later, under the influence of Peirce, Royce reinterpreted his idealism as absolute pragmatism, and applied Peirce's triadic theory of interpretation to knowledge. On this view, the self, meaning, and knowledge reveal a social structure that can be illustrated as follows. In communicating an idea, one does not merely signal another self, rather one self who has an idea interprets that idea to another self, which is, of course, a community of interpretation. This result led many to think that Royce, in the end, abandoned absolute idealism; though not all share this view.

Absolute idealism remained influential well into the twentieth century, but not without its critics. Fellow idealists criticized absolute idealism as being deterministic, pantheistic, and unable to account for individual selves. Borden Parker Bowne, in particular, developed a viable alternative in his personalistic idealism, which emphasized the worth and significance of the plurality of individual persons. Others, such as John Dewey, who once embraced a version of idealism advanced by his teacher, G.S. Morris, gradually abandoned it in favor of his instrumental naturalism on the grounds that the identification of the real with the ideal, typical of absolute idealism, neglected the open possibilities characteristic of our experience of nature. Versions of idealism are still defended today, but not in the form of the grand metaphysical systems of Hegel or Royce. Other important idealists, after Royce, are W.E. Hocking and Brand Blanshard.

Further reading

Fichte, J.G. *The Science of Knowledge*, trans. Peter Heath and John Lachs. Cambridge: Cambridge University Press, 1982.

Hegel, G.W.F. *Phenomenology of Spirit*, trans. A.V. Miller. Oxford: Oxford University Press, 1977.

—— *Science of Logic*, trans. A.V. Miller. London: George Allen and Unwin, 1969.

Kant, Immanuel. *Critique of Pure Reason*, trans. and ed. Paul Guyer and Allen W. Wood. Cambridge: Cambridge University Press, 2000.

—— *Critique of the Power of Judgment*, trans. Paul Guyer and Eric Matthews. Cambridge: Cambridge University Press, 2001.

Royce, Josiah. *The Religious Aspect of Philosophy: A Critique of the Basis of Conduct and Faith*. New York: Harper Books, 1958.

—— *The World and the Individual*, 2 volumes. New York: Dover, 1959.

—— *The Problem of Christianity*. Chicago, IL: University of Chicago Press, 1968.

Gary L. Cesarz

IDEALISM: MORAL

Idealism is a complicated philosophical position, but, in general, idealism involves the central claim that the mind is a fundamental aspect of the world as a whole. Moral idealists, in addition, stress the moral and spiritual aspects of reality. Indeed, idealism, in American thought, tended to be a social or moral idealism that included efforts to realize ideals in practice. Thus, Transcendentalists like Emerson and Thoreau worked to bring about an ideal lifestyle and to reconcile the speculative and the practical. Idealism in America reached its zenith in the work of Josiah Royce whose thought contains a strongly pragmatic flavor with an emphasis upon ideas as plans of action, on thought and will and ultimately on establishing a universal community through semiotic, triadic interpretation.

A key issue for idealism is the position of mind in relation to nature. Is mind outside or behind nature, or is it some sort of nature-pervasive power of rationality? For moral idealists such as Royce the emphasis is on purposive will as well as thought. Another relational question for idealism is that of individual minds vis-à-vis some absolute mind. Some idealist positions, i.e. *social* idealists, speak of a collective social mind of individuals in general while others, often cited as *personal* idealists, posit a distributive collection of individual minds. Moral idealists generally are concerned about individual freedom as key to moral action.

Idealism is also often characterized in terms of its opposition to other metaphysical points of view such as naturalism, namely, the view that mind and spiritual and moral values emerge from or are reducible to material and/or natural things and processes. It is also viewed as opposed to realism, i.e. the view that material objects exist externally to us, our minds and our language and have properties not entirely or even mind-dependent. However, some philosophers claim that idealism need not be opposed to this common-sense realist view and the description "*objective* idealism" has been applied to a position that is anti-naturalist without being anti-realist.

A major form of idealism called *immaterialism* involves the central thesis that there is no such thing as material substance. Berkley is the best-known exponent of this type of idealism with his claim that "to be is to be perceived." He argues that what we call physical things are orderly collections of sensations or ideas and hence mind-dependent like the sensations or ideas which compose them.

Immanuel Kant, in his *Critique of Pure Reason*, describes his philosophical view as critical or transcendental idealism. His view is that space and time and categories like cause–effect are conditions of the possibility of experience rather than features of things as they are in themselves; without these conditions we could not have knowledge of an objective world. What makes this necessary synthesizing of experience possible is another condition of knowledge, namely, a transcendental self; and since this self is a condition of knowledge rather than an object of knowledge, we can know nothing about it. Despite his claim to idealism, Kant strongly critiqued idle metaphysical speculations and held fast to the idea that sense experience cannot lead us beyond the natural world. He argued that any attempt to prove a First Cause or an Absolute or the immateriality of a soul leads to insoluble antinomies.

However, aspects of Kant's philosophy did lead other philosophers who followed him to forms of absolute idealism. Drawing upon Kant's emphasis on the elements of activity and spontaneity in knowledge, some of his successors came to regard knowledge as a form of construction or making. Kant's ethical writings were also very influential on the development of idealism. Kant argued that our knowledge of and respect for the moral law presupposed freedom of will. Though he did not believe freedom of will, the existence of God or the immorality of the soul could be theoretically (metaphysically) proven, Kant argued that we are justified in accepting these ideas as what morality presupposes. He also introduced a faculty of reason he called *Vernunft*, a faculty dissatisfied with the confinement of the understanding to the ordering of sense experience and thus one which constantly strove for completeness and totality. Successors of Kant such as Fichte, Schelling and Hegel used these ideas to claim that reason reveals a real totality, not a desired or methodological one. Fichte, for example, argues that thought and intelligence, because they comprehend cause and effects, necessarily go beyond it. Thus, a free, intelligent ego must be the starting point of all philosophy from which everything else must be deduced. Schelling placed more stress on will than thought and saw free activity as basic in the world. He argued for a system of active moral beings as fundamental to reality. Schelling's idealism was labeled *moral idealism.*

Although his philosophical system is complex and has many dimensions, the idealism of Hegel is often taken to be a model of the view known as *objective or absolute idealism.* Hegel asserts that only mind is real for it alone is free and thus infinite. However, he did not mean that material things do not exist and only minds do. Mind was, for Hegel, a system of individuals actively developing their potentialities by embodying them in increasingly complex forms. He tries to show rudimentary mind working in the natural world as well as in human society and history. For Hegel, a fundamental feature of mind is freedom and since nothing that is partial or finite can be wholly free, mind is the only reality that is therefore infinite. Further, freedom involves consciousness of what one is doing and thus infinite mind is therefore self-conscious mind.

In America, Hegel's philosophy became particularly influential on a group of philosophers in Ohio. A school of idealism also developed in St Louis in the 1860s. Like the Transcendentalists, two philosophers of this school, Brokmeyer and Harris, were active in promoting ideals in social, political and educational circles.

In the United States the philosopher most associated with idealism was Josiah Royce. Royce was well acquainted with German and British idealism and his work *The World and the Individual* followed a careful study of Kant, Fitche, Schelling and Hegel as well as the English idealist, Bradley. In addition, he was intimate with the persons and work of William James, an empiricist and pragmatist, and with the logic and philosophy of C.S. Peirce. Royce also reflected critically upon various metaphysical views including mysticism, realism, and Kant's critical idealism, labeling them as the first, second and third conceptions of Being, and ultimately developing his own view which he called the "fourth conception of Being."

Royce was very concerned to make his idealism as realistic as possible. When we undertake to know, argues Royce, what we intend to know, is precisely that which is independent of us. Yet, for Royce, an idea is a partial expression of a purpose; and it is true or not in case it agrees or not with its object. Further, ideas are selective and unique in that no one else can determine for me what object I mean by my idea. The truth of propositions is, for Royce, the expression of meanings. Thus, the world in its wholeness, in its finality, is the complete expression of the meaning of every significant finite idea, so far as that idea has significance. The world is a world of interpretation, a process of expressing significance, a temporal, gradual process of expressing meaning. It is a purposive world since, for Royce, meaning is fully expressed when purpose is fulfilled. Though the world, for Royce, is essentially purposive, this does not rule out evil, conflict, or tension. Rather, argued Royce, conflict and tragedy belong to the expression and fulfillment of meaning both for the individual and for the community, both for nature and for private individuals. What we all seek, argues Royce, is the interpretation of life. The real, he argues, is that which answers this quest, which deals with the life of spirit, the life of unity, the community, the experience of wholeness.

Idealism, for Royce, must acknowledge the unique significance of the individual. The world must be seen as a realm of individuals, self-possessed, morally free, and significantly independent of one another to make their freedom of action possible and finally significant. The world must be an expression of moral, rational Will. His ultimate view is indeed properly labeled as a *moral idealism* for his conception of being is a teleological one that regards the real as explicable in terms of value and, like Schelling, his system involves active, free, individual, moral beings. In his last course on metaphysics given at Harvard, Royce declared that one cannot view the world as real without viewing it in a teleological manner; the essence of the real is the interpretation of experience. The very recognition of being, says Royce, is itself an estimate. The categories of metaphysics are from the beginning teleological.

At the close of the nineteenth century idealism was considered the dominant Western philosophical position

Further reading

Marsoobian, Armen and Ryder, John (eds) *The Blackwell Guide to American Philosophy.* New York: Blackwell, 2004. See especially the chapter on "Idealism in America."

Rescher, Nicholas. *Ethical Idealism: An Inquiry into the Nature and Function of Ideals.* Berkeley, CA: University of California. 1987.

Royce, Josiah. *Metaphysics.* His Philosophy 9 course of 1915–16 as stenographically recorded by Ralph W. Brown and complemented by Bryon F. Underwood. William Ernest Hocking, Initial Editor. Co-edited Richard Hocking and Frank Oppenheim. Albany, NY: SUNY Press, 1998.

—— *Lectures on Modern Idealism.* New Haven, CT: Yale University Press, 1967 [1919].

JACQUELYN ANN KEGLEY

IDEALISM: NATURALISTIC

Idealism and naturalism represent distinct yet often intertwining perspectives within classical American philosophy. There are many modes of naturalism just as there are distinctively different kinds of idealism. What is especially interesting is the way in which otherwise naturalistic perspectives incorporate idealistic commitments that move key concepts away from nature toward the supernatural or the atemporal. On the other side, many idealisms insist on an embeddedness within nature that puts pressure on the classical doctrine of *creatio ex nihilo* or the creation of being out of absolute nonbeing. When naturalism admits idealistic components the concept of the nonsupernatural is stretched to its limit.

In doing a taxonomy of naturalism five distinctive types emerge as encompassing the broad trajectory of American philosophy. There are strong family resemblances among them and they share some basic presuppositions. We will examine these presuppositions, of which there are three, before analyzing the five types of naturalism. The first presupposition is the view that nature is all that there is. There is one and only one nature and there are no entities, divine or otherwise, that somehow exist independently of the innumerable orders of the world. That is, everything that can be encountered in any way is connected to some other orders within the world. However, no entity is connected to *all* orders of the world but remains relevant to a given, if shifting, realm of orders. Naturalism generally believes that there are breaks and tears within the fabric of nature; that is, spheres of nonrelevance and nonrelation.

Second, naturalism affirms the extreme littleness of the human process. The human self is but one circumscribed product of nature and has no special status within the innumerable orders that surround and penetrate it. Nature is indifferent to its most complex known creature. For most naturalisms there is no place for the doctrine of a soul that continues its subjective consciousness after bodily death. In the language of John Dewey the human being is an organism interacting with an immediate environment in a Darwinian mode of adaptation to antecedent conditions. The belief in a soul or in an absolute self-consciousness is held to be a supernaturalist holdover that has no role in a robust naturalism.

Third, naturalism affirms a kind of immanentism concerning the origin of nature. The doctrine of a unique and special divine creation is rejected in favor of the view that nature creates itself out of itself alone. The key distinction here is the classical one between *nature naturing* and *nature natured. Nature naturing* is the overwhelming force by which the innumerable orders of nature emerge into their place within the world. *Nature natured* is the orders themselves as they unfold into innumerable forms of interaction. *Nature naturing* and *nature natured* are wedded together in a seamless fabric that works in what might be called the unconscious of nature.

The five types of naturalism are: descriptive, honorific, pluralistic, process, and ecstatic. Idealistic components are central in the honorific, pluralistic, and process forms. The descriptive and ecstatic forms are more immanent in their understanding of the self and the religious sphere.

Descriptive naturalism is deeply Darwinian with a view of the self that is instrumental and focuses on efficient causality as the motor force within nature. There is no realm that locates nature in some larger super order and there is no center within nature that could be the fulcrum point for a totalistic perspective. There is a kind of darkness surrounding the self in process but a moderate form of light within the sphere of self/world interaction. The three primary descriptive naturalists are John Dewey, George Santayana, and Justus Buchler.

Honorific naturalism, most fully expressed by Ralph Waldo Emerson, sees nature as the seed bed for self-transcending potencies that enlarge and divinize the human self. There is a muted role for a kind of cosmic consciousness whenever the self encounters a potency of nature. Efficient causality is downplayed while formal and final causality assume center-stage. Nature is infinite and filled with moral lessons that can be decoded through metaphor. A potency is a power that emerges from *nature naturing* and impacts on the human process making it spiritual and religious, but in a nonsupernatural sense.

Pluralistic naturalism, whose chief exemplar is William James, privileges the notion of consciousness even though it remains within the orbit of Darwin. For James nature consists of centers of vitality that work to provide meaning in a world that has genuine tragic components. For the individual there is a constant struggle between a kind of materialistic and pessimistic naturalism and a more idealistic view of absolute mind. His pragmatism represents the naturalistic solution to this dyad. Meanings can transcend the individual and are rooted in a finite but growing god who helps the self find stable meaning.

Process naturalism is also pluralistic but posits an absolute (primordial) mind of god that represents stability and the principle of creative growth within the universe. Alfred North Whitehead and Charles Hartshorne are the two key figures in this movement. This god transcends nature in some senses but is connected to it with its second nature which is called the "consequent" nature. This second nature is immanent and grows with the creatures in the universe.

Ecstatic naturalism works out of the key distinction between *nature naturing* and *nature natured* and sees all of nature as a product of its own self-fissuring. The orders of the world long to return to the unconscious of nature (*nature naturing*) and participate in a nonsupernatural form of religious awareness. History is cyclical and makes no absolute progress to some kind of transcendent sphere. The self is a foundling that must attain fitful kinds of homecoming within a nature that has neither center nor circumference.

Idealism has a cluster of intertwined commitments: (1) there is an atemporal mind that contains all relations and all things in relation; (2) all of the world is experience (the doctrine of panpsychism); (3) everything is related to everything else (the doctrine of internal relations); (4) human consciousness is capable of absolute consciousness; and (5) history is moving toward an ideal convergence within either the near future or in the infinite long run.

Idealism becomes naturalistic when it lets go of some of its supernaturalism while shifting its emphases to meaning structures within nature. The doctrine of the absolute mind becomes transformed to that of the beloved community, as in the work of Josiah Royce. History is still seen in progressive terms but the focus is more on finite human energy, as in William James. The doctrine of internal relations is rejected or transformed into the infinite long run as in the thinking of Charles Sanders Peirce for whom the universe is growing toward greater degrees of connectedness when thirdness (law and reason) becomes more manifest. Naturalistic idealism combines the richest parts of each trajectory and in the end affirms an evolutionary social and cosmic history in which the self can grow in consciousness and meaning within finite parameters. The principle of hope replaces that of the infinite mind as the human mode of comportment that brings us closest to the endlessly self-creative orders of *nature naturing*.

Perhaps the best way to understand the notion of a naturalized idealism is in terms of the tension between the finite and the infinite. Idealisms posit a number of forms of infinity, each funded by a robust web of internal and external relations and by a sense of evolutionary expansion. For an idealist the infinite is knowable and the structures of human self-consciousness are set up in such a way as to ride the waves of the infinite and overcome finite limitations. When idealism encounters the more chaste perspective of naturalism, it is compelled to recognize two things: (1) that the finite is more prevalent than the infinite (if the infinite is seen as a series of internal relations without end), and (2) that the infinite is not knowable. The second claim needs some refinement. For the naturalist, nature is indeed infinite in scope and complexity yet its infinitude is precisely not knowable to finite beings like ourselves. We can see tendencies, leanings, prospects, openings, but we have no means of access to the infinite in itself. There is a kind of agnosticism in naturalism, especially evident in Santayana, which disallows piggybacking on some alleged infinite sign series.

Panpsychism, the doctrine that matter is to some degree mental, no matter how primitive, is replaced with a view that insists that mentality is limited in nature and that much that we encounter has no mentality. The remaining idealistic piece is that human semiosis, that is, the use of signs that refer to the world independent of the human sign user, has a hunger toward the kind of internal relations that idealism posits within a divine mind.

A full-blown naturalistic idealism will combine the best of both trajectories and will mark out a terrain that is unique among world philosophies. It will affirm a growing infinite while remaining reticent about infinite knowledge; it will place mind within nature not outside nature in an absolute atemporal cosmic consciousness; it will see limits to all sign series and thus see breaks within the one nature that there is; and it will have a chastened role for religious consciousness as a comportment to sacred impulses within nature but never beyond – thus producing a theology of what could be called "sacred folds," i.e. semiotically dense foldings of meaning within the one nature that there is.

Further reading

Buchler, Justus. *Metaphysics of Natural Complexes*, second expanded edition. Albany, NY: SUNY Press, 1990.

Ryder, John. *American Philosophical Naturalism in the Twentieth Century.* Amherst, NY: Prometheus Books, 1994

Shea, William M. *Naturalists and the Supernatural*. Atlanta, GA: Mercer University Press, 1984.

ROBERT S. CORRINGTON

IDEALISM: SUBJECTIVE

Subjective idealism is the doctrine that admits the existence only of ideas and the minds of which those ideas are the content. It might be disputed whether anyone truly embraced such a view. Still, the designation "subjective idealism" is used in two overlapping ways, as a term of demarcation and as a mark of criticism. It often is used to distinguish the early versions of idealism of George Berkeley and Arthur Collier from later versions of idealism such as transcendental idealism, absolute idealism, and personalistic idealism. These later forms of idealism invoke various objective conditions or criteria of the ideal that insure its objectivity. Kant employs validity, necessity and universality characteristic of formal logic, mathematics and natural science. Finding a clue in the types of judgment formal logic deals with, Kant further derives transcendental logic, which details twelve categories of the understanding, necessary conditions for the possibility of objects of experience. Hegel has his system of categories and Absolute Spirit; and personalism appeals to social conditions necessary for intersubjectivity and self-consciousness.

Subjective idealism commonly rides on the epistemological thesis that all that one can know are one's ideas and one's own awareness of those ideas, and is taken to imply the metaphysical position that all that can be justifiably admitted to exist are ideas and minds. Though it is misleading to conflate the two, one might be tempted to infer that subjective idealism is a thoroughgoing Protagorean subjectivism, which leads to skepticism, relativism, and solipsism. At most, Protagoras' "*homo mensura*" doctrine is a type of subjectivism, not idealism. In contrast to idealism, to maintain that whatever counts as existing or true is relative to or holds only for an individual perceiver and only in a quotational sense, scarcely rises, as Plato demonstrated long ago in the *Theaetetus*, to a full-fledged metaphysics or epistemology.

Berkeley preferred to describe his philosophy as "immaterialism," by which he meant to deny the existence of matter as an independent self-subsistent being, and never used the label, "subjective idealism." Still, to many, Berkeley is the most famous example of a subjective idealist given his enunciation, "*Esse es percipi et percipere*," which implies that subjects and the contents of subjective awareness, minds and their ideas, are all that exist. The axiom is not the argument for Berkeley's thesis, but its summation. His arguments for his position derive from his empiricist theory of knowledge, rejection of representationalism, and nominalism concerning language and ideas. Berkeley accepted Locke's claim that all knowledge is of ideas of sensory qualities derived from one or more of the five senses. As such, all ideas are particular instances of definite qualities or clusters of qualities; i.e. an idea of "cat" is of a particular cat of definite breed, color and so on. Berkeley thus held that there could be no general abstract ideas, hence no abstract idea of matter or material substratum as distinct from but the bearer of qualities (even Locke referred to matter as "something, he knew not what"). He argued that since ideas of primary qualities (e.g. shape, motion) are perceived in precisely the same way as ideas of secondary qualities (e.g. blue, sweet), there is no empirical basis for distinguishing the two, and no way to verify that the former "resemble" and are "in the bodies" to which they are attributed, while the latter bear no such resemblance. After all, since ideas of primary and secondary qualities are derived from the senses, both types exist only insofar as they are perceived. It is unverifiable contradictory nonsense, Berkeley reasoned, to claim that one type of idea resembles and exists in an unperceived and unperceiving material substratum while the other type does not, when both are indistinguishable as sensory ideas that exist only as perceived by a perceiver. Berkeley further argued that objects we perceive (e.g. a tulip) do not cease to exist simply because there might be no finite passive perceivers (minds or spirits) available to perceive them, for they continue to be perceived by God, an infinite active perceiver and active cause of the ideas. Since he must appeal to an infinite perceiver existing independently of finite subjective awareness, some scholars have argued that Berkeley is not a subjective idealist.

Two American contemporaries of Berkeley, Samuel Johnson and Jonathan Edwards, are sometimes considered subjective idealists. Johnson was clearly influenced by Berkeley's immaterialism, visited him in Rhode Island when Berkeley came to America (1728–31), and corresponded with Berkeley after he returned to Ireland. Johnson accepted Berkeley's arguments against the existence of material substance, but attempted to combine immaterialism with a form of Platonism. Johnson held that all that exists are ideas in the minds of perceivers, but the ideas perceived in finite minds are copies of archetypal ideas in the mind of God. Edwards is more original and his similarity to Berkeley more circumspect, having independently discovered the same problems in Locke that Berkeley found. Edwards sought a new synthesis of Calvinism, Scottish Platonism and the new science presented in the works of Newton and Locke. However, Edwards resembles Berkeley primarily in that he denies the existence of an external self-subsistent material substance, and affirms that all that exists are ideas perceived and perceivers. Edwards differs from Berkeley, though, in that he accepts Locke's distinction between primary and secondary qualities, and Newtonian atoms. All of these, however, exist only as ideas ordered according to the laws reflected in nature as perceived by God, the only substance and ultimate cause of all that exists. Their appeal, however, to an eternal substantial God and refusal to base their conclusions on human subjectivity alone seems to count against their being subjective idealists.

As noted above, some philosophers use the designation as a form of criticism. For instance, Shelling distinguished his system of idealism from Fichte's by criticizing the latter as having not gone sufficiently beyond subjective idealism. Ralph Barton Perry and James Edwin Creighton, in America, criticized several idealistic philosophies, arguing that they reduce to subjective idealism and are open to some common objections. Perry criticized subjective idealism as being subject to but misunderstanding the "egocentric predicament," the thesis that "one cannot conceive things to exist apart for consciousness, because to conceive is *ipso facto* to bring within consciousness." This amounted to the charge that subjective idealism results in a highly implausible denial of the existence of anything beyond the contents of an individual consciousness, which is tantamount to solipsism. Perry further maintained that all forms of idealism involve the egocentric predicament. Creighton described subjective idealism to be a type of psychological idealism or "mentalism," which he distinguished from his own objective or speculative idealism. He then grouped idealists as diverse as Berkeley, Kant and Royce under the same heading and criticized the group as representing variations of mentalism. Today, some of the arguments that once were labeled subjective idealism, and later, phenomenalism, have been reformulated under the heading of anti-realism.

Further reading

Berkeley, George. *The Works of George Berkeley, Bishop of Cloyne*, 9 volumes, ed. A.A. Luce and T.E. Jessop. Edinburgh: Thomas Nelson, 1949, Vol. 2.

Edwards, Jonathan. *Scientific and Philosophical Writings. Edited by Wallace E. Anderson*, Vol. 6 of *The Works of Jonathan Edwards*, 10 volumes, ed. John E. Smith. New Haven, CT and London: Yale University Press, 1980.

Johnson, Samuel. *Elementa Philosophia: Containing chiefly, Noetica, or Things relating to Mind or Understanding: and Ethica, or Things relating to the Moral Behaviour*, Vol. 2 of *The Works of Samuel Johnson, President of King's College: His Career and Writings*. 4 volumes, ed. Herbert Schneider and Carol Schneider. New York: Columbia University Press, 1929.

Gary L. Cesarz

IDEAS: REFLECTIVE

In *An Essay Concerning Human Understanding* (1690), the British empiricist John Locke (1632–1704) introduced a distinction between those "Objects of the Understanding" (*Essay* I.i.8), or *ideas*, that originate in sensation and those that originate in reflection upon "the Internal Operations of our Minds" (*Essay* II.i.2). Examples of the former include our ideas of red or of cold. Examples of the latter include our ideas of comparing, abstracting, dreaming, and, most fundamentally, perception, memory, and will.

Lauding Locke's emphasis upon the representational or sign function of ideas, the American philosopher and founder of pragmatism Charles S. Peirce (1839–1914) nevertheless took issue with Locke's account of the mechanics of reflection, finding it to be not only "vaguely explained" (EP 1.96) but to illustrate what Peirce disparaged as "the chief intellectual characteristic of the English." This is the "wish to effect everything by the plainest and directest means" (EP 1.85). In particular, Peirce considered simplistic and mistaken Locke's attempt to explain our awareness of the differences between mental operations in terms of the same sort of recognitional capacity that Locke believed allowed us to distinguish between sensible ideas.

Peirce's own explanation of our cognizance of such mental actions as sensing, imagining, believing, conceiving, and willing is set forth in the first essay of his 1868 Cognition Series, "Questions Concerning Certain Faculties Claimed for Man." He begins by separating "the objective element of cognition," or "the something represented," from "the subjective element of cognition." Roughly paralleling Locke's conception of reflective ideas, Peirce defines the latter as "some action or passion of the self whereby [the objective element] becomes represented" (EP 1.21).

For Peirce, there is no need to postulate the existence of a faculty that immediately distinguishes, or directly recognizes, the subjective element of cognition. Rather, we *infer* that we are, say, sensing rather than imagining on the basis of differences in their objective elements: "the very fact of the immense difference of the immediate *objects* of sense and imagination, sufficiently accounts for our distinguishing these faculties" (EP 1.22). This is likewise true for the all-important ability to distinguish believing – an action of the self that requires that we *know* that we are believing – from conceiving, or merely entertaining a hypothesis. This is because only the object of a belief is colored by "a peculiar feeling of conviction." As Peirce insists, "This sensation, like any other, is an object of consciousness; and therefore the capacity for it implies no intuitive recognition of subjective elements of consciousness" (EP 1.22). Finally, this explanation holds for our awareness of volition. Once differentiated from desiring, Peirce claims that willing is simply "the power of concentrating the attention or abstracting" (EP 1.22). And so, just as we infer our ability to see based upon our awareness of color, we infer that we are willing based upon our awareness of abstract objects. As an example of this, Peirce follows Locke's lead and points to the fact that we can think of a triangle "without thinking if it is equilateral, isosceles, or scalene" (EP 1.48).

Further reading

Locke, John. *An Essay Concerning Human Understanding*, ed. John Yolton. New York: Dutton, 1965 [1690].

Peirce, Charles S. *The Essential Peirce*, Volume 1, ed. the Peirce Edition Project. Bloomington, IN: Indiana University Press, 1991. Cited by EP 1.

MARY MAGADA-WARD

IDENTITY, NATIONAL

The national identity of the United States has been a topic of controversy and passionate declamation since the early seventeenth century when European settlers first invaded and set out to conquer the land and civilizations of the Native American inhabitants. Since its founding the United States has been for many, and perhaps most, as a city on a hill, the envy of many generations; for others the American dream has been a nightmare.

The progenitor of jazz and blues, pragmatism and process philosophy, as well as the largest and most radically diverse population in the history of humanity, the United States of America would seem to resist the concept of national identity. An attempt to articulate America's national identity must take account of a population comprised of tens of millions of immigrants, the mass movement of several generations of its citizens several thousand miles from the east coast to the west, as well as modes of thought and culture that emphasize movement and innovation in direct opposition to definitions aiming to fix an identity or an essential character.

Both proponents and opponents of the concept of the national identity of the United States must also take account of its profoundly conflicted and paradoxical history. A beacon of the bright light of freedom for much of the world, America's history casts several dark shadows, including especially slavery of Africans and racism toward African Americans, as well as the direct and largely unacknowledged holocaust of millions of Native peoples. At the beginning of the twenty-first century, ever in denial of its shadow, America has again activated its latent penchant for military and economic imperialism.

On the positive side – and scarcely any historical event has been so universally acknowledged as unqualifiedly positive – the nation was founded in the last quarter of the eighteenth century primarily by a group of courageous, far-sighted, and gifted individuals – Washington (justifiably considered first in the hearts of his countrymen), Franklin, Adams, Jefferson, Hamilton, and Madison. They laid the foundation for an honored constitution and a governmental structure that has survived unbroken for more than two centuries. It must be acknowledged, however, that its founders imagined a nation by and for Protestant white males and not at all its current population that includes enfranchised blacks and women. America now includes more Muslims than Episcopalians (the dominant religion of the founders) as well as millions of Jews, Hindus, Buddhists, and more than fifty million Roman Catholics – approximately one-sixth of the population.

Many of the texts considered distinctively American and profoundly influential on American thought and culture are to be found in the essays of Ralph Waldo Emerson, perhaps the most famous of these being the following: "Why should not we also enjoy an original relation to the universe?" Prophet and exemplar of original thinking and the active soul, in the early to mid-nineteenth century, Emerson gave to America, and thereby to the world, a vision of a people creating a culture based on ideals thoughtfully reviewed and freely affirmed. When the pressure of conflicting value commitments proved unsustainable, Abraham Lincoln provided the language and the deeds that enabled the divided nation to refound itself. As Emerson is America's sage, Lincoln is its avatar.

To the extent that the United States has a national identity, it is surely characterized by its radical pluralism and evolving character. It is appropriate, and perhaps necessary, that these qualities should also characterize the philosophies of William James and John Dewey, the most representative of American philosophers. Cheerfully extending the Romantic vision and epistemology of Emerson, at the turn of the twentieth century James celebrated every form of pluralism – varieties of religious experience, philosophical perspectives, and psychological types. Like America, James was open to possibilities and alternatives, determinedly resisting any one metanarrative that would exclude others. His definition of philosophy, "the habit of seeing alternatives," has a distinctively American ring.

For James's younger colleague, Josiah Royce, born in a mining town in northern California, America represented a sublime reconciliation of what he considered to be life's three great values – individuality, community, and the ideals by which a community of free individuals can render itself beloved. The preeminent philosopher of democracy, John Dewey, celebrated the wisdom of shared experience. He exposed and opposed privilege and certainty. While the great arc of classical American philosophy, which can be said to include the third period of A.N. Whitehead's brilliant philosophical career, seemed to have come to an end at mid-twentieth century under the near total domination of British analytic philosophy, American philosophy (not merely philosophy in America) has been in a promising resurgence since the 1970s.

Perhaps the most distinctive and influential expression of American character and values, and hence national identity, is to be found in the brief inspiring life and enduring message of Martin Luther King, Jr. The Presidential Medal of Freedom, awarded to King posthumously, expresses the extent to which America is a work in progress:

> Martin Luther King, Jr, was the conscience of his generation. A southerner, a black man, he gazed on the great wall of segregation and saw that the power of love could bring it down. From the pain and exhaustion of his fight to free all people from the bondage of separation and injustice, he wrung his eloquent statement of his dream of what America could be.

Steadily by the decade, the legacy of King, like that of Lincoln, can increasingly be seen to be at the core of America's national identity. King is the latest, and perhaps the greatest, in the tradition of American religious and social reformers – and martyrs – committed to the realization of the American mission on behalf of individual freedom and social justice.

America's national identity has been primarily a commitment to, if not yet an adequate realization of, the proposition that all persons are created equal. It has been an experiment in multi-ethnicity and a form of government intended to ensure the freedom of individual conscience and freedom from religious and government oppression.

Further reading

Carroll, Andrew (ed.) *Letters of a Nation*. New York: Broadway Books, 1997.

Commager, Henry Steele. *The American Mind: An Interpretation of American Thought and Character since the 1880s*. New Haven, CT: Yale University Press, 1950.

Takaki, Ronald. *A Different Mirror: A History of Multicultural America*. New York: Little, Brown, 1993.

Zinn, Howard. *A People's History of the United States: 1492–Present*. New York: HarperCollins, 1999.

Robert McDermott

IDENTITY, POLITICS OF

Contemporary political life has witnessed the emergence and development of different social movements for the liberation of marginalized and oppressed identity groups (racial and ethnic minorities, women, sexual minorities, etc). These movements have articulated their legal and social demands and their political claims through the notion of *recognition*, that is, in terms of the due recognition that the identity of their members deserves and is not given by society and its institutions. Different forms of recognition (legal, economic, social, political, and cultural) are demanded by these movements; and they concern different aspects of identity, such as race, ethnicity, gender, and sexual orientation. Racial and ethnic movements, the women's movement, and the gay movement are often conceived as different fronts of the struggle for the liberation and empowerment of those whose identity has been subject to oppression; and they are subsumed under the label of *identity politics*. The philosophical foundation of these movements is a dialectic of recognition (of Hegelian origins) that brings to the fore the social dynamics that supports the formation and development of identity. The ethical and political significance of recognition is often grounded in the rights of individuals and groups to have their identities properly recognized and in the corresponding duties of society and its institutions to provide proper recognition. In this sense, it is argued that the absence of recognition or the *misrecognition* of certain identities constitutes a particularly insidious form of oppression and injustice. As Taylor (1994), for one, has put it, "due recognition is not just a courtesy we owe people" but "a vital human need"; and "misrecognition shows not just a lack of due respect", but "it can inflict a grievous wound, saddling its victims with a crippling self-hatred" (p. 26).

Identity politics has been praised by many (e.g. Alcoff, Lugones, Medina) as a fruitful source of solidarity and a necessary site for coalition across different forms of oppression, but it has also been criticized by others (e.g. Fraser, Hollinger, Rorty) as the source of divisions, antagonisms, and political derailments. The critics of identity politics can be divided into two different groups. On the one hand, there are those radical critics who think that identity politics is a political dead-end because it involves, unavoidably, a partisan politics based on narrow group interests that stand in the way of broader forms of solidarity. For these critics, identity politics is socially and politically detrimental and intrinsically divisive. These radical critics (such as Hollinger and Rorty) see no future in identity politics and contend that the social and political movements under this rubric should be overcome or superseded by other movements. On the other hand, there are those critics who think that identity politics can make a positive contribution to political life but find it problematic in its present form. In this vein, Nancy Fraser has argued that identity politics presents a misguided order of priorities by focusing on cultural battles of recognition and disregarding the unequal distribution of resources which is the root of the most fundamental forms of oppression and which calls for redistribution, not recognition. In the so-called *recognition versus redistribution* debate with Axel Honneth, Fraser argues that the core political value of liberation movements should be (legal, political, and more fundamentally economic) equality, because there is "no recognition without redistribution." Judith Butler has replied to Fraser that the battles of identity politics are not "merely cultural," and that the politics of recognition are distorted (or *misrecognized*) if we ignore how lack of recognition and socio-economic subordination are bound up with each other. While insisting that identity politics must be critically interrogated and deepened or supplemented, in her recent work Fraser brings together redistribution claims and recognition claims in her account of the principle of *participatory parity*, which recasts the value of equality in terms of equal power and agency in society and its practices and institutions.

The questioning of identity categories has taken place as an internal process of critical interrogation within each identity movement. Critical voices within racial and ethnic movements, the women's movement, and the gay movement have argued that those forms of solidarity that are predicated on a shared identity are problematic because they erase or marginalize differences and become oppressive. The very labels used as banners in these movements ("woman," "African-American," "Hispanic," "gay," "lesbian," etc.) have been deemed oppressive because they tacitly impose a common identity on a diverse group, overlooking internal differences. Within each of these political movements we find a good number of its members protesting that their differences are not being acknowledged, sometimes to the point of being forced to strip themselves of these differences in order to participate in the shared identity postulated by the movement. Responding to these internal criticisms, Race Theory, Feminist Theory, and Queer Theory have entered a new, *minimalist* phase in which new (more minimal or deflated) notions of solidarity have been proposed. Thus contemporary critical race theorists (such as Tommie Shelby) have argued for a minimalist conception of black identity and black solidarity that does not require shared properties, but only common problems and interests. Similarly, recent Feminist and Queer Theory contain many views that argue for the formation of networks of solidarity organized around overlapping gender and sexual concerns without presupposing homogeneous gender and sexual identities. Drawing on these minimalist views and underscoring the heterogeneity of identity categories, some identity theorists (such as Alcoff and Medina) have argued that it is possible to form alliances across different movements of liberation without sacrificing the specificity and heterogeneity of particular identity groups and their internal differences.

The debates about identity politics have resulted in a strong division within the discipline of American Studies. On one side of this divide there are Americanists (such as David Hollinger and Richard Rorty) who argue that "our country's ideals have been betrayed" and that American culture and American identity cannot be pursued and achieved unless we overcome the divisions created and reinforced by identity movements. On the other side of the divide we find Americanists (such as Nikhil Pal Singh and Cornel West) who are more sympathetic to identity politics and argue that the project to construct an identity-blind (post-ethnic, post-racial, etc.) America rests on a naïve patriotism that hides racial and class conflicts and different forms of oppression (economic, political, legal, cultural, etc.).

Further reading

Alcoff, Linda. *Visible Identities: Race, Gender, and the Self.* New York: Oxford University Press, 2005.

Fraser, Nancy and Honneth, Axel. *Redistribution or Recognition? A Political–Philosophical Exchange.* London and New York: Verso, 2003.

Gates, Henry Louis, Jr and West, Cornel. *The Future of the Race.* New York: Vintage, 1997.

Gould, Carol and Paquino, Pasquale (eds) *Cultural Identity and the Nation-State.* New York: Rowman and Littlefield, 2001.

Hollinger, David. *Post-Ethnic America: Beyond Multiculturalism,* revised and updated edition. New York: Basic Books, 2000.

Lugones, María. *Pilgrimages/Peregrinajes: Theorizing Coalition against Multiple Oppression.* New York: Rowan and Littlefield, 2003.

Medina, José. "Pragmatism and Ethnicity: Critique, Reconstruction, and the New Hispanic," *Metaphilosophy 35*, 1–2 (2004): 115–46.

Shelby, Tommie. *We who are Dark: The Philosophical Foundations of Black Solidarity.* Cambridge, MA: Harvard University Press, 2005.

José Medina

IMAGINATION

Imagination is a capacity of internal visualization, concept creation and manipulation not directly dependent upon sensation. Imagination is associated with a range of phenomena: mental imagery, fancy, inventiveness, insight, counterfactual reasoning, pretence and simulation and conceivability. Products of the imagination are sometimes considered false or fantastical, e.g. the phrase, "I must have imagined it" is applied to explain a mistake in conversation. The term "imagine" is also used in countless idiomatic ways that do not imply any use of an imaginative faculty; for example, a person might exclaim "Imagine that!" to an unusual news item.

In the history of western philosophy, the term "imagination" often relates to mental imagery or imagistic representation: that is, how mental "pictures" could be "in the head" and how those "pictures" can have intentionality. However, there is also epistemological concern regarding inventiveness, especially what kind of knowledge arises from the imagination and whether conceivability impacts on possibility. Contemporary cognitive science is focused on the cognitive architecture underlying imaginative thought and suggests connections between imagination, counterfactual reasoning and understanding other people's mental states. This approach has impacted broader philosophical areas such as ethics, where the imagination plays a role in invoking moral responsibility through simulation, role-play and empathy. Non-visual sense modalities (e.g. hearing) have received much less attention in the imagination literature (Currie and Ravenscroft 2003). Because of the range of uses of the term "imagination" it is illuminating to look at the history of the faculty of mental imagery.

Imagination as a mental faculty

The "imagination" has been considered a faculty of the mind since ancient Greek times. Plato described this faculty as a perceptual capacity to imprint images from the senses. Since then, its role has increased from a tool of perception to one of creativity, and insight. In the twentieth century the existence of an imaginative faculty has been challenged with behaviorism and then resurrected by contemporary cognitive science as a faculty of supposition and pretence.

Imagination as a faculty of perception

The history of imagination in western philosophy begins with ancient Greek discussions of *phantasia* (Latin translation *imaginatio*). Plato explained *phantasia* as the faculty of imagery which operated during perception as well as during dreaming and recollection. Thus it was both an active and a passive faculty depending on the context of use. Unlike modern conceptions of imagination which explicitly contrast its role with perception, the ancient Greek *phantasia* was an integral part of perception. That is, the *phantasia* interpreted perceptual information (*aisthesis*) into sensory judgments about the world (*phantasma*). In *de Anima*, Aristotle explained this by considering our notion of the sun. Through *phantasia* we sense that the sun is a small disk in the sky. Yet we believe that the sun is in reality much bigger and located in the heavens. Aristotle illustrates how *phantasma* informs but does not dictate knowledge. This ancient Greek faculty is analogous with Kant's concept of *reproductive imagination.* Kant describes reproductive imagination as a reconstructive capacity of humans and animals which completes fragmentary data of the senses. For example, it is utilized when we perceive a cube as a three-dimensional object, even though we only *see* three sides of it.

Because Plato viewed empirical knowledge as inherently flawed, and *phantasia* was informed by the senses, he took beliefs informed by this faculty to be a poor sort of knowledge. He supposed that real knowledge of the world was restricted to the Gods and perhaps a few superior human beings who had access to the forms. Aristotle was more moderate and took *phantasma* to be one of the two key elements in thinking, the other being judgment. In contrast, the stoics and epicureans took sense judgments to be the superior form of knowledge. They argued that all knowledge is simply the development and extension from sense knowledge, thus they claimed that *phantasia* was crucial to understanding. Regardless of its epistemological role, phantasia in early Greek thinking was securely tied to perception. The extension of *phantasia* from a faculty of perception to one of creation or divine insight came hundreds of years later.

Imagination as a creative faculty

Creative imagination is the ability to construct new ideas from those previously experienced. This kind of imagination first appeared in Philostratus in 300 AD and was a philosophical syncretism probably attributable to a Platonizing stoic who believed that through the manipulation of *phantasma* all knowledge of the world arose. This was also the view of the British Empiricists, e.g. Hume made the imagination the central faculty of cognition which freely created and combined ideas according to three principles of association: resemblance, contiguity, and cause and effect. Hume's imagination was responsible for categorizing things into kinds, story-telling and creative thinking. Kant also considered creative imagination a central faculty of cognition. He called this ability to combine experiences the *productive imagination* and it played a crucial role in the mind's ability to create a coherent understanding of the world.

The American pragmatists were great advocates of the creative imagination. Charles Peirce considered imagination the fundamental capacity of the intellect. He argued that scientific progress was made by an imaginative inductive leap which fueled the search for truth. This imaginative induction, or amplitative logic, he called abduction. Abductive reasoning was a source of both scientific insight and inference. John Dewey argued that creative or artistic expression drawn from the imagination deepened and intensified thought and ideas. William James thought the imagination was a tool to create new objects, ideas and possibilities.

Although Hume had many positive roles for imagination, he also warned of the danger of flights of fancy to solid philosophical inquiry. He argued that imagination can lead to error because once ideas have been formulated they can come to have greater sway over belief than is warranted by their genesis. Hume's concern has led to imaginings being associated with falsehood or fiction. Because imagined ideas are not limited by either natural or social laws, they have been viewed as a dangerous departure from epistemological success. Nevertheless, Jean-Paul Sartre welcomed the freedom of the mind brought by the imagination. E.J. Furlong also championed the originality, creativity, freedom and spontaneity of the faculty.

Imagination as a faculty for divine inspiration

The imagination became associated with religious revelation due to neo-Platonic interpretation. Even though Plato did not suggest this connection, he did locate *phantasia* in the soul near the faculty for divination, visions of warning and consolidation. Neo-Platonists consequently interpreted *phantasia* as a transmission device for divine inspiration. This notion was heartily endorsed by the early Christian church and went on to substantially influence the romantic view of imagination as a redemptive act analogous to and a part of the infinite creative act of God (Coleridge *Biographia Literaria*, 1817). The neo-Platonic imagination of the nineteenth century was a poetic source of deeper truth about the world. Vedic and Sufi traditions also considered imagination a faculty through which humans could connect with the spiritual world, hence ultimate reality. This view is sharply contrasted by the treatment of imagination by twentieth-century analytic philosophy.

Imagination as a faculty of supposition

In the late nineteenth century Dewey argued that a key role of the imagination was counterfactual reasoning and the consideration of possibilities because imaginative thinking could be isolated from behavior. James compared the function of imagination with language. He thought that both capacities enable thought about objects not present to the senses and the ability to disregard present objects as though they were absent. However, James thought imagination differed from language in that imagined objects are vague and holistic, whereas language is precise and analytic. James concluded that imagined objects, like those of perception, were fleeting experiences in the stream of consciousness, never to truly be repeated on subsequent consideration, whereas ideas fixed in language could be revisited as the same.

The rise of behaviorism in the twentieth century reduced philosophical discussion of imagination and obliterated of all talk of mental faculties. Gilbert Ryle argued that the term "imagination" did not designate a mental capacity, but instead related to a multitude of creative behaviors such as pretending and fancying. He argued that many of the activities called "imaginative" were really connected with hypothetical reasoning and supposition. He denied any necessary connection with mental images at all. Indeed, Ryle denied the existence of mental images. Ryle's persuasive arguments substantially influenced materialist philosophers of the late twentieth century. Cognitive science has since tried to explain Ryle's imaginative behaviors as products of the functional architecture of the mind.

Recent philosophy of mind has acknowledged Ryle's criticisms against mental imagery and generally avoids commitment to "mental images." Instead, philosophers investigate the imagination as functional faculty concerned with many of the behaviors Ryle sought to explain such as pretence and supposition. Current theorists suggest that this faculty gives rise to pretend behavior and the ability to simulate other people's mental states (Nichols 2006). Currie and Ravenscroft (2003) have dubbed this ability "recreative imagination." Recreative imagination is an empathetic skill which enables people to take perspectives other than their own and to contemplate possibilities. To this end, imagining may be mental faculty where the will can consider ideas "offline" without concern for truth makers. Contemporary philosophical debate about recreative imagination is interdisciplinary and seeks to reveal the underlying cognitive architecture and neurological basis of imagining.

Another recent debate focuses on imagination as a tool of conceivability. These philosophers discuss whether the ability to imagine or conceive of something provides any justification to believe in its possibility or likelihood. This line of inquiry stems from Hume's argument that whatever can be imagined is possible. Hume used this claim to buttress his argument against causality. He said that because we can imagine a cause without a particular effect or vice versa, there is no necessary link between them. Similarly, contemporary philosophers often judge the reasonableness of thought experiments based on whether they have difficulty imagining the scenario presented. Nevertheless, it is important to be clear exactly what is implied by this notion of "imagine." If "imagine" is restricted to instances of mental imagery, then things deemed impossible by modern science – such as whales the size of the earth or humans with five heads – can be visualized without any commitment to their likelihood of existence. If "imagine" is extended to logical conceivability, then inconceivable objects such as round squares may be rendered less likely in virtue of the difficulty in understanding what such an object could be. Because of the myriad of issues brought up by mental imagery it is important to deal with it separately as a topic.

Imagination and mental imagery

Even though contemporary philosophy of mind no longer focuses on mental imagery as a necessary component of imaginative thought, the history of imagination has been dominated by discussions of imagery (Tye 1991). This history begins with Descartes. Descartes took images as a necessary part of imagination. To investigate the usefulness of mental images he invited his readers to contrast the experience of imagining a chiliagon (a thousand-sided figure) versus conceiving of one. He noted that while it is clear that we can conceive an object with one thousand sides, he doubted whether we can create a mental image of one. Because of this, Descartes argued that the imagination must be a separate faculty to reasoning or consideration and is clearly a less impressive tool of thought.

Contrary to Descartes, some philosophers have argued that mental imagery solves many problems *better* than reason alone. For example, when imagining the number of windows in our home, we seem to move through the house using our "mind's eye," examining and counting the windows as they appear in the images of rooms we "see." The usefulness of mental imagery for solving cognitive tasks has been used to support a resurgence of the picture theory of the imagination. Imagery enthusiasts argue that the reason that mental imagery is useful in solving particular problems is because there really are spatially distributed, image-like representations in the brain which graphically correspond to the objects they represent, and this distribution behaves differently to ordinary thoughts. They point to neuroscientific evidence which shows similarities between the parts of the brain active during visual perception and those activated during imagining

Detractors of the picture theory do not deny that visual centers of the brain are active during both perception and imagining. However, they do deny the existence of mental images. They consider talk of "mental images" to be metaphorical, arguing that mental "images" are not *really* imagistic because they are neither *really* seen with an internal eye and nor do they have objective colors, shape or texture or any other properties that actual pictures have. They argue that images are indeterminate in a way that pictures are not. For example, we can imagine a tiger without representing a definite number of stripes, yet an ordinary picture of a tiger will have a determinate number of stripes as will the tiger itself. Other philosophers emphasize that subjective experiences are no guide to underlying representation. That is, the properties of visual representations during ordinary perception do not have pictorial properties, so it is unlikely that the properties of imagined representations have them either. To assume that a representation has the same properties as the object represented is to make what Daniel Dennett calls "the intentional fallacy." This does not mean that the *conscious experience* of mental images does not exist, merely that the properties of the *underlying representation* do not need to mimic the objects they represent.

The intentionality of mental images

The conscious experience of mental images has lead philosophers to try and understand what they are about, i.e. their intentionality. When we imagine, we always imagine *something*, either actual or fictional, e.g. we can imagine ourselves climbing the Eiffel Tower or Santa Claus riding a unicorn. Because imaginings frequently have a pictorial phenomenology, the intentionality of imagination has focused on how mental images could be the bearers of intentionality. One way to explain the intentionality of mental images is in terms of the intrinsic properties of the images themselves. Unfortunately, as Gilbert Ryle pointed out, pictures themselves cannot exhibit intentionality because a mental image of twins might look the same for each person, yet we can easily think about each twin as an individual. Another problem is that we seem to be able to imagine things that have no pictorial qualities to them. We are also capable of imagining very complicated pictorial qualities, e.g. a thousand-sided figure, which is almost impossible to construe with images. Due to these criticisms, accounts of intentionality for imagination have appealed to features other than the properties of the images themselves, such as the thoughts behind the images. Also because "imagination" and "imagining" are used colloquially in idiomatic ways, perhaps it is unfair to hold philosophers of imagination accountable for non-imagistic counterexamples. If we limit the use of "imagine" to experiences involving images, then unique problems in intentionality arise, e.g. how do mental images refer to the objects in the world they represent, rather than just themselves? For example, a mental image of the Eiffel Tower could be about the tower itself or about the representation of the tower. How does the image itself distinguish between these intentions? It seems that a combination of thinking *about* our subjective experiences and the world give mental images their elusive intentionality, not the experience itself. Thus, intentionality comes from propositional thoughts and objects in the world, not internal perceptions of objects such as mental images.

Further reading

Currie, Gregory, and Ravenscroft, Ian. *Recreative Minds: Imagination in Philosophy and Psychology.* New York: Oxford University Press, 2003.

Nichols, Shaun (ed.) *The Architecture of the Imagination: New Essays on Pretence, Possibility, and Fiction.* New York: Oxford University Press, 2006.

Tye, M. *The Imagery Debate.* Cambridge, MA: MIT Press, 1991.

S. Kate Devitt

IMMEDIACY

The concept of immediacy has had a long history in philosophy. The rationalists used it as an appeal to self-evident truths in the seventeenth century, and the empiricists used it to allude to simple atomistic sensations or impressions. Both of these were supposed to bring a sort of certainty with them. In the nineteenth century the quest for certainty took a different form, appearing as Hegelian idealism. In this outlook reality was mediated by knowledge, specifically by dialectical reasoning. One went from the dualistic stage of "thesis" and "antithesis" to a more incorporating stage, through "synthesis." The emphasis was on knowledge-in-general rather than contextual knowledge. Rather than stressing the process undergone or transacted, this outlook stressed from the beginning the idea that "being" was co-extensive with "being-known." Or, put slightly differently, that "the real is the rational and the rational is the real."

The American tradition rejected both the type of immediacy found in the rationalists and the empiricists, as well as the claims for certainty found in the idealist tradition. Since it was not looking for certainty in any traditional sense, it tended to use the term "immediacy" in a somewhat different manner

Charles Sanders Peirce

For Charles Sanders Peirce, there are three modes of being: firstness, secondness, and thirdness. These have to do with, respectively, qualitative possibility, actual fact, and law or habit (CP 1.23). Firstness is the mode most closely associated with immediacy for Peirce. It is what consciousness is aware of immediately, before one is conscious of being conscious. It is a feeling, i.e. a positive qualitative possibility, not an event or a happening. There is no resemblance of feeling to object here, for this is the realm of just possibility, not actuality (CP 1.284–7). The idea of firstness is predominant in freshness, life, and freedom.

In sum, firstness is not something and it is not nothing. Second, it is not dependent on an observer in order to exist. It does not describe a mere subjective psychological feature only, but rather a metaphysical feature of reality. Third, firstness possesses generality, i.e. it is not totally dependent upon individual sensation.

On the other hand, while the qualities, as unmaterialized possibility, represent firstness, it is also the case that, "rightly understood it is correct to say that we immediately perceive matter" (CP 1.418–20). "To say that we only infer matter from its qualities is to say that we only know the actual through the potential" (CP 1.418–20). In neither the case of firstness nor the case of secondness, however, do we have meaning. Pure possibility is equivalent to feeling and facticity to brute sensation, but the meaning of the sensation comes with the tendency of a group of secondnesses or sensory facts to exhibit a pattern, or set of habits in the long run. This does not culminate in certainty; the result remains "fallible," though exhibiting synechistic continuity.

William James

William James, in *The Principles of Psychology* (1890), distinguished between knowledge-by acquaintance and knowledge-about. Knowledge-by acquaintance is immediate, knowledge about, mediate. Knowledge-about occurs as the result of classifying an object known by direct acquaintance. Knowledge-by acquaintance is the more simple of the two; however, "simple" is a relative term, so what might seem knowledge by acquaintance in one context might not be in another. In other places James distinguished between sensation and perception by saying that the first of these is more simple or immediate. Third, he uses the same criterion to distinguish percepts from concepts. The fact that the distinction could only be made in a relative manner is of utmost importance. In *The Principles*, James had argued that there is no such thing as a perfectly simple or immediate sensation. What we hear is not "thunder" pure and simple, but rather "thunder-breaking-in-on silence-and-contrasting-with it." In other words, what is immediately present to consciousness is a "stream", i.e. a passing flow. Later, James extended this viewpoint from the topic of consciousness in psychology to his view of reality. His metaphysics, termed "radical empiricism," had postulated that the only things discussible in philosophy had to be capable of being experienced, and added that relations as such, i.e. not just atomistic sensations, were so experienced. Reality as such contains both substantive and transitive parts. James called what really exists "pure experience"; This is what immediately exists before the subject–object or consciousness–content dichotomy is drawn. The latter comes about through language, which "freezes" pure experience. In *Essays in Radical Empiricism* (1912) James writes that "The instant field of the present is at all times what I call the 'pure experience'." But he also adds that "Experience in its immediacy seems perfectly fluent." Going further, he states that "'Pure experience' is the name which I give to the immediate flux of life which furnishes the material to our later recollection with its conceptual categories." Here James tries to present the immediate to us, but, ironically, what is immediately given is not immediate, it is flux. In *Essays in Radical Empiricism*, when asked "to whom is pure experience available," James's answer is rather harsh: only new-born babes, or people in a coma from drugs, illness, etc., could have such an undiluted experience – a "that" as opposed to a "what." Later, however, he modifies this. Pure experience is not pre-conscious experience. It is rather pre-conceptual or pre-linguistic experience. Language or concepts cannot capture reality in all its richness, but this does not mean that we cannot experience reality, at least occasionally. In *A Pluralistic Universe*, he adds that logic, a form of idealized language, can touch the surface of reality, but it cannot plumb its depths, and this insufficiency is a permanent one. "Reality, life, experience, concreteness, immediacy, use what word you will, exceeds our logic, overflows and surrounds it." Unlike his fellow pragmatist Peirce, James seems to give the world as experienced a cognitive dimension. Experience as had or undergone is not just brute facticity. It has meaning, even if that meaning cannot be linguistically articulated.

John Dewey

Dewey tried to reclaim the term "immediacy" from its traditional use as equivalent to "knowledge" at least as early as in "The Postulate of Immediate Empiricism" in 1905. "Immediate experience," he says, "postulates that things – anything, everything, in the ordinary or non-technical sense of the term 'thing' – are what they are experienced as." Going further, Dewey argues that "knowing is only one mode of experiencing," and that things can also be experienced aesthetically, morally, economically and technologically. Because something is "True" therefore, in terms of being known, does not mean that something is more "real." Going further, because something is "cognitive" does not mean that it has been "cognized." For this to occur a process must take place. Dewey later admitted that he had been unsuccessful in reclaiming "immediate," and that the term was too entrenched in traditional literature as synonymous with "knowledge."

In *Experience and Nature*, Dewey argues that "things in their immediacy are unknown and unknowable ... For knowledge is ... concerned ... with sequences, coexistences, relations. Immediate things may be pointed to by words, but not described or defined." Immediacy of experience is ineffable, but there is nothing mystical about this. It has to do with immediate enjoyment or suffering – not relational as in cognition, but terminal and exclusive. The occurrence of emergent immediate events is one that is affectionately and appreciatively had, but they are not themselves known. To know anything we must go beyond what is immediately present – and classify these occurrences. Qualitative immediacy exists, i.e. we can have direct experiences, but they are not directly known. Once again, there is an important distinction between "knowing" and "having." Going further, "values" are directly experienced as immediate occurrences. But values can be "evaluated," i.e. subjected to inquiry and criticism.

In "Immediate Knowledge: Understanding and Inference" in *Logic: the Theory of Inquiry*, Dewey again argues against the belief that there is such a thing as immediate knowledge – in the form of either atomic sensations or self-evident first principles. First of all, what appears as immediate knowledge oftentimes isn't. "The immediate use of objects known in consequences of previous mediation is readily confused with immediate knowledge." Second, there is a difference between immediate "apprehension" of an object or idea and the justified assertion that such an item actually exists. But even seemingly apprehended knowledge is a product retained through previous questioning and investigation, and now retained through habit. Dewey says,

> It has been usual for some time in philosophy (1) to view the common sense world in its distinction from the domain of scientific objects as strictly perceptual in character; (2) to regard perception as a mode of cognition; and (3) what is perceived whether object or quality, to be therefore cognitive in status and force. None of these assumptions is warranted.

While the common-sense world does contain directly perceived objects, these are understood only in the context of an "environment." "An environment is constituted by the interactions [or as Dewey later put it, the "transactions"] between things and a living creature." The distinction between acquaintance-knowledge and knowledge-about is rejected. Acquaintance-knowledge is either not primitive but acquired, or not really knowledge in the sense of warranted assertability. For Dewey then, as for Peirce, all knowledge is "mediated."

In conclusion, all three thinkers develop a notion of immediacy. But for Peirce and Dewey, experience becomes meaningful only through mediation, i.e. through thirdness or inquiry. Experience as immediately had is not cognitive in nature. For James experience as had or undergone seem to possess a meaningful or cognitive dimension, and there is more of a suspicion of language or concepts to deal with the richness of reality than exists in Peirce or Dewey.

Further reading

Dewey, John. *The Collected Works of John Dewey*, ed. Jo Ann Boydston. Carbondale, IL: Southern Illinois University Press, 1969–91, and published as *The Early Works: 1882–98* (EW), *The Middle Works, 1899–1924* (MW), and *The Later Works, 1925–53* (LW). See especially "The Influence of Darwin on Philosophy," in *The Influence of Darwin on Philosophy: And Other Essays in Contemporary Thought*, in Vol. 4 of *The Middle Works*; "Nature, Ends and Histories," from *Experience and Nature*, in Vol. 1 of *The Later Works*, and "Immediate Knowledge: Understanding and Inference" from *Logic: the Theory of Inference*, in Vol. 12 of *The Later Works*.

James, William. *The Principles of Psychology*, 2 volumes. New York: Henry Holt, 1890, Especially Ch. 8, "The Relations of Minds to Other Things"; and Ch. 9, "The Stream of Thought."

—— *Essays in Radical Empiricism*. New York: Longmans, Green, 1912, especially Ch. 3, "The Thing and Its Relations."

—— *A Pluralistic Universe*. New York: Longmans, Green, 1909, especially Lecture 5, "The Compounding of Consciousness"; and Lecture 6: "Bergson and His Critique of Intellectualism."

Peirce, Charles Sanders. *The Collected Papers of Charles Sanders Peirce* (CP), 8 volumes, ed. Charles Hartshorne and Paul Weiss (Vols 1–6), and Arthur W. Burks (Vols 7–8). Cambridge, MA: Harvard University Press, 1931–58, especially Vol. 1, Section 23ff and Section 417ff.

WILLIAM J. GAVIN

IMPULSE

Influenced heavily by Darwin's *The Expression of the Emotions in Man and Animals* (1872), William James and John Dewey viewed impulse and habit as instruments necessary for an organism's adaptation to its environment. Impulse keeps the organism in step with a continually changing environment by providing the impetus for both the development of old habits and the formation of new ones. In keeping with the "instinct psychology" of the time, James and Dewey viewed impulse and instinct synonymously as the root of non-purposive conduct, that is, conduct that does not presuppose any specific idea regarding a desired end or outcome. Instead, the ends that a particular instinct or impulse actualizes are determined by the environment. The term "organism" was used in this context since its generality preserved the continuity between human beings and other species; however, James observed that human beings are distinct from other species since they have a greater variety of impulses and can do more with them and, further, memory increases the significance of impulse since it allows human beings to learn from and predict impulsive behavior. Hence, many species act on impulse/instinct, but human beings are characterized by the capacity to reflect upon and control the expression of impulse.

To mark a point of contrast, in his *Principles of Psychology* (1890) James catalogued a wide array of human instincts that range from simple motor responses such as grasping, sucking, and imitation to more complex affective instincts such as fear and sympathy. On the other hand, Dewey argued that instincts should not be classified in this manner since there are no separate instincts. This is because, for Dewey, in lived experience impulses always have distinct qualities that are influenced by the situation in which they unfold. Hence, "aggression" can be classified as a particular instinct, but in experience "aggression" is always "aggression-toward-x" where "x" is a component of one's physical and/or social environment. The quality of a particular instance of aggression is influenced by context: where and when it is expressed and toward whom it is directed (boss, colleague, lover, wrongdoer, etc.). Generalizations can be made, but it is essential, on this view, not to confuse the generalization with the experiences that it is drawn from.

Another point of contrast concerns the context in which James and Dewey addressed impulse: James addressed it as a psychologist whereas Dewey focused on the implications that impulse has for ethics, art, and, more generally, growth. Impulse has ethical import since it is the psychological force that can influence the course of habit and custom (e.g. widely practiced habits). On this view, when habits can no longer mitigate problems, pressure is exerted on the individual and this pressure elicits impulse. The next phase is key, for it is there that impulse can be consciously guided in order to alleviate this pressure and to actualize desired ends. For Dewey, intelligence lies in tempering impulse so that problematic situations can be solved, whether they are ethical, political, or artistic in nature. On its own, impulse will not go far enough in modifying existing habits; however, if it is guided in light of the problem at hand, then it will effect change and consequently render experience more meaningful since, in the process, the environment is controlled and the self-affirmed through a creative response to the problem. On this account, then, the central ethical problem in both childhood and adulthood is the utilization of impulse in order to modify or create new habits in the face of novel circumstances. Further, the transformation of spontaneous energy also takes place in the practice of art, for artists too consciously guide impulses toward specific ends. Here also, impulse cannot be "expressed" in its raw state but must be administered, that is, the impulse "that seethes as a commotion demanding utterance must undergo as much and as careful management in order to receive eloquent manifestation as marble or pigment, as colors and sounds" (*The Later Works* 10:81). This management entails the use of artistic technique which just is habit that has been developed in order to actualize characteristically aesthetic ends.

Further reading

Darwin, Charles. *The Expression of the Emotions in Man and Animals.* Chicago, IL: University of Chicago Press, 1965.

Dewey, John. *Human Nature and Conduct* in *The Middle Works: 1899–1924, Vol. 14, 1922*, ed. Jo Ann Boydston. Carbondale, IL: Southern Illinois University Press, 1983.

—— *Art as Experience* in *The Later Works: 1925–1953, Vol. 10, 1934*, ed. Jo Ann Boydston. Carbondale, IL: Southern Illinois University Press, 1987.

Eldridge, Michael. *Transforming Experience: John Dewey's Cultural Instrumentalism.* Nashville, TN: Vanderbilt University Press, 1998.

Hocking, William Earnst. *Human Nature and its Remaking.* New Haven, CT: Yale University Press, 1923.

James, William. *Principles of Psychology in Two Volumes.* New York: Henry Holt, 1890.

Senchuk, Dennis M. *Against Instinct: From Biology to Philosophical Psychology.* Philadelphia, PA: Temple University Press, 1991.

Wilm, Emil Carl. *The Theories of Instinct: A Study in the History of Psychology.* New Haven, CT: Yale University Press, 1925.

ERIC C. MULLIS

INCOMMENSURABILITY

The concept of incommensurability entered the philosophic arena with the publication of Thomas Kuhn's *Structure of Scientific Revolutions* (1962), one of the most influential books of the twentieth century. A central theme of this work is that a stage of science guided by or developed under one paradigm is "incommensurable" with that guided by or developed under another. Incommensurability means that there is no common measure for comparing the different theories. As a result, theories from different periods suffer from certain deep kinds of failure of comparability and certain kinds of translation are impossible.

During periods of "normal science" scientists operate in accordance with a "paradigm" which structures the kinds of issues, questions, or problems which arise and provides the direction for their resolution. But, when there develops a deep erosion of confidence in the ability of the paradigm to solve certain types of problems or "anamolies," a crisis arises and a revisionary "scientific revolution" may take place, under the guidance of a new paradigm.

The concept of incommensurability brings in the importance of history of science for philosophy of science, challenging the static analytical framework which had dominated the field. It also challenges what had been the widely held belief that later scientific theory builds on the corpus of knowledge housed within the earlier science.

This view further rejects the claim that later theories are closer approximations to the truth than earlier theories, denying not only that theories can be regarded as more or less close to the truth but even that any sense can be made of the notion of nearness or approximation to the truth. In the change to a new paradigm, not all of the achievements of the preceding period of normal science are preserved. In fact, a later period of science may not have an explanation for a phenomenon that an earlier paradigm was considered to successfully explain. Revolutions and the new paradigms which emerge do in general house an increase in overall problem solving ability, but this in no way implies increases in truth or nearer approaches to truth.

The usual understanding of a straightforward comparison between paradigms and the theories or solutions they generate by the use of common methods of comparison and evaluation is not possible for several reasons. First, the standards of comparison and evaluation themselves are subject to change with changing paradigms, for these standards are housed within the existing paradigm.

Before this time, the standard of evaluation was that of abstract rationality following strict rules. But the incommensurability thesis holds that scientists do not make their judgments through rational rule following – either consciously or unconsciously. There are no rules for deciding the significance of the problems, issues, questions or solutions raised by a paradigm or comparing one paradigm with another. Nor are purely rational factors at issue.

During periods of normal science, scientific judgments to a large degree are constrained by a guiding paradigm, and theories or solutions to problems are judged by comparison to the paradigm. When revolutions occur, however, the confinements or constraints on scientific judgments structured by the given paradigm are broken and other factors important in scientific judgment come into play as dominating factors. While there is a certain agreement on what criteria enter paradigm changes, many of these features, such as elegance, simplicity, or fruitfulness bring into play the functioning of human capacities such as informed imagination or creative intelligence. Moreover, all the generally agreed-to criteria are imprecise, and allow for disagreement about the degree to which they hold as well about how to balance one against the other in cases of conflict. Advocates of competing paradigms may not even agree on which problems a new paradigm should solve. Furthermore, there are other factors than the generally agreed-to criteria that enter into paradigm choice.

Nor can perceptual or observational evidence provide a common basis for theory comparison. Indeed, even if there were agreed methods of procedure or comparison, incommensurability could still arise because scientists can disagree on the nature of the observational data themselves. The standard position had held that observation provides the neutral determinant between competing theories. A vital point of the incommensurability thesis is that observation or perceptual experience is theory-dependent, that there are no neutral observations that can be used to resolve the merits of incommensurable frameworks. What a scientist observes changes as a result of a scientific revolution.

What one observes is influenced throughout by one's beliefs and past experience, and two scientists observing the same data may not make the same observations. Using Kuhn's example, when a Galilean and an Aristotelian are both looking at a pendulum, each will see something different, for they are practicing in "different worlds."

Observations as theory dependent are part of a meaning holism. The incommensurability thesis incorporates the view that the meanings of terms are intertwined in such a way that changing the meaning of one term results in changes in the meanings of related terms. The languages of theories from different periods of normal science may not be inter-translatable. For example, the physical referents of Newtonian concepts are not identical to Einsteinian concepts that have the same name. "Mass" as used by Newton cannot be translated into "mass" as used by Einstein. The paradigm change from Newton to Einstein requires a replacement of the entire conceptual network.

The incommensurability thesis negates central positivist doctrines which constituted the entrenched view at that time, challenging the positivist views of scientific progress, rule structured rationality, scientific analysis, a permanent and neutral observation language, and a neutral epistemological framework for evaluating competing theories and paradigms. At the same time it presents a challenge to the realist conception of scientific progress which holds that later science improves on earlier science, and does so by approaching closer to the truth. These factors, combined with the notion of the imaginative or creative, non-measurable features at play in the scientific enterprise, and the radical claim that at the most fundamental level of incommensurability scientists are practicing in different worlds and seeing different things, has led to charges of subjectivism, relativism, irrationalism, and the denial of scientific progress. Kuhn himself recognized the dilemma of rejecting long-held foundationalist interpretations of scientific method while having no developed philosophical alternative to replace them.

Some contemporary philosophy, however, and most notably American pragmatism, does offer such a developed alternative, providing the metaphysical and epistemic underpinnings for Kuhn's understanding of science.

For pragmatist philosophy, the indeterminate character of the universe in its indefinite richness and "thickness," which "intrudes" within and constitutes one dimension of experience, combined with the creatively interpretive nature of all experience, undercuts the long-held dichotomies of foundationalism or non-foundationalism and, along with it, the closely related dichotomies of realism or anti-realism, and objectivism or relativism since each, in its own way, represents the alternatives of an absolute grounding of knowledge or skepticism. All that need be acknowledged is, from within the confines of our conceptual webs, a resistance that is not itself concepts, language, or beliefs, even though our grasp of it develops within these interpretive contexts and truths can arise only with these contexts. It is that which instigate changes in networks of beliefs and constrains the way our networks of beliefs develop. The constraining, resisting element within experience allows pragmatism to forge a new understanding of the meaning of truth as the engagement with reality in fruitful ways. We do not *think to* a reality to which language or concepts conform but rather we *live through* a reality with which we are intertwined and the creative intertwining with which constitutes experience. Different ways of reflectively engaging reality involve different "worlds" as the holistic horizons of our meaningful engagement with it, and these worlds may well be incommensurable.

Yet, for the pragmatist, incommensurable perspectives, whether at the level of common sense or science, though in a sense structuring differing worlds, cannot, by the very nature of our conceptually structured worlds as opening onto a natural universe with which we must successfully interact, be closed to rational discussion. The adequacy of any world is ultimately judged by a vague sense of workability embodied in our everyday engagement with the universe at its most primal level, and such judgment, at any level of its functioning, is holistic in nature and irreducible to rigid "rules of rationality." Further, rationality is no longer in conflict with imagination and creativity for rationality, whether at the level of common sense or science, is itself inherently creative and imaginative rather than rule driven.

Moreover, for the pragmatist position knowledge as cumulative and knowledge as changing need not lie in opposition, for any novel world emerges from a cumulative process or history which yields enrichment of intelligibility both of the old and of the new. Such a process is not a straightforward building upon the old, nor does it tend toward "the truth," but it nonetheless is cumulative or progressive, and radical changes in world views are neither arbitrary nor irrational.

Regardless of the stand one takes toward the incommensurability thesis, it remains a powerful force in shaping the direction of philosophy and contouring philosophic debates.

Further reading

Horwich, P. (ed.) "World Changes" in *Thomas Kuhn and the Nature of Science.* Cambridge, MA: MIT Press, 1993.

Kuhn, Thomas. "The Essential Tension: Tradition and Innovation in Scientific Research" in Ed. C. Taylor (ed.) *The Third University of Utah Research Conference on the Identification of Scientific Talent.* Salt Lake City, UT: University of Utah Press. 1959.

—— *The Structure of Scientific Revolutions*, second edition with postscript. Chicago, IL: University of Chicago Press. 1970 [original 1962].

—— "Reflections on my Critics" in I. Lakatos and A. Musgrave (eds) *Criticism and the Growth of Knowledge.* London: Cambridge University Press. 1970.

—— "Rationality and Theory Choice," *Journal of Philosophy*, 80, 10 (1983): 563–70.

Lewis, C.I. "A Pragmatic Conception of the A Priori" in *Collected Papers of Clarence Irving Lewis*, ed. John Goheen and John Mothershead, Jr. Stanford, CA: Stanford University Press. 1970.

Sandra B. Rosenthal

INDETERMINACY OF TRANSLATION

Imagine that a linguist is researching the language of a previously unexplored island, trying to learn the meaning of sentences and words in the country's language by observing the behavior of the locals. If, whenever a rabbit is present, the residents of the island reliably remark, "*Gavagai!*" how ought this utterance to be translated? Does *Gavagai* mean "There goes a rabbit"? Or, given that whenever a rabbit is present, undetached rabbit parts are present, might the expression *Gavagai* mean "There goes an undetached rabbit part" in the local language? An instantiation of rabbithood is also present: perhaps *Gavagai* could be translated "There goes an instantiation of rabbithood." While we might find translation of *Gavagai* as "There goes a rabbit" as most plausible, is there any determinate fact of the matter to decide between the competing translations?

According to W.V. Quine, in the widely discussed chapter "Translation and Meaning" in *Word and Object*, there is no determinate fact of the matter to decide on the correct translation of this remark. For the available behavioral evidence is fully consistent with translating *Gavagai* either as "There goes a rabbit!" or as "There goes an undetached rabbit part."

The linguist might think that some progress could be made by translation of other sentences and words in the language. Perhaps, through further investigation of the native language, the linguist can discover equivalents in the island language to expressions in her native language of English, such as "is," "one," "part," and "whole," as well as the local equivalent to English pronouns and pluralizations, that might serve to decipher the proper translation of *Gavagai.* In making conjectures on the translation, we would be developing a system of what Quine calls "analytical hypotheses," translations of these sentence, words, and devices into English. As Quine points out, however, we have not yet reached a determinate translation of *Gavagai* on the basis of our analytical hypotheses, for there are a multitude of systems of analytic hypotheses, each fully consistent with all of the available behavioral evidence. Whether we translate *Gavagai* as "There goes a rabbit" or "There goes an undetached rabbit part" is going to depend on our choice of a system of analytic hypotheses, and no determinate system of analytic hypotheses can be chosen in light of what we can observe. In light of this indeterminacy of translation, Quine contends that there are no facts of the matter regarding the meanings of linguistic expressions.

Quine's conclusion regarding the indeterminacy of meaning is a controversial one, and philosophers have rebutted Quine's skepticism about meaning in a number of ways. Philosophers have contended that there is an alternative conception of meaning that is not susceptible to the indeterminacy of translation; or there are ways to find a determinate translation in the example Quine provides; or there is no reason to accept Quine's assumption that we need to resolve this problem in order to explain facts about meaning.

An influential argument for the last of these responses to Quine was given by the linguist Noam Chomsky. Chomsky famously argued that the indeterminacy of translation ought not to lead us to Quine's skepticism regarding the meaning of linguistic expressions. When all relevant evidence is taken into consideration, Chomsky contends, the indeterminacy in linguistics is no different from the well-known underdetermination of physics in light of the available evidence, a result that does not lead to a kind of skepticism about physics along the lines of Quine's skepticism regarding theories of meaning.

As Hartry Field has pointed out, there may be cases of indeterminacy of translation that do not depend on Quine's translation thought experiment. Isaac Newton's use of the word "mass" in his physics could be translated in one of two ways in contemporary physics: "rest mass" or "relativistic mass." Neither translation would make Newton's theory entirely true – the theory is partially true if "mass" is translated "rest mass," and partially true if "mass" is translated "relativistic mass." In light of this evidence, it seems best to say there is no determinate fact whether the term "mass," as used by Newton, should be translated in either of these two ways. If the indeterminacy of translation is restricted to examples of this kind, it may not be as widespread a phenomenon as Quine claimed.

Further reading

Chomsky, Noam. "Quine's Empirical Assumptions" in *Words and Objections: Essays on the Philosophy of W.V. Quine*, ed. Donald Davidson and Jakko Hintikka. Dordrecht: D. Reidel, 1969, pp. 53–68.

Field, Hartry. *Truth and the Absence of Fact*. Oxford: Clarendon, 2001.

Quine, W.V. *Word and Object*. Cambridge, MA: MIT Press, 1960.

FRITZ J. MCDONALD

INFERENCE

There are two fundamental conceptions of inference. One is a psychological, descriptive conception involving acts and modes of reasoning, i.e. actual inferences that people make. The second is a logical, normative conception involving formal implication of sentences, i.e. standards and criteria of valid or correct inferences. The fact that some people actually infer the conclusion that "All saints are priests" from the premises that "All saints are men" and "All priests are men" is an example of the first conception, but not of the second (because the conclusion is not implied by the premises). This difference is captured by the notion that people often make unwarranted inferences, i.e. inferences that are not actually implied.

Philosophers usually distinguish between deductive and inductive inferences. This distinction is often characterized as deductive inferences involving more general premises implying a more particular conclusion and inductive inferences involving more particular premises implying a more general conclusion, where "general" and "particular" refer to the size of the classes of objects under discussion. For example, in a purported deductive inference, from the more general premise that "All humans are mortal," along with the premise that "Greeks are human," the more particular conclusion that "Greeks are mortal" follows. This conclusion is more particular than the premise because "Greeks" denotes a smaller class of objects than does "human." On the other hand, in a purported inductive inference, the conclusion that "All humans are mortal" is said to follow from the premises that "Greeks are human" and "Greeks are mortal." This characterization of deductive and inductive inference as involving class sizes, however, is inadequate, as the following example shows: "All cats are mammals" therefore "All non-mammals are non-cats." The distinction between deductive and inductive inferences, then, is that with the former (deduction) the nature of the relationship between the premises and the conclusion is such that the structure of the argument entails that the conclusion is warranted on the basis of the premises while in the latter (induction) the structure of the arguments does not entail, but makes more probable that the conclusion is warranted on the basis of the premises. In a technical sense, deductive inferences and inductive inferences are not two types of inferences or argument forms, but are different standards or criteria for evaluating the warrant of support that the premises give to the conclusion.

With respect to actual inferences that people make and to informal norms of inference, the American pragmatist Charles Peirce claimed that inference was a response to an "irritation of doubt," that response leading to inquiry in order to settle that irritation and establish, or fix, belief. This fixation came about, he claimed, by a method of tenacity (by which one simply held to a belief no matter what), a method of authority (by which one appealed to some authority or other to settle a question), a method of aprioricity (by which one appealed to some method of reason or theory), or – his prescribed method – a method of science (by which beliefs were subject to collective testing against empirical information).

Restricted to the formal (implication) conception of inference, Peirce argued that deductive and inductive inferences do not completely encompass all modes of reasoning. Peirce distinguished deductive inferences from ampliative inferences, i.e. those in which new information or knowledge is obtained, or amplified. Ampliative inferences include both inductive inferences and also what Peirce called abductive inferences. He argued that all inferences involve a rule, a case, and a result, with the following example illustrating the different kinds of inferences:

Deduction: All beans from this bag are white (Rule)
These beans are from this bag. (Case)
Therefore, these beans are white. (Result)

Induction: These beans are from this bag. (Case)
These beans are white. (Result)
Therefore, all beans from this bag are white. (Rule)

Abduction: All beans from this bag are white. (Rule)
These beans are white. (Result)
Therefore, these beans are from this bag. (Case)

While Peirce stressed the value and importance of all three kinds of inference, he emphasized the significance of abduction in the context of practical and scientific reasoning.

Perhaps even more than Peirce, John Dewey housed an understanding of inference, in both the descriptive and normative senses, in the context of a larger theory of inquiry. All inference, for Dewey, begins from a "felt difficulty," which is the genesis of any inquiry. Even though in a given case that felt difficulty might be fairly abstract and intellectualized, no inquiry is disinterested. It is always purposive and it always involves the recognition of and attempt to resolve some problem. If the process of inquiry is successful, what was anomalous and not unified with previous knowledge and expectation (i.e. what was the felt difficulty) becomes so unified. Inference, then, is "a coherent commitment of diverse images to a common focus, to a comprehensive result." Knowledge, as the objective of any inquiry, is what is warranted by norms and methods of inquiry that have been proven via experience. Dewey saw the very norms and methods by which inferences are evaluated as themselves subject to the tribunal of collective human experience. That is, the very standards of deductive and inductive logic are neither foundational nor fixed; they are revisable in light of how well they resolve the felt difficulties. This view of inquiry and inference holds that particular inferences as well as norms of correct inference are corrigible, corrective, and naturalistic. Such a view has been adopted and expanded upon by later philosophers, such as Nelson Goodman, Thomas Kuhn, and W.V.O. Quine. Goodman, for instance, claimed that there is a "reflective equilibrium" between what actual inferences and what norms of valid inference we are willing and justified in accepting. Kuhn, concurring with Dewey's insistence on a problem-solving basis for inquiry, claimed that scientific practice is largely a matter of addressing empirical and conceptual puzzles posed by our collective experiences. Quine, renowned for his work in formal logic, argued that even the laws of logic are revisable.

Further reading

Dewey, John. *Logic: The Theory of Inquiry.* New York: Irvington, 1980.

Goodman, Nelson. *Fact, Fiction, and Forecast*. Indianapolis, IN: Bobbs-Merrill, 1955.

Kuhn, Thomas. *The Structure of Scientific Revolutions.* Chicago, IL: University of Chicago Press, 1962.

Peirce, Charles S. *Collected Papers of Charles Sanders Peirce, Volumes 2 and 5*, ed. Charles Hartshorne and Paul Weiss. Cambridge, MA: Harvard University Press, 1931–5.

Quine, W.V.O. *The Methods of Logic*. New York: Holt, Rinehart and Winston, 1950.

David Boersema

INFINITY

The infinite has played an important role in philosophy since the ancient Greeks. The theory of the infinite remained pretty much the same from Aristotle to the development of the calculus (see Rucker 1995). The development of the calculus triggered the modern exploration of the infinite. Among the early modern explorers of the infinite, Leibniz worked out a highly detailed theory of infinite sequences and infinite division (see Levey 1998). However, Leibniz strongly denied the real existence of either infinitely large quantities or infinitely small quantities (infinitesimals).

Mathematicians and philosophers did not remain content with the Leibnizian foundations for the calculus. The modernists in the nineteenth century were forced to move beyond the denials of the infinitely large and infinitely small. They showed how to develop positive theories of infinitely large numbers, infinitely small numbers, and infinitely complex structures. They showed that some infinities are larger than others. Charles Sanders Peirce helped to develop the modern notion of infinity, and he made extensive use of that notion in his work. Josiah Royce is notable for his early incorporation of the modern notion of infinity into his metaphysics.

The modern theory of the infinite depends on the notion of a set. A set is any collection of things. For instance, {Socrates, Plato, Aristotle} is a finite set. But what is an infinite set? An Aristotelian might say that you can never finish counting off the members of an infinite set or that any list of members of such a set goes on forever. But an intuitive notion like "going on forever" is not mathematically precise.

Peirce was among the first to have shown how to precisely distinguish between finite and infinite sets. In 1881, he used De Morgan's syllogism of transposed quantity to develop the distinction between finite and infinite sets (Peirce 3.288). Consider various sets of possible Texans. Peirce portrays them as violent. Suppose Texans shoot at each other and they shoot to kill. Before dying, a Texan has some time to shoot some other Texans. Now consider these two premises: Every Texan kills a Texan; No Texan is killed by more than one Texan. If the set of Texans is finite, the following conclusion holds: Every Texan is killed by a Texan. But if the set of Texans is infinite, the conclusion need not hold. For suppose T1 kills T2, T2 kills T4, T4 kills T6, and so on. The two premises are true; but this spree leaves every odd numbered Texan alive. The syllogism composed of the two premises and the conclusion is thus valid for finite sets but not for infinite sets. Peirce says that he sent a copy of his 1881 work to Dedekind. Dedekind would later say (in 1888) that a set is infinite if and only if it can be put into a 1–1 correspondence with one of its proper subsets. For example, the whole numbers can be put into a 1–1 correspondence with the even numbers. Peirce claimed that Dedekind's definition is derived from his work (Peirce 4.331; see 3.564). Although it is not easy to see the derivation, it is clear that Peirce has correctly distinguished the infinite.

Peirce wrote extensively on infinite sets (see Dauben 1977). During the 1890s, Peirce was deeply influenced by the work of Georg Cantor. Cantor showed in 1891 that the infinity of real numbers is greater than the infinity of rational numbers. He also showed that there is an endless series of ever-greater transfinite sets. Specifically, for any set S, the power set of S has more members than S. The power set of S is the set of all subsets of S. For instance, the power set of {A, B} is {{}, {A}, {B}, {A, B}}. For finite sets, it is obvious that the power set has more members than the set. But Cantor showed that for infinite sets, the power set also has more members than the set. To generate an endless series of ever-greater infinite sets, we start with the set of whole numbers {0, 1, 2, … }. Let this set be N. Let N* be the power set of N; N** be the power set of N*; and so on. We thus obtain a precisely defined endless series of increasingly greater infinite sets. Peirce followed Cantor in affirming the existence of this infinite series (Peirce 3.547–3.549; 4.200–4.217).

Peirce made surprising use of this endless series. He argued that for any set S in this Cantorian series, a continuous line can be divided into parts so that the parts can be put into a 1–1 correspondence with the members of S. Since there is no upper bound to the size of the sets in the Cantorian series, there is no upper bound to the number of parts into which a continuous line can be divided (Peirce 3.563–570). A line is thus a true continuum. There is no division of the line into distinct particular points that exhausts its continuity. Peirce was thus led to affirm the existence of infinitesimal quantities. Two points can be at an infinitesimal distance from one another (less than any finite distance but greater than 0). It has consequently been said that Peirce's notion of infinitesimals anticipates Robinson's non-standard analysis (1996) and Conway's surreal number line (2001). Herron (1997) provides a detailed study of Peirce's theory of infinitesimals.

The concept of an infinitely inexhaustible continuum plays a central role in Peirce's evolutionary cosmology (Peirce 1.175, 6.33, 8.317). According to this cosmology, reality is undergoing a continuous growth from non-existence to full existence. The logical start of this growth in the infinite past is a chaos of pure potentiality (6.215). This chaos self-actualizes and self-organizes to form increasingly stable and complex structures (including times, spaces, natural laws, and substances – 1.413–1.416, 6.189–6.220, 8.318). The process of self-organization is self-strengthening (1.409, 6.490). The logical end of this growth in the infinite future is a maximally ordered and complex structure. Since the continuum of potentiality is inexhaustible, there is always an element of chance in the growth of order. We are currently somewhere in the middle of this growth. The laws of our universe are highly regular but still statistical. Strikingly, Peirce allows the process of self-actualizing potentiality to branch (1.412). Each branch generates its own plurality of (branching) universes. It may thus be said that Peirce's cosmology anticipates Linde's inflationary cosmology in which reality organizes itself into a branching tree of universes (Linde 1994).

Royce often used mathematical concepts in his writings (Hocking 1955). Royce was among the first thinkers to apply the modern notion of infinity to philosophical problems. Royce discusses the infinite in the Supplementary Essay to the First Series of lectures in *The World and Individual*. He continues to use the infinite in the Second Series of those lectures. Royce credits Peirce as well as Dedekind.

Royce uses the notion of a self-representative system to introduce the infinite. A self-representative system contains a perfect image of itself. An approximate example can be constructed with two mirrors. If you put the mirrors facing one another, each mirror contains an apparently endless series of reflections of itself in the opposite mirror. Of course, the reflections only go on finitely. But Royce wants us to think about the case of perfect self-reflection. Royce asks us to think of a perfect map of England drawn somewhere on the surface of England. Royce says we should not think of the map as a drawing that has to be made in time but as a perfect picture that simply exists. Since the map occupies a place in England, that place must be represented on the map. The map contains a representation of itself. And this representation contains a representation of itself. So the map contains an infinite series of self-nested copies. The map is an example of a self-representative system. It is infinitely complex. Royce thus anticipates the notion that a whole is infinitely complex if and only if it contains a part that is not identical to itself but that has exactly the same structure as itself.

According to Royce, self-representative systems play important roles in metaphysics and religion. Royce argued that a perfectly self-conscious mind would be a self-representative system and so would be infinitely complex. Since the Absolute (according to Royce) is a perfectly self-conscious mind, the Absolute is a self-representative system and is infinitely complex. It is possible for England to contain many perfect self-maps. Each of these maps is located at a distinct place in England and thus maps England from its own perspective. These distinct perspectives are distinct non-absolute selves in the Absolute Self.

The modern Cantorian conception of the infinite develops and matures during the first half of the twentieth century. During this period, awareness of the modern concept of the infinite slowly spreads through the American philosophical community. A typical example is the notion of the infinite abstractive hierarchy developed by Whitehead (1925: Ch. 10). Such a hierarchy is a collection of abstract objects stratified into levels according to their degrees of complexity. After World War II, as American philosophy takes an analytic turn, the modern concept of the infinite is used extensively.

Further reading

Conway, John. *On Numbers and Games*, second edition. Natick, MA: A.K. Peters, 2001.

Dauben, Joseph. "C.S. Peirce's Philosophy of Infinite Sets," *Mathematics Magazine* 50, 1 (1977): 123–35.

Herron, Timothy. "C.S. Peirce's Theories of Infinitesimals," *Transactions of the Charles S. Peirce Society* 33, 3 (1997): 590–645.

Hocking, Richard. "The Influence of Mathematics on Royce's Metaphysics," *Journal of Philosophy* 53, 3 (1955): 77–91.

Levey, Samuel. "Leibniz on Mathematics and the Actually Infinite Division of Matter," *The Philosophical Review* 107, 1 (1998): 49–96.

Linde, A. "The Self-Reproducing Inflationary Universe," *Scientific American* 271, 11 (1994): 48–55.

Peirce, Charles Sanders. Cited by volume number and section number from *Collected Papers of Charles Sanders Peirce*, ed. Charles Hartshorne and Paul Weiss Cambridge, MA: Harvard University Press, 1965.

Robinson, Abraham. *Non-standard Analysis*, revised edition. Princeton, NJ: Princeton University Press, 1996.

Royce, Josiah. *The World and the Individual*, First Series, Supplementary Essay. New York: Macmillan, 1899.

Rucker, Rucker. *Infinity and the Mind*. Princeton, NJ: Princeton University Press, 1995.

Whitehead, Alfred. N. *Science and the Modern World*. New York: The Free Press, 1925.

Eric Charles Steinhart

INQUIRY

This article will neglect Whitehead and Royce who are more aligned with European philosophy than American philosophy and will concentrate on the two principal American pragmaticists, Peirce and Dewey, as opposed to the Jamesian pragmatists, who tended not to emphasize inquiry. It is noted that W.V.O. Quine, an analytical philosopher, and other twentieth-century pragmatists, have continued the American inquiry tradition.

The foundation of American philosophy

It is possible to argue that inquiry and its related concepts form the foundation of American philosophy, distinguishing it from other schools of philosophy. Besides inquiry, these related concepts include doubt, final authority, truth, and reality; however, this entry will concentrate on the concept of inquiry.

"Inquiry" is treated as the resolution of "doubt", while the correctness of this resolution must be adjudicated by some "final authority." The results of inquiry, as agreed to by the final authority, lead to a knowledge of "truth"; and "reality" is that which has been found to be true. However, our philosophic understanding of each of these concepts, along with our understanding of the scientific method, has evolved constantly from as early as the Scholastic Age and is still continuing even today, with our understanding of inquiry evolving along with them.

Evolution of the concept of doubt

One example of this evolution concerns the concept of doubt. Throughout the Scholastic Age, about 1000 to 1500, philosophic doubt consisted of a mixture of random doubt and curiosity. If two philosophers attempted to resolve our doubts regarding the same question in contradictory ways, the acceptability of each solution was judged by an appeal to either Aristotle or the Catholic Church. However, by early in the seventeenth century, Descartes (1596–1650), father of the Modern Age, about 1500 to 1900, revolutionized our ways of thinking by systematizing the approach to inquiry with what he called "complete doubt," but what Peirce later called "radical" or "extreme" doubt. Descartes appealed all questions of final authority to the individual inquirer. He claimed that if an inquirer had a clear and distinct understanding of the problem he could not fail to arrive at the truth.

By the nineteenth century many problems had been found with Modern philosophy and many philosophers looked for ways to correct them or get around them. Charles Peirce (1839–1914), founder of American Pragmatism, was especially dissatisfied with the many dualisms of Cartesian philosophy and the infallibility that it required of man. He sought for a way to complete the program of Modern philosophy, eliminate its dualisms, compensate for fallibility, and make a complete breakthrough to better ways of doing inquiry. He found them all in a method he first called "pragmatism," and later "pragmaticism." Peirce regarded inquiry as the process of resolving genuine doubt, and truth as the goal of inquiry.

Among the principles of Pragmatism, as Peirce formulated it, fallibilism required that any suitable method of inquiry must allow for the existence of human errors and provide for ways of correcting them. In "The Fixation of Belief" (1877), he examined methods of inquiry (fixation of belief) and determined that the only method of inquiry that had the built-in power for self-correction was the scientific method. Since all human behavior is fallible, he concluded that all inquiry should employ the scientific method.

Peirce also chided Descartes for "pretending to doubt what cannot be doubted," concluding that only genuine doubt had the ability to lead inquiry to a successful conclusion. A better understanding of the scientific method led Peirce to believe that scientific evidence cannot be a matter solely for the individual inquirer, as Descartes had claimed, but must be public in the sense that all inquirers trained in the particular discipline must be able to examine and subject it and its implications to critical review. Therefore, the final arbiter of any philosophical inquiry is the entire community of inquirers.

Since inquiry is itself fallible, the results of inquiry are always subject to further doubts, thus generating further inquiry. Thus truth, which is the conclusion of inquiry, is not the conclusion of this particular inquiry, nor even of any finite set of inquiries, but the final conclusion agreed upon at the end of all time by all investigators who enter upon inquiry with an open mind using the best scientific methods. Thus the determination of truth and the results of inquiry can even outlast the human race. Finally, reality is defined simply as the object of the true results of inquiry.

John Dewey (1859–1952) was a student of Peirce at the Johns Hopkins University for one full course of logic and part of another. But it may have been only coincidently that he developed his logic along Peircean lines. His so-called "logic" could be viewed as a generalization and elaboration of Peirce's theory of inquiry and his greatest work of logic was titled *Logic: The Theory of Inquiry* (1938). Whereas Peirce renamed his approach to philosophy "Pragmaticism," Dewey called his version of pragmatism "Instrumentalism." Both relied on the notions of process and purpose to guide the conduct of inquiry. Dewey generalized the Peircean concept of genuine doubt to what he called the "problematic situation" because he felt that genuine doubt applied only to intellectual inquiry and Dewey wanted his results to apply to all inquiry. Thus he also had to generalize Peirce's concept of truth to that of warranted assertion and Peirce's concept of the community of inquirers to the entire democratic community.

In addition to American philosophy's break with European philosophy in the conception of doubt and the adoption of fallibilism, two other changes mark major breaks between Modern philosophy and Postmodern philosophy. They are Peirce's change from Aristotelian "thing"-oriented languages to his own process-oriented language, and his new insight into the role that teleology plays in the process of inquiry.

Purpose of inquiry

For the new American philosophy, now called "Classical Pragmatism," the main purpose of inquiry was the settlement of belief. Another important purpose of inquiry was the advancement of science and our philosophical understanding of it. Peirce had an Aristotelian, or scientific, conception of inquiry as a means of understanding the world. Dewey had a Baconian, or engineering, conception. For him, inquiry was a means of *controlling* the world.

For Dewey, inquiry starts as an effort to get out of a problematic situation. Sleeper (1986) argues that Dewey considers inquiry more a matter of logic than epistemology. Hickman (1990) interprets this to mean that "Dewey was not so much interested in a theory of certain knowledge as he was in a method of inquiry by means of which perceived problems could be solved."

Methodology: the process of inquiry

For more than forty years, Peirce was a close student of the methods of inquiry. Even his most famous quote concerns inquiry and its methodology: "Do not block the way of inquiry." Peirce found four common roadblocks to inquiry. These are: (1) absolute assertion; (2) maintaining that the object of inquiry can never be known; (3) maintaining that a given element is basic in that there is nothing beneath it to be known; and (4) maintaining that a result is the final and most perfect formulation of inquiry.

In his instrumentalism, Dewey came to emphasize the role of experiment for inquiry of all forms, but Peirce, himself a professional experimental scientist, also saw the role of experiment. Peirce came to think of Synechism, his principle of continuity, not as a doctrine of metaphysics, but as a methodological principle of inquiry. As a regulative principle, Synechism is the idea that an hypothesis should be accepted only if it does not "block the way of inquiry." Another methodological principle of inquiry that Peirce insisted upon was the essential role of musement, the free play of the mind. This was further explicated in his 1908 paper "A Neglected Argument for the Reality of God," which also spelled out the role of induction, abduction, and deduction for inquiry.

Peirce sought a method of verification to test the truth of inquiry in a way that goes beyond the Modern alternatives, namely:

- Deduction from self-evident truths, or *rationalism*;
- Induction from raw experiential sensation, or *empiricism*.

He found it in a method of reasoning discovered by Socrates but almost totally neglected ever since,

- Abduction from the conclusions of induction, and tested by coupling the results of deduction back again to induction, or *pragmaticism*.

However, Peirce's greatest contribution to the methodology of inquiry was his development of the science of semiotics. The subsumption of inquiry within reasoning in general and the inclusion of thinking within the class of sign processes allows us to approach the subject of inquiry with a new methodology: The semiotic approach views inquiry as a genus of semiosis, an activity taking place within the more general setting of sign relations and sign processes. It has already been mentioned that rather than semiotics, Continental philosophers use a Saussurian semiology which does not have this power to analyze inquiry.

The instrumentalist pattern of inquiry was developed by John Dewey as a deepening and expansion of Peirce's radical conception of inquiry. Dewey felt that Cartesian, or "armchair," inquiry had a fatal defect. It did not begin with genuine doubt, "and so tended toward speculation about matters that were not part of anyone's experience. Since there was no problem, no 'resistance' to test proposed solutions against, it was not possible, save by accident, to produce concrete, testable consequences" (Hickman 1990).

For Dewey, logic meant simply inquiry into inquiry. Dewey suggests that science was his model for analyzing inquiry and that logic, as the study of inquiry, is a study of the scientific method. In his treatment of Dewey's theory of technology, Hickman claims that "Nowhere is Dewey's treatment of technology more insightful than in his radical reconstruction of traditional theories of knowledge and his replacement of them with a theory of inquiry" (1990).

One of Dewey's most important contributions to the concept of inquiry was to eliminate the dualistic distinction between a thing and its environment. A thing together with its environment is called an organism. He also expanded on Peirce's development of process language and philosophy by emphasizing the important role of time in inquiry. An inquiry conducted in this "instrumentalist" way is called a transaction.

Dewey expanded on Peirce's conception of the role of teleology in inquiry by eliminating the dualistic distinctions between ends and means. Teleology is a balance between ends, means, and their interactions. Dewey refused to place means in a secondary position with respect to ends. To do so, he said, would "block the road to inquiry."

Dewey insisted that the results of inquiry do not exist prior to the successful completion of inquiry. Assuming the existence of the result before completing the process, he called the "philosophic fallacy."

Dewey's corresponding generalization of Peirce's concept of truth was "warranted assertion" (1938). He suggested reserving this term for what he called competent and controlled inquiry. But he noted that inquiry is a continuing process that is never completely settled, thus recognizing Peirce's infinite limit concept of truth.

Although Dewey hesitates to use Peirce's word "semiotics," he nevertheless attests to its importance in both inquiry and the study of inquiry. When the things of our common experience function as signs, their semiotic qualities must arise from a reflective situation, and it is this semiotic function that finally allows them to function as evidence in inquiry.

For Dewey, once the meanings of a situation have been ascertained, it is possible to ask about the meaning of the "truth" of the inquiry. For this, he used Peirce's pragmatic maxim, which he characterized as the difference it would make if this, rather than something else, were the case (MW 4.103).

Willard Van Orman Quine (1908–2000) is sometimes treated as America's best-known representative of the analytical tradition in philosophy, but is also the inheritor of the Peirce–Dewey inquiry tradition of pragmaticism. As such, Quine made several notable contributions to the methodology of inquiry. Due to space limitations, only three will be discussed here, but it should be mentioned that other twentieth-century pragmatists, such as Robert Nozick, have continued the American inquiry tradition.

In attempting to explain ordered pairs, Quine (1960) enunciated a theory of explication for concepts used in inquiry that was in part adumbrated by Carnap: "*explication is elimination*." We have, to begin with, an expression that is somehow troublesome, but also serves certain purposes that are not to be abandoned. Then we find a way of accomplishing those same purposes using other and less troublesome forms of expression.

When new evidence indicates that an old, accepted theory no longer explains all of the pertinent facts, how does one go about revising the theory in such a way as to make it most useful for inquiry? Quine's conclusions were to adopt those changes that caused the least impact to the most settled parts of theory, leaving most of the impact to fall on the "don't cares."

Quine analyzed referential opacity and discussed it to the extent that he is often given credit for discovering the effect. That this is not the case is attested by the fact that it was extensively discussed in scholastic logic, and was also discussed in modern times by both Frege and Russell. Nevertheless, Quine's (1960) is the best-known and the most popular discussion of the parsing of referential opacity and its use in inquiry.

Further reading

Burke, Tom. *Dewey's New Logic*. Chicago, IL: University of Chicago Press, 1998 [1994].

Dewey, John. *Logic: The Theory of Inquiry*. New York: Henry Holt, 1938.

—— *John Dewey: The Middle Works, 1899–1924*, Vols 1–15, ed. Jo Ann Boydston. Carbondale, IL: Southern Illinois University Press, 1976–80. Cited as MW.

Hickman, Larry. *John Dewey's Pragmatic Technology* (First Midland Book Edition). Bloomington, IN: Indiana University Press, 1992 [1990].

Peirce, Charles S. "The Fixation of Belief," *Popular Science Monthly* 12 (1877): 1–15. Reprinted in *The Collected Papers of Charles S. Peirce*, Cambridge, MA: Harvard University Press, 1958, 5.358–87.

—— "A Neglected Argument for the Reality of God," *Hibbert Journal* 7 (1908): 90–112.

—— *Chronological Writings of Charles S. Peirce*, 6 volumes to date, ed. the Peirce Edition Project. Bloomington, IN: Indiana University Press, 1982–. Cited as X: yyy, where X is the volume and yyy is the page number.

Quine, W.V.O. *Word and Object*. Cambridge, MA: MIT Press, 1960.

Sleeper, Ralph. *The Necessity of Pragmatism*. New Haven, CT: Yale University Press, 1986.

Charles Pearson

INSCRUTABILITY OF REFERENCE

Consider the problem raised by W.V. Quine in *Word and Object* (1960). According to Quine, translation is indeterminate in light of all behavioral evidence. If we were to try to translate another language into our own, without knowing the meaning of any of the words and sentences in this foreign language, a number of different translations might fit the behavioral evidence equally well. In Quine's most famous example, if the speakers of the unknown language typically say "*Gavagai!*" in the presence of rabbits, all of the available evidence would not give us a basis for deciding among "There's a rabbit!" "There's an undetached rabbit part!" and "There is a temporal stage of a rabbit!" as the proper translation of the sentence "*Gavagai!*" Given this indeterminacy of translation, Quine contends that there are no facts of the matter regarding the meanings of linguistic expressions.

In "Ontological Relativity," Quine notes that this very same example raises a problem not only for theories of meaning, but also for theories of reference. For, in light of this example, it is also clear that there are many possible assignments of referent to a given expression, each of which will make the expression true in the appropriate circumstances. By observing the behavior of the speakers of this foreign language, we have learned that the expression "*Gavagai!*" is true whenever there is a rabbit present. It would thus seem fairly obvious that the term "*gavagai*" refers to rabbits. However, the sentence "*Gavagai!*" would be true in the appropriate circumstances if the referent of the term is "undetached rabbit parts" or "a temporal stage of a rabbit." Whenever a rabbit is present, undetached rabbit parts and a temporal stage of a rabbit are also present, so when it is true that a rabbit is present, it will also be true that undetached rabbit parts are present, and it will also be true that temporal stages of rabbits are present. Given that multiple assignments of referent to the expression work equally well for assigning truth values to the sentence, reference is inscrutable in light of the available evidence.

Quine's theory of inscrutability of reference is often confused with the thesis of the indeterminacy of translation, for, as I noted above, Quine uses the same example to motivate both theses. The problem of the inscrutability of reference, however, can be motivated without discussion of Quine's example of radical translation. According to Quine, the problem of inscrutability applies to one's own native language and one's own idiolect as well. I may think that the word "rabbit," when I utter it, refers to rabbits. What evidence do I have that determines that my first-person perspective on my reference to rabbits is correct? According to Quine, I have no evidence that would decide, even in the case of my own idiolect, that I am referring to rabbits as opposed to undetached rabbit parts or temporal stages of rabbits. It would not be possible to test one or another hypothesis for whether the referent is "rabbit" or one of these alternatives, given that, as noted above, rabbit stages and undetached rabbit parts are always present when rabbits are present.

Quine attempted to resolve the problem of the inscrutability of reference through his thesis of ontological relativity. On this thesis, our terms do have determinate referents, but only relative to a certain background theory. When we take ourselves to be referring to rabbits with the term "rabbit," this is unproblematic relative to a background theory according to which rabbits are the referent of "rabbit" in my idiolect. There is no possibility of a non-relativized notion of reference. It is difficult to see how this relativization to a background theory is supposed to resolve the problem, given that (as Quine grants) the referents of terms in the background theory are themselves inscrutable in light of all available evidence.

In his later book *Pursuit of Truth*, Quine suggests that there is an unproblematic, disquotational notion of reference along the lines presented in Tarski's work on truth. Thus all that needs to be said in order to spell out the notion of reference in a language are trivial truths like the following: "is a rabbit" is satisfied by rabbits. Resolving the problem of inscrutability remains a problem for philosophers who seek an account of reference beyond this disquotational account.

Further reading

Fodor, Jerry. *The Elm and the Expert*. Cambridge, MA: MIT Press, 1994.

Quine, W.V. *Word and Object*. Cambridge, MA: MIT Press, 1960.

—— *Ontological Relativity and Other Essays*. New York: Columbia University Press, 1969.

—— *Pursuit of Truth*, revised edition. Cambridge, MA: Harvard University Press, 1992.

FRITZ J. MCDONALD

INSTRUMENTALISM

The term "instrumentalism" has suffered from negative connotations within some circles, including various strands of European philosophy and colloquial American speech. An earlier generation of Critical Theorists, for example, condemned instrumentalism as a type of praxis in which ends justify means.

For William James and John Dewey, however, the terms "instrument" and "instrumentalism" took on meanings that were both more positive and integral to their versions of Pragmatism. In 1907 James related instrumentalism to functionalism, arguing that an idea, when functionally considered, is an instrument that improves our ability to deal with the object of that idea and to act in ways that effectively take it into account. James thus viewed theories as tools or instruments for making a difference in future experience. On more than one occasion he characterized inquiry as a tool or instrument with which to "remodel" nature. For the most part, however, James was interested in the moral aspects of instrumentalism; he never fully developed its logical aspects.

Logical aspects of instrumentalism

Instrumentalism received its fullest expression in the work of Dewey. Applying the term "instrumentalism" to his theory of inquiry, he argued that standards and ideals are not given as valid a priori, but are instead instruments that are under continual review as they enter into experiments related to the control of particular situations. In properly controlled inquiry, ends do not dominate means. Ends and means inform and justify one another as a part of the process of intelligent production of new tools and artifacts – both tangible and intangible – that Dewey at one point termed "technology."

Dewey identified *Studies in Logical Theory*, a volume of essays that he and his colleagues at the University of Chicago published in 1903, as the first statement of instrumentalism. He thought that the unique contribution of that volume lay in its development of the idea that there is a close association of normative logic with actual processes of thought as determined by an objective or biological psychology. Among the volume's critics was Charles S. Peirce, who argued Dewey had effectively abandoned normative logic for psychologism, or the view that logic principally concerns psychological processes. Dewey acknowledged that the roots of instrumentalism lay in the work of William James, especially in *The Principles of Psychology*, but defended the normative aspects of his instrumentalism.

The first instance of the term "instrumentalism" in Dewey's published work occurs in a 1905 essay in which he characterized ideas, and even sensations, as tools for producing objective knowledge of things. His purpose in this remark was to stress that Pragmatist theories of inquiry involve satisfaction of objective as well as subjective conditions, and to reject the idea that recondite, intervening states of consciousness are required in order to know things as they are.

During the same year, 1905, Dewey provided a clear statement of the ways in which instrumentalism, functionalism, the genetic method, and experimentalism are related as aspects of his wider philosophy. Functionalism treats ideas not as facts or states of affairs, but as functions of mind; the genetic method is a way of analyzing such functions that takes into account the considerable instability of things as experienced; instrumentalism is a theory of the significance of "the knowledge-function"; and experimentalism is a theory of how the value of ideas may be tested.

In a 1917 essay Dewey elaborated on the relation between Pragmatism and instrumentalism. Pragmatism demands that thinking be tested by consequences that, far from being the narrowly utilitarian, "bread and butter" type, may be aesthetic, moral, political, or religious in quality. As a behaviorist theory of thinking and knowing, instrumentalism thus treats meanings in their logical roles as ways of behaving with respect to data. Dewey thought that instrumentalism was rooted in the soil of Aristotle's *Organon*, but also noted that great advances in the theory of inquiry had resulted from the seventeenth-century invention of a logic of scientific discovery, which incorporated the Aristotelian empirical protosciences of definition and classification as elements or "auxiliary tools."

In an even more precise statement in 1925, Dewey defined instrumentalism as "an attempt to establish a precise logical theory of concepts, of judgments and inferences in their various forms, by considering primarily how thought functions in the experimental determinations of future consequences." This remark contains a restatement of Dewey's conception of the relation of instrumentalism to Pragmatism (as the theory that the meaning of ideas lie in their conceivable practical consequences) and experimentalism (as the process by means of which the value of ideas may be tested).

Instrumentalism is closely related to Pragmatic theories of truth. Both James and Dewey rejected standard correspondence and coherence theories of truth. For James, an idea is made true by events. For Dewey, a judgment is true when it enjoys a background of experimentally based warrant that allows it to be assertible in future cases that are relevantly similar. Such judgments may then become instruments that function within further processes of inquiry. Both theories – instrumentalism and the Pragmatic theory of truth – emphasize the instrumental function of ideas: true ideas work, or cohere, within a behavioral network and they correspond to emerging situations, not as a mirror corresponds to what is before it, but as a key corresponds to a lock.

The instrumentalism of Josiah Royce and Dewey's reply

Josiah Royce embraced a thin version of instrumentalism that characterized true ideas as effective tools. He viewed instrumentalism as a more or less acceptable account of the ways in which human organisms engage in seeking truth. But he rejected the broader claims of instrumentalism on the grounds that it failed to provide an explanation for how verification or satisfaction of conditions could be anything more than subjective or personal. He thought that instrumentalism required an Absolute Spirit to transcend subjective or personal experience and to create community.

Dewey's reply to Royce focused on the relation of instrumentalism to experimentalism: he pointed out that experience and verification are not private but public matters. In neglecting this point, he argued, Royce had failed to get the point of instrumentalism as he and James had formulated it. Ideas are not tools to be deployed in the interest of personal satisfaction alone; objective conditions importune and therefore must also be satisfied. Since instrumentalism embraced philosophical naturalism, and since human communities of inquiry are naturally occurring phenomena, there is no need to posit supernatural or other types of transcendent support for objectivity.

Dewey was not always clear about the relationships among the various elements of his wider philosophy. Consequently, many of his critics failed to grasp the meaning of his instrumentalism. In 1934, however, Dewey characterized his instrumentalism in terms that were both simple and clear: "Knowledge is instrumental to the enrichment of immediate experience through the control over action that it exercises."

Further reading

Dewey, John. "The Reflex Arc Concept in Psychology" in Vol. 5 of *The Collected Works of John Dewey: The Early Works, 1882–1898*, ed. Jo Ann Boydston. Carbondale, IL: Southern Illinois University Press, 1972.

—— *Experience and Nature*, Vol. 1 of *The Collected Works of John Dewey: The Later Works, 1925–1953*, ed. Jo Ann Boydston. Carbondale, IL: Southern Illinois University Press, 1981.

—— *Studies in Logical Theory*, Vol. 2 of *The Collected Works of John Dewey: The Middle Works, 1899–1924*, ed. Jo Ann Boydston. Carbondale, IL: Southern Illinois University Press, 1976.

Hickman, Larry A. *John Dewey's Pragmatic Technology*. Bloomington, IN: Indiana University Press, 1990.

James, William. *The Principles of Psychology* in *The Works of William James: The Principles of Psychology*, ed. Frederick Burkhardt and Fredson Bowers. Cambridge, MA: Harvard University Press, 1981.

Royce, Josiah. *William James and Other Essays*. New York: Macmillan, 1911.

—— *The World and the Individual*. New York: Dover, 1959.

—— *Studies of Good and Evil*. New York: Kessinger Publishing, 2003.

LARRY A. HICKMAN

INTELLIGENCE

Among the American philosophers, John Dewey most extensively examined the concept of intelligence. He conceived of intelligence as the fundamental difference between living and non-living things. Intelligence, for Dewey, is the process of voluntarily bringing about results in activity and, in future experience, exhibiting a preference for some results over others. Intelligence, therefore, is found in the efforts of living things to bring about preferred conditions. Rocks are incapable of avoiding results, but mice can. Intelligence in human beings, for Dewey, is continuous with basic forms we see in animals and plants, but with the added or more advanced ability of refining the methods of inquiry we employ to more effectively bring about our preferred conditions.

Intelligence, according to the Pragmatists, was characterized as a process more than a property. American philosophers generally see continuities where other schools of thought see breaks, or static things. Intelligence, like belief, can be conceived of statically as a thing. But, American philosophers consider both belief and intelligence as inextricably related to action. The ordinary notion of a person who is intelligent, but never makes use of his or her talents would not suit the American philosophical context. We would say instead that the person has potential, but that intelligence and beliefs are exhibited in what we do. Intelligence, like belief, is not something that gets dusty on the shelf for Pragmatists. It is the activity and use of methods and principles to aid in forming and achieving goals.

Dewey considered the history of philosophy in terms of the development of intelligence. He explained that there are two aspects to the development of intelligence, one negative, one positive. The first, he explains in *Ethics*, involved the process of removing the impediments to inquiry. In ancient Greece, Socrates was the most famous of the philosophers to pave the way for intelligence through negative development, which is a clearing away of our presuppositions, myths, and superstitions – impediments to inquiry. Only once we let go of our superstitions and unsupported assumptions can we be ready for the positive endeavor of looking into the problems we face. The Greeks also brought a positive development of intelligence, Dewey explains, when they then began to build a body of scientific practices.

Dewey explains that the negative and positive developments of intelligence occurred side by side during the Renaissance and then in the Enlightenment, though not without setbacks. During the Enlightenment, he tells us, the negative development reached its zenith in the movement known as "rationalism." It was the philosophical outlook which attempted to reject all prior assumptions, exploring reason itself as the basis for knowledge and authority. With this movement came a look inward, to the experiences of human beings, rather than to the heavens. This fundamental shift of focus to reason as a source of authority came about not only with reference to science, but also to the moral life. Kant, Rousseau, and others famously considered all human beings to possess a worth of great importance, given humanity's special faculties. The individual, Dewey explained, was believed to attain his or her "highest reach only as a member of a moral society. But it is one thing to point out the need and meaning of a moral society, it is another thing to bring such a society into being" (Dewey 1908: 156). In this context we can better understand Dewey's aims in focusing so extensively on the notion of intelligence, and on the scientific methods which most carefully make use of it. Intelligence is fundamental not only for our selfish preferences, but also for advancing the moral life.

Charles Peirce also studied intelligence as an important scientific and social concept. In *Elements of Logic*, he characterized intelligence of the scientific sort as one that can learn from experience (Peirce 1965: 2.227). It is important to note the sense in which scientific intelligence is not static, therefore. Intelligence is a growing process, given that it is learning. Elsewhere, Peirce explains the value of intelligence more generally. In "What is the Use of Consciousness?" Peirce claims that "intelligence does not consist in feeling intelligently but in acting so that one's deeds are concentrated upon a result" (Peirce 1965: 7.559). Here we see Peirce's Pragmatism in his attention to action, aims, and results. And, for Peirce, among the important things one can learn through intelligent action is how to form good habits of action generally. If we focus intelligent action on reforming and refining our habits, we can make powerful tools for social and scientific progress.

Intelligence as inquiry might be conceived as a process of seeking out fixed ends. This is not what Dewey had in mind. The process of inquiry itself is formative of its ends. For, if a person does research, although she might have a hypothesis in mind, the process of inquiry will inform her goals. And, thus, the scientific inquiry does not just determine whether or not the hypothesis is true, but also which direction she might look, which ends she might pursue, as one of the central products of the inquiry. Dewey claims that intelligence is a reformulation of ends or goals, rather than the effort to attain antecedent ones. He writes that "the pragmatic theory of intelligence means that the function of mind is to project new and more complex ends – to free experience from routine and from caprice" (Dewey 1980: 44–5).

One of Dewey's central contributions toward the Enlightenment goal of the just society, of intelligent moral life, came in the form of his philosophy of education. Education, he believed, is fundamental to democracy and moral life insofar as it develops the faculties of individuals to pursue social harmony. Dewey argued that "The problem of bringing about an effective socialization of intelligence is probably the greatest problem of democracy today" (Dewey 1985: 365). So although Dewey sought to move beyond the Enlightenment project of negative developments of intelligence, he embraced the goals of forming the just society through positive developments of free and open inquiry.

Further reading

Dewey, John. "The Need for a Recovery of Philosophy" in *The Middle Works, 1899–1924, Vol. 10, 1916–1917*, ed. Jo Ann Boydston. Carbondale, IL: Southern Illinois University Press, 1980, pp. 3–48.

—— *Ethics* in *The Middle Works, 1899–1924: Volume 5, 1908*, ed. Jo Ann Boydston, Carbondale, IL: Southern Illinois University Press, 1985 [1908]; with revisions in *The Later Works, 1925–1953: Volume 7, 1932*, ed. Jo Ann Boydston. Carbondale, IL: Southern Illinois University Press, 1986.

—— *A Common Faith* in *The Later Works, 1925–1953: Volume 9, 1933–1934*, ed. Jo Ann Boydston. Carbondale, IL: Southern Illinois University Press, 1986, pp. 3–58.

James, William. *The Principles of Psychology* in *The Works of William James*, ed. Frederick H. Burkhardt, Fredson Bowers, and Ignas K. Skrupskelis. Cambridge, MA: Harvard University Press, 1981.

Peirce, Charles Sanders. *The Collected Papers of Charles Sanders Peirce*, ed. Charles Hartshorne and Paul Weiss, Cambridge, MA: The Belknap Press, 1965.

ERIC THOMAS WEBER

INTENTIONALITY

Intentionality is *aboutness.* Mental or linguistic things have intentionality just in case they are *about* real or unreal objects or states of affairs. My belief that *Nixon resigned* is intentional because it is *about* Nixon. Intentionality seems essential to thinking, action, and language. The intentionality of thoughts enables them to carry information or misinformation. Actions have motives, which include mental states with intentionality such as beliefs and desires. Intentionality is puzzling, however. Natural objects do not seem to be *about* anything, especially that which does not exist. The knowledge of every natural fact about a person, including facts about that person's brain states, would seem not to include the knowledge of what that person's mental states are about. It is tempting, therefore, to suppose that intentionality and the mind are not natural. This, however, leads to stubborn problems. One project in American philosophy has been to avoid these problems by naturalizing intentionality.

First, some distinctions. The mental states we call "intentions" have intentionality but so do other mental states. Intentionality must also be distinguished from *intensionality*, which is a semantic property declarative sentences have just in case their truth values (true, false) are not fixed by the referents of their non-logical terms. *It is necessary that* 7 + 5 = 12 is true but *it is necessary that* 7 + 5 = *Joe's favorite number* is false even if "12" and "Joe's favorite number" refer to the same thing. So these sentences are *intensional*. If "Joe's cat" and "Tiger" refer to the same object, then the extensional (i.e. non-*intensional*) sentences *Joe's cat is fluffy* and *Tiger is fluffy* have the same truth value, but *Sally believes that Joe's cat is fluffy* and *Sally believes that Tiger is fluffy* need not. So these sentences about beliefs are *intensional*. Intentionality and *intensionality* are connected, however, for intentional mental states are most perspicuously described by *intensional* sentences. For person S, individual terms "*a*" and "*b*," and predicates "*P*" and "*Q*," *S believes that a is P* can have a different truth value than *S believes that b is Q* even if *a* is *b* and *P* is *Q*. That intentional states are most perspicuously described by *intensional* sentences is, I think, no accident, since it is essential to intentional states that they represent their objects under some descriptions and not others, even if the descriptions in question are logically equivalent and refer to the same objects and properties.

The dominant position in early modern philosophy was that intentional states – "ideas" and the mental states they constitute – are mental contents that mediate our awareness of other things and function as reasons for actions. This raises problems. If our awareness of the world is mediated by ideas, how can we know that our ideas accurately represent the objects they are about or that they are about anything at all? If thinking is a non-physical activity of a non-physical substance, how can mental states have any effect on the physical world? Important strands in American philosophy can be understood as different attempts to provide naturalistic alternatives to this conception.

The classical American pragmatists C.S. Peirce and John Dewey insist that the intentionality of ideas is a product of the more fundamental aboutness of external signs such as language and tools. This changes the focus of questions about intentionality from "inner" to "outer" states, but can the intentionality of outer states be explained in non-intentional terms? In an important exchange, Wilfrid Sellars and Roderick Chisholm sharpen a key issue: Sellars maintains, while Chisholm doubts, that the intentionality of language can be analyzed without reference to the irreducible intentionality of thoughts. The focus of much subsequent debate has thus been on language, but a central question remains whether intentionality – wherever it be – is reducible to non-intentional, natural properties.

To reduce one property to another is to show that they, or the sets of objects that have them, are identical. Reduction has worked in other areas of inquiry – *being water* is *being H_2O*, *heat* is *mean molecular kinetic energy*, etc. – so we might conjecture that mental properties can be reduced to non-mental properties. To complete the reduction we need a non-mental, natural property Φ for every mental property Ψ such that, necessarily any object has Ψ if, and only if, it has Φ.

Intentionality raises problems for reduction. On the one hand, it is difficult to see that there is a physical property Φ such that whatever has Φ has some intentional property Ψ. Putnam's Twin Earth case is designed to show that what a person's mental states are about is not a function of the non-relational properties of that person. Twin Earth is like Earth except for containing a complex substance XYZ instead of H_2O. Since XYZ and H_2O are indistinguishable under normal conditions, inhabitants of Twin Earth have thoughts about XYZ just in case their counterparts on Earth have thoughts about H_2O, not about XYZ, despite the fact that persons in both places have all of their non-relational properties in common. So it seems that the aboutness of thoughts cannot be explained in terms of the non-relational natural states of thinkers. A promising suggestion is that what distinguishes thoughts about XYZ from thoughts about H_2O is some natural relation. Perhaps thoughts about XYZ are *caused by* XYZ while thoughts about H_2O are *caused by* H_2O, for example. Such causal views and their kin face the formidable challenge of accounting for thoughts about what does not exist (e.g. unicorns) or about things that cannot be causes (e.g. numbers). On the other hand, it is difficult to see that all things with a given mental property Ψ must have a single natural property Φ in common. For we can readily conceive of cases in which complex beings with very different physical constitutions – advanced robots or Vulcans, say – can think.

Problems with reductionism have prompted a large number of American philosophers to adopt *property dualism*, the view that mental properties, including those involving intentionality, are not reducible to other natural properties but that they are somehow – the accounts vary widely – explainable in natural terms. A smaller group promotes *eliminativism*. Eliminativists hold that nothing has intentional mental properties since there are no such things as the beliefs, desires, choices, and so on postulated by "folk psychology." I conjecture that a resolution of these issues will turn on the logical coherence and descriptive, predictive, and explanatory power of the *intensional* sentences we use to pick out intentional mental states.

Further reading

Churchland, Paul M. *Scientific Realism and the Plasticity of Mind*. New York: Cambridge University Press, 1979.

Dennett, Daniel. *The Intentional Stance*. Cambridge, MA: MIT/Bradford, 1987.

Dewey, John. *Experience and Nature*, second edition. LaSalle, IL: Open Court, 1929.

Putnam, Hilary. "Meaning and Reference," *Journal of Philosophy* 70, 19 (1973): 699–711.

Rorty, Richard. *Philosophy and the Mirror of Nature*. Princeton, NJ: Princeton University Press, 1979.

Searle, John. *Intentionality*. New York: Cambridge University Press, 1983.

Sellars, Wilfrid, "'Intentionality and the Mental,' a Correspondence with Roderick Chisholm" in H. Feigel and M. Scriven (eds) *Minnesota Studies in the Philosophy of Science*, Vol. II. Minneapolis, MN: University of Minnesota Press, 1957, pp. 521–39.

ANDREW D. CLING

INTERNAL REALISM

Internal realism is a doctrine defended by the contemporary American philosopher Hilary Putnam. In Putnam (1981) he introduced the doctrine as an alternative to what he called metaphysical realism, in his view a commonly held but seriously erroneous metaphysical theory. As he understood this latter theory, the world consists of a fixed totality of mind-independent objects. There is exactly one true and complete description of this fixed totality, according to the theory, because the truth of such a description consists in a correspondence between the individual words of the description and the components of the totality. A true and complete description embodies a "God's Eye view" of the world.

An internal realist holds that the question "What objects does the world consist of?" makes sense only in relation to a theory or description of the world, not in relation to the world itself. We can meaningfully say "According to theory A, the world consists of objects X, Y, and Z, and according to theory B, the world consists of objects M, N, and O," but we cannot meaningfully say "The world itself consists of objects C, D, and E." We cannot meaningfully say the latter, Putnam says, because the objects of a world "do not exist independently of a conceptual scheme." A conceptual scheme or a scheme of description constructs the objects of a world, he said; a scheme of this kind is not constructed to fit an independently existing world of objects.

Putnam supported his internal realism by arguments about reference and truth. If objects in the world were not human constructions, he said, they would collectively constitute a world of Kantian things-in-themselves. But we could not successfully refer to such things or attach descriptions to them. They would be incomprehensible to us. The fact that we can comprehend them and know facts about them shows us, Putnam thought, that they are not mind-independent objects and that ascertainable truths about them cannot consist in a correspondence, or fit, between what we think and what they are like. Such truths consist rather in warrantedly assertible beliefs, ones whose assertion is warranted under optimal conditions by creatures with our sensible natures.

Although mutually compatible theories may identify different constituents of the world – miles rather than kilometers and liters rather than quarts – critics of Putnam deny that such constituents are thereby mind-dependent entities. Conceptions are obviously mind-dependent, they say, but the reality to which they apply is not. As a general matter, entities singled out from a distinctly human point of view are not thereby mind-dependent, nor are the objects of inventory. If Sarah refers to certain people as her aunts and uncles, the subjectivity of her means of reference in no way limits the independence of the people she refers to. Truths about them need not, inconsequence, be understood as merely warrantedly assertible beliefs; they are propositions that describe reality as it actually is. For arguments supporting these criticisms, see Aune (1985: 126ff, 157ff).

Further reading

Aune, Bruce. *Metaphysics: The Elements.* Minneapolis, MN: University of Minnesota Press, 1985.

Putnam, Hilary. *Reason, Truth, and History.* Cambridge: Cambridge University Press, 1981.

BRUCE AUNE

INTERPRETANT

The concept of interpretant is certainly the most important, if not also the most difficult, of all semiotic concepts. Perhaps this explains why it has also been one of the most controversial and confused concepts since it was introduced into semiotics by the American philosopher Charles S. Peirce (1839–1914), nearly a century and a half ago. It turns out that he may have had to define the concept of sign in terms of the interpretant in order to guarantee the real possibility of being able to interpret every sign. This marked a definite step on his road from nominalism to realism. That step was the introduction of the real possibility of interpreting all future signs, since this requires the reality of "mere" possibilities. His definition of the sign was, in turn, partly necessitated by his desire, as a working scientist, to avoid dealing with a world of metaphysical fictions, such as Kant's neumenal realm, while at the same time explicating and justifying scientific methodology.

Peirce's original definition of interpretant was for a particular purpose – the advancement of science nominalistically conceived. His definition, in terms of the mental sign that interprets the same object, suited the needs of a philosophy of science wonderfully since many of the processes of science involve obtaining a better understanding and explication of a fixed object. However, there are many other sign processes involving interpretation in which some other sign component is held fixed. For instance, in philosophical analysis, the goal is to expand the interpretation keeping the ground the same. Thus, this Peircean concept appears to be only one of many possible generalized concepts of the interpretant.

An understanding of the interpretant concept is necessary for many purposes, such as a better understanding of the nature of arguments, for as Peirce said, an argument is "intended to refer to an interpretant" (W1: 477; 1866). For Peirce, the definition of argument makes explicit reference to interpretants. Terms and propositions are defined without reference to interpretants. But although terms and propositions are essential components of arguments – they secure the reference to objects and grounds that arguments require – they contribute to the meaning of arguments only by contributing to the determination of interpretants (W2: 431; 1870). Paul Forster explained this by saying, "For Peirce ... an argument is the principled determination of an interpretant by an interpreted symbol" (Forster 2003: 530).

Early on, Peirce defined the interpretant simply as an idea: "the idea to which a sign gives rise is called its interpretant" (CP 1.338). But later, he expanded on this by defining the interpretant as the sign of the same object, produced in the mind of the interpreter, as a result of interpreting the original sign. Peirce also realized that if inquiry were due only to genuine doubt, interpretation must come to a halt when genuine doubt ends, and hence there must be some kind of final interpretant. He was later able to determine that the concept of final interpretant that made all of semiotics and all of pragmaticism consistent was a habit of action.

Further reading

Forster, Paul. "The Logic of Pragmatism: A Neglected Argument for Peirce's Pragmatic Maxim," *Transactions of the Charles S. Peirce Society* XXXIX, 4 (2003): 525–54.

Ketner, Kenneth L. *A Thief of Peirce.* Jackson, MS: University Press of Mississippi, 1995.

Peirce, Charles S. *The Collected Papers of Charles Sanders Peirce*, 8 volumes, ed. Charles Hartshorne. Cambridge, MA: Harvard University Press, 1931–58. Cited in standard notation as CP X.yyy, where X stands for volume and yyy stands for paragraph number.

—— *The Chronological Writings of Charles S. Peirce*, 6 vols to date, ed. the Peirce Edition Project. Bloomington, IN: Indiana University Press, 1982–. Cited in standard notation as WX: yyy, where X stands for volume and yyy stands for page number.

CHARLS PEARSON

INTUITIONISM

Theories of knowledge are intuitionistic if they give a special or foundational role to intuition in their accounts of knowledge. "Intuition" may be used to refer to (1) the intellectual faculty or process that allows us to grasp particular truths or true principles non-inferentially or immediately and/or (2) the non-inferential or immediate truths or true principles so grasped.

Intuitionisms are typically proposed by foundationalists in epistemology. According to foundationalism, knowledge (justified true belief) has a two-tiered structure with non-inferential, immediately known truths as the foundation that guarantees the certainty of whatever further truths we infer from or on the basis of those foundational truths. However, not all foundationalist theories are intuitionistic. The term "intuitionism" is normally restricted to those versions according to which non-inferential truths are grasped by the mind independent of our external senses, etc. Thus foundational theories of knowledge that appeal to sense-perception or experience as the ground of basic, non-inferred true beliefs about the world would not count as intuitionisms. Intuitionism as a theory of knowledge is distinct from metaphysical accounts of the things or propositions intuitively known. Thus intuitionists can be metaphysical realists or idealists. Intuitionism about our knowledge of the external world or other minds does not entail intuitionism about values (or vice versa) though often the two go hand in hand.

American philosophy has produced no homegrown schools of intuitionism, although intuitional theories popular in various periods of Western philosophical thought have been influential. For example, various versions of Platonism have incorporated intuitionism in their accounts of knowledge. Plato held that true knowledge is immediate intellectual acquaintance with the eternal ideal Forms of things. Our beliefs about things in the experiential world approach the status of knowledge to the extent that experiential objects partake of the Forms. Since none do completely, inferences about them based on their incomplete instantiation of the Forms are merely probabilistic, lacking the certainty of true knowledge. The Cambridge Platonists, widely read in North America during the seventeenth and eighteenth centuries were also intuitionists, although their Christianized metaphysics departed substantially from Plato's in reinterpreting the Forms as eternal ideas of in the mind of God, copies of which exist in and are thus present to our own finite minds

During the same period, Cartesian Rationalism was sometimes taken to provide an alternate form of intuitionism, divorced from Platonic metaphysics. This was because in Descartes' epistemology, the foundation of our knowledge of the world and ourselves is provided not by mere sensory experience but by an inner power of perception or discernment of the clearness and distinctness of ideas. That is, ideas can or cannot be not immediately perceived clearly and distinctly by rational insight. If perceived clearly and distinctly, they may be judged indubitable or absolutely certain on that evidence alone. If perceived vaguely or indistinctly, their meaning and truth is doubtful, and inference from further evidence will be required.

By the nineteenth century, the dominant form of intuitionism in America was Scottish Common Sense Realism. Following Thomas Reid, this school held that as we manifestly possess knowledge of things, events, and other minds, we must possess immediate, intuitive knowledge of concepts and principles (such as causality) that make this possible – concepts and principles that (as Hume had shown) were not themselves objects of experience or derivable from sensory experience alone. Reid argued that these fundamental concepts are products of the mind's own faculties, employed in its interpretation of sense experience. Our minds are structured so as to generate the fundamental concepts and principles necessary to transform sensations into coherent ordered knowledge of the world. While the inferences we make about externalities by means of these concepts and principles may sometimes be mistaken, our knowledge of the concepts and principles themselves is immediate and certain.

Scottish Common Sense Realism gradually lost favor in part because of the inability of later members of the school to answer Kant's objection that what the mind immediately apprehends are merely phenomena of its inner operations. If Kant was correct, then what we intuit gives us no insight at all into how the mind or external reality is in itself. This objection was exploited by intuitionism's neo-Hegelian and pragmatist opponents in American philosophical debates throughout the nineteenth and early twentieth century.

Moral intuitionisms have never been as popular in America as in Britain where novel forms continue to be produced. In America, Scottish Common Sense Realism, which held moral principles to be directly intuitable by the mind, was arguably the last widely influential school.

However, the term "intuitionism" was used very loosely in moral debates in the nineteenth and twentieth centuries, so caution must be exercised in accepting the designation of a moralist's position as intuitionistic. For example, British Moral Sense theorists (e.g. Francis Hutcheson, David Hume) were sometimes called intuitionists because they held that our moral "ideas" or "impressions" were products of an inner sensibility that reacts to our perceptions of others' conduct or character with feelings of approbation or disapprobation. While we are immediately aware of these feelings, they do not give us knowledge of or about the properties or qualities of the acts or persons to which we react. Thus such theories are not theories of moral knowledge per se and so not species of moral intuitionism.

Similarly, Kant was sometimes labeled an intuitionist by utilitarian and pragmatic opponents in this period because he held the fundamental concepts of moral practical reason to be a priori. However, a priori status is not sufficient in Kant's philosophy to establish that what is grasped a priori is true – transcendental deduction is required to establish the validity of what we grasp a priori. So again, that moral concepts or principles are inwardly determined does not by itself guarantee their truth or the validity of inferences about acts or persons we might employ them to make. Thus Kant's ethics should not be considered a species of intuitionism.

In the twentieth century, British philosopher W.D. Ross's intuitionist theory of moral knowledge was probably the most influential in America. Ross held that acts and persons possess directly intuitable moral qualities from which true principles can be derived by inductive induction from a single case. Using these principles one can determine the good and right-making qualities of any act, qualities that *prima facie* determine our duties regarding it (although where these conflict, further judgment is required to determine what our actual duty may be). Though much discussed in America, Ross did not inspire acceptance of intuitionism. Among contemporary American philosophers, Robert Audi is notable (in part) for his defense of moral intuitionism.

Further reading

Audi, Robert. *The Good in the Right: A Theory of Intuition and Intrinsic Value*. Princeton, NJ: Princeton University Press, 2004.

Broadie, Alexander. *The Cambridge Companion to the Scottish Enlightenment*. Cambridge: Cambridge University Press, 2003.

Dancy, Jonathan. "Intuitionism" in Peter Singer (ed.) *A Companion to Ethics*. Oxford: Blackwell, 1993.

Flower, Elizabeth and Murphey, G. Murray. *A History of Philosophy in America*, 2 vols. New York: Capricorn Books, 1977.

Kuklick, Bruce. *The Rise of American Philosophy*. New Haven, CT: Yale University Press, 1977.

Moser, Paul K. *Oxford Handbook of Epistemology*. Oxford: Oxford University Press, 2002.

Ross, W.D. *The Right and the Good*. Oxford: Oxford University Press, 1930.

Stratton-Lake, Philip. *Ethical Intuitionism: Re-Evaluated*. Oxford: Oxford University Press, 2003.

JENNIFER WELCHMAN

IRONISM

Ironism is a central component in Richard Rorty's pragmatist version of liberalism. It refers to a distinctive manner of holding one's beliefs and attending to one's values. The *aim* of ironism is to allow us to fully embrace our moral and political convictions while at the same time realizing that these convictions are crucially shaped by natural and historical contingency. Its *method* is to uncouple the sustenance of these convictions from the demand for a certain kind of philosophical justification, viz. one that reaches beyond our particular historico-cultural location and latches onto supposedly suprahistorical features of the human being and the human situation. If this reconceptualization is successful, we shall no longer feel intellectually crippled by the fact that such "skyhooks" are not within our cognitive reach, and that any justification of our moral beliefs must necessarily proceed by reference to what is palpably just more such beliefs. Ironism can thus be seen as an application to our moral–political convictions of the anti-foundationalist stance that Rorty has urged that we adopt with respect to our scientific and philosophical beliefs quite generally: While truth is absolute, its very absoluteness is what keeps us from making epistemic use of it. Instead, what guides our inquiries are norms of justification. Justification, forever defeasible and distinct from truth, is a suitably pragmatic measure, but, as such, also necessarily relative to our beliefs. The justification of our deepest convictions will thus inevitably be circular, although "only in the sense that the terms of praise used to describe liberal societies will be drawn from the vocabulary of the liberal societies themselves" (IPPI: 29).

The recognition that we can never have an objective vocabulary of epistemic and moral assessment should not lead to any facile form of relativism. Indeed, Rorty's point is precisely to encourage us to abandon this particular dialectic, since relativism is entirely parasitic upon the objectivism it supposedly provides an alternative to. Instead, the pragmatist reminds us that justifying our moral beliefs and political institutions is a responsibility we bear not to a timeless, non-human reality, but precisely to the transient communities of our fellow human beings. Thus, Rorty's slogan is that we substitute *solidarity* for *objectivity*: we vindicate our moral convictions in the first instance by "enlarging our acquaintance" (1989: 80), by increasing the scope and variety of communities to whom we recognize that justification is due. This task is a matter of "sentimental education" (1998: 181), proceeding not by amassing steadily greater insight into human nature in the abstract, but rather by increasing our ability to recognize and be moved by the suffering of others. As such, it is better entrusted to "genres such as ethnography, the journalist's report, the comic book, the docudrama, and, especially, the novel" (1989: xvi) than to philosophical theory.

The *liberal ironist* embraces this challenge, and develops her moral convictions by addressing an ever-expanding range of human experience, choice, and existence. She subjects the validity of her beliefs to constant query, while also harboring a deep-seated suspicion of the very notion of validity to which her convictions are at any given point being held. This suspicion turns moral justification into constant existential effort. Meanwhile, she maintains a working moral perspective precisely by "enlarging her acquaintance" – by moving into different vocabularies, developing new self-descriptions, and appropriating the possibilities that acculturation affords.

Further reading

Rorty, Richard. *Philosophy and the Mirror of Nature*. Princeton, NJ: Princeton University Press, 1979.

—— *Contingency, Irony, and Solidarity*. Cambridge: Cambridge University Press, 1989.

—— *Objectivity, Relativism, and Truth: Philosophical Papers Vol. 1*. Cambridge: Cambridge University Press, 1991.

—— *Truth and Progress: Philosophical Papers Vol. 3*. Cambridge: Cambridge University Press, 1998.

ENDRE BEGBY
BJØRN T. RAMBERG

J

JAMES, HENRY, SR

Henry James, Sr (1811–82), religious philosopher, Christian socialist, sometime transcendentalist, and founder of his own private religion, was father to Henry James the novelist and William James the psychologist. Raised in a strict Irish Presbyterian and Calvinist household, Henry James, Sr, rebelled and at an early age took up instead the ideas of the Scottish minister Robert Sandeman, who preached vegetarianism, communal living, and the shunning of morality, considering egotism the greatest sin of Christians. As a young man, James Sr then became a follower of Charles Fourier, French utopian thinker whose communal phalanxes were spread throughout the US. James Sr later co-financed several Fourierist communes, notably Eagleswood in Rahway, New Jersey. Though a New Yorker, after 1842 he became a member of the Transcendentalist circle in Concord, Massachusetts. Through his close friend Ralph Waldo Emerson, James Sr was then led to Carlyle's dinner table in England, where he met Bain, Mill, and other of the foremost philosophers of utilitarianism and British Empiricism of his day. In England he also experienced a spiritual crisis that cast him into total despair, until, through the English physician and homeopath James John Garth Wilkinson, he was led to the writings of the eighteenth-century scientist and philosopher of religion Emanuel Swedenborg. Thereafter, he wrote some dozen pamphlets and books interpreting Swedenborg's writings, helping to elevate Swedenborg to one of the most important influences in popular American thought in the nineteenth century.

Among his several works, James Sr's *Church of Christ Not an Ecclesiasticism* (1856) was a book-length letter to a Swedenborgian challenging the theology of the Church of the New Jerusalem, the Christian denomination that followed Swedenborg's writings, when Swedenborg's vision of 1758 described a transformation of all Christiandom and a falling away of the denominations. *Substance and Shadow* (1863) emphasized Swedenborg's claim that the overt thoughts expressed in the Bible concealed throughout an inner spiritual meaning related to the transformation of the individual. *The Secret of Swedenborg* (1869) was the insight that the natural world is derived from the spiritual, not the other way around, while *Society the Reformed Form of Man* (1879) dealt with the problem of egotism, claiming that we are one with God in the beginning, but fall out of that relationship through the development of selfhood. The purpose of selfhood was to lead us to the edge of the abyss, to total self-abnegation, where we abandon egotism and find God again, but now in human relationships, called the Divine Natural Humanity. James Sr had only a few followers, among them his sons, William and Henry. Corroborated by the late Max Fische, Charles Sanders Peirce, the founder of pragmatism, was another. Yet another was the Rev. Charles Holbrook Mann, rogue New Church minister, ardent disciple of James Sr's writings, and father of noted New York Jungian Kristine Mann, whose library forms the core of the C.G. Jung Center in New York City.

Further reading

Hebegger, A. *The Father: A Life of Henry James Sr.* New York: Farrar, Strauss, and Giroux, 1994.
James, H. *Lectures and Miscellanies.* Clinton Hall, NY: Redfield, 1852.
—— *The Church of Christ Not an Ecclesiasticism: A Letter of Remonstrance to a Member of the Soi-disant New Church.* London: William White, 1856.
—— *Christianity, the Logic of Creation.* London: William White, 1857.
—— *Substance and Shadow: Morality and Religion in their Relation to Life. An Essay on the Physics of Creation.* Boston, MA: Fields and Osgood, 1863.
—— *The Secret of Swedenborg: Being an Elucidation of his Doctrine of the Divine Natural Humanity.* Boston, MA: Fields and Osgood, 1869.
—— *Society, the Redeemed Form of Man and God's Omnipotence in Human Nature, Affirmed in Letters to a Friend.* Boston, MA: Houghton Mifflin, 1879.
James, William (ed.) *The Literary Remains of the Late Henry James.* Boston, MA: Houghton Mifflin, 1884.

EUGENE TAYLOR

JAMES, WILLIAM: INFLUENCE

William James was not a systematic philosopher and for this reason did not have followers who could bill themselves as Jamesians in the way in which there were, for example, Deweyites and Whiteheadians. Nevertheless, his influence was very extensive, both within and outside of philosophy, but it occurred on the retail level, doctrine by doctrine. Because this essay is doctrinally driven, it will not consider the astounding number of book-length accounts of James's philosophy that have appeared in recent years, with there being no end in sight. One of the reasons that James has been and continues to be a growth industry is that every major subsequent movement in philosophy can find its roots in his writings, his philosophy being a vast ocean out of which can be fished whatever the angler desires.

Religion

James's extensive writings on religion have had the deepest and most widespread influence of all his work. In his *The Varieties of Religious Experience*, which is his most beloved and widely read book (even Wittgenstein carried a copy of it with him during World War I), he defends the thesis that religious experience, especially of a mystical sort involving a complete or partial union with some higher spiritual power, is the essence and life-blood of religion. This has the ecumenical upshot of radically deemphasizing, maybe too much according to critics like John Smith, religious institutions and especially their exclusivist creeds that have proven to be a breeding ground for so much evil – holy wars, inquisitions, persecution, and intolerance. James's effort to find a vital common denominator of all religions, which he relegated to the "science of religion" in *Varieties,* helped to bring about, if only indirectly, the numerous contemporary efforts, most notably by John Hick, to find such an ecumenicalism.

In recent years William Alston, William Wainwright, Richard Swinburne, Gary Guting, Jerome Gellman, and Keith Yandell have defended the cognitivity of mystical experiences on the basis of their being analogous to ordinary sense experiences, which, admittedly, give evidence for the existence of their apparent object. Some of them, Alston for instance, rightly credit James as the source for this argument, since he treated mystical experiences in *Varieties* as perceptual and held that there are background tests, such as agreement among observers and coherence with subsequent experiences, such as favorable moral and spiritual growth by the subject as a result of the experience, for determining their veridicality that are analogues to those for sense experiences.

James's eloquent account of the religion of healthy-mindedness has been highly influential in subsequent religions based on positive thinking, as well as optimistic New World psychotherapy. This influence is found even in places in which one might not expect to find it. For example, Masaharu Taniguchi, the founder of Seich-No-le in Japan, who has 3,000,000 followers, often cites James as one of his major influences. James's doctrine of the will to believe, which licenses us to believe a proposition upon insufficient evidence when doing so will have desirable consequences, works hand in glove with the religion of healthy-mindedness since by getting ourselves to believe in the goodness of people and the universe, we can help to make good win out over evil in the long run. This doctrine continues to be hotly disputed. James's critics, such as Dickenson Miller, Bertrand Russell, and A.J. Ayer, think that allowing ourselves to acquire an evidentially nonwarranted belief is a betrayal of our duty to realize what is distinctive and best about us – our rationality. Some of these critics, such as Louis Pojman, implausibly try to make do with merely hoping in place of believing. If one agrees with James's trashing of natural theology, the only option for theists is to base their faith on a will-to-believe basis. James, along with Pascal and Kierkegaard, will continue to be the major inspiring forces behind this perennial pragmatic justification of faith.

Psychology

James's 1890 *The Principles of Psychology* attempted to make psychology into a legitimate natural science by bringing together all of the notable work by psychologists up to that date, a truly Herculean feat. On the one hand, its German-based emphasis on the need for laboratory controlled experiments had a strong influence on American psychologists, such as Munsterberg, Titchener, and Cattell, all of whom were critical of James's subsequent abandonment of clinical psychology in favor of paranormal psychology. There also was a strong physiological and neurological emphasis, as for example in its treatment of emotions, which is captured by the slogan "No psychosis without neurosis," which helped to spur behavioristic and neural scientific approaches to the mind. The most influential aspect of the book was its Darwinian-based functional view of the mind, which inspired Dewey and his Chicago school of psychology. Nothing came of the Deweyan functionalistic approach in psychology, no doubt because it was metaphysics posing as psychology. James's multi-dimensional approach has made him a man for all seasons, which explains why, in the words of George Miller, "even as the very definition of scientific psychology swung violently from functionalism to behaviorism and back to cognitivism, William James's *Principles of Psychology* has continued to hold a living place in everyone's thinking."

Pragmatism

James's pragmatic theory of meaning and truth based on the successful working of an idea had a cautionary influence on his fellow pragmatist John Dewey. There were passages in James that seemed to countenance psychological satisfactions as counting for the successful working of an idea. Dewey's account of the successful working of an idea in terms of its ability, when acted upon, to transform an indeterminate into a determinate situation was supposed to escape this unwanted subjectivism.

Dewey felt very much indebted to James's biological psychology for leading him out of his bondage in the dark land of Hegel and into the sunshine of the wonderful land of naturalism and attempted to repay this debt by passionately expounding and defending James's philosophy over a period of fifty-one years, extending from 1897 to 1948. Unfortunately, his account, although well intentioned, gave a blatantly distorted account that attempted to make James into a good naturalist like himself, thereby overlooking all of the mystical and spiritual aspects of James's philosophy. He also read into James's text a socializing of all things distinctly human, again remaking James in his own image.

Richard Rorty has perpetuated Dewey's legacy of giving distorted, self-serving accounts of James. In Rorty's case it is his attributing the same sort of deconstructionist proclivities to James that he rightly attributed to Dewey, at least when Dewey explicitly said what philosophy should be, though his practice as a philosopher was in sharp variance with this deconstructionism, as Rorty has correctly pointed out. Rorty claimed that "as long as we see James or Dewey as having 'theories of truth' or 'theories of knowledge' . . . we shall get them wrong." Instead, James had a "therapeutic conception of philosophy familiar from Wittgenstein's *Philosophical Investigations*" that showed us a way of avoiding the fruitlessness of doing philosophy in the traditional manner. *Pace* Rorty, James repeatedly claimed to have a theory or account of truth and even devoted an entire book, *The Meaning of Truth*, to expounding and defending it against criticisms.

The influence of James's pragmatism was also felt in Italy by a group in Florence led by Giovanni Papini that was known as "Leonardo." Papini's "*pragmatisi magica*" version of pragmatism stressed intoxication with the creative spirit. His take on James's account of what makes a "life worth living" is based on the heroic moments of one's life. This placed him in sympathy with a cult of violence and danger that favored revolution and dictatorship. In a 1926 interview, Mussolini named James, along with Nietzsche and Sorel, among his inspiring influences. According to Ralph Barton Perry,

> there can be no doubt of the broad fact that pragmatism and Fascism (as well as Bolshevism) held some ground in common . . . That [James] would have had the least sympathy with either Bolshevism or Fascism is unthinkable. We have to do, then, not with a coherent revolutionary philosophy of which James was the forerunner, but with a group of ideas and sentiments, shifting and often unrelated, which here and there overlap the ideas and sentiments of pragmatism.

James enjoyed considerable popularity in Russia prior to the Stalin era, influencing, among others, Maxim Gorky, Nikolai Berdyaev, Semyon Frank, and Lev Shestov. Some saw him as offering a third way between positivism and idealism. During the Stalin era, James, along with Dewey, was lampooned as being "the Wall Street pragmatist." In the *Great Soviet Encyclopedia*'s second edition he is said to be an "American reactionary philosopher and psychologist, ideologue of the imperialist bourgeoisie, one of the founders of the anti-scientific philosophy pragmatism, defender of religion ... James fully justified the expansionist plans of the American bourgeoisie, its fight against Socialism and the workers' movement." James became resurrected after the collapse of the Soviet Union in 1991, with new translations appearing of some of his important works. P.S. Gurevich claimed that the republication of James's *Varieties* helped Russians to reconnect with mysticism after decades of cultural isolation.

Phenomenology

James's chapter on "The Stream of Thought" in *The Principles of Psychology* exerted a strong influence on both the young Husserl and the later Wittgenstein. Husserl, in his *Logische Untersuchungen*, credits James with his being able to overcome psychologism, and, in *Krisis*, with supplying an accurate phenomenological description of the horizontal structure of consciousness based on its fringes, which is also developed in James's doctrine of the specious present. Of special importance to Husserl was James's development of Brentano's theory of the intentionality of consciousness. Bruce Wilshire makes this aspect of James the central feature in his account of how James's phenomenology distributed "consciousness across the face of the lived-world." John Wild's study on James's phenomenology makes use of a fuller range of James's philosophy and justifies classifying him as a phenomenologist because he was primarily interested in "mental phenomena and their patterns as we are directly familiar with them and live through them." Issues of *Philosophy and Phenomenological Research,* during the 1950s and 1960s, contains essays by Alfred Schutz, Herbert Spiegelberg, and Aron Gurwitsch that give a detailed account of James's influence on Husserl, stressing both the similarities and dissimilarities between them.

Process philosophy

James's phenomenological description of the stream of consciousness eventually blossomed into a full-scale process philosophy in his final two books, *A Pluralistic Universe* and *Some Problems of Philosophy.* Immediate temporal neighbors coalesce so that sharp numerical distinctions cannot be made between successive states in the stream of time (see the entry on "Relations"), this being the only way to escape Zeno's paradoxes. This spurred Dewey and Alfred North Whitehead to develop a similar type of process philosophy. In the Preface to his *Process and Reality,* Whitehead wrote, "I am also greatly indebted to Bergson, William James, and John Dewey. One of my preoccupations has been to rescue their type of thought from the charge of anti-intellectualism."

Wittgenstein

One of the most fascinating chapters in the history of philosophy concerns the deep influence, both positive and negative, that James had upon Wittgenstein. But the proper telling of it had to await the publication of Russell Goodman's *Wittgenstein and William James.* In the 1930s, when Wittgenstein was developing ideas that eventually turned into his *Philosophical Investigations*, the only philosophy book on Wittgenstein's bookshelves was *The Principles of Psychology.* There are numerous explicit and implicit references to James in the *Investigations.* James's subjective theory of meaning and, in particular, his commitment to an in principle private language, was Wittgenstein's declared polemical targets. James's "Principle of constancy in the mind's meaning" – that "the same matters can be thought of in successive portions of the mental stream, and some of these portions can know that they mean the same matters which the other portions meant" by the thinker intending that they do so – involves the use of a private rule, since no one other than the thinker can determine whether it is being correctly followed. Wittgenstein's famed private language argument attempts to discredit such a rule. But, as Goodman points out, it would be a mistake to surmise that James exerted only a negative influence on Wittgenstein, for they shared commitments: "to antifoundationalism, to the description of the concrete details of human life, to the priority of practice over intellect, and to the importance of religion in understanding human life."

Neutral monism

James's doctrine of "pure experience," subsequently called "neutral monism" by Bertrand Russell, held that reality is composed of percepts or pieces of pure experience that are neither intrinsically mental nor intrinsically physical but qualify as one or the other on the basis of what sort of a temporal succession of events they are placed in, a physical ordering being a law-like one whereas a mental ordering is rhapsodic and disjointed, memory being the glue that bundles the successive events together to form the history of a single mind. This, supposedly, eliminates the unbridgeable gap between the mind and the body, the mental and the physical, that had so tormented traditional epistemology. Bertrand Russell and Hilary Putnam have given sympathetic expositions of James's doctrine. Russell's major objection is that the doctrine is not true of every particular, since some are irreducibly mental, his favored example being facts reported through the use of "emphatic particulars" such as "now" and "here."

Ontological relativism

According to James there are many possible worlds, such as those composed of ordinary sensible objects, the theoretic entities of science, abstracta such as numbers and properties, mythical entities, supernatural beings, etc. No one of these worlds qualifies as the actual world simpliciter but acquires this coveted title only in relation to the passing interest of some subject. Nelson Goodman, in *Ways of Worldmaking,* makes explicit use of this Jamesian doctrine of ontological relativism. Putnam's "realism with a human face" also is indebted to James, because it denies that there is a ready-made reality that our true concepts must copy and instead holds that reality is what we make of it on the basis of the interest-based concepts that we adopt for the purpose of helping us to get around successfully in the world. Rudolf Carnap's distinction between "internal questions," which concern the existence of entities within a given world or linguistic framework, and "external questions," which concern which one of them to adopt, is another example of James's ontological relativism.

Further reading

Dewey, John. *The Collected Works of John Dewey. The Middle Works, Vol. 6 (1910–11)* and *The Later Works, Vol. 15 (1942–8)*, ed. Jo Ann Boydston. Carbondale, IL: Southern Illinois University Press (1976–91).

Donnelly, Margaret E. (ed.) *Reinterpreting the Legacy of William James.* Washington, DC: American Psychological Association, 1992.

Edie, James E. *William James and Phenomenology.* Bloomington, IN: Indiana University Press, 1987.

Goodman, Nelson. *Ways of World Making*. Indianapolis, IN: Hackett, 1978.

Goodman, Russell. *Wittgenstein and William James.* Cambridge: Cambridge University Press, 2002.

Grossman, Joan Delaney and Rischin, Ruth (eds) *William James in Russian Culture.* New York: Lexington Books, 2002.

Putnam, Hilary. *Realism with a Human Face.* Cambridge, MA: Harvard University Press, 1990.

Wild, John. *The Radical Empiricism of William James.* New York: Doubleday, 1969.

Wilshire, Bruce. *William James and Phenomenology.* Bloomington, IN: Indiana University Press, 1968.

Wittgenstein, Ludwig. *Philosophical Investigations.* Oxford: Blackwell, 1958.

RICHARD M. GALE

JAMES, WILLIAM: LIFE

William James (1842–1910) was born in New York City in 1842. His father's father had made a great deal of money, having, among other things, invested in the Erie Canal. James's father inherited a good deal of that money, and, due to an early physical accident where he was forced to have part of a leg amputated, spent his time doting on the education of his children, especially William and Henry. William traveled to Europe five times before he was twenty-one. He was fluent in French at fourteen and German by eighteen years of age. James initially wanted to be an artist, and showed some talent in that area, but this was not a vocation endorsed by his father. Indeed, James spent considerable time trying, with only limited success, to please his father. James did enter Harvard Medical School in 1864, receiving an MD in 1869 – the only degree received by the man subsequently called the "father" of American psychology, and who became one of the three great pragmatists in Philosophy. He was, in fact, a truly interdisciplinary thinker.

James's biography discloses a person who underwent several personal crises, including a threat of serious depression between 1868 and 1870. Never robust in health, he lost the use of his eyesight twice, suffered from insomnia and neurasthenia, and went through a serious personal conflict with nihilism in the late 1860s. *The Letters of William James*, edited later on by his son Henry, indicate this clearly. Writing to his father from Berlin on 5 September 1867, James wrote:

> Although I cannot say that I got low-spirited, yet thoughts of the pistol, the dagger and the bowl began to usurp an unduly large part of my attention, and I began to think that some change, even if a hazardous one, was necessary.

The *Letters* also indicate that this personal conflict with nihilism and subsequent temptation to despair continues into 1870, when James "touches bottom" in February. By April of that year, however, he had read the works of Charles Renouvier, and wrote in his diary:

> I think that yesterday was a crisis in my life. I finished the second part of Renouvier's second "Essais," and see no reason why his definition of Free Will – "the sustaining of a thought *because I choose* to when I might have other thoughts" – need be the definition of an illusion. . . . My first act of free will shall be to believe in free will.

In other words, James realized that he could marshal an argument for freedom and one for determinism. Both arguments are coherent and correspond to some available data. The issue is "vague" or ambiguous, and because of this very vagueness or ambiguity, James is compelled to commit himself, to take a stand. This personal or existential experience of the vague receives its textual equivalent some twenty-six years later, in an essay by James entitled "The Will to Believe," where James argues that there are some situations in life where the options are "forced, living, and momentous," thereby compelling us to respond – to "leap," as it were. These issues are not confined to the so-call "soft" or personal areas of morals and religion. They ultimately apply to one's entire metaphysical outlook. Being, or existence, in other words, is not a "problem" to be solved but rather "attested to." Finally, James's own writing, i.e. his works, constitute his own personal exercise of the will to believe. He would "save himself" through his writing. It was a way of proving that he existed, or "made a difference."

Having overcome the worst moments of his state of depression by the early 1870s, James taught a course in Physiology at Harvard in 1873 – thus beginning his lifelong career as a professor. He taught the first modern psychology course there in 1875, and was appointed full time as an assistant professor of physiology in 1876. In July of 1878, he married Alice Howe Gibbens, and also signed a contract with Henry Holt to write *The Principles of Psychology* (1890). This was supposed to take two years to complete, but it actually took twelve. When it was published, it assured James's international reputation. A briefer version, consisting of one volume, was published as a textbook in 1892.

In the meantime, James had taught his first course in Philosophy in 1879, and also published an important essay entitled "The Sentiment of Rationality" in that year. He continued to travel extensively to Europe, but also purchased a summer home in Chocorua, New Hampshire, in 1886.

Many of James's most philosophical texts were published in the latter part of his life, although a neat division cannot be set up between his philosophical and psychological works. *Talks to Teachers on Psychology and to Students on Some of Life's Ideals* was published in 1899. *The Will to Believe and Other Essays in Popular Psychology* had been published in 1897. James's religious interests, especially in mysticism, were apparent in the Gifford Lectures he gave at Edinburgh in 1901–2, published as *The Varieties of Religious Experience.* His most complete metaphysical efforts are contained in two volumes: *Essays in Radical Empiricism*, containing several articles published in 1904–5, was published posthumously in book form 1912. Second, *A Pluralistic Universe*, published in 1909, consisted of the Hibbert Lectures given at Manchester College on "the Present Situation in Philosophy." Finally, on the epistemological level, *Pragmatism*, a series of lectures given at the Lowell Institute, again at Columbia University, was published in 1907. *The Meaning of Truth*, an attempt to explicate and correct some misunderstandings of pragmatism, was published in 1909. James's last major work was entitled *Some Problems in Philosophy.* It was published in 1911, and James saw it as "the beginning of an introduction to Philosophy." In a way, he seemed unwilling or unable to "sum up" the universe once and for all in language. Once again, it was a case of "life exceeding logic."

James had tried several times to resign from teaching at Harvard, but each time his resignation was refused. He was, by then, too famous to be let go. He finally managed to resign from teaching in 1907. James died at his summer home on 26 August as a result of angina problems. He had injured his heart badly while climbing in the mountains (Adirondacks) of New York in 1898 and again in 1899.

In sum, James's writing is his own form of exercising "the will to believe." His text is his own form of continuing the personal choice made in 1868. "Writing the text" is keeping the faith, so to speak. For us readers, his texts exist as an invitation or a spur; they are "directional" in nature, and they point beyond themselves, back to the world of "lived experience," where the reader can try them out to see if they "make a difference," pragmatically speaking.

Further reading

Allen, Gay Wilson. *William James, A Biography.* New York: Viking, 1967.

Gavin, William Joseph. *William James and the Reinstatement of the Vague.* Philadelphia, PA: Temple University Press, 1992.

James, Henry (ed.) *The Letters of William James*, 2 vols. Boston, MA: Atlantic Monthly Press, 1920.

Myers, Gerald. *William James, His Life and Thought*. New Haven, CT: Yale University Press, 1986.
Simon, Linda. *Genuine Reality, A Life of William James*. New York: Harcourt, Brace, 1998.

William J. Gavin

JAMES, WILLIAM: PRAGMATISM

The accessible, vivid and picturesque writings of William James (1842–1910) made him the popular and prominent spokesperson of the classical American philosophy of pragmatism. James popularized a technical philosophical position that was first articulated by C.S. Peirce (1839–1914) and that was later made expansive and systematic by John Dewey (1859–1952). *Pragmatism* (1907), James's most influential work, was a reprinting of a series of public lectures which, as he notes in the Preface of the book, "were delivered at the Lowell Institute in Boston in November and December, 1906 and in January, 1907, at Columbia University, in New York. They are printed as delivered, without developments or notes." There is little doubt that James's lectures captured the attention of his audience, illuminating his first listeners and subsequently generations of readers of *Pragmatism.* (The book has never gone out of print.) But the flamboyant and breezy flair of his remarks left little room for technical precision, rigor or careful distinctions with an eye to strict consistency. Predictably, then, *Pragmatism* generated considerable heat among professional philosophers who pressed James to address the ambiguities, confusions, contradictions and fallacies that they thought they found in his lectures. For example, A.O. Lovejoy counted thirteen pragmatisms in James's volume. Responses from the British philosophers G.E. Moore and Bertrand Russell were especially vigorous. Rejoinders to logical technicalities and responses by way of semantic niceties were not a priority for James. Instead, he remained adamant that his calling was to respond to a general audience of men and women who were understandably concerned with the inroads that science and the rise of Darwinism seemed to be making on the secure place that religion, free will and personal responsibility had had in the traditional wisdom regarding the significance and meaning of human lives. James's training in science, along with his own long-standing interest in the perennial, big-picture concerns of philosophy, made him the ideal candidate to mediate between the apparently incompatible claims of philosophy and science.

Early on, James was interested in art and anatomy. At nineteen he enrolled in the Lawrence Scientific School and, three years later, the Harvard School of Medicine. His medical studies were briefly interrupted when he joined a scientific expedition to Brazil led by Louis Agassiz (the leading biologist of the day) to collect zoological specimens. James passed his MD exams in 1869 and began teaching at Harvard, first in anatomy and comparative physiology and then in psychology, leading to the publication of *The Principles of Psychology* in 1890. Gradually James thought of himself primarily as a philosopher, and he delved into ethical and religious issues, culminating in the publication of *The Will to Believe and Other Essays in Popular Philosophy* (note the second half of his title) in 1896, whence he paid even more attention to epistemology and metaphysics, resulting in the appearance of *Pragmatism* and then, in 1909, *The Meaning of Truth* and *Essays in Radical Empiricism.* Both the public and his fellow philosophers paid attention to all of James's works, and even though his *magnum opus* is *The Principles of Psychology*, *Pragmatism* is his important book.

The tasks that James took upon himself in the eight lectures that make up *Pragmatism* were bold and comprehensive: laying out pragmatic theories of meaning and truth and then applying those theories to many of the vexing and perennially significant issues that thoughtful humans confront, notably free will vs determinism, personal identity, immortality, divine creation and providence vs chance and idealism vs materialism.

James begins by proposing pragmatism as a theory of meaning, offering it as a method for determining the "practical cash-value" (32) of beliefs. His recommendation is to translate the meaning of an idea into its practical consequences:

> What difference would it practically make to anyone if this notion rather than that notion were true? If no practical difference whatever can be traced, then the alternatives mean practically the same thing, and all dispute is idle. Whenever a dispute is serious, we ought to be able to show some practical difference that must follow from one side or the other's being right.
>
> (28)

A strenuous application of this procedure has striking and significant results. Some interminable philosophical disputes are set aside because no difference in practice accrues to them and, when examined concretely, other pairs of positions long thought to be contrary will be shown to prompt identical conduct. The remaining real controversies comprise the agenda for philosophers. Accordingly, pragmatism, as a theory of meaning, serves as a sorting mechanism to generate a roster of disputes whose meanings make measurable and practical differences in human lives.

Once we are clear about what a belief means, that is, the behavior that it prompts, we can pragmatically test its truth. Since true beliefs lead to fruitful interactions with reality and false beliefs bring frustration, assessing the success or failure of our actions is, for James, determining their truth or falsity.

James, and pragmatists in general, challenge the traditional view that ideas duplicate, correspond with or agree with reality. In addition, pragmatism dismisses the contention that Truth is a single, complete and unchanging copy of a fixed, permanent and independent Reality. James begins Lecture VII, "Pragmatism and Humanism," by noting that

> what hardens the heart of everyone I approach with the [pragmatic] view of truth … is that typical idol of the tribe, the notion of *the* Truth, conceived as one answer, determinate and complete, to the one fixed enigma which the world is believe to propound.
>
> (115)

Pragmatism, heavily influenced by the natural sciences, is content with the modest task of generating testable and revisable philosophical claims. In Lecture II, "What Pragmatism Means," James comments:

> But as the sciences have developed farther, the notions has gained ground that most, perhaps all, of our laws are only approximations … investigators have become accustomed to the notion that no theory is absolutely a transcript of reality, but that any one of them may be from some point of view useful.
>
> (33)

While James's recasting philosophy as a practical endeavor is, paradoxically, both revolutionary and non-controversial, his redefinition of truth and his relocating it as "*one species of good*" (42) is, ironically, both radical and plausible. The compelling force of James's pragmatic theories of meaning and truth can be efficiently conveyed by way of an uncomplicated simile: ideas functions as maps. Consider ideas as trustworthy tools that facilitate our living with and within an environment. Thus understood, ideas neither duplicate nor picture external reality; instead, they (like maps) guide us. Maps are extraordinarily compact digests of past experiences that literally lead us. Reliable ones get us to our destination; faulty ones get us lost. Recall James's relocation of truth under the good; it is both telling and appropriate that we call maps good or bad, instead of true or false. And so, too, James asserts that true ideas help us and false ideas hinder us.

James's explication of the pragmatic theories of meaning and truth is the central concern of Lecture II: "What Pragmatism Means" and the lectures that follow apply these theories to standard philosophical problems. For instance, Lecture III: "Some Metaphysical Problems Pragmatically Considered" begins with the sorting exercise noted above, seeking whether the difference between free will and determinism is merely semantic or theoretical or whether it is a "genuine metaphysical debate [involving] some practical issue" (52). James explains that "free-will pragmatically means *novelties* … [so] the future may not identically repeat and imitate the past" (60) while determinism "assures us … that necessity and impossibility between them rule the destinies of the world" (61). Having pointed out the vast attitudinal and behavioral differences between the two beliefs, James leaves it to his listener/reader to assess which belief has superior benefit for life. This last point is crucial. James does not prove the existence of free will or determinism; his interest is in seeing what is at stake in the controversy and thereafter appraising the costs and benefits of believing (that is, of acting) one way or the other.

Many of James's critics and some readers with traditional expectations about the nature of philosophy find the analyses in *Pragmatism* incomplete and inconclusive. For example, in an especially memorable examination of whether God exists or not, James contends that, pragmatically speaking, belief in God gives us "a right ever and anon to take a moral holiday, to let the world wag in its own way, feeling that its issues are in better hands than ours" (41). Note that James does not address whether God exists, but whether it is beneficial for humans to believe that He does. In effect, James has turned a classical philosophical question about the nature of reality into a modest and tractable query dealing with what is meaningful for humans. Pragmatic philosophy thus understood recasts the renaissance philosophy of humanism. Recalling the subtitle that James gave *Pragmatism*, even while many find it *the* distinctively American philosophy, it is also "A New Name for Some Old Ways of Thinking."

Further reading

Dooley, Patrick K. *Pragmatism as Humanism: The Philosophy of William James.* Chicago, IL: Nelson-Hall, 1974.

James, William. *Pragmatism.* Cambridge, MA: Harvard University Press, 1975 [1907].

Lovejoy, A.O. "The Thirteen Pragmatisms," *Journal of Philosophy* 5 (1908): 5–12, 29–39.

Moore, G.E. "Professor James' 'Pragmatism'," *Proceedings of the Aristotelian Society* 8 (1907–8): 22–77.

Russell, Bertrand. "Pragmatism," *Edinburgh Review* 209 (1909): 363–88.

Suckiel, Ellen Kappy. *The Pragmatic Philosophy of William James.* Notre Dame, IN: Notre Dame University Press, 1987.

PATRICK K. DOOLEY

JAMES, WILLIAM: PSYCHOLOGY

William James was one of the founders of psychology in the late nineteenth century. James's psychology appears primarily in *The Principles of Psychology* (James 1890/1950). This brought together German experiments on sensory perception, French research on psychpathology, British associationist psychology, and much of what was known of neurological structure and function. In forging the new discipline James faced a central issue in the tension between mechanistic and voluntaristic accounts of mental life. This issue appeared in many guises: in the relation of mind and matter, free will and determinism, individual uniqueness and scientific uniformity, among others. It was also evident in conflict between associationist theories of mind drawn from British empiricism, and "spiritualistic" theories deriving from German idealism. James felt this tension particularly acutely himself, it being the central motif in all of his work (Dewey 1946). Nonetheless, James adopted a fruitful method, which was to adopt strict mechanism provisionally and seek modifications when it came up short.

Evolutionary model

The inspiration for a middle way between mechanism without purpose and purpose without mechanism came from evolutionary theory. If human mental abilities evolved naturally, then consciousness is likely to be of adaptive utility, and not a mere epiphenomenon of mechanical action. It must be an active "fighter for ends," and not a mere passive spectator, contra the associationists. On the other hand, it must also be adapted to the specific features of this world, contrary to the abstract conceptions of the ego of the idealists. The notion that "consciousness" is a functional activity rather than a spectator or inner entity was the core premise of philosophical pragmatism and functional psychology.

The reflex arc

If the Darwinian organism provided a metaphor, the "reflex arc" provided a structure. It had been found that the nervous system is organized such that sensory neurons carry electrical signals into the spinal cord from one side and motor neurons carry them out from the other (the "Bell–Magendie law"). The spinal cord, in turn, carries sensory impulses up to the brain and from there back down to motor centers. This suggested that a model of "reflex action" based on a linear sequence of sensory input, central reflective process, and motor response, could describe both neurophysiological structure and mental function (James 1892: 7). Using this model, matter and mind could be given parallel description.

This model appeared to be entirely deterministic: given a stimulus the response is "fatally" determined. However, organisms differ in the kinds of "objects" to which they respond, some responding only to immediately present objects, while others, like humans, responding to spatially and temporally distant objects. James argued that such differences are "only a difference in degree" that "does not change the reflex type" (James 1892: 101).

What made such different forms of behavior possible is the fact that the nervous system is organized in a hierarchy such that higher level centers, like the cerebral hemispheres, modulate the behavior of those at a lower level, sampling sensory input from them and sending "orders" back down. Such higher-level centers function as "an organ added for the sake of steering a nervous system grown too complex to regulate itself" (James 1890/1952: 94). James argued that each "level" also exhibits its own implicit preferences, some preference being necessary in mental or intelligent behavior, whose "characteristic feature" is selection of means for future ends (James 1890/1952: 5–7). Since all the nervous centers have one essential function, intelligent action, "they feel, prefer one thing to another, and have 'ends'" (James 1890/1952: 51).

The effect of this analysis was to break down the dichotomy between mechanistic and voluntaristic accounts. If lower centers respond to immediately present objects, while higher centers use more complex "considerations" to respond to those that are spatially or temporally distant, then immediate determinism becomes a matter of degree. Similarly, if every level has its own implicit preferences, then he stark contrast between machinery without purpose versus purpose without machinery is softened.

Habit

James saw habit as a mechanized form of behavior that helps free conscious attention for other tasks. Habit is simply a name for the fact that organic materials are to some degree "plastic," their structure being affected by repetitive use the way a book is affected by being frequently opened to the same page. The underlying cause of "habit" is the plasticity of the brain that allows a "new pathway of discharge" to be formed (James 1892: 134).

While James's treatment of habit was quite conventional, two aspects of his treatment related to the determinism/voluntarism contrast. In habitual behavior each response creates conditions that sensed by the next habitual response. Thus "processes of inattentive feeling" go on along side of more conscious intellectual processes (ibid.: 142). In other words, there is "feeling" or implicit preference even in the most mechanical forms of behavior.

The stream of consciousness

James's chapter on conscious thought, his most famous, was also an attempt to find a *via media* between the naturalistic but passive psychology of the associationists and the active but unnatural psychology of the idealists. The problem was to find an account of the experience of conscious thinking that does not divide it into artificial bits or presuppose an inner ego to do the thinking.

James tackled this problem by proposing a dynamic rather than static model of thinking. A thought is like a "wave" or "pulse" in a succession of waves or pulses characterizing a dynamic process (presumably oscillations in the cerebral hemispheres). Thought of a given object may be relatively stable, like a standing wave, while thinking searching for its object may be relatively unstable. Thus thinking flies like a bird from relatively stable "perches," through unstable "flights," to other "perches."

This metaphor gave James a way of conceiving of thoughts as individually unique waveforms, each a complex whole, though possibly about the same object, unlike the assembled fragments posited in associationistic theory. It also gave a way of bringing relationships into experience without positing an inner ego to do the relating. Since each waxing or waning wave of thought is part of the same dynamic process, each has components of those coming before and after in its form. These resonances give feelings of relationship, much as an utterance's tone unites it dramatically with what comes next. Each thought also comes with a "fringe" of related thoughts that are part of the same process. As a result, distinctions between objects are relative rather than absolute, and structured anticipation is possible without positing a fixed inner schema. One sees in this account the seeds of James's later "radical empiricism" (James 1971).

The self

James viewed the "self," a further control process involving knowledge of one's own interests, as a reflective process rather than a thing. Since self-consciousness involves an implicit knower and object known it must have two aspects or phases. But how can one know about one's self without a knower existing inside to do the knowing? And how can successive thoughts be had by the "same" knower without a substantial ego inside that remains the same? James appealed to his dynamic wave model to solve these riddles. Each thought could know a prior thought because its dying ripples continued in the present thought's form. Successive thoughts could also be felt to be part of the "same" self because of emotional feelings of affinity among them. Each, in effect, "greets" the next, "saying: 'Thou art mine, and part of the same self as me'" (James 1892: 204). What makes a "self" seem to be the "same" over time, even while the person changes, is the fact that this process has intrinsic continuity. As James concluded, "in this book the provisional solution which we have reached must be the final word: the thoughts themselves are the thinker" (ibid.: 216).

Emotion

His theory of emotion, which nears the overt response phase of the sequence, was also quite influential. The conventional view of emotion was that perception of an "exciting" object causes an inner emotional feeling, which in turn causes a visible bodily response. This was Darwin's account when he argued that expressive behavior, like a dog's baring its teeth, was originally simply a preparatory phase of biting that over time gained the new function of "expressing" emotion to other animals (Darwin 1889/1904).

The philosophical problem with this account is that it takes a description of a form of behavior, "anger," and turns that description into a reified inner entity that is presumed to the same behavior. It also makes emotional expression a form of show or pretense. James argued that it could be corrected by reversing the causal sequence:

> My theory, on the contrary, is that the bodily changes follow directly the perception of the exciting fact, and that our feeling of the same changes as they occur IS the emotion ... the more rational statement is that we feel sorry because we cry, angry because we strike, afraid because we tremble.
>
> (James 1892: 375–6

Will

Tensions between freedom and determinism came to a head in James's discussion of conation or "will." Here he argued that there is no such thing as "freedom" from a scientific standpoint. The closest one can get to it is the notion of "chance." Assuming that the universe is not a tightly coupled whole one set of events may happen independently of another, at least for all practical purposes. This was the essence of Darwinian theory – that variation and environmental are independent of one another. In similar fashion, James argued that the complex oscillations in the cerebral hemispheres involved in thinking have considerable independence from the immediate environment. The chance responses they introduce relative to blind, deterministic habit correspond to all that "free will" can possibly mean, interpreted scientifically. James did not think the scientific interpretation the ultimate one, however. An interpretation emphasizing free will was equally valid, and more so when it comes to making moral decisions. Interpreted from an inner, subjective standpoint, will is a process of voluntary, effortful, attention. It occurs when the mind cannot sustain a constant focus of attention, and has to be brought back to it intentionally time and again. The resulting feeling of inner mental effort is what we call "will."

Conclusions

James accepted a deterministic reflex arc model as the basis for his psychology, but only provisionally, his commitment to voluntarism and moral agency leading him to chip away at it. At the same time he also proposed possible mechanisms whose dynamics might account for aspects of voluntaristic behavior. The resulting model suggested a number of ways in which an organism's activity affects the stimulations to which it responds.

Habitual responses are constructed through unconscious sensory feelings or "preferences." Cognitive processes selectively attune the organism to different sensory inputs. Feelings of relationship, flow, and development lead to sequential thoughts or arguments being accepted as "rational." Processes of voluntary attention, evidently related to self-consciousness awareness of interest, further select aspects of stimulation to which response is made. And emotional bodily reactions create emotional feelings, which affect conscious interest and attention.

Despite this emphasis on inner activity, the reflex model tended to presuppose a given environment to which the organism passively adapts. Dewey subsequently suggested a correction to this view, noting that organisms alter their environments rather than merely adapting to them (Dewey 1896). Thus organism–environment dynamics need to be considered as well, and not merely cerebral and bodily dynamics. Recent work in evolutionary theory suggests a similar correction to the classical adaptationist view is needed (Odling-Smee *et al.* 2003).

Despite this limitation, James's approach was highly productive (Allport 1968) and humbly aware of its own limitations. In James's approach all viewpoints are partial and provisional. The attempt to resolve conflicts between them is the job of metaphysics, but that, too, must inevitably be partial and provisional – James's own metaphysics suggested (James 1971).

Further reading

Allport, G.W. "Traits Revisited" in *The Person in Psychology.* Boston, MA: Beacon Press, 1968, pp. 43–80.

Clark, A. *Being There: Putting Brain, Body and World Together Again.* Cambridge, MA: MIT Press, 1997.

Darwin, C. *The Expression of the Emotions in Man and Animals.* London: John Murray, 1889/1904.

Dewey, J. "The Philosophy of William James" in *Problems of Men.* New York: Philosophical Library, 1946, pp. 379–95.

Gobar, A. "The Phenomenology of William James," *American Philosophical Society* 114, 4 (1970): 294–309.

James, W. *The Principles of Psychology*, New York: Dover, 1890/1950.

—— *Psychology: Briefer Course.* New York: Henry Holt, 1892.

—— *Talks to Teachers on Psychology: And to Students on Some of Life's Ideals.* New York: W.W. Norton, 1899/1958.

—— *Essays in Radical Empiricism and A Pluralistic Universe.* New York: E.P. Dutton, 1971.

Odling-Smee, F.J., Laland, K.N., and Feldman, M.W. *Niche Construction: The Neglected Process in Evolution.* Princeton, NJ: Princeton University Press, 2003.

Powers, W.T. *Making Sense of Behavior.* New Canaan, CT: Benchmark Publications, 1998.

Reed, E.S. "The Fringing Reef: Applying Darwin to the Mind," *Times Literary Supplement* 6 December (1996), p. 6.

ERIC BREDO

JAMES, WILLIAM: RADICAL EMPIRICISM

For William James, "radical empiricism" functions as both the limiting feature of and a liberating approach to philosophical discourse. His first overt discussion of radical empiricism appears in his introduction to his collection *The Will to Believe and Other Essays* (1897). Therein James calls radical empiricism an empirically minded "attitude" that concerns the hypothetical nature of conclusive judgments which must respond to experience itself. He qualifies this empiricism as radical,

> because it treats the doctrine of monism itself as an hypothesis, and, unlike so much of the half-way empiricism that is current under the name of positivism and agnosticism or scientific naturalism, it does not dogmatically affirm monism as something with which all experience has got to square.
>
> (1979 [1897]: 5)

For James, the radically empirical attitude undermines the "intellectualism" of both traditional "rationalism" and "empiricism" that demand that "evidence" be had before belief (or "faith") is warranted. This intellectualism "is the belief that our mind comes upon a world complete in itself and has the duty of ascertaining the world's contents; but has no power of re-determining its character, for that is already given" (1979 [1911]: 111). Instead, James insists on a melioristic alternative where "work is still doing in the world-process, and that in that work we are called to bear our share. The character of the world's results may in part depend upon our acts" (1979 [1911]: 112). Radical empiricism, then, is just this "melioristic" alternative to both traditional empiricism and rationalism.

However, radical empiricism mediates more than just the philosophical debate between empiricists and rationalists. James understands "radical empiricism" to be a meliorist position that attempts to steer between the conflicting elements of life itself. Thus, radical empiricism, though metaphysically pregnant, is ultimately a deep human psychological and philosophical commitment to two claims: (1) one must not deny anything that is experienced; and (2) one must not deny the potency of human action.

On the latter, James insists that experience, his own "radical empiricism," and, for that matter, philosophy itself demand connection to human activity, pursuit, even courage. Mere speculation, bare theory, simple words, which ground much of so-called "intellectualism," cannot meet the conditions of human living. James's commitment to experience is evident in a later definition he offers of radical empiricism:

> To be radical, an empiricism must neither admit into its constructions any element that is not directly experienced, nor exclude from them any element that is directly experienced. For such a philosophy, *the relations that connect experiences must themselves be experienced relations, and any kind of relation experienced must be accounted as "real" as anything else in the system.* Elements may indeed be redistributed, the original placing of things getting corrected, but a real place must be found for every kind of thing experienced, whether term or relation, in the final philosophic arrangement.
>
> (1976 [1912]: 22)

To put this view in philosophical context, the history of modern Western thought can be viewed as a debate between two metaphysical and epistemological positions. On the one hand rationalism argues that the most basic stuff is spiritual or mental in nature, and that experience is the rational operation of a mind that is prior to and necessary for the possibility of experience. In contrast, empiricists believe that we have to start from experience itself. So, whereas Descartes argued that our perceptions only serve to implicate a mind that perceives, empiricists believe that perceptions tell us little if anything about what perceives, but about perceptions themselves. This is most evident in the philosophy of David Hume whose empiricism takes a skeptical turn on the very possibility of the perceiving self. In fact, for Hume perceptions are so discrete that even the acceptance of causal relations is a "fiction" of the imagination. The most that we can say about how (or if) our impressions hang together is that there seems to be a relation of "constant conjunction" for some parts of our experience. This take on experience, a direct outcome of the path begun by John Locke and carried forth by George Berkeley, had uncomfortable consequences for many philosophers.

With the empiricists before him, then, James insists that experience is all we have and that no ability to "get behind" or "beyond" experience is possible. As such, we can only start from experience as we find it – namely, in its rich plurality. Unlike those same empiricists, however, James does not believe that experience reduces to atomic sensations, and thus makes no room for the experience of relations themselves. Instead, James insists that a commitment to radical empiricism demands that we recognize as "real" any experienced relation. Such a commitment, then, not only undermines atomic empiricism, it need not rely on any idealist's notion of a transcendental metaphysic either. Simply put, relations as part of experience need no extra-experiential apparatus to support them.

A final definitive account of "radical empiricism" solidifies this commitment.

> Radical empiricism consists first of a postulate, next a statement of fact, and finally of a general conclusion.
>
> The postulate is that the only things that shall be debatable among philosophers shall be things definable in terms drawn from experience . . .
>
> The statement of fact is that the relations between things, conjunctive as well as disjunctive, are just as much matters of direct particular experience, neither more so nor less so, than the things themselves.

> The generalized conclusion is that therefore the parts of experience hold together from next to next by relations that are themselves parts of experience. The directly apprehended universe needs, in short, no extraneous trans-empirical connective support, but possesses in its own right a concatenated or continuous structure.
>
> (1975 [1909]: 6–7)

James postulates that only and all experience matters to philosophy, and any/every experience is real in so far as it is experienced. James's radical empiricism establishes an attitude, an approach to philosophy writ large. Once such a vision of philosophy is postulated, a "fact" about experience itself is put forth – namely, the "parts" of experience include both "disjunctive" *and* "conjunctive" elements – and this "fact" leads to the "conclusion" that while experience is individuateable, it is also constitutively self-supporting in and through its content. Ours, accordingly, is a "pluralistic universe," but rather than merely consisting of atomic sensations (as Hume argued), James claims this plurality includes the connections among sensations as well.

Further reading

Berkeley, George. *A Treatise Concerning the Principles of Human Knowledge*, ed. C.M. Turbayne. Indianapolis, IN: Bobbs-Merrill, 1957 [1710].

Descartes, René. *Meditations on First Philosophy* in *The Philosophical Writings of Descartes*, Vol. II, ed. J. Cottingham, R. Stoothoff, A. Kenny and D. Murdoch. Cambridge: Cambridge University Press, 1948 [1641].

Hume, David. *A Treatise on Human Nature*, second edition, ed. P.H. Nidditch. Oxford: Clarendon Press, 1978 [1740].

James, William. *Will to Believe and Other Essays*. Cambridge, MA: Harvard University Press, 1979 [1897].

—— *The Meaning of Truth*. Cambridge, MA: Harvard University Press, 1975 [1909].

—— *A Pluralistic Universe*. Cambridge, MA: Harvard University Press, 1977 [1909].

—— *Essays in Radical Empiricism*. Cambridge, MA: Harvard University Press, 1976 [1912].

Locke, John. *An Essay Concerning Human Understanding*, ed. P.H. Nidditch. Oxford: Clarendon Press, 1975 [1689].

D. Micah Hester

JAMES, WILLIAM: RELIGION

William James was one of the founders of the psychology of religion. Fascinated by individual religious experience, he was one of the first to study it systematically. His classifications of the various types of religious experiences have been very influential in the study of religion.

In an age when many scientists and other scholars were extremely critical of religion, James defended the right of individuals to believe in religion and documented the value of religious experience for human flourishing. While he himself was not a member of a church, found prayer impossible, and claimed to be an outsider in the study of the most profound types of religious experience, he was very respectful of religion. He was strongly influenced by his father Henry James, who was a deeply religious, free-thinking theologian. William James himself was for many years a regular attendee of the Harvard chapel services, and he has left behind accounts of a few very meaningful religious experiences he had. Toward the end of his life, he articulated what he called his "overbeliefs" about religion – his personal views on God and on the relation between God and humankind.

"The Will to Believe"

In an essay called "The Will to Believe," which he first published in 1896, James defended the right of individuals to believe in the truth of religion. While some of James's fellow scientists argued that it is wrong to believe in religion since no one has sufficient evidence for doing so, James responded that religion belongs to a class of beliefs about which we must decide on non-evidentiary grounds. James pointed out that to require agnosticism in the face of our intellectual inability to prove religion true or false is practically the same as requiring atheism. This is because the consequences of remaining agnostic about religion are, in the practical realm, nearly the same as rejecting it. Agnostics, James argued, are unlikely to hold religious beliefs or to engage in religious practices; thus, they will not be in a position to reap (either in the present or in the future) any potential benefits from these beliefs and practices.

James's critics argued that his position opened the way for irresponsible beliefs in all kinds of things. Some even suggested he should have titled his essay "The Wish to Believe" or "The Will to Make-Believe." They contended that his argument could be used to defend any religious belief – no matter how outlandish – so long as it would have practical consequences if it *were* true.

The Varieties of Religious Experience

James elaborated his position further in the prestigious Gifford Lectures he was invited to give at the University of Edinburgh in 1901 and 1902. Published in book form under the title *The Varieties of Religious Experience*, these lectures have become a foundational classic in the psychology of religion.

James here argued that there are three criteria we use to judge the value of religious beliefs and experiences: immediate luminousness (how they make us feel in the moment), philosophical reasonableness (how well they connect with other things we hold to be true) and moral helpfulness (how well they address our moral needs). For James, outlandish religious beliefs should be held in check by noting their incommensurability with other beliefs we hold to be true.

James's larger aim in *Varieties* was to examine different types of religious experiences. For the purposes of his lectures, he gave a provisional definition of religion as "the feelings, acts, and experiences, of individual men in their solitude, so far as they apprehend themselves to stand in relation to whatever they may consider the divine" (p. 34, italics deleted). James proposed to focus on the experiences of those he called "religious geniuses," since he believed their religious experiences would be more extreme and easier to study. Furthermore, James believed that the experiences of religious geniuses are primary and that churches and theologies are secondary developments based on these experiences.

James made a distinction between morality and religion, where morality is based on self-sufficiency and religion is based on self-surrender. While moralists emphasize the importance of voluntary human effort, religionists emphasize the importance of surrendering the will. James argued that this surrendering of the will takes different forms, depending on the temperament of the religionist. He distinguished between "healthy-minded" and "sick-souled" religious persons and argued that they need different types of religions. On his definition, healthy-minded persons believe that the world is basically good; such persons need religions like New Thought or Mind Cure (or more contemporarily, Norman Vincent Peale's "power of positive thinking") to help them maintain and live out that belief. Sick-souled persons, by contrast, see evil to be an essential part of the world. Such persons may well turn to the more traditional world religions like Buddhism, Hinduism, Islam, and Christianity for help in finding ways to triumph over this evil, even if it cannot be completely eliminated.

In spite of the different mind-sets of healthy-minded and sick-souled religions, James pointed out similarities in the religious experiences to which they lead. Both healthy-minded and sick-souled persons can experience religious conversions. James was careful to point out that not all religious people seem temperamentally capable of experiencing a conversion and that persons who have had such an experience are not necessarily better off psychologically or religiously than those who have not had them. He did note, however, that converted persons seem to be better off than they were prior to conversion. He concluded that, for those who are susceptible to them, conversions seem to be a good thing, but that – at least for many people – moral and religious development can take place without them.

James noted that saintliness and mysticism seem to be commonalities across religions. While saints and mystics sometimes go to pathological extremes that vitiate the moral usefulness of their experiences, beliefs, and behaviors, for the most part saintliness seems to lead to exemplary moral living and mysticism leads to deep moral conviction.

James was critical of the role philosophy typically plays in religion, pointing out that it encourages the development of elaborate systematic theologies that often seem very disconnected from the practical domain of human experience and conduct. He suggested that philosophy can make itself useful to religion, not by encouraging the development of elaborate theologies, but by establishing a "science of religions." Philosophy would not then provide the foundation for religious beliefs; instead, it would help prune the religious beliefs that naturally grow up out of concrete religious experience. It would help make sure these beliefs are formulated in such a way that they are as consonant with science and as morally useful as possible. Although James admitted that this would not prove the truth of religion, he argued that it would take away inessential elements of religions that oftentimes constitute obstacles to their acceptance.

While *Varieties* has been enormously influential in the study of religion, it is also open to criticism. One key criticism is the degree to which James relied on the individual experiences of religious geniuses. His dismissal of ecclesiastical experiences as secondary downplays the fact that most religious geniuses have been deeply influenced by careful religious training prior to having their own experiences. Furthermore, corporate religious experience seems both important and significantly different from individual religious experience.

Pragmatism and *A Pluralistic Universe*

James was also interested in the scientific study of psychical experience. He served as the president of the Society for Psychical Research and was instrumental in the founding of the American Society for Psychical Research. The aim of these societies was to investigate claims to the paranormal by using rigorous, scientific methods.

In his later writings, James spent more time going beyond an examination of religious and psychical experience to the articulation of some of his own personal beliefs about religious truths. He was critical of theological and philosophical views that made God too big and abstract to be of concrete relevance in the world of everyday experience. Instead of accepting the God of scholastic theology or the Absolute of Hegelian philosophy, that are represented as guaranteeing the final salvation of the world, James preferred what he believed was a more realistic, if less stable, view of the divine. James called his position "pluralistic pantheism." It is a type of pantheism, since he held that God is the divine spark within us and that we form one continuous soul and body with God. And it is pluralistic, since he held that God is finite and includes the good but not the evil parts of experience. In this way, James believed in a God that was both large enough and small enough to accompany and aid human beings in an ongoing process of evolutionary development.

Further reading

James, William. *The Varieties of Religious Experience.* Cambridge, MA: Harvard University Press, 1985.

Pawelski, James O. *The Dynamic Individualism of William James.* Albany, NY: SUNY Press, 2007.

Taylor, Charles. *Varieties of Religion Today: William James Revisited.* Cambridge, MA: Harvard University Press, 2002.

JAMES O. PAWELSKI

JAMES, WILLIAM: WILL TO BELIEVE

William James's *The Will to Believe and Other Essays in Popular Philosophy* (1896) is a loose aggregation of ten pieces written and /or presented over nearly twenty years between 1879 and 1896. The volume's title underscores that key to this collection is the often misunderstood but seminal essay, "The Will to Believe." Further, James's subtitle "essays in popular philosophy" calls attention to his desire to engage issues that ordinary persons identify as philosophical: that is, ultimate questions dealing with morality, human freedom, personal responsibility, the existence of God, the reality of soul and the afterlife.

James's title essay argues that our intellectual and active lives follow the lead of our emotional natures. His thesis is bold and wide-ranging:

> Our passional natures not only lawfully may, but must, decide an option between propositions, whenever it is a genuine option that cannot by its nature be decided on intellectual grounds; for to say, under such circumstances, "Do not decide, but leave the questions open," is itself a passional decision – just like deciding yes or no – and is attended with the same risk of losing the truth.
>
> (20)

In working out the implications of his thesis, James insists that one has the right to take risks in the face of inconclusive evidence, in part, because sometimes acting on faith produces crucial evidence that would not otherwise exist. His critics promptly accused him of encouraging a "will to make-believe" and promoting irrational risk-taking. His defenders stress two critical qualifications made by James: he endorses believing (and acting) upon insufficient evidence only when one is faced with a forced, living and momentous "genuine option," and, also (being a pragmatist) he is confident that all beliefs, both those with ample evidence and "overbeliefs" with less justification, will be corrected by the pressure of experience.

Much of the seminal influence of this essay is due to its examination of the phenomenon of "self-fulfilling prophesies," or as James put it, situations wherein faith can become father to fact. First, he gives attention to cooperative situations where percussive faith is a crucial factor in outcomes, "a government, an army, a commercial system, a ship, a college, an athletic team, all exist on this condition, without which not only is nothing achieved, nothing is even attempted" (29). Next, in the third essay of the volume, "The Sentiment of Rationality," he examines how faith-before-fact also applies to individual situations. In his famous example, a mountain climber whose only escape is by a "terrible leap" needs to believe that he will succeed if he is to have a chance, "in this case (and it is one of an enormous class) the part of wisdom clearly is to believe what one desires; for belief is one of the indispensable preliminary conditions of the realization of the object" (80).

More generally, James's "will to believe" doctrine lays the groundwork for the distinctive meliorisitic strain in his philosophy. James's second essay asks "Is Life Worth Living?" His resoundingly affirmative answer is due, in large part, to his confidence that believing that improvement is possible encourages us to work hard enough to make it a fact.

The middle essays of the volume examine the moral life and the nature of ethical judgments, including the connection of the ethical with the religious. In this connection, brief attention needs to be made paid to the tightly reasoned analysis of "The Dilemma of Determinism" chapter which offers a vigorous and thoroughgoing defense of the prerequisites of the moral life. James argues that only an open universe with tragedy and triumph can support our experiences of ethical choice and personal responsibility. To test this assertion, he examines reactions to a vicious murder in a determined world. The key difference between an indeterminate, open world and a determined, block universe hangs on saving or abandoning judgments of regret:

> The judgment of regret calls the murder bad. Calling a thing bad means, if it means anything at all, that the thing ought not to be, that something else ought to be in its stead. Determinism, in denying that nothing else can be in its stead, virtually defines the universe as a place in which ought be is impossible.
>
> (125–6)

Determinists attempt to rebut by saying that what we thought to be evil was a neutral event, even a good thing. Even so, asks James, what of the original judgment of regret? Since it, too, was determined, we would live in a world of theoretic absurdities and necessary errors. On the contrary, concludes James, the line of least resistance is to exercise our will to believe in a pluralistic, theistic and melioristic universe.

Further reading

Dooley, Patrick K. "The Nature of Belief: 'The Proper Context for James' 'The Will to Believe'," *Transactions of Charles S. Peirce Society* 8 (1972): 141–51.

James, William. *The Will to Believe and Other Essays in Popular Philosophy.* Cambridge, MA: Harvard University Press, 1979 [1897].

O'Connell, Robert J. *William James on the Courage to Believe.* New York: Fordham University Press, 1984.

PATRICK K. DOOLEY

JORDAN, ELIJAH

Raised in southern Indiana, Elijah Jordan (1875–1953) earned an MA from Cornell University and a PhD from the University of Chicago. From 1913 to 1944 he taught at Butler University in Indianapolis. One of the last systematic philosophers of his era, Jordan's metaphysics is reminiscent of Hegel's in its quest for an integrity of the categories of quantity and quality. In reducing reality to the quantitative analysis of physical matter, Jordan believed science fails to provide an adequate ground for a philosophy of culture, which should be equally steeped in aesthetic values. Although his metaphysics and aesthetics were neglected, their practical application to the crassness of power politics and the dehumanizing practices of big business found an audience. Max H. Fisch praised *Forms of Individuality* (1927) and *Theory of Legislation* (1930) as "in some respects the greatest" contributions to American social philosophy. Though reminiscent of Thoreau's iconoclasm, Jordan's work also anticipates the qualitative existentialism of Robert M. Pirsig.

Further reading

Barnett, George. *Corporate Society and Education: The Philosophy of Elijah Jordan.* Ann Arbor, MI: University of Michigan Press, 1961.

Jordan, Elijah. *Forms of Individuality: An Inquiry into the Grounds of Order in Human Relations.* Indianapolis, IN: Progress Publishing, 1927.

—— *Theory of Legislation.* Indianapolis, IN: Progress Publishing, 1930.

—— *Business Be Damned.* New York: H. Schumann, 1952.

—— *Metaphysics.* Evanston, IL: Principia, 1956.

FRANK X. RYAN

JUDGMENT

What distinguishes judgment from such functions as perception, intuition, sensation, action, and a myriad of other possible functions? Historically, in philosophy, judgment has been associated with conscious, mental reflection that culminates in an explicit assertion, typically a proposition of some kind, that is thought to contribute to knowledge and that can be assessed as true or false. It is sometimes thought of as *the* unit of thought, whereby thought has an active and self-conscious character to it, unlike, for example, the passivity or receptivity that is attributed to perception and sensation for example. Kant distinguishes between a priori and a posteriori judgments and analyzes them as units of thought with different bases and that hence contribute to the possibility of knowledge in very different ways.

The classic American philosophers took a variety of approaches to the notion of judgment. For instance, Royce and Peirce remain close to the description given above while Dewey and Buchler attempt to reconstruct the notion of judgment in broader terms.

Peirce distinguishes between judgment and proposition, with the former being the psychical act itself of affirming or recognizing a belief, and the latter as the matter or content of thought that is affirmed or recognized. Royce defines judgment as the undertaking to express the objective validity of any truth. Every judgment involves a conscious intention to be in significant relation to the real. Therefore, hypothetical, universal and negative judgments all say something determinate about the real, and that may consist in an assertion about what the future will include or it may consist in an assertion of what the real excludes. For Royce, a judgment is a step towards Truth and valid determination of the character of the Real.

Dewey attempts to broaden the notion of judgment by arguing that judgment is much wider than has historically been recognized. For one, practical judgments (propositions about agendas or about things to be done) are contributory to cognitive endeavor no less than are descriptive judgments. Dewey points out that practical and descriptive judgments are not so different as they have been supposed to be. A practical judgment may be a factor in the completion of the situation which the proposition is about, and in that respect it appears to be different from contingent descriptive judgments. For example, the practical judgment, "I'm going to purchase that house tomorrow," states my intention in its propositional content; its subject matter (my intention or agenda) is a factor in the ultimate completion of the indeterminate state of affairs that the judgment is about. In contrast, a judgment "It will probably rain" is a descriptive judgment and its propositional content does not appear to contribute to the completion of the indeterminate state of affairs that the judgment is about. On the other hand, as a settled outcome of inquiry, even the descriptive judgment is not merely a psychological act, but an event that is existential and modifies an existential situation, for example by giving it definiteness or in so far as the judger then resolves to take an umbrella. Dewey was concerned to argue against those (such as Russell) who argued that judgment always takes or is reducible to the propositional form of predicate attribution (e.g. SP) or of relational assertion (e.g. mRn), as well as those who thought of judgments as primarily psychological or mental acts. In Dewey's view, judgments are existential events which reconstitute a situation. As he put it in *The Quest for Certainty*: "Intelligence is associated with *judgment*; that is, with selection and arrangement of means to effect consequences and with choice of what we take as our ends."

Buchler defines judgment as any discrimination or appraisal; it need not be a thought or a component of a reflective, intellectual act. An action (e.g. the act of buying a piece of property) is as much a judgment as is a verbal statement or the mental formulation of an intention that one will buy a piece of property. The action is an appraisal of the property in relation to the judger, as much as the mental formulation is, but in a different mode. Buchler distinguishes three modes of judgment: assertive (judgments which can be true or false), active (judgments which can be good or bad) and exhibitive (judgments which are concerned with the character or quality of ordering, arranging or structuring). These modes are functional distinctions. Thus, a statement could function as an assertive, active or exhibitive judgment; as assertive, its concern would be with accuracy, or truth or falsity; as active, its concern would be with enactment; as exhibitive, its concern would be with the ordering or structuring of the statement per se. Thus, a statement, "A house is worth $500,000," may be an utterance that functions as a true or false assessment of market conditions (assertive judgment), or it may be an utterance in a negotiation that functions to move the process in a particular direction (active judgment); it could also be both, that is, could function as both modes of judgment. A statement could also function exhibitively, as for example in poetry where it plays a role in the verbal structure or ordering that is the poem. Drawing inspiration from Dewey, Peirce and Royce, Buchler aims (1) to remove judgment from the confines of mentalistic and cognitivist theories, which, he argues, fail to do justice to the broadly judicative character of human experience, and (2) to extend judgment beyond its primary association with inquiry and truth and falsity. Rather, judgment occurs in any of the three modes and has three distinct orientations and criteria for validation, although any given judgment may occur in more than one mode, and hence be subject to more than one scale of evaluation. The tripartite theory of judgment affirms the parity of the three modes of judgment in human experience, while at the same time allowing that one mode may be preferable or more desirable than another in a particular context or for a particular purpose. Nonetheless, all three modes are equally judicative and equally valid in their particular respects.

Further reading

Buchler, Justus. *The Main of Light: On the Concept of Poetry.* Oxford: Oxford University Press, 1974.

—— *Toward a General Theory of Human Judgment*, second, expanded edition. New York: Dover, 1979.

—— *Nature and Judgment.* Lanham, MD: University Press of America, 1985.

Dewey, John. *Essays in Experimental Logic*, ed. D. Micah Hester and Robert B. Talisse. Carbondale, IL: Southern Illinois University Press, 2007.

—— *Experience and Nature.* New York: Dover, 2000.

—— *The Quest for Certainty.* New York: Minton, Balch, 1929.

Peirce, Charles Sanders. *Collected Papers of Charles Sanders Peirce*, ed. Charles Hartshorne and Paul Weiss. Cambridge, MA: Belknap Press, 1965.

Royce, Josiah. *The World and the Individual First Series: The Four Historical Conceptions of Being*. New York: Macmillan, 1927.

KATHLEEN WALLACE

JUSTICE

In keeping with their practical treatment of normative concepts such as truth or the good generally, pragmatists do not seek to provide the universal, necessary and sufficient conditions for justice, nor even a "theory" of justice based on a few basic principles. Rather, pragmatists understand justice practically in terms of a more comprehensive moral, social and political ideal: the ideal of democracy. The rights, equality, and freedoms that are constitutive of the democratic ideal are substantively related to various ends of justice, including self-development, peace, and self-government. Democracy is thus not only a means to achieving justice, but also constitutive of its ends, and the institutional form that it takes must best realize the proper means and ends under the current circumstances (Dewey 1991). Rawls' conception of justice as fairness as "political and not metaphysical" is in part a continuation of this pragmatic approach. Along with Rawls' emphasis on institutions, pragmatists add the important role of actual deliberation and ongoing institutional reform, especially in cases of conflict and disagreement. Democracy does not aim to settle such disagreements once and for all, but to make them fruitful for the ends of justice.

Rather than defining justice in terms of democracy, pragmatists take the two terms to be mutually dependent practical ideals: a democracy becomes just only by becoming more democratic, so that democracy and justice can only be realized together. The core idea of this practical interrelationship of means and ends could be put in terms of Jane Addams's well-known adage: "the only solution to the problems of democracy is more democracy," to which John Dewey immediately adds an interesting proviso: democracy can remedy its ills only by becoming "genuinely different in kind" (Dewey 1988). Such reform shows that new circumstances of injustice provide the impetus for democratic transformation, as new publics come to outstrip the normative constraints of the very institutions that formed them. The mutual dependence of democracy and justice provides the basis for seeing both as embodied in a dynamic process of learning and change through communication and deliberation.

As aiming at developing the form of practical knowledge needed to realize such ends, pragmatism is often thought of as a form of consequentialism. Indeed, Dewey, James, and Peirce all speak about judging claims to truth or goodness in terms of their practical consequences. This idea is so central to pragmatism that Dewey, following Peirce, calls it the pragmatic rule or maxim: "in order to discover the meaning of an idea, ask for its consequences" (Dewey 1983). Dewey argues further that the pragmatic idea of truth has practical worth only if it carries over an experimental approach and method from the sciences into political and social institutions. Such an open-ended method of inquiry is integral to democracy itself. But what are the consequences that are salient in this context? This is determined by public deliberation about means and ends, a process that defines and solves problems by engaging citizens in cooperative forms of inquiry in which to exercise practical intelligence (Dewey 1991).

The first task of such inquiry is to ascertain the social facts relevant to the practical realization of democracy, in order to determine how best to realize the conditions of justice. Pragmatic social inquiry is concerned not merely with elaborating an ideal in convincing normative arguments, but also with its realizability and its feasibility. In this regard, any political ideal must take into account general social facts if it is to be feasible. These facts about democracy in modern societies include expertise and the division of labor, cultural pluralism and their accompanying deep conflicts and disagreement, social complexity and differentiation, and globalization and interdependence, to name a few. In cases in which the "facts" challenge the very institutional basis of modern political integration and democratic practices of public deliberation, practical inquiry must seek to extend the scope of political possibilities rather than simply take the facts to fix the limits of political possibilities once and for all. If, as Rawls believes, "the fact of pluralism," of diverse comprehensive moral doctrines among citizens, is permanent, then it is likely that liberal democracies will become increasingly more, rather than less, pluralistic as they become more democratic (Rawls 1996). For pragmatism and recent critical social theory inspired by pragmatism, a robust and deliberative democracy is the relevant ideal and an important part of the wider historical ideal of human emancipation and freedom from domination is a necessary condition of justice and democracy. Accordingly, democracy is a mode of inquiry in which human beings exercise their basic freedoms and powers, fallibly revising the means and ends of their common life.

An important contribution of Dewey's *Logic* to such an account of democratic inquiry is precisely its practical interpretation of social facts as "problematic situations," even if these problems are more felt or suffered than fully recognized as such (Dewey 1986). The way to avoid seeing facts as mere constraints is to see them practically: facts are such only if they serve "to delimit a problem in a way that affords indication and test of proposed solutions." For example, in response to Lippmann's insistence on the fact of expertise, Dewey criticizes "existing political practice" for ignoring the distribution of social knowledge, and sought to show how to make it a resource for public deliberation (Dewey 1988). In response to Lippmann's elitist view of majority rule, Dewey held on to the possibility and feasibility of democratic participation by well-informed citizens who are able to distribute deliberative labor across social roles and institutions.

How might democracy be organized as a mode of inquiry or procedure for selecting new institutions in response to the open possibilities of problematic situations? Pragmatists have a remarkably robust conception of democracy as a form of social inquiry that must be counted as one of the sources of the ideal of deliberative democracy. According to the pragmatic account, democracy is a form of deliberative problem solving typical of cooperative social activity. But what makes deliberation democratic is that it is "multiperspectival," to the extent that it incorporates the perspectives of all the social actors into the investigation of the problematic situation. According to this conception of deliberative democracy, citizens do not deliberate as abstract individuals who join together in a collective will, but rather as diverse actors with a variety of epistemic competences and social perspectives. Standing in opposition to those forms of liberalism that take such matters as boundaries, jurisdictions and constituencies as given, pragmatism sees reflexivity as the main practical virtue of deliberative democracy and thus leave open the scope and extent of deliberation as the circumstances require (Dorf and Sabel 1998). This reflexivity is a requirement of justice, to the extent that it is a constitutive condition for the exercise of basic freedoms and human powers that are necessary to transform unjust circumstances by transforming democratic practices and institutions.

Besides Dewey, George Herbert Mead provides the most innovative arguments and conceptual resources for the development of such a multiperspectival conception of deliberative democracy. In cases of injustice and exclusion, deepening and widening democracy may also mean the emergence of new institutions and even new rights, and these may require that the community be able to adopt new perspectives in order to undermine the legitimacy of current democratic injustice. Mead names this sort of critical normative perspective the "Generalized Other," which he understands not as a single "We" but as all the different perspectives available in the community (Mead 1934). A democratic community might institutionalize this perspective of the Generalized Other in its practices that test the justification of the terms of democracy. Understood in this distributive rather than the usual impartial sense, the Generalized Other is the perspective of "an enlarged mentality" or of "enriched and enlarged experience" that is a requirement of taking up claims to justice. Kant sees such a mentality in a distributive fashion, as thinking and judging from "the standpoint of everyone else." Such reflexivity is part of the ongoing process of realizing a universal ideal compatible with multiple perspectives without dissolving them into a single impartial perspective or a higher unity.

Mead understood the perspective of the Generalized Other as the cosmopolitan and universal core of democratic practice, in which the Generalized Other consists of the normative attitude that we take when addressed by others in the human political community. These "others" are thus normatively entitled to exercise their communicative powers to change political norms anywhere. As Mead puts it, a "universal society" exists to the extent that "all can enter into relations with others through the medium of communication." In this respect, Mead takes as his starting point that any socialized modern individual is "always a member of a larger community," in which her more immediate relations are embedded. More generally, critical reflexivity is achieved "only by individuals taking the attitude of the Generalized Other *toward themselves*" so that each views her membership "from any one of the different standpoints in which he belongs to the community." In response to the question of the applicability of such norms and institutions internationally Mead is optimistic: "Could a conversation be conducted internationally? The question is a question of social organization" and the realistic extension of current possibilities (Mead 1934).

In the case of international society, democratic institutions once again have a special claim to be able to achieve the ends of global justice, such as the full realization of human rights. The pragmatist faith in democracy came from the commitment to deliberation as an impetus for the reform of existing democratic institutions. But deliberation can also do more in more deeply problematic situations, especially if democracy today includes a mode of creative inquiry into democratic renewal in light of global publics' demands for justice (Bohman 2007). With their emphasis on widening and deepening democracy, the pragmatists anticipated current discussions of expressive freedom and of forms of democracies that extend beyond the boundaries of existing communities. Pragmatism suggests that justice can be realized only if its means and ends are set by inclusive deliberation. Thus, democracy remains the best mode for multi-perspectival inquiry into the conditions for global justice.

Further reading

Aboulafia, Mitchell. *The Cosmopolitan Self: George Herbert Mead and Continental Philosophy.* Chicago, IL: University of Illinois Press, 2001.

Bohman, James. "Realizing Deliberative Democracy as a Mode of Inquiry," *Journal of Speculative Philosophy* 18 (2004): 23–41.

—— *Democracy Across Borders.* Cambridge, MA: MIT Press, 2007.

Dewey, John. "Reconstruction in Philosophy" in *The Middle Works, 1899–1924, Vol. 12, 1920*, ed. Jo Ann Boydston. Carbondale, IL: Southern Illinois University Press, 1983.

—— "Liberalism and Social Action" in *The Later Works, 1925–1937, Vol. 11, 1935–1937*, ed. Jo Ann Boydston. Carbondale, IL: Southern Illinois University Press, 1991.

Dorf, Michael and Sabel, Charles. "The Constitution of Democratic Experimentalism," *Columbia Law Review* 98 (1998): 267–473.

Mead, George Herbert. *Mind, Self and Society.* Chicago, IL: University of Chicago Press, 1934.

Rawls, John. *Political Liberalism.* New York: Columbia University Press, 1996.

Westbrook, Robert. *John Dewey and American Democracy.* Ithaca, NY: Cornell University Press.

JAMES BOHMAN

JUSTIFICATION

"Justification" is a normative term with multiple meanings. On the one hand "justified" is used in a moral sense in "The German citizen was justified in lying to the Nazi guard." One might also use "justifiable" in a distinctly prudential or pragmatic sense in saying "His high bet was justifiable given the stakes." There is a third sense of justification, however, that we may call the *epistemic* sense, since the study of this form of justification has traditionally been central to the branch of philosophy known as "epistemology." When used in the epistemic sense, the word "justified" applies to beliefs, such as my belief that there is a computer before me, or your belief that dinosaurs roamed the earth many years ago. With a few exceptions (James 1956), American philosophers have been primarily concerned with stating the necessary and sufficient conditions for a belief's being justified in the *epistemic* sense, and with determining the structure of epistemic justification exemplified by systems of justified beliefs.

Internalism and externalism

In attempting to state the necessary and sufficient conditions for a belief's being justified, philosophers are, colloquially, attempting to state "what it takes" for a belief to be justified. For example, a plausible first statement of these conditions might run as follows: "a belief, b, is justified if and only if the relevant believer's evidence appropriately supports b." What constitutes one's evidence, and what it takes for one's evidence to appropriately support a belief, would need to be spelled out here. But the important point for present purposes is that, on this view, whether one's belief, b, is justified depends only on one's evidence and the relation that her evidence bears to b. It does not depend on the belief's truth-value, or on the reliability of the method by which she formed it, for instance. A believer could be highly reliable at forming true beliefs, but fail to be justified in holding any of them on this account (if her evidence failed to appropriately support any of them). And a believer could, equally, be hugely unreliable at forming true beliefs, and yet be justified in holding all of them on this account (if her evidence did appropriately support those beliefs).

The last view of what it takes for a belief to be justified is an example of what are standardly known as *internalist* accounts of justification. On standard formulations, internalism is the view that whether a believer's belief is justified is fixed by her internal psychological states, such as her beliefs and sensory experiences. Some internalists additionally hold that such states must be introspectively accessible, or even introspectively recognizable as supportive of the relevant belief (BonJour 1985; Chisholm 1989). Internalism about justification is contrasted with *externalism* about justification, according to which the conditions that must obtain in order for a belief to be justified are outside of the head of the believer. Prominent examples of externalism share the vague theme that whether a belief is justified is a function of whether or not the belief was formed in a truth-conducive way (Goldman 1986). In stark contrast to the view sketched above, then, strict versions of these latter views are generally consistent with a believer's belief being justified independent of what kind of evidence she has for it. Finally, some American philosophers have endorsed synthetic views of justification, which incorporate both internalist and externalist themes (Dewey 1903; Lewis 1946).

The very radical variance in views regarding the necessary and sufficient conditions for a belief's being justified has led some American philosophers to doubt that there is a single concept of epistemic justification at issue (Alston 1993). Thus, some have argued that there are multiple epistemic goods that go by the name "justification," some having more to do with responsiveness to evidence, and others having more to do with truth-conduciveness. To try to figure out which of these goods is "really" epistemic justification, the thought runs, is like trying to figure out whether a bank is really a monetary institution or a land mass that borders a stream.

The architecture of justification

Virtually all internalists about justification – or philosophers interested in "internalist" epistemic goods – agree that when one is justified in holding at least many ordinary beliefs, there are other beliefs – "justifiers" – that serve to *justify* them. Thus, it is thought that if I am justified in believing that the Iraq war will last at least another year, then some of my other beliefs justify my holding this belief. Perhaps, for example, my belief that the Bush administration fears leaving Iraq in disarray, in tandem with some other beliefs about recent history, justifies my belief that the Iraq war will last at least another year. Agreeing with this much, internalists disagree vehemently as to whether *all* beliefs require justifiers in order to be justified.

Some philosophers, known as *foundationalists*, maintain that certain beliefs, such as beliefs about one's current experiences, require no justifiers in order to be justified – such beliefs are thought to be *self-justifying* or to be justified by something other than beliefs, such as sense-experiences (Chisholm 1989). These beliefs are thought to be "foundational" in the sense that all other justified beliefs "inherit" their justification from them – all other justified beliefs are linked by a continuous chain of justifiers to these self-justifying beliefs.

Foundationalists face a serious difficulty in attempting to explicate the new notions that they invoke like "self-justification" (BonJour 1986). This has led many American philosophers to endorse a quite different picture of the architecture of justification known as *coherentism*. Coherentists usually maintain, in opposition to foundationalists, that all justified beliefs do require justifiers in order to be justified. And rather than seeing the chain of justifiers that leads up to any one justified belief as exhausting in a "foundation" of beliefs which are justified independent of justifiers, coherentists see such chains as proceeding in a kind of "virtuous circle" – A1 is justified by A2, and A2 by A3, until eventually a belief, An, is reached that is itself justified by A1. A worry for this view is that the notion of "virtuous circle" at play is obscure, and that any viable elucidation of that notion would suggest that people could be justified in having what seem to be unjustified beliefs (if those beliefs formed a "virtuous circle" of justification).

The regress problem

Foundationalism and coherentism naturally afford distinct responses to a longstanding skeptical problem that has come to be known as the "regress" problem of justification. Roughly speaking, the regress problem arises from the not obviously fallacious assumptions that every belief requires a justifier in order to be justified, and that no belief can be justified if the trail of justifiers leading up to it tracks back to itself – i.e. is circular. The problem is that it seems to follow from these assumptions that either none of our beliefs is justified, or that there are infinite chains of justifiers "sustaining" each of our justified beliefs. Some American philosophers have endorsed the second of these consequences (Peirce 1868). But, much more often, American philosophers have invoked a foundationalist or coherentist account of the architecture of justification to deny the first or second assumption, respectively. Foundationalism tells us that not all justified beliefs require justifiers (so the first assumption leading to the regress problem is false), and coherentism tells us that circular chains of justification are possible (so that the second assumption leading to the regress problem is false).

Further reading

Alston, William. "Epistemic Desiderata," *Philosophy and Phenomenological Research* LIII, 3 (1993): 527–51.

BonJour, Laurence. *The Structure of Empirical Knowledge*. Cambridge, MA: Harvard University Press, 1985.

Chisholm, Rodrick. *The Theory of Knowledge*, third edition. Englewood Cliffs, NJ: Prentice-Hall, 1989.
Dewey, John. *Studies in Logical Theory.* Chicago, IL: University of Chicago Press, 1903.
Goldman, Allen. *Epistemology and Cognition*. Cambridge, MA: Harvard University Press, 1986.
James, William. *The Will to Believe and Other Essays in Popular Philosophy.* New York: Dover, 1956.
Lewis, C.I. *An Analysis of Knowledge and Valuation* (The Paul Carus Lectures, Series 8, 1946). La Salle, IL: Open Court, 1946.
Peirce, Charles S. "Questions Concerning Certain Faculties Claimed for Man," *Journal of Speculative Philosophy* 2 (1868): 103–14.

JUSTIN CLARKE-DOANE

K

KALLEN, HORACE MEYER

Horace Meyer Kallen was an American philosopher and leading public intellectual. Born in Berenstadt, Germany, into an Orthodox Jewish family, Kallen moved to Boston in 1887. He earned his BA in 1903 and his PhD in 1908, both at Harvard. He studied with George Santayana, Josiah Royce, and William James, and edited the manuscript of James's *Some Problems of Philosophy* (1910). In 1918 he resigned his teaching position at the University of Wisconsin to protest the trampling of academic freedom during the patriotic fervor of the First World War. In 1919 he joined the original core faculty of the New School for Social Research, where he remained for his entire career, teaching his last course in 1973. Freedom loomed large in his career, and he wrote eight major books and numerous articles with the word "free," "freedom," or "liberty" in the title. He called his philosophical approach "aesthetic pragmatism." The arts, literature, and religion were central to his philosophical outlook. He was a committed Zionist who embraced a secular Judaism. From early in his career, he argued that cultural diversity and the "American Idea" were compatible with each other. He coined the term "cultural pluralism" while a teaching assistant to Santayana. His 1915 essay "Democracy Versus the Melting-Pot" thrust him into the public debate about immigration and assimilation. Critical of those who contended that assimilation was essential for the preservation of American democracy, he argued that respect for ethnic and racial difference strengthened America.

Further reading

Kallen, Horace Meyer. "Democracy Versus the Melting-Pot: A Study of American Nationality," *The Nation* (18 and 25 February 1915): 190–4, 217–20.

—— *Art and Freedom: A Historical and Biographical Interpretation of the Relations Between Ideas of Beauty, Use and Freedom in Western Civilization from the Greeks to the Present Day*, 2 volumes. New York: Duell, Sloan and Pearce, 1942.

—— *Cultural Pluralism and the American Idea: An Essay in Social Philosophy.* Philadelphia, PA: University of Pennsylvania Press, 1956.

—— *Liberty, Laughter and Tears: Reflections on the Relations of Comedy and Tragedy to Human Freedom.* De Kalb, IL: Northern Illinois University Press, 1968.

Armen T. Marsoobian

KING, MARTIN LUTHER, JR

Martin Luther King, Jr (1929–68), born Michael King, Jr, in Atlanta, GA, was a minister and one of the most prominent leaders of the Civil Rights Movement, and the youngest winner of the Nobel Peace Prize (1964). He was the first son of Michael (later Martin) King, Sr, a prominent Baptist minister, and Alberta Williams King. King Sr was pastor of the prominent Ebenezer Baptist Church, which was founded by King Jr's maternal grandfather, Rev. A.D. Williams, who, like King Sr, was a social gospel activist. Williams was instrumental in forming the Georgia Equal Rights League and was a founder of the Atlanta division of the NAACP. King Sr was president of the NAACP in Atlanta and fought "in Atlanta to equalize teachers' salaries and was instrumental in the elimination of Jim Crow elevators in the courthouse"

(King 1998: 5). King excelled in segregated schools. He entered Morehouse College (1944–8) at the age of fifteen, graduating with a BA in sociology. King went on to attend Crozer Theological Seminary in Pennsylvania (1948–51), where he came under the theological and avuncular tutelage of Joseph Pius Barbour and where he obtained his Bachelor of Divinity degree. While at Crozer, King took philosophy courses (one on Kant and another one on aesthetics) at the University of Pennsylvania (Burrow 2006: 30). King then attended Boston University (1951–5), where he developed the Dialectical Society. After the sudden death of his advisor, the preeminent personalist philosopher Edgar S. Brightman, King "shifted his registration from the graduate school's philosophy department to the School of Theology" (Branch 1988: 100), where he eventually received his PhD in systematic theology. While in Boston, King met and fell in love with Coretta Scott, a classical singer and student at the New England Conservatory in Boston. They were married by King Sr in 1953 and had four children together.

In terms of his philosophical world-view, during his first year at Crozer, King read Walter Rauschenbusch's *Christianity and the Social Crisis*. Rauschenbusch's work functioned as a formal theological underpinning of the importance of not only being concerned with man's "soul but his body; not only his spiritual well-being but his material well-being" (King 1998: 18). More fundamentally, it was the impact of the social gospel activism of King's father and maternal grandfather that provided King with an early example of how religion and the galvanizing power of a rich Black homiletic tradition might be used to instigate social movement and challenge injustice. While at Morehouse, King came under the activist ministry of College President Dr. Benjamin E. Mays, Dr. George D. Kelsey, professor of philosophy and religion, and Samuel W. Williams, Chairman of the Department of Philosophy and Religion.

In Mays and Kelsey, King "could see in their lives the ideal of what I wanted a minister to be" (King 1998: 16). Through Mays and Kelsey, King also came to appreciate how both united religion with critical scholarship. King's social gospel activism was shaped by his philosophy of active non-violent resistance. Although King heard a lecture on pacifism given by A.J. Muste, a socialist activist who later became King's advisor during the Civil Rights Movement, it was after hearing Mordecai Johnson, President of Howard University, lecture on Gandhian non-violence in terms of *Satyagraha* or soul force/love force, that King voraciously began reading books on Gandhi.

For King, non-violent resistance was a way of life. King believed that if he met hate with hate, then he would become depersonalized, "because creation is so designed that my personality can only be fulfilled in the context of community" (Washington 1986: 20). His active non-violent resistance was predicated upon *agape*, which "is a willingness to forgive, not seven times, but seventy times seven to restore community" (Washington 1986: 20). Consistent with his active non-violent approach to social change and his belief in the significance of community is King's Personalist philosophy, which he adopted under the philosophical guidance of Edgar S. Brightman and Harold L. De Wolf. According to King,

> Personalism's insistence that only personality – finite and infinite – is ultimately real strengthened me in two convictions: it gave me metaphysical and philosophical grounding for the idea of a personal God, and it gave me a metaphysical basis for the dignity and worth of all human personality.
>
> (King 1998: 31–2)

In his dissertation, King came to reject the theological and philosophical views of God as propounded by theologians Henry Nelson Wieman and Paul Tillich. Although King's criticism of Hegel is Kierkegaardian and existentialist, for he saw Hegel's system as tending "to swallow up the many in the one" (King 1998: 32), he did accept Hegel's view that truth is the whole. Hence, King used Hegel's conception of *Aufhebung*, the view that a higher unity results from processes of negation and preservation, to concede that "Wieman is right in emphasizing the goodness of God, but wrong in minimizing his power. Likewise, Tillich is right in emphasizing the power of God, but wrong in minimizing his goodness" (Carson 1994: 171). The concept of *Aufhebung* also formed the framework in terms of how King came to think through and resolve tensions between such extremes as violence and non-violence, liberal and neo-orthodox conceptions of the goodness of human persons, and the tension that often emerged between being both American and African living in the US. King argued, "The old Hegelian synthesis still offers the best answer to many of life's dilemmas. The American Negro is neither totally African nor totally Western. He is Afro-American, a true hybrid, a combination of two cultures" (Washington 1986: 588). Growing out of his Personalist philosophy, King believed that "God is able to conquer the evils of history" (Washington 1986: 507). While King acknowledged that existentialism is a useful philosophical lens through which to understand the world as filled with angst, alienation, and meaninglessness, he maintained that "the ultimate Christian answer is not found in any of these existentialist assertions" (Washington 1986: 37). Rejecting an existentialist ethics, King was a moral realist. He believed that there is an arc in the moral universe that bends toward justice. It is through human effort, however, that social justice obtains. Hence, to be in community while fighting for justice is to be on the side of the universe and God (Burrow 2006: 187). It is his conception of the moral universe that buttressed King's faith in the eventual manifestation of the beloved community. On this score, war, hatred, racism, and segregation are enemies of the beloved community, of God, of "the principle of the sacredness of human personality" (Ansbro 2000: 22) and of the natural order of the universe.

Further reading

Ansbro, John J. *Martin Luther King, Jr: Nonviolent Strategies and Tactics for Social Change.* Lanham, MD: Madison Books, 2000.

Burrow, Rufus, Jr. *God and Human Dignity: The Personalism, Theology, and Ethics of Martin Luther King, Jr.* Notre Dame, IN: University of Notre Dame Press, 2006.

Carson, Clayborne. "Martin Luther King, Jr, and the African-American Social Gospel" in Paul E. Johnson (ed) *African-American Christianity: Essays in History.* Los Angeles, CA: University of California Press, 1994.

King, Martin Luther, Jr. *The Autobiography of Martin Luther King, JR*, ed. Clayborne Carson. New York: Warner Books, 1998.

Washington, James M. (ed.) *A Testament of Hope: The Essential Writings of Dr. Martin Luther King, Jr.* New York: HarperCollins, 1986.

George Yancy

KLINE, GEORGE LOUIS

George Kline (1921–) has contributed significantly to an understanding of Russian and Soviet thinkers in philosophy and religion – especially with respect to their use of Benedict Spinoza, G.W.F. Hegel, Karl Marx, and Friedrich Nietzsche. His numerous philosophic translations from Russian include V.V. Zenkovsky's classic two-volume *A History of Russian Philosophy.* He has also translated and commented extensively on Russian poetry, and was an early translator and remains an important interpreter of the poetry of 1987 Nobel laureate Joseph Brodsky.

Kline has published important interpretive essays not only in Slavic studies but also in the metaphysics of Hegel and of Alfred North Whitehead. He is noted for his meticulously detailed concern with the often systematically ambiguous ways in which philosophers use their key terms, but Kline's terminological focus always serves broader and deeply humanistic ends. For example, his work in the ontology of time in Hegel and Whitehead, and in the thought of Russians such as Alexander Herzen and Nicholas Berdyaev, focuses on their critique of what he calls the "Fallacy of the Actual Future" in which a "spatialized" future is taken as a concrete settled reality, the coming of which justifies destroying present communities, cultural practices, and – especially – individual persons who might prevent or merely retard its realization.

Further reading

Kline, George Louis. *Spinoza in Soviet Philosophy.* London: Routledge and Kegan Paul, and New York: Humanities Press, 1952; reprinted Westport, CT: Hyperion Press, 1981.

—— *Religious and Anti-Religious Thought in Russia* (The Weil Lectures). Chicago, IL: University of Chicago Press, 1968.

—— "Form, Concrescence, and Concretum" in Lewis S. Ford and George L. Kline (eds) *Explorations in Whitehead's Philosophy.* New York: Fordham University Press, 1983, pp. 104–46.

—— "'Present,' 'Past,' and 'Future' as Categoreal Terms and the 'Fallacy of the Actual Future,'" *Review of Metaphysics* 40, 3 (1986): 215–35.

—— "The Myth of Marx's Materialism" in Helmut Dahm, Thomas J. Blakeley, and George L. Kline (eds) *Philosophical Sovietology: The Pursuit of a Science.* Boston, MA: Reidel, 1988, pp. 158–203; reprinted in Scott Meikle (ed.) *Marx.* Burlington, VT: Ashgate-Dartmouth, 2002, pp. 27–72.

—— "The Use and Abuse of Hegel by Nietzsche and Marx" in William Desmond (ed.) *Hegel and his Critics.* Albany, NY: SUNY Press, 1989, pp. 1–34.

—— "The Potential Contribution of Classical Russian Philosophy to the Building of a Humane Society in Russia Today" in *XIX World Congress of Philosophy (Moscow 22–28 August 1993): Lectures*, Moscow: n.p., 1993, 34–50.

George Allan

KNOWLEDGE: A PRIORI

For a subject to know that p, that subject must believe that p and p must be true. Further, the subject must have justifying reasons for p. Reasons derived from sensory evidence yield a posteriori justification. Reasons not derived from empirical sources yield a priori justification. On this rough description, we seem to know many things a priori – inference rules of deductive logic, mathematical truths, some truths about our concepts and their relations, and perhaps some truths of philosophy. Characterizing a priori justification in a positive fashion beyond merely saying it is not empirical is notoriously difficult. One feature may be that the belief is incorrigible, though many a priori reasons have been revised in light of current research (e.g. the axioms of Euclidean geometry) and it is often claimed that many empirical beliefs are incorrigible (e.g. beliefs about current first-person experience). Another feature may be that the belief is self-evident, in that it does not derive its justification from anything other than itself. Upon understanding the proposition, subjects intuitively see that the proposition is true. However, there is wide disagreement not only over which propositions have this feature and which do not, but also over how understanding yields justification. A further feature could be, as C.I. Lewis argues, that a priori knowledge is independent of experience in a pragmatic sense, in that it is a scheme that organizes and classifies experiences.

A priori knowledge is often associated with knowledge of necessary truths. A proposition is necessarily true if and only if it is not possible that it is false, or the proposition is true in all possible worlds. Logical and mathematical truths are clearly candidates for this status. Contingent truths are those that are possibly false, or are true in this world but not in all possible worlds. Kant may be plausibly read as holding that all a priori knowledge is knowledge of necessary truths and that all knowledge of necessary truth is a priori. He argued that because the truths of mathematics are necessary, and because we cannot know necessary truths on the basis of experience, it follows that we cannot know mathematical truths a posteriori. Given that we do know mathematical truths, their necessity proves their a priority. The connection between the necessity and a priority has been challenged on a variety of fronts. First is Saul Kripke's example of knowing that the meter bar in Paris is one meter long. The bar fixes the reference of the term "one meter," so we know a priori that the bar is one meter long. Given that we could have used another bar of another length as the standard, it is contingently true that the bar is one meter long. Second, Kripke argues that we know that the morning star is the evening star, and we know this on the basis of empirical research. Identities, though, are necessary. So we know something necessary but a posteriori. Third, Philip Kitcher has argued that, in Cartesian fashion, I know I exist independently of experience. I do not exist in all possible worlds, so I know a contingent truth a priori. The upshot of these difficulties is that the metaphysical distinction between necessity and contingency does not bear directly on the distinction between the a priori and a posteriori.

The semantic distinction between analytic and synthetic propositions has regularly been taken to be relevant to the epistemic distinction between a priori and a posteriori justification. Analytic propositions are roughly those true in virtue of their meanings. For example, bachelors are unmarried. Such propositions are denied on pains of self-contradiction. Synthetic propositions are true by virtue of something other than their meaning. Those propositions may be denied without self-contradiction, though they may contradict standing evidence. Empiricists limit a priori knowledge only to analytic propositions, so that such knowledge is strictly formal. Hume's fork was that human knowledge is divided between that of relations of ideas and matters of fact. Kant, however, held that there were cases of synthetic a priori knowledge. The empiricist conception of a priori knowledge has been further challenged by Quine's argument that analyticity is an empty notion and, as such, cannot answer the question as to how one knows such propositions. However, if the Kantian tradition is correct, Quine's argument does not touch a priori knowledge *per se*, since a priori justification is independent of the semantic features of the proposition at issue.

In the American pragmatist tradition, claims to a priori knowledge have generally been treated with skepticism. Charles S. Peirce argued against the existence of a priori justification by noting that a priori reasons are ones agreeable to reason, but this agreeableness to reason is more a matter of taste than a matter related to the truth of the propositions considered. John Dewey similarly held that a priori principles were disguised empirical generalizations reflecting a subject's interests. C.I. Lewis's pragmatic notion of the a priori was designed to accommodate these concerns in that Lewis held that a priori knowledge was concerning truths of how experience is structured. This significantly pares back the range of such knowledge. In the wake of Quine's criticism of analyticity, pragmatists steered well clear of countenancing a priori justification. However, questions still remain as to how to analyze paradigmatic cases of a priori knowledge, for example knowledge of mathematical or logical principles, or knowledge of the relations between our concepts.

Further reading

Casullo, Albert. "A Priori Knowledge" in Paul K. Moser (ed.) *The Oxford Handbook of Epistemology.* New York: Oxford University Press, 2002.

Dewey, John. *Experience and Nature.* Vol. 1 of *Later Works*, ed. Jo Ann Boydston. Carbondale, IL: Southern Illinois Press, 1988.

Hume, David. *An Enquiry Concerning Human Understanding*. Oxford: Oxford University Press, 1902.
Kant, Immanuel. *The Critique of Pure Reason*, trans. Norman Kemp Smith. New York: St Martin's Press.
Kitcher, Philip. "A Priority and Necessity," *Australasian Journal of Philosophy* 58 (1980): 89–101.
Kripke, Saul A. *Naming and Necessity.* Cambridge, MA: Harvard University Press, 1972.
Lewis, Clarence Irving. "A Pragmatic Conception of the A Priori," *Journal of Philosophy* 20, 7 (1923): 169–77.
Peirce, Charles Sanders. "The Fixation of Belief" in *Collected Papers*, Vol. 5, ed. C. Hartshorne, P. Weiss, and A.W. Burks. Cambridge, MA: Harvard University Press, 1931–58.
Quine, Willard Van Orman. "Two Dogmas of Empiricism" in *From a Logical Point of View.* Cambridge, MA: Harvard University Press, 1953.

SCOTT FORREST AIKIN

KNOWLEDGE: AND BELIEF

The distinction between knowledge and belief applies only to propositional knowledge (or knowledge-that) and not to either objectual knowledge (knowledge-of) or operational knowledge (knowledge-how-to). Each kind of knowledge involves the other two kinds. My propositional knowledge that no square number is twice a square number involves among other things my objectual knowledge of the system of numbers (positive integers) and my operational knowledge how to square numbers. It also involves further operational knowledge: my ability to perform other arithmetic operations, my ability to understand propositions, my ability to make judgments, and my ability to deduce conclusions from premises – to mention a few of the skills used acquiring arithmetic knowledge.

In the strict sense of *know*, the sense used in this essay but rarely used outside of mathematics and philosophy, every proposition known to be true actually is true, and, except in rare cases, was true before it was known. Truth is a precondition to propositional knowledge, and propositional knowledge is objective in that it is of objective reality. Moreover, every proposition known to be true is known to be true by a person. Propositional knowledge is personal: it is subjective in the sense of being achieved by a knowing subject. Knowing requires that the knower accurately judge based on conclusive evidence. Philosophers may agree to use the words *know* and *knowledge* in the strict sense and yet disagree on whether a given proposition is known to be true by a given person or whether there is any knowledge outside of mathematics or even whether anyone has ever known any proposition to be true.

The word *believe* has broad and narrow senses. In the narrow or exclusive sense – sometimes signaled by a word such as "mere" – no proposition is known to be true and believed to be true by the same person: "beliefs exclude knowledge." In the narrow sense, belief is partly or entirely subjective: it includes a component of personal faith going beyond evidence. However, nothing precludes subjective beliefs from being true – in some cases by accident, so to speak. However, in the broad or inclusive sense used in this essay – sometimes signaled by suffixing words such as "in the broad sense" – every proposition known to be true is believed to be true: "beliefs include knowledge."

Certitude is the subjective feeling of assurance of the truth of a proposition. Certitude can be the result of thorough objective investigation which started from a suspension of belief or even from doubt or disbelief, and it can also arise without investigation or be the result of deception, rationalization, indoctrination, or hallucination, to mention a few. O.W. Holmes, Jr, reminded us that "Certitude is not the test of certainty." Absolute certainty is the state of having knowledge in the strict sense. Even absolute certainty is not always accompanied by certitude – especially in cases where the knower is at first surprised, delighted, or dismayed to find out that the proposition is true. As implied above, philosophers disagree on whether absolute certainty is achievable. John Stuart Mill had certitude that "There is no such thing as absolute certainty." Belief spans the spectrum starting with groundless belief, the limiting case of faith, and ending with absolute certainty, the limiting case of *cognition* (knowledge in the broad sense).

Many of my beliefs, including all those based on testimony, are not *my* knowledge, and some are not knowledge for anyone. An example that is knowledge for others is the famous Fermat proposition: given any three numbers that are all the same power exceeding two, no one is the sum of the other two. This implies that no cube is a sum of two cubes; that no fourth power is a sum of two fourth powers; and so on. I think that I am fully justified in believing this – mathematicians I have reason to respect have testified that it has been proved to be true by a proof that has been carefully studied and found to be cogent by qualified experts. Here is a justified and true belief of mine that is not my knowledge. But the proposition in question is a justified true belief of many mathematicians for whom it *is* knowledge. With regard to the Fermat proposition, while I have certitude but not certainty, some mathematicians have certitude and certainty.

How does a person go about arriving at knowledge of the truth of a proposition even if, in at least some cases, knowledge in the strict sense is the ideal limit of a process that can never be completed – except perhaps in mathematics? Let us use the word *hypothesis* for a proposition not known to be true and not known to be false by a given knower. In the first place, it is necessary to understand the hypothesis to be investigated. Next, it is necessary to investigate – to connect with the reality that the proposition is about in order to acquire from it evidence sufficient to ground a judgment that the proposition is true. Third, it is necessary to marshal the evidence, to bring the evidence to bear on the hypothesis. Finally, it is necessary to see that the evidence is conclusive and to accurately judge on the basis of the understanding and marshalling that the proposition is true. A belief that resulted from successful completion of this four-step process is said to be *cognitively* grounded or justified.

In the case of the proposition that no square number is twice a square number, which was probably known to be true by Socrates, Plato, Aristotle, Leibniz, Pascal and many others, the evidence phase included review of previously known arithmetic propositions and the marshalling phase included inferring the hypothesis from them by logical deduction.

Knowledge is cognitively justified true belief. In this context the word "true" is redundant in the sense that every cognitively justified belief is true. My belief that a given proposition is true is cognitively justified once I have successfully completed the four-step method or its equivalent. Moreover, a proposition that is a true belief of mine not now knowledge can become cognitively justified and thus knowledge if I successfully complete the four-step method.

The verb *to justify* is ambiguous. In other senses the word "true" is not redundant in the sentence "knowledge is justified true belief," which then expresses false and misleading propositions. In some of the other senses, justifying a belief involves explaining something to others: perhaps why I should not be blamed for having the belief or why other people in my circumstances would have come to the same conclusion. No matter how these explanatory senses of justification are spelled out, it is clear that knowledge is not justified true belief. Gaining knowledge that a proposition is true does not require explaining anything to anyone. More generally, in any sense of "justify" in which a false belief of mine is justified there are indefinitely many propositions that could become justified true beliefs without becoming my knowledge. The reason is based on the fact that from any false proposition indefinitely many true propositions are deducible.

In the cognitive sense of "justify" every justified belief is true and, in the strict sense of "knowledge," justified belief is knowledge; knowledge is justified belief.

Background

It might be supposed that discussion of knowledge versus belief took center-stage in American philosophy with the 1877 publication by Charles Sanders Peirce of his seminal paper "The Fixation of Belief," which has justly become somewhat a *locus classicus* for the issue. It is evident to scholars that the above discussion is heavily indebted to the Peirce paper both in spirit and in particular views. The above resonates with several of Peirce's points including his "method of science," his supposition that "there is some one thing to which a proposition should conform," and his view that what is believed is in no way determined or changed by our thinking – to mention only three.

In terms of the present discussion, roughly speaking, "The Fixation of Belief" presents four methods that can be used to increase *certitude* in a proposition already believed. One of those methods, the method of science, increases *certainty*. Nevertheless, Peirce does not explicitly raise the issue of distinguishing "knowledge" from "belief." Perhaps surprisingly, he does not even use the word "knowledge" or a synonym, and he does not make a distinction analogous to certitude/certainty.

However, the above discussion does not relate to certain later "pragmatic themes" in Peirce in which focus on the *nature* of truth as "conforming to facts" gives way to focus on the *criterion* of truth as leading us to fulfilling our aims. *A fortiori*, the above does not relate to other classic American philosophers such as William James and John Dewey who worked in paradigms that might even be incommensurable with those currently flourishing in the United States. James and Dewey would dispute that "truth is a precondition to knowledge" and that "the proposition known is not changed by becoming known."

The present discussion of the knowledge/belief distinction addresses the more analytic side of post-World War II American philosophy. One of the most accessible of relevant texts is the 1978 monograph *The Web of Belief* by Quine and Ullian. An excellent contemporary American treatment of propositional knowledge is the 1991 treatise *Knowledge and Evidence* by Paul Moser. This book explicitly treats the knowledge/belief distinction.

Further reading

Moser, P. *Knowledge and Evidence*. Cambridge: Cambridge University Press, 1991.

Peirce, C.S. *The Fixation of Belief* in *The Essential Peirce: Selected Philosophical Writings (1867–1893)*, Vol. 1, ed. N. Houser and C. Kloesel. Bloomington, IN: Indiana University Press, 1992 [1877].

—— *The Essential Peirce: Selected Philosophical Writings (1867–1893)*, Vol. I, ed. N. Houser and C. Kloesel. Bloomington, IN: Indiana University Press, 1992.

Quine, W.V. and Ullian, J.S. *The Web of Belief*. Cambridge, MA: Harvard University Press, 1978.

JOHN CORCORAN

KNOWLEDGE: BY ACQUAINTANCE

In the classic American philosophical tradition, the notion of knowledge by acquaintance is usually deployed in bold contrast with "knowledge about" or "descriptive knowledge" or "propositional knowledge," and it marks that tradition's insistence on immediacy as a touchstone in human life. This terminology is often associated with Bertrand Russell, in whose book *Problems of Philosophy* appeared a chapter called "Knowledge by Acquaintance and Knowledge by Description"; he also discussed the topic in *Our Knowledge of the External World* (1914). But though Russell's name has acquired a reflexive association with "knowledge by acquaintance," William James wrote of it as early as 1884 ("Meaning of Truth: The Function of Cognition"), and summarized his view in *Principles of Psychology* (1890) and its chapter entitled "The Relations of Minds to Other Things." There he distinguishes our "knowledge of acquaintance" of (for example) colors, flavors, and feelings of duration, effort, and attention, from "knowledge-about" that cannot be described or communicated. "At most, I can say to my friends, Go to certain places and act in certain ways, and these objects will probably come."

James continues in this vein, noting how very much of our most basic understanding must be "known in this dumb way of acquaintance without knowledge-about." The less we know of a thing's relations, and the less we can describe it, the more must we lead and point one another toward independent recognition, if there is to be any mutuality of shared insight and communication at all. But these are relative conditions: "the same thought of a thing may be called knowledge-about in comparison with a simpler thought, or acquaintance" compared to a more articulate one. By "rallying our wits" we can attain knowledge, or we can choose instead to "relapse" into entranced, inattentive acquaintance. Here James seems to side with those "intellectualists" he and others in the American grain would later sharply criticize for errantly dichotomizing thoughts from feelings and knowledge from acquaintance.

In his later, more explicitly philosophical works, James would return to the theme of inarticulate acquaintance. "The philosophy which is so important in each of us is not a technical matter; it is our more or less dumb sense of what life honestly and deeply means," he announced in *Pragmatism* (1906**). In *A Pluralistic Universe* (1909) he apologized for trying to give voice to something whose acquaintance he was sure we would have to make non-verbally, if at all, and solicited "inner sympathy" to acknowledge a vital core of life that words alone cannot reach. "I must deafen you to talk, or to the importance of talk."

Gone from these later works is any hint that a "rallying of wits," or definitions, might in such instances carry us beyond "mere acquaintance." Gone as well is any implication that acquaintance as such is to be viewed as a deficiency or failure – even if it fails to satisfy the conditions of propositional knowledge. Overall, James typifies a recurrent strain in American philosophy that emphasizes, embraces, and celebrates the human condition as one in which knowledge per se is inevitably partial, but in which the vastly larger class of perceptual experience is richly pluralistic and compensatory.

The point of mentioning "knowledge by acquaintance" typically, and perhaps misleadingly, is not to advance sweeping and generalized knowledge claims based on non-linguistic or prelinguistic forms of experience, but rather to spotlight the ranges and varieties of experience that evade linguistic expression but that nonetheless stand as markers of significant, actionable relations within the totality of personal and communal life. "Knowledge about" is relatively impersonal, mediated by verbal description and based on reports of the experiences of others. "Knowledge by acquaintance" refers to qualities of experience and relations that are personal, intimate, and immediate or first-hand. For James especially, to speak of such "knowledge" is to acknowledge the distinctiveness or "subjectivity" of persons, in the intimacy, immediacy, and felt-but-not spoken texture of incommunicable conscious life.

Philosophers in the classic American tradition contend that there is much more to reality than is dreamt of in the philosophies of those who would treat knowledge as an exclusively intellectual relation, or who claim that it can be captured and translated or expressed in terms of definite descriptions and logically transparent propositions without significant unexpressed remainder. The spirit of this tradition is pithily suggested by John Dewey's declaration, in his *Essays in Experimental Logic* (1916), that "thinking or knowledge-getting is far from being the arm-chair thing it is often supposed to be." For James and Dewey and their confreres and successors, propositional knowledge built on description and inference may have a seductively armchair sort of appeal that is insufficiently engaged in all the processes of living. Knowledge does not occur exclusively in the brain, but is an ongoing and shifting record of the transactions of living organisms attempting to navigate, ameliorate, extend, and transmit their respective natural and social environments.

For humans these transactions are inseparable from the qualities of direct and firsthand experience that we do not merely keen from a distance and impersonally, but that we enjoy with absorbed attention. This is nowhere more strongly expressed in American philosophy than in the first chapter of *Art as Experience* (1934), where Dewey exalts "the delight of the housewife in tending her plants" and "the zest of the spectator in poking the wood burning on the hearth and in watching the darting flames and crumbling coals." We are far from "cold spectators" of our lives and their arresting qualities, far from abstract knowers in the strictly descriptive armchair sense.

Charles Sanders Peirce offers another important analytical perspective with his notion of "firsts," or simple qualities of experience considered apart from any relations into which they might enter. Thus regarded, these qualities announce the presence of purest possibility and spontaneity in our lives: the possibility of fresh, unmediated perception.

Against Russell's insistence that sensory acquaintance with the environing world yields no significant knowledge because "it does not imply knowledge of any proposition concerning the object with which we are acquainted," philosophers in the tradition of James, Dewey, and Peirce remind us that the immediacy of embodied experience perpetually harvests something potentially much more valuable than mere propositional or descriptive observation shorn of its existential context and analyzed in isolation: it yields what neurologist Antonio Damasio has called "the feeling of what happens." Perceptual immediacy, viewed in this light, is the self-renewing seed of a naturalistic faith that can motivate us to intelligent and reconstructive action. George Santayana, often but not always accurately regarded as the antithesis of a pragmatic philosopher, seems to harmonize with the larger American tradition on this point when he writes in *Realms of Being: The Realm of Truth* (1938) that "all the sensuous colour and local perspective proper to human views" are conditions of human knowledge, not barriers to it, "supply(ing) instruments for exploration." Color and context are precisely what James found missing from Russell's account, in uncharacteristically caustic language scoring "Bertie Russell trying to excogitate what true knowledge means, in the absence of any concrete universe surrounding the knower and the known. Ass!"

Philosophers in the classic American tradition champion the immediacy of acquaintance, then, not in lieu of knowledge about but as its complement and sometime-corrective against the casual willingness of some philosophers to construct elaborate philosophical houses floating free of a concrete surrounding universe of real events and real resistances. They insist on the centrality for us all of what James (in *Varieties of Religious Experience*) called "something in the living act of perception that glimmers and twinkles and will not be caught, and for which reflection comes too late" ... but without which reflection and its peculiar form of knowledge would likely not come at all.

Further reading

Dewey, John. *The Essential Dewey*, 2 volumes, ed. Larry A. Hickman and Thomas M. Alexander. Bloomington, IN: Indiana University Press, 1998.

James, William. *The Writings of William James: A Complete Edition*, ed. John J. McDermott. Chicago, IL: University of Chicago Press, 1977.

Lachs, John. *Intermediate Man*. Indianapolis, IN: Hackett, 1981.

Oliver, Phil. *William James's "Springs of Delight": The Return to Life*. Nashville, TN: Vanderbilt University Press, 2001.

Peirce, Charles Sanders. *The Essential Peirce: Selected Philosophical Writings*, 2 volumes, ed. Nathan Houser and Christian Loesel. Bloomington, IN: Indiana University Press, 1992.

Philip Oliver

KNOWLEDGE: BY DESCRIPTION

The distinction between knowledge by description and knowledge by acquaintance is associated with Bertrand Russell; however, a form of the distinction is clearly used as early as Descartes' distinction between deduction and intuition. When one has knowledge of some fact or object by description, one's relation to the known thing is mediated by the descriptions that justify and comprise that knowledge. When one knows something by acquaintance, no such intermediaries obtain. For example, take the proposition that you are in pain. You will know you are in pain just by directing your attention, when you are in pain, to your pain. Someone else, though, would know about your pain on the basis of your non-verbal behavior, your accounts of the pain, or by inferring that you are in pain from some visible physical injury. Both you and someone else can know you are in pain, but these cases of knowledge are different on two fronts. First, the source of their justification is different. The other person relies on inference from your cues and testimony, while you make no inferences – you are directly aware. Second, what the other person believes about your pain is a set of descriptions about your pain dependent on what she can infer. You, though, know your pain not as a set of descriptions, but as a felt fact of the matter. You could describe it (say, to the other person) but your descriptions are descriptions of something prior – namely, your direct awareness of the pain.

Knowledge by description, opposed to knowledge by acquaintance, is mediated in two respects. First, it is epistemically mediate. The justification for the knowledge is derived from something other than the fact that is known – experience, memory, testimony of a fact is different from the fact, and there are cases where our knowledge of facts is held entirely on the basis of these. Second, it is propositionally mediate. What is believed is held in terms of the concepts and descriptions one has of the fact or the object. Descriptions are phrases that carry information about objects that distinguish them from other objects. The information that marks off these objects is information about the objects' properties. So, the phrases "the first man on the moon" and "inventor of bifocals" pick out Neil Armstrong and Benjamin Franklin respectively, and they do so by way of the objects' unique properties. The content of knowledge by description is comprised of a combination of descriptions picking out objects with predicates so that an object with specified properties is known to have other specified properties.

There is a variety of strengths of commitment to knowledge by description. On the one hand, one may hold that knowledge by acquaintance and knowledge by description are distinct and one does not semantically or epistemically precede the other. On the other hand, one may hold that the two are distinct, but one has priority to the other. Russell held that all descriptions are ultimately analyzable into acquaintances and that all cases of knowledge by description are epistemically supported by cases of knowledge by acquaintance. These two theses are those of *semantic* or *logical atomism* and *epistemic foundationalism* respectively. Further, one may be committed to the epistemic or semantic priority of descriptions to acquaintance. For example, classic cases of acquaintance are often articulated with demonstratives (e.g. I now see *this*). But, as Robert Brandom has argued, such demonstratives, in order for them to be relevant to the rest of our cognitive lives, must be sortal. So every *this* that one knows by acquaintance is already something known determinately under some description – it must always be a *this something*. So demonstratives, if they are to play epistemic roles, must always be demonstratives of a certain class of objects and that their meaning is determined in terms of what inferences one can draw about belonging to that class. This thesis is usually termed *inferentialism*, that cases of purported acquaintance are mediated by concepts or descriptions and the inferences they license.

In the American pragmatist tradition, Charles S. Peirce argued that there are no cases of acquaintance or intuitions, because were cognitions intuitive, it would be intuitive that they are intuitive. Were they intuitively intuitive, the second order intuitions themselves must be intuitive, and so on. As such, all knowledge must be knowledge by description. John Dewey extended this inferentialist argument by noting that there must be no conscious experience without inference; reflection is native and constant. Clarence Irving Lewis rebutted this line of argument by showing that without direct knowledge, judgment could not have any specifiable content or epistemic status. Wilfrid Sellars and Richard Rorty have argued that Lewis' case falls into the Myth of the Given; however, without such direct knowledge, human cognition risks being disconnected from the world.

Further reading

Brandom, Robert. *Making It Explicit*. Cambridge, MA: Harvard University Press, 1994.

Descartes, René. *Rules for the Direction of the Mind*. New York: Bobbs-Merrill, 2000.

Dewey, John. "The Need for the Recovery of Philosophy" in *Essays and Articles: Middle Works, Vol. 10, 1916–1917*, ed. Jo Ann Boydston. Carbondale, IL: Southern Illinois University Press. 1985 [1917].

Fumerton, Richard. *Metaepistemology and Skepticism*. Boston, MA: Rowman and Littlefield, 1995.

Lewis, Clarence Irving. *Mind and the World Order: Outline of a Theory of Knowledge*. Mineola, NY: Dover, 1929.

McDowell, John. *Mind and World*. Cambridge, MA: Harvard University Press, 1994.

Peirce, Charles Sanders. "Questions Concerning Certain Faculties Claimed for Man" in *Collected Papers*, Vol. 5,

ed. C. Hartshorne, P. Weiss, and A.W. Burks. Cambridge, MA: Harvard University Press, 1931–58.
Rorty, Richard. *Philosophy and the Mirror of Nature*. Princeton, NJ: Princeton University Press, 1979.
Russell, Bertrand. *The Problems of Philosophy*. Oxford: Oxford University Press, 1912.
—— "On Denoting," *Mind* 14 (1905): 479–93.
Sellars, Wilfrid. *Science, Perception, and Reality*. New York: Humanities Press, 1963.

SCOTT FORREST AIKIN

KNOWLEDGE: PROBABLE

Knowledge is standardly defined as justified true belief. The precise type of justification required for genuine knowledge needs to be properly qualified in order to avoid counterexamples. Among the ways in which beliefs can be justified within these parameters, there are *a priori* and *a posteriori* methods. Justification *a priori* prominently includes appeal to the theorems of pure logic and mathematics, together with analytic truths in which the property predicated of an object is included in the concept of the object, as when we say, for example, that green is a color. If we set aside *a priori* justification as a method of validating knowledge as a term of epistemic appraisal, then all remaining knowledge is *probable*. Probable knowledge in turn is also *empirical*, relying on observation and inference from sensory evidence. It is therefore fallible and defeasible in a way that the absolutely certain knowledge thought to obtain *a priori* from logic, mathematics, and the implications of conceptual analysis is not.

Probable knowledge encompasses all the correct information about the state of the world to which common sense, philosophy and science can possibly aspire. All such knowledge in turn is subject as such to the *problem of induction*. If we compare inductive with deductive reasoning, inductive appears weaker and hence in need of special justification. Deductively valid inferences guarantee the truth of their conclusions conditionally on the truth of their assumptions. If the assumptions of a deductively valid inference are true, then it is logically impossible for their conclusions to be false. Deductive reasoning as a result is said to be *monotonic*, meaning that its conclusions when validly derived always have the same truth value as its assumptions.

As an example, consider that if today is Tuesday, then tomorrow is Wednesday; today is Tuesday, therefore tomorrow is Wednesday. The assumptions might not be true; but if they are, then the conclusion cannot possibly fail to be true. In contrast, inductive reasoning is said to be *nonmonotonic*, meaning that even when the assumptions of an inductive inference are true, the conclusion is not guaranteed to be true, but is only at best inferred thereby to be probably true. If I sample a population of entities in order to determine their properties, I might then try to generalize beyond the sample, concluding that all objects of that certain type have the property I have observed in every member of the sample, or, at least, that all objects of the type have the same percentage of distribution of the property discovered in the sample. This, other things being equal, is a reasonable conclusion to draw, but it bears no guarantee of truth, and it might turn out to be false. If I survey every swan in reach, I might conclude that all swans are white, failing to discover within the limits of my empirical experience that there are Australian swans that are black. Similarly if I apply inductive reasoning on the basis of repeated patterns of past events to conclude that most probably events in the future of similar kind are likely also to display the same features.

Bertrand Russell in his 1912 book *The Problems of Philosophy* famously mentions a chicken who concludes on the basis of a firmly established pattern of events in which every day the farmer offers food that the next day the farmer will do so also; when, in fact, the following day the farmer comes to wring the chicken's neck. The same is true, if, on the basis of past experience, we conclude that the sun is increasingly likely to rise every day, given that it has done so indefinitely in the past. For we know that one day the sun will burst into supernova, after which there will be no more risings or settings of the sun, and no more witnesses of solar phenomena on planet Earth.

The probable truth, and hence probable knowledge, supported by inductive reasoning, being weaker than that of deductive reasoning, seems to require special justification. This is where the problem of induction gets its grip. First remarked by David Hume in *A Treatise of Human Nature* (1739–40), the problem of induction has since been discussed by every major philosopher of science, knowledge theorist, and probability specialist. The problem can be formulated as a dilemma. It would appear that induction, and with it probable knowledge, can only be justified either deductively or inductively. Induction, however, cannot be justified deductively, because deductive grounds for the truth of an inductively inferred probable truth are necessarily deductively invalid. The truth of deductively supported propositions are necessarily true, while an inductively inferred proposition is at most and at best only probably true. Thus, it will always be logically possible for the assumptions of an attempted deductive justification of inductive reasoning to be true while the probable conclusion is false, which is the mark of a deductively invalid inference. On the other hand, an attempt to justify induction inductively is evidently viciously circular.

Some epistemologists and philosophers of science have hoped to avoid the problem of induction by appeal to C.S. Peirce's concept of abductive reasoning as a third choice that potentially might go between the horns of the deductive–inductive dilemma in seeking an adequate justification for probable knowledge. Inference to the best explanation strikes many theorists as different than either deductive or inductive thinking, and, if probable knowledge can be justified as the best explanation for inferences in which knowledge is extended by inductive methods, then it appears promising to avoid the problem of induction and secure the justification of probable knowledge by reference to a mode of reasoning that is neither strictly deductive nor inductive. The difficulty here is to establish abduction as distinct from rather than merely a specific type of inductive reasoning. For, if it is the latter, then it will be just as circular to try to justify induction abductively as more directly by standard inductive considerations.

Another, radically alternative, approach to the problem of justifying probable knowledge is to consider a *transcendental* justification similar to that proposed by Aristotle for the principle of non-contradiction, or by Immanuel Kant for the principles of his transcendental philosophy. By this method, probable knowledge is justified by inductive reasoning if we must presuppose induction even to question its justification. If such a rationale can be supported, then, within the limits of its merely probable implications, probable knowledge can be just as firmly validated and defended as the *a priori* knowledge upheld by logic, mathematics, and conceptual analysis.

In American philosophy, William James emphasizes the importance of probable knowledge in his posthumously published 1912 collection of *Essays in Radical Empiricism*. James defines a quasi-epistemic concept of "pure experience" constitutive of both minds and matter. As such, James' notion of pure experience represents a kind of potentiality, also characterized as "the immediate flux of life" that provides the substance of reflection and further conceptualization. James had previously explained the concept of radical empiricism in his 1911 book, *The Meaning of Truth*. There he defines the basis of knowledge as consisting of a postulate according to which anything capable of philosophical discussion must be drawn from experience, a statement of fact, that relations are just as directly experienced by knowing subjects as the objects the relations relate, and the conclusion that the components of experience hold together by virtue of relations that are themselves experienced. Thus, in James' radical empiricist epistemology, contrary to and even more extreme than Hume's, causal relations themselves are experiential. Empirical experience, for James, is consequently not only the basis of knowledge, but pure experience in his technical sense serves as a surrogate for the ultimate building blocks of material and psychological metaphysical reality. The nature of experience in turn assures that all knowledge of mind and matter for James is probable.

The experiential and hence probable nature of knowledge is central also to John Dewey's pragmatic theory of knowledge. Dewey's early idealism was supplanted by empiricism already in the mid-1890s during his years at the University of Chicago, and which eventually resulted in the publication of four essays on pragmatic epistemology published in 1903 as *Studies in Logical Theory.* In his 1929 *Quest for Certainty: A Study of the Relation of Knowledge and Action*, Dewey confronts an established model for certain knowledge, taking logic and mathematics as its paradigm. Dewey considers this the fundamental mistake of modern philosophy, beginning with the rationalist thinkers G.W. Leibniz and René Descartes, confusing the distinction between knowledge and belief with the distinction between certain and uncertain knowledge. Dewey further equates the misguided quest for certainty as opposed to merely probable empirical knowledge with the desire to separate theory from practice, in trying to penetrate beyond the appearances of things to a higher transcendental knowledge of ultimate reality, such as Kant's or Arthur Schopenhauer's thing-in-itself (*Ding an sich*). Against the grain of these trends, Dewey advocates instead a model of practical knowledge as a realistic human way of interacting with the empirical world in which knowledge is defined pragmatically and experimentally as the practical activity of trying to discover facts about the nature of phenomenal change.

Further reading

Cooke, Elizabeth F. *Peirce's Pragmatic Theory of Inquiry: Fallibilism and Indeterminacy.* London: Continuum Press, 2006.

Dewey, John. *The Quest for Certainty: A Study of the Relation of Knowledge and Action*. New York: Minton, Balch, 1929.

Hume, David. *A Treatise of Human Nature*, third edition, ed. L.A. Selby-Bigge and P.H. Nidditch. Oxford: Clarendon, 1978.

James, William. *The Meaning of Truth*. New York: Longman, Green, 1911.

—— *Essays in Radical Empiricism*. New York: Longman, Green, 1912.

Peirce, C.S. *Collected Papers of Charles Sanders Peirce*, new edition, ed. Charles Hartshorne, Paul Weiss and Arthur W. Burks. London: Thoemmes, Continuum Press, 1998.

DALE JACQUETTE

KNOWLEDGE: SENSIBLE

Sensible knowledge concerns sensory experiences and the objects perceived by means of such experiences. An example of the former is the experience of seeing and smelling a rose; an example of the latter is the rose that is seen and smelled. Although there is no question that sensory experiences and perceived objects both exist, influential American philosophers have had serious disagreement about how the two of them enter into perceptual knowledge. The basic points at issue are well illustrated by the sharply contrasting views of Roderick Chisholm and Wilfrid Sellars.

Chisholm acknowledged that his philosophy was deeply indebted to Descartes. As he saw it, the most secure empirical knowledge concerns our nature as thinking, sensible creatures (Chisholm 1989). When we think or have some sensory experience, our thoughts or sensations are "self-presenting": we have direct, non-inferential knowledge of what they are like, and there is no possibility of our being wrong about them. Chisholm described sensible experiences as states of sensing or "being appeared to." These states do not contain or involve sensory objects, as many of his predecessors thought; they are best described adverbially – as in saying that someone "senses redly." Our knowledge of these states is not only direct or immediate; it is epistemically fundamental. Together with our knowledge of what we are thinking, believing, or supposing, our knowledge of our sensory experiences provides the foundation of our empirical knowledge. If we are subjected to persistent Socratic questioning about how we know some contingent matter of fact, we shall eventually arrive at propositions that we know to be certain because they assert that we have some self-presenting mental or sensible property.

Chisholm expended much effort attempting to show how knowledge of self-presenting sensible states can provide a rational justification for believing that mind-independent objects of sensing, roses or garden sheds, actually exist. His view of how this is done changed significantly over the years. In the first two editions of his *Theory of Knowledge* (1966, 1977), he held that the justification is given by special rules of evidence, which we can know to be sound because they yield exactly the knowledge of external objects that we intuitively accept. In his third edition of the book (1989), he abandoned this view and argued that the general presuppositions from which the desired justification is directly inferable are ultimately justified by the self-trust or faith in their own cognitive abilities that epistemologists naturally possess. Such epistemologists (who are not skeptics) are committed, he thought, to accepting those presuppositions. A justification of this kind does not show that the presuppositions are true or likely to be true, however. For this reason, his revised view of empirical justification is disappointing to many contemporary philosophers.

Sellars

The self-presenting character of sensible properties that Chisholm spoke of is substantially the same as the "giveness" of sensory experiences that was assumed by philosophers of an earlier generation. In a very influential essay, "Empiricism and the Philosophy of Mind," Wilfrid Sellars argued that the entire category of giveness is a "myth." Sellars's argument is complicated and difficult to summarize, but its upshot is that no contingent assertion is inherently credible and that even sensory experiences can in principle be misrepresented by a subject's beliefs. Accepting the current conviction urged by followers of the later Wittgenstein, Sellars in fact turned Chisholm's position on its head, contending that assertions about objects of sensation (flowers or street lamps) are actually more basic, epistemically, than assertions about sensations themselves. Instead of having to support beliefs about public objects by beliefs about one's sensory experiences, one obviously needs to do the opposite when dealing about the experiences of others, and one in fact learns to identify and describe one's own experiences in relation to the publicly accessible contexts in which they occur. This is why we describe our experiences indirectly, as in using such words as "the experience of seeing a red rose." If someone should say that he or she is seeing red when looking at something blue, another person would probably object, saying the speaker could hardly be using the right words in a case like this.

In sharp contrast to Chisholm, Sellars explicitly rejected the view that empirical knowledge rests on a foundation of sensible certainty. In his view it does not rest on any foundation at all. Instead of adopting the Hegelian alternative that empirical knowledge consists in some kind of coherence among one's beliefs, he adopted a third position, which he did not fully elaborate. As he put it,

> we do not have to choose between the picture of an elephant resting on a tortoise (what supports the tortoise?) and the picture of a great Hegelian serpent of knowledge with its tail in its mouth (where does it all begin?).

The alternative we should accept, he said, is that "empirical knowledge, like its sophisticated extension, science, is rational, not because it has a foundation, but because it is a self-correcting enterprise that can put any claim in jeopardy, though not all at once" (Sellars 1963: 170).

Sellars also differed from Chisholm in not making use of special rules of evidence or an unsupported faith in one's cognitive abilities for the justification of beliefs about the experiences of others or the unobservable objects of chemistry or physics. He relied instead on the scientific method of postulation, prediction, and verification or refutation. He did not attempt to describe the logic of this method in any detail: what he did say is consistent with an endorsement of the so-called hypothetico-deductive method (see Earman 1983) or the method of Inference to the Best Explanation (see Lycan 1988). His claim was that science is just an "extension" of common sense and that common-sense reasoning about other people's experiences and such things as germs or electricity is basically the same as the reasoning carried out by scientists in the laboratory. It is less mathematical, to be sure, but it has essentially the same logical structure.

Further reading

Chisholm, R.M. *Theory of Knowledge*. First edition 1966; second edition 1977; third edition 1989. Englewood Cliffs, NJ: Prentice Hall, 1996.

Earman, John (ed.) *Testing Scientific Theories*, Vol. X of *Minnesota Studies in the Philosophy of Science*. Minneapolis, MN: University of Minnesota Press, 1983.

Lycan, William G. *Judgment and Justification*. Cambridge: Cambridge University Press, 1988.

Sellars, Wilfrid. "Empiricism and the Philosophy of Mind" in his *Science, Perception, and Reality*. London: Routledge and Kegan Paul, 1963, pp. 127–96.

BRUCE AUNE

KNOWLEDGE: SPECULATIVE

On the face of it, the term "speculative knowledge" is an oxymoron. Knowledge is commonly taken to require rational certainty, but speculation is associated with conjectures, guesses, and hypotheses. Kant, in his *Critique of Pure Reason*, a work that strongly influenced generations of American philosophers, went so far as to claim that speculation is the main source of false thinking in metaphysics. Human beings, he said, are naturally disposed to speculate about three "transcendental" subjects: the existence of God, the freedom of the will, and the immortality of the human soul. But because we cannot in his view have genuine knowledge of things that transcend our experience, our speculation about these transcendental subjects must be futile. Fortunately, our practical concerns as rational beings justify us in believing that God, freedom, and personal immortality are not illusory. In place of speculative knowledge, we have rationally grounded faith. Charles S. Peirce, the originator of pragmatism, appears to have shared this view (see Peirce). For him, religion is a matter of faith, not knowledge.

A closer look at speculation reveals a connection with knowledge that Kant, at least, overlooked. When we wonder how some phenomenon may be explained, we speculate about explanatory factors. Many contemporary American philosophers suppose that Inference to the Best Explanation is a basic source of a posteriori knowledge (see Harmon, Lycan). If they are right, speculation is therefore important for empirical knowledge. This method of inference is not accepted, however, by all American philosophers; some insist that there is really no good reason to suppose that the best explanatory hypothesis anyone can think of in a particular case is generally true or even close to the truth. As they see it, mere speculation can uncover hypotheses that may deserve testing, but it is successful testing rather than speculation that actually delivers knowledge (see van Fraassen). Of course, if the speculation did not occur, the subsequent testing would not have occurred either. Thus, fruitful speculation makes at least a necessary contribution to what we know.

Reflection shows that speculation has a further connection with knowledge. Sometimes scientists speculate about the possible causes of some phenomenon. When they do this, they are not concerned with abstract possibilities; they are concerned with what is consistent with existing evidence. An example concerns the origin of life in our solar system. Scientific evidence about the age of this system convinced some thinkers that there was insufficient time for life to have evolved in it; life must have evolved elsewhere, they thought, and somehow found its way here. But recent discoveries support a more likely hypothesis. It is now known that the kind of molecules found in interstellar clouds, when dosed with ultraviolet light, form a variety of organic molecules whose further interactions can produce amino acids and other biochemical molecules. If these organic molecules had drifted to earth when it was about 600 million years old, there would have been ample time for life to evolve here (see Gribbin). This kind of speculation rests on scientific evidence, and its connection with actual knowledge is very close.

Further reading

Gribbin, John. *Stardust*. London: Penguin, 2000.
Harman, Gilbert. "Inference to the Best Explanation," *Philosophical Review* 74 (1965): 88–95.
Kant, Emmanuel. *Critique of Pure Reason*, trans. and ed. Paul Guyer and Allen Wood. Cambridge: Cambridge University Press, 1997. (German original first published in 1781.)
Lycan, William G. *Judgment and Justification*. Cambridge: Cambridge University Press, 1988.
Peirce, Charles S. "Critique of Positivism" in *Writings of Charles S. Peirce*, Vol. 2, ed. Edward C. Moore. Bloomington, IN: Indiana University Press, 1984, pp. 122–30.
van Fraassen, Bas C. *The Empirical Stance*. New Haven, CT: Yale University Press. 2002.

Bruce Aune

KUHN, THOMAS

Thomas Samuel Kuhn (1922–96) was an American historian and philosopher of science and the author of *The Structure of Scientific Revolutions* ("*Structure*" for short), the one book that has, since its 1962 publication, most shaped scholarly discussion about, and understanding of, science. Although he received bachelor's, master's, and doctorate degrees in physics (in 1943, 1946, and 1949, respectively, from Harvard University), and was professionally an historian of science for most of his career, Kuhn is frequently cited as the twentieth century's most influential philosopher of science. He began his academic career at Harvard, moving to the University of California-Berkeley in 1957, Princeton University in 1964, and the Massachusetts Institute of Technology in 1979, where he was Laurence S. Rockefeller Professor of Philosophy at the time of his retirement in 1991.

Structure was Kuhn's attempt to replace an "image of science" by which (as he put it) philosophers, historians, and sociologists of science, as well as scientists, had been "possessed" with a competing image, one Kuhn took to be consonant with science's history. On Kuhn's image, science is a social enterprise in which a community attempts to solve puzzles involving the natural world, inspired and guided by a set of puzzle-solutions Kuhn called a "paradigm." Such "normal science," however, inevitably produces "anomalies" – puzzles that resist solution despite repeated attempts by the community's best minds. Anomalies cause crisis in the community which is resolved in the course of "revolutionary science," a period in which a new paradigm – one that handles its predecessor's anomalies and is incompatible with it – is adopted. Normal science resumes under this paradigm, until it too is beset by anomalies, crisis, and revolution.

Structure's influence is reflected in the issues it brought to the fore in philosophy of science. Kuhn claimed, for example, that scientific observations necessarily reflected a paradigm (they were, in Norwood Russell Hanson's phrase, "theory-laden"), and that new paradigms were *incommensurable* with their predecessors. From these claims Kuhn drew the conclusion that adherents to different paradigms lived, literally, in different worlds. Kuhn further argued that science accumulates puzzle-solutions, not truths, and this only in periods of normal science (although in *Structure's* comparatively sober final chapter argues that puzzle-solutions accumulate even over revolutions).

Debate over paradigms, theory-ladenness, incommensurability, and progress dominated philosophical discussion about science for decades after *Structure*, motivating philosophers and historians of science to collaborate, and leading various disciplines to assess their own disciplines along Kuhnian lines. Kuhn pursued subsequent research in the history and philosophy of science, seeking through a series of essays to develop themes introduced in *Structure* (abandoning the term "paradigm," for example, in his 1970 "Postscript" to *Structure* in response to the term's overuse) and, increasingly, distance himself from approaches to science that looked to *Structure* for arguments that science was not just a social enterprise but ultimately an irrational one as well. A book manuscript, systematically developing his mature philosophy of science, was unfinished at the time of his death.

Further reading

Bird, Alexander. *Thomas Kuhn*. Princeton, NJ: Princeton University Press, 2001.
Horwich, Paul (ed.). *World Changes: Thomas Kuhn and the Nature of Science*. Cambridge, MA: MIT Press, 1993.

Hoyningen-Huene, Paul. *Reconstructing Scientific Revolutions: Thomas S. Kuhn's Philosophy of Science*, trans. Alexander T. Levine. Chicago, IL: University of Chicago Press, 1993.

Kuhn, Thomas S. *The Copernican Revolution: Planetary Astronomy in the Development of Western Thought*. Cambridge, MA: Harvard University Press, 1957.

—— *The Road since Structure: Philosophical Essays, 1970–1993, with an Autobiographical Interview*, ed. James Conant and John Haugeland. Chicago, IL: University of Chicago Press, 2000.

Gary L. Hardcastle

L

LAMONT, CORLISS

Corliss Lamont (1902–95) was born in Englewood, New Jersey, to Florence C. and Thomas W. Lamont. He was educated at Harvard College, later at New College, Oxford, and finally earned a Ph.D. at Columbia University under the guidance of Frederick J.E. Woodbridge. He wrote a doctoral thesis on the subject of human immortality, and remained preoccupied with that subject until the end of his life. A crusading spirit, Lamont was deeply concerned with the safeguarding of civil liberties. He was elected to the Board of Directors of the American Civil Liberties Union in 1932, and remained a member of the Board for twenty-three years.

Because he advocated strenuously on behalf of Socialist ideals, and because his 1946 book *The Peoples of the Soviet Union* found its way into the bibliography of a United States Army pamphlet, Lamont was questioned before the Senate Permanent Subcommittee on Investigations by Senator Joseph McCarthy in September 1953. McCarthy claimed the pamphlet included Communist propaganda. Lamont finally defeated his indictment, which was dismissed by a Federal District Judge in July 1955, on the substantial grounds that the Senate Permanent Subcommittee had no authority to investigate him. It was a signal victory against the abuse of power by Congressional committees.

The centerpiece of Lamont's intellectual bequest is the philosophy of naturalistic humanism, which he unflaggingly championed and tried to popularize. His most famous book, *The Philosophy of Humanism*, now in its eighth edition and originally published in 1949 under the title *Humanism as a Philosophy*, is thought to be a standard text on the subject. As its name indicates, naturalistic humanism professes to combine the main tenets of two long-standing philosophical positions.

Naturalism is the metaphysical thesis that our universe and everything in it amounts to a single vast system governed by laws. In such a universe, any purportedly supernatural event must either (A) enter into the system from without, in which case it would be fundamentally unintelligible, or (B) arise from within the system itself, in which case it would, at least in principle, be explainable in terms of the laws of the system. In the case of (B), to call the event "supernatural" would be misleading at best. Hence, according to naturalism, there are no such things as supernatural events.

Humanism is the value-theoretical view that human beings and our ideals have a certain kind of priority in the universe, either ontological, or epistemic, or moral priority. Naturalism suggests a boundless universe governed by extra-human laws in which human beings and our ideals are comparatively insignificant. By contrast, humanism suggests that human beings are cosmically pre-eminent.

Exactly how Lamont can manage to marry the two positions is unclear. What is clear about Lamont's positions is mainly negative. We know what he did not believe. He did not believe in either a personal or an impersonal divinity and was eager to confute, if not to convert, religious believers of every type. He did not believe in personal immortality, even though the issue so possessed him that he penned a study of more than 250 pages on the subject entitled *The Illusion of Immortality.* The original edition includes a selection of poetry on the subject of death and the possibility of immortality. Lamont was strongly influenced by the work of Bertrand Russell, John Dewey, and George Santayana, with all of whom he occasionally corresponded.

Further reading

Lamont, Corliss. *The Peoples of the Soviet Union.* New York: Harcourt, Brace, 1946.
—— *A Humanist Funeral Service.* Buffalo, NY: Prometheus Books, 1977.
—— *Freedom of Choice Affirmed.* New York: Continuum, 1990.
—— *The Illusion of Immortality.* New York: Continuum, 1990.
—— *The Philosophy of Humanism.* Amherst, NY: Humanist Press, 1996.

MICHAEL BRODRICK

LANGER, SUSANNE

Susanne Knauth Langer (1895–1985) was, at once, a philosopher's philosopher and an author with the facility to contribute pieces to such publications as *Fortune* or *Saturday Evening Post*. She was also one of the first women in the United States to pursue a career as a philosopher and, unquestionably, the first one to garner an international reputation. Almost immediately upon her divorce in 1942, Langer resigned her position at Radcliffe and left Cambridge, MA, for New York, for the next twelve years taking a series of temporary positions, including ones at NYU (1945–6), Columbia (1945–50), and the New School for Social Research (1950), later ones in the Midwest (Northwestern, Ohio State, and University of Michigan) and for one year on the west coast (University of Washington). In 1954, Langer at the age of sixty secured her first permanent position in the Department of Philosophy at Connecticut College, though a grant in 1956 freed her from the responsibilities of teaching for the remainder of her life. She nonetheless remained formally affiliated with Connecticut College.

The trajectory of her intellectual life can be traced from her early work on logic (including the philosophy of logic), through a phase in which the topic of symbolization became the pivotal concern of her philosophical investigations, to one in which the distinctive features of artistic symbols became her central preoccupation, culminating in the period in which she undertook the daunting task of articulating in painstaking detail a thoroughly naturalistic account of the human mind. While her first philosophical work, *The Practice of Philosophy* (1930), praised by Whitehead (with whom she as a graduate student studied) for being "an admirable exposition of the aims, methods, and actual achievements of philosophy," defended her conception of philosophy as the clarification of various kinds of meaning, her next book, *An Introduction to Symbolic Logic* (1937), more clearly indicated the principal focus of the years immediately following the receipt of her Ph.D. But her conception of logic (logic being the study of the "types and relations among abstracted forms"), deeply influenced by her teacher Henry Sheffer, was broad and, in a sense, flexible, allowing "as much scope for originality as metaphysics." Along with C.I. Lewis, Alonzo Church, and W.V. Quine, and others, she helped found the Association for Symbolic Logic and her own *Introduction* was one of the first textbooks in this relatively new field. From technical questions in logic, her philosophical attention shifted to broader questions about symbolization, a shift dramatically signaled by the publication of *Philosophy in a New Key: A Study in the Symbolism of Reason, Rite and Art* (1942). The conclusions regarding music and art put forth in Chapters VIII ("On Significance in Music") and IX ("The Genesis of Artistic Import") were generalized and developed in detail in Langer's following books – *Feeling and Form: A Theory of Art developed from Philosophy in a New Key* (1953), *Problems of Art: Ten Philosophical Lectures* (1957), and to some extent also in *Philosophical Sketches* (1962). Then, after immersing herself in the research of biologists, psychologists, anthropologists, and other scientists, she brought forth the fruits of her own research in the three successive volumes of *Mind: An Essay on Human Feeling* (1967; 1973; 1982; 1988, abridged edition edited by Gary Van Den Heuvel). From these titles alone, it is evident that her contributions range from logic to epistemology, semiotics to aesthetics, the philosophy of culture to philosophy of mind. The paperback edition of *Philosophy in a New Key: A Study in the Symbolism in Reason, Rite, and Art*, the work for which she is still best known, was a bestseller. Her first publication ("Confusion of Symbols and Confusion of Logical Types," a critique of Bertrand Russell's theory of types) was an article in *Mind*, then under the editorship of G.E. Moore. Her last was the third and unfinished volume of *Mind: An Essay on Feeling.* The defining marks of an indefatigably inquisitive intellect are evident from first to last.

The thread running from her earliest work in logic to her culminating investigation of mind is a preoccupation with meaning in its most generalizable form and its myriad species (meaning being closely allied with form). While she never was narrowly interested in technical questions of symbolic logic, such questions were ones of intense interest in her. Indeed, she saw the work of philosophy to be principally the task of clarifying meaning, including the reflexive task of becoming clearer about the meaning of meaning itself. Her concern with this topic was already evident in her dissertation, *A Logical Analysis of Meaning* (Radcliffe, 1926). But her MA thesis from the same institution, *Eduard von Hartmann's Notion of Unconscious Mind and Its Metaphysical Implications* (1924) foreshadowed by more than four decades her mature attempt to formulate a naturalistic account of mind, consciousness, and feeling, one in which the work of Freud and other defenders of the unconscious is judiciously considered. (Hartmann convinced C.S. Peirce of the reality of unconscious mind, while he served as a foil for James's spirited critique in the *Principles* of various attempts to render meaningful such expressions as "unconscious mental states"). Langer judged *Mind* to be her most significant contribution to the intellectual world, but these volumes were at the time of their publication the subject of only qualified praise. In recent years, however, the relevance of her treatment of mind to contemporary developments, including cognitive science, has won increasing recognition. It is conceivable that her last work will in time come to illuminate our understanding of mind, consciousness, and emotion as earlier ones have influenced our thinking about symbols, art, and culture. Whether or not this turns out to be true, her multifaceted and deep-cutting contribution to philosophy and other disciplines cannot be gainsaid.

Further reading

Berthoff, Ann E. "Susanne K. Langer and the Process of Feeling" in her *The Mysterious Barricades: Language and Its Limits*. Toronto: University of Toronto Press, 1999, pp. 112–24.

Campbell, James. "Langer's Understanding of Philosophy," *Transactions of the Charmless Peirce Society* 33, 1 (1997): 133–47.

Nelson, Beatrice K. "Susanne K. Langer's Conception of 'Symbol': Making Connections through Ambiguity" in Cecile T. Tougas and Sara Ebenreck (eds) *Presenting Women Philosophers*. Philadelphia, PA: Temple University Press, pp. 71–80.

Reichling, Mary J. "Susanne Langer's Theory of Symbolism: An Analysis and Extension," *Philosophy of Music and Education Review* 1 (1993): 3–17.

Royce, Joseph R. "The Implications of Langer's Philosophy of Mind for a Science of Psychology," *Journal of Mind and Behavior*, 4 (1983): 491–506.

VINCENT COLAPIETRO

LANGUAGE

Philosophic accounts of language have often been undertaken with the expectation that an understanding of language will contribute to an understanding of the nature of mind. Language has also been studied by philosophers in connection with investigations of logic and epistemology. At the end of the nineteenth and the beginning of the twentieth century, however, some American philosophers became interested in language per se – in its defining characteristics, its origin and nature. The idea that language needs philosophic delineation may itself count as a new development. Many philosophers had simply assumed, many continue to assume, that the capacity for language is a self-evidently distinctive feature of the human mind, and many philosophers have participated in a cultural tradition that sees this capacity as a divine gift or a unique invention.

Pragmatic, evolutionary accounts

George Herbert Mead and John Dewey were among those who came to see language as evolved, not bestowed or invented, and they wanted to find a naturalistic explanation for this evolution. Darwinian theory set the context for this new perspective. If human beings were understood as part of nature, not as separate and above nature, as continuous with other biological organisms, not utterly distinctive, then it became reasonable to try to understand language in a wider biological context. The evolutionary standpoint also suggested the appropriateness of a revised teleological inquiry, one that looked for the point of language in its usefulness, its functional qualities, and its survival advantages.

All the classic pragmatic philosophers noted the affinities, not just the differences, between human language use and non-human animal communication. William James, in *The Principles of Psychology,* described language as a system of signs associated with objects, and he compared communicative processes of signification in "brutes" with those undertaken by human children and "primeval man." According to James, the animal signals begin "involuntarily." For example, a dog, overflowing with energy from impeded desire, barks before a closed door. The dog's master lets the dog out. Repetition of this process leads the dog to associate the bark with the opening of the door, and soon the dog manages to produce the bark intentionally, as a signal. The rat terrier learns the human word "rat," as it is uttered repeatedly in conjunction with the culmination of an activity of great natural interest to the terrier. Human speech too begins with emotional interjections, James claimed, but the greater human capacity for vocalization, the great imitativeness of humans, and, most importantly, the human ability to abstract the idea of a *sign* together lead to a vast generalization of this process. Humans develop "a deliberate intention to apply a sign to everything," James said, and this leads to the proliferation of signs that, to James, indicated true language.

James's account of signification was in many ways close to the traditional theories of language he took himself to be criticizing, and his discussion was not wholly evolutionary. (Indeed, the discussion of animal communication adverts to neither biology nor ethology, but is focused on a domesticated animal interacting with modern man, "its master.") Charles Sanders Peirce offered an evolutionary theory of signs, but his was a very general theory, with no specific emphasis on language per se. Peirce's triadic division of signs (icon, index, and symbol) suggested basic modes of representation (reference by resemblance, by modification or connection, and by law or convention), and anything – a photograph, a plume of smoke, a word in a natural language – could be understood as a sign. Because every sign has an interpretant, according to Peirce's theory, and because the interpretant is itself a sign, with, in turn, its own interpretant, and so on *ad infinitum*, there is a dynamism in Peirce's account that seemed to mirror the life of natural language. Peirce insisted, too, on the growth and development of symbols, and illustrated this growth by pointing to the spread of words in natural languages and words' changing meanings over time. Language use was just one example of sign functioning, however, not the central focus of Peirce's semiotic, which was meant to be a formal doctrine of all signs.

Mead and Dewey

Among the classical pragmatists, it was Mead who tried most directly to give a detailed evolutionary account of the development and nature of language. He suggested continuity with the signaling behavior of non-human animals, and he presented language as an emergent feature of basic social interactions tied to biological or physiological impulses. Analyzing meaning in terms of response, Mead sketched the mutual modifications that animals might undergo in a cooperative or a hostile social act – e.g. a dogfight. The growl and bared teeth of a dog protecting its territory provoke some response of the part of the interloper – either turned tail and retreat or bared teeth and a lunge. The interloper's lunge provokes further action, say a jump and bite from the first dog, and so on. Various segments of the dogfight can be understood as stimuli from one dog eliciting responses from the other, and each response can be understood as an interpretation – as the meaning – of the stimulus. Mead called these mutual modifications "a conversation of gestures," and he thought that eventually, in some animals, such conversations could proceed intentionally. Language requires not just intentional control of gestures, however, but, according to Mead, shared meanings. If meaning is understood in terms of response, what is then required for language is shared responses to gestures. The "vocal gesture" is an ideal vehicle for the development of language, Mead claimed, because it is heard by its maker just as it is heard by the one to whom it is addressed. It is a stimulus that can provoke a shared response. Changes in breathing patterns that accompany sudden action – action to which others must adjust – unconscious, involuntary grunts and cries could, Mead suggested, evolve into self-consciously controlled vocal communication among social animals that shared basic needs, basic urges, and hence basic reactions.

Mead also offered an ontogenetic account of language acquisition, again in terms of social context, viz. the interactions required for nurturance and survival. Again he relied on the idea that the similar physiology of human beings – not imitativeness – allowed for shared responses from one generation to the next, and thus the transmission of language. Dewey endorsed the rough outlines of Mead's theory of the social construction of language and the intertwined account of the evolution of mind. Both philosophers embraced an interactionist understanding of the relation between individuals, language, and society. Language may have evolved from contingent circumstances, and may with each generation begin again with instinctive babbling and gestures; but, Dewey claimed, language once in existence molds and modifies the forces that produced it. A child learns the language spoken by those around him or her. Those particular linguistic customs shape the babblings, form the linguistic habits of the young child, because it is only by conforming to the customs of the surrounding community that the child can articulate the full range of his or her needs and better secure their satisfaction. At the same time, each generation, each individual will contribute to the renewal and the reconstruction of language. We may say, Dewey noted, that French, Spanish, Italian, and so on have been derived from a Latin mother tongue, and yet there was never a time at which the changes that led to these separate languages were intentionally or explicitly introduced. Constitutive growth and differentiation work reciprocally between language, on the one hand, and, on the other, individual human minds as well as functional human groups.

Historical linguistics vs structuralism

As the pragmatists were incorporating the Darwinian perspective into their approach to philosophical problems, the separate field of linguistics was also being transformed by evolutionary theory. Language changes over the course of time were being meticulously charted, and historical linguistics came to dominate the field. Other new, or newly, differently understood, social sciences – anthropology, psychology, sociology – were also contributing to philosophers' conceptions of language. At the end of the nineteenth century, however, and throughout much of the twentieth, interest revived in thinking of language formally and synchronically, as a complete system at a moment of time. The Swiss linguist Ferdinand de Saussure was the pivotal figure in the emergence of this new structural linguistics, and Leonard Bloomfield was the leading American structuralist. Adherents of structuralism held that each element of a language could be understood only in the context of its relationship to every other element. Though a structural analysis of language was formal, structural linguistics was also descriptive, and Bloomfield's methodology was rigorously empirical. He insisted that observable data ground all structuralist accounts.

The Sapir–Whorf hypothesis

Bloomfield's positivistic, behavioristic, formal approach to language was compatible with the dominant philosophical outlook in Anglo-American philosophy in the first half of the twentieth century, but speculative interest in the relation between language and mind never disappeared. The anthropologist–linguist Edward Sapir, along with his student Benjamin Whorf, suggested that there might be a relationship of mutual and reciprocal influence between a particular natural language and the thought and behavior of native speakers of that language. The systematic descriptive study of non-Indo-European languages – e.g. Hopi, and other native American languages – and the discovery of their categorical differences from most languages of Western Europe suggested to Sapir and Whorf that, from a flux of sensations and phenomena, different cultures might organize, see, and understand the world differently, with these differences reflected in each language, and with each language in turn shaping the cognition, perception, and behavior of its native speakers.

Chomsky and generative grammar

In the mid-twentieth century, another development in linguistics had an extraordinary impact on philosophy. Noam Chomsky's 1957 *Syntactic Structures* and his 1965 *Aspects of the Theory of Syntax* suggested not just a new way of analyzing syntax but a new view of language. Chomsky asserted that any language can generate an infinite number of novel sentences, so no matter how many instances of actual language use are described and analyzed, the proportion of the language thus understood will always be trivially small. Instead of linguistic performance, then, linguistic competence should be the subject matter of linguistic science. Competence – that which allows the native speaker to speak and understand the language – is not, however, directly observable. Chomsky claimed that a distinction could be made between the "surface structures" of linguistic expressions and the "deep structures" underlying those expressions. An adequate theory of language, according to Chomsky, would involve identification of the deep structures of language and articulation of the transformational rules that can, from those deep structures, generate any fully grammatical sentence.

Chomsky argued, in addition, that available theories of learning, behaviorism in particular, could not account for the speed and facility with which a child acquires language. Infants hear a very limited sample of language, yet very quickly, with little apparent effort or training, all normal children learn language, learn to construct novel but grammatical sentences. To grasp the grammar of their native languages so easily, on the basis of so little evidence, children must have, Chomsky claimed, "innate schematisms" for grammar. Because this process of rapid natural language acquisition holds for children born into any language community, the "tacit knowledge" must be of a universal grammar. Thus Chomsky seemed to resuscitate rationalism, and he took himself to be endorsing a theory of innate ideas.

Behavioristically inclined philosophers, such as Willard Van Orman Quine, criticized both the methodology and the conclusions of Chomsky's theories. A speaker's behavior might be captured by grammatical rules or principles posited by Chomsky, but that would not show that that particular set of rules, rather than another extensionally equivalent one, exists in the mind of the speaker or actually guides the behavior. Quine pointed to the problem of evidence for the linguistic universals posited by Chomsky, given that behavioral criteria do not indicate either the existence or the identity of the elements of those universals. John Searle, a philosopher sympathetic to speech-act theory, found the Chomskian idea of competence impoverished, as it focused on the production and understanding of utterances, but neglected language's communicative force and the role of speakers' intentions. Still, the Chomskian revolution in linguistics has helped fortify the currency of interdisciplinary cognitive science as an approach to the philosophic study of language. Other methodologies persist, however, and in a variety of ways, from a variety of perspectives, philosophy remains interested in the relation between language, logic, and mind.

Further reading

Bloomfield, Leonard. *Language*. Chicago, IL: University of Chicago Press, 1984.

Chomsky, Noam. *Syntactic Structures*. Berlin: Walter de Gruyter, 2002.

Lepore, Ernest and Smith, Barry (eds) *The Oxford Handbook of Philosophy of Language*. New York: Oxford University Press, 2006.

Peirce, Charles S. "Speculative Grammar" in *Collected Papers of Charles Sanders Peirce*, ed. Charles Hartshorne and Paul Weiss, Vol. II. Cambridge, MA: Harvard University Press, 1960.

Quine, Willard Van Orman. *Word and Object*. Cambridge, MA: MIT Press, 1964.

Sapir, Edward. *Language: An Introduction to the Study of Speech*. New York: Dover, 2004.

Searle, John. *Speech Acts: An Essay in the Philosophy of Language*. Cambridge: Cambridge University Press, 1969.

Skinner, B.F. *Verbal Behavior*. New York: Appleton-Century-Crofts, 1957.

Whorf, Benjamin. *Language, Thought, and Reality: Selected Writings*. Cambridge, MA: MIT Press, 1964.

KAREN HANSON

LAVINE, THELMA Z.

Thelma Z. Lavine (1915–) was born in Boston, Massachusetts. She received a BA from Radcliffe College and an MA and PhD from Harvard University. Lavine studied psychology as well as philosophy at Harvard and her first teaching position, at Wells College, was in both fields. She taught philosophy at Brooklyn College from 1946 to 1951 and at the University of Maryland from 1955 to 1965, and in 1965 she was given their Outstanding Faculty Member Award. Later that year she was appointed Elton Professor of Philosophy at George Washington University, and she received their Outstanding Professor Award in 1968. In addition to teaching philosophy, she attended seminars at the Washington School of Psychiatry from 1965 to 1970. In 1985 she was appointed Clarence G. Robinson Professor of Philosophy and American Culture at George Mason University and she held that chair until she retired from teaching in 1998. Among the courses she taught were Philosophy of the Social Sciences, Nineteenth-Century Philosophy, and Habits of the American Heart and Mind in which she located American Philosophy in an economic and political context.

A prolific writer, Dr. Lavine has lectured and published on a wide variety of topics, notably the ideas of the Founding Fathers, women's studies, Judaic studies, psychoanalysis, biomedical ethics, metaphysics, modernism, and postmodernism, as well as pragmatism and other schools of thought in American philosophy. In 1991, at a meeting of the Central Division of the American Philosophical Association, she gave the fifth Patrick Romanell Lecture on Philosophic Naturalism. The title of the lecture was "Modernity and the Spirit of Naturalism" and in it she discussed American naturalistic pragmatism within a historical framework.

Among the American philosophers about whom Lavine has written are Charles S. Peirce, John Dewey, C.I. Lewis, Morris R. Cohen, John Herman Randall, Jr., Arthur Bentley, Richard Rorty, Charles Frankel and John J. McDermott. In addition to American philosophy she has written about European philosophy, including articles about Kant, Karl Mannheim, Jacques Derrida and Paul Ricoeur, and she has also written about Sigmund Freud.

Writings by Lavine have been published in several other countries, including the Netherlands, the Federal Republic of Germany, and Japan. While continuing to teach and to write, she gave thirty lectures on television in a series, *From Socrates to Sartre: A Historical Introduction to Philosophy*. The series, which was first presented in 1979 appeared numerous times on commercial as well as university television stations, and students could earn college credit for it. She also wrote a book on the same topic, *From Socrates to Sartre: The Philosophic Quest*; 250,000 copies were published in the

United States and the book was translated into Japanese and published in Japan.

Thelma Lavine has been active in philosophy organizations. She was a founding member of SOPHIA, the Society of Philosophers in America, which was organized in 1987, and she was President of the Society for the Advancement of American Philosophy from 1992 to 1994. In 2000, at the Annual Meeting of this organization, she received the Herbert W. Schneider Award for Distinguished Contributions to the Understanding and Development of American Philosophy.

Further reading

Lavine, Thelma Z. "Naturalism and the Sociological Analysis of Knowledge" in Yervant H. Krikorian (ed.) *Naturalism and the Human Spirit*. New York: Columbia University Press, 1944.

—— *From Socrates to Sartre: A Historical Introduction to Philosophy*, New York: Bantam Books, 1984; in Japanese, *Koshiva Chiba*, Japan: Riso-Sha, 1988

—— "Judaism in the Culture of Modernity" in William O'Neill (ed.) *Philosophy, History, and Social Action*. Dordrecht: Reidel, 1988.

—— "Modernity and the Spirit of Naturalism," Fifth Annual Romanell Lecture on Philosophic Naturalism, *Proceedings and Addresses of the American Philosophical Association* 65 (1991).

—— "The Case for a New American Pragmatism," in A. Kurtz and T. Madigan (eds) *Challenges to the Enlightenment*. Amherst, NY: Prometheus Books, 1994.

—— "Modernity, Interpretation Theory, and American Philosophy", in Robert W. Burch and Herman J. Saatkamp, Jr. (eds) *Frontiers in American Philosophy*, Volume II. College Station, TX: Texas A&M University Press, 1996.

BETH J. SINGER

LAW: LEGAL POSITIVISM

The position of the nineteenth-century English legal theorist John Austin is taken to be the essence of *classical* legal positivism. Jurisprudence is the science of positive law, and the positive law of a political community consists of the general commands of the sovereign. While the command-sovereignty theory was generally rejected, Austin's "separability thesis" was adopted by such American writers as John Chipman Gray in his seminal work *The Nature and Sources of the Law* (1909, 1921):

> [T]he Law of a State is not an ideal, but something which actually exists. It is not that which is in accordance with religion, or nature, or morality; it is not that which ought to be, but that which is. To fix this definitely in the Jurisprudence of the Common Law, is the feat that Austin accomplished.

In other terms, there is a conceptual distinction between the law that *is* and the law that *ought to be*. The existence of law in a society depends on social facts, the activities of legislatures and judges, that can be described in value-neutral terms. Though positivists may disagree on details, they all accept the separability thesis.

From a different angle, Justice Oliver Wendell Holmes, Jr., also separated law and morality, which he claimed to be constantly confused with each other. The purpose of the criminal law is to impose "external" patterns of conduct on the citizen. The criteria of liability, therefore, are also external (behavioral) rather than "internal." The state of mind of the agent, which is central to moral judgment, will therefore often be irrelevant to legal liability.

Positivism was attacked by Lon L. Fuller in his book *The Law in Quest of Itself* (1940). He argued that in the dynamic world of law a sharp separation between *is* and *ought* cannot be maintained, in fact a confusion between the two should be tolerated. Morris R. Cohen responded that positivism merely required that *is* and *ought*, law and morality or ethics, should be distinguished, not separated. It is still possible to evaluate the law; moreover, such evaluation becomes impossible if a confusion between the two is allowed.

Austin's positivism, or rather what passed for his positivism, went under the heading of analytical jurisprudence. Legal systems contain certain necessary concepts such as rights, duties, property, and possession, which can be understood independently of social facts and context. According to its critics (Roscoe Pound, Morris R. Cohen) analytical jurisprudence conceived the law as a complete and closed formal system which a judge can apply without considering the ideals and purposes of the law ("mechanical jurisprudence," "formalism"). This conception reinforced the view that it is not within the judge's function to enlarge or improve or change the law, a position probably held more by practicing lawyers than by legal theorists. For Gray, all law is judge-made, and while morality is not law, it is a source of law. From the 1920s on, much of American legal philosophy is concerned with the nature of judicial decision-making. Positivism is in fact compatible with a variety of theories of judicial decision.

While much of American legal philosophy is concerned with US constitutional law, it is now part of a wider Anglo-American discussion. The leading influence is the Oxford University professor H.L.A. Hart (*The Concept of Law*, 1961, 1994). Hart criticized Austin on crucial points, but he accepted the separability thesis. For though there is a contingently necessary overlap of law and social morality, this overlap is consistent with a system's containing immoral and unjust laws. Each developed legal system contains a "rule of recognition," which consists of the practice of officials, principally the courts, in using certain criteria in determining the valid laws of the system.

On the rule of recognition there is some division among legal positivists. Hart himself leaned toward soft or "inclusive" positivism, which allows that the criteria may incorporate substantive moral principles. Thus Jules Coleman argues that there can be socially constructed criteria of legality that make moral merit a necessary or sufficient condition for something to count as law.

"Exclusive" positivists deny that moral principles can be binding law or that there can be moral criteria of legality. This position is not based on the separability thesis, but rather on the nature of *authority*, as Joseph Raz maintains. Legal systems claim authority over those who are subject to them, and this authority would be undermined if there were moral criteria of legal validity. Whether a purported law is valid depends on its "pedigree"; the criteria of legality are source-based. Still, legal systems can be morally evaluated, and a claim of authority might not in fact be morally justified.

Opposition to legal positivism comes from natural law theories (Aquinas), as traditionally understood, such contemporary secular versions as that put forward by Lon L. Fuller, and more recently the theory expounded by Ronald Dworkin, who criticizes Hart. Federal judge Richard Posner claims to be a legal pragmatist in contrast to a positivist. He maintains a strong role for economics in judicial decision. Yet Posner has often been called a legal positivist. It would seem that the designation "legal positivist" may have outlived its usefulness.

Further reading

Campbell, Tom D. (ed.) *Legal Positivism*. Aldershot: Ashgate, 1999.

George, Robert P. (ed.) *The Autonomy of Law*. Oxford: Oxford University Press, 1996.

Gray, John Chipman. *The Nature and Sources of the Law*, second edition. Boston, MA: Beacon Press, 1963.

Hart, H.L.A. *The Concept of Law*. Oxford: Clarendon/Oxford University Press, 1961, second edition 1994.

Raz, Joseph. *The Authority of Law*. New York: Clarendon/Oxford University Press, 1979.

Sebok, Anthony J. *Legal Positivism in American Jurisprudence*. Cambridge: Cambridge University Press, 1998.

MARTIN P. GOLDING

LAW: LEGAL REALISM

Legal realism has been characterized as a movement (rather than a school) or even as a mood. It had its heyday in the United States during the 1920s and 1930s, but it has an influence until today. According to Karl Llewellyn, a main figure, what united the realists was their "negation" of the traditional focus on legal rules, principles and doctrines.

An important influence on realism was Justice Oliver Wendell Holmes, Jr., who, however, never explicitly identified himself with it. Holmes has been seen as part of the late nineteenth-century "revolt against formalism" in American thought (Morton White). As early as 1880, Holmes rejected the declaratory theory of judicial decision, that the law always preexists the case, and that the principle of legal growth is that of logical development out of fundamental doctrines and concepts. He also maintained that the law is prophecies of what courts will do in fact. The task of the lawyer is to predict the decisions of judges. This position seems to turn legal norms into empirical statements of fact about judicial behavior, though it is doubtful that Holmes meant to deny the existence of rules binding on the judge.

This article will deal with a few of realism's exponents of the "negation" of the traditional focus, who approached the issue in different, but usually complementary ways.

Joseph W. Bingham was interested in the nature of the "science" of law, which was influenced by his views on the nature of science. A highly original thinker, he rejected as "fundamentally erroneous" the idea that the field of law consists of rules and principles enforced by political authority. Writing in 1912, he maintained that rules and principles are only "mental tools" for the classification of knowledge of the concrete causes and effects of external governmental phenomena. It is an easy step from this to the view that the law consists of the individual decisions of judges, a position held by some realists. Thus, Jerome Frank stated that rules are "merely words." Bingham's position was sharply criticized by Morris R. Cohen as a version of medieval nominalism.

Herman Oliphant was influenced by behaviorist psychology in his approach to judicial decision-making. He criticized the traditional doctrine of *stare decisis*, standing by the precedents. Rule-governed cases are rarer than is assumed; the law is largely indeterminate. The idea of extracting a rule from a prior decision is beset by the logical difficulty that any set of facts is classifiable in an indefinite number of ways, a point widely accepted by the realists. Still, it is possible to determine what courts have done in response to the concrete cases before them. Since there often is no prior rule, courts should decide cases on the basis of policy rather than principle. How this is to be done is basically left unexplained by Oliphant.

Jerome Frank, who cites Bingham with approval, was influenced by psychoanalysis. Frank endorsed Oliphant's analysis of *stare decisis*, while rejecting the latter's stimulus–response approach. Frank attacked the "myth" of legal certainty, which he attributed partially to a childish wish for father authority. He popularized the idea that judicial deliberation begins with a "hunch." The written opinions of judges, which contain references to rules and principles, are "rationalizations." No useful distinction can be drawn between rule and discretion. Frank's name is particularly associated with "rule skepticism," though in later writings he said he was more of a fact skeptic. The real indeterminacy of the law is mainly at the trial court level, where facts are in dispute and outcomes are unpredictable.

John Dickinson, a critic of realism, argued that rules of law serve a discretion-minimizing function. Felix S. Cohen, the son of Morris R. Cohen, responded to Dickinson. The critic mistakenly assumes that a judge's duty is to find the law rather than mold it. When realists expressed themselves on the issue, they adopted the "separability" thesis of the legal positivists, that law and morality are conceptually distinct. Felix was anxious that the temporary severance of Is and Ought, as Llewellyn called it, not repudiate in practice the question of what the law ought to be. He developed a "functional" jurisprudence that was both critical and constructive. While realists generally asserted the necessity of policy judgments in judicial decision, Felix Cohen tried to show how a kind of hedonistic utilitarianism could answer questions of legal policy (Morris was skeptical).

The contribution of Roscoe Pound to American legal thought, and to his own thought, is acknowledged by Karl Llewellyn, though they engaged in a heated exchange over the realists' "negation" of the centrality of rules. Llewellyn insisted that he never denied the existence of rules, principles, and doctrines; he took exception to Frank's exaggerated claims about uncertainty in the law. The limitation of the traditional study of law was that it focused on words rather than functions, what the law was doing. Relying on John Dewey's pragmatic theory of meaning, Llewellyn maintained that rules *are* what they *do*. He saw legal order as a set of institutions with a variety of functions, toward which he adopted a "behavior approach."

In political terms, the realists tended to be reformers and liberals. Some adherents worked in various capacities in Roosevelt's New Deal. The 1970s saw the development of the Critical Legal Studies movement which was influenced by legal realism. It was also influenced by Marxism and tended to be more radical than realism. Some critics considered it to be "nihilist."

A longstanding theme in legal realism was the relation between law and the social sciences. Recently, Brian Leiter has reinterpreted realism in line with philosophical naturalism. Naturalism holds that a variety of philosophical problems should be treated in terms of natural science. Thus, the conceptual analysis of law should be replaced by social scientific explanations of legal phenomena and that normative theories of adjudication should be replaced by empirical theories.

Further reading

Bingham, John W. "What is the Law?" *Michigan Law Review* 11, 1 and 2 (1912): 1–25, 109–121.

Cohen, Felix S. *Ethical Systems and Legal Ideals.* Ithaca, NY: Cornell University Press, 1959 [1933].

Cohen, Morris R. *Reason and Law.* Glencoe, IL: Free Press, 1950.

Dewey, John. "Logical Method and Law," *Cornell Law Quarterly* 10, 1 (1924): 17–27.

Dickinson, John. *Administrative Justice and the Supremacy of Law.* New York: Russell and Russell, 1959 [1927].

Frank, Jerome. *Law and the Modern Mind.* New York: Cowan-McCann, 1949 [1930].

Holmes, Oliver Wendell. *The Common Law.* Boston, MA: Little, Brown, 1963 [1881].

Leiter, Brian. "Rethinking Legal Realism: Toward a Naturalized Jurisprudence," *Texas Law Review* 76, 2 (1997): 267–315.

Llewellyn, Karl N. *Jurisprudence: Realism in Theory and Practice.* Chicago, IL: University of Chicago Press, 1962.

Oliphant, Herman. "A Return to Stare Decisis," *ABA Journal* 14, 2 (1928): 71–6.

Pound, Roscoe. *Jurisprudence*, 5 volumes. St Paul, MN: West Publishing, 1959.

White, Morton Gabriel. *Social Thought in America, the Revolt Against Formalism.* New York: Viking Press, 1949.

Martin P. Golding

LEWIS, CLARENCE IRVING

C.I. Lewis (1883–1964), logician, epistemologist, value theorist, and systematic philosopher, was born in Stoneham, Massachusetts and educated at Harvard University (AB 1905; PhD 1910). He taught at the University of California from 1911 to

1919 and at Harvard from 1920 until retirement in 1953. He gave the Carus Lectures, Woodbridge Lectures, and Powell Lectures. He was appointed Edgar Pierce Professor of Philosophy at Harvard. Stanford University has a philosophy professorship in his name. Lewis spent his entire career working systematically toward a defense of value judgments and ethics as part of the rational enterprise; as he says in the Woodbridge Lectures, "In all the world and in all of life there is nothing more important to determine than what is right."

Lewis's early work was in logic and philosophy of logic. In 1918, he published *The Survey of Symbolic Logic*, a classic work on the history and development of modern extensional logic that challenged the extensional nature of the widely adopted logical system developed by Bertrand Russell and A.N. Whitehead in *Principia Mathematica*. In *Principia*, only simple subject–predicate statements describe the world; the truth of compound statements such as conditionals is merely a function of the truth-values of the component simple statements. Lewis would later argue that contrary-to-fact conditionals, such as "If you fuse hydrogen, you will generate energy," are not truth-functional and can present causal truths that describe the world. *Principia* acknowledged only material implication, expressed by a material conditional extensionally relating antecedent and consequent; a conditional is contingently false if its antecedent is true and its consequent is false. Lewis contended we actually reason deductively using logical implication; a conditional whose true antecedent is an argument's premise and whose false consequent is the argument's conclusion instead is necessarily false. In his 1932 *Symbolic Logic* (with Langford), he worked out a modal approach to logic that incorporates necessity and that is intensional in that it depends on the meaning (versus truth-values) of premises and conclusion.

The modern empiricist tradition has had to account for the a priori character of math, logic, and metaphysics. The philosophy of logic from Boole through *Principia* tried to reduce mathematical truths to logical truths. Lewis's account of the a priori therefore focused on logic and philosophy. Lewis had worked out several equally good systems of modal logic, convincing him that no logic therefore is true and that logic does not tell us about the world. The choice of which logic to apply turns on its use as a reasoning tool, which helps us act in the world. In *Mind and the World-Order* (1929), he held that a priori truths are in some sense analytic. He contended that philosophical truths tell us how we must experience the world but not about the world in itself. But both logical and philosophical a priori truths can tell us only about the logical or conceptual relationships holding between the concepts that we use to shape up experience. The mind imposes a conceptual scheme, ordered by a set of fundamental categories, on sensory data in order to produce an experience of the world. Contra Kant, though, this conceptual and categorial scheme is a function of which way of ordering belief we find works pragmatically in the area of human action that meets human needs. We could change even our basic categories and logical truths on pragmatic grounds. Lewis called this position "conceptualistic pragmatism." These kinds of a priori truths constitute one kind of foundation in his system.

His *Analysis of Knowledge and Valuation* (1946) presented his account of empirical knowledge. One traditional problem with knowledge was how to avoid an infinite regress, since what justifies a knowledge claim must itself need justification, ad infinitum. A traditional strategy was to identify some self-justifying, regress-stopping foundation. Sense datum theorists such as Russell had contended that sense data constituted that foundation by being known infallibly. Lewis instead argued that any knowledge claim must be subject to epistemic appraisal as correct or incorrect and justified or unjustified, and since sense data cannot be incorrect, they do not constitute knowledge. But he held that knowledge is generated from this sensory given. This "given" is not conceptually delineated, and so does not even constitute a judgment, though it can be reported in "expressive" language. Nevertheless, it is the basis from which we form predictive judgments about sense data. These conceptually structured judgments take the form of contrary-to-fact conditionals: given some sensory data, if one were to act in a particular way, one would expect a particular experience. Lewis called these "terminating judgments;" since they can be conclusively verified within experience, they provide the certain knowledge that stops the regress. Judgments about physical objects are non-terminating and can be analyzed into an infinite number of terminating judgments. So, all empirical knowledge of objects rests on terminating judgments; this knowledge is only probable, since further terminating judgments could in principle falsify the non-terminating judgment.

Lewis was in the pragmatist tradition, holding that knowledge aims at helping us act, while action in turn is guided by choices and therefore valuations. His value theory accounts for empirical value knowledge roughly parallel with empirical factual knowledge. The value "given" is a feeling or emotion – including likes, dislikes, pain, satisfaction, dissatisfaction, and so forth. These can be reported in expressive language but are not in the form of judgments. They cannot be in error and so cannot be knowledge. But they do form the basis for predictive judgments about feelings: given sensory data, if one were to act in a particular way, one would feel a particular way. Actually feeling that way would verify the judgment, so these are terminating value judgments. They give rise to non-terminating judgments about the objective value of something. Empirical knowledge of objective value is only probable.

In *The Ground and Nature of the Right* (1955) and in *Our Social Inheritance* (1957), Lewis turns to ethics. The individual can reach knowledge about the good, but this does not address how to decide which "good" to pursue. Ethics is needed to help one order one's judgments of the good and weigh them. Lewis argues that all areas of rational deliberation – including logic, epistemology, and ethics – are constrained by rational imperatives, such as "Be consistent." Any attempt to deny such imperatives would employ those very imperatives, producing a "pragmatic contradiction." Ethical imperatives have a social dimension, in contrast with prudential imperatives, which speak to what is better for one in the larger context of one's life. Unfortunately, Lewis never finished his work in the area of ethics.

Further reading

Firth, Roderick, and Brandt, R.B. "Commemorative Symposium on C.I. Lewis," *Journal of Philosophy* 61 (1964): 545–70.

Goheen, John D. and Mothershead, John L., Jr (eds). *Collected Papers of Clarence Irving Lewis.* Stanford, CA: Stanford University Press, 1970.

Haack, Susan. "C.I. Lewis" in Marcus G. Singer (ed.). *American Philosophy.* Cambridge: Cambridge University Press, 1986, pp. 215–38.

Lewis, Clarence Irving. *A Survey of Symbolic Logic*. Berkeley, CA: University of California Press, 1918.

—— *Mind and the World-Order: An Outline of a Theory of Knowledge.* New York: Charles Scribner's Sons, 1929; reprinted New York: Dover, 1956.

—— *An Analysis of Knowledge and Valuation* (The Paul Carus Lectures, Series 8). La Salle, IL: Open Court, 1946.

—— *The Ground and Nature of the Right* (The Woodbridge Lectures, V, 1954). New York: Columbia University Press, 1955.

Lewis, C.I. and Langford, C.H. *Symbolic Logic*. New York: Appleton-Century, 1932; reprinted New York: Dover, 1951.

Murphey, Murray G. *C.I. Lewis: The Last Great Pragmatist* (SUNY Series in Philosophy). Albany, NY: SUNY Press, 2005.

Parry, William Tuthill. "In Memoriam: Clarence Irving Lewis (1883–1964)," *Notre Dame Journal of Formal Logic* 11, 2 (April 1970): 129–40.

Saydah, J. Roger. *The Ethical Theory of Clarence Irving Lewis.* Athens, OH: Ohio University Press, 1969.

Schilpp, Paul Arthur (ed.) *The Philosophy of C.I. Lewis.* La Salle, IL: Open Court, 1968.

Seth Holtzman

LIBERALISM

Liberalism is many things to many people. Some think of it as a political position, others a political philosophy, and still others a comprehensive philosophy with ethical, metaphysical, epistemic, and political commitments. This entry will survey these various perspectives, and see if they share anything in common.

Liberalism as a political position

People think of liberalism first and foremost as a family of views on various political issues. For example, we think of someone as liberal on abortion if she favors a woman's right to choose, or on euthanasia if she favors a patient's right to die. One might infer from these and other examples that liberalism seeks to maximize liberty – that it holds that the more freedom one has, the better off we all are. But other liberal views subvert this inference. For example, we think of someone as liberal on guns if she favors restricting access to them. Therefore, the challenge for political theorists is to determine whether liberalism is a real philosophical position, or an arbitrary collection of views that changes with the political winds.

Some evidence suggests the latter interpretation. Liberalism takes different shapes in different countries. For example, in America liberals emphasize civil liberties at the expense of capitalism, whereas in Australia the opposite is the case. Moreover, as Ronald Dworkin points out, liberal views have changed over time: New Deal liberalism was a different collection of views than, say, Cold War liberalism (Dworkin 1978: 116). But despite these problems, most theorists, Dworkin included, think there is an underlying philosophy that makes coherent these seemingly random families of views.

Liberalism as a political philosophy

Dworkin thinks that liberalism is based on a constitutive morality, and that liberal views change over time not because liberals trade in this morality for a new one, but rather because they reconsider which policies best promote it. Dworkin thinks this morality is as follows: Liberalism, like conservativism, holds that the state should treat its citizens as equals; but unlike conservativism it holds that the best way to do that is by adopting a neutral stance regarding the good life. In other words, whereas conservativism holds that the state should choose the right ends, and then equip its citizens with the means necessary for them, liberalism holds that the state should equip its citizens with means necessary for whatever ends they choose (Dworkin 1978: 127).

John Rawls agrees with Dworkin on this score. Rawls argues that the state should remain neutral on comprehensive conceptions of the good, and seek instead to pursue policies that any reasonable citizen could endorse. This means that the state should avoid presupposing any philosophical position – moral, metaphysical, epistemic, and so on – that citizens could reasonably disagree on.

Rawls proposes that we determine which policies to endorse through a thought experiment known as "the original position." An agent in the original position dons the "veil of ignorance," with the result that she has ideal rational capacities and complete information about the world she lives in, but no information about who she is in that world. She then determines a set of policies that would be reasonable for her no matter who she turns out to be (Rawls 1999: 118). Rawls thinks that an agent in the original position would settle on his two principles of justice, which are as follows:

1 Each person is entitled to as much liberty as is consistent with equal liberty for all.
2 Social and economic inequalities are permissible on two conditions: first, that they attach to offices open to all under fair equality of opportunity; and second, that they provide the greatest benefit to the least-advantaged members of society (the difference principle.
(Rawls 2003: 42–3).

Since the state must remain neutral on conceptions of the good, it should aim for an equal distribution of primary goods, or goods that all "citizens need as free and equal persons living a complete life" (Rawls 2003: 58). These goods include basic rights and liberties, freedom of movement and occupation, powers of office, income and wealth, and the social bases of self-respect (Rawls 2003: 58–9). And if the state distributes these goods according to the two principles of justice, it will deviate from equal distribution only to compensate for the unequal distribution of natural and social endowments, such as birthright, intellect, talent, and so on (Rawls 1999: 87).

Many consider Rawls's theory of justice the best available expression of political liberalism. But it is not without problems. For instance, some charge that it is not as neutral about comprehensive conceptions of the good as Rawls claims: e.g. it may be neutral about the good life for the individual, but not about the priority of the individual over the community. Similarly, others charge that no political philosophy, liberalism included, can have *no* substantive philosophical commitments. To see why, recall that Rawls argues that the state should pursue policies that all citizens could reasonably endorse. The problem is: How can we tell what "reasonably" means here without presupposing a theory of epistemic or practical rationality? Jeremy Waldron makes a related point: One cannot be neutral all the way down. As he puts it, "neutrality as a policy is never, in any context, self-justifying: one is always neutral in a particular conflict for a reason, and it is obvious that one cannot then be neutral about the force of that reason" (Waldron 1993: 165).

Liberalism as a comprehensive philosophy

These considerations have compelled some theorists to embrace liberalism not as a political philosophy, full stop, but rather as a comprehensive philosophy with various moral, metaphysical, epistemic, and, of course, political, commitments. In what follows, I will outline some of the moral commitments liberals accept, because these tend to receive the most attention in the literature.

Obviously, liberals treats liberty as valuable, and consequently they hold that any state action that restricts liberty must be justified. But there is disagreement about how to construe the value of liberty.

First, there is disagreement about what liberty is. Some, such as Isaiah Berlin, argue that liberty is *negative*, and thus present whenever one is free from coercion; whereas others, such as Jean-Jacques Rousseau, argue that liberty is *positive*, and thus present whenever one acts on free will. Other theorists employ some combination of these views, and even add new conditions entirely. John Dewey, for example, argues that liberty is present whenever one is free from coercion, acts on free will, engages in social interaction (because, according to Dewey, the individual is not merely something social institutions *benefit*, but also something they *create*), and, finally, *exercises* these freedoms (as opposed to merely having the opportunity to).

Second, there is disagreement about why liberty is good. We have considered the Kantian claim (endorsed by Dworkin and Rawls) that liberal principles should not presuppose any conception of the good. Other theorists, however, argue that liberal principles *should* presuppose a conception of the good, and they offer various takes on what that good is. Some say that liberty is good in itself, whereas others say that it is good insofar as it contributes to other good things. These theorists are known as "perfectionists." John Stuart Mill, for example, contends that liberty is good because it helps us to develop our talents and become individuals. Joseph Raz, similarly, claims that liberty is good because it promotes autonomy. And Josiah Royce suggests that liberty is good because it helps us to set goals for ourselves, find "communities of loyalty" that share these goals, and then pursue these goals from within those communities. In short, perfectionists generally agree that liberty is good insofar as it helps individuals to flourish, but they disagree about what that flourishing involves.

Third, there is disagreement at a more abstract level about the nature of value. Of course, this issue pertains to normative theory as a whole, but it has direct application to liberalism. Putting nihilism to the side, there are three general positions liberals take on the nature of value. The first is monism. Monists believe that there is one thing that is good, and everything else is good insofar as it contributes to that thing. The perfectionists we considered above are monists: they believe that human flourishing is good (though of course they have different conceptions of what human flourishing amounts to). The second position is pluralism. Pluralists believe that there are many things that are good, and it is impossible to rank them objectively, or show that one is more deserving of promotion than another. Berlin is an example of a pluralist. The third position is subjectivism, which is sometimes construed as relativism, and sometimes collapsed into monism, pluralism, and even nihilism. Subjectivists believe that the good is determined by our tastes and preferences.

Monism, pluralism, and subjectivism are distinct in many ways, but they share one important thing in common: They all imply that there is not a single "good life" that applies to all. Monism implies this because people with different capacities will flourish in different ways; pluralism because if there are many things that are good, then people can choose among them however they wish; and subjectivism because tastes and preferences can vary across cultures and throughout time. Each of these theories of value, therefore, provides the justification for political neutrality we were seeking in our discussion of Rawls.

Further reading

Berlin, Isaiah. "Two Concepts of Liberty" in Michael J. Sandel (ed.). *Liberalism and Its Critics*. New York: New York University Press, 1984.

Dworkin, Ronald. "Liberalism" in Stuart Hampshire (ed.). *Public and Private Morality*. Cambridge: Cambridge University Press, 1978.

Mill, John Stuart. *On Liberty*. New York: Barnes and Noble Books, 2004 [1859].

Rawls, John. *A Theory of Justice: Revised Edition*. Cambridge, MA: Harvard University Press, 1999.

—— *Justice as Fairness: A Restatement*, ed. Erin Kelly. Cambridge, MA: Harvard University Press, 2003.

Waldron, Jeremy. *Liberal Rights: Collected Papers 1981–1991*. Cambridge: Cambridge University Press, 1993.

Jeff Sebo

LIBERATION THEOLOGY

Most academic theologians who are familiar with liberation theology equate "liberation theology" with "Latin American liberation theology." Accordingly, these theologians would consider Gustavo Gutiérrez's *A Theology of Liberation* (1971) to be the first systematic articulation of liberation theology. And they would be partially correct because Latin American liberation theology is arguably the most influential liberation theology in the world.

Unfortunately, these theologians tend to downplay, if not neglect outright, the fact that there has been a liberation theology indigenous to the United States since the mid-1960s. That indigenous liberation theology is black theology of liberation (BTL). Like Latin American liberation theology, BTL seeks to articulate theologically the sociopolitical plight of those people who are most economically and politically disadvantaged. Nevertheless, Latin American liberation theology and BTL combat different yet interrelated types of oppression. Latin American liberation theology combats sociopolitical injustice caused by economic oppression whereas BTL combats sociopolitical injustice caused by anti-black racism and white supremacy, or the network of sociopolitical and economic institutions and practices that maintain white privilege.

Although BTL can trace its historic origins back to antebellum black Christianity, its immediate historic origins can be traced back to some African American clergy's support of the black power movement in the mid-1960s, as evidenced in the National Committee of Negro Churchmen's theological statement on the Black Power movement published in the *New York Times* on 31 July 1966. Academically, BTL can trace its origins back to the first sustained attempt of some African

American theologians in the 1960s to develop a theological language that supports the liberation of poor African American communities. The first systematic expressions of BTL were James H. Cone's *Black Theology and Black Power* (1969) and *A Black Theology of Liberation* (1970).

Following Dwight N. Hopkins' periodization of BTL in *Introducing Black Theology of Liberation*, this article describes the two-staged development of BTL.

The first stage of Black Liberation Theology's development

The pioneers of BTL (e.g. Cone, Gayraud S. Wilmore, and Major J. Jones) sought to interpret biblical Scripture in such a manner that Jesus's earthly ministry revealed God as God of the oppressed. Accordingly, a central motif of the gospel for BTL is Jesus's liberatory mission to uplift the downtrodden and the social outcast. In 1960s America, the African American poor qualified as the most downtrodden and socially outcast. Additionally, these early black liberation theologians sought to re-imagine the Christian tradition so that it could properly portray the beauty, dignity, worth, and humanity of African Americans, especially in a socio-historical milieu where "being black" was regarded as ugly, debased, unworthy, and inferior. That is why these first-generation black liberation theologians often built their theologies upon the sermons, prayers, music, and folktales of the very African Americans they purport to represent.

Nevertheless, these pioneers did not limit their attention to the plight suffered by poor African Americans. During the 1970s, they allied themselves with Third World theologians, especially African theologians, as participants in the Ecumenical Association of Third World Theologians (EATWOT). They also critiqued what they regarded as American imperialism in Vietnam and attacked South African apartheid. BTL, then, could be considered a particular manifestation of the decolonization movements and struggles of oppressed people worldwide.

The second stage of Black Liberation Theology's development

Jacquelyn Grant's critique of BTL for neglecting African American women and their experiences and Cornel West's critique of BTL for not having a sufficient Marxist critique of America's oppressive economic system in the late 1970s and early 1980s mark the beginning of the second generation of BTL. West's early works, especially *Prophesy Deliverance!* (1982), enabled black liberation theologians to perform Marxist critiques of America's economic and social exploitation of poor African Americans without delegitimizing their religious (usually Christian) commitments. Grant's critiques of sexism in BTL eventually led to the birth of womanist theology as a distinct liberation theology in the 1980s. Womanist theology is a liberation theology which reinterprets central Christian dogmas from the vantage point of African American women's life experiences. Indeed, Delores S. Williams, a womanist theologian, has written one of the best systematic articulations of liberation theology: *Sisters in the Wilderness* (1993).

Like first-generation black liberation theologians, second-generation black liberation theologians have continued cross-cultural dialogues with liberation theologians from the Third World by participating in such forums as EATWOT. Unlike many first-generation black liberation theologians, though, many second-generation black liberation theologians have willingly used numerous European and Euro-American philosophical approaches to construct their theologians. These philosophical approaches include neo-pragmatism, Whiteheadean process metaphysics, Foucauldian poststructuralism, and phenomenology.

Among the more notable appropriations of philosophy by second-generation black liberation theologians is Henry J. Young's ongoing conversation with Whiteheadean process metaphysics. Young thinks that Whiteheadean metaphysics is compatible with BTL because it promotes a cultural pluralism that could liberate people from the social ills that maintain an oppressive social order, such as classism, ethnocentrism, imperialism, racism, and sexism. Whiteheadean metaphysics promotes such a liberatory cultural pluralism because it attacks the very metaphysical foundations of an oppressive social order, namely, a static essentialism that reifies otherwise impermanent ethnic, racial, and social identities.

Furthermore, Young thinks that Whiteheadean process metaphysics gives BTL an additional theoretical vantage point from which to assert that genuine spiritual liberation cannot be divorced from the ending of sociopolitical and economic oppression. Moreover, he thinks that Whiteheadean metaphysics is compatible with BTL since both of them advocate that one's theoretical reflections should originate from one's experiences of the world.

Another notable appropriation of philosophy by second-generation black liberation theologians is

Hopkins's critical dialogue with European and Euro-American postmodernism. Hopkins thinks that BTL can have a fruitful dialogue with European and Euro-American postmodernism since both BTL and postmodernist theorists are efforts to deconstruct the illusory universalism of Western religious and political thought, which masks the white supremacy operative in American society. He also thinks that postmodernism is beneficial to BTL because it opens an intellectual space for black liberation theologians to delve into the traditions, folklore, and music of the formerly voiceless and, in many cases, illiterate African American poor. Hopkins's own BTL, as articulated in *Shoes that Fit Our Feet* (1993) and his contribution to *Liberation Theologies, Postmodernity, and the Americas* (1997), is a testament to the possibilities available to black liberation theologians to construct a viable BTL in a postmodern and pluralistic America.

Further reading

Batstone, David, Mendieta, Eduardo, Lorentzen, Lois Ann and Hopkins, Dwight N. (eds). *Liberation Theologies, Postmodernity, and the Americas.* New York: Routledge, 1997.

Burrow, Rufus, Jr. *James H. Cone and Black Liberation Theology.* Jefferson, NC: McFarland, 1994.

Cone, James H. *Risks of Faith: The Emergence of a Black Theology of Liberation, 1968–1998.* Boston, MA: Beacon Press, 1999.

Hopkins, Dwight N. *Black Theology of Liberation.* Maryknoll, NY: Orbis Books, 1999.

Mitchem, Stephanie Y. *Introducing Womanist Theology.* Maryknoll, NY: Orbis Books, 2002.

West, Cornel. *Prophesy Deliverance! An Afro-American Revolutionary Christianity.* Philadelphia, PA: Westminster Press, 1982.

Williams, Delores S. *Sisters in the Wilderness: The Challenge of Womanist God-Talk.* Maryknoll, NY: Orbis Books, 1993.

Young, Henry J. *Hope in Process: A Theology of Social Pluralism.* Minneapolis, MN: Fortress Press, 1990.

DWAYNE A. TUNSTALL

LIBERTY

The Age of Enlightenment in the eighteenth century brought about a profound reversal of the relationship between the individual and the state. Where both Greco-Roman and subsequent Christian philosophies emphasized the subjugation of the individual to a temporal or divine authority, the English philosopher John Locke argued that the role of government should be limited to rectifying "deficiencies" in relations that arise naturally among humans. Individuals are endowed with both reason and a moral sense by which they may determine what best suits their interests, and they are entitled to own and enjoy whatever they produce pursuant to such interests. Beyond arbitrating contracts and the protection of lives and property, government is obligated to educate citizens capable of participating in the democratic stewardship of the community. Thus for Locke, as for successors such as Rousseau and Voltaire, "liberty" acquired the double sense of a *negative* prohibition of undue constraints and coercion, and a *positive* entitlement to rights and skills individuals may use to procure what they desire.

Roots and branches of Jeffersonian democracy

The influence of the Enlightenment upon the Founding Fathers is strikingly manifest in the Declaration of Independence, where basic civil liberties are deemed "self-evident." Thomas Jefferson took office in 1800 bent upon keeping the American presidency from sliding into the decadence of power and patronage common among European monarchies. Alarmed at the centralization of government promoted by the Federalist Congress, and the erosion of civil liberties under the Adams administration, Jefferson insisted that power remain close to the people by promoting states' rights and a central government "rigorously frugal and simple."

For Jefferson, the ideal society is fundamentally grounded in a "noble agrarianism." The farmer and frontiersman most fully exemplify the virtues of self-reliance, practical know-how, simplicity, and an appreciation of nature – traits Jefferson saw as promoting a civil society of individuals working together to pursue common interests rather than indulging in selfish desires. The Jeffersonian ethos remained robust throughout the first half of the nineteenth century, especially among Southern agrarians wary of Yankee industrialization and federal meddling on the question of slavery. In the upper Midwest, the granger movement gave farmers political and economic leverage against railroads and food processors well into the latter decades of the century.

Another base of support arose with New England transcendentalism. Loosely rooted in Kant's effort to overcome the alienation of mind from its objects by showing the interdependence of perception and conception, Ralph Waldo Emerson believed a deep aesthetic appreciation of nature unveils the literal unity of the individual and the divine. At Walden Pond Emerson's one-time handyman, Henry David Thoreau, realized the full liberation of the self in the embrace of wilderness. According to Thoreau, mercantile interests perpetuate lives that are venial, empty, and inauthentic. Like Jefferson, who thought a "little rebellion" from time to time was good for the nation's psyche, Thoreau both advocated nonviolent civil disobedience and practiced it himself by refusing to pay taxes to support slavery and the Mexican War. He dissented, however, from Jefferson's confidence in majority rule – to act upon one's heartfelt convictions, and be willing to accept the consequences of such actions, is to constitute a "majority of one."

Captains of industry and social crusaders

"We are sleeping on a volcano," Tocqueville wrote in 1848 as the Industrial Revolution was transforming the cultural landscape on both sides of the Atlantic. In the aftermath of the Civil War, America became increasingly industrial and urban as workers left farms for better-paying factory jobs and blacks migrated from the rural south to northern cities in the wake of Reconstruction and the Jim Crow backlash. Both were soon joined by waves of immigrants seeking political and economic freedom. Though the Jeffersonian ideal did not completely vanish, "captains of industry" supplanted "noble agrarians" as heroes of popular culture. John Jacob Astor, Sr, the first self-made American mogul, amassed twenty million dollars from the fur trade by the 1830s. But within five decades Andrew Carnegie in steel, Cornelius Vanderbilt in railroads, and John D. Rockefeller in oil each would eclipse Astor's fortune by more than tenfold. In such feats economist Thomas Nixon Carver perceived Adam Smith's "invisible hand" whereby the creation of wealth benefits owners, workers, and consumers alike. For Social Darwinists such as William Graham Sumner, laissez-faire capitalism is the economic manifestation of the doctrine of the "survival of the fittest," where the exploitation of the weak by the strong is both natural and cleansing. On both accounts, liberty is viewed primarily in the negative sense as freedom from governmental constraints on property and productivity.

One person's "captain of industry" is another's "robber baron," of course, and many regarded the "liberty" of unbridled capitalism as abandoning even the modest positive constraints of classical liberalism. For such reformers, neither Jeffersonian republicanism nor laissez-faire capitalism did much to promote "liberty and justice for all." The former, after all, had been used to perpetuate slavery and the oppression of women, and the latter had created intolerable working conditions, a grossly inequitable distribution of wealth, monopolies and corruption, and perilous cycles of boom and bust. With industrialization egalitarian movements grew from grassroots movements such as the Ephrata Colony and Shakers into a large but unsteady alliance of immigrant socialists, labor activists, populists, and progressives. Pioneer sociologist Lester F. Ward disputed Sumner's interpretation of Darwin, arguing that cooperation and social cohesiveness typically predict evolutionary success better than the "red fang and claw" of popular myth. Ward further insisted that inequities of wealth and social class are artificial rather than natural. True liberty cannot be enjoyed by all until barriers to equality of gender, race, and economic opportunity are removed by positive governmental intervention.

The pragmatism of James and Holmes

Despite the efforts of Ward, Edward Bellamy's galvanizing novel *Looking Back,* and the union-building of Eugene Debs and Daniel De Leon, American's reception of socialism remained lukewarm. Moderate reformers had difficulty separating themselves from communists and anarchists who, or so their critics claimed, brought not just "foreign" ideas but the insinuation of sedition. The entire debate between the bourgeois and the proletariat seemed better suited to European class struggles than the youthful American dream of prosperity. Those equally suspicious of big business and big government found the alternatives of capitalism and socialism equally unattractive.

This changed with William James and the advent of a distinctively home-grown philosophical perspective – pragmatism. In his youth this most public, and most personal, of American philosophers struggled mightily with the question of free will versus determinism. Do humans have genuine freedom of choice, or, as both physics and psychology suggest, are our decisions wholly molded by nature or society? James ceded that neither philosophy nor science could settle the question, but reasoned that we are justified to presume free will given that we couldn't make genuine decisions or otherwise function effectively without it. That *workability* trumps metaphysical speculation became the touchstone of his pragmatism – the significance of any term or concept is its *cash value* for inquiry.

Although there are often multiple paths to any given end, James's pluralism led him to embrace views others have deemed inconsistent: the consolation of religious faith with an unwavering humanism, the exemplary virtues of the working class with the transformative power of history's "great men," and an optimistic faith in moral and technological progress with a sense of pathos bordering upon the tragic. For James, liberty is not so much a societal ideal but a project of self-realization based upon creativity, innovation, and broad-mindedness.

In some respects James' darker side is reflected in the life of his Harvard companion Oliver Wendell Holmes, Jr., who frequented the "Metaphysical Club" gatherings that mark the informal birthplace of pragmatism. Holmes returned from the Civil War wounded in body and devoid of spiritual beliefs. He came to reject the natural laws and rights of the Enlightenment, and upon joining the Supreme Court in 1902 opposed conservative justices who used legal formalism and strict Constitutional constructivism as a pretext for judicial activism. What we come to hold as "self-evident" truths or rights are really deep-seated customs or preferences we "can't help" believe and defend. From a Darwinian supposition of inevitable conflict, what becomes hypostatized as a "natural law" is really a majority opinion that "can lick all others." Though attacked as a nihilist who undermined the notion of liberty, Holmes was actually intent upon converting its ground from "self-evidence" to *experience.* A law promoting or constraining freedom is justified not by its conformance to *essential* human nature, but due to its *predictive* success in adjudicating conflicting desires and interests. Though Holmes himself advocated judicial restraint, younger colleagues such as Louis D. Brandeis eagerly incorporated the progressive and interpretive implications of his legal philosophy into their own opinions, thus setting the precedent for the expanded role of the judiciary in the twentieth century.

Dewey's new individualism

No one integrates the theoretical reach of James and Holmes with the practical aims of the progressives and reformers more fully than John Dewey. What began in Chicago in the 1890s as an experimental school and advocacy of Jane Addams's Hull House became a lifelong commitment to the empowerment of women, immigrants, and minorities – the social realization of James's pragmatic pluralism. But unlike James, who rather enjoyed the tensions between his "soft-hearted" idealism and "hard-headed" empiricism, Dewey was driven to search for the underlying unity between the ideal and the real.

Dewey agreed with James that life itself is the manifestation of successful problem-solving activity, and that human reason and technology is continuous with simpler forms of "doing-undergoing." He further agreed that pragmatism is primarily concerned with the form or method of such activity, and not with cosmological or metaphysical disputes. Nevertheless, since any account of *what* the world *is* is coincident with *how* it is determined to be so, the ultimate inseparability of methods and facts is indeed a cornerstone of a pragmatic "world view."

The general pattern of this *how* is what Dewey calls the "method of inquiry," in which working ideas or hypotheses – Holmes's "predictions" – are transformed into attained objectives by successful experimentation. Appeal to this pattern, where idea and object are integrated phases of activity, circumvents the traditional epistemological problem of how a "mind" gains access to a "mind-independent reality," but it is equally applicable to the presumed dualism of "facts" and "values." Since it designates the fulfillment of a desire or interest, an attained objective of inquiry that in one context is a "fact," in different circumstances may be called an attained value or constructed "good."

Although Dewey rejects the dualism of facts and values, he fully realizes that dissent and disputation naturally arise when we focus upon values. Because values are vested in social and political institutions more complex than those of the natural sciences, and because the social sciences are still in their infancy, such conflicts are unavoidable. They cannot be remedied by appeals to an absolute good, but neither should we resign ourselves to relativism or Social Darwinism. Failure to see beyond these alternatives is a consequence of what Dewey calls the "old" individualism. The metaphysical mistake that a "mind" or "self" has an "inner" reality apart from the world is the basis for the mistaken ethical appeal to natural rights or laws. The classical view that liberty means the absence of social constraints is thus literally incoherent, whether the outcome is Hobbes's savage world of each against all or Locke's competitive world ameliorated by charity; whether it is Sumner's world of "beasts of prey" or Marx's world heralding the extinction of such predators.

Dewey believed that big business, mass media, and rampant consumerism were pushing America toward complacency and conformity where "liberty" becomes little more than a commercial gimmick and consoling palliative. But he was equally distrustful of bureaucracies and planning by "experts" or central committees. Dewey's "new" individualism fully acknowledges that a "self" is a social construct: the quest for one's self arises within a web of language, customs, and acquired habits we can modify but not step beyond. And where the only authentic "good" is a *constructed* good, to contribute to the growth of others fulfills both a moral imperative and an opportunity for self-realization. However, we equally understand that the world is precarious, and often in unexpected ways. As such it is imperative to cultivate the Jamesian virtues of innovation, creativity, and broad-mindedness, and to assure those who aspire to them both a hearing and an opportunity for just compensation.

Dewey's "new" individualism, in short, acknowledges the ongoing reciprocity of obligation and opportunity. Unpredictable problems are most successfully resolved by an engaged and enfranchised citizenry that (1) generates a broad range of possible solutions, (2) employs compromise and consensus-building to select testable hypotheses from these, and (3) evaluates the success of attained outcomes with an eye toward revision and improvement. In an educational environment that encourages the lifelong development of such practices, and a democratic political environment where their exercise is protected and rewarded, Dewey's "new" individualism culminates in "social intelligence" – the unification of personal development and cultural flourishing.

Fairness and freedom

The second half of the twentieth century saw a diversification of views about freedom and liberty. Whereas some, such as Richard Rorty and Jürgen Habermas, advanced Dewey's optimistic progressivism, more radical existentialists and deconstructionists returned to the struggle between freedom and oppression, often manifest in forms specific to race, gender, or culture. In a very different direction, yet equally robust, is the recovery of traditional approaches as diverse as utilitarianism, naturalism, libertarianism, communitarianism, virtue ethics, and spirituality.

Despite this proliferation, the distinctively American clash between "social crusaders" and "rugged individualists" on the question of liberty remains alive and well in the debate between Harvard philosopher John Rawls and his colleague and critic Robert Nozick. Rawls's point of departure is Kant's observation that each rational being, no matter what station in life, regards himself or herself as a being of incalculable worth – an end rather than a means. And in realizing that all other rational beings avow this, we conclude that any theory of distributive social justice, if it is to be fair, may consider various allotments of wealth, income, and abilities among individuals affected, but not one's *personal* circumstances.

Rawls incorporates this idea into what he calls the "original position," which may be illustrated by two (oversimplified) ways of distributing the same total income. In scenario A, the most advantaged individuals each get one million dollars a year, whereas the least advantaged get nothing. In scenario B, the highest permitted income is $100,000, whereas the lowest is $10,000. Faced with the equal likelihood of being among the most or least advantaged, Rawls thinks almost every rational being would choose scenario B over A: the advantage of receiving a large versus a moderately high income is not worth the risking a subsistence income for an alternative so desperate that survival itself would be in jeopardy.

Rawls thus believes he has offered a model of a social contract agreeable to reason, and not based upon fear or privilege. It favors a distribution of wealth that, though the details could vary widely, is generally supportive of welfare, affirmative action, and additional "entitlement" programs that effectively expand the notion of liberty to include economic and social opportunities. However, Rawls claims his theory of justice is not simply a rehash of the utilitarian appeal to the "greatest good for the greatest number," nor does it place an amorphous "public interest" above the rights and opportunities of individuals. Concurrent with this, Rawls allows (1) each person may enjoy maximum liberty so long as it does not reduce the liberty of another, and (2) inequality is permitted insofar as it benefits everyone and is achieved under conditions of equal opportunity.

Critics such as Nozick complain that the "original position" is artificial, and misrepresents what actually constitutes property. In refusing to consider individual assets, income, and abilities, we eliminate those very acts of "mixing with our labor" Locke insists is constitutive of property ownership and use. The problem of the distribution of wealth is posed without consideration of who *generated* that wealth or how it was produced. As such, Rawls has not shown that justice requires or is even served by discounting the inequitable distribution of assets, especially talents and abilities. Nozick agrees that a theory of justice should specify how property is properly acquired and transferred, and to rectify violations of either. But he insists, with Locke, that the individual has the right to own what he makes, and to appropriate anything not already owned so long as others are not injured in the process.

Further reading

Dewey, John. *The Public and Its Problems.* New York: Henry Holt, 1927.

—— *Individualism Old and New.* New York: Minton, Balch, 1930.

Hofstadter, Richard. *Social Darwinism in American Thought*. New York: G. Braziller, 1959.

Nozick, Robert. *Anarchy, State, and Utopia*. New York: Basic Books, 1974.

Page, Charles H. *Class and American Sociology, from Ward to Ross.* New York: Schocken Books, 1969.

Rawls, John. *A Theory of Justice*. Cambridge, MA: Harvard University Press, 1971.

White, G. Edward. *Justice Oliver Wendell Holmes: Law and the Inner Self.* New York: Oxford University Press, 1995.

Wilentz, Sean. *The Rise of American Democracy: Jefferson to Lincoln*. New York: Norton, 2005.

FRANK X. RYAN

LIEBER, FRANCIS

Francis Lieber (1798–1872) was born 8 March 1798, in Berlin. As a young man, Lieber studied botany and medicine in hopes of a career as a military surgeon. His studies were cut short with Napoleon's return to command from exile in Elba. Lieber then joined the Colberg Regiment in hopes of defeating the French. During his short military career, Lieber was present at the Battle of Waterloo and later wounded in the neck at the Battle of Namur. Although barred from other Prussian universities due to his friendship with Karl Sand, the assassin of August von Kotzebue, in 1819 Lieber matriculated at the University of Jena. In 1820 Lieber received a PhD from Jena, based on a dissertation in the field of mathematics. Lieber then studied applied mathematics at the Universities of Halle and Dresden, and studied privately in Berlin. Lieber's life during this time was complicated. He was implicated in the Strasbourg affair of 1821, the aborted French uprising against Louis XVIII. He took part in the Greek Revolution, and he later became a tutor in Barthold Niebuhr's household in Rome. He served as a language tutor in London, and became personally acquainted with John Stuart Mill and Jeremy Bentham. Although Lieber did not become a utilitarian, the group befriended him and helped arrange for a position in the United States as director and swimming instructor of a Boston gymnasium in 1827.

Lieber soon after became editor of the *Encyclopaedia Americana*, the country's first and most widely used general encyclopedia. Lieber used his notoriety as its editor to help him attain a professorship at the South Carolina College (now the University of South Carolina) from 1835 until 1856. Lieber then served as a Professor at Columbia College (now University) from 1857 until his death.

Lieber made contributions in several fields. He wrote the plan for Girard College. He was an early translator and advisor on the American political system to Alexis de Tocqueville. He was an innovator in the area of prison reform. He was the chief author of the "General Orders No. 100," the first code of war, adopted by the United States military in 1863, and later used as the basis of The Hague and Geneva Conventions. After the war, he saved and archived all of the captured Confederate papers at the request of Secretary Stanton. Francis Lieber was known for his contributions to several disciplines, but should also be known for his contributions to American philosophy, especially for his works on ethics and his innovative work on hermeneutics.

Lieber's *Manual of Political Ethics* presented a qualified version of Kantian ethics that is summarized by Lieber's admonition, "Do or omit that which thou desirest that others do or omit." His ethics incorporated the works of Adam Smith, Aristotle, John Stuart Mill, and Friedrich Schleiermacher, but primarily as a means of making Kant relevant and workable within the American institutions and political system that Lieber had come to value. The real importance of this work is as a summary of the discipline of ethics as taught and studied in American universities during the early nineteenth century.

Lieber's *Legal and Political Hermeneutics* was written as an introduction to his *Manual of Political Ethics.* It was a general theory of hermeneutics as applied to the fields of politics and law. It served as the foundation for the study of those disciplines and as the cornerstone for his views. This work should be seen as a landmark in American philosophy. Lieber's unique advantage was his ability to combine German theory and American principles. He was the first to use any form of the word *hermeneutics* in a book title published in the United States. He was the first to use the word *hermeneutics* in the fields of politics or law in the English language. He was the first in this country to try to apply the art of hermeneutics to a discipline other than religious interpretation. His rules-based approach to the art of hermeneutics was an innovation within the field. Another innovation was his distinction between the terms *construction* and *interpretation* with rules and justifications for each. Lieber's analysis of signs, of which language is the most important, would seem outdated to many. Lieber warned that any text can have but one true meaning and that any interpretations must be true to the whole text (to the letter of the text and to the spirit of the text) as well as to the utterer. His discussions of signs, symbols, meaning, language, mind, and sense antedate similar discussions that have defined American philosophy. He saw hermeneutics as an indispensable part of one's relationship with others. Signs, of which language is the most important, are intricately tied to our psychological being. Lieber should be remembered as a man of remarkable talents and as the first American advocate of the study of hermeneutics as it applies to political theory and law.

Further reading

Cardozo Law Review. "A Lieber Bibliography, with Annotations." *Cardozo Law Review* 16, 6 (April 1995): 2321–51.

Catalano, John. *Francis Lieber: Hermeneutics and Practical Reason*. Lanham, MD: University Press of America, 2000.

Freidel, Frank. *Francis Lieber, Nineteenth Century Liberal*. Gloucester, MA: Peter Smith, 1947, 1968.

Lieber, Francis (ed.) *Encyclopaedia Americana*, 13 volumes. Philadelphia, PA: Carey, Lea, and Blanchard, 1829, 1835.

—— *Manual of Political Ethics, Designed Chiefly for the Use of Colleges and Students at Law*, 2 volumes. Boston, MA: Little, Brown, 1838–9.

—— *Legal and Political Hermeneutics*, enlarged edition. Boston, MA: Little, Brown, 1839.

—— *On Civil Liberty and Self-Government*, enlarged edition. Philadelphia, PA: J.B. Lippincott, 1859.

—— *The Miscellaneous Writings of Francis Lieber*, 2 volumes. Philadelphia, PA: J.B. Lippincott, 1880.

Mack, Charles M. and Lesesne, Henry H. (eds) *Francis Lieber and the Culture of the Mind*. Columbia, SC: USC Press, 2005.

JOHN CATALANO

LITERARY PSYCHOLOGY

Literary psychology is best understood as distinguished from scientific psychology. It is an idea derived from George Santayana's philosophy, an idea he got from Aristotle. In the *Realm of Matter*, Santayana says that Aristotle distinguished two sorts of psychology, the scientific and the literary. Aristotle says that you can speak of anger in a scientific sense as a boiling of the humors, and speak of it dialectically as a desire for revenge. In the former sense, Santayana says the mind is understood in a biological/behavioristic sense. In the latter sense, the mind is understood verbally and dramatically, i.e. in terms of "motives, memories, likes and dislikes, and delicate juxtapositions of images and words" (345). In more current terms, Santayana is making a distinction between the mind as the subject of scientific, i.e. materialistic/experimental study, such study as is performed under the controlled conditions in the neuroscience/psychology laboratory, and mind expressed in the vocabulary of folk psychology. Mind in the latter sense, says Santayana, is "non existent in the realm of matter" (346).

In making the distinction between scientific and literary psychology, Santayana is not interested in epistemologically or metaphysically elevating the status of one at the expense of the other. He is making the distinction for the sake of clarity in order that we appreciate and understand the benefits and limits of each approach to the mind. Parallel to Santayana's distinction here between scientific psychology and literary psychology is his distinction between "psyche" and "spirit," i.e. considering the mind biologically/behavioristically or in an intuitive/contemplative sense.

The scientific approach is an extension of the methodologies of physics. In this respect, scientific psychology is strictly speaking a study of nature. Scientific psychology like all scientific endeavor is materialistic and reductionist; like all scientific endeavor it aims at causal explanation and prediction. Of course, as philosophers of science are inclined to remind us, scientific endeavor also has its scope and limits.

The literary approach to mind is not a record of animal morphology and behavior. As Santayana says in *Scepticism and Animal Faith*, it is the "art of imagining how they (animals) feel and think" (252). Santayana uses a variety of terms in discussing the idea of literary psychology in order to hammer home both the point that mind in this sense is "non-existent" materially, and that we come to "know" ourselves by other than scientific means. Perhaps one might say that we develop an understanding of ourselves in both cognitive and imaginative senses. Hence in addition to using terms such as, "dialectically," "verbally," and "dramatically," Santayana also in his discussion of literary psychology employs "imitative sympathy," "morally," "mythologically," and "imaginatively." Such is essentially the phenomenological and poetic vocabulary of "what it is like to be . . . ."

One might say that scientific psychology needs no advocate; its results are clear and quantifiable. Santayana, however, is an advocate for literary psychology as long as it functions as an imaginative expression of the underlying material processes of the animal; as Santayana would say, as long as it is pious. Without the imaginative expression of ordinary folk psychology, we not only lose the dramatic character, and, one might add, the spiritual character of mind, but concomitantly we sacrifice a sense of the mind's profundity and dignity. It is only through the fine arts in the broad sense that the study of mind maintains its human appearance. However, as a note of caution, Santayana reminds us that myths (and by extension all the arts) cannot be true. Or we might say: scientific psychology employs propositions which are *true about* the mind, i.e. true in a propositional sense; literary psychology employs expressions which are *true to* the mind, i.e. true in a metaphorical sense in so far as myth may suggest and disclose aspects of the world and self about which we were previously unaware.

In his discussion of literary psychology, Santayana anticipates some of the discussion current in philosophy of mind: physicalism, epiphenomenalism, supervenience, and reductionism

Further reading

Lachs, John, "Santayana's Philosophy of Mind" in John Lachs (ed.) *Animal Faith and Spiritual Life*. New York: Appleton Century-Crofts, 1967.

Santayana, George. *Realms of Being*. New York: Charles Scribner's Sons, 1942.

—— *Scepticism and Animal Faith*. New York, Dover, 1955.

Sprigge, Timothy L.S. *Santayana: An Examination of his Philosophy*. London and Boston, MA: Routledge and Kegan Paul, 1974.

CHRISTOPHER PERRICONE

LIVED EXPERIENCE

Lived experience, in the Classical American Pragmatist tradition, refers to the experiences we have that make up, nourish and transform our lives. The lived experience is the part of experience that we are most attuned to. This idea necessarily implies that experience is larger than our lived experience. In order to clarify what this means we will focus on the ideas of two American philosophers: William James (1842–1910) and John Dewey (1859–1952).

William James on the lived experience

The lived experience for James opposes the metaphysical subject/object dichotomy of the modern period. This way of splitting up the world into the experiencing subject and the object experienced is, James believes, nothing more than a functional and theoretical description. For James, our experience of the world is not intrinsically dichotomized in this manner; it is not intrinsically dichotomized at all. He tells us that "pure experience" is "unqualified actuality," or a "simple *that*." Our most immediate encounter with the world is not yet dichotomized. This dichotomy is a theoretical abstraction from our experience. James wants to call our attention to the primacy of experience. Not only is experience a "simple *that*," but it is also where we find ourselves, where we take off from in theoretical flight and where we should, James stresses, come back to. In other words, our theories must stem from problems found in experience and our answers and theories about such problems must be checked against experience for verification.

James also opposes the substance view of metaphysics. In his *Essays in Radical Empiricism*, James writes: "Life is in the transitions as much as in the terms connected" (James 1912). The lived experience for James is what continuously makes us; we are not complete substances before we experience our lives. Experience is forever always becoming. James explains this process by telling us that "experience grows by its edges" which means that our experiences bleed into each other and expand.

James believes that everything in experience is in some form of relationship to everything else. Whether the relationship is one that brings things together or one that separates them, unification and separation are both a type of relationship. A relationship is not merely one that connotes unification, addition, conjunction, "and"; its opposite, separation, subtraction, disjunction, divorce, "or," is also a type of relationship. *Flights and perchings*, *substantive* and *transitive parts*, clear and vague are all types of relationships we find in experience. James believes that in our lived experience, the more relationships we have, the richer our experience will be. Also, and more importantly, each relation on its own can be a source of further relationships. These relationships besides making experience cohesive, also allow for its expansion. Experience is continuously reaching out and expanding. The continuous expansion of experience is the progress of time and change, the conjunction and disjunction of substantive parts into transitive parts.

Experience is fundamentally more complex than what we can at any given point in space and time experience. For James, different experiences are all ontologically equal and equally valid. He believes in the plurality of experiences. There are different ways of experiencing the world. In our lived experience we have access to some ways of experiencing the world, but James believes that ultimately we do not have the final say as to what experience is.

John Dewey on the lived experience

Much of Dewey's thought resonates that of James. Although their insights are complementary in nature, their terminology and the manner in which each articulates his ideas is different. In agreement with James, Dewey also believes in the primacy of experience. The subject/object distinction, the emphasis on substance at the expense of quality and abstraction from experience into theoretical isolation are what Dewey calls philosophical fallacies.

For Dewey, we are most fundamentally organisms in an environment. Dewey, like James, believes that our lived experience has the potential to provide us with nourishment. Dewey believes that we encounter resistance from our environment and this resistance is directly linked to pain, suffering or some discomfort, which in turn irritates us or stimulates us into either death or growth. According to Dewey, resistance from our environment makes us aware of ourselves. The lived experience is the affirmation of life not in spite of but in acknowledgment and appropriation of the uncertainty, pain, doubt and fear that are contained within our experiences.

Dewey stresses two ideas: One, experience is infinitely more complex than what we are able to experience. Cognitive awareness of our experience is only one type of experience; there are many others, some are emotional, religious, aesthetic, ethical, etc. Two, each of these different experiences provide us with knowledge about our environment.

An experience for Dewey is a continuous process that hangs together cohesively by a particular quality. Otherwise, it is not *an* experience, but a "distracted dispersion." An experience, though of a continuous quality, has places of emphasis; Dewey calls these *inception, development* and *fulfillment*. Some of the examples Dewey provides to illustrate what constitutes an experience are: "that meal in Paris," "that conversation," "that storm." The lived experience has a rhythm which Dewey calls *doing and undergoing*. The doing is the action; the undergoing is the taking in, the reconstruction of what preceded. This is how our lived experience has the potential to become intelligent and allow us the opportunity to grow from our struggles. Dewey tells us that when we meet resistance from our environment and we are stimulated to think about our precarious situation, we can use our imagination to solve our problem and ameliorate our situation. Our problems are grounded in our lived experience, and in turn our solutions (imaginative answers or theories) should be checked against experience. If we are successful we will have ameliorated our situation and experienced growth. Dewey's idea of the lived experience states that our moments of struggle have the potential to be turned into *working capital*. This working capital of previous experiences can nourish us and allows us to grow, to experience qualitative transformations of struggle into deeper appreciations and meanings.

The lived experience dovetails with some aspects of phenomenology, particularly with the ideas of Edmund Husserl and Wilhelm Dilthey. Since phenomenology considers things to be already there, before reflection begins, phenomenology and the Classical American Pragmatist tradition agree that a world exists previous to our theoretical reflections of it. In other words, both schools of thought agree that there is a difference between the way in which we immediately experience things – the lived experience – and a theoretical stepping back to reflect upon such experiences.

Further reading

Dewey, John. *Experience and Nature.* New York: Dover, 1925.

—— *Art as Experience.* New York: Perigee, 1934.

James, William. *The Varieties of Religious Experience.* New York: Longmans, Green, 1902.

—— *Essays in Radical Empiricism.* New York: Longmans, Green, 1912.

McDermott, John J. (ed.) *The Philosophy of John Dewey.* Chicago, IL: University of Chicago Press, 1973.

—— (ed.) *The Writings of William James.* Chicago, IL: University of Chicago Press, 1977.

KIM DÍAZ

LOCKE, ALAIN

Alain Locke (1885–1954) was an African-American philosopher, cultural critic, and aesthete venerated as the chief architect of the Harlem Renaissance. Locke received his bachelor's degree in philosophy *magna cum laude* from Harvard University in 1907. He was subsequently awarded a Rhodes Scholarship, which allowed him to study philosophy and classics at Oxford University's Hertford College from 1907 to 1910. He was the first African-American to receive this award. During 1911 and 1912, Locke studied at the University of Berlin, taking particular interest in the value theory and empirical psychology of Franz Brentano, Alexius Meinong, and Christian Freiherr von Ehrenfels. In 1912, Locke joined the faculty at Howard University, where he would remain for the rest of his academic career. Locke wrote his dissertation, "Problems of Classification in Theory of Value," under the directorship of Ralph Barton Perry and was awarded his doctorate in 1918. He was the first African-American to receive a doctoral degree from Harvard's Department of Philosophy.

Locke, like William James, was engaged in an all-out battle against monism and absolutism. Focusing on axiology, Locke rejected value monism – the view that there are metaphysical value essences to which all forms of valuing are reducible. On such a view, there is only one proper value scheme to which we ought to give our loyalty. Locke found such attempts to establish one single categorical criterion of value to be arbitrary, provincial, and dogmatic. In opposition, Locke proposes value relativism. On this view, values pertain to functional psychological categories rooted in feeling, rather than natural kinds. As such, values are subject to intermittent change and tend to vary across cultures, locations, and times. Locke recognized that transvaluations – the revaluations of prior values – are natural and entirely legitimate occurrences in the sphere of values. Locke distances value relativism from value anarchism, i.e. the view that each person is the measure of value on a case-by-case basis. Locke argues that functional value ultimates/imperatives must be established, for human beings rely heavily upon them to regulate their everyday interactions. Moreover, Locke maintains that an empirical psychology of values reveals common-denominator values (e.g. parity, reciprocity, and tolerance), which are pragmatically confirmed by common human experience.

Locke's value relativism serves as the bedrock to his own variant of pragmatism – critical pragmatism. Critical pragmatism is chiefly concerned with transforming the lived world through intelligent action so as to promote cultural pluralism and cross-cultural communication. Locke maintains that the toleration and reciprocal cultural exchange of diverse social groups within a society strengthens that society. Obstacles to this include absolutism, provincialism, prejudice, and racial hatred. Much of Locke's work (e.g. *The New Negro*) is an attempt at achieving a transvaluation of the worth and dignity of marginalized cultures. One key aspect of this was the rejection of the notion that races are rooted in inherent hereditary traits of a biological nature. Locke argues that races are socially defined groups which always possess the potential to change and be changed.

Further reading

Harris, Leonard (ed.) *The Critical Pragmatism of Alain Locke*. New York: Rowman and Littlefield, 1999.

Locke, Alain. *The Philosophy of Alain Locke: Harlem Renaissance and Beyond*, ed. Leonard Harris. Philadelphia, PA: Temple University Press, 1989.

—— (ed.) *The New Negro*. New York: Touchstone, 1997 [1925].

Lee A. McBride III

LOGIC: DEDUCTION

From the time of Aristotle, deduction was taken as a mode of reasoning in both descriptive and prescriptive senses. Descriptively, deduction was held to be a mode of reasoning in which a conclusion was inferred on the basis of information contained in the premises that gave warrant to that conclusion. Prescriptively, deduction was held to be not synonymous with inferences that were actually made, but with conclusions that followed validly (i.e. according to a set of syllogistic patterns). In either case, deduction was seen as involving an inference to a more particular conclusion on the basis of warrant from more general premises. For example, from the more general premise that "All humans are mortal," along with the premise that "Greeks are human," the more particular conclusion that "Greeks are mortal" follows. This conclusion is more particular than the premise because "Greeks" denotes a smaller class of objects than does "human." This was held as being true even for syllogistic argument forms that contained only general statements, i.e. "All cats are mammals, all mammals are warm-blooded, therefore all cats are warm-blooded," since "cats" denotes a more particular class of objects than does "mammals." Deductive modes of reasoning were held as distinct from inductive modes of reasoning, in which more general conclusions were said to follow from more particular premises.

This conception of deduction changed in the late nineteenth and early twentieth centuries when deduction was held as a syntactic entity in which a set of formal vocabulary terms is specified, along with formation rules (for formulating "grammatical" statements), transformation rules (for stipulating appropriately derived statements), and a set of axioms. Under this push for a syntactic conception of logical systems, deduction was seen by logicians such as George Boole, Gottlob Frege, and Bertrand Russell as removed from the psychology of reasoning and concerned primarily (and even exclusively) with rules for valid derivations. The work of Alfred Tarski in the 1920s and 1930s was seen as crucial for providing a legitimate semantics to such syntactic systems. The earlier conception of the relative generality or particularity of the content of sentences was dropped under this strictly formal, syntactic conception of deduction.

A particularly significant advance in the construction and analysis of formal logical systems was the advent of a logic of relations, often associated with Frege, but formulated independently by Charles S. Peirce. A logic of relations was seen as an advance over traditional syllogistic logic because it allowed the formulation of sentences beyond the pale of syllogistic logic (such as "Portland is between Seattle and Sacramento") as well as derivations using such sentences. Along with the introduction of quantifiers as a means of fully expressing a logic of relations, formal quantificational (or predicate) logical systems became much more powerful and robust, subsuming both the syllogistic logic of classes and propositional logic. Later American philosophers, most notably Willard Van Orman Quine, extended Peirce's advances to a fuller understanding of formal systems and related topics, such as recursion, predication, necessity, and meaning.

Further reading

Aristotle. "De Interpretatione" in *The Complete Works of Aristotle*, ed. Jonathan Barnes. Princeton, NJ: Princeton University Press, 1984, pp. 25–38.

Boole, George. *The Laws of Thought*. New York: Dover, 1958.

Frege, Gottlob. *The Frege Reader*, ed. Michael Beaney. Oxford: Blackwell, 1997.

Peirce, Charles S. *Collected Papers of Charles Sanders Peirce, Volume 2*, ed. Charles Hartshorne and Paul Weiss. Cambridge, MA: Harvard University Press, 1931–5.

Quine, W.V.O. *Methods of Logic*. New York: Holt, Rinehart and Winston, 1950.

Russell, Bertrand. *Introduction to Mathematical Philosophy*. New York: Dover, 1993.

Tarski, Alfred. *Logic, Semantics, Metamathematics*. Indianapolis, IN: Hackett, 1981.

David Boersema

LOGIC: DEMONSTRATIVE

Demonstrative logic is the study of *demonstration* (apodictic proof) as opposed to persuasion. It presupposes the Socratic knowledge/belief distinction – between beliefs that are known to be true (or that have been cognitively established) and those that are not known (or that have not been cognitively established even though they might perhaps be true). Demonstrative logic is the subject of Aristotle's two-volume *Analytics*, as he said in the first sentence of the first volume, the *Prior Analytics*. Every demonstration produces *knowledge* of the truth of its *conclusion* for every person who can comprehend it. Persuasion merely produces *belief*.

However, shortly after having announced demonstration as his subject, Aristotle turned to *deduction*, the process of extracting information implied by given premises – regardless of whether those premises are known to be true or even whether they are true. After all, we can determine that a premise is false by deducing from it a proposition we already know to be false. In the beginning of Chapter 4 of Book A of *Prior Analytics*, Aristotle wrote the following: "Deduction should be discussed before demonstration. Deduction is more general. Every demonstration is a deduction, but not every deduction is a demonstration."

Demonstrative logic is temporarily supplanted by deductive logic, the study of deduction.

He did not revisit demonstration per se until the *Posterior Analytics*, the second volume of the *Analytics*. Deductive logic is the subject of the first volume, *Prior Analytics*. It has been said that one of Aristotle's greatest discoveries was that deduction is *cognitively neutral*: the same process of *deduction* used to draw a conclusion from premises known to be true is also used to draw conclusions from propositions whose truth or falsity is not known, or even from premises known to be false. Another of his important discoveries was that deduction is *topic neutral*: the same process of *deduction* used to draw a conclusion from geometrical premises is also used to draw conclusions from propositions about biology or any other subject. His point, using the deduction/demonstration distinction, was that as far as the process is concerned, i.e. after the premises have been set forth, demonstration is a kind of deduction: demonstrating is deducing from premises know to be true. Deduction is formal in the sense that no understanding of the subject matter *per se* is needed. Theoretically, diagrams, constructions, and other aids to imagining or manipulating subject matter are irrelevant hindrances to purely logical deduction. In fact, in the course of a deduction, any shift of attention from the given premises to their subject matter risks the fallacy of *premise smuggling* – information not in the premises but evident from the subject matter might be tacitly assumed in an intermediate conclusion as a *non sequitur*.

For Aristotle, a demonstration begins with premises that are known to be true and shows by means of chaining of evident steps that its conclusion is a logical consequence of its premises. Thus, a demonstration is a step-by-step deduction whose premises are known to be true. For him, one of the main problems of logic (as opposed to, say, geometry) is to describe in detail the nature of the deductions and to say how the deductions come about.

Thus, at the very beginning of logic we find what has come to be known as *the truth-and-consequence conception of demonstration*: a demonstration is a discourse or extended argumentation that begins with premises known to be *truths* and that involves a chain of reasoning showing by evident steps that its conclusion is a *consequence* of its premises. The adjectival phrase "truth-and-consequence" is elliptical for the more informative but awkward "*established*-truth-and-*deduced*-consequence."

Over and above the premises and conclusion, every deduction and thus every demonstration has a chain-of-reasoning that shows that the (final) conclusion follows logically from the premises. An Aristotelian *direct* demonstration based on three premises p1, p2, and p3, having the conclusion fc, and having a chain-of-reasoning with three intermediate conclusions ic1, ic2, and ic3, can be pictured as below.

p1
p2
p3
?fc
ic1
ic2
ic3
fc

QED

Note that in such an Aristotelian demonstration the final conclusion occurs twice: once as a goal to be achieved and once as it has been inferred. This picture represents only a direct demonstration.

The picture is significantly different for *indirect* demonstrations, for *reductio ad impossibile* or proof by contradiction. In such a deduction, after the premises have been assumed and the conclusion has been set as a goal, the contradictory opposite of the conclusion is assumed as an auxiliary premise. Then, a series of intermediate conclusions are deduced until one is reached which contradicts a previous proposition. To represent a simple indirect demonstration, ~fc (the contradictory opposite of the final conclusion) is added as a new assumption and the X indicates that the last intermediate conclusion ic3 contradicts one of the previous intermediate conclusions or one of the premises.

p1
p2
p3
?fc
~fc
ic1
ic2
ic3
X

QED

It is difficult to understand the significance of Aristotle's logic without being aware of its historic context. Aristotle had rigorous training and deep interest in geometry, a subject that is replete with direct and indirect demonstrations and that is mentioned repeatedly in *Analytics.* Aristotle spent twenty years in Plato's Academy, whose entrance carried the motto: *Let no one unversed in geometry enter here.* The fact that axiomatic presentations of geometry were available to the Academy two generations before Euclid's has been noted often. David Ross pointed out "there were already in Aristotle's time *Elements of Geometry.*" According to Thomas Heath, "The geometrical textbook of the Academy was written by Theudius of Magnesia . . . [who] must be taken to be the immediate precursor of Euclid, and no doubt Euclid made full use of Theudius . . . and other available material".

Following the terminology of Charles Sanders Peirce (1839–1914), America's most distinguished logician, a belief that is known to be true may be called a *cognition*. Cognitions that were obtained by demonstration are called *theorems* and are said to be *demonstrative* or *apodictic*. Those that were not obtained by demonstration are called *intuitions* and are said to be *intuitive.* In his 1868 paper on cognitive faculties reprinted in the 1992 Houser-Kloesel volume, Peirce has a long footnote on the history of the words "intuition" and "intuitive." Shortly after introducing the noun, he wrote (1992: 11–12), "*Intuition* here will be nearly the same as 'premise not itself a conclusion'." It is impossible to have demonstrative knowledge without intuitive knowledge. This point was made by Plato, Aristotle, and many others including Leibniz and Pascal. However, it is difficult to determine with certainty exactly which cognitions are intuitive and which are demonstrative. Peirce said in the 1868 paper that there is no evidence that we have the ability to determine, given an arbitrary cognition, whether it is an intuition or a theorem (1992: 12).

Deductive logic has made immeasurable progress since Aristotle. In retrospect, the explosive increase in the field reported in the 1854 masterpiece by George Boole (1815–64) merely served to ignite a chain reaction of further advances that continues even today (Corcoran 2006). Aristotle's system did not recognize compound terms or equations. Boole's system recognizes both. Unlike other revolutionary logical innovators, Boole's greatness as a logician was recognized almost immediately. In 1865, hardly a decade after Boole's 1854 *Laws of Thought* and not even a year after Boole's tragic death, his logic was the subject of a Harvard University lecture "Boole's Calculus of Logic" by C.S. Peirce, America's most creative native logician. Peirce opened his lecture with these prophetic words:

> Perhaps the most extraordinary view of logic which has ever been developed with success is that of the late Professor Boole. His book ... *Laws of Thought*. ... is destined to mark a great epoch in logic; for it contains a conception which in point of fruitfulness will rival that of Aristotle's *Organon*.
>
> (Peirce 1982: 223–4)

Peirce was among the earliest logicians to discern Boole's achievement.

Aristotle's system recognized only four logical forms of propositions, each involving exactly two (non-logical) terms; today infinitely many are recognized, with no limit to the number of terms occurring in a single proposition. In fact, as early as his famous 1885 paper "On the Algebra of Logic: A Contribution to the Philosophy of Notation," also reprinted in the 1992 Houser-Kloesel volume, Peirce recognized in print simple propositions having more than two terms (1992: 225–6). Examples are the triadic proposition that the sign "7" denotes the number seven to the person Charles and the tetradic proposition that one is to two as three is to six. Peirce revisits the topic in his 1907 manuscript "Pragmatism," printed in the 1998 Houser-Kloesel volume (1998: 407–8), where he presented his now well-known triadic analysis of propositions about giving as "The person Abe gives the dog Rex to the person Ben."

Aristotle's system recognized only three patterns of immediate one-premise deductions and only four patterns of immediate two-premise deductions; today many more are accepted. In particular, he never discerned the fact pointed out by Peirce that to every pattern of deduction there is a proposition to the effect that its conclusion follows from its premises. Peirce (1992: 201) called them *leading principles*. It never occurred to Aristotle to include in his system such propositions as, for example, that given any two terms if one belongs to all of the other then some of the latter belongs to some of the former.

The simple linear chain structures of Aristotle's deductions have been augmented by complex nonlinear structures such as branching trees and nested linear chains. Moreover, his deductive logic has been subjected to severe criticism. Nevertheless, the basic idea of his demonstrative logic, the truth-and-consequence theory of demonstration, which was fully accepted by Boole, has encountered little opposition in its more than 2,000-year history. It continues to enjoy wide acceptance in the contemporary logic community. Perhaps ironically, Peirce never expressed full acceptance and, in at least one place, he seems to say that diagrams are essential not only in geometrical demonstrations (1998: 303) but in all demonstration (1998: 502).

Further reading

Corcoran, J. "Aristotle's Prior Analytics and Boole's Laws of Thought," *History and Philosophy of Logic* 24 (2006): 261–88.

Peirce, C.S. *Writings of Charles S. Peirce: A Chronological Edition*, Vol. I. Bloomington, IN: Indiana University Press, 1982.

—— *The Essential Peirce: Selected Philosophical Writings (1867–1893)*, Vol. I, ed. N. Houser and C. Kloesel. Bloomington, IN: Indiana University Press, 1992.

—— *The Essential Peirce: Selected Philosophical Writings (1893–1913)*, Vol. II, ed. N. Houser and C. Kloesel. Bloomington, IN: Indiana University Press, 1998.

JOHN CORCORAN

LOGIC: EXPERIMENTAL

"Experimental logic" is a name that John Dewey gave to his theory of inquiry, especially as it was developed in *Essays in Experimental Logic* (1916), *How We Think* (1910), and *Logic: The Theory of Inquiry* (1938). In the preface to his 1916 volume Dewey indicated that his experimental logic contained "psychological phases" and that those phases were written from the standpoint of behaviorism. This statement deserves special attention on two counts.

First, some of Dewey's critics, including Charles S. Peirce, accused Dewey of confusing logical method (how people ought to think) with an analysis of psychological processes of thinking (how people do in fact think). For Dewey, however, logical forms are normative for inquiry in the sense that they have arisen within the context of inquiry into inquiry and have been demonstrated to be capable of producing judgments that are true in the sense of being both warranted and assertible. Just as farm machinery has developed as a result of inquiry into farming practices, the "machinery" of logic is the product of inquiry into the practice of inquiry. The tools of logic, like the tools of farming, are constructed artifacts; they are neither discovered as entities that existed prior to inquiry nor are they invented out of nothing. In each case there is modification, and modification of modification, of naturally occurring existents.

Second, experimental logic must be understood from the standpoint of behaviorism. Inquiry is public, organic behavior. Moreover, because inquiry involves signs, abstract entities, and other cultural artifacts, it is social behavior. Inquiry is also social behavior in the moral sense that it allows individuals to "rehearse" courses of action before committing themselves to decisions that might be harmful to themselves and others. This type of behaviorism was thus quite different from that of John B. Watson, which depended on what Dewey regarded as a discredited account of stimulus–response (S–R) theory, an unwarranted reduction of psychology to physiology, and treatment of psychology as if it were a science of the behavior of individuals.

Dewey argued that there is continuity within inquiry. Methods utilized by control of inquiry in the sciences and control of inquiry in common-sense affairs are basically the same: they differ only in degree of complexity and type of subject matter. Both types of inquiry are concerned with adjustment to situations that are social in nature.

Experimental logic is thus more comprehensive than symbolic or mathematical logics, which have tended to separate formal systems of proof from the broader concerns of scientific method. Dewey considered formal logic an essential part of the broader processes of inquiry, but rejected attempts to identify inquiry with formal logic *simpliciter*.

Dewey noted that experimentation is neither simply a practical convenience nor just a means of modifying states of mind. Experiment is required to organize and deploy the data that are employed to warrant inferences, since experiences per se are not sufficient to this task. Experiment is also required to eliminate irrelevant existential material and to seek additional material that may be relevant to the problem at hand.

More specifically, Dewey thought that the process of inquiry – quotidian as well as scientific – involves a more or less well-defined sequence. Once an indeterminate situation has become determinate in the sense that it is recognized as in need of reconstruction in a manner that settles doubt, four types of relations enter into the process. In the first there is recognition of involvement of existential conditions with other existential conditions. In the second, some existent is treated as a sign or symbol of another existent, giving rise to inference. In the third, there is a relationship of implication between symbols in their role as symbols. It is at this level of *abstracta* relating to other *abstracta* that symbolic logic and scientific hypotheses operate and are developed. Finally there is the relation of symbols (hypotheses and other *abstracta*) to existential affairs that Dewey terms "reference." This is the stage at which hypotheses are tested against existential conditions that initiated the problem under consideration.

The process just described is Pragmatic in the sense that it involves inquiry into the practical consequences that the inquirer conceives the object of his or her conceptions to have; it is instrumental in the sense that logical entities, hypotheses, and other *abstracta* are treated as tools or instruments of inquiry (and not as having independent ontological status as essences), and it is experimental in the sense that it involves "the art of conducting a sequence of observations in which natural conditions are intentionally altered and controlled in ways which will disclose, discover, natural subject-matters which would not otherwise have been noted."

Further reading

Dewey, John. *Essays in Experimental Logic*. Chicago, IL: University of Chicago Press, 1916.

—— *Studies in Logical Theory, The Collected Works of John Dewey: The Middle Works, 1899–1924, Vol. 2*, ed. Jo Ann Boydston. Carbondale, IL: Southern Illinois University Press, 1976.

—— *How We Think, The Collected Works of John Dewey: The Middle Works, 1899 1924, Vol. 6*, ed. Jo Ann Boydston. Carbondale, IL: Southern Illinois University Press, 1978. Revised edition in *The Collected Works of John Dewey: The Later Works, 1925–1953*, Vol. 8, ed. Jo Ann Boydston. Carbondale, IL: Southern Illinois University Press, 1986.

—— "Introduction to *Essays in Experimental Logic,*" *The Collected Works of John Dewey: The Middle Works, 1899–1924, Vol. 10*, ed. Jo Ann Boydston. Carbondale, IL: Southern Illinois University Press, 1980.

—— *Experience and Nature, The Collected Works of John Dewey: The Later Works, 1925–1953, Vol. 1*, ed. Jo Ann Boydston. Carbondale, IL: Southern Illinois University Press, 1981.

—— *Logic: The Theory of Inquiry, The Collected Works of John Dewey: The Later Works, 1925–1953, Vol. 12*, ed. Jo Ann Boydston. Carbondale, IL: Southern Illinois University Press, 1986.

LARRY A. HICKMAN

LOGIC: INDUCTIVE

Logic is the study of the quality of arguments. An argument consists of a set of premises and a conclusion. The quality of an argument depends on at least two factors: the truth of the premises, and the strength with which the premises confirm the conclusion. The truth of the premises is a contingent factor that depends on the state of the world. The strength with which the premises confirm the conclusion is supposed to be independent of the state of the world. Logic is only concerned with this second, logical factor of the quality of arguments.

Deductive logic classifies arguments into two kinds: those where the truth of the premises guarantees the truth of the conclusion, and those where they do not. The former are called deductively valid, and the premises are said to logically imply the conclusion. The latter arguments are called deductively invalid. So the deductive-logical explication of the logical factor of the quality of an argument is the qualitative yes-or-no concept of deductive validity.

Inductive logic aims at a more lenient explication of the logical factor of the quality of an argument. It comprises deductive validity as a special case. The reason is that the conclusions we are normally interested in are too informative to be logically implied by premises we can know. For instance, no set of premises about the past and present logically implies a conclusion about the future. Inductive logic usually aims at a quantitative explication of the logical factor of the quality of an argument, viz. the degree to which the premises confirm the conclusion.

Hempel (1945) made one of the earliest attempts to develop a formal logic of qualitative confirmation. His goal of constructing a purely syntactical definition of confirmation is shared by Carnap (1962), who goes beyond Hempel by aiming at a quantitative concept of degree of confirmation. Carnap bases his inductive logic on the theory of probability (Kolmogorov 1956). Due to Goodman's (1983) "new riddle of induction" there is consensus nowadays that a purely syntactical definition of (degree of) confirmation cannot be adequate. However, the use of probability theory has been a central feature of inductive logic ever since.

A "probability measure" is a real-valued function on a language or field of propositions that is (1) non-negative, (2) normalized, and (3) additive. So every proposition receives a non-negative probability; the tautological proposition receives probability 1; and the probability of the union or disjunction of two disjoint or incompatible propositions is the sum of the probabilities of the two propositions. The conditional probability of one proposition given another proposition is defined as the ratio of the probability of the intersection or conjunction of the two propositions divided by the probability of the second proposition. Obviously this makes sense only if the second proposition receives positive probability.

In inductive logic conditional probability is usually put to use in the following way (Carnap 1962; Hawthorne 2005; Skyrms 2000). The "degree of absolute confirmation" of a conclusion by a set of premises relative to a probability measure on a field of propositions is defined as the conditional probability of the conclusion given the (conjunction of the) premises. For more see Huber (2005).

It is important to note that this definition renders degree of confirmation relative to a probability measure on a language or field of propositions that include the premises and the conclusion. The difference between the Carnapian approach (Carnap 1962) and more modern approaches (Hawthorne 2005; Skyrms 2000) now can be put as follows. Carnap sought to come up with one single logical probability measure, whereas modern writers consider (almost) any probability measure as admissible from a purely logical point of view.

The notion of deductive validity is a three-place relation between a set of premises, a conclusion, and a language that includes the premises and the conclusion. By trying to define a unique logical probability measure for each language, Carnap in effect tried to define degree of confirmation in a similar fashion as a three-place relation between a set of premises, a conclusion, and a language. Modern theories of confirmation differ in this respect, because they construe confirmation as a four-place relation, thus making explicit the probability measure. Fitelson (2005) still considers this to be a logical relation.

Carnap (1962) also proposed a definition of qualitative confirmation, where the idea is that premises confirm a conclusion if they raise the probability of the conclusion. A conclusion is incrementally confirmed by a set of premises relative to a probability measure on a field of propositions if and only if the conditional probability of the conclusion given the premises is higher than the unconditional probability of the conclusion.

As indicated by the qualifiers "absolute" and "incremental," we have here two different concepts of confirmation. The quantitative concept of absolute confirmation is explicated by the conditional probability of the conclusion given the premises. Absolute confirmation thus consists in high conditional probability, and the qualitative concept of absolute confirmation is to be defined as follows. A conclusion is absolutely confirmed by a set of premises relative to a probability measure on a field of propositions if and only if its degree of absolute confirmation is sufficiently high. Incremental confirmation, on the other hand, focuses on increase in probability. Therefore the quantitative concept of incremental confirmation is to be defined as the degree to which the premises increase the probability of the conclusion, i.e. the difference between the unconditional probability of the conclusion and the conditional probability of the conclusion given the premises.

As noted by Fitelson (1999), there are many non-equivalent ways to measure degree of incremental confirmation. Earman (1992) discusses the distance measure, which subtracts the unconditional probability of the conclusion from its conditional probability given the premises. Joyce (1999) and Christensen (1999) propose a measure which subtracts the conditional probability of the conclusion given the negation of the premises from its conditional probability given the premises.

In a different context, Carnap and Bar-Hillel (1952) propose to measure the informativeness of a conclusion by the probability of its negation. Hempel and Oppenheim (1948) suggest measuring the extent to which the conclusion informs us about the premises by the conditional probability of the negation of the conclusion given the negation of the premises. This is relevant since it turns out that the above-mentioned measures of incremental confirmation are aggregates of the degree of absolute confirmation and the informativeness in the respective senses. More precisely, incremental confirmation is proportional to expected informativeness. Different measures of incremental confirmation differ in the way they measure informativeness.

We have thus detected a third factor of the quality of an argument: the informativeness of the conclusion. This is not surprising. After all, the informativeness of the conclusion was the very reason why we were considering more lenient standards than deductive validity in the first place. Note also that the informativeness of the conclusion is as much a logical factor as is the degree to which the premises confirm the conclusion. For both factors are determined once the premises, the conclusion, and the probability measure on the field of propositions are specified. In fact, this opens the door to render all factors of the quality of an argument to be logical; for we can now also consider the probability that the premises are true.

So far we have been engaged in conceptual analysis, where we appeal to intuitions as the data against which to test various proposals for a definition of confirmation. The assumption is, of course, that the concept we are explicating is important. Surely it is a good thing for a hypothesis to be confirmed by the available data. Surely we should strive to list premises that confirm the conclusion we are arguing for. Inductive logic is important, because it is a normative theory. Yet conceptual analysis does not provide the resources to justify a normative theory. Appeals to intuitions do not show why we should prefer "well-confirmed" hypotheses to other hypotheses, and why we should provide inductively strong rather than any other arguments.

The analogy to deductive logic again proves helpful. The rules of deductive logic are norms that tell us how we should argue deductively. As any other set of norms, it needs to be justified. Contrary to Goodman (1983), the rules of deductive logic are not justified, because they adequately describe our deductive practices. They do not. The rules of deductive logic are justified *relative to* the goal of arguing truth preservingly, i.e. in such a way that the truth of the premises guarantees the truth of the conclusion. The results that provide the justification are known as soundness and completeness. Soundness says that every argument we obtain from the rules of deductive logic is such that truth is preserved when we go from the premises to the conclusion. Completeness states the converse. Every argument that has this property of truth preservation can be obtained from the rules of deductive logic. So the rules of deductive logic are justified relative to the goal of truth preservation. The reason is that they further this goal insofar as all and only deductively valid arguments are truth-preserving.

What is the goal-inductive logic supposed to further – relative to which it can be justified? Surely it includes truth. However, as Hume (1739) argues, it is impossible to justify induction relative to the goal of truth. His argument assumes that justifying induction means providing a deductively valid or an inductively strong argument with knowable premises for the conclusion that induction will always lead to true conclusions. As noted by Reichenbach (1938), there are deductively valid arguments for other conclusions that may show that induction furthers the goal of truth to the extent this is possible. Similar results obtain for absolute confirmation, where it can be shown that the conditional probability of a conclusion given the premises converges to its truth value when more and more premises are learned.

However, if obtaining true conclusions were the only goal induction is supposed to further, induction could be replaced by deduction. All that is logically implied by what we know is guaranteed to be true. We do not need to go beyond the premises to satisfy the goal of truth. The reason we nevertheless do go beyond what is logically implied by the premises is that we aim at more than mere truth: we aim at informative truth. It is this very feature that makes us strive for a more lenient explication of the logical factor of the quality of arguments in the first place; and without it Hume's problem of the justification of induction would not even get off the ground. Thus, the important question is whether and in which sense inductive logic can be justified relative to the goal of informative truth. One answer is given by Huber (2005). There it is shown that incremental confirmation in the sense of the above-mentioned measures converges to the most informative among all true conclusions when more and more premises are learned.

Further reading

Carnap, Rudolf. *Logical Foundations of Probability*, second edition. Chicago, IL: University of Chicago Press 1950/1962.

Christensen, David. "Measuring Confirmation," *Journal of Philosophy* 96 (1999): 437–61.

Earman, John. *Bayes or Bust? A Critical Examination of Bayesian Confirmation Theory*. Cambridge, MA: MIT Press, 1992.

Fitelson, Branden. "Inductive Logic" in J. Pfeifer and S. Sarkar (eds) *The Philosophy of Science. An Encyclopedia*. London: Routledge, 2005.

Goodman, Nelson. *Fact, Fiction, and Forecast*, fourth edition. Cambridge, MA: Harvard University Press, 1983.

Hawthorne, James. "Inductive Logic" in E.N. Zalta (ed.) *Stanford Encyclopedia of Philosophy*. Stanford, CA: Stanford University Press, 2005.

Hempel, Carl Gustav and Oppenheim, Paul. "Studies in the Logic of Explanation," *Philosophy of Science* 15 (1948): 135–75.

Huber, Franz. "What Is the Point of Confirmation?" *Philosophy of Science* (Proceedings) (2005): 1146–59.

Hume, David. *A Treatise of Human Nature*, ed. D.F. Norton and M.J. Norton. Oxford: Oxford University Press, 1739/2000.

Joyce, James F. *The Foundations of Causal Decision Theory*. Cambridge: Cambridge University Press, 1999.

Kolmogorov, Andrej N. *Foundations of the Theory of Probability*, second edition. New York: Chelsea, 1956.

Reichenbach, Hans. *Experience and Prediction. An Analysis of the Foundations and the Structure of Knowledge*. Chicago, IL: University of Chicago Press, 1938.

Skyrms, Brian. *Choice and Chance. An Introduction to Inductive Logic*, fourth edition. Belmont, CA: Wadsworth Thomson Learning, 2000.

Franz Huber

LOGIC: INFORMAL

Informal logic is, as the name of the subject suggests, not formal logic. Unlike formal logic, it does not consist of precise techniques for determining whether an argument is valid, i.e. whether the truth of the premises of an argument necessitates the truth of the conclusion of that argument. Informal logic, taught primarily in critical thinking courses, consists of a number of techniques – other than those techniques studied in formal logic – for identifying arguments as either flawed or successful arguments.

The most well-known technique in informal logic, historically, has been the use of descriptions of common fallacies. A fallacy is a form argument that generally contains premises that do not give adequate support to the conclusion of the argument. Informal logic allows one to use descriptions of common fallacies to identify arguments as flawed. Among the most common and well-known fallacies are ad hominem fallacies, and ad populum fallacies.

Ad hominem fallacies contain premises that are not directed toward the issue in question, but rather directed toward the person who raises the issue. A critic of the war in Iraq, for example, who supports her anti-war position on the basis of the claim that George W. Bush is an unintelligent person, is committing an ad hominem fallacy.

The premises of ad populum fallacies concern the popularity of the conclusion to argue for that conclusion. If one argues that it is permissible for corporations to use sweatshop labor on the basis of the claim that the majority of US citizens are unconcerned regarding the conditions in factories making inexpensive clothes, then one has appealed to ad populum to make this point.

It would be a mistake to think that informal logic consists solely of the technique of identifying fallacies. Courses in informal logic also typically cover issues related to clarity in writing and speaking, teaching students how to avoid vagueness, ambiguity, and obscurity. A central concern of informal logic is the structure of arguments. Techniques such as diagramming of arguments are employed for the purpose of identifying which statements in a discourse are premises, which statements are conclusions, and whether the premises support their conclusions separately or in conjunction with each other. A related technique is identifying enthymemes, arguments with unstated premises or conclusions. An example of an enthymeme is the following: Iran poses a threat to the security of the United States, therefore the United States ought to invade Iran. The unstated premise is that if a country poses a threat to the security of the United States, the United States ought to invade that country.

Informal logic also involves techniques for identifying the premises of arguments as acceptable premises. Whereas formal logic only studies the relationship between premises and conclusions, informal logic studies whether a given premise ought to be accepted or rejected in light of the available evidence. To cite a fairly simple example, premises from an unreliable source, such as a celebrity tabloid magazine, ought not to be given as much credence as a premise that is obtained from a (generally) reliable source, such as the *Washington Post*.

Through the study of these topics, informal logic contributes to the study of logic generally, the study that distinguishes good and bad arguments.

Further reading

Copi, I.M. *Introduction to Logic*, seventh edition. New York: Macmillan, 1986.

Freeman, James B. "The Place of Informal Logic in Logic" in Ralph A. Johnson and J. Anthony Blair (eds) *New Essays in Informal Logic*. Windsor, ON: Informal Logic, 1994.

FRITZ J. MCDONALD

LOGIC: MATHEMATICAL

Mathematical logic is a field of mathematics that includes the study of symbolic logic and its metatheory. The latter includes proof theory (the study of deducibility relations among sentences in a formal language, where deducibility is defined syntactically) and model theory (the study of interpretations of formal languages, where interpretations are specified in extensional settheoretic terms suited for the study of the language of mathematics). Key metatheoretic questions regarding a given formal language concern correspondences between syntactic deducibility relations among sentences in that language and semantic consequence relations among sentences as determined by interpretations of the language. A proof system for the given language is *complete* with respect to a given class of interpretations just in case any semantic consequence of a set of premises in those interpretations is syntactically provable from those premises. Conversely, the proof system is *sound* with respect to a given class of interpretations just in case any sentence that is syntactically provable from a given set of premises is respectively a semantic consequence of those premises. Besides issues of soundness and completeness, mathematical logic is also concerned with the expressive capabilities of formal languages (what concepts they can and cannot explicitly distinguish; what properties and relations they can and cannot categorically define).

Computability theory falls within the scope of mathematical logic insofar as certain classes of algebraic grammars are associated with respective computational capabilities. Inductive logic, if there are such logics, involves the use of statistics and probability theory; but while statistics and probability theory employ sophisticated mathematical machinery, this does not place inductive inference within the scope of mathematical logic as such. Mathematical logic is restricted rather to a study of formal systems of deductive inference and algorithmic computation, particularly as such formal systems provide potential mathematical models of the expressive and *deductive* capabilities of natural language.

While sometimes characterized as a science of correct reasoning, formal logic is in fact at best a study of correct deductive reasoning. A standard development of formal deductive logic begins with propositional logic and proceeds to introduce various refinements. The primitive elements in *propositional logic* are sentential variables along with an expressively complete set of truth-functional connectives. The main concern here is with arguments (provability and/or consequence relations) whose validity depends on truth-functional operations such as negation, conjunction, disjunction, material implication, and the like. Semantically, one assumes that the world consists of facts and that sentences will be true or false relative to a given domain, insofar as they do or do not express facts in that domain. Various modifications are possible: e.g. truth-value gaps or multiple truthvalues are possible; or one may permit infinitely long well-formed sentences.

One the other hand, firstorder predicate (quantificational) logic allows that sentences will have internal structures reflecting more detailed ontological commitments. The assumption here is that the world consists of objects having various properties and standing in various relations. Facts are at bottom determined by which objects have what properties or stand in which relations. The language of firstorder logic in this case requires predicate (relational) symbols, names, individual variables, perhaps functional symbols, and quantificational operators (esp. *all* and *some*) to reflect this kind of ontological scenario. The new concern here is with arguments that involve quantificational as well as truthfunctional operations. Firstorder logic is the strongest finitary logic that is both complete and has the Löwenheim–Skolem property. The latter indicates the expressive weakness of firstorder logic insofar as many key mathematical concepts (infinity, continuity, etc.) are therefore not categorically definable in any firstorder language.

The quantifiers in firstorder logic only range over the objects in a given domain of quantification. Secondorder logic allows quantification over properties and relations as well. (Thirdorder logic allows quantification over properties of and relations among firstorder properties and relations, etc.) Unlike firstorder logic, secondorder logic is neither complete nor compact, nor does it have the Löwenheim–Skolem property. But while firstorder logic is expressively very weak, standard secondorder logic has greater expressive power, whereby most key concepts in mathematics are categorically definable.

On a different front, modal logic introduces operators to accommodate logics of necessity and possibility, introducing possible worlds into the underlying ontology. This permits a straightforward extension of propositional logic, where one treats possible worlds as distinct universes of possible facts. Meanwhile, interactions between modal operators and quantificational operators in first-order logic present problems (concerning substitution into modal contexts, identity of objects across different worlds, etc.) whose solutions remain unclear. Variations of modal logic include temporal logic, epistemic logic, deontic logic, and dynamic logic. Relevance and paraconsistent logics also exploit a possibleworlds ontology to handle difficulties with material implication and inconsistency, respectively.

Logic is an old subject that developed slowly but surely in the works of Aristotle, the Megarians, the Stoics, and various medieval logicians. Mathematical logic on the whole is a recent revolutionary advance, having begun to emerge in its present form in the middle of the nineteenth century. George Boole, Augustus De Morgan, Gottlob Frege, Ernst Schröder, Giuseppe Peano, and a host of others pioneered this work in Europe, laying the groundwork for Whitehead and Russell's *Principia Mathematica* and subsequent developments throughout much of the twentieth century.

A number of American philosophers have contributed to these developments. First and foremost was Charles Peirce who introduced the algebraic notation for predicate calculus that is the basis for what has become the most widely used notation for logic today. Peirce also developed a graphical notation for propositional and predicate logic, including techniques capable of handling proofs in modal logic. Modal logic as developed by classical and medieval logicians had been mostly forgotten until C.I. Lewis revived interest in it early in the twentieth century in an attempt to address the peculiar problems with ordinary truthfunctional material implication. W.V. Quine (one of Lewis's and Whitehead's students) did as much as anyone to move formal logic into center-stage in mid-twentieth century analytic philosophy, largely by way of espousing a tight integration of first-order logic with philosophical conceptualization and argumentation. Saul Kripke and others took Lewis's work with modal logics to new heights by showing how it may be given a Tarski-style semantics. The list could go on beyond the few mentioned here; but one cannot help but notice that mathematical logic has been dominated largely by European mathematicians and philosophers, many of whom worked in the United States after fleeing war-torn Europe early in the twentieth century.

Further reading

Gabbay, Dov and Guenther, Franz. *Handbook of Philosophical Logic*, second edition, 18 volumes. Berlin: Springer Science+Business Media, 2001–.

Gamut, L.T.F. *Logic, Language, and Meaning*, 2 volumes. Chicago, IL: University of Chicago Press, 1991.

Hopcroft, John E., Motwani, Rajeev, and Ullman, Jeffrey D. *Introduction to Automata Theory, Languages, and Computation*, second edition. Boston, MA: Addison-Wesley, 2001.

Kripke, Saul. *Naming and Necessity*. Cambridge, MA: Harvard University Press, 1980.

Lewis, C.I. *Collected Papers of Clarence Irving Lewis*, ed. John D. Goheen and John L. Mothershead, Jr. Stanford, CA: Stanford University Press, 1970.

Manzano, María. *Extensions of First Order Logic*. Cambridge: Cambridge University Press, 1996.

Peirce, Charles Sanders. "On the Algebra of Logic," *American Journal of Mathematics* 7 (1885): 180–202.

Quine, Willard Van Orman. *Selected Logic Papers*. New York: Random House, 1966.

Roberts, Don D. *The Existential Graphs of Charles S. Peirce*. The Hague: Mouton, 1973.

van Heijenoort, Jean. *From Frege to Gödel: A Source Book in Mathematical Logic*. Cambridge, MA: Harvard University Press, 1967.

Whitehead, Alfred North, and Russell, Bertrand. *Principia Mathematica*, 3 volumes. Cambridge: Cambridge University Press, 1910–13.

TOM BURKE

LOGIC: MODAL

Modal logic is logic of alethic modalities, viz. actuality, possibility, and necessity. As early as 1918, dissatisfied with the dominant treatment of conditionals as material implication ("'If *P* then *Q*' is true just if either *P* is false or *Q* is true"), C.I. Lewis proposed an alternative treatment: "If *P* then *Q*" is true just if *P* strictly implies *Q*. In 1932, Lewis, with C.H. Langford, defined strict implication in terms of possibility: *P* strictly implies *Q* just if it is not possible for P to be true and Q false, or in symbols, $\sim\Diamond(P \,\&\, \sim Q)$, where $\sim$ is the negation operator and $\Diamond$ is the possibility operator. Alternatively, P strictly implies Q just if it is necessarily the case that if P then Q. Symbolizing the necessity operator as $\Box$, P strictly implies Q just if $\Box(P \supset Q)$, where $\supset$ is the material implication operator. It is easy to see that $\Diamond$ and $\Box$ are inter-definable: $\Diamond P \equiv_{df} \sim\Box\sim P$; $\Box P \equiv_{df} \sim\Diamond\sim P$. Modal logic began as a syntactic system governed by axioms for $\Diamond$ and $\Box$, has been developed extensively since, and now provides important tools in all areas of philosophical investigation.

Modal logicians follow Leibniz and relativize truth to possible worlds. Moreover, they speak of the accessibility relation, R, between possible worlds and lay out the following truth conditions for $\Diamond$ and $\Box$:

$\Diamond P$ is true in a possible world w just if P is true in at least one possible world bearing R to w;
$\Box P$ is true in a possible world w just if P is true in every possible world bearing R to w.

The most comprehensive system of modal logic is known as S5 and consists of the following axioms:

PL. All truths of propositional logic;
T. $\Box P \supset P$;
K $\Box(P \supset Q) \supset (\Box P \supset \Box Q)$;
5 $\Diamond P \supset \Box\Diamond P$.

There are two rules of inference:

Modus ponens Infer Q from $P \supset Q$ and P;
Necessitation Infer $\Box P$ from P.

S5 is widely regarded as the standard system for logical possibility and necessity. The axiom T requires R to be reflexive (for every w, wRw), and 5 requires R to be euclidean (if w_1Rw_2 and w_1Rw_3, then w_2Rw_3). Any relation that is reflexive and euclidean is an equivalence relation. This means that S5 partitions the space of possible worlds into subspaces within each of which every world is accessible from every world. In the simplest such model, the entire space of possible worlds is the only such subspace, i.e. every world is accessible from every world.

If we combine S5 with first-order predicate logic, the result is quantified modal logic (QML). Ruth Barcan (Marcus) and Rudolf Carnap pioneered rigorous investigations of QML, and Saul Kripke gave a definitive treatment of the semantics for QML. QML yields two controversial theorems: $\forall x\Box Fx \supset \Box\forall xFx$ (the Barcan Formula) and $\Box\forall xFx \supset \forall x\Box Fx$ (the Converse Barcan Formula). The Barcan Formula says that if everything actual is necessarily F, then necessarily everything is F. Let F mean "is physical" and assume physicalism to be actually true. Also assume that every physical thing is necessarily physical. Then everything actual is necessarily physical. But at the same time, it is also possible for there to be a non-physical thing, say, a Cartesian ego or an abstract object of some kind. So, it is not necessarily the case that everything is physical. Therefore, it appears, the Barcan Formula is false. Let F mean "exists." Then since in every world everything in that world exists, and not everything in the actual world exists in every world, the Converse Barcan Formula appears false. Various attempts to overcome these problems – some syntactic, others semantic – constitute important parts of the development of QML.

Further reading

Barcan, Ruth. "A Functional Calculus of First Order Based on Strict Implication," *Journal of Symbolic Logic* 11 (1946): 1–16.
Kripke, Saul. "A Completeness Theorem in Modal Logic," *Journal of Symbolic Logic* 24 (1959): 1–15.
Lewis, Clarence I. and Langford, Cooper H. *Symbolic Logic*. New York: Appleton-Century, 1932.

TAKASHI YAGISAWA

LOGIC: SYMBOLIC

Symbolic logic explores the symbolic abstractions that get hold of the formal features of logical inference. Symbolic logic is comparatively new in the long history of logic, and its ongoing development has close ties to mathematical abstractions and reasonings.

In 1910 Alfred North Whitehead and Bertrand Russell published *Principia Mathematica*, a three-volume work on the foundations of mathematics which is generally considered a vitally important work for symbolic logic and for philosophy in general. It attempted both to derive all mathematical truths from axioms and inference rules in symbolic logic and to avoid some contradictions in earlier logical developments.

The relation of "material implication," which served as the basis for the work and as a paradigm for logical deduction, is truth conditional, and housed what are known as the paradoxes of material implication. These had far-ranging consequences for epistemology in general. According to the "if–then" relation of material implication, a false proposition implies any proposition, while a true proposition is implied by any proposition. Or, in other terms, if the antecedent or "if" clause is false the entire statement is true, no matter what the consequent or "then" clause, while if the consequent clause is true, the entire statement is true no matter what the antecedent clause.

This does not allow for the significance of contrary to fact conditionals, for the significance of claims concerning what would happen if one were to perform a certain action even if that action has not been or ever will be performed. For example, the claim that if I were to jump out the window I would float upward and the claim that if I were to jump out the window I would fall to the ground are equally true, since I did not jump out of the window. But if the two contradictory claims can both be true, the claim has no significance. Material implication cannot allow for the meaningfulness of unactualized possibilities and potentialities, but only for actual facts, and thus it renders senseless the ordinary meaning of causal connections or real connections. Moreover, it undermines the entire concept of verification, for if a true proposition is implied by any proposition, then an observational truth technically verifies any hypothesis whatsoever; if the consequent is true, the statement is true regardless of the truth of the antecedent. In short, material implication wreaks havoc with our ordinary claims and inferences.

To counter what he saw as these destructive implications for the direction of epistemology in general, C.I. Lewis developed his logic of strict implication, which is a modal symbolic logic. Modal logic is not truth conditional but allows for the various modalities of possible and impossible, contingent and necessary, consistent and inconsistent. Strict implication captures the meaning of ordinary inference or deducibility, with meaningful implications holding whether the antecedent is true or false, and allows for meaningful assertions involving potentialities and possibilities.

Lewis held that the choice among alternative logical systems answers to criteria best called pragmatic. We choose that which works best in answering our interests and needs. The problem of alternative logics is similar to the problem of alternative geometries. The question in the latter is which geometry applies to real space, and the question of the former is which applies to ordinary inference.

Further reading

Gabbay, D.M. and Guenthner, F. (eds) *Handbook of Philosophical Logic*, second edition, 13 volumes. Dordrecht: Kluwer. 2001–5.

Kneale, W. and Kneale, M. *The Development of Logic*. Oxford: Oxford University Press. 1962/1988.

Lewis, C.I. and Langford, C. H. *Symbolic Logic*. New York: Dover. 1959.

Putnam, Hilary. "Is Logic Empirical?" in *Boston Studies in the Philosophy of Science*, Vol. V. Boston, MA: Boston University Press. 1969.

Russell, Bertrand, and Whitehead, A.N. *Principia Mathematica*. Cambridge: Cambridge University Press. 1910.

SANDRA B. ROSENTHAL

LOVE

A topic most philosophers place outside mainstream Western philosophical discourse, love has a long history in the West including treatments that resulted in complex distinctions. Yet love has rarely been given much thought by many famous philosophers in their systematic speculations as it has seemed to most to somehow exist outside intellectual discipline. For many, love has been a human emotion or situation beyond the rational: an a-rational, counter-rational, anti-rational mode of being related to others in the world.

Still resonant senses of traditional Western subcategories of love remain with us in distinctions between *eros*, *philia*, *agape*, and *caritas*: lustful desire, friendly or parental care, disinterested generosity, and compassion directed towards strangers and neighbors (a Christian alteration of *agape*), respectively. Vibrant sub-topics have included courtly love and chivalry, the former a love situated among high-status individuals with time for socially frivolous yet sometimes serious, highly formulaic interactions between men and women (to some twenty-first century sensibilities, with striking, coded examples of love between women or between men). Patterns of this behavior denoted and reinforced aristocratic class, including internal, subtle distinctions among nobles, including exciting transgression across social differences. Chivalric love derived from the courtly, and extended notions of adherence to stylized forms of language, gesture, social posture, and vows to another, before others, often of another gender, but sly tales of subversive gender manipulation and sexual identity.

These traditions of love usually are reported as coming more from fiction, music, and the arts than from philosophy. Ovid, a Roman poet, deployed a sense of love as enchaining, a psychic state for the lover analogous to enslavement (an insight later amplified by de Beauvoir). Such a lover felt bound to his (less often, *her*) desire for privileged attention, desire, and commitment from the beloved. Related realms of "being in love," including, for the modern reader, ironic versions of "needing to be in love" or "loving love," have an extraordinarily broad and well-populated history within literature. Besides Shakespeare's plays and sonnets, many shorter lyric poems have been devoted to what becomes "romantic love" (Andrew Marvell's "To His Coy Mistress"). Similar breadth of topics within all the arts demonstrates long-standing consensus that such expression *should* reside outside philosophy as a discipline.

Especially in medieval times, and fundamental to Christianity, the idea of loving God as savior of humanity advanced in ways the Old Testament did not generally promote. The humanity of Christ was seen as opening a path to a kind of all-enveloping love by believers directed toward God, self, and others (particularly leaders and members of God's community). Such love demonstrated or could secure salvation and, depending on the imagery and ideology, transformed believers in this life as well. Early Christian-era and medieval thinkers often went to great lengths to report on their personal devotion or to advance approvingly the example of saintly behaviors that demonstrate illumination through piety rooted in love of the Divine. This feature of stressing devotional love appears in saintly yet still popular figures such as Augustine, Teresa of Avila, and even Thomas Aquinas, each of whom contributed importantly to later traditions of philosophical questions, movements, methods, and practices.

An exception to the American history of avoiding love in philosophy is Peirce's concept of "evolutionary love." Peirce advances a cosmological notion of things tending to seek integration into large wholes. One feature is a kind of *liking* that mimics the dialectics of analogy: things progressively relate to others. When such liking is especially strong, then it evolves towards an overarching integration of the world (and the people in it).

Despite Sappho's "love is bittersweet," romantic love became for English literary studies a spectacular source of inspiration, values, images, and meanings. Romanticism connected to a deeper evolution in the West, the appearance of individualism as the definer of the person. Coupled with Protestant notions of the personal path of Christian salvation, this confluence emphasized love for another as not just transforming but as self-definitional within modernity.

By the mid-nineteenth century, relations previously associated with the emotions and their exploration through artistic expression became of increased interest to some thinkers. The most obvious movement of philosophic attention into previously off-limit regions of exposition and witness was existentialism. Following Nietzsche, Kierkegaard, and Dostoevsky, writers such as Sartre, Camus, and the Spanish Basque Miguel de Unamuno made literary expression part of their philosophical meditations. Modernists like Picasso also transported romantic love into images defining of experimentation and innovation in the painterly plastic arts. Much drama and film focused on personal relationships.

In their speculations on projects and methods, thinkers often reformulated the philosophical to include topics once left to the arts and humanities. Such thinkers became promoters of the introduction of the irrational into philosophy, as William Barrett famously detailed. In the English-speaking world, this transformative turn did not capture academic philosophical practice. In the United States and Great Britain, counterforces successfully resisted and marginalized the introduction of the irrational as a topic in mainstream philosophy. Ironically, early exemplars or advocates of the inclusion of the contrarational into philosophy tended not to emphasize romantic love or its antecedents, but darker, more bleak, agonic modes of experience. In recent decades, psychology, biology, and even neurology have become popularly associated with theory about the roles, appearances, modes, motives, and styles of love.

If topics of love challenge philosophy and its long-standing biases against the irrational as grounds for systematic thinking, such resistance seems odd considering the global, evocative nature of love. Existentialism stressed personal and cultural centralities, impressed by art's interpretative powers and open to taking transformational emotion into philosophy for critical investigation, reflection, rigor, and report. The embrace of criticism, which thinkers as different as Plato, Augustine, Pascal, Sor Juana Inés de la Cruz, Mary Wollstonecraft, John Stuart Mill, Nietzsche, William James, and Octavio Paz advocate, seemingly still can evoke and contest fruitfully the authority and roles of the irrational, especially love, a deeply serious, joyous, and conflictive major theme.

Further reading

Feder, Ellen K., MacKendrick, Karmen, and Cook, Sybol S. (eds) *A Passion for Wisdom: Readings in Western Philosophy on Love and Desire*. Upper Saddle River, NJ: Pearson/Prentice Hall, 2004.

Fromm, Erich. *The Art of Loving*. New York: Harper Perennial Modern Classics, 2006.

Weinstein, Michael A. *Culture/Flesh: Explorations of Post-civilized Modernity*. Lanham, MD: Rowman and Littlefield, 1995.

John A. Loughney

LOVEJOY, ARTHUR

Besides being a pivotal architect for the history of ideas movement and instrumental in establishing academic freedom and the professionalization of philosophy, Arthur Lovejoy (Oncken Schauffler) (1873–1962) was also an engaged and active philosopher in his own right. He studied at the University of California and Harvard University under William James and Josiah Royce, taught at Washington University, Columbia, the University of Missouri, and spent the majority of his career at Johns Hopkins University from 1910 to 1938.

As philosopher, Lovejoy focuses on the theory of knowledge, and his developed position of Critical Realism responds to Idealism, Pragmatism, and Neo-Realism, all prominent philosophical perspectives in America in the early twentieth century. His Critical Realism offers a dualism between an object of knowledge and an external, physical object to counter Neo-Realism's epistemological monism that connects an object with the medium of knowledge, resulting in his emphasis on the independence of physical objects.

The dualism involved in Lovejoy's Critical Realism is related both to an epistemological dualism between the perceived content and the object behind the content, as well as a psychophysical dualism between the realm of the mind and the physical world. The former suggests that objects are always mediated and hence distinct from the object perceived, while the latter reflects a clear separation between the mental and physical worlds. *The Revolt Against Dualism* – his most philosophically acknowledged work – contains his critique of Idealism, Pragmatism, and Neo-Realism. Lovejoy was opposed to the idea that we only know our ideas about objects (the claim of Descartes as representative realist); he contended that we know objects directly through ideas (a "mentalistic realism").

Due to Lovejoy's difference between the reality of the physical world and the world of ideas, he valorizes the world of abstract ideas, connecting his philosophical perspective with his interest in historical examination. The history of ideas focuses on core themes and concepts ("unit-ideas") that motivate and condition thought through an empirical, textual study that looks for unit-ideas across a wide range of sources. This method is best exemplified in *The Great Chain of Being*, which contributed to establishing the history of ideas as a valid sub field through its investigation of the concepts of plenitude, continuity, and gradation from their Greek origins through to their influence on Enlightenment and Romantic thought. His conclusion ultimately denied the intelligibility of static, monistic, absolute models of the universe due in part to the rise and acceptance of evolutionary ideas. As a result of his efforts, *Journal for the History of Ideas* first came to print in 1940 and has enjoyed success ever since.

Lovejoy served the academy by helping to establish the American Philosophical Association and the American Association of University Professors in 1913 (along with John Dewey). He played an essential role in early efforts at academic freedom (although with limitations during the McCarthy Era) and helped initiate the professionalization of philosophy in America by lobbying to establish rigorous methods and standards to ensure philosophical intelligibility – the overriding criterion of all his work.

Further reading

Kuklick, Bruce. *A History of Philosophy in America, 1720–2000*. Oxford: Clarendon Press, 2001.

Lovejoy, Arthur. *The Revolt Against Dualism*. Chicago, IL: Open Court, 1930.

—— *The Great Chain of Being: A Study of the History of an Idea*. Cambridge, MA: Harvard University Press, 1936.

Wilson, Daniel J. *Arthur Lovejoy and the Quest for Intelligibility*. Chapel Hill, NC: University of North Carolina Press, 1980.

David Perley

LOYALTY

Though "loyalty" is not a mainstay in the philosopher's lexicon, the word has special significance in American philosophy because of its use by Josiah Royce. Royce's mature philosophy of loyalty is notable, not merely for its own considerable merit and importance, but also because it develops certain ideas originally championed by Charles Sanders Peirce.

Royce's initial discussion of loyalty was founded on his absolute idealism – which Royce developed prior to detailed study of Peirce. Royce the absolute idealist held that every thing that is (including our human ideas and their objects), is part of, and directly comprehended by, an absolute consciousness that constitutes reality. Ideas about what is true are purposeful attempts to express certain connections pertaining within the absolute unity. They are true when they succeed, and false when they fail (though failure is presumably temporary insofar as it leads to revisions). Certain potent "leading ideas" exhibit a kind of continual evolution, in which progressively deeper layers of insight are achieved as they intermingle with other ideas.

Loyalty is one such leading idea. In *The Philosophy of Loyalty*, Royce begins with the hypothesis that loyalty, properly defined, is both a first principle of ethics and also "the fulfillment of the whole moral law." His preliminary definition of Loyalty is "the willing and practical and thoroughgoing devotion of a person to a cause" (Royce 1995: 9). In the subsequent discussion, he argues that loyalty, thus conceived, constitutes the ultimate good for individual persons because it enables them to construct an adequate life plan (a person being "a human life lived according to a plan"). Unlike other moral ideals, loyalty adequately addresses two fundamental but apparently countervailing prerequisites for the construction of a satisfactory individual life plan: (1) the personal ideal must be self-legislated, and (2) the personal ideal must adequately respond to the individual's social context. In order to address the first prerequisite (self-legislation), it is crucial that loyalties be freely undertaken (they are "willing" devotions). If they are to adequately structure a life plan, they must be practical and thoroughgoing. Finally, if they are to adequately address the second prerequisite (social responsiveness), while also withstanding the sometimes arbitrary vicissitudes of social change and fashion, loyalties must be directed toward a social cause that is both transpersonal (a shared devotion) and superpersonal (valued for more than its utility for particular individuals or particular aggregates of individuals). Loyalty is never devotion to an individual or group of individuals; it is devotion to an ideal that binds them.

Royce held that loyalties are elaborate truth claims about the good and the right. Lower forms of loyalty address themselves to what is good or right within a small circle of loyalists. More enlightened loyalties, on the other hand, are concerned with the unity of causes (loyalty to universal loyalty) and the meaning of good and right within this unity. They are attempts to live in accordance with ethical truth. The ultimate sanction for Royce's enlightened loyalty resided in the consciousness of his Absolute. Hence, for Royce enlightened loyalty ultimately became "the Will to Believe in something eternal, and to express that belief in the practical life of a human being" (Royce 1995: 166).

In his later years, Royce emphasized the manner in which the cause of the loyalist constitutes the ideal and interest of a moral community. This led him to focus on another formulation of the definition of loyalty – loyalty as devotion to a community. Royce distinguished ethically good loyalties from ethically bad ones on the basis of his moral estimate of the communities the loyalties serve. Particular communities that prey on other communities are ethically good insofar as they provide a substrate for loyalty; but they are ethically blameworthy to the extent that they obstruct the loyalty of those who are not their members (see the discussion in "Royce, Josiah: loyalty/community"). Loyalty to such flawed communities is degenerate. Enlightened loyalties, on the other hand, always strive to align themselves with other loyalties, ultimately serving a universal community or "Great Community" of all humanity.

Of particular interest to the later Royce was the manner in which communities of enlightened loyalty function as a communities inquiry. His efforts to elucidate the characteristics of loyalty as a mode of ethical inquiry brought him into deeper dialogue with American pragmatists, especially Peirce and William James. In explicating "the will to interpret," Royce contrasts James's dyadic notion of a leading idea (as a psychological process that ideally culminates in a specific fulfillment) with Peirce's more expansive, triadic conception. A leading idea, according to Royce's characterization of the latter, is one that mediates between contrasting ideas.

Royce's basic conception of "loyalty" is a leading idea of the Peircean variety, first of all because it mediates the contrasting ideas of individual autonomy and social responsiveness. But that is just the beginning. This triad of ethical concepts (loyalty–autonomy–social responsiveness) has parallels in epistemology, metaphysics and religion. Like Peirce, Royce conceives truth as the ultimate destination of interpretation within an inclusive community of inquiry. In epistemology, then, loyalty to a community of interpretation is a leading idea that mediates the contrast between individual theorization or discovery, on one hand, and social experience or verification, on the other. Reality, again for Peirce and Royce alike, is the true interpretation of human experience. Hence in metaphysics, loyalty to a universal community mediates the contrast between the distinctness of present experience and the self-conscious unity of all experience over an infinite process of interpretation. Finally, in religion, loyalty to a Beloved Community – expressed not merely as simple devotion, but also through acts of atonement – mediates the contrast between the ethically burdened, detached individual and the ultimately vindicated and unified community of believers (which itself is the highest individual, i.e. God). Loyalty to the Beloved Community is equated with love of God, and Royce elaborates the Holy Trinity in accordance with his triadic account of human inquiry, as (1) God, the conscious, infinite, eternal unity of the universal community, (2) Jesus Christ, the redeemer whose atoning acts provide ethical inspiration for the religion of loyalty, and (3) the Holy Spirit, who through Grace manifests the Will to Interpret in individual inquirers.

Charles Sanders Peirce, for his part, portrayed the character of the ideal inquirer in terms that evoke images of Roycean loyalty to a community of interpretation. Specifically, Peirce held that inquiry required "identification of one's interests with those of an unlimited community" (Peirce 1992: 150). Peirce's conception of musement provides the interpretive framework for Royce's account of loyalty as a leading idea, though the most pristine forms of musement, on Peirce's account, involve a "play" of the intellect without proximate purposes. Still, it is musement that brings Peirce to his hypothesis of "God's Reality" – suggesting that anyone who muses on three suggested leading ideas with "scientific singleness of heart" will be led to the God hypothesis, and come to be

> stirred to the depths of his nature by the beauty of the idea and by its august practicality, even to the point of earnestly loving and adoring his strictly hypothetical God, and that of desiring above all things to shape the whole conduct of life and all the springs of action into conformity with that hypothesis.
>
> (Peirce 1998: 440)

The three leading ideas in question are Peirce's three "Universes of Experience:" (1) "mere Ideas," (2) "Brute Actuality of things and facts," and (3) "everything whose Being consists in active power to establish connections between different objects, especially objects in different universes" (Peirce 1998: 435). Peirce's playful musings on these ideas ultimately begets an attitude of reverence and moral resolve – and something very much akin to Royce's notion of enlightened loyalty.

Further reading

Oppenheim, Frank M. *Royce's Mature Philosophy of Religion.* Notre Dame, Indiana, IN: University of Notre Dame Press, 1987.

Peirce, Charles S. *The Essential Peirce: Selected Philosophical Writings: Volume 1 (1867–1893)*, ed. Nathan Houser and Christian Kloesel. Bloomington, IN: Indiana University Press, 1992.

—— *The Essential Peirce: Selected Philosophical Writings: Volume 2 (1893–1913)*, ed. the Pearce Edition Project. Bloomington, IN: Indiana University Press, 1998.

Royce, Josiah. *The Problem of Christianity.* Chicago, IL: University of Chicago Press, 1968 [1918].

—— *The Philosophy of Loyalty.* Nashville, TN: Vanderbilt University Press, 1995 [1908].

—— *Metaphysics*, ed. William Earnest Hocking, Richard Hocking, and Frank Oppenheim. Albany, NY: SUNY Press, 1998.

Trotter, Griffin. *On Royce.* Belmont, CA: Wadsworth, 2001.

GRIFFIN TROTTER

M

MADDEN, EDWARD H.

Edward Harry Madden (1925–2006) was born in Gary, Indiana on 18 May 1925. He received his BA in 1946 and his MA in 1947 from Oberlin College. In 1950 he received his PhD at the University of Iowa with a dissertation entitled "An Examination of Gestalt Theory" directed by Gustav Bergmann. His early teaching positions in philosophy were at the University of Connecticut from 1950 to 1959, and at San Jose State University from 1959 to 1964. From 1964 until his retirement in 1980 he taught at the State University of New York at Buffalo. He also held visiting positions at Brown, Amherst, Toronto, American University of Beirut, Linacre College (Oxford), and the Institute for Advanced Study, Princeton, NJ. In retirement he lived in Wilmore, Kentucky, where he was a visiting research fellow at Asbury College in 1981–2. From 1982 to 1994 he was an adjunct professor at the University of Kentucky. In 2000 he moved to White River Junction, Vermont, where he died at home on 25 November 2006.

Although Madden's main interests were philosophy of science, history of American thought, and philosophy of religion, he also wrote on topics as various as Islamic art, Aristotle, history of science, Scottish philosophy, nineteenth-century American religious movements, Irish history, metaphilosophy, French philosophy, social philosophy and ethics. He authored or co-authored nine books, and edited or co-edited five books. His journal articles and contributions to books number more than a hundred. Over the course of his career he collaborated with twenty different scholars. It would be hard to imagine a philosopher who more enjoyed collaboration.

Madden's reputation in philosophy of science was first established by the publication of *Philosophical Problems of Psychology* (1962). His most discussed book in philosophy of science is *Causal Powers* (1975, co-authored with Rom Harré), in which a realist ontology and epistemology is defended against the Humean tradition. In 1963 he published his classic study in the history of American philosophy, *Chauncey Wright and the Foundations of Pragmatism.* His mastery of transcendentalism and the common-sense tradition in America is demonstrated in *Civil Disobedience and Moral Law in Nineteenth-Century American Philosophy* (1968) and *Freedom and Grace: The Life of Asa Mahan* (1982, with James Hamilton). His studies in the history of American thought were extended into the middle of the twentieth century with *Causing, Perceiving, and Believing: An Examination of the Philosophy of C.J. Ducasse* (1975, with Peter Hare). Most notable of his publications in philosophy of religion is *Evil and the Concept of God* (1968, with Peter Hare), in which what is now known as the evidential argument from evil is advanced against theism, including process theism.

Often scholars speak figuratively of their doctoral students becoming members of their families. In Ed's case it was almost literally true. For many hours each week a dissertation student met with him in his home study and shared meals with his wife and sons. After graduation, the life of a student (and his or her family) was closely followed with affectionate concern.

Ed's lecturing style was rooted in his early success as an actor in high school dramas. Without an outline or note before him, he could deliver word for word, pause for dramatic pause, anecdote for anecdote, the same riveting lecture that he had last given many years before.

At his death Ed left two noteworthy manuscripts unpublished. One is a book on Thomas Reid and the Scottish common-sense tradition edited by his student Todd Adams. In the other manuscript Ed shows his Irish-American roots and command of lyrical prose in a series of short stories about his childhood.

In 1946 Ed married Marian Canaday, who survives him. In addition to co-authoring many of his articles, Marian supported him in countless other ways, ways that Ed never tired of acknowledging. Two sons, Kerry and Dennis, and two grandchildren, Erin and Ryan, also survive him.

PETER H. HARE
MICHAEL L. PETERSON

MADDEN, EDWARD H.: AUTOBIOGRAPHY

The early influence of logical positivism is reflected in my early articles and introductory essays, in *The Structure of Scientific Thought*, and in *Philosophical Problems of Psychology.* While not abandoning the Humean regularity viewpoint, I began to see its weaknesses, and in a series of articles in *Philosophy of Science* I argued that every Humean effort to account for counterfactual inference failed. I was undecided what to believe until I read the works of Thomas Reid, C.J. Ducasse, and Roderick Chisholm, after which in various articles and in *Causal Powers* (with R. Harré) I formulated a singularist view of causality according to which a physical explanatory system could not exist without necessary connections; though, since the competing systems which might be exemplified in our world must be determined by aposteriori means, there is less than definite assurance which of the competing systems is the correct one. While I do not wholly reject my early work, since other issues than causality were involved, I have clearly rejected my early regularity views. I would change nothing in one of the early books, namely, *Theories of Scientific Method: The Renaissance through the Nineteenth Century* (with R.M. Blake and Ducasse).

My contributions to the history of modern philosophy have grown out of my discontent with the Humean tradition. Contributions to this area include articles on Reid, Dugald Stewart, Sir William Hamilton, Victor Cousin, and Theodore Jouffroy, all members of the Scottish realist tradition, a sane alternative, I argue, to the dustbowl empiricism of Hume, on the one hand, and the thriving jungle of absolute idealism, on the other. Reid seems to me one of the outstanding modern philosophers; his embryonic adverbial view of perceiving influenced both Ducasse and Chisholm.

In *Causing, Perceiving, and Believing* (with Peter Hare) I reject the view that adverbial appearings are incorrigible but defend the adverbial view as a natural realism which avoids the pitfalls of sense data theory.

My work in American philosophy was influenced by Herbert Schneider, Joseph Blau, and Morton White with their commitment to studying the whole spectrum of American philosophy and not concentrating solely on one figure who anticipated current thought and must be defended at all costs. I by no means reject "doing philosophy historically" and believe that much good work is done by showing the relevance of a favorite figure to the contemporary scene. My only concern here is whether we can adequately understand individual philosophers without some knowledge of their historical location. My work in American philosophy includes Jonathan Edwards, the Scottish realism of Francis Wayland, Asa Mahan, Henry Tappan, James McCosh *et al.*; the Unitarians, the transcendentalists, especially Emerson, Parker, and Thoreau; Chauncey Wright (*Chauncey Wright and the Foundations of Pragmatism*), C.S. Peirce, William James, and Ducasse; and social and moral problems, discussed in *Civil Disobedience and Moral Law in Nineteenth Century American Philosophy.*

The problem of evil, I have urged, in *Evil and the Concept of God* (with Peter Hare) is not simply a problem of logical consistency but an existential and evidential problem of real importance which must be pursued by philosophical dialectic, not by a posteriori probability judgments. It is not only an existential and evidential problem but also a moral one. How could one bear to face a God whose higher morality transgresses the whole spectrum of ordinary morality? On this issue, close to my heart, there were no external influences. When nine years old I felt something had gone wrong with the game plan. At thirty, I concluded that there had never been a game plan.

EDWARD H. MADDEN

MADISON, JAMES

James Madison, born 16 March 1751, held many significant public offices, including the fourth

President of the United States, but his most celebrated achievements surround the Constitution of 1787 and the subsequent Bill of Rights. Like almost all the other founders, Madison never left a systematic statement of his political theory, yet it is possible to locate the pieces of it in his numerous public and private writings. In many ways, it is appropriate to see him as a classic eighteenth-century Anglo-American liberal who believed that through reason individuals could avoid the state of nature by creating a social compact, a pluralistic society, and sound government based on individuality, reason, equality, natural rights, and a strict separation of church and state. He is best known for his contributions to *The Federalist*, eighty-five essays, the bulk of which were written by Alexander Hamilton and Madison; these writings were designed to persuade Americans to ratify the Constitution. Although Madison never claimed originality for any of his theoretic contributions to the design of the American political system, he advocated the virtue of an extended commercial republic where the multiplicity of "factions" (interest groups) would tend to counterbalance each other and help bring about social stability. This was particularly important with religion: Madison hoped that a plurality of religious sects would keep any one from dominating the others. In addition, he wanted an amendment to keep religion and government separate. Madison had serious reservations about the ability of the people to govern directly, so his system relied on indirect participation by citizens that allowed elected elites to make policy decisions. To this end, he supported a trustee model of representation where those elected would act as a filter on the views of the voters. He also supported a system of checks and balances, or a separation of powers, where every actor had to have a "defense armor" to protect itself from encroachments by other political actors or institutions. Lastly, Madison was critical of the concept of implied powers and argued that the Constitution granted only "enumerated" powers. If the Constitution did not explicitly grant a power, its silence meant the government lacked that power. Consequently, he initially thought there was no need for a Bill of Rights: the Constitution itself was one. Nevertheless, in order to secure ratification by the states he endorsed the idea of an explicit Bill of Rights and helped secure its passage in the first Congress. While Madison tended to be a consistent thinker, he made a few alterations. Prior to the constitutional convention of 1787, Madison favored a "legislative veto" by the central government over all state legislation and proportionate representation in both the House and Senate. Neither of these ideas made it into the Constitution. During the 1790s, when he thought the executive branch was exceeding its constitutional limits, he helped construct a political party to check the government and now advocated a strong federal system, where the states could act as a check on a chief executive. Upon retirement from office, he slowly began to accept the idea of universal (male) suffrage, a basic prerequisite of democracy. To that end, he argued for public education as well as a free and rigorous press to create an enlightened and informed citizenry that could check government through public opinion. Madison died on 29 June 1836.

Further reading

Banning, Lance. *The Sacred Fire of Liberty: James Madison and the Founding of the Federal Republic*. Ithaca, NY: Cornell University Press, 1997.

Matthews, Richard K. *If Men Were Angels: James Madison and the Heartless Empire of Reason*. Lawrence, KS: University Press of Kansas, 1995.

Rakove, Jack N. (ed.) *James Madison: Writings*. New York: Library of America, 1999

RICHARD K. MATTHEWS

MARGOLIS, JOSEPH

Joseph Margolis (1924–), an American philosopher, earned his PhD at Columbia University, and has since taught in the US and Canada, and for many years at Temple University. Margolis, who has been very active professionally, is past president of the American Society for Aesthetics, and honorary president and lifetime member of the International Association of Aesthetics. He has lectured widely in the US and abroad and serves on the editorial board of many philosophy journals. During his long career, he published more than forty books on a wide span of topics, whose center lies in the philosophy of culture in a very broad sense.

Margolis did his initial work, for which he is still most widely known, in the philosophy of art. He is perhaps best known for his distinctive thesis that there is in principle no difference between problems as they arise within the wider scope of the philosophy of art and in philosophy in general. He has continued to write within this field while extending his domain to areas in continental philosophy and particularly American pragmatism.

Margolis consistently favors an ontology of flux over an ontology of invariance. This leads to the replacement of rigorous methodologies by open-ended, critical and explanatory practices, a view of any form of objectivity as an artifact of habitual practices, a conception of human selves as themselves emergent and constituted by historical and enculturational process, a conception of human thinking as profoundly historicized, suspicion about reliance on bivalent logic leading in the direction of relativism, and related doctrines.

In *The Truth about Relativism* (1991), he contends that relativism is not an inadmissible but rather a necessary doctrine that in a certain sense we cannot avoid. Clearly inspired by the model of cultural interpretation of all kinds, he maintains that we can safely deny excluded middle without contradiction. Relativism is not incompatible with truth since truth claims are themselves always relative. The truth, then, about relativism is that truth is relative, not a property of first-order determinations, but rather the result of a second-order consensus among individuals concerned to reflect on the status of what we think we know.

Margolis worked out the implications of this doctrine in more recent books. In *The Flux of History and the Flux of Science* (1993), he showed that we can take history seriously and yet maintain our belief in natural science as a highly successful source of knowledge. In *Interpretation Radical but Not Unruly* (1995), he contends that interpretation replaces epistemology in the old sense of a theory of knowledge based on a two-valued logic. For if, as a result of invoking a many-valued logic, there can be no single correct answer to some or indeed most questions, then we cannot avoid the inference that our views of what is true, or what is the case, in short what we take as knowledge and truth, are embedded in different perspectives. In *Historied Thought, Constructed World* (1995), perhaps his most impressive effort, he contends that thinking is a history, roughly the claim that we need to begin our discussion from real finite human beings, lodged in social reality, who are shaped by and in turn shape the social context in which we live.

Further reading

Margolis, Joseph. *The Truth about Relativism*. Oxford: Blackwell, 1991.

—— *Flux of History and the Flux of Science*. Berkeley, CA: University of California Press, 1993.

—— *Historied Thought, Constructed World: A Conceptual Primer for the New Millennium*. Berkeley, CA: University of California Press, 1995.

—— *Interpretation Radical but Not Unruly: The New Puzzle of the Arts and History*. Berkeley, CA: University of California Press, 1995.

Tom Rockmore

MATERIALISM

Materialism is belief that everything real is either a form or a function of matter – spatially extended stuff having mass and motion. Contradicting longstanding belief that thinking and sensing are the doings of invisible and intangible *minds*, materialists maintain that these are the work of visible and tangible *brains*.

Materialism had little following in America until the twentieth century, when influential philosopher/psychologist John Dewey proclaimed that the mind is not a thing but a bevy of functions. Dewey's most famous Chicago pupil J.B. Watson soon turned this *functionalism* into *behaviorism*, belief that the sole and proper subject of scientific psychology is the publicly observable behavior of physical organisms.

To oppose behaviorist dismissal of privately discerned mental processes, Harvard psychologist E.G. Boring published his provocatively titled *The Physical Dimensions of Consciousness* in 1933. This book declared that even consciousness could become an object of scientific study if sufficient attention were paid to the brain. Joining Boring in this stance were the so-called American new realists, and the critical realists Roy Wood Sellars and George Santagane.

Santayana put forward the proposition that states of consciousness are mere epiphenomena of brain processes. Although these evanescent states have neural causes, they are themselves causally impotent, so do not figure in any science. Sellars agreed with Boring that thoughts and sensations are as yet unspecified brain processes.

In the second half of the century, two Australians, Jack Smart and Ullin Place, attempted to give precision to Boring's idea by defending the hypothesis – declared by die-hard believers in mind–body dualism to be unintelligible – that sensations, if not also thoughts, are identical with processes in the brain. In America, this identity theory was embraced by influential philosopher of science Herbert Feigl and his famed Minnesota colleague Wilfrid Sellars, a son of Roy Wood Sellars.

Though widely accepted, the identity theory was soon qualified. In a 1967 essay, Max Hocutt of Alabama pointed out that the theory was more plausible regarding tokens than regarding types of mental phenomena. The same insight led Hilary Putnam of Harvard to urge "multiple realizability," meaning that in different brains functionally equivalent sensations might be identical with processes having different physical descriptions.

On this plinth, and inspired by some observations of Harvard's Willard Quine regarding the logical irregularity (the "referential opacity") of psychological talk, Donald Davidson of Berkeley erected *anomalous monism*, the thesis that, although sensations and thoughts are indubitably dependent on the brain, neurophysiology will never be able to explain them. Psychology will remain an autonomous enterprise that, like medicine, makes use of science without becoming a science.

In a mirror image of Davidson's thesis, Paul Churchland, a Pittsburgh pupil of Wilfrid Sellars and a professor at San Diego, has taken the position that the prized categories of "folk psychology" will have no more use in a finished science than do earth, air, fire and water, the primitive entities of "folk physics."

Churchland's *eliminative materialism* has not diminished materialist enthusiasm for the proposition that thought and sensation are dependent on the brain; but it has diminished confidence in what Tufts philosopher and Quine pupil Daniel Dennett denigrates as *Cartesian materialism*, meaning belief that the introspectively discerned "contents" or "qualities" of so-called states of mind will eventually be reflected in the categories and concepts of neural science. Now the reverse is thought to be more likely. Increased knowledge of the workings of the brain will cause revisions in the way we talk and think about consciousness and cognition.

Materialism is now the dominant philosophy in America, but in recent years it has undergone challenges by Saul Kripke and Thomas Nagel.

Further reading

Churchland, Paul M. *Matter and Consciousness: A Contemporary Introduction to the Philosophy of Mind.* Cambridge, MA: MIT Press, 1988.

—— *A Neurocomputational Perspective: The Nature of Mind and the Structure of Science.* Cambridge, MA: MIT Press, 1989.

MAX HOCUTT

MATTER

"Matter" is a term that frequently refers to the physical world in general, and stands in contrast with "mind." In his objective idealism, Charles Peirce envisages the two drawing closer together, with matter evolving toward law-like mind. William James asks what we mean by "matter" and looks to practical differences arising from possible answers. The notion of a hidden material substance with attributes of space-occupancy and impenetrability is discredited and must be supplanted; he praises Berkeley for finding the cash value of the term "matter" pragmatically in sensations. For James, one can plausibly be a materialist in the sense of explaining higher phenomena by lower ones, something that does not require a belief in material substance. In this wider sense, materialism is opposed to theism or spiritualism. One argument against materialism in this sense holds that "gross, coarse, crass" matter cannot account for the "pure, elevated, noble" mental. This is wrong; the matter postulated by modern science is "inconceivably quick and fine." A more telling argument for him is that materialism entails the denial of an eternal moral order. John Dewey also seeks to avoid the metaphysical notion of matter through a pragmatist account; he declares that matter must be understood as the conditions of what it does and how it functions.

George Santayana is one American philosopher who accepts matter as a fundamental category in his system. He rebels against any treatment of the external world purely in terms of human experience, and makes matter into one of four basic ontological categories, along with essence, truth, and spirit. The realm of matter is distinct from the realm of spirit, and he takes every occasion to separate the two. In the latter he places all felt experience; spirit is merely consciousness, as experienced presumably by humans and other forms of organic life. Questions about how spirit emerged in animal life and how it supervenes on material existence are difficult and perhaps unsolvable; but they are problems about the realm of matter for science to investigate. Among Santayana's Harvard colleagues, the idealist Josiah Royce eliminated external matter; and Santayana felt that, although James had a good feeling for the ever-changing material flux in his early scientific writings, he lost this with the later advocacy of pragmatism. In a critique of the pragmatist John Dewey, Santayana finds a philosophy of the foreground in which matter is seen as the experience of matter. Dewey is a naturalist, in his eyes, but one who is too tied to the idealist tradition. In response, Dewey sees a failure in Santayana to avoid the evils of dualism.

Santayana agrees with his former professor James that matter is sufficiently complex to explain mind, and goes beyond this to distinguish in animal life a material psyche, which for humans is the ultimate source of moral interests. He accepts matter as a substance; to do so for him is merely physics, not metaphysics, which arises precisely when some substance other than matter is chosen as basic. Santayana is not a substance dualist, since spirit is unsubstantial and the realm of matter is the sole source of change in the world; spirit is a wholly original emanation created by matter within organic life. Nor is he a property dualist; properties are essences in his system, something entirely different from moments of spirit. Inasmuch as he gives to the physical world all causal powers and admits an impotent consciousness, he can be called an epiphenomenalist, although he prefers to call himself a materialist. A certain duality does remain in his system and is evident in his treatment of the self. Psyche is a configuration in the realm of matter found in organic life that powers all action. As well, it generates spirit within that animal life. Because psyche is a part of the realm of matter, humans are capable of initiative. They have psychic freedom, which may be exercised intelligently in case spirit attains a true understanding of psychic needs and genuine opportunities. This understanding, like spirit itself, has psyche in the realm of matter as its ultimate source. However, without spirit there can be no value to life, so any treatment of morality will have spirit as a crucial factor. In regard to our interaction with matter, we can be identified with our psyches; but in regard to self-image we might, as Santayana does, prefer to be identified by the spiritual fruits of our life.

The notion of matter as a substratum whose true nature is unknown is alien to pragmatists. Remote from experience and lacking in conceivable practical effects, the concept is seen as redundant and metaphysical. It does not meet their criterion of meaningfulness, and is little seen in their writings.

Further reading

James, William. "Some Metaphysical Problems Pragmatically Considered" in *Pragmatism*. New York: Meridian Books, 1955, pp. 65–86.

Santayana, George. *The Realm of Matter.* New York: Charles Scribner's Sons, 1930.

ANGUS KERR-LAWSON

McDERMOTT, JOHN J.

John J. McDermott (1932–), an American philosopher and educator, was born in New York City on 5 January 1932. He was educated at St Francis College in Brooklyn, and at Fordham University in the Bronx. He has taught at St Francis College (1954–7), Queens College/CUNY (1957–77) and at Texas A&M University (since 1977), where he is Distinguished Professor of Philosophy and Humanities, and Abell Professor of Liberal Arts.

McDermott is a prolific and catholic author who, beginning with his 1959 dissertation: *Experience is Pedagogical: The Genesis and Essence of the American Nineteenth Century Notion of Experience*, has striven to bridge American philosophy and culture. His primary contributions as a writer have been twofold. First, he has worked to help us better understand the figures in classical American philosophy. Part of this task was making available accurate and well-introduced editions of their works. He has assembled three examples: *The Writings of William James: A Comprehensive Edition* (1967), *The Basic Writings of Josiah Royce* (1969), and *The Philosophy of John Dewey* (1973). McDermott was also co-founder of the nineteen-volume Harvard edition of *The Works of William James* and general editor of the twelve-volume edition of *The Correspondence of William James.*

McDermott's second contribution has been to write extensively about the themes with which contemporary American philosophers, and others interested in the larger questions of existence, should deal. These themes include: the nature and importance of American culture; the role of embodiment, of life and death, in our attempts to understand our existence; the aesthetic power of our environment to offer nutrition to our bodies and spirits; the means of establishing a morality that will connect us with our fellows; the ways that education, and especially teaching, can foster human growth; and the naturalizing of the religious quest of humankind into the establishment of community. McDermott's essays on these and other themes have been gathered into three volumes: *The Culture of Experience: Philosophical Essays in the American Grain* (1976), *Streams of Experience: Reflections on the History and Philosophy of American Culture* (1986), and a third to be announced.

McDermott's work is part of the American philosophical tradition that has always taken the aim of philosophical inquiry to be the interpretation of the meaning of experience. As did Ralph Waldo Emerson and William James and John Dewey, he takes our novel situation at face value and refuses to reformulate it to satisfy the assumptions of inherited doctrines. For McDermott, the meaning of experience is open and growing. He rejects all pretense of having ultimate explanations which, however comforting psychologically, have no scientific or logical merit. The human journey is a personal project within which adequate explanations must be created and meanings developed. Similarly, the self is not a given substantial entity. Rather, the self is relational, with a kind of loyalty to its natural place. Third, philosophy is not an exclusively cerebral endeavor. The wisdom that philosophy seeks is a fuller experiential matter, incorporating intellectual and affective aspects.

McDermott believes that we can and must create for ourselves a world in which we can find meaning. Still, he admits that "in so far as our being human naturals, we find ourselves in a situation which, in its most profound sense, does not work" (1994: 11). This is a hard message to accept, he admits, and philosophy has long attempted to disguise it with all sorts of comforting stories. He views the history of philosophy as "a long prose poem, evoking the extraordinary, brilliant, provocative and contentious efforts to work out speculatively what does not work experientially, namely, totality, finality or answers, once and for all" (1994: 12). It is our task as humans to create meaningful social and natural places. Although

> loneliness ... is our ontological state of being human, and natural processes both offer us support and promise us extinction, we are still able to create, by forging contexts, situations and attitudes, each of which opens us to possibilities not given to simply being here or there.
>
> (1994: 23)

Further reading

Campbell, James and Hart, Richard E. (eds) *Experience as Philosophy: On the Work of John J. McDermott*. New York: Fordham University Press, 2006.

McDermott, John J. *The Culture of Experience: Philosophical Essays in the American Grain*. New York: New York University Press, 1976.

—— *Streams of Experience: Reflections on the History and Philosophy of American Culture*. Amherst, MA: University of Massachusetts Press, 1986.

—— "Ill-at-Ease: The Natural Travail of Ontological Disconnectedness", *Proceedings and Addresses of the American Philosophical Association* 67, 6 (June 1994): 7–28.

JAMES CAMPBELL

MEAD, GEORGE HERBERT

George Herbert Mead (1863–1931), American philosopher and social psychologist, is widely regarded as one of the most important figures in the pragmatic tradition in the first half of the twentieth century. In sociology he is considered the father of the School of Symbolic Interaction. Mead was born on 27 February 1863 in South Hadley, Massachusetts. His father, George Hiram Mead, was a Congregationalist minister and a professor of homiletics at Oberlin Theological Seminary. Mead's mother, Elizabeth Storrs Billings, served as the president of Mt Holyoke College. Mead matriculated at Oberlin College in 1879 and graduated in 1883. As a young man he considered Christian social work as an occupation, but found it impossible to follow this course because he had lost his belief in God. Nevertheless, even when he could no longer believe in the supernatural, he adhered to notions of charity and public service often associated with liberal Protestant sects.

After holding positions as a teacher and then as a surveyor with the Wisconsin Central Railroad, Mead enrolled at Harvard in 1887, where he lived in William James's house and tutored his children. At Harvard Mead studied with George H. Palmer, Francis Bowen, and Josiah Royce. In 1888 Mead went to Germany to study. At the time his main interest appears to have been physiological psychology. In 1891, before completing his doctoral work, Mead joined the faculty at the University of Michigan, where he met John Dewey. The two became life-long friends, and when Dewey took the position of chair of the Department of Philosophy at the University of Chicago, he invited Mead to join the department in 1894. Mead spent the remainder of his academic career at the University of Chicago. Along with his friend Jane Addams, he was active in civic causes in Chicago, which perhaps in part explains why he never published a book in philosophy. He did publish a good number of articles, but his most important and well-known works – for example, *Mind, Self, and Society from the Standpoint of a Social Behaviorist* (1934) – were drawn from notes, those of Mead and his students, and were published after Mead's death in 1931. In 1891 Mead married Helen Castle, the sister of his close friend Henry Castle. They had one child, Henry Castle Albert Mead, whose wife, Irene Tufts Mead, became a psychiatrist in Chicago. Mead was very supportive of Irene Tufts Mead's decision to have a career, which was consistent with his advocacy of women's causes.

Mead was well read in the history of Western philosophy and had a special affinity for Hegel's thought, which he shared with Dewey. However, both broke with Hegel's idealism and methodology, and were deeply influenced by William James's *Principles of Psychology*. While it is accurate to say that Hegel's influence on Mead was lasting, it is also true that the British empiricists left a permanent imprint. In fact, Mead synthesized elements of Hegel, James, British empiricism, and Darwin to develop a novel account of the self, for which he is most widely known. Mead's philosophical and scientific interests were wide-ranging. The last decade of his life found him attempting to address the implications of Relativity Theory for metaphysics in *The Philosophy of the Present* (1932).

Mead shares a commitment to the importance of habit, practice, and problem solving behavior with other pragmatists. Most of the time the world is unproblematic, and our habits and unconscious beliefs allow us to manage our affairs. We rely on what Mead calls the world that is there. However, when we encounter a problematic situation, perhaps due to a novel event, or when we purposely create a situation that is problematic – for example, in scientific experimentation – we move to a level of reflective problem-solving behavior that entails anticipating alternative courses of action. This view is not original to Mead. What is original is his account of the development of the self. In the latter he explains for the first time within the pragmatic tradition how the development of language and the self make possible the kinds of anticipatory experience that we take for granted when we solve problems.

To understand Mead's developmental account of the self and anticipatory behavior, we need to address the importance of the gesture for language development. Animals can gesture. For example, a dog growls, which is a gesture, and a second dog runs away. In this situation the first dog is not aware of the "meaning" of its gesture. The growl does not mean "run or fight." It simply produces a behavioral response in the second dog. However, vocal gestures or significant symbols can have the same functional meaning for different human beings. When I speak, I can hear myself at virtually the same instant that another person can hear me, and I can anticipate how the other person will respond to my vocal gesture, for it calls out a similar response in both of us. I become reflexively aware of the symbol. And in becoming reflexively aware of the meaning of significant symbols, I learn to talk to myself.

The reflexive behavior that we see in simple linguistic exchanges parallels the way in which we engage in social roles, which can be thought of as proto-selves. For Mead, with the assistance of language, we internalize complex patterns of behavior. These patterns are roles, and they arise in social settings. To be able to play the role of a store clerk, for example, there must be another to play the role of patron. To be able to play the role of doctor, someone must take the role of patient. In order to take these roles the actors must be able to anticipate the responses of each other. Children become so accomplished at learning to anticipate the responses of others that they can imaginatively take roles when others aren't present, in a fashion analogous to the way in which they learn to talk to themselves. Anticipatory experience, then, is as fundamental to role-taking as it is to language.

However, for a self to develop there must be more than roles for Mead. We must not only take the role of the other, but the perspective of the "generalized other." Selves entail more complex behaviors than we associate with roles and require generalized others, which arise in relationship to groups, for example, one's family or a corporation. There are numerous possible selves for Mead. Whether there is a moral self that unifies all of these different selves is an open question. Be this as it may, an important qualification must be introduced at this juncture. We have been discussing the development of the self, but properly speaking we have been addressing what Mead refers to as the "Me," the self that arises in relationship to generalized others. The individual, however, is not only a "Me," but an "I." The "Me" can be thought of in terms of repertoires of learned behaviors. The "I" is the spontaneous responses of the individual. For example, I may be a pitcher on a baseball team who has learned a standard repertoire of pitches. But I may very well throw a pitch in an unexpected and novel fashion. Actions of this sort are not planned. We do not decide in advance to behave in novel ways, although we can set up situations – for example, scientific experiments – that increase the probability of doing so. Yet for Mead novelty should not to be understood solely in terms of the "I." Novel events are part and parcel of the fabric of the cosmos, and they help transform the world. And here a connection to Darwin should be noted. Evidence of novelty in nature can be found in the mutations that exist in the biological world. They are unplanned and yet can have lasting consequences.

Mead's social and political philosophy and his ethics support a notion of individual and collective self-determination and self-actualization. Individuality is not viewed as antithetical to sociality. While there must be functional similarities in our responses if we are to communicate, the spontaneity of the "I" and the complexity of our social life lend themselves to individuation. The best political order should consider both of these elements, that is, similarity and difference. It should also help to meet basic human needs, for without proper food, shelter, and education, individuals will not be in a position to realize themselves. Mead's political progressivism is linked to a vision of a democratic society that fosters individuation as well as collective action.

Further reading

Aboulafia, Mitchell. *The Cosmopolitan Self: George Herbert Mead and Continental Philosophy.* Urbana, IL: University of Illinois Press, 2001.
Cook, Gary A. *George Herbert Mead, The Making of a Social Pragmatist.* Urbana, IL: University of Illinois Press, 1993.
Joas, Hans. *G.H. Mead: A Contemporary Re-examination of his Thought*, trans. Raymond Meyer. Cambridge, MA: MIT Press, 1985.
Mead, George Herbert. *The Philosophy of the Present*, ed., with an Introduction, by Arthur E. Murphy and Prefatory Remarks by John Dewey. La Salle, IL: Open Court, 1932.
—— *Mind, Self and Society: From the Standpoint of a Social Behaviorist*, ed., with an Introduction, by Charles W. Morris. Chicago, IL: University of Chicago Press, 1934.
—— *Movements of Thought in the Nineteenth Century*, ed., with an Introduction, by Merritt H. Moore. Chicago, IL: University of Chicago Press, 1936.
—— *The Philosophy of the Act*, ed., with an Introduction, by Charles W. Morris. Chicago, IL: University of Chicago Press, 1938.
—— *Selected Writings: George Herbert Mead*, ed., with an Introduction, by Andrew J. Reck. Chicago, IL: University of Chicago Press, 1964.
Miller, David L. *George Herbert Mead: Self, Language, and the World.* Chicago, IL: University of Chicago Press, Phoenix Edition, 1980.

MITCHELL ABOULAFIA

MEANING

Questions around the concept of meaning acquired a certain prominence in Anglo-American philosophy during the twentieth century, particularly after the so-called "linguistic turn" which suggested that many questions traditionally associated with epistemology, metaphysics, and even ethics could be resolved by a proper analysis of the meaning of various expressions in our language. These analyses in turn called for general accounts of meaning, and while such theories initially took a theory of meaning to be like, say, a theory about hydrogen or some other sort of object, more recent approaches to meaning focus instead on what it takes for the use of a word to be considered meaningful.

Meanings as objects

We unreflectively talk and think about word meanings as if they were objects, and so it can be natural to start one's theorizing about meaning by wondering just what sorts of objects meanings are. Three prominent approaches to meaning take meanings to be objects of various types. These are:

Meanings as external objects

An obvious choice for the meanings of our words were the external objects that they intuitively seem to be about, so that the meaning of "Julius Caesar" is the man himself, the meaning of "Horse" is the class of horses, the meaning of "red" the set of red things, etc. In spite of its lasting appeal, this view faces a number of serious problems. First of all, the account seems inappropriate for terms such as "and," "then," "quickly," "because" which make up a large portion of the language and yet do not clearly refer to any objects. Second, while it is easy to see what external objects (some) words could refer to, it is far less clear what could serve as the meaning of sentences (especially false ones). "Facts" are often suggested here, but the idea that sentences correspond to facts has proven notoriously hard to spell out, and one can very quickly find oneself endorsing Frege's conclusion that there are only two things for sentences to refer to, the true and the false (Frege 1984). Third, even in cases where the account seems at its best – say, proper names – it seems that meanings of names have properties that the external objects don't have. For instance, Julius Caesar can be destroyed, but the meaning of "Julius Caesar" is not destroyed with it. The meaning of a term can't *be* the object it refers to if one can be destroyed while the other remains unchanged (Wittgenstein 1953). Fourth, there are names such as "Atlantis" or "Santa Claus" that seem to be meaningful in spite of having no object to refer to. Finally, the suggestion that meanings are external objects seems to leave meaning too coarse-grained, because two terms that intuitively mean different things can refer to the same object or class. For instance, "the Morning Star" and "the Evening Star" both refer to Venus, but the two terms do not seem to have the same meaning. This becomes especially clear when the terms are incorporated into sentences such as "Everyone knows that the Morning Star is the Morning Star" and "Everyone knows that the Morning Star is the Evening Star" which do not, intuitively, say the same thing at all (Frege 1984).

Meanings as internal objects

Almost as old as the idea that the meanings of our words are the *external* objects that they stand for is the suggestion that words are meaningful in virtue of standing for certain *internal* objects, namely, our ideas. (The view finds a particularly clear expression in empiricists like Hobbes and Locke.) Language is, among other things, a medium for communicating our thoughts, and if it is understood *primarily* in this way, the suggestion that the meanings of our words simply *are* the ideas we make them stand for can seem natural. The view can deal with some of the problems that faced the previous account. In particular, it explains both how words that don't succeed in referring to anything in the external world can still be meaningful (because they still refer to the internal ideas), and why two words that refer to the same external object could have different meanings (because the associated ideas may be different). However, the view faces serious difficulties stemming from the fact that (since each of us has our own ideas) it seems to suggest that we each mean something different by each of our words. Further, the idea theory seems to miss out on the "objectivity" of language, since if what we mean is determined by our ideas, it seems as if we could never misapply our words (Royce 1885; Wittgenstein 1953). Further, like the previous theory, it is only plausible for a limited range of words, since it is not at all obvious that there are ideas corresponding to words like "and," "however," "economic," and the like, and even if there were, it would be hard to see such ideas as the meaning of the terms in question.

Meanings as senses

Finally, there is the suggestion that the meaning of a word is something halfway between the external object referred to and the psychological states of the speaker using the word. In the 1880s Frege explicitly took his "senses" to have this intermediate status, and his views have had a lasting influence on subsequent thought about meaning. Senses were to be "objective" and independent of thinkers, but still have the fineness of grain needed to explain cases of reference failure and co-designative terms (Frege 1984). Unfortunately, no real progress has ever been made in specifying what these senses could be without turning them into something more psychological than Frege would have wanted. Indeed, while the Fregean account faces fewer clear objections than those that identify meanings with physical objects or ideas, this may simply stem from the fact that it's very hard to get a clear idea of what the view is supposed to be. Finally, positing objective senses seems at odds with a type of naturalism about meaning that can be traced back to James's *Pragmatism* (James 1907), and that has dominated philosophical thought about meaning since Quine's influential *Word and Object* (Quine 1960).

Meaning as use

Because of problems such as those mentioned above, most philosophers have given up on the idea that meaning-talk requires that there actually be "meanings" out there to be talked about. There needn't be anything more to meaning than what must be captured in order to know what the expressions in our language mean, and this knowledge need not be knowledge of any type of *object*. The philosophically relevant question then becomes not "What are meanings?" but rather "What do you need to know to count as knowing the meaning of a sentence?" or "What do you need to understand to count as understanding the meaning of a word?"

Within this framework, there is still room for debate, but the most popular approach has been to understand meaning in terms of *use*. That is, to endorse something like: Knowing the meaning of a sentence is knowing the use of that sentence, and knowing the meaning of a word is knowing the use of that word.

The above can seem like something of a truism, but it becomes more controversial whenever "use" is spelt out in some substantial way. All plausible specifications require two qualifications: (1) the use we are concerned with is how our words and sentences *should be* rather than *are* used, since a mistake that is systematic does not thereby become part of a word's meaning; and (2) some aspects of even *proper* use are not relevant to meaning in the sense that they reflect the *pragmatics* rather than the *semantics* of our language, so it is not part of the *meaning* of a word not used in polite company that it not be so used. With these in mind, the most popular three approaches to the aspects of use that account for meaning are:

Inferential role semantics

According to this view, knowing the meaning of a sentence is knowing the inferential role of that sentence (what entails it, what follows from it, what is incompatible with it), and knowing the meaning of a word is knowing the contribution that word makes to the inferential role of the sentences in which it occurs. Such accounts tie meaning directly to a recognizable aspect of our usage that do seem to correlate with knowing the meanings of our terms. Such inferential roles can be defined narrowly so that they only include sentence-to-sentence inferences, but more plausible accounts understand the notion of inference more generously so as to include, say, our applying observation terms in the face of perceptual stimuli. The details of such accounts can be difficult to specify, and such difficulties have made others more sympathetic to:

Truth-conditional semantics

According to truth-conditional semantics (e.g. Davidson 1984), knowing the meaning of a sentence is knowing the conditions under which it is true, and knowing the meaning of a word is knowing what the word contributes to the truth conditions of the sentences in which it occurs. This approach gets at much of what was plausible in those accounts that tried to identify meanings with external objects, but one might wonder whether, if we understand truth realistically (that is as verification-transcendent), we can both identify meaning with truth conditions and claim that it is a function of use, since our own use can only manifest distinctions that are within our power to recognize. This problem would be resolved if we understood truth as being non-verification-transcendent, which would in turn leave us with:

Verficationist semantics

According to the verificationist, knowing the meaning of a sentence is knowing the conditions under which it is verified, and knowing the meaning of a word is knowing what the word contributes to the verification conditions of the sentences in which it occurs. Verificationist semantics can seem better placed to explain how we know the meanings of our terms, but this only seems clear if we tie the meaning with what we currently *take* to verify it, and this loses out on meaning's *normative* character, while if one ties the meaning of a sentence to what one *should* take to verify it, then it is less clear that the verificationist is better placed to claim that we know the meanings of our terms than the truth-conditionalist. Further, verificationists were notorious for having an overly narrow conception of what could be considered meaningful with, for instance, ethical statements being viewed as meaningless because they could not be verified.

These faults were mitigated in the pragmatist tradition which kept the verificationist's "forward-looking" conception of meaning (Dewey 1925), but accounted for the "narrowness" objection by tying the meaning of a sentence to what *practical* difference it would make to us if it were true (James 1907), which, unlike the purely "evidential" conception of verification typical of the positivists, would allow for ethical claims to be meaningful. Further, in tying the meaning of a sentence to what one *would ultimately* take to verify it (Peirce 1878), the pragmatist is able to explain meaning's normative character while still insisting that it is not, in principle, recognition transcendent.

All three approaches still have their defenders, as do others which try to understand meanings more mentalistically, and one may suspect that the meaning of "meaning" is open enough that a consensus on how it is to be understood will not be reached any time soon.

Further reading

Davidson, D. *Inquiries into Truth and Interpretation*. Oxford: Oxford University Press, 1984.

Dewey, J. *Experience and Nature*. Carbondale, IL: Southern Illinois University Press, 1981 [1925].

Frege, G. *Collected Papers*. Oxford: Blackwell, 1984.

James, W. *Pragmatism*. Cambridge: Harvard University Press, 1975 [1907].

Peirce, C.S. "How to Make Our Ideas Clear" in *The Writings of Charles S. Peirce, Volume 3: 1872–1878*. Bloomington, IN: Indiana University Press, 1986 [1878].

Quine, W.V.O. *Word and Object*. Cambridge, MA: MIT Press, 1960.

Royce, J. *The Religious Aspect of Philosophy*. Boston, MA: Houghton Mifflin, 1885.

Wittgenstein, L. *Philosophical Investigations*, third edition. Oxford: Blackwell, 1953.

HENRY JACKMAN

MEDITATION

"Meditation" is a vague term that has been used to designate a wide variety of practices, frequently religious in origin and purpose, but sometimes having explicitly secular objectives. The word has ancient Greek and Latin roots with meanings that include "care" and "exercise." Whatever diverse forms it might take, meditation is typically a practice of paying attention to something (some person, object, text, idea, etc.) that one cares a great deal about. It can be conceived as an exercise because one of its primary purposes is self-transformation, the effecting of specific cognitive, emotional or spiritual changes within the person who meditates. This exercise is a bringing into play of the intellect, feelings and imagination as a form of self-discipline, rather than for purposes like recreation or problem-solving.

Within the context of American life and thought, the art of meditation has deep roots, as the practice is clearly displayed in the writings of New England Puritans during the colonial period. Edward Taylor's (1644–1729) poetic meditations on Christian themes represent one noteworthy example; the theologian Jonathan Edwards's (1703–58) contemplation of the beauty of nature, rendered in prose that shades into poetry, represents another.

During the nineteenth century, Henry David Thoreau (1803–82) supplied the recipe for a vigorous type of meditative exercise in his essay on "Walking."

The sort of walking that Thoreau prescribed ("sauntering") was to be distinguished from any merely physical activity the objective of which is to arrive at some particular destination. This type of walking typically has no pre-established goal or itinerary, nor is it engaged in for the purpose of physical exercise. Nevertheless, Thoreau did conceive of it as a kind of meditative exercise, since the person who saunters "ruminates when walking," continuously growing in moral awareness, as well as in appreciation of the natural environment.

Early in the twentieth century, the American philosopher Charles S. Peirce (1839–1914) portrayed in one of his writings a type of activity that he called "musement" and explicitly identified as a form of meditation. It is a kind of reasoning that can best be described as "pure play." Musement has no purpose "save that of casting aside all serious purpose." Nevertheless, it is not like daydreaming; rather, it involves a "lively exercise of one's powers." The essay in which Peirce's account of musement appeared was an argument for the reality of God, and he explored there the possibility that musement might "flower" into religious meditation. But he also conceived of musement, in secular terms, as the important first phase of any scientific inquiry, the kind of disinterested, playful thinking that can result in the generation of new insights and the formulation of useful hypotheses.

No twentieth-century thinker wrote more extensively about the art of meditation than the Roman Catholic poet, monk, and religious philosopher Thomas Merton (1915–68). As a young man, Merton's thinking was significantly shaped by the philosophy of existentialism. Later in his life, Merton blended insights from his own Christian tradition with those gleaned from his ongoing study of Zen Buddhism and other Asian religious traditions.

The secularization of the practice of meditation has continued in the late twentieth and early twenty-first centuries, for example with the employment of meditative techniques for purely medical reasons, such as pain mitigation or stress-reduction for the purpose of preventing cardiovascular disease.

Further reading

Edwards, Jonathan. *A Jonathan Edwards Reader*, ed. Harry S. Stout, John E. Smith, and Kenneth P. Minkema. New Haven, CT: Yale University Press, 2003.

Merton, Thomas. *Contemplative Prayer*. New York: Doubleday, 1996.

Peirce, Charles S. "A Neglected Argument for the Reality of God" in *The Essential Peirce: Selected Philosophical Writings*, Volume 2, ed. the Peirce Edition Project. Bloomington, IN: Indiana University Press, 1992, pp. 434–50.

Taylor, Edward. *Edward Taylor's God's Determinations and Preparatory Meditations: A Critical Edition*, ed. Daniel Patterson. Kent, OH: Kent State University Press, 2003.

Thoreau, Henry David. *Walking*. New York: HarperCollins, 1994.

MICHAEL L. RAPOSA

MELIORISM

The idea of meliorism is crucial to pragmatic philosophy. Its most well-known formulation comes from William James in his *Pragmatism* lectures, which have been influential to philosophers such as Josiah Royce, John Dewey, Jane Addams, Cornel West, and Richard Rorty. Meliorism is more of an attitude than a metaphysical doctrine. The foundation of a meaningful human life, meliorism is a heart-felt belief that human action can mitigate suffering in the world.

In describing meliorism, James identifies two types of philosophers. On the one hand, there are the "tender-minded" philosophers, who are more religious and rationalistic in temperament, and who find the most satisfying universe to be one in which all supposed differences are resolved into a higher unity. For them, instances of suffering are disregarded, getting lost within a greater Good. The result of this attitude is that one can say – as people often do during times of tribulation – that "everything happens for a reason." On the other hand, there are the "tough-minded" philosophers, who are more scientific and empirical in temperament, and who are drawn to the idea of a world in which differences are fully recognized. For them, suffering is an inescapable reality, the affirmation of a belief in an essentially inhospitable universe.

Pragmatically speaking, each of these philosophers has a bad attitude: The tender-minded ones ignore suffering for the sake of their unifying scheme; the tough-minded ones readily accept suffering so that they can condemn the universe. In neither case is anything *done* about the suffering. Suffering is either just an insignificant nuance in a heavenly view of the universe, or an irremediable fact justifying a bleak world-view. This is the difference between the attitudes of optimism and pessimism. Ordinarily, optimism and pessimism are understood as relative terms referring to the tendency to look at the good things in life more than the bad things – the proverbial half-glass of water. James, however, presents these attitudes as they would be understood by philosophers, namely as intellectual systems in stark opposition. Optimists believe that the triumph of the Good is inevitable, while pessimists believe that such a triumph is impossible. Each view prevents meaningful action on the part of the believer. If encountering, for example, a neighbor who is wrongly accused of a crime, the optimist might suggest that if the person just looks at the situation differently, he will see himself as a victim, take solace in his own righteousness, and count himself victorious in the end. The optimist is positively dismissive of the fact that others do not share the man's view, while the pessimist is negatively dismissive of this fact. The pessimist would merely shrug and note that the universe is an unfair place, so there is little use fighting against it.

It is only the meliorist who would make a place in the universe for her own actions, which can minimize the instances and effects of injustice. James offers meliorism as an alternative to optimism and pessimism in the same way that he offers pragmatism as an alternative to the exclusively tender-minded and exclusively tough-minded views. "Meliorism treats salvation as neither inevitable, nor impossible," says James. "It treats it as a possibility, which becomes more and more of a probability the more numerous the actual conditions of salvation become." Probability is increased but certainty is never attained. Our actions are without guarantee, our successes incomplete. This is an important point for Dewey, who argues that nature's mixture of the stable and the hazardous affords the possibility of meliorism and real ends to human effort. As he explains in *A Quest for Certainty*, the kind of "block universe" favored by those who desire certainty is "either something ended and admitting of no change, or else a predestined march of events." There is no room for human effort here.

Meliorism and social action

Meliorism is perhaps most relevant to pragmatic social philosophy. James, for example, uses it in "The Moral Equivalent of War" when making his proposal for curtailing the human tendency for violent conflict. To mitigate humanity's warlike behavior, one cannot optimistically assume that the progress of intelligence will triumph over humanity's brutal, impulsive history. Yet one also cannot pessimistically assume that this brutality is an ineluctable part of human nature. James' proposal is that humanity enlist its warlike instincts into building projects such as the creations of roads, skyscrapers, etc. He likens these projects to a war on nature, a sublimated form of aggressive activity that transforms a problematic past into a better future.

James's proposal was followed up by Jane Addams, who put practices of social reconstruction in place of activities of aggressive human action toward the environment. In *Newer Ideals of Peace*, she adopts James' position that war-sentiments should be mitigated, and like James, she argues against what she calls "the goody-goody attitude of ineffectiveness" that characterizes sentimental peace-lovers. She argues for a profound readjustment of social attitudes, and finds a model for this ideal in the interactions of immigrant communities within American cities, where there is both a tough-minded acknowledgment of difference, and a tender-minded sympathy for common struggles. If we were to work toward universalizing this "cosmopolitan affection" that is found in American cities, "we may then give up war, because we shall find it as difficult to make war upon a nation at the other side of the globe as upon our next door neighbor."

Meliorism also informs the philosophy of Cornel West. In "Subversive Joy and Revolutionary Patience in Black Christianity," West describes how African-American Christianity developed a tragicomic attitude out of the absurdity of slavery. Against hopeless pessimism and tragedy, West asserts that "Black Christian eschatology focuses on praxis against suffering, not reflection upon it." And against naïve optimism and comedy, it focuses on "personal and collective resistance to suffering, not a distancing from it." In *Race Matters,* West advocates that African Americans think of themselves not as victims of, but as people *victimized* by, a racist system. To assume that economically and spiritually impoverished people can be encouraged to ignore their suffering is to be naively optimistic. Yet to refer to such people as victims is to be pessimistic, making people into permanent objects of an oppressive system. To consider oneself victimized is both to acknowledge the suffering and to be motivated to work productively to minimize it. This tragicomic attitude would have been appreciated by Josiah Royce. Royce says that the loyalty that attends lost causes – such as that of the early Christians who expected their Savior to triumph on earth – involves both grief and imagination. "The imagination," as he describes it in *The Philosophy of Loyalty*, is "chastened by this grief," and "not only reforms the story of the past, but builds wonderful visions of what is yet to come" (132).

No less melioristic than West and Royce is Richard Rorty, who argues that the Christian prophecy regarding the coming of God's kingdom of social justice, and the Marxist prophecy regarding the coming of a secular utopia, have been literal failures. Rorty is not advocating the hopeless belief that maximal human flourishing is impossible. He is saying rather that the prophecies of each world-view should be read as expressions of what their authors *hoped* would happen, not as expressions of what they *knew* will inevitably happen. "Hope often takes the form of false prediction," he writes in "Failed Prophecies, Glorious Hopes," "but hope for social justice is nevertheless the only basis for a worthwhile human life." To despair at the failed forecasts is to give in to pessimism; to rest assured of the coming of the Good is to be seduced by optimism. The meliorist will eschew both these attitudes for one of meaningful action – and uncertainty.

Further reading

Addams, Jane. *Democracy and Social Ethics*, Introduction by Charlene Haddock Seigfried. Urbana, IL: University of Illinois Press, 2001.

Addams, Jane. *Newer Ideals of Peace* in *Jane Addams's Writings on Peace*, ed. Marilyn Fischer and Judy Whipps. London: Thoemmes Continuum, 2005.

Dewey, John. *The Late Works, Volume 4: 1929: The Quest for Certainty*, ed. Jo Ann Boydston. Carbondale, IL: Southern Illinois University Press, 1988.

James, William. *Pragmatism*. Cambridge, MA: Harvard University Press, 1978.

—— "The Moral Equivalent of War" in *Essays and Religion and Morality*. Cambridge, MA: Harvard University Press, 1982.

Rorty, Richard. "Failed Prophecies; Glorious Hopes" in *Philosophy and Social Hope*. New York: Penguin, 1999.

Royce, Josiah. *The Philosophy of Loyalty*, Introduction by John J. McDermott. Nashville, TN: Vanderbilt University Press, 1995.

West, Cornel. *Race Matters*. New York: Random House, 1994.

—— "Subversive Joy and Revolutionary Patience in Black Christianity" in *The Cornel West Reader*. New York: Basic Civitas Books, 2000.

TADD RUETENIK

METAPHILOSOPHY

Metaphilosophy is a field or branch of philosophy that investigates the aims, methods, and nature of philosophy. While there is no agreed-upon definition of metaphilosophy, current usage identifies an issue as metaphilosophical if it raises questions *about* philosophy. In this sense, some have called it a philosophy of philosophy. Its primary question is "What is philosophy?" Western philosophy from its beginnings in ancient Greece has always questioned itself. For example, what makes a question philosophical as opposed to empirical, historical, or factual is itself a metaphilosophical question.

Historically, most philosophers have had conceptions of the nature of philosophy, though for many these conceptions have been inchoate. The twentieth century evidenced an increased metaphilosophical questioning of the discipline of philosophy by professional philosophers. Some have identified the later writings of Ludwig Wittgenstein as one of the chief catalysts for this trend. In the American philosophical tradition, John Dewey raised important metaphilosophical questions about the direction and categories of philosophy in the beginning decades of the twentieth century. In a 1913 letter he identified his desire to write a metaphilosophical essay in which he would examine "the nature of philosophy and how the pragmatic conception affects philosophy if the pragmatist philosopher applies his conception faithfully to himself" (Dewey 1985a: 436). Dewey's seminal essay "The Need for a Recovery of Philosophy" (1917) was the result. In it Dewey raised important metaphilosophical questions concerning the problems that philosophy traditionally attempted to answer. He explicitly eschewed proffering solutions to the traditional problems of epistemology and metaphysics and questioned the fundamental assumptions upon which these problems had been formulated: "This essay … is not in intent a criticism of various solutions that have been offered, but raises a question *as to the genuineness, under present conditions of science and social life, of the problems*" (Dewey 1985b: 4). His critiques of an epistemology industry based upon a spectator theory of knowledge and of the invidious consequences of the search for the "really real" are guiding themes of much of his subsequent philosophizing. Dewey made explicit his metaphilosophical concerns near the conclusion of his essay:

> What are the bearings of our discussion upon the conception of the present scope and office of philosophy? What do our conclusions indicate and demand with reference to philosophy itself? For the philosophy which reaches such conclusions regarding knowledge and mind must apply them, sincerely and whole-heartedly, to its idea of its own nature.
>
> (Dewey 1985b: 37)

Such metaphilosophical questioning guides much of Dewey's most important work in philosophy. In *Reconstruction in Philosophy* (1920) he revisits some of the central criticisms raised in his earlier essay. *Experience and Nature* (1925) and *The Quest for Certainty* (1929) continue these concerns. Of particular relevance here is Chapter 10 of *Experience and Nature*, in which he offers a formulation of philosophy's nature as a "criticism of criticisms."

The 1940s and 1950s saw a diminished interest in metaphilosophical questions among many professional philosophers. Then Richard Rorty's work in the 1960s and 1970s, culminating in such books as *The Linguistic Turn* (1967) and *Philosophy and the Mirror of Nature* (1979), explicitly raised metaphilosophical questions about the direction of philosophy and in the latter case hearkened back to some of the themes of Dewey's earlier work. A growing interest in metaphilosophy led to the establishment of the philosophy journal *Metaphilosophy* in 1970. Terrell Ward Bynum attributes his motivation to establish such a journal to his experience in Rorty's seminars in the 1960s at Princeton University. He was "most impressed with Rorty's ability to 'stand back' and get an overview of philosophy – to see it in perspective, relate it to other fields of knowledge, interrelate its various schools and methods" (Bynum 1989: 201). Bynum and his co-editor, William L. Reese, wrote in their inaugural issue that

> a growing number of books and articles have appeared, which consider topics such as the justification or characterization of philosophical methods and arguments, the foundation and scope of philosophy, the relation between philosophy and other disciplines.

This "new cluster of problems and interests – often termed 'metaphilosophical'" warrants calling "the emerging field 'metaphilosophy'" (Bynum and Reese 1970: 1)

While the editors deferred giving a definition of the term, preferring to keep it open-ended and subject to further articulation, they published a note by Morris Lazerowitz (1970) in which he took credit for coining the term "metaphilosophy" in 1940. In this note Lazerowitz claimed that he devised the term in order to "refer unambiguously to a special kind of investigation which Wittgenstein had described as one of the 'heirs' of philosophy." He went on to claim that the term "metaphilosophical" first appeared in print in his July 1942 book review in *Mind* of C.J. Ducasse's *Philosophy as a Science: Its Matter and Its Method.* Lazerowitz concluded his note by stating his general agreement with the notion that metaphilosophy is an investigation into the nature of philosophy.

In recent years this interest in metaphilosophy has continued, in part fueled by the controversies generated by clashes among analytic, Continental, and pragmatist philosophers as to what counts as philosophy. The critical question – What is philosophy? – still remains.

Further reading

Bynum, Terrell Ward. "Editor's Introduction," *Metaphilosophy* 20, 3 and 4 (July/October 1989): 201–2.

Bynum, Terrell Ward and Reese, William L. "Editors' Introduction," *Metaphilosophy* 1, 1 (January 1970): 1.

Dewey, John. "Excerpt from Letter to Boyd Bode dated 24 October 1913," quoted in "Textual Commentary" in *The Middle Works, 1899–1924, Vol. 10: 1916–17*, ed. Jo Ann Boydston. Carbondale, IL: Southern Illinois University Press, 1985a [1913], p. 436.

—— "The Need for a Recovery of Philosophy" in *The Middle Works, 1899–1924, Vol. 10: 1916–17*, ed. Jo Ann Boydston. Carbondale, IL: Southern Illinois University Press, 1985b [1917], pp. 3–48.

Lazerowitz, Morris. "A Note on 'Metaphilosophy.'" *Metaphilosophy* 1, 1 (January 1970): 91.

ARMEN T. MARSOOBIAN

METAPHOR

Metaphor does not explicitly appear as a topic of central importance in American philosophy until the middle of the twentieth century. Before that time, metaphor is studied as a poetic and rhetorical device, but there is no extended philosophical analysis of its nature or its role in philosophy. With the 1955 publication of his essay, "Metaphor," Max Black almost single-handedly succeeded in putting metaphor on the philosophical map in America, when he argued that metaphor plays a crucial role, not just in language, but primarily in conceptualization and reasoning. Black challenged the dominant literalist idea that the basic unit of human meaning is a proposition consisting of combinations of literal concepts that correspond to aspects of the world. According to this traditional literalist view, a metaphor does nothing more than highlight pre-existing literal similarities between different kinds of objects or events, as if to say "Notice that domain *X* is similar to domain *Y* in the following respects." In contrast with this traditional Comparison Theory of metaphor, Black introduced his Interaction Theory, which construed the meaning of a creative metaphor as resulting from the complex interaction of two systems of implications. We use our knowledge of a source domain to structure our conceptual understanding of some target domain. In the metaphor of mind-as-container-for-ideas, for example, the source domain is our conception of the nature and logic of physical containers and the target domain is mental operations. The source domain becomes a "filter" or "screen" through which we draw inferences about the target domain. In the mind-as-container metaphor, ideas are construed as quasi-objects or mental entities that can be held in the mind or else can move from one mind to another, and that can be manipulated by mental operations (such as, "She turned the idea over in her mind"). Black tantalizingly asserted that creative metaphors are not reducible to literal similarities, so that "It would be more illuminating in some of these cases to say that the metaphor *creates* the similarity than to say that it formulates some similarity antecedently existing" (Black 1995: 285). Black thus boldly argued that metaphor is a matter of meaning, a distinctive intellectual operation that uses one complex system of implications to select, emphasize, and organize relations in another domain of implications, in a way not reducible to the comparison of literal similarities.

Black's essay made metaphor not just philosophically respectable, but henceforth a required part of any adequate theory of language, concepts, knowledge, and reasoning. Today no serious philosopher can avoid giving some account of the role of metaphor, not just in poetry and literature, but equally in philosophical, religious, and scientific worldviews. Black's work thus framed the fundamental philosophical issues in contemporary discussions of metaphor as centering on three related questions: (1) Is metaphor a fundamental constituent of human meaning and thought? (2) Can the cognitive content of a metaphor be reduced to literal concepts? (3) What are the implications of metaphor for the practice of philosophy?

Among the more recent influential philosophical developments, John Searle grants that metaphors can have cognitive content, but often not a content that can be reduced to literal similarity statements. Conceiving of language-use as a system of practices guided by conventional constitutive rules, Searle tries to specify a set of rules by which we could determine *that* some expression is meant metaphorically and *what* precisely it means. The problem to explain how someone might utter a statement "*S* is *P*" (which has a literal *sentence* meaning) and intend thereby to communicate a different literal *utterance* meaning "S is R." Searle claims that the values or meanings of *R* for a metaphor might be based on definitions of the term *P*, on what is contingently true of *P*, or on what is generally believed to be true of *P*, but he also (following Black) argues that for certain cases there are no underlying similarities that will explain the metaphor's meaning. For these special irreducible cases, "it is a fact about our sensibility, whether culturally or naturally determined, that we just do perceive a connection, so that *P* is associated in our minds with *R* properties" (Searle 1979: 108). It has not gone unnoticed by Searle's critics that this fourth principle is more an assertion than an explanation of how such irreducible metaphors actually work.

Donald Davidson gained notoriety by challenging the fundamental assumption (shared by Black, Searle, and most theorists) that metaphor is a semantic phenomenon – a matter of meaning. Davidson insists that there is no such thing as metaphorical meaning, beyond the strict literal meanings of the sentences used in making the metaphorical expression. He treats metaphor as exclusively a matter of pragmatics (use) rather than semantics (meaning) – metaphor is a use of words (with their literal senses) to "intimate" or "suggest" something to a hearer. However, when a metaphor leads us to notice something, "What we notice or see is not, in general, propositional in character" (Davidson 1978: 47). Davidson is thus a Literalist about meaning, but he differs from Searle by denying metaphor any distinctive semantic content.

Richard Rorty immediately saw the startling implications of Davidson's limiting of metaphor to pragmatics. If metaphors have no distinctive cognitive content, then they are merely tools for drawing our attention to some feature or aspect of the world:

> In his [Davidson's] view, tossing a metaphor into a conversation is like suddenly breaking off the conversation long enough to make a face, or pulling a photograph out of your pocket and displaying it, or pointing to a feature of the surroundings, or slapping your interlocutor's face, or kissing him . . .
>
> All these are ways of producing effects on your interlocutor or your reader, but not ways of conveying a message.
>
> (Rorty 1989: 18)

Rorty champions the use of metaphor by "strong Poets" like Nietzsche, who supposedly destabilize our dominant conceptual systems by creating metaphors that institute new "vocabularies", which eventually, if they catch on, become our new literal understanding. Rorty thus sees metaphors as tools for imaginative restructuring of our literal conceptual systems via a process based on a non-rational creative leap.

Black, Davidson, Rorty, and to a lesser extent, Searle, regard metaphor primarily as a device for creatively remaking our understanding of the world. George Lakoff and Mark Johnson argue that metaphor is a pervasive constitutive mode of ordinary human understanding, and not just a device for novelty and creative insight. They draw on empirical evidence from linguistics, psychology, and cognitive science to show that virtually all of our abstract concepts are defined by multiple, typically inconsistent systems of metaphors. Like Black, Lakoff and Johnson present evidence that these conceptual metaphors are part of meaning, insofar as they define concepts and support inferences. Moreover, metaphors are not based on similarities, but rather on experiential correlations between the source and target domains. For example, our metaphorical conception of understanding-as-seeing (as in, "I see your point," "Could you shed more light on your argument?" and "The facts are not clear") is based on the experiential correlation (and neural co-occurrence) between the sensory-motor experience of seeing and the experience of gaining understanding, As Black and Searle claimed, the meaning of such metaphors is not reducible to any core literal concepts or propositional contents.

Although John Dewey did not explicitly give a theory of the nature and bodily grounding of metaphor, he sketched a naturalistic, non-dualistic account of mind, thought, and language that is supported by contemporary cognitive neuroscience and that includes embodied metaphoric processes of thought as one crucial part of abstract thinking. In one especially prescient passage, Dewey explains that our abstract concepts are grounded in aspects of our bodily experience:

> Every thought and meaning has its substratum in some organic act of absorption or elimination of seeking, or turning away from, of destroying or caring for, of signaling or responding. It roots in some definite act of biological behavior; our physical names for mental acts like seeing, grasping, searching, affirming, acquiescing, spurning, comprehending, affection, emotion are not just "metaphors."
>
> (Dewey 1925/1981: 221)

Metaphor is seen to be philosophically important, then, because it is our primary means for extending our sensory-motor, body-based meaning as the basis for our abstract conceptualization and reasoning, in a manner that preserves the continuity of "body" and "mind", perception and conception.

One important implication of this view is that all our abstract concepts – such as those for causation, events, mind, knowledge, ideas, morality, justice, democracy, politics, religion – are irreducibly metaphoric. This entails that analysis of any philosophical system or view must investigate the metaphors used to frame the issues, to define the key ideas, and to structure the arguments. Without metaphor, there would be no philosophy as we know it.

In less than half a century, metaphor has thus moved from the periphery to the center of philosophical concern. It is no longer dismissed as poetic word-play. Instead, converging evidence from many fields of cognitive science and philosophy recognize that metaphor is a pervasive, constitutive principle of human understanding and reasoning. We cannot think abstractly without it. To know ourselves and our world, we must understand the metaphors that define our reality and the ways in which those metaphors are grounded and grow.

Further reading

Black, Max. "Metaphor," *Proceedings of the Aristotelian Society*, NS 55 (1954–5): 273–94.

Davidson, Donald. "What Metaphors Mean," *Critical Inquiry* 5, 1 (1978): 31–47.

Dewey, John. *John Dewey: The Later Works, 1925–53, Vol. 1, 1925*, ed. Jo Ann Boydston. Carbondale, IL: Southern Illinois University Press, 1981 [1925].

Johnson, Mark (ed.) *Philosophical Perspectives on Metaphor*. Minneapolis, MN: University of Minnesota Press, 1981.

Lakoff, George and Johnson, Mark. *Metaphors We Live By*. Chicago, IL: University of Chicago Press, 1980.

Ortony, Andrew (ed.) *Metaphor and Thought*, second edition. Cambridge: Cambridge University Press, 1993.

Rorty, Richard. "The Contingency of Language" in *Contingency, Irony, and Solidarity*. Cambridge: Cambridge University Press, 1989, pp. 3–22.

Searle, John. "Metaphor" in *Expression and Meaning*. Cambridge: Cambridge University Press, 1979, pp. 76–116.

MARK JOHNSON

METAPHYSICS

The term "metaphysics" derives from the classical Greek expression *meta ta phusika* (meaning "after the things of nature"), which in turn derives from the phrase *ta meta ta phusika biblia* ("the books after the books on nature"), a reference to selected writings of Aristotle (384–322 BCE) that had been compiled and that dealt with topics not covered in his writings on the things of nature. These "metaphysical" writings concerned topics that were more removed from observation and sense perception, such topics as causation and being *qua* being.

Metaphysics is concerned primarily with the kinds of things that constitute reality. This would include investigating not only empirical, physical things, but also things outside of the senses, like abstract entities. It also includes an investigation of questions about broader conceptions of things and reality, such as whether what is real is constituted by such things as objects or events, properties or relations. For example, common physical objects, such as cats, are taken to be real. But events, such as "the battle of Waterloo," are not equivalent to the physical objects, e.g. horses, cannons, etc., that engaged in the battle. Events, then, seem to be real, but not reducible to physical objects. Alfred North Whitehead (1861–1948) and Charles Hartshorne

(1897–2000) in particular argued for an ontology of events, under the label of "Process Philosophy," claiming that change, creativity, and becoming, not permanence and being, are the genuine constituents of reality. Events as a fundamental kind of reality were also later advocated by Donald Davidson (1917–2003).

While physical objects such as cats are real, so, too, are properties of physical objects, e.g. the color or weight or shape of cats. Likewise, we speak of cats as being smaller than houses, that is, that there is a "smaller than" relation between cats and houses. A long-standing issue among metaphysicians is the nature and status of relations. In his writings on radical empiricism, William James (1842–1910) argued that relations are as real, i.e. just as much a part of our experiences, as are objects or properties.

In addition, seeing metaphysics as primarily concerned with the things that constitute reality can lead to questions about the very nature of being(s) and existence: for example, what "being" means and what it could mean for something not to exist or for there to be non-being. Finally, some have taken metaphysics to be the study not directly of things themselves, but rather of how things are and should be categorized. It is ultimately the study of categories or classificational schema (and whether those schema are discovered or constructed) that distinguishes metaphysics from other philosophical concerns. Among American philosophers, Nelson Goodman (1906–98) was especially noted for arguing that there are many "ways of worldmaking," i.e. that no single set of categories or descriptions match or mirror an independent world.

Besides focusing on the content of metaphysics, that is, on metaphysics as concerned with the things that constitute reality, philosophers often emphasize the methods and processes of metaphysical investigations. If metaphysics is the study of the nature of ultimate reality, then just what type of study is it? Here the emphasis is not on the nature of ultimate reality (i.e. things), but on the epistemic nature of metaphysics itself. For example, must metaphysical inquiry be non-empirical? There might be no sharp boundary between basic questions of physics and basic questions of metaphysics about the nature of time and space, but one thing that physicists insist upon is the empirical nature of their questions. If metaphysical questions can be addressed empirically, then what, if anything, distinguishes them from basic scientific questions? On the other hand, if metaphysical inquiry can be conducted non-empirically, how can it be done and what standards or criteria are relevant to the understanding and evaluation of metaphysical claims? How can, and should, metaphysics be conducted? Some have argued that it is a matter of intuition, others that revelation is relevant, still others that it follows the standards of logic, but each of these suggestions has generated controversy among philosophers about the veracity and reliability of its method. Indeed, much of the history of philosophy has been an on-going dispute about such varying and competing methodologies (for example, what, if anything, can be known a priori).

The result of these complexities is that metaphysics is often treated not as a single, coherent discipline or field of study, but as a collection of separate, though perhaps related, topics. These topics include broad, abstract issues such as the nature of existence (including questions such as: what does it mean for something to exist or to come into or go out of existence; what can it be for something to exist non-corporeally) or the nature of modality (i.e. actuality vs possibility vs necessity). It can also include more specific issues such as what things there are vs what can be truly said or known about those things, and what is the nature of the relationship between reality and our thought (or language or theories) about reality. Often these topics are treated as dichotomies: for example, whether there is a difference – and, if so, what it is – between appearance and reality or between what is essential and accidental (or incidental) or between what is permanent and transient. Finally, metaphysical topics can include even more specific issues such as the nature of causation or the nature of consciousness or the nature of personal identity.

Beyond concerns about the content of metaphysics and the method(s) of metaphysics, philosophers and others have raised questions about the aim and value of metaphysics. Because of the abstract nature of the content and method(s) of metaphysics, it appears to have little value or interest beyond philosophical speculation and argumentation. This view, however, is mistaken, as is illustrated by the issue of personal identity (or, the self). This issue revolves around two questions: what makes something a person and what makes a person the same person over time (that is, in what lies a person's identity)? One reason that personhood is important is that the notion of rights is generally held to apply to persons, entities that have interests and projects, entities who are moral agents, who can properly be said to bear duties and have goals and hold rights. To this extent, then, the concept of rights, or having rights, rests in part on what constitutes persons. In even more practical terms, the issue of the abortion of human fetuses rests on the concept of personhood. In purely biological terms, a human fetus is, of course, a human (i.e. it has the appropriate genetic structure). But having a particular genetic structure is not what seems morally relevant, or at least morally sufficient, for basing theories of rights and duties. What matters more is the status of being a person. Philosophers have generally taken personhood to be either a property of certain entities or a relation between certain entities. Wilfrid Sellars (1912–89), for example, spoke of two competing images of who we are, a scientific image and a manifest, or common sense, image, each with differing assumptions and implications. Of the views that take personhood to be a property, one is a materialist view: that is, what constitutes being a person is having a particular type of material or bodily existence. What, then, constitutes personal identity (being the same person) over time is some acknowledged bodily continuity over time. A different view, but one that still sees personhood as being a property, albeit a different property, is a mentalistic view. On this view, what constitutes being a person is having (at least potentially) certain acknowledged mental capacities or abilities. Personal identity under this view is a matter of mental continuity, especially memory. While both the materialist and mentalist views take personhood to be a property of entities, an alterative view takes personhood to be a relation between entities. This view sees entities as becoming persons over time, and doing so because of their interactions with other entities. Simply having a particular physical structure or a particular mental state is insufficient for personhood under this view. Indeed, supporters of this relationist view deny that there is some sort of essential self, some substance (whether physical or non-physical) that underlies actions and beliefs. We do not live in vacuums, and who we are is a matter of social construction. Our personal identity is derivative upon our social identity. This relationist view that denies the notion of an essential self, that there is some property that constitutes personal identity, was held by George Herbert Mead (1863–1931). The African-American philosopher W.E.B. DuBois (1868–1963) also championed a relationist view of the self with particular emphasis on the social construction of the identities of racial minorities.

With the rise of empiricist thought in the late eighteenth century, philosophers challenged the meaningfulness of metaphysical claims, suggesting that since they can't be established either empirically (as matters of fact) or purely conceptually (as relations of ideas), they were nonsensical. Immanuel Kant (1724–1804) took up this challenge and asked the meta-metaphysical question of what could make metaphysics possible. Identifying metaphysical claims as synthetic a priori (i.e. as conveying information about existence yet being knowable prior to experience of the world), he argued that basic metaphysical structures must be understood as being necessary in order for experience to be possible. By focusing less on the objects of our experience and more on the subject and conditions of the possibility of our experience, Kant shaped much of nineteenth-century metaphysical thought, including that of American philosophers. In particular, Kant argued that since our experience is necessarily mediated by various categories, we never experience things in themselves (noumena) but only as they seem to us (phenomena). This generated a wave of varieties of idealism throughout the following century, most notably among American philosophers through the writings of the St Louis Hegelians, Josiah Royce (1855–1916), and Brand Blanshard (1892–1987). Both idealism as a metaphysical view and, more broadly, metaphysical speculation itself came under intense scrutiny and criticism early in the twentieth century. Rudolf Carnap (1891–1970) and Ralph Barton Perry (1876–1957), among others, argued that metaphysical claims cannot be tested to determine if they are true or false; as such they are nonsensical. In addition, the rise of ordinary language philosophy in the mid-twentieth century brought another version of rejection of metaphysics. Metaphysical problems were said to be pseudo-problems, generated by philosophers in the context of their misuse and misunderstanding of language. By the end of the century, under the influence of John Dewey (1859–1952), George Santayana (1863–1952), W.V.O. Quine (1908–2000) and others, many philosophers adopted a stance they termed "naturalism," a stance dedicated to understanding philosophical issues via scientific methods and in which only natural objects are real. Critics of this stance see it as merely insisting on a particular metaphysical set of commitments, which these critics label as "scientistic," rather than as solving or resolving any metaphysical issues.

From the beginnings of American philosophy, metaphysical issues have been paramount. Jonathan Edwards (1703–58) wrote passionately on the nature of the mind and free will, denying that the latter could contradict God's nature and insisting that both natural necessity and moral necessity determined a person's choices. Philosophical attention to traditional metaphysical concerns waned during the latter half of the eighteenth century, with issues of social and political philosophy becoming more pronounced. But with the rise of Trancendentalism in the early 1800s, metaphysical questions of the nature of reality once again came to the forefront. Writers such as Ralph Waldo Emerson (1803–82) and Henry David Thoreau (1817–72) explicitly addressed issues of the metaphysical nature of persons and of the reality of relations. By the late 1800s, an important focus of philosophical concern among American philosophers was the question of metaphysics itself. Chauncey Wright (1830–75) emphasized the need for verifiability as a criterion of meaningfulness and he, along with others, challenged the verifiability of many metaphysical claims. Charles Peirce (1839–1914), though bemoaning what he saw as the gibberish nature of most metaphysics, insisted on the fundamental importance of metaphysical questions, so long as they were understood pragmatically. For example, while the special sciences offer explanations of empirical phenomena, the question of the very nature of explanation is a metaphysical one and is a legitimate and fruitful point of investigation as long as that investigation follows the pragmatic maxim. By the latter half of the twentieth century, much of the focus on metaphysics was less about metaphysics itself and more on metaphysical topics, such as the nature of mind and consciousness; language, categorization, and ontology; and the nature of agents and persons.

Further reading

Davidson, Donald. *Essays on Actions and Events.* Oxford: Oxford University Press, 1980.

Eldridge, Michael, "Naturalism" in Armen T. Marsoobian and John Ryder (eds) *The Blackwell Guide to American Philosophy.* New York: Blackwell, 2004, pp. 52–71.

Goodman, Nelson. *Ways of Worldmaking.* Indianapolis, IN: Hackett, 1978.

Gracia, Jorge J.E. *Metaphysics and Its Task.* Albany, NY: SUNY Press, 1999.

Mackinnon, Barbara. *American Philosophy: A Historical Anthology.* Albany, NY: SUNY Press, 1985.

Mead, George Herbert. *Mind, Self, and Society.* Chicago, IL: University of Chicago Press, 1967.

Quine, W.V.O. *Ontological Relativity and Other Essays.* New York: Columbia University Press, 1969.

White, Morton. *Science and Sentiment in America.* Oxford: Oxford University Press, 1972.

Whitehead, Alfred North. *Process and Reality.* New York: Macmillan, 1929.

DAVID BOERSEMA

MILLER, JOHN WILLIAM

John William Miller (1895–1978) received his AB from Harvard in 1916, served in World War I, and then returned to Harvard for both his MA (1921) and PhD (1922), studying as a graduate student with R.B. Perry, E.B. Holt, C.I. Lewis, and William Ernest Hocking. As an undergraduate he studied with Josiah Royce. Very early in his career he secured a position at Williams College, where he became a legendary teacher and Socratic presence. Though he wrote voluminously, he published very little. Much of what he wrote took the form of letters to former students who became close friends, letters often more than a hundred pages. On the eve of his death, George Brockway, one of these students, who had become the CEO of W.W. Norton, brought out *The Paradox of Cause and Other Essays* (Norton, 1978). Four other posthumous volumes followed in rather quick succession: *The Definition of the Thing* (1980), Miller's 1922 dissertation; *The Philosophy of History* (1981); *The Midworld of Symbols and Functioning Objects* (1982); and *In Defense of the Psychological* (1983).

His deepest intellectual sympathies were with the idealistic tradition, especially the post-Kantian German philosophers Fichte and Hegel as well as his own teachers Royce and Hocking. Miller's creative appropriation of the idealistic tradition centers on the idea of history in his distinctive sense, a fateful (though not fatalistic) process in which self and world are entangled in a mutually constitutive and transformative engagement with one another. His mature thought drove toward a radical reorientation of philosophical reflection, wherein the task of viewing human existence and its cosmic setting *sub specie aeternitatis* was abandoned for that of depicting them *sub specie temporis.* But he rejected what others took to be the nihilistic and relativistic implications of a thoroughgoing espousal of the historicist approach. Such ideals as truth, objectivity, and freedom were not for him precluded by this espousal; rather their meaning and authority as ideals could only be established by appeal to their actual function in our ongoing historical experience. Far more than M.R. Cohen, the author of *The Meaning of Human History* (1947), J.H. Randall, Jr, *Nature and Historical Experience* (1958), and other roughly contemporaneous thinkers in America and elsewhere, Miller made history the central object of his philosophical concern, though one closely allied to a variety of traditional concerns (e.g. science, education, politics, and aesthetics). Like C.S. Peirce, S.K.

Langer, and Charles Morris, also such Europeans as Karl Bühler, Jakob von Uexküll, and Ernst Cassirer, he stressed the role of symbols and what he called "functioning objects" (e.g. numbers, yardsticks, clocks, and other instruments of measurement) in the institution and development of every distinctively human undertaking (e.g. mythology, religion, art, science, and philosophy itself). In sum, Miller took the semiotic turn as decisively as he took the historical turn; the former is more profound than the linguistic turn taken by so many of his contemporaries, while the latter is in his case less nihilistic and anti-metaphysical than the turn toward history taken by Nietzsche, Foucault, and the legion of thinkers influenced by them.

Further reading

Colapietro, Vincent. *Fateful Shapes of Human Freedom: John William Miller and the Crises of Modernity.* Nashville, TN: Vanderbilt University Press, 2003.

Fell, Joseph P. (ed.) *The Philosophy of John William Miller.* Lewisburg, PA: Bucknell University Press, 1990.

McGandy, Michael J. *The Active Life: Miller's Metaphysics of Democracy.* Albany, NY: SUNY Press, 2005.

Tyman, Stephen. *Descrying the Ideal: The Philosophy of John William Miller.* Carbondale, IL: SIU Press, 1993.

VINCENT COLAPIETRO

MILLER, PERRY

Perry Miller (25 February 1905–9 October 1963) was born in Chicago and received his BA and PhD from the University of Chicago. But Miller left the university after his freshman year in 1923 for the road, the sea, and exotic places. He lived in a cabin in Colorado, tried acting in Greenwich Village, and worked as a seaman on an oil tanker to the Belgian Congo, now Zaire. In Africa, Miller writes that he determined that his life mission was "expounding what I took to be the innermost propulsion of the United States. ..." Africa was the scene of an "epiphany" – the realization of "the pressing necessity of expounding my America to the twentieth century" (*Errand into the Wilderness*: vii–viii).

Miller was an important force in the then relatively new field of American Intellectual History. His interests in theology, literature, science, and philosophy are integrated in all his works, although some are more narrowly focused such as *The Raven and the Whale.* But even here Miller is concerned with the larger social context and impact of his literary characters. Miller published extensively on Puritanism, beginning with his revised doctoral dissertation *Orthodoxy in Massachusetts.* But the more important works are his two volumes titled *The New England Mind.* Miller also edited important anthologies of original documents including *The American Puritans: Their Prose and Poetry. The Transcendentalists* collected the works of the lesser-known figures. Miller was honored in 1966 with the Pulitzer Prize in History for *The Life of the American Mind*, a posthumous publication of a projected larger work.

Jonathan Edwards captures the theologian's sense of the majesty of creation and the kinship between the sense of beauty and religious affections. Miller's Edwards declares the supremacy of passion and recognizes that "even in abstract reasoning the mind is sensible of the beauty and amiableness of things, and in the presence of the idea of them, experiences sweetness and light" (p. 184). An important essay in *Errand*, "From Edwards to Emerson," contrasts their attitudes toward the relation of mind, both human and divine, to nature while observing that certain basic continuities persist in a culture. In this case, what persists is the "Puritan effort to confront, face to face, the image of a blinding divinity in the physical universe" (p. 185). Edwards is hard pressed to maintain the separation of God and Nature while Emerson is happy to equate the two.

"Nineteenth-Century New England and Its Descendents" highlights Thoreau as the major transcendentalist. Miller writes, "There really isn't anything you can say about him except that he is the ultimate in subversion, because he would subvert even the reformers, let alone the conservatives" (*The Responsibility of Mind*, p. 161). This interesting posthumous collection also includes Miller's musings on being a solitary scholar out of step with the times, "The Plight of the Lone Wolf," and an intriguing essay on social class, educational standardization, and the academic profession, "What Drove Me Crazy in Europe." Students interested in American philosophy will also profit from his extended introductory essay on Benjamin Franklin and Jonathan Edwards in *Major Writers of America.* There Miller illustrates his view that the intellectual history of the United States is a prolonged drama featuring a series of contrasting personalities engaged in creating a national identity.

Further reading

Crowell, John and Searl, Stanford J., Jr (eds). *The Responsibility of Mind in a Civilization of Machines: Essays by Perry Miller.* Amherst, MA: University of Massachusetts Press, 1979.

Miller, Perry. *Errand into the Wilderness*. Cambridge, MA: Belknap Press of Harvard University Press, 1956.
—— "Introduction to Benjamin Franklin and Jonathan Edwards" in Newton Arvin (ed.). *Major Writers of America*, Vol. 1, New York: Harcourt, Brace and World, 1962, pp. 83–98.
—— *The Life of the Mind in America: From the Revolution to the Civil War*. New York: Harcourt, Brace and World, 1965.

ANTHONY J. GRAYBOSCH

MILLS, C. WRIGHT

A prominent sociologist and social critic, C. Wright Mills (1916–62) rose to national acclaim in the 1950s with the publication of three seminal works: *White Collar* (1951), *The Power Elite* (1956), and *The Sociological Imagination* (1959). Mills's work, influenced heavily by Max Weber and Thorstein Veblen, highlights the ways in which the middle class moves toward ever greater forms of bureaucratic rationality. The powerlessness found within bureaucratic thinking is compounded by the concentration of power in the hands of military, corporate and political elites. These threats to democratic society are further heightened by the failure of intellectuals to address fundamental social problems of the day. Mills calls for a new sociological imagination that works toward overcoming various forms of false consciousness by closely examining the relationship between history and biography. Such an engagement, he argues, would bring a greater awareness of the relationship between individual problems and the current socio-cultural apparatus.

Further reading

Horowitz, Irving L. *C. Wright Mills: An American Utopian*. New York: The Free Press, 1983.
Mills, C. Wright. *The Sociological Imagination*. New York: Oxford University Press, 1959.
—— *Power, Politics, and People: The Collected Essays of C. Wright Mills*. New York: Ballantine Books, 1963.
—— *Sociology and Pragmatism: The Higher Learning in America*. New York: Oxford University Press, 1966.
—— *The New Men of Power*. Chicago, IL: University of Illinois Press, 2001 [1948].
Tilman, Rick. *C. Wright Mills: A Native Radical and his American Intellectual History*. London: Pennsylvania State University Press, 1984.

MATTHEW J. FITZSIMMONS

MIND

The mind figured prominently in the thought of classic American philosophers. William James (1842–1910) gave center-stage to the discussion of mental phenomena, introducing philosophical issues concerning *consciousness*, underscoring the importance of *affects* and *temperaments*, and connecting philosophy with the empirical study of psychological realities. At the core of his philosophy of mind is a constructivist conception of the self as *Promethean*, as the result of its own activity and spontaneity, rather than as a mere product of biological inheritance or of the social context. In *The Principles of Psychology* (1890) James examined empirical studies of psychological phenomena (including "the stream of consciousness") and offered a systematic review of the experimental data available at the time. He argued that the central problems studied in psychology could only be properly understood by a philosophical approach. His *pluralistic* approach underscores the richness and diversity to be found in human *experience* (in the relational manifolds given to us in streams of consciousness). Like James, John Dewey (1859–1952) also developed an experiential account of individuality and the creative power of the mind. In *Experience and Nature* (1925) he defined the mind as "an agency of novel reconstruction of a pre-existing order". Dewey is heavily critical of the mind–body problem that has dominated the philosophical discussions of the mind, creating unnecessary and distorting divisions and polarizing the different elements and aspects of our life in an artificial way. For Dewey, in the life of the human organism the mental and the corporeal, far from being separate poles, are in fact inextricably intertwined elements that cannot be understood independently of one another. He develops a naturalistic account of the mind that dissolves the traditional mind–body problem and overcomes the distorted conceptions of the mind that had been developed in the philosophical tradition as responses to this misconceived problem. In Dewey's naturalistic account, the mind involves a set of faculties that emerge from natural processes in the interactions between the human organism and the world. Dewey's account distinguishes different layers or aspects of our mental life. On the one hand, he articulates an *objective* concept of mind with Hegelian undertones that goes beyond the individual and is shared by an entire collectivity that participates in the same meaning structures. On the other hand, he also articulates a *subjective* concept of mind as a center of consciousness – of immediate and qualitative experiences – in which inputs are reconstructed into outputs in the organism's transactions with the environment. It is in this sense that Dewey contrasts *mind* with *consciousness*: while "consciousness denotes the totality of actualized immediate qualitative differences," the "actualized apprehensions of meanings," "mind denotes the whole system of meanings as they are embodied in the workings of organic life; . . . the field of mind – of operative meanings – is enormously wider than that of consciousness."

Dewey's account of the mind as a creative agency emphasizes both its individual and its social aspects as being mutually supportive and equally necessary. In this sense, Dewey argues that "the mind that appears *in* individuals is not as such an individual mind". For the individual mind is "a system of belief, recognitions, and ignorances, of acceptances and rejections, of expectancies and appraisals of meanings"; and these meanings that constitute the contents of the mind are social products "which have been instituted under the influence of custom and tradition". Dewey's dialectical approach to the mind and the self focuses on the social dynamics underlying our interactions or transactions with the environment and with each other. This social and naturalistic view was also developed by another classic American philosopher, G.H. Mead (1863–1931), the creator of *symbolic interactionism*. The theoretical foundations of symbolic interactionism are laid out in *Mind, Self, and Society* (1934) where Mead offers an account of the genesis of the mind and the self in terms of language development and role playing. In this account the defining feature of the mental is *reflective intelligence*, a kind of interactive intelligence through which the organism relates simultaneously to the environment and to the community. Reflective intelligence requires the capacity of *taking the role of another toward oneself*, that is, of adopting the perspective that others have on one's own behavior. Mead argues that this kind of intelligence requires interpersonal communication mediated by symbols and that, therefore, mentality arises "when the organism is able to point out meanings to others and to himself." His account of the mind is thus essentially *linguistic* and *social*: "Out of language emerges the field of mind"; "We must regard mind, then, as arising and developing within the social process, within the empirical matrix of social interactions." The central element in Mead's account is *reflexiveness*: "It is by means of reflexiveness – the turning-back of the experience of the individual upon himself – that the whole social process is thus brought into the experience of the individuals involved in it." Through the notion of reflexiveness Mead articulates an account of self-consciousness as arising from symbolically mediated interaction. Mead referred to himself as a *social behaviorist*. But, although his discussions of mental processes often take the form of stimulus-and-response explanations of behavior, he is not a reductive behaviorist (such as John B. Watson) who dismisses the reality of mental processes that are not publicly observable.

The mind received increasing theoretical attention in American philosophy in the second half of the twentieth century. Of special importance in inaugurating the philosophical discussion of mind in this period was Wilfrid Sellars's "Empiricism and the Philosophy of Mind" (1956). In this essay Sellars developed a critique of what he termed the *myth of the given*, the spurious thesis that our knowledge of the world is inferred from a foundational form of sense experience which is not itself a form of conceptual cognition. Against this doctrine Sellars formulates Kantian arguments to the effect that there are no contents that are simply *given* in experience without the mediation of concepts. He offered an *inferentialist* account of the mind and its contents which results in a holistic view of mental states that has deep affinities with the holistic views of the mind of other American philosophers (especially Quine and Davidson). On Sellars's holistic view, the mind is conceptualized as an inferential network in which everything is interrelated. This inferential network is composed of propositional attitudes (beliefs, desires, intentions, etc.) and their propositional contents. According to Sellars, an inferential network of mental states operates in "the space of reasons" and is subject to three sets of rules which connect linguistically articulated contents with each other ("intralinguistic rules"), with percepts ("language entry rules"), and with actions ("language departure rules"). This Sellarsian inferentialism about the mind has been further developed in recent years by Robert Brandom.

Another holistic view of the mind, developed in the 1960s, is *functionalism*, which was instrumental in the development of Cognitive Science. Functionalism contends that what defines the psychological type of a mental particular is the causal role it plays in the mental life of the organism or system. Mental state types are thus holistically defined by their causal interconnections with other state types: input state types, output state types, and other internal state types. An influential version of functionalism was the *machine-state functionalism* proposed by Hilary Putnam, among others. According to this view, mental states are types of Turing machine states. A Turing machine is a mechanism whose inputs and outputs are written on a tape divided into squares containing symbols from a finite alphabet. The machine scans the tape one square at a time, performing simple mechanical operations on it: printing a symbol, erasing a symbol, moving the tape and changing state. According to machine-state functionalism, every mental function can be computed by a Turing machine. A corollary of this view is that all mental states can in principle be mechanically implemented since they can be fully specified in terms of the program states of Turing machines. Machines and their abstract programs provide the perfect illustration for functionalist specifications of mental states. While functionalism is compatible with token physicalism, it is in tension with type physicalism because it argues that mental state types can be physically realized in different mechanical and biological systems. Functionalism created problems for strong versions of *central state materialism* and *identity theory*, such as the one defended by Richard Rorty. Functionalist accounts of the mind undermine any strict identification of mental states with brain states insofar as it shows that mental state types are *independent of the medium* in which they are realized and can be *multiply realizable* by different physical (or even non-physical) state types. With the thesis of *medium independence* and *multiple realizability*, functionalism suggested that the mind operates at a higher level of abstraction than the brain and that mental states require abstract and formal specifications that are beyond the scope of the brain sciences, thus providing a rationale for Cognitive Science as an autonomous domain for the description and explanation of mental phenomena.

The dominant approach in Cognitive Science has been to reduce cognitive processes to *computational* processes, that is, to rule-governed symbol manipulations. This computational approach conceptualizes the mind as a formal symbol manipulator or *syntactic engine*. This formalist perspective views mental representations as participating in computational processes solely in virtue of their syntactic or formal properties. As a result, semantic content has become a difficult problem for Cognitive Science. Some have argued that semantic content cannot be explained computationally and it constitutes a recalcitrant problem that reveals the limitations of the computational paradigm. The most famous argument to this effect was provided by John Searle in *The Chinese Room* thought experiment, which shows that a rule-follower can be a successful symbol manipulator by applying syntactical rules on the formal aspects of the Chinese symbols she is given, but without having any understanding of the contents that these symbols are supposed to express. This thought experiment is supposed to show that meaning and the intentional aspects of the mind cannot be captured in a purely formal or syntactic account of mental processes, thus undermining the widely held view in Cognitive Science that the study of the mind should take care of syntax while semantics will take care of itself. Jerry Fodor has explicitly argued for *content parallelism*: the view that syntactic mental processing preserves semantic coherence because it runs parallel to semantic mental processing. According to Fodor, the cognitive architecture of the human mind requires a *language of thought* with a combinatorial syntax and semantics that run parallel to one another, so that formal computational processes are at the same time content-sensitive reasoning processes. Many have argued that functionalist accounts have to be supplemented with a psychosemantic theory that is sensitive to the material and biological aspects of cognition. Fred Dretske and Ruth Millikan, among others, have articulated naturalistic accounts of mental representation in terms of causal and evolutionary processes of adaptation to the environment, providing the foundations for a naturalized theory of mental content. But not everybody agrees that computational accounts of the mind need to be supplemented with a psychosemantic theory of mental content. Stephen Stich, for one, has argued that Cognitive Science should restrict itself to the syntactic properties of mental representations.

Another serious difficulty for functionalism and computationalism has been the problem of *consciousness* and *qualia*. It has been objected that functional and computational models cannot account for the conscious and qualitative aspects of mental phenomena because two mental states can have the same causal role – thereby realizing the same functional state – and yet be quite different from the point of view of consciousness and subjectivity: conscious and subjective aspects may be present in one state but not in the other (the problem of *absent qualia*); or these aspects may become systematically distorted when we go from one state to the functionally equivalent one (the problem of *inverted qualia*). Thomas Nagel has argued that consciousness and subjectivity are the essential features of the mental, so that, in order to understand mental states, one must understand *what it is like* to be in them, which one can only do by taking up the experiential point of view of the subject who has them. This view claims to reveal the insurmountable limitations of physicalism: if the mental is intrinsically subjective, it remains, of necessity, beyond the scope of physical descriptions that eliminate the experiential point of view of the subject. Others have argued, *pace* Nagel, that consciousness and subjectivity can be explained in physicalistic accounts of the mind. Some, like Daniel Dennett and William Lycan, have tried to explain consciousness functionally. Others, like Paul and Patricia Churchland, have proposed an *eliminative materialism* that explains away conscious phenomena, replacing the subjective concepts of folk psychology with the objective concepts of neuroscience. But there are also different versions of *non-eliminative materialism*. Among these views of the mind, Davidson's anomalous monism has been especially influential, arguing that mental properties supervene on physical properties and that the mental emerges from the physical but cannot be reduced to it.

Further reading

Brandom, Robert. *Making it Explicit: Reasoning, Representing, and Discursive Commitment*. Cambridge, MA: Harvard University Press, 1994.

Dennett, Daniel. *The Intentional Stance*. Cambridge, MA: MIT Press, 1987.

Dewey, John. *Experience and Nature* in *John Dewey. The Later Works, 1925–1953, Vol. 1, 1925*, ed. Jo Ann Boydston. Carbondale, IL: Southern Illinois University Press, 1988.

Dretske, Fred. *Explaining Behavior: Reasons in a World of Causes*. Cambridge, MA: MIT Press, 1988.

Fodor, Jerry. *Psychosemantics: The Problem of Meaning in the Philosophy of Mind*. Cambridge, MA: MIT Press, 1987.

James, William. *The Principles of Psychology*. Cambridge, MA: Harvard University Press, 1981.

Loewer, Barry and Rey, Georges (eds) *Meaning in Mind: Fodor and his Critics*. Oxford: Blackwell, 1991.

Mead, G.H. *Mind, Self, and Society*. Chicago, IL: University of Chicago Press, 1934.

Putnam, Hilary. *Mind, Language and Reality: Philosophical Papers, Volume 2*. New York: Cambridge University Press, 1975.

Rorty, Richard. *Philosophy and the Mirror of Nature*. Princeton, NJ: Princeton University Press, 1979.

Searle, John R. *Mind, Language and Society*. New York: Basic Books, 1998.

Sellars, Wilfrid. *Science, Perception and Reality*. Atascadero, CA: Ridgeview, 1963.

José Medina

MIND-DUST

After the emergence of Darwin's evolutionary theory, psychologists began to apply genetic methodology to psychological phenomena. However, Darwin's theory struggled to explain the "appearance" of consciousness. One early attempt to solve this problem posited a direct continuity in which material development gives rise to mental processes. Unfortunately, such an approach begs the traditional ontological question about how one kind of substance (matter) can produce a different kind (mind).

To address this ontological concern, some evolutionary psychologists suggested that along with primordial material elements (atoms) there must also exist primordial mental elements. These hypothesized elements of consciousness are what William James calls, in the sixth chapter of *The Principles of Psychology* (1890), "mind-dust" (152). Under mind-dust theories, consciousness evolves analogous to the evolution of material beings, and thus, just as the body is an evolved arrangement of material atoms, the mind is explained as an evolved arrangement of simple mental elements, or "mind-dust." The theories, thus, are expressions of psychological, atomistic empiricism (found, for example, in the British philosophical psychology of Herbert Spencer (1855), the French psychology of H.A. Taine (1871), as well as the German physiology of Adolf Fick (1864)), building up complex "consciousness" through the combination of elemental "mental" particles (153–6).

The mind-dust theories succeed in retaining the evolutionary postulate that nothing novel is required for the development consciousness, and the parallel character of the mind-dust theories to material evolution avoids the "relation of substances" problem. However, as James argues, "such an interpretation flies in the face of physical analogy, no less than on logical intelligibility" (158). Under physical analogy, the theory purports to explain that all complex mental sensations reduce to simple ones, of which the former is an amplified composite. James, points out, however, that positing such a developmental picture cannot be proved directly, and as an indirect proof it fails to follow observed behavior in physical processes (156–60). On the logical side, the theory fails as well, since internally any two distinct elements (whether mental or physical) always remain as they are – simple and unrelated to each other; to unify simple elements requires a third, external entity in order to conjoin the distinct elements into an experienced unity. The mind-dust theory, however, is unable to support the presumption of an external "third" entity (160–4). James's own position in the *Principles* explains consciousness as genetically and constitutively stream-like and whole, only admitting of division through purpose-driven analysis ex post facto. (See "The Stream of Thought," Chapter IX.)

Further reading

Fick, Adolf. *Lehrbuch der Anatomie und Physiologie der Sinnesorgane*. Lahr: Schauenburg, 1864.

James, William. *The Principles of Psychology*. Cambridge, MA: Harvard University Press, 1981 [1890].

Spencer, Herbert. *Principles of Psychology.* London: Longman, Brown, Green, and Longmans, 1855.
Taine, H.A. *On Intelligence*, trans. from the French by T.D. Haye. London: L. Reeve, 1871.

D. MICAH HESTER

MONTAGUE, WILLIAM PEPPERELL

William Pepperell Montague (1873–1953) was born in Chelsea, Massachusetts. He was educated at Harvard College where he worked as a teaching assistant for George Herbert Palmer, and enjoyed the legendary tuition of William James. Santayana's courses confirmed his native belief in a world of independently existing substances. He wrote a doctoral thesis on the subject of practical reason under the benevolent guidance of Josiah Royce, even though the two men disagreed on almost every philosophical issue.

Montague possessed a primarily scientific intelligence, and was acutely interested in mathematics, but he was not ill disposed toward speculation, and even held it up as an ideal. In the spirit of William James, he encouraged his students and readers to think of philosophy as a visionary adventure in quest of expansive vistas. He authored a book titled *Great Visions of Philosophy* and proclaimed earnestly in its prologue that where it has no vision philosophy must perish. In point of fact, however, his philosophical method was decidedly analytical. He proudly mimicked the procedures of physical scientists, preferring to collaborate with colleagues on creative projects rather than work alone, and microscoping philosophical problems, hoping to make progress by isolating crucial details the better to examine them.

In a textbook called *The Ways of Things*, Montague developed a metaphysical position he called "animistic materialism." According to animistic materialism, continuous quantitative growth can explain the emergence of organic life out of inorganic matter, of animal life out of plant life, and of persons out of animal life. Think of a teapot full of tepid water sitting on a hot stove; as more and more heat is added to the system, the water verges closer and closer on boiling. When the water boils, we can say that continuous quantitative growth has brought about a qualitative development, a phase change. Analogously, as more and more energy is added to an inorganic system, the system comes closer and closer to becoming organic until eventually the threshold is crossed and an organism emerges. Montague distinguishes between kinetic energy, which predominates at the inorganic level, and potential energy, which is kinetic energy organized and stored, but how this distinction helps to elucidate his position is unclear. The analogy between boiling water and the emergence of organic life is obviously dubious.

His most useful book by far, *The Ways of Knowing*, is less an original contribution to epistemology than it is a clear and fair-minded survey of competing epistemological methods. In epistemology, Montague was at the leading edge of a movement called New Realism, which included Ralph Barton Perry. New realists maintained that objects of knowledge exist independently of being known by any mind. Consciousness is like a flashlight; the world of objects is like a dark room full of many things. When present, consciousness illuminates the objects in proximity to it. Objects in the far corners of the room may remain in the dark for a long time, but all of the objects exist just the same in the dark as they do in the light. The immediate object of consciousness and the surface of the ontological object are identical. But then how can we account for erroneous perceptions? In the case of a straight stick partly immersed in still water, the immediate object of perception looks bent, but the surface of the ontological object is perfectly straight. Nevertheless, Montague insisted that the fact of error is not incompatible with a world of mind-independent objects.

Further reading

Montague, William Pepperell. *The Ways of Knowing*. New York: Macmillan, 1928.
—— *The Ways of Things.* New York: Prentice-Hall, 1940.
—— *Great Visions of Philosophy.* La Salle, IL: Open Court, 1950.

MICHAEL BRODRICK

MORALITY

Moral philosophy in the Western tradition has been largely a function of reason. As Denise, White and Peterfreund (*Great Traditions in Ethics*) observe, "To seek, with the aid of reason, a consistent and correct ideal of life is the traditional goal of moral philosophers," and further, "once we go beyond immediate action to a consideration of the reasons for our actions, we are in reason's territory, and there, logic rules" (1–2). Such exercise of rational analysis has allowed for (1) the delimiting of moral issues, namely defining what is a moral issue and what is morality; (2) the derivation of moral theories or principles; and (3) the application of such theories or principles to moral decision-making and action. As moral philosophy developed, two principal influences provided most of the concepts with which Western theorists have dealt. One emerged from ancient Greece and focused on the "good life" and how human happiness, properly understood, contributed to it. The other grew out of the Judeo-Christian tradition, and became an ethics of righteousness before God that contrasted with the happy or pleasant life. The latter emphasized duty and an absolute sense of right, whereas the former concerned itself with individual happiness.

Specific moral theories or systems that followed tended to fall roughly into this dual pattern. The intersection of morality and religion has yielded, for example, pervasive Christian ethics and various strains of natural law theory. Virtue ethics, as first developed in Aristotle, stressed moral character and the good life. Social contract theories (such as Hobbes) presumed the rational need to agree to social rules for survival. Kant's absolutist deontology shows how formal reason yields an unquestionable sense of duty, whereas Mill's utilitarianism is a form of moral consequentialism that seeks the greatest good or happiness for the greatest number. For Marx morality is inseparable from social ideology and for many feminist ethicists morality often involves empathy and care for others. In each case, the specific theory of morality tends to result from an exercise of reason, each adhering to some ultimate value, goal or principle considered the "end" of moral philosophizing. Some are absolutist, and seek to transcend everyday experience, while others are more attached to the lived situation. Each provides its own concepts and models, while establishing norms that it considers necessary to the conduct of moral living.

American philosophy (notably Pragmatism) is cognizant and respectful of such traditions and uses of reason, yet parts company with its antecedents, charting its own course in a number of important ways. It emphasizes the centrality of moral experience and societal improvement. With the rise of "applied ethics" in the past forty or so years, so-called "case-based reasoning" has become useful in business, medical and other professional settings. This approach is perhaps closest to the spirit of Pragmatism in that it shuns the idea of a pre-conceived, universally applicable morality for all cases in favor of specific deliberation within a context and employment of current understandings from various fields. It seeks a provisional moral resolution in response to the exigencies of any unique situation or case.

Pragmatism

Pragmatism consciously moved away from moral absolutes and the rule of logic in favor of immediate experience and behavioral response. Abstract contemplation and conceptual analysis were replaced by an experientially based program for action. Pragmatism concerned itself not with what is ultimately true or right but with what we can know and what will work to advance human needs and societal improvement. It is, thus, a kind of consequentialism. Values (including moral values) are to be considered relative, but this need not entail a negative arbitrariness, but rather a constructive engagement with the here and now.

For Pragmatism human life (and philosophy) is seen as continual problem-solving, wherein no long-held distinction between fact and value obtains. Indeed, science and morality are fundamentally interconnected and must evolve together. The reflective methods of science, and particularly the tenets of Darwinian evolution, become fundamental for Pragmatism.

Pragmatism seeks to overcome all outworn dualisms (subject–object, mind–world, theory–practice, fact–value) because it believes that scientific discoveries simply rendered them obsolete. It holds to no particular doctrine about the nature of moral value, subscribing rather to a notion of fallibilism wherein there is a downgrading of the eternal and transcendent in favor of the imperfect contingent, the living, the experiential. While there can be no knowledge of eternal truth this need not hamper human endeavor or moral aspirations. Philosophy, indeed, should simply stop asking about the ultimate nature of reality or ultimate moral values and focus on the common aim of all human inquiry, which is human flourishing.

Pragmatism's concentration on practical deeds rather than lofty ideals imbued it with a profound social dimension. Through cooperative inquiry the aim of moral philosophy should be to help clarify the moral problems of the day while assisting with change that leads toward greater freedom and stronger communities. Such general notions are central to the work of Pragmatism's two most important figures in relation to morality, William James and John Dewey. Other American moral philosophers of note include Ralph Barton Perry and C.L. Stevenson, whose work focused on ethical situations and disagreements.

William James

William James, pioneering American psychologist and philosopher whose ideas stirred considerable controversy, wrote several important essays on morality (such as "The Moral Philosopher and the Moral Life"). James focused on the individual in relation to philosophy. It is the individual after all who must face difficult moral choices regarding, for example, religion and how to live one's life. Accordingly, philosophy (and moral philosophy) is never a detached, objective search for Truth but rather a very personal attempt to find a world view that lends purpose and meaning to one's life. Thus, Pragmatism for James was a basic method of inquiry, not a fixed set of conclusions. In an important sense, philosophy *is* one's life in that it gives significance and direction to one's efforts as a moral agent.

For James each person is free to live as she sees fit. Every human desire or need has a right to be fulfilled unless a competing desire or need (perhaps of another) provides reason not to satisfy it. James thereby introduced radical notions concerning needs, truth, beliefs, philosophical method and the will.

James's method of "radical empiricism" was thoroughly open-minded, not confined to so-called "facts," but instead took seriously all human experience, including the powerful role of emotions. It turned toward concreteness and the centrality of action. Beliefs took on seminal importance for James. Our beliefs (including moral beliefs) are nothing more than guides to action, and they are to be forever experimentally tested in terms of whether or not they are lived out and make an actual difference in the way one lives. When the pragmatic method is applied to questions of religion or moral concern the individual simply cannot wait for scientific or logical certitude (which is impossible in any case). One must decide on value questions and operationalize them before all the evidence is in. While there is contingency and at times an emotional leap into the dark in conducting our moral lives, for James valuing and the "will to believe," both essential to human nature, are not purely arbitrary. The measure of truthfulness and value is always based on whether beliefs make a difference in one's life and conduct. The pragmatic test for truth must, therefore, directly appeal to experience. For instance, does a belief in God, and all that it requires, lend emotional satisfaction, a moral steadiness and purpose to one's life? If so, it is true and morally justifiable regardless of skeptical questions about God's existence or possible contradictions in moral teaching. What should one do to help others, become a better person and improve the world? These are not abstract questions for James, but, indeed, intensely practical. Individuals will, of course, answer such questions differently. In this sense, that which is morally right is, for anyone, simply that which is expedient in the way of believing and behaving. In sum, for James the workability of ideas and values is forever individual, personal and, in a sense, private. This differs significantly from the other great pragmatist of morality, John Dewey.

John Dewey

Whereas James focused chiefly on the individual in relation to morality, Dewey, the humanist, concentrated on the individual *and* society or the individual *in* society. He emphasized social and public criteria of truth and value. Furthermore, his ethics was correlated with scientific method. For Dewey reflective thinking (or intelligence) was equivalent to scientific inquiry. He sought to apply the method of science to problems of morality. This was his way of claiming that scientific study of nature (including human nature) must be united with a philosophical interest in values. Science and morality should progress together, each serving as a check on the other. Regrettably, this rarely occurs. Historically, science and technology race ahead without the restraining balance of moral scrutiny. When a mess is made, morality has to enter to clean it up, as with the rapid proliferation of nuclear science and technology or the internal combustion engine and the myriad social and health problems that each has precipitated. Moral concerns generally enter after the fact and try to mitigate the damage.

For Dewey, the self (or individual) is not a Cartesian substance or reality that exists prior to language and culture. The self is an emergent product of social practices and interactions. In the absence of society, there simply are no individuals. Our species-unique language, values and cultural practices function as tools (instruments) that help us coordinate our activities, constitute new social and institutional orders, in general allowing us to enlarge human possibilities.

For Dewey the principal task of philosophy is to help clarify the social and moral issues of the time and place, the sorts of factors that frustrate human growth and fulfillment. His fundamental moral commitment involves the elimination of any distinction between moral deliberation (typically conceived in abstract or technical terms) and proposals and activities aimed at progressive advances in education and socio-political institutions. Dewey was convinced that human history has always been about the expansion of freedom, democracy, inclusiveness and community. All efforts to change attitudes and public policies are essentially aimed at the gradual realization of freer, more democratic communities that in turn have the capacity to create a better, more moral sort of human being. Philosophical progress inevitably involves problem-solving, that is, constant efforts to overcome obstacles to freedom and the satisfaction of human needs. For Dewey persons have no basic need for ultimate Truth, but rather for freedom and strengthened community. Morality, the exercise of freedom and democracy, and the building of community are all inextricably bound together in practice. Humans must come together and engage in the sorts of cooperative inquiry that lead to scientific, social and moral progress.

Dewey introduced a number of novel ideas relating to morality. For him the "means" of moral decision and action and the "ends" of morality are united in practice and experience, just as theory is in reality inseparable from action, from doing. Further, there are no ultimate or final ends just as there are no universally binding absolutes in morality. We have only what he called "ends-in-view" or steps taken in incremental ways toward solutions. Once an end-in-view is achieved it simply becomes the means to the next end-in-view. In morality, as well as all other realms of inquiry, we must give up our obsession with ultimate (or final) goals or ends. Instead of fixating on the generation of absolute moral rules or principles we must accept (using the model of scientific method) that any moral concept or rule is but a hypothesis to be tested against experience, including most notably new strains of knowledge and experience. In so doing, we realize that each and every moral situation is unique, context defined and driven. If, for example, a society morally determines that patient autonomy and dignity require the possibility of physician-assisted suicide in selected cases of terminal illness, then such a provision must be enacted and tested out in terms of its consequences. Are patient rights enhanced under such a program? Are people, including doctors, willing to freely participate? What problems arise? If, upon thoughtful examination, the policy is deemed a practical and moral success, what would be the next step? Should the criteria for patient eligibility be expanded? Should more doctors be certified as appropriate providers of such services? This basic pattern of inquiry is, in principle, to be applied to any moral question.

Dewey's moral theory is not something deduced from principles of logic, from philosophical argumentation in a broader sense or from the requirements of religion. His theory involves individuals cooperating, in their mutual self-interest, to seek reconstruction of economic, political and religious institutions that powerfully affect all persons. The overriding goal is to stimulate human flourishing, bring about greater self-awareness, self-determination and creative problem-solving. Under this approach the operative notion of what is "good" (morally good) will evolve and change as society changes and as knowledge in all areas increases. Obsolete, non-workable values and presuppositions must simply be discarded. Values must be adapted to human needs and changing environments, but this can only happen as reflective methods of inquiry are applied to human experience and the social orders in which and through which we live. Simply stated, intelligence *and* experience must be actively combined in the conduct of moral life.

Pragmatism's contribution to morality is not a new ethical theory or set of guidelines. It is more like the outline of a social program, an active process in which persons utilize all their resources and tools in confronting and tentatively resolving the most important concerns of any human life: who am I to be, what am I to do, how can I help society advance? Experience and critical reflection, not logic, always serve as the beacon and guide in such a process.

Further reading

Denise, Theodore C., White, Nicholas P., and. Peterfreund, Sheldon P. (eds) *Great Traditions in Ethics*, tenth edition. Belmont, CA: Wadsworth, 2002 (includes a chapter on Dewey).

Dewey, John, "Morality is Social" in *Human Nature and Conduct: An Introduction to Social Psychology*. New York: Modern Library, 1930 [1922].

Dewey, John and Tufts, James H. *Ethics – Revised Edition*. New York: Henry Holt, 1932.

—— *Theory of Valuation*. Chicago, IL: University of Chicago Press, 1939. Published originally in the *International Encyclopedia of Unified Science*, II, 4.

—— "Three Independent Factors in Morals," *Educational Theory* (July 1966): 197–209.

James, William, "The Moral Philosopher and the Moral Life," in *The Will to Believe and Other Essays in Popular Philosophy*, New York: Dover, 1956 [1927].

—— *Pragmatism and Four Essays from the Meaning of Truth*, ed. Ralph Barton Perry. New York: Meridian, 1955.

—— *Essays In Religion and Morality*. Cambridge, MA: Harvard University Press, 1982.

RICHARD E. HART

MUMFORD, LEWIS

Lewis Mumford (1895–1990) was one of America's leading public intellectuals for almost six decades. Extraordinarily diverse in his interests and prolific as an author, Mumford made major contributions to literary criticism, architectural studies, the study of technology, and urban studies (for which he remains best known). A professional writer throughout his life, Mumford was architectural critic of the *New Yorker* magazine for over thirty years. His book *The City in History* (1961) received the National Book Award in 1961. But he was also the author of four major works of philosophy (broadly conceived) on the "renewal of life" in which he developed his doctrine of "organic humanism."

Mumford was born in New York City and always regarded his experiences there as his true education, having dropped out of New York's City College early on. From the start he was interested in the relation between culture, especially in its imaginative dimensions, and the environment – both natural and human-made. He was deeply influenced early in life by the eccentric Scottish urbanist J. Patrick Geddes. Though he and Geddes were never personally close, Mumford always admired him as a model of a synthetic theorist and practitioner. Mumford would merge activism and theorizing in his own life. He was a co-founder with Benton MacKaye and Henry Wright of the Regional Planning Association of America, and was a lifelong advocate limited urban growth and balancing urban development with its regional environment. These commitments have led him to be identified as an early voice for the importance of ecological concerns. He remained a persistent observer and critic of modern urban development to the end of his long life. One of his last writings was a critique of the new World Trade Center while it was being built. (See *The Pentagon of Power* text to illustration 20, "Homage to Gigantism.")

The focus of Mumford's first books was the development of a distinctly American culture in the nineteenth and early twentieth centuries. These works have placed him as one of the founders of American studies. His *The Golden Day* (1926) and *Herman Melville* (1929) were key to the rediscovery of literary transcendentalism, a fact that F.O. Matthiessen acknowledged in *The American Renaissance. The Golden Day* marked the inception of Mumford's lifelong love affair with Emerson, whose work he regarded as a pinnacle of cultural achievement. His subsequent *The Brown Decades* (1931) explored post-Civil War culture in all its dimensions, including the architecture of Henry Hobson Richardson and Louis Sullivan. Mumford was also an influential champion of Frank Lloyd Wright's work.

The Golden Day drew attention – and some harsh criticism – from philosophers for its chapter on "The Pragmatic Acquiescence" in which Mumford portrayed William James as a philosopher of accommodation to his times rather than the critic he should have been. He voiced similar criticisms of Dewey's thought as a philosophy of expediency incapable of providing a truly critical perspective on the world due to its lack of an adequate value theory. Robert Westbrook in *John Dewey and Democracy* has maintained that Mumford's criticisms of Dewey were influential in their day. (Dewey responded to Mumford in "The Pragmatic Acquiescence" (1927), see *Later Works* 3.147–51.)

Mumford's doubts about pragmatism were deeply influenced by Randolph Bourne and Bourne's similar criticisms of Dewey. Indeed, in his study of the two thinkers, *Beloved Community*, Casey Blake has portrayed Mumford's subsequent work as carrying on the legacy of Bourne (who died in the 1919 flu epidemic). Bourne famously linked the horrors of World War I to the rise of the centralized nation-state; much of Mumford's later writings can be seen as seeking to identify a form of community less centralized and more pacific than the state, a community that can provide a countervailing power to it. Mumford was also deeply influenced in this regard by the nineteenth-century political tradition of "mutualism."

But from today's perspective Mumford's value theory seems less a true alternative to pragmatism than another way to develop a naturalistic account of human values in relation to human purposes. His "organic humanism" was developed in such works as *Technics and Civilization* (1934), *The Condition of Man* (1944), *The Conduct of Life* (1951) and *The Transformations of Man* (1956). These books were notable for their strong historical sense, their deep appreciation of the interactions between technology and human culture, and their stress on the creative dimensions of the human personality. A key to that personality in Munford's view was "balance": balance between the practical and spiritual, and the emotional and the intellectual. Such balance was key to human growth in its fullest sense.

Throughout his life Mumford voiced concern about pragmatism's ability to account for the aesthetic realm. Yet the aesthetic theory sketched in his *Art and Technics* (1952) bears interesting similarities to Dewey's in *Art and Experience.* Both regard the arts as essential to sustaining humanity's higher purposes in the face of modernity's impersonality and violence. Mumford's short text provides a genealogy of the aesthetic realm's emergence from everyday practical activities and concerns. Art, in his view, does not constitute a separate distinct realm; rather, art's concern with creation informs all realms of human interaction, beginning with the most primitive languages, and reaches its highest achievement in the creation of the human personality itself. In the face of a fractured depersonalized society the aesthetic realm offers our greatest hope for human fulfillment and cultural integration. "If modern man does not recover his wholeness and balance, if he doesn't regain his creativity and freedom, he will be unable to constrain the destructive forces that are now conspiring to destroy him" (*Art and Technics*: 151).

These words were written in the shadow of the Cold War and the nuclear arms race, which turned Mumford's thought in a decidedly more pessimistic direction. Mumford played a heroic role in seeking to organize the public in general and the scientific community in particular against the dangers of nuclear weapons. His *In the Name of Sanity* (1954) is a landmark in the campaign against nuclear weapons that Mumford saw as embodying all that was pernicious in modern culture. Strains of this pessimism were evident in his magisterial *The City in History* (1961) which traced the story of urbanism from the very start of civilization to the present, paying special attention to the city's role as both a product of culture and a shaper of culture. Looming over it all was the specter of the "megalopolis" – that oversized impersonal urban monstrosity whose triumph would mean the death knell of all that was deeply human. To prevent this, Mumford wrote,

> We must restore to the cities the maternal, life nurturing functions, the autonomous activities, the symbiotic associations that have long been neglected or suppressed. For the city should be an organ of love; and the best economy of cities is the care and culture of man.
>
> (*The City in History*: 575)

The pessimism achieved full voice in his two last major works, *Technics and Human Development* (1967) and *The Pentagon of Power* (1970), collectively titled *The Myth of the Machine*. The "machine" in this case was both a technological fact and a neurotic human aspiration – to a large, inhuman, machine-like formal organization that increased our practical powers at the cost of destroying our truly human creative capacities. Mumford's story began once again at the dawn of human civilization and the origins of collective life, which he saw as responsive to our emotional and creative needs as much as to our more practical ones. The earliest forms of human organization were among the healthiest and most balanced in his view (leading his critics to charge him with romanticizing the past). With the emergence of large cities, history became a struggle between the human impulses to balance creativity and the *in*human impulses to exaggeration and destruction. These works were written in the shadow of the Vietnam War, of which Mumford was an early and sharp critic. They conclude with an epilogue on "The Advancement of Life" that sought to strike a hopeful note. He wrote,

> There are already many indications, though scattered, faint, and often contradictory, that a fresh cultural transformation is in the making; one which will recognize that the money economy is bankrupt, and the power complex has become, through its very excesses and exaggerations, impotent.
>
> (*The Pentagon of Power*: 429)

But everything Mumford had said suggested that those indications were faint indeed; he remained hopeful but not optimistic.

Mumford's' last productive years were spent anthologizing his life's writings with a special emphasis on the autobiographical. His life was not without its deep tragedies: his son, Geddes, was killed in the Second World War while serving as a rifleman in Italy. He memorialized him fondly in *Green Memories: The Story of Geddes* (1947). Though Mumford was a strong supporter of the effort against Hitler, the loss of his son undoubtedly contributed to his lifelong aversion to modern warfare. Mumford married Sophia Wittenberg while a young man in New York and they eventually moved together to Duchess County where he spent his final fifty years.

Lewis Mumford's intellectual fate is strange, to say the least. He was a renowned public figure influential enough to grace the cover of *Time* magazine and receive the Presidential Medal of Freedom 1964. Moreover, his works were received with high seriousness by the leading intellectuals of his day. As noted, figures like John Dewey felt compelled to answer his views. Yet today he is hardly remembered outside of urban studies and some corners of the environmental movement. His standing among philosophers has no doubt been harmed by his complete lack of interest in epistemological issues and the sort of "foundational" concerns that have traditionally defined what it means to be a "philosopher." But this is why one might expect him to be admired – or at least remembered – by those who are skeptical of such traditional concerns.

Further reading

Blake, Casey. *Beloved Community The Cultural Criticism of Randolph Bourne, Van Wyck Brooks, Waldo Frank, and*

Lewis Mumford. Chapel Hill, NC: University of North Carolina Press, 1990.
Miller, Donald. *Lewis Mumford: A Life*. New York: Weidenfeld and Nicolson, 1989.
Mumford, Lewis. *The Story of Utopias*. New York: Boni and Liveright, 1922.
—— *The Brown Decades: A Study of the Arts in America, 1865–1895*. New York: Harcourt Brace, 1931.
—— *The Condition of Man*. New York: Harcourt Brace, 1944.
—— *The Transformations of Man*. New York: Harper and Row, 1956.
—— *The Myth of the Machine: Vol. I, Technics and Human Development*. New York: Harcourt Brace Jovanovich, 1967; *Vol. II, The Pentagon of Power*. New York: Harcourt Brace Jovanovich, 1970.
—— *Sketches from Life: The Autobiography of Lewis Mumford*. New York: Dial Press, 1982.

CHEYNEY RYAN

MÜNSTERBERG, HUGO

In 1885 Hugo Münsterberg (1 June 1863–16 December 1916) earned his PhD in psychology as a student of Wilhelm Wundt at the University of Leipzig, followed by his MD at the University of Heidelberg two years later. While teaching at the University of Freiburg, he attended the First International Congress of Psychology in Paris, where he met William James, who eventually invited him to Harvard. He later oversaw the development of Harvard's experimental psychology laboratory.

Münsterberg lectured both in psychology and in philosophy, and in fact served as president of both the American Psychological Association (1898) and the American Philosophical Association (1908). Wundt had seen psychology as an empirical method for approaching questions that are philosophical in origin, but for Münsterberg it seems that the two disciplines worked to constitute two sets of objects out of the same world, each with its own questions and answers. This is not an unfamiliar thought to philosophy; Kant and Fichte clearly hold something similar, and yet it is with a distinctively Hegelian maneuver that Münsterberg attempts the reconciliation of the two. That is to say, he comes closest to a synthesis of his psychological and philosophical "worlds" when he engages social questions at the highest degree of abstraction.

In spite of a persistent tension between his philosophical interests in questions of value and freedom and his psychological interests in human malleability, the aim of his work in applied psychology is clearly motivated by his philosophical commitment to the priority of community, culture, and commerce at the highest level. By treating the community as subject (or "over-subject"), he reconciles the thoughts of freedom and determination, since then nations and communities act as both agents and sources of value. What others would criticize as a potentially manipulative approach to individual subjects is justified, as he sees it, by the fact that the aim all of us ought to share is that of furthering the economic and cultural good of the whole. Thus, his work in applied psychology – in criminal psychology, industrial and organizational psychology, and in the psychology of education – aims to serve the abstract authorities of state and culture. He also treated individuals, of course, and his use of suggestion and auto-suggestion in those treatments was a precursor of today's cognitive-behavioral therapies.

As the first World War approached, this commitment to the state and the power of patriotism, coming from a German, brought him sharp criticism and repudiation, although he did not limit himself to trumpeting German patriotism. He did, however, ultimately ally himself with the German cause. During that time, in addition to publishing his only textbook, he turned his attention to film, writing his 1915 *The Photoplay: A Psychological Study*, sometimes cited as the first philosophical monograph on the subject. There, he argues against the then-current conception of film as simply a medium of reproduction as he investigates on the one hand its analogies with psychological processes and on the other its aesthetic value. Throughout his life, he published on a surprising array of topics, and his works ranged from spirited popular essays on topics like Prohibition to the principles of art education. He died in 1916, collapsing at the lectern as he prepared to give a talk at Radcliffe.

Further reading

Carroll, Noël. "Film/Mind Analogies: The Case of Hugo Münsterberg," *Journal of Aesthetics and Art Criticism* 46, 4 (1988): 489–99.
Hale, Matthew. *Human Science and Social Order: Hugo Münsterberg and the Origins of Applied Psychology*. Philadelphia, PA: Temple University Press, 1980.
Münsterberg, Hugo. *On the Witness Stand: Essays on Psychology and Crime*. Boston, MA: Houghton Mifflin, 1923 [1908].
—— *American Patriotism and Other Social Studies*. Freeport, NY: Books for Library Press, 1968 [1913].
—— *American Problems from the Point of View of a Psychologist*. Freeport, NY: Books for Library Press, 1969 [1910].
—— *The Americans*. Kila, MT: Kessinger Publishing, 2005 [1905].
Münsterberg, Margarete Anna Adelheid. *Hugo Münsterberg, His Life and Work*. New York: Appleton, 1922.

KATHLEEN EAMON

MURPHEY, MURRAY

Murray Murphey (1928–) received his BA from Harvard University in 1949 and his PhD from Yale University in 1954, and two years later began his teaching career as an assistant professor of history at the University of Pennsylvania, where he remained until he retired. A few years after being promoted to full professor he became Chairman of the Department of American Civilization, keeping that position on and off until 1994. In 2000 he retired as Professor Emeritus of History.

Along with other honors he was awarded a Fulbright Fellowship as well as a Rockefeller Fellowship, and was the 1993 recipient of the Herbert W. Schneider Award of the Society for the Advancement of American Philosophy for his distinguished contributions to the understanding and development of American philosophy. He has served as president of the Charles Peirce Society, as editor of *American Quarterly*, and as director of several summer institutes and seminars.

Among his numerous books, one in particular, *The Development of Peirce's Philosophy*, has had a large and lasting impact on the understanding and furtherance of interest and scholarship in, the philosophy of Charles Sanders Peirce. Published in 1961, it remains today a classic in the field. His work ranges from lengthy studies of single philosophers to sweeping examinations of American thought, from its European sources in the seventeenth century through the twentieth-century work of C.I. Lewis. In both types of studies he combines a decidedly historical approach with in-depth, comprehensive, and insightful analyses of his subject matter.

Further reading

Murphey, Murray. *The Development of Peirce's Philosophy.* Cambridge, MA: Harvard University Press. 1961. Reprinted with new preface and appendix, Indianapolis, IN: Hackett, 1993.

—— *Philosophical Foundations of Historical Knowledge.* Albany, NY: SUNY Press. 1994.

—— *C.I. Lewis: The Last of the Great Pragmatists.* Albany. SUNY Press. 2005.

Murphey, Murray and Flower, Elizabeth. *A History of Philosophy in America*, 2 volumes. New York: Putnam's, 1977.

SANDRA B. ROSENTHAL

MURPHY, ARTHUR E.

Arthur E. Murphy (1901–62) was born in Ithaca, New York, raised and educated in California, and died in Austin, Texas. He took his PhD at the University of California in December 1925, and held positions consecutively at the University of California, University of Chicago, Cornell University, University of Chicago, Brown University, University of Illinois, Cornell, University of Washington, and University of Texas, in these last four positions serving as Head of Department. He was a Fellow of the American Academy of Arts and Sciences, served as President of the American Philosophical Association, was twice a Matchette lecturer, and gave the Carus Lectures in 1955. His main philosophical interests early in his career were in metaphysics, epistemology, speculative philosophy, and the nature and importance of philosophy itself; later on he developed a strong interest in moral and political philosophy, and throughout his career he retained an interest in contemporary philosophy, especially American philosophy, philosophy in relation to culture, and the ways in which reason can operate in obtaining knowledge and in the ordering of human affairs. He edited the Prentice-Hall Philosophy series for twenty-six years, served as a book editor of *The Journal of Philosophy* for several years, in which capacity he reviewed an extraordinary number of books, and later was editor of *The Philosophical Review*.

During his lifetime Murphy had a considerable reputation among American philosophers, partly derived from his fame as a lecturer, a reputation that diminished sharply after his death. He acquired a national reputation with the publication of his first papers, in 1926, in which he developed a theory he called objective relativism (later repudiated), which he claimed to find in the writings of Dewey and Whitehead. His first book, *The Uses of Reason*, provides an account of how reason operates in gaining truth about matters of fact, in the context of morality, in the area of social action, and in philosophical inquiry itself, and attempts to show how reason can itself be used to justify the use of reason. His Carus Lectures, *The Theory of Practical Reason*, published posthumously, are a sustained attempt to refine and develop the theory of practical reason presented in *The Uses of Reason* and in some later papers; also published posthumously was a collection of his essays, *Reason and the Common Good.* His *Reason, Reality, and Speculative Philosophy*, derived from a longer unpublished manuscript on "Contemporary Philosophy" completed in 1940 and never brought to publication, was only recently published; enough unpublished papers remain to make another collection of essays.

Murphy constantly emphasized the importance of good sense, good judgment, and good will in understanding the world and in dealing with matters of fact and with moral and social problems. This emphasis comes out repeatedly in *The Uses of Reason* and *The Theory of Practical Reason* and in many of the essays in *Reason and the Common Good.* He was especially impressed with the early work of Peirce, Moore, Dewey, Santayana, and Whitehead, but came to think that all these philosophers departed from their moorings in good sense and solid thought in their later work. *Reason, Reality, and Speculative Philosophy* constitutes a critique of speculative philosophy, especially that of the period from approximately 1890 to 1940, and provides an account of what a reasonable, sound, and adequate philosophy would be and do. It was intended as "a study of what a philosophy in operation amounts to and what comes out of it." Along with Dewey, Murphy was concerned that philosophy was divorcing itself from the problems of common life and was becoming culturally irrelevant. Unlike Dewey, Murphy believed that there are genuine and legitimate problems of philosophy that are not problems of common life and need to be dealt with philosophically. His four books, and especially his last, bring out the nature of his concerns and his prescriptions and arguments for dealing with them. They also manifest his subtle sense of humor, his extraordinary wit, and his uncanny ability to get at the essence of someone else's thought and state it in a nutshell, all encased in an elaborate, and often extremely funny, style of writing. He was convinced that a sense of humor is an essential trait of philosophical wisdom, and manifested this in his teaching and in his writings.

Further reading

Murphy, Arthur E. *The Uses of Reason*. New York: Macmillan, 1943.

—— *Reason and the Common Good: Selected Essays*, ed. W.H. Hay and M.G. Singer. Englewood Cliffs, NJ: Prentice-Hall, 1963. Contains a bibliography of Murphy's writings.

—— *The Theory of Practical Reason*, ed. A.I. Melden. La Salle, IL: Open Court, 1965.

—— *Reason, Reality, and Speculative Philosophy*, ed. Marcus G. Singer. Madison, WI: University of Wisconsin Press, 1996, with a memoir, introduction, and bibliographical notes.

MARCUS G. SINGER

MYSTICISM

A classic analysis of mysticism – and the most famous one undertaken by an American philosopher – is to be found in William James's *Varieties of Religious Experience*. James there wrote that "personal religious experience has its root and centre in mystical states of consciousness" (p. 301). He argued that these mystical states have certain characteristics that mark them off from other types of experiences. He claimed that all mystical states are ineffable and have a noetic quality, since they cannot be adequately described for those who have never felt them and since they seem to those who experience them to reveal deeply significant, nondiscursive truths. In addition, he claimed that most mystical states are marked by transiency (typically lasting only a few minutes) and passivity (with mystics reporting their wills being overcome during these experiences).

James pointed out that all the major world religions have mystical traditions within which mystical states are methodically cultivated. Hindu yoga, Buddhist meditation, Sufi practices, and Christian orison (meditation) are examples James cited. He observed that (despite their associations with religious traditions having widely diverging theologies) mystical states seem to lead to worldviews that are pantheistic, optimistic, anti-naturalistic, and other-worldly. He argued, further, that well-developed mystical states tend (legitimately) to convince the individuals experiencing them of the truth of these views, but that they do not seem to have the same effect for those who do not experience them. Yet even for these persons, James held, mystical states are valuable in that they open up new possibilities beyond the merely rationalistic consciousness.

Since James, Americans of widely divergent religious persuasions have continued to report mystical experiences, and researchers have made finer and finer distinctions among them. In academic philosophy, though, the general drift has been away from mysticism and supernaturalism toward naturalism.

Further reading

Bridges, Hal. *American Mysticism from William James to Zen*. New York: Harper and Row, 1970.

James, William. *The Varieties of Religious Experience*. Cambridge, MA: Harvard University Press, 1985.

JAMES O. PAWELSKI

MYTH OF THE GIVEN

The Given is the brute element of conscious experience. As an example, imagine someone seeing an apple. In her visual field, there is a red, apple-like impression. On the basis of this impression, this person may believe she sees an apple or that there is an apple before her. The Given is brute, then, in two ways: it is not a belief, but an experience, and it is something that the subject does not infer or otherwise derive, but is rather something she receives. The Given has significant intellectual consequences, since it is on the basis of our awareness of it that we know anything about the world.

The classic case for the Given proceeds on two fronts. The first front is the regress argument. In order to know, one must have good reasons. For those reasons to be good reasons, they must be true, and in order for us to reasonably believe they are good reasons, we must have further reasons. If reasons may not go on infinitely or in circles, there must be legitimate stopping places for reason-giving. There must be Givens in order for there to be knowledge. Experience provides these Givens in that subjects do not need to give further reasons for claims that they are having certain experiences – the fact of having the experience is not something one infers but is something one simply knows.

The second line of argument for the Given is the argument from illusion. For example, the subject may see a pencil half submerged in a glass of water. The pencil looks bent to her, and on the basis of that she may believe that the pencil is bent. She may be wrong about the pencil, but she is not wrong about how it looks to her. It may even be said that she cannot be wrong about how it looks to her, and that because she knows the way it looks, she believes that it is that way. So her awareness of how things appear to her precedes and grounds her knowledge of how things are.

A commitment to the Given, then, amounts to the following complex of theses: there is a brute element to experience that (1) is not a belief or something inferred, (2) is necessary for, or at least is a condition for, knowledge, and (3) is known more securely than and prior to our knowledge of the world.

Clarence Irving Lewis presented his views on the Given in *Mind and the World Order* (1929) and *An Analysis of Knowledge and Valuation* (1946). Lewis advanced the classic case for the Given in two areas. First, Lewis updated the regress argument with a technical argument that because our knowledge of the world is probabilistic, there must be a ground of certainty to give those probabilities definite values. Probabilities are not determined independently, but against a background of other things known. Those things known are either certain or probable, and if they are probable, they must also be determined by something else. Until these probabilities are determined by a certainty, they simply are not. Hence Lewis's dictum, "If anything is to be probable, then something must be certain." The Given element of experience, according to Lewis, is the source of these certainties.

Lewis's second advancement of the case for the Given was his account of how beliefs about the world are interpretations of the Given. That is, awareness of the Given not only yields reasons for our beliefs about the world, it is the very content of those beliefs. Lewis's thesis here is not only an epistemological thesis (one about the grounds for knowledge), but is a semantic thesis that all statements about the world are translatable into statements about future or possible experiences. What we mean when we talk about the world is entirely renderable in terms of statements about experience. The Given, then, was regularly associated with a program of phenomenalism as a theory of meaning for object terms. Those who reject phenomenalism, of course, question whether Lewis's innovation here is a real advancement.

Wilfrid Sellars criticized the theory of the Given in "Empiricism and the Philosophy of Mind" (1963). His argument was that the theory was an inconsistent set of theses: (1) sense experience is the ground for beliefs about the world, (2) sense experiences are not beliefs, and (3) beliefs are supported by reasons by being inferred (or inferable) from them. The problem, according to Sellars, is that (2) and (3) are in tension. If experiences are not beliefs, then how can they support beliefs as premises for inferences? That is, if experiences just are (but are not true or false like beliefs are), then they cannot play a role in an inference, since inferences are defined in terms of relations between the truth values of premises and conclusions. The very bruteness of experience prevents it from furnishing reasons. On the other hand, if experiences did have truth values, they would fail to be brute. The question, then, would be whether these are experiences or are our interpretations. Thereby, they could no longer end the regress of reasons.

Sellars' case against the Given further calls to question the thesis that knowledge of the Given is more secure than other knowledge. Sellars' challenge is that this security is bought less by the status of what is known in the two cases of knowledge and more by the content of what is claimed in the two cases. Seems-talk is highly attenuated talk, and as such is much more secure than is-talk, because much less is at stake with it. Seems-talk, in order to be certain, reduces claims to the point of being knowledge of effectively nothing.

Willard Van Orman Quine's case against the Given was that it was a consequence of the two driving dogmas of empiricism – that of the cleavage between analytic and synthetic statements and that of reductionism. In the place of these commitments Quine places holism, where sentences are not individually confirmed or disconfirmed, but rather face the tribunal of sense experience as a corporate body. There are not individual beliefs separately supported by discrete experiences. Donald Davidson argued that a third dogma drove commitments to the Given – that of a dualism between conceptual schemes and empirical contents. Such dualisms have experience stand in logical relations to beliefs. But the question is how they can. Experiences can certainly stand in causal relations to beliefs, but the only thing that can justify a person holding a belief is another belief. Experiences may explain our beliefs about the world, but they do not justify them.

Is the Given a myth? The primary defense of the Given is that if a version of the regress argument is right, then holding that the Given is a myth amounts to a general skepticism. If our beliefs cannot be brought to account before something other than our beliefs, then we have no reason to take our beliefs as accurate about the world. We live entirely within a circle of our beliefs. The Given, if objectivity is to be salvaged, is indispensable.

The role the Given plays in justifying a belief is the central concern of the challenges to the theory. One response is to take the justifying relation to be interpretive – there is some brute event in experience that we interpret, and our beliefs about what we have experienced are justified on the basis of the quality of the interpretation. The question, then, would be whether the quality of interpretation of the Given can be articulated independently of how that interpretation fits with our beliefs. If it is not, the Given cannot play the role required to solve the regress problem. A second strategy is to take the justifying relation between the Given and the belief to be internal. Experiences, as experiences, are not beliefs but are reasons to believe. The question, again, is how experiences can play the role of reasons without being beliefs. The only answer is that the requirement that only beliefs can be reasons is wrong – experience rationally constrains our beliefs not because of our beliefs about it, but because of its own intrinsic authority. We may have theories about the reliability or veracity of our experiences, but those theories come much later in the game of giving and asking for reasons. And our beliefs about the world, though often coordinated with those theories, clearly do not directly depend on them for all cases. The two determining factors for accepting or rejecting the Given, then, are whether conscious states other than beliefs can play the role of reasons, and, if so, whether brute experience lives up to the requirements of being such a source for reasons.

Further reading

Alston, William. "Sellars and the 'Myth of the Given'," *Philosophy and Phenomenological Research* 65, 1 (2002): 69–86.

Chisholm, Roderick. "Theory of Knowledge" in Richard Schlatter (ed.) *Philosophy*. Englewood Cliffs, NJ: Prentice Hall, 1964.

Davidson, Donald. "A Coherence Theory of Truth and Knowledge" in Ernest Leplore (ed.) *Truth and Interpretation*. New York: Blackwell, 1986, pp. 307–19.

Lewis, Clarence Irving. *Mind and the World Order: Outline of a Theory of Knowledge*. Mineola, NY: Dover, 1929.

—— *An Analysis of Knowledge and Valuation*. La Salle, IL: Open Court, 1946.

Quine, Willard Van Orman. "Two Dogmas of Empiricism" in *From a Logical Point of View*. New York: Harper, 1963.

Sellars, Wilfrid. "Empiricism and the Philosophy of Mind" in *Science, Perception, and Reality*. New York: Humanities Press, 1963.

Scott Forrest Aikin

N

NAGEL, ERNEST

Ernest Nagel was born in 1901 in Slovakia, then a part of Hungary. Nagel arrived in the United States in 1911 and became a citizen in 1919. He was for years one of the editors of *The Journal of Philosophy.* During the latter part of the twentieth century, Ernest Nagel was considered (by a British reviewer of one of his books) as one of America's two or three foremost philosophers. Because he was considered dispassionate and objective, he was chosen to moderate a projected (but never realized) national debate on the Viet Nam War.

Nagel's philosophy was distinguished by two phases. The earlier phase showed an emphasis on the rational structure, the objectivity, and the test of scientific conclusions. The later phase of Nagel's career found the logic, the method of inquiry, the objectivity, and the warrant for the conclusions of inquiry under attack.

Nagel's philosophy reflected the influence of Morris Cohen and John Dewey. Although he avoided calling himself a pragmatist, he did adhere to the pragmatist views of inquiry as propounded by Peirce and Dewey, where inquiry was begun by response to a problem. After reading Dewey's *Logic*, Nagel accepted Dewey's substitution of "warranted assertability" in place of "truth." Nagel, however, preferred to speak of "reliably warranted conclusions" and similar variants, avoiding the use of "truth," except when speaking in contexts (where others had introduced "truth") which required him to respond in conceptual kind.

The nineteenth-century view of science emphasized observation and eschewed hypotheses as frivolous speculation. With Cohen as co-author, Nagel produced *Logic and Scientific Method* which argued against a view that science was based solely on observation and that scientific laws are shorthand summaries derived from observations. As against the admonition to "study the facts, nothing but the facts," they pointed out the need for hypotheses. Second, they explained the deductive pattern of scientific explanation, distinguishing it from historical and genetic explanations and showed how scientific explanations function logically, enabling the deduction of the-fact-to-be-explained from the explanation. They also showed that the appropriate place for experience was in experimentally testing and verifying hypotheses. Much of this has become commonplace but in those days it was an important advance.

Nagel became interested in the logic of induction. His *Principles of the Theory of Probability* (1939) clarified probability, identifying it with the limits of relative frequencies. The warrant for any claim to knowledge involved the weight of evidence construed in terms of probability. Russell, Woodbridge, and Cohen thought that the laws of logic implied something about reality. On the other hand, some other empiricists like Mill believed that the laws of logic were generalizations from experience. Nagel refuted both claims.

If the laws of logic said something about an underlying reality, then they should be subject to empirical test and possible falsification. Nagel's analysis showed there was no way to specify the conditions for such a test that does not assume the laws being tested. If, as Mill and others thought, the laws of logic were empirical generalizations, then one should be willing to countenance that the laws *could be false*. But, followers of Mill were not willing to countenance that the laws of logic could be refuted by further experience. Hence the laws were not empirical.

Nagel's essay examined some of the so-called "laws of logic," namely, the Laws of Non-Contradiction, Excluded Middle, and Identity and interpreted them in terms of sentential logic, demonstrating *logically* that they were not three laws, but, instead, were variants of one tautology: namely, "If any sentence p is true, then the sentence p is true." His conclusion was that the laws of logic were just rules for intelligibly conducting discourse. You *ought not say* something was both true and was not true (at the same time and in the same respect). If you did, you would not be understood.

Nagel discussed science as an institutionalized art of inquiry, resulting in the achievement of generalized theoretical knowledge concerning fundamental determining conditions for the occurrence of various types of events and processes; the emancipation of men's minds from ancient superstitions in which barbarous practices and oppressive fears are often rooted; weakening the protective cover that the hard crust of unreasoned custom provides for moral and religious dogmas which support social injustices; and adopting, in domains previously closed to critical thought, logical methods for reliably assessing matters of fact or desirable policy.

Nagel again analyzed – but more intensively – the logical organization of scientific knowledge. Nagel discussed the difference between laws and theories, making a useful distinction between laws and theory; laws explain *facts*, whereas theories explain *laws*. This distinction was not arbitrary; it rested upon the different function each one performs. Unfortunately, this distinction has not taken hold, and (as Nagel himself noted) one can find indiscriminate use of "theory," even among scientists.

Nagel then ventured into the problem of counterfactual conditionals, the cognitive status of theories, and the problem of causality and indeterminism in physical theory arising from quantum theory.

According to Nagel, a scientific theory is "deterministic" with respect to a set of properties; if given a specification of the set at any initial time, a unique set of the properties for any other time can be deduced by means of the theory. He granted that quantum theory was not deterministic with respect to a state-description assumed to be defined in terms of positions and momenta as the state variables. But it did not follow that the theory is not deterministic with respect to a state-description differently defined. The Psi-function was of special importance. Given the values of the function for each point of a region at some initial instant, the Schrodinger wave-equation determines a unique set of values for the function at any other instant. Quantum mechanics was therefore a fully deterministic theory with respect to the quantum-mechanical state-description defined by a Psi-function.

Nagel's second phase

During the last quarter of the century there had been a many-pronged attack on the claim that the logic of scientific inquiry was the paramount instrument for achieving intellectual mastery of nature. Critics had produced arguments for doubting that "objective" and soundly based knowledge was really achieved in theoretical science; they doubted that scientific theories are ever accepted or rejected on the basis of *a "rational" evaluation of the evidence* for them. According to these critics, the belief in an "absolute" distinction between observation and theory was untenable. Observation statements are not unbiased formulations of supposedly "pure" materials of sensory experience, but involve interpretations placed on the sensory data. Nagel replied that the evidence for such a view is far from compelling. It would be idle to pretend, however, that there are no difficulties in drawing a distinction between observational and theoretical statements. For example, the observation reported by means of a telescope, theoretically assumes the laws of optics. Nagel did not know how to make such a distinction precise. Nevertheless, he said, because no sharp line can be drawn to mark off day from night does not make this, or similarly the other, distinction empty and useless.

Critics, moreover, doubted that there actually is anything like an identifiable "scientific method." Nagel also examined claims whose general import was to deny that scientific inquiry ever achieves genuine knowledge or employs determinate rules for evaluating the cognitive worth of its intellectual products. Feyerabend thought the growth of knowledge was best served by *rejecting* definite rules for the conduct of inquiry, For Nagel, however, these studies do not vitiate his contention that there was a certain logic to science. The task of logic is to make explicit *the structures of methods* and *assumptions employed* in the search for reliable knowledge in all fields of inquiry. So understood, logic articulates the principles implicit in *responsible critiques* of cognitive claims; but it also *assesses the authority* of such principles, and weighs the merits even of special postulates and intellectual tools (such as "instantaneous velocity" and other idealized conditions) that may be used in quests for knowledge.

The fallible character of scientific inquiry had become a commonplace. But, in the hands of Popper, this commonplace was being transformed into a paradox. The fallibility of inquiry became the basis for denying that claims to knowledge about any matter of fact are *ever* justified. The proper task of research was said by Popper to be "sincere" efforts to refute proposed answers to the problem initiating research. Nagel dubbed this as "*the search for uncertainty.*" There was a growing tendency, said Nagel, for scientists, as well as philosophers, to argue from the fallibility of scientific inquiry to a denial that claims to knowledge are *ever* warranted. Popper, a proponent of such a view, denied that science achieves genuine *knowledge* of any matters of fact, and claimed on the contrary that every assertion of science was "merely a guess" or "conjecture." Indeed, science was said to be "not interested" in establishing its conjectures or theories as either secure, certain, or probable, but only in criticizing them and testing them.

Nagel's response was two-fold. It consisted of: (1) an analysis of the criticisms and (2) a general judgment about the worth of the criticisms. His analyses showed idiosyncratic meanings given to terms like "hypotheses," "observation," "theoretical," and "knowledge"; and also showed unwarranted generalizations and unwarranted skepticism. Nagel found it perverse to inquire into an annoying problem with the intent to refute any proposed solution that might be offered, to be not interested in establishing its answers as secure, but only in criticizing and testing them. Nagel defended the view that in many domains of inquiry *we can and do possess genuine knowledge.*

Nagel's naturalism and humanism

Nagel said that philosophy at its best was a critical commentary upon existence and upon our claims to have knowledge of it. Its mission was to illuminate what is obscure in experience and its objects. Nagel added that there was no one "big thing" which, if known, would make everything else coherent and unlock the mystery of creation.

Naturalism merely formulates what centuries of human experience have repeatedly confirmed. It was a sound generalized account of the world encountered in practice and in critical reflection, and what he thought was a just perspective upon the human scene.

Two theses seemed to him central to naturalism. One was the existential and causal primacy of organized matter in the executive order of nature. It was one of the best-tested conclusions of experience. There was no place for disembodied forces, no place for an immaterial spirit directing the course of events, no place for the survival of personality after the corruption of the body. Nagel insisted that the variety of things, their qualities and their functions, are an irreducible feature of the cosmos, *not a deceptive appearance* cloaking some more homogeneous "ultimate reality,"

Naturalism had been repeatedly charged with insensitivity, with a Philistine blindness toward the ineradicable miseries of human existence. It seemed to Nagel singularly inept to indict naturalism as a philosophy without a sense for the tragic aspects of life. Naturalism offers no cosmic consolation for the unmerited defeats and undeserved sufferings which all men experience. As to the sorrows and evils to which we are now heirs, human reason is potent only against evils that are remediable, but it is impossible to decide antecedent to inquiry, which of the many human ills can be mitigated. Naturalism, although not a philosophy of renunciation, recognizes that it is wiser to be equably resigned to what, in the light of available evidence, cannot be avoided. The actual limitations of rational effort do not warrant a romantic philosophy of general despair and they do not blind naturalism to possibilities implicit in the exercise of disciplined reason for realizing human excellence.

Nagel explained that *philosophical* atheism is the denial of a belief in God as creator, omniscient, omnipotent, and benevolent. Nagel reformulated some of Hume's atheistic arguments within a Darwinian context. But his strongest criticism was of those who speak of the necessity of evil, or that evil is an illusion, or at worst only the "privation" or absence of good. Accordingly, evil is not "really real." Evil was only the product of our limited intelligence which fails to plumb the true character of God's creative bounty. But, said Nagel, facts are not altered by re-baptizing them. Evil may indeed be only an appearance and not genuine. But this does not eliminate from the realm of appearance the suffering which men so frequently endure. And it raises once more the problem of reconciling evil in the realm of appearance with God's alleged benevolence. It is small comfort to anyone suffering a cruel misfortune, to be told that what he was undergoing was only the absence of good. It was a gratuitous insult to mankind, a symptom of insensitivity to human suffering, to be assured that all the miseries men experience are only illusory.

Nagel said that atheists, pursuing the values of a liberal civilization, have played effective roles in attempts to rectify social injustices. Atheism cannot offer the incentives and consolations which theistic religions supply – no hope of personal immortality, no threats of Divine chastisement, no sure salvation. For on its view of the place of man in nature, human excellence and human dignity must be achieved within a finite lifespan or not at all, so that the rewards of moral endeavor must come from the quality of civilized living. Accordingly, atheistic moral reflection at its best is a vigorous call to intelligent activity for the sake of realizing human potentialities. Never pretending that human effort can invariably achieve the heart's every desire produces a tragic view of life in atheistic thought. This ingredient does not invite lamentation. But it does touch the atheist's view of man and his place in nature with an emotion that makes the philosophical atheist a kindred spirit to those who, within the framework of various religious traditions, have developed a serenely resigned attitude toward the inevitable tragedies of the human estate.

Further reading

Nagel, Ernest. *Sovereign Reason: And Other Studies in the Philosophy of Science*. Glencoe, IL: Free Press, 1954.

—— *Logic without Metaphysics: And Other Essays in the Philosophy of Science*. Glencoe, IL: Free Press, 1956.

—— *Teleology Revisited and Other Essays in the Philosophy and History of Science*. New York: Columbia University, 1979.

Nagel, Ernest and Cohen, Morris R. *Introduction to Logic and Scientific Method*. New York: Harcourt, Brace, 1934.

Angelo Juffras

NATURAL COMPLEX

In Justus Buchler's ontology, "natural complex" is the term of universal identification for any being. "Natural complex" enables reference to whatever is without assimilating it to a particular model of being (in contrast with, for example, "entity" or "a being," each of which assimilates what is referred to the model of a substance or an individual). Any being can be identified in more specific terms – such as entity, substance, process, individual, society, object, event, possibility, actuality, or relation – but in the most general or fundamental ontological terms it is a natural complex.

In characterizing every being as natural, the ontology affirms that all beings (complexes) are continuous with other complexes, that whatever is is not bifurcated into fundamentally disconnected and different realms of being (supernatural versus natural, spiritual versus material, mental versus physical, reality versus fiction). This is not a rejection of distinction between different kinds of beings, but rather, a claim that simply *qua* being, every kind of being is on a par with every other being; every being is a natural complex. This is not a rejection of the divine, although it is a rejection of a claim that God is more real than other beings. "If God were understood in part as that *complex of nature* [emphasis ours] which preserves overwhelming contrast with the finite, then to God might be ascribed perpetual consummations of a related kind" (Buchler, *Metaphysics of Natural Complexes*: 7). Theology, like biology and any other specific type of inquiry, discriminates a particular kind of subject matter (complex) in a particular way. But, if we want to know what it means to be, whatever the kind of being and however it exists, the answer on this view is, "to be is to be a natural complex." Nature encompasses whatever is – the divine, fictional entities, physical objects, relations, numbers, etc. "Natural" as an ontological term does not have a meaningful opposite. The history of the term has given it several contrasting terms (supernatural, non-natural, unnatural, artificial), not all of which are compatible with one another. But, in Buchler's view, anything designated as falling into one of those contrasting categories is, ontologically, a natural complex.

In characterizing every being as complex, the ontology affirms the indefinite ramifiability of whatever is. This is not a universal affirmation of vagueness. It is a claim that complexity is irreducible. When some particular kind of complex, for example an atom, can be broken down into sub-atomic parts (e.g. protons, electrons, neutrons), and those in turn to yet smaller parts, the claim of complexity entails: (1) that no part is ever purely simple (if it were, it would be traitless, and therefore unrelatable and unable to be a part of a composite); (2) that the allegedly simpler part is only simpler in relative terms; it will still have its own complexity (meaning plurality of traits, relations and locations); and (3) that complexity will obtain however far "down" the analysis goes. "Natural complex" signifies potential diversity and manyness within the unity of its reference (Buchler, *The Main of Light*: 104).

Further reading

Baeten, Elizabeth M. "An American Naturalist Account of Culture," *Metaphilosophy* 27, 4 (1996): 408–25.

Buchler, Justus. *The Main of Light: On the Concept of Poetry.* Oxford: Oxford University Press, 1974.
—— *Metaphysics of Natural Complexes*, second, expanded edition. Albany, NY: SUNY Press, 1990 [1966].
Corrington, Robert S. "Conversation between Justus Buchler and Robert S. Corrington," *Journal of Speculative Philosophy* 3 (1989): 261–74.
Marsoobian, Armen, Wallace, Kathleen, and Corrington, Robert S. *Nature's Perspectives: Prospects for Ordinal Metaphysics.* Albany, NY: SUNY Press, 1991 (contains bibliography of secondary literature through 1991).
Singer, Beth J. "Systematic Nonfoundationalism: The Philosophy of Justus Buchler," *Journal of Speculative Philosophy* 7, 3 (1993): 191–205.
Wallace, Kathleen. "Ontological Parity and/or Ordinality?" *Metaphilosophy* 30, 4 (1999): 302–18.

KATHLEEN WALLACE

NATURAL RIGHTS

In the history of political thought natural rights theory is most closely associated with John Locke, although as Brian Tierney has shown, the idea had been formed much earlier and some, for example Fred D. Miller, Jr, even hold that Aristotle was already considering certain issues in terms of them. The crucial function of the qualifier "natural" is that these rights, however understood, are supposed to derive from an understanding of human nature. Given that human beings are basically free and independent, argued Locke, they all (in virtue of their human nature) possess the right to their person and estate within human communities – what we would now call to life and property. As he put it,

> there being nothing more evident, than that creatures of the same species and rank, promiscuously born to all the same advantages of nature, and the use of the same faculties, should also be equal one amongst another without subordination or subjection.

He adds,

> The state of nature has a law of nature to govern it, which obliges every one: and reason, which is that law, teaches all mankind, who will but consult it, that being all equal and independent, no one ought to harm another in his life, health, liberty, or possessions: for men being all the workmanship of one omnipotent, and infinitely wise maker; all the servants of one sovereign master, sent into the world by his order, and about his business; they are his property, whose workmanship they are, made to last during his, not one another's pleasure: and being furnished with like faculties, sharing all in one community of nature, there cannot be supposed any such subordination among us, that may authorize us to destroy one another, as if we were made for one another's uses, as the inferior ranks of creatures are for our's.

A right then, in this context, is a sphere of personal authority or jurisdiction, wherein someone is supposed to be sovereign or self-governing. Accordingly, having such rights by virtue of their human nature would imply that no one may violate them with impunity. The American founders succinctly expressed this idea in the Declaration of Independence by noting that everyone is created equal in so far as everyone – "all men" – have the right to, among other things, life, liberty, and the pursuit of happiness. The inclusion of a Bill of Rights in the US Constitution – and subsequently, in terms of "human rights," in numerous other political and legal documents across the world – shows the strong influence of Locke's theory, even though in time the type of rights ascribed to people changed somewhat from those Locke believed everyone possesses. (See "Rights.")

Locke's idea was that because human beings are distinctive living beings by virtue of their capacity for free choice and independent conduct – they can govern themselves and need to do so properly, as guided by reason – everyone in a community needs what another, contemporary natural rights theorist, the late Robert Nozick, called, "moral space." This is a sphere or region of personal jurisdiction, one which others may only enter with the rights possessor's permission.

The idea of these natural rights came to dominance in political theory along with the idea of individualism, the notion that it is not the society, family, tribe, race or nation that needs to be guarded most by legal institutions but individual human beings. Given that these human beings are subject to moral evaluation – their conduct can be deemed ethically or morally right or wrong – such moral evaluation would be distorted if other people had the legitimate power over them, interfering with how they conduct themselves. So even in the course of political affairs, every individual must give his or her consent so that others will be properly authorized to govern them. (Again, the Declaration of Independence has significant wording indicating this implication of natural rights theory.)

As it is now explained, John Locke understood rights as involving mostly that they are prohibitions on other people interfering with what someone is doing. Both oneself and one's property – anything from nature with which one has mixed one's labor, according to Locke – may only be treated by the person, not others, unless these others gained one's consent or agreement. In a complicated society the legal system – first the basic law or constitution and following it all the great variety of laws – must accord with the basic rights everyone possesses. Although matters can become very complex, the idea is that if these basic, natural rights are something everyone does in fact possess, then these implications can be worked out by legislatures and the courts and a society developed in which all citizens will be treated as free and independent, as their nature requires.

Natural rights theory was very influential as well as widely criticized, especially by those who believed that society's laws must serve the common or general good and not focus on protecting individuals and their liberty. Among the critics, one who is most remembered is the English jurist and philosopher Jeremy Bentham, who said, famously,

> Right is the child of law; from real law come real rights; but from imaginary laws, from "law of nature," come imaginary rights ... Natural rights is simple nonsense; natural and imprescriptible rights (an American phrase) ... [is] rhetorical nonsense, nonsense upon stilts.

Other prominent political thinkers agreed. For example, David Hume believed that both natural law and natural rights are mythical, "metaphysical" fictions.

More importantly, there were those, such as Thomas H. Green and later many defenders of the welfare state, who believe that Locke failed to make room for positive rights, meaning rights to provisions from others, especially important to those who were not favored by circumstances, who were poor and needy. For example, while the rights Locke spelled out, to life and property, would secure for the reasonably well-off a sphere of liberty, others, such as members of the working class, would need special rights to being provided with care and consideration – for example, a minimum wage, health care, education – so as to enjoy a fruitful, flourishing life.

In America two influential voices, Josiah Royce's and John Dewey's, also found fault with the individualist natural rights stance that came from John Locke and found such favor with the American founders. Royce's position was the more radical challenge because of its emphasis on the greater importance of the "whole," which could be interpreted as a kind of anti-individualism or even collectivism whereby individuals must be loyal to a greater entity, humanity or society, instead of to the best prospects in their lives. Dewey, in turn, believed that individualism in this tradition is a kind of ideology or even dogma, disguising certain motives as universal truths. By "ideology" Dewey had in mind a notion that arises from Hegel and Marx, namely, a kind of rationalization for certain special interests, so in a sense Dewey is questioning the authenticity of Locke and others, just as Marx did. This is done, often unintentionally, by the thinker. Yet it serves a purpose that is quite different from what it appears to serve, namely, the general or common good or unacknowledged interests.

Defenders of the Lockean idea responded to these kinds of criticisms by noting, first of all, that any talk of positive rights amounted to undermining the rights to liberty and property and that if some in a society required special care, this must come from voluntary help, not labor that is conscripted and property that's confiscated. It is especially Locke's and his followers' support of an unqualified, basic right to private property that divided the two factions, those supporting negative rights and those favoring positive rights. And the dispute has surfaced most prominently within the context of political economy and those societies that have found inspiration in the American experience. Should they follow the stricter Lockean idea that can be used to support a substantially, even completely, laissez-faire capitalist political economic order or should they follow a modified version we call today the welfare state or, in Europe, "the Third Way" (one between capitalism and socialism)?

There is no doubt that the natural rights tradition of political thought rejects the idea that some great whole such as humanity or society is of superior value to the value of the individuals who make up that whole. Society is not some entity, nor is humanity. They are concepts usefully deployed in certain circumstances, but when they are fully unpacked what emerges is that they refer in reality ultimately to large groups of human individuals. The individual, the natural rights defenders will claim, is still the fundamental being and value in political theory.

As to the charge of "ideology" when it comes not only to natural rights theorizing but theorizing of any type, it has the problem of self-referential inconsistency – those making the claim that some viewpoint is no more than ideology (an expression of some hidden or not so hidden special agenda of, say, the rich or the powerful) can also be indicted for laying out a position that advances some special interest – e.g. of idealists, revolutionaries, the power hungry, *et al.* In more general terms, calling some view an ideology fails to come to terms with its arguments and indulges in a kind of psychologizing or even character assassination. If one finds fault with natural rights theory, why not compare it with other theories and consider which is the more successful for purposes of guiding human community life? Natural rights theorists tend to hold that their theory rests on a realistic conception of human nature, that human beings are indeed primarily individuals, which means mainly that they must use their own minds to address problems in the world, including the problem of how best to relate to one another.

Although during the twentieth century the pure capitalist system fared badly, because many historians, rightly or wrongly, have linked the great depression and other economic ills in society to it, by the end of the twentieth and beginning of the twenty-first centuries capitalism, with its idea of strict protection of private property rights (privatization) and freedom of contract, resurfaced because of socialism's demise in the Soviet bloc and the faltering economic performance of some Western European welfare states.

The Lockean tradition has continued to enjoy some strong support among prominent economists – Ludwig von Mises, F.A. Hayek, Milton Friedman – and some political philosophers – the late Robert Nozick, Ayn Rand, Anthony Flew, John Hospers, *et al.* – but in practical, public policies issues the welfare state – supported by a far larger number of thinkers, such as the late John Rawls and most of his followers (e.g. James P. Sterba) – has had greater presence throughout Western liberal countries.

More recently the Lockean idea has come under criticism and out-and-out hostility from those who have criticized Western political and legal institutions for failing to promote traditional Christian, Muslim or related religious virtues, for their so-called licentiousness and official indifference to abuses of the right to liberty (for example, gambling, divorce, homosexuality, drug abuse, hedonism, etc.). With the stress on protecting the individual's rights to life, liberty, property, pursuit of happiness, privacy and so forth, Western countries supposedly encourage atheism, infidelity, and vice, and governments look the other way when people become corrupt and violate God's laws.

This line of criticism of Western liberalism is resisted by the more or less Lockean liberals among contemporary political thinkers on such grounds that vice and virtue have no meaning in a society in which there is no individual liberty – only free men and women have the chance at morally significant conduct. If one denies people their Lockean rights, they are no moral agents but merely followers of the commands of others, something that deprives them of the chance to do either what is morally right or wrong conduct.

It is difficult to imagine a future in which the natural rights tradition will have no influence, at least as a standard of political and legal institutions serving as a source of serious debate and criticism of various societies. The era when legal systems, governments, law and order amounted to a fully top-down regime, with the population kept silent and inert by powerful monarchs, dictators, families, and even parties, seems to be largely past, although there is, of course, considerable evidence of them in many parts of the world. But those parts are seriously threatened as viable human institutional arrangements by developments in thinking and institutions that have been clearly influenced by the Lockean natural rights position. Globalization, women's equality, the abolition of slavery in all of its forms, the limitation on government power and similar trends are among these and it is difficult to imagine them not continuing to make an impact across the world.

Further reading

Bentham, Jeremy. *An Introduction to the Principles of Morals and Legislation*, ed. J.H. Burns and H.L.A. Hart. London: Athlone Press, 1970.

Dworkin, Ronald. *Taking Rights Seriously*. Cambridge, MA: Harvard University Press, 1977.

Locke, John. *The Second Treatise of Government*. New York: Barnes and Noble, 1966.

Machan, Tibor R. *Individuals and Their Rights*. Chicago, IL: Open Court, 1989.

Miller, Fred D., Jr. *Nature, Justice, and Natural Rights in Aristotle's Politics*. Oxford: Clarendon Press, 1995.

Nozick, Robert. *Anarchy, State, and Utopia*. New York: Basic Books, 1974.

Rasmussen, Douglas and Den Uyl, Douglas. *Norms of Liberty*. University Park, PA: Pennsylvania University Press, 2005.

Shue, Henry. *Basic Rights: Subsistence, Affluence, and U.S. Foreign Policy*. Princeton, NJ: Princeton University Press, 1980.

Tierney, Brian. *The Idea of Natural Rights: Studies on Natural Rights, Natural Law and Church Law*. Atlanta, GA: Scholars Press, 1997.

TIBOR MACHAN

NATURAL SELECTION

Natural selection is an essential feature of biological evolution depicted in Darwin's theory of the evolution of biological species (1859), and can be contrasted with artificial selection in agriculture and animal husbandry. Post-Darwinian biology theorizes that evolution of species progresses by means of three essential processes: variation, inheritance, and selection. Darwin did not fully understand genetic variation and inheritance. It was only in the early twentieth century, with the rediscovery of Gregor Mendel's research into genetic inheritance (1866), that genetic variation and inheritance were incorporated into modern evolutionary theory. Nevertheless, to Darwin's credit, his conception of evolution was based on the view that selection takes place only within populations of reproductive individuals that are slightly different from one another. Individuals with characteristics that give them an advantage in staying alive long enough to reproduce are those that pass on their traits more readily to subsequent generations whereby their traits become more common. A population will evolve to the extent that inherited traits are new and different from past characteristic traits of members of the population. Entirely new species may eventually emerge if these cumulative modifications are sufficiently substantial.

Darwin's view of natural selection was keyed to his observation of populations of Galápagos finches distributed over different isolated environments. His assumption was that variations exist among South American finches as a matter of course, and the different environments on the islands afforded lesser reproductive potential to individuals whose peculiar anatomical traits were not well suited to specific food sources available in those respective environments. Over many generations, these different isolated environments exerted respectively different selection pressures that favored different anatomical traits (e.g. different beak shapes).

In general, while not as efficient as carefully controlled artificial selection (namely, culling and segregation of individuals so that they are not able to reproduce), the mechanism of natural selection is largely the same. The selection pressures are instead effected by natural processes such as predation, disease, and abundance or scarcity of accessible food, water, and other resources needed for survival. These natural selection pressures may be particularly subtle; for example, in a given island environment, abundant foods may be accessible to long-beaked finches but not to short-beaked finches so that shortness-of-beak would be culled from the characteristic traits of the island population over the course of many generations.

It is important to note that Darwin neither originated nor ever used the phrase "survival of the fittest" in his theory of natural selection. That idea was first used by Herbert Spencer as an evolutionary metaphor in economics (1851). Darwin's concept of natural selection might be better sloganized as a theory of "non-survival (for better or worse) of the ecologically unlucky."

A significant challenge for this view of evolution has been to give a naturalistic account of the evolutionary origins of traits like thought and self-consciousness as it occurs in human beings. Among American philosophers, an early attempt to meet this challenge was made by Chauncey Wright (1873). A later attempt is found in George Herbert Mead's evolutionary social psychology (1956). This challenge was not so salient for Charles Peirce's evolutionary cosmology (1888, 1893). His concern with natural selection was rather to ascertain its consistency with his triadic system of categories, which he does at one point by associating variation with chance, hence firstness; inheritance with compulsion, hence secondness; and selection with generalization, hence thirdness.

Further reading

Darwin, Charles. *On the Origin of Species by Means of Natural Selection*. London: John Murray, 1859.

Dewey, John. *The Influence of Darwin on Philosophy, and Other Essays in Contemporary Thought*. New York: Henry Holt, 1910. Critical edition with an introduction by Douglas Browning, Carbondale, IL: Southern Illinois University Press, 2007.

Mead, George Herbert. *On Social Psychology*, ed. Anselm Strauss. Chicago, IL: University of Chicago Press, 1956.

Mendel, Gregor, "Versuche über Pflanzen-Hybriden," *Verhandlungen des naturforschenden Vereines in Brünn* 4 (1866): 3–47. First English translation, *Journal of the Royal Horticultural Society* 26 (1901): 1–32; reprinted in *Experiments in Plant Hybridization*. Cambridge, MA: Harvard University Press, 1967.

Peirce, Charles S. "A Guess at the Riddle," unpublished notes, 1888. Reprinted in *The Essential Peirce*, Vol. 1, ed. Nathan Houser and Christian Kloesel. Indianapolis, IN: University of Indiana Press, 1992, Ch. 19.

Spencer, Herbert. *Social Statics, or The Conditions Essential to Happiness Specified, and the First of them Developed*. London: John Chapman, 1851.

Wright, Chauncey. "The Evolution of Self-Consciousness" in his *Philosophical Discussions*. New York: Henry Holt, 1877. Originally published in the *North American Review*, April 1873.

Tom Burke

NATURALISM

American naturalism is one of the most distinguished accomplishments in philosophy in more than a century, and it might in time prove to be one of the great achievements in all the modern era. It began, indeed, largely as a response to the incoherencies endemic to modern philosophy, principally as propagated by the philosophy of Descartes. It was also ignited by developments in science, above all those occasioned by the theories of Charles Darwin, which demanded a rethinking of our assumptions about the nature of man and the nature of nature. Perhaps most fundamentally, naturalism grew out of the emerging intellectual temper that demanded of any cognitive claim, including those of philosophy, that it be testable in publicly experimental conditions.

Its two greatest exponents have been George Santayana, especially in his five-volume masterpiece, *The Life of Reason* (1905–6) and John Dewey, whose philosophy is most systematically set forth in the magisterial *Experience and Nature* (1925, 1929). The works of both these men largely define American naturalism, and they have had a profound impact on hundreds of successors and many thousands of readers. (Among the most conspicuous precursors and successors are Ralph Waldo Emerson, C.S. Peirce, William James, F.J.E. Woodbridge, J.H. Randall, Jr., and Justus Buchler.)

Both thinkers strived to develop a comprehensive theory of the nature of nature and of man's status within this encompassing whole. Each insisted that any such theory be faithful to the disclosures of science and to the fullness of life experience. Neither meant by "experience" the contrived and theoretical abstractions that enfeebled modern philosophy, where it had been portrayed as a mass of inherently unrelated and subjective atoms of sensation. They meant the vital activities undergone and undertaken by living human beings through all phases of their endeavor and aspiration. Accordingly, even a remotely adequate philosophy of nature must deliver an account of mind, science, art, religion, language, social and political life, moral life and striving as emergent of nature; and the range and depth of the qualities exhibited in all such endeavors must be fully intelligible as traits of nature – not as subjective phenomena wholly other than nature.

In the terms of modern philosophy, however, such ambitions are inherently impossible to satisfy. Cartesian philosophy holds that nature is nothing but matter in motion. Hence all characteristics of experience are expelled from nature. The putative external world can have none of the swarm of glories, horrors, moral and aesthetic affections, loves, hatreds, miseries, aspirations and triumphs that define and give meaning to human existence. Experience has no access to nature; so science itself becomes an insoluble mystery. To compound the obfuscations, the experience of any given individual has no access to any other individual. What a fine mess this is! – at least for any philosopher who would bring intelligibility and the possibility of direction to human life. Both Santayana and Dewey held that the entire point of philosophy is to bring clarity, resource, wisdom, and ideal values within the ken of human existence. So they recounted the insuperable difficulties of modern philosophy and argued that they were owing to the unwarranted assumptions basic to the entire enterprise. Hence each of the two philosophies is an epochal undertaking.

Inspired by Plato and Aristotle, *The Life of Reason* is devoted to the discernment of ideal goods as they might occur and be fulfilled in all of the main endeavors of human practice. The entire project cannot begin without ridding ourselves of the prevailing philosophies of nature. Santayana brings to the task what he calls the Aristotelian principle, according to which ". . . everything ideal has a natural basis and everything natural an ideal development." (*Reason in Common Sense,* vol. I of *The Life of Reason,* Triton edition of *The Works of George Santayana,* vol. III, p. 28.) In stark contrast to modern dualisms, this is an assertion of continuities in nature; at the same time it is a principle of resource, for it implies that there are specific relations in nature from origins to fulfillments. Hence ideals become the object of experimental inquiry and enabling practice.

Throughout the five volumes, Santayana is brilliant in the discrimination of ideal values and the disciplines needful for their achievement. To be sure, ideal outcomes could not be declared ideal if there were no human beings with love for deeply fulfilling ends, but this fact does not make ends unnatural or non-natural. Rather, ends (and all other qualities) exhibit nature's potentialities under distinctive conditions. So it is with all events in nature: their existence is dependent upon a particular confluence of natural processes. Without such a confluence, the existence would not occur. Except for his metaphor, when Santayana says "Nature is a perfect garden of ideals" (Ibid., p. 216.), he speaks literal truth and remains wholly naturalistic.

Likewise, in his naturalism, Santayana does not resort to the postulation of inherently complete faculties in human nature. True to the Aristotelian principle, he contends in some detail that the distinctive functions and excellences of human nature are derivative of the instincts of a living creature attempting to survive in a perilous but potentially supportive environment. In sum, the ideas of nature and human nature have become unified. Just as Dewey would later propound in greater detail, the two do not stand in lonely isolation from each other. Human being emerges from the womb of mother nature and is thereafter nurtured and shaped by the natural environment. Such budding ideas in American naturalism have proved richer and more fecund by far than any that could be derived from the Cartesian legacy; and the idea of nature has become far more efficacious in conduct.

Although greatly admiring the Greeks, Dewey also found in them the source of the fundamental problems of modern philosophy: the assumption that the object of rational knowledge, as such, alone constitutes the really real. Here, "rational knowledge" means "attained by reason alone, free of any contribution by the senses." The really real is complete, changeless, and perfect being; all else is appearance. Dewey came to regard this assumption as the defining constituent of the entire classic tradition, as he called it. Not only is such "rational" knowledge unverifiable, but in constituting complete being it is bound to lead to a reductive and incomplete philosophy of nature. Notoriously, Descartes takes it as rational knowledge that nature is extension in motion. Therefore, in accordance with the classic tradition, it can be nothing else, and all the unresolvable perplexities of modern philosophy follow abjectly. A naturalist, in contrast, embraces the overwhelming evidence that nature is unimaginably prolific and varying.

Dewey's tasks were several: to overturn the classic tradition, to digest the profusion and luxuriance of nature into a few salient and especially fateful traits (each of which would receive extensive analysis), to discern the instrumentalities of nature with a view to the enhancement of human life, and to identify and celebrate the most conspicuous goods that nature affords. He does not use the expression "Aristotelian principle," but the principle is operative in all his work.

There are many similarities and some differences between Santayana and Dewey, and they can be examined with great benefit. American naturalism owes much to these progenitors, but as any naturalist will gladly affirm, this is a philosophy that can be pursued much further, that can introduce themes not hitherto prominent, and that can contend with the novelties and surprises that appear in history. We may reasonably expect that the heritage will continue to fructify.

JAMES GUINLOCK

Further reading

Dewey, John. *Experience and Nature,* in *John Dewey: The Later Works, 1925–195.* Volume I: 1925, edited by Jo Ann Boydston with an Introduction by Sidney Hook. Carbondale and Edwardsville, IL: Southern Illinois University Press; London and Amsterdam: Feffer and Simons, Inc.: 1981.

Krikorian, Yervant H. (ed.). *Naturalism and the Human Spirit*. New York: Columbia University Press, 1944.

Santayana, George. *The Life of Reason.* Triton edition, 5 volumes. New York: Charles Scribner's Sons, 1936.

NATURALIZED EPISTEMOLOGY

Naturalized epistemology is the theory that epistemology and science are continuous with each other. Generally, this means that science can help address traditional epistemological problems, particularly concerning the justification of true beliefs. Naturalized epistemology therefore rejects the traditional idea that epistemology can be done a priori, or without some sort of empirical data. Still, not all naturalists agree on the best way of applying science to epistemology and, as a result, naturalized epistemology includes a range of different projects.

While naturalistic themes can be traced to the pragmatism of Peirce, James, and Dewey, among others, contemporary naturalized epistemology arose in response to two developments in the 1960s. One was the need to analyze the concept of knowledge, sparked by Gettier's celebrated problem; the second was the publication of Quine's essay "Epistemology Naturalized" (1969).

Emergence of contemporary naturalized epistemology

In 1963, Edmund Gettier published "Is Justified True Belief Knowledge?" In concluding that knowledge requires more than simply having a justified true belief, Gettier spawned numerous alternative accounts of the concept of knowledge. Among these was Alvin Goldman's "A Causal Theory of Knowing" (1967). Here Goldman argued that knowledge requires a causal connection between a particular belief and the circumstances that make that belief true. For example, on Goldman's account, if a person knows that it is raining, then this is because the fact that it is raining caused the person to form this belief. (Of course, in many cases the causal chain will be more complex and less direct.) Later, Goldman refined his theory to require that specific belief-forming processes reliably, and not just accidentally, produce true beliefs. Such a reliabilistic theory defines knowledge in terms of reliable belief-forming processes which psychology and cognitive science can describe. Thus, these solutions to Gettier's problem point to a naturalized epistemology which incorporates results from scientific fields.

At the same time W.V.O. Quine was also proposing that epistemology be naturalized, although for different reasons. In his influential essay "Epistemology Naturalized" (1969), Quine noted that epistemologists seemed incapable of refuting the skeptical claim that knowledge is impossible. In particular, Quine argued, epistemologists had failed to provide science with an incontrovertible foundation: for example, they had failed to show how scientific statements could be logically deduced from sense experience. For this reason, Quine claimed, epistemologists should abandon the search for incontrovertible foundations and instead examine how, in fact, scientific theories arise out of particular experiences. Once again, this would be a job for psychology and related fields. Once epistemology stops trying to refute skepticism, Quine concluded, it can pursue empirical questions that are best answered scientifically.

Responses to naturalized epistemology

As it emerged in the late 1960s, naturalized epistemology was a radical departure from traditional epistemology. By focusing on the actual processes that generate true beliefs, naturalized epistemology changed how traditional epistemological problems were addressed. Naturalized epistemology suggested that the methods of traditional epistemology, and in particular its reliance on a priori theorizing, were either incapable of solving epistemological problems or complicit in their apparent insolubility. Not surprisingly, this provoked a number of strong responses to naturalized epistemology.

For one thing, causal and reliabilist theories of justification would imply that, if justification depends solely on how a belief is produced, then it does not matter if the believer has any conscious reason for thinking that belief is true. In other words, all that matters is whether the belief is properly connected to some external state of affairs, and it would not matter whether the believer is aware of these connections. This would mean that a person could have a justified belief even if she had no reason to think the belief justified, and even if she had reasons to think it unjustified – just so long as her belief was, in fact, the result of a reliable belief-forming process. But this implication strikes many as deeply mistaken since it would separate justification from the process of giving reasons and citing evidence that has been a central epistemological concern. This problem is at the center of the debate between internalists, who emphasize the epistemological importance of internally accessible factors (such as reasons), and externalists, who emphasize instead the importance of objective, external relationships between particular beliefs and actual states of affairs.

Quine's naturalized epistemology faces a similar objection. Traditionally, epistemology has been a normative discipline: for example, it has attempted to identify the conditions under which one *should* hold a certain belief. From this perspective, a scientific description of how people do come by their beliefs sheds little light on how they should. Quine's proposal, that epistemology become a "chapter of psychology" that studies "inputs" and "outputs," eliminates the normative questions of whether a belief is reasonable, permissible, or responsibly held. But these still appear to be valid and important questions. As a result, Quine's naturalized epistemology apparently goes too far in its rejection of traditional epistemology.

Varieties of naturalized epistemology

As a result of these and related criticisms it is important to distinguish between different versions of naturalized epistemology. Some naturalists are willing to embrace naturalism's most radical and controversial implications. These naturalists, often called "eliminativists," follow Quine in claiming that epistemology, as a philosophical discipline, can and should be eliminated in favor of scientific studies of human cognition.

Other naturalists take a less radical position and argue that epistemology must be reducible to science even if it should not be entirely eliminated. According to these naturalists, often called "reductivists," it should be possible to define normative epistemological terms in a descriptive scientific language. If that were so, epistemology and cognitive science would run parallel with, and frequently cross over into, each other. A variation on reductivism is to show that epistemological concepts supervene on naturalistic concepts.

Finally, some naturalists take an even more modest position and argue only that science may be relevant, in some circumstances, to addressing epistemological questions. These naturalists (whom we might call "minimalists," in contrast to the naturalists described above) argue that scientific evidence showing how humans do reason is relevant to deciding how humans should reason. For example, if an epistemological theory were to set the standard for knowledge so high that no human, given the empirical limits of the human brain, could ever have knowledge, then these naturalists would argue that this epistemological theory is fatally flawed. Similarly, recent empirical work has shown that many of the intuitions supporting contemporary epistemology are not, in fact, as intuitive as many epistemologists suppose. For instance, variants of the Gettier problem seem to elicit different intuitions depending on one's ethnicity and socioeconomic status. If that is so, then it is futile to draw normative conclusions based on "our" intuitions. In these ways minimalists question the distinction between normative epistemology and descriptive empirical science, though without reducing one to the other.

Historical roots of naturalized epistemology

Looking at the American philosophical tradition, pragmatists developed versions of naturalized epistemology well before that term came into use, thus making pragmatism one of the historical precursors of contemporary naturalized epistemology. Like contemporary naturalists, pragmatists distrusted a priori theorizing, valued the results of scientific inquiry, and paid attention to actual practice as a way of addressing philosophical problems. Peirce, for example, is famous for his attack on the "a priori method" of justifying beliefs and for his support of the empirical "scientific method." Other pragmatists, such as James and Mead, used science, particularly psychology, to address traditionally philosophical questions of perception, cognition, and knowledge. Dewey's *Logic: The Theory of Inquiry*, published in 1938, is a full-blown naturalized epistemology. In it Dewey argues that epistemological principles are the product of specific inquiries designed to solve real-life problems. According to Dewey, not only do these epistemological principles emerge in response to specific concrete problems, and are thus not a priori, but we accept these principles because they succeed in solving these and other problems. For this reason epistemology and science are continuous with each other: both are fundamentally concerned with finding ways of solving real problems and improving human lives.

A pragmatic naturalized epistemology, such as the one Dewey defended, avoids many of the problems associated with eliminativism and reductivism. In particular, because it stresses the instrumental character of both science and epistemology, it avoids eliminating or reducing epistemological concepts to a supposedly more real level of scientific concepts. Instead, a pragmatic naturalized epistemology argues for the non-reductive continuity between epistemology and science, and in this way augments a minimal naturalized epistemology. On the one hand, this means that descriptive science can have normative implications: for example, by setting limits on what we should reasonably require of responsible human knowers. So, since science is one of our most effective means of gaining knowledge, epistemology can learn much by studying its results and methods. On the other hand, the continuity of epistemology and science still leaves an important role for epistemology. Because the ultimate purpose of science is to recognize and solve concrete problems, and not simply accumulate true beliefs, epistemology can shed light on how science can best address a wide range of natural, social, and practical problems. The flipside of naturalizing epistemology is therefore recognizing the normative potential already implicit in scientific practice. In this way a pragmatic naturalized epistemology can encourage both epistemology that is scientifically informed and science that is explicitly concerned with improving human lives.

Further reading

BonJour, Laurence. "Externalist Theories of Empirical Knowledge" in Peter French, Theodore E. Uehling, and Howard Wettstein (eds) *Midwest Studies in Philosophy*, Vol. 5. Minneapolis, MN: University of Minnesota Press, 1980, pp. 53–73.

Dewey, John. *Logic: The Theory of Inquiry.* New York: Henry Holt, 1938.

Goldman, Alvin. "What is Justified Belief?" in George Pappas (ed.) *Justification and Knowledge.* Dordrecht: Reidel, 1979, pp. 1–23.

Kim, Jaegwon. "What is 'Naturalized Epistemology'?" in Hilary Kornblith (ed.) *Naturalizing Epistemology*, second edition. Cambridge, MA: MIT Press, 1994, pp. 33–55.

Kitcher, Philip. "The Naturalists Return," *Philosophical Review* 101, 1 (1992): 53–114.

Kornblith, Hilary. *Naturalizing Epistemology*, second edition, Cambridge, MA: MIT Press, 1994.

Putnam, Hilary. "Why Reason Can't Be Naturalized," *Synthese* 52 (1982): 1–23.

Quine, W.V.O. "Epistemology Naturalized" in his *Ontological Relativity and Other Essays.* New York: Columbia University Press, 1969, pp. 69–90.

Weinberg, Jonathan M., Nichols, Shaun, and Stich, Stephen. "Normativity and Epistemic Intuitions," *Philosophical Topics* 29, 1 and 2 (2001): 429–60.

John Capps

NATURE

Two views of nature dominated early America: the broadly economic picture of a land waiting to provide resources to the industrious, and the religious vision of nature as a dark, ominous place from which the Elect must shelter their souls. Though at variance, these pictures rarely clashed. While the broadly economic approach continued unabated, however, the religious vision became transformed. The cities of man (perhaps through their commitment to raw commerce) began to appear as dark and invidious places while nature assumed high, transcendent value. Previously negated, nature had come full circle. It was now sacred.

This transformation was in part engendered by the Enlightenment concept of nature as constrained by universal laws and thus devoid of miracles or evil presences. Nevertheless, it was against this Enlightenment view (stressed by the founders of the American constitution) that those who came to sacralize nature rebelled. The Transcendentalist movement, whose chief proponents were Ralph Waldo Emerson (1803–82) and Henry David Thoreau (1817–62), denied the scientific standpoint and focused instead on a broadly poetic and idealist concept of nature. The Transcendentalists, though educated in philosophy, wrote outside of universities and came to be considered (somewhat narrowly) as literary thinkers.

The Transcendentalists reached a remarkably broad, diverse public. The result was a mixed attitude towards nature. Nature romanticism marched hand in hand with the goals of economic exploitation. Given the vastness of the continent, a relatively small population and the limits of technology, only slowly did it become clear that the nation's economic thrust was in sharp conflict with wilderness and the religious values now associated with it. Awareness of this conflict was created by artists like John James Audubon (1785–1851) and writers like John Burroughs (1837–1921), who acted as the environmental educators of the American people. Activist environmentalists like John Muir (1838–1914) functioned as prophets, waking the public from its slumber, pleading for the saving of nature's cathedrals.

The end of the land frontier and exhaustion of forest and other resources around 1890 finally sparked the first broadscale environmental moment in the United States. This movement, termed Resource Conservation Environmentalism, is linked with the names of Teddy Roosevelt (1858–1919) and Gifford Pinchot (1865–1946). Though criticized as "anthropocentric," this view led to the creation of both the National Park Service and the National Forest Service and marked a real change in commonsense attitudes toward nature, which was no longer viewed as inexhaustible. A consensus emerged, according to which, if for economic reasons alone, nature's resources would have to be looked after.

Environmental and economic views of nature were to compete again in the twentieth century. During World War I and in the extended boom which was to follow it, environmentalism was once again submerged. The coming of the Great Depression, however, brought with it a renewed interest in the environment. The ideas behind "New Deal" environmental programs, however, were little different from those of Theodore Roosevelt and Pinchot. Nature's resources were to be conserved for human benefit alone. Dams and hydroelectric plants appeared alongside new national parks.

After the Second World War, under the pressures of a new, massive production technology, increasing world population and spiraling pollution, this emphasis changed. This shift can be found in many writers at this time (around and following 1950). The most influential of these was Aldo Leopold (1887–1947).

Leopold's *A Sand County Almanac* (1949) in several ways broke with prior environmental axioms. He expressed his views in broadly anthropological terms. Arguing that environmental problems now constituted a crisis for the human race, he proclaimed that technology alone could not resolve pressing dilemmas and insisted that a new ethics was needed. This ethics involved a concern for the land *per se*, a thesis which moved beyond anthropocentrism towards an "ecocentric" viewpoint. Leopold's views were more strongly influenced by the new science of ecology than were those of previous environmentalists.

Others were to proceed similarly. The Norwegian philosopher Arne Naess (1912–) was to sharpen the distinction between man-centered ("shallow") and "deep" (nature-centered) ecology. The church historian Lynn White, Jr (1907–87) in a famous essay argued that the deepest roots of our environmental problems lie in the radically anthropocentric nature of Western religion. These ideas, as they began to attract a popular audience, were to have repercussions among philosophers. The first book of purely philosophical essays on man and nature, William T. Blackstone's (edited) *Philosophy and Environmental Crisis*, appeared in 1974. The first philosophical journal to deal exclusively with broadly environmental issues, *Environmental Ethics*, appeared in 1979. Not until the seventh decade of the twentieth century did academic philosophy in the United States begin to take nature seriously.

The first academic environmental philosophers, in spite of their disagreements, were united in the belief that environmental problems were the result of a fundamental philosophical error: that of placing man above and outside of nature while viewing nature as essentially valueless. This green axiom was to be debated and by many to be modified or abandoned. Nonetheless, it provided a rallying-point for the environmental "isms" which emerged in the 1980s: ecofeminism, green economics, ecoanarchism, green mysticism, environmental ethics, bioregionalism. It also provided a viewpoint from which the history of Western philosophy could be reexamined in terms of its treatment of man–nature relationships. In general René Descartes was criticized, Baruch Benedict Spinoza valorized.

A developing environmental movement in league with the diversity of environmental thinkers was to achieve significant successes in the protection of species, ecosystems, air and water. But both the successes and the rhetoric of the environmentalists led to a strong backlash. The far right responded angrily that environmentalists were "green terrorists," frightening the public with ill-founded doomsday scenarios. The far left quickly typed environmentalist thinkers as "green bigots", protecting wilderness without concern for the people who live there. Social constructivists objected that the very notion of nature is a human fabrication having no counterpart in fact.

The United States had passed through and in part assimilated various concepts of nature. In each case these concepts competed with, sometimes fought against, and sometimes coincided with economics-centered views of the physical world. None of these "environmental" views achieved complete dominance. Economics-centered and environmentally centered concepts continue to play themselves out in American life, taking on new forms in every epoch.

Further reading

Oelschaeger, Max. *The Idea of Wilderness: From Prehistory to the Age of Ecology.* New Haven, CT: Yale University Press, 1991.

Shabecoff, Phillip. *A Fierce Green Fire: The American Environmental Movement*. New York: Hill and Wang, 1993.

Thoreau, Henry David. *Walden and Resistance to Civil Government*, second edition. New York: W.W. Norton, 1992.

PETE A.Y. GUNTER

NECESSITY

The concept of necessity, like the corresponding modal notion of possibility, has been examined by American philosophers from different perspectives. Logicians and philosophers of language study its logico-semantic aspects, while metaphysicians construct ontological theories about necessity. Classical American thinkers, including the pragmatists, also critically discussed necessity, but modal investigations have particularly flourished in the analytic tradition.

Logical necessity

From a logical point of view, necessity (like possibility) is a logical operator used to prefix a sentence: "Necessarily, *p*." What exactly such sentences state, and how they logically behave, has been a matter of dispute. Twentieth-century American philosophers made lasting contributions to modal logic and possible worlds semantics, uncovering crucial logical features of modal sentences and languages. C.I. Lewis's, Saul Kripke's, Jaakko Hintikka's, Alvin Plantinga's, and David Lewis's well-known theories continue to be examined.

The logical approaches to necessity, which historically go back to Leibniz, employ the notion of a possible world. The sentence (or proposition) *p* is necessarily true, in a narrow sense, if its denial is self-contradictory; in a broader sense, *p* is necessarily true if true in all possible worlds. Correspondingly, *p* is necessarily false (expresses an impossible proposition) if false in all possible worlds, i.e. if there is no possible world in which it is true. However, it is controversial which system of modal logic should be preferred. Moreover, necessity should not be conflated with epistemic concepts such as self-evidence or a priori knowability; complex mathematical truths, for instance, are far from self-evident, yet necessary.

Metaphysical necessity

The logico-semantic properties of modal notions have robustly metaphysical bearings, though not all philosophers are willing to extend the scope of their modal analyses from logic to ontology. The distinction between *de re* and *de dicto* modalities has been debated in American philosophy. *De re* necessities are properties a thing necessarily (essentially) has, properties it has in every possible world (where it exists), while *de dicto* necessities are necessarily true sentences (propositions). Thus, *de re* necessities are ascribed to properties (attributes) of things, whereas *de dicto* necessities are ascribed to what is said. However, a necessary proposition can be said to have (*de re*) the property of being true essentially.

The sentence, "The number of apostles is necessarily greater than ten" (given that there were twelve apostles) is false if read *de dicto*, because it is contingent that there were twelve apostles, but true if read *de re*, as a statement about a necessary property of the number twelve, which could not have failed to be greater than ten. In cases like this, it is crucial to notice the difference between *de re* and *de dicto* modalities.

Contrary to metaphysicians like Plantinga who endorse *de re* necessities and individual essences, American thinkers preferring more austere ontologies, most notably W.V. Quine, attack the very idea of *de re* necessity, also rejecting modal logic and possible worlds semantics, because they fail to satisfy the requirements of extensionalism (viz. the substitutability *salva veritate* of any constituent expressions of any sentence by coreferential ones). Quine finds ontologically seriously intended talk about the necessary properties of things conceptually muddled. Only *de dicto* necessity is allowed in his philosophy of science. Things can be specified in different ways by means of different descriptions; there are no properties that metaphysically belong to an exclusive set of those essential to a thing.

Among modal metaphysicians, David Lewis held a bold theory asserting the existence of all possible worlds, characterized as comprehensive concrete entities spatiotemporally and causally distinct from each other. This possibilist view is very different from the actualist modal realism defended by Plantinga, for whom possible worlds are actually existing abstract entities, maximally comprehensive possible states of affairs. Plantinga argues that Lewis's possibilism does not make sense of modal notions any more than Quine's rejection of them does.

While the distinction between logical and metaphysical problems of necessity seems clear, it is debatable whether there are interesting differences (and if so, what kind) between logical, conceptual, metaphysical, and physical (causal, nomic) necessities. Logical necessity can simply be defined as logical truth (in some system of logic), while physical necessities are something that the laws of nature nomically necessitate. It is physically but not logically necessary that heavy bodies fall. Are there, between these forms of necessity, intermediary ones, such as "metaphysical" or "conceptual" necessities? Kripkean necessary identities, e.g. "Water is H_2O," are paradigmatic examples of allegedly metaphysical necessities, derivable from neither logical rules (or the meanings of words) nor mere contingent laws of nature. Philosophers disagree, however, over whether, say, the sentence "Every human person has a body" expresses a necessary truth, and if so, which kind of a necessary truth.

Further issues

A perennial problem, examined voluminously by American thinkers, is the question concerning the existence of a necessary being. The existence of such a being, traditionally identified with God, has sometimes been regarded as demonstrably true. (There might be necessary beings other than God, e.g. numbers, universals, or the world itself.) Among American philosophers, Plantinga is one of the few who defends a version of the ontological proof of the existence of God, an argument traceable to the eleventh-century thinker St Anselm. In a modal formulation in Plantinga's style, the proposition that there is a necessary being is reached through a reasoning starting from the concepts of necessity and possibility. If it is acknowledged that a necessary being possibly exists, then there is a possible world in which it exists. However, to be a necessary being is to exist in all possible worlds. Consequently, if there is a possible world in which a necessary being exists, then, necessarily, this being exists in all possible worlds. *Ergo*, a necessary being exists.

The argument is controversial. Even if one accepts its premises, including the definition of a necessary being as a being existing in all possible worlds, it demonstrates only that the existence of such a being is either necessary or impossible. In any case, the metaphysics of necessity has often been studied in close relation to the philosophy of religion.

Among classical American thinkers, Charles Peirce rejected what he called necessitarianism, arguing that there are real chances in the evolutionary development of the universe. This anti-necessitarian view is known as his tychism. The dispute over necessitarianism – better, determinism – is, however, only indirectly related to the concept of necessity, as discussed by analytic philosophers.

A critique of various kinds of necessity assumptions extends throughout the tradition of pragmatism. American pragmatists, early and late, have argued that the necessary (metaphysical) truths philosophers have traditionally defended are contingent, historically contextualized assumptions that may be given up. Richard Rorty's neopragmatism is a case in point; it is no accident that Rorty's attack on the necessity assumptions of the metaphysical and epistemological tradition is partly derived from Quine's criticisms of essentialism and *de re* modalities. For pragmatists generally, necessity is something that arises out of the practices of inquiry, instead of being either a logical or a metaphysical principle prior to inquiry.

Further reading

Hintikka, Jaakko. *Models for Modalities*. Dordrecht: Reidel, 1969.

Kim, Jaegwon and Sosa, Ernest (eds) *Metaphysics: An Anthology*. Malden, MA: Blackwell, 1998.

Kripke, Saul. *Naming and Necessity*. Cambridge, MA: Harvard University Press, 1980.

Lewis, David. *On the Plurality of Worlds*. Oxford: Blackwell, 1986.

Loux, Michael J. *Metaphysics: A Contemporary Introduction*, second edition. London and New York: Routledge, 2002.

Peirce, Charles S. *The Essential Peirce: Selected Philosophical Writings*, 2 vols, ed. the Peirce Edition Project. Bloomington, IN: Indiana University Press, 1992–8.

Plantinga, Alvin. *Essays on the Metaphysics of Modality*, ed. Mathew Davidson. Oxford: Oxford University Press, 2002.

Quine, W.V.O. *Word and Object*. Cambridge, MA: MIT Press, 1960.

Rorty, Richard. *Philosophy and the Mirror of Nature*. Princeton, NJ: Princeton University Press, 1979.

Sleeper, Ralph W. *The Necessity of Pragmatism: John Dewey's Conception of Philosophy*. New Haven, CT: Yale University Press, 1986.

SAMI PIHLSTRÖM

NEO-PRAGMATISM

After the flourishing of classical pragmatism early in the twentieth century, the American pragmatist tradition almost disappeared from the philosophical scene during the mid-century heyday of logical empiricism and its descendant, analytic philosophy. After the 1970s, pragmatism made a comeback, however. It has become customary to refer to this revival of pragmatism – a revival by no means restricted to the work of American philosophers – as "neo-pragmatism." The leading figures of this new pragmatism are Hilary Putnam (1926–) and Richard Rorty (1931–). These neo-pragmatists' writings have also stimulated new scholarly interest in the classical pragmatists, whom the neo-pragmatists are sometimes argued to misinterpret, though.

An important background for neo-pragmatism is W.V. Quine's article, "Two Dogmas of Empiricism" (1951). Quine argued, through his famous criticism of *the analytic/synthetic distinction*, for a "shift toward pragmatism," claiming to represent a "more thorough pragmatism" than his teachers Rudolf Carnap and C.I. Lewis had done in their essentially pragmatic treatments of the "external" (contextually a priori) questions about the choice of a linguistic framework. Quine's place in the pragmatist tradition is unclear, and he seldom mentions pragmatism in his later works, but he did influence most of the later neo-pragmatists. Also, his *naturalism*, urging a continuity between science and philosophy, was Deweyan in spirit, if not in letter.

Rorty: pragmatism as anti-representationalism

Rorty's *Philosophy and the Mirror of Nature* (1979), as well as his subsequent collections of papers (e.g. 1982, 1998), articulate a radical neo-pragmatist vision of a *"post-philosophical" culture* in which an "edifying" discussion has replaced the traditional systematic, argumentative pursuit of theoretical solutions to well-defined philosophical problems. This is not the end of philosophy as an intellectual activity, but it is meant to be the end of a certain conception of philosophy, the ancient ideal of a search for eternal truths. According to Rorty, we just have to live within our contingent, temporary, insecure human projects and practices without having epistemological or metaphysical guarantees of their success – of our ever being able to reach final truths about reality *per se*. No vocabulary is more intimately connected with the way the world is "in itself" than any other.

Rorty's pragmatism is flatly *anti-representationalist*: neither language nor the mind can (or should) accurately represent the independent world; it cannot even be meaningfully asked whether they do or do not. Such questions belong to the history of systematic, epistemology-centered philosophy, which should now be over. The notion of representation, yielding traditional philosophical puzzles such as skepticism and the problem of realism vs idealism, ought to be given up. The philosophical problems of the past are "optional," not necessarily forced on us. The Rortyan pragmatist follows thinkers like John Dewey and Ludwig Wittgenstein in treating language as a tool, serving a variety of human purposes, rather than a means for accurate representation, a "mirror" of reality. Our task is to cope with the world, not to represent it. Dewey and Wittgenstein (among others) have also taught us how to live without the Cartesian problems of securing a foundation for knowledge and understanding the metaphysical nature of the mind.

Traditional philosophical concepts, including *truth* and *reality*, require revision in Rortyan neo-pragmatism. Truth cannot be understood in terms of the correspondence theory but must be thoroughly deflated. Rorty follows another influential American philosopher, Donald Davidson (controversially reading him, too, as a pragmatist), in regarding truth as an unanalyzable notion which should not be "defined" at all. The basic virtue of pragmatist accounts of truth, for Rorty, is that they abandon age-old philosophical attempts to uncover the timeless essence of truth.

The Rortyan pragmatist, then, celebrates active experimental efforts to find previously unforeseen ways of speaking, new innovative vocabularies, instead of efforts to accurately represent "the way things are." Thus, the scientific pursuit of truth is also seen as a search for new innovative descriptions, not a matter of getting closer to privileged representations about the World or Nature itself. Science no more mirrors reality than any other human practices or vocabularies do. Still, vocabularies can be compared in terms of their ability to help us cope with the world we live in.

Philosophy, for Rorty, is not (as Plato, Descartes, and Kant in their various ways thought) a transcendental "super-science" critically and normatively systematizing all other forms of culture, laying metaphysical and methodological foundations for other forms of inquiry, but only one way of using language among others. There is no specifically philosophical methodology apart from the "method" of open, unbiased conversation. The pragmatist philosopher's aims are deconstructive and therapeutical rather than constructive or theoretical.

Putnam: pragmatic realism

Rorty has several followers, but many neo-pragmatists are critical of his program. A major neo-pragmatist dialog in the 1980–1990s was the one between Rorty and Putnam. Against Rorty's anti-representationalist pragmatism, Putnam (1994, 1995) argues that while metaphysical realism and the correspondence theory of truth must be rejected (and the tradition of pragmatism is full of insights that should be taken into account here), the notions of truth and representation cannot be deflated in Rorty's manner. On the contrary, we pragmatically need a substantial notion of truth.

Putnam agrees with Rorty that there is no humanly meaningful way to speak about a reality absolutely independent of our languages, vocabularies, concepts, or practices, and that correspondence-theoretical notions of truth and accurate representation ought to be abandoned. However, he wants to steer a middle course between metaphysical realism and the kind of *relativism* or *anti-realism* he sees as the inevitable result of Rorty's neo-pragmatism. In particular, Rortyan anti-representationalism sacrifices the crucial *normative* aspects of language-use. In defending the irreducible normativity of linguistic practices, Putnam's neo-pragmatism is also indebted to Wittgenstein's later philosophy. For a Putnamian pragmatist, truth, representation, and epistemic justification are always tied to our historically changing practices – that is, the metaphysically realist dream of a "view from nowhere" is absurd. Yet, they are not immanent to any particular practice but require transcending one's own point of view.

Having frequently changed his opinions on the realism issue, Putnam continues to defend a "pragmatic realism" which in his view maintains everything that is worth maintaining in both realism and pragmatism. The pragmatic realist acknowledges the phenomenon of *conceptual relativity*, i.e. that there is no metaphysically privileged way of using existential expressions (e.g. "there is/are" or the existential quantifier), while defending the moderately realist and anti-relativist view that the truth of sentences is *not* determined by a paradigm, a culture, or the consensus of language-users. We are answerable to a reality distant from us – even if there is no "ready-made world" metaphysically pre-categorized independently of our practice-embedded categories and conceptualizations. Putnam also insists on applying the concept of truth to ethical and more generally normative statements, thus defending a pragmatically articulated moral realism.

Rorty's views, according to Putnam, lead to relativism, or even to "cultural solipsism." The Rortyan cannot in the end distinguish "being right" from thinking that one is right. Rorty, however, has responded that his pragmatism is not relativistic but *ethnocentrist*, simply admitting that "we have to start from where we are," from within our present framework – which, for Rorty, is the cultural situation of "us Western liberals." From Putnam's perspective, this leads to a kind of cultural imperialism, making normative, critical discussion across cultures impossible; according to Rorty, Putnam's attempt to save, albeit in pragmatist terms, a culture-invariant notion of truth is a remnant of the philosophical tradition that has exhausted itself. Hence, Rorty's pragmatism is, for Putnam, too extreme, whereas Putnam's is, for Rorty, only half-baked.

Other neo-pragmatists

The Putnam–Rorty exchange has largely mapped the territory of neo-pragmatism. Some neo-pragmatists defend and elaborate on Rortyan views, while others try to synthesize pragmatism and realism in a manner closer to Putnam's.

Joseph Margolis's complex neo-pragmatism, closely related to his *constructivism* and *historicism*, emphasizes the irreducible normativity of "second-order" questions of legitimation, resisting the kind of deflationary assimilation of philosophy to "first-order" (empirical) inquiry typical of both Rortyan pragmatism and radical (Quinean) naturalism (e.g. Margolis 2002). Susan Haack (1998), in turn, has charged Rorty for giving up the very concept of inquiry. Nicholas Rescher (2000) defends a *methodological pragmatism* based on an underlying realist metaphysics and idealist epistemology. Morton White has, for more than half a century, defended a *pragmatic holism* similar to Quine's but more inclusively and tolerantly incorporating ethical sentences in the holistic web of empirical testing (see White 2002).

Although neo-pragmatism gradually emerged, through Quine's and his followers' work, as a synthesis of pragmatism and analytic philosophy (even Putnam and Rorty were originally purely analytic philosophers), the standard division between "analytic" and "Continental" thought has largely been overcome in neo-pragmatism (cf. Eggington and Sandbothe 2004). Neo-pragmatists sometimes describe themselves as "post-analytic" thinkers, equally responsive both to analytic discussions of realism, truth, reference, etc., and Continental, particularly French, treatments of postmodernism, deconstruction, etc. Another distinction, the one between the history of philosophy and systematic philosophy, is also criticized by a number of neo-pragmatists. Instead of taking such a sharp dichotomy for granted, it is possible to philosophize historically, making pragmatic use of the ideas of past philosophers, including the old pragmatists.

The influence of Wittgenstein on neo-pragmatism also demonstrates the richness and versatility of the pragmatist tradition – and has even led to new scholarly interest in Wittgenstein's historical relations to the pragmatist tradition. By taking seriously the Kantian background of both Wittgenstein and classical pragmatism, neo-pragmatism might fruitfully integrate, in a reinterpreted manner, very different philosophical orientations, including philosophical anthropology and transcendental philosophy (cf. Pihlström 1998, 2003). Several as yet unexplored philosophical and/or historical comparisons (from a neo-pragmatist perspective) between pragmatism and other philosophical schools are possible. Neo-pragmatism must, thus, still be pragmatically evaluated.

Neo-pragmatism and classical pragmatism

It must be asked whether the neo-pragmatists, especially Putnam and Rorty, have further developed the central concepts and conceptions of the American pragmatist tradition, or whether they misrepresent the classical pragmatists' views. That they have done the latter rather than the former has been claimed by several scholars of pragmatism. Critics argue that the basically sound ideas of classical pragmatism, such as its attack on metaphysical realism and foundationalist epistemology, are carried into implausibly radical extremes in Rorty's "postmodern" pragmatism.

The major division in twentieth-century philosophy known as the "linguistic turn" is also crucial here: the old pragmatists, working before this mid-century shift of focus, primarily discussed experience and cognition, while neo-pragmatists like Rorty and Putnam talk about language, vocabularies, or conceptual schemes. Pragmatists more faithful to the classics have tried to restore the old pragmatists' richer, less language-bound conception of experience (see Hildebrand 2003 for a defense of Dewey against Putnam's and especially Rorty's mischaracterizations). Rorty, on the other hand, is satisfied with developing a merely "hypothetical" (post-linguistic-turn) Dewey, caring little about the historical accuracy of his interpretations.

Some contemporary philosophers seem to have a mission of defending characteristically Peircean realist neo-pragmatism, criticizing the more Jamesian and Deweyan – relativist or constructivist rather than realist – brands of pragmatism on offer in the on-going evaluation of Putnamian and Rortyan neo-pragmatisms (e.g. Haack 1998; Rescher 2000). The debate over the significance of neo-pragmatism, and more generally of pragmatism as such, old and new, thus continues – inspired by (and inspiring) both historical interpretations of classical pragmatists' and their critics' views and systematic philosophical treatments of issues such as realism, relativism, and truth. A tension between realism and anti-realism might even be claimed to be *a* (not *the*) unifying theme in the entire pragmatist tradition.

Accordingly, the tradition of pragmatism, far from being closed or fixed once and for all, stays open and evolves through the continuing argumentative telling and retelling of the story of pragmatism (Bernstein 1995), including the debates over how pragmatism ought to be properly defined, who should be included in the pragmatist camp, and on which grounds. While it remains unclear whether, say, Rorty's neo-pragmatism is "really" a form of pragmatism, the very fact that this question is often asked in philosophical studies of the pragmatist tradition already partly (re)articulates this tradition by regarding its identity open for innovative redescriptions.

Neo-pragmatism has been institutionalized by a journal, *Contemporary Pragmatism* (inaugural issue in 2004), and the website "Pragmatism Cybrary" (www.pragmatism.org), both largely thanks to John Shook's initiatives.

Further reading

Bernstein, Richard. "American Pragmatism: The Conflict of Narratives" in Herman J. Saatkamp, Jr (ed.) *Rorty and Pragmatism: The Philosopher Responds to His Critics.* Nashville, TN: Vanderbilt University Press, 1995.

Dickstein, Morris (ed.). *The Revival of Pragmatism: New Essays on Social Thought, Law, and Culture.* Durham, NC: Duke University Press, 1998.

Eggington, William and Sandbothe, Mike (eds). *The Pragmatic Turn in Contemporary Philosophy: Contemporary Engagements between Analytic and Continental Thought.* Albany, NY: SUNY Press, 2004.

Haack, Susan. "Pragmatism, Old and New," *Contemporary Pragmatism* 1 (2004): 3–41.

Hildebrand, David L. *Beyond Realism and Antirealism: Dewey and the Neopragmatists.* Nashville, TN: Vanderbilt University Press, 2003.

Kuklick, Bruce. *A History of Philosophy in America: 1720–2000.* Oxford: Oxford University Press, 2001.

Margolis, Joseph. *Reinventing Pragmatism: American Philosophy at the End of the Twentieth Century.* Ithaca, NY: Cornell University Press, 2002.

Pihlström, Sami. *Naturalizing the Transcendental: A Pragmatic View.* Amherst, NY: Prometheus/Humanity Books, 2003.

Putnam, Hilary. *Pragmatism: An Open Question.* Oxford: Blackwell, 1995.

Rescher, Nicholas. *Realistic Pragmatism: An Introduction to Pragmatic Philosophy.* Albany, NY: SUNY Press, 2000.

Rorty, Richard. *Truth and Progress.* Cambridge: Cambridge University Press, 1998.

Shook, John R. (ed.). *Pragmatic Naturalism and Realism.* Amherst, NY: Prometheus Books, 2003.

White, Morton. *A Philosophy of Culture: The Scope of Holistic Pragmatism.* Princeton, NJ: Princeton University Press, 2002.

Sami Pihlström

NEO-REALISM

By the end of the nineteenth century both idealism and the Cartesian dualism of mind and matter were in marked eclipse. The ascendance of natural science in general, and empirical psychology in particular, helped naturalistic and realist accounts of perception and cognition overthrow the specter of "mind-stuff." The dominant realism, representational realism, traced its lineage from Locke to Russell, who argued that mind-independent reality is accessed only indirectly, via "sense-data" or "appearances." Notoriously vulnerable to skepticism and charges of subjectivism, some pursued a direct approach where knowledge requires no such intermediaries. The American counterpart to G.E. Moore's "naïve" realism, neo-realism gained popularity during the first two decades of the twentieth century.

The neo-realists were Ralph Barton Perry and Edward B. Holt from Harvard, W.P. Montague and Walter B. Pitkin from Columbia, Walter T. Marvin from Rutgers, and Princeton's Edward Gleason Spaulding. Inspired by the collaborative practices of physics and chemistry, in 1910 they issued a "Program and Platform of Six Realists" – a series of separately signed statements expressing a common view.

The position itself is disarmingly simple. While admitting that anything known must be known in relation to a knower, neo-realism insists the act of knowing is "eliminable." As Perry phrases it, the act of cognition is "transparent" – consciousness *selects* from a field of existences it does not *create.* Traditional realists trap themselves in the "egocentric predicament" by trying to get a known sense datum to "correspond" to its unknown (and perhaps unknowable) object, when in fact "one knows truly because one's knowledge merges into its object." They further grope for an "epistemology" capable of connecting mind-independent existences to mind-dependent percepts, when in fact only a logic of *external relations* is needed: For any relation (R) *a*R*b*, *a*R does not constitute *b,* R*b* does not constitute *a,* and R does not constitute *a* or *b.* Having explicated this formal relation, the philosopher readily yields to the scientist: epistemological problems thus become empirical questions about how a real external object relates to a real central nervous system.

In advancing the claims of external relations, the neo-realists were specifically targeting the ubiquitous *internal* relations of idealists such as Bradley, for whom Relation, as self-consciousness, "penetrates" both cognition and its objects. Yet the most trenchant criticism came not from idealists but from pragmatists such as John Dewey and representational realists such as Durant Drake. Dewey initially accused the neo-realists of forcing a formal theory of relations onto actual objects or events, and assumed *a* and *b* were like unalterable Leibnizian monads. Spaulding denied this, insisting that neo-realism agrees with pragmatism that one entity can causally affect another, and that inquiry can help bring about such changes. Nonetheless, inquiry must presuppose certain brute existential "givens" and at least one logical "given" – the theory of external relations. Dewey balked at this – to posit a priori ontological and logical "givens" not only smacks of the purportedly discredited idealism, but creates a new refuge for "epistemology." According to Dewey, the pragmatist who affirms that existential and logical relations alike are determined *within* patterns of inquiry – and for whom there are no reals beyond experienceable reals – is the authentic direct realist.

Drake deployed classic objections to common-sense realism against its newest instantiation. He argued, first, that for all its devotional claims to science, neo-realism is out of step with both physics and physiology. The perceived light of a distant star is not just given as it is in the star itself, it is the relic of an object that left its object years ago and perhaps no longer even exists. Second, neo-realism defies our empirical understanding of cause and effect by permitting the "reverse projection" of phenomena: where common sense and science both tell us that, e.g. a dark room only appears to grow brighter as our eyes adjust to the light, if reality is exactly as it is perceived the room itself must be getting brighter! And the same, of course, would hold for any experience normally dismissed an illusion or hallucination. Finally, and the culmination of these difficulties, is the problem of truth: If reality is always perceived exactly as it is, then how could we be wrong about anything or ever entertain false beliefs?

By the mid 1920s, neo-realism was overtaken by critical realism – a view that retains the representational axiom that cognition is *interpretive* but leans toward naturalism and physicalism to avoid charges of subjectivism. Neo- or "new" realism has enjoyed periodic revivals, however. In 1990 Hilary Putnam traded at least part of his internal realism for one directly inspired by the "program and platform" realists. Elements of neo-realism are also evident in blind realism, which holds that some of our beliefs must grasp how things actually are, though in deference to the problem of truth we are never certain which beliefs these are. It also survives in reliabilist claims that a belief factually aligned with a state of affairs is sufficient for knowledge, without the further requirement of having to justify the relation.

Further reading

Conant, James, and Zeglen, Urszula M. *Hilary Putnam: Pragmatism and Realism*. London and New York: Routledge, 2002.

de Waal, Cornellis (ed.). *American New Realism: 1910–1920*. Bristol: Thoemmes Press, 2001.

Dewey, John. "The Short-Cut to Realism Examined," *Journal of Philosophy, Psychology, and Scientific Methods* 7 (1910): 553–7.

Drake, Durant. "A Cul-de-Sac for Realism," *Journal of Philosophy, Psychology, and Scientific Methods* 14 (1917): 365–73.

Holt, Edwin B., Marvin, Walter T., Montague, W.P., Perry, Ralph Barton, Pitkin, Walter B., and Spaulding, E.G. "The Program and Platform of Six Realists," *Journal of Philosophy, Psychology, and Scientific Methods* 7 (1910): 138–42.

Frank X. Ryan

NEVILLE, ROBERT CUMMINGS

Robert Cummings Neville was born 1 May 1939 in St Louis, Missouri. He received a PhD in philosophy at Yale University (1963). Neville has held teaching and administrative positions at Yale (1963–5), Fordham University (1965–71), SUNY Purchase (1971–7), SUNY Stony Brook (1977–87), and Boston University (1987–). He served as a Hastings Institute Associate for behavioral sciences specializing in behavior control and psychosurgery (1968–71). Neville has been President of the Metaphysical Society of America (1989), President of the American Academy of Religion (1992), President of the International Society for Chinese Philosophy (1993), and a member of numerous other professional and service groups. He was ordained as Deacon in the United Methodist Church in 1963, and as an Elder in 1966.

Development of Neville's thought

Neville's work has revolved around metaphysics and themes in philosophical theology. In his first book, *God the Creator* (1968), he articulated a theory of divine creation *ex nihilo* that interprets divine transcendence in terms of God being wholly indeterminate apart from creation and immanence as creativity within the determinate harmonies of creation. While this theory is well suited to solving many classical metaphysical problems, especially the problem of the one and the many and the problem of divine transcendence and immanence, the radical immanence of God in creation presents a challenge to human freedom. Neville's work in the social sciences through the Hastings Center and the philosophical influences of Whitehead and Dewey led him to a theory of freedom in three parts: personal, social, and spiritual freedom. This was published in *Cosmology of Freedom* (1974) and applied in *Soldier, Sage, Saint* (1978). Complementing these works was his critique of the metaphysics of process thought in *Creativity and God* (1980).

In 1981, Neville began his "Axiology of Thinking" series, a three-volume work of systematic philosophy articulating the thesis that all thinking is valuing. The series begins with a critique of modern philosophy's attempts to be value-free and postmodern philosophy's futile attempts to avoid theory construction. Neville offers detailed treatments of four kinds of valuing-thinking: imagination, interpretation, theorizing, and the pursuit of responsibility. The Axiology of Thinking evolves symbiotically with a philosophy of nature that treats the natural world as intrinsically valuable, leading to causal theories of imagination and interpretation. The accounts of theorizing and responsibility integrate Confucian and Western philosophical themes.

Neville's interest in comparative religion, already evident in the argument of *God the Creator*, has produced a series of writings. These works continue the metaphysics of his first book while exploring the connections between abstract metaphysics and social-political philosophy. They exhibit a special interest in Chinese philosophy. *The Tao and the Daimon* (1982) examines many East–West themes in comparative fashion, including the problem of multiple religious identities. *Behind the Masks of God* (1991) continues this project with special emphasis on the treatment of religious thought in the field of religious studies. *The Puritan Smile* (1987) is a work at the intersection of comparative metaphysics and practical philosophy. *Boston Confucianism* (2000) epitomizes Neville's attempt to synthesize Western and Confucian thought.

The Highroad around Modernism (1992) argues that the pragmatic tradition of American philosophy has no need to escape from the problems of modernist, foundationalist philosophy because its founders (especially Peirce and Dewey) diagnosed and avoided them. *Eternity and Time's Flow* (1993) furnishes an account of a major religious theme while continuing the interest in freedom by situating the problem of personal responsibility in the context of the theory of creation. *The Truth of Broken Symbols* (1996) uses a naturalistic epistemology to develop an interpretation of religious experience and the practice of religion. It applies a semiotic theory in the style of Peirce to the problem of religious symbolism. *Symbols of Jesus* (2001) and *The Scope and Truth of Theology* (2006) begin a long-term project, as yet unfinished, aiming to interpret the symbols of major religious traditions in a demythologized way that does full justice to their practical imaginative power.

Central ideas

Neville's system of philosophy addresses many of the central Western philosophical problems of metaphysics, epistemology, ethics, aesthetics, political theory, and philosophical theology. The chief characteristics of the system are its engagement of East Asian and South Asian philosophical traditions; its concern to do justice to conditions of plausibility drawn from the sciences and religion; its stylistic range from highly abstract metaphysics to concrete applications in religion, education, and bioethics; its thoroughgoing naturalism; and its indebtedness to pragmatic and process philosophical traditions.

Neville centralizes the idea of valuing, which indicates his indebtedness to the various Platonic traditions of philosophy. At the same time, he maintains contact with science and scientific canons of intelligibility. Neville's metaphysics is neutral to particular scientific outcomes, making it less liable to collapse as scientific knowledge advances (though it loses some of the concrete intelligibility that a theory has when it clearly indicates what scientific discoveries might count against it). Yet, he frames ethical and political problems in explicit dialogue with knowledge derived from the social and natural sciences, and requires of his metaphysics that it account for the world as the social and natural sciences disclose it to be.

Four aspects of Neville's system are particularly notable. First, his theory of God as determinate Creator but as wholly indeterminate apart from creation solves many conundrums in the philosophical problem of the one and the many. It answers the question of "Why is there something rather than nothing?" with reference to the divine will (in the fashion of Duns Scotus) and in such a way as to permit fruitful engagement with ontological theories in non-Western religious and philosophical traditions. It is problematic in relation to traditional forms of theism, which picture creation as reflecting the divine nature, but Neville argues that this kind of theism cannot finally solve the problem of the one and the many.

Second, Neville's metaphysics is naturalistic and yet capable of registering a wide range of phenomena. His account of space, time, motion, and causation leads to a theory of intentionality rooted in patterns of causation, thus remaining consistent with naturalist commitments. This yields a theory of truth as causal (and so properly naturalistic) yet non-mechanistic, thereby avoiding a weakness of many naturalistic theories of truth. Neville argues that truth is the carryover of value from an object to an interpreter. This carryover is by means of signs, so a semiotics is presupposed. The respect in which a sign stands for an object determines the way value is carried over. This non-foundationalist theory of truth is not a part of major analytic or continental projects but has a predominantly American heritage running through Edwards, Emerson, Peirce, and Dewey (along with the Scottish common-sense philosophers, such as Dougald Stewart and Thomas Reid), and a far older heritage in Platonic philosophy through the concept of participation.

Third, Neville's cross-cultural study has yielded a theory of comparison. He argues that the comparison of religious and philosophical ideas across cultures requires an array of comparative categories linking the most specific ideas (such as the view of a human person in a particular religious text or practice) by means of categories of intermediate vagueness to extremely general categories (such as "human condition"). Each category of comparison is simultaneously vague in respect of the specific things compared by means of it, and specific in respect of some encompassing category of which it is a specification. Neville's theory provides the theoretical framework needed to avoid both of the distortions plaguing cross-cultural comparison: insufficient sensitivity to details and the surreptitious predominance of the perspective of the comparativist. This was worked out in practice through Neville's Comparative Religious Ideas Project, which produced three volumes of results in 2001.

Fourth, Neville's interest in religious symbols is coordinated with his semiotic theory and his theory of truth. A symbol is true in an objective sense when it rightly engages its object and true in a subjective sense when it rightly orders the symbol wielder in relation to the symbol's object. This double analysis resists both one-sided dismissals of religion and the uncritical habits of religious superstition. Neville regards religion as a major test for the adequacy of a philosophical interpretation of reality. Philosophy need not confirm the truth claims of religion but it must account for the details of religion's imaginative potencies and social functions.

Further reading

Chapman, J. Harley and Frankenberry, Nancy K. (eds). *Interpreting Neville*. Albany, NY: SUNY Press, 1999.

Neville, Robert Cummings. *God the Creator: On the Transcendence and Presence of God*. Chicago, IL: University of Chicago Press, 1968. Corrected edition with a new preface, Albany, NY: SUNY Press, 1992.

—— *Soldier, Sage, Saint*. New York: Fordham University Press, 1978.

—— *Creativity and God: A Challenge to Process Theology*. New York: Seabury Press, 1980. Corrected edition with a new preface, Albany, NY: SUNY Press, 1995.

—— *Behind the Masks of God: An Essay toward Comparative Theology*. Albany, NY: SUNY Press, 1991.

—— *Eternity and Time's Flow*. Albany, NY: SUNY Press, 1993.

—— *The Truth of Broken Symbols*. Albany, NY: SUNY Press, 1996.

—— *Symbols of Jesus: A Christology of Symbolic Engagement*. Cambridge: Cambridge University Press, 2001.

—— *Religion in Late Modernity*. Alban, NY: SUNY Press, 2002.

—— *The Scope and Truth of Theology*. New York: T. and T. Clark, 2006.

Yong, Amos and Heltzel, Peter G. (eds). *Theology in Global Context: Essays in Honor of Robert Cummings Neville*. New York: T. and T. Clark, 2004.

WESLEY J. WILDMAN

NEVILLE, ROBERT CUMMINGS: AUTOBIOGRAPHY

After attending public schools in St Louis, Missouri, I had the great good fortune to attend Yale University on scholarship for both undergraduate and graduate work. In our freshman philosophy class we were told that we were to read the great philosophers of the Western tradition and consider ourselves as aspirants to be their peers. Though the likelihood that any of us would become peers of the greats was small, that project defined authentic philosophy, thence theology, for me.

My dissertation and first book, *God the Creator*, started as a study of Duns Scotus' theory of divine creation. But because I thought his fundamental distinction between infinite and finite modes of being was a mistake, I transformed the topic to be the development of my own theory of divine creation that drew from many additional sources and addressed the classic problem of the one and the many. My conclusion was that God is not a being but rather the singular eternal act that creates everything determinate. But if God creates everything determinate, is human freedom possible? My next book, *The Cosmology of Freedom*, analyzed issues of personal freedom, such as free choice and disciplined action, as well as those of social freedom, treating freedom of opportunity, of culture, and of participatory democracy, among others. The cosmology for this affirmed temporal indeterminacy, and it showed how God could create a temporal world that unfolds with free agents making decisive choices within it. *Soldier, Sage, Saint* developed these ideas with respect to spiritual freedom.

Influenced by Whitehead and Dewey, I next undertook a three-volume project called *Axiology of Thinking* that showed (1) how thinking should be regarded as a part of nature, not a separate mental process; (2) how all thinking is valuation, not representation of facts by means of forms alone; and (3) how four main families of thinking are important – imagination, interpretation, theorizing, and the pursuit of responsibility. This required developing a critique of the Western scientific tradition's fact-value distinction (in *Reconstruction of Thinking*), a rather fulsome cosmology (in *Recovery of the Measure*), and a theory of theoretical and practical reason (in *Normative Cultures*). By this time my thinking was much influenced by comparative philosophy and the last volume is as Confucian as it is Western in its fundamental argument.

Comparative philosophy and theology has been a strong interest, exhibited in several books of essays, in *Boston Confucianism*, and in the exciting collaborative project I directed that resulted in the edited volumes, *The Human Condition*, *Ultimate Realities*, and *Religious Truth*. My interest has turned to semiotics and theories of religious symbolism, which tie in closely with my theological work. *The Truth of Broken Symbols* and *Symbols of Jesus* develop the theory that symbols connect us with reality so that it can be grasped, with tests for the truth of such grasping being delicate and long range. My next project is a systematic theology drawing upon all the world's religions, as well as some of the sciences and arts.

ROBERT CUMMINGS NEVILLE

NEW RIDDLE OF INDUCTION

The problem of induction is to justify inferences about the future on the basis of evidence of the past, or more generally to justify inferences about a wider class of cases on the basis of evidence in a narrower class. In *Fact, Fiction, and Forecast* (1984), Nelson Goodman demonstrates that this is a trickier problem than it seems. Define the predicate *grue* as follows:

> *X* is grue if and only if *X* is examined before future time *t* and is found to be green or *X* is not so examined and is blue.

Now, consider emeralds. Since *t* is in the future, every emerald that has been examined, being green, is also grue. If induction consists simply in projecting from examined cases to unexamined cases, "grue" presents a problem. Although the evidence consists of emeralds that are both green and grue, we cannot predict that future emeralds will be both green and grue. If any emeralds remain unexamined at *t*, the two predictions diverge. To predict that emeralds first examined after *t* will be grue is to predict that they will be blue, not green. What justifies our conviction that we should predict that all future emeralds will be green, none will be blue, hence none will be grue? This is the new riddle of induction. Since grue-like alternatives can be constructed for any predicate, the problem threatens all ampliative reasoning.

Whatever its solution, the grue paradox reveals something significant about induction: both the constitution and the characterization of the evidence class figure in the validity of an inductive inference. It matters how the evidence is described.

No one doubts that "green" is preferable to "grue." But what makes it so? One seemingly obvious answer is that "grue" is defined in terms of "green." Hence "green" is the more basic predicate, perhaps indicating that *green* is the more natural property. But "green" can be defined in terms of "grue" as easily as "grue" in terms of "green." First define a predicate "bleen":

> *X* is bleen if and only if *X* is examined before future time *t* and is found to be blue or *X* is not so examined and is green.

Taking "grue" and "bleen" as primitive, then define "green":

> *X* is green if and only if *X* is examined before future time *t* and is found to be grue or *X* is not so examined and is bleen.

Which predicate is primitive is a function of where we start. And we could as easily start with "grue." Definitional priority affords no basis for saying that "green" is more fundamental than "grue."

Another suggestion is that "grue" is illicit because it is *positional*; its definition makes essential reference to a time. The interdefinability of "grue" and "bleen" undermines this proposal too, since if we start with "grue" and "bleen," "green" is positional. Moreover, one can contrive grue-like predicates that are manifestly non-positional.

> Momentum = mass times velocity.
>
> Schmomentum = mass times velocity up to the threshold of measurement and twice mass times velocity thereafter.

No appeal to positionality explains why we should take the evidence to confirm the law of momentum rather than the law of schmomentum.

A third suggestion appeals to evolution. It contends that our survival is evidence that our predicates are the proper ones for induction (successful induction being critical to survival). The difficulty here is that the extensions of "green" and "grue" have not yet diverged. Up to now, "grue"-projectors and "green"-projectors would be equally adapted to their environment. Until the predicates diverge, any evolutionary advantage that attaches to "green" is shared by "grue."

Goodman maintains that the solution is pragmatic. We cannot ground our solution in an assurance that future emeralds will be green, not grue. We have no such assurance. That was Hume's insight. And it would be question-begging to provide an inductive argument for the validity of our inductive practice. But we still have a sound practical reason to prefer "green" to "grue." Projecting "green" and its cognates fits with our past inductive practice. Projecting "grue" and its cognates does not. Since our past inductive practice is deeply enmeshed in our daily lives and in sophisticated science, we should abandon it only if it fails us. There is no guarantee that it will not fail us, but so far it has not. Until it does, we should project "green."

Further reading

Elgin, Catherine Z. (ed.). *Nelson Goodman's New Riddle of Induction*. New York: Garland, 1997.
Goodman, Nelson. *Fact, Fiction, and Forecast*. Cambridge, MA: Harvard University Press, 1984.
Hullett, Jay and Schwartz, Robert. "Grue: Some Remarks," *Journal of Philosophy* 64 (1967): 259–71.
Stalker, Douglas (ed.). *Grue*. Chicago, IL: Open Court, 1994.

CATHERINE Z. ELGIN

NIEBUHR, REINHOLD

The son of a pious and politically liberal German immigrant, Reinhold Niebuhr (1892–1971) followed his father's footsteps in graduating from Eden Theological Seminary in St Louis. Ordained into the German Evangelical Synod, he earned Bachelor's and Master's degrees at Yale Divinity School. The monotonous toil of automobile workers he witnessed as a young minister in Detroit led Niebuhr to socialism, though he later supported Roosevelt's New Deal. From 1928 through 1960 Niebuhr taught at the Union Theological Seminary in New York, combining an academic career with a lifelong dedication to social activism.

Niebuhr's theory of human nature, Christian realism, is captured in the title of his masterwork, *Moral Man and Immoral Society.* Individuals, he argues, are naturally endowed with both selfish and unselfish impulses. The former can be partially suppressed by (1) *Reason*, which opens the possibility of self-transcendence by bidding us to consider the interests of others, and (2) *Religious imagination*, where contemplating our finitude before the infinite allows us to surrender our selfish impulses to the Absolute Will, a boundless love exemplified in the life and ethic of Jesus.

Niebuhr warns, however, that the individual's ability to modify egoism cannot be replicated in the social order. A group is merely an aggregate of individual desires and impulses, and it runs against its nature to value the interests of other groups or contemplate its own self-transcendence. Groups are thus more susceptible to violent conflict. Although social turmoil can be lessened by individual acts of love and by prudent governmental intervention, perfect harmony is not realizable in this world. Although he shared John Dewey's progressive views, Niebuhr thought Dewey's notion of "social intelligence" was dangerously naïve.

Further reading

Brown, Charles C. *Niebuhr and His Age: Reinhold Niebuhr's Prophetic Role in the Twentieth Century.* Philadelphia, PA: Trinity Press International, 1992.
Brown, Robert McAfee (ed.). *The Essential Reinhold Niebuhr: Selected Essays and Addresses.* New Haven, CT: Yale University Press, 1992.
Niebuhr, Reinhold. *Moral Man and Immoral Society.* New York: Charles Scribner's Sons, 1932.
—— *The Nature and Destiny of Man*, Vols 1 and 2. New York: Charles Scribner's Sons, 1941, 1943.

FRANK X. RYAN

NORMAL SCIENCE

The concept of normal science was developed by Thomas Kuhn and utilized in his *The Structure of Scientific Revolutions* (1962). According to Kuhn the development of a science is not uniform but has alternating "normal" and "revolutionary" or "extraordinary" phases. The revolutionary phases are not merely episodes of accelerated progress, but differ qualitatively from normal science.

Normal science resembles the standard cumulative picture of scientific progress, indicating the relatively routine work of scientists experimenting within what Kuhn calls an accepted "paradigm" or "disciplinary matrix." This work involves filling in details within the framework of established fundamental theory, but it does not challenge or test the underlying assumptions of the theory. Kuhn describes this mode of science as being a form of "puzzle-solving." When solving crossword puzzles, jigsaw puzzles, or chess puzzles, the methods of solution are highly familiar and one expects, if one has the ability, to have a good chance of solving the puzzle.

Puzzle-solving in science does not involve completely uncharted waters but assumes some familiarity with the parameters of the puzzle, and normal science is intent on finding an increasing number of puzzle-solutions within the parameters of established theory. In normal science the scientific community is committed to shared theories, beliefs, values, instruments and techniques, and may even share, implicitly or explicitly, similar metaphysical beliefs. The assumptions that comprise the paradigm or disciplinary matrix are kept fixed, permitting the cumulative generation of puzzle-solutions. This commitment to the shared paradigm or disciplinary matrix underlies the scientific training of the period and structures the way of thinking of the scientists. It structures the kinds of issues, questions, or problems which arise and provides the direction for their resolution.

According to Kuhn there is an essential tension between the inherently conservative attitude of most scientists and the drive for innovation in science. Kuhn's strong emphasis on the conservative attitude inherent in what he calls normal science runs contrary to the claims of some philosophers of science, such as Karl Popper, who understands science in general as an enterprise which is continually attempting to refute its key theories.

Normal science, according to Kuhn, is and must be fundamentally conservative. It does not attempt to refute its most significant theories, and tends to explain away any anomalies that may occur. Because of this conservative resistance to theory refutation, scientific revolutions occur only in extreme situations. The accumulation of particularly worrisome anomalies may make it difficult for scientists to remain committed to fundamental theory, and when this occurs normal science will not continue with cohesion and confidence.

When the practice of normal science is undermined through a widespread failure of such confidence a "crisis" occurs. The most dramatic, and most interesting result of such a crisis is the search for a new paradigm. This leads to a scientific revolution in which the old paradigm or disciplinary matrix is replaced with a new one which allows for the solution of the major anomalies that disrupted the secure progress of the normal scientific period. When revolutions occur the confinements or constraints on scientific judgments structured by the given paradigm are broken. The decision to opt for a revision of a disciplinary matrix is not one that is rationally compelled, nor is the particular choice of revision rationally compelled. With the entrenchment of a new paradigm, a new period of normal science begins.

Further reading

Kuhn, Thomas. "The Essential Tension: Tradition and Innovation in Scientific Research" in C. Taylor (ed.) *The Third University of Utah Research Conference on the Identification of Scientific Talent*. Salt Lake City, UT: University of Utah Press, 1959.

—— *The Structure of Scientific Revolutions*, second edition with postscript. Chicago, IL: University of Chicago Press, 1970 [1962].

—— "Reflections on my Critics" in I. Lakatos and A. Musgrave (eds) *Criticism and the Growth of Knowledge*. London: Cambridge University Press, 1970.

Popper, Karl. *The Logic of Scientific Discovery*. London: Hutchinson Press, 1959.

Toulmin, S. 1970 "Does the Distinction between Normal and Revolutionary Science Hold Water?" in I. Lakatos and A. Musgrave (eds) *Criticism and the Growth of Knowledge*. London: Cambridge University Press, 1970.

SANDRA B. ROSENTHAL

NORMS

A norm is a standard for behavior of some kind. Norms can be social, legal, moral, or procedural. Norms can be codified, be a matter of custom or convention, or be a combination. Ethical or moral norms, it might be argued, are universal, reflecting the prescription of nature, or universal reason, or divine authority, whereas social, procedural and legal norms are relative to a particular society, time, legal structure or process. Norms might be conceptualized as rationalized or customary byproducts of other more basic biological or evolutionary processes, or as independent products of human inventiveness, or as somehow embodied in the nature of things or as articulated by the divine. Norms can be thought of as instrumental, that is, guidelines or standards for behavior or judgment that is in the service of another goal. For example, food safety standards are norms that govern the production, processing, packaging and distribution of food for the sake of promoting human health. Norms can also be thought of as being for the sake of an activity or judgment itself. For example, a poetic definition of a sonnet is a norm that guides the process of producing poetry itself. Or, a Kantian-type moral norm that says that moral duties must be universalizable is conceptualizing the norm as one which fulfills the meaning of rational consistency in ethics in contrast to a utilitarian approach which would conceptualize ethical norms, rules and guidelines, in terms of their instrumental value for promoting happiness and minimizing pain. The distinction between these two types of norms need not be mutually exclusive. For example, a Kantian-type moral norm might also have an instrumental function (for instance, observing it might also promote happiness). The American philosophical tradition has been associated with the notion of instrumental reasoning and norms, but both approaches to norms can be found in the tradition.

For a number of philosophers in the American philosophical tradition, norms are conceptualized within a naturalistic and pragmatic framework which is characterized by the idea that progress is achieved through ongoing intelligent adaptation to new circumstances and problems in the community. For John Dewey, ethical judgments and norms are in principle no different from scientific judgments and practices; each is a culmination and expression of intelligence as it aims to solve the social and practical problems that a community faces. George Herbert Mead argued that norms are produced in so far as individuals are able to import social life into their own growing consciousness and in turn are able to use their social intelligence to solve the problems of everyone. C.S. Peirce took a more formalistic, although still pragmatic approach, and distinguished what he called "phenomenology" (the study of qualities of experience) from the normative sciences, aesthetics, ethics and logic, which prescribe our foundational aims and responses to experience. Josiah Royce rejected empirical bases (e.g. emotional responses, instincts, factual evidence, science) for normative claims and argued that norms are developed through commitment and abstraction in the process of interpretation. In Justus Buchler's theory norms may be individually or collectively produced and in any of three modes of judgment, assertive (e.g. formulation of a principle), active (e.g. action as articulation of or embodiment of a norm) and exhibitive (e.g. poetic license as a norm for exhibiting linguistic poetic possibilities).

Further reading

Dewey, John. "Valuation and Experimental Knowledge" in *The Middle Works (1899–1924), Vol. 13, 1922*, ed. Jo Ann Boydston. Carbondale, IL: Southern Illinois University Press, 1976.

Royce, Josiah. *The Philosophy of Loyalty*. Nashville, TN: Vanderbilt University Press, 1995 [1908].

—— *The Problem of Christianity*. Washington, DC: Catholic University Press of America, 2001 [1913].

KATHLEEN WALLACE

O

OBJECTIVE RELATIVISM

The term "objective relativism" was coined by Arthur E. Murphy in 1927 in reference to a "genuinely new philosophy" that rejects the traditional "bifurcation" of reality into two incommensurable kinds: the objective and the relative, independently existing facts and the relationships into which they enter. For example, since the perception of an object is relative to the perceiver's standpoint, it cannot be objective. The perception is subjective, an idea in a mind, whereas the object itself is a physical part of the external world. Objective relativism, in contrast, holds that objective facts are directly disclosed in perception and are therefore always relative to perceivers' perspectives. Murphy identifies Alfred North Whitehead and John Dewey as the primary exponents of this approach.

The apparent oxymoron of a fact being both objective and relative is overcome, Murphy argues, by inverting the traditional understanding of objects and events. An event is a network of relations concretely actualized, and an object is a character or meaning that the event exhibits. Thus for Whitehead the fundamental units of reality are events, processes by which various perspectives of the antecedent determinant world and derivatives therefrom are integrated into a single new determinate outcome, the primary character of which is spatio-temporal volume. A star or stone or organism is a vast collection of events identified by the shared characteristics it exhibits and perpetuates. Each fundamental Whiteheadian event is a relationally constituted unity, the features of which are objective.

Whitehead never called himself an objective relativist, although George Herbert Mead accepted the term as a proper label for his own as well as Whitehead's philosophy of nature, both of which Mead thought consonant with Albert Einstein's theory of relativity. If times and distances are functions of some specified reference system, and if any and every standpoint uniquely defines such a system, then there can be no single non-relative overarching spatio-temporal system, and hence no single objective world and no single metaphysically ultimate reality. Post-Newtonian science entails an objective relativist ontology.

Another form of objective relativism is epistemological rather than metaphysical. The events at issue are limited to human acts of sense perception and the claim is that the objects of these perceptions are what the world is. Reality, argues Dewey, is the system of events disclosed in direct experience. A particular event can have as many different meanings as the perspectives determining it. What the rain means to the farmer differs from what it means to the tourist, but both are warranted meanings, objective perspectives on the rain, each a function of the differing experiential contexts out of which they emerge.

Although Dewey also rejected the objective relativist label, other epistemologists have embraced it. Lewis White Beck, for instance, argues that we only know objects in their relation to our knowing consciousness, and that each object is therefore a unique consequence of those relations, concretely relative to them. Nonetheless, such objects all have a similar invariant relational structure: their potential for further relationships. Hence, C.I. Lewis argues, a thing's objectivity lies not in it independence from our experiencing it but rather in the accuracy of the predictions made about future experiences to which it is likely to lead. Because these arguments are forms of the claim that truth is not a matter of correspondence but of warranted assertability, objective relativism is sometimes associated with American pragmatism in general: with the thought of Charles Sanders Peirce and William James as well as that of Dewey and Mead.

Since 1940, those using the term "objective relativism" have been limited to value theorists. Theodore Lafferty and John Clark, in differing ways, specify general empirical criteria for determining the validity of contextually dependent judgments about moral values. Jerome Stolnitz makes similar arguments with respect to aesthetic judgments. Paul Kurtz finds in culturally relative ethical principles objective criteria for their assessment, criteria that even justify a claim about universal human rights. Whereas these thinkers locate objective norms in structurally general features of culturally relative practices, John Herman Randall, Jr. simply equates objective relativism with historical relativism. The ideas of a thinker can only be understood in terms of the historically contextual problems they were devised to address.

So Murphy's "new philosophy," promising to overcome traditional bifurcations, itself bifurcated into two strands, neither of which Murphy found acceptable: forms of speculative metaphysics postulating unverifiable fundamental relational events in nature, and forms of value theory that ignore the ontology of events altogether. Indeed, the term is now used mainly in theological circles where it is attacked as a stalking horse for moral relativism.

Further reading

Beck, Lewis White. "Secondary Quality," *Journal of Philosophy* 43, 21 (1946): 599–610.

Clark, John. "An Ethical Objective Relativism," *Philosophical Review* 49, 5 (1940): 515–36.

Dewey, John. *Experience and Nature*, revised edition. Carbondale, IL: Open Court, 1986.

Kurtz, Paul. *Forbidden Fruit: The Ethics of Humanism*. New York: Prometheus Books, 1988.

Lafferty, Theodore. "Empiricism and Objective Relativism in Value Theory," *Journal of Philosophy* 46, 6 (1949): 141–54.

Mead, George Herbert. "Fragments on Whitehead" in Charles W. Morris (ed.) *Philosophy of the Act*. Chicago, IL: Chicago University Press, 1938, pp. 523–48.

Murphy, Arthur E. "Objective Relativism in Dewey and Whitehead," *Philosophical Review* 36, 2 (1927): 121–44. Reprinted in *Reason and the Common Good: Selected Essays of Arthur E. Murphy*, ed. William H. Hay, Marcus G. Singer, and Arthur E. Murphy. Englewood Cliffs, NJ: Prentice-Hall, 1963, pp. 49–66.

Robischon, Thomas. "What is Objective Relativism?" *Journal of Philosophy* 55, 26 (1958): 1117–31.

Stolnitz, Jerome. "On Objective Relativism in Aesthetics," *Journal of Philosophy* 57, 8 (1960): 261–76.

Whitehead, Alfred North. *Science and the Modern World*. New York: Free Press, 1967.

GEORGE ALLAN

OBJECTIVITY

The problems ensuing from the subject/object dichotomy emerged most clearly in the mid-seventeenth century, when Descartes published his celebrated *Meditations.* In that work he divided the world into two different parts: one part was the mental field of the subject-knower, and the other was the external world to be known. The problem of bridging the gap between the world of matter (the objective side of the knowing process) and the knower (the subjective experience of the knower) has been debated within philosophy ever since. How does one go from "inside" to "outside" without contaminating one or the other side of the dichotomy? A final resolution was offered in the eighteenth century by Immanuel Kant, who argued in *The Critique of Pure Reason* for the presence of *a priori* forms of sensibility and *a priori* categories of pure reason that organized our world into patterns that made sense (in terms of space and time) and in terms of non-contradictory ways of reasoning. He argued that human beings also contributed to the knowing process and in so helping to construct our world made it impossible for us to know "the thing-in-itself" (*noumenon*). After Kant we would have to be content with knowing how the thing known appeared to us (*phenomenon*). While this did not solve all the issues involved in the question of objectivity, it allowed science to regard its method as grounded in universal and necessary (*a priori*) knowing structures that were in fact the very conditions of the possibility of knowing.

After Kant, objectivity was secured through the presence of the transcendental sources guiding its inquiries. Here "transcendental" means "always already there." Kant had secured a foundation for the empirical methods used by science. Henceforth only facts will be allowed primary place within the scientific world. Facts prove theories. Theories need to be proved by facts. Laws are made certain because they rest on facts and are in accord with the laws of reasoning.

Still, great issues remained. All other forms of human inquiry such as poetry, philosophy, the arts and so forth are to be banned from science's laboratory. To capture the drama underlying this division of thought and its methods, consider what happens when subjective thinking is considered. It stresses by reason of its own commitments, passions, emotional fire, feelings, a sense of the beautiful, immediately felt reactions to life and its situations, joy, sorrow, depression, elation, freedom, fear, and a thousand other qualities. It is the opposite of objectivity. Where the objective is impersonal, the subjective is personal. Where the objective looks for the facts, the subjective concerns itself with values. Thus we are faced with another form of the dualism undergirding objectivity and subjectivity as rival forms of knowing: call one science, call the other humanism.

No matter what cultural terms are used to describe these different ways of knowing, one thing does keep them together. Even though they are split on the methods they use, it is the case that both are committed to method as a way of inquiry. It is this allegiance to method that American philosophy in the form of pragmatism uses in order to bring about a rapprochement between these different arms of human culture. There is no escaping value; it is everywhere. We could not perform a single action without some feeling of interest in what is to be done. Interest is another word for value; therefore, science's insistence on a bloodless methodology called objectivity is fundamentally at odds with real-world experience. At the same time, one must be truly grateful to science's insistence on an objective methodology, as it challenges assertions blocking the road to genuine inquiry.

It is useful to recall William James's description of the method of pragmatism. He uses the fruitful image of a corridor off which many rooms are set. Behind each door is a different subject matter of human concern and interest. Pragmatism has respect for each of these academic pursuits. When it leaves the corridor and enters each room, it only asks a single question, "What difference does it make?" Now this word "difference" in practice comes to signify what is the meaning of the results achieved by the methods in question. Applying this pragmatic maxim to the question of objectivity, we are able to see its strengths as well as its weaknesses. As a way of gaining access to the actual facts of a matter of interest, objectivity is indispensable. But there is often more to a situation than the facts that make it up. Motivation, belief, interests, personal and social values – to list but a few potential variables – are not simply facts. They are also values. The pragmatic solution for dealing with objectivity involves a new understanding of scientific investigation that John Dewey called "inquiry."

Inquiry is the effort to unravel all strands of a situation that has become problematic. The first step in inquiry is to identify these problems. The second is to feel how it affects those under their sway. This requires something much more than an objective survey of data relating to income, housing, children, nutrition and so forth. It demands that the investigator actually enter into the concrete lives of these human beings and see, feel, taste, smell and listen to the various dimensions of their environment. What Dewey is encouraging is the dropping of the antiseptic robes of laboratory science so that the subjective domain and the method of objectivity become part of the problems to be addressed. What Dewey fought against most strenuously were the separations that tear apart the seamless cloak of experience. By bringing together objectivity and subjectivity under the umbrella of inquiry, Dewey achieved two important cultural improvements. He made science drop its pretense of omniscience, which of course was only operative in the laboratory. At the same time he compelled philosophy to come down from its Olympian heights and get to work in the streets. For Dewey it was the experience of the streets that would heal all fissures, bind up all separations and inspire human beings to further acts of intelligence in order to ensure justice for their fellow citizens. This act of applying the results of inquiry has come to be called praxis. Inquiry and praxis are the great gifts of American philosophy to the poor, the forgotten, the blind, the lame, the halt and the deaf.

Further reading

Bernstein, Richard. *Beyond Objectivism and Relativism*, Philadelphia, PA: University of Pennsylvania Press, 1983.

Dewey, John. *Essays in Experimental Logic*. New York: Dover, 1916.

Whitehead, Alfred North. *Science and the Modern World*. New York: Free Press, 1967.

JOSEPH GRANGE

ONTOLOGICAL COMMITMENT

Ontology is the study of reality. Consequently, to determine "ontological commitment" is to work out what objects we commit ourselves to by virtue of what we say. The term was coined by Willard Van Orman Quine in his 1948 essay "On What There is." There, Quine studies the Platonic riddle of non-being: the difficulty of denying that something exists without thereby affirming its existence: when we say "Pegasus doesn't exist," we seem to be committing ourselves to Pegasus – by virtue of talking about *him*.

Quine resolves this dilemma with his criterion for ontological commitment. Quine's criterion works as follows. First, our statements are translated into first order logic. Then, we look at what falls under the existential quantifier: the quantifier ∃x, translated by the English words "there is an object x such that ..." (Quine, *Philosophy of Logic*). Any logical statement of the form (∃x)**S**x – there is an object x such that x is **S** – which we believe commits us to **S**s. If (∃x)**S**x is also true, then **S**s exist. A statement such as "Pegasus doesn't exist" is translated as ~(∃x)**P**x – it is not the case that there is an object x that Pegasizes ("Pegasizes" is what Pegasus, if he existed, would uniquely do), and therefore does not commit us to Pegasus.

Quine's criterion also rids us of other entities, such as universals: "There are red houses" commits us to houses, but not to redness. Other abstract entities, however, appear more stubborn: "There are at least three numbers greater than seven," by Quine's criterion, commits us to the number seven, unless that sentence can be paraphrased to avoid quantification over numbers.

Quine's argument for his criterion relies on how we use "there is" in English. He argues that since the existential quantifier is a translation of "there is" into logic, and in English we use "there is" in an ontologically committing way, then ∃x must be ontologically committing as well.

Quine's criterion has dominated the philosophical scene since its introduction, but in 1990 his views began to be challenged. Stephen Yablo, in "Does Ontology Rest on a Mistake?" (1998) argues that "there is" and other existential phrases are sometimes used metaphorically, and that one cannot always rewrite statements to eliminate this metaphorical use. Jody Azzouni, in *Deflating Existential Consequence: A Case for Nominalism* (2004), addresses Quine's argument about ordinary language. He claims that "there is" phrases are often and naturally used in an ontologically innocuous way. Example: "There are fictional mice that talk." Azzouni then argues that such statements cannot be paraphrased to avoid their apparent ontological commitments.

If Azzouni turns out to be right, how should ontological commitment be determined? Azzouni suggests that we look at the use of predicates such as "is causally efficacious" or "is concrete." Such predicates may serve the role of committing us to the objects to which they apply. Since, for instance, neither "is causally efficacious" nor "is concrete" applies to Pegasus in the true statement "Pegasus can fly," Pegasus doesn't exist.

Further reading

Azzouni, Jody. *Deflating Existential Consequence: A Case for Nominalism.* New York: Oxford University Press, 2004.

Quine, W.V. "On What There is" in W.V. Quine (ed.) *From A Logical Point of View.* Cambridge, MA: Harvard University Press, 1980 [1948], pp. 1–20.

Yablo, Stephen and Gallois, Andre. "Does Ontology Rest on a Mistake?" *Proceedings of the Aristotelian Society,* supplementary volume 72 (1998): 229–61.

YVONNE RALEY

ONTOLOGY

Ontology is the branch of metaphysics concerned with existence or being. Some philosophers, including Alexius Meinong and George Santayana, have argued for a distinction between being and existence. Most philosophers, however, have rejected such a distinction. So the central question of ontology tends to be "What really exists (or might exist)?"

Typically, ontology is concerned with whether a given *kind* or *category* of entity, as opposed to any particular entity, exists (or could exist). For example, ontology asks whether there are or might be numbers, sets, properties or universals or Platonic Forms, macro-level material things (like tables and chairs), unobservable material things (like quarks), events, processes, societies, past or future entities, holes (like the holes of Swiss cheese), immaterial minds or souls, God, fictional entities (like Sherlock Holmes), and impossible entities (like round squares).

Ontology is also concerned with the natures of what exists (or could exist). This concern is closely related to the first. Whether entities of some kind can or do exist turns on what their nature would be if they existed.

Given the generality and diversity of the topics covered by ontology, it is perhaps easiest to understand what is distinctive of ontological disputes by focusing on a few representative examples: whether there are abstract entities (like numbers and properties or universals), what kinds of material objects there are and whether they compose or are composed by further material objects, and whether there are processes or events.

One of the most fundamental and general ontological disputes is over the existence of *abstract* entities. Roughly, abstract entities are located neither in space nor in time and lack causal powers, whereas concrete entities are located in both and do have causal powers. Paradigmatic examples of concrete entities are people, plants, animals, tables, chairs, and so on, whereas paradigmatic examples of abstract entities are properties or universals, numbers, sets, propositions, and so on. Some philosophers, often called *nominalists* (though the term has other uses), deny the existence of all abstract entities. They have typically been motivated by epistemological worries: if abstract entities are unobservable because they lack causal powers and are located neither in space nor in time, then it is mysterious how we could know what we appear to know about them. Other philosophers, often called *Platonists* (though the term also has other uses), remain unmoved by these epistemological worries and affirm the existence of some abstract entities, though they might disagree over which kinds of abstract entities exist and how to respond to the epistemological worries.

Another fundamental ontological dispute is that over the nature of material objects and their composition. Intuitively, we think there are tables, chairs, people, plants, and animals. But science says that these macro-level material things are composed of micro-level material things: tables are composed of molecules, molecules of atoms, atoms of sub-atomic particles, and so on. Philosophers disagree over whether this list terminates: that is, whether or not all macro-level things are ultimately composed of material things, or *mereological atoms*, which have no material parts.

Either way, we might still wonder whether the macro-level material things exist in their own right, or whether there are really only the micro-level material things that compose them. Peter Unger's Problem of the Many suggests that there may be no macro-level material things at all. Consider the billions of particles that make up a cloud. A cloud remains if any one of these particles is destroyed. A cloud still remains if yet another particle is destroyed. Continuing the reasoning suggests that there are trillions of clouds overlapping each other. If that result is intolerable, the arbitrariness of choosing any one of the collections of cloud particles as being the one and only cloud seems to require denying that there is even one cloud there at all.

Another question is whether or not wholes are, in some sense, identical to their material parts. A statue, during its existence, is materially composed of the clay. But when the statue exists, is it just identical to the clay that composes it? Intuitively, it seems not, because the statue can exist even if some of the clay is destroyed (e.g. perhaps by replacing the destroyed clay with some new clay). This suggests that the statue and the clay are distinct things. If so, what more needs to be added to the clay to yield the statue? And if the clay and the statue are distinct things, how is it that they can sometimes occupy the same place at the same time?

Perhaps the most general question about composition is Peter van Inwagen's Special Composition Question, which asks: under what conditions is some or other thing composed by some class of other things? The intuitive view is that not just any class of things composes some or other things, e.g. while your limbs, torso, and your head might compose something (you), these things together with the Space Needle compose nothing. But it has proven difficult to isolate plausible conditions for this restricted sort of composition. Doubtful of the prospects for the intuitive view, some have adopted one of two extreme views. *Mereological nihilists* have said that there are no such conditions: there are no wholes composed of parts. *Mereological universalists* have said that the conditions are vacuous: every class of things composes a whole.

Ontology has largely focused upon the existence and nature of things and properties. Some have rejected this focus. For example, adherents of process philosophy, including American pragmatists like C.S. Peirce, John Dewey, and William James, have argued for the primacy of an ontology of change, events, or processes over that of an ontology of things and properties. It is not always clear whether such an ontology denies the existence of things and properties or rather affirms their existence but conceives their natures somehow in terms of processes. Either option would seem to affect the evaluation of ontological disputes as traditionally conceived.

Philosophers have also been interested in questions, sometimes grouped under the label "meta-ontology", about the nature of ontological disputes themselves. Under what conditions are we ontologically committed to the existence of a kind of entity? What is the correct methodology for settling ontological disputes? Are ontological disputes significant or even intelligible?

Various modern innovations in logic have been incorporated in standard methods for determining ontological commitments. Peirce's pioneering use of logic to distinguish categories and, especially, Frege's and Peirce's existential quantifier have been particularly influential. For example, W.V.O. Quine influentially argued that someone is ontologically committed just to the ontological commitments of a theory he or she accepts, where a theory is ontologically committed to *F*s if and only if, when translated into first-order logic, it implies sentences of the form "$\exists xFx$." Quine's view, though controversial, has achieved the status of orthodoxy. Notable dissenters include proponents of truth-maker theory, including D.M. Armstrong, who hold that someone is ontologically committed to *F*s if and only if a truth-maker of his or her beliefs requires that *F*s exist.

Views about the correct methodology for ontological inquiry can be grouped into two main traditions. The "rationalist" tradition holds that, at least sometimes, ontological disputes can be settled on *a priori* grounds alone (few have held that all such disputes can be settled on *a priori* grounds alone). For a recent example, Neo-Fregeans, like Crispin Wright and Bob Hale, have revived Frege's logicist project of deriving mathematical truths from logic alone. This has involved arguing for the existence of numbers on the basis of *a priori* premises alone.

Some have doubted the possibility of *a priori* ontology. Both the American pragmatists and the logical positivists held versions of the view that the meaning of a statement is the conditions under which it could be empirically verified. The claims of *a priori* ontology appear empirically unverifiable and, therefore, meaningless. Rudolph Carnap influentially argued that the question "Do *F*s exist?" might be asked either dependently or independently of a linguistic framework. The former, *internal* questions have objective but trivial answers: for example, it is a trivial consequence of our mathematical framework that numbers exist. To the extent that ontological questions are not trivial, they are *external* questions, independent of any framework. But Carnap argued that because the meaning of the word "numbers" is given by a mathematical framework, it is meaningless to ask whether numbers exist independently of that framework. External questions, and therefore ontological questions, are meaningless.

Whereas logical positivists, like Carnap, tended to regard ontology as impossible because meaningless, others influenced by Peirce, Dewey, James, and Quine reconceived ontology as an *a posteriori* discipline. The resulting "empiricist" tradition holds that ontological disputes can only be settled on *a posteriori* grounds. Quine influentially argued that our ontology ought to be that of our best empirical theory. This view partially motivates the indispensability arguments for the existence of various entities, especially abstract entities. For example, Quine and Hilary Putnam have argued that because numbers are indispensable to our best empirical theory, we should believe that they exist.

Some have had more radical doubts about the significance of ontology, whether conceived in the "rationalist" or "empiricist" tradition. Quine himself argued that empirical evidence underdetermines what our best empirical theory is and therefore our ontological commitments may be to that extent indeterminate. More radically, Nelson Goodman's irrealism rejects the widespread assumption, common to both traditions, that there is a unique correct ontology, even if we are unable to discern what it is. Different ontologies, according to Goodman, reflect different world-views and it is either incorrect or pointless to suppose that the ontologies of these world-views are incompatible. Putnam and Richard Rorty have also recently defended related views.

Despite that ontology is abstract, difficult, and subject to the preceding philosophical doubts, interest in it has remained. One reason why pertains to its bearing on realist/antirealist disputes. For example, a realist construal of a given subject (e.g. mathematics) may be challenged by denying the existence of its objects (e.g. numbers) or by construing their nature in unobvious ways. Thus the intelligibility of realist/antirealist disputes about a given subject seems to presuppose the intelligibility of ontological disputes about the existence of its objects. So if we wish to defend the intelligibility of the former, it seems we must defend the intelligibility of the latter.

Further reading

Armstrong, D.M. *Truth and Truthmakers.* Cambridge: Cambridge University Press, 2004.

Carnap, Rudolph. "Empiricism, Semantics, and Ontology" in *Meaning and Necessity: A Study in Semantics and Modal Logic*, second edition. Chicago, IL: University of Chicago Press, 1956.

Chalmers, David, Manley, David, and Wasserman, Ryan. *Metametaphysics.* Oxford: Oxford University Press, forthcoming.

Goodman, Nelson. *Ways of Worldmaking*. Indianapolis, IN, IN: Hackett, 1978.

Hale, Bob and Wright, Crispin. *The Reason's Proper Study: Essays Toward a Neo-Fregean Philosophy of Mathematics.* Oxford: Clarendon Press, 2001.

Laurence, Stephen and Macdonald, Cynthia (eds). *Contemporary Readings in the Foundations of Metaphysics.* Oxford: Blackwell, 1998.

Mellor, D.H. and Alex Oliver, Alex (eds). *Properties.* Oxford: Oxford University Press, 1997.

Peirce, C.S. *Collected Papers*, ed. Charles Hartshorne and Paul Weiss. Cambridge, MA: Harvard University Press, 1933.

Quine, Willard Van Orman. "On What There Is" in *From a Logical Point of View*, second edition, revised. Cambridge, MA: Harvard University Press, 1980.

Santayana, George. *The Realms of Being*, 1-volume edition. New York: Charles Scribner's Sons, 1942.

Unger, Peter. "The Problem of the Many," *Midwest Studies in Philosophy* 5 (1980): 411–67.

van Inwagen, Peter. *Material Beings.* Ithaca, NY: Cornell University Press, 1990.

Wright, Crispin. *Frege's Conception of Numbers as Objects.* Aberdeen: Aberdeen University Press, 1983.

MICHAEL J. RAVEN

OPERATIVE RIGHTS

The central thesis of my 1993 book, *Operative Rights* is that rights are social institutions and exist only in communities where there are norms governing them. For a right to exist – to be operative – the norms must establish both an entitlement and the obligation to respect it. Entitlements are called rights but properly understood a right is the entitlement together with the correlative obligation of respect.

This thesis is based on George Herbert Mead's analysis of norm-governed social interaction. According to Mead all individuals who participate in a social institution share a common perspective, a general attitude in terms of which they understand that institution and the meanings of the behaviors and communicative gestures involved. Such a perspective governs the institution of rights. Everyone in a community in which it exists should know to respect the entitlements of others and to expect them to respect his or her own entitlements.

Individuals who share a perspective constitute a community and everyone belongs to many communities. "Community" is used in two general senses. A "perspectival community" is any collectivity of individuals who have a common perspective or similar perspectives. A "normative community" is a species of perspectival community, its definitive perspective consisting of social norms.

Since rights are only operative in normative communities, there are no universal "natural" rights. But are there or can there be rights that are universally operative? The book puts forth the theory that there are rights that ought to be operative in every normative community. These are "generic rights" and there are two fundamental generic rights. They are rights to the necessary conditions of normative community: the right of members of a community to participate in the establishment, perpetuation, and revision of the norms that govern the community – the right of authority – and the right to judge when and how the norms ought to be applied in particular situations – the right of autonomy.

Communities as well as individuals can have rights. The question is how this is possible. For communities to have rights they must belong to inclusive communities that confer those rights and they must be able to act as communities in implementing them. In the United States, states' rights are an example. But not every community can act as an entity. An ethnic minority, for instance, cannot. However, since its members have its perspective as a constituent of their individual perspectives, when they apply that perspective in acting, the ethnic community acts through them.

There are norms that govern communities' relations with one another, including rights norms. These are also norms of an inclusive community, established and implemented by the member communities. For individuals to treat their own community as having rights, they must understand that the norms of that community apply to the other member communities as well as their own.

Communities that can act (agential communities) should have rights analogous to the generic rights of individuals and the rights that these presuppose and entail. As rights of communities these are "communal rights." Nonagential communities cannot have communal rights, but insofar as the members of such a community share a collective identity they can jointly have comparable rights as well as others. These are all "collective rights."

Further reading

Singer, Beth J. *Operative Rights.* Albany, NY: SUNY Press, 1993.

BETH J. SINGER

OPTIMISM

Optimism is the view that the world is essentially good. The term can also be used to indicate that some part of the world is essentially good or that some future outcome will be good.

The concept can be found in ancient texts as disparate as the Hebrew Bible (where God sees that His entire creation is "very good"), the *Timaeus* (where Plato concludes that the universe is the "greatest, best, fairest, most perfect"), and the works of Mencius (where the claim is made that human beings are innately good).

The term itself is relatively new, having been coined in the eighteenth century to describe the views of the German philosopher Gottfried Leibniz. Leibniz claimed that this is the "best of all possible worlds." That is, of all the worlds God could have created, He chose the one that contains the maximum amount of good and the minimum amount of evil. On Leibniz's view, optimism about the world is justified based on the benevolence of its creator.

Optimism has played an important role in the shaping of America. The explorers, pioneers, and immigrants, as well as the entrepreneurs and industrialists, who have done so much to define American culture were driven by the hope that life could be better in a new world. While not all of them realized the American dream, millions left their homes to try to find it. For them the goodness of the world was not a guarantee made by a benevolent deity as much as a possibility depending on the effectiveness of human action.

This distinction between the metaphysical guarantee of the goodness of the world and the real possibility that it can be made better is a key theme in American philosophy. While both of these views can be thought of as optimistic in a general sense, the term "optimism" is most properly applied to the former view, the sense in which it will be used here.

William James was very critical of this type of optimism, seeing it as a type of intellectualism. For James, intellectualism is the belief that the world is essentially complete and independent of us. Human minds can seek to know the world but have no capability of changing it. If optimism is true, then the moral quality of the world is already predetermined and there is nothing we can do to change it. (The same, incidentally, holds true for pessimism, which James also saw as a kind of intellectualism.) James used the term "meliorism" to refer to the alternative view that the world can be made better through effective human action. Meliorism (from the Latin *melior*, meaning "better") is the view that the moral quality of the world is yet to be determined. Meliorists hold that the world is not already complete and that human minds can not only seek to know it but can also change it. For James and other meliorists, the goodness of the world is not dependent on some metaphysical guarantee, but rather on the joint actions of human beings.

John Dewey was critical of optimism for similar reasons. He saw optimism as inimical to human action. If the world is already good (or at least as good as it can get), then why should we seek to fight against the evils we find in it? Optimists, he argued, are less likely to notice the sufferings of others, and if they do notice them are less likely to work to relieve them. In this way, he held that optimism can be just as paralyzing as pessimism.

Contemporary American philosophers also tend to be critical of optimism. The horrors experienced by so many during the various wars and massacres of the last one hundred years make it difficult for many to believe that the world is basically good. But instead of using the term "meliorism," contemporary thinkers tend to use the word "hope."

Richard Rorty, for example, uses the term "social hope." For Rorty, the most positive human capacity is the ability to trust others and to work cooperatively with them to make the future better than it otherwise would be. For him, the ideal future consists in the creation of a global, democratic, and egalitarian society. Although Rorty sees as pretty small the chances that such a utopia will ever actually be realized, he argues that there is no better way to spend our lives than in working toward this ideal.

While the specifics of Rorty's ideal world may differ in significant ways from the ideals of James and Dewey and from those of various American immigrants and entrepreneurs, his notion of social hope puts him squarely in the American tradition they helped to fashion. Instead of seeing the world as essentially good as it is, they tended to see the world as essentially improvable through human effort. So it may be more accurate to think of American optimism in terms of meliorism or hope; that is, of a belief that the world is as yet unfinished and that our cooperative efforts can help bring about its goodness in the future.

Further reading

Dewey, John. *A Common Faith*. New Haven, CT: Yale University Press, 1960.

James, William. "Lecture VIII: Pragmatism and Religion" in *Pragmatism*. Cambridge, MA: Harvard University Press, 1975.

Rorty, Richard. *Philosophy and Social Hope*. New York: Penguin, 1999.

JAMES O. PAWELSKI

ORGANISM

Just as the concept of the machine played a dominant role in the thought of seventeenth- and eighteenth-century Europe, so the concept of the organism plays a dominant role in the thought of nineteenth- and twentieth-century America, especially after the publication of Charles Darwin's *The Origin of Species* in 1859.

One crucial issue introduced by Darwin's work was with regard to whether species were fixed, and thus instantiations of Platonic forms, or whether all characteristics of a species were subject to change. If the species are not fixed, but merely groups of individual organisms such as plants, animals, bacteria, closely related through common ancestry, then change is from individual to individual, not across the entire species. A related issue pertained to randomness in the natural world.

Natural selection operated on random changes in subsequent generations of organisms. In the mechanistic worldview, there are no random events. Furthermore, where change is biologically passed from parent to offspring, the process of change is irreversible. A mechanical universe is repetitive; an organic universe is unidirectional.

Two years after the publication of *The Origin*, William James entered Harvard and became a student of the anti-Darwinian Louis Agassiz. As he grew away from this early mentor, James began to emphasize the uniqueness of the individual, the priority of function over form, indeterminacy, the contingency of knowledge claims, and the priority of experience over knowledge, all elements of pragmatism that can be traced back to the debates over the nature of the organism initiated by the publication of *The Origin*.

Charles Sanders Peirce, rather than focusing specifically on the nature of the organism, generalizes evolutionary theory to include physical law. The cosmos itself is moving from homogeneity to heterogeneity. Physical law is the result of change, not the cause of it. For Peirce, the greatest lesson learned from Darwin is that intelligibility does not require determinism.

John Dewey incorporates Darwin's analysis of the interaction of organism and environment into the analysis of experience. Organisms, including the human organism, are both shaping their environment and being shaped by their environment.

The most forceful rejection of the concept of the machine in favor of that of the organism is by Alfred North Whitehead. Whitehead claims that evolution would be impossible if materialism were true for the basic unit, a material particle in a simple location, is incapable of change. Whitehead's metaphysics utilizes both a macrocosmic and a microcosmic concept of organism. At the macrocosmic level, the universe itself is evolving and expanding. At the microcosmic level, each "actual entity" is an organic process.

Whitehead, like the pragmatists, emphasizes indeterminacy, the priority of experience, the evolution of physical law, and the interaction of the organism with the environment. He goes well beyond the pragmatists, however, in raising the concept of organism to a metaphysical level. The universe as a whole is organic, as is each level down to the "actual occasion," the fundamental event that is the building block of Whitehead's cosmology. Each actual occasion is a prehension of previous occasions, organically, internally related. Only contemporary events do not enter into the constitution of the actual occasion.

Further reading

Dewey, John. *On Experience, Nature, and Freedom*, ed. with an introduction by Richard J. Bernstein. Indianapolis, IN: Bobbs-Merrill, 1960.

Menand, Louis. *The Metaphysical Club: A Story of Ideas in America*. New York: Farrar, Straus and Giroux, 2001, especially Chs 4–8.

Peirce, Charles Sanders. "Design and Chance" in *Writings of Charles Sanders Peirce: A Chronological Edition, Volume 4, 1879–1884*. Bloomington, IN: Indiana University Press, 1986.

—— "The Triad in Biological Development" in *Writings of Charles Sanders Peirce: A Chronological Edition, Volume 6, 1886–1890*. Bloomington, IN: Indiana University Press, 2000.

Whitehead, Alfred North. *Science and the Modern World*. New York: Free Press, 1925.

—— *Process and Reality: Corrected Edition*, ed. David Ray Griffin and Donald W. Sherburne. New York: Free Press, 1978.

Wilson, R. Jackson (ed.). *Darwinism and the American Intellectual: An Anthology*. Chicago, IL: Dorsey Press, 1989.

David L. Rouse

OVER-SOUL

"The Over-soul" is an essay in Ralph Waldo Emerson's first volume of *Essays*, published in 1841. The term "over-soul" is used only once in the essay and never again in Emerson's published works, although a series of related terms (Universal Mind, Unity, wise silence, Ideal, Soul) play similar roles in his essays. "The Over-Soul" focuses on mystical experience, which is short-lived, ineffable or inexpressible in words, yet also seemingly authoritative, a state of deep knowledge. "There is a difference between one and another hour of life," Emerson states at the beginning of the essay, "in their authority and subsequent effect." In some of these hours, Emerson finds, the deepest questions of life are answered, but not "by words" – rather, by "the thing itself that is inquired after."

Although the over-soul cannot adequately be described, Emerson speaks of it with some specificity: as a "great nature in which we rest," something within which we are all contained, as a "Unity" and "the eternal ONE." His debt to Neoplatonism is apparent in such language and in quotations from Plotinus, but he also cites as sources "the trances of Socrates," St Paul, George Fox, and Jacob Boehme. The experience of the over-soul is thus not confined to one religious or philosophical tradition. Without a specific creed (except perhaps for "Unity"), without a church or priests, that experience is not best thought of as "religious," Emerson holds, but simply as "innocent . . . glad, young, and nimble."

The over-soul is not an entity, and not just a great consciousness among others. It is better understood as "the background of our being." Although it is "original" and in some sense always here, it is also "forever . . . new." In such descriptions Emerson blends Platonic and romantic elements: like Plato's Forms, the over-soul is "Perfect" and "Universal," but it is newly established in the creations of poets and philosophers, and in the creative moments of each person's life.

The "over" in over-soul construes the self as aspiring to a higher version of itself, to an "unattained but attainable self," as Emerson puts it in "History." Emerson's use of "over" also suggests that we mostly live "under" or below ourselves, beneath our best possibilities. In our social relations, for example, we mostly "descend to meet," forsaking our "native nobleness" for "trivial conversation." Emerson finds models for a more elevated society in certain memorable conversations, when all participants share the "common thought," and in the education of his child, when he abandons his attempts to control the child's experience and "reveres and loves" together with him.

Emerson's over-soul is a forerunner of Nietzsche's overman (Uebermensch). Each requires the creation of something genuinely new, but also a return to something authentically one's own; each embodies a striving for something better, greater, higher, nobler. The first edition of *The Gay Science* (1882), where the word "overman" was initially used, carries an epigraph from Emerson's essay "History"; and Nietzsche was rereading Emerson in the summer before he composed *Thus Spoke Zarathustra* (1891), where the concept of the overman is most extensively developed. For Nietzsche the mystical insight, attained at the heights, is into the truth of eternal recurrence, and it is the overman who is able to will (or affirm) that truth.

Further reading

Cavell, Stanley. *Emerson's Transcendental Etudes*. Stanford, CA: Stanford University Press, 2003.

Emerson, Ralph Waldo. *The Collected Works of Ralph Waldo Emerson*, ed. Robert B. Spiller. Cambridge, MA: Harvard University Press, 1971–.

Goodman, Russell B. "Emerson's Mystical Empiricism" in John J. Cleary (ed.) *The Perennial Tradition of Neoplatonism*. Leuven: Leuven University Press, 1997, pp. 456–78.

Nietzsche, Friedrich. *The Gay Science*, ed. Walter Kaufmann. New York: Vintage, 1974, pp. 7–12, 191–2.

Russell B. Goodman

P

PANENTHEISM

Panentheism is the view that everything is in God. It is perhaps best understood in contrast to pantheism and traditional theism. Pantheism says that all is God, and God is all, such that reality and divinity are identical (e.g. Spinoza). Traditional theism, on the other hand, makes a strong distinction between the creator and the created, such that they are utterly separate. Panentheism is a middle path. It states that everything is in God, but that God is more than everything. The analogy often given is that between mind and body: God is the mind of the world, and the world is God's body.

The term itself was coined by the German philosopher Karl Christian Friedrich Krause (1781–1832). It was brought firmly into the American philosophical lexicon in the 1950s by Charles Hartshorne (1897–2000), who, in the twentieth century, was its leading advocate. On Hartshorne's view, given that God is both the world and more than the world, God must be dipolar, having both eternal and temporal aspects. God's eternal aspect is reflected in God's divine nature, which is absolute, immutable, and independent. God's temporal aspect is consequent upon the passage of time, and in this aspect God is supremely relative, supremely mutable, and supremely dependent.

Advocates of panentheism argue that this account of God is superior both to pantheism and to traditional theism, taking the best of both while rejecting their problematic aspects. They view traditional theism as being incoherent. On the one hand, it asserts that God is completely other than the world, transcendent, eternal, and immutable. On the other, it conceives of God as all loving and all knowing. Yet, to love and to know are to be related to and to be affected by, thereby requiring the lover and the knower to change. An immutable being cannot love, change or be affected in any meaningful sense of those terms. Panentheism avoids this incoherence by including the world within God. In this way, panentheists can assert both divine immanence (since the world is included in God) and divine transcendence (since God is more than the world).

This dual assertion, they maintain, also shows the advantages of panentheism over pantheism. The latter admirably avoids the complete otherness of the God found in traditional theism, but it does so at a large price. Pantheism totally denies any transcendence to God, again making it impossible for God to love and know the world. To know and to love imply that the knower and the lover is at least in some respect other than are their objects. Even the notion of self-love requires a degree of self-transcendence, at least in some respect, in order to recognize the self as a self. Thus, pantheists have to deny that God can know and love the world, unless they want to assert some sort of divine transcendence. Once that move is made, however, the pantheist has moved from pantheism to panentheism.

Further reading

Cobb, John. *God and the World*. Philadelphia, PA: The Westminster Press, 1969.

Hartshorne, Charles. *The Divine Relativity.* New Haven, CT: Yale University Press, 1948.
McFague, Sallie. *The Body of God.* Minneapolis, MN: Augsburg Fortress Press, 1993.

WILLIAM T. MYERS

PANPSYCHISM

Panpsychism ("all mind" or "mind everywhere") is the theory that entities within the physical world are in some way sentient or conscious. More specifically it is the belief that sentience or the mind is located throughout the world to some degree. Theories of panpsychism vary according to the use and definiteness of terms denoting mentality. There is a resemblance between panpsychism and forms of hylozoism and animism, but in the context of panpsychism the attribute extended beyond the human entails some sense of the mind, as opposed to a principle of life or spirit. For example, consciousness might be present in the world, even if only as a mere "proto-mentality," i.e. something less than fully conscious. The varieties of panpsychistic theories can be visualized as lying along a spectrum, where mentality has a range of applicability. At an extreme end of such an idealized spectrum, mentality is attributed to ultimate physical units, whether they are a part of an animate object or not. Such mentality can denote the ability of a unified natural body to possess a sense of environment and withstand detrimental effects therein.

Panpsychism is not reliant on a metaphysical explanation of the nature of mentality, but simply includes mentality as a component of the physical world: therefore it does in fact say something about the nature of the physical world, i.e. it is partly comprised of sentience. While both idealism and panpsychism take some form of mind as a basic component of reality, idealists view the physical world as an appearance, whereas the panpsychist views mentality as existing alongside of and within the physical world. The question becomes how to integrate this notion of a fundamental sentience with the physical world, and in fact it is a question that simultaneously fuels the rival views of panpsychism and emergentism. Emergentism refers to the theory that out of substantially similar elements of the physical world comes a new element: consciousness. The panpsychist asks: how could something so novel arise from the physical world as a result of reconfiguring the already familiar to become something brand new? Emergentism is impossible, according to this view, because something as distinct as consciousness cannot have emerged from nothing. The panpsychist resolves the problem of emergentism by placing an earlier form of mentality within the world prior to the emergence of "consciousness proper" that is the basis of our own mentality.

Through analogical inference, beginning with the mentality we all feel to exist in our own experience, panpsychists extend a similar form out into the world and project it onto other entities or natural bodies. Maintaining sentience as indefinite, i.e. keeping indefinite the projected attribute of the analogical inference (sentience, mentality, etc.), merely suggests that basic units in the world have some measure of mentality. This responds to the criticism that it sounds absurd to say that inanimate objects should have sentience (feeling, pleasure, pain, etc.) like human beings. Panpsychists avoid the argument from common sense by stressing that they do not claim that units or bodies within the physical world literally have "pains," so mentality is maintained as something indefinite, not immediately analogous to any particular nuance of human experience. A stronger critique of the analogical inference comes from Wittgenstein's declaration that there is no analogical inference even from one human being's experience to another, but rather an immediate judgment (when I see you stub your toe I know you are in pain), hence there is no sense in suggesting we make an analogical inference between something extremely remote and ourselves. The emphasis shifts to the meaning of sentience and its cognates and the criteria for their use.

Within the historical context of the nineteenth century and early twentieth century, important Americans linked with panpsychism include Charles Sanders Peirce (1839–1914), William James (1842–1910), and Josiah Royce (1855–1916). Peirce's philosophy maintains both a naturalistic emphasis and a belief that all relations in the world require a mental basis (feelings, signs, etc.); i.e. all matter is a subdued form of mind. His theory of thirdness (that mediation is an element of reality), rejection of a purely materialistic view of the world, and refutation of a physical–mental dualism all express Peirce's panpsychism. Given William James's theory of radical empiricism, which grounds all reality in experience, he sees the world as a panpsychistic conglomeration of interacting, experiencing agents, regardless of the grade or sophistication of this experience. In *Principles of Psychology* (1890) James rejects the specific "mind-dust" theory that holds consciousness to be a collection of smaller units of consciousness; however, in his later works James explicitly links together his views of experience and reality with panpsychism.

Royce's absolute Idealism utilizes a rationalistic top-down perspective that need not require that all things be attributed with mind, while mind remains the primary feature of reality. It is in this context that Royce propounds an implicit panpsychistic theory, because mind becomes part of the building blocks of reality, while at the same time it does not ascribe mentality directly to material objects. In the later twentieth century and beyond, panpsychism continues to attract historical interest and new proponents (for introductions to the topic see, e.g., D.S. Clarke 2004, Seager and Allen-Hermanson 2005, and David Skrbina 2005). Panpsychism is interpreted in an informational context, where information is analogous to consciousness; other philosophers have returned to idealism and Jamesian philosophy for further renewed interpretations of panpsychism.

Emergentism and panpsychism were both eventually overlooked by the physical sciences and the logical positivist perspective of most American philosophy. The ultimate issue taken up with the panpsychists' analogical inferences is that the conclusions derived from them are not subject to testing and empirical confirmation. Without empirical science to back it up, logical positivism maintained little interest in panpsychism. Nevertheless, metaphysics provides a necessary context for science, enabling science to join up with a larger worldview as well as encouraging new research. New directions in panpsychism build a self-critical understanding through a historical appreciation of earlier theories, and if panpsychism is able to inspire and motivate reformulations and proponents then it will most certainly continue to contribute to the history of American philosophy.

Further reading

Clarke, D.S. *Panpsychism: Past and Recent Selected Readings.* Albany, NY: SUNY Press, 2004.

Kuklick, Bruce. *A History of Philosophy in America, 1720–2000.* Oxford: Clarendon Press, 2001.

Nagel, Thomas. "Panpsychism," reprinted in his *Mortal Questions*, Cambridge: Cambridge University Press, 1979.

Skrbina, David. *Panpsychism in the West*, Cambridge, MA: MIT Press, 2005.

David Perley

PANTHEISM

Pantheism is a doctrine maintaining that all creatures are either part of God or in God. Conversely, it states that God or the Supreme Being possesses as part of its being all finite creatures. It is a complex doctrine, and therefore there are many subtle differences in the ways God and creatures are related. One of the more basic problems is the question of determinism – that is, if God is every creature and is a necessary being, then there is no room for freedom of any kind. If this is taken seriously, then massive conundrums concerning responsibility, creativity and destiny are sure to emerge.

This type of classical pantheism has its roots in a monistic view of the universe. Only God truly exists and everything else is either a reflection or shadow of that supreme power. Theisms of this sort must come to grips with the question of divine domination. For this reason many classical approaches to pantheism have stalled in the twentieth and twenty-first centuries.

A truly comprehensive description of American pantheism would have to begin with Native American spirituality. In this ancient way of understanding the world, the divine ultimate is often called "Wankan Tonka," which expresses the idea that there are no gaps in the universe. As detailed in Joseph Neihardt's *Black Elk Speaks* (1991), this type of thinking about the relation between God and the universe manifests the ways in which a pantheistic worldview can have significant ecological impact. Mining this vein of the American experience may renew our appreciation for nature, and provide a powerful foundation for developing an American environmental ethics. However, much present-day consumerism has forgotten the values of nature; a revival of interest in this very old doctrine of the continuity of humans, nature and divinity may be the spark needed to reconstruct our approach to planetary environmentalism.

It can be argued that from its beginnings American thought and culture acknowledged an interconnection between divinity and the rest of nature. The Puritan divines brought to America a severe God whose omnipotence stood opposed to forms of pantheistic thinking. But from the 1830s to the Civil War Ralph Waldo Emerson – in the essays contained in his book *Nature* (1836) and his other essays such as "The Over-Soul," "History," and "Circles" – limned a non-systematic portrait of pantheistic experience that formed the basis of the powerful intellectual and religious movement called New England Transcendentalism. Rooted in an affinity for the sense of the divine pervading all forms of existence, this alternative view softened the divine glare and brought forth a more intimate way of experiencing God and nature.

Twentieth-century American philosophy developed a compelling systematic doctrine of the concept of God that is called panentheism. This school of thought found in the process cosmology of Alfred North Whitehead new sources for expressing with great nuance some of the important implications of pantheism for contemporary American religious experience. Finally, the fascination with all things Asian so prevalent in New Age religions and philosophies promises a renewed appreciation for the value and merits of pantheism as a way of thinking about the relations between ultimate realities and human beings.

Further reading

Emerson, Ralph Waldo. *Nature*, in *Nature and Selected Essays*. New York: Penguin, 2003 [1836].

Hartshorne, Charles and Reese, William L. *Philosophers Speak of God*. Amherst, NY: Humanity Books, 1972.

James, William. *Pragmatism and Other Essays*. New York: Penguin, 1978.

Miller, Perry. *The American Transcendentalists: Their Prose and Poetry*. Garden City, NY: Doubleday Anchor, 1957.

Neihardt, Joseph. *Black Elk Speaks*. Lincoln, NE: Nebraska University Press, 1991.

JOSEPH GRANGE

PAPINI, GIOVANNI

Giovanni Papini (1881–1956), an Italian journalist, writer and philosopher, is considered one of the most controversial Italian literary figures of the early and mid-twentieth century, and the earliest and most enthusiastic representative of Italian pragmatism. As a critic of the Italian cultural environment of his day, tainted with pedantic academism and second-hand positivism as he saw it, Papini introduced pragmatism in Italy as the "gospel of a new age hopefully relieved from the burden of empty metaphysical questions, and heading to a more positive knowledge able to free the most productive energies of humanity." In 1903, together with Prezzolini, he started the journal *Il Leonardo*, which was the official voice of Italian pragmatism until 1907. "Gianfalco" was Papini's pseudonym, with which he signed his articles in *Il Leonardo*. The journal hosted both of the opposing factions of Italian pragmatism: the "magical" pragmatism inspired by W. James (Papini–Prezzolini) and the "logical" pragmatism descending from C.S. Peirce (Vailati–Calderoni).

In 1904 Papini met William James at the International Congress of Psychology in Rome. This marked the beginning of an intense correspondence between the two thinkers. Papini revered James as the most eminent spokesman of the new philosophy and James considered Papini as one of the few who fairly understood the pragmatist notion of truth as a tool to "unstiffen" theories and caught the spirit of pragmatism as a doctrine promoting the enhancement of human ability and action (William James, *Pragmatism*, Cambridge, MA: Harvard University Press, 1975, pp 43, 78, 123). In fact Papini's "magical" pragmatism overstressed the irrationalist and voluntaristc side of James's doctrine and twisted it into a wishful mystic of unreflexive action and power of belief (Giovanni Papini, *Sul Pragmatismo*, 1913). In 1906, due to quarrels with the "logical" pragmatists, Papini and Prezzolini, still holding onto their view of pragmatism, stopped the publication of *Leonardo*. That same year, Papini published his first philosophical book, *The Sunset of Philosophers* (*Il crepuscolo dei filosofi*), which James hailed as "the work of a genius" (letter from James to Papini, 27 April 1906). In the book Papini criticizes the thought of the "six lighthouses" of contemporary philosophy (Kant, Hegel, Schopenhauer, Comte, Spencer, Nietzsche) and claims the death of philosophy on behalf of irrationalist vitalism.

Papini's pragmatist leanings did not last long. In 1913, Papini embraced Futurism. In 1921 Papini underwent a religious conversion and published *Life of Christ* (*La storia di Cristo*). Papini would eventually count himself among Mussolini's supporters and become one of the official writers of Fascism. The decade after the end of World War II was the most difficult period of Papini's life. He found himself isolated, and his work discredited and dismissed, because of his previous commitment to Fascism.

Through *Leonardo*'s pages Papini and the other contributors introduced in Italy several important thinkers such as Kierkegaard, Nietzsche, James, Peirce, Poincaré and Russell. Moreover, Papini personally translated or encouraged the translation into Italian of several works of American philosophers such as James, Royce and Santayana.

Further reading

Di Biase, Carmine. *Giovanni Papini. L'anima intera*. Napoli: Edizioni Scientifiche Italiane, 1999.

Invitto, Giovanni. *Un contrasto novecentesco: Giovanni Papini e la filosofia*. Lecce: Ed. Micella, 1984.

Papini, Giovanni. *Tutte le opere*, ten volumes. Milano: Mondatori, 1959–66.

—— *Un uomo finito*. Firenze: La Voce 1912; new edition Firenze: Ponte alle Grazie, 1994; English edition *The Failure*, Whitefish, MT: Kessinger Publishing, 2005.

—— *Passato remoto* (Conversations with Bergson, Nietzsche, James and others). Firenze: L'Arco, 1948; new edition Firenze: Ponte alle Grazie, 1994.

Santucci, A. *Il pragmatismo in Italia*. Bologna: Il Mulino, 1963.

Spirito, Ugo. *Il pragmatismo nella filosofia contemporanea*. Firenze: Sansoni, 1920.

SERGIO FRANZESE

PARADIGM

The word "paradigm" came into popular use after the 1962 publication of Thomas S. Kuhn's book *The Structure of Scientific Revolutions*. The work itself has had lasting influence, not only in philosophy and science and philosophy of science, but in many other disciplines as well, such as those associated with postmodernism, the social sciences, history, art, and economics.

Originally, as used by Kuhn, "paradigm" referred to that which all members of a community of scientists have in common that allows them to engage in productive "puzzle-solving activity." The communities of scientists are the groups comprising the various disciplines of science, for example, astronomy, biology, chemistry, physics, and botany.

One good way to understand paradigm is to focus on the period in history which Kuhn refers to as *pre-science*. This is a time, according to Kuhn, when groups of people in various places were studying the stars, winds, light, motion, and so on but not studying these phenomena in a uniform, or united, way; not necessarily asking the same questions, using the same instruments, engaging in the same experimental methods and not communicating with one another. In other words, the disparate groups were not a community. Another way of characterizing this would be to say that science was in a *pre-paradigm period* because, following our initial characterization, there was nothing these groups had in common that allowed for sustained research and experimentation.

Perhaps the dominant use of paradigm today is as a "way of looking at the world." While this idea is extremely broad, the example of Ptolemy believing that the Sun, the planets and the stars revolve around the Earth and Galileo believing that the Earth, the other planets and the stars revolve around the Sun is telling. Ptolemy and Galileo had very different ways of looking at the world, or universe. They did not embrace the same paradigm. Another example from the history of science involves the idea of motion; Aristotle believed that an object must be constantly pushed in order to stay in motion whereas Newton believed that an object would remain in motion until or unless some other object or force interfered with the moving object. Aristotle and Newton were not working within the same paradigm and they therefore did not see the world in the same way.

This specific use of paradigm can be seen in a host of disciplines. In psychology, cognitivism, functionalism, and behaviorism, for example, each have different perspectives on how to explain the workings of the human mind. Come to that, even within a specific school of thought, such as behaviorism, it is possible that there are different conceptions and methods adhered to by the psychologists themselves. This has, in fact, been one of the most recurrent criticisms of the social sciences, namely that they are not a community committed to any one dominant paradigm. Kuhn argued that this is the most important aspect, a defining aspect even, of a mature science, that the group of individuals working in the discipline will accept one, and only one, paradigm at any given time to do the puzzle-solving work that is, in Kuhn's view, *science*.

Very quickly after the publication of *The Structure of Scientific Revolutions*, Kuhn was roundly criticized for his multiple uses and definitions of paradigm. Margaret Masterman put the count at twenty-one. Subsequently, Kuhn was obliged to attempt an explication of paradigm to stave off charges that the term was unhelpful because of the many different uses to which it had been put. There are two primary senses in which paradigm is to be understood. One is called "disciplinary matrix." "Disciplinary" is used to indicate that the reference is to a specific area of science, e.g. botany, astronomy, chemistry. Each discipline embraces its own paradigm or set of paradigms (some disciplines will have some paradigms in common). "Matrix" is used to indicate ordered elements of three sorts: (a) symbolic generalizations, (b) models, and (c) exemplars. The last of these Kuhn picks out as the second, and more fundamental, sense of paradigm.

With science having been defined by Kuhn as "puzzle-solving activity," and with exemplars being "concrete problem solutions," it is easy to understand why Kuhn would see exemplars as the main sense in which paradigm is to be understood and used. To take an example, we can point to the fact that physics, as a discipline, has embraced one set of acceptable solutions to solve the question/problem of whether light travels faster in air than in water. The way(s) of solving this problem is simply part of what all physicists hold in common that allows them to do the work needed as well as to communicate clearly among themselves. Excellent examples of the use of exemplars can be seen in the teaching of students in any area of science, where the textbook being studied has a section of exercises at the end of each chapter containing questions and problems the student is to answer and solve. These "problem sets" have particular methods, answers and solutions that the student comes to understand by studying the chapter material. The chapter examples exemplify "how we do it in [physics]" and the student is to apply the lessons of the chapter to the exercise sets.

While it may be more or less clear just what paradigms are thought to be, the literature on this concept is vast. For any given discipline, within science or not, it seems the term "paradigm" can apply. In philosophy, for example, it is simply part of the Cartesian paradigm that the mind is private and the body is public. In the study of predicate logic, to take another example, the Law of Excluded Middle is unquestioned. It is part of the paradigm and is one aspect that logicians won't question unless forced to do so by discipline-related problems that become intractable and in need of solution.

What has been called a "paradigm shift" is a topic that one could spend a great deal of time explaining and giving various examples of. For most people, a paradigm shift is a turning away from one way of looking at the world to another, presumably very different, way of looking at the world. So, at the point when the scientific community established that the Earth revolves around the Sun, instead of the other way around, this was a major paradigm shift. On the other hand, midway through the twentieth century, when psychology became enamored with Skinnerian behaviorism, there was an important, though somewhat limited, paradigm shift. One prominent theory has it that through paradigm shifts science makes progress, that scientists working in the new paradigm solve many of the old problems, as well as both expand and change the problem and solution landscapes for that discipline, and provide new ways of looking at the world.

Further reading

Bird, Alexander. *Thomas Kuhn*. Princeton, NJ: Princeton University Press, 2000.

Horwich, Paul (ed.). *World Changes: Thomas Kuhn and the Nature of Science*. Cambridge, MA: MIT Press, 1993.

Kitcher, Philip. *The Advancement of Science*. Oxford: Oxford University Press, 1993.

Kuhn, Thomas S. *The Structure of Scientific Revolutions*. Chicago, IL: University of Chicago Press, 1962, second edition 1970, third edition 1996.

—— *The Road Since Structure*. Chicago, IL: University of Chicago Press, 2000.

Laudan, Larry. *Science and Values*. Berkeley, CA: University of California Press, 1984.

Nickles, Thomas (ed.). *Thomas Kuhn*. Cambridge: Cambridge University Press, 2003.

Sharrock, Wes and Read, Rupert. *Kuhn: Philosopher of Scientific Revolution*. Cambridge: Polity Press, 2002.

Thagard, Paul. *Conceptual Revolutions*. Princeton, NJ: Princeton University Press, 1992.

MICHAEL F. GOODMAN

PARTICULARS, NATURE OF

The terms "particular" and "universal" are correlatives. Corresponding to the traditional problem of universals is a problem of particulars. Central to the former problem is the question: what is the ontological status of universals? Correspondingly, central to the latter problem is the question: what is the ontological status of particulars? Hence the subject of the nature of particulars belongs to metaphysics, and, more specifically, to ontology. For instance, one sort of anti-realism about universals, resemblance nominalism, holds that a universal is nothing but a set of resembling particulars (Armstrong 1989: 39–58). Analogously, a sort of anti-realism about particulars, once advocated by Bertrand Russell, holds that a particular is nothing but a bundle of compresent universals (Armstrong 1989: 70–1). Indeed, the history of philosophy is replete with theories of universals and particulars (most dramatically, Plato's), but it is appropriate to focus here on two American exemplars, the trope theory of Donald Cary Williams and Alfred North Whitehead's theory of eternal objects and actual occasions. (Born in England, Whitehead developed his theory at Harvard.) Of course, other American philosophers have considered the problem of particulars. For example, John Dewey remarked that the "recurrent problems" of "classic philosophy" include that of "the comprehending universal" and "the recalcitrant particular" (Dewey 1929: 41–2). And George Santayana claimed that the problem of "particulars and universals" is "scholastic and artificial" (Santayana 1923: 90). However, in an article of this brevity, it is best to focus on two American philosophers whose conceptions of particulars are especially original.

The ontological category of particulars is exemplified most obviously by concrete things of ordinary experience – e.g. dogs and rocks. But what is particularity? What is meant by "particular"? A frequent answer is that "what is peculiar to particulars is that each occupies a single region of space at a given time" (Loux 2002: 23). But what is the ontological status of spatial (or spacetime) regions? An absolutist (or substantivalist) about space might hold that regions are themselves particulars, albeit abstract ones. In addition to concrete particulars, the ontological category of particulars is thus exemplified controversially by a type of abstract particulars. But what is meant by "abstract particular"? To illustrate how the nature of particulars is problematic, this specific question will be emphasized. On the other hand, a relationalist about space might hold that talk about regions is to be understood in terms of relations between concrete particulars. Apparently, the term "particular" has a meaning that is quite basic, a meaning that cannot be so readily analyzed in terms of the notion of occupying a region. (Similar remarks hold about times.)

Adhering to a foundationalist conception of philosophical analysis, we might conclude that the concept of particularity is "unanalysable" (Campbell 1990: 69). Alternatively, adhering to a conception of "coherence" – i.e. that the basic concepts of metaphysics "presuppose each other so that in isolation they are meaningless" (Whitehead 1978: 3) – the basic concept of particularity might be elucidated through its relationships with other basic concepts. Whichever alternative wins our adherence, we should expect that the question of the ontological status of particulars will be answered somewhat differently by different metaphysicians. This article focuses on the answers of Williams and Whitehead.

Williams's conception of abstract particulars

Traditionally, the history of the problem of universals is portrayed as a debate between realism (e.g. Plato) and nominalism (e.g. Hume). Contrastingly, the history of the problem of particulars may be portrayed as a debate between substance theories (e.g. Aristotle) and bundle theories (e.g. Hume) (Loux 2002: 96–105). "The idea of a substance," Hume maintained, "is nothing but a collection of simple ideas"; and "all general ideas are nothing but particular ones" (1978: 16–17). The key words here are "collection" and "particular." Most fundamentally, simple impressions are particulars, albeit abstract ones. Thus the ontological category of particulars is again exemplified controversially, but by a quite different type of abstract particulars than regions. For example, a simple impression of red is not a perception of the universal redness. Instead, it is a perception of a particular red. In other words, it is a perception of an instance of red. More exactly, it is a perception of an instance of a determinate shade of red.

Williams's nominalistic theory of tropes may be interpreted as a generalization of Hume's nominalistic theory of substances and general ideas. However, rather than being primarily epistemological, Williams's theory is primarily metaphysical. Metaphysics is, he asserted, an "empirical science" (1953: 3), a core aim of which is to discern the basic constituents of reality. The concrete particulars of ordinary experience are complex, and thus have constituents. According to standard scientific theories, these concrete particulars (e.g. a rock) have concrete particulars as constituents (e.g. molecules). But at the heart of Williams's metaphysical theory is the thesis that there is a radically different method of ontological analysis, the analysis of a concrete particular into its constituent abstract particulars. Furthermore, in addition to instances of phenomenal qualities, there are instances of scientific properties. For an illustration, let us consider electrons, particles which the standard model of particle physics regards as elementary (i.e. an electron has no internal structure, it is not composed of anything). Each electron has constitutive properties: for example, an electric charge of minus one and a spin of one half. According to Williams's theory, each electron is nothing but a bundle of instances of these constitutive properties: for example, an instance of the electric charge of minus one and an instance of the spin of one half.

Instances of properties are termed by Williams "tropes" (1953: 7). Tropes are, he asserted, "the primary constituents of this or any possible world, the very alphabet of being" (1953: 7). Accordingly, he answered the question of the ontological status of universals roughly as follows: an "abstract universal" – e.g. "a definite shade of Redness" – is nothing but "the set or sum of tropes precisely similar to a given trope" (1953: 9). This answer is roughly stated especially because it presupposes a "relation of *precise similarity*" (1953: 9). Correlatively, he answered the question of the ontological status of concrete particulars roughly thus: a concrete particular is nothing but "the set or sum of tropes concurrent with a trope" (1953: 9). And this answer is roughly stated especially because it presupposes a metaphysical "relation of *concurrence*" (1953: 9). (The term "sum" in both answers expresses a mereological concept, but this complication has to be ignored.)

But what is a property instance? What is meant by "instance"? Why should such instances be ontologically categorized as abstract particulars? To grasp how Williams would answer these questions, let us consider what he called his "chief proposal" – namely, "that to say that *a* is partially similar to *b* is to say that a part of *a* is wholly or completely similar to a part of *b*" (1953: 4). The term "part" is used ontologically. In effect, the proposal is that conceptual analyses of partial similarity should be grounded on ontological analyses into exactly similar parts. In addition to "ordinary concrete parts" (1953: 4), there are "thinner or more diffuse parts" (1953: 5). The thinnest parts – the primary constituents – are property instances (or tropes) (e.g. a "color component") (1953: 6). Typically, a concrete particular has more than one property (e.g. a rock has shape and weight), and so two concrete particulars can be similar in some ways and dissimilar in others. But a primary constituent is an instance of just one determinate property: it is maximally thin. Suppose that two primary constituents are instances of the same determinate property. Then they are precisely similar. They cannot be dissimilar in other ways, because they do not have other determinate properties.

Whatever the merits or weaknesses of Williams's theory of tropes (a theory that is developed further in Campbell 1990), our study of it should help us to recognize that particularity is as problematic as universality, and that the problem of universals is best explored conjointly with the problem of particulars.

Whitehead's conception of relational particulars

Since much of this brief article is devoted to Williams's theory of tropes, there is only room to sketch very incompletely Whitehead's extraordinarily complicated theory of eternal objects and actual occasions. (For an introduction to Whitehead's metaphysics, see Lango 2004.) Whitehead held a realist theory of universals (which are termed "eternal objects") and a bundle theory of ordinary concrete particulars. Individual events (as distinguished from event types) are particulars. The particulars that are most concrete are temporally evanescent and spatially minute events (which are termed "actual occasions") (cf. the point events of relativity theory). Most fundamentally, eternal objects "ingress" into actual occasions, and ordinary concrete particulars are "societies" of actual occasions.

And, most fundamentally, causal relations between complex events involving ordinary concrete particulars can be "reduced" to elementary causal relations between actual occasions (the latter relations being termed "prehensions" that are "causal") (Whitehead 1978: 236). Hence the primary bundling relation between actual occasions is a relation of *prehension*. An ordinary concrete particular is a collection of actual occasions which are interrelated through their causal prehensions of one another. Indeed, each actual occasion has constitutive properties – namely, eternal objects which ingress into it – but it also has constitutive relations – namely, its causal prehensions of past actual occasions.

Should causal prehensions be ontologically categorized as abstract particulars that are inherently relational? To answer this question, it is instructive to compare Whitehead's metaphysics with trope theory (for a fuller comparison, see Lango 2002). Although it has been argued that a trope theory should include "particularized relations" (Bacon 1995), it also has been argued that relations are supervenient on property tropes (Campbell 1990: 101). In Whitehead's metaphysics, "'relatedness' is dominant over 'quality'" (1978: xiii), and prehensions are both "particulars" (1978: 48) and "Concrete Facts of Relatedness" (1978: 22). Hence causal prehensions are not supervenient on nonrelational particulars, and may be ontologically categorized as relational particulars. Furthermore, an actual occasion comes into being through a process involving a succession of phases of prehensions, and the initial phase is one of causal prehensions. And, in the final phase of becoming, the actual occasion is itself "one complex" prehension (1978: 26). In brief, an actual occasion is a concrete relational particular, and its constituent causal prehensions are abstractions from it.

Even if somewhat unusual, Whitehead's metaphysics exhibits one way in which basic concepts of particularity and relationality can be interlinked.

Further reading

Armstrong, D.M. *Universals: An Opinionated Introduction*. Boulder, CO: Westview Press, 1989.

Bacon, John. *Universals and Property Instances: The Alphabet of Being*, Aristotelian Society Series Vol. 1. Oxford: Blackwell, 1995.

Campbell, Keith. *Abstract Particulars*. Oxford: Blackwell, 1990.

Dewey, John. *Experience and Nature*, second edition. La Salle, IL: Open Court, 1929.

Hume, David. *A Treatise of Human Nature*, second edition. Oxford: Oxford University Press, 1978.

Lango, John W. "Relational Particulars and Whitehead's Metaphysics," in George W. Shields (ed.) *Process and Analysis: Whitehead, Hartshorne, and the Analytic Tradition*. Albany, NY: SUNY Press, 2002, pp. 119–37.

Loux, Michael J. *Metaphysics: A Contemporary Introduction*, second edition. London and New York: Routledge, 2002.

Mertz, D.W. (ed.). "Nominalism and Realism: The Ontology of Unit Attributes," *The Modern Schoolman* 79, 2/3 (January/March 2002): 99–252.

Santayana, George. *Scepticism and Animal Faith*. New York: Dover, 1955 (reproduction of original 1923 edition).

Whitehead, Alfred North. *Process and Reality*, corrected edition. New York: Free Press, 1978.

Williams, Donald C. "On the Elements of Being," parts I and II, *The Review of Metaphysics* 7, 1 (September 1953): 3–18; 7, 2 (December 1953): 171–92.

JOHN W. LANGO

PEIRCE, C.S.: EPISTEMOLOGY AND CATEGORIES

In 1905, Charles Sanders Peirce reflected on his epistemology and the development of his categories, writing to Signore Calderoni that "after three years of almost insanely concentrated thought, hardly interrupted even by sleep, I produced my one contribution to philosophy in the 'New List of Categories.'" This new list, first presented for the American Academy of Arts and Sciences in 1867, represents Peirce's early attempts to classify the elements of thought and consciousness according to their formal structure. It exposes his budding desire to formalize the various modes of human inquiry, and along these lines, reflects his early investigations of epistemology. This desire draws Peirce to develop the "Fixation of Belief" (1877), in which he highlights the three categories of thought in the movement from doubt to certainty.

In arriving at these categories, Peirce follows in the footsteps of Hegel's analysis of phenomenon; Peirce explains to Calderoni that he begins this investigation of thinking by examining *phaneron* which he defines as "all that is present to the mind in any sense or in anyway whatsoever." From this undifferentiated phaneron, he sorted out its elements according to the complexity of their structure. Peirce concludes: "Thus I came to my three categories." Peirce's categories may have "sorted out" the elements of formal logic or mental phenomenon, but by the 1890s, as Peirce begins to reconsider the connection between epistemology and ontology, the categories of thought come to define the Law of Mind that underpins not only the nature of human consciousness, but also the growth and development of nature on the whole. Throughout his career, Peirce's discussion of the categories doubles as an investigation of the epistemological and ontological concepts he would call Firstness, Secondness and Thirdness. A brief account of these concepts seems warranted in order to shed light on the character of the categories and on Peirce's epistemology more generally.

Firstness is, by definition, the slipperiest of categories. Peirce describes it at various points as the momentary, wholly unrelatable presence that gives rise to any phenomenon. Peirce writes, "Stop and think of [firstness] and it has flown! … [It is] present, immediate, fresh, new initiative, original, spontaneous, free, vivid, conscious, evanescent. Only remember that every description must be false to it" ("The Categories in Detail," Peirce 1958: 1.318)

In terms of phenomenology, Peirce suggests that Firstness could be understood as bare feeling, stating:

> Contemplate anything … Attend to the whole and drop the parts out of attention all together. One can approximate nearly enough the accomplishment of that to see that the result of the perfect accomplishment would be that one would have in his consciousness at the moment nothing but a quality of feeling.
>
> ("The Categories in Detail," Peirce 1958: 1.318)

This feeling would be bare in the sense that it would be unlike any prior moments of feeling and would defy comparison and resemblance. In 1894, Peirce reiterates an earlier suggestion that Firstness should be conceptualized as a moment of free chance. "The free is that which has not another behind, determining its actions." It is worth noting that Firstness, framed as both free chance and an immediate quality of feeling, is always present in Peirce's notion of inquiry. This point will be appropriated with little modification by William James and John Dewey in their investigations of epistemology.

While Firstness appears as unrelated presence, Secondness emerges in, and as, a reaction to this immediate sensation. It stands in relation and opposed to Firstness. It is in this sense that Peirce writes in 1903 that "the second category that I find, the next simplest feature common to all that comes before the mind, is the element of struggle." He elaborates: "By struggle I mean mutual action between two things regardless of any sort of third or medium." In the "Guess at the Riddle," Peirce is sure to emphasize that the category of the second cannot be without the first and "meets us in such facts as another, relation, compulsion, effect, dependence … negation … and result." As opposed to bare chance, the category of Secondness comes to be in brute reaction; at other points, Peirce describes it as brute or necessary law. He remains intrigued by the role this reaction-law plays in the development of human thought. He writes: "[Secondness] is the idea of the other, of not. This becomes the very pivot of thought." According to Peirce, Secondness is often the prominent feature of human inquiry; individuals often run up against opposing facts that serve as the pivot, or impetus, in any turn of human thought. Peirce underscores the situation of Secondness in

"The Architecture of Theories," writing, "besides feelings [Firstness], we have Sensations of reactions [Secondness]; as when a person blindfold suddenly runs against the post, when we make a muscular effort, or when any feeling gives way to a new feeling." John Dewey makes a similar point in his discussion of the way in which "problematic situations" give rise to human ways of knowing.

While Secondness might provide the impetus in human knowing, it is Thirdness, the final and most complex category of Peirce's thought, which characterizes the *movement* and development of human knowing. Peirce situates Thirdness in his understanding of epistemology:

> Very different both from feelings and from reaction-sensations or disturbances of feeling are general conceptions. When we think, we are conscious that a connection between feelings is determined by a general rule, we are aware of being governed by habit. Intellectual power is nothing but facility in taking habits.
> ("The Architecture of Theories," Peirce 1958: 6.20)

It is important to note that this general rule of taking habits, this order of Thirdness, is not a determinate law of thought. In the "Categories in Detail" (1894), Peirce is emphatic on the point that Thirdness is "the mediating element between chance, which brings forth First and original events, and law which produces sequences or Seconds." The complexity of Thirdness is due to its mediating character that encompasses Firstness and Secondness and draws together these opposing elements of phenomena. Peirce's investigation of Thirdness corresponds to his abiding interest in the character of continuity in the evolution of thought. For Peirce, as well as Royce, James and Dewey, habits of thought develop over time and through a process of adaptation. Similarly, truth progresses through the three categories that Peirce defines and through the community of inquiry that is itself continuous with these three elements of thought.

Further reading

Anderson, Douglas. R. *Strands of System: The Philosophy of Charles S. Peirce.* West Lafayette, IN: Purdue University Press, 1995.

Kent, Beverly. *Charles S. Peirce and the Classification of Science.* Montreal: McGill-Queen's University Press, 1987.

Peirce, Charles Sanders. *Collected Papers of Charles Sanders Peirce*, ed. Charles Hartshorne and Paul Weiss. Cambridge, MA: Harvard University Press, Vol. 6, 1958.

Potter, Vincent. *Charles S. Peirce: On Norms and Ideals.* New York: Fordham University Press, 1997.

John J. Kaag

PEIRCE, C.S.: LIFE

Charles Sanders Peirce (1839–1914) was a prodigious, protean, and productive intellect, who lived a tragic and humiliating life. Peirce, judged by many scholars and intellectuals to be the most important American thinker, holds a unique place in American philosophy. He is the founder of pragmatism, the only American contribution to philosophy. With Augustus de Morgan, he is one of the founders of the logic of relatives. His pioneering work in semiotics (the theory of signs) provides, in the judgment of such contemporary figures as the philosopher Hilary Putnam, the novelist Walker Percy, and the physicist Karl Popper, a fruitful matrix of inquiry for the sciences and humanities alike. Peirce, a polymath, made important contributions to philosophy, logic, mathematics, geodesy, geology, metrology, computing, photometrics, spectroscopy, astronomy, cartography, psychology, metaphysics, phenomenology, and the history, philosophy, and logic of science.

Peirce was born into the privileged world of well-bred Cambridge and Boston. His family was well connected in politics, trade, and the professions. His father Benjamin (1809–80) was the most distinguished American mathematician of the time, and held the chair of mathematics and astronomy at Harvard University. At Harvard, Peirce graduated seventy-ninth out of ninety in the class of 1859, in part because his father conducted his son's education himself, with little regard for academic requirements. Aiming his son for greatness, Benjamin schooled Charles rigorously in mathematics, science, and philosophy. At college, Peirce earned a reputation for arrogance, brilliance, iconoclasm, dangerous mood swings, and dissipation – behaviors due, in part, to two neurological pathologies: trigeminal neuralgia and manic depression. This reputation remained with him until old age, and undermined both his personal and professional life, resulting in two disastrous marriages, and dismissal from both the faculty of Johns Hopkins University in 1884 and the United States Coast Survey, his employer of thirty years, in 1891, and in 1903 in the failure of the Carnegie Institution to approve his request for a grant to write and publish his philosophy.

Peirce was an experimental scientist and his lifelong pursuit of the nature of inquiry into truth derived from this source. At twenty-five, he began conducting experiments on star brightness at the Harvard Observatory. These studies resulted in his publication of *Photometric Researches* (1878), which was the first modern compilation of star magnitudes and a work which was among the first to suggest a disc shape for the Milky Way galaxy. In 1872, his father, then superintendent of the Coast Survey, appointed Peirce to head the measurement of gravity at the Coast Survey. In 1877, he became the first American scientist to participate in a major European scientific meeting, the International Geodetic Association, where his work was recognized as an important advance in gravimetrics. In the early 1880s, he pioneered the application of spectroscopy to use a wave-length of light to determine the length of the meter, a major refinement in metrology.

Peirce integrated this thorough grounding in exact science with a thorough knowledge of philosophy and its history. He was well aware of his indebtedness to Aristotle, Plato, medieval realism, Leibnitz, Berkeley, Boole, de Morgan, Scottish commonsensism, Schelling, Hegel, and especially to Kant, whose concept of "pragmatic belief" he extended to mean that truth is the ultimate opinion that would survive all possible logical scrutiny and experiential evidence. Peirce is best known for his series of essays "Illustration of the Logic of Science" (1877–8), the first two of which ("The Fixation of Belief" and "How to Make Our Ideas Clear") William James, in 1898, called "the birth certificates of pragmatism."

He published, jointly with his students, only one volume of philosophy, *Studies in Logic* (1883) while at Johns Hopkins. Peirce spent his last twenty-five years in increasing isolation and poverty, working obsessively and successfully on his philosophy. He left more than 80,000 pages of unpublished philosophical manuscripts, from which the Peirce Edition Project is selecting a projected thirty volumes for publication.

Peirce's influence on William James, John Dewey, and Josiah Royce was immediate and fundamental. It was indirect but significant for many subsequent thinkers, including Clerence I. Lewis, Ilya Prigogine, Jacques Derrida, Umberto Eco, Jürgen Habermas, Jacques Lacan, Richard Rorty, and others.

Since about 1970, Peirce's philosophy has become an important source of stimulation for philosophers and scientists internationally. For these thinkers, he is a point of departure for new approaches to issues in the philosophy of science, and in physics, mathematics, logic, language, computer design, consciousness, artificial intelligence, anthropology, sociology, psychology, law, literature, and cultural studies.

Further reading

Brent, Joseph. *Charles Sanders Peirce: A Life*, revised and enlarged edition. Bloomington, IN: Indiana University Press 1998.

Hookway, Christopher. *Peirce*. London and New York: Routledge, 1992.

Peirce, Charles Sanders. *The Essential Peirce: Selected Philosophical Writings Volume 1 (1867–1893)*, ed. Nathan Houser and Christian Kloesel. Bloomington, IN: Indiana University Press, 1992.

—— *Reasoning and the Logic of Things*, ed. Kenneth Lane Ketner. Cambridge, MA: Harvard University Press, 1992.

—— *The Essential Peirce: Selected Philosophical Writings Volume 2 (1893–1913)*, ed. the Peirce Edition Project. Bloomington, IN: Indiana University Press, 1998.

JOSEPH BRENT

PEIRCE, C.S.: METAPHYSICS AND COSMOLOGY

Metaphysics

Charles Peirce's metaphysics underpins his architectonic system in that it seeks to explain what he saw as the three fundamental modes of reality. Unlike many of his predecessors, Peirce did not seek a metaphysics that was *a priori*; he sought one that was far more developmental and beholden to logical, mathematical, and scientific observation. Peirce thought his categories to be the three most general aspects of existence, each irreducible to the other and each fundamentally necessary to a holistic explanation. On the medieval question that concerned Duns Scotus, whether laws or types were real or merely definitional figments of the imagination, Peirce came out squarely on the side supporting realism. He considered laws ontological continuities that did not merely exist but provided the backbone for the shape of cosmic development *and* human understanding. He differed from other modern philosophers, though, because most of the moderns, according to Peirce, accepted only one kind of existence: the individual fact, the single, isolated, extant entity. The actual, for Peirce, is subsumed into the probable, as continuity creates the conditions for further manifestations of whatever actuality is in question. For Peirce, who acknowledged the reality of the singular, the saturated reality of the repeatable, the continuous, trumped, in the end, this modern predilection toward singularity. What is verifiable and therefore what is real is that which is repeatable and testable in the future.

Peirce believed that the deep structure of reality was triadic and had three distinct though complimentary elements: Firstness, Secondness, and Thirdness. Firstness is the dimension of chance and quality, variegated heterogeneity flush with the virtual variety of spontaneity, pure possibility. Peirce considered a quality merely an eternal possibility, almost, but not exactly, a set of conditions. Firstness can behave, though, both actually and potentially, as an actual quality that can set parameters for the appearance of future qualities.

Secondness is the dimension of fact, of actual energetic reaction of either the causal or contiguous variety. Secondness, or dyadic relation, is not in itself repeatable. In a famous chalkboard example that Peirce was known to use on his students at Johns Hopkins, he drew a white line on the black chalkboard and explained that Secondness was the exact limit between the two which is essentially discontinuous and completely unique. Secondness is *this here*; it is a slap on the shoulder, a car crash, the division in time when the lunch whistle blows. Though essential for scientific observation, science and reality do not stop with Secondness, however. Science needs more than the "this here." Science is interested in the conditions under which the "this here" might reappear in the future and thus become verifiable and predictable, might become the proper object of study. Peirce's three categories of existence take his readers from the possible (Firstness) to the probable (Thirdness) by means of the actual (Secondness).

Reality exists for Peirce in the future and repeatable past and the continuous nature of reality is the last metaphysical category: Thirdness. Thirdness or ontological continuity gives us real existence or regularity. Peirce believes that the continuous movement of the cosmos is built on the principle of cosmic habit-taking, a type of movement in which the specific becomes the general and the possible becomes the probable. Cosmic habits, for Peirce, eventually turn into cosmic laws and are evidence of the work of mind – the definition of which eschews embodiment for cosmic regularity and uses matter but is not coequal to it. Matter is, for Peirce, merely mind that has lost its vivacity, mind that has forgone possibility and become sterile and ceased to change. Peirce called matter "effete mind" because it lacks the vitality and fecundity present in mind as the purposive, habitual combination of chance, fact, and habit. Mind consists of chance-driven regularity. Human consciousness is, then, a Third-Thirdness in which cosmic regularities have become somewhat aware of their own existence and have become reflexive.

Cosmology

Peirce readily admitted that his cosmology was hypothetical and that his explanation of the origin of the cosmos and of his different metaphysical categories was more than anything an explanatory tool for the comprehension of his system. However, Peirce held firm to his hypothetical explanations until the end of his life, believing that they offered a grain of truth about the origins and nature of mind, matter, and reality. Cosmology was important for Peirce's system because in it came his most complicated question: since no law in particular can explain law in general, then how does law itself evolve? The answer to this turned out to be an ongoing explanation of the function of his three metaphysical categories.

Peirce's cosmology starts before time, before matter, and before mind in a state of ultimate Firstness: pure chance, pure potentiality, where there is not such a thing as thing-ness or substance. In this state qualities exist only potentially, and due to their strictly potential existence they exist as perfect possibilities (there cannot be two possibilities of redness, for example). Peirce believed that this pure Firstness was a state where all potential qualities existed *sui generis*. They are potential but absolutely of their own kind, completely self-similar. These qualities-as-possibilities exist prior to their own embodiment.

Importantly, Peirce unifies chance and possibility into the category of Firstness because he believes that qualities are mere possibilities, eternal chances. Original Firstness, while empty of things, is full of chance, completely saturated with possibility. Peirce proposed a logic of chance called tychism. Tychism (a principle that seems to echo Spencer's cosmology) is the belief that chance is self-annulling, that chance brings about order. Tychistic evolution, then, is the type of evolution by fortuitous variation that Darwin upheld and out of which certain types of order are developed. Eventually, as thread of the cosmos is drawn out by the pull of chance, this ordering becomes a principle itself. Peirce calls this ordering principle synechism, or the belief that the universe contains self-generating continuous phenomena. This cannot happen, though, without the development of Firstness into Secondness and both of these into an irreducible continuity, Thirdness.

After this unbounded potentiality becomes, to a certain degree, unified into qualities or metaphysical unities, these unities are brought into relationship with each other and come into existence as such. In Firstness, qualities do not exist as such;

they only exist as potentialities, but in Secondness they are brought into dyadic relation with one another. The qualities of Firstness are ever-present in Secondness, but Secondness is the category of reaction or relation of two qualities. This reaction or relation is only absolutely singular, and though it does exist in one place at one time, it does not exist for the future. Pure Secondness, then, does not exist as fully as it would through Thirdness or continuity because it cannot be brought into the future and made repeatable. The qualities of Firstness and the singular facts of Secondness are ordered and rendered comprehensible, repeatable, by Thirdness. Cosmologically, Firstness and Secondness necessarily precede Thirdness.

Since Thirdness is the irreducible dimension of continuity that includes the former two categories (quality and fact, respectively), it is the category out of which reality is born. That is, Secondness is real but could never be acknowledged as such due to its lack of repeatability. Peirce saw in the cosmos movement from the homogeneous to the heterogeneous, and he saw in that principle the fact that chance works itself "out" into repeatable habits, then out of habits into laws until the cosmos enters into a state where no chance remains, a state of what Peirce called concrete reasonableness.

In this state continuity doesn't cease; it marches on. The movement of Firstness to Secondness to the all-encompassing Thirdness is an attempt to explain the development of law out of purely singular elements, as no law in particular can explain law in general. The development of the rule-governed, continuous cosmos served, along with a serious phenomenological and semeiotic explanation of verifiability, to bolster Peirce's realism. Peirce believed that once elements of fact, of Secondness, entered into these repetitions of growth or habit-taking, the development of mind, or Thirdness was a necessary outcome, a greater complexity out of which matter creates some sort of consciousness of itself or, at least, the ability to act as though consciousness existed. A plant's phototropism, turning toward the nourishment of the sun, is an example of this completely material quasi-consciousness. Late in his life, Peirce worked ferociously on a system he called his semeiotic that would explain the workings of mind in principles consistent with his metaphysics and cosmology.

Further reading

Anderson, Douglas R. *Strands of System: The Philosophy of Charles Peirce*. West Lafayette, IN: Purdue University Press, 1995.

Reynolds, Andrew. *Peirce's Scientific Metaphysics: The Philosophy of Chance, Law, and Evolution*. Nashville, TN: Vanderbilt University Press, 2002.

Robin, Richard and Moore, Edward C. (eds). *From Time and Chance to Consciousness: Studies in the Metaphysics of Charles Peirce*. Oxford: Berg, 1994.

Sheriff, John. *Charles Peirce's Guess at the Riddle*. Bloomington, IN: University of Indiana Press, 1994.

JASON BARRETT-FOX

PEIRCE, C.S.: SEMIOTICS

Although the special sciences (or what, following Jeremy Bentham, C.S. Peirce frequently called *idioscopic* investigations) depend upon "special observation, which travel or other exploration, or some assistance to the senses, either instrumental or given by training ... has put into the power of its students" (CP 1.242), philosophical investigations (or *cenoscopic* inquiries) appeal mainly to "observations such as come within the range of every man's normal experience, and for the most part in every waking hour of his life" (CP 1.241). Even though most Americans are likely to call everyday experience or familiar phenomena "squeezed lemons," thereby indicating they need "recondite experiences" to awaken theoretical curiosity, Peirce insists it is impossible for familiar experiences to have "their juices sucked out of them" entirely (CP 6.565).

One such phenomenon is the operation or function of signs (i.e. semiosis) evident not only in human conduct but also throughout the natural world (e.g. the formation of a fossil, the flight of a deer upon hearing what is instinctually taken to a sound indicative of predation, and perhaps even the sunflower turning toward the sun). Accordingly, Peirce in a relatively late manuscript recommends that it would be a promising scientific undertaking, "for those who have both a talent and a passion for eliciting the truth of such matters, to institute a cooperative attack upon the problems of nature, properties, and varieties of Signs, in the spirit of twentieth-century science" (EP 2.462). In fact, he had almost five decades earlier laid the foundations, or opened the field, for such an investigation. Moreover, he devoted sustained, intense philosophical attention to these problems. Even so, he felt forced to confess: "I find the field too vast, the labor too great, for a first-comer." But, even as "a pioneer, or rather a backwoodsman, in the work of clearing and opening up ... the doctrine of the essential nature and fundamental varieties of possible semiosis" or sign-functions, we are still not in the position to take the full measure of Peirce's monumental contributions to what he called *semeiotic* and what we more commonly designate *semiotic*.

He transformed the classical, dyadic definition of the sign as *aliquid stat pro aliquo* (something standing for something else) into his dynamic, triadic definition, first, by proposing the irreducibly triadic structure or signs and, then, shifting attention away from the individual unit of the sign to the ongoing *process* of semiosis (Short 2004: 216). The triadic structure is evident in what is arguably his most famous definition: "A sign, or *representamen*, is something which stands to somebody for something in some respect or capacity" (CP 2.228). That for which the sign stands is called by Peirce its *object*. That to whom the sign stands for something (e.g. this gesture signifies to me friendship) is ordinarily taken to be the interpreter, but that to which the sign gives rise is identified by Peirce as the *interpretant* (a term not synonymous with *interpreter*). While the interpretant of a sign might be in some cases the mental response of a mindful agent (the thought or feeling evoked by an utterance or phenomenon), it need not be. Indeed, in order to establish a truly general theory of signs, Peirce deliberately formulated a definition in which the functioning of signs is characterized without any necessary reference to mind or consciousness. Signs in their most rudimentary forms are not explicable in terms of mind; rather, mind is itself an emergent, semiotic function. That is, mind is what evolves when semiosis reaches a level of complexity wherein the functional integration of semiotic processes allows for the remarkable forms of stability, growth, and reflexivity we observe in, say, the conduct of various mammals. In the text quoted, the respect in which the sign stands for the object (e.g. the object might be represented insofar as it is a piece of furniture from a particular period in Chinese history) is identified by Peirce as the *ground*. But this is not to be counted as a fourth factor, since it is reducible to the way the object functions in the process of semiosis.

The dynamic character of semiosis most clearly comes into focus when Peirce stresses that this process does not terminate in the generation of a single interpretant, or even finite set of interpretants, but continues by producing at least a potentially endless series of interpretants. Thus, Peirce's theory of signs is concerned with semiosis as an open-ended process, not signs as separable entities. Just as there are for him no isolated signs, there are no static ones: evolving systems of evolving signs, such as natural languages, human cultures, and scientific traditions indisputably manifest themselves to be, are the phenomena for which the definitions, distinctions, and classifications articulated in his doctrine of signs were crafted to illuminate.

Above all else, he designed his semeiotic to assist in offering a normative theory of objective inquiry, i.e. an account of how we ought to comport ourselves when striving to discover truths not yet known. The focus of his concern was to ascertain "what *must be* the characters [or traits] of all signs used by 'scientific intelligence,' that is to say, by an intelligence capable of learning by experience" (CP 2.227). Such intelligence is defined by a commitment to fallibilism. In reference to semeiotic, this necessitates the distinction between the immediate and the dynamical object, i.e. the object as it is represented at a particular juncture in the actual development of a sign (e.g. the identity of the burglar at this phase of the investigation) and the object as it really is (the identity of the individual who was really, or truly, responsible for the crime). The immediate object is potentially a misrepresentation of the reality being sought. The dynamic object is functionally what in the course of development serves to constrain or direct the process toward the disclosure of truth. Although its presence is effectively exerted in the traces that, when properly interpreted, would lead to its discovery, its principal locus is neither at the origin nor along the course of inquiry, but at the end of the process (when, for example, the real perpetrator is identified). When inquiry is successful, when truth is discovered, the immediate and dynamical objects coincide. For most of the investigations conducted by natural scientists are others engaged in historically evolving forms of objective inquiry, however, there is, in practice, difference between the immediate and the dynamical object, the object as we conceive it to be and the object as it really is.

The drive to ascertain what must be characteristic of the functioning of signs, beginning at the most rudimentary level (the level at which semiosis is conceived in abstraction from mind) makes of Peirce's semeiotic "a quasi-necessary, or formal, doctrine of signs." But his lifelong investigation of the relevant phenomena and also his inherent fascination with semiosis in its myriad forms resulted in reflections on signs having relevance far beyond the focal concern of this inaugural figure.

One glimpses the range of this relevance only by appreciating the explanatory power of Peirce's various classifications of semiotic functions. The most famous and fecund of these is the trichotomy of icon, index, and symbol. It is imperative to understand this as a set of functional distinctions; so, rather than speak of the iconic sign it is more appropriate to speak of the iconic function of signs, suggesting thereby that virtually every actual sign is a complex one in which various functions are integrated. Anything functions iconically insofar as it signifies its object by virtue of a resemblance or similarity to that object. In turn, anything functions indexically insofar as it signifies its object by virtue of a physical or causal connection to that object. Finally, anything functions symbolically insofar as a habit or disposition (be it conventional or instinctual) serves to relate a sign to its object. The example of a photograph shows clearly how the iconic, indexical, and symbolic functions are fused together to make a complex sign capable of serving diverse purposes (e.g. as documentary evidence, or aesthetic object, or psychological portrait).

The heuristic function of Peirce's three categories of firstness, secondness, and thirdness is nowhere more apparent in his writings than in his investigation of signs. At every turn, they serve to guide and goad this inquiry, suggesting possibilities for classification and the necessity for distinctions. One might even say that his categories and semeiotic were born twins. We have in "On a New List of Categories" (1867) Peirce's earliest published presentation of both his categories and the outline of his theory of signs, including a variant of his trichotomy of icon, index, and symbol. In contrast, the pragmatic aspects of his semeiotic and, in turn, the semeiotic form of his pragmatism only come into sharp focus in the last decade of his life.

Peirce insisted: "Symbols grow" (2.302). It seems appropriate that his own reflections on symbols and other signs grew over the course of a lifelong study of their nature, defining characteristics, and myriad forms. This makes it necessary to be attentive to the date when a particular formulation was written. Here as much as anywhere else the chronological development of Peirce's actual thought is of the utmost pertinence to the accurate interpretation of his evolving thought. In not only the "New List" but also the cognition series in the *Journal of Speculative Philosophy* (the first article of which is "Certain Faculties Claimed for Man") and other early writings, some of Peirce's most basic insights are already articulated, not least of all his conception of semiosis as an open-ended process and his vision of the human person as an evolving sign of an irreducibly complex character. The self is not simply a user of signs; s/he is a sign in the process of development, even if the significance of the self-as-sign mostly transcends the comprehension of this self. For this reason, Peirce was fond of quoting Shakespeare's lines:

> proud man,
> Most ignorant of what he's most assured,
> His glassy essence.
> (*Measure for Measure* 2.2.117–20)

The notion of infinite semiosis so prominent in many of the early texts is, however, dramatically modified around 1907 when Peirce introduced in a decisive manner habit or habit-change as the "ultimate logical interpretant" of sign-activity. Thus, the extent to which his mature doctrine of habit being the "ultimate logical interpretant" of the signs employed by scientific intelligence modifies his early view regarding "unlimited semiosis" (to use Umberto Eco's expression) has been insufficiently appreciated by many of Peirce's most sympathetic and influential expositors, including Eco. Semiosis generates habits and habits in their status as interpretants mark the appropriate closure, not the premature or arbitrary arrest, of potentially infinite processes. But the dissolution of habits, hence the eruption of doubt, itself marks the renewal of semiosis. Yet, apart from the specification of habits or habit-changes as the ultimate logical interpretant of semiosis, the connection between Peirce's semeiotic and pragmatism is obscure, if not invisible (Alston 1956; Short 2004).

Further reading

Apel, Karl-Otto. *Charles S. Peirce: From Pragmatism to Pragmaticism*, trans. J. Krois. Amherst, MA: University of Massachusetts Press, 1981.

Benedict, George. "What are Representamen?" *Transactions of the Charles S. Peirce Society,* 21, 2 (1985): 340–70.

Colapietro, Vincent. *Peirce's Approach to the Self.* Albany, NY: SUNY Press, 1989.

Liszka, James J. *A General Introduction to the Semeiotic of Charles Sanders Peirce.* Bloomington, IN: Indiana University Press, 1996.

Nöth, Winfried. *Handbook of Semiotics.* Bloomington, IN: Indiana University Press, 1990.

Oehler, Klaus. "An Outline of Peirce's Semiotic" in Martin Krampen, Klaus Oehler, Roland Posner, Thomas A. Sebeok, Thure von Uexküll (eds) *Classics of Semiotics.* New York: Plenum Press, 1987, pp. 1–21.

Peirce, C.S. *The Collected Papers of Charles Sanders Peirce* (CP,) ed. C. Hartshorne and P. Weiss (Vols. 1–6) and A. Burks (Vols. 7–8). Cambridge, MA: Harvard University Press, 1931–58.

—— *The Essential Peirce: Selected Philosophical Writings*, 2 volumes, ed. N. Houser and C. Kloesel. Bloomington, IN: Indiana University Press, 1998.

Ransdell, Joseph. "C.S. Peirce and American Semiotics" in *The Peirce Seminar Papers*, Vol. 2, ed. Michael Shapiro. Oxford: Berghahn Books, 1994.

Shapiro, Michael. *The Sense of Grammar: Language as Semeiotic*. Bloomington, IN: Indiana University Press, 1983.
Short, T.L. *Peirce's Theory of Signs*. Cambridge, Cambridge University Press, 2007 [2004].

VINCENT COLAPIETRO

PEIRCE, C.S.: TRUTH, MEANING, INQUIRY

Charles Sanders Peirce (1839–1914) made numerous significant contributions to astronomy, mathematics, and logic, as well as to philosophy; prominent among the latter are his accounts of truth, of meaning, and of inquiry.

Truth

Peirce typically equated truth with the final opinion towards which inquiry, if pushed sufficiently far, would ultimately lead us. Thus, in 1871 he wrote:

> There is ... to every question a true answer, a final conclusion, to which the opinion of every man is constantly gravitating ... The arbitrary will or other individual peculiarities of a sufficiently large number of minds may postpone the general agreement in that opinion indefinitely; but it cannot affect what the character of that opinion shall be when it is reached. This final opinion, then, is independent, not indeed of thought in general, but of all that is arbitrary and individual in thought; is quite independent of how you or I, or any number of men think.
>
> (CP 8.12)

This is evidently a communitarian and a dialogical conception, which defines truth with reference to a social process of inquiry, the aim of which is the gradual elimination of all that is individual and arbitrary in human opinion. But it is not a consensus theory of truth, as is clear from Peirce's simultaneous insistence that truth is the agreement of a statement with its object, and that the truth of a matter is what it is independently of what you or I or any number of people may think about it (CP 5.408). No actual consensus, therefore, is a test or criterion of truth. The concept of truth as the final opinion of inquiry is, on the other hand, not empty of pragmatic content. Truth as agreement with the object of belief can be equated with the final opinion of inquiry because inquiry is – or, if pushed far enough, will be – governed by a method that is specifically designed to let the content of belief be determined by its object. We have no idea on which questions the final opinion may already have been reached. But to make a truth claim is, on this account, to predict that it will be upheld by further inquiry and thus in effect to invite inquiry by others. This conception has also, and famously, been expressed as an ideal limit towards which inquiry will converge in the long run, as in this dictionary entry from 1901:

> Truth is that concordance of an abstract statement with the ideal limit towards which endless investigation would tend to bring scientific belief, which concordance the abstract statement may possess by virtue of the confession of its inaccuracy and one-sidedness, and this confession is an essential ingredient of truth.
>
> (CP 5.565)

Whatever scope Peirce intended this definition to have, this is recognizably the statistical concept of the true value of a parameter, as distinct from an estimated value. Thus, given certain conditions (random sampling, etc.) a population mean μ is the limit towards which the sample mean $\overline{X}$ converges as you enlarge the sample indefinitely, *and* you can express the numerical value of μ only by specifying the probable error (the "confession of inaccuracy and one-sidedness"); leave out the probable error and what you will express is not μ, but the estimated mean $\overline{X}$. As Peirce's limit theory may be best known from Quine's famous objection that the concept of a limit is defined for measurements, but not for theories, it should be noted that Peirce himself made it clear in 1903 that he did not think we know precisely what it means for a theory to be "true" (CP 7.119). Qualitative induction, Peirce there held, differs in this respect sharply from statistical induction, where approximation to truth is quantifiable and thus precisely understood.

Meaning

Peirce's account of meaning is part and parcel of his "semiotic," or general theory of signs, according to which a sign is something which stands for something to some other sign in some respect (CP 5.283). Every sign is thus connected to three things: its ground, its object, and its interpretant – i.e. the sign which interprets it, not the interpreting mind – and the irreducibly triadic nature of this relation is what characterizes the sign relation and distinguishes it from causal relations. Since the interpretant of a sign is itself a sign, every interpretant is in turn capable of further interpretation, so the process of sign-interpretation is open-ended, and the meaning of no sign is determined once and for all (CP 2.303; Deledalle 2000: 60) What enables us to break out of the circle of signs, as has been emphasized by T.L. Short (2004: 228–30), is Peirce's pragmatism which, in its mature form, holds that the meaning of a sign, at any given time, consists in its mediation between perception and purposive action. A sign can always take on a new meaning through further interpretation, but in "real time" its meaning consists in the interpretation which *now* predisposes us to act one way rather than another.

Peirce's account of meaning is undoubtedly best known from his pragmatic maxim, published in 1878, albeit not yet under that name: "Consider what effects, that might conceivably have practical bearings, we conceive the object of our conception to have. Then, our conception of these effects is the whole of our conception of the object" (CP 5.402). This maxim has been widely interpreted, and not entirely without justification, as a reductive definition of meaning, closely akin to the verifiability criterion of meaning later formulated by the logical empiricists. It can never really have been so intended, as Peirce early and late professed a metaphysical commitment to a moderate scholastic realism not compatible with strict verificationism. But Peirce himself encouraged such an interpretation by saying, in his 1878 article that, since to call an object "hard" only means that it resists scratching, there would be no *falsity* in saying that all objects remain perfectly soft until brought under pressure; in other words, the hardness consists only in the observable phenomena. Later, in 1903, Peirce came to realize that subjunctive conditionals are not reducible to material conditionals, and that therefore a disposition, such as hardness, is not reducible to its observable manifestations (CP 4.546; 4.580). In his later restatements of pragmatism, accordingly, Peirce explicitly rejected his earlier equation of hardness with resistance to scratching (CP 5.457). While continuing to insist that discourse is meaningful only to the extent that we can relate its terms to possible actions and their consequences, the mature Peirce did not intend to eliminate metaphysical speculation, only to subject it to the rigorous discipline of restricting it to what could be explicated in terms of potential actions and their consequences.

Inquiry

The struggle to dispel doubt and attain belief is what Peirce dubbed "inquiry," paradigmatic of which is the scientific method, which he explicated as consisting of three stages, corresponding to the three basic modes of reasoning: abduction, or the inference from a set of puzzling facts to an explanatory hypothesis; deduction, or the derivation of observable consequences of our hypothesis; and lastly induction, whereby our hypothesis is tested through observation and experiment. Like Karl Popper and others later, Peirce stressed that observations can only refute hypotheses, not prove or confirm them, he formulated the outlook he dubbed "fallibilism," according to which the conclusions of science at any one time must be regarded as fallible and provisional, and, while he analyzed the logic of statistical inference in great detail and formulated a propensity theory of probability, he stressed that no numerical probability could be attached to laws of nature – something which would make sense only "if universes were as plentiful as blackberries" (CP 2.684).

Inquiry, in Peirce's view, is inherently social. Its impulse comes from disagreement over matters of fact, and its methods are designed to produce consensus. However, only lasting consensus is worthy of the name consensus and, as Peirce explains in his 1877 article "The Fixation of Belief," a consensus reached by "direct" methods, methods that are designed *only* to produce consensus, such as the burning or exiling of heretics, will be too transparent and arbitrary to last. People will too quickly realize that the very same methods could be used to yield the opposite conclusions from those favored by the powers that be. A lasting consensus requires indirect methods, methods which produce consensus by allowing the objects of our beliefs to determine the content of our beliefs:

> To satisfy our doubts, therefore, it is necessary that a method should be found by which our beliefs may be determined by nothing human, but by some external permanency – by something upon which our thinking has no effect . . . Such is the method of science.
>
> (CP 5.384)

This method, Peirce goes on, proceeds on the assumption that real things exist, and that sufficient experience and reasoning will ultimately lead any inquirer to the same true opinion as any other inquirer. This method, finally, is self-corrective, in that any error it leads us into can only be, and in due course will be, corrected by the further application of the scientific method itself (CP 2.729; 2.781; 5.582). From this recognition derives Peirce's insistence on the autonomy of scientific inquiry from religious and philosophical systems, frequently expressed in what Peirce called the First Rule of Reason: "Do not block the way of inquiry" (CP 1.135).

Further reading

CP. *The Collected Papers of Charles Sanders Peirce*, ed. C. Hartshorne and P. Weiss (Vols. 1–6) and A. Burks (Vols. 7–8). Cambridge, MA: Harvard University Press, 1931–58.

Deledalle, G. *Charles Peirce's Philosophy of Signs: Essays in Comparative Semiotics.* Bloomington, IN: Indiana University Press, 2000.

Misak, C.J. *Truth and the End of Inquiry: A Peircean Account of Truth.* Oxford: Clarendon Press, 1991.

Short, T.L. "The Development of Peirce's Theory of Signs" in C.J. Misak (ed.) *The Cambridge Companion to Peirce.* Cambridge: Cambridge University Press, 2004, pp. 214–40.

Skagestad, P. *The Road of Inquiry: Charles Peirce's Pragmatic Realism.* New York: Columbia University Press, 1981.

—— "Peirce's Conception of Truth: A Framework for Naturalistic Epistemology?" in *Naturalistic Epistemology: A Symposium of Two Decades*, ed. A. Shimony and D. Nails. Dordrecht: D. Reidel, 1987, pp. 73–90.

PETER SKAGESTAD

PERRY, RALPH BARTON

In the early decades of the twentieth century, a neo-realist movement responded sharply to the idealism of such American philosophical figures as Josiah Royce and W.E. Hocking, a movement led by Harvard philosopher Ralph Barton Perry (1876–1957). Perry was born 3 July 1876 in Poultney, Vermont, attended Princeton as an undergraduate, and earned his doctorate in philosophy from Harvard in 1899, where he was a favorite student of William James. After a brief stint at Williams and Smith Colleges, Perry became a professor in the Harvard philosophy department (1902) until his retirement in 1946.

Author/editor of over twenty books, and hundreds of addresses and articles, Perry's scholarship developed a realism that, while ultimately unsuccessful at capturing a long-term central place, proved transitional for philosophy in America. Specifically, Perry's attack on what he called the "ego-centric predicament" took on the idealists' emphasis on objects as necessarily cognitive and epistemic. In fact, according to Perry, objects need not be "known" at all, but just "are." Metaphysics, then, is strictly separate from epistemology; existence stands outside cognition and consciousness; and data exist independent of our "knowing" them. Instead of introspection and speculative concepts, Perry exhorted that mathematics and natural science be employed in the pursuit of philosophical aims. What is required is accurate use of language, strict employment of logic, and careful analysis of concepts. It is these emphatic elements of the movement that survive as central to the Anglo-American analytic philosophy of the late twentieth century.

Although Perry's initial work focused on the metaphysical and epistemological concerns raised by idealism, his most important contribution to the philosophical landscape is in the area of value theory. With Perry's insistence on a functional behaviorism, where beliefs and purposes can be analyzed entirely through one's acts, this led to the construction of a theory of value in terms of observed interests. As argued in his most famous book of original scholarship, *A General Theory of Value* (1926), "That which is an object of interest is *eo ipso* invested with value. Any object, whatever it be, acquires value when any interest, wherever it be, is taken in it" (115–16). In order to avoid subjectivism, Perry, relying on naturalism, describes interest as a feature of the "motor-affective" life of organisms, while objects, independent of interests, gain value in the conjoining of a particular interest to a specified object.

The influence of James on Perry is obvious throughout Perry's corpus. James's writings in functional psychology – emphasizing the physiological and habitual basis of thought – his radical empiricism – delimiting philosophical thought to the realm of experience – and ethical nominalism – developing a theory of the good from the building-blocks of expressed human interests – is at the heart of Perry's own realist positions. Perry himself saw his work as contiguous with "the spirit of William James." However, Perry's deep admiration and debt to James is most evident in his Pulitzer Prize-winning two-volume work, *The Thought and Character of William James* (1935). Therein the student crafts an insightful intellectual biography of his teacher, not only offering personal details with extensive excerpts for James's correspondence, but penetrating analysis of James's psychological and philosophical writings.

Perry became emeritus professor at Harvard in 1946, continuing to write and edit until his death on 22 January 1957.

Further reading

Perry, Ralph Barton. *The Approach to Philosophy.* New York: Charles Scribner's Sons, 1904.

—— *Present Philosophical Tendencies: An Outline of European and American Philosophy since 1860.* New York: Longmans, Green, 1912.

—— *General Theory of Value: Its Meaning and Basic Principles Construed in Terms of Interest.* New York: Longmans, Green, 1926.

—— *Philosophy of the Recent Past.* New York: Charles Scribner's Sons, 1926.

—— *The Thought and Character of William James, in two volumes.* Little, Brown, 1935; briefer version, abridged to one volume, 1948.

—— *In the Spirit of William James.* New Haven, CT: Yale University Press 1938.

—— *Realms of Value: A Critique of Human Civilization.* Cambridge, MA: Harvard University Press, 1954.

D. MICAH HESTER

PERSONALISM

Personalism is a philosophy that claims person to be the ontological ultimate. With roots in European philosophy, the American form of personalism began in the late nineteenth and developed in the twentieth century. Other forms of personalism that appeared in Great Britain, Europe, Latin America, and the Orient will not be discussed in this article.

"Person" stems from the Greek *prosopon*, face, mask; Etruscan *phersu*, mask; Latin *persona*, mask, actor, part in a play, the character one sustains in the world. Boethius associated person with "hypostatis" from standing under and *ousia*, substance, in his definition of person as an individual substance of a rational nature. Boethius' definition deeply influenced Christian theological understanding of God and human persons.

In America "personalism" is recent, but the concept is rooted in the work of eighteenth- and nineteenth-century European thinkers, such as Friedrich Heinrich Jacobi (1743–1819), Johann Gottlieb Fichte (1762–1814), George Wilhelm Friedrich Hegel (1770–1831), and Friedrich Wilhelm Joseph Schelling (1775–1854). Schleiermacher (1768–1834) used the term casually. In France Charles-Bernard Renouvier (1815–1903), a teacher of William James, used "personalism" in 1903 to designate his philosophic system. In America "personalism" was used in 1901 by George Holmes Howison (1847–1910), Mary Whiton Calkins (1863–1930) in 1906, and Borden Parker Bowne (1847–1910) in 1908. Earlier, both Walt Whitman (1819–92) and Bronson Alcott (1799–1888) used the term in the 1860s. Howison and Bowne employed it to distinguish their pluralistic philosophical systems from the absolutism of Josiah Royce (1855–1916). American personalists have followed either Howison, Bowne, or Royce in their understanding and philosophical use of the term.

Historical roots

American Personalism developed under the influence of the western philosophical tradition. Philosophers who decisively influenced personalists ranged from late roman and early medieval through the nineteenth century. Augustine's (354–430) analysis of free will contributed significantly to later philosophical understanding of the moral life of persons. Boethius' (470–525) view of person as substance became the centerpiece of the metaphysical view of persons. Both free will and substance appeared in Descartes' (1596–1650) thought, to which he added directness, primacy, and indubitability of first person experience. Leibniz (1646–1716), considered by some the founder of personalism, argued that reality is composed of psychic entities (momads) that are centers of activity. His view influenced both pluralistic and panpsychistic idealistic personalists. Berkeley's (1685–1753) view that material substance is mental, the "language" of the Divine Person, deeply influenced personalistic idealism.

Immanuel Kant (1724–1804) and Hegel were the major influences on the development of American personalism. Kant distinguished between the phenomenal and noumenal world, reinforcing Berkeley's view of "material" substance, and emphasized that the only path to the reality is through practical reason of persons. Kant exerted the single most important influence on ethical personalists. This occurred largely through the work of Hermann Lotze (1817–81), under whom Royce and Bowne studied. Hegel's view of logic as the dialectical movement toward wholeness, the individual as a concrete universal, and Spirit as ultimate influenced both Royce and Edgar Sheffield Brightman (1884–1953).

Branches of personalism

These historical roots found their way into American philosophy and formed at least four distinctive branches of personalism. They are idealistic, realistic, naturalistic, and ethical.

Idealistic personalism is the most distinctive form of personalism in America. Excluding Platonism or Kantianism, this form of idealism is expressed in three different forms: absolutistic, panpsychistic, and personalistic.

Absolutistic idealists contend that reality is quantitatively and qualitatively one absolute mind, spirit, or person. All other beings, including physical and human ones, are ontologically manifestations of the absolute mind. Josiah Royce, William Ernest Hocking (1873–1966), and Calkins represent this view.

Panpsychists are deeply influenced by Leibniz, who held that God, the supreme monad, created all other monads in a pre-established harmony. Rejecting absolutistic idealism they hold that reality is composed of psychic entities of varying degrees of consciousness. Both A.N. Whitehead

(1861–1947) and Charles Hartshorne (1897–2000) can be called, with qualification, panpsychists.

Finally, for personalistic idealists reality is personal. Quantitatively, reality is pluralistic, a society of persons. Qualitatively, reality is monistic; it is persons. The Infinite Person or God is the ground of all beings and the creator and sustainer of finite persons. In that sense personalistic idealists are theistic. Representatives of this branch of personalism include Bowne, Brightman, Bertocci, and Leroy Loemker (1900–85).

Realistic personalists agree with idealistic personalists that Reality is spiritual, mental, personal. They disagree about the ontological status of the natural order. Nature is neither intrinsically mental nor personal. Realistic personalism is most notably expressed by Neo-Scholastics in Europe such as Jacques Maritain (1882–1973), Emmanuel Mounier (1905–50), and Pope John Paul II (1920–2005), and in America W. Norris Clarke (1915–), and John F. Crosby (1944–). In America some realistic personalists stand outside the scholastic tradition, notably Georgia Harkness (1891–1974).

Naturalistic personalism is a recent form of personalism that has been developed by Frederick Ferre (1933–). Rejecting panpsychism and personalistic idealism and influenced by Whitehead's philosophy of organism, Ferre argues for a personalistic organicism. He claims in *Living and Values* that persons are "organisms with especially well-developed mental capacities leading to special needs and powers." By these powers they can perceive and manipulate the world, can vocalize and socialize, can create language, can imagine and plan by use of symbols freed from the immediate environment, and can guide behavior by ideal norms.

Ethical personalists stress the crucial role of values in ontology and the moral life. Ontological ethical personalists are well represented by Howison who focuses on the Ideal or God toward which all uncreated persons move and the standard by which they measure the degree of their individual self-definition. Practical ethical personalists concentrate on the dignity and value of persons in moral decision-making.

Major figures

Josiah Royce's thought was motivated by a religious view of life and reality, with an emphasis on the self and community. He sought to realize his philosophical goals through a synthesis of two traditions: the rationalistic system-building of philosophers in the West, and the pragmatic emphasis on experience and practice, distinctive of American philosophical activity since the late nineteenth century. Royce also had a long and abiding interest in science and scientific inquiry. These strands were woven together during his long and productive career.

At the root of his system is a concept of the self. Early in his career the self appears as the Absolute, as Being who knows in one synoptic vision. Rejecting realism, mysticism, and critical rationalism, his central thesis is that to be real is to be a determinate, individual fulfillment of a purpose. Later he focused more on mediation and the idea of system. Toward the end of his career, the self appears as social. He developed a social theory of reality, a community of interpretation. He called this community the Beloved Community whose goal is to possess the truth in its totality.

One of the first American philosophers to employ the term personalism was Howison. Early in his career he was one of the St Louis Hegelians. A thorough discussion of Hegel, however, led Howison to champion the finite individual and reject the absorption of the individual in the Absolute. In this way, Howison opposes Royce's absolutism.

Howison succinctly stated his position, quoted by Buckman and Stratton in *George Holmes Howison*,

> All existence is either (1) the existence of minds, or (2) the existence *of the items and order of their experience*; all the existences known as "material" consisting in certain of these experiences, with an order organized by the self-active forms of consciousness that in their unity constitute the substantial being of a mind, in distinction from its phenomenal life.

Devoted to empiricism, Howison rejected creation. "These many minds … have no origin at all – no source in *time* whatever. There is nothing at all, prior to them, out of which their being arises. … They simply are, and together constitute the eternal order." Collectively they move toward their own fulfillment as measured by the eternal standard to God.

Borden Parker Bowne claimed to be the first personalist in any thoroughgoing sense, having developed a systematic metaphysics, epistemology, and ethics. He taught at Boston University from 1876 until his death. Metaphysically Bowne was a pluralistic idealist like Howison. But his theism distinguishes his personalism from Howison's. God, the Divine Person, is both creator and world ground. Finite selves are created, and nature is the energizing of the Cosmic Mind. As world ground, the Divine Mind is the "self-directing intelligent agency" that accounts for the order and continuity of the phenomenal world.

Bowne was not only a systematic philosopher but also a caustic critic of Hegel's absolutism, the evolutionism of Spencer, and all forms of materialism. These criticisms were expressed in his famous chapter in *Personalism*, "The Failure of Impersonalism." In addition, any form of dogmatism or fundamentalism was the target of his searing attacks, especially when held by religious leaders in the Methodist Church.

Bowne's teaching at Boston University attracted many young talented philosophers, some of whom formed the second generation of personalists in America. The most important among them were Albert Knudson (1873–1953), who continued the personalist tradition in the Divinity School of Boston University; Ralph Tyler Flewelling (1871–1960), who developed the School of Philosophy at the University of Southern California; and Brightman, who led the Philosophy Department at Boston University from 1919 until his death in 1953.

A creative, brilliant, original philosopher, Edgar Sheffield Brightman, in agreement with other Boston University personalists, sought truth in the most empirically coherent interpretation of experience to guide creative living. Rejecting the skepticism of Descartes, beginning the search for truth within experience, and advancing and testing hypotheses, Brightman developed the distinction between the shining present and the illuminating absent. Pointing beyond itself, the shining present is unintelligible without reference to an illuminating absent. Though the shining present does not prejudice the nature of the illuminating absent, the hypothesis that most coherently illumines the present is Person.

Brightman contended that "everything that exists [or subsists] is in, of, or for a mind on some level." In *Person and Reality* he defined personalism as "the hypothesis that all being is either a personal experience (a complex unity of consciousness) or some phase or aspect of one or more such experients." Nature is an order generated by the mind of Cosmic Person. Finite persons are created and grounded by the uncreated God, and as such possess free will. Reality is a society of persons.

Brightman's most impressive work is his *Moral Laws*, in which he works out along lines heavily indebted to Hegel a thoroughgoing ethical theory. In his thought values occupy a central place, which he believes are grounded in God and provide evidence for God's existence. Values have a central place in his philosophy of religion.

Central to his philosophy of religion is his well-known revision of the traditional view of God. If personality is the basic explanatory model, God must be seen as temporal. As temporal, God is not timeless but omnitemporal. Brightman agrees with the traditional view of God as infinite in goodness, but he disagrees that God is infinite in power. To maintain that God's power is infinite seriously compromises the goodness of God. If evil is to be taken seriously, the will of God must be understood as limited by the nonrational Given within God's nature. This nonrational condition in God is neither created nor approved by God, but God maintains constant and growing control of it. This controversial view was debated within personalist circles. For example, L. Harold DeWolf (1905–6) followed Bowne's traditional theism rather than Brightman's, and Peter A. Bertocci (1910–89) found in Brightman's revisions a cogent and intelligible theism.

Following Brightman as the leading personalist at Boston University, Bertocci enriched the understanding of person through his work in psychology. In "Why Personalistic Idealism?" Bertocci claims that the person "is a self-identifying, being-becoming agent who maturing and learning as he interacts with the environment, develops a more or less systematic, learned unity of expression and adaptation that we may call his personality." Bertocci is well known for his view that the essence of person is time. He is best known in the field of philosophy of religion for his wider teleological argument that provided increased evidence for God's existence.

Among Afrikan personalists the best known was Martin Luther King, Jr (1929–68). Following closely its major themes, King translated personalism into social action by applying it to racism, economic exploitation, and militarism. However, the precedent for King's social personalism was set by John Wesley Edward Bowen (1855–1923), a student of Bowne's, whom Burrows cites in *Personalism* as the "first Afrikan American academic personalist." Rufus Burrow, Jr (1951–) argues for a militant personalism that takes into consideration the Afrikan American experience. Holding firmly to central personalist themes, he argues in *Personalism* for the sanctity of the body, the dignity of women, "we-centeredness plus I-centeredness," preference for the poor and oppressed, immediate and radical social change, and respect for non-human life forms.

Current trends

Personalists in America carry on a vibrant philosophical discussion. They are developing, modifying, and challenging concepts and themes central to twentieth-century personalism. Erazim Kohak (1933–), drawing on the early work of Edmund Husserl (1859–1938) and Max Scheler (1874–1928), developed a personalistic view of nature. John Howie (1929–) developed an environmental ethics along personalist lines. Randall Auxier's (1961–) work on time is a rethinking of a category central to Brightman's thought. And Thomas O. Buford's (1932–) work on education, social ontology, and God manifests the influence of Giambattista Vico as well as of Bowne, Brightman, and Bertocci.

Further reading

Auxier, Randall E. *Hartshorne and Brightman on God, Process, and Persons: The Correspondence, 1922–1945*. Nashville, TN: Vanderbilt University Press, 2001.

Bertocci, Peter A. *Introduction to the Philosophy of Religion*. New York: Prentice-Hall, 1951.

Bowne, Borden Parker and Brightman, Edgar Sheffield. *Person and Reality*, posthumous edition, ed. Peter A. Bertocci with Janette E. Newhall and Robert S. Brightman. New York: Ronald Press, 1958.

Buford, Thomas O. and Oliver, Harold H. (eds). *Personalism Revisited, Its Proponents and Critics*. New York: Rodolpi, 2002.

Burrows, Rufus R. *Personalism, a Critical Introduction*. St Louis: Chalice Press, 1999.

Deats, Paul, and Robb, Carol (eds). *The Boston Personalist Tradition in Philosophy, Social Ethics, and Theology*. Macon, GA: Mercer University Press, 1986.

Ferre, Frederick. *Living and Value. Toward a Constructive Postmodern Ethics*. Albany, NY: SUNY Press, 2001.

Flewelling, Ralph Tyler. *Creative Personality*. New York: Macmillan, 1926.

Harkness, Georgia. *The Providence of God*. New York: Abingdon Press, 1960.

Hartshorne, Charles. *The Divine Relativity, A Social Conception of God*. New Haven, CT: Yale University Press, 1948.

Hocking, William Ernest. *The Meaning of God in Human Experience*. New Haven, CT: Yale University Press, 1912.

Howison, George Holmes. *The Limits of Evolution and Other Essays Illustrating the Metaphysical Theory of Personal Idealism*. New York: Macmillan, 1901.

Knudson, Albert C. *The Philosophy of Personalism*. New York: Abingdon Press, 1927.

Muelder, Walter G. *Foundations of the Responsible Society*. New York: Abingdon Press, 1960.

Royce, Josiah. *The Philosophy of Loyalty*. New York: Macmillan, 1908.

Steinkraus, Warren E. and Beck, Robert N. (eds). *Studies in Personalism. Selected Writings of Edgar Sheffield Brightman*. Utica, NY: Meridian, n.d.

THOMAS O. BUFORD

PERSONALITY

As a technical term, "personality" is more widely used in psychology than philosophy. In ordinary usage, it indicates the set of traits which makes an individual distinctive, different from others. The psychological use is continuous with the ordinary. Personality theory, drawing upon several sciences, attempts to distinguish and classify the personality types which human beings exhibit. Emphasis is on causal factors, the physiological and environmental conditions which favor particular types.

The ordinary sense is found in philosophy, for example, in Sidney Shoemaker's claim that "personality, character" is not a condition of personal identity, since personality can change over a lifetime. But more commonly, the term is used to emphasize the defining characteristic of persons, namely, the capacity to initiate action. To have personality is not simply to react to stimuli, but to initiate in accordance with ideals. A powerful personality is one which transforms his or her surroundings in accordance with consciously chosen values. A personality is generally seen as also free and unified.

For an important but dormant tradition, personality is the key to a truer understanding of reality. For philosophers such as Josiah Royce, Mary Whiton Calkins, George Holmes Howison, Border Parker Bowne, science remains on the surface, while metaphysics penetrates deeper and reveals reality to be personal.

Outside metaphysics, the term often occurs on the border between the descriptive and the normative, indicating both a trait found among certain beings and a moral good to be achieved. Apart from striving, human beings would remain subject to diverse influences and lack unity, thereby remaining less than complete personalities. Unified personality as an ethical ideal is prominent in Royce's philosophy of loyalty, where it grounds morality. For Royce, the loyal service of a single, overarching, freely chosen cause unifies a person and is the highest moral good.

A distinctive conception of personal unity as the integration of interests is offered by Ralph Barton Perry. To be integrated, to have a "personal will," is to act on each interest in the light of all the rest. Integration is the "locus of responsibility" and enables one to become a rational participant of human society.

Perry's emphasis on personality as social continues a theme found in Royce for whom loyalty not only unifies persons but builds communities as well. The social aspect is also prominent in George Herbert Mead.

The link between personality and ideals is emphasized by Harry Frankfurt. For him, persons can have second-order desires, that is, can want to have other preferences and purposes than the ones they have. Frankfurt would like to see, alongside epistemology and ethics, a third area of philosophy devoted to what we should "care about."

The concept of personality is closely linked to freedom. Discussion has moved away from free will – analysis of the causal antecedents of actions – to view freedom as the capacity for informed choices between values. For Daniel Dennett, freedom is a capacity acquired by certain complex organisms in the course of evolution to achieve what is of value. This sense is central to his project to develop, within naturalism, a conception of personality as a moral good.

Further reading

Dennett, Daniel C. *Freedom Evolves.* New York: Viking, 2003.

Frankfurt, Harry G. *The Importance of What We Care About: Philosophical Essays.* Cambridge: Cambridge University Press, 1988.

Perry, Ralph Barton. *Realms of Value: A Critique of Human Civilization.* Cambridge, MA: Harvard University Press, 1954.

Royce, Josiah. *The Philosophy of Loyalty.* New York: Macmillan, 1908.

Shoemaker, Sidney. *Self-knowledge and Self-identity.* Ithaca, NY: Cornell University Press, 1963.

IGNAS K. SKRUPSKELIS

PERSONS

Reflection on persons by American philosophers encompasses a wide range of issues and approaches; some of this reflection is quite theoretical, and some more practically grounded. For those historical figures most prominently associated with a distinctive American philosophy, however, a philosophy of persons tends to develop out of a dialectic between theory and practice.

In mainstream professional philosophy in America, much theoretical work on persons rests on the assumption that persons cannot be radically different in their metaphysical constitution from the rest of the universe. For many, this means that the challenge is to account for the personal quality of conscious experience in impersonal, physicalist terms. Some respond to this challenge by adopting a reductionist strategy that aims to translate claims about the mental, emotional, and social aspects of personal experience into the more impersonal language of the natural sciences. The claim that someone feels sad, on this view, is really a claim about his or her neurophysiological condition, or about various observable bodily behaviors he or she displays, or about the computational functions currently being carried out by his or her brain. There are also physicalists, however, who are dubious that "folk psychological" descriptions of our inner lives are eliminable in this way. For them the challenge is to develop a non-reductionist strategy for assigning meaning to these descriptions that grants their utility in everyday life without requiring an ontology of mental states as different in kind from physical states.

Another option is to take folk psychological ascriptions at face value, and, setting aside theoretical worries about how to square these ascriptions with a scientific account of human persons, focus on more practical concerns. Because we tend to think of persons as possessors of rights and responsibilities, determining who counts as such has serious moral and legal implications. Many American philosophers working in applied ethics have made it their business to explore these implications. Does a fetus count as a person? And if so, what are the implications for the morality and legality of abortion or fetal cell research? Is a comatose patient who displays no detectable brain activity a person? And if so, what are the implications of removing that patient from life-support systems? Does a corporation, which has legal responsibilities, count as a person? And if so, to what rights can it lay claim? Were there a machine that gave every sign of possessing intelligence in its interactions with us, would it count as a person? And if so, what should be its moral and legal status in the community? Do racial injustice, gender inequality, and abusive treatment of the environment rest on faulty accounts of who counts as a person? And if so, what would a more adequate account of persons look like?

Although dealing with practical conundrums such as these may not require a settled ontology of persons, it does require some workable account of personal identity. Emphasis on the "workable" sends us back to classical American pragmatism, where we find an approach to persons that takes seriously the science of its day, but, in its attention to actual scientific practice, avoids the sharp dichotomy between the personal and impersonal that gives rise to reductionist quandaries. For thinkers such as William James and John Dewey, science is not an impersonal mode of knowing incompatible with persons; rather, from the pragmatist point of view, the sciences grow out of the interaction of human persons with their surrounding environment, forming part of an elaborate coping mechanism whereby we actively engage the natural world. Consciousness, on this view, develops through interaction between organism and environment, so that personal identity emerges out of cognizance of one's own actively engaged responses to the world as they define one's own particular location in and contribution to a larger intersubjective network of relations.

Contemporaneous with the birth of American pragmatism was the birth of the American personalist movement as well as the beginnings of an American interest in process philosophy. The account of persons in both these movements bears striking resemblance to the pragmatist view, but is reached by a more explicitly metaphysical route in which theological conviction plays a more prominent role. For process philosophers, personal identity, including the identity of the Divine Person, resides in the continuity over time of a complex network of interrelated processes of doing, apprehending, and responding, as opposed to sameness of underlying substance over time. For personalist philosophers, the concept of the personal is not derived from the more metaphysically basic notion of a process, but is, rather, treated as itself metaphysically basic. Our experience only makes sense, it is argued, if we take reality to be personal in character, recognizing its ultimate source in a Divine Person. This subsumption of the impersonal under the personal directly inverts the assumption shared by so many contemporary mainstream accounts of persons. It is, however, a vision that has had a significant practical impact on American life through the work of Dr. Martin Luther King, Jr, whose transformative vision of civil rights was significantly shaped by his study of personalist philosophy.

Although much American thought about persons has pursued agendas set by Europeans – by Cartesian dualism, Newtonian and Darwinian science, British empiricism and German idealism – the practical concerns peculiar to the American experience have also contributed significantly to shaping an American sensibility regarding persons. As the range of experience explicitly taken into account in scholarly philosophical work expands to include the voices of women, of Native Americans, of African Americans and of other groups whose perspectives have not traditionally been represented in academic discourse, a host of new ideas about persons is taking shape. Recent historical scholarship, furthermore, suggests these voices may have had more impact along the way than has been acknowledged. The pragmatist vision of the person as continuous with as opposed to divergent from the natural world, for example, echoes themes in much Native American thought, and may have been indirectly influenced by such in ways that are only beginning to be appreciated.

Further reading

Auxier, Randall and Davies, Mark Y.A. (eds). *Hartshorne and Brightman on God, Process, and Persons: The Correspondence, 1922–45*. Nashville, TN: Vanderbilt University Press, 2001.

DeGrazia, David. *Human Identity and Bioethics*. Cambridge: Cambridge University Press, 2005.

Kim, Jaegwon. *Philosophy of Mind*. Boulder, CO: Westview Press, 1996.

Margolis, Joseph. *Persons and Minds: The Prospects of Nonreductive Materialism* (Boston Studies in the Philosophy of Science). Dordrecht: Reidel, 1978.

Meyers, Diana Tietjens (ed.). *Feminists Rethink the Self*. Boulder, CO: Westview Press, 1997.

Rorty, Amelie. *The Identities of Persons*. Berkeley, CA: University of California Press, 1976.

PATRICIA A. SAYRE

PESSIMISM

Pessimism is the view that the evil in the universe outweighs or triumphs over the good. While it can be considered an attitude or disposition, it is more commonly treated as a doctrine according to which human efforts to secure goods are judged futile or temporary at best, since suffering and the tooth of time undermine our positive achievements. The nineteenth-century German philosopher Arthur Schopenhauer offered the classic defense of systematic pessimism, arguing that life (or the will to live) is by its very nature a matter of incessant striving and suffering. American thinkers have rarely embraced pessimism as a doctrine but more commonly considered it a challenge that helps sharpen our appreciation of moral values or objective truth.

George Santayana was influenced by Schopenhauer, with whom he shares some metaphysical beliefs, but it is an exaggeration to characterize his philosophy as a thoroughgoing pessimism. Material existence and animal life, Santayana argues, are characterized by conflict and change. Santayana offers no consolatory belief in God or an afterlife and rejects any ultimate salvation for us as individuals or a race. An epiphenomenalist, he denies that spirit or consciousness helps secure the cause of the good, for spirit is an inefficacious product of animal life that impartially enjoys what is immediately presented to it. Unlike traditional philosophers, Santayana finds in spirit not the promise of a new kind of life but rather a momentary and optional achievement of animal life. Hence, Santayana is neither an optimist who believes in the cause of an ultimate ideal nor a pessimist like Schopenhauer who calls us to extinguish the will to live.

William James judges pessimism in light of its practical effects on our action. He argues that pessimism threatens to quell strenuous capacities such as our ability to act courageously in the face of uncertainty. Pessimism attends a condition he calls the "sick soul" which finds an incurable evil in the very nature of things. James characterizes the pessimistic view of the world as deterministic, leaving no room for chance or genuine novelty to interrupt the fateful course of events. For the pessimist, possibility and actuality coincide perfectly so that this is the *only* possible world, despite the evil within it. James rejects deterministic pessimism in favor of a meliorist view according to which good *might* triumph over evil if we dedicate our efforts to its cause. Meliorism, James argues, calls forth the strenuous mood, while pessimism quiets it.

Other authors argue that pessimism provides valuable insights we are remiss to neglect. Josiah Royce contends that an analysis of individual consciousness can lead to pessimism, especially insofar as it uncovers the condition of detached individuals who, acting in isolation from one another, can never attain salvation. Fortunately, Royce argues that the life of the individual is not our only possibility. An unselfish life of devotion to loyalty unites the individual self with larger causes and ultimately with the whole of conscious life. Bruce N. Waller argues that while optimism may be productive in focusing our energies, belief in pessimism promises its own fruits, chief of which is a more realistic appraisal of our conditions and abilities. Waller recognizes the benefits of both optimism and pessimism and contends that pessimism offers us a better path to the truth. Joshua Foa Dienstag argues that pessimism as a modern position results from the modern conception of linear time. He denies the popular assumption that pessimism is associated with a depressing attitude that paralyzes us and instead claims it represents a particular understanding of humans as creatures aware of their relation to time. Moreover, Dienstag argues that we can rebel against the burden of time not by fostering hopes of overcoming its eradicating force but by living in it with self-respect. Pessimism, then, need not lead to passivity and resignation.

There is also an epistemological version of pessimism, especially in the context of antifoundationalism and anti-realism. An example is what has been called the "pessimistic induction," attributed to such thinkers as Hilary Putnam, which holds that the erroneous nature of past scientific theories suggests that our current theories are probably false as well. Similarly, thinkers such as Thomas Kuhn, W.V.O. Quine, Wilfrid Sellars, and Richard Rorty – each of whom has dismantled the traditional foundationalist scaffolding in the theory of knowledge – have been thought to accept pessimism with respect to truth and meaning. Whether these views are pessimistic depends in part on whether the absence of a foundation or the denial of realism bankrupts the pursuit of truth and the possibility of meaningful action.

Further reading

Dienstag, Joshua Foa. "The Pessimistic Spirit," *Philosophy and Social Criticism* 25 (1999): 71–95.

James, William. "The Dilemma of Determinism" in *The Will to Believe and Other Essays in Popular Philosophy.* New York: Dover, 1956, pp. 145–83.

Lewis, Peter J. "Why the Pessimistic Induction is a Fallacy," *Synthese* 129 (2001): 371–80.

Putnam, Hilary. *Meaning and the Moral Sciences.* London: Routledge and Kegan Paul, 1978.

Royce, Josiah. "Pessimism and Modern Thought" in *Fugitive Essays.* Cambridge, MA: Harvard University Press, 1925, pp. 155–86.

—— "The Practical Significance of Pessimism" in *Fugitive Essays.* Cambridge, MA: Harvard University Press, 1925, pp. 133–54.

Santayana, George. *Realms of Being.* New York: Cooper Square Publishers, 1972.

Waller, Bruce N. "The Sad Truth: Optimism, Pessimism, and Pragmatism," *Ratio* 16 (2003): 189–97.

PATRICK SHADE

PHENOMENOLOGY

For most interested persons in the late twentieth and early twenty-first centuries, Edmund Husserl is the paradigmatic phenomenologist. Indeed, he provided the most complete and systematic account of what a phenomenological philosophy would look like. Moreover, with his rallying cry, "To the things themselves!" he focused much of the fresh look at the world that followed in the wake of Immanuel Kant.

But Husserl's very prominence obscured much of phenomenological importance in the years following Kant. In the face of totalizing skepticism issuing from several quarters, Kant took the radicalizing step of grounding reason by limiting it (*begründen ist begrenzen*). If the scope of reason is limited to how things appear to, or in, the mind – that is, limited to phenomena – then if we discover mind's structure, discover how things *must* appear in mind, we will discover how the *world* must appear to us. First, this will be all that is needed to ground science; second, morality will be grounded by freeing it from all dependence on how things appear; third, the study of the beautiful and the sublime is grounded by allowing the full play of the productive imagination, that is, the free play of sensuousness and the understanding, without the constraints of concepts for objects. Independent of both the power and limits of science, the arts – e.g. symbolical imagery and metaphor – can throw free-floating phenomena into unexpected and revealing connections. Mind facilitates disinterested pleasure – trans-egological and trans-utilitarian experience. Post-Kantian philosophers were greatly interested in this third Critique.

But Husserl's retrieval of Kant was also a critique of Kant, one that had resounded variously in the important philosophers of the nineteenth century. Husserl's phenomenological ideal for philosophy was what has been called "a presuppositionless beginning." By that he meant a beginning that does not allow any *unacknowledged and unclarified* assumptions. But it was seen by many (e.g. F.H. Jacobi), that Kant's very framing of the idea of phenomenon contained an unclarified assumption. It was a kind of mentalistic assumption inherited from Descartes as well as the British Empiricists. It was the assumption that phenomena appear "in the mind." But there must be something somehow outside the mind that accounts for them getting into the mind in the first place.

But here lies the grave unclarity. How could we specify or know what this could possibly be, since it lies, somehow, outside the mind? And how could we know how it produced phenomena in the mind: since Kant had grounded and limited phenomena by demonstrating that the concept of cause in all its guises applies only between phenomena, not between phenomena and what Kant was forced to call noumena, unknowable "things in themselves"?

Hegel put the critique most brazenly and forcefully. To claim to know the supposedly unknowable noumenon is to contradict oneself. Hegel himself is assuming that we must have some idea of *what* it is in order to say that we can't know what it is. A mere *that* – or something-or-other – is for him unintelligible. In any case, for the prominent post-Kantian philosophers, the very meaning of phenomenon is altered significantly, for it is untethered from its supposed polar opposite, noumenon. Things appear, not just in private consciousnesses, but to the mind of the race in general.

But these post-Kantian philosophers don't pretend to throw out all of Kant's restrictions on reason. They are very wary of the highflown abstractions of pre-Kantian rationalist metaphysics. No doubt Spinoza, say, continues to exercise a strong influence (particularly on J.G. Herder and F.W.J. Schelling). But they are wary of what they take to be his quasi-deductive method, and his reliance on supposedly self-evident axioms, such as his definition of Substance as that which is conceived in and through itself, cause of itself, the only true individual and free Being, the Whole.

These post-Kantian philosophers are all phenomenologists in some sense (they all repudiate Descartes' phenomenalism), and they all accept the challenge of beginning "presuppositionlessly," that is, beginning philosophizing without cheating, as we might say. Tellingly enough, Hegel's first major philosophical work, his "voyage of discovery" is *Phenomenology of Mind* or Spirit. He disciplines himself to focus his attention on what actually presents and shows itself in the actual here and now situation in which bodily knowers find themselves – to lay himself open to piercing actuality (*Wirklichkeit* – as William Barrett liked to emphasize). Come to find out, in the dynamic universe, phenomena have a life of their own, they develop themselves. As we look closely, things as phenomena first present themselves as independent of mind, as not mind. Then, allowing our attention to dilate a bit, they present themselves as *not* not mind. That is, as they present themselves here and now, they present themselves as particular instances of hereness and nowness. They present themselves caught up in these universals, these mind-dependent beings. Finally a synthesis forms: things that on one level of phenomenological description and analysis are seen to function as having their own integrity, independence, reality, are seen on another level to also involve mind, the *very same things*.

F.W.J. Schelling's phenomenologies are at least as important as Hegel's, and, as Schelling ages, they increasingly diverge from Hegel's and throw ever more light on the human enterprise of philosophy. Schelling believes that Hegel hurries off too fast to the universals that animate Hegel's Absolute Mind. While it is understandable to want to ground reason, this desire can try to realize itself prematurely. There are depths in phenomena that we must patiently await and release. Schelling cautions us against Hegel's presumption to think God's thoughts after Him, to presume to grasp the course of the development of Absolute Mind to an inevitable fruition in the life of Europe, to Europe's formulation of the essence of human life as a certain sort of rational autonomy and freedom. Schelling delves in world-myth as sources of the constitution of things in their being. In his never finally completed *Ages of the World*, the ever-maturing Schelling reasons and feels his way to the inescapable *Abgrund* and *Ungrund* of all beings that can vouchsafe themselves to us sensuous organisms in this actual world. Yes, in our struggles and artistic and scientific creations we achieve a degree of illumination of the world, but the ground of this illumination cannot itself be completely illuminated. Schelling is a source of what has come to be called existential phenomenology in contrast to the dominant themes of the Husserlian variety. (Allotted space does not allow treatment of Martin Heidegger or Jean-Paul Sartre.)

The "classical" American thinkers are greatly indebted to this phenomenological tradition that has been somewhat misleadingly labeled "idealist" – indebted are Emerson, Peirce, James, Royce, Hocking, Dewey. C.S. Peirce declared that he himself might be called a Schellingian much influenced by modern physics. Moreover, most perceptively, he declared that the first business of philosophy is phenomenology (what he called idiosyncratically phaneroscopy). He also declared that the first business of philosophy is to jettison the so-called father of modern philosophy, Descartes, and his phenomenalism. These declarations come to the same thing pragmatically: they generate the same consequences for experience.

Peirce first tried to generate a long list of categories for thought and experience somewhat in the Hegelian manner. He failed. Probably influenced by Schelling, and incubating his own doctrine of fallibilism, Peirce settled on merely three: firstness, secondness, and thirdness. He believed that any thorough description of phenomena finds these categories embedded in them – indissociable, inescapable, self-evident. Briefly, some sensuous quality, actual or possible, or firstness; also some element of impact and resistance, sheer obduracy, or secondness; finally – necessarily usually – some degree of interpretation via sign-action, or thirdness (though Peirce asserts that a residuum of the ineffable flows throughout all experiencing). On this phenomenological basis, Peirce developed his dynamical, evolutionary, "agapastical" and "synechistical" philosophy. His role for musement, for intellectual play, provides his version of what Husserl called fictive or free variation: what cannot be thought-away, imagined-away, from a phenomenon – what proves to be indissociable – is essential to it, is of its essence. And Peirce came to agree with Emerson: the heart is a cognitive organ – what we cannot empathize with we cannot understand. When we empathize with the evolving cosmos, we have an argument (not an argumentation) for God.

To my knowledge, William James never used the term "phenomenology." Yet he employed its principles in his thought, one of them being to describe phenomena before one attempts to explain them. He confirmed this principle arduously in his massive *The Principles of Psychology.* He planned what he thought to be a scientific psychology: to discover laws of functional co-variation between mental states and brain states, i.e. to explain mental states. But he gradually finds that he must first specify or describe them. Yet when he attends closely to them he finds only what they are of, or about, together with certain movements of his own body. "Mental states" (or events of experiencing) turn out finally to be particular contexts of characteristics, which, in other contexts, constitute the world itself experienced. The characteristics themselves are "neutral between mind and world." This becomes key to his metaphysics of radical empiricism. For example, in "The Experience of Activity" he maintains that it is bootless to try to explain the immediately evident human quality of our motivations in terms of scientific causes "hidden in the cubic deeps," because such putative causes must partake of some of the same sorts of characteristics that appear in our close descriptions of our sensuously evident motivations. No detour of the phenomena can succeed.

Like James, John Dewey is more a de facto phenomenologist than a thematic, self-advertising one. His protracted, lifetime's work was spent deconstructing polar oppositions, e.g. between the mental and the physical. What emerges is an idea of experience that must involve Nature, and an idea of Nature as experienceable in various ways. The nerve of his momentous theories of education is the induction of students into ever more ramifying and involving networks of experiencing and the world-experienced that catch students up and entice them to explore.

In the case of W.E. Hocking, say, the connection to phenomenology is more nearly explicit. He spent three crucial months under the tutelage of Husserl himself in Germany. This is a necessary clue in navigating the heights and depths of his monumental, *The Meaning of God in Human Experience* (see my essay in *A William Ernest Hocking Reader*, Vanderbilt University Press, 2004).

Further reading

Dewey, John. *Essays on School and Society.* Carbondale, IL: Southern Illinois University Press, 1976 [1899].

Heidegger, Martin. *The Basic Problems of Phenomenology*, trans. A. Hofstadter. Bloomington, IN: Indiana University Press, 1982 [1975].

Hocking, William Ernest. *The Meaning of God in Human Experience.* New Haven, CT: Yale University Press, 1912.

Husserl, Edmund. *Ideas: General Introduction to Pure Phenomenology,* trans. W.R. Boyce-Gibson. New York: Crowell-Collier, 1962.

Peirce, C.S. "Critical Commonsensism" in *Philosophical Writings of Peirce,* ed. Justus Buchler. New York: Dover, 1955. (See Buchler's assemblage of Peirce on phenomenology.)

Sartre, J.-P. *The Transcendence of the Ego,* trans. F. Williams and R. Kirkpatrick. New York: Noonday Press, 1957.

Schelling, F.W.J. *The Ages of the World,* trans. J.M. Wirth. Albany, NY: SUNY Press, 2000.

Wilshire, Bruce. *William James and Phenomenology: A Study of "The Principles of Psychology".* Bloomington, IN: Indiana University Press, 1968 (AMS reprint, 1979).

BRUCE WILSHIRE

PHILOSOPHY, CONCEPTIONS OF

Conceptions of philosophy and philosophical practice have taken many diverse forms in the history of America. This diversity in philosophical outlook is due to the various intellectual, professional, and social challenges that have been part of American life and which accordingly have influenced philosophical thought. Some examples might include Jonathan Edwards's placing of Calvinist theology within the scientific framework provided by Newtonian physics, or later developments in the early nineteenth century where Scottish commonsense realism became the dominant philosophy in American universities. It is after the traumatic events of the Civil War, and the publication of Darwin's *Origin of Species* that we witness a set of philosophical perspectives that lay some claim to being distinctly American, resulting in the so-called Classical period of American philosophy stretching from the 1860s until the 1930s. It is during this period that pragmatism emerges as a distinct and influential contribution to philosophy, and various forms of realism and naturalism begin to challenge the idealist orthodoxy that dominated the second half of nineteenth-century American thought.

Pragmatism famously emphasizes a close relationship between theory and practice and human thought and action. This basic claim is developed in diverse ways within Charles Sanders Peirce's scientific conception of pragmatism, William James's voluntaristic epistemology and John Dewey's later "experimentalism" and naturalism. At the end of the nineteenth century, the fundamental intellectual challenge faced by these three classical pragmatists revolved around the issue of philosophy's relation to science, and the more specific question of whether philosophy is or could be a science (Wilson 1990: 56–75). Pragmatism was then explicit in its attempt to clarify the nature of philosophy in relation to both the nature and scope of the empirical, *a posteriori* methods of science. These intellectual issues were made more acute by the further challenges of specialization and professionalization that occurred with the expansion of American higher education. One significant response to these various challenges was the need for greater cooperation and consensus within philosophy. Such attempts at cooperative philosophy find expression in the work of the Chicago school of pragmatism, the new and critical realists, and later at mid-century with the Columbia University naturalists.

W.V. Quine's early training in logic in the 1930s and his later promotion of themes from logical empiricist philosophy helped set the stage for the influence of analytic philosophy within America. His emphasis on the technical, scientific aspects of pragmatism and naturalism, at the expense of their social and moral orientation, fed into the increasing pressure for professionalization in philosophy. In the aftermath of the Second World War, Quine's understanding of the discipline prevailed, with conceptions of scientific philosophy and various forms of scientific naturalism reaffirming the model of the professional philosopher as empirical technician, rather than as moral and social visionary. Other analytically trained philosophers such as Richard Rorty and Hilary Putnam have returned to the ideas of classical pragmatism in an attempt to counter what they perceive as the harmful excesses of analytic philosophy. Their reinterpretations of the virtues of classical pragmatism diverge, but they both highlight the possibility of a conception of philosophy that is once again more socially and politically engaged.

Three pragmatist philosophers: James, Dewey and Peirce

Although idealist philosophy would maintain an active place through the early part of the twentieth century (Murphey 2005: 106) it began to lose its predominance in the face of alternative conceptions of philosophy. It is roughly at this time that pragmatism emerges with James's popular expression of its main tenets in his public lectures of 1906 and 1907, later published as *Pragmatism* (1981). Here, James highlights a core feature of pragmatist thought with its view that philosophical inquiry be grounded in concrete experience. Within this shared methodological outlook, the pragmatists offered differing responses to the question of the scientific status of philosophy, and thus illustrated the diversity present within pragmatist conceptions of philosophy.

James's pragmatism sought the middle ground between the extremes of a scientistic materialism and the demands of spiritual faith. He recognized the power of science and tied its success to its method, yet remained skeptical that it could take the place of faith and belief. James was then highly critical of those advocates of scientific materialism that he thought neglected the nonscientific aspects of thought and life. He offered a broader conception of philosophy, emphasizing its importance in developing a wider vision and more flexible frame of mind than can be found in specialized scientific training. Central for this view is James's emphasis on how one's intellect, will, tastes, passions, and temperaments all play a central role in the development of a philosophical vision. Philosophy develops out of our practical human need to make sense of our world and provides a vision for life that impacts our most immediate interests and activities. James thinks it central that we recognize how these philosophical demands are not met through focused scientific study, and how they are importantly not in conflict with the interests of modern science. Consequently, he argued that philosophical issues surrounding the justification of religious belief cannot be effectively addressed by the *a posteriori* methods of empirical science.

Dewey's attempt to reconcile the competing demands of science and philosophy led to his own pragmatist conception of philosophy, which he called "experimentalism." On this view, science was presented as a concrete and practical methodology of action that can be applied to human conduct. Like James, Dewey thought of philosophy as offering a broader kind of perspective where we are concerned with finding meaning and giving meaning to our lives. While Dewey thus distinguished between the proper domains of science and philosophy, this did not result in a dualistic picture of their relationship, since they achieved their synthesis within the context of social action. Science remains the methodological means through which knowledge is gained and problems solved. However, science and philosophy must work together in order to direct social activity towards the improvement of the human condition. This basic conception of the point and purpose of philosophy in its relation to science was to remain central for Dewey's mature thought of the 1920s and 1930s, where he more explicitly urges the reconstruction of philosophy, and a view of philosophy as criticism. Dewey's broader social and cultural conception of philosophy depicts its central function in moral terms: philosophy is concerned with questions of human value and in defending specific ways of life always with an eye to improving society. This requires understanding what science teaches us about ourselves and the world, and the further application of this knowledge to questions concerning how we should address our moral and social problems. Philosophy then becomes a generalized form of criticism, where philosophers seek to uncover and evaluate the various assumptions at work within our culture. This critical perspective on all aspects and phases of our society provides philosophy with the chief intellectual task of determining more intelligent ways for effectively dealing with the problems of modern life.

Of the three classical pragmatists Peirce is the most willing to conceive of pragmatism as scientific philosophy, and his own technical work in the philosophy of science inspired his view that philosophy must find its basis in the theory of logic. Peirce also stressed the importance of scientific method as central to its success, and emphasized the central role of the scientific community in achieving continued progress. He thought of philosophy as contributing to this scientific pursuit of truth when pursued with the same scientific spirit, and through adherence to the same method. He further argues that the scientific philosopher is interested in truth for truth's sake and not for practical human ends, since such considerations are distractions that would block the road to scientific inquiry. Importantly, this did not result in the crude scientific materialism that distressed James, since Peirce thought that religion and science were compatible, and that his philosophy would allow us to view science as the study of God's works.

Attempts at cooperative philosophy: realism and naturalism

While the pragmatists were struggling with the question of philosophy's relation to science, other professional challenges emerged with the development of the modern research university. Psychology's gradual separation from philosophy occasioned a "crisis of confidence" within philosophy resulting in an inability to precisely define scientific practice and its relation to philosophic inquiry (Wilson 1990: 121–49). The founding of the American Philosophical Association (APA) in 1901 provided a further opportunity to debate whether philosophy should align itself closer to science and what this might entail for both the practice of philosophy and its place within the larger intellectual community. No general consensus was found concerning the scientific or non-scientific status of philosophy. However, the organizational successes of the APA provided a broad professional home for philosophers of varying stripes, which further solidified its professional status and helped to resolve philosophy's crisis of confidence.

Within the context of these challenges emerged a desire for greater cooperation among philosophers. This was seen by some as a prerequisite for philosophy's claim to scientific status. By adopting a shared vocabulary and set of problems, it was thought that philosophy could partake in the sort of progress found in scientific research. Dewey's Chicago school of pragmatism, which included such thinkers as George Herbert Mead, James R. Angell and James H. Tufts, provided an early example of this trend with their publication of *Studies in Logical Theory.* A later attempt at "cooperative philosophy" was promoted with the new realist movement, which consisted of the philosophers Ralph B. Perry, Edwin B. Holt, Walter T. Marvin, W.P. Montague, Walter B. Pitkin and E.G. Spaulding. Their collaborative spirit was witnessed in their joint publication of "The Program and First Platform of Six Realists" and later in their *The New Realism: Co-operative Studies in Philosophy.* The new realists questioned the idealist view that the knowing process conditioned the known object, and argued that objects known are directly present to consciousness while still being independent of the knowing relation. By rejecting the need for a mental state mediating our awareness of objects, the new realists abandoned what they thought inexorably led to idealism. The main pitfall for this view was its inability to account for such phenomena as error, illusion and perceptual variation. Such issues were further discussed by the group known as the critical realists: Durant Drake, A.O. Lovejoy, J.B. Pratt, A.K. Rogers, George Santayana, R.W. Sellars, and C.A. Strong. These philosophers outlined the main lines of their position in the collaborative volume *Essays in Critical Realism: A Co-operative Study of the Problem of Knowledge.* Critical realism agrees with the new realists' claim that the object of knowledge is an independent physical world, but differs by acknowledging the need for mental states mediating our awareness of objects. It was thought that only by describing the knowledge process in terms of such "mental" mediation could perceptual illusion and variability be explained. While such attempts at cooperative philosophy did not result in the programs of constructive philosophy envisioned by its participants, they fostered conceptions of philosophy that in many respects emulated science, while promoting forms of analysis that foreshadowed later philosophical perspectives.

During the 1930s and 1940s a third group of like-minded philosophers centered in the New York City area, many educated or teaching at Columbia University, comprised the movement known as Columbia naturalism. This group described their perspective in the volume *Naturalism and the Human Spirit* (1944), which included articles by John Dewey, Sidney Hook, Abraham Edel, Herbert W. Schneider, Ernest Nagel and John Herman Randall, Jr. The naturalists were united in viewing nature as all-inclusive and sufficient, and they promoted scientific method as an appropriate model for philosophical inquiry. With this basic platform in place, they offered their joint work as, in part, a technical project in philosophy, but also as an active response to those religiously minded philosophers who claimed that naturalism was a threat to American society. The main aim of their volume was to demonstrate that, properly understood, the experimental method of modern science could apply to the full range of human experience and provide useful resources for addressing the problems of modern America. This vigorous response to the religious enemies of science indicates the larger cultural significance of these debates and how the naturalists represented those philosophers who saw science as a vehicle for moral and social progress in America.

Quine and the emergence of analytic philosophy

The migration of intellectuals and philosophers from Europe during the 1930s had a significant impact on conceptions of philosophy in America. The logical empiricism of such philosophers as Rudolf Carnap, Philip Frank, Carl Hempel, and Hans Reichenbach advocated the use of logical, *a priori* resources in addressing fundamental epistemological questions. This form of what would later be called "analytic philosophy" gradually displaced the conceptions of philosophy offered by pragmatism and naturalism, at least in the socially and morally engaged versions offered by James and Dewey. The Harvard-trained logician and philosopher Willard Van Orman Quine was an important conduit of these changes.

With the completion of his dissertation in 1932, Quine traveled to Europe to study recent advances in logic and philosophy. With the work of the leading logical empiricist, Rudolf Carnap, Quine found the conception of technical, scientific philosophy, which was to inform his own mature thought. On his return to America, Quine began actively promoting the view of scientific philosophy he imbibed from logical empiricism, and which would influence the professional conception of philosophy after World War II. Although the social-political orientation of logical empiricism survived its American transplantation and led to fruitful interaction with homegrown conceptions of pragmatism and naturalism, such as Dewey's, this eventually became a casualty of the Cold War (Reisch 2005: 83–95). Quine never saw the social-political aspects of logical empiricism as part of its importance, but took its criticism of metaphysics and its marshaling of logical techniques in philosophy as central to the development of a scientific, naturalist conception of philosophy (Isaac 2005: 226). His later influential criticism of the analytic–synthetic distinction resulted in an empirical reconfiguration of philosophy, where all knowledge claims become susceptible to the same general empirical methods that animate empirical science. The result was Quine's naturalistic conception of philosophy, which rejected any epistemologically significant understanding of the *a priori*, and which synthesized elements of pragmatist epistemology with the technical outlook of logical empiricism while removing the social-political orientation of both projects.

The return of pragmatism: Richard Rorty and Hilary Putnam

While Quine used pragmatist and naturalist ideas to promote his own scientific conception of philosophy, other thinkers have looked to the classical pragmatists for resources to question many of the assumptions and distinctions present within analytic philosophy. Trained in both the history of philosophy and analytic philosophy, Richard Rorty has developed a version of pragmatism that shares the pragmatist's suspicion over the categories and language used in modern thought. The distinctions between mind versus matter, and appearance versus reality have defined the central problems of modern philosophy, and by questioning these problems Rorty follows James's and Dewey's criticisms of the metaphysical assumptions underlying these distinctions. In his *Philosophy and the Mirror of Nature* Rorty locates the aspirations of analytic philosophy within the epistemological program of modern philosophy, which argued for the necessity of philosophy for justifying our knowledge claims. By using ideas from analytic philosophy itself, notably Quine's and Wilfrid Sellars's, Rorty develops a general critique of the defining project of modern epistemology, where the mind structures experience into thoughts that are claimed to mirror reality. By coupling Quine's attack on the structure–content distinction with Sellars's questioning of the notion of empirical givenness, Rorty seeks to undermine this general project of clarifying how thoughts accurately mirror an outside reality. Rorty views these arguments as reintroducing the blurring of philosophical distinctions that comprised the core achievement of American pragmatism. By dismantling the project of modern epistemology, analytic philosophy has promoted the reappearance of pragmatism, and forced us to rethink what our society can achieve once freed from the debilitating features of modern thought.

Hilary Putnam's analytic training led him to affirm many of the central distinctions that had been questioned by classical pragmatism. Putnam now sees his early perspective as largely mistaken, and he argues that pragmatism's greatest achievement was the recognition of the connection between theoretical and practical discourse, and the interdependent nature of facts and values. By defending these central ideas of classical pragmatism, Putnam questions the assumption of many analytic and logical empiricist philosophers who affirm a strict distinction between factual, scientific statements and non-scientific normative claims. He further indicates the way science depends on judgments of value, and how it cannot proceed without making such evaluative judgments. This leads him to reconsider the question of the objectivity of value claims, which he defends by arguing for the objectivity of judgments of coherence and simplicity that are presupposed by science. These reflections involve the further controversial denial of any significant methodological divide between science and ethics. By developing these and related points, Putnam's pragmatic conception of philosophy appeals to central elements of James's and Dewey's philosophy, and further shares the Deweyan conviction that scientific "intelligence" can be extended to matters of social and moral concern.

Further reading

Dewey, John. *Reconstruction in Philosophy.* Boston, MA: Beacon Press, 1948.

Haack, Susan and Lane, Robert. *Pragmatism, Old and New: Selected Writings.* Amherst, NY: Prometheus Books, 2006.

Isaac, Joel. "W.V. Quine and the Origins of Analytic Philosophy in America," *Modern Intellectual History* 2, 2 (2005): 205–34.
James, William. *Pragmatism*. Indianapolis, IN: Hackett, 1981.
Krikorian, Yervant (ed.). *Naturalism and the Human Spirit*. New York: Columbia University Press, 1944.
Kuklick, Bruce. *A History of Philosophy in America: 1720–2000*. Oxford: Clarendon Press, 2001.
Murphey, Murray. *C.I. Lewis: The Last Great Pragmatist*. Albany, NY: SUNY Press, 2005.
Reisch, George. *How the Cold War Changed the Philosophy of Science*. Cambridge: Cambridge University Press, 2005.
Schneider, Herbert W. *Sources of Contemporary Philosophical Realism in America*. New York: Bobbs-Merrill, 1964.
Wilson, Daniel. *Science, Community, and the Transformation of American Philosophy, 1860–1930*. Chicago, IL: University of Chicago Press, 1990.

Robert Sinclair

PLATONISM, INFLUENCE OF

Platonism had developed in many ways for nearly two millennia after the death of Plato before its influence on the rise of American philosophy. Because of this, Platonism has come to mean many different and sometimes conflicting ideas. Three principal ideas found in Plato's texts, however, have played important roles in American philosophy, enriched by the intervening history. They are (1) the importance of formal understanding, especially in mathematics; (2) the conception of nature as becoming or in process, as contrasted with Aristotle's conception of substance; and (3) the conviction that, because of the roles of form in natural processes, value is a part of nature.

Form and mathematics

Plato was convinced that formal ideas, logical structures, and mathematical notions are completely understandable in themselves, in principle, although their application to concrete realities is often uncertain. Formal ideas, especially mathematical ones, have a kind of beauty to them that Plato appreciated. He hoped that mathematics would supply the conceptual language for understanding the world, a hope that differed from Aristotle's conviction that understanding is mainly by classification in genus/species hierarchies. The rise of astronomy and physics in early modern European science, with its emphasis on mathematics, gave impetus to Plato's hope, and the final transformation of biology in the middle of the twentieth century from classification to mathematical biochemistry gave the Platonic project a clean sweep over the Aristotelian project in the natural sciences.

Philosophy in America felt this aspect of Platonism as early as Jonathan Edwards (1703–58). Although Edwards was not a mathematician, he approached the study of nature through appreciation of its formal symmetries. He conceived of *being* as a matter of harmony and consent, and articulated the aesthetic aspects of beauty in his analysis of nearly all things, from spiders to human virtue, to the relation between God and the world.

The enthusiasm for mathematics in science was no more prominent in America than in Europe during the modern period. One of the earliest important American contributions, however, was made by Charles S. Peirce (1839–1914), known mainly as the originator of pragmatism. Peirce was the son of Benjamin Peirce, a famous Harvard mathematician, and he developed a philosophy of mathematics based on the analysis of diagrams. He was an early founder of symbolic logic and was convinced that all relations could be analyzed into monadic, dyadic, and triadic ones, as explained further below.

One of the greatest achievements in philosophy of mathematics and formal thinking was the collaborative work, *Principia Mathematica*, by Alfred North Whitehead and Bertrand Russell, both Englishmen. After completing this work and expanding his range of philosophical interests, Whitehead (1861–1948) came to America for a distinguished career in the Harvard Philosophy Department. More at home in America with its pragmatists and idealists than in the foundationalist and modernist philosophical world of Great Britain, Whitehead developed an explicitly Platonic metaphysical system. He undertook that project because of his conviction that the Aristotelian substance metaphysics presupposed in most modern science simply could not account for how the relational intricacies of mathematical language could apply to the real world. In his magnum opus, *Process and Reality*, Whitehead developed a metaphysical model that demonstrated how things can be related as mathematical science says they are. Most directly, he argued that mathematics defines the way the world is experienced in patterns, which he called "morphological analysis." He contrasted this with the way the world is experienced as in process, as becoming, which he called "genetic analysis" (reflecting the genesis of things).

Interest in symbolic logic and philosophy of mathematics was reinforced by Whitehead and his position at Harvard, although it was fed by many other currents of philosophical interest, especially by logical positivism. Two of Whitehead's students, Clarence Irving Lewis and Frederic Brenton Fitch, made important advances in symbolic logic, illustrating Plato's point that systems with different premises can be consistent while lifting up different elements for recognition, the former training generations of students at Harvard, the latter at Yale.

Process and form

In contrast to Aristotle's theory that physical reality consists of substances, Plato took physical reality to be something like a maelstrom of intersecting processes. A concrete reality for Plato is never a thing with a fixed identity or nature, but is always a process moving from one form to some other form; reality is always becoming something else. Whereas forms or ideas can be identified with "being," because they are self-identical, physical and social processes are always changing forms or "becoming." The function of ideas or theories for Plato, as developed in *The Republic* for instance, is to give us a handle for measuring processes, for lifting out what is important to notice, ultimately with a practical purpose of guiding life better.

Ralph Waldo Emerson (1803–82) thought of himself as a Platonist, for whom the forms or ideas embodied in the Oversoul, his conception of God, are more real than the passing processes that hold them fleetingly. He was not a Neo-Platonist, however, who believed that one should hope to ascend from the hurly-burly of physical and social processes to a purer and higher realm. On the contrary, he was convinced that the hyper-reality of the ideal forms is present in that hurly-burly, if only we have eyes to see it. Emerson did not develop these notions with much metaphysical precision.

Charles Peirce was a superb metaphysician on these points. Enthusiastic about ideas of evolution, he asked: what are the simplest things that do not need explanation? Order, he answered, is what needs explanation, and chaos does not. Nothing in pure chaos exists to be explained. Insofar as things are "Firsts," they simply are what they are, not related to one another by being similar or different, not distinguishable from one another. The next simplest move in evolution is to suppose sheer difference, "Secondness." At the level of Secondness, things are not different in any respect, they are not comparable, just different. For us to say they are different, however, we suppose that they differ in some respects, and those respects of difference are what he called "Thirds." Thirds are mediators, which in physical and social reality means habits. The determinate character of a thing is its habit of behaving or relating in some way. Habits connect earlier and later phases of the same thing, and also the relations among things that allow them to be discriminated and compared. The cosmos, Peirce thought, has many chancy elements – things not connected with other things by natural laws or habits of any sort. Chance events do not connect with other things enough to make much difference, unless they fit into an evolutionary scenario in which they can be connected with what is reinforced in the environment. In these cases, chance events alter habits into which they play. Further, habit has a tendency to grow, Peirce said. Things in the universe, he argued, are getting more regular and connected. He called this tendency of habits to generalize, "evolutionary love."

While Peirce's metaphysical language was somewhat idiosyncratic and not much developed by his followers, his ideas about process and form were elaborated by many of the pragmatists, notably John Dewey (1859–1952). For Dewey, the central category was not nature but experience. Experience is an interaction between intentional organisms and their environments. The experience is shaped both by human purposes (of many kinds) and by the real structures of the environment, and it is articulated by ideas that we use as instruments to note the distinctions that are important for our well-being and purposes. Unlike Plato and Peirce, Dewey did not dwell on the formal qualities of our ideas, although he acknowledged them. His most important Platonic theme, however, was that inquiry, philosophic and otherwise, is devoted to determining which ideas are best for articulating and guiding experience. He agreed with Plato that ideas, while resident in nature as experienced in some sense, are best understood as human constructions that we try out as instruments for discernment. For Dewey, the most elementary kinds of experiential ideas are qualities. When experience is unproblematic, it is a tissue of qualities enjoyed. But enjoyment in experience is extremely precarious, and when things become doubtful we have to start thinking about how to sustain and enrich the qualities that give life meaning and value. Then we have to think with ideas constructed in more formal way. Dewey, like Plato, looked to science to offer ideas that would be instrumental in guiding life.

The great metaphysician of process and form in American philosophy, however, was not Dewey or Peirce but Whitehead. With technical precision Whitehead defined process according to what he called the Category of the Ultimate, which combines three notions: one, many, and creativity. In any situation in which many things exist, creativity causes them to be integrated into a new unity or singular thing, thereby increasing the original many by one and thus calling forth yet another integrative process. He defined an event of integration as an "actual entity" or "actual occasion," and provided a detailed analysis of how such an occasion begins with many actual things, eliminates many of their elements so as to make them compatible, and actualizes a new finished thing that is ready to enter into a subsequent event of integration. The genesis of a new actual occasion is Platonic "becoming." Its conclusion or realization is Platonic "being." Following Plato, Whitehead defined "being" as the power to affect something, in the sense that every finished occasion necessarily must be taken up into a subsequent occasion and integrated with others.

Integration requires patterns or forms according to which past actual things are integrated. Whitehead called forms "eternal objects," and argued that they exist absolutely as the primordial nature of God. For an actual occasion to integrate its primary data, it must do so with a complex eternal object that articulates its completed structure. Having done that, the subsequent actual occasions that include that one also pick up the eternal objects actualized in it. Because every actual occasion includes previous actual occasions with their eternal objects, which in turn have included yet prior actual occasions with their eternal objects, the array of eternal objects that get passed down in the world, and sometimes get used in novel ways, is extremely complicated. In philosophy, as mentioned above, genetic analysis is how we understand the eternal objects being passed down, altered, and used in new contexts; morphological analysis is how we understand those eternal objects that articulate the field in which we experience things as integrated. From the inside of an emerging actual occasion, eternal objects feel like qualities, with aesthetic appeal or revulsion. From the perspective of a finished actual occasion on the other occasions of its environment, eternal objects take the form of structures, laws, and mathematical relations. Thus Whitehead combined the formal structural themes of Platonic forms with the experiential, qualitative, aesthetic themes of Platonism.

Natural value

The most important influence of Platonism on American philosophy has been the theme of value. For Aristotle, value was something like the completion or fulfillment of a goal or structure, which he called a "final cause." Value, for him, lay in actualizing a thing's potential as defined by its substantial form. By contrast, Plato had a far more aesthetic notion of value, which he characterized in terms of symmetry, balance, proportion, and harmony, say in his *Philebus*. For Plato, value is dependent on things fitting together in harmony. Given the pressures of various physical and social processes, valuable harmonies are always in jeopardy. The environment suffers drought or floods, the wrong kinds of personality are thrust into positions of leadership, and the barbarians might be just over the hill. So Plato conceived the function of philosophy to be to discern just what the processes of nature and society are, to understand their contributions or threats to human value, and to guide both personal and social life so as to enhance value and deal with disasters.

That theme was directly evident in Jonathan Edwards' philosophy. As noted above, he defined being in terms of symmetry and proportion, just as Plato did. As a good Calvinist, he saw all of the world to be a beautiful creation, although some parts could conflict with other parts. Even his theology defined the being of God as the supreme harmony. Moreover, he defined human experience pragmatically (a century and a half before pragmatism) as the aesthetic response to beauties in nature and humanity. Unlike the British empiricists, with whom he had some affinities, he described thoughts as intentional and then distinguished mere "wouldings," what I would do if I ever got around to acting on my intent, from real action. Human virtue, for Edwards, was the practice of the "consent to being" in things. Emerson continued the aesthetic interpretation of experience and elaborated it as a kind of alternate reading of both Kantian transcendentalism and British romanticism.

For Peirce, like Edwards and Emerson, value consists in a kind of connection or harmony, as he detailed in his discussions of Thirdness. Peirce said that logic is a species of ethics, namely, the ethics of thinking; and ethics is a species of aesthetics, namely, the aesthetics of acting. More than Edwards and Emerson, Peirce subscribed to the ethos of science, and therefore employed a rhetoric that assumed a huge distinction between facts, which science might know, and value. Most practitioners of the scientific project came to believe that values are not in things, rather are only human subjective projections. But Peirce did not. When pressed, he was firmly committed to the conception of value as resident wherever relations are made. Supreme value, he thought, lies in "concrete reasonableness," when all connections are made with aesthetic harmony and Thirdness ties up all the loose ends of Firstness and Secondness. Whitehead's metaphysical theory lays out in detail a theory of value as harmony, resident in every actual occasion. The very motive for integration is the achievement of value, which he described as the subjective harmony in definiteness. Whitehead's expression of the ubiquity of value, along with the technical tools to analyze what the value consists in within nature, provides a powerful tool for environmental ethics.

The Platonic theme of the aesthetic character of natural value played out in two closely related projects in the first half of the twentieth century. George Santayana (1863–1952), a Harvard professor at the time of William James, developed a philosophy of life modeled on a theory of art. He explicitly elaborated a theory of essences, which he related to Plato's theory of forms, in his early work, *The Sense of Beauty: Being an Outline of Aesthetic Theory.* Throughout his work he acknowledged his indebtedness to Plato, as in *Platonism and the Spiritual Life.* Moreover, he focused on how the aestheticism of human experience is continuous with "animal life." Whereas Santayana's philosophy was a Platonized aestheticism, John Dewey's was a naturalized Platonism. Dewey held that, because our experience is valuational all the way through, even our most scientific inquiries are shaped by the values we seek or flee. For Dewey, we do not discriminate the world at all, in science, common sense, or in any other way, save by the selective processes shaped by our purposes. But, contrary to the suggestion that these purposes are mere subjective projections onto reality, Dewey argued firmly that they are responses to what is found to be valuable in reality. We might be mistaken about what we think we find, but then the correction of our response to reality's values is the very purpose of inquiry.

Further reading

Dewey, John. *Experience and Nature* in *John Dewey: The Later Works, Vol. 1*, ed. Jo Ann Boydston. Carbondale, IL: Southern Illinois University Press, 1981 [1925].

—— *Art as Experience* in *John Dewey: The Later Works, Vol. 10*, ed. Jo Ann Boydston. Carbondale, IL: Southern Illinois University Press, 1987 [1934].

Hartshorne, Charles, and Weiss, Paul (eds). *The Collected Papers of Charles Sanders Peirce*, Vols 3 and 4. Cambridge, MA: Harvard University Press, 1933.

Santayana, George. *The Sense of Beauty: Being the Outline of Aesthetic Theory.* New York: Charles Scribner's Sons, 1896; New York: Dover, 1955.

—— *Winds of Doctrine* and *Platonism and the Spiritual Life*, in one volume. New York: Harper Torchbook, 1957.

Whitehead, Alfred North. *Process and Reality: An Essay in Philosophical Cosmology*, revised edition, ed. David Ray Griffin and Donald Sherburne. New York: Free Press, 1978 [1929].

ROBERT CUMMINGS NEVILLE

PLEASURE

Philosophers think about words or concepts and the realities, if any, to which they refer; so it is with "pleasure." To cover all its complexities, "pleasure" should be defined as "any quality of feeling that we normally desire to cultivate and sustain for its own sake." Hedonists claim that pleasures either are or should be the only things that we value and desire to cultivate and sustain as ends. Quantitative hedonists like Jeremy Bentham think that there is only one such pleasant feeling, and though pleasures have diverse sources and effects, they differ as such only with respect to quantitative intensity and duration. Qualitative hedonists like John Stuart Mill claim that pleasures differ also in quality, that, for example, "physical pleasures" are not exactly the same agreeable feelings as "mental pleasures." Best understood, physical or bodily pleasures are those directly experienced as being located in some definite part or region of the body, such as the Freudian genital, anal, or oral erogenous or pleasure zones. Though they have physiological concomitants, mental pleasures like enjoying music, reading, socializing, good conversation, friendship, interpersonal intimacy, or loving children and friends, are not directly experienced as being located in some specific bodily place. With respect to such enjoyments, "Where does it feel good?" has no exact or obvious answer. Is the quality of agreeable feeling from a back rub or sexual arousal exactly the same as that derived from philosophizing or hearing beautiful music, differing only in intensity and duration? If not, there are many kinds or qualities of pleasure.

Do we desire only pleasures, as psychological hedonists contend? Yes, we can desire pleasures, but do we desire nothing else? Psychological hedonism is doubtful for many reasons. Pleasures usually accompany activities, both physical and psychological; and a vast plethora of natural and artificial desires for things other than pleasure undergird enjoyable activities. As William James indicated, impulses or desires for things other than pleasure must first be present before we can derive pleasure from activities that satisfy them. James wrote, "The pleasure of successful performance is the *result* of the impulse, not its cause" (James 1950: II, 557). When hungry, we desire food, not pleasure, though eating gives pleasure. Pleasure normally accompanies the satisfaction of desires and reinforces efforts to fulfill desires, but that does not mean that we desire only pleasure. James called psychological hedonism "a premature philosophy" that "has decided that these [pleasures and pains] are our only spurs to action" (II, 550). The "pleasure-philosophy," James said, offers only "an illusory simplification at the cost of half the facts" (II, 551, 552).

Should we desire only pleasures for their own sake, even if we don't? Ethical or normative hedonists claim that pleasure is the only thing desirable or valuable for its own sake, and getting pleasure is the only rational end or goal, the only intrinsic good, even if we mistakenly believe and behave otherwise. The cheap way to "prove" that pleasure is our only good is simply to define "good" as meaning "pleasant," but for many reasons philosophers now generally reject this "naturalistic fallacy," as G.E. Moore called it. John Dewey refused to identify the "satisfying" with the "satisfactory," or "enjoyment" with "value." Values are more than feelings; they must satisfy criteria of goodness, and not all likings or enjoyments do this (Gouinlock 1976: 150–2). William James recognized that both pleasures and pains have significant survival value and can be powerful reinforcers and motivators. According to James, "It is a well known fact that pleasures are generally associated with beneficial, and pains with detrimental, experiences" (I, 143) and "present pleasures are tremendous re-enforcers" (II, 550). However, he refused to identify goodness with pleasure, claiming that "The class 'goods' contains many more generally influential motives to action than the class 'pleasants'" (II, 553).

Kinds of pleasure can be distinguished from one another only by their intentional objects, from which experience, thought, and imagination cannot separate them. If so, pleasures could never be the only ingredients in intrinsically desirable states of affairs. The pleasures of thinking are inseparable from thinking, just as the pleasures of sex are not available apart from sex; distinct pleasures cannot be identified, much less valued, in total isolation from their intended objects. Pleasant experiences exist only in individuated consciousness, apart from which they cannot be separated, isolated, or evaluated; and, say many non-hedonists, their real value is that they enrich the lives of conscious individual persons and animals, which are the true ends in themselves.

Is pursuing pleasure always selfish? It need not be; unselfish people might just try to create pleasure or happiness for others. We can want both ourselves and others to be happy, and happiness is nothing more than prolonged pleasures with minimal or zero pains, hedonists contend. John Dewey accepted a more complex non-hedonistic kind of "happiness that comes from lively and ever-renewed interests in others and in the conditions and objects which promote their development" (Gouinlock 1976: 119).

Non-hedonistic ways of relating pleasure and the good or happy life are available. John Dewey repudiated "fixed ends" and claimed that "ends are only endings," only "ends in view." Nevertheless, he ranked "consummatory experiences" as inherently satisfying, enjoyable, and intrinsically worthwhile, and he held that they include far more than mere pleasure. Happiness is not just sustained pleasure; it involves "a fulfillment that reaches to the depths of our being – one that is an adjustment of our whole being with the conditions of existence" (Gouinlock 1976: 93). Its objects are "enjoyable in themselves," but they "also reinforce and enlarge the other desires and tendencies which are sources of happiness;" whereas "in a pleasure there is no such harmonizing and tendency" (Gouinlock 1976: 100).

Pleasure may be one, but not the only, good-making property in every inherently desirable state of affairs; it may be just one good thing amid many others that are also valuable or desirable as such, even if we don't always enjoy them, though we usually do. In addition to pleasures, knowledge, truth, moral virtue, creativity, conscientiousness, desire-fulfillment, self-realization, and individual persons have been regarded as valuable for their own sakes, or at least for the sake of conscious individuals; and many concepts of "happiness" or "well-being" include a rich plurality of good-making properties. If we enjoy these, that is "icing on the cake," but it isn't the whole cake.

Further reading

Edwards, Rem B. *Pleasures and Pains: A Theory of Qualitative Hedonism*. Ithaca, NY: Cornell University Press, 1979.

Gouinlock, James. *The Moral Writings of John Dewey*. New York: Hafner Press, 1976, pp. 58–61, 90–4, 99–100, 150–2.

James, William. *The Principles of Psychology*. New York: Dover, 1950, Vol. 1, 143–4 and Vol. 2, 549–59.

REM B. EDWARDS

PLURALISM

Pluralism, in the most literal sense, marks the belief that there are "many things," in contrast to monism, the view that there is one thing. What makes pluralism a problem is that the "many" are also incommensurable. The general issues of how to understand the relation between one and many and between many and many were long a part of the European philosophical tradition. These issues and an emphasis on the "many" emerged early in the American tradition, in part, as a response to the distinctive environment of the Americas and, in part, due to an indigenous commitment to pluralism already present among the people of America before the first Europeans arrived. The lived experience of the border between European and Native America helped to reinforce the experience of diverse ways of thinking, acting, making judgments, and organizing communities. Early American philosophers such as Roger Williams, Cadwallader Colden, Benjamin Franklin, Lydia Maria Child, Margaret Fuller, Ralph Waldo Emerson and others developed conceptions of experience and nature that recognized plurality as a starting point and, by degrees, generated ways of thinking systematically about the world that accepted the value and inevitability of pluralism. By the end of the nineteenth century, American philosophy as it developed in colleges and universities had fully embraced the importance of the general problem of the relation between monism and pluralism and sought ways of finding in favor of one view or the other. In the time since, American philosophy has developed a variety of pluralisms: ontological, epistemic, cultural, and interactional.

Ontological pluralism, represented by diverse philosophers including Mary Whiton Calkins, A.O. Lovejoy, and C.I. Lewis, holds that reality is many irreducible things. Calkins argued that the universe is composed of individual persons or agents, human and otherwise, whose behaviors generate the experience of diversity but whose existence as agents depends upon the universe as a whole. Lovejoy adopted a traditional dualism of material things and ideas. Lewis took reality to be "constituted of facts and their relations" where facts are plural and can be compatible or incompatible. Such facts are not made by human knowers but rather are given in human experience and can be systematized by the logic of propositions. In ontological pluralism, plurality in experience is taken to present the character of reality not dependent upon human experience.

Although some pluralists begin with ontology, others argue for epistemic pluralism as the starting place. From this angle, pluralism is "the doctrine that any substantial question admits of a variety of plausible but mutually conflicting responses," as Rescher observes. In some cases, this diversity of knowledge is understood in relation to a single independent world; in others, it is taken as a mark that there are multiple worlds related to each system of responses. Peirce, for example, held that finite human inquiry necessarily leads to diverse sets of knowledge claims, not all compatible with one another. The inquiries that produced such claims, however, can never, at least in human experience, be final, and so epistemic pluralism is an inevitable condition. At the same time, Peirce held that the nature of the universe was such that there is a single reality. "The opinion which is fated to be ultimately agreed to by all who investigate," he says, "is what we mean by the truth, and the object represented in this opinion is the real. That is the way I would explain reality." The tension between finite inquiry and reality provides not only for epistemic pluralism, but a requirement for fostering inquiry which generates new systems of knowledge and overturns others.

Dewey, in contrast, offers an epistemic pluralism bound to an ontological pluralism. Dewey expressed this pluralism early in his work through his postulate of immediate empiricism, "things are what they are experienced *as* being." In this case, if experience is diverse, then what there *is*, is equally so. To the extent that experience produces knowledge, the resulting knowledge is diverse as well. Later, in his theory of inquiry, Dewey conceives the process of inquiry as beginning in the context of uniquely real situations. The process of inquiry emerges out of a situation and proceeds in a way that transforms the situation into one "*so determinate in its constituent distinctions and relations as to convert the elements of the original situation into a unified whole.*" There is, in this case, no ultimate reality in terms of which new knowledge is generated, only new situations that serve as their own origin and standard.

In more recent work in American philosophy, these two poles of epistemic pluralism continue to have advocates. Sandra Harding, in her work *Is Science Multicultural?* develops a feminist standpoint theory of knowledge as a means of recognizing diverse methods of knowing framed by practices and by social structures. These distinct standpoints have the potential to provide diverse knowledge claims about a shared world such that the more standpoints involved in processes of knowing, the more knowledge is possible as well as better critical resources to correct what is known. Both the standpoints of women within societies and culturally determined standpoints have the potential to make a significant contribution to human knowledge. As in Peirce's pluralism, epistemic pluralism of this sort has the advantage of taking into account diverse viewpoints in the context of an ontologically stable world in terms of which knowledge can be evaluated in the long run. At the other pole, Nelson Goodman in *Ways of Worldmaking* follows Dewey by proposing a pluralism of worlds that are generated as versions of the old. Just as inquiry begins in a unique situation and then is transformed into a new whole, Goodman asserts "Worldmaking as we know it always starts from worlds already on hand; the making is a remaking" and the result, he says, is a "mad proliferation of worlds" each distinct and whole.

Cultural pluralism was proposed by Horace Kallen, among others, as a view in which diverse cultures generate both knowledge and realities. While they intersect politically in the context of American democracy, they are best recognized as deep and irreducibly different. On this view, the "melting pot" vision of America is destructive of these cultures and counter to the commitments of democracy that require the presence of diverse and competing ideas. Alain Locke also accepted a form of cultural pluralism he called cultural relativism in which cultural commonalities or functions serve to foster democratic interactions among cultures that can overcome conflicts while maintaining cultural differences.

These pluralisms share a common emphasis on recognizing the things taken as plural – systems of knowledge, substances, persons, situations, worlds or cultures. While the emphasis is useful in framing the experience of diversity, it overlooks the idea that regardless of what things (or kinds) are taken as different, the character of these emerges only in their interactions. Although William James is sometimes identified with Dewey as favoring both epistemic and ontological pluralism, James can also be seen as focusing on an alternative model. In his last book, *Some Problems of Philosophy*, he says

> pluralism need not be supposed at the outset to stand for any particular kind or amount of disconnection between the many things which it assumes. It only has the negative significance of contradicting monism's thesis that there is absolutely *no* disconnection.

Pluralism, in this sense, focuses on what connects and disconnects, that is, on what is *between*. In his description of consciousness, James observes that it is like the behavior of a bird, a series of flights and perchings. A focus on the perchings leads to a conception of consciousness as a series of disconnected moments. Pluralism does not only recognize the disconnections, however, but the possibility of connections as well. In this case, perchings are understood in relation to one another through the process of flight and the flights are understood as well in terms of the perches that mark their beginnings and endings.

Interactional pluralism is a matter of what links and divides, a matter of what Josiah Royce called "betweenness." Among those who adopt this sort of pluralism are Jane Addams, Mary Parker Follett and more recently Michael Lynch and Karen Barad. Addams's conception of pluralism recognizes diverse cultures and that their interaction leads to the development of a middle ground that connects groups while maintaining their boundaries. In *Creative Experience*, Follett argues that reality is in the "activity-between" that make possible the distinct "things" involved and generates something new in the interaction. The generative process also leads, for Follett, to a conception of purposive agents who engage in the activities-between and to a conception of two kinds of power relations. The first, "power over," suppresses interaction in favor of isolation and assimilation while the second, "power with," fosters interactions and new possibilities. In more recent philosophy, Michael P. Lynch developed a version of James's pluralism in relation to theories of truth while Karen Barad developed a view she calls agential realism in which she argues for a plurality of agents whose characters emerge in the process of inter-activity.

Further reading

Goodman, Nelson. *Ways of Worldmaking*. Indianapolis, IN: Hackett, 1976.

Harding, Sandra. *Is Science Multicultural? Postcolonialisms, Feminisms, and Epistemologies*. Bloomington, IN: Indiana University Press, 1998.

James, William. *A Pluralistic Universe*. New York and London: Longmans, Green, 1909.

SCOTT L. PRATT

PLURALIST REVOLT

The American Philosophical Association (APA) in the 1970s had become an increasingly diverse group of several thousand members from many different parts of the country, public and private universities, church-related institutions with interests in a wide variety of fields and orientation to a number of different traditions. But the leadership, drawn from a relatively small number of areas, institutions and orientations, were associated with the so-called "better schools" that took an analytic approach to philosophy. Or so the Committee on Pluralism in Philosophy alleged in the late 1970s.

Representing non-Ivy Leaguers, Catholic schools, phenomenologists, classic American philosophy, process philosophy, metaphysicians, and those who emphasized undergraduate instruction, the Pluralists organized a challenge to the leadership of the APA's Eastern Division, the largest of the three regional divisions

Claiming that the leadership was essentially a self-perpetuating group that denied, through the program committees that it appointed, access by anyone who did not adopt an analytic approach, the Committee overwhelmed the 1979 Business Meeting, a usually staid, poorly attended affair. The insurgents succeeded, in a contested vote, to elect three of their candidates to positions, including John Smith of Yale University as vice-president. This was a key position, for it meant that he would then become president the following year.

The analysts, who still controlled the Nominating Committee, succeeded the next year, 1980, in electing Pittsburgh's Adolf Grünbaum, who had been defeated in 1979, as vice-president. In a flyer circulated a month before the December 1980 meeting in Boston, "under the banner of maintaining 'high professional standards' and resisting 'factional pressures,' the letter argued for support of Grünbaum . . . in order to 'counteract the effects of last year's election.'" Signed by several previous Eastern Division presidents, the letter continued:

> The Committee on Pluralism seeks to obtain, through political means, a position of influence which its members have not been able to obtain through their philosophical work. We believe that the Committee favors the suppression of serious scholarly and intellectual standards under the false banner of openmindedness.
>
> (quoted in Wilshire 2002: 60)

John Lachs, one of the leaders of the Pluralist revolt, writing some fifteen years later, judged the insurgency a mixed success:

> Many of the narrow political goals of the pluralists were never achieved. The hold of rich and established graduate departments on the Board of the APA has been weakened but not eliminated, APA divisional presidencies are still viewed as rewards for excellence unconnected to practical sense or the ability to lead, and elections continue largely as popularity contests based on name recognition and current assessments of technical publications. Yet it is clear that academic philosophy is profoundly different today from what it was a couple of decades ago, and of this change ongoing pluralist agitation was both symptom and part cause.
>
> (Lachs 2004: 11)

Ruth Marcus, one of the APA's leaders at the time, and a colleague of Smith's at Yale, thought that, on the whole, the APA ultimately handled the pluralist challenge well. She is also reported to have said at the time, "You keep the conventions, we'll keep the graduate schools" (Wilshire 2002: 62). While a shrewd strategy, this is not in fact what happened. The divisional meetings have become more pluralist, as have the graduate schools, but the APA can hardly be said to be a transparently democratic organization. So the profession has opened up some philosophically even as its professional organization continues to be less open politically than the challengers sought.

Clearly there was intense conflict between the analysts and pluralists in the 1970s and 1980s and it continues to some extent even today, but the issues were as much about access to power as they were about what counts as philosophy.

Further reading

Eldridge, Michael. Conversation with Ruth Barcan Marcus, Eastern Division, APA, 28 December 2005.

Gross, Neil. "Richard Rorty's Pragmatism: A Case Study in the Sociology of Ideas," *Theory and Society* 32 (2003): 93–148.

Lachs, John. "The Future of Philosophy," Letter to the Editor, *Proceedings and Addresses of the American Philosophical Association* 78, 2 (November 2004): 5–14.

Wilshire, Bruce. "The Pluralist Rebellion in the American Philosophical Association" in *Fashionable Nihilism: A Critique of Analytic Philosophy.* Albany, NY: SUNY Press, 2002, pp. 51–64.

MICHAEL ELDRIDGE

POETRY

American philosophers have made important contributions to aesthetics, the most notable being John Dewey's *Art as Experience* (1934), although much of their work has yet to be recognized. It may nonetheless seem odd to consider poetry in the context of a philosophical tradition that emphasizes directness and practicality: the prosaic, as it were. Yet poetry does have a place in that tradition and offers a perhaps unexpected perspective on it.

The relation of poetry to philosophy suggests a complex of interconnected issues. To begin, it would be worthwhile to consider American poets whose work reflects a strong philosophical bent and to study the aesthetic ideas most strikingly reflected in their poetry. An outstanding example of such poets is Wallace Stevens. Then one might consider important American philosophers who wrote poetry, such as Emerson, Thoreau, Santayana, and even Dewey, and the relation of their poetry to their philosophical views. Another facet of the subject would be to examine the work of philosophers in whose writing poetry occupies a noticeable place. A fourth approach, and probably the one most directly relevant, is writing on the aesthetics of poetry that Americans have contributed to the philosophical literature. All these would be included in a thorough study of the place of poetry in American philosophy, but this article will consider only the last of them, and its brief length will allow only an overview.

Here, too, the question is more complex than might be thought at first, for important work on the aesthetics of poetry has been done not only by philosophers but by poets. One of the first was Edgar Allen Poe, whose "The Poetic Principle" (1850) reflects a romantic yearning for an intense, ethereal poetic aspiration, an elevating excitement of the soul, which we might, in modern terminology, call a powerful imaginative experience. In *The Necessary Angel* (1951), a century later, Wallace Stevens wrote of the living, sensuous presence of words, but he insisted that "the all-commanding subject-matter of poetry is life," which is its source. In the best poetry, he held, imagination and reality are interdependent, imagination responding to the pressure of reality, and poetry illuminating life. Ultimately, imagination is bound up with our very self-preservation.

Like Stevens, Archibald MacLeish pressed for the knowledge that poetry brings us, not in abstract form but by the direct presence it gives us of what is real in our experience. He claimed in *Poetry and Experience* (1960) that the poem stands as the great alternative to knowledge of the world by abstraction, for poetry does not abstract but brings us into an intimate relation with things. Poetry is thus capable of a different kind of knowledge from that of science. It is an action in the world through sounds, their referents, the images they make, and their interrelationships, "to the feel of meaning." In this way, we come to know, that is to discover, ourselves.

In "Projective Verse" the poet Charles Olson found the source of poetry in the body's vital center. The poem pulsates with a special life, as the line, the objects, the total field of a poem are infused with the vitalizing breath of speech. Olson insisted on the critical place of breath: poetry is for the ear, not the eye. Is this a distant echo of Thoreau's comment that "poetry is nothing but healthy speech" when he wrote that the poet, in his best lines, "simply saw or heard or felt what seems the commonest fact in my experience"? For Thoreau the true theme of poetry is "to describe the common."

Philosophers find in poetry a way of grasping experience. Emerson claimed that the poet, perhaps unexpectedly, ranges over the full scope of experience and, through words that are themselves a kind of action, articulates the richness of the natural world in symbols and tropes, and identifies the beauty that lies in it. The poetic imagination, he wrote, is a liberating force; it converts our immersion in daily affairs into universal symbols, and educates us by elevating us.

Despite his literary gifts, Santayana did not write extensively on poetry, yet he gave it a significant place in the life of reason. As incantation or charm, primitive poetry underlies all discourse. Pre-figuring Stevens, he held that poetry is based on human experience and is always faithful to nature, even though dominated by imagination. For Santayana, moreover, both poetry and religion are grounded in imagination and approach the world imaginatively. But while religion inhabits the ideal world of poetic imagination, its aspirations lead it beyond those of poetry, so that it mistakes its myths, which should be interpreted imaginatively as poetry, as literal, scientific truth and assigns moral authority to them. Poetry, on the other hand, remains in its true realm, enlivened by vivid feeling and imaginative expression. Poetry is also bound up with human life and labor, whose demands give the arts a moral function. "Works may not be aesthetic in their purpose, and yet that fact may be a ground for their being doubly delightful in execution and doubly beautiful in effect."

More recent philosophical work on the theory of poetry has been contributed by Suzanne Langer and Justus Buchler. One might question whether Langer merits inclusion in a discussion of poetry in American philosophy inasmuch as her work is informed by a different tradition and follows the neo-Kantian idealism of Ernst Cassirer's philosophy of symbolic forms. Working in this context, she considered the poet to be using language to create an illusion of life as a non-discursive symbolic form.

The most recent and extensive of all American philosophical considerations of the meaning and significance of poetry is undoubtedly Justus Buchler's *The Main of Light*. Like Dewey's *Art as Experience*, *The Main of Light* is a monument with two faces: a major contribution to the philosophy of art and at the same time an extraordinary summation of the author's overall philosophical vision. Buchler devoted this, his last major work, to the concept of poetry, beginning with a penetrating critique of conventional accounts of poetry based on imagination, reality, unity, inner experience, and form and content. In their place he developed a theory that endeavors to ascertain what it is to be an instance of poetry and, further, reflects the practice and variations of poetry. This entails a metaphysics of the human process and indeed a general ontology. For poetry, Buchler states, is a form of judgment, using that term in an extended sense that encompasses "the makings, sayings, and doings of everyday habit and impulse." Like all art, poetry is the particular mode of judgment he called "exhibitive," a mode that is fashioned here in language. Buchler develops this claim and illuminates it both within a metaphysical context and through poetic examples.

It may be more surprising to discover that poets have recognized the intimate bond poetry has to the active, physical engagement in the world of living experience than that philosophers have made that connection. Both, however, reflect that dominant strand in American culture.

Further reading

Buchler, Justus. *The Main of Light: On the Concept of Poetry.* New York: Oxford, 1974.

Emerson, Ralph Waldo. "Poetry and Imagination" (1872) in *Letters and Social Aims.* Boston, MA: James R. Osgood, 1875.

—— "The Poet" (1844) in *Essays: Second Series.* New York: J.W. Lovell, 1844.

MacLeish, Archibald. "Why Do We Teach Poetry?" *Atlantic Monthly* 197 (March 1956): 48–53.

—— *Poetry and Experience.* Boston, MA: Houghton Mifflin, 1961.

Santayana, George. *Interpretations of Poetry and Religion.* Boston, MA: MIT Press, 1989 [1900].

—— *Reason in Art*, Vol. 4 of *The Life of Reason.* New York: Charles Scribner's Sons, 1905.

ARNOLD BERLEANT

POLARITY

Polarity is a prominent concept in American Transcendentalism which drew heavily upon British and German Romanticism. The poet William Wordsworth (1770–1850) highlights polarity in his 1802 preface to *Lyrical Ballads* (1798), defining poetry as "the spontaneous overflow of powerful feelings from emotions recollected in tranquility." Samuel Taylor Coleridge (1772–1834) gives polarity a central metaphysical role as the dynamic force behind all temporal existence. Physical and mental or spiritual events occur as a result of the tension between opposite concepts. And so if we grant that a physical event can be poetic, a landscape perhaps, then we can imagine that both the poem about the landscape and the landscape itself emerge as a result of polarity.

Ralph Waldo Emerson (1803–82) takes his cue from these British Romantics, finding the authentic individual life emerging in the middle ground between sensation and reflection. The rejection of social conformity is a rejection of a scientific or common polarity embodied by institutions. Instead an individual life emerges by embracing the uniqueness of experience offered by Nature.

Emerson's connection of individualism and polarity is clearest in later essays. In "Fate" (1860), Emerson uses the bill of a bird as an example of its fate. And he remarks, "When each comes forth from his mother's womb, the gate of gifts closes behind him." The impulse to act and choose is a part of Fate. And intellect annuls the determining aspect of Fate. The presence of an impulse to act, the particular direction of choice, and the extent of intellect are a function of each individual's fated polarity.

Henry David Thoreau (1817–62) explicitly makes polarity the basis of self-culture and healthy civilization. Thoreau comments favorably on Coleridge's presentation of polarity as the principle of individuation and practices polarity in his writing. "Walking" (1851) treats man as part of Nature rather than society since there are enough people already concerned with civil society. Instead, Thoreau highlights absolute freedom or wildness and yearns for a "people who would begin by burning fences and letting the forest stand." He tells us that the founders of every eminent state have drawn upon a wild source.

Process philosophy emphasizes polarity as a metaphysical principle, as with Alfred North Whitehead (1861–1947) and Charles Hartshorne (1897–2000). For Whitehead, polarity is a pervasive principle but perhaps most importantly figures in his distinction of the primordial and consequent natures of God. Hartshorne defended a dipolar view of God against what he labeled a monopolar theism which by privileging one of a pair of opposites, such as permanence over change, privileged a classical Greek vision of the deity and generated unsolvable "theological mistakes" when combined with more historical views of God.

The naturalist Morris Cohen (1880–1947) took polarity as the metaphysical principle of our existence emerging from opposites which mutually require and attract each other. The German philosophers Johann Wolfgang Goethe (1749–1832) and Friedrich Wilhelm Joseph von Schelling (1775–1854) treated polarity as an important metaphysical principle. Scholars regard both as influences on Emerson and Thoreau.

Further reading

Cohen, Morris R. *Reason and Nature.* New York: Harcourt, Brace, 1931.
Coleridge, Samuel Taylor. *Biographia Literaria.* Princeton, NJ: Princeton University Press, 1985 [1817].
Emerson, Ralph Waldo, *Essays and Lectures.* New York: Library of America, 1981.
—— *The Works of Ralph Waldo Emerson*, http://rwe.org
Hartshorne, Charles. *Omnipotence and Other Theological Mistakes.* Albany, NY: SUNY Press, 1983.
Robinson, David M. "Emerson, Thoreau, Fuller, and Transcendentalism," *American Literary Scholarship* 1 (2002): 3–27.
Thoreau, Henry David. *The Essays of Henry D. Thoreau*, ed. Lewis Hyde. New York: Farrar, Straus and Giroux, 2002.
Whitehead, Alfred North. *Religion in the Making.* Cleveland, OH: Meridian Books, 1960.
Wordsworth, William and Coleridge, Samuel Taylor. *Lyrical Ballads.* New York: Routledge, 1991 [1798].

ANTHONY J. GRAYBOSCH

POSSIBILITY

Systematic study of possibility began with the invention of modal logic by C.I. Lewis. Semantics of modal logic postulates possible worlds and defines possible truth as truth in some possible world. In the United States, the study of possibility has been closely intertwined with the study of conditionals ("If *P* then *Q*"). C.I. Lewis's modal logic was inspired by considerations of strict implication. *P* strictly implies *Q* just if there is no possible world in which *P* is true and *Q* false. Later, Robert Stalnaker proposed the following semantics for counterfactual conditionals: "If *P* were the case, then *Q* would be the case" is true just if *Q* is true in the closest *P*-world, i.e. *Q* is true in the possible world in which *P* is true and which is closer to the actual world than any other world in which *P* is true. Shortly thereafter, David Lewis offered a more generalized treatment without the assumption of the existence of the closest *P*-world, along with extensive discussions of the closeness relation.

As the metaphysical foundations for his theory of counterfactual conditionals, David Lewis proposed a realist theory of possible worlds and *possibilia* (possible individuals). On his theory, the actual world is a maximal whole made up of all individuals spatiotemporally related to us, and a non-actual possible world is a maximal whole made up of spatiotemporally related non-actual *possibilia*. Every *possibile*, actual or non-actual, exists in just one world. Hubert Humphrey could have won the presidential election in 1968. So, in some possible world Humphrey did win. But if Humphrey does not exist in any world other than the actual world, how did he manage to win in any other world? Lewis resorts to counterpart theory. For Humphrey to win in a non-actual world *w* is for there to be someone who is his counterpart in *w* who wins. To be Humphrey's counterpart is to resemble Humphrey in relevant respects, where what is relevant varies from one context of discourse to another, depending on the pragmatics of the discourse.

Truth in at least one possible world is possibility in the absolute sense, or logical possibility. Truth in at least one possible world in which a particular proposition *P* is true is possibility in a restricted sense. Let *P* be the conjunction of all laws of nature, and we have nomological possibility. If *P* is the totality of all that is known, we have epistemic possibility. If *P* lays out all law-like generalizations of politics, we have political possibility. And so on.

Further reading

Lewis, David. *Counterfactuals.* Cambridge, MA: Harvard University Press, 1973.
—— *On the Plurality of Worlds.* London: Blackwell, 1986.
Stalnaker, Robert. "A Theory of Conditionals" in Nicholas Rescher (ed.) *Studies in Logical Theory.* Oxford: Blackwell, 1968, pp. 98–112.

TAKASHI YAGISAWA

POSSIBLE WORLDS

There are numerous ways the world might have been different. Gore might have become president, for example. Possible worlds provide a way of making sense of this. The possibility that Gore could have become president is represented by a possible world where Gore (or his counterpart – see below) *did* become president. Possible worlds have been introduced primarily to deal with modal notions, such as necessity and possibility. "Necessary *P*" is true iff *P* is true in all possible worlds, and "Possibly P" is true iff P is true in at least one possible world. They have also proved fruitful in dealing with a number of other philosophical issues, such as properties, propositions, causation, and counterfactuals. For example, propositions might be conceived of as sets of possible worlds, and properties as sets of objects in these worlds (Lewis 1986). Accounts of possible worlds can be divided into two types: possibilist and actualist. Possibilists believe that possible worlds are non-actual, merely possible entities, whereas actualists believe that everything that exists is actual, so that possible worlds consist of, or are constructs of, actual entities.

Possibilism

A version of possibilism has been developed in detail by Lewis (1986). Possibilists seem to assert a contradiction: that there exist things that do not exist. Lewis avoids this contradiction by arguing that possible worlds exist in just the same way that the world around us exists. The world we inhabit is just one among a plurality of worlds, each spatio-temporally and causally isolated from one another. The worlds are so plentiful that for every way a world might be there is a world that is that way. There is nothing metaphysically special about the world we inhabit. Other possible worlds contain physical objects that are just as real as the physical objects around us. We just happen not to live in these other worlds. We call this world "actual" simply because it is the one we inhabit. "Actual" is interpreted as an indexical term relative to the world in which the term is uttered. Each world is actual from the perspective of speakers in that world. On Lewis's account, no object can exist in more than one world, so when we say that Gore might have become president we mean that there is another possible world with a counterpart for Gore who did become president. An object in another possible world, *w*, is a counterpart for Gore if that object resembles Gore in relevant respects more closely than any other object in *w*.

Lewis's account has faced a number of criticisms. Given that other possible worlds are spatio-temporally isolated from us, how can we gain knowledge of particular modal claims or even knowledge that there *are* other possible worlds? It has also been argued that his account misrepresents what is possible, since it precludes the possibility of an empty world or a particular world with spatio-temporally isolated parts (Bigelow and Pargetter 1990: 189–93). In other cases, his account appears able to accurately represent what is possible only by relying on modal notions, which he is trying to analyze (Bigelow and Pargetter 1990: 193–203; Divers 2002: 114–21). His account has also been accused of leading to paradox, and a number of criticisms have been raised for his counterpart theory (see Divers 2002). However, the most common complaint is that his account defies common sense. For discussions of these and other criticisms, see Lewis (1986) and Divers (2002).

Actualism

According to actualist accounts, possible worlds consist of, or are constructs of, entities (typically abstract entities) that are actual. Some (e.g. Carnap) conceive of possible worlds as sets (or conjunctions) of propositions (or sentences) that are maximally consistent, where a set of propositions is maximal iff for every proposition, *P*, either *P* or *Not P* is contained in (or derivable from) the set. A set represents the actual world iff it contains all and only true propositions. Plantinga (1974), in contrast, argues that possible worlds are possible maximal states of affairs, where a state of affairs, *S*, is maximal iff for every state of affairs, *S**, *S* includes or precludes *S**. The actual world is the possible world that obtains. Others (e.g. Bigelow and Pargetter 1990) conceive of possible worlds as complex world properties – *ways* the world might have been. All but one of these is uninstantiated; the actual world is the world property that is instantiated. A similar view can be found earlier in the work of Santayana, who views possible worlds as complex essences. He conceives of the entire history of the world around us as a complex event. This complex event exemplifies a complex essence, which he calls a "trope." Possible worlds are extremely complex tropes, one of which is exemplified by the entire history of the world around us. There are also combinatorial accounts, attributed most famously to Wittgenstein's *Tractatus Logico-Philosophicos*, according to which possible worlds are constructs created by recombining actual entities, such as actual individuals and instantiated properties.

Each of the above actualist accounts have been accused of having some or all of the following problems. While they seem metaphysically and epistemically less problematic than Lewis's possible worlds, they are still committed to abstract entities many find objectionable, such as uninstantiated universals in the case of the world-property account or individual essences in the case of Plantinga's account. Moreover, given the abstract nature of possible worlds on these accounts, it is still unclear how we would gain modal knowledge, since we cannot causally interact with such entities. Actualist accounts have also been accused of having paradoxical implications (see Divers 2002). Furthermore, it is unclear whether they have the resources to represent all the possibilities there are, and they are only able to exclude all impossibilities (such as being entirely red and entirely green) by relying on primitive modal notions, such as consistency (see Lewis 1986). For an overview of responses to some of these criticisms, see Divers (2002).

Alternatives

Because of these and other problems, some, most famously Quine, have argued that we ought to dispense with talk of possible worlds, while others have attempted to provide antirealist interpretations of such talk, for example by conceiving of possible worlds as fictions. The question faced by these alternatives is whether the benefits provided by the realist accounts discussed in the previous two sections can be maintained without the realist commitment to the existence of possible worlds.

Further reading

Bigelow, John and Pargetter, Robert. *Science and Necessity.* Cambridge: Cambridge University Press, 1990.

Divers, John. *Possible Worlds.* London: Routledge, 2002.

Lewis, David. *On the Plurality of Worlds.* Oxford: Blackwell, 1986.

Plantinga, Alvin. *The Nature of Necessity.* Oxford: Clarendon Press, 1974.

JESSICA PFEIFER

POSTMODERNISM

Depending on the context, postmodernism refers to either a new era of history or a successor to modernism in the various arts. In the arts, the question is whether artistic and cultural projects known as modernism have been replaced by postmodernism. In history it concerns whether the project of modernity, begun roughly in the fifteenth or sixteenth century, has been superseded by a new postmodern era or whether, as in Lyotard's view (1984), it is an intrinsic feature of modernism, the incredulity to narratives that pushes modern science forward even as modern science constantly appeals to an overarching narrative. Postmodernism in the arts concerns whether a particular modernism – e.g. the high modern literary era of Ezra Pound and T.S. Eliot – is over; the question of postmodernism as an historical epoch concerns whether there is something decidedly and decisively diferent about the current era as opposed to modernity. The two are connected in so far as modernism in one art or another can be understood as a moment when the ideals of modernity finally take hold. As such, postmodernism in an aesthetic field is not merely a rebuke of a previous modern aesthetic but on the ideals of modernity itself.

History and meaning

Postmodernism is not so much a reversal of modernism as it is a critique and outgrowth of it, perhaps even the underside or incompleteness of modernity. One of the most trenchant critiques began at the end of the nineteenth century with Friedrich Nietzsche's attack on some of modernity's central values: the notion of the progress of reason in history, the ideals of dispassionate search for truth, the link between democracy and a better life for humanity. On the heels of some of modernism's most vocal spokesmen, Hegel and Marx, Nietzsche lashed out at what he took to be modernity's great errors. His ideas of perspectivalism, his critiques of the Cartesian subject, his notions of metaphor, of nominalism, and of truth as a will to power all prefigured the postmodern attitude to modernity. Also in Europe, Ludwig Wittgenstein in the trajectory of his own writings, moving from a picture (correspondence) theory of truth to the idea of language games, pointed to the unsustainability of the modern project and the undecidability of truth in the coming era. In the United States, William James and John Dewey anticipated postmodernism with their critiques of many of modernity's presuppositions and their calls for pluralism and the reconstruction of philosophy. German émigrés to the United States, notably Horkheimer and Adorno, lashed out at modernity in their *Dialectic of Enlightenment* (1944), though they did not have anything more than a pessimistic notion of the future to follow it. By the middle of the twentieth century, writers from a variety of disciplines and perspectives (history, economics, sociology, literature) began to comment on a momentous change taking place, largely due to transformations in the economy and culture (namely through new media). Daniel Bell in the United States described what he saw as a new post-industrial society. In France Guy Debord described the "society of the spectacle." Marshall McLuhan saw a new "global village," anticipating today's ideas of globalization.

The term "postmodernism" first emerged in the late nineteenth century. The English painter John Watkins Chapman spoke of post-impressionist painting as "postmodern" and in 1917 Rudolf Pannwitz complained of the rising nihilism and collapse of values in contemporary Europe and he called for "postmodern" men who would bring about new elite (and rather fascistic sounding) values (Best and Kellner 1991). The renowned historian Arnold Toynbee used the term in his six-volume study of history (1947), marking the postmodern era as beginning in 1875. Yet none of these early uses of the term captured the sense that is current today. Subsequent historians and sociologists (Bernard Rosenberg, C. Wright Mills, Peter Drucker) came closer, picking up the term to note apparent historical breaks between modernity and a new era. Starting in 1971, the literary critic Ihab Hassan developed a theory of literary postmodernism that began to develop a language of the postmodern still in circulation today; he described postmodernism as a "decisive historical mutation" from industrial society (Best and Kellner 1991), all the while writing in the new grammar of the postmodern: in a "non-linear, playful, assemblage-like style that constructs a pastiche text comprised largely of quotations and name-dropping" (Best and Kellner 1991). By the 1980s, the term *postmodernism* was in full flower in France, with philosophers such as Jean Baudrillard and Jean-François Lyotard radically departing from Cartesian philosophy and even the more recent existential and structuralist philosophies. By the late 1980s, postmodernism became a subject of extensive philosophical and aesthetic discourse and debate, largely dividing along questions of whether we were truly in a new era and whether this was something to be celebrated or overcome.

Throughout the rise of the idea of the postmodern and fully in the height of postmodern discourse, the idea of postmodernism became a site of debate: some theorists saw it negatively; others championed it. Generally, those who saw modernity and the Enlightenment as a good, even if unfinished, era for humankind tended to view what seemed to be a new, postmodern era as a terrible development leading to nihilism, relativism, and an abandonment of democratic, liberatory ideals. In such criticism, cultural conservatives found themselves agreeing with critics on the left, especially the new generation of the Frankfurt School, namely Jürgen Habermas. On the other side, those like Susan Sontag, Leslie Fielder and others who thought Enlightenment rationality was oppressive looked forward to the potentially liberating aspects of postmodernism. Early advocates of postmodernism were of two orientations, social and cultural, with social theorists optimistically anticipating how a new society might break with an obsolete and oppressive industrial order. Cultural critics of modernity looked forward to new postmodern forms of popular culture, less elitist and formal than modern culture, more playful, spontaneous, and participatory.

By the mid-1980s, the major postmodern theorists – including Gilles Deleuze, Felix Guattari, Baudrillard, Lyotard, Fredric Jameson, Ernesto Laclau, Chantal Mouffe, Donna Haraway, Judith Butler, and Jane Flax – had taken as a given that we were in a new era and they began working out what it meant for theory, subjectivity, history, the arts, and politics. Yet even among these theorists there is no unified and uncontested understanding of what postmodernism means. Some observers offer rough characterizations. Richard Shusterman finds the following features:

> transfigurative appropriation of older materials, eclectic mixing, an embracing of new media technology and mass culture, an emphasis on the local and temporal rather than the universal and eternal, and a challenging of modernity's notions of aesthetic autonomy and artistic purity.
>
> (Shusterman 1995: 154)

Still there are very different views about what postmodernism is, what has brought it about, and whether it is a good thing. The Marxist critic Fredric Jameson, for example, sees what can be alluring about postmodernism, but is at the same time critically aware of how it is an outgrowth of an inhumane economic order, namely late capitalism. Nonetheless some general features emerge:

First, it is antifoundational. Like many American pragmatists, postmodernists hold that there are no external foundations – or bedrock ways of knowing or transcendental truths – that can support or back up our claims. Most other philosophies hold on to something by which a theory can be measured, whether metaphysical notions like God or reason or truth or more contemporary measures like reality or referents (e.g. Tarski's statement that the statement "snow is white" is true if and only if snow is white). Both pragmatists and postmodernists eschew correspondence theories of truth, but postmodernists might also avoid the notion that "the truth is what works," because they might even shy away from making a claim about "what works." Despite this discrepancy, pragmatists and postmodernists, with their antifoundationalism, suffer from the same criticism (often levied by Habermasian critical theorists, including Habermas himself): that their own discourses are subject to a performative contradiction – that to theorize that there can be no overarching foundational theory is to use theory to undermine theory or, worse, to speak babble. Or, as John Stuhr puts it,

> Their opponents charge that a philosophy without a foundational epistemology and/or a transcendental metaphysics cannot justify its own critical content. These opponents claim that pragmatism, like postmodernism, historicizes all claims, relativizes all values, and legitimizes all sides of all struggles.
>
> (Stuhr 2003: 128–9)

To such charges, pragmatists will point critics to look at the effectiveness of pragmatic inquiry, to judge it by what it accomplishes rather than to dismiss it for lack of putative foundations. Postmodernists such as Jacques Derrida, the seeming exemplar of relativism and postmodernism, actually have a much more subtle position, that there is a far distance between antifoundationalism and nonsense. Derrida's view, as laid out in a very direct rebuke of Habermas's (mis)reading of his texts (Derrida 1988: footnote 9, pp. 156–8), seems more like a coherence theory of truth that is extremely cautious about how language might hang together coherently yet does not avoid making claims and arguments. Of his critics he writes, "exposed to the slightest diffculty, the slightest complication, the slightest transformation of the rules, the self-declared advocates of communication denounce the absence of rules and confusion" (Derrida).

Second, there is a focus on difference, both the differentiation of the postmodern era from modern (looking for breaks and discontinuities, though some postmodern theorists such as Lyotard will look for continuities and connections as well) and the way in which "difference" operates in language, in peoples (as in the postmodern feminist notion that the category "woman" no longer suffices to explain the heterogeneity of actual women), in time (preferring a diachronic rather than synchronic lens) and space (as in the way in which postmodern buildings rupture the distinction between inside and outside). As opposed to modernity and even recent structuralist theory, postmodernists focus on difference because they are suspicious of any theoretical search or claim for unity and totality, seeing these as oppressive and totalitarian tendencies.

Third, postmodernism tends to decenter things and take issue with modernity's claim to the possibility of objective truth. Like Nietzsche, postmodernists are perspectivalists. By decentering they mean that the subject or author loses its point at the center of things; authors do not write texts, cultures and languages do. Also, they mean that power and energy can flow in multiple directions all at once (Foucault, *Archaeology of Knowledge*). The Cartesian subject, following Nietzsche's critique, is roundly routed from authority; it is just a grammatical illusion, a fiction fabricated from our language with its grammar of subject and predicate. Poststructuralist theorists in particular (poststructuralism being one of many strands within postmodernism) notice the ways in which language and signs constitute the subject and other identities. Simone de Beauvoir's famous axiom, "A woman is made not born," prefigures postmodern feminists' understanding that both sex and gender are fabrications, identities that come about through performance (Butler) or through many ages of sexist metaphysics (Irigaray).

Fourth, postmodernism gives rise to historicism; cultural artifacts become unmoored from history: where Hegel led modernity into the ideal that history is the march of progress, however dialectical, postmodernism sees the shift from one era to another as arbitrary and not necessarily an improvement. One era is just different from another, but not in a necessarily meaningful way. Where modernists created the credo that form follows function, that, for example, the purpose and use of a building should inform what its architecture is, postmodernism does away with the link between form, function, and history. A postmodern building is a pastiche of styles, with form seeming to follow whim, and function sidelined by the play of images and facades. It may appropriate elements from an earlier era in order to make a new point, in keeping with the postmodern attitude that form can be stripped of history and context.

The postmodern era seems to be an era of reruns, sequels, and remakes, with endless appropriations of past cultural productions. Fredric Jameson chalks this up to "the collapse of the high-modernist ideology of style" which had been able to continue producing new artifacts because "stylistic invention and innovation" drew from the creator's uniqueness (Jameson 1991: 17). With the collapse of modernism,

> the producers of culture have nowhere to turn but to the past: the imitation of dead styles ... This situation evidently determines what the architecture historians call "historicism," namely, the random cannibalization of all the styles of the past, the play of random stylistic allusion, and in general what Henri Lefebvre has called the increasing primacy of the "neo."
>
> (Jameson 1991: 17–18)

These imitations of past modes, these "neo-this, that, and the other," however, do not actually refer back to some place and time and moment. These referents float beyond the reach of the artefact. The problem with postmodernism's historicism is that it is cut off from history and meaning and caught up in the variations themselves, for breaks and discontinuities, for "when it all changed" (Jameson 1991: ix). For Jameson, this is what is most salient about postmodernism: "It is safest to grasp the concept of the postmodern as an attempt to think the present historically in an age that has forgotten how to think historically in the first place" (Jameson 1991: ix).

The future of the postmodern

As a philosophical discourse that seemed to sweep the academy, postmodern theory is already twenty-five years old and has the earmarks of a well-worn theory that can be spoken of in the past tense. The last key texts were written in about 1990, oddly, just at the cusp of a truly postmodern break in culture, history and the economy. Fredric Jameson's points about postmodernism being the logic of late capitalism seem more apropos than ever in an era when a peasant in Tibet can access more information now than an Ivy League college student could have ten years ago. Today anyone anywhere with a computer and a credit card number can shop for anything anywhere. Today people from all parts of the world are participating in global conversations through weblogs; they are sharing stories and information with new digital media including podcasts, videocasting, and social software such as "wikis" (websites that multiple people can edit). The hallmarks of postmodernity have, to a new generation, become second nature: becoming extensions of media and technology; mixing high and low culture; appropriating history and information for new purposes; rendering obsolete spatial and temporal boundaries; operating twenty-four hours a day, seven days a week, 365 days a year from any point on the globe. Postmodernism today may be more of a fact than ever, even if oddly today it causes less theoretical interest.

Further reading

Baudrillard, Jean. *Symbolic Exchange and Death*, trans. Ian Hamilton Grant. London: Sage, 1993.

Best, Steven and Kellner, Douglas (eds). *Postmodern Theory.* New York: Guilford, 1991.

Cahoone, Lawrence (ed.). *From Modernism to Postmodernism: An Anthology*, second edition. London: Blackwell, 2003.

Deleuze, Gilles and Guattari, Felix. *Anti-Oedipus: Capitalism and Schizophrenia*, trans. Robert Hurley, Mark Seem, and Helen R. Lane. Minneapolis, MN: University of Minnesota Press, 1983.

Habermas, Jürgen. *The Philosophical Discourse of Modernity*, trans. Frederick Lawrence. Cambridge: Cambridge University Press, 1987.

Irigaray, Luce. *This Sex Which Is Not One*, trans. Catherine Porter. Ithaca, NY: Cornell University Press, 1985.

Jameson, Fredric. *Postmodernism or, the Cultural Logic of Late Capitalism*. Durham, NC: Duke University Press, 1994.

Lyotard, J.-F. *The Postmodern Condition: A Report on Knowledge*, trans. Geoff Bennington and Brian Massumi. Minneapolis, MN: University of Minnesota Press, 1984.

Shusterman, Richard. "Rap Remix: Pragmatism, Postmodernism, and Other Issues in the House," *Critical Inquiry* 22, 1 (Autumn 1995): 150–8.

Stuhr, John. *Pragmatism, Postmodernism, and the Future of Philosophy.* New York: Routledge, 2003.

Taylor, Victor E. and Winquist, Charles E. *Encyclopedia of Postmodernism*, London: Routledge, 2001.

Vattimo, Gianni. *The End of Modernity: Nihilism and Hermeneutics in Postmodern Culture*, trans. Jon R. Snyder. Baltimore, MD: Johns Hopkins University Press, 1988.

NOËLLE MCAFEE

POWER

Power is both a principal and a collateral theme in the American philosophical tradition. It is an essentially multidimensional concept and plays different roles in the great figures of American philosophy in shaping their views on the individual, their accounts of the trans-individual spaces opened by community, society, and the polity, and their conception of the processes of nature.

American philosophy's focus on the power of the individual is most clearly exemplified and emphasized in the work of Emerson and James. Emerson's meditative essays, with their engaged exercises in self-reflection and the repudiation of merely external authorities, carry the theme of the intrinsic power of the individual to reach truth and attunement with the universe to great length. The wide-ranging phenomenological and radical empiricist reflections of James, with their constant appeals to powers of selection, will, and choice are frank and open commitments to the power of the individual to take life in hand over against a cosmos that is not unambiguously meaningful or favorable to human desires, but which is not, at any rate, deterministic. Emerson's "Self-Reliance" and James' "Will to Believe" are classic statements of the power, indeed, the duty, of the individual to determine not only the truth of life but also the life of truth. Their maxim is, "dare to do what is in your power to do."

In essential and constant tension with the ascription of power to the self-reliant and self-determining individual is the recognition of the dependence of the individual upon community, understood as the primary "local" groups into which the individual is born, upon the wider "society" which is composed of multiple communities, and upon the more formal and institutionalized political order. The power of these groups is, indeed, ought to be, not just "over" the individual but also "for" the individual. While the primary community certainly can constrain the individual and can force an individual to conform to its essentially "local" norms and prescriptions, it is clearly an "enabling" condition for the development of distinctively human powers and skills: language, affective relations, and the moral sense that make it possible for the individual to function within the wider social and political domains. The power of education is rooted in the community dimension of power, without, however, exhausting it. This theme of community power through education was developed, applied, and criticized throughout a lifetime of reflection by John Dewey, with his focus on the power of experiencing and not just on the experiencing of power. A constant theme of Dewey's work was that society and the polity were to be measured by their capacities to expand, stabilize, and deepen the powers of the individual and the individual's capacities for rich and permanent experiences, and not by their recourse to "force" and various forms of violence. In this respect American philosophy did not engage in a kind of "rhetoric of suspicion" or support reactionary forces in society and the polity that marked certain strands of European philosophy exemplified by such thinkers as Nietzsche and his heirs.

Another dimension of the trans-individual aspects of power was developed by Josiah Royce, with reliance on the semiotic theory of C.S. Peirce. Royce's concern was the nature of interpretation and the power of signs to mediate a person's adherence to a community or tradition of meaning. The paradigm case of such a community was Christianity as a trans-generational process of constituting the "beloved community" through interpretations and the ethical actions flowing from them. The sign processes that generate the continuity of the community have a distinctive kind of power, but they do not operate automatically, because they are dependent upon those who also carry the interpretation community. Peirce, upon whom Royce relied, had shown that sign-action, or semiosis, is something that we find ourselves in and cannot completely control. Semiosis is an event that transcends the power of an individual subjectivity. The power of semiosis is exemplified and concretized in Peirce's theory of interpretants, which are what he calls the proper significate effects of signs (and sign actions).

Peirce foregrounded the power of signs to shape subjectivity on three distinct levels: the affective, the behavioral, and the intellectual or "logical." While the knowledge that we are using signs is a defining mark of humans, as opposed to other sign-using animals, and consequently the ultimate source of human power, engagement with sign systems structures our modes of feeling, steers and constrains our courses of action, and enables and carries our conceptual systems. Sign systems "touch" us at every level of our being and cannot be put on or taken off by mere whim. It is the ability to consciously and systematically use signs that marks power, as an example of thirdness, as opposed to force, an example of secondness. For Peirce, Royce, and Dewey it was this power of meaning and power of unrestricted communication that was of overarching concern. G.H. Mead foregrounded the social-psychological consequences of the power of signs to shape the self. For him, mind, self, and society form a kind of triadic structure of interdependent variables, inseparable from one another. Here the power of society becomes the critical matrix for the rise of the powerful self. American philosophy has perhaps not been as aware as it could be of the social and ideological forces embodied in the social role of signs, contrasting in this way with such intellectual projects as Michel Foucault's which have foregrounded the subjectivity shaping powers of those who control the means of discourse and the exchange of signs.

Classical American philosophy had a deeply naturalistic dimension, even while it was defined by variously conceived dimensions of transcendence. Nature, ultimately understood not as product, *natura naturata*, but as process, *natura naturans*, was the ultimate locus of the power of creativity and spontaneity. This essentially open power of nature as process became explicitly conscious of itself in human beings. The paradigm case of this power of nature was to be found in the imagination, which is the realm of possibilities *par excellence*. The theme of natural imaginative powers and the imaginative power of nature plays a central role especially in Emerson's transcendental naturalism, in Dewey's critique of an otherworldly transcendentalism, and in Santayana's formulation of a poetically structured semi-Spinozistic "ultimate religion." In these three thinkers the development of a religious naturalism is deeply intertwined with a naturalist aesthetics, albeit with very different emphases and philosophical commitments. Nature for them bears witness to its powers of transcendence, and not just to its ineluctable destructive tendencies. A recognition of the role of natural powers or powers of nature is also found in James's development from a naturalistic psychology to his radical empiricism, with its experiential monism, and in Peirce's doctrine of synechism or continuity and in his reformulation of Schelling's objective idealism. It is in the work of Peirce that a metaphysics of natural powers is most worked out, although Dewey made considerable contributions in that direction, as did Whitehead with his development of a full-fledged categorial scheme of natural processes and his thesis of the ultimacy of creativity in nature. American philosophy has clearly established the creativity of nature as the essential locus and engine of power, in all its forms, as well as the essential standard that distinguishes it from all forms of brute force and meaningless occurrences in the individual and in the various groups to which the individual belongs. The ultimate lesson of American philosophy is that the culmination and fruition of power is the power of the free imagination and all its works.

Further reading

Dewey, John. *The Moral Writings of John Dewey*, revised edition, ed. James Gouinlock. Amherst, NY: Prometheus Books, 1994.

Emerson, Ralph Waldo. *Nature*, in *The Selected Writings of Ralph Waldo Emerson*, ed. Brooks Atkinson. New York: The Modern Library, 2000.

James, William. "The Will to Believe" in *Pragmatism and Other Writings*, ed. Giles Gunn. New York: Penguin, 2000.

Peirce, Charles S. "Evolutionary Love" in *The Essential Peirce*, Vol. 1, ed. Nathan Houser and Christian Kloesel. Bloomington, IN: Indiana University Press, 1992, pp. 352–71.

Royce, Josiah. "The Will to Interpret" in *The Problem of Christianity*, with a Foreword by Frank M. Oppenheim, SJ. Washington, DC: Catholic University of America Press, 2001 [1913].

ROBERT E. INNIS

PRAGMATIC MAXIM

The *locus classicus* of the pragmatic maxim is an 1878 paper by Charles S. Peirce entitled "How to Make Our Ideas Clear," where it is presented as the third and highest grade of clearness an idea can attain. The conception of meaning that Peirce here developed follows directly from the doubt–belief theory he set out in the "Fixation of Belief," where he argued that to establish belief is the sole purpose of inquiry (CP 5.394). With the added notion that belief is a disposition to act, the *meaning* of a word, sentence, theory, or road sign is how it leads us to act. Consequently, the meaning of anything is the *habits* it elicits. In line with this, Peirce devised the following principle, which is now called the "Pragmatic Maxim": "Consider what effects, that might conceivably have practical bearings, we conceive the object of our conception to have. Then, our conception of these effects is the whole of our conception of the object" (CP 5.402). Peirce considered this maxim an imperative of logic: it tells us how we should define our terms.

After stating the maxim, Peirce gave several examples on how to apply it. Best known is its application to the concept "hardness" where Peirce gave an overly nominalistic reading of the maxim that proved damaging to the way it was later received. Because of this, Peirce spent much effort defending his realist interpretation of the maxim against the nominalist interpretations of other more popular authors, arguing that what he had intended with "effects" are, as he put it, "consequences for deliberate, self-controlled conduct" (CP 8.191), and that by "practical" he meant "apt to affect conduct" – meaning with the latter "voluntary action that is self-controlled" (CP 8.322). Peirce's later formulations clearly show the maxim's realist import. For instance, in 1905, he writes: "The entire intellectual purport of any symbol consists in the total of all general modes of rational conduct which, conditionally upon all the possible different circumstances and desires, would ensue upon the acceptance of the symbol" (CP 5.438).

It was William James who, in 1898, brought the maxim into the limelight during a lecture called "Philosophical Conceptions and Practical Results." James paraphrased the maxim as follows:

> To attain perfect clearness in our thoughts of an object . . . we need only consider what effects of a conceivably practical kind the object may involve – what sensations we are to expect from it, and what reactions we must prepare. Our conception of these effects, then, is for us the whole of our conception of the object.
>
> (1977: 348)

Thus, whereas Peirce sought to derive the meaning of an object of thought from the habits it evokes (which are *generals*, not particulars), James related meaning strictly to particulars, namely, anticipated sensations and reactions. Peirce rejected this reading, believing this view to be as absurd as claiming that the purpose of a musical movement is the few bars at the end. There is a further difference in how the two interpret the practical effects that are referred to by the maxim. Whereas Peirce related these effects strictly to the object conceived, James preferred to relate them to the believer, arguing that something is meaningful if it has conceivable practical consequences in the lives of those who believe it. Moreover, inspired by his own arguments in "The Will to Believe," James broadened the maxim not only by making it a criterion of meaning but also by linking truth with what works, a criterion of truth.

The course that was set by James was taken further by Ferdinand Schiller, who in his 1911 *Encyclopaedia Britannica* pragmatism entry solidly declared the maxim a criterion of truth: "every truth has practical consequences, and these are the test of its truth." In Italy, Giovanni Papini gave the following rendition, tying the maxim closely to James's will-to-believe argument: "The meaning of theories consists entirely in the consequences which their followers may expect from them" (1907: 352). John Dewey related the maxim to his own notion of an indeterminate situation, arguing that our responses to sensory stimuli determine our conceptions. To get a clear conception, Dewey observed, is to consider the differences it would make in practice if the idea were true (1912). C.I. Lewis gave the following rendition in a letter of 19 September 1944 to W.T. Stace:

> A statement is meaningful if and only if there is a criterion in mind by reference to which we should, under appropriate and specifiable circumstances, be able to recognize some empirical presentation as affording confirmation or disconfirmation of it in some degree.

More recently, Richard Rorty briefly captured the maxim by stating that, "the meaning of a concept is the sum of its possible effects upon conduct" (1961: 198).

The pragmatic maxim differs from the *verificationist principle* of the logical positivists in that it does not tie meaning narrowly to sensory input. Early versions of the principle professed that a statement has meaning only insofar as it can be translated into a conjunction of statements each of which merely expresses direct observations. Because this would also count as the statement's verification, the verificationists, like some pragmatists, drew a tight connection between meaning and truth. One rather obvious problem with the verification principle is that applying the principle to itself shows it to be meaningless. The pragmatic maxim is not similarly self-defeating.

Further reading

Dewey, John. "Pragmatism" in Paul Monroe (ed.) *A Cyclopedia of Education*. New York: Macmillan, 1912.

James, William. *The Writings of William James: A Comprehensive Edition*. Chicago, IL: University of Chicago Press. 1977.

Papini, Giovanni. "What Pragmatism is Like," *Popular Science Monthly* 71, 10 (1907): 351–8.

Peirce, Charles S. *The Collected Papers of Charles Sanders Peirce*. Cambridge, MA, 1958 [1931–5] (referred to as CP, with volume and section number).

Rorty, Richard. "Pragmatism, Categories, and Language" *Philosophical Review* 70, 2 (1961): 197–223.

CORNELIS DE WAAL

PRAGMATISM

Pragmatism is the philosophical perspective most often uniquely associated with the "classic" age of American academic philosophy (1860–1940). While that association is certainly valid, we must distinguish between the precise sense of "pragmatism" as a philosophical *doctrine* of meaning and/or truth, and the global sense of pragmatism as a general *philosophy*. As the former, pragmatism was invented by Charles Peirce as a theory of meaning, and inevitably came to imply a theory of truth. This was the pragmatism that became most famous among twentieth-century philosophers as one of three canonical accounts of truth (the others being the "correspondence" and the "coherence" theories). In the global sense "pragmatism" serves as shorthand to label the distinctive approaches of the classical Americans as a group, not only Peirce, James, and Dewey, but William Ernest Hocking, George Herbert Mead, Josiah Royce, and George Santayana, "second-generation" students like Max Fisch, Horace Kallen, Sidney Hook, Ralph Barton Perry and Herbert W. Schneider, related philosophers like F.J.E. Woodbridge, C.I. Lewis, Wilfrid Sellars, Alfred North Whitehead, John Herman Randall, Paul Weiss, and Justus Buchler, and finally pragmatist thinkers long neglected by philosophers, like Jane Addams, W.E.B. DuBois, Charlotte Perkins Gilman and Alain Locke. We are free to use the term in this global way, but must remember that these thinkers espoused many ideas not "pragmatic" in the narrow sense, just as others have endorsed the pragmatic doctrine without accepting other ideas of the Americans.

Birth of pragmatism

The pre-history of pragmatism, both as doctrine and philosophy, can be attributed to the Scottish and German Enlightenments. The former evolved various forms of empiricism, influenced by English empiricism, in reaction to speculative philosophies, the skeptic David Hume being the greatest example. However, pragmatism was more influenced by other Scots, like Thomas Reid, whose "common sense" philosophy especially influenced Peirce, Alexander Bain (about whom more later), and perhaps by Adam Ferguson and Adam Smith, who were largely responsible for the notion of "spontaneous order," that order and even virtuous order could emerge from an accumulation of uncoordinated acts, rather than design. Later, nineteenth-century English empiricism, primarily John Stuart Mill, had a significant impact, particularly on Dewey. From the German side, pragmatism inherited what we may call the "philosophy of the act," expressed in Goethe's line, "*Im Anfang war die Tat*" ("In the beginning was the deed"). Kant regarded the *a priori* order of experience as the product of the transcendental activity of the human mind. He also claimed that the rational will provided presuppositions about the world that we can never know to be true but must believe both in order to act aright (*a priori* morality) and to discover order in the world (regulative ideals of knowledge). Such constitutive mental activity became the hallmark of German thought after Kant, from Fichte's Absolute Idealism through Schelling's evolutionary cosmology – Peirce more than once called himself a Schellingian – and Hegel's dialectics through Schopenhauer's metaphysics of will to the "will to power" of Nietzsche (who, interestingly, admired Ralph Waldo Emerson). The inspiration for pragmatism was thus largely Scots–German.

Its motivation was more complex. Kant was Peirce's guide to the problem of knowledge. But Peirce concluded that the experience-forming components of cognition are signs, not transcendental mental categories. Peirce was a strict fallibilist, holding that there are no "first principles," no "first thoughts," and that no thought or perception has an immediate, hence incorrigible, relation to its object. This left his semiotic theory of thought and knowledge in difficulty. He had denied that there is any beginning or end to a sign's – hence a thought's – interpretation; signs are defined recursively as giving rise to other signs *ad infinitum*. If inquiry cannot find *a priori* principles and its signs are defined via relations to others signs without end, how can the meaning of any concept be delimited?

His answer emerged in the discussions of "the Metaphysical Club," a group that met in the early 1870s in Cambridge, Massachusetts, frequented by Peirce, William James, Nicholas St John Green, Chauncey Wright, Oliver Wendell Holmes, Jr, and Joseph Warner. Green in particular is credited with alerting Peirce to Scotsman Alexander Bain's remark that "belief is that upon which a man is prepared to act." Peirce delivered a paper expounding a method of clarifying concepts to the club in 1871–2, which he called "pragmatic." It became the basis for two papers he published in November 1877 and December 1878 ("The Fixation of Belief" and "How to Make our Ideas Clear," respectively). Those essays argue that the meaning of an idea, term or belief is "our idea of its sensible effects," and hence the difference its affirmation or assertion makes to the guidance of our conduct. In effect, the meaning of a thought is "the habits it involves." What Peirce has in mind is the experimental scientist's conception of meaning. A term means what the experimenter must do in order to study what it refers to. Although not yet clear, in saying the idea of a thing is "our idea of its sensible effects" Peirce meant the effects it *would* or *could* have, not merely the effects it once had or now has.

Even in this early presentation, the new doctrine of meaning broached a more portentous topic, truth. This application is entirely natural; after all, "truth" is a term whose meaning needs to be clarified. In the second essay Peirce asserted his famous "convergence theory," that, "The opinion which is fated to be ultimately agreed to by all who investigate, is what we mean by the truth, and the object represented in this opinion is the real" (Peirce, para. 402). This need *not* deny correspondence. Peirce later agreed that truth is "nominally" defined as correspondence to reality. The question is, what does "correspondence" *mean*? Convergence is his pragmatic answer to that question. Notice that it entailed a communitarian approach to knowledge, logic, and even reality, since reality is defined in terms of the goal of the community of inquirers. This idea would later be taken up by Josiah Royce, most Idealist and religious of the canonical American philosophers, under his "absolute pragmatism."

Thus was the pragmatic doctrine born. But remarkably, while it played an important role in Peirce's thought over the next twenty years, he never identified it by name in print during this time. So went the anonymous childhood phase of pragmatism's strange life history.

Troubled adolescence

Pragmatism's coming out party occurred in 1898, in Berkeley, California, where William James gave a lecture entitled "Philosophical Conceptions and Practical Results." As a result it was James' notion of pragmatism, later formulated in a series of 1906 lectures and published in the little book *Pragmatism*, that defined the doctrine for other philosophers and the public. Ascribing the doctrine to Peirce, James wrote about the "truth" of an idea "agreeing" with reality that

> *To "agree" in the widest sense with a reality can only mean . . . to be put into such a working touch with it as to handle either it or something connected with it better than if we disagree.* Better either intellectually or practically!
>
> (James 2000: 93, his emphasis)

He further explained that "purely objective truth," truth devoid of the human function of "marrying previous parts of experience with newer parts" to achieve "human satisfaction," is unavailable. In fact, truth "means only to perform this marriage-function." Globally put, "The trail of the human serpent is over all." He went as far as to say that "Truth is one species of the good" (a plausible rendition of Peirce's later doctrine that logic, as a "normative science," is a subspecies of ethics). In his most provocative formulation, James claimed that, "'The true' ... is only the expedient in the way of our thinking, just as 'the right' is only the expedient in the way of our behaving ... expedient in the long run and on the whole of course" (James 2000: 97–8).

It is from such Jamesian remarks that the notion of a specifically pragmatic conception of truth became common and was generally regarded as an "antirealist" denial of the possibility of objective truth. James did not intend antirealism, however; he says that truth literally is agreement with reality. Furthermore, the final quotation above shows him hastening to add something like Peirce's notion of convergence in the long run. Nevertheless his view was widely taken to mean that truth is "what works," that a proposition is true when the results of believing it or acting on it are satisfactory. This was criticized by some as relativism, by others as confusion (most famously by A.O. Lovejoy in his sarcastically titled essay, "The Thirteen Pragmatisms"). Later on, European philosophers would see such pragmatism as an uncultured, parochial expression of American capitalism and self-interest. This was unfortunate, not only because the American philosophers were as a group disapproving of pecuniary individualism, but because they were all thoroughly versed in European culture, James perhaps above all.

We may pause here for a brief critical analysis. It is possible to distinguish (1) what truth itself *is*, (2) what *makes* an idea or belief true, and (3) how we *know* it is true. The first says what the word "true" means, the second says what conditions must hold for a belief to be true (whether we know it or not), and the third concerns our knowledge of the evidence or reasons which "justify" it. We may fairly say that James sometimes failed to distinguish (2) and (3), allowing their conflation to serve as an adequate analysis of (1). But it is also true that critics were unfair in not recognizing his continued attempt to maintain a realist definition of truth as agreement with reality. The underlying problem may be that, while accepting a nominal correspondence theory (1), James yet wanted to say that a belief is made true *by us* (2), that our activity *does* the "marrying" of idea to event, in effect *establishing* the correspondence. Since our actions aim to satisfy purposes, this led James to conceive of a belief's truth as achieving a "satisfactory" working relationship with objects that results from affirming it (3). He argued this in his famous 1896 essay "The Will to Believe," rightly noting that sometimes the assertion of a hypothesis is a necessary condition for the hypothesis being (or becoming) true – e.g. only if I believe "I *can* leap across that gorge" am I likely to be able to do so. But such cases, in which our activity not only reveals but makes truth, are rare. My predictions of what will happen to me based on my actions may be entangled in the future consequences that will prove them true, but not my predictions of what will happen to *you* based on *your* actions. Even in the most likely cases, e.g. leaping across the gorge, belief in my success is only *one necessary* condition for making it true, not the only necessary one nor a sufficient one, along with distance, leaping ability, and wind speed.

Despite, or because of, these controversies, pragmatism became a subject of significant national and international debate. After James' Berkeley lecture, Peirce was roused to clarify his doctrine, finally using the term in print in an entry in 1902 (in Baldwin's *Dictionary of Philosophy and Psychology*) and giving a famous series of lectures at Harvard in the spring of 1903. John Dewey at Chicago, later Columbia, and Ferdinand Canning Scott Schiller at Oxford, joined the pragmatist circle; Dewey formulated "instrumentalism," a naturalistic theory of logic as the method an intelligent organism follows to rectify problematic situations, and Schiller promoted pragmatism as a humanistic epistemology. Peirce went on to conceive pragmatism in numerous ways as he evolved novel doctrines in other areas, for example as defining a concept's role in "the development of concrete reasonableness," the spreading or generalization of embodied rationality, and as the logic of "abduction" or hypothesis-making. His most precise later definition held that pragmatism defines the "intellectual" meaning of a sign as "equivalent to declaring that a certain operation, corresponding to the concept, if performed upon that object would (certainly, or probably, or possibly, depending on the mode of predication) be followed by a result of a definite general description" (Peirce: para. 483). But this period of growth witnessed another bizarre twist in pragmatism's checkered history. In a 1905 essay, "What Pragmatism Is," Peirce declared that the now public – i.e. Jamesian – understanding of pragmatism was so wrong-headed that he renamed his own version "pragmaticism," a name "ugly enough to be safe from kidnappers." In saying this Peirce was characteristically ill-tempered and prescient; his new term was quickly relegated to an aesthetically deserved anonymity. His early and late formulations, together with those of James and Schiller, have ever since, with rare scholarly exceptions, been known by the single name "pragmatism."

Youthful travels

In the early twentieth century pragmatism was an important, international philosophical doctrine. Schiller was for a time equal with James as the public face of pragmatism in Europe. In France Maurice Blondel, Edouard Le Roy, the radical syndicalist Georges Sorel, and the great sociologist Emile Durkheim all lectured or wrote on pragmatism. The greatest enthusiasts were arguably the Italians Giuseppe Prezzolini, Giovanni Papini, Mario Calderoni, and Giovanni Vailati. But along with theirs came the dubious affections of Bennito Mussolini who, seeing in pragmatism the primacy of the will, named James, along with Sorel and Nietzsche, the philosophers most congenial to Fascism! German philosophy was less interested, but even so, pragmatism was explored in print by Günther Jacoby, Eduard Baumargarten and Jürgen von Kempski. Later American pragmatists would sometimes find a pragmatist sensibility among European philosophers, e.g. the existentialist phenomenology of Martin Heidegger and Maurice Merleau-Ponty, but their invitations were largely refused. So the positive early European impressions dissipated, overwhelmed by the more common dismissal of pragmatism as the product of a "philistine" American culture.

In contrast, among British and American analytic philosophers there has always been a minority receptive to pragmatism. It seemed a natural fellow-traveler to the anti-idealism of analysis (e.g. G.E. Moore's "A Defense of Common Sense") and the anti-metaphysics of logical positivism (e.g. the work of the Vienna Circle, especially Rudolf Carnap). Still, between the world wars the only open devotee of pragmatism working in this area was Frank Ramsey, a brilliant philosopher of mathematics at Cambridge and friend of Wittgenstein, who read Peirce and identified himself as a pragmatist (see "Truth and Probability," 1926). Ramsey died tragically in 1931 at the age of twenty-six, but his turn to pragmatism was prescient. For as Richard Rorty would later argue, analytic thought was to undergo a sea-change immediately following the Second World War from "ideal" to "ordinary language" philosophy, logical atomism to epistemic holism, drawing even the most prominent of analysts in a pragmatist direction.

Wittgenstein's turn from his early positivism to ordinary-language philosophy in the 1940s was crucial. In the process he flirted with pragmatism and pragmatists, reading James (on religion) and at one point employing Peirce's notion of "normative science" (probably told him by Ramsey). His late theory of linguistic meaning as based in contexts of social activity or "language games" was very like the pragmatic view of meaning. In the posthumously published *On Certainty* he wrote of his position, "So I am trying to say something that sounds like pragmatism" (Wittgenstein 1969: para. 422). But, he continued, "Here I am thwarted by a kind of *Weltanschauung*," presumably meaning that pragmatism seemed concerned to improve the conditions of a community rather than grapple with "fundamental" questions (Wittgenstein believed that of Ramsey, once calling him a "bourgeois" philosopher). In 1950 Rudolf Carnap, a seminal figure for logical positivism, allowed that the decision as to which semantical system to employ, hence which embedded ontology to accept – for example, a description of the world as phenomenal data or physical objects – was a "practical" decision over which language is most "expedient and fruitful for the purpose for which semantical analyses are made" (Carnap 1987: 221). Most explicit in recognizing his own pragmatism was the American philosopher W.V.O. Quine. He acknowledged that his behaviorist view of linguistic meaning had been anticipated by Dewey. In 1951 in the essay "Two Dogmas of Empiricism" he closed his famous denial of the analytic–synthetic distinction – the distinction between truths of definition and those of experience – by insisting that:

> Carnap, [C.I.] Lewis, and others take a pragmatic stand on the question of choosing between language forms, scientific frameworks; but their pragmatism leaves off at the imagined boundary between the analytic and the synthetic. In repudiating such a boundary I espouse a more thorough-going pragmatism. Each man is given a scientific heritage plus a continuing barrage of sensory stimulation, and the considerations which guide him in warping his scientific heritage to fit his continuing sensory promptings are, where rational, pragmatic.
>
> (Quine 1961: 46)

Despite analytic philosophy's arguably "pragmatic" turn, Quine remained rare in accepting his kinship with the American pragmatists. Pragmatism was then displaced by European imports from its natural place as an alternative to mainstream analysis. Pragmatism was virtually absent from the main venues of American philosophy from the 1950s through the 1970s.

Mature philosophy

Despite their marginal status in professional philosophy, pragmatists throughout the twentieth century evolved and maintained a distinctive philosophical approach to matters extending beyond meaning and truth. We may list six traits as definitive of that approach, some of which are unique in the history of Western philosophy.

The pragmatists were always *methodologically integrative*. Unlike the other innovations of late nineteenth to mid-twentieth century Western philosophy – Marxism, analysis, logical positivism, ordinary language, existentialism, phenomenology, fundamental ontology and hermeneutics – pragmatists made less of a break with the history of philosophy and other methods. They never declared "traditional" philosophy *dead*. There is no major sub-discipline of philosophy that pragmatism disowned – not metaphysics or ethics or history or politics or religion or epistemology or science or aesthetics. Pragmatists continued to find congenial ideas in Anglo-American, French, German, and other European philosophers (not to mention Dewey's forays to China and Japan). While developing their own characteristic perspective, they found no area of contemporary or historica philosophy *discontinuous* with their tasks.

The second feature is arguably the most basic, and from it all others flow: pragmatists tend to understand whatever is under consideration in the *context of human action*. This does not mean that pragmatism conceives everything as a human action, or reality as humanly constructed. It means that all we know and encounter emerges in a process of our embodied interaction with things that is at least partly purposive, even if those emergents express an independent reality. It means that experience is active, that knowing is not mere representation, that evaluation of things is not disinterested, that truth, rather than being static, emerges from events. And if meaning and knowing lie in the guidance of conduct, they must be oriented toward the future, and must accept that they swim in a sea of uncertainty.

Third, and consequently, the pragmatists reject one of the hallmarks of ancient Greek and Christian medieval philosophy, often maintained by the moderns, namely the *priority of disinterested contemplation*. Dewey put this in a political-economic way: until the modern period, most philosophy was done by priests or aristocrats, or patronized by them, in societies where practical work with one's hands was relegated either to slaves or peasants. Peirce and Dewey argued in reverse that knowledge and inquiry are practical, that inquiry is motivated by the need to reform habits that recalcitrant experience has shown unsatisfactory. We inquire only when our extant habits of conduct prove inadequate to the real world, generating doubt; we then seek knowledge to get rid of this doubt and establish more adequate patterns of behavior. Thought and knowledge arise in practical dealings with the world. Dewey argued that philosophy itself is practical in the sense that it serves the "reconstruction" of the conditions of experience.

Fourth, as this implies, pragmatists are notoriously *anti-dualist*, and the form this takes is primarily *naturalistic*. Their anti-dualism rejects the opposition between matter and mind, nature and society, contemplation and practice, head and hand, science and art. Pragmatism is in a sense a reaction against transcendentalism. Ideas and things inhabit a continuous reality; all ideas, mental or spiritual aspects of human existence, including logic and mathematics, are to be understood as continuous with nature or bodily activity. The continuity holds whether the pragmatist in question understands physical nature as the ultimate reality (like Dewey) or places physical nature in the context of a more fundamental psychic existence (like Peirce and Royce). In either case human mentality is located in nature, and the processes of nature accepted as real – even if, for the idealists, metaphysically *pen*ultimate. Particularly important, pragmatists renounce any rigid or ontological version of the fact–value distinction; values, including moral and aesthetic values, are emergent upon states of affairs. One can reasonably argue that the American pragmatists thus created a *virtually unique synthesis of naturalism and idealism* by transposing the idealist notion of formation through human activity into the context of a *physical nature itself conceived as a dynamic, non-mechanical system.*

Fifth, pragmatist philosophy tends to regard reality, like practice itself, as *process*. Phenomena have their existence and their significance in dynamic processes of interaction. Indeed, life itself and consequently biology have had a special place in pragmatism. This is not to say that pragmatists are solely concerned with the living, but that the processes of life are the exemplary model for the integration of matter with higher-order complexity and functioning, ultimately with mind itself. *Life disproves Cartesianism.* This emphasis on process, when applied to particular situations rather than cosmology as a whole, presents an antidote to dualism. For wherever ideal and real, *a priori* and *a posteriori*, concept and percept, thought and action are dichotomized in traditional philosophy, the pragmatist retorts that these apparently opposite realities are in fact *phases* in a process rather than substantive antipodes. In one of his earliest contributions, Dewey argued that the common understanding of the stimulus–response model in behaviorist psychology reified stimulus and response into a passive mental impression and an active physical response. Instead, Dewey claimed, "stimulus" and "response" are functional terms that can hold for either sensory or motor events, both types of events being phases in an evolving sensori-motor circuit, a "transactional" process of exchange between organism and environment.

Sixth and last, in their philosophical anthropology the centrality of practice as opposed to inner contemplation or private experience imposes a *social* perspective on pragmatists. Pragmatists reject "subjectivism," the notion of private meaning, and the Cartesian isolation of the conscious subject. Rather than logic, mind, and self being the source of socio-cultural interaction, socio-cultural interaction is the source of logic, mind, and self. This does not imply conventionalism – the view that all truth and moral goodness depend upon social agreement – but that social interaction is the ontological basis for meaning and mind. And with this, in its conception of society and politics American philosophy tends toward egalitarianism and away from individualism. (Indeed, it is here that the European dismissal of pragmatism as the philosophical expression of *laissez-faire* capitalism was most wrong-headed.) The Americans nevertheless maintained a robust endorsement of individuality and individual freedom, which, they claimed, can only be formed by, and maintained through, social relations. Arguably they were in this, too, unique, that *rather than accept the apparent opposition of individual and community, they made the two symbiotic.*

Middle-aged rebirth

In the 1980s pragmatism experienced what John McDermott has rightly called a "renascence." Certainly this was enabled by the continuing work of philosophers who had identified themselves with the American pragmatic tradition in the interregnum (1950–80) when Americanist philosophy was far outside the mainstream. But the new receptivity arose when other philosophers turned to classic pragmatism as providing resources unavailable in the dominant schools of thought.

The problem driving this turn was how, or whether, to justify the validity of human knowledge of reality without foundationalism. The idea that some knowledge of things, either intellectual or perceptual, is self-evidently true and so available to "ground" all other knowledge, increasingly seemed unsustainable. Without it, realism, the claim that our true judgments are made true by their relation to a reality independent of those judgments, seemed unsupportable. Some turned from realism to relativism, others denied the cogency of the problem, others sought an answer, but neither language, nor logic, nor experiment, nor subjectivity seemed promising as a possible source of support. The catalyst came when two prominent American analytic philosophers turned to pragmatic doctrine for an answer.

Hilary Putnam's "pragmatic realism" (also called "internal realism") staked out a position between "metaphysical" (foundationalist) realism and relativism, arguing that while all truth is in fact relative to our conceptual schemes – hence there is no "God's eye view" of the world – reality as grasped by any conceptual scheme places intersubjective constraints on judgment, making truth independent of desire and power. Putnam argued that pragmatism provided precisely this middle ground, "humanizing" knowledge by discovering, as James said, that "the trail of the human serpent is over all," but without destroying objectivity. More controversially, Richard Rorty claimed in *Philosophy and the Mirror of Nature* (1979) that analytic philosophy, from Frege, Russell, and Moore to the later Wittgenstein, and continental philosophy, from Husserl to the later Heidegger and Derrida, were in the process of dismantling their earlier transcendental-foundationalist projects – logical positivism and Husserlian phenomenology, respectively – and turning to what is in effect a pragmatic position. He applauded their transformation, but chided them for failing to recognize that James and Dewey had beaten them to their destination. His was a "postmodernist" pragmatism – in effect, if not style, akin to French post-structuralism – arguing that pragmatism was not after all a theory of truth but the *denial of the usefulness of any such theory.* "True" is simply the compliment we pay to beliefs that have passed our culture's confirmatory procedures. No further philosophical exploration is needed or justified.

The spectacle of the dominant debate of the day being conducted as the argument between two different versions of pragmatism returned pragmatism to the center of the philosophical stage in the United States. But remarkably, at the same time, German philosophy made its greatest foray into pragmatism, in the work of Karl-Otto Apel in epistemology, and Jürgen Habermas in social philosophy, leavening the Kantian–Hegelian tradition with the non-foundational realism, communitarian concept of self, and democratic affiliations of Peirce, Mead, and Dewey. This drew pragmatic philosophy in the broad sense into international debates over modernity, democratic individualism, and postmodernism.

The result was a general resurgence of interest in the classical pragmatists. But it also led pragmatists to discover heretofore neglected members of their own tradition, and generate a host of new applications, from Cornel West's reconstruction of the social gospel of "prophetic pragmatism," to Charlene Haddock Seigfried's rediscovery of the feminist role in early pragmatism, the affinities of pragmatism with the "deconstruction" of Jacques Derrida, Scott Pratt's unearthing of the Native American connection to pragmatist thought, and the interpretation of Chinese philosophy as embodying a kind of pragmatism by David Hall and Roger Ames. A hundred years after its father sent it into the world nameless, to be widely misunderstood, nearly disowned, and virtually abandoned, pragmatism had regained a recognizable and respectable public identity in the land of its birth. As to its future employment and evolution, that remains, as pragmatism teaches us to accept, uncertain.

Further reading

Apel, Karl-Otto. *Charles Peirce: From Pragmatism to Pragmaticism*, trans. John Michael Krois. New York: Prometheus, 1995.

Carnap, Rudolf. "Empiricism, Semantics, and Ontology" in *Meaning and Necessity*. Chicago, IL: University of Chicago Press, 1987.

Dewey, John. "The Development of American Pragmatism" in *The Later Works of John Dewey. Vol. 2, 1925–1927*, ed. Jo Ann Boydston. Carbondale, IL: Southern Illinois University Press, 1981.

Hall, David, and Ames, Roger. *Democracy of the Dead: Dewey, Confucius, and the Hope for Democracy in China*. Chicago, IL: Open Court, 1999.

James, William. *Pragmatism and Other Writings*, ed. Giles Gunn. New York: Penguin, 2000.

McDermott, John J. "The Renasence of American Philosophy" in Armen T. Marsoobian and John Ryder (eds) *The Blackwell Companion to American Philosophy*. Malden, MA: Blackwell, 2004.

Mead, George Herbert. *Mind, Self, and Society from the Standpoint of a Social Behaviorist*, ed. Charles W. Morris. Chicago, IL: University of Chicago Press, 1962.

Mouffe, Chantal. *Deconstruction and Pragmatism*. London and New York: Routledge, 1996.

Pratt, Scott L. *Native Pragmatism: Rethinking the Roots of American Philosophy*. Bloomington, IL: Indiana University Press, 2002

Putnam, Hilary. *Pragmatism: An Open Question*. Cambridge, MA: Blackwell, 1995.

Quine, W.V.O. "Two Dogmas of Empiricism" in *From a Logical Point of View: Nine Logico-Philosophical Essays*. New York: Harper and Row, 1961.

Ramsey, Frank. "Truth and Probability" in *The Foundations of Mathematics and Other Logical Essays*. New York: Harcourt, Brace, 1931.

Rorty, Richard. *Philosophy and the Mirror of Nature*. Princeton, NJ: Princeton University Press, 1979.

Royce, Josiah. *The Problem of Christianity*. Washington, DC: Catholic University Press, 2001.

Seigfried, Charlene Haddock. *Pragmatism and Feminism: Reweaving the Social Fabric*. Chicago, IL: University of Chicago, 1996.

West, Cornel. *The American Evasion of Philosophy: A Genealogy of Pragmatism*. Madison, WI: University of Wisconsin, 1989.

Wittgenstein, Ludwig. *On Certainty*, trans. Denis Paul and G.E.M. Anscombe. New York: Harper, 1969.

LAWRENCE CAHOONE

PRIMARY EXPERIENCE

Primary experience is both a term and a concept that overlaps – but is not equivalent to – what might be called the primacy of experience viewpoint in the history of philosophy. With respect to the latter, some preliminary comments will help to clarify the usage of primary experience in the philosophy of John Dewey.

Despite its apparent simplicity, the phrase "what experience shows" is a complex concept. In certain respects, it embodies or compresses many of the central issues of philosophy. Whether, and how, and why experience can show anything are questions left unexamined in commonly used phrases such as: "foundation in experience," "based on experience," "product of experience." This primacy of experience thesis extends backwards and forward. Experience as a whole may be considered the privileged or foundational starting point for knowing and acting, or experience may be a collective term for other foundations – structures and processes – that are the most primordial, the most necessary starting points. The appeal to experience is not limited to ultimate beginning or starting points. Indeed, when experience is thought of as basis or foundation for what is or can be shown, then it has been used as the basis for pointing to ultimate ends and highest goods. Experience has been regarded as the determiner of not just where we start, but also of where we end or conclude. The matter of starting point and of ultimate end or realization has found expression in American, Western, and world philosophy. That experience has some sort of authority in thinking of first and last things is not an unfair characterization of its place in the history of philosophy. Neither is it incautious to note that the exact nature of its authority in grounding beginnings and endings has been the subject of considerable reflection and debate in historical, philosophical, and cultural contexts.

The primacy of experience outlook functions centrally in American writers such as Thoreau, Emerson, James, Peirce, Lewis, and Dewey. It also functions somewhat differently in each of them. In Dewey, "primary experience" has fairly well-defined contours, and this enables one to see in what ways it is specification, refinement, and reconstruction of the primacy of experience standpoint. Its most concentrated as well as extensive expression (appearing over two dozen times) is found in the 1929 revised first chapter of *Experience and Nature*, "Experience and Philosophic Method." Dewey begins his consideration of method with a distinction that does not immediately seem methodological. He contrasts what he calls "gross, macroscopic, crude subject-matters in primary experience" and the "refined, derived objects of reflection." The subject matter of primary experience is the starting point for reflection and through reflection the meaning of subject matter is "enriched and expanded." Reflection of course is not an intruder into a primary experience that is barren, lacking continuity with the results of prior acts of reflection. Reflective meanings endure through habits of mind and are present in primary or direct experience. Caution is necessary when considering some of Dewey's equivalent terms for primary experience. For example, "crude experience" is "crude" only by comparison to "refined" objects of reflection, and the latter is able to be refined because it can take advantage of the meanings that endure in primary experience. Likewise, "direct experience," another of Dewey's equivalent terms for primary experience, is "direct" not in the sense of offering meaning unmediated by prior experience. What he calls "funded" meanings from prior experiences are constitutive of present experience and are so with a "minimum of incidental reflection."

Primary, concrete, or ordinary experience for Dewey is both subject matter and method. It perhaps is easier to see the sense in which it is subject matter than it is to grasp how it is a method. A direct route to grasping its methodological dimension, and indeed of grasping a great deal about Dewey's empiricism, is contained in his contention that experience "is capable of developing from within itself methods which will secure direction for itself and will create inherent standards of judgment and value." Primary experience as both starting point and final end, as both content and warrant, is at the center of Dewey's empiricism. Primary experience permits and authorizes ways – methods – of articulating the meaning of its objects by the "secondary objects" of reflection. Dewey includes philosophical reflection in the category of "secondary objects" and he is insistent that philosophical theory must be reinserted back into primary experience. Philosophy is not more prone to what he calls an "arbitrary intellectualism" than other forms of articulation, but philosophy stands to lose its relevance and authority if it forgets – or denies – its basis in what he calls "life-experience."

The centrality of primary experience in Dewey's philosophy can be judged by the weight and scope of three fallacies that he attributes to non-empirical philosophies. The first is the separation, "complete separation" Dewey notes, of what is experienced from how it is experienced. The what and the how, the object and the subject, are distinctions made by reflection out of what he calls the "unanalyzed totality" of primary experience. This dualism has a very long philosophical history, and there have been many attempts to overcome the dualism, sustain it, and, recently, to reconstruct it along lines influenced by the cognitive and neurosciences. Dewey's account of the relationship between subjects (as "centers of experience") and objects of nature rejects rather than endorses the view that primary experience can be reduced to acts of experiencing, i.e. ways of experiencing. It also is not compatible with the view that the subject has no effect on, is not contributory to, the qualities of experienced things. Similarities, not exact but rather suggestive, may be found in Husserl's treatment of the "life-world" and Heidegger's understanding of "being-in-the-world."

The second fallacy Dewey attributes to the neglect of primary experience is the identification of known objects and real objects. Knowing is one mode of experience. The traits and characteristics of nature are revealed in ways other than knowledge, including ways other than scientific knowledge. The identification of knowing and being has an important corollary: the tendency to neglect, deny, or explain away what Dewey variously calls the obscure, the vague, the dark, the twilight. His insistence that things are "had" before they are "known" is a cogent formulation of how he believes meaning appears in experience before its specification into distinct objects of reflection.

The third and last fallacy Dewey discusses is what he calls "selective emphasis." Selectivity or choice is not of course, in itself, a flaw or fallacy. Rather, the fallacy consists in the attribution of ultimate reality and superior value to selected properties and elements of primary experience. If primary experience is "loaded with the tangled and complex," then the search for logical and phenomenological elements is not only permissible, but necessary. Primary experience invites selection and choice, but it also demands that the philosopher "prove the honesty of choice." This expectation of proving the honesty of choice encourages, Dewey believed, philosophy's closer attention to the problems and possibilities of primary experience.

Further reading

Alexander, Thomas M. *John Dewey's Theory of Art, Experience, and Nature: The Horizons of Feeling*. Albany, NY: SUNY Press, 1987.

Dewey, John. "The Postulate of Immediate Empiricism" in *John Dewey: The Middle Works, 1899–1924, Vol. 3, 1903–6*, ed. Jo Ann Boydston. Carbondale, IL: Southern Illinois University Press, 1977.

—— "Introduction" to *Essays in Experimental Logic, John Dewey: The Middle Works, 1899–1924, Vol. 10, 1916–17*, ed. by Jo Ann Boydston. Carbondale, IL: Southern Illinois University Press, 1980.

—— *Experience and Nature* in *John Dewey: The Later Works, 1925–53, Vol. 1, 1925*, ed. Joseph Ratner. Carbondale, IL: Southern Illinois University Press, 1981.

VICTOR KESTENBAUM

PROCEPTION.

Justus Buchler (1914–91) introduced proception, a central category in his metaphysics of the human process, in *Toward a General Theory of Human Judgment* (1951) and elaborated it in *Nature and Judgment* (1955). Buchler deemed the term "experience" to be metaphysically inadequate because it often implied a narrow mentalistic connotation (see his 1979 Introduction to the second, revised edition of *Toward a General Theory*), and he chose the archaic word "proception" to capture his reconceptualization of experience.

Buchler introduces the concept with these words:

> The interplay of the human individual's activities and dimensions, their unitary directions, constitutes a process which I shall call *proception*. The term is designed to suggest a moving union of seeking and receiving, of forward propulsion and patient absorption. Proception is the composite, directed activity of the individual.
>
> (Buchler 1979: 4)

An object or event is a procept if it "modifies or reinforces" an individual's powers or functions, or what Buchler terms her "proceptive direction." The term "direction" highlights the forward motion of the individual through her world and captures the force of her historicity within the givens of her present world.

> To say that an individual necessarily has a proceptive direction means, then, that certain potentialities of doing, making, and saying, and certain potential relations to other things, are excluded from his future while others are included in it, all by virtue of the cumulative power of his past in total relation to his world.
>
> (Buchler 1955: 114)

Buchler makes clear that this directedness does not imply purposiveness to all human experience or a teleological order to the universe.

Proception is characterized as both directedness and content. Any natural complex that modifies or reinforces an individual's proceptive direction is a procept and part of the self's proceptive domain. The proceptive domain is the individual's world. Not every complex in the actual world is related to the individual proceiver, though potentially all complexes may be. "The depth of a crater on the moon" may "fall outside the proceptive domain" of most individuals, but for an astronomer examining images of the surface of the moon, it may be highly significant to the character of her proception (1979: 7). This does not mean that awareness is a prerequisite for proception. "To be a procept is not necessarily to be noticed, felt, or attended to in awareness" (1979: 7). One may never be aware of an innuendo spread by a colleague, but it may profoundly affect the direction of one's career and thus be part of one's proceptive domain. Buchler further distinguishes three levels of relevance or perspectives within the proceptive domain: the gross, the floating, and the imminent domains. These are concentrically related to each other, with the gross domain encompassing everything that belongs to the individual's living make-up, while the floating domain "represents the summed-up self or proceiver within a given situation." The imminent domain comprises all that is available to the proceiver at any given moment; "it is the gross domain represented in minimal cross section" (1979: 8–9). Buchler denies that this domain suggests immediacy or awareness, for what is available to the proceiver may not be part of her conscious awareness. In the same light, proceiving is not a transitive verb. One does not proceive pain as one would perceive or feel pain. The perception of pain is encompassed by the proceptive process, which is more generic.

Buchler identifies two generic dimensions to proception: manipulation and assimilation. Manipulation identifies the individual as the actor or agent, while assimilation identifies her as the spectator, sufferer, or patient. The two dimensions are not separable metaphysically, but one dimension may be emphasized for purposes of a specific interpretation. Manipulation, unlike Dewey's notion of doing, is not instrumental. There is no conscious ordering of means to ends. Nor should Buchler's notion of assimilation be equated with Dewey's "undergoing," for Buchler avoids the association with felt immediacy that Dewey's notion sometimes implies. As Buchler writes: "We assimilate not just sensible qualities, but advancing age, changing modes of thought, and the ethical temper of society" (1979: 18). As co-dimensions, assimilation and manipulation are simultaneously evident in all proceptive processes.

Buchler's concept of proception sets the stage for his theory of communication and his tripartite theory of judgment or utterance. The latter theory marks Buchler's major contribution to the American philosophical tradition.

Further reading

Buchler, Justus. *Toward a General Theory of Human Judgment*, second, revised edition. New York: Dover, 1979. First edition New York: Columbia University Press, 1951.

—— *Nature and Judgment*. New York: Columbia University Press, 1955.

Marsoobian, Armen T., Wallace, Kathleen, and Corrington, Robert S. *Nature's Perspectives: Prospects for Ordinal Metaphysics*. Albany, NY: SUNY Press, 1991.

Wallace, Kathleen. "Justus Buchler, 1914–91" in Armen T. Marsoobian and John Ryder (eds) *The Blackwell Guide to American Philosophy*. Oxford: Blackwell, 2004, pp. 271–86.

ARMEN T. MARSOOBIAN

PROCESS PHILOSOPHY

Process philosophy is the metaphysical view that stresses the process of becoming and perishing as having the same ontological value as that of being. Among the philosophers who have held this view are Heraclitus, Henri Bergson, Charles Sanders Peirce, William James, John Dewey, George Herbert Mead, Alfred North Whitehead and Charles Hartshorne. In order to provide as full a picture as possible of what process philosophy entails, the ideas of Heraclitus, James, Dewey and Whitehead will be considered. James, Dewey and Whitehead are within the Classical American Pragmatist tradition. Heraclitus was a pre-Socratic philosopher and widely considered to be the first philosopher to articulate the fundamental ideas that characterize process philosophy.

One way to understand process philosophy is to first acknowledge what is the most common and also pervasive substance view of metaphysics. According to this view, reality is made up of substances with qualities. Here, that which is, is favored against that which is not. This means that we prefer to notice things and speak of them in terms that bind them in existence, for example "my shoes are dirty," "the food is ready," "the dog barks." Some substance (shoes, food, dog) exists that has qualities (dirty, ready, barking).

Heraclitus

Heraclitus of Ephesus (b. ca. 540 BCE) is famous for his phrase: "You cannot step twice into the same river, for other waters and yet others go ever flowing on" (Wheelwright 1966). Heraclitus believed that the most fundamental characteristic of reality is change. Due to his belief that everything is always changing, you and the river will change so that though you stepped in the river once, if you were to step in it again, you would be a somewhat different person and the water in the river will be a different water.

The roots of process philosophy can be traced back to Heraclitus due to his emphasis on flux. Heraclitus believes that the universe did not begin at one point in time, but rather that it has always existed. For Heraclitus there is harmony in strife and change is the order of the universe. The universe did not come into being for Heraclitus, because this would mean that suddenly something took place. Instead, Heraclitus believes the universe has always been coming into being, and by the same token, it has always also perished. He compares the universe to an ever living-changing fire that kindles itself into being and also goes out by regular measures. Change is pervasive throughout all time.

Although Heraclitus believes that everything is always in a state of flux, he does not believe that change happens randomly. Heraclitus does not think of change as being chaotic, he thinks of change as being regular, consistent and pervasive. It is precisely through this pervasive change that the universe is able to maintain its order.

William James

William James's (1842–1910) ideas are considered to be the most original and insightful in the field of process philosophy since the time of Heraclitus. James called his approach to philosophy *Radical Empiricism*. He distinguished his *Radical Empiricism* from the empiricism of the modern philosophers by emphasizing the primacy of unabstracted experience. Experience is primordial for James. He describes experience as "unqualified actuality," a "simple *that*." The empiricism of the moderns dichotomizes experience into an experiencing subject and into the objects experienced. James believes that we do not inherently experience the world this way. Traditional empiricism is already an abstraction from experience; it is a theory about experience.

James's process philosophy attributes the same ontological value to change as to permanence. In other words, the changing and the permanent are both equally real. There is a continuous process of things coming into and out of being. To illustrate his idea, James compares the flow of experience to the activity of birds. He tells us that "life is an alternation of flights and perchings." Experience is encompassed by both moments of rest and moments of transition, or as James calls them, *substantive moments* and *transitive moments*. Unlike the traditional substance view of metaphysics which attributes existence to a static substance, James believes the process of becoming and perishing are as important as the substantive moments. The substantive moment is for James not a static substance as such, but only a moment in the process of becoming. Our *stream of thought* (James's epistemological parallel to his metaphysics of experience) reflects the same idea. In the stream of thought we have moments of uncertainty where we are not able to distinguish differences among things; we do not know, we are either ignorant or uncertain. There are also moments of certitude when we understand the nature of a concept or grasp something with clarity. James believes that in the stream of thought we experience moments of certitude (substantive moments) until we become dislodged from them and move into moments of uncertainty (transitive moments). James's philosophy of process exists in an open-ended universe. This means that James believes that there is no ultimate answer or explanation, no arche. James tells us that the processes of becoming and perishing involve change. Change of any kind entails uncertainty and novelty. Due to the uncertain nature of change there exists an element of freedom. James is therefore not a determinist. His notion of freedom is rooted in uncertainty but this does not mean that uncertainty and freedom are equal to random chaos. James believes that there is a cohesive order to experience. This order is provided by the different relations into which things enter. James calls relations the "glue of experience." He believes that every entity, including ourselves, is in an infinite number of relations to other entities or people around. For James relations do not merely constitute unification, addition, conjunction, "and," but rather, its opposite, separation, subtraction, disjunction, divorce, "or" is also a legitimate way of being in relation to something else. In the process of experience, James tells us that each relation on its own can be a source of further relations. The more relations we have throughout our experience, the richer our experience will become. Experience is continuously reaching out and expanding.

The last idea to stress about James's metaphysics is that it is pluralistic. James believed that we are unable to give an ultimate and exhaustive explanation or account of reality.

John Dewey

John Dewey's (1859–1952) philosophy of process also denies the existence of the substance/qualities and subject/object dichotomies in our immediate experience. He believes it is a mistake on the part of philosophy to insist on the substance view of metaphysics and the subject/object dichotomy. He calls these ideas philosophical fallacies, which he outlines as the separation between the subject and object, the emphasis on the substance at the expense of the qualities, and the abstraction of theories from experience that fail to meet back with their ground of inception.

Instead of thinking of ourselves as being subjects with objects around us, as modern philosophers describe our being in the world, Dewey believes we are organisms having transactions with our environment. We are constantly in transaction with our environment and other organisms which form part of our environment. This transaction is not a mere interaction. We affect it and it affects us, we are both changed through and due to our transactions. For Dewey, the key characteristic of the process of life is growth of the organism. In the process of life there is struggle, there is inherent resistance from our environment. Dewey tells us that resistance causes us to become aware of ourselves. If the resistance overwhelms us, we fall out of step with our environment and perish, but if we are able to overcome the struggle we experience growth from the experience. Furthermore, we never go back to the same place where we started from before our struggle. Though we may go back to a stable place, our lives and our environment have changed, they have been enriched by our experiences.

Life is the continuous development of past experiences leading us into new ones. According to Dewey each experience has the following rhythm: Inception, development, and fulfillment. The process rather than the substance view of metaphysics is embraced: An experience comes into being by a gradual development until it comes to an end, a fulfillment.

Dewey's process of inquiry reflects a similar pattern. He believes that the purpose of inquiry is to lead us from an indeterminate situation into a determinate one. Life is inherently precarious for Dewey. Still, we do enjoy moments of stability, that is until we encounter resistance from our environment. Something goes wrong, or not as we had expected, and this resistance irritates us to think, to engage in inquiry to ameliorate our situation. Through the use of our imagination and our previous knowledge of past experiences we can formulate theories that might help us move from an indeterminate situation into a determinate one where our process of inquiry is fulfilled.

Dewey calls our previous experiences our "working capital" because we draw nourishment, knowledge, strength and confidence from them. He believes that our moments of struggle are turned into working capital, which in turn allows us to grow, to have qualitative transformations of struggle into deeper appreciations and meanings. The process philosophy of Dewey is meliorative. Dewey is aware that at any point in our process of becoming we might fall out of step with our environment to the extent of death. Every experience for Dewey comes to a fulfillment and he believes that any attempt on our part to perpetuate that particular experience will only result in alienation from our environment. He emphasizes the organism's process of growth from its experiences, its ability to ameliorate its situation and continue on with its process of becoming. Dewey believes that unless our lives have come to a final fulfillment, we never stop growing and learning new things about ourselves, other people and our environment.

Alfred North Whitehead

Alfred North Whitehead (1861–1947) is the philosopher of process who most clearly formed a metaphysics of process into a system. Though Whitehead shares similar insights about process philosophy with James and Dewey, Whitehead uses original terminology to articulate his ideas. Like Dewey and James, Whitehead is also a pluralist. Whitehead also believed that the substance view of metaphysics is incomplete and misguided for choosing to focus only on static ontological instances.

In his book *Process and Reality*, Whitehead outlines his project, which he calls *speculative philosophy*, as being "the endeavor to frame a coherent, logical, necessary system of general ideas in terms of which every element of our experience can be interpreted" (Whitehead 1929). Whitehead believes that entities move continuously from disjunction to conjunction. Entities come together to create a new entity which in turn comes apart into many entities that go on to create new ones. This is his *category of the ultimate*, Whitehead's fundamental metaphysical principle. Whitehead calls the moment of conjunction *concrescence*. At the moment of concrescence we have what he calls *actual occasions*, which are the most basic ontological units of existence. Everything that is, is an actual entity, a concrescence of unique togetherness. True to his category of the ultimate, however, these actual occasions come apart and become further *prehensions*. There are three aspects to every prehension: First, the actual occasion which prehends; second, the datum prehended; and third, the manner in which (how) the actual occasion prehends the datum. Whitehead distinguishes two types of prehensions, physical and conceptual. Physical prehensions refer to the concrescing of the past into an actual occasion. A conceptual prehension is the prehension of eternal objects. Eternal objects are characterized by Whitehead as being pure potential. These do not exist apart from their becoming in an actual occasion. Actual occasions are related to each other through their prehensions. A group of actual occasions with prehensions in common is a *nexus*. Actual occasions come into being by grasping previous prehensions. For Whitehead, becoming is a continuous process where actual occasions are the conjunction of prehensions which develop on to further actual occasions.

Whitehead is not a determinist. He believes that although the past plays an influential role in how actual occasions come about, there is an element of freedom and novelty in every concrescence.

As we have seen, the roots of process philosophy are in the ancient Greek tradition, but it has also been appropriated by other philosophers throughout history. Georg Wilhelm Friedrich Hegel (1770–1831) believes that reality in a process of becoming as well. His idea of process involves the development of individual freedom through a historical unfolding towards absolute Spirit (Geist). Unlike James and Dewey, Hegel believes that change has a definite and logical pattern which is dialectical – not open-ended. The process of historical unfolding is described by Hegel as a dialectic between existence and nonbeing. Existence (thesis) is in a dialectical relationship to nonbeing (antithesis). The process of becoming is the synthesis of existence and nonbeing. Change is necessary for Hegel and moving towards a definite end – Absolute freedom. Hegel also believed that the traditional dichotomies such as subject/object, universal/particular, for example, were not inherent dichotomies, but incomplete understanding of the dialectical process of becoming.

The notion that reality is in a state of continuous flux has led philosophers to different conclusions. In the case of David Hume (1711–76), the idea that reality is continuously changing led him to become skeptical of any metaphysical claims to certainty. He tells us that any claims by philosophy to know ultimate qualities about human nature are at best presumptuous. Like Dewey, the role of the imagination is important for Hume. It is through the imagination that we come to have an unreliable coherence between external objects that are not necessarily linked and our own self-identity.

Further reading

Browning, Douglas (ed.). *Philosophers of Process.* New York: Random House, 1965.

Dewey, John. *Experience and Nature.* New York: Dover, 1925.

James, William. *Essays in Radical Empiricism.* New York: Longmans, Green, 1912.

Lowe, Victor. *Understanding Whitehead.* Baltimore, MD: Johns Hopkins Press, 1966.

Myers, William T. "The State of Dewey's Metaphysics," dissertation. The University of Texas at Austin. 1996.

Wheelwright, Philip (ed.). *The Presocratics.* Upper Saddle River, NJ: Prentice Hall, 1966.

Whitehead, Alfred N. *Process and Reality.* New York: Free Press, 1929.

KIM DÍAZ

PROPHETIC PRAGMATISM

Since the 1980s, Cornel Ronald West (1953–) has been commonly recognized as one of America's leading black intellectuals and as one of academia's most outspoken, controversial, and influential public voices. As one of its most notable contemporary interpreters, he has been among those centrally responsible for renewed interest in the classical American pragmatist tradition. West sees this tradition, which spans back to Ralph Waldo Emerson, as an evasion of epistemology-centered philosophy, and, hence, as focused on actual social, political, and cultural circumstances and practices, instead of on insular quests for foundations and certainty. For West, pragmatism can be rightly viewed as a historically conscious method for future-looking deliberation aimed at ameliorating practical problems that everyday people face. West offers his own version of pragmatism – "prophetic pragmatism" as he calls it – which is designed to be religiously compatible, politically engaged, and a culmination and corrective extension of the pragmatist tradition. He means for prophetic pragmatism to combine the insights of the classical pragmatists – such as C.S. Peirce, William James, John Dewey, and Sydney Hook – with certain religious sensibilities and with Karl Marx's criticism of socio-economic structures and W.E.B. DuBois's analysis of racial injustice. The point is for prophetic pragmatism to overcome what West regards as the biggest obstacles to the full achievement of democracy and to the promotion of personal growth in America. Prophetic pragmatism aspires to liberate and empower specifically the "wretched of the earth" – people who have been historically and systematically exploited, oppressed, and/or marginalized – and thereby to augment democracy by creating participatory space for those people in the public square. West intends for prophetic pragmatism to call attention to the extent to which the pragmatist tradition up to this point has generally neglected matters of race when it comes to cultural criticism.

According to West, leftist, progressive intellectuals often undermine their own attempts to bring about reform, since many of them rely on decidedly anti-religious strategies for bringing it about. Strategies of that sort, on his view, overlook the extent to which religious traditions are an entrenched aspect of society. In order to be practically effective, prophetic pragmatism incorporates the religious within the scope of the political by appropriating the spirit in which Jewish and Christian prophets criticized surrounding social and political practices and, in so doing, brought particularly urgent attention to the plight of oppressed peoples. West argues that a responsive awareness to these prophetic traditions is crucial to achieving our democratic goals insofar as it better enables us to ask how legislation and public opinion should be shaped and affected by the needs of the least powerful, and often underrepresented, individuals in society.

While it seeks to capitalize on the potential benefits of particular religious traditions, prophetic pragmatism is not itself a religion-specific enterprise; it is religiously pluralistic. However, West admits, the prophetic pragmatist will most likely have to stay on the outskirts of any particular religious tradition. For certain aspects of the pragmatist's chosen religion will need to be dropped or reinterpreted through the modern lens of a democratic agenda so that it can be readied for political engagement. That prophetic pragmatism can remain religiously pluralistic means that certain differences – metaphysical and theological doctrines specific to a particular tradition – can be deemed irrelevant to the religious traditions in question. What each tradition offers by way of certain narratives capable of promoting and motivating the liberal democratic agenda is of key relevance and importance. As such, the essence of religion for the prophetic pragmatist is to be found in the motivational potential of religious narratives and beliefs within the socio-political realm, not in theology or metaphysics. At least in this respect, West's treatment of religion mimics that of his pragmatist predecessor William James. For James, the core of religion is to be seen in the melioristic cash-value in the moral life of religious believers – that is, its ability to "let loose in us the strenuous mood" – and not in metaphysical or theological doctrine concerning the existence and nature of any particular God. Taken pragmatically, a religious belief is not interpreted as a belief *that* something exists in some literal sense, such that a religious proposition corresponds to some objective reality. Instead, a religious belief is interpreted more as a *belief in* something, or the adoption of an ideal or aspiration.

West's own version of prophetic pragmatism – which does not have to be the only version, he admits – is positioned specifically within the Christian tradition. He gives two reasons for this. He says that, on the one hand, he finds "existential sustenance" in many of the narratives of Christianity and, on the other hand, locating his own version of prophetic pragmatism within this particular tradition allows him to remain in solidarity with the African-American community. In West's estimation, the black community has had strong ties to the Christian church, and if he is to remain a politically effective player within this particular community, his prophetic pragmatism must maintain some affiliation with the institutions integral to the community's experience and unique history. Further, staying affiliated with those institutions also gives him insight into, and a fuller appreciation of, the manner in which the African-American community both conceptualizes its predicament and articulates its concerns, goals, and proposed solutions. What this implies for West is that religious vocabulary, particularly Christian vocabulary, must be incorporated into the scope of public deliberation and political advocacy in order to facilitate the political agenda of empowering black Americans.

One concern with prophetic pragmatism is that it runs the risk of manipulating religious believers by means of equivocation when it employs the claims of traditional religious believers. Whereas traditional religious believers generally interpret their religious beliefs in a manner consistent with metaphysical realism and a correspondence theory of truth, prophetic pragmatism semantically reconstructs those beliefs in accordance with pragmatist theories of meaning and truth. Clarifying the interpretation of the religious claim employed by the prophetic pragmatist would diminish its motivational force and potentially humiliate the traditional religious believer.

Further reading

West, Cornel. *Prophesy Deliverance! An African American Revolutionary Christianity.* Louisville, KY: Westminster Press, 1982.

—— *Prophetic Fragments: Illuminations of the Crisis in American Religion and Culture.* Grand Rapids, MI: Eerdmans, 1988.

—— *The American Evasion of Philosophy: A Genealogy of Pragmatism.* Madison, WI: University of Wisconsin Press, 1989.

—— *Race Matters.* Boston, MA: Beacon Press, 1993. Reissued in hardcover with new introduction, 2001.

—— *The Cornel West Reader.* New York: Basic *Civitas* Books, 1999.

—— *Democracy Matters.* New York: Penguin, 2004.

West, Cornel and Gates, Henry Louis, Jr. *The African-American Century: How Black Americans Have Shaped Our Century.* New York: Simon and Schuster, 2000.

West, Cornel and Unger, Roberto. *The Future of American Progressivism.* Boston, MA: Beacon, 1998.

J. Caleb Clanton

PROPOSITION

In its linguistic form, a proposition consists of a subject, predicate, and connecting copula, typically "is." It differs from other forms of language such as questions or commands by making a factual claim that, on the classical conception, is either true or false. Aristotle held that propositions have metaphysical significance inasmuch as predicates can express essential properties that fix subjects within kinds or classes. Realists and nominalists disputed this from the late middle ages, but the rejection of essentialism in the twentieth century prompted the rise of formal systems where *reference* takes precedence over the contentious notion of *sense.* Thus Frege devised a functional logic where the meaning of propositions containing common, singular, or general terms is its *semantic value.* Russell further urged the conversion of common and proper nouns, where essences might lurk, into referential descriptive predicates.

While helpful in avoiding essentialism and other vagaries of sense, the emphasis on reference has generated its own share of problems. One obstacle is *indexicality* – the truth value of e.g. "I have blue eyes" will vary from speaker to speaker, suggesting that for such claims reference is sensitive to a context of utterance. A related difficulty arises in statements such as "The Morning Star is bright" and "The Evening Star is bright," made by someone unaware that both are observations of Venus. Here though both statements are true (they have the same referent) and also believed and justified, we would be pressed to say they have the same "meaning," as commonly construed. But perhaps the most intractable obstacle has been *referential opacity.* Since Brentano, propositions in the analytic tradition have been regarded as *intentional* – literally the *objects* of beliefs or desires. Yet in the statement, "Smith believes Washington was assassinated," it is unclear whether the intensional object is the false embedded statement or the true ascription of Smith's mental state. As intentional objects, moreover, propositions seem to occupy a nether realm between subjective attitudes and objective facts, thus prompting J.L. Mackie's complaint that they are "ontologically queer."

Whereas the nature, and even the existence, of propositions is still disputed among analytic philosophers, from the outset the classical pragmatists adopted a strikingly different attitude and approach. Neither bearers of self-contained essences nor correspondents of "truth," Charles S. Peirce argued that propositions are disguised *hypotheticals* whose function is to identify potential *operations* through which meaning originates and evolves. "Diamonds are hard," for example, encapsulates an open set of conditional statements such as: "If this is a diamond, then it will cut glass," "If this is a diamond, then it will not be scratched by steel," "If this is a diamond, then its molecular weight is 12.01," etc. The meaning of "diamond," then, would be the sum of all possible effects resulting from operations involving all applicable predicates, including not only physical attributes but economic and cultural characteristics as well. The dictum that the meaning of any object is the sum of its potential operationally derived effects is one formulation of Peirce's "pragmatic maxim."

John Dewey's *Logic: The Theory of Inquiry* may be the most ambitious attempt to articulate a pragmatic theory of propositions. In this 1938 work Dewey paints an expansive picture of logic as "inquiry into inquiry" attentive to the broad biological and social matrices of human problem-solving activity. In this endeavor Dewey distinguishes *propositions,* which as Peirce realized are hypotheses for engaging problems, from *judgments* that reflect the settled outcomes of such activities. In this sense, then, a proposition is literally a *proposal* for action, and meaning the *means* by which a present idea is realized in a future outcome. More specifically, a logical subject denotes something requiring modification, the predicate a possible adjustment or response, and the copula their operative intersection. Dewey further distinguishes *generic* from *universal* propositions. Generic propositions are either *particular* ("this is gray"), *singular* ("this gray thing is a cat") or a *relation of kinds* ("some cats are gray"). Universal propositions are existential *ways of being* ("all cats are mammals") or nonexistential *logical or mathematical relations* ("all cats are not not cats"). Although superficially resembling the traditional dichotomy of "synthetic" and "analytic" propositions, generic and universal propositions actually signify (1) *phases* of inquiry from the onset of a problem to the most general principles applicable to its solution, and (2) *progressions* from brute sensory shock to regulative scientific laws. The first of these contends that a proposition consists of the operational integration of an intentional idea and existential conditions that ultimately confirm or reject it, not a "no man's land" between the two. The latter, which Dewey elsewhere calls the "denotative principle," states that the subject and predicate at each step be *rigorously operationally equivalent*, and that each of these in turn be *productive* of a subsequent step of greater generality. Like "rungs in a ladder," rigor and productivity lead from raw sensory reports to general explanatory laws, and from such laws back to their ground in everyday experience.

Though less radically than Dewey, other philosophers have thought about propositions in broadly pragmatic or operational terms. C.I. Lewis, who admired Peirce, rejected representational realism for "conceptual pragmatism." Empirical truth claims arise not from a "likeness to reality," but from tacit conceptual schema that are necessary, and thus a priori, yet culturally forged and revisable, thus *pragmatically* a priori. Propositional meaning, moreover, evolves in predictive relations between present and future experiences. Where Lewis accepted a weakened notion of the "given" in experience, Wilfrid Sellars challenged even this. It is a myth, he claimed, to believe that ordinary empirical propositions are built up from primitive "observation reports" of directly given sensations, for our theories affect what is to *count* as such reports. For Sellars, the whole notion of "propositional content" creates a dilemma: either such content is unjustifiable, in which case it cannot be known, or it requires justification in the form of *another* proposition, which generates a regress. Other American philosophers who have emphasized the pragmatic content of propositions include W.V. Quine, Donald Davidson, Nelson Goodman, Richard Rorty, Susan Haack, and Robert Brandom.

Further reading

Burke, Tom. *Dewey's New Logic: A Reply to Russell*. Chicago, IL: University of Chicago Press, 1994.

Dewey, John. *Logic: The Theory of Inquiry*. New York: Henry Holt, 1938.

Haack, Susan. *Philosophy of Logics*. Cambridge: Cambridge University Press, 1978.

Lewis, C.I. *Collected Papers of Clarence Irving Lewis*, ed. John Lange. Stanford, CA: Stanford University Press, 1970.

Miller, Alexander. *Philosophy of Language*. Montreal and Kingston: McGill-Queen's University Press, 1998.

Peirce, Charles S. "How to Make Our Ideas Clear," *Popular Science Monthly* 12 (1878): 286–302.

Sellars, Wilfrid. *Science, Perception, and Reality*. London: Routledge and Kegan Paul, 1963.

FRANK X. RYAN

PROVINCIALISM

In 1908 Josiah Royce saw concentrations of power expanding so much that they tended to reduce individuals to ciphers. These negative forces might appear legitimate – governments, businesses, and media – or function like mob-like groups, blinded by ignorance, prejudice, or passion. Against all of these, Royce envisioned his kind of "wise provincialisms" as pluralistic opponents. After revision, he published his study, "Provincialism." (To its pages internal references are made below.)

Since Royce's unique term "provincialism" presupposes some kind of province, he described what he meant by "province" as "any one part of a national domain, which is, geographically and socially, sufficiently unified to have a true consciousness of its own unity"(61). He contrasted his "province" chiefly with a nation, yet also with corporations and any "spirit of sectionalism." With its distinctive language, customs, and self-awareness an English county might well be a province in Royce's sense. Yet it might swell to include smaller cities, larger regions, or become as large as northern California, or even New York City.

On this basis Royce offered a three-tiered description of his kind of provincialism, as

> first, the tendency of such a province to possess its own customs and ideals; secondly, the totality of these customs and ideals themselves; and thirdly, the love and pride which leads the inhabitants of a province to cherish as their own these traditions, beliefs, and aspirations.
>
> (61)

For Royce, "the better aspect of our provincial consciousness is always its longing for the improvement of the community" (102). The heart of his wise provincialism, then, lies in this yearning for what is truer, better, and more beautiful for the community and thus for its members.

Royce saw his provincialism as wholesome, higher, and wiser than uncritical or self-prioritized groups. It opposes disloyalty to the nation and promotes genuine patriotism. Unwise provincialisms came across as sickening, less morally disciplined, and foolish enough to tend into self-centered enclaves or "communities of hate." Although his term "provincialism" has an elastic use, Royce wanted it used only for communities of the genuinely loyal. He distanced himself from complacent crowds and power-pushing politicos, as well as from narrow-mindedness, jealousies, and antipathies.

He hoped his healthy provincialism would reunify polarized groups. It certainly had to contend against three evils. First, against estrangement in province-members who become too alienated to partake consciously in province life or who exclude minorities from real participation. True, a flood of un-assimilated newcomers can threaten a province's self-identity. Accordingly, a centralized portion of the community needs to develop a strong sense of its province's spirit so that the community gains a sense of its identity and dignity, which newcomers can appreciate and identify with.

The second evil lies in the "leveling tendency of modern civilization" which reduces everyone to a "dead level of harassed mediocrity" (74). Giant corporations, big government, and mass media tend to render individuals just more dots on the page like every other dot. This leveling tendency stifles creativity, responsible criticism, and initiatives from below.

The third evil lies in such peer pressure to conform either to the larger group or to a mob tendency which can overwhelm the individual's identity. A partly sentimental sympathy promotes this urge to imitate and conform. It leads to fears of being seen as an outsider or a critic of the majority. Under this influence "the individual may come to be, as it were, hypnotized by his social group" (83).

Against all three tendencies, not evil in themselves but pushing toward social evils, Royce championed his "wise provincialism." These three tendencies – the estrangement of province-members, the leveling "tendency" of modern civilization, and peer pressure to conform – are good psycho-social realities when viewed simply as a-moral existents. Yet given time and social dynamics these tendencies will surely work harm, unless checked. And that "checking" is what Royce's groups of provincialist members are recognized as doing if they are healthy and wise "loyalists." Royce's wise provincialism grows in groups who possess their own unique wisdom generated and guided by shared beliefs. These strengthen selfhood and direct people to fulfill their mission.

To foster this healthy provincial consciousness, Royce suggested four steps: (1) rather than boast about your community, yearn to improve it through deeds; (2) make sure each individual in the province is treated as of unique and irreplaceable worth; (3) even while keeping yourself open to influences from abroad, emphasize investing your talents, time, and treasure in the local province (4) make sacrifices so that your community's ideals get embodied in its beautiful surroundings, its architecture, and its great institutions. Each of these steps will signal to your local members how valuable is your province.

Further reading

Clendenning, John. *The Life and Thought of Josiah Royce*, revised and expanded edition. Nashville, TN: Vanderbilt University Press, 1999.

Royce, Josiah. *Race Questions, Provincialism, and Other American Problems*. New York: Macmillan, 1908.

Frank M. Oppenheim, SJ

PSYCHE

In the American tradition, materialist George Santayana (1863–1952) made extensive use of the concept of psyche, giving it original meaning while remaining mindful of its historical origins. In the Greek tradition *psychê* (ψυχη; "soul") designated the essential, animating principle of all living things. Santayana's use of the term is closest to that of Aristotle, though with a key difference. Aristotle employed *psychê* to indicate the substantial form of a natural body as it has potentiality to develop (*De Anima*: 412a, 20). Santayana agreed that psyche is the "form" of the body, but in a different sense; he aligned his understanding more with contemporary science by calling psyche a "hereditary trope" rather than a substance. By "trope" he meant a dynamic pattern or order of activity which develops over time and through diverse instances. According to Santayana, psyche displays itself in activity as a "substantialized mind": a seat of preferences, latent habits, and impulses whose existential proof is posited in the living emotional experience of sudden shock or surprise.

In another context Santayana explains his meaning of psyche in terms of a *refusal to admit the possibility of mental machinery*, referring to the attributions of mental identity one person makes to another through observation of his or her natural behaviors and characteristics. Humans are individuated through aptitudes their psyches dynamically reveal across time and those modes of individuation, for Santayana, are natural (i.e. attributable to underlying natural processes rather than to supervening conscious acts or states). In this respect psyche was for Santayana the material manifestation of the mind while spirit, the other conspicuous theme of his mature ontology, was its immaterial manifestation.

Though they avoided extensive use of the term, other Classical American philosophers such as C.S. Peirce (1839–1914), William James (1842–1910), and John Dewey (1859–1952) provided kindred, notions of psyche. Under "idioscopy" Peirce distinguished the "psychical" or human sciences from the physical. Psychical sciences were understood by Peirce to extend beyond sheer mental phenomena, as they continually draw from the physical sciences (though he claimed that the physical sciences draw little from the psychical). In this sense Peirce perhaps reserved an understanding of psyche very similar to that of Santayana, though he worked out this understanding in terms of a semiotic rather than materialistic framework. As for James, despite the fact that the most widespread retail of the term "psyche" occurs in the field of psychology, he avoided any endorsable use of the term in his discipline-founding text *The Principles of Psychology* (1890). Nonetheless John Dewey, in his autobiographical "From Absolutism to Experimentalism" (1930) identified James's "return" to the Aristotelian conception of psyche (with the advantage of the advances of modern biology) as a major influence. James presents a view of consciousness incorporative of – and clearly inspirational to – the meaning indicated in Santayana's work. James's famous 1904 essay "Does 'Consciousness' Exist?" ends by associating consciousness with bodily, physiologic phenomena – breathing, internal muscular adjustments and so forth – which specifies an embodied self similar to that indicated in Santayana's concept of psyche. Around the time he credited James's biological conception of psyche Dewey wrote *Experience and Nature* (1925) in which he employed the term "psycho-physical" to denote animate nature as a function of *the conjunctive presence in activity of need-demand satisfaction.* "Psycho-physical" was for Dewey an adverbial-descriptive means of avoiding the problems of substance dualism bequeathed by the Cartesian tradition. So, while in his use of the descriptive Dewey attempted to capture much the same meaning Santayana tried to evoke with his own use of "psyche," and derivatively of James in his biological understanding of consciousness, the term itself was avoided probably because of worries about dualism.

These worries seem to have been prophetic. After Dewey the philosophical treatment of issues connected with the traditional conception of "psyche" were, due to the larger turn to linguistic analysis, appropriated by the burgeoning industry of the philosophy of mind. In 1974 Thomas Nagel published his field-founding article "What Is It Like to Be a Bat?" which set down the problematic as one of determining the demarcation of conscious from non-conscious life, and reaffirmed belief that the Cartesian mind–body problem, in the absence of an objective science of mind, was "intractable." This would have perplexed the Classical American philosophers, whose various endorsements of the traditional notion of psyche were aimed precisely at resolving this allegedly intractable dualism.

Further reading

Aristotle. *De Anima*. New York: Penguin, 1987.

Dewey, John. *Experience and Nature* in *The Later Works, 1925–1953, Vol. 1*, ed. Jo Ann Boydston. Carbondale, IL: Southern Illinois University Press, 1981 [1925].

James, William. *The Principles of Psychology*. New York: Dover, 1972.

Nagel, Thomas. "What Is It Like to Be a Bat?" *Philosophical Review* 83 (1974): 435–50.

Peirce, C.S. *Charles S. Peirce: The Essential Writings*. Amherst, NY: Prometheus Books, 1998.

Santayana, George. *Skepticism and Animal Faith*. New York: Dover, 1977.

MATTHEW CALEB FLAMM

PSYCHOANALYSIS

Psychoanalysis is both a clinical practice and a theoretical approach to understanding human conduct, agency, and culture. Moreover, it is commonplace to speak of the psychoanalytic movement, a broad and diffuse cultural development radiating from the work of artists, scholars, and humanists as much as from the writings of trained psychoanalysts. In his famous poem written on the death of Sigmund Freud, W.H. Auden characterized the originator of psychoanalysis himself as "a whole climate of opinion" ("In Memory of Sigmund Freud"). Indeed, ordinary consciousness and language are in Western cultures suffused with such psychoanalytic terms as denial, repression, projection, and ambivalence, so much so that Jacques Derrida has gone so far as to assert, "we inhabit psychoanalysis, living with it, in it, around it, beside it" (*The Post Card*, p. 262) – and, indeed, *against* it. The degree and nature of the *resistance* to psychoanalysis seem to invite a psychoanalytic interpretation. But opponents will most likely resist having their resistance to psychoanalytic practice or theory being construed in this manner, arguing that psychoanalysis "wins" too easily, taking every criticism of it and interpreting it as a confirmation of its validity. From the perspective of Adolf Grünbaum, it is, thus, a pseudo-science, for nothing is allowed by its defenders and practitioners to count as evidence against psychoanalysis. The controversy born with the movement itself continues, with remarkable intensity, to this day. What psychoanalysis as a therapeutic practice, as a theoretical perspective, and as a cultural "climate" all have in common is a commitment, or at least openness, to interpreting mental and cultural phenomena in terms of unconscious processes, whereas its critics suppose the explanatory power of the unconscious in its psychoanalytic sense is on a par with that of phlogiston in a different context.

The theory grew out of the practice and, in turn, the practice underwent several dramatic alterations in the course of a brief time. The extent to which Sigmund Freud, the originator of psychoanalysis, understood the character of his own therapeutic and theoretical undertaking is, like virtually everything else about him and his endeavor, a matter of intense controversy. In particular, his typically mechanistic, reductivist, and deterministic depictions of his theory often seem to be at odds with the hermeneutic, humanistic, and voluntaristic facets of his approach (see, e.g., Ricoeur and Bettelheim). In any event, there are, at the center of psychoanalytic practice and theory, descriptions and interpretations referring to the *unconscious* motivations of human actors: what distinguishes psychoanalysis is, above all else, a distinctive conceptualization of the unconscious dimension of the human psyche (Freud's word typically being *Seele* rather than *Geist*). The unconscious in its dynamic sense (i.e. in its strictly psychoanalytic sense) is any number of a cluster of tendencies strenuously resisting being brought to consciousness; in addition, ones only brought to light in an indirect or circuitous manner. Hence, Freud stressed he and his colleagues derived their understanding of the unconscious in its dynamic sense from their clinical experience with patients who, in their judgment, could best be described as engaged in processes of repressing some part of what these persons thought, experienced, or incorporated in their psyches in some form. One of his most famous and succinct definitions of psychoanalysis, as a clinical practice, underscores this fact: "The work by which we bring the repressed mental material into the patient's consciousness has been called by us psycho-analysis" (quoted in Laplanche and Pontalis, p. 368).

As a clinical practice, it grew out of a series of endeavors on the part of Sigmund Freud to assist his patients transforming their hysterical or neurotic misery into ordinary human unhappiness ("Studies in Hysteria" [1895]: *SE*, 2, 351). "Psychoanalysis developed," as Jonathan Lear points out, "in response to people who were in pain and unintelligible to themselves" (1995: 863). It aims to alleviate or lessen their pain by deepening their self-understanding. It is premised on the suspicion that human beings are frequently their own worst enemies, more often than not in ways they disavow or refuse to countenance. The task of enabling agents to discern the personally specific and almost always highly idiosyncratic ways in which this is so characteristic is a protracted, arduous one, continuously short-circuited by the re-enactment of deeply ingrained patterns of resistance. The function of the psychoanalysts is, at bottom, maieutic, assisting others to interpret their lives and actions in light of unacknowledged or disavowed conflicts, identifications, desires, attractions, antipathies, and numerous other factors. The validity of psychoanalysis as a therapeutic practice depends ultimately on that of portraying human agents as being, in some instances, inevitably their own worst enemies, of being unconsciously complicit in making themselves unhappy. While the specific articulations of the psychoanalytic perspective certainly require painstaking examination and critical assessment, the center of Freud's vision is that humans desperately need to come to know themselves in ways they strenuously resist. For this reason, contemporary defenders and practitioners such as Jonathan Lear (who is also a trained philosopher), Adam Phillips, Jean Laplanche and countless others emphasize the Socratic character of the psychoanalytic exchange.

While it was characterized by one of Freud's earliest patients as the "talking cure" and has often been disparaged as worse than idle expensive talk, one of its most knowledgeable expositors and astute critics, J.B. Pontalis (a trained and practicing psychoanalyst), confesses, "I like the fact that Freud characterized psychoanalysis as 'ordinary conversation'" (1993: 154). He is quick to point out, however, that the exchange between analyst and analysand is not so much what our ordinary conversations actually are as what they would be were the ordinary constraints of everyday life suspended, were the mind allowed to engage in an open-ended process of free association. In such a process there is allegedly an inevitable re-enactment of deep-rooted yet energetically disavowed patterns or habits. Moreover, there is in the exchange between analyst and analysand the transference of unconscious wishes from the original objects or occasions of those wishes to the analyst and the occasion of psychoanalysis. In such transference, the psychoanalyst catches glimpses of the primordial, unresolved conflicts calling for analysis. Indeed, Freud's insistence upon analysis for the name of this process is rooted in the exigency of using processes of transference to disentangle habitual associations and thereby to generate opportunities to form new habits:

> in mental life we have to deal with trends [or tendencies] that are under a compulsion towards unification and combination. Whenever we succeed in analyzing a symptom [of breaking it apart into its most important elements], in freeing an instinctual impulse from one nexus [or set of habits], it does not remain in isolation, but immediately enters into a new one.
>
> (quoted in Laplanche and Pontalis, p. 368)

Where analysis is an arduous, protracted task, synthesis is on Freud's account an immediate, spontaneous achievement (ibid.).

At times Freud identifies the goal of psychoanalysis to be that of strengthening the ego and, accordingly, the role of the psychoanalyst to be that of an ally to the ego.

> The analytic physician and patient's weakened ego, basing themselves on the real external world, have to band themselves together into a party against the enemies, the instinctual demands of the id and the [tyrannically] conscientious demands of the super-ego.
>
> (*An Outline of Psycho-Analysis*, SE 50)

The objective is to give back to the patient's ego "its mastery over lost provinces of his mental life" (ibid.). But, in one of the most famous passages in Freud's entire oeuvre, he portrays himself as the latest in a sequence of scientists who shattered the naïve self-love of human beings: first, Copernicus removed humanity from the center of the cosmos, then, Darwin, Wallace, and their predecessors demonstrated that humans constitute but one species of animal among countless others and, finally, Freud and his colleagues have proven that the ego "is not even master of its own house" (p. 353). Nor, given the nature of the psyche, does it seem could the ego ever be master. One therapeutic tradition has tended to appropriate that side of Freud wherein he stresses the allegiance between psychoanalysis and the ego in its struggle against the tyrannical demands of both its instinctual tendencies and internalized ideals, whereas another tradition (e.g. Jacques Lacan) takes the task of therapy to be the ongoing deconstruction of the ego itself.

William James was generally ambivalent toward Sigmund Freud and the psychoanalytic movement, though decidedly hostile to some of the central claims of the Freudian approach (e.g. the interpretation of dreams and the reductivist treatment of religious experience). On the one hand, he was convinced that "Freud and his pupils . . . can't fail to throw light on human nature" (Perry, II, 122). James even encouraged his friend James Jackson Putnam to win a hearing in the United States for the Freudian approach, since Putnam found so much of value in psychoanalytic theory and (though he himself had deep misgivings about the inherent biases of this particular orientation) James thought insight would result from psychoanalysts pushing "their ideas to their utmost limits" (Perry, II, 122 On the other hand, Freud made on James "the impression of a man obsessed with fixed ideas." James' ambivalence toward Freud's project is summed up in a letter to Mary W. Calkins: "I strongly suspect Freud, with his dream theory, of being a regular *halluciné.* But I hope that he and his disciples will push it to its limits, as undoubtedly it covers some facts, and will add to our understanding of 'functional' psychology" (Perry, II, 123). In the background of James' encounter with Freud in 1909 was his critique in the *Principles* of the unconscious and his ongoing interest in psychical research (an interest engendering a deep skepticism in his Viennese counterpart). Of equal importance there were James' efforts to craft in the *Varieties of Religious Experience* and elsewhere a thoroughly experiential conception of the subconscious. The deep, obvious differences between the Freudian unconscious and the Jamesian subconscious should not prompt us to overlook entirely possible, unnoticed affinities. The differences are undeniable, but the affinities or connections might be (for just that reason) quite significant.

If anything, George Santayana's relationship to Freud and psychoanalysis is even more complex. On the surface, he is, whenever treating the unconscious, quick to mark his distance from other theories (readers of the time would readily know that he had Freud in mind, even if he is characteristically less than explicit about the theorists to whom he is reacting). Underneath the surface, however, Santayana appears to articulate a conception of the psyche at least remotely akin to the one defended by psychoanalysts. Moreover, his qualified advocacy of "literary psychology" (as distinct from scientific psychology) seems to allow room for the sort of imaginative discourse so prominent in psychoanalytic theorizing. As the influence of psychoanalysis as both a theory and practice was extending to the United States, Great Britain, and other places beyond Austria, John Dewey in *Human Nature and Conduct* (1922) noted: "A psychology based upon habits (and instincts [or impulses] which become elements in habits as soon as they are acted upon) will . . . fix its attention upon the objective conditions in which habits are formed and operate." Then he immediately added, "The rise at the present time of a clinical psychology which revolts at traditional and orthodox psychology is *a symptom of ethical import.* It is a protest against the futility . . . of the psychology of conscious sensations, images and ideas" (emphasis added) (MW 14.61). Such a psychology (and from the context there is no question Dewey has psychoanalysis in mind) "exhibits a sense for reality in its insistence upon the profound importance of unconscious forces in determining not only overt conduct but desire, judgment, belief, idealization" (ibid.). But psychoanalysis undermines itself by retaining "the notion of a separate psychic realm or force." Even so, it points to "facts of the utmost importance" and does so in a manner clearly indicating "practical recognition of the dependence of mind upon habit and of habit upon social conditions" (ibid.). But this question in truth remains an open one: Can one incorporate *within* a broadly pragmatist account of mind, with its definitive emphases on habits and on the actual, historical conditions in which habits are formed and operate, a psychoanalytic understanding of the specific *workings* of our habits of (say) disavowal and resistance, transference and projection? That is, what if the Freudian unconscious is reconstructed along pragmatist lines, rather than strictly psychoanalytic ones, to refer not to a supposedly separate psychic realm but to an inchoate mass of unconscious habits, ones often involved in processes or acts by which human agents serve as unwitting accomplices in their own unhappiness?

Further reading

Bettelheim, Bruno. *Freud and Man's Soul*. New York: Vintage Books, 1984.

Freud, Sigmund. *Five Lectures on Psycho-Analysis*, trans. James Strachey. New York: W.W. Norton, 1989 [1909].

—— *The Standard Edition of the Works of Sigmund Freud* (SE), ed. James Strachey. New York: W.W. Norton, 2000.

Lear, Jonathan. *Freud*. New York: Routledge, 2005.

MacIntyre, Alasdair. *The Unconscious: A Conceptual Analysis*, revised edition. New York: Routledge, 2004.

Malcolm, Janet. *Psychoanalysis: The Impossible Profession*. New York: Vintage Books, 1982; London: Karnac Books, 1999.

Roth, Michael S. *Psycho-Analysis as History: Negation and Freedom in Freud*. Ithaca, NY: Cornell University Press, 1995.

Wollheim, Richard. *Sigmund Freud*. New York: Cambridge University Press, 1971.

VINCENT COLAPIETRO

PSYCHOLOGISM

Psychologism with respect to a given branch of knowledge, in the broadest neutral sense, is the view that the branch is ultimately reducible to, or at least essentially dependent on, psychology. The parallel with logicism is incomplete. Logicism with respect to a given branch of knowledge is the view that the branch is ultimately reducible to logic. Every branch of knowledge depends on logic. Psychologism is found in several fields including history, political science, economics, ethics, epistemology, linguistics, aesthetics, mathematics, and logic. Logicism is found mainly in branches of mathematics: number theory, analysis, and, more rarely, geometry.

Although the ambiguous term "psychologism" has senses with entirely descriptive connotations, it is widely used in senses that are derogatory. No writers with any appreciation of this point will label their own views as psychologistic. It is usually used pejoratively by people who disapprove of psychologism. The term "scientism" is similar in that it too has both pejorative and descriptive senses, and its descriptive senses are rarely used any more. It is almost a law of linguistics that the negative connotations tend to drive out the neutral and the positive. Dictionaries sometimes mark both words with a usage label such as "Usually disparaging." In this article, the word is used *descriptively* mainly because there are many psychologistic views that are perfectly respectable and even endorsed by people who would be offended to have their views labeled psychologism.

A person who subscribes to logicism is called a logicist, but there is no standard word for a person who subscribes to psychologism. "Psychologist," which is not suitable, occurs in this sense. "Psychologician," with stress on the second syllable as in "psychologist," has been proposed.

In the last century, some of the most prominent forms of psychologism pertained to logic; the rest of this article treats only such forms. Psychologism in logic is very "natural." After all, logic studies reasoning, which is done by the mind, whose nature and functioning is studied in psychology – using the word "psychology" in its broadest etymological sense.

One convenient way to evade the charge of psychologism is to regard epistemology not as a branch of psychology but as an entirely separate field and to understand logic as formal epistemology. In order to leave room for alternative views, this option is not taken in this article.

Consider one form of the principle of excluded middle stated using the ambiguous word "proposition": every proposition is either true or false. One *ontological* point at issue is the nature of the entities that are the subject of this law. How should the word "proposition" be taken in order for the above sentence to express the law of logic known as *the* principle of excluded middle? Views that this law is about judgments, thoughts, beliefs, ideas, assertions, statements, or any other mental or partly mental entities can be called psychologistic. Every such entity depends for its existence on some one person's mind. For example, every belief exists only in a limited time interval. It comes into existence at a particular time in the life of its believer and perishes no later than the believer does.

Other ontological forms of psychologism in logic arise by taking truth and falsity to be mind-dependent. Views that define a proposition to be true if and only if it is or will be believed by a certain person or group can be called psychologistic.

Psychologicians tend to regard logic as an empirical science that studies mental entities. Logicians such as George Boole who refer to principles of logic as laws of thought invite being interpreted psychologistically, unless of course they explicitly distance themselves from psychologism as Gottlob Frege did.

What are alternatives to psychologism? Gottlob Frege, Edmund Husserl, Kurt Gödel, Alonzo Church, and others have taken the principle of excluded middle to be about what Church calls propositions – tenseless, abstract, non-mental entities that are true or false and can but need not be meanings of sentences and contents of beliefs. For them, the principle of excluded middle is one proposition that is about all propositions. It is a single proposition that can be expressed in many different languages and can be the content of many different beliefs believed by different people at different times and places. This view has been called *Platonism*, *Platonic realism*, and *Platonic idealism* – even though it is doubtful that Plato held it.

Tadeusz Kotarbinski, Alfred Tarski, Willard Van Orman Quine, and others have taken the principle of excluded middle to be about sentences in the sense of sentence-tokens, physical objects composed of such things as sounds or bits of ink. Tarski is quite clear that this requires certain laws of logic to be dependent on laws of physics. Perhaps for this reason, the Kotarbinski–Tarski–Quine view has been called *physicalism*. In contrast, America's pre-eminent logician, C.S. Peirce (1839–1914), was quite clear that logic was not about tokens (1998: 311). In the process of interpreting the writings of philosophers to determine their views of the nature of the entities dealt with in logic, it is important to realize that one and the same writer may hold different views at different times, and even in different parts of one and the same work.

There are different kinds of psychologistic theses: ontological, foundational, and epistemological, to mention three. Ontological psychologism, treated above, says that logic is about mental entities or that truth and falsehood are mind-dependent. Foundational psychologism addresses the ground or foundation of logic, why it is that logical laws are true. For example, to the question of why a given conclusion follows from given premises a psychologician might refer to the nature of thought or the nature of the mind. Epistemological psychologism concerns how we "know" that logical laws are true. One psychologician might answer that it is impossible to think otherwise; another might appeal to psychological empirically based induction. For reasons of space, the last two kinds of psychologistic theses have not been treated.

Peirce died before the issue of psychologism was debated in the United States. He never wrote about the various forms of psychologism in logic. He did nothing to distance himself from it in his famous 1880 paper "On the Algebra of Logic," reprinted in the 1992 Houser-Kloesel volume. It is open to a psychologistic interpretation. It begins with an embarrassing psycho-physiological preamble characterizing rules of inference as habits. Peirce asserted that "the logician" maintains that "the process of inference or the spontaneous development of belief" is evolving according to a law, and he wrote that "the process of inference" is "adapted to an end, that of carrying belief, in the long run, toward certain predestinate conclusions which are the same for all men". Almost a quarter-century later, he distanced himself from another form of psychologism in logic by saying that his principles debarred him "from making the least use of psychology in logic" (1998: 210), without being very explicit about the principles or how they "debarred" him. In an unpublished manuscript written about the same time (1998: 300–24), he made a detailed attempt to construct a non-mental concept of proposition (1998: 308–12). For a discussion of psychologism in Peirce, see Kasser 1999.

Another quarter-century later Morris Cohen, one of the most important and respected philosophers in America at the time and one of the earliest to recognize Peirce's greatness, vigorously attacked psychologism in his logic lectures at City College of New York. These lectures were worked into book form by his energetic student Ernest Nagel and published in 1934 as *Introduction to Logic and Scientific Method*. The formal logic part is still in print with the original pagination. The anti-psychologistic remarks are in a subsection, "Logic and Psychology", on pages 18–20. Throughout the book, Cohen and Nagel continue to distance themselves from psychologism and, for that matter, from physicalism. For example, their still fresh discussion of propositions explicitly warns on page 28 against confounding propositions "with the mental acts required to think them" or with the sentences that express them.

Further reading

Cohen, M. and Nagel, E. *Introduction to Logic and Scientific Method*. New York: Harcourt, Brace, 1934.

Cohen, M. and Nagel, E. *Introduction to Logic*, second edition with new exercises, indexes, bibliography, and editor's introduction by John Corcoran. Indianapolis, IN: Hackett. 1993 [1934/1962].

Kasser, J. "Peirce's Supposed Psychologism," *Transactions of the Charles S. Peirce Society* XXXV (1999): 501–26.

Peirce, C.S. *The Essential Peirce: Selected Philosophical Writings (1867–1893)*, Vol. I, ed. N. Houser and C. Kloesel. Bloomington, IN: Indiana University Press, 1992.

—— *The Essential Peirce: Selected Philosophical Writings (1893–1913)*, Vol. II, ed. N. Houser. Bloomington, IN: Indiana University Press, 1998.

John Corcoran

PURE EXPERIENCE

William James's concept of "pure experience" is introduced as both "datum" for and "field" of cognition and consciousness. As such, it has been interpreted as the metaphysical underpinning for James's own "radical empiricism." And while several of his own characterizations of the concept lend themselves to this metaphysical emphasis, and while philosophy itself is, according to James, strictly limited and fed by "pure experience," an emphasis on the metaphysical importance of pure experience is ultimately an unsatisfying interpretation.

Arising from the desire to undo his own frustrations with the traditional metaphysical dualism between consciousness and content, knower and known (see James 1890 [1981]), James explains in his 1904 essay, "Does 'Consciousness' Exist?" that substantive notions of "consciousness" must be abandoned and the traditional metaphysics that accompany such substantive notions are illusory. James states pointedly, "I believe that 'consciousness' . . . is on the point of disappearing altogether. It is the name of a nonentity, and has no right to a place among first principles" (1912 [1976]: 3). However, if consciousness is illusory, then what is left of knowledge and the relation between the "knower" and the "known"? James's response? Consciousness, while not an entity, "does stand for a function . . . That function is *knowing*" (1912 [1976]: 4). He explains,

> My thesis is that if we start with the supposition that there is only one primal stuff or material in the world, a stuff of which everything is composed, and if we call that stuff "pure experience," then knowing can easily be explained as a particular sort of relation into which portions of pure experience may enter.
>
> (1912 [1976]: 4)

Thus initially introduced, pure experience is described as prior to and datum from which "knowing," as a relation, is crafted. The adjective "pure" concatenated with the concept of "experience," thus, seems to indicate a "primal" condition of experience as an undifferentiated substance out of which our concepts arise. Importantly, though, only a few pages later James attempts to undo just such a reading stating,

> Although for fluency's sake I myself spoke early in this article of a stuff of pure experience, I have now to say that there is no *general* stuff of which experience at large is made. There are as many stuffs as there are "natures" in the things experienced.
>
> (1912 [1976]: 14)

From this confusion concern arises whether pure experience is truly a substantive monistic metaphysics or, as James seems to want to argue, a collective metaphor of the plurality of "natures."

In many places throughout his corpus, James discusses his own deep concern for the metaphysical conflict between "the one and the many," sometimes calling it the conflict between monism and pluralism. James's concern to delineate his take on "pure" experience from such a monism is evident not only in the passage above, but also in the fact that nowhere does James come down solely on the side of "the one," stating that "The world is One just so far as its parts hang together by any definite connexion. It is many just so far as any definite connexion fails to obtain" (1907 [1975]: 76). *Exclusive* monism and *radical* pluralism are, for James, forms of pernicious "intellectualism" to be eschewed by philosophy.

Of course, James's own claims to the contrary do not by themselves settle the problem, and he continues the confusion in his essay of 1905, "The Thing and Its Relations" when he says that

> Pure experience is the name which I gave to the immediate flux of experience of life which furnishes the material of later reflection with its conceptual categories. Only new-born babes, or men in semi-coma . . . may be assumed to have an experience pure in the literal sense.
>
> (1912 [1976]: 46)

Such a description leads us again to ask whether or not pure experience denotes the "material" available to reflection. Alternately, though, we might contend that it is essentially metaphorical description – a philosophical device to shift metaphysical perspective to the function of cognition and away from the "reality" of consciousness. The former reading suggests a more substantive metaphysical category while the latter makes pure experience instrumental, rather than elementary, to his philosophy.

While not succeeding at putting the controversy to rest, pure experience taken as metaphorical allows a deeper focus on experience as the source and content of philosophy, without positing – even explicitly eschewing – a priori what experience is. Experience is what we might call *phenomenal reality*, initially undifferentiated, though infinitely differentiatable. By "phenomenal" we mean pre-reflective immediacy (not reducible and prior to theories and categories), and by "reality" we mean that experience is real and that reality is objective (not essentially subjective and private) – and no *other* reality exists for philosophy to pursue. Experience, for James, admits of infinite possibility, thus it admits of infinite plurality. It is not one thing that mutates, but infinite undifferentiated somethings. "It is made of *that*, of just what appears ... Experience is only a collective name for all these sensible natures" (1912 [1976]: 14). In what James calls a "world of pure experience" plurality abounds, but it abounds in an undifferentiated way. Differentiation is a *post hoc*, functional act which arises out of life's continuing flow as a way to control the inherent vagueness and quasi-chaos long enough to accomplish things.

Further, experience is also importantly organic. As James tells us, experience grows; and in particular, it grows "by its edges" (1912 [1976]: 42). In his famous analogy, James relates experience (what he originally called by more cognitive terms such as "thought" or "consciousness") to a flowing stream. The center of the stream carries water come what may, but the bottom and sides wear away the soil, shifting the landscape. James's philosophy of experience is thereby conservative. The world, though historically contingent and malleable, is neither arbitrary nor capricious. By growing "by its edges," it protects the center from catastrophic disruption in most cases. What James says in the context of a discussion of "habit" could easily be said of experience itself: "[It is] weak enough to yield to influence, but strong enough not to yield all at once" (1890 [1981]: 110).

Like habit itself, then, "pure experience" is functional, the delimitation of philosophical inquiry; the field and content of agency and object, knowing and known – contracting and expanding, flowing and growing.

Ultimately, "pure experience" moves away from substantive metaphysics, through metaphor, to play methodology. As James says in 1909,

> The principle of pure experience is also a methodological postulate. Nothing shall be admitted as fact, it says, except what can be experienced at some definite time by some experient; and for every feature of fact ever so experienced, a definite place must be found somewhere in the final system of reality. In other words: Everything real must be experienceable somewhere, and every kind of thing experienced must somewhere be real.
>
> (1912 [1976]: 81)

In this way, James makes the final connection between pure experience and radical empiricism when we come to find that the principle of pure experience is simply the methodological postulate of radical empiricism itself.

Further reading

James, William. *The Principles of Psychology.* Cambridge, MA: Harvard University Press, 1890 [1981].

—— *Pragmatism: A New Name for Some Old Ways of Thinking*. Cambridge, MA: Harvard University Press, 1907 [1975].

—— *Essays in Radical Empiricism*. Cambridge, MA: Harvard University Press, 1912 [1976].

D. Micah Hester

PURITANISM

The term "Puritanism" applies originally to the religious doctrines of the Nonconformist Christians in England in the early sixteenth century. Many Puritans emigrated to America in the seventeenth century, and their views were very influential in later developments in American philosophy. Among the most important figures in American Puritanism are John Winthrop (1587–1649), Cotton Mather (1663–1728), and Jonathan Edwards (1703–58).

The flourishing of American Puritanism runs roughly from the founding of the Massachusetts Bay Colony in 1629 until the death of Edwards in 1758. During this period Puritanism was not a static doctrine but evolved considerably. Nevertheless, some consistent themes can be identified. Among these are an espousal of Congregationalism in religious polity and a concomitant rejection of mysticism; a theologically constrained humanism and promotion of universal literacy; a Platonistic belief in an essential correspondence between being and knowledge; and the notion that politics, religion, and nature are best understood in terms of covenants.

One of its major sources is the philosophy of the French logician Peter Ramus (aka Pierre de la Ramée, 1515–86). Ramus argued against the Aristotelian Scholasticism that dominated European thought in his time. He viewed Scholasticism as too arcane, too interested in demonstrations, and too detached from ordinary human practice. Ramus argued for Congregationalism, which holds that local church congregations should be self-governing associations, not subject to the hierarchical authority of an episcopate or of presbyters. Ramus's Platonistic logic championed the essential unity of knowledge and viewed objects in the phenomenal world as signs or archetypes of another world.

In politics, the Puritans were anti-monarchical and male-egalitarian but not democratic. They generally espoused a theocratic state governed by a non-hereditary aristocracy, where fitness to govern was tied to church membership. Puritans held to the notion of "visible sainthood," namely that the invisible justification of a sinner by God would be made manifest in outward and visible signs, so that it was to some degree possible to examine a person's soul by means of tests applied to that person's life. In a sermon given around the time of the founding of the Massachusetts Bay Colony in 1629, Governor John Winthrop (1587–1649) described the new settlement as a "city on a hill." The colony was to exemplify Christian ethics, with its public life serving as a visible sign of the invisible covenant between God and humanity. The Puritan covenantal notion of voluntary association and obligation is akin to contemporary social contract theory.

This emphasis on the covenantal community points to a key theme in their epistemology, namely the importance of testing knowledge in a community. Puritan theology eschewed mysticism and private revelation, as may be seen in the 1637 trial of Anne Hutchinson over her claims of mystical communion with the Holy Spirit. It was feared that admission of private revelation would allow people and the state to be governed by private emotion rather than by publicly reasoned law.

Puritan sermons show the degree to which Puritans took philosophy to be relevant and a matter of public concern. Intricately crafted and logically rigorous, sermons were the main philosophical forum in Puritan life, touching on politics, ethics, metaphysics, and science.

Harvard University is an enduring testament to the high value Puritans placed on learning. Most Puritan ministers were highly educated. Each member of the community was responsible for adherence to both civic and divine covenants, making universal literacy and logical skills imperative. Puritan education was humanist, modified somewhat by theology. Instruction in Latin, Greek, and Hebrew was emphasized for all ministers, and broad education in classical literature was encouraged.

Puritans held that nature was a sign of God's benevolence and power. A number of Puritans, notably Mather and Edwards, kept journals of their observations of natural phenomena and of their readings in natural philosophy, anticipating the later writings of Emerson and Thoreau. Although natural science was not as important as religious study, Puritans held that nature, like classical Greek and Roman texts, communicated much of value for the conduct of life.

While the Puritanism of the early seventeenth century was theologically rigid, eighteenth-century Puritans like Edwards took the scientific advances of Bacon, Newton, and Locke seriously, and attempted to wed modern science to traditional Christianity. In Puritanism one may see some seeds of later Unitarianism and Evangelical Revivalism, as well as of nineteenth-century Utopianism, Transcendentalism, and Pragmatism.

By the late 1600s Puritanism's emphasis on common religious belief and communal covenants proved too cumbersome in the face of growing religious and political pluralism. In the 1700s Puritanism yielded to increasingly democratic and naturalistic doctrines in politics, religion, and science.

Further reading

Edwards, Jonathan. *Works of Jonathan Edwards.* New Haven, CT: Yale University Press, 1957–present.

Mather, Cotton. *Selections from Cotton Mather*, ed. Kenneth Murdock. Whitefish, MT: Kessinger, 2003.

Miller, Perry. *The Puritans.* New York: Dover, 2001.

Morgan, Edmund S. *Visible Saints: The History of a Puritan Idea.* Ithaca, NY: Cornell University Press, 1965.

DAVID L. O'HARA

PURPOSE

Questions about purpose – Does life have a purpose, and if so, what is it? How and to what extent do purposes figure into human actions? Does nature have a purpose? – have long been central issues of philosophical concern, but American philosophy, because of its specific influences and mode of development, has tended to emphasize purpose more than many other philosophical movements.

It was a strong sense of Divine purpose that led the Puritans, the first philosophers of European descent in North America, to settle in the New World. They sought to make spiritual ideals manifest in the temporal world through the founding of New Canaan and believed that God had a special purpose in mind for their individual lives and for their settlement as a whole. The Puritans believed that each person has a particular role to play and it was by the grace of God that he or she would find it. This belief was illustrated, for example, in Cotton Mather's *Life of His Excellency Sir William Phips.* Indeed, the Puritan belief in the irresistible power of Grace and Divine sovereignty was so strong that at times it seemed to threaten to crowd out the role of human purposes in history. Consequently, inspired to reconcile conflicting concepts of the role of human purposes found in, on the one hand, the Calvinist doctrine of predestination and the deterministic model of Newtonian physics, and, on the other, those dictated by the need to form specific plans to survive and thrive on a new continent, Jonathan Edwards penned a number of philosophical essays including "On the Freedom of the Will," published in 1753.

Setting the context for debates about the significance of human purposes was the received view that nature as a whole exhibited a cosmic purpose or purposes, a notion inherent in the classical ideas of species (*eidos*) and purpose (*telos*). The ancient Greeks and Aristotle, in particular, believed that each proper thing, living and non-living, was of a natural kind and that, as such, its development proceeded according to a plan or pattern found within it. An acorn develops into an oak tree because of the sort of thing that it is, because its development is governed by the idea of an oak tree with the purpose of becoming an oak. In addition, philosophers into the Middle Ages reasoned that not only did individual kinds of things exhibit particular purposes but that nature as a whole must follow some grand plan and strive toward some unified purpose. American pragmatist John Dewey, in an essay entitled "The Influence of Darwin on Philosophy," put the matter this way: "Purposiveness accounted for the intelligibility of nature and the possibility of science, while the absolute or cosmic character of this purposiveness gave sanction and worth to the moral and religious endeavors of man" (MW 4.9). Purpose was a means of understanding not only the development of individual organisms and events but the cosmos as a whole and the role of human beings within it.

For a time this view was strengthened by discoveries in natural philosophy (physical science) and natural history (biology) and, in particular, improved understanding of the function of biological organisms. For example, the development of the science of optics coupled with a more precise understanding of the eye showed how the precise positioning of the lens relative to the retina produced an image. No other arrangement would do and just the precise parts were included in the eye to generate this effect. Thus, natural philosophers reasoned, the parts of the eye must have been for the purpose of seeing, and eyes, in turn, for the purpose of perception, and so on. Nothing besides purpose could explain the order of the universe. Or so it seemed to most philosophers, until the publication in 1859 of *The Origin of Species* by British naturalist Charles Darwin.

According to Darwin, structural features of living organisms that seem purposive are actually the result of random variation under environmental pressure over very long periods of time. Organisms vary naturally and if a variation tends to favor an organism's chances to survive long enough to reproduce, that variation will get passed to the organism's offspring and will tend to spread through the population over time, as long as conditions remain the same. Moreover, if features are not designed to serve one particular purpose, organs or parts of organs can serve different functions over time. Thus the retina, a highly complex light-sensitive organelle that in conjunction with a lens can provide a highly refined visual image, evolved from a more primitive antecedent organelle that provided simple detection of light and dark in absence of a lens or other supporting mechanisms.

Darwin's discovery was to find a way to account for order and seemingly purposive systems without any appeal to purpose. As Dewey points out, even the title of the book *The Origin of Species* was earthshaking since, given that species had been thought to be permanent and unchanging, the very idea that a species could have an origin (or an end) fundamentally transformed the concept. Moreover, if the order found in individual organisms could be accounted for without appealing to divine or other purpose, it became reasonable to suppose that appeals to cosmic purposes might be superfluous as well. The cosmos itself might be thought of evolving though toward no specific, preordained end, as Charles Sanders Peirce thought, or it might not, as Chauncey Wright thought (Wright thought that apparent examples of directional development were mere fluctuations in *cosmical weather*). In either case, cosmic purpose was no longer deemed necessary to explain the order of nature at the individual or cosmic scales.

But given the prior relation between cosmic purpose and the "sanction and worth [of] the endeavors of man," the disappearance of Purpose as a necessary explanatory factor at a cosmic level threw into question the meaning and value of purely human endeavors. If I can no longer find my purpose in some sort of divine plan, as the Puritans believed, what is there that can guide my own actions? One response was to look even harder for spiritual purpose and to relate that to human endeavor in the context of evolutionary thought: thus, the rise in popularity of several varieties of neo-Hegelianism in the latter half of the nineteenth century in Britain and the United States. Another response was despair followed by an embrace of the absurd nature of existence. This was the response of the twentieth-century European existentialists.

The pragmatists responded to the eclipse of transcendent purposes differently. First, rather than seeking supernatural sources of meaning or simply accepting the alleged meaninglessness of human life once deprived of cosmic purpose, the pragmatists (and Dewey in particular) shifted their inquiries to focus more squarely on the natural order and concluded that lack of fixed, pre-given, transcendent purposes actually rendered life (a) more meaningful, and (b) more subject to human control. Human life is more meaningful because in the absence of a fixed, pre-given order, our choices count for that much more. (This implication pragmatism shares with existentialism.) Human life becomes more subject to control because a shift of intellectual focus "from an intelligence that shaped things once and for all to the particular intelligences which things are even now shaping" highlights the way that purposes can and ought to be modified in light of experience. Purposes came to be seen, by the pragmatists not as pre-packaged plans, but as features of human life that were themselves subject to modification and control, in light of other purposes (also modifiable) and changing environmental conditions. Rather than simply accepting purposes as they come – an approach called *straight line instrumentalism* – the pragmatists argued that we can change and adapt our purposes to conditions on the ground. Ends in the Aristotelian sense of final perfections became *ends in view*, tentative, temporary goals subject to modification and, more importantly, the application of intelligence.

Finally, the pragmatic shift in the role of purposes in human life shifted focus from a search for transcendent, antecedent causes and explanations for the way things are or ought to be back to local, specific conditions that could be subjected to empirical inquiry, thus reestablishing philosophy as the handmaiden of science and servant of human interests.

Further reading

Wright, Chauncey. *Philosophical Writings of Chauncey Wright: Representative Selections*, ed. Edward Madden. New York: Liberal Arts Press, 1958.

PHILLIP MCREYNOLDS

Q

QUALITATIVE THOUGHT

"Qualitative thought" is John Dewey's term for the non-cognitive, pervasive, felt meaning of a situation that guides all cognitive and instrumental thinking. "Qualitative Thought" (1930), one of Dewey's most important and difficult articles, is absolutely essential in understanding his instrumentalism and theory of logic; both *Art as Experience* (1934) and *Logic: The Theory of Inquiry* (1938) amplify many of the ideas found here. The world itself is primarily experienced in a qualitative way, as lived or felt or undergone. With Galileo and Descartes, qualities were treated as non-physical "mental" events, i.e. as subjective, with the resulting dualism between propositions about the world of experience and those about the world of science. Both classical and contemporary relational logic treat subjects of propositions simply as given; what is needed is a logic of inquiry. Subjects and predicates only emerge in relation to each other in the process of experience. Prior to quality as a definite predicate, there is a more elusive quality that pervades any given experience, which can be recognized in the way we encounter a work of art, a person, or an historic event, giving each an expressive individuality. This is not an "attribute" or "predicate": it is constitutive, and all our conceptual analyses rely upon it. It is "the quality of the subject-matter as a whole" that controls inquiry (LW 5.246; see *Logic: The Theory of Inquiry*, LW 12, Ch. 4).

The pervasive nature of quality in thinking leads Dewey to a metaphysical conclusion. Instead of beginning with discrete individuals, essences or bare particulars as the ultimate subjects, Dewey makes "situations" primary. Individual objects are functional designations within a larger situation of interaction, portions of the environment selected by interest and given form by coordinated bodies of habits. A chair is something that has a designated meaning for a human being looking for a place to sit. But it is not ontologically primary; it exists only as a "chair" in relation to human beings. Situations are not "objects," but conditions within which objects are possible. Because of this "The situation as such is not and cannot be made explicit. It is taken for granted, 'understood,' or implicit in all propositional symbolization" (LW 5.247; see LW 12.72f). It forms the "context" or "universe of discourse" within which explicit discourse occurs, giving it a constitutive, tacit "sense." A situation may become an object of thought, but only as an object within another situation. It is an ultimate ground of reference.

Moreover, "the situation controls the terms of thought, for they are *its* distinctions" (LW 5.247; see LW 12.74, 109). In art, especially, we note the way a pervasive quality provides the unifying "sense" to the experience, making each part fit and take on meaning in relation to the others. This tacit, pervasive sense-giving quality operates in all experience to the extent it does "make sense," and is the basis for all cognitive deliberation and choice. Rationality and intelligence depend on a continuum of feeling that can, at best, be intuited. For Dewey, the "logic of artistic construction" has great bearing on logic itself and the logic of the artist is "the logic of qualitative thinking" (LW 5.251). "Artistic thought is not however unique ... but only shows an intensification of a characteristic of all thought" (LW 5.251–2; see *Art as Experience*, LW 10, Ch. 1). As far as logic itself is concerned, it is conceived as a "logic of inquiry," i.e. of turning an indeterminate situation into a determine one (*Logic: The Theory of Inquiry*, Ch. 6).

Dewey thinks that this approach clears up some traditional logical problems, especially the theory of predication (LW 5.252 f.; see *Logic: The Theory of Inquiry*, LW 12, Ch. 7, esp. p. 128f). "Sugar is sweet" is, as a proposition, traditionally viewed as a tautology, derived from the meaning of "sugar," or descriptive of someone's experiential discovery, like an infant learning about the meaning of the word in relation to taste. But viewed as a statement in the process of trying to organize a field of experience, subject and predicate are correlative. An infant mistaking sugar for salt, tasting it, and experiencing the result is reconstructing a whole set of dispositions toward the world: this white thing *is* sweet like a cookie or candy; it is a new object of desire and its nature can be explored. The correlation of subject and predicate is the result of inquiry. In this sense, Dewey claims "The logical force of the copula is always that of an active verb" whose temporal and existential reference is only disguised when considering the formal relationship between terms (LW 5.253; see LW 12.135f). Our effort to classify sugar within the genus of "sweet things" is a subsequent endeavor based on this primary experience, as would be an analysis of its chemical makeup. In other words, "The sentence or proposition is not an end in itself, but a directive of future activities" (LW 12.124).

Philosophers who want to see logic as a mirror of the way things are prior to inquiry either break the world up into hypothetical discrete units like sense data, bare particulars, or "states of affairs" – the route taken by empiricism and positivism – or amalgamate everything into a completely determinate, absolute whole which is then the "real" subject of all reference – the route taken by absolute idealism. By taking logic as a dynamic, organizing process, Dewey makes it responsive to a qualitative, lived world that has degrees of clarity and structure, but also inherent vagueness. To avoid the "intellectualist fallacy," philosophers should follow the *denotative method* (q.v.). Logical relations and concepts are refinements of ordinary experience and can be used in a variety of contexts, but they are no more the basic ontological furniture of existence than hammers and nails are the true nature of a house. To conceive of a world in which any given proposition is automatically true or false is to think of a different world than the one in which we live. Such, indeed, was the later Wittgenstein's judgment on his earlier thought.

Further reading

Burke, E. Thomas, Hester, D. Micah, and Talisse, Robert B. *Dewey's Logical Theory.* Nashville, TN: Vanderbilt University Press, 2002.

Dewey, John. "Qualitative Thought" in *Later Works, Vol. 5*, ed. Jo Ann Boydston. Carbondale, IL: Southern Illinois University Press, 1984, pp. 243–62.

—— *Logic: The Theory of Inquiry* in *Later Works, Vol. 12*, ed. Jo Ann Boydston. Carbondale, IL: Southern Illinois University Press, 1986.

Sleeper, R.W. *The Necessity of Pragmatism.* New Haven, CT: Yale University Press, 1987.

THOMAS M. ALEXANDER

QUALITIES

Prior to World War I, most references to qualities by American philosophers reflect their attitude toward British empiricism. In order to understand what British empiricism meant for American philosophers in the eighteenth and nineteenth centuries, their own characterizations are more useful than recent historical studies reflecting the influence of Frege, Wittgenstein, and logical empiricism; these aimed at a theory of knowledge based on logic or conceptual analysis rather than on psychology.

Two chapters in Francis Bowen's *Modern Philosophy, From Descartes To Schopenhauer and Hartmann* provide a helpful perspective on British empiricism. The first, Chapter VIII, "Realism, Nominalism, and Conceptualism," remarks:

> Surely, the most extravagant of all philosophical theories is that doctrine, first taught on English ground by Hobbes, and since too much favored by J.S. Mill and other Positivists and ultra Nominalists, that all our knowledge begins with particulars, and is derived from mere sensations, so that, to quote Hobbes's own language, "there is no conception in a man's mind, which hath not at first, totally or by parts, been begotten upon the organs of sense"; and "a man can have no thought representing anything not subject to sense."
>
> (Bowen 1878: 139ff)

This philosophical theory within which qualities were identified and divided was a theory about the mental operations from which all knowledge was said to arise. The laws governing these psychological operations were said to be laws of association. The last elements of these associations were said to be the words or thoughts constituting human knowledge. The first elements were supposed to be sensations deriving from operations of our senses.

Robert Boyle and John Locke divided the cognitive content of sensations into primary and secondary qualities. Locke's "An Essay Concerning Human Understanding" (1690) is widely regarded as the most important foundational work in the history of British empiricism. The fact that Bowen mentioned Hobbes rather than Locke deserves an explanation.

From Locke's point of view primary qualities such as number, shape, size, impenetrability and motion differed from secondary qualities such as color, taste and smell in having a causal foundation in properties of the object. But Berkeley's early criticism of Locke argued that our knowledge of primary qualities is inconceivable if these are abstracted from our experience of secondary qualities. Berkeley's own position is the subject of Bowen's Chapter IX, "Berkeleyanism." It describes an idealism in which the world of material objects and their properties have been replaced by a world of minds, their thoughts and their sensations. Bowen interpreted this result as a victory for nominalism, in which individual qualities present in or, at least, presentable to, individual minds have replaced the robust realism of substances and properties.

American philosophy only developed a distinctive tradition of its own after the Civil War. Earlier, serious thinking and writing about qualities was done by authors whose motives were primarily either religious or political. For them, the nominalism–realism issue trumped the problem of analyzing the powers of the mind. America's first important theologian, Jonathan Edwards, illustrates this effect of religion as a motive. His use of the language of qualities in very early writings does show the influence of Locke. (Edwards 1966: 56, 60, passim; the text is taken from *The Works of President Edwards*, Vol. 1, ed. S.B. Wright). And his conclusion is a position with a striking resemblance to Bowen's "Berkeleyanism." But, unlike Berkeley, Edwards' attachment to Newton was earlier than and perhaps more profound than his attachment to Locke. One point capturing his imagination was Newton's description of space as infinite. Infinity is a property that cannot be given through any sensory quality. For both Edwards and Newton, it was a property reserved to divinity. From Edwards to Emerson, thinkers trained in theology in America tended to be hostile to British nominalism. So, for example, Frankena in his preface to Edwards's important work, *The Nature of True Virtue* can identify it as "a profound restatement of the New Testament law of love in terms borrowed from the metaphysics of the Platonists" (Edwards 1960: vii).

One strand of American political thought did find the empiricists' streams of sense qualities a useful solvent in which to dissolve traditional talk about persons and their properties. Persons, with the properties belonging to them de jure, belong to a Roman law tradition that mirrored the Greek metaphysics of physical substances and their de facto properties. In the British common law, characteristic of most jurisdictions in colonial America, these de jure properties were understood to include a set of ancient and imprescriptable rights. Whitehead once observed that "There seems no obvious reason why one flux of impressions should not be related to another flux of impressions in the relative status of master to slave" (Whitehead 1967: 30). He was writing without polemical intent and excused Hume from holding any such view. But Bentham, another defender of sensory qualities, made a frontal assault on talk about rights (of the sort found in the Declaration of Independence), declaring it "nonsense on stilts." And John C. Calhoun had made extended use of the British empiricist tradition in his influential defense of Southern slavery, "A Disquisition on Government" (Calhoun 1853). In this context Bowen's association of British empiricism with Hobbes clearly served the author's polemical purposes. Hobbes was almost as unpopular then as Calhoun would be today.

Purely philosophical reflection on the problem of qualities hardly appears in America before the advent of pragmatism. Of the two founders of the movement, William James remained closer to British empiricists. His mature position in his *Essays in Radical Empiricism* is recognizably related to the philosophies of Berkeley and Hume. But James believed that his position is saved from fatal objections by altering their doctrine of sensible qualities. The view which James rejected had been noted by Bowen, quoting from Adam Smith: "'Qualities,' says Adam Smith, 'are almost always the objects of our external senses; relations never are.' . . . Hence, similarity as such, distinguished from similar objects, cannot be imagined, but can only be conceived, or thought" (Bowen 1878: 136). James argued that by admitting such relations as causation into the world of sensible qualities we preserve radical empiricism from a host of difficulties.

The other founder of pragmatism, Charles S. Peirce, was a committed realist from an early age. But, if one carefully compares Peirce's doctrine of the categories to James Mill's *Analysis of the Phenomena of the Human Mind*, one sees the relationship is more complicated. In particular, if one classifies the contents of consciousness by considering what the items are to which Mill's three laws of the association apply, one will find items "which are connected in three principal ways: 1st as cause and effect; 2dly, as resembling; 3dly, as included under the same name" (Peirce 1869: 186). Generalizations of these three classes give us what Peirce's mature system calls Secondness, Firstness, and Thirdness. (For details Smyth 1997: 13ff.) However only Firstness, described as "positive qualitative possibility," approaches the earlier doctrine of sensory qualities. And Peirce attributed the laws of association to Aristotle rather than the British empiricists.

The doctrine of primary qualities in British empiricism was intended to isolate those elements in our experiences that would account for the truth of our judgments about objects in the real world. Some parts of that project survived within logical positivism. By contrast, John Dewey offered a reconstruction of philosophy which not only challenged the search for isolated elements within experience, but, more radically, challenged the idea underlying talk about primary properties, namely the idea that the end of philosophy is truth about the real objects causing the impressions of sensation. An analogy might be of use here. Imagine a disaster involving dozens of cars on a superhighway. One legal system might require litigation to establish the truth about the causes and culpability in each separate collision. Another legal system might adjust its legal concepts of what has occurred in such cases to the more pragmatic issue of how we best can go forward in dealing with the effects of the collisions. Dewey's idea of the goal of philosophy would allow it to be more useful for the second system. As to qualities, they have a role in his account of experience quite different from their role in the earlier empiricism. Their function is to account for integration within the experience, rather than to isolate causal factors in the understanding of the experience. Dewey's *Art as Experience* (1934) develops these views about experience.

Further reading

Bowen, Francis. *Modern Philosophy, from Descartes to Schopenhauer and Hartmann*, second edition. New York: Scribner, Armstrong, 1878.

Calhoun, John C. *The Works of John C. Calhoun*, Vol. 1. New York: Appleton, 1853.

Edwards, Jonathan. *The Nature of True Virtue*. Ann Arbor, MA: University of Michigan Press, 1960.

—— *Jonathan Edwards: The Basic Writings*. New York: New American Library, 1966.

James, William. *Essays in Radical Empiricism*. New York: Longmans, Green, 1912.

Peirce, Charles S. *Analysis of the Phenomena of the Human Mind*, Vol. 1. London: Longman, Green, 1869 [1829].

Smyth, Richard. *Reading Peirce Reading*. Lanham MD: Rowman and Littlefield, 1997.

Whitehead, Alfred North. *Adventures of Ideas*. New York: Free Press, 1967 [1933].

RICHARD SMYTH

QUEST FOR BEING

There have been many religious revivals in American history, but the revival of religion that Sidney Hook (1902–89) witnessed was one of intellectuals turning to religion. For the most part, observed Hook, these intellectuals, primarily literary and political ones, "had never earned their right to religious disbelief." They "had inherited it as a result of a struggle of an earlier generation." So they were unprepared for the Holocaust, totalitarian terror and the development and use of the atomic bomb. Rather than reacting with greater skepticism, they became "more credulous, abandoning beliefs never properly understood, for others understood even less" ("Religion and the Intellectuals," in Hook 1991 [1961]: 95–6). Hook, in *The Quest for Being*, attempts to understand what he regards as an irrational response and to counter it with a restated "pragmatic naturalism," which he identifies in the Introduction as a reliance on the various scientific disciplines to understand what there is and the way things behave. This approach is "continuous with, although sometimes critical of, common-sense experience." The philosopher's special task when tensions develop between science and common sense is to help the latter adjust to the findings of the former (xi–xii). Accordingly most of the essays reprinted in *Quest for Being* were not written for professional philosophers but for the intellectuals whom he thought were not handling well the traumas of mid-century.

In these various essays Hook tackles a whole variety of misconceptions and bad arguments, attempting to state anew the case for democracy, the scientific method and the sufficiency of a naturalistic perspective.

The title essay, however, was originally published in a philosophical journal. Here Hook sets out to show that "being" in the sense favored by its various proponents – Martin Heidegger, Nicolai Hartmann, Thomists, Paul Tillich – is an empty term. There is nothing to which it refers. Moreover, ontology, or the study of being, is problematic also, for some would treat it as a science with its own subject-matter, yet the subject-matter is that which is common to all subject-matters. Yet Hook does not reject all uses of "ontological." He concludes with a proposal as to how it should be used. There are an "indeterminate number of truths" that are taken for granted by the sciences and are not the province of any one discipline. They may be "loosely called common-sense statements about the world which all scientists take for granted" (168). "Recognition of their truth provides the fundamental tests of normal perception and sanity of behavior" (169). The clearest indication of what these "truisms" are is found in his discussion of John Dewey's "generic traits of existence": "The traits to which Dewey pays the greatest attention" are "individuality and constant relations; contingency and need; movement and arrest; the stable and precarious." Hook then comments, "These are not the categories of science but of the cosmic theatre of human destiny" (171). And he soon makes clear, once again following his teacher Dewey, that real wisdom consists not in identifying these truisms, but in spotting them in actual situations.

Hook thus relocates the subject-matter of ontology from "Being" to what there is that is not itself a subject of scientific investigation, from the impenetrable mysteries of clouded philosophies to the stuff of everyday life that can be examined by all different sorts of people in an intelligent manner. He concludes the essay with this declaration:

> No verbal bars or taboo will prevent people from discussing questions such as these. The only legitimate goal in this connection is to ask that the questions first make sense, and then to find out whether the answers make good sense.
>
> (171)

This is the activity of wisdom.

Further reading

Hook, Sidney. *The Quest for Being*. Buffalo, NY: Prometheus Books, 1991. Originally published by St Martin's Press, 1961.

Michael Eldridge

QUEST FOR CERTAINTY

John Dewey coined the phrase "quest for certainty" – also the title of one of his most influential books – to characterize a pivotal factor in the development of western philosophy which led, among other things, to the proclivity to explicate and justify human knowing in terms of the pursuit of certitude. According to Dewey, the consequences of this conception of knowing ramify throughout the western intellectual tradition.

Dewey held that the quest for certainty has its roots deep in the pre-history of human experience. Mankind found itself in a hazardous world where one's very survival was often imperiled. In the face of such danger, humans sought security. One mode of response was the propitiation of the powers thought to determine our lot: the realm of religion and magic was born. Another mode of response was the development of the arts of controlling nature: this is the realm of practical action. Practical action seeks to bring about change in the world, and so contrasts with mere change in self – with change in *attitude toward* the (external) world. But practical action ineluctably involves contingency; mere probability of outcome is attainable, in contrast to the greater assuredness thought attainable through the operation of pure intellect. Given humanity's powerful desire for security, intellectual activity became elevated over the practical.

The consequences of the elevation of intellection over practice, argues Dewey, played themselves out over the course of western philosophy. At the hands of the Greeks, the terms of the debate – epistemological, metaphysical, valuational *et al.* – are set for the millennia: Since practical activity involves change, thus instability, whatever man touched brought unpredictability and insecurity. Only the immutable, the completely stable and secure, is fully knowable; the world of flux with which the practical arts deal is not. The quest for certainty, then, gives rise to a world that is metaphysically and valuationally bifurcated into (1) the immutable, "higher," and *better* realm of "the Real," thought to manifest perfect Being; and (2) unstable, "lower," and *inferior realm* of nature, thought to be (more or less) devoid of Being. Only the mind in its own independent, abstract operations could grasp this static Reality, and according to Dewey, a Spectator Theory of Knowledge was the inevitable result.

Issuing, according to Dewey, from the radical separation of knowing and doing, theory and practice, the Spectator Theory of Knowledge is a conception of human knowing shared by all (traditional) epistemologies. Roughly, it is the thesis that knowing is a passive beholding relation between a knowing subject and an object known. Plato, for example, manifested commitment to the Spectator Theory – and motivation by the quest for certainty – when, in *The Republic*, he held that genuine knowledge, *episteme*, is gained by the soul's grasp of the eternal Forms. Anything less, as we see in the Allegory of the Cave, is inferior to genuine knowing. This general conception of knowing is carried down through the history of philosophy: The rationalist Descartes is motivated by the quest for certainty, and is committed to the Spectator Theory, in holding that genuine knowledge is indubitable or incorrigible, and is only attainable through clear and distinct perceptions of simple natures. The empiricist Locke was similarly motivated, and similarly committed to the Spectator Theory, in holding that certitude is attainable only in the agreement (or disagreement) of ideas "immediately" given to the mind (analogous to how the visual object is "given" to the eye). Contemporary epistemologists, in the effort to meet skeptical challenges to empirical knowledge by finding its "proper ground," have appealed to sense data as the basis of (strong) foundationalism, holding that the direct object of perceptual awareness, a sense datum, is passively viewed by the epistemic agent, and is indeed known with certitude.

Dewey rejected this whole cluster of consequences of the quest for certainly. He rejected the duality between Reality and nature, between higher and lower, better and worse spheres of existence. Where his predecessors saw bifurcation, Dewey saw continuity: the world is of one broad ontic and valuational type, and should be conceived of *naturalistically* through and through. And he also rejected the Spectator Theory of Knowledge (and so the special theories of knowledge committed to it), which he considered fatally flawed for a number of reasons, though largely owing to what he considered its misconception of the relation between knowledge and action. Dewey sought to replace the Spectator Theory with his own pragmatic theory of knowledge, one that takes seriously the lessons of contemporary scientific method, and thus emphasizes the connection of knowing with practical activity. For Dewey, knowing is emphatically *not* a matter of passively grasping what exists prior to inquiry – the "antecedently Real" – but rather a matter of applying action directed by thought to resolve a problem situation. What is known, then, is the consequences of such inquiry.

Dewey's critique of the quest for certainty has been widely influential in American philosophical circles. Whether he succeeds in overturning the legacy of traditional, non-pragmatic philosophy is, however, a matter that remains under dispute. Still, it is interesting to note that many contemporary Anglo-American epistemologists, even those not generally sympathetic to Dewey's views, have come to reject the notion that knowing requires certitude.

Further reading

Dewey, John. *The Quest for Certainty: A Study in the Relation of Knowledge and Action. John Dewey: The Later Works, 1925–1953, Vol. 4, 1929*, ed. Harriet Furst Simon. Carbondale, IL: Southern Illinois University Press, 1984, pp. 1–250.

Dicker, Georges. *Dewey's Theory of Knowing*. Philadelphia, PA: Philosophical Monographs, Temple University Press, 1976.

Kulp, Christopher B. *The End of Epistemology: Dewey and His Current Allies on the Spectator Theory of Knowledge.* Westport, CT: Greenwood Press, 1992.

Rorty, Richard. *Philosophy and the Mirror of Nature.* Princeton, NJ: Princeton University Press, 1979.

CHRISTOPHER KULP

QUINE, WILLARD VAN ORMAN

W.V. Quine (1908–2000) studied philosophy as an undergraduate at Oberlin College, and earned his PhD at Harvard University. Quine's dissertation, written under Alfred North Whitehead, was on Whitehead and Russell's *Principia Mathematica*, and aimed to fix some problems with the system presented in that work, most notably confusion between the use of a term and the mention of that term. Interested throughout his life in travel and maps, Quine traveled to Europe after finishing graduate school, and met a number of major figures in philosophy and logic, including Gödel, Reichenbach, Tarski, and the figure who had the greatest influence on Quine's work, Rudolf Carnap. Upon his return from Europe, Quine was named to the first group of Society of Fellows at Harvard, and he continued to work at Harvard for the rest of his philosophical career, where he taught a number of students, many of whom went on to become significant figures in philosophy.

Quine wrote a number of influential articles and books, and was also the author of logic textbooks, an autobiography, and a Voltairean philosophical dictionary. Quine is the rare philosophical writer whose works have the virtues of being clear and full of wit.

Quine is the most influential American philosopher of the twentieth century. The most significant, enduring contribution of Quine to philosophy is his revival of philosophical naturalism, an approach whose most prominent proponent prior to Quine was the eighteenth-century Scottish philosopher David Hume. Naturalism (roughly) is the view that the methods of science are to be used in solving certain philosophical problems. Quine appealed to naturalism to address a number of significant metaphysical, epistemological, semantic, and psychological issues that had traditionally been approached in an *a priori*, nonnaturalistic fashion.

In Quine's naturalized epistemology, for example, appeal is made to the methods and results of psychology in order to answer questions regarding the nature and scope of our knowledge of the external world. Philosophers who are dubious of the promise of naturalism might find such an account unsatisfying. Naturalized epistemology, for example, takes for granted a number of facts that the traditional Cartesian skeptic would consider contestable. Quine is presenting a theory that is supposed to explain how we are eventually able to make reference to physical objects on the basis of information derived (in part) from the impact of light rays upon our retinas. The Cartesian skeptic would not grant one the right to assume that there are in fact light rays or retinas – these assumptions would be called into question by the skeptical problem. An epistemic naturalist, in response to the skeptic, could claim, as Quine did, that the Cartesian project of seeking an indubitable foundation for knowledge is a "lost cause" (Quine 1969: 74), and thus the only way to properly account for knowledge is within the framework of science.

Support for Quine's naturalism can be found in what is probably his best-known philosophical thesis, the thesis that there is no distinction between analytic truths and synthetic truths. Analytic truths are, in a definition due to Frege, statements that are true in virtue either of being (1) logical truths or (2) capable of being transformed into a logical truth by substitution of synonymous terms. "All vixens are vixens" is a logical truth, and is hence analytic on this definition. If "vixen" and "female fox" are synonymous, then the following sentence is also an analytic truth: "All vixens are female foxes." In "Two Dogmas of Empiricism," Quine considers a number of ways to account for the notion of synonymy, and finds them all lacking. Without a way to clarify the notion of synonymy, there is no way to draw the Fregean analytic/synthetic distinction.

If this view is correct, and there is no distinction between analytic and synthetic truths, there are wide repercussions for philosophy. The nonexistence of the distinction provides support for philosophical naturalism, for without an analytic/synthetic distinction, one cannot draw a distinction between conceptual disputes and factual disputes. There are also consequences for our understanding of epistemology: One could not characterize the distinction between *a priori* and *a posteriori* knowledge on the basis of the analytic/synthetic distinction.

Quine's denial regarding the analytic/synthetic distinction led him to a kind of skepticism regarding the prospects for a theory of meaning along the lines of Gottlob Frege's theory of sense. Further grounds for Quine's skepticism regarding meaning result from his thesis of the indeterminacy of translation, according to which there are many translations of words and sentences from one language to another that are equally good, in light of the available evidence. In his essay "Ontological Relativity," Quine also voiced doubt regarding the theory of reference, arguing for the thesis of the inscrutability of reference. According to this thesis, it is impossible to determine on the basis of all available evidence what the referent of a term is. These two skeptical theses have generated a great deal of discussion in the philosophical literature, and many philosophers have attempted to save the notions of meaning and reference from Quine's critiques by rebutting his arguments. Other philosophers have attempted to show that there are unproblematic notions of meaning and reference that are not susceptible to Quine's arguments.

Quine has had a great deal of influence on subsequent discussion in philosophy not only for his doubts regarding accounts of meaning and reference, but also for his positive accounts of matters such as truth. In *Philosophy of Logic*, Quine proposes a disquotational account of truth, an account that has had a great influence on subsequent discussion of deflationary theories of truth. The account is called a "disquotational" one, due to the fact that it characterizes truth based on a trivial schema, a schema that quotes a sentence on the left-hand side of a biconditional, and "disquotes" the same sentence on the right-hand side of the biconditional. On the disquotational theory of truth, for any meaningful, context-independent sentence S, the following schema applies: S is true if and only if s. An example of an instance of this schema would be: "Quine is a naturalist" is true if and only if Quine is a naturalist. The sole purpose of the notion of truth is to serve as a device of generalization, to form generalizations such as "All sentences of the form 'p or not p' are true."

Further reading

Quine, W.V. *Mathematical Logic*, revised edition. Cambridge, MA: Harvard University Press, 1951.

—— *Word and Object*. Cambridge, MA: MIT Press, 1960.

—— *From a Logical Point of View*, revised edition. Cambridge, MA: Harvard University Press, 1961.

—— *Ontological Relativity and Other Essays*. New York: Columbia University Press, 1969.

—— *Philosophy of Logic*. Englewood, NJ: Prentice Hall, 1970.

—— *Pursuit of Truth*, revised edition. Cambridge, MA: Harvard University Press, 1992.

FRITZ J. MCDONALD

R

RADICAL EMPIRICISM

Radical empiricism is an epistemological and metaphysical view developed in the late nineteenth and early twentieth century, though it may have been anticipated by earlier figures. It is associated with the American pragmatists William James and Charles Sanders Peirce.

Traditional rationalism tells us that if we want true knowledge we have to ignore our transient sensations and use reason. We will then discover the invisible conscious self, sensation-independent matter, and the abstract forms and principles that connect all things but exist beyond our experience. Traditional empiricism responds that in fact all our human thought and knowledge originate in sensory experience. All the things we can think of are perceivable things; we cannot even entertain the hypothesis that there are unperceivable things apart from experience. Moreover, sensory experience tells us about particular things rather than relations among them, and so the world we know and think of must be a world of particular items, perhaps even of "atomic" sensation-particles that we observers string together with our habitual expectations and fictional categorizations. Even we human selves may be no more than the fictional constructions of our fellow fictional constructions.

But radical empiricism argues that this traditional empiricism was not empirical enough. James argues that if empiricists had paid more attention to experience, they would have observed that whole objects, whole selves, and even relations among objects and selves are in fact experienced by observers. Experienced qualities and things often present themselves to us with real, and in some cases developing, feelings of conjunction with or transition to other experiences. But the whole objects we experience are not made of mind-independent matter and the connected-together selves we experience do not have the transcendent quality of "consciousness." Instead, subjects and objects alike are made of "pure experience."

"Experience," says James, "… has no … inner duplicity; and the separation of it into consciousness and content comes, not by way of subtraction, but by way of addition" (1912: 9). Under the influence of the old rationalists and empiricists, we think of the perception of an object, say Memorial Hall on the Harvard campus, as the holding of a material object in the mind by means of a mental representation. But James says that my experience starts out involving no representing sensation in my conscious mind and no represented material thing independent of my perception. It begins as a pure event of experience belonging to no subjects or objects. It is only after that experience is contextualized or added to other experiences of expectation and satisfaction that it becomes *both* my experience of Memorial Hall *and* Memorial Hall as experienced by me.

As past and future experiences link themselves transitionally to other experiences, both Memorial Hall and the beings who experience it construct themselves. The single pure experience comes to belong to both the subjective world of my thought and perception and the objective "material" world just as a single point can belong to two lines, and there is nothing more to either me or Memorial Hall than those ongoing histories. Of course, the hall-history, as the history of an "objective" thing, will intercept other selves besides mine, and it will also meet new coats of paint, fire and reconstruction, and the like, while my "subjective" self-history intercepts other buildings, other selves, my own self and its thoughts, and so on.

This view is understood by some interpreters to be anticipated in the metaphysics of Spinoza, who argued that spirit and nature were two names for the same reality (1677). Moreover, Hume may have been on the same track when he used the terms "object" and "perception" indifferently for the same "single existence" (1739: 366). Ernst Mach argued that things like colors were physical in one domain of investigation and psychical in another (1886: 17–18). And though Henri Bergson rejected traditional idealism, he argued that matter and spirit differed only in degree, not in kind (1911).

Bertrand Russell at one point adopted James's anti-dualistic metaphysics and renamed it "neutral monism," though James would have associated the term "monism" with the "block universe" of his arch-foes the Hegelians (1907). James called radical empiricism "a more comminuted *Identitätsphilosophie*" (1912: 134–5), meaning that it broke up the monistic block-world into sundry particular experiences that could then become the experiences of individual persons. This was crucial because James thought that individuals could not freely struggle to make their experiences and their world better in the Hegelian picture, and the possibility of this free struggle is at the root of James's philosophy. (See Cormier 2000: *passim.*)

Charles Sanders Peirce identified himself as a "pragmatist or radical empiricist," and he claimed that James had kidnapped the label "pragmatism" for his own position when he saw that "[James's] 'radical empiricism' substantially answered to [Peirce's] definition of pragmatism." (1857–86: 5.414, 7.617; and see Hookway 1997: 147). But while Peirce did see correctly that his understanding of reality was the same as that expressed in radical empiricism, James distinguished what he called "pragmatism" from radical empiricism more than once (1907: 6 and 284–5). Radical empiricism was, for James, a theory of reality, while pragmatism was a way of deciding which theory of reality to adopt. In fact, James used pragmatism as a way of arguing for radical empiricism (1912: 10–12 and 72–4). Thus, unless James was arguing circularly, these were two different ideas.

But whoever was or was not a radical empiricist, how plausible is a world of pure experience? As time passes, readers seem less skeptical of James's attack on transcendent consciousness, but one enduring question is just how radical empiricism can account for real physical objects that existed before there were human beings. These "objects" would seem as if they have to be made of experience – but whose? Or, if there is (or was) nobody to have these pieces of pure experience, how can they exist?

Here James contrasts real things with merely mental things:

> Mental triangles are pointed, but their points won't wound. With "real" objects, on the contrary, consequences always accrue; and thus the real experiences get sifted from the mental ones ... and precipitated together as the stable part of the whole experience-chaos, under the name of the physical world.
>
> (1912: 33)

Thus, much as pragmatic "truth" is belief with good consequences in experience, the "reality" of radical empiricism is experience with other stable experiences that come along after it as consequences. Our thoughts are the fanciful experiences that operate according to no fixed rules, and our true thoughts sort themselves out as the experiences that lead us, sometimes against our will, to the steady, strong experiences we know as reality. But were there no real objects before this process of sorting took place?

Yes and no. Yes, in that the Big Bang, the accretion of the planets, and the rise of the prokaryotes obviously took place before anyone was around to know about them. No, in that the separation of those objective, real physical phenomena from our subjective knowledge of them took place long after those physical things happened. These ancient physical phenomena are indeed parts of our present experience; we wouldn't and couldn't so much as think of them without our experiences of background cosmic radiation, other planets, and geological evidence of increasing oxygen in the early atmosphere. Thus, we who now know about these things have wound up owning the pure experience that makes up the ancient objects. These experiences have sorted themselves out as realities rather than mere imaginings by leading to further experiences; and as they did, they built both the persons who know them and the past times and spaces that they inhabited. If those past times and spaces are real, they are also parts of experience with steady and stable consequences, and they are nothing more than that. They have had no existence apart from their having been teased out of our experiences – along with the physical objects they contained and the subjects who own those experiences.

Further reading

Bergson, H. *Matter and Memory*, trans. Nancy Margaret Paul and W. Scott Palmer. New York: Zone Books, 1988 [1911].

Cormier, H. *The Truth Is What Works*. Lanham, MD: Rowman and Littlefield, 2000.

Hookway, C. "Logical Principles and Philosophical Attitudes: Peirce's Response to James's Pragmatism" in Ruth Anna Putnam (ed.) *The Cambridge Companion to William James*. Cambridge: Cambridge University Press, 1997.

Hume, D. *A Treatise of Human Nature*, ed. L.A. Selby-Bigge, Oxford: Clarendon Press, 1975 [1739].

James, W. *Essays in Radical Empiricism*. New York: Longman, Green, 1912.

Mach, E. *The Analysis of Sensations and the Relation of the Physical to the Psychical*, fifth edition 1906, trans. C.M. Williams and S. Waterlow. New York: Dover, 1959 [1885].

Peirce, C.S. *Collected Papers of Charles Sanders Peirce*, ed. Charles Hartshorne and Paul Weiss. Bristol: Thoemmes Press, 1998 [1857–86].

Russell, B. "Review of William James' *Essays in Radical Empiricism*," *Mind* 21 (1912): 571–5.

Spinoza, B. *Ethics*, edited and translated by G.H.R. Parkinson. New York: Oxford University Press, 2000 [1677].

HARVEY CORMIER

RAMSEY SENTENCE

In the midst of the mathematico-formalist heyday of Cambridge philosophy, epitomized by the work of Bertrand Russell and Ludwig Wittgenstein, Frank P. Ramsey (1903–30) proffered a strongly pragmatist-oriented approach to the analysis and understanding of philosophical concerns regarding ontology and epistemology, as well as of philosophical methodology. Drawing on the distinction between the observational terms of a theory (that is, terms that denote ontological entities that are in fact observable, e.g. a bird's red plumage) and the theoretical terms of a theory (that is, terms that denote ontological entities deemed non-observable, e.g. faster-than-light particles), Ramsey developed a logically formal means of construing theoretical terms in empirically acceptable ways. He did this by treating theoretical terms not as logical constants, which denote specific entities, but as existentially bound variables. For example, a sentence in physics might speak of tachyons (faster-than-light particles) in such a way as, "Tachyons exhibit both particle-like and wave-like properties." Ramsey's formulation would treat such a sentence as, "$x (x exhibits particle-like and wave-like properties." The theoretical term "tachyon" now is defined as "an x such that x exhibits … ," where particle-like properties and wave-like properties are observables. Carl Hempel dubbed such a formal construal a *Ramsey Sentence*. The point of such a sentence is not to eliminate or reduce theoretical terms to observational ones, but to allow empirical theories meaningfully to incorporate such terms.

A consequence of this sort of logical move, for Ramsey, is that there is no given sharp dichotomy between individuals and predicates. A given term can be represented as either. Quine made use of such a move in his argument that proper names can be treated as predicates. So, the name "Pegasus" could be treated as the predicate "pegasize," as in the sentence, "$x (x is a flying horse)" or "$x (x pegasizes)." While many philosophers, particularly those with allegiance to nominalism, balk at such a move, Ramsey found such treatment to be a pragmatic decision regarding a theory's ontological commitments.

David Lewis made one application of Ramsey Sentences in his articulation of a functionalist view of mind, or mental terms. In an existentially quantified sentence, whatever entities can be substituted for the quantified variable x turn out to satisfy the sentence and make it true. That is, whatever fulfills that function makes the sentence true. In the case of a functionalist view of mind, whatever entities fulfill the functions associated with mentality satisfy the variable's value. Mind, then, is not some particular substance or thing, but whatever functions in appropriate ways. This has led some philosophers to speak of a Ramsey/Lewis method of defining terms.

While Ramsey's means of treating theoretical terms was formal in a logically technical sense, his concerns were more pragmatist. He emphasized the anticipation of future experience over the simple assignment of truth-values in his analysis. Theories, he claimed, are construed with a view to supplementation by discovery of further facts; they are always attitudes of expectation for the future.

Further reading

Hempel, Carl. *Aspects of Scientific Explanation*. New York: Free Press, 1965.

Lewis, David. *Counterfactuals*. Oxford: Blackwell, 1973.

Ramsey, Frank P. *The Foundations of Mathematics and Other Essays*, ed. R.B. Braithwaite. London: Routledge and Kegan Paul, 1931.

—— *Philosophical Papers*, ed. D.H. Mellor. Cambridge: Cambridge University Press, 1990.

Quine, W.V.O. *Ontological Relativity and Other Essays*. New York: Columbia University Press, 1969.

DAVID BOERSEMA

RANDALL, JOHN HERMAN

Randall was born on Valentine's Day 1899, the son of a liberal Protestant minister. Studying under Woodbridge at Columbia, and bearing his influence, he had definite views about Greek philosophy. Although Dewey was away when Randall was a student, Randall nevertheless came under Dewey's influence by reading him. Woodbridge's influence turned Randall to Aristotle. Consequently, Randall always presented himself as a follower of both Aristotle and Dewey.

Despite his father's calling, Randall was, like many American philosophers from William James onward, unable to believe in the traditional conceptions of deity. Nevertheless, he thought that one could not ignore religion's pervasive presence. One had to understand how religion functioned in the world. Unlike James, who was concerned with religion as experienced by the individual, Randall was concerned with it as social phenomenon and criticized James for ignoring that part of it.

When looked at world-wide and historically, religion, according to Randall, has three distinctive functions: (1) consecration to an ideal, (2) celebration (most religions, he thought, celebrate the important secular activities of their society) and (3) clarification of those ideals. He thought it important that in most religions outside of the West and Islam, religion has never been a body of beliefs.

For Randall, religion is neither true nor false; it is adequate or inadequate in its functions. He thought there was no conflict between religion and science; rather, the conflict was between older scientific beliefs enshrined in religion and new science.

Randall's metaphysics reflects both Aristotle and Dewey. He equated Aristotle's *ousia* with Dewey's "situation" as that which is encountered in all existence. Some philosophers had avoided the use of powers as a metaphysical notion, thinking it to be too "spooky." But Randall found it indispensable.

A thing is its powers. But powers are known only through their operations. Powers are never completely known. Knowledge of what things can do in various situations is inexhaustible and the reason why knowledge can never be final and is the best reason for a fallibilistic view of knowledge. The experimental, self-corrective temper of science is suited to the inexhaustible powers of things, which new situations can bring to light.

In contrast to those who put an emphasis on science as a body of logically organized system, whose purpose is theoretical comprehension, Randall emphasized the importance of experimental science. This attitude followed from his metaphysics of "the situation."

A situation has many factors as ingredients (causes in Aristotle). A variation in one factor affects the kind of outcome that can emerge in a situation. These factors *operate jointly* to enhance or limit an outcome. They have potentialities which can be realized under appropriate circumstances. The extent of these powers, their universality or their limits cannot be determined except by experience or experiment. You can never tell in advance how factors operate conjointly with other factors and whether this joint operation augments or inhibits the powers each factor has. It is something that calls for experimentation. The role of science is to find out what things can do, how they function. But functioning, simply put, is not the object of inquiry. Rather, it is how functioning takes place – how something is or can be done. But the ultimate object of inquiry is how best to do it. Evaluation, the determination of the better and the worse ways of acting is fundamental. To be anything is to function.

Nature is plural and diverse but can become unified in human vision. Men have seen the world whole through the great creation myths of primitive cultures. More recently, some have tried to see it entire through the vision that is knowledge and science.

Randall sees history as a branch of metaphysics – a study of how something came to be. For Randall, history is an explanation of how something came to be. Factors that contribute to that outcome are relevant. The historian chooses what outcome is to be explained, but the factors that affect and the causes that effect that outcome can be objectively inquired into and are publicly verifiable. As we learn more in the future about the consequences of that outcome, we revise our histories.

As a historian of philosophy, Randall's notion of what constitutes modern and post-modern philosophy does not follow current literary and artistic views. Modern philosophy can be defined, in other than chronological terms, as the conflict between two types of knowledge. Such "modern philosophy" ends when one type has won out, as science in the twentieth century had. Even after the passing of modern philosophy, it can still be revived, whenever the problem of knowledge reasserts itself as a central problem. The central problem for Randall was how to attain the good life – an inquiry which has been deflected by modern philosophy.

Randall said that the historical treatment of philosophy illuminates the intellectual reaction of outstanding minds to culturally significant events. It displays ideas in the process of being worked out and as they intervene in human activities, and as they influence the course of institutional development.

As a historian of philosophy, he gave a penetrating criticism of the Newtonian scientific ideal, that philosophy came to seek a broader and deeper intellectual method that would do greater justice to the manifold areas of man's cultural experience. He showed how in the Romantic era the main impulses to philosophizing came from the non-scientific areas of man's cultural experience: how the central thread of science ran underground, until it re-emerged with Marx, Comte, and Mill.

After Darwin, said Randall, science returned to serve as a central thread but Romanticism was still there; and science was no longer taken as itself offering a satisfactory philosophy of life.

In ancient philosophy, Randall had doubt that Plato seriously entertained a Theory of Ideas. His historical view of the Hellenistic world saw the Trinity as a philosophical solution to intellectual problems. Randall also told of the fortunes of Greek philosophy in Rome, and emphasized the importance of Cicero for subsequent philosophizing in the West, along with the influence of Augustine.

Further reading

Randall, John Herman, Jr. *The Making of the Modern Mind: A Survey of the Intellectual Background of the Present Age*, revised and enlarged edition. New York: Houghton Mifflin, 1940.

—— *Nature and Historical Experience: Essays in Naturalism and in the Theory of History.* New York: Columbia, 1958.

—— *The Career of Philosophy: Volume I: From the Middle Ages to the Enlightenment.* New York: Columbia University, 1962.

—— *How Philosophy Uses Its Past.* New York and London: Columbia University, 1963.

—— *The Career of Philosophy: Volume II: From the German Enlightenment to the Age of Darwin.* New York: Columbia University, 1965.

—— *Hellenistic Ways of Deliverance and the Making of the Christian Synthesis.* New York and London: Columbia University, 1970.

—— *Plato: Dramatist of the Life of Reason.* New York: Columbia University, 1972.

—— *Philosophy after Darwin: Chapters for The Career of Philosophy: Volume Three, and Other Essays*, ed., Beth J. Singer. New York: Columbia University, 1977.

ANGELO JUFFRAS

RATIONALISM

Rationalism in its most standard sense is defined as a position about the sources of human knowledge, and as one of two contrasting ways of doing philosophy in the "modern" era. On this construal, both rationalism and its counterpart, empiricism, share certain assumptions that mark them as modernist yet diverge where the proponent of empiricism holds that sense experience is the source of knowledge concerning propositions of all sorts, while the rationalist holds that some propositions are knowable by rational insight or intuition. There are also looser connotations of philosophical rationalism that apply the term to Greek thought at least as far back as Plato and to later philosophers who have shared the Platonic vision of an ideal unchanging structure of reality which intellectual insight can grasp. An as extension of the rationalist's optimism that the natural order of things is intelligible to reasoned inquiry, some forms of rationalism go beyond supposing that analytic, logical, and mathematical knowledge is grounded in rational intuition, to including propositions of an ethical or of a metaphysical character. Since among these are propositions such as that God exists, philosophers of religion often distinguish "religious rationalism" from its philosophical counterpart in order to characterize the position that God's existence (or other claims of a religious nature) can be rationally supported by evidential and/or *a priori* arguments.

Returning to the primary or standard construal, empiricism has been the dominant of the two streams of epistemological thought over the past two centuries. Mainstream empiricists in Anglo-American philosophy have often conceded the existence of *a priori* reasons, but sought to undercut their significance by showing that they reflect only linguistic or conceptual conventions, such as those involved in matters of definition. In American academics during the first half of the twentieth century, when schools of thought such as pragmatism and logical empiricism enjoyed successive periods of influence, their proponents often questioned the existence or significance of a faculty of rational insight. Pragmatism became one way in which Emerson's vision of American intellectual independence came to be fulfilled, and when it did, the influence of Charles Darwin was greater than of any particular empiricist philosopher in leading the classical pragmatists to reject what William James called the "rationalistic temperament" in philosophy. Yet James would agree with the rationalists about the value of the great metaphysical systems, against the narrower logical empiricism which attempted to ground an anti-metaphysical theory of meaning upon Hume's division between matters of fact and relations of ideas.

William James understood pragmatism as "the attitude of looking away from first things, principles, 'categories,' supposed necessities; and of looking towards last things, fruits, consequences, facts" (1907: 54–5). He often presented Josiah Royce's religious epistemology as a rationalism to which the pragmatist attitude is adverse. John Dewey's version of pragmatism is arguably more qualified and more thoroughly developed, but "intelligence" and "critical intelligence" were words he used to avoid rationalism while still conveying the importance of thought and reflection. Because it roots in praxis – in problems encountered in actual human practices – pragmatism is presented by both authors as avoiding pitfalls identified with rationalism.

The logical empiricists influential through the 1950s generally followed Hume in rejecting *a priori* synthetic knowledge and insisting that *a priori* knowledge concerns only relations of ideas rather than matters of fact. W.V.O. Quine's holistic empiricism (1951) and Morton White's holistic pragmatism, despite being critical of the analytic–synthetic distinction upon which the logical empiricist account of meaning depended, both continued support for empiricism by indicating that the only reasons relevant to retaining or giving up a claim within one's "web of belief" have to do with accommodating experience.

Such examples illustrate how the empiricist temperament has remained dominant; yet interest in it as an epistemological view re-emerged with Noam Chomsky's work on innate elements in language in the 1960s. Chomsky describes his account as a "rationalist conception of the nature of language" (1966) because it posits certain innate constraints on language learning not adequately explained on empiricist assumptions. Coming at a time when interest in innate ideas and *a priori* knowledge had largely evaporated, yet positivist conceptions of meaning were discredited, Chomsky's work became influential across a variety of academic fields. Saul Kripke's further contributions to restructuring philosophy of language, especially in *Naming and Necessity* (1980), where he challenges received views about the relationship between the *a priori* and the necessary, are sometimes said to have "made metaphysics respectable again."

Today, much of the urge to reassess empiricist views about the *a priori,* the necessary, and the analytic come as a result of developments in American philosophy specific to the final decades of the twentieth century. Repeated calls to "naturalize epistemology," together with widespread rejection of epistemic internalism in favor of externalism, are seen as *tested* by their ability to explain the appearance of *a priori* knowledge/reasons. In recent years, proponents of reliabilist externalism have been among the critics of *a priori* knowledge, so that their own critics have in turn used this denial in order to expose inadequacies of reliabilist externalism. Epistemologists such as Lawrence BonJour (1998) and George Bealer have argued against empiricist accounts of human knowledge and in favor of rationalist alternatives. Bonjour argues that only a rationalist view of justification can provide the basis for a non-skeptical account of human knowledge: in order to have any genuine knowledge or justification there must be *a priori* justification that fits the original rationalist conception (Casullo 1999: 121–2). Bealer argues that the capacity for intellectual insight is fundamental and irreducible, and that it supports a thesis of the "autonomy of philosophy" that undermines the motivation to replace traditional philosophical projects with scientific surrogates. The "*a priori* disciplines," under which Bealer includes not only logic and mathematics but also philosophy, can be largely autonomous from the empirical sciences (Boghossian and Peacocke 2000).

In summary, the rationalist side of the rationalist/empiricist debate remains vibrant in contemporary philosophy, even as and in part *because* the internalist and foundationalist assumptions associated with philosophical modernism have themselves come to be widely challenged in recent decades. Whatever the fate of modernism itself, some form of this perennial conflict is likely to remain important in the theory of knowledge, since rationalist and empiricist perspectives often provide needed counterpoint by drawing attention to aspects of human knowledge and reflective reason that the other tends to neglect.

Further reading

Boghossian, Paul and Peacocke, Christopher (eds.). *New Essays on the A Priori.* New York: Oxford University Press, 2000.

BonJour, Lawrence. *In Defense of Pure Reason: A Rationalist Account of A Priori Justification.* New York: Cambridge University Press, 1998.

Casullo, Albert (ed.). *A Priori Knowledge.* Brookfield, VT: Ashgate, 1999.

Chomsky, Noam. *Cartesian Linguistics: A Chapter in the History of Rationalist Thought.* New York: Harper and Row, 1966.

Dewey, John. "What Pragmatism Means by Practical" in *Essays in Experimental Logic.* Chicago, IL: University of Chicago, 1916, pp. 303–29.

James, William. *Pragmatism: A New Name for Some Old Ways of Thinking*. New York: Longmans, Green, 1907.
Kripke, Saul. *Naming and Necessity.* Cambridge, MA: Harvard University Press, 1980.
Quine, W.V.O. "Two Dogmas of Empiricism," *Philosophical Review* 60, 1 (1951): 20–43.

GUY AXTELL

RAWLS, JOHN

John Rawls (1921–2002) was born 21 February 1921 in Baltimore, Maryland. After he graduated from Princeton University, he served in the infantry in the Pacific theater during World War II. At the end of the war, he returned to Princeton and completed a PhD in 1950 under the supervision of Walter Stace. While writing his thesis, in 1948 Rawls met Margaret Warfield Fox, then a senior at Pembroke College (now part of Brown University). Married June 1949, together they spent the summer in Princeton, producing an index to Walter Kaufmann's book *Nietzsche: Philosopher, Psychologist and Anti-Christ* (Princeton, 1950).

Rawls taught at Princeton for two years. He spent 1952–3 as a Fulbright Fellow at Oxford, where he was deeply influenced by Isaiah Berlin and H.L.A. Hart. When he returned to the United States, Rawls accepted a position as an assistant professor of philosophy at Cornell. He moved to MIT in 1960 and to Harvard in 1962. In 1979, he succeeded Kenneth Arrow as the James Bryant Conant University Professor at Harvard. He remained a member of the Harvard Philosophy Department until his retirement in 1992. In 1999, President Clinton awarded him a National Humanities Medal with the citation noting his success in helping women enter the ranks of a male-dominated field. He died in Lexington, Massachusetts on 24 November 2002 at the age of eighty-one.

John Rawls's greatest achievement as a philosopher was that he opened doors through which many other philosophers were then able to pass. This was primarily the effect of the publication of his best-known book, *A Theory of Justice.* Prior to *A Theory of Justice*, contemporary ethical theory in the Anglo-American tradition was primarily meta-ethics and contemporary political philosophy was virtually nonexistent. When Rawls published *A Theory of Justice*, situated as he was at one of the US premier educational institutions, he made it possible for others to write dissertations in political philosophy and to publish in the field, even helping to give rise to a number of new journals.

In his book, Rawls attempts to generalize and carry to a higher level of abstraction the social contract theory of Locke, Rousseau, and Kant. In Rawls's version of social contract theory, people are to select the principles of justice they are to live by in imagined ignorance of whether natural or social contingencies have worked in their favor. Rawls argues that the principles of justice they would select would be significantly different from the classical or average principle of utility.

Almost immediately, there was a utilitarian challenge to Rawls's work led by R.M. Hare and Richard Brandt; soon after there was a libertarian challenge led by Robert Nozick, and later a communitarian challenge led by Michael Sandel and Michael Walzer, an Aristotelian challenge led by Aliastair MacIntyre, a feminist challenge led by Susan Okin, among others, and a multicultural challenge led by a diverse array of Western and non-Western philosophers. Since Rawls was reluctant to respond directly to his critics, these challenges created opportunities for others to step in and respond to them or to suggest ways that Rawls's work needed to be modified in order to best deal with these criticisms.

There was also the important question of the practical implications of Rawls's work for how we should live our lives individually and collectively. Rawls had always claimed to be developing primarily an ideal moral theory. *A Theory of Justice* only touched briefly on nonideal theory to provide an account of civil disobedience. But the more removed one's society is from having ideally just institutions, the more need there is to spell out the practical requirements of justice for one's time, otherwise one might be thought to legitimate the unjust institutions and practices that exist. By deciding to focus his work on ideal moral theory, Rawls created opportunities for others either to work out the practical implications of his own view or to work out the practical implications of views developed in opposition or as a corrective to Rawls's view for the nonideal world in which we live.

Rawls's second book, *Political Liberalism*, was written to correct a fundamental problem that Rawls perceived in *A Theory of Justice.* Rawls believed that his earlier book assumed a relatively complete Kantian conception of the good. In *Political Liberalism*, Rawls tries to ground his same theory of justice on a more minimal foundation – an overlapping consensus of reasonable comprehensive conceptions of the good. According to Rawls, citizens were to conduct their fundamental discussions within a framework of a conception of justice that everyone, irrespective of their particular comprehensive conceptions of the good, could be reasonably expected to endorse. An important implication of Rawls's view is that religious considerations were generally ruled out in public debate over fundamental issues in society. This feature of Rawls's view has engendered considerable debate among theologians, political scientists, and lawyers, as well as philosophers, but it has not had any discernable effect on public policy, at least in the US, where religious considerations continue to have an impact on public policy beyond anything that could be justified by a reasonable overlapping consensus.

Rawls's third major book, *The Law of Peoples*, attempts to extend his theory of justice to the international realm. Rejecting any straightforward application of his principles of justice to the international realm, Rawls favors more minimal obligations to other peoples. According to Rawls, there is virtually "no society anywhere in the world ... with resources so scarce that it could not, were it reasonably organized and governed, become well-ordered." Rawls also allows for exceptions to international principles of justice, specifically a requirement of noncombatant immunity, in order to attain "some substantial good," while at the same time disallowing any comparable exceptions to intersocietal principles of justice. Here again, Rawls's views have given rise to a wide-ranging discussion, which has now become even more important given the connection that exists between terrorism and international justice.

It is very hard to overestimate the impact that John Rawls has had on contemporary political philosophy. He is undeniably the most influential political philosopher of the twentieth century in the Anglo-American tradition.

Further reading

Rawls, John. *A Theory of Justice*. Cambridge, MA: Belknap Press, 1971, revised edition 1999.

—— *Political Liberalism*. New York: Columbia University Press, 1993. The paperback adds a valuable new introduction and an essay titled "Reply to Habermas."

—— *The Law of Peoples* with "The Idea of Public Reason Revisited." Cambridge, MA: Harvard University Press, 1999.

—— *Collected Papers*, ed. Samuel Freeman. Cambridge, MA: Harvard University Press, 1999.

—— *Lectures on the History of Moral Philosophy*, ed. Barbara Herman. Cambridge, MA: Harvard University Press, 2000.

—— *Justice as Fairness: A Restatement*, ed. Erin Kelly. Cambridge, MA: Belknap Press, 2001.

JAMES P. STERBA

REALISM

Realism is the most protean of all philosophical terms; its meaning in the context of American philosophy is no less multi-faceted. There are four distinctly realist movements in the history of American thought since the eighteenth century: Natural Realism, New Realism, Critical Realism and Pragmatism. All four take the problem of realism to have an epistemological cast: the issue is whether and how we know anything about reality outside our own minds.

Natural Realism purports to embody the "natural" opinion of the common man about the answer to the problem of realism. The doctrine reflects the powerful influence of the Scottish Common Sense approach to philosophy – particularly the work of Thomas Reid – on its advocates. Natural Realism arose in America through figures such as John Witherspoon (1723–94) and Samuel Stanhope Smith (1751–1819), the sixth and seventh Presidents of Princeton respectively. Writers of the time typically characterize the view in these terms: we are in direct perceptual and epistemic contact with external objects; we can know about the existence and properties of external objects without recourse to reasoning or inference (see McCosh 1887). Opposition to Natural Realism was initially confined to religious figures such as Jonathan Edwards, among whom Berkeleyan Idealism was popular. This opposition steadily grew, however, along with dissatisfaction with the apparent dogmatism and naiveté of Natural Realism.

Many philosophers critical of Natural Realism turned to German Idealism, particularly the works of Kant, Fichte, Schelling, and Hegel. The champion of the resulting Idealist movement was Josiah Royce, who in 1899 published his Gifford Lectures under the title *The World and the Individual*. The work contained a sustained critique of realism, and an elaborate argument to the effect that the doctrine made all relations impossible and was self-contradictory.

Eventually the dominance of Idealism attracted challengers, and the first distinctively American forms of realism began to arise at the beginning of the twentieth century. The first of these was "New Realism," which successfully challenged Idealist doctrine, even if it did not yet provide a complete or compelling alternative. One proponent, Ralph Barton Perry (a student of Royce) attacked what he called "The Cardinal Principle of Idealism." This was the argument that because all objects are known, knowing therefore constitutes all objects. Perry noted that this "argument" is an example of the fallacy *post hoc ergo propter hoc* (literally "after, therefore because of"). We may only have access to an object's existence *after* coming to know it, but it does not follow that our knowing it *causes* or brings about its existence.

The canonical statement of New Realism is "The Program and First Platform of Six Realists" (1910), in which Perry, W.B. Pitkin and others propose a new, collaborative realist agenda for philosophy. Although each writer lists several distinct theses, they are in broad agreement about the following:

- The "doctrine of internal relations" is false. The doctrine states that all relations are "internal" or essential to the nature of their bearers. It entails that no object can change any of its relations to other objects without thereby becoming a different object or changing its essential nature.
- The relation of knowing is not an internal relation; it neither constitutes nor "conditions" its objects.
- Objects exist and have their natures fixed independently of our knowing them, and our knowing about them does not affect their existence or essential natures.

New Realists commonly cite two claims in support of their views: (1) New Realism represents the views of the common man, and therefore constitutes the default philosophical position, in arguing against which the idealist or subjectivist bears the burden of proof; (2) the truth of New Realism is a necessary presupposition for the success of science, so those who argue against it threaten to undermine scientific knowledge and practice.

Critics of New Realism argued that the doctrine had one overriding weakness; it could not offer a satisfactory account of how error was possible, given our supposed direct contact with the objects of perception. These critics agreed that the problem was the New Realists' "immediatism," or their insistence that knowledge of the world must be achievable immediately or directly, rather than through a medium of representation. The resulting consensus among New Realism's critics became "Critical Realism," whose chief advocates were J.B. Pratt, R.W. Sellars, A.O. Lovejoy and George Santayana. Because Critical Realists posited an interface between the mind and the external world, they were able to explain error as the malfunctioning of this interface. Divisions among Critical Realists were deep, however, and focused on the difficulty of specifying whether something like sense data or a logical entity such as a universal constituted the datum of knowledge. Controversy also arose over whether Critical Realism had *dualist* implications (knower/known or mind/body). As a result, Critical Realism also failed to make a substantial constructive impact.

This is not so with pragmatism, which has been arguably the most successful and influential American philosophy. Pragmatism's relationship with realism is complex. Many critics object to pragmatist ideas – especially its account of truth – because they consider it incompatible with realism. Pragmatists certainly offer a variety of arguments against what they call "metaphysical realism," though in doing so they may only be arguing for a subtler alternative. Pragmatism's founder C.S. Peirce, for example, shows clear realist inclinations: in his early work he vehemently opposes nominalism and in his later work advocates an extreme form of realism, by asserting the reality of what he calls "secondness" and "thirdness." Peirce's fellow pragmatists take a somewhat different stance, however, and Dewey's work, if not also James's, seems to many to undermine the very kinds of question to which realism provides an answer (see e.g. Hildebrand 2003; Rorty 1991).

Contemporary "neo-pragmatists" continue to disagree about the appropriate relationship between pragmatism and realism. Hilary Putnam, for example, has long drawn inspiration from pragmatist thinkers in constructing his arguments for "internal realism" (Putnam 1981) and later "pragmatic realism" (Putnam 2004). Richard Rorty on the other hand has drawn on Dewey's work to advance what critics regard as a radical relativism, and which he calls "ethnocentrism" (Rorty 1991).

Further reading

Hildebrand, D. *Beyond Realism and Anti-Realism: John Dewey and the Neopragmatists.* Nashville, TN: Vanderbilt University Press, 2003.

Holt, E.B., Marvin, W.B., Montague, W.P., Perry, R.B., Pitkin, W.B., and Spaulding, E.G. "The Program and First Platform of Six Realists," *Journal of Philosophy, Psychology and Scientific Methods* 7, 15 (1910): 393–401.

Pratt, J.B. "Critical Realism and the Possibility of Knowledge" in Durant Drake, Arthur O. Lovejoy, James B. Pratt, Arthur K. Rogers, George Santayana, Roy W. Sellars and C.A. Strong, *Essays in Critical Realism.* New York: Macmillan, 1920.

Andrew W. Howat

REALISM: SCHOLASTIC

One of two major positions developed during medieval times regarding the problem of universals (ultimately, the question of the ontological status of concepts and hence of our knowledge of the world). Considered by many to have reached its maximum expression in John Duns Scotus's (c. 1266–1308) version, scholastic (moderate) realism is intermediate between two extremes: at one end is Platonic realism, which claims that only universals (the Forms, e.g. "Horseness," Beauty, etc.) are real, inhabiting a separate realm from the one in which individual things (e.g. horses, beautiful statues), mere copies of the Forms and therefore not real, reside. At the other end is nominalism, famously advocated by William of Ockham (c. 1287–1347), claiming that only individual things exist and are real, and that universals, since they are words or concepts, do not exist, and are not real. Scotus strikes a compromise: while agreeing with nominalists that universals are mind-dependent, that only individual things have actual existence, and that individual things are real, he maintains, against nominalists, that universals are also real. This involves the claim that there is an actual repeatable structure, an entity called a "nature," in the individual things themselves, which, through the complicated process of abstraction, is imprinted on the intellect by means of the senses. This abstracted nature is the basis for the universal concept (e.g. horse), which, although a product of the mind, is not mere fiction since it actually originates in the real existent thing and is henceforth recognized in all particular instances of it (e.g. this particular object is a horse). Scotus's elaborate theory allows for the relation of predicability, guaranteeing the truth of our conceptions, thereby safeguarding our claims to knowledge about the world. Scotus also preserves the integrity of the individual thing: this common nature is "contracted" into one unique singularity (its "haecceity") in each individual thing (e.g. although horseness is common to both Bucephalus and Trigger, it is manifested in Bucephalus as his "haecceity," which is non-repeatable, just as Trigger's is unique to Trigger). In this way Scotus avoids the extremism of Platonic realism by denying that the nature can exist by itself apart from individual things.

Charles Sanders Peirce (1839–1914), the founder of pragmatism, claimed that what distinguishes his theory (which he eventually dubbed "pragmaticism") from rival versions is his insistence on the truth of scholastic realism. Crediting Scotus with recognizing another kind of real being besides existence, Peirce's metaphysical categories of Firstness (possibility), Secondness (existence), and Thirdness (law, or regularity), as well as his definition of "reality" reflect Scotus's influence. Also sharing Scotus's epistemological concern about the truth of our conceptions, Peirce claims that science is based on the assumption that universals ("generals" as Peirce called them) are real; i.e. that general laws really operate in nature. Though initially siding with Scotus's brand of realism, Peirce eventually distanced himself from it, claiming he was more of an "extreme scholastic realist" than Scotus. Although Peirce never said explicitly what he meant by this, he did not side with the Platonic kind (he claimed the latter to be nominalistic since it posed the existence of universals). Rather, Peirce's objection seems to be centered on Scotus's theory of contraction, since grounding the nature of things in the individual is too limiting and does not recognize the continuity or open-endedness of laws.

Further reading

Duns Scotus, John. *Questions on the Metaphysics of Aristotle*, trans. Girard J. Etzkorn and Allan B. Wolter, OFM. St Bonaventure, NY: Franciscan Institute Publications, 1998.

Gracia, Jorge. *Individuation in Scholasticism*. Albany, NY: SUNY Press, 1994.

Haack, Susan. "Extreme Scholastic Realism: Its Relevance to Philosophy of Science Today," *Transactions of the Charles S. Peirce Society* XXVIII (1992): 19–50.

Hookway, Christopher. *Truth, Rationality, and Pragmatism*. Oxford: Oxford University Press, 2000.

King, Peter. "Duns Scotus on the Common Nature and the Individual Differentia," *Philosophical Topics* 20 (1992): 51–77.

Mayorga, Rosa M. "The Hair: On the Difference between Peirce's Nominalism and His Realism," *Transactions of the Charles S. Peirce Society* XL, 3 (summer 2004): 433–55.

Wolter, Allan. *The Philosophical Theology of John Duns Scotus*. Ithaca, NY: Cornell University Press, 1990.

Rosa Maria Mayorga

REALITY

Reality is that which is unaffected by what you, or I, or anyone in particular thinks it to be. This conception may be called the Scotistic conception of reality, as John Duns Scotus (1266–1308) originally introduced its Latin origin (*realis*) as a technical term into philosophy. Reality is contrasted with products of the understanding, such as dreams, or figments of the imagination.

From the Renaissance on, the Scotistic conception of reality has been interpreted predominantly in terms of the outward constraints on which the understanding has no control. On this interpretation, only the absolute external causes of perception are real, and reality is taken to be equivalent with existence. In short, only what exists is real. With his notion of *substratum*, John Locke presents a prime example of this view in the second book of his *Essay* (1975: 298). This interpretation of Scotus's conception of reality is a driving force behind the metaphysical position called *nominalism*. The nominalist denies the reality of universals precisely because they cannot be experienced as direct outward constraints. As a result, universals, natural laws, etc., must be products of the mind, inspired by our sensory experience, and to be confirmed or falsified by the latter.

However, as Charles Peirce discovered, this modern nominalistic reading of "reality" is too restrictive as there are other ways in which objects of thought can be independent of what anyone in particular thinks them to be. For instance, a conclusion we are forced to draw when all the facts are known, and the idiosyncrasies of individual minds are filtered out, meets the Scotistic conception in that this conclusion will be independent of what anyone in particular thinks it to be. Consequently, besides outward constraints, some products of the understanding may be real as well as they too can be independent of what anyone *in particular* thinks them to be. This second interpretation of reality – which does not require that everything that is real must also exist – allows for a *realist* interpretation of universals, natural laws, possibilities, etc., thereby avoiding the nominalist's predicament of having to classify them all as mere figments of the imagination. On this realist interpretation everything that exists will be real, but not everything that is real needs to exist. The distinction between reality and existence also allows Peirce to argue for the reality of God while denying its existence (1998: 434). The realist conception of reality also plays a central role in Peirce's theory of inquiry in which reality is what would be the object of the opinion that all who investigate ultimately are fated to agree upon if their inquiry were to continue sufficiently long.

As the above reveals, existence falls in a category more restrictive than reality in that anything that exists is not merely independent of what anyone in particular thinks about *it*, but is independent of what anyone in particular thinks about *anything*; that is to say, no matter what we think about anything, the absolutely external causes of our perception remain wholly unaffected. Moreover, on the Scotistic conception, reality consists in *an independence of thought*; it is not a mode of being, like existence or possibility. Hence, one cannot really fault the realist for a lack of ontological parsimony. The Peircean approach differs in this respect from the approach of Alexius Meinong (especially in the interpretation of Bertrand Russell), which is largely ontological.

Reacting against those who hold that reality is fixed and complete from all eternity, and which is represented in knowledge very much like an object being reproduced in a mirror, William James and F.C.S. Schiller maintain that the universe itself is both unfinished and open-ended, and that we humans are makers of reality. Schiller explicitly argues that we *make* reality out of what is given to us in the same way a carpenter *makes* a chair out of the materials that are available to him. The material given to us is uninterpreted sensation – what James identifies with the blooming buzzing confusion as it appears to a child when it first opens its eyes. A similar view is found in C.I. Lewis, who considers reality a product of the application of an a priori conceptual scheme to what he calls, with occasional references to James, "the given."

Further reading

De Waal, Cornelis, "Peirce's Nominalist-Realist Distinction: An Untenable Dualism" *Transactions of the Charles S. Peirce Society* 34, 1 (1998): 183–202.

Lewis, C.I., "The Pragmatic Conception of the A Priori" *Journal of Philosophy* 20, 7 (1923): 169–77.

Locke, John. *An Essay Concerning Human Understanding*. Oxford: Clarendon Press, 1975.

Meinong, Alexius. "Existence and Being" in *Logic and Philosophy*, ed. Gary Iseminger. New York: Appleton-Century-Crofts, 1968, pp. 116–27.

Peirce, Charles S. *The Essential Peirce*, 2 vols. Bloomington, IN: Indiana University Press, 1992, 1998.

CORNELIS DE WAAL

RECONSTRUCTION

The theme of reconstruction is almost entirely absent in early American philosophical writings. Puritans and Calvinists from John Winthrop and Cotton Mather to Jonathan Edwards were focused on revelation and the next world rather than reconstruction in this one. Similarly, Deists and American Enlightenment writers from Benjamin Franklin to Thomas Paine and Thomas Jefferson were concerned (in their writings, if not in their politics) more with the recognition by reason of eternal and universal natural law than with the ongoing reconstruction of merely temporal realities and local values.

In nineteenth- and twentieth-century American transcendentalism and pragmatism, however, the theme of reconstruction emerged as central. In the philosophy of Ralph Waldo Emerson, William James, and John Dewey, and in the poetry of Walt Whitman, the legal theory of Oliver Wendell Holmes, Jr, and the social theory of W.E.B. DuBois and Jane Addams, for example, wide-ranging cultural changes, new experiences, and pressing problems were seen as demands for reconstruction *in* philosophy so that it could account adequately for these new realities. In turn, this effort paralleled a reconstruction *of* philosophy, such that philosophy itself came to be considered properly an intellectual agent of progressive change and critical adjustment rather than a passive compendium of unchanging wisdom.

In "The American Scholar," the essay Holmes called America's declaration of intellectual independence, Emerson proclaimed that America's long dependence on the philosophies of other lands and other times must end. He called on the country's "sluggard intellect" self-reliantly to sing its own, new life. For Emerson, because reality itself is an ongoing process of reconstruction, accounts of reality must also constantly be reconstructed. The experience of one person, country or age differs from, and does not capture, that of all others. Genius, Emerson argued, looks forward – in philosophy as in life – and so each generation must rewrite or reconstruct the books of earlier generations.

This same commitment to an unfinished, open, always in-the-making, pluralistic universe pervades the philosophy of William James. Like Emerson, James didn't view philosophy as an impersonal account of permanent truths, but instead as personal vision and expression of individual character and preferences in response to the whole drift of one's life. In this light, offering his pragmatism as an alternative both to traditional tough-minded empiricism and to equally traditional tender-minded idealism, James sought not to solve old problems but rather to dissolve them and, so to reconstruct philosophy itself.

This notion is most fully developed in the work of John Dewey. In writings such as the 1917 "The Need for a Recovery of Philosophy" to the 1920 *Reconstruction in Philosophy* to his 1948 new introduction to this book, "Reconstruction as Seen Twenty-Five Years Later," Dewey set forth two interrelated theses. First, he argued that changes in social life, including science, had rendered obsolete old philosophical problems – not just various proposed solutions to the problems, but the whole problems. Intellectual advance in philosophy, he held, required that these problems be abandoned – and this is the destructive component in all reconstruction. Instead, he advocated a naturalistic orientation and an experimental approach. Rejecting old-fashioned speculative responses to problems generated by supposed metaphysical dualisms – God and nature, mind and matter, fact and value, means and ends, self and others, experience and nature, and so on – Dewey sought to reconstruct philosophy by treating it as the culturally situated articulation of the values to which persons are most deeply attached and as an organ for dealing intelligently and imaginatively with conflicts among these attachments. It proceeds, he continued, not by positing dualisms, but by identifying and evaluating the values realized and the interests served by thinking in some way rather than others.

Dewey's second main thesis was that this reconstruction in philosophy must be accompanied by the reconstruction of philosophy itself. Philosophy is cultural criticism, and as criticism it concerns values and meanings. The need for this criticism is immense: Rapid and far-reaching material and physical changes have outstripped, but have not replaced, our traditional values. Philosophy accordingly must develop the values and meanings and the direction of these new realities. This task, Dewey stressed, always takes place on behalf of some interests; an honest philosophy must acknowledge rather than deny these interests. In Dewey's own work, and in that of many philosophically oriented social philosophers and activists in America, this reconstruction of philosophy made it an instrument for social criticism on issues such as labor, women's rights, race and civil rights, the environment, and war and violence.

Further reading

Dewey, John. "Philosophy and American National Life," *John Dewey: The Middle Works, 1899–1924, Vol. 3* ed. Jo Ann Boydston. Carbondale, IL: Southern Illinois University Press, 1977 [1905], pp. 73–8.

—— "The Need for a Recovery of Philosophy" in *John Dewey: The Middle Works, 1899–1924, Vol. 10*, ed. Jo Ann Boydston. Carbondale, IL: Southern Illinois University Press, 1980 [1917].

—— *Reconstruction in Philosophy* (including the 1948 "Introduction: Reconstruction as Seen Twenty-Five Years Later") in *John Dewey: The Middle Works, 1899–1924, Vol. 12*, ed. Jo Ann Boydston. Carbondale, IL: Southern Illinois University Press, 1982 [1920, 1948 reprint].

Emerson, Ralph Waldo, "Nature: Introduction," "The American Scholar," and "The Divinity School Address," *Nature, Addresses, and Lectures*, Vol. 1. Boston, MA: Houghton Mifflin, 1904 [1836, 1837, 1838].

Gavin, William J. *In Dewey's Wake: Unfinished Work of Pragmatic Reconstruction*. Albany, NY: SUNY Press, 2003.

James, William. "The Types of Philosophic Thinking" in *The Works of William James: A Pluralistic Universe*, ed. Frederick Burkhardt. Cambridge, MA: Harvard University Press, 1977 [1903].

Stuhr, John J. (ed.). *Philosophy and the Reconstruction of Culture: Pragmatic Essays after Dewey.* Albany, NY: SUNY Press, 1993.

JOHN J. STUHR

REFLEX ARC

A reflex arc is a neural pathway of incoming sensory nerves and outgoing motor nerves that facilitates reflex action, one of the basic processes in the nervous system. Reflex arcs can pass through the spinal cord or the brain and, in their simplest forms, result in automatic neuromuscular action. An understanding of the role of the reflex arc developed slowly over the course of the nineteenth and twentieth centuries through the work of many anatomists, physiologists, psychologists, and philosophers.

For many, the reflex arc supported a mechanistic view of the nervous system. T.H. Huxley, for example, argued that animals, and human beings as well, are conscious automata. Often aware of the activity taking place along the reflex arcs, consciousness is incapable of intervening to change it. Although he initially accepted this mechanistic view, William James soon rejected it, arguing that consciousness would not have evolved if it did not play some important adaptive function. James argued that this adaptive function was to select which of many possible responses to incoming sensations would be most helpful to the organism.

It would be difficult to overestimate the impact the reflex arc theory had on William James's thought. In an early lecture, he approvingly observed that most physiologists would agree that all actions – not just automatic ones – follow the reflex type. The reflex arc makes an important explicit or implicit appearance in each of his subsequent books, with the entire second volume of his *Principles of Psychology* organized around it.

D.C. Phillips has pointed out that there is a close connection between James's views on reflex action and his pragmatism. In describing the reflex arc, James argued for a teleological relation among its three interdependent components. He wrote, "The sensory impression exists only for the sake of awakening the central process of reflection, and the central process of reflection exists only for the sake of calling for the final act," and argued that if reflection "led to no active measures, it would fail of its essential function, and would have to be considered either pathological or abortive" (James 1979: 92). James's pragmatism, too, emphasized the practical importance of thought, with both meaning and truth determined by the world of experience.

John Dewey, too, was deeply influenced by the reflex arc theory, although he was critical of certain aspects of it. He agreed with James that it represented an important advance in physiology and psychology, but he thought the reflex arc should be thought of as more of a circuit, since behavior influences perception just as surely as perception influences behavior. Given this complexity of influence, he suggested that the relation is less reflex than organic.

Further reading

Dewey, John. "The Reflex Arc Concept in Psychology" in *The Essential Dewey*, 2 vols, ed. L.A. Hickman and T.M. Alexander. Reprint, Bloomington, NY: Indiana University Press, 1998 [1896], pp. 3–10.

James, William. "Reflex Action and Theism" in *The Will to Believe and Other Essays in Popular Philosophy.* Cambridge, MA: Harvard University Press, 1979, pp. 90–113.

Phillips, D.C. "James, Dewey, and the Reflex Arc," *Journal of the History of Ideas*, 32, 4 (1971): 555–68.

JAMES O. PAWELSKI

REFORM (V. REVOLUTION)

Revolution means fundamental changes from one political or economic system to another. Revolutions can be either total or partial and either violent or peaceful. Reform means lesser or incremental changes, improvements within the system without jettisoning or exchanging the system. The question is: Should those suffering from the deficiencies of a political or economic system, and those who sympathize with them, settle for piecemeal reforms or demand fundamental revolution? Following are seven different, important answers to this given in the American experience since the Civil War.

Karl Marx and his followers are absolutists who demand violent political and economic revolution. To Marx, democratic capitalism is spurious democracy in which the majority of the rich rule, and capitalism means the exploitation by the bourgeoisie of the working class. According to Marx's dialectical materialism, there are laws of the historical development of society. These necessitate violent revolution by the exploited classes until politics disappears and a classless socialism arrives to endure permanently as the end or goal of history. Any attempts at or grants of reform would be useless attempts of exploiters to delay the dialectical changes that will disempower them.

John Dewey rejects absolutism and believes Marx misunderstands science. Dewey also wanted the advent of socialism, though of a non-Marxist sort. So he sometimes voted for the Socialist Party presidential candidates, Eugene V. Debs and Norman Thomas. That is, Dewey wanted the peaceful revolution of exchanging capitalism for socialism that he hoped our democratic procedures would allow. He thought Marx's predictions of violent revolution dangerous self-fulfilling prophesies.

Dewey thought democratic elections might allow the peaceful but revolutionary change to socialism. It is also the case that our democratic Constitution's amendment process would allow this change so that a large majority here could achieve revolutionary ends without violence.

The Progressive movement of the late nineteenth and early twentieth centuries sought and achieved reforms without revolution, without fundamental changes in our political or economic systems. Democratic elections were enough to achieve, for instance, referendum and recall, the Pure Food and Drug Act and Meat Inspection Act, and the thirteenth to nineteenth Amendments to the Constitution.

Like Dewey and the Progressives, the pragmatist William James eschewed absolutism in favor of the provisional. Not revolution but reform is human in scale. Improvements, incremental changes, piecemeal amelioration, gradual betterment, is the way. He called his moderating doctrine *meliorism* (from the Latin *melior*, better) to distinguish it from optimism (from *optime*, best) and pessimism (from *pessime*, worst).

Again like Dewey and the Progressives, Reverend Martin Luther King, Jr, helped direct the black civil rights movement of the 1960 to seek and achieve peaceful reforms. Revolution was unnecessary. He estimated correctly that, as long as blacks were non-violent, our democratic politics would grant even civilly disobedient blacks federal and court reforms of state and county policies and laws.

The first six items here assume American citizens feeling, at the worst, oppressed by the American government. But what if the American government oppresses the citizens of other countries? The historian Walter LaFeber wrote a book, *Inevitable Revolutions: The United States in Central America*. The title is meant to say that because the United States' foreign policy made reforms in Central America impossible, it made revolutions there inevitable. His story is an unpleasant one for Americans to hear. Our governments have so feared socialism that they have made impossible the democratic reforms desired by the poor majorities in Central America. Reforms blocked, these desperate people sought change by violent revolutions, revolutions that the United States then helped crush.

Further reading

Hofstadter, Richard. *The Age of Reform*. New York: Vintage Books, 1955.

King, Martin Luther, Jr. *Why We Can't Wait*. New York: Signet Books, 1963.

LaFeber, Walter. *Inevitable Revolutions: The United States in Central America*. New York: W.W. Norton, 1984.

McDermott, John J. (ed.). *The Writings of William James*. New York: Modern Library, 1968.

McLellan, David, (ed.). *Marxism: Essential Writings*. New York: Oxford University Press, 1988.

Westbrook, Robert B. *John Dewey and American Democracy*. Ithaca, NY: Cornell University Press, 1991.

JOSEPH BETZ

REICHENBACH, HANS

Hans Reichenbach (1891–1953) earned degrees in physics and philosophy, was a professor of philosophy of physics at the University of Berlin (1926–33) and of philosophy at the universities of Istanbul (1933–38) and Berkeley Los Angeles (CA) (1938–53). He was sympathetic to logical positivism and is considered the most representative member of the Circle of Berlin, the physicalist German equivalent of the Circle of Vienna.

Among Einstein's first students (1919), Reichenbach focused his studies on philosophy of science and epistemology. Reichenbach's first essay, *The Theory of Relativity and a Priori Knowledge* (*Relativitaetstheorie und Erkenntnis a priori*) (1920), objects Kant's doctrine of a priori forms of experience as at odds with the scientific account of space and time as stated in Einstein's theory of general relativity. Later on, Reichenbach's studies of the problem of space and time find a more extensive and technical account and solution in the fundamental work *The Philosophy of Space and Time* (*Raum-Zeit Lehre*) (1928): space and time are not intuitions but a system of relations able to describe the physical world. Reichenbach generally rejects altogether the idea of a priori principles or conditions of knowledge since the materials of knowledge are to be found through experience only. Along this line he approaches logical positivism and becomes the leading member of the Berliner Kreis, namely, the German equivalent of the Wiener Kreis (Vienna Circle). The rejection of the a priori leads Reichenbach to a second set of problems concerned with causality, induction and truth. Although connected to the other members of the Wiener Kreis, in particular Rudolf Carnap, with whom he was the co-editor of *Erkenntnis*, the official journal of logical positivism, Reichenbach rejects the positivist *truth theory of meaning* based on two-valued logic (True/False) and adopts a probability theory of meaning based on his own general theory of probability as expounded in *The Theory of Probability* (*Wahrscheinlichkeitslehre*) (1935).

Reichenbach attains an holistic view according to which probability is not to be referred to a single proposition but to more comprehensive logical items called "propositional series." Such a development of the theory of probability allows Reichenbach to try a solution of David Hume's classical problem of induction. Hume's skepticism is justified insofar as we are bound within the domain of two-valued logic, yet it is to be overcome, for life as well as the practice of science in order to generate useful predictions. Prediction, however, is possible and has a degree of *weight* only if we use the logic of probablility of which two-valued logic and truth theory of meaning are but special instances. An effective prediction is the result of the application of inductive inference to a "probability lattice" of events: "The aim of induction is to find a series of event whose frequency of occurrence converges toward a limit."

Reichenbach's stress on the practical value of prediction and his account of experience as probability inference leads him closer to pragmatism, namely to Peirce's theory of chance and James's doctrine of belief and holistic empiricism, as it is suggested in *Experience and Prediction* (1938). Science and knowledge always entail *voluntary decisions* about their preliminary conditions and aims and the system of science is but a system of concatenated wages that as a whole has no foundation.

Further reading

Reichenbach, Hans. *Experience and Prediction: An Analysis of the Foundations and the Structure of Knowledge*. Chicago, IL: University of Chicago Press, 1938.

—— *The Rise of Scientific Philosophy*. Los Angeles, CA: University of California Press, 1951.

—— *The Philosophy of Space and Time*. New York: Dover, 1958.

—— *Hans Reichenbach, Logical Empiricist*. Boston, MA: D. Reidel, 1979.

—— *Logic, Language, and the Structure of Scientific Theories: Proceedings of the Carnap-Reichenbach Centennial, University of Konstanz, 21–24 May 1991*. Pittsburgh, PA: University of Pittsburgh Press, 1991.

SERGIO FRANZESE

RELATIONS

Relations posed both a metaphysical and an epistemological problem for classical American pragmatists. The former concerns how relations are possible at all and the latter how they can be known. Since the manner in which William James and John Dewey dealt with these problems were the most searching and influential, the focus will be on their writings.

The metaphysical problem

James claimed that the ultimate parting of the ways between philosophers was due to their rival "sentiments of rationality" concerning what constitutes an intellectually satisfying explanation. One prominent example of this is the perennial clash between the Humean atomizers and the Spinozistic unifiers. The atomizers explain a given subject matter by breaking it up into its atomistic constituents, whatever they might be, each of which is capable of existing independently and separately from all of the others. There is no problem of explaining how relations are possible. They just are, and that's all there is to it. End of story. In contrast, the question of how things can get connected together is a profound one for the unifiers, and they are prepared to give a metaphysical explanation of how this is possible.

James and Dewey, along with their absolute idealist opponents, ascribed to what could aptly be called the Humpty Dumpty Principle: If you ever allow reality to fall apart into numerically distinct individuals (as do the Humeans), there is no way in which they can be reassembled into relational complexes. In stating this Principle, Dewey even alludes to the fate of poor Humpty Dumpty.

> [Nonempirical] methods begin with results of a reflection that has already torn in two the subject-matter [organism and environment] experienced and the operations and states of experiencing. The problem is then to get together again what has been sundered – which is as if the king's men started with the fragments of the egg and tried to construct that whole egg out of them.

The same Humpty Dumpty Principle informs James's claim that "immediate feeling possesses a native wholeness which conceptual treatment analyzes into a many, *but can't unite*." He said that for Humean atomists, "there is no discrimination without separation; no separation without absolute 'independence' and thereupon impossibility of union."

Both men agree that the way to prevent Humpty Dumpty from falling off the wall is to deny that the relata in a direct (nonmediated) relation are numerically distinct from each other. Relata in a mediated relation will be connected by a chain of such direct relations. James claimed, in particular, that adjacent neighbors in space and time mush together in a way that makes each the Hegelian other of the other.

> every individual morsel of the sensational stream takes up the adjacent morsels by coalescing with them ... that no part absolutely excludes another, but that they compenetrate and are cohesive; that if you tear out one,

> its roots bring out more with them; that whatever is real is telescoped and diffused into other reals; that, in short, every minutest things is already its hegelian "own other," in the fullest sense of the term.

James's descriptions of this "Hegelian" coalescing relation are rich in gaseous and watery metaphors of "melting, merging, fusing, and flowing together," "undergoing endosmosis," "compenetrating," as well as "telescoping" and "diffusing" into each other.

James realized that his mushing together relation defies the ordinary logic of identity, since it gives us an "identity" that is not really an identity because it is non-transitive – that x is "identical" with y and y is "identical" with z does not entail that x is "identical" with z – and for this reason characterized his doctrine of relations as "pluralistic mysticism" in *A Pluralistic Universe.* James realized that his concept of a nontransitive identity "will sound queer and dark" but claimed that it had good phenomenological credentials since our experience of change vouchsafed that successive stages "are their own others, and indeed are so in the self-same sense in which the absolute is maintained to be so by Hegel." Spatial neighbors also behave like Playdoh. "What is true here of successive states must also be true of simultaneous characters. They also overlap each other with their being." "You can't confine content." James seems to be saying, if I may paraphrase the punch line to the old shaggy dog joke, that these immediate neighbors, be they in space or time, are identical but not that identical.

When Dewey, circa World War II, was preoccupied with the challenge to democracy posed by totalitarianism, he appealed to James's pluralistic mysticism to show how a society can be both unified and yet contain genuine individuals. The needed unification could be realized if immediately conjoined neighbor-citizens were fused together by James's nontransitive "identity" relation.

Throughout his long career, Dewey staunchly adhered to the Humpty Dumpty Principle. It took the form of a methodological principle that enjoins us, whenever we are confronted by an apparent dualism, that is, numerically distinct objects, to show how they emanate out of some background unity in terms of how they function within inquiry. His 1884 doctoral dissertation charged Kant with committing the cardinal sin of beginning with a dualism between the subject of experience and its numerically distinct object, thereby rendering it impossible to show how the subject and object can stand in epistemic relations to each other, such as the subject's perceiving and knowing the object. He tells us:

> The relation of subject and object is not a "transcendent" one, but an "immanent," and is but the first form which Reason manifests that it is both synthetic and analytic; that it separates itself from itself, that it may thereby reach higher unity with itself.
>
> (EW 1.41)

There is an all-enveloping background Consciousness or Reason, which is Hegel's Absolute Idea, that "differentiates itself so as to give rise to the existence within, that is for, itself of subject and object." Therefore, "The relation of subject and object is one which exists within consciousness." This sounds a lot like the traditional mystical doctrine of emanations and could earn Dewey the sobriquet of "The Plotinus of Burlington."

When Dewey made the transition from Hegelianism to instrumentalism, also called "experimentalism" and "pragmatism," he changed the background unity out of which the subject and object emanate from universal consciousness or Reason to "experience," with the subject and object now being called respectively "organism" and "environment." Herein he was pouring old wine into a new bottle, and it is no wonder that no one ever understood what Dewey meant by "experience," for it has ceased to be a contrastive term since it now is the totality of what is.

In a 1915 letter to Scudder Klyce he writes that "the 'one' is always pluralizing and recovering its diversities before they escape (or become plural) and thereby keeping itself going." In 1929 Dewey wrote that

> To non-empirical method . . . object and subject, mind and matter . . . are separate and independent. Therefore it has upon its hands the problem of how it is possible to know at all; how an outer world can affect an inner mind; how the acts of mind can reach out and lay hold of objects defined in antithesis to them. Naturally it is at a loss for an answer.
>
> We have no ready-made distinction between the individual agent and the world of experience over against him . . . each is built up out of a common material by contemporaneous processes.

One can recognize in these later, mature comments of Dewey the same Humpty Dumpty Intuition that informs his very early views.

The epistemological problem

The bane of Humean psychological atomism is that it cannot account for how we derive our concept of relations, especially temporal ones, given that, for him, our concepts must be derived from sense experience. For a succession of discrete impressions is not an impression of succession.

Kant, in basic agreement with Hume's atomistic account of sense experience, made the relational categories part of the a priori machinery of a transcendental ego. James and Dewey, in an attempt to avoid having to countenance such a non-natural ego, countered that both Hume and Kant had inaccurately introspected their own sensory experience because they failed to note that relations are given in the same immediate and direct way that sensory ideas are, which is one of the three tenets that compose James' Radical Empiricism. James wrote that "if there be such things as feeling at all, then so surely as relations between objects exist in rerum natura, so surely, and more surely, do feelings exist to which these relations are known." Dewey gave a similar diagnosis: "For, making clear the non-empirical character of the alleged manifold of unconnected particulars [of Hume and Kant], it would render unnecessary the appeal to the functions of the understanding [of Kant] in order to connect them."

The dispute between James–Dewey and Hume–Kant over what is given in introspection is a queer one. It is made to appear as if it concerns whose introspective eyesight is superior. I think that the disputants are engaging in a Jack Horner type of introspection in which they can pull out of their introspective pie whatever is philosophically required. The disputants begin with their own a priori criteria as to what can be a possible object of introspection. James agrees with Hume that we do not have a sensory image or "idea" of a relation but insists that nevertheless we have a "feeling" or "thought" of a relation, which are James's most generic terms for consciousness. Would Hume or Kant want to challenge James's contention? Is not their dispute a purely verbal one?

Further reading

Dewey, John. *John Dewey: The Early Works, Vol. 1* (EW), ed. Jo Ann Boydston. Carbondale, IL: Southern Illinois University Press, 1969, pp. 9, 34–47, 122–43.

—— *John Dewey: The Middle Works, Vol. 10* (MW), ed. Jo Ann Boydston. Carbondale, IL: Southern Illinois University Press, 1985, pp. 3–48.

—— *John Dewey: The Later Works, Vol. 1* (LW), ed. Jo Ann Boydston. Carbondale, IL: Southern Illinois University Press, 1988.

James, William. *A Pluralistic Universe.* Cambridge, MA: Harvard University Press, 1977.

—— *Some Problems of Philosophy.* Cambridge, MA: Harvard University Press, 1979.

—— *The Principles of Psychology.* Cambridge, MA: Harvard University Press, 1981.

Richard M. Gale

RELATIVITY, THEORY OF

Traditionally, spacetime has been thought of as a continuum of events. An event is uniquely characterized by four numbers – three numbers for its spatial position and one for its time. The Newtonian picture further assumes that spacetime has the following structure: Given some event p, the set of events that are simultaneous (i.e. "at the same time") as p is defined independently of any observer. In particular, the simultaneous events to p form an absolute three-dimensional surface in spacetime.

Special relativity theory rejects the assumption of observer-independent simultaneity (in fact, one might say that it demonstrates this since the observer-dependence of simultaneity is not actually one of the theory's two postulates). The observer can still define the notion of simultaneity with respect to some event, but the three-dimensional surface so defined will depend on the state of motion of the observer. To derive the consequences of this radical shift in the way we conceptualize simultaneity, we can consider an inertial observer *O* (an observer who is not subjected to any external forces) who is passed by another inertial observer *O*'. How will *O*' label (with coordinates) an event p relative to the way *O* labels *p*? Given the constancy of the speed of light and some elementary geometrical considerations, one can derive a set of coordinate transformations – known as Lorentz transformations – that reduce to the usual Newtonian transformations at low speeds while differing markedly at speeds significant to the speed of light. At such high speeds, two physical effects have been predicted by special relativity and experimentally verified, viz. the Lorentz contraction and time dilation. The former concerns the length contraction of material bodies and the latter concerns the slowing down of clock measurements (and is sometimes described as the "slowing down of time").

Many philosophers claim to have found support for their favorite metaphysical theses in special relativity. Among the issues on which special relativity is said to bear is the question of how objects persist through time. Roughly speaking, do they exist as temporal extensions with temporal parts (four dimensionalism) or do they exist as wholly present at a point in time (three dimensionalism)? A familiar strategy in arguing for the former is to capitalize on the notion of observer-relative simultaneity that is inherent in special relativity; I provide a brief sketch in what follows (the exact argument requires some careful setting-up and qualification). Suppose that the set of events simultaneous with an event p form the present for an observer – these events are thus equally real/determinate. Furthermore, suppose that reality is an observer-independent notion. Now, given the existence of at least two observers and the observer-dependence of simultaneity, one can try to force the conclusion that the future is already real/determinate for any observer. The moral then drawn is that the present of an observer is just a three-dimensional cross-section of his four-dimensional existence. However, there has been no lack of objections to this argument in contemporary literature. At any rate, it is unclear that arguments based on physical theory should result in skepticism or revisionism about our common-sense concepts of persistence through time, at least in the domain of everyday experience.

Given the success of special relativity, it is natural to ask if our formulations of physical laws are consistent with this theory. Maxwell's theory of electromagnetism is consistent with special relativity. Newtonian gravitation, however, is not. In particular, the instantaneous force exerted by one body on another violates special relativity by allowing one to construct a notion of absolute simultaneity. Einstein's solution to this problem was to construct a completely new theory of gravitation: general relativity.

General relativity is based on two principles. First, the Equivalence Principle says that all bodies are influenced by gravity and that they all fall in the same way. This motivates the idea that gravity is not really a "separate" field but is part of the structure of spacetime; e.g. a curved spacetime geometry can dictate the manner in which bodies fall (this statement is made precise by the apparatus of differential geometry). Second, Mach's principle expresses the idea that the structure of spacetime is influenced by the presence of material bodies. As John Wheeler's famous maxim puts it, "Matter tells space how to curve. Space tells matter how to move." More precisely, the fundamental equation of general relativity – Einstein's equation – relates the curvature of spacetime to the matter distribution in spacetime.

Admittedly, Einstein's achievement was not the only effort made to generalize special relativity. For largely philosophical reasons, Alfred North Whitehead sought to develop a theory in which the gravitational field was independent and ontologically distinct from the geometry of spacetime. He was especially critical of the founding principles of general relativity because he thought they contained the following circularity: Length and time are only defined after one has solved the Einstein equations. But to solve the equations, one has to plug in initial conditions in terms of length and time.

Although the initial calculations made with Whitehead's theory yielded results that were fairly similar to those of general relativity, gravitational redshift experiments have shown that the theory requires major modifications if it is to be tenable. General relativity – having thus far faced the tribunal of experiment successfully – is now accepted as orthodoxy by mathematicians, physicists, and philosophers.

If special relativity can be thought of as a playground of sorts for the metaphysician, then general relativity is still very much uncharted territory that awaits philosophical exploration. Here is a brief sampling of some issues in general relativity that might be of interest to philosophers:

1 The hole argument: Is spacetime a substance that exists independently of the processes that go on in it, or is its existence dependent on such processes? The mathematical framework of general relativity, as well as its physical interpretation, readily lends the theory to an analysis of this problem.
2 The definition of mass and energy: Concepts such as mass and energy in general relativity are radically different from their classical counterparts. Furthermore they do not seem to admit of a general definition; a proliferation of different definitions is currently on offer, depending on the application to which the concept is put.
3 Evolution from initial data: The Einstein equation is a system of very complex nonlinear partial differential equations and their analysis yields many philosophical conundrums. E.g. an analysis of certain black hole solutions shows that there are regions where evolution is undetermined by the equations. How ought one to interpret such results?
4 Topology-change: There are classical results in general relativity that permit spatial topology-change only at the cost of causality violation. How strong are these results? Is there any way of avoiding them? Shouldn't we also be concerned about change in differentiable structure?

Historically, the theory of relativity has left its mark on American philosophy through its influence on John Dewey and Ernest Nagel. Dewey drew from it the moral that theoretical abstraction is made in the service of inquiry and has no ontological reference apart from the inquiry. So, for instance, he saw the absolute character of Newtonian space and time as an attempt to secure ontological reference; whereas relativity theory rendered spacetime as itself the subject matter of inquiry. Nagel – who was Dewey's student – did important work on the relationship between geometry and physics, emphasizing the transition between classical physics and general relativity.

Further reading

Putnam, Hilary. "Time and Physical Geometry," *Journal of Philosophy* 64 (1967): 240–7.

Stein, Howard. "On Relativity Theory and the Openness of the Future," *Philosophy of Science* 58 (1991): 147–67.

Wald, Robert. *General Relativity.* Chicago, IL: University of Chicago Press, 1984.

Whitehead, Alfred N. *The Principle of Relativity with Applications to Physical Science.* Cambridge: Cambridge University Press, 1922.

NICHOLAS J. TEH

RELIGION

Understanding the term "religion" is itself one of the main problems of religion, and what has passed for religion in America has had a troubled past. One of the ways that has been used to chronicle religion's development has been to trace the generational changes in its family tree. On this strategy, elements such as beliefs and religious practices play heavily in the discussion along with cataloguing the emergence of new denominations and sects. However, another way of tracing the development of religion in America is to view it from the standpoint of the integration of values; on this strategy, what is underscored is how each change registered in the history of religion contributes to, or detracts from, the movement toward the integration of human and religious values. It is in this vein that America's contribution to religion stands out as particularly distinctive and unique; indeed, it is as a direct result of the thought of key American philosophers and religionists that America has given birth to a peculiarly American religious tradition.

This contribution to religion was made almost entirely during the period of time from roughly the early/mid-1800s to the mid/late-1900s and continues into today. As a result of this inauguration, the understanding of religion in America underwent a radical change owing to the efforts of such as Phineas Parkhurst Quimby, Ralph Waldo Emerson, Mary Baker Eddy, William James, Myrtle Fillmore, and John Dewey, producing a distinctively American rendering of religion; one which, even today, stands in stark contrast to the traditional orthodox rendering. Indeed, John Dewey, in his *A Common Faith*, declared that the view he was presenting went

> contrary to traditional religions, including those that have the greatest hold upon the religiously minded today. The view announced will seem to cut the vital nerve of the religious element itself in taking away the basis upon which traditional religions and institutions have been founded.
>
> (Dewey 1934: 2)

There were, of course, many others who contributed to this development, but the realization of the aim of this entry must be done within the assigned limits; accordingly, I can only hope to suggest much of what a more detailed account of this subject would make explicit; nevertheless, what is presented here I take to be at the heart of the matter as it pertains to the more general interests of American philosophy.

The campaign mounted against the traditional rendering of religion, although not explicitly contrived, occurred on two fronts; the first was philosophical and the second was experiential. These two influences worked in concert with one another to effect what Dewey referred to as the taking away of the "basis upon which traditional religions and institutions have been founded." The coordination of the offensive, however, is probably more attributable to *der Zeitgeist* than it is to any particular intent of the individuals involved; consequently, there is not a linear chronology that would disclose a "chain of events" that finally culminated in the aforementioned change. However, it is generally agreed that, on the philosophy side, Emerson figured prominently as a fulgurating influence and Quimby was his counterpart on the side of experience. These two men, born only a year apart, greatly influenced those who came after them in their respective traditions, and can be considered as the originating agents in the change. It is the aim of this entry to sketch the broad contours of these two influences and introduce the reader to the resulting religious tradition.

In Emerson's time, and still today, orthodox views of God in American thought and religion merely echoed the strains of European Christianity and, consonant with that view, held to a model in which the theme of separation prevailed. This, of course, is simply the continuation of a trend that started in 1607 with the establishment of the first Anglican Church in the American colonies and continued through the dismissal of Jonathan Edwards from his post as minister of the Congregational Church in Northampton, Massachusetts; and right up to today. Edwards had been at that particular post for twenty-three years, but his ultra-conservative theology never relented; and nine years after his famous "Sinners in the Hands of an Angry God" sermon was delivered, his stringent theology and his rigidity on administrative matters became too much for the congregation and they dismissed him on 22 June 1750.

Edwards, however, is usually credited with the beginning of what has come to be known as the Great Awakening; the name given to the period of time from around 1725 to 1776 and characterized by such national themes as a religiously oriented sense of mission, an abundant land, and a favoring Providence (Ahlstrom 1972: 2). It was also a time characterized by the presence of a great many itinerant preachers who traveled into the backwoods and frontier of America to carry the message of a more personal and inner religion, stressing one's own personal responsibility. This emphasis on personal responsibility, no doubt, played equally well in the political arena, as the American Revolution was coming on apace.

The logic of sin and separation that characterizes much of orthodox Christianity, and which was especially noticeable in the preaching of Jonathan Edwards, creates an economy of guilt that many find not only intolerable but also inconsistent with the nature of God, as it is revealed to them in the dialogue carried out between how they understand their daily experiences in life and how they understand the Scripture. The dismissal of Edwards for the reasons given demonstrates that there was a strong spirit of individualism beginning to appear in the American psyche; a spirit that would be immortalized in two famous documents penned just twenty-six years hence.

Quimby and Emerson were born in 1802 and 1803 respectively, while the spirit of revolution was still fresh in the air; and shortly after the individualism promoted during the Great Awakening had run its full course, swelling every citizen with pride in a new nation. This spirit of the times was not lost on Ralph Waldo Emerson and he incorporated much of it into his writings and lectures; among the works that proved especially influential are: "The American Scholar," an address delivered to the Phi Beta Kappa Society, at Cambridge, 31 August 1837; the "Divinity School" address, delivered before the Senior Class in Divinity College, Cambridge, Sunday evening, 15 July 1838; the essay on "Self-Reliance" (1841), "The Transcendentalist", a lecture read at the Masonic Temple in Boston January, 1842; and the essay, "Nature" (1849).

When Emerson concluded "The American Scholar" address to the Phi Beta Kappa Society in 1838, he concluded it with these words:

> We have listened too long to the courtly muses of Europe ... We will walk on our own feet; we will work with our own hands; we will speak our own minds ... A nation of men will for the first time exist, because each believes himself inspired by the Divine Soul which also inspires all men.
>
> (Emerson 1983: 70–1)

The central theme of this passage became a springboard, not only for a renaissance in philosophy, but in religion as well; that central theme is represented by Emerson's phrase "the Divine Soul which also inspires all men." The apparently innocuous reference to the Divine Soul, with which Emerson peppers so much of his writing, strikes at the very foundation of religious orthodoxy by denying the very separation between God and humankind which is orthodoxy's stock-in-trade. Emerson's frequent references to the "Divine Soul" or "Divine Spark" within each person are a continual reminder that, in his own words from "The Transcendentalist," "The height, the deity of man is, to be self-sustained, to need no gift, no foreign force ... Everything real is self-existent. Everything divine shares the self-existence of Deity" (Emerson 1983: 195). In such statements Emerson repudiates the claim that we are separated from the Divine, insisting, instead, that we are One with it.

The separation characteristic of traditional religion is held to be the cause not only of eternal damnation, but of sickness and death as well. So, when Phineas Parkhurst Quimby, known as "Park," began to heal people, this created some cognitive dissonance and acted as a catalyst for the re-examination of religious doctrine and texts. Quimby might have been hailed as a "savior" owing to his unique gift of healing had it not been for the fact that he taught his technique to others and demonstrated that they, too, could heal. One such beneficiary of the healing was Mary Baker Eddy, who went on to found the Church of Christ Scientist; and who subsequently taught Myrtle Fillmore, who in turn also experienced a healing, as did her husband, Charles Fillmore; the Fillmores founded the Unity School of Christianity. The main import of Quimby's teachings (and an explicit element of Emerson's thought) is that the individual is, in an important sense, Divine; hence, the mind can create health. In this regard, it is claimed that the mind's healing and creating strength comes from affirming the truth about oneself, i.e. that one is Divine; and from thinking Divine thoughts, i.e. kind and loving thoughts. Indeed, in his *Varieties of Religious Experience* (James 2004), William James referred to these groups as "The Religion of Healthy-Mindedness," and contrasted them with the more orthodox religions, which he categorized in the very next chapter entitled "The Sick Soul."

One of the later contributors to this transformation is John Dewey, whose contribution comes as the Terry Lectures delivered at Yale University from 1933 to 1934. What is interesting about these lectures is that during his day, Dewey was perceived as being a secular humanist with little or no interest in religion. But in these lectures, published as *A Common Faith*, he recast his pragmatic naturalism as a religious way of life. He begins by addressing a presupposition held in common by believers and unbelievers alike; the presupposition is that the notion of the supernatural is inextricably bound up with the notion of the religious. In the pages that follow he argues that these notions are not logically committed to one another and, indeed, the notion of the religious must be emancipated from the notion of the supernatural.

In Christian theology, sin is the vehicle, and guilt the symptom, of separation; however, separation is present in other major world religions as well; in those religions it is conveyed by the notion of the supernatural – a notion which is itself implicit in the Christian concept of sin. Dewey takes aim at the notion of the supernatural in his *A Common Faith* by drawing a distinction between religion, *a* religion, and the religious. He dismisses any attempt to assign meaning to the term "religion" as futile; claiming that

> "religion" is a strictly collective term and the collection it stands for is not even of the kind illustrated in textbooks of logic. It has not the unity of a regiment or assembly but that of any miscellaneous aggregate. Attempts to prove the universality prove too much or too little.
>
> (Dewey 1934: 7–8)

For the most part, the distinction between *a* religion and the religious can be distilled to the difference between two different purposes. Dewey noted that a particular religion is committed to "a special body of beliefs and practices" that pertains to the supernatural; and it always has "some kind of institutional organization," whereas the religious aspect of experience "denotes attitudes that may be taken toward every object and every proposed end or ideal." The former has as its veiled motive the defense of the supernatural, while the latter involves a positive attitude toward certain experiential values that ought to be enhanced.

By making a distinction between "religion" and "the religious," Dewey proposed that one could, without reference to or dependence upon the supernatural, develop a meaningful life of passionate intelligence. This life would be one in which the values achieved by social effort could be intelligently furthered and expanded in the life of the individual. In effect, Dewey's distinction between "religion" and "the religious" exposed the misleading distinction between sacred and secular as the result of flawed reasoning; and as being a distinction that is representative of the very separation implicit in traditional religions. Another way of putting this is to say that Dewey's distinction between "religion" and "the religious" made explicit what was already implicit in Emerson's thought; and the movement from Emerson to Dewey, as well as the movement from Quimby to Fillmore, describes a path in which idealized values find a "human abode" and are integrated with actual human experience instead of relegated to the realm of the supernatural, where they are orphaned from the very human experience that gave them birth. In other words, the path describes experiences in which there occurs an integration of human and religious values in a way that does not involve an appeal to the supernatural.

The importance of the philosophic thought and the experiential healings to religion is that, probably, neither one of them taken alone would have influenced religion much at all. However, taken together at that particular time, they created a whole new religious understanding – indeed, a whole new religious tradition. The contributing factors include: a sense of personal initiative in deciding what was to count as good theology, demonstrated by the dismissing of Jonathan Edwards; the development of a sense that it was important to have a personal and responsible relationship with God, a sense brought about by the message of the itinerant preachers of the Great Awakening; the reasoned position explaining the Divinity of humankind, taught by Emerson and Quimby and borne out by healings; and the emancipation of the "religious" from the supernatural. All of these influences came together at the right time, a *kairos*, to lay the foundation for a uniquely American religion.

As a result of this confluence of effort and in contradistinction to the prevailing religious views, a set of beliefs emerged from the teachings of Emerson, Quimby, Dewey, and others in which there was no dual nature of humankind promoted; instead, the "Deity of man" was claimed, affirmed, and demonstrated. There was no longer any "sacred" and "secular": rather, the world was one world and awaited the hard work of dedicated individuals for the communally achieved values to be realized. The "sin" that was characteristic of traditional religion's belief in separation was seen as simply a mistake that could be intelligently corrected; people were taught that they were not punished *for* their sins; they were punished *by* them. As the Divine children of a Loving God, all things were possible; healing, health, and wealth all were within reach. By emphasizing the Deity of humankind, promoting thoughts of the mind that are consistent with love, and by allowing the logic of those attributes to play out their implications, these philosophers and religionists made it possible for a new way of thinking about religion to emerge: a new way of thinking that promotes positive thought and love instead of sin, guilt, and shame. This "New Thought" religion, as it has been termed, is distinctively American; it was bred of American thought and American feeling by American men and American women; it has made its way into the everyday philosophy of everyday citizens and has "assumed among the powers of the earth a separate and equal station"; it has dissolved the religious bands that have connected it with traditional religion; it is, indeed, the truly American brand of religion.

Further reading

Ahlstrom, Sydney. *A Religious History of the American People*. New Haven, CT: Yale University Press, 1972.

Cady, H. Emilie. *Lessons in Truth*. Unity Village, MO: Unity School of Christianity, 2003.

Emerson, Ralph Waldo. *Emerson: Essays and Lectures*. New York: Library of America, 1983.

Quimby, Phineas Parkhurst. *The Complete Writings*, ed. Ervin Seale, Vols 1–3. Marina Del Rey, CA: DeVorss Publishing, 1988.

JOHN M. COGAN

RESCHER, NICHOLAS

Nicholas Rescher (1928–) is an unusually prolific American philosopher, the author of more than a hundred books. Rescher, who was born in Germany, migrated to the US as a young boy, received all his education in the US, and took his PhD at Princeton. He has taught at Lehigh and then for more than forty years at the University of Pittsburgh. He has held many honors, too numerous to mention here.

Rescher has written on an unusually wide range of topics, including logic, epistemology, the philosophy of science, metaphysics, and the philosophy of value, as well as historical studies on Leibniz, Kant, Peirce, and Arabic philosophy and logic. He is especially interested in knowledge, especially scientific knowledge. A consistent theme in his writings over many years is the limits of natural science. For Rescher, science is open-ended, without possible closure. Beginning with *Scientific Progress* (1976), he has often taken a quantitative approach to science, culminating in *Epistemetrics* (2005), which inaugurates the project of a general theory of knowledge from a quantitative point of view.

Rescher, who is sensitive to the many overlapping strands between idealism and pragmatism, has often defended idealism, as in *Conceptual Idealism* (1973) and many other works. He depicts idealism as the philosophical doctrine that real objects comprising the "external world" are not independent of cognizing minds, but in some way correlated to mental operations. By "minds" he means separate individual minds equipped with socially engendered resources. He believes the strongest argument for idealism is that any characterization of the real is mind-constructed, since our only access to it is through mind. He sees this view as fully consistent, not inconsistent, with a realism according to which reality decides our claims about it.

Over the years, Rescher has described pragmatism in different ways. In a recent work, *Value Matters: Studies in Axiology* (2004), he returns to the theory of truth from the point of view of methodological pragmatism. He rejects efforts by such pragmatists as W. James to "soften" the meaning of truth to avoid skepticism in favor of a theory of "criteriology." We should not define "truth" in terms of success. We should rather validate methods leading to truth in terms of their success, in relying on such methods to validate truth claims.

He has expounded his systematic position, under the heading of *Pragmatic Idealism* (1992–4), a trilogy emphasizing both its idealist and pragmatic aspects. The system, which aims at knowledge of reality, has three main aspects, as concerns idealism, fallibilism, and pragmatism. It is idealistic, since the mind contributes to what it knows, and because the criterion of truth is systematic coherence. This view of idealism is distantly related to Kant's interest in constructivism, the central insight in his Copernican revolution, as well as his insistence on system. Unlike Kant, Rescher favors a coherence rather than a correspondence view of truth with emphasis on what Dewey calls warranted assertibility. Second, his system is fallibilistic since it denies we can provide more than an imperfect approximation of reality. Rescher's form of fallibilism has an obvious link with Peirce's idea of the long run, only at the end of which we reach reality. Finally, his system is pragmatic since it invokes utility as the standard for judging the validity of knowledge claims. By "utility," Rescher has in mind general usefulness for human purposes however defined.

Further reading

Rescher, Nicholas, *Conceptual Idealism*. Oxford: Blackwell, 1973.

—— *Scientific Progress: A Philosophical Essay on the Economics of Research in Natural Science*. Pittsburgh, PA: University of Pittsburgh Press, 1978.

—— *A System of Pragmatic Idealism*. Princeton, NJ: Princeton University Press, 1992–4, including: Vol. 1: *Human Knowledge in Idealistic Perspective*, 1992; Vol. 2: *The Validity of Values: A Normative Theory of Evaluative Rationality*, 1992; Vol. 3: *Metaphilosophical Inquiries*, 1994.

—— *Value Matters: Studies in Axiology*. Frankfurt: Ontos Verlag, 2004.

—— *Epistemetrics*. Cambridge: Cambridge University Press, 2005

TOM ROCKMORE

RESCHER, NICHOLAS: AUTOBIOGRAPHY

Nicholas Rescher was born in 1928 in Hagen, Germany, where his father had established a law practice after serving as a German army officer during World War I. His family emigrated to the USA in 1938, and he was educated there, receiving the PhD at Princeton University in 1951, while still twenty-two years of age. Since 1961, he has taught at the University of Pittsburgh, where he serves as University Professor of Philosophy and also as Co-Chairman of the Center for Philosophy of Science. He has published over 300 articles in scholarly journals, has contributed to many encyclopedias and reference works, and has written some hundred books in various areas of philosophy, including epistemology, metaphysics, value theory and social philosophy, logic, the philosophy of science, and the history of philosophy.

After first working primarily on topics in formal logic and in the history of logic, Rescher has, since the late 1960s, increasingly devoted himself to problems of metaphysics and the theory of knowledge. In his writings, he has sought to revive and refurbish the idealistic tradition in epistemology and metaphysics in the light of approaches drawn from American pragmatism. His work on this program combines a nineteenth-century concern for large-scale systematizing with a twentieth-century Anglo-American penchant for specialized investigations using the modern formal tools of philosophical analysis. His approach to philosophy is comprehensively expounded in a trilogy entitled *A System of Pragmatic Idealism* published by Princeton University Press in 1991–3. Rescher also has diversified interests in the history of philosophy, and has written extensively about medieval philosophy as well as about Leibniz, Kant, and Peirce.

From 1964 to 1993 Rescher edited the *American Philosophical Quarterly* and for many years the *History of Philosophy Quarterly* as well. During 1969–75 he served a term as Secretary General of the International Union of History and Philosophy of Science (an organ of UNESCO). He has served as a President of the American Philosophical Association, the American Catholic Philosophical Association, and the Metaphysical, and also of the Charles S. Peirce Society and the Leibniz Society of America.

Rescher's contributions to philosophy have primarily involved: the rehabilitation of idealism in general and the coherence theory of truth in particular, the revival and reconstruction of pragmatism; the development of inconsistency-tolerant logic, and the development of an exponential retardation theory of scientific progress. In several cases, a particular concept on principle has come to be associated with his name, including Rescher's Law of Logarithmically Diminishing Returns in scientometrics; the Rescher Quantifier in symbolic logic; Rescher's Effective Average Standard in the theory of distributive justice; the Dienes–Rescher Inference Engine in nonstandard logic; the Rescher–Manor Consequence Relation in non-monotonic reasoning theory; and the Gaines–Rescher implication in many-valued logic. Characteristic of Rescher's work – especially in the theory of knowledge – is the development of a quantitative standpoint under the title of *epistemetrics*. He has directed much attention to exploring the limits of science and of human knowledge in general, stressing in particular the impracticability of gaining a present understanding of future cognitive progress.

Some dozen books devoted to various aspects of Rescher's philosophical work have been published in recent years and six honorary degrees have been awarded to Rescher by universities on three continents. A member of several learned academies, its fellows elected him an honorary member of

Corpus Christi College, Oxford, and in 1983 he received an Alexander von Humboldt Humanities Prize, awarded "in recognition of the research accomplishments of humanistic scholars of international distinction." A vivid picture of his personal and intellectual development is given in his autobiographical, *Enlightening Journey* (Lexington Books, 2002).

In epistemology and philosophy of science, Rescher is best described as an analytic pragmatist in placing epistemic priority on the methods of the natural sciences as a source of both understanding the empirical world and directing our action within it. It is part of Rescher's coherentism that he regards science as seeking the best fit between the data of experience and the conjecture we make in our attempts to resolve questions.

Rescher's theory of knowledge differs from the original "utilitarian" pragmatism, which takes a theory to be true (or justified) if its acceptance is useful. Instead, Rescher's pragmatism is methodological: a theory is taken to be true (or justified) if it is based on the application of methods which have proved themselves by their usefulness – for instance, by successful predictions.

Yet, while Rescher ascribes a certain primacy to induction and the methods of natural science as natural products of cultural evolution, he nevertheless denies that the only legitimately answerable questions are those that admit of answer under the methods of science. He defends metaphysics as a philosophical venture seeking to examine and elucidate the presuppositions of natural science, which natural science cannot do without viciously circular reasoning. He has also claimed that such presuppositions find their ultimate justification in the consequences of accepting them as instrumentalities of need-satisfaction. An emphasis on the role of commonsensical presumptions in the development of knowledge is yet another characteristic feature of Rescher's work. On the question of scientific realism, Rescher has argued for a particular form of instrumentalism in science without endorsing instrumentalism as a whole on the issue of factual knowledge. For Rescher, commonsense beliefs (those beliefs so obviously true that we cannot even imagine factual conditions under which they would be false) do succeed in correctly describing the physical world because such beliefs are sufficiently vague not to be likely to suffer truth value revision. However, our scientific beliefs forego any such protection imprecision.

Rescher's approach is idealistic because it prioritizes and because it regards systematic coherence as the criterion of truth; fallibilistic because it denies that knowledge can provide more than an imperfect approximation of reality; and pragmatic because it maintains that the validity of knowledge-claims depends on their utility in furthering human purposes. Rescher's pragmatism envisions an objective pragmatism of what works impersonally, rather than a subjective pragmatism of what works for me or for us. It is applied not only in our factual commitments but also to our value commitments. As he sees it, values secure objectivity because our emplacement in reality imposes upon us certain basic projects not constructed or freely chosen, but simply given. About these we cannot properly deliberate.

A persistent theme in Rescher's philosophy is human limitations and the imperfection (and imperfectability) of human knowledge. However, he does not succumb to skepticism, nihilism, or relativism, all of which he roundly rejects. He argues on pragmatic grounds that there is an objective reality that is intelligible, the truth of which can be obtained by human reason; and though perfect knowledge is impossible, adequate knowledge for the realization of human ends is not.

A further characteristic feature of Rescher's epistemology is its systematic integration of matters of value (that is, norms – be they cognitive or affective) and matters of experientially determined fact. For Rescher morality is basically a matter of safeguarding the real or best interests of people and while the identification of such interests involves an irreducibly normative element, the processes of their effective cultivation are something we can only learn about empirically. Morality thus weaves issues of fact and value into a seamless whole. Moreover, the axiology of Rescher's system aims at deriving values from human needs and purposes and evaluating knowledge-claims in the light of them.

As of the 1980s Rescher worked increasingly on issues of metaphilosophy and philosophical methodology. He has argued in considerable detail for an aporetic and dialectical perspective on the development of philosophy.

Rescher espouses a metaphysical view he calls *philosophical standardism*. He thinks, for example, that human knowledge is fundamentally and standardly a matter of belief that is justifiably held to be true. Prevalent counterexamples to the classical definition of knowledge as justified-true-belief ignore the fact that our concepts are based on limited generalizations that are subject to revision and thus reflect what is normally and typically the case rather than what is unexceptionally and necessarily so. In consequence traditional philosophy is too preoccupied with abstract necessities of general principle which do not capture our understanding of the world as it is actually experienced, and the price we pay for this more modest construal of philosophical generalizations is to acknowledge the essential open-endedness of our philosophically relevant concepts.

However, Rescher strongly opposes the fashionable nihilism of a "post-philosophical" age. Notwithstanding concession to the pervasive pluralism of the times he maintains a traditionalistic dedication to a philosophical search for truth, granting that people's views are of course bound to reflect differences in backgrounds of experience and that they are also bound to differ constitutionally as well. The undeniable diversity of human circumstances do not support skepticism or indifferent relativism because objectivity is preserved through the circumstances that certain issues resolutions are impersonally and objectively appropriate once those circumstances are given.

Further reading

Almeder, Robert (ed.). *Praxis and Reason: Studies in the Philosophy of Nicholas Rescher*. Washington, DC: University Press of America, 1982.

Bottani, Andrea. *Verità e Coerenza: Suggio sull' epistemologia coerentista di Nicholas Rescher*. Milano: Franco Angeli Liberi, 1989.

Carrier, Martin, Massey, G., and Ruetsche, G. (eds). *Science at the Century's End: Philosophical Questions on the Progress and Limits of Science*. Pittsburgh and Konstanz: University of Pittsburgh Press and University of Konstanz Press, 2000.

Coomann, Heinrich. *Die Kohaerenztheorie der Wahrheit: Eine kritische Darstellung der Theorie Reschers von Ihrem historischen Hintergrund*. Frankfurt: Peter Lang Verlag, 1983.

Marsonet, Michele. *The Primacy of Practical Reason: An Essay on Nicholas Rescher's Philosophy*. Lanham, MD: University Press of America, 1995.

Murray, Paul D. *Reason, Truth and Theology in Pragmatic Perspective*. Leuven: Peeters, 2004.

Nabavi, Lotfallah. *Avicennan Logic Based on Nicholas Rescher's Point of View*. Tehran: Scientific and Cultural Publications, 2003.

Sosa, Ernest (ed.). *The Philosophy of Nicholas Rescher*. Dordrecht: D. Reidel, 1979.

Weber, Michel (ed.). *After Whitehead: Rescher and Process Philosophy: Critiques and Replies*. Frankfurt: ONTOS Verlag, 2004.

Wüstehube, A. and Quante, M. *Pragmatic Idealism: Critical Essays on Nicholas Rescher's System of Pragmatic Idealism*. Amsterdam: Rodolpi, 1998.

Nicholas Rescher

RESPONSIBILITY

Most of the dictionaries and encyclopedias repeat that responsibility means accepting the results of one's actions, very often choosing its commonsense understanding in which the problem is to establish who, for what, and to whom should be responsible. Human beings find themselves related to responsibility only as performers of certain actions. Such a point of view is applied to explain moral and legal responsibility. Moral responsibility is discussed as a relation of a subject to his conscious and free actions. It considers moral obligation, which is connected with satisfying criteria, which prescribe praise or rebuke for morally meaningful actions and behavior. In turn, legal responsibility arises when certain premises are fulfilled, regarding for example an obligation to right somebody's wrongs or the necessity to punish. However, if one starts from legal and moral understanding of responsibility, there is no chance to reach the notion of it, which would refer to a more basic phenomenon of responsibility. The issue is thus responsibility understood not as a legal or moral notion, but as a basic philosophical notion, functioning on the ontological and metaphysical level. If understood in such a way, responsibility is inherent, not dependent on man's will or choices. It is a responsibility understood in a positive sense. It is not directed at the past but at the future. Such responsibility creates a fuller possibility for describing human entity. This possibility appears with transition from the ancient paradigm of the third person, subject–object relation, objectivity and truth – and from the modern one of the first person, of subjectivity and freedom – to the paradigm of the second person and You–Me relation, i.e. to the dialogical one, to listening and answering. This change becomes a transition from truth and freedom to responsibility as the essence of the You–Me relation. And in this way the philosophy of modern times, being the philosophy of freedom, becomes in the twentieth century the philosophy of responsibility. However, freedom, which is so important for responsibility, is not negated but gains a new dimension. It becomes defined by responsibility, which fits into a certain path of the development of philosophy from the notion of truth, through freedom, to responsibility.

Tracing the change in the understanding of responsibility, we can see it already e.g. in the philosophy of Søren Kierkegaard. Its basis is constituted by an obligating bond, which binds a human with the world. To become conscious of this responsibility, we cannot drown in the anonymity of the crowd. Human beings who truly chooses themselves accepts to a great extent responsibility for everything that concerns them. In spite of differences regarding the issue of faith, we find a similar approach in the philosophy of Friedrich Nietzsche. Responsibility in his understanding takes a form towards oneself and is necessary to liberate ourselves from being slaves to the tradition, from our previous selves. Denying obedience to any authority, he writes the famously controversial "God is dead." Liberating a human being from the chains of traditions, habits and proclaiming "God's death," might be, however, perceived as something that destroys the responsibility of a human being. The man who connects responsibility with the existence of God is Martin Buber. However, Jean-Paul Sartre is of a different opinion. From his perspective a human being is absolutely responsible for himself, for his behavior, for the world. It is a consequence of having absolute freedom. A human being is sentenced to freedom because there is no God. He himself has to make choices, with only himself and others – and not some higher truth – as the point of reference. This is convergent with Hans Jonas's point of view, presenting the immense responsibility of a human being for the world and for mankind's existence in it. There is no divine providence that watches over the world. A responsible subject cannot use it to justify his actions. We have to understand that God will not help us, and this is not Nietzsche who says so but Jonas – a believer. Responsibility is ours. Jonas does not believe that we are alone, but it is a human being who makes decisions and is responsible for them. In a similar spirit Sartre ends his *Is Existentialism a Humanism?* writing that no matter whether God exists or not, choices have to be made by us.

Yet who or what do we answer to? As Jonas points out, we are responsible for the future and towards the future, for history and towards history. We are responsible "towards good" and towards "the other." He describes the relation between me and the other as a vertical relation of "face to face" in which it is me who is responsible towards the other and for the other. Does such responsibility limit our freedom? Levinas's answer is negative. In his account we can see a new understanding of the relation between freedom and responsibility. Another human being is not perceived as someone who limits my freedom, but only by calling me to be responsible does he establish it.

The philosophers mentioned above have prepared the basis for a new understanding of freedom as the relation of one person toward another and toward the world. An alternative explanation of the nature of responsibility – convergent with the former explanation and the above-mentioned paradigm of a second person – is provided in the classical pragmatism of such philosophers as William James, Josiah Royce, John Dewey or Richard Rorty. While pragmatism perceives a person to a great extent as a social being, his features as a product and not something innate, this philosophy also forcefully stresses the dialogical relation with the other based on the responsibility towards him and for him. For Royce, communication and openness are the basic elements of a healthy society. Shutting the other out is a sin. Association of the individual to community is essential. Dewey also believes in this; for him, to learn to be human is to develop through the give-and-take of communication and being an individually distinctive member of the society. Through such a communication we are allowed to shape the conditions we live in. And because there is no one-sided accommodation of individual needs and powers to any fixed environment but mutual adjustment, freedom of mind is central in maintenance of a society. Such freedom rests in the trained power of thought, in the ability to look at matters deliberately. This is not freedom from involvement but free and full participation. It is a responsible participation and struggle for conditions that will make individuals effective members of the community. We are not left opposing our moral values to a universe governed by blind physical forces. Such a perspective as offered by Hegelianism, which James cheerfully described as a "moral holiday," was not the one to agree on. The moral weight is on our shoulders. For Dewey the individual becomes a social being at the moment when he or she undertakes the responsibility of acting for the good of the community. Everything that contributes to the development of the individual must also contribute to the development of the community. As he says in *The Public and its Problems*, on the side of the individual it consists in having a responsible share in forming and directing the activities of the groups one belongs to and in participating according to need in the values which the groups sustain. On the side of the groups, it demands liberation of the potentialities of members in harmony with the common good and interests. The truly moral man is interested in the welfare of others, to expand their autonomous activity, but such an interest is essential to his own self-realization. So this is not a call for authoritarian social engineering, of which James was aware, pointing to the neo-Hegelian concept of freedom leading to the image of a "buttoned-up" society. In Dewey's view either social goals take precedence over the individual or individual goals assume importance over social ones. A personal desire for happiness is also a desire for the happiness of the community. Because of that, in his view self-realization is "in the service" of a "Great Community" or democracy as a way of life, and not merely a way of public life but an ideal that must affect all modes of human association. This is what Dewey shared with T.H. Green and Josiah Royce: that all idealism must be of future goals in which all can participate. Democracy for him is more than a form of government. It is primarily a mode of associated living, of conjoint communicated experience based on the free exchange of ideas and responsibility that we take for our future. Rorty, who walks in the footsteps of Dewey, agrees. He believes that human coexistence depends on mutable forms of egalitarian unforced communication based on mutual free exchange of thoughts. All these motives in their thought argue for a democratic society in which, as Dewey says, a free social action would be inseparable from living communication. In doing so, drawing our attention to responsible communication, pragmatic philosophers join the trend of philosophical thought which not only shows a person his responsibility toward the other and for the other, but also can strengthen the sense of responsibility.

Further reading

Dewey, John. *The Public and Its Problems* in *Collected Works of John Dewey 1882–1953, Vol. 2*. Carbondale, IL: Southern Illinois Press, 1991, pp. 235–373.

Hart, H.L.A. *Punishment and Responsibility: Essays in the Philosophy of Law.* Oxford: Oxford University Press, 1978.

Hart, H.L.A. and Honoré, A.M. *Causation in the Law.* Oxford: Oxford University Press, 1959.

Jonas, Hans. *The Imperative of Responsibility. In Search of an Ethics for the Technological Age*, trans. Hans Jonas with David Herr. Chicago, IL: University of Chicago Press, 1984

Levinas, Emmanuel. *Totality and Infinity: An Essay on Exteriority*, trans. Alphonso Lingis. Pittsburgh, PA: Duquesne University Press, 1969.

Nietzsche, Friedrich. *On the Genealogy of Morals*, trans. Walter Kaufmann and R.J. Hollindale. New York: Random House, 1969.

Sartre, Jean-Paul. *Is Existentialism a Humanism?* in *Essays in Existentialism*. New York: Citadel, 1993.

Rorty, Richard. "On moral obligation, truth, and common sense" in *Debating the State of Philosophy: Habermas, Rorty, Kołakowski*, ed. Jozef Niżnik and John T. Sanders. Westport: Greenwood, 1996, pp. 48–52.

Marcin Kilanowski

REVOLUTION

Revolution means the process of making radical and fundamental change in the political, economic and social systems of a country. For instance, there was the American Revolution's violent change from English rule to independence. It need not be violent change, but the word tends to suggest it, and the word "rebellion" makes most explicit this idea of violence in a revolution. However, a phrase like "the industrial revolution" means only that sharp break from the past in the average worker's occupations due to the invention of machine production, and of itself suggests nothing violent. The Glorious Revolution of 1688, in which the British substituted a Protestant monarch for a Catholic one, was a non-violent revolution whose justification derived from the British philosopher John Locke (1632–1704).

The American Revolution

The Declaration of Independence. adopted 4 July 1776, was written to begin, explain, and justify the American colonies' revolution or rebellion against their mother country, England. The first Continental Congress, 1775, demanded reforms from Great Britain in accordance with the colonists' rights as English subjects, for British soldiers and colonists were already engaged in violent exchanges. But in 1775 King George III's proclamation declared the colonies in rebellion, and Parliament prohibited trade with the Americans. Thus, in reaction, the second Continental Congress, 1776, meeting in Philadelphia, appointed a committee to draw up a declaration of independence. The committee members were John Adams, Benjamin Franklin, Roger Sherman, Robert R. Livingston, and their chosen penman, Thomas Jefferson.

There was general consensus in the committee and the Congress about what Jefferson was to write. The document would have two parts. The first part was a statement of the general, philosophical theory justifying revolution. This was basically Locke's social contract theory. All humans have unalienable natural rights such as the rights to life, liberty, property and the pursuit of happiness. To secure these rights, humans institute a government that contracts to safeguard them in exchange for the subjects' allegiance and obedience. If the government fails to safeguard these rights or violates them, the subjects' contractual obligations to that government are dissolved and they have the right to establish a new government.

The second part was the list of about twenty-seven "repeated injuries and usurpations" by the King, the reasons why the theory applied to the situation of the American colonists. It is worth noting that the harms were all ascribed to King

George III and none to Parliament, and this was the model the British themselves had used in their Glorious Revolution a century before.

The American Revolution inspired and influenced many other modern revolutions, starting with the 1789 French Revolution.

Jefferson's own ideas about revolution

Jefferson's personal views on revolution were even more radical than those of the Declaration. His letters offered the opinion that a little rebellion now and then is desirable, for it usually means that the government is encroaching on its citizens' rights, and so the government should be mild in punishing rebellion. He coupled this with the opinion that, since the earth and its fruits are for the living, every generation has a right to its own new constitution and laws. If the old constitution and laws are enforced longer than for nineteen years, this is an act of force and not of right, and something approaching rebellion is the citizenry's appropriate response. However, since the US Constitution allows for its complete replacement in the amendment process it contains, it would theoretically allow complete revolution without violence and even allow it every twenty years.

John Dewey on revolution

The greatest philosopher of American democracy, John Dewey, wanted changes in the United States which would have been revolutionary had they been achieved. He wanted our apparent democracy of contending political parties to give way to a real participatory democracy in which everyone subject to an institution has the opportunity to help shape the values of that institution. He wanted our capitalism to be replaced by socialism. However, since most of the public in Dewey's day understood revolution to be only violent, and socialism to be only autocratic, largely because of the prominence of Karl Marx's understanding of both, Dewey would not employ or accept the terms "revolutionary" or "socialist" for his position. His doctrine of the interdependence of means and ends meant that the only way to achieve a peaceful socialistic democracy was by employing the peaceful and democratic means of discussion, persuasion, and experimentation.

Hannah Arendt on revolution

The German Jewish refuge from Nazism, Hannah Arendt, became one of America's greatest political philosophers. Her 1963 book, *On Revolution*, argued that revolutions have two phases: (1) the liberation from the necessity that comes with poverty, and (2) the foundation of freedom or creation of a guaranteed and permanent space in which all may act. She holds that both the French and the Russian Revolutions failed in the first phase. She holds that the American Revolution succeeded in the first phase because of the blessing of natural abundance here, especially of land that any and all could take and cultivate. Thus, only the American Revolution could move on to and partly succeed in the second phase, the foundation of freedom. This freedom is founded in our Constitution's principles of the separation of powers and checks and balances, and its guarantees in the Bill of Rights. Thus our Constitution is the longest enduring constitution on any nation in the modern world.

Twentieth-century American hostility to revolution

During the Cold War, most Americans came to understand that any revolution outside the Iron Curtain that was trying to achieve liberation from necessity, from poverty, was the work of communists or was certain to fall under their influence. Consider the Latin American revolutions since World War II. Arendt thought that this understanding was wrong. Nevertheless, we typically believed that these "communists" were trying to establish a totalitarian socialism hostile to American democratic capitalism. Arendt would say that we wrongly came to think of our sort of democracy and capitalism as the sole possible conditions for political and economic freedom.

However, as the 1990s got underway, there were peaceful revolutions behind the Iron Curtain that led to the dissolution of the Soviet Union. These revolutions resulted in the establishment, led by Russia, of many democratic capitalistic imitators of the United States. Dewey would have preferred that they experiment with democratic socialism, not democratic capitalism, which would have been less revolutionary and more freedom-enhancing for them. Still, since Americans are no longer suspicious that Soviet totalitarian communism is behind revolutions, Americans should be free from the prejudice of thinking of revolutions in unfavorable terms. This would please Arendt.

The ward, town meeting, workers' council, *soviet*

It is remarkable that Jefferson, Dewey and Arendt agree that any true revolution would yield a sort of institution that inevitably arises in the revolutionary process but has never been properly preserved. This is that aspect of participatory democracy and genuine freedom seen in New England's town meetings, in Jefferson's wards, in Dewey's industrial autonomy through workers' councils, or in the USSR's soldiers' or workers' *soviets*. These three theoreticians agree that some wrongly supposed necessity has always led to the unfortunate obliteration of these small examples of genuine democracy by big, power-monopolizing, freedom-denying governments.

Further reading

Arendt, Hannah. *On Revolution*. New York: Viking Press, 1965.

Dewey, John. *The Living Thoughts of Thomas Jefferson*. New York: Premier Books, 1963.

Lipset, Seymour Martin. *The First New Nation*. New York: Doubleday Anchor Books, 1963.

Locke, John. *Two Treatises on Civil Government*. London: A. Millar, 1784 [1690].

Westbrook, Robert B. *John Dewey and American Democracy*. Ithaca, NY: Cornell University Press, 1991.

JOSEPH BETZ

RICE, PHILIP B.

Philip Blair Rice (1904–56) was a philosophy professor at Kenyon College and influential editor of the *Kenyon Review* in its mid-twentieth-century heyday. At the *Kenyon Review*, he worked with John Crowe Ransom and edited the poetry of Marianne Moore, John Berryman, Dylan Thomas, *et al*. He was a Rhodes Scholar (1925–8), and President of the American Philosophical Association (1952–3).

Rice's philosophical interests lay in questions of value. In respect to aesthetics, like George Santayana and T.S. Eliot, Rice argued in "The Philosopher as Poet and Critic" that emotions evoked by the aesthetic object (especially by the literary work) needed to find or feign their "correlative objects." In respect to morality, Rice, in *On the Knowledge of Good and Evil*, was critical of much of twentieth-century Anglo-American moral theory and argued for an affective theory of value. An affective theory of value asserts that experience is the final arbiter of value; something is good only in so far as it serves as an immediate or eventual means to the production of an activity or experience enjoyed.

Further reading

Brandt, Richard. "Review of *On the Knowledge of Good and Evil*," *Journal of Philosophy* 41, 7 (30 March 1944): 184–90.

Rice, Philip Blair. "The Philosopher as Poet and Critic" in Paul Arthur Schilpp (ed.) *The Philosophy of George Santayana*. Chicago and Evanston, IL: Northwestern University Press, 1940.

—— *On the Knowledge of Good and Evil*. New York: Random House, 1955.

—— Foreword to George Santayana, *Sense of Beauty*. New York: Modern Library Book, 1955.

CHRISTOPHER PERRICONE

RIGHT

The notion of a right figures prominently in the writings of eighteenth-century revolutionaries such as Thomas Jefferson and Thomas Paine, who articulated a conception of natural rights similar to the one which the English philosopher John Locke had proposed. Their conception is rooted in the idea, central to the natural law tradition, of a natural moral order more fundamental than any that humans might create. Natural rights on their view, in contrast with civil or legal rights, are not created or granted by society or government. They are moral rights, often described as God-given, to freely exercise certain powers or capacities without interference from others; and they are possessed equally by all men from birth, independently of and prior to the involvement of men in society or government. Since rights are vulnerable to violation, however, men enter into society and institute governments in order to secure them: consenting to be governed in order to obtain protection of their rights. The people have a right to alter or abolish and replace a government that fails to live up to that social contract.

In the nineteenth century the influence of the revolutionaries' emphasis on rights was evident in a number of social movements. Abolitionists, for instance, appealed to the notion of rights in arguing for the liberation of slaves, while leaders of the women's movement worked to secure the right to vote and equal property rights for women. Various aspects of the doctrine of natural rights began to be subjected to philosophical criticism, however, in the nineteenth and early twentieth centuries. Josiah Royce, for example, rejected the view that individuals possess rights independently of their involvement in society. Men are social beings shaped and defined by their social relations, according to Royce, whose highest good is loyalty: the willing devotion of a person to a cause. Loyalty unites individuals through their commitment to causes greater than their private selves, and rights are outcomes of their loyalty to those causes.

John Dewey evaluated the natural rights doctrine from an instrumentalist perspective. He acknowledged that the doctrine was beneficial at the time of its development: the view that all men possess rights that are more fundamental than the dictates of government was instrumental in securing individual liberties against tyrannical government. During and following the industrial revolution, though, natural rights – especially property rights – were increasingly associated with a laissez-faire approach to government and economics, providing a rationale for restricting the role of government to minimize its interference with individuals in general and with economic activity in particular. In that context, Dewey argued, appeals to natural rights contributed to the development and persistence of enormous inequalities, with great wealth becoming concentrated in relatively few hands while many earned low wages under terrible conditions. In the absence of government involvement designed to prevent or reduce the disparities, individuals were left with their negative freedom from interference intact, according to Dewey, but without positive or effective freedom in the form of genuinely equal opportunities to develop their abilities and capacities.

Concerns of the kind raised by Dewey have prompted some philosophers to advocate what are often called positive rights, and have contributed to the emergence of egalitarian liberalism. Ralph Barton Perry, writing during a period of heightened emphasis on rights in the aftermath of World War II, maintained that the purpose of rights is the promotion of the interests of members of society, and that restricting interference with individuals is often insufficient to achieve that purpose. He therefore noted with approval an increasing tendency to recognize not just negative rights securing freedom from interference, but also positive rights, correlated with duties on the part of organized society to enable (and not merely allow) individuals to fulfill interests.

In *A Theory of Justice*, John Rawls presented a version of egalitarian liberalism, in which rights (and duties) are to be assigned on the basis of principles of social justice. He proposed two such principles: the first requires equality of basic rights and duties; the second specifies that social and economic inequalities must be to the greatest benefit of those least advantaged, and attached to positions open to everyone under conditions of equality of opportunity. In contrast with Rawls, Robert Nozick rejects egalitarian theories of justice, on the grounds that implementing them violates rights by redistributing justly acquired property holdings in order to promote equality. He adopts a more libertarian version of liberalism similar to the laissez-faire political and economic positions of the nineteenth century, in which state interference with individual liberties is minimized. Dworkin, however, shares Rawls's emphasis on equality, and his conception of rights is rooted in that value. Rights, according to Dworkin, are "trumps" held by individuals over general utility or welfare. They prevent individuals from being treated, for the sake of general utility or welfare, without equal respect and concern.

Recent work on rights has focused on a variety of issues, including: (1) the nature of rights (rights have commonly been characterized, for instance, as certain kinds of claims, liberties, or entitlements); (2) the justification of rights (some philosophers have grounded rights in an aspect of human nature, or appealed to the consequences of recognizing rights, while others such as Richard Rorty regard the justification project as outmoded or misguided); (3) the bearers of rights (human beings, nonhuman animals, future generations, etc.); and (4) the existence or scope of specific rights (e.g. the right to health care). Given that rights have become firmly entrenched in political and ethical discourse, interest in those and other rights-centered issues is likely to remain strong.

Further reading

Dewey, John. *Ethics*. New York: Henry Holt, 1908.

—— *Liberalism and Social Action*. New York: Capricorn Books, 1963.

Paine, Thomas. *The Rights of Man: Being an Answer to Mr. Burke's Attack on the French Revolution*. Buffalo, NY: Prometheus Books, 1987.

Winston, Morton E. (ed.). *The Philosophy of Human Rights*. Belmont, CA: Wadsworth, 1989.

Andrew Piker

RIGHTS

A number of American philosophers have developed theories of rights although not all their theories are equally comprehensive. More important is the fact that they have diverse views of the nature and function of rights.

Judith Jarvis Thomson takes rights to include claims, privileges, powers and immunities and understands claims to be rights in the strictest sense. She denies that legal and moral rights are different species of rights. She also introduces another kind of rights that she calls cluster-rights. Cluster-rights are not rights in the strictest sense as they may contain privileges, powers or immunities as well as claims. But Thomson denies that all claims are absolute. She suggests what she calls the

Tradeoff Idea, namely that it is sometimes permissible to infringe a claim, but is so if and only if infringing it would be much better for those for whom infringing it would be good than not infringing it would be for the claim holder. In developing her theory of rights, Thomson maintains that we may cease to have rights and points out that we can give our word that we will not exercise a right that we have. We can also consent to someone else's doing something that entails our ceasing to have a right. We can waive a right, either actively or by not exercising it. To do so by not exercising it, she says, can be to forfeit it. Acting so as to harm another person violates a claim of theirs and can be grounds for the denial of rights.

Rex Martin, another American philosopher, takes rights to be institutional practices, socially recognized and secured ways of acting or being treated. He maintains that human rights call for legal recognition and promotion by government as well as moral justification. In view of this he takes them to be not simply moral rights but civil rights. Taking civil rights, including human rights, to be political rights, he holds that such rights can most reliably be determined by democratic institutions. The civil rights in a society and the democratic institutions that produce and maintain them comprise what Martin calls a system of rights. He holds that individuals have a duty to conform to democratically established civil rights laws but civil disobedience for the sake of an important moral or social purpose can be justified.

Carl Wellman identifies and compares several different kinds of rights. He takes legal rights to be institutional in that laws are practices of a functional legal system, but he notes that there are other institutional rights such as the academic rights conferred by the rules and regulations of a university.

He understands the conventional morality of a society to confer what he calls morality rights, which are also institutional because they are established in and by an organized community. Moral rights, in contrast, are based on rationally justified moral norms. Nevertheless, Wellman points out that most moral rights are possessed by specific classes of individuals, for example parents, children, employers, employees, etc. He also holds that corporate bodies such as states, organizations, and other kinds of groups can have moral rights.

Moral rights possessed by the citizens of a particular society he calls civic rights, and he contrasts these not only with civil rights, which are legal rights, but with human rights, rights possessed by all human individuals.

Alan Gewirth takes rights of freedom and well-being to be necessary conditions of purposive action. To deny that one has these rights is therefore contradictory, but they are not held by Gewirth to be absolute since there are circumstances under which they may be justifiably overridden. Gewirth takes human rights to include economic and political rights and he holds political democracy to be an expression of the right to freedom.

Moral rights are central to A.I. Melden's theory of rights. But he contends that any moral rights that persons have by virtue of their relations or transactions with one another presuppose human rights, which they have as human beings. To demand one's rights is to assert oneself as a moral agent, to demand that one be dealt with as a member of the human community and as a participant in the life of a moral community who expects to be dealt with on terms of moral equality. As a moral agent, Melden says, one has an inalienable right to pursue one's own affairs in accordance with one's own interests and he takes the right to pursue one's own interests to be a basic or human right of persons as agents. Any social practices or institutions that limit or restrict the pursuit of their interests by the members of any social group violate this right.

Melden notes that this is the case with regard to women in a male-dominated society. According to him, the fundamental human right to pursue one's interests implies the right to life and the right of the young to the kind of education that will prepare them for membership in the moral community.

Ronald Dworkin is especially concerned with issues concerning rights of and against governments. According to his theory, if someone has a right to something it is wrong for the government to deny it even if doing so would be in the general interest. Dworkin holds that government should treat all whom it governs with equal concern and respect. He does not mean by this the right to equal treatment in the sense of entitlement to the same goods and opportunities, but rather the right to be treated as equals in the making of political decisions and the formulation of policies. He stresses that this applies to minorities, whose rights must be respected. Dworkin contends that one sometimes has the right to disobey a law, for instance when the law violates a right that should be respected. In addition, he argues that when a law is unclear or is thought to be of questionable validity citizens have the right to follow their own judgment, which may in some cases require civil disobedience.

For Virginia Held, as for A.I. Melden, moral rights are fundamental, but she defines them as stringent entitlements yielded by valid moral principles and says that we can claim our rights even if society doesn't recognize them. She holds that rights should be respected just because they are yielded by moral principles, not for the sake of any good or benefit. Held contends that the primary moral and human rights a legal system ought to assure are those of persons to life, liberty, justice and equality. Using "freedom" in the sense of liberty, she maintains that the exercise of freedom presupposes having at least the basic necessities, rights to which should be assured by law. An important feature of Held's theory of rights is that she maintains that not only individuals but also collective entities, from nations to groups such as American blacks, can and should have rights. Also because it is central to the workings of a democratic society, she sees the right of persons to know what their government is doing to be very important and the right of the press to inform them of this to be equally important.

The concept of community is central to Martin P. Golding's theory. He holds that every right exists in relation to a community. One can only have a right, he says, in a community whose members recognize that right and would not usually resist or object to its being exercised. If anyone threatens to do so the right would ordinarily be acknowledged on demand; if necessary, members of the community would be ready to aid the right-holder. According to him the concept of human rights implies the notion of a human community at large.

As defined by Joel Feinberg, a right is a kind of claim but only valid claims are rights. To be valid a right must be justified within a system of rules.

A legal right is justified when it is officially recognized; a moral right is a claim the recognition of which is called for by moral principles or the principles of an enlightened conscience. But no right is more of a right than any other and all rights entail the duty to respect them. Noting that in practice rights can be demanded, affirmed or insisted upon as well as claimed, Feinberg holds that claiming rights gives them moral significance because it makes for self-respect and respect for others and conveys a sense of personal dignity.

Richard Wasserstrom provides several arguments for what he and other theorists call natural or human rights. He uses racial discrimination as an example of the denial of human rights. Wasserstrom conceives rights as entitlements that do not require anyone's consent and cannot properly be denied. Human rights are possessed equally by all human beings regardless of any particular status or relationship and they can be claimed or asserted equally against any and every human being. Nevertheless, he holds that no such rights are self-evident and they are not absolute in the sense that there are no conditions under which they can properly be overridden.

David Braybrooke writes about personal rights. He holds such rights to be individualistic in that all persons who have rights must decide for themselves whether to exercise them. Unlike many other theorists, Braybrooke doesn't take moral and legal rights to be different categories of rights. He points out that rights can be both morally endorsed and legally affirmed and holds all others to be approximations of those that are. To say that someone should be accorded a right is to treat the right as if it had the force of law. He counts as legally established rights not only those conferred by governments but also those conferred by other institutions such as universities.

Further reading

Braybrooke, David. *Three Tests for Democracy: Personal Rights, Human Welfare, Collective Preference.* New York: Random House, 1968.

Dworkin, Ronald. *Taking Rights Seriously.* Cambridge, MA: Harvard University Press, 1982.

Feinberg, Joel. "The Nature and Value of Rights," *Journal of Value Inquiry* 4 (Winter 1970): 243–57.

Gewirth, Alan. *The Community of Rights.* Chicago, IL: University of Chicago Press, 1996.

Golding, Martin P. "Towards a Theory of Human Rights," *The Monist* 52, 4 (October 1968): 543–44.

Held, Virginia. *Rights and Goods: Justifying Social Action.* New York: Free Press, 1984.

Martin, Rex. *A System of Rights.* New York: Oxford University Press, 1993.

Melden, A.I. *Rights and Persons.* Berkeley, CA: University of California Press, 1977.

Thomson, Judith Jarvis. *The Realm of Rights.* Cambridge, MA: Harvard University Press, 1990.

Wasserstrom, Richard. "Rights, Human Rights, and Racial Discrimination," *Journal of Philosophy* LXI (29 October 1964): 641–5.

Wellman, Carl. *A Theory of Rights: Persons Under Laws, Institutions, and Morals.* Totowa, NJ: Rowman and Littlefield, 1985.

Beth J. Singer

RORTY, RICHARD

It is unlikely that any living American thinker is more widely identified with Pragmatism than Richard Rorty (1931–). And yet, more than anyone, Rorty is scorned by self-identified "American" philosophers. This has produced an odd situation. For some, Rorty champions Pragmatism, while to others, he subverts it. In fact, he does both. Like all original thinkers, Rorty reads selectively, espousing and eschewing, and therein lies his achievement. Through remarkable readings of Dewey and James, Davidson and Derrida, Rorty has helped an entire generation find dialogue where contempt ruled, conversation where derision reigned. Moreover, he works outside the academy, writing in dailies and monthlies, thus living Emerson's charge: speak with, not at, the citizenry. Ever candid, lucid, and controversial, Rorty fits grandly into the tradition of American philosophy.

Taking leave from Wittgenstein's therapeutic orientation, Dewey's anti-essentialism, and an erosion of the "philosophy/literature" distinction in Heidegger, Gadamer, and Derrida, Rorty developed, throughout the 1970s, theses concerning the end of philosophy and a post-metaphysical culture. After the publication of his major work, *Philosophy and the Mirror of Nature* (1979), in works such as *Contingency, Irony, and Solidarity* (1989) he has focused upon the political import of the claim that cultural discourse proceeds without the benefit of a well-defined method or metaphysics. Viewed as a whole, Rorty's thought runs along three axes: inquiry, metaphysics, and community. Each should be taken in turn.

Inquiry

According to Rorty, neither science nor culture can claim a method which ensures validity. First, there are a plurality of sciences, and no one method can hope to capture the range of their practices. But might a special method not govern an exemplary science? Rorty rejects this view given the work of Dewey and Kuhn. When one looks closely at a given science, one does not find "a method," but a pattern of inquiry or paradigm, what Rorty terms a "vocabulary." Actual inquiry, he argues, employs culturally bound belief and habit clusters which overdetermine data collection, evidence assessment, and theory adjustment. In other words, inquiry proceeds holistically, and thus one cannot speak of "a method" vindicating particular beliefs. While one might locate method in general traits of experimentation, following Dewey's *Logic* (1938), such theories, Rorty argues, wax platitudinous, invoking the obvious: define problems, gather evidence, revise theories.

If one abandons a rhetoric of "method," "truth" might appear jeopardized. If some method does not validate a particular belief, how can it be "true"? Rorty believes this concern involves a misunderstanding. If "truth" denotes some special relation between beliefs and the world, then "truth" does come into question once inquirers can no longer appeal to the fidelity of a method which secures that relation. According to Rorty, however, following James, "true" neither denotes nor explains any relations, but is "a term of praise used for endorsing" certain rules for action, e.g. "stove tops can be hot, so watch out," or "electrons can just leap from one shell to another, so watch out" (Rorty 1991: 127). One should eschew all theories of truth, therefore, for they contain nothing to theorize about; rather, there are beliefs that are successful rules of action, and beliefs that are not.

One might think that a theory of truth is needed to explain why certain beliefs are successful, but Rorty, following Davidson, warns against such a project, arguing that one only needs a theory of truth if beliefs are made "true" in virtue of mapping on to the world. Such an idea is unintelligible, however. Holism in inquiry makes plain that beliefs are generated and tested only within vocabularies, and thus the praise of "true" makes sense in virtue of one's goals and patterns of action, i.e. one's vocabulary, and not in virtue of the way the world is. One might suppose that beliefs are thus made true by "cohering" with our vocabularies, but given that a belief can cohere and still not be a successful rule of action, and thus not be praiseworthy, coherence theories are misleading. True beliefs work, and that is all there is to say about them: that is, their being "true" doesn't tell us why they work, only that they do. "Truth," like "method," therefore, is philosophically unproblematic from the standpoint of inquiry.

What, then, is problematic for inquiry? Rorty's answer: fields of action in need of governance. For Rorty, inquiry engages indeterminate situations. Astronomy tracks the heavens, oncology tumor reproduction, and sociology behavioral patterns, and quite well. Various disciplines do not need support from philosophical theories about the nature of truth or method. Instead, they take care of themselves.

Metaphysics

Given the minimalism of Rorty's theory of inquiry, one wonders about his metaphysics. If one accepts his vision of inquiry without method, what is one to say about the "real," given that not only do subjects contribute to what can be termed "objects," but no a priori inquiry will be able to determine where subjects fall off and objects begin. In place of a transactional metaphysics, however, Rorty, after Davidson, rejects the scheme/content distinction. If we cannot engage the world except under a description, why retain the distinction between "the world as it is given under a description" and "the world as it is in itself"? The latter plays no role in inquiry, and given that the former is all there is to engage and explore, the qualification "given under a description" is unhelpful and misleading, for it suggests that "the world" might be given in some other way.

If one forgoes philosophical talk of the real, aligned projects seem imperiled. For many, the "real" (like "truth") keeps inquiry honest, and its removal may hearken a descent into dogmatism. Rorty disagrees. What drives inquiry is not some sense of the "real" apart from inquiry, for there is no such sense. Instead, inquiry is driven by action, and nothing calls for revision like disappointment and frustration. Moreover, forsaking the category of the real allows one to avoid the idealism implicit in those theories which posit "realities" for every vocabulary.

Another concern involves human meaning. In the absence of metaphysics, what guides projects of self-realization? Rorty finds this anxiety misplaced. Metaphysics chains human growth to ends which supposedly have roots in nature, and such chains have damaged people on the margins of various vocabularies, e.g. women and people of color. Relinquishing projects of self-realization should help free humanity from its history of violent marginalization. Moreover, the end of metaphysics empowers projects of self-creation. With essentialism out of the way, one can turn to creating oneself without the worry that one may be living at odds with one's "nature."

Rorty terms his position "metaphysical ironism." His stance is ironic because it refuses to regard any vocabulary as essential. The vocabularies which govern human inquiry, even those "final vocabularies" which articulate how humans ought to live, are always subject to revision: that is, they might fail to facilitate human projects or those projects might change. One thus affirms vocabularies knowing well that one may have to revise or give them up. Along with tempering totalitarian urges, Rorty's ironism would dissolve conundrums sparked by incompatible descriptions of the same object. On Rorty's view, we need not answer the question: which of Eddington's two tables is the real one, the one he writes upon, or the one he studies as a physicist? That question only arises if one can ask the "real" table to stand up. Given one cannot, the question admits of no solution and thus, like metaphysics itself, should be dropped.

Community

No longer a tribunal concerning truth, method, or "the real," philosophy, Rorty evinces, is at an end. But if it is, how does one ground a politics? Given the fragility of all vocabularies, Rorty abandons the idea that the public might be governed by a shared sense of the good life. He thus privatizes pursuits of the good, and advocates a democratic politics which, in the spirit of Mill and James, ensures that everyone be granted the opportunity to create themselves as they wish so long as they do not thereby prevent others from creating themselves. Rorty's public is a progressive one, however, and thus his politics, like Dewey's, demands that projects of human growth be protected and enabled, through mechanisms of education and distributive justice.

While many are drawn to pluralist forms of progressive liberalism, one wonders whether Rorty can philosophically ground his position. For Rorty, this is the wrong question to ask. On his view, a commitment to progressive liberalism, or "solidarity," is inescapably ethnocentric. It cannot be legitimated through arguments which transcend the culturally bound vocabularies of the disputants, e.g. through appeals to natural rights or rational agency. Instead, one explains how things are done "around here," and proceeds to convince one's interlocutors that they will find these conditions satisfying. One could disagree, of course, arguing that another way of running things would prove more satisfying, but such confrontations always prove circular, coming down to goods which one party finds prima facie desirable, or, to reinvoke the rhetoric of legitimation, intrinsically good.

Although he eschews the rhetoric of "legitimation crisis," Rorty does not believe that public life should go without social critique. He does believe, however, that such is not the business of a special kind of intellectual, i.e. the political philosopher. Instead, this task is best left to novelists, poets, and social visionaries. On Rorty's view, social progress, like individual growth, does not involve collective realization of overarching goods. Instead, progress involves extending and empowering opportunities of self-creation. And literature, or the arts in general, mark the vanguard of this project. On the one hand, it helps one understand others, thus building solidarity. On the other hand, it allows individuals to imagine different selves and different futures. And on a third hand, consider Adrienne Rich, it may inspire and provoke us to remedy situations we would rather not confront. But one should not construe the category of "literature" too narrowly, for, on Rorty's terms, social visionaries such as John Dewey and Martin Luther King enlarge democracy like great writers do: by opening its doors, by admitting more people to its dream than had been thought possible. As with inquiry, however, such work neither has nor needs a method or metaphysics. Instead, like all forms of human activity, it gropes about in the hope of meting out mortal happiness to mortal selves.

Further reading

Malachowski, Alan. *Reading Rorty.* Oxford: Blackwell, 1990.

Rorty, Richard. *Philosophy and the Mirror of Nature.* Princeton, NJ: Princeton University Press, 1979.

—— *Consequences of Pragmatism.* Minneapolis, MN: University of Minnesota Press, 1982.

—— *Contingency, Irony, and Solidarity.* Cambridge: Cambridge University Press, 1989.

—— *Objectivity, Relativism, and Truth*, Vol. 1 of *Philosophical Papers*, 2 vols. Cambridge: Cambridge University Press, 1991.

—— *Essays on Heidegger and Others*, Vol. 2 of *Philosophical Papers.* 2 vols. Cambridge: Cambridge University Press, 1991.

Saatkamp, Herman. *Rorty and Pragmatism: The Philosopher Responds to His Critics.* Nashville, TN: Vanderbilt University Press, 1995.

John Lysaker

ROSENTHAL, SANDRA B.: AUTOBIOGRAPHY

My enthusiasm for philosophy began almost the first day I entered a required freshman philosophy course, while my interest in pragmatism began through an exposure to C.I. Lewis's work in an undergraduate independent reading course. I later realized that my way of reading Lewis was contrary to the accepted analytic interpretation and bore the marks of classical American pragmatism, to which I had not yet been exposed. As my interests turned in that direction, what unfailingly struck me was not differences among the pragmatists but their underlying similarities, and the way each seemed to complement and clarify the others. A general skeletal framework of classical pragmatism emerged for me in the very process of becoming acquainted with the texts. A brief exposure to phenomenology convinced me, to my astonishment and the skepticism of virtually everyone else, of its underlying compatibility with pragmatism, and guided me in locating and developing some of pragmatism's very embryonic doctrines.

Throughout my career there were three crucial and ongoing personal influences. Peter Hare, from the backdrop of a history of encouragement and support, argued long and hard to convince me that while my writings were in keeping with classical pragmatism, they were going beyond its present development in a way which demanded a book. This gave me a sense of intellectual freedom which resulted in *Speculative Pragmatism.* Through a long history of exposure to the writings and personal vitality of John Lachs and John McDermott, I developed a more vivid sense of the relevancy of pragmatism for issues of daily life.

The direction of my writings was guided by several interests. I wanted to present pragmatism not as an historical episode but as a living position capable of adding a unique vitality to the contemporary philosophic scene. I thought it important to see the classical pragmatists in terms of their underlying unity rather than their more superficial differences, and show how this in turn yields a full-blown philosophic system that provides an integrated paradigmatic novelty – including a paradigmatic novelty for understanding process metaphysics and the nature of philosophic system itself – which undercuts, and provides a shattering attack upon, virtually all the assumptions governing the philosophical tradition and the kinds of alternatives and dilemmas to which they give rise, as well as similar assumptions, alternatives, and dilemmas, offered in seemingly new fashion, by what is often considered "mainstream" philosophy. To do this it was also necessary to lay bare the way in which this unique paradigm is lost if it is not kept clearly distinct from the neo-pragmatisms which are engaged in something very different. On more specific notes, I also wanted to show the mutual enrichment to be gained for both pragmatism and continental thought by an ongoing encounter between them; and finally, to put pragmatism to work in throwing a unique light on the issues and debates within the field of business ethics. To what extent I have succeeded remains an open question for me.

Further reading

Rosenthal, Sandra B. *Speculative Pragmatism.* Amherst, MA: University of Massachusetts Press, 1986. Paperback edition Peru, IL: Open Court, 1990.

—— *Charles Peirce's Pragmatic Pluralism.* Albany, NY: SUNY Press, 1994.

—— *Time, Continuity, and Indeterminacy: A Pragmatic Engagement with Contemporary Perspectives.* Albany, NY: SUNY Press, 2000.

Rosenthal, Sandra B. and Buchholz, Rogene A. *Rethinking Business Ethics: A Pragmatic Perspective.* New York: Oxford University Press, 2000.

Sandra B. Rosenthal

ROYCE, JOSIAH: EPISTEMOLOGY

Unlike many contemporary philosophers Royce does not make a rigid distinction between metaphysics and epistemology. That is, for Royce, the theory of knowledge is part of the larger question of the nature of the Absolute Mind or Self that is fully aware of the finite particulars of the world and its orders. There is a shift of emphasis in Royce, moving from a fairly static understanding of the Absolute (1885–1912) to a more pluralistic and time-bound understanding of the Spirit as the agent of interpretation. The later Royce, c. 1912–16, writes under the influence of Peirce's semiotics and the biblical writings of St Paul.

In his first major book, *The Religious Aspect of Philosophy* of 1885, Royce develops his idealistic epistemology along hermeneutic lines. He rejects realism with its view that a given thought intends and corresponds to an external object by insisting that only an internally coherent and finite/infinite parallel structure for thought exists. The finite thoughts of my mind are coherent in their own right insofar as they emerge from volition and attention to realities that transcend the empirical. From his dissertation on Kant he unfolds the idea of what he calls the "postulates" that are thought forms that reach beyond the empirically given into values, norms, and categorial structures that are linked to the Absolute. We are creatures of will and the core of our self is rooted in the Absolute Self that is a Will beyond time and space. Finite ideas standing alone leave us with epistemological chaos until they are woven into the fabric of the Absolute.

The hermeneutic dimension of his idealistic epistemology is seen in the problem of psychological interpretation. He gives the example of two people, John and Thomas, who must come to an understanding of each other, that is, to correctly interpret the substantive self with whom they are in dialogue. But this process soon fissures into six selves; namely, John's idea of Thomas, Thomas's idea of John, John's idea of himself. Thomas's idea of himself, and the real John and the real Thomas. Royce argues that there is no possibility for genuine knowledge in the finite realm of psychological projection and reciprocity, only an entanglement of delusion. The way out of this morass is through an attunement to the Absolute Mind for whom the real John and the real Thomas are fully known outside of the vicissitudes of time. Structurally, Royce argues, my thought a:b must be isomorphic with the Absolute thought A:B. However, we get few clues at this stage (1885) as to how the isomorphism is to be accomplished by finite minds.

In his next major work, based on his Gifford Lectures of 1899, *The World and the Individual* (1901), Royce refines his analysis of the correlation between finite ideas and the world of the Absolute by introducing the mathematical idea of the self-representative system as explicated by Richard Dedekind. The finite willing world of the human self lives in what he calls the world of description while the divine mind lives in the realm of appreciation. The link between mere external description and full internal appreciation is through the self-representative system that links finite to infinite knowledge. Royce gives the example of someone who is asked to draw a perfect map of England. They are to represent everything in England on this map. When they are finished they find that they have left out one element, namely the map itself which is now a part of England. So they must draw the map on the map, but now this leaves the project incomplete yet again as the second map is now also part of England, so a third map must be drawn inside of the second one. This process continues to infinity. The important point is that any one map in the self-representative system can stand for the series as a totality through a projection outward and downward simultaneously. In our finite epistemological and hermeneutic moves we catch a piece of the infinite series through a kind of epistemic grace whereby the Absolute bestows its plenitude upon us. Yet it remains a mystery of how, phenomenologically, we actually encounter the self-representative series and know when we have done so.

A major turning point for Royce took place around 1912 when he carefully works through the semiotic writings of the early Peirce. The idea of the self-representative system becomes more "earth-bound" by becoming transfigured into the idea of sign series as they unfold within the structure of community. His earlier idealistic epistemology becomes reshaped into a communitarian and more fully hermeneutic model in which finite selves unite to work in and through the Spirit Interpreter to create and sustain what he calls, following his understanding of St Paul, the "Beloved Community." In *The Problem of Christianity* (1913) he works through Christian scriptures and Peirce's semiotics to unfold a semiotic epistemology that places priority on how finite minds, each loyal to the semiotic processes of other selves, unite to forge a spirit-filled community in which genuine knowledge takes place. The atemporal Absolute of 1901 is modified into the Spirit that lives and moves through communitarian and earth-bound structures.

We traffic in signs and know that we do so. Like Peirce, Royce argues that signs come in series with neither beginning nor end in view. We interpret a sign whenever we encounter it in any modality and this encounter creates a new sign that functions to amplify and deepen the original sign. Sign structures are triadic in several senses. Whenever a perception and a conception come together we get an interpretation (again pointing to the hermeneutic dimension of his epistemology). Second, whenever we, for example, translate a text we have three terms: the text, the interpreter, and the interpretee. Third, we see the present self interpreting its past self to its future self. All three modalities are epistemological dimensions of semiosis. In the mature Royce knowledge is semiotic and interpretive. The energy within these triads comes from the Spirit Interpreter who coaxes signs into birthing further and deeper meanings. Here there is a kind of grace that is even more evident than in the earlier Royce as the structure of knowledge is tied to the Spirit that infuses the community with its infinite powers. In the Beloved Community we are known as we truly are and we know other loyal selves as they are. The finite and the infinite have now come together in the time process.

Further reading

Royce, Josiah. *The Religious Aspect of Philosophy.* New York: Harper Torchbook, 1958 [1885].

—— *The World and the Individual.* New York: Dover, 1959 [1901].

—— *The Problem of Christianity*, ed. John E. Smith. Chicago, IL: University of Chicago Press, 1968 [1913].

—— *The Basic Writings of Josiah Royce*, 2 vols, ed. John McDermott. Chicago, IL: University of Chicago Press, 1969.

ROBERT S. CORRINGTON

ROYCE, JOSIAH: EVIL

Josiah Royce (1855–1916) struggled with the problem of evil throughout his life, exploring it from various approaches and with different refinements throughout his career. For Royce evil was a genuine philosophical problem as well as a practical one.

Royce believed that one could account for the moral world only by a form of metaphysical idealism and thus evil was a metaphysical problem. However, he equally saw evil as a fact of the world and he knew the pessimism it could invoke. Further, as a native Californian and historian of early California, he described ways in which evil manifested itself in social relations among persons, in social bodies infected with racism, greed, a variety of harmful prejudices, expressions of hate, and mob violence.

In, *Studies of Good and Evil* (1899) Royce provides an overview of the problem of evil. Thus he asks how far the knowledge of evil contributes to moral perfection. Seeing physical life and the moral life as balancing opposing tendencies, Royce posits that moral goodness, unlike innocence, is only won through struggle with the forces of evil and it involves a rather deep knowledge of evil – a knowledge that unfortunately can lead to sin. This thesis is further explored in his essay, "The Case of John Bunyan" (1894), where Royce presents a case of an actual good man triumphantly struggling with his own profound problem of evil. Royce continually stresses the personal and experiential in dealing with the problem of evil. A consistent theme, both philosophicaly and practically, is the necessity of a courageous struggle against evil in all its forms. For Royce, individuals could only achieve genuine spirituality and morality by detesting and subordinating evil. Thus, for Royce, good is not a simple concept but rather an idea inseparable from the idea of evil. Further, the essence of moral life is not to seek a pure good or a distant ideal God but rather to find God in the present within the mix of good and evil and to see the truly good man as one who takes his part in the struggle with evil.

In "The Problem of Job," (1897) Royce presents a fairly succinct overview of the traditional statement of the problem of evil and various standard solutions. Job views God traditionally, namely as wise, omnipotent, all powerful, and all good, and sees his own situation as one of universal unearned ill-fortune, and a reigning down of evils on a good man. For Royce, Job represents the fundamental psychological fact about the problem of evil, namely the universal experience of unearned ill-fortune. This, asserts Royce, is the experience of every person, the kind of evil that each person can see for themselves every day if they choose, and this fundamental experiential and psychological perspective grounds Royce's own answers to the problem of evil as well as his dismissal of the various traditional answers. Thus, for example, there is the view that the purpose of the world is "soul making," that pain teaches us the ways of the world and helps us develop our higher potentialities. Royce believes this answer inadequate because it presupposes a greater evil, namely a world which allows evils as the only way to reach given goals. Such an answer Royce believes unacceptable to a sufferer of evil and undeserved ills.

Another answer to the problem of evil is the infinite worth of agents with free will. Royce finds value in this view in that it acknowledges evil as a logically necessary part of a perfect moral order, but he believes this answer ultimately fails, and particularly for the innocent sufferer. Such unearned ills may be partly due to free will actions, but, asserts Royce, the unearned ills are also due to a God who declines to protect the innocent.

Royce believes that as long as one views God as an external power, as Job did, the problem of evil cannot be solved. Rather, one must recognize God as internally present to us and as suffering with us to produce the higher good. When we suffer, our sufferings are God's sufferings and this is the case because without suffering, evil, and tragedy, God's life could not be perfected. Further, asserts Royce, personally overcoming evil is the essence of the moral life. Thus, in his 1912 book *The Sources of Religious Insight*, Royce presents man as a destroyer of evil, a being who uses every effort to get rid of evil. Conquering evils and oppressions provides man's greatest opportunities for loyalty and here is the source of religious insight and spiritual triumph. The encounter of human selves with the problem of evil is, for Royce, the most important moral aspect of the world. One must see the problematic situation into which human selves are immersed as part of the atoning process which tends toward an ultimate reconciliation of finite conflicts. Confronted with evils, one needs to trust within one's limited view that the Spirit of the Universal Community reconciles.

The relations of life are of ultimate significance and good persons are called to build community, seeking to interpret and reconcile diverse views. In his *The Problem of Christianity* (1913) Royce focuses on the idea of "atonement," the work of individuals and community to restore unity to aggrieved and shattered relationships. Indeed Royce saw the universe as an ongoing interpretative, reconciling process, and each individual as a courageous pilgrim overcoming evil and engaging in creative, reconciling deeds while placing trust in a far wider and deeper wisdom of the Interpreter-Spirit of the Universal Community. Royce believed such a teleological and purposive universe necessary to account for a moral point of view. It is because he holds to this belief that he finds evil, represented in the anti-teleological elements of the world, a serious metaphysical problem.

Ultimately, Royce sees evil as an eternal part of both human and divine life and the human conquering of evil step by step as the most important moral fact of the universe.

Further reading

Oppenheim, Frank M., SJ. *Royce's Mature Ethics.* Notre Dame, IN: University of Notre Dame Press, 1993.

Royce, Josiah. *The Religious Aspect of Philosophy: A Critique of the Bases of Conduct and of Faith.* Boston, MA: Houghton Mifflin, 1885. Reprinted as a Harper Torchbook, New York: Harper, 1958.

—— *The Philosophy of Loyalty.* New York: Macmillan, 1908.

—— *Race Questions, Provincialism, and Other American Problems.* New York: Macmillan, 1908.

—— *The Problem of Christianity*, 2 vols. New York: Macmillan, 1913.

JACQUELYN ANN KEGLEY

ROYCE, JOSIAH: INFLUENCE

Royce left no cadre of absolute idealists to fulfill his program and founded no school that bears his name. Moreover, since his younger contemporaries who once embraced idealism later abandoned it in favor of versions of realism, naturalism, and scientism, many expected absolute idealism to fade away in silent neglect. Others expected that, since Royce came toward the end of a movement of foreign origin, absolute idealism would not survive his death. However, Royce deeply inspired his colleagues and students, if not as much by his doctrine of the Absolute, as by his rigorous philosophic method, penetrating criticism, encouragement of original thought, and his anticipation of the future course of philosophy. In fact, Royce influenced James and Peirce and prepared his students for future movements in western philosophy. For embedded in Royce's idealism are two lines of reasoning that anticipated the two dominant streams of twentieth-century thought. Royce's work in mathematics, logic and the analysis of knowledge inspired C.I. Lewis and C.J. Ducasse, while his moral and religious thought was re-appropriated in Gabriel Marcel's phenomenology.

Throughout their long friendship, James and Royce mutually influenced each other. James was one of the first to acknowledge Royce's influence on his philosophical and psychological work. In *The Principles of Psychology*, James credited Royce's psychological studies on self-consciousness, memory, and attention, and approvingly quoted *The Religious Aspect of Philosophy* where Royce describes the "law of least effort." James' famous chapter on the "stream of thought" is profitably reread in light of Royce's account. Philosophically, James was deeply impressed by Royce's argument for absolute idealism based on the possibility of error, and reluctantly accepted its conclusion for he could find no way to overturn it. If James ever fully embraced absolute idealism, it was short-lived, for he never stopped struggling against the doctrine. This led to their fruitful exchanges over James' pragmatic conception of truth. Royce argued that James' early statements on pragmatism and truth involved an equivocation on two distinct concepts of truth and led to subjectivism and solipsism. In time, Royce compelled James to successively refine his notion of truth, moving him ever closer to C.S. Peirce's views on truth and meaning toward which Royce himself was moving.

It is well known that Peirce reinvigorated Royce's abiding interests in logic and mathematics. This eventually led to Royce's System Σ and his work on infinite series. Peirce also imparted a spirit of "pragmaticism" to Royce's idealism and convinced him of the necessity of the triadic structure of interpretation. In fact, toward the end of his life, Peirce commented that, among those who espoused pragmatism, Royce's was closest to his own. Recently, Frank Oppenheim has argued that the influence between Peirce and Royce was mutual. It was Royce, Peirce acknowledged, who convinced him of an ethical basis and richness of logic that escapes its formalism. Just after reading Royce's *The Problem of Christianity*, Peirce wrote:

> As for my Pragmatism, though it is all very well as far as it goes, it chiefly goes to improve the *security* of inference without touching, what is far more important, its Uberty [rich potential]. It doesn't for instance have anything to say as to our exaltation of beauty, duty, or truth … I am going to insist upon the superiority of Uberty over Security.
>
> (Oppenheim 2005: 32)

Peirce's longing here is not fully explained, but perhaps he meant to acknowledge the extent to which Royce succeeded in giving logic a metaphysical embodiment that attempted to do justice to truth and value. If so, then a similar lesson impressed many of Royce's students.

As noted above, Royce founded no school; personality, example, and style were other modes of influence that greatly mattered to Royce, especially in regard to his students. His teaching style suggests that he would have thought it a failure had he left a school of followers. His students fondly recalled how he urged them to independent original thought. Once, a doctoral candidate who sought Royce's approval by seasoning his oral examination with Roycean ideas was instead reproved by a bemused Royce who proposed to award the student the RD (Doctor of Royce) rather than the PhD. Among his most important students were George Santayana, Henry Sheffer, A.O. Lovejoy, C.J. Ducasse, G.H. Mead, T.S. Eliot, W.E. Hocking and C.I. Lewis. The diversity of thought represented in this small sample underscores Royce's success as a teacher.

Of his students, Hocking and Lewis most notably found ways to reformulate Royce's teachings and produced original idealistic theories. Both were drawn to Royce's logical studies, but only Lewis, who considered Royce his "ideal of a philosopher," nurtured the seeds planted by Royce and became one of the most important logicians and epistemologists of the twentieth century. Royce introduced his students to *Principia Mathematica*, the paradoxes of which (material implication) motivated Lewis to develop his theory of strict implication and establish modal logic. Though Lewis never embraced Royce's metaphysics, he appreciated his teacher's treatment of the *a priori* and pragmatic elements of knowledge and scientific method. From Royce's concept of "leading ideas," Lewis developed his concept of the "pragmatic *a priori*," the key concept in his *Mind and the World Order*. Another consequence of Royce's emphasis on logic materialized when Ducasse founded the *Journal of Symbolic Logic*.

Hocking took his lead from Royce's struggle to preserve the significance of the individual person in the context of absolute idealism. In the late 1890s, Royce developed an account of the social context of individual self-consciousness in several psychological papers first presented at Berkeley when he delivered his famous lecture, "The Conception of God," further developed in *The World and the Individual*. Hocking rejected Royce's arguments, and offered alternative arguments for the interdependence of self and society. If nature is that-which-is-experienced-in-common, Hocking held, then, to experience nature is to experience other minds, finite or divine; for one could only experience nature as that-which-is-experienced-in-common if that experience included others experiencing nature. From this, he inferred that reality is a society of selves experiencing the world-in-common, a conclusion with social and political consequences. Royce's theory of the social context of the self-conscious individual also shaped the work of G.H. Mead.

In Europe, Marcel found the beginnings of his own phenomenology of hope in Royce's ethics of loyalty, his social conception of the self, and the triadic structure of interpretation. Specifically, Marcel's principle of "fidelity" has its roots in Roycean loyalty, and Marcel's notion of "communicative being" in the "I–Thou" relationship traces to Royce's concept of the "Beloved Community" of interpretation. Through Marcel, these ideas made their way to Paul Ricoeur. Royce's theories of community and interpretation received one of their clearest expositions in the work of John Smith. In *Royce's Social Infinite*, Smith traces Royce's struggle with the relation between individuals and the Absolute and its eventual resolution in his doctrine of the community of interpretation. In doing so, Smith established the value and relevance of Royce's moral philosophy and his interpretation of Christianity to twentieth-century issues. Most recently, the writings of Kegley and Trotter in social theory and biomedical ethics prove the relevance of Royce's moral philosophy to contemporary medical and communitarian questions. But even in mathematics and logic, Royce's work on systems of order has received renewed appreciation in the historical research of Grattan-Guinness.

Further reading

Cesarz, Gary L. "A World of Difference: The Royce-Howison Debate on the Conception of God," *The Personalist Forum* 15, 1, special issue (Spring 1999): 84–128.

Grattan-Guinness, I. *The Search for Mathematical Roots, 1870–1940: Logics, Set Theories and the Foundations of Mathematics from Cantor through Russell to Gödel.* Princeton, NJ: Princeton University Press, 2000.

Kegley, Jacquelyn. *Genuine Individuals, Genuine Communities: A Roycean Public Philosophy.* Nashville, TN: Vanderbilt University Press, 1997.

Lewis, C.I. *Mind and the World Order: Outline of a Theory of Knowledge.* New York: Dover, 1956.

Marcel, Gabriel. *Royce's Metaphysics*, trans. Virginia and Gordon Ringer. Chicago, IL: Henry Regnery, 1956.

Oppenheim, Frank M., SJ. *Reverence for the Relations of Life: Re-imagining Pragmatism via Josiah Royce's Interactions with Peirce, James and Dewey.* Notre Dame, IN: University of Notre Dame Press, 2005.

Smith, John E. *Royce's Social Infinite: The Community of Interpretation.* New York: Liberal Arts Press, 1950; New York: Archon Books, 1969.

Trotter, Griffin. *The Loyal Physician: Roycean Ethics and the Practice of Medicine.* Nashville, TN: Vanderbilt University Press, 1997.

GARY L. CESARZ

ROYCE, JOSIAH: LIFE

Josiah Royce (1855–1916) was born in the small mining community of Grass Valley, California. His parents, Josiah and Sarah Eleanor Bayliss Royce, had migrated there in the unfulfilled hope of finding gold. Royce proved precocious and enrolled in the University of California in Oakland at the age of fourteen. In 1875, Royce received a Bachelor of Arts degree in classics from the university, which had relocated to Berkeley.

He immediately left for a year of study in Germany. Leaving the deepest impressions on him were Wilhelm Wundt, who taught Royce anthropology and logic, and Rudolf Hermann Lotze, who introduced Royce to post-Kantian idealism. Royce continued his engagement with these ideas at Johns Hopkins University in Baltimore, commencing study in 1876. Among the requirements of the program was that students formulate and deliver their own lectures to one another; Royce offered courses on Schopenhauer and Kant. Royce received one of the first four doctorate degrees awarded by Johns Hopkins, awarded in 1878.

Prospects of employment being bleak, with some dissatisfaction Royce returned to the University of California as an assistant instructor of English where he joined numerous clubs and organizations, and wrote, delivered, and published several articles, as well a textbook for use by his logic students. In 1880 Royce married Katharine Head. In 1882, their first son, Christopher, was born.

In the spring of 1882, Royce received a letter from William James, with whom he had developed a friendship over summers in Boston and Cambridge, asking Royce to temporarily replace him at Harvard while on a sabbatical leave. Royce agreed to the appointment and following two one-year extensions to his contract, Royce was promoted to assistant professor at Harvard in the spring of 1885. He would spend the rest of his career there.

In addition to his promotion, in 1885, Royce met success with the publication of his *The Religious Aspect of Philosophy*, featuring the introduction of his theory of the Absolute, an all-encompassing intelligence of which each individual intelligence is a part. In addition to the birth of his second son, Edward, in 1886, Royce published his history, *California*, which would be followed in 1887 by his novel, *The Feud of Oakfield Creek*, also set in his home state. Though some consider these projects digressions, in them Royce grapples with tensions between individuals and communities; this struggle pervades most of his philosophical thought.

In 1888, Royce suffered a nervous breakdown, and upon returning from recuperative travel, learned of the recent death of his father. The birth of his third son, Stephen, in 1889, was one of relatively few occasions for joy in the following few years. In 1890, the notorious "Abbot Affair" was ignited by Royce's searing review of F.E. Abbot's *The Way Out of Agnosticism*. A dogged contestation unraveled, with the duo battling in print for two years. In the midst of the quarrel Royce's mother died in 1891.

Royce became chair of the Department of Philosophy at Harvard in 1894, a post he retained for four years. Within that span, *The Conception of God* and *Studies of Good and Evil* were published. The former recapitulated Royce's argument for the Absolute, while the focus of the latter was "The Problem of Job" (the problem of evil). From 1899 to 1900, Royce delivered the prestigious Gifford Lectures at the University of Aberdeen; these were published in two volumes as *The World and the Individual*, Royce's major work in metaphysics.

Of his work to follow, two collections of essays published in 1908 demand explicit attention. In the popular *The Philosophy of Loyalty*, Royce adumbrated an ethics centered upon devotion to causes. In the prescient *Race Questions, Provincialism, and Other American Problems*, Royce applied this ethics to concrete situations, several of which are particularly pressing even today. "Loyalty," which Royce sometimes interchanges with "love," emerges again as one of *The Sources of Religious Insight* in 1912, and figures prominently in his signature work, *The Problem of Christianity*, published in 1913. In this text, implementing Pauline doctrine, Royce incisively argues that human salvation lies in loyal "communities of interpretation" in which triadic unities are accomplished through the mediation of conflicts of two combatant parties by an interpretive third.

Royce died in 1916, as the First World War wore on. Much of the end of his life had been consumed with coping with this conflict. Published posthumously, "The Hope of the Great Community" is one manifestation of this effort. It has been said that Royce's use of the word "hope" affirmed the creative possibility of the life of humanity. This affirmation is demonstrably a part of Royce's philosophical vision and is, moreover, thematic of Royce's life.

Further reading

Clendenning, John. *The Life and Thought of Josiah Royce*, revised and expanded edition. Nashville, TN: Vanderbilt University Press, 1999.

Hine, Robert V. *Josiah Royce: From Grass Valley to Harvard*. Norman, OK: University of Oklahoma Press, 1992.

Kuklick, Bruce. *Josiah Royce: An Intellectual Biography*. Indianapolis, IN: Hackett, 1985.

McDermott, John J. "Introduction" in *The Basic Writings of Josiah Royce*, 2 vols, ed. John J. McDermott. New York: Fordham University Press, 2005 [1969].

Oppenheim, Frank M., SJ. *Reverence for the Relations of Life: Re-Imagining Pragmatism via Josiah Royce's Interactions with Peirce, James, and Dewey*. Notre Dame, IN: University of Notre Dame Press, 2005

MATHEW A. FOUST

ROYCE, JOSIAH: LOYALTY/ COMMUNITY

"Loyalty" and "community" are the centerpieces of Josiah Royce's ethics. For Royce loyalty is a comprehensive moral virtue and also a self-revising moral ideal through which persons constitute themselves ontologically and integrate themselves into communities and the world. Loyalty is always fidelity to a community. The most enlightened loyalties are loyalties to communities that align themselves with other communities, forming higher-order communities of communities. Ultimately, genuine loyalty is directed to a universal community of all persons. This ideal, universal community is the fundamental reality in the universe, the source of all being and truth; yet it is never fully actualized in human experience. It manifests through the spirit of interpretation, which animates the spirit of loyalty in each person and hence constitutes the deepest motive for human morality.

The concept of loyalty permeates writings in Royce's middle (1896–1911) and late (1912–16) periods, but receives its most focused treatment in the 1908 treatise, *The Philosophy of Loyalty*. Natural loyalty, on Royce's account, arises through the efforts of individuals to establish a personal identity. Royce holds that "a person, an individual self, may be defined as a human life lived according to a plan" (Royce 1995: 79). To formulate such a plan is to make determinate one's own will. This process involves, among other things, specification of the individual's duties and moral commitments. Thus, Royce reinterprets Kant's "Principle of Autonomy" by linking individual fulfillment with ethical responsibility.

This principle is impotent, however, when conceived in purely individual terms. Apart from training and other social influences, the individual has only a collection of disparate impulses from which to draw. But these sources are insufficient for establishing a durable individual will. In fact, Royce holds that we begin to develop a will only by imitating the wills of various role models, and then at times contrasting our will with that of others.

Royce regards the apparent incompatibility between the principle of autonomy and the social determinants of the individual will as a paradox that is best resolved through an attitude of loyalty. His provisional definition of loyalty is "a willing and practical and thoroughgoing devotion of a person to a cause" (Royce 1995: 9). Loyalty resolves the paradox, first of all, because the loyalist's cause is neither wholly personal, nor something merely inherited from a collective "other." It is transpersonal in the sense that it binds a multiplicity of persons who have constructed their life plans (and thus constituted their personhood) around it. It is "superpersonal" insofar as it is valued for more than its utility for any individual or collection of individuals. Loyal individuals conceive the cause as something that survives their own demise – indeed, as something worth dying for. Furthermore, the principle of autonomy is satisfied by loyalty insofar as: (1) service to the cause is "willing" – i.e. chosen freely among various possible causes, without overweening social influence, and (2) each individual serves the cause in her own unique way. A cause that is simply dictated by an external source produces, on Royce's account, at best only a degenerate form of loyalty.

Beyond its paradox-resolving attributes, loyalty is effective as a source of personal identity because of its practical, thoroughgoing nature. As the criterion of right and wrong, and good and bad, loyalty becomes a kind of meta-criterion for other choices (such as career moves and political alliances) that impact the formation of individual personality, moral values and the formation of a life plan.

Loyalties are community-forming in the sense that the cause loyalists serve is a mutual interest they share. According to Royce, communities are defined by such interests. As he points out, one can never be loyal to an individual person, but rather to a "tie that binds" persons (Royce 1995: 11). In essence, the "cause" is the interest or value that defines a moral community – where the "defining" occurs not just abstractly, but through past events and anticipated outcomes that community members mutually recognize as aspects of their personal histories and personal destinies. Hence, Royce's preliminary definition of loyalty yields a second, fuller definition: loyalty is love of a community.

Natural loyalties arise in natural communities such as families, churches and polities. Because these loyalties untangle the primary problem of human life – the problem of personal identity – and provide individuals with comprehensive personal ideals, Royce believes that they constitute the ultimate good for each individual. Just as clearly, loyal lives embody the good for moral communities, which are higher-order persons.

In conceiving loyalty as a moral ideal, however, a problem arises. Some natural communities subscribe to destructive, hateful, or false doctrines that pit natural loyalties against one another. If loyalty is to serve as a satisfactory ethical ideal, it must contain a means of sorting out these conflicts and channeling natural loyalties to better ends.

Hence, Royce believes that a philosophy of loyalty must offer guidance about how to choose a good cause. If the source of the problem is that loyalties conflict, and destroy one another, then the solution, Royce holds, is to live in the spirit of universal loyalty, in which particular causes are aligned with a higher-order cause that recognizes the prima facie value of all loyalties. Devotion to this higher-order cause, according to Royce, is "loyalty to loyalty:"

> In so far as it lies in your power, so choose your cause, and so serve it, that, by reason of your choice and of your service, there shall be more loyalty in the world rather than less. And, in fact, so choose and so serve your individual cause as to secure thereby the greatest increase of loyalty amongst men.
>
> (Royce 1995: 57).

The concept "loyalty to loyalty" thus completes Royce's preliminary development of loyalty as a personal and ethical ideal. Royce's enlightened loyalty to loyalty devotes itself to the creation of a universe in which all loyalties cohere. Several features of this enlightened loyalty bear particular attention: (1) it recognizes the universe of cohering loyalties as a cause; (2) it recognizes that this cause is shared by all who are loyal to loyalty; (3) it recognizes therefore that, by virtue of this common devotion, those who are loyal to loyalty join together in a single "Great Community" of all humanity; (4) it recognizes that loyalty to the Great Community is the ultimate source of ethical content in their particular, natural and individual human loyalties; and, hence, (5) it recognizes that the Great Community is a universal community and an object of all genuine human loyalty.

The remaining problem for Royce is to show that the universal community is a "fact" of the universe – i.e. that it exists – and hence that the philosophy of loyalty is no mere wishful fancy, but indeed an expression of ethical truth. We know, from our description of the loyal life, that the universal community is not fully actualized, or even adequately conceived, in human experience. Based on reasoning exhibited in his earlier *The World and the Individual*, Royce held that we also know the same to be true of all other human ideas. That is, no idea is fully actualized or adequately conceived in human experience (which is to say, also, that its truth or falsity is never fully exhibited). Because the objects of ideas – "facts" or "truths" – mutually interpenetrate one another, the fulfillment or proper interpretation of one idea would entail the fulfillment or proper interpretation of all. Hence, the "truth" about the universal community mingles with all the facts and truths of the universe. Loyalty to the universal community, then, is loyalty to a community of interpretation – dedicated to rendering the universal community into a determinate "fact."

Genuine "facts" and "truths" – like communities – are transpersonal. That is, they are identical, and equally true, for all persons; and they are what they are apart from the perception of any individual person. Individual human ideas, including loyalty, aim at expressing facts or truths. But the perceivable linkages between human ideas are never sufficiently determinate fully to manifest a given fact or truth. If there is any ultimate truth, or even any ultimate meaning in human life, then it must issue from a source beyond humanity. On the basis of such considerations, the "middle Royce" tried to demonstrate that a fact or truth fully exists, as fact or truth, only insofar as it is the object of a universal consciousness that both enacts and perceives all facts/truths in their fullness and relatedness. Royce called this universal consciousness "God." On the basis of such reasoning, Royce concluded that the universal community fully exists, if at all, as both an object and an act of God. If there is any truth at all, in ethics or elsewhere, then there is a universal community; and it is part of God.

In the "mature" Royce, efforts at demonstrating God's existence give way to the project of interpreting human experience and inquiring about whether, and to what degree, God manifests within it. In his analysis of the "Problem of Christianity" – i.e. the problem of whether or not contemporary persons can be Christians without contradicting what they've learned from forms of inquiry that do not presuppose a "Christian" viewpoint – Royce employs a triad of leading Christian ideas. These include: (1) community, (2) the lost state of the detached individual, and (3) atonement. The lost state of the individual manifests as the tangible inevitability that each person at some point will betray her loyalties. Conceived broadly, this means that she will interpret poorly or erroneously – betraying the community of interpretation. Atonement provides for the remediation of these failures by a third person (outside the dyad of wrongdoer–person wronged), who helps not only to get things right, but also to render an ultimate outcome that is something better, and more effective at inspiring loyalty, than what pertained prior to the betrayal. In his mature Trinitarian Christian vision, Royce portrays Jesus as the redeemer – the one whose atoning acts inspire the religion of loyalty. The Father is the universal community. And the Holy Spirit is the spirit of interpretation – imparting Grace that enables fallen loyalists to recognize their true ideal, bit by bit, as they undertake the arduous task of enacting the universal community on earth.

Further reading

Oppenheim, Frank M. *Royce's Mature Philosophy of Religion*. Notre Dame, IN: University of Notre Dame Press, 1987.

—— *Royce's Mature Ethics*. Notre Dame, IN: University of Notre Dame Press, 1993.

Royce, Josiah. *The Problem of Christianity*. Chicago, IL: University of Chicago Press, 1968 [1918].

—— *The World and the Individual*, 2 vols. Gloucester, MA: Peter Smith, 1976.

—— *The Philosophy of Loyalty*. Nashville, TN: Vanderbilt University Press, 1995 [1908].

Trotter, Griffin. *The Loyal Physician*. Nashville, TN: Vanderbilt University Press, 1997.

GRIFFIN TROTTER

ROYCE, JOSIAH: RELIGION

From boyhood, Royce found religion his deepest interest. His ideas about religion developed, became richer after 1907, and were deepened by his 1912 insight into C.S. Peirce's ideas. Accordingly, this article focuses on the late Royce's thought, relying chiefly on his *Philosophy of Loyalty* (1908), *Sources of Religious Insight* (1912), and *The Problem of Christianity* (1913).

In his *Philosophy of Loyalty,* Royce presented religion as transcending morality by gaining beliefs through the emotion-laden symbols and legends of the higher religions. Through sufferings and creative imagination, humans eventually distill the beliefs which form the "creed of the Absolute Religion." These five factual truths are that the divine World-Life is: one good rational Whole; truly near us, although invisible; full of meaning despite our barren present experience; personally interested in our destiny as moral beings; and meeting us in our truly loyal deeds just as certainly as Moses experienced in his face-to-face encounters with God.

Of his *Sources of Religious Insight*, Royce wrote that it contained the whole sense of himself in a brief compass. In it Royce presented religion in a far richer way than previously. Like William James in *The Varieties of Religious Experience* 1902, Royce now held that a person discovers religion most profoundly when experiencing a two-sided interest. People want union with their highest genuine good and also escape from shipwrecking their lives through failure to prize this good at its real worth. Religion centers, then, on establishing a felt union with one's Deliverer – that is, with that Reality which *frees* a person from being entrapped in one's narrow viewpoint and moral baseness. No human self can achieve this liberation by itself alone nor by any other human means.

Royce took issue, however, with William James' belief that individual religious experience was adequate. Instead, such experience needed the enrichments of social, rational, and volitional insights insofar as these become synthesized into true "loyalty to universal loyalty." Only then does the religious insight become genuine, valid, and hence reliable. Loyalty's religious insight is further enhanced by sorrows that transform the mind with still deeper insights and by the recognition of "the unity of the spirit," found in the invisible Church.

Royce cautioned against imagining that one's institutional religion is the only genuine religion. If one does so, one entraps oneself within such a particular view that it blocks one from reaching a universal grasp of religion and its definition. Instead, Royce called upon his almost entirely Christian audience to set aside for the present their particular Christian associations of salvation with ideas about the fall of the human race, its process of redemption, and the human soul's destiny in a future life. He called them to generalize their idea of salvation in such a way that they could hear that deep universal cry which arises in the darkness of this world at any time or place from any wanderer who seeks some saving light.

Realizing that each human being is infinitely needy in its yearnings for food, pleasures, power, peace, and love in all its forms, Royce focused on a still deeper need at work in every person. Not to fulfill this need renders one's life altogether meaningless and a radical failure. Hence, what human selves need above all is to be saved from the pervasive and overmastering danger of failing to reach their paramount goal. A human self can and often does recognize the object of this deepest need as its "pearl of great price," since gaining it means salvation, while losing it means utter ruin. If one recognizes this radical two-sided interest, that person can gain at least a general idea of salvation. In fact, said Royce, all peoples have agreed, *in this general way*, that human life has a paramount meaning, however dimly appreciated, which humans are in danger of missing.

Within a person's truth-seeking power lies an inner light which images God, like that human, divine spark of Meister Eckhart, the late medieval theologian and spiritual writer. By this inner light one discerns the Spirit of Truth's coming and light, in contrast to the light that arises from one's own spirit or from some misleading spirit. As so aided, one's inner light can discern spirits. It can solve that "religious paradox" which struggles to understand how a so fallible human self can reliably know the advent of the divine Spirit. This paradox functions as the vital and critical center of Royce's *Sources*.

Religion in *The Problem of Christianity*

Before creating this late masterpiece, Royce gained his "Peircean insight." It transformed his thought even as much as did his 1883 insight into the truth of an All-knower. In the *Problem* Royce united historical study and philosophical reflection on what he called Christianity's three most essential ideas. These were the ideas of a universal Community (or invisible Church), the moral burden of the sinful individual, and the atonement process. These three ideas were integrated by the idea of Grace.

Royce found a prime instance of the idea of a universal community in the early Christian communities of the apostle Paul. In these assemblies Royce found a love for each individual Christian and a loyalty to the divine community of all the faithful. These realities, however, so combined with a gracious sentiment and orderly discipline that, as signs, all these ingredients were interwoven directly with each other and each sign helped interpret and appraise the other. Such interpretation discovered the real and divinely significant, spiritual community to which all must belong if they are to reach life's true goal.

Yet human nature is tainted and persons are weighed down by guilt. For example, misunderstandings between people and the tragedies which they produce make clear the moral defects and guilt in both Jews and non-Jews alike, as the apostle Paul saw clearly. Thus a moral burden presses so heavily on the guilt-laden individual that a person cannot bear this burden by oneself.

Grace can heal the moral burden of even the basest individual and can raise that person into the new realm of the Beloved Community. Here appears a sine qua non in Royce's late view of religion, his doctrine that life and consciousness operate on two basic levels: that of the human individual and that of the graced community. As inescapable, the human individual's social dimension binds the human self both to other human selves and especially to communities. In ordinary human living these two levels are intertwined as distinct but not separate factors.

Atonement effects the transition of the morally "lost individual" to this second level in which one becomes a member of a genuinely loyal community. Working in and with the Interpreter-Spirit, either some human community or one of its heroic members generates a process of atonement. It consists in such actions as offset the treasonous deed of some lost individual by rendering the overall situation of the treason-scarred community better than it would have been if the traitor's act had never been committed.

Overall, then, the late Royce did not think that religion could be defined wisely if one omitted the divine Other to which each human self is related. Similarly, he maintained the view that ethics could not be defined wisely if one omitted God (or the Absolute) to which ethics is ultimately related.

Eventually, Royce's thought interpreted God through a pair of ideas: first, as the Universal Community of Interpretation, and then, above all, as the Spirit-Interpreter who

> interprets all to all and each individual to the world, and the world of spirits to each individual ... [who as] servant to all and chief among all, [is] expressing his will through all, yet, in his interpretations, regarding and loving the will of the least of these his brethren.
>
> (*Problem* 2: 219)

Royce was convinced that the history of religions made at least one lesson clear. The ruins of the earth's ancient temples prove that the "needs of the worshippers determine, in the long run, the historical fate of religions." Psychologically, human evolution changes the needs of worshipers for spiritual sustenance. So, religions must change to meet these altered needs, or else die.

Finally, concerning his monotheistic "divine Other," Royce attended to three historical forms of monotheism. Its Greek form focuses on God as the source of the cosmos, a God that the intellect can clearly detect. Its Hebraic form sees God as the Righteous Ruler who requires free ethico-religious obedience from its human creatures. Its Hindu form stresses God as mystery beyond human grasp, as the Unspeakable "not this and not that." Royce foresaw that religion's future challenge lies in so interpreting the religious meaning of God that a synthesis of all three forms should guide people's religious life in the coming centuries. Toward this goal Royce called thinkers to integrate intellect and will under beauty's leadership. He insisted that this triadic ideal of intellect, will, and aesthetic affect is one from which philosophy cannot escape.

Further reading

Clendenning, John (ed.). *The Life and Thought of Josiah Royce*, revised and expanded edition. Nashville, TN: Vanderbilt University Press, 1999.

Oppenheim, Frank M., SJ. *Royce's Mature Philosophy of Religion*. Notre Dame, IN: University of Notre Dame Press, 1987.

—— *Reverence for the Relations of Life*: *Re-imagining Pragmatism via Josiah Royce's Interactions with Peirce, James, and Dewey*. Notre Dame, IN: University of Notre Dame Press, 2005.

Royce, Josiah. *The Philosophy of Loyalty*. New York: Macmillan, 1908.

—— *The Sources of Religious Insight*. New York: Charles Scribner's Sons, 1912.

—— *The Problem of Christianity*, 2 vols. New York: Macmillan, 1913.

—— "Monotheism" in James Hastings (ed.) *The Encyclopaedia of Religion and Ethics*. New York: Charles Scribner's Sons, 1916, Vol. 8, pp. 817–21.

—— *The Letters of Josiah Royce*, ed. John Clendenning. Chicago, IL: University of Chicago Press, 1970.

FRANK M. OPPENHEIM, SJ

S

SANTAYANA, GEORGE: ANIMAL FAITH

Animal faith refers primarily to the natural and abiding conviction that we are part of and confronted with a dynamic physical world. This is a principal doctrine in Santayana's philosophy, one that marks the intersection of his epistemology and ontology. His official presentation of the doctrine is found in his 1923 work *Scepticism and Animal Faith* and its full implications are set out in the 1930 sequel *The Realm of Matter*, the second book of his magnum opus *Realms of Being*. But like many central ideas in Santayana's philosophy, the basic elements of the doctrine are evident in his earliest writings.

To see the significance of animal faith and its rationale it helps to consider the constituent terms. Take, first, the word *faith*. It is not intended to invoke theological notions. Instead it denotes the fact that the Cartesian search for beliefs that attest to their own truth or justification is futile. In the opening chapters of *Scepticism and Animal Faith* Santayana argues that since methodological doubt rigorously carried out terminates in solipsism of the present moment, the Cartesian project, and every other search for certainty, must be abandoned. For Santayana it then follows that if we are to recognize the fact that we do have knowledge we must admit that our knowledge necessarily includes beliefs that cannot be rationally justified. By way of comparison, we can note that it is not uncommon for philosophers to hold that knowledge based on inductive reasoning or memory involves beliefs that are groundless. For Santayana, an element of groundless presumption pervades every area of knowledge, including, for instance, knowledge about our own mental states.

Santayana did not think the act of faith involved in knowledge is voluntary. He admits that it is a psychological fact that some individuals (himself included) are able through skepticism to suspend all of their beliefs. However, this can only be done momentarily. The exigencies of life and the body's reactive attitudes disallow anything but the most fleeting moments of suspended belief.

Accepting that all knowledge rests on faith, the question then becomes exactly what our faith is directed upon. For Santayana it is the material world. Hence the second term of his phrase: *animal*. His position is that insofar as we are biological centers of activity our thoughts are spontaneously directed upon the physical environment. Animal faith thus marks a complete break with all subjectivist accounts of knowledge that claim that mental states and not physical things are the primary objects of belief.

To the objection that animal faith amounts to the dogmatic assertion that the material world exists, Santayana replies that all philosophical systems must begin by admitting some kind of reality and the existence of that reality will also rest on faith. Granting that faith in the existence of the material world is unavoidable if we are alive and thinking, it does not follow that disputes about fundamental ontology will always end at an impasse. In support of his position Santayana argues that all of our actions manifest our faith in the existence of matter. Moreover, Santayana claims that animal faith is the prerequisite for scientific inquiry. It is implicated in the framing of hypotheses and having perceptual beliefs. For these among other reasons Santayana was keen to emphasize that his doctrine is not put forward as a theory. Rather it is intended to express the universal and inevitable convictions of a human animal living in a physical world. Santayana regards all rival positions that fail to express these convictions as sophistical or arbitrary.

Santayana elaborates his doctrine of animal faith within the context of his philosophical system. For example, his claim that we believe in the material world because we must act, rather than act because we believe, points towards his epiphenomenalist account of consciousness by affirming the primacy of the biological over the mental. Our interaction with the physical environment is reflected at the level of consciousness as the spontaneous convictions of animal faith. Similarly, the biological basis of animal faith generates intent and turns the essences given to consciousness into signs of things. Without animal faith the intuition of essences would be purely aesthetic rather than indicative of the surrounding environment. Thus for Santayana animal faith is a type of conscious attitude with a material basis in bodily activity.

Further reading

Santayana, George. *Scepticism and Animal Faith.* New York: Dover, 1955 [1923].

—— *Realms of Being* (one-volume edition which contains Santayana's four books: *The Realm of Essence* (1927); *The Realm of Matter* (1930); *The Realm of Truth* (1938); and *The Realm of Spirit* (1940)). New York: Charles Scribner's Sons, 1942.

GLENN TILLER

SANTAYANA, GEORGE: INFLUENCE

Santayana's broad influence reflects the large body of work he produced over a long life. He expressed his philosophy in poetry, essays, a novel, literary and cultural criticism, autobiography, and systematic treatments of an array of philosophical issues. By the 1920s Santayana was an internationally famous philosopher inside professional circles and beyond. His reputation, however, was based largely on his early writings. The comparative neglect of his later philosophy is partly explained by his decision at the age of forty-nine to retire from teaching, return to Europe permanently, and distance himself from the academic environment and movements of the day.

Santayana's first book of philosophy, *The Sense of Beauty* (1896), a work on aesthetics, set his career in motion. Although he later played down the significance of the book and claimed that it was written primarily to meet professorial demands, it nevertheless sold well and remained in print throughout his life and well after his death. In 1905–6 he published the multi-volume *Life of Reason or the Phases of Human Progress.* In this work the organizing role of reason, in the areas of common sense, society, religion, art, and science, was presented in naturalistic terms. *The Life of Reason* was Santayana's most influential book and it received high praise from luminaries such as John Dewey. It was embraced by, among other scholars, the philosophers Frederick J.E. Woodbridge of Columbia, the co-founder and editor of *The Journal of Philosophy*, and Morris R. Cohen of City College of New York. These men viewed Santayana as a powerful spokesman for philosophical naturalism and the spirit of pragmatism. The *Life of Reason* consequently became part of the curriculum at their respective universities and a generation of students grew up studying and discussing Santayana's ideas.

As a professor of philosophy for over twenty years Santayana had his own opportunities to make his mark on students both at Harvard and at the other universities in America and Europe where he lectured. He was, by virtually all accounts, a masterly teacher and his Spanish heritage and great range as a commentator on philosophy and religion made him a unique presence at Harvard. While it is difficult to determine precisely Santayana's influence on his students, we know that he had a number of distinguished pupils, including Conrad Aiken, James B. Conant, T.S. Eliot, Felix Frankfurter, Robert Frost, Horace Kallen, and Walter Lippmann, to name a few. Former students frequently remained in contact with Santayana and those who became publishers and editors often invited him to contribute to their projects.

In 1911, Santayana published a three-part review of Bertrand Russell's philosophy. In the third part, "Hypostatic Ethics", he challenged Russell's views on ethics. Russell advocated the position that "good" was unanalyzable and objective. Like G.E. Moore, Russell argued that there was no relation between what is and what ought to be. But he abandoned his position after considering Santayana's objections. In a separate development around the same time, Santayana was enlisted as a leader of the Critical Realist movement, which included the philosophers Arthur O.

Lovejoy and Roy Wood Sellars. Santayana's general notion of an essence as a qualitative character was integral to the Critical Realists' account of perception and critique of rival epistemological positions. The collaborative efforts of the group resulted in the publication of *Essays in Critical Realism* (1920) to which Santayana contributed the paper "Three Proofs of Realism".

For the last half of his life Santayana concerned himself with writing the five-volumes that make up *Scepticism and Animal Faith* and *Realms of Being*. While these works received praise from prominent American and European philosophers, many critics nevertheless came to the conclusion that Santayana had moved away from his earlier naturalism and affinities to pragmatism. This perception, in addition to the fact that Santayana refused offers of appointment from several major universities, reduced his philosophical currency in America. By 1936 Santayana was, arguably, most famous for his novel *The Last Puritan*. This book, a bestseller that was translated into several languages, secured Santayana a place on the front cover of *Time* magazine (3 February 1936).

After Santayana's death in 1952 and the subsequent dominance of analytic philosophy in North American and British universities, his star went into near total eclipse. Recent decades have brought a resurgence of interest in his work in both North America and Europe, notably with the formation of the Santayana Society in 1980 as well as the ongoing publication of *Overheard in Seville: Bulletin of the Santayana Society*, a yearly publication devoted to Santayana scholarship, and *The Works of George Santayana*, a critical edition of his writings.

Further reading

Kuklick, Bruce. *A History of Philosophy in America, 1720–2000*. Oxford: Oxford University Press, 2001.

McCormick, John. *George Santayana: A Biography*. New York: Alfred A. Knopf, 1987.

GLENN TILLER

SANTAYANA, GEORGE: IRONY

Santayana employs a playful irony (the discrepancy between the expected and the actual), free of sarcasm, as a philosophical tool. With a serious purpose, but also for his own amusement, he derives radically new conclusions from the traditional philosophical arguments. Santayana is an American philosopher: the goal for mankind, in Santayana as in the other Americans, is no approximation to a static standard, but rather continuous activity. The activity which is the goal of his aspirations is, to be sure, idiosyncratic: it is the peaceful intuition of essences.

His metaphysical masterwork, *Realms of Being* (1927–40), is an immense prose poem, where with deadpan irony separate "realms" actually represent the various types of philosophical activity. Thus the "realm" of spirit is phenomenology, treated from the point of view of consciousness. The "realm" of matter is physical science, from the point of view of an omniscient observer. This is his rejection of idealism. His rejection of nominalism is the "realm" of essences; ironically naming these "a term in scepticism", he slips in that essences are actual. Thus these three "realms" are really ways of describing what there is.

But what is the "realm" of truth? This is the only "realm" to which he has given a name referring to discourse, and with a stroke of irony it is the only actual realm in the system: it is the world of facts – where certain essences and not others are instantiated in matter; certain essences and not others are intuited in minds.

Santayana said that he was a materialist, and joked that he might be the only materialist living, to distinguish himself specifically from the German Idealists when they held that sense data inform us about the "sensor," the mind, and not the "sensed." For the Idealists, spirit "posits" the physical world, sets it up. Santayana's ironic redefinition agrees that the sensor posits the sensed; but his sensor is not the mind, but a material organization, a "habit" in matter, which he calls the "psyche." For the psyche, "positing" a physical object merely means behaving with the confidence that it is there. What he, then, ironically calls "spirit" turns out to be merely a sum of private appearances, the epiphenomenal products of the physical psyche. Spirit can do nothing.

The natural state of matter is motion and continuous change; it tends to become more and more complex, moving into patterns that develop more and more complexity, until at last they spin off seeds that reproduce the parent pattern and matter has become alive. The active pattern of events driving each organism he calls a "habit" in matter, and such a habit in matter it is that he calls the physical "psyche." Consciousness, what he calls "spirit," is the voice of the psyche talking to itself about the predicament of being alive. It is an emotional exclamation.

Santayana's aesthetics and moral philosophy flow smoothly from his metaphysics: so beauty is an exclamation of joy on the part of the beholder.

By the "moral" point of view Santayana intends the subjective view of a caring physical psyche. The moral point of view is the point of view of a conscious self, which is always emotional. The "moral" is so from a specific view at a time.

In using the device of the implicit ironic redefinition of terms, as we have shown, Santayana lends a term a meaning which is different from its customary one in some philosophically important respect, signaling by the use of this device that traditional philosophy has had the matter in question wrong end to.

Traditionally, the term "moral" carries with it the aura of solemnity, momentousness. Santayana's ironic redefinition retains this solemnity and urgency. Its irony and power consist in pointing to what he sees as their only possible source: the vital needs of each personality. Not only do the self's deep needs deserve the solemn appellation of "moral": nothing else does.

A Spaniard educated in Boston and writing in English, Santayana kept a simultaneously insider's and outsider's perspective on both societies. He wrote two autobiographical works whose subtitles signal, with a smile, that neither is to be taken as a full account of his life. *Persons and Places* (1944, 1947, 1953, 1986) bears the subtitle "Fragments of Autobiography"; *The Last Puritan* (1936) is subtitled "A Memoir in the Form of a Novel." Although the two books tell very different stories, their characters are related in important ways.

George Santayana's mother was cold and withholding. It was his much older half-sister Susannah who gave him the affection that helped him grow up as a loving person. In the novel, two separate mothers represent these two women: Oliver, the "last Puritan," bottle-fed as a baby, has an indolent, cold and rather stupid mother. His friend Mario was breastfed by his opera-singer mother: he loves her and all her women friends, and women in general.

When we set the portrayal of Santayana's mother side by side with that of Oliver's mother, we note the similarities at once, but we see also that in the novel the cold brutality of description is exacerbated by irony. What he seems unable to forgive his own mother is that, being something so much better, being Spanish, she aspired to be a New England matron. Her caricature in the novel is not even a Boston snob, but a snob from a completely insignificant Connecticut town.

His richest revenge upon his mother comes in the final twist of the screw: in his Boston childhood, where money mattered, it was his mother who had the moneyed connections; the money itself, tantalizingly all around him, was just out of reach of his immediate family's genteel poverty. His father had no money to educate the boy.

In the novel, by contrast, the money belongs to the father, who puts it at the mother's disposal with a sardonic noblesse oblige.

This was Santayana's ultimate personal, ironic myth. Plain speech was hazardous in his boyhood home. His response was to laugh up his sleeve and to develop the irony that is the voice of his philosophy.

Further reading

Hahn, Lewis Edwin and Schilpp, Paul A. (eds). *The Philosophy of George Santayana*. La Salle, IL: Open Court, 1991.

Reck, Andrew J. and Lachs, John (eds). *Southern Journal of Philosophy* 10, 2 (1972), Special Issue on Santayana.

Santayana, George. *Realms of Being*. New York: Charles Scribner's Sons, 1942.

—— *Persons and Places*, critical edition, ed. William G. Holzberger and Herman J. Saatkamp, Jr. Cambridge, MA: MIT Press, 1986.

—— *The Last Puritan*, critical edition, ed. William G. Holzberger and Herman J. Saatkamp, Jr. Cambridge, MA: MIT Press, 1994.

Sprigge, Timothy L.S. *Santayana. An Explanation of his Philosophy*. London: Routledge and Kegan Paul, 1974.

HENNY WENKART

SANTAYANA, GEORGE: LIFE

George Santayana (1863–1952) was a philosopher of Spanish birth, brought up and educated in the United States, and is a principal figure in Classical American philosophy. He was a professor at Harvard and a prolific writer of philosophical texts, literary essays, cultural criticism, poems, and a best-selling novel. He perceived himself as a perpetual student and observer of the world, a characterization that is attested to by the breadth and tone of his work.

Santayana was born in 1863 in Madrid to Agustín Santayana and Josefina Sturgis, widow of George Sturgis and mother to his three children. The family lived briefly in Avila, Spain, but in 1869 Josefina chose to return to Boston, the origin of her previous husband, with the Sturgis children. Santayana and his father followed in 1872, with Agustín returning permanently to Avila some months later. Santayana was raised by his mother and her family, particularly his elder sister and godmother Susan, who Santayana referred to as "Susana" and with whom he was especially close. He kept in touch with his father but did not travel to visit him until completing his first year of college.

Growing up in New England, Santayana was educated at the Boston Public Latin School and attended Harvard for both his undergraduate and graduate degrees, where he studied with William

James and Josiah Royce. During his graduate education, he studied in Germany on a Walker Fellowship and wrote his dissertation on Hermann Lotze. After completing his doctorate, he was hired to teach at Harvard, first as an instructor and eventually as a professor. Early in his career he spent a year studying in England as an advanced student at King's College, Cambridge, where he became acquainted with Bertrand Russell, G.E. Moore, and J.M.E. McTaggart. Santayana wrote his first book of philosophy under academic pressure to define himself as a specialist, reworking lecture notes from a course he taught in aesthetics. The result was *The Sense of Beauty* (1896). He continued to produce work in philosophy and poetry during this period, most notably a series of five books under the heading *The Life of Reason* (1905–6).

Santayana was not happy with professional life. He perceived himself to be a classical mind among moderns in both his philosophical and pedagogical outlook. He found himself at odds with academic philosophy's trend toward specialization and what he referred to as its "psychologistic" focus. Santayana's discordance with the dominant strains in academia increased his already poignant sense of alienation. He had always considered himself a detached and solitary figure, though he had enjoyed many friendships during his school days and with his students during the earlier part of his career. In 1893, upon reaching thirty years of age, he experienced what he described as a *metanoia*, a change of heart. A confluence of forces – Susana's marriage, his father's death, and the untimely death of a young friend, Warwick Potter – combined with growing older in a professional world in which he did not feel at home led Santayana to become resigned from his emotional and professional attachments to the world. In 1912, during one of his many trips to Europe, Santayana's mother died, leaving him a small inheritance. This, combined with his savings, enabled him to resign his position at Harvard and live independently in Europe for the remainder of his life.

Santayana was perhaps most productive as a writer during his retirement. In the first ten years alone he published *Winds of Doctrine: Studies in Contemporary Opinion* (1913), *Egotism in German Philosophy* (1915), and *Character and Opinion in the United States* (1920). During his travels, he spent a good deal of time in England, including the duration of the First World War, which led to a series of reflections, *Soliloquies in England* (1923). Santayana published throughout the remainder of his life, including his major philosophical system, *Realms of Being* (a series of four separate volumes spanning 1927–40), to which *Scepticism and Animal Faith* (1923) serves as the introduction. He also produced a bestselling novel, *The Last Puritan* (1936).

In 1939, at the onset of World War II, Santayana found himself in Italy and unable to leave the country, as he lacked the proper papers. Two years later, at seventy-seven years of age, he moved into a convent-clinic, the Clinica della Piccola Compagna di Maria, where he spent the remainder of his life. During this period, he wrote his autobiography, *Persons and Places*, in three volumes, the last of which, *My Host, the World* (1953) was published posthumously. He died 26 September 1952.

Further reading

Santayana, George. *Persons and Places: Fragments of Autobiography*, Volume I of *The Works of George Santayana*, ed. Herman J. Saatkamp, Jr (General Editor) and William G. Holzberger (Textual Editor). Cambridge, MA: MIT Press, 1986.

—— *The Letters of George Santayana, Volume 5, Book One: [1868]–1909 (2001), Book Two: 1910–1920 (2002), Book Three: 1921–1927, Book Four: 1928–1932 (2003), Book Five: 1933–1936 (2003), Book Six: 1937–1940*, ed. Herman J. Saatkamp, Jr, and William G. Holzberger. Cambridge, MA: MIT Press, 2004.

JESSICA WAHMAN

SANTAYANA, GEORGE: LIFE OF REASON

"Life of reason" is an ideal advanced by George Santayana in the early major work of the same title, consisting in five volumes dealing with reason in common sense, society, religion, art, and science. His advocacy of philosophical naturalism in *The Life of Reason* had a considerable impact on American thought from its publication in 1905–6. The life of reason, as he understands it, is described in the first volume, *Reason in Common Sense*. It arises as a coherent accommodation in action of the genuine interests of a person or society which advances the more dominant ones, and relinquishes any that are entirely incompatible with these. The interests of a person are determined by a combination of that person's nature and the possibilities open to that person. The life of reason itself is an ideal, not compulsory but one with a persuasive advocate. His text is fully naturalistic while at the same time dealing at length with the ideal, according to his happy formulation: "In Aristotle the conception of human nature is perfectly sound; everything ideal has a natural basis and everything natural an ideal development." In this volume, he deals with issues concerning knowledge. This lacks the focus of the later *Scepticism and Animal Faith*, although anticipations of the main themes are found in it. As the title of the second volume would suggest, *Reason in Society* deals less with the exercise of power in various political systems than with forms of human association. Beginning with topics like family, love, and friendship, he ends with his notion of an ideal society. Neither an aristocratic nor a democratic society is satisfactory, although he seems to prefer the former. The third volume, *Reason in Religion*, has been found especially interesting. Religion is false and misleading where it makes factual claims about the nature of things, but when these claims are interpreted symbolically and poetically, religion is valuable – indeed essential – for a life of reason. He has a marked allegiance to the Catholic Church stripped of its dogmas. Christ was an exceptionally spiritual Jew whose teachings were merged with Greek philosophy. This yielded an uneasy mix of the two chief aspects of a religion: the piety of the practical-minded Hebrew religion and the worship of the ideal found in Plato. Santayana's love for the arts is evident in the fourth volume, *Reason in Art*, and indeed his literary flair is evident throughout the five volumes. Any operation that humanizes and rationalizes objects is called art. He has little sympathy for purely abstract art, and favors as more fruitful art that arises from practical needs. He continued to write about religion in later years, but this is less true of art. Although his first book, *The Sense of Beauty*, continued to be used as course text for many years, in his later years he had decided that aesthetics was not a genuine field in philosophy. Themes that might have touched on art and its value were sometimes dealt with in his more general context of spirit. *Reason in Science* deals with themes like mechanism and psychology, but also with history and ethics; it has neither the narrow scope nor the precision expected today in the philosophy of science. He sees two forms of science, physics and dialectic. Rational ethics is for him a dialectical science. While the entire *Life of Reason* has a moral aim, the explicit treatment of morality appears, rather surprisingly, in this final volume. He presents a notable trichotomy, with the science of rational ethics lodged between the disorganized absolute claims of a pre-rational morality and a perhaps disillusioned post-rational morality.

Santayana's later major work, *Realms of Being*, culminates in a final fourth volume, *The Realm of Spirit*; some have suggested a shift to the ideal of a spiritual life from the earlier allegiance to a life of reason. In fact, he claims to adhere always to a life of reason. Still, he admits a change in attitude. The later writings introduce an ontology not found in the earlier, and a shift within naturalism to a more explicitly materialist and harder version. The humanism remains, but is lodged in what for him is a more satisfactory ontological setting. One considerable shift does come in his treatment of society: he later felt that the earlier embrace in *Reason in Society* of English and especially Greek ideals was too narrow and too dependent on a personal bias. In the very late political tract *Dominations and Powers* he has a "more modest intention" and no longer seeks to judge which institutions are best. This text also shows that he continued to value reason in society, and did not turn exclusively to contemplation and the life of the spirit.

Further reading

Santayana, George. *The Life of Reason: Or, The Phases of Human Progress*, 5 volumes. New York: Charles Scribner's Sons, 1905–6. Republished in paper by Dover, 1980.

ANGUS KERR-LAWSON

SANTAYANA, GEORGE: ONTOLOGY

Some see ontology as merely the question of what exists and what few items must be added to physical objects to make up a universe of discourse. For George Santayana, the physical world calls for its own category, the realm of matter. Whatever else there is will be radically different and out of place there. Thus universals are gathered together in a vast separate realm of essence; the realm of truth is a comprehensive ideal record of what happens to matter; and the realm of spirit consists of all mental experiences. While the latter is tied to sentient organisms, the other three are ontologically independent of experience. The term "ontology" is appropriate since the four realms answer to the question of what there is, where being is a larger category than existence. Meant to be common-sense categories, the four are first broached explicitly in *Scepticism and Animal Faith*, an epistemological introduction to the four volumes of *Realms of Being*. In the preface to the former, he discusses briefly his appeal to an ontology of realms. For an appreciation of the late ontology, see Timothy Sprigge (1995).

In the first instance, essences are the contents of experience. When we perceive things, we have an intuition of essence. As well, essences arise in a second equally important way: each thing or event or fact embodies its own essence, seen as the full objective nature of that object. This essence is not limited to certain special properties of the object, but is understood to include *all* its properties; Santayana is not an essentialist. The kind of being admitted to essences is extremely thin; they have no property other than that of self-identity. Nothing should be inferred from his use of substantives in speaking of them. A thing must have an essence inasmuch as it has some nature; similarly, every experience has its own individual character, also an essence. When philosophers debate whether to include in a universe of discourse intensions, sets, numbers, propositions, they already accept these as essences by singling them out and having an understanding of what they are; nothing further is needed for them to be essences. However, it would be a confusion to adjoin selected ideal entities like sets to the realm of matter. What is admitted to a universe of discourse is subjective and variable and not a question of ontology. Any or all essences could be referred to and quantified over in discourse; Santayana says that they can be named, and only through this is reasoning possible. He treats these and other issues against a stable double background: the realm of existing things; and an entirely disjoint realm of non-existent, non-material, possible forms of being. Both are independent of human discourse, in which terms for the description of the former are drawn from the latter. Whereas many analysts admit universals reluctantly, Santayana is under no such constraint with essences. These do not belong to the universe of existing things and are not subject to the demand for parsimony proper to theorizing within the realm of matter. Indeed the situation is quite the opposite, and the realm of essence is full and boundless in all directions. Would the golden mountain be a genuine object? For Santayana the notion is a mere neutral essence, presumably not embodied anywhere as an existing object. However, as essence it is available as an object of thought. He would accuse both Meinong and Meinong's critics of using "object" in a double sense that his ontology disambiguates.

In *Scepticism and Animal Faith*, Santayana accepts the external world with animal faith as the only available confirmation, and admits valid and useful symbolic knowledge of it similar to that of pragmatism. He retains a notion of absolute truth which would arise as literal knowledge if the essence intuited corresponded exactly to the essence of the thing perceived. Our intuitions in the realm of spirit permit us to negotiate our way effectively in matter, without at all requiring access to this literal truth.

Essences for him are merely his chosen means for understanding issues and discussing them: "they do not form a world but a vocabulary." His main philosophical themes concern the other realms, each of which can be seen as the manner in which essence comes to be realized. Material existences, things and events, are embodiments of essence; the truth is treated as the collection of those essences that are realized in events and the realm of spirit consists in actual intuitions of essence. Although the exposition of Santayana's philosophy must deal at length with essence, its fruits lie elsewhere. He is more successful in capturing common-sense categories with the other three realms than with essence. The arguments he makes turn again and again on the radical differences among the four realms. Essences are eternally fixed, while matter is change itself. Changing matter is captured in truth, but the change is frozen. Spirit is powerless but is of the first importance.

With the realm of matter he presents a robust naturalism. Any philosophy with claims to knowledge will presuppose substance in some form, where this initially means only that something beyond the given must always be assumed. In *The Realm of Matter* the development is continued; he argues that, in order to explain human action, substance must be the spatio-temporal, physical cosmos, and an appropriate designation for it is "matter." Assumed as a prerequisite to action rather than demonstrated (and indeed imposed by animal faith), it is the sole source of dynamical change. Natural laws are prevalent but not necessary; they are prerequisites of action and of life itself. The realm of matter is everywhere contingent; something he derives from the abundance of essences. A major concern throughout is the separation of physical entities from human representations of them through essences. According to his account of knowledge, the latter cannot be expected to mirror exactly the former. Thus physical time is a real constituent of matter, in contrast with sentimental time and mathematical time which are mere representational essences. A discussion that identifies time with a mathematical definition will be more precise and rigorous, and perhaps seem better qualified for legitimate argumentation; but physical time would be lost in abstractions, and the dynamic vision of a time determined by the flow of substance through events would be replaced by a detached quasi-substantial mathematical continuum. Human initiative arises through a psyche, which he defines as a recurring form or trope lodged in matter and found in all organic life. Humans can exert power intelligently insofar as through spirit they attain self-knowledge of their psyches; they achieve psychic freedom when action is in harmony with the deepest psychic impulses. This is neither absolute nor dependent upon indeterminism.

We all unthinkingly posit a truth as something independent of humankind. Truth is defined as the ideal record of all that happens in the realm of matter – past, present and future. This includes brain events and the fact that sometimes there is an intuition of essence accompanying these events. He speaks of *the truth* and describes it as "a comprehensive standard description for every fact." An account of truth as a feature of language would be more precise and more open to logical treatment. However, in his eyes this would not be a faithful account of the subtle reality of truth, which is independent of human influence and is eternally unchanging. A definition dependent on language or knowledge fails in these two respects.

Santayana deals at length with spirit, something unusual for a materialist philosopher, and presents what he calls a personal lay religion. A moment of spirit is an act of awareness, a felt experience, the "inner" difference between being asleep and awake. Nothing different from spirit can explain what spirit is; one can only appeal to a felt consciousness, assumed in others, to elicit what is meant. Santayana is clear that spirit is *only* the experience; agency stems from psyche. This must be seen as definitional. He argues that mere awareness cannot be a physical cause, and by spirit he means no more than awareness. The manner in which spirit is generated by psyche raises difficult questions for science, but he sets aside this question in his lengthy discussion of impotent spirit. In action, intuition of essence is accompanied by animal faith in significant external objects of immediate interest. Here the content is secondary and is passed over; little attention is directed to the essence intuited. However, pure intuition without intent is possible also. Psyches, some more than others, have an affinity for contemplation. In *The Realm of Spirit*, he deals at length with spirituality. Other late works show that he does not abandon the broader ideal of a life of reason. Indeed, he appears to prefer some combination of the two.

Further reading

Santayana, George. *Scepticism and Animal Faith*. New York: Charles Scribner's Sons, 1923.

—— *Realms of Being*, 4 volumes (*The Realm of Essence* [1927]; *The Realm of Matter* [1930]; *The Realm of Truth* [1938]; *The Realm of Spirit* [1940]). New York: Charles Scribner's Sons. Reprinted as a one-volume edition with a new preface, *Realms of Being*. New York: Charles Scribner's Sons, 1942.

Sprigge, Timothy L.S. *Santayana: An Examination of His Philosophy*. London: Routledge and Kegan Paul, 1974. A revised and expanded edition in paper, *Santayana*, was published by Routledge in 1995.

ANGUS KERR-LAWSON

SANTAYANA, GEORGE: SPIRITUAL LIFE

The phrase "spiritual life" plays a central role in the philosophy of George Santayana. Spirit is Santayana's name for consciousness, that "inner difference between being asleep and being awake." Consciousness is always intentional; the object of consciousness Santayana calls an essence. The intuition of essences both simple and complex constitutes mental life. Thus, spirit is the necessary condition of any mental life. Since spirit is an ontological idea, Santayana wants to stress that spirit has its origins in matter.

Spirit contains no principle of selectivity. It cannot choose which essences it intuits. What determines the character of one's mental life is the psyche which is the material aspect of personhood. If it were not for the psyche, our mental lives would be a "booming, buzzing confusion" in William James' terms. The unity of consciousness is determined by the unity of the psyche. Material life involves change, the exchange of qualities on a background of permanence. Spirit does not undergo internal change; it remains the same throughout its existence. It is the pure unchanging intuition of essences. In the spiritual life the *act* of consciousness does not change but the objects of consciousness are changing.

As an astute observer of Nature and the human condition, Santayana wants to distinguish between two attitudes of spirit. There is the type of spirit which entertains the world as a means to an end, and, then, there is a form of spirit which takes the world as an end in itself. In the latter case, the rainbow is enjoyed for what it is and nothing else.

The spiritual life consists only of those moments when the intuition of an essence remains pure, untainted by the cares of the psyche beneath it. Although it is different from matter, spirit can adopt, from time to time, its true nature as transcendental witness to the material aspect of our lives. It can adopt a position of pure intuition of essences devoid of any taint of the material life. This stage of spirit can result, for the time being, in it achieving a harmony with its material conditions. In stressing the spiritual life, Santana wants to maintain that "spiritual life" is a moral ideal as well as an ontological idea. Human life can achieve for a time an existence which is more than the continual pursuit of one end after another. Santayana believes that it is possible to escape, for a time, the everyday "rat race" of the continual pursuit of means to ends.

In one sense the "spiritual life" is a misnomer for it has no changing life without the material psyche beneath. It arises from beneath when a material psyche reaches a certain degree of complexity. In material life its successive phases are generated from one another; however, spirit has no internally generated phases. One instance of spirit is not successively different from another. The spiritual life is not life lived by spirit alone, for spirit has no causal power and no principle of selectivity. These are properties of the material world and not spirit. Thus the spiritual life is not a life of pursuing a given set of values. This is the task of the psyche.

In the spiritual life one transcends the cares and preferences which are common to the life of the psyche and serve as the basis of all values. In the spiritual life there is an absence of passion and preferences; thus, it cannot be an appropriate life for the psyche. For value to accrue to any object or any lifestyle, the person must have some interest, preference, or proattitude toward the object. The object must be impulse-appeasing, and finally, the essence goodness must attach itself to the object. Therefore, if the psyche were devoid of all preference and passions, it would cease to exist. Spirit does not seek to impose its apprehension of the essence "goodness" on any other person or thing. Spirit is absolutely devoid of material dogmatism. It represents true tolerance and appreciation of all forms of divergent life.

Many philosophers down through the ages have espoused varieties of the life of reason as the ideal form of life. Santayana, while he admires many forms of this lifestyle, is prevented from deeming it the sole good or highest form of existence for persons. All claims for value superiority lie at the level of the psyche. In the spiritual life, spirit loves all things for their own sake and not for the sake of another. Thus, in the spiritual life, intuition is the pure apprehension of essence devoid of any ulterior interest. The spiritual life is an end in and of itself, not a means to an end, Hence, it does not hold any form of life to be superior to any other form of life.

The question becomes how one can attain the spiritual life. The answer is that there is no specific way that can be prescribed that will ensure the attainment of the spiritual life. It may occur by chance, or it may be the attainment of a life's pursuit by the psyche. One of the best ways to reach the spiritual life is by achieving a harmony of desires within the psyche. Desires tend to disturb the internal harmony of spirit. In the life of reason, harmony means that the maximum number of desires can be satisfied with minimum effort.

Santayana is appreciative of the Indian philosophy which stresses a recognition of and appreciation for diverse ways of achieving this harmony. An individual may choose a life of isolation from society and a pairing down of the number of desires in his psyche so that there is a greater chance one may satisfy at least the minimum number. On the other hand, a person may choose a form of the life of reason which seeks to maximize satisfaction of desires with a minimum amount of effort. The resulting satisfaction will mean the psyche is less distracted by the cares of the body and may achieve those moments or series of moments of the pure intuition of essences. For those who value the spiritual life, it will add a different dimension to a life normally devoted to one's own good.

Douglas M. MacDonald

SATISFACTION

A prevailing theme of American philosophy is a vivid sense of experience as a field of interaction and feeling. An important consequence is an emphasis on *satisfaction* as the culmination or completion of experience. Two examples of such an understanding can be found in Alfred North Whitehead (1861–1947), where satisfaction represents the final feeling of the becoming of an actual occasion, and in John Dewey (1859–1952), where the fulfillment of a process of inquiry and the culmination of an aesthetic experience are both described as *satisfactions.*

Whitehead describes his *Process and Reality* as an essay on speculative philosophy, with eight categories of existence. Among these are "'actual entities' – also termed 'actual occasions'" (Whitehead, *Process and Reality*: 18). An actual occasion is an event of experience that originates in feelings or prehensions of past occasions and culminates in its feeling of satisfaction in which it perishes to be prehended by future actual occasions. Whitehead describes this complete relation in feeling from the past to the future as *subject/superject*.

Satisfaction is the culmination of the becoming of an actual entity – including the becoming of

God whose consequent nature is an infinite, ongoing satisfaction – in which all the elements that constitute it are received through feeling or prehension, augmented in its own becoming (by the Category of Conceptual Reversion) as governed by its subjective aim, and fulfilled in its felt, determinate satisfaction.

Dewey takes inquiry to be a process that begins in doubt and ends in a satisfaction in which the conditions that initiated the inquiry are resolved. Satisfaction here is both emotional and situational, a quality of the entire situation. Similarly, an aesthetic experience is constituted by a feeling of satisfaction that is both unifying and consummatory.

Further reading

Dewey, John. *Art and Experience.* New York: Putnam, 1934.

—— *Experience and Nature*, second edition. New York: Dover, 1958.

Whitehead, Alfred North. *Adventures of Ideas.* New York: Macmillan, 1933.

—— *Modes of Thought*. New York: Capricorn, 1938.

—— *Process and Reality*, corrected edition, ed. D.R. Griffin and D.W. Sherburne. New York: Free Press, 1978.

STEPHEN DAVID ROSS

SCHEFFLER, ISRAEL

Israel Scheffler (1923–) is one of the premier American philosophers of science and education. Scheffler received his undergraduate and master's degrees at Brooklyn College, and completed his PhD at the University of Pennsylvania in 1952 where Nelson Goodman was his dissertation director. In that same year Scheffler joined the philosophy faculty at Harvard University, retiring in 1992 as Victor S. Thomas Professor of Education and Philosophy, Emeritus.

Scheffler's writings combine philosophical interests in general pedagogy with detailed investigations of scientific methodology. In this respect, Scheffler joins company with some of the most respected figures in classical American philosophy, including William James, C.S. Peirce, and John Dewey. Scheffler's philosophy of science is remarkable for its sound treatment of objectivity, properly interpreted and qualified, as a realistic aim of scientific inquiry. His *Anatomy of Inquiry* seeks to explain the "confrontation" between experience and scientific principles. He characterizes science as a human enterprise in which truth is sought and hypotheses confirmed or rejected inductively. Accordingly, he addresses in detail David Hume's concerns about the justifiability of induction itself, dividing the main topics of his treatise into treatments of explanation, significance, and confirmation. In *Science and Subjectivity*, Scheffler portrays science as a rational enterprise under attack from sociological accounts of its purpose and methods. He considers the arguments by which science is set adrift from its moorings in observation and experiment and seeks to restore a measured balance between recognizing science as evolving in response to a variety of challenges while functioning within a framework that is not subject in its essentials to individual caprice or cultural trends.

Equally (and in some circles better) known for his contributions to philosophy of education, Scheffler over the years has endeavored to make philosophy a vital component in teacher education. As in his work in philosophy of science, Scheffler emphasizes the rationality of thought and the importance of teaching as a rational enterprise with rational methods and goals, which he sees as a continuation of Dewey's pioneering experience-based philosophy of education. Scheffler has been deeply involved for more than half a century in education theory and practice as a continuation of the quest for knowledge and understanding in philosophy, science, and everyday life.

Further reading

Scheffler, Israel. *In Praise of the Cognitive Emotions and Other Essays in the Philosophy of Education*. London: Routledge, 1991.

—— *Symbolic Worlds: Art, Science, Language, Ritual.* Cambridge: Cambridge University Press, 1997.

—— *Gallery of Scholars: A Philosopher's Recollections* (*Philosophy and Education*). Dordrecht: Springer, 2005.

Siegel, Harvey. *Reason and Education: Essays in Honor of Israel Scheffler*. Dordrecht: Kluwer Academic Publishers, 1997.

DALE JACQUETTE

SCHEMA

The schema (plural: schemata, or schemas) or scheme (plural: schemes) has played important but long-unrecognized roles in logic since Aristotle: the syllogistic figures and moods can be taken to be or to presuppose argument schemata. Likewise, the axioms and rules of the Stoic propositional logic can be taken to be or to presuppose sentence schemata and argument schemata, respectively. Modern philosophers know the role of schemata in explications of the semantic conception of truth through Tarski's Schema T. The systematic investigation of schemas and their roles in the history and philosophy of logic is in its infancy.

The word "schema" is ambiguous even in logic. In some of several closely related senses, a schema is a complex system having several components, one of which is a *template-text* or *scheme-template*, a syntactic string composed of one or more "blanks" and usually also words and/or symbols to which meanings are assigned. The template-text of a schema is used as a "template" to specify a multitude, often infinite, of linguistic expressions such as phrases, sentences, argument-texts, or proof-texts called *instances of the schema*. The template-text of *Tarski's Schema T* is the following eight-word two-blank string:

... is a true sentence if and only if ...

The following two strings are instances – the first uses a quotes-name of the sentence filling the second blank, the second uses a phonetic descriptive name.

"zero is one" is a true sentence if and only if zero is one
zee-ee-ar-oh-space-igh-es-space-oh-en-ee is a true sentence if and only if zero is one

More revealing instances are obtained by using a sentence not known to be true and not known to be false.

"every perfect number is even" is a true sentence if and only if every perfect number is even
"some perfect number is odd" is a true sentence if and only if some perfect number is odd

Each schema is accompanied, implicitly or explicitly, with a *side condition* specifying how the "blanks" (dummies, placeholders, or ellipses) are to be "filled in" to obtain instances – and, sometimes, also how the other words or symbols are to be understood. The side condition may also be regarded as another component of the schema or *schematic system*, as it may appropriately be called. Some logicians sometimes seem to use the word "schema" for the scheme-template alone, and a few even insist that no other usage is acceptable. No uniform terminology has gained wide acceptance.

Mathematical logicians recognize schemata in first-order number theory: lack of finite-axiomatizability is finessed by the *mathematical induction schema*. This schema is used to specify effectively an infinite number of axioms. Its template-text is a 22-word, 4-blank string.

If zero is such that ...

and the successor of every number such that ... is also such that ... ,
then every number is such that ...

Its side condition requires that the four blanks be filled in with (occurrences of) one and the same first-order arithmetic *semi-sentence* or "open sentence" such as "it is zero or it is a successor," "it precedes its own successor" or "it is finite." Notice that the semi-sentences and the scheme-templates are strings that are not sentences; they do not have truth-values and they cannot coherently be asserted or denied. Every instance of the mathematical induction schema is a true sentence implied by the *second-order principle of mathematical induction*: every property that belongs to zero and that also belongs to the successor to every number to which it belongs, also without exception belongs to every number. In other words, the principle of mathematical induction is that in order for a given property to belong to every number it is sufficient for it to belong to zero and for it to belong to the successor of every number to which it belongs.

However, as is well known, the principle of mathematical induction is not implied by the set of its first-order instances, an infinite set that is coextensive with the set of instances of the schema. Here we have a schema that is associated with a universal sentence having the same instances. It is typical in such cases that the universal sentence is not logically implied by the instances of the schema, and thus information is lost by replacing the universal sentence by the schema.

Besides the template-text and the side condition, the collection of specified instances of the schema may be regarded as another component of the schema. The instances are considered to be in a previously identified language (whether formal or natural), which is often considered to be another component.

In order to see the ontological and epistemological advantages and disadvantages of replacing a universal sentence with the set of instances of a schema, it is necessary to sharply distinguish placeholders, or schematic "blanks," from variables in the context of interpreted languages. This distinction is almost explicit in Peirce's 1885 paper (Peirce 1992: 228), where he said, "the x, y, z, etc. of a general formula, such as $(x + y) z = xz + yz$, are blanks to be filled up with tokens, they are indices of tokens."

There are expository advantages to be gained by considering cases of schemata that correspond closely to *implicitly quantified* sentences from the underlying language. Consider a simple arithmetic sublanguage of English containing generalizing variables, ecks and wye, ranging over the natural numbers beginning with zero. Assume that the only verb is "equals" as in "(1 plus 2) equals 3." Because the generalizing variables are implicitly quantified, the following sentence expresses a universal truth, not simply a relational condition: (X plus Y) equals (Y plus X).

The truth is a law of arithmetic, namely the *Law of Additive Commutativity*: given any two numbers, the first plus the second equals the second plus the first. Now consider the following scheme-template, a three-word, four-blank string: (... plus ...) equals (... plus ...)

We get the *Schema of Additive Commutativity* by adding the following side-condition: the first and fourth blanks are to be filled with occurrences of one and the same natural-number word and the second and third blanks are to be filled with occurrences of one and the same natural-number word, not necessarily the same as used in the first and fourth.

The Law may be regarded as referring to the entire infinite collection of natural numbers. The two variables in its implicitly quantified expression range over that infinite collection. Moreover, although it is expressed in English and its instances are the same as the instances of the Schema; it is about numbers. It is not about English expressions. In particular, the Law does not refer to the infinite collection of number words – although they are its *substituents* – expressions that may be substituted coherently for its variables. In contrast, the blanks in the template-text of the Schema are meaningless placeholders. The template-text does not express a Law; it does not even have a truth-value. Any attempt to assert or deny a template-text of a schema would be incoherent. Moreover, although each of the substituents of a blank refers to a number; the blanks themselves do not refer to anything and they do not range over anything.

This should give some idea of the ontological and epistemological tradeoffs involved in the decision whether to formulate a theory in an object-language using variables ranging over an infinite collection of objects or to avoid object-language variables by using schemas that in effect presuppose meta-language variables ranging over an infinite collection of strings. These issues are dealt with in detail, at greater length, and with more precision in my 2006 paper. Although there are several encyclopedia articles on schemata, the above is the only full-length treatment of this topic I know of. As said above, the study of schemata is in its infancy. It does not even have a name; *schematology*, *schematography*, or *schematics* are obvious candidates.

Further reading

Corcoran, J. "Schemata: the Concept of Schema in the History of Logic," *Bulletin of Symbolic Logic* 12 (2006): 219–40.

Peirce, C.S. *The Essential Peirce: Selected Philosophical Writings (1867–1893)*, Vol. I, eds N. Houser and C. Kloesel. Bloomington, IN: Indiana University Press, 1992.

John Corcoran

SCHILLER, FERDINAND CANNING SCOTT

F.C.S. Schiller was born on 16 August 1864 in Schleswig-Holstein, Denmark; he died in Los Angeles on 9 August 1937. He attended Rugby School before moving on to Oxford's Balliol College, which was at that time a hotbed of idealism. In 1893, he became an instructor in logic and metaphysics at Cornell University. Schiller returned to Oxford in 1897 to join the faculty of Corpus Christi College. After his retirement, in 1926, he became a professor at the University of Southern California, where he taught until 1935. Having developed views akin to pragmatism in his 1891 *Riddles of the Sphinx*, Schiller became the most vocal proponent of pragmatism in Europe. A staunch opponent of the absolute idealism of F.H. Bradley and others, Schiller used pragmatism as a springboard for his own philosophy, called humanism. Schiller was predominantly influenced by James, especially the latter's notion of the will to believe, which remained a driving force behind Schiller's pragmatism and humanism.

In *Riddles of the Sphinx,* which was published under the pseudonym "a Troglodyte" or cave dweller (the reference is to Plato's allegory of the cave), Schiller defends a non-skeptical relativism, arguing that knowledge is always a product of particular human interests. For Schiller, all our thoughts and actions are unavoidably a product of individual human beings who are always guided by human needs and desires from which they cannot be abstracted. Consequently, Schiller considered himself the modern equivalent to Protagoras, the Sophist who maintained that man is the measure of all things.

Schiller's campaign for humanism began with his 1902 essay "Axioms as Postulates," which contains a vigorous attack on the notion of a priori knowledge. The essay was followed by *Humanism* (1903), and *Studies in Humanism* (1907). Schiller's humanism is a reaction against attempts to "dehumanize" knowledge by artificially eliminating the human aspects of knowing. For Schiller, knowledge is always a product of the whole person with all his limitations, desires, fears, hopes, plans, and purposes. Thus the humanist will always be a pragmatist. By dehumanizing thought, Schiller argues, philosophers have inadvertently severed the link between knowledge and reality.

In 1908, Schiller published *Plato or Protagoras*, in which he examines Protagoras's speech in Plato's *Theaetetus*. In 1924, he published *Problems in Belief*, in which he traces the epistemological implications of different varieties of belief. In the area of logic, Schiller's first major contribution was his *Formal Logic: A Scientific and Social Problem* (1912). In this polemical work, he presents a humanist critique of traditional logic, arguing that the material of logic cannot be meaningfully abstracted from actual use and interest. Seventeen years later, in 1929, Schiller published a second volume on logic, *Logic for Use: An Introduction to the Voluntarist Theory of Knowledge*, which was intended as a constructive sequel to *Formal Logic*.

Schiller, who was a founding member of the English Eugenics Society, published three books on eugenics: *Tantalus or the Future of Man* (1924), *Eugenics and Politics* (1926), and *Social Decay and Eugenic Reform* (1932). Schiller's defense of eugenics as the savior of society – which was accompanied by distinctive antidemocratic sentiments – set him wide apart from the American pragmatists. It could be argued, however, that Schiller's proactive stance toward eugenics is at least in part a logical outcome of his humanism.

Further reading

Abel, Reuben. *The Pragmatic Humanism of F.C.S. Schiller*. New York: King's Crown Press, 1955.

De Waal, Cornelis. *On Pragmatism*. Belmont, CA: Wadsworth, 2005.

Schiller, F.C.S. "Axioms as Postulates," in Henry Sturt (ed.) *Personal Idealism*. London: Macmillan, 1902, pp. 47–133.

—— "Why Humanism?" in J.H. Muirhead (ed.) *Contemporary British Philosophy: Personal Statements*, 1924, pp. 385–410.

—— *Humanistic Pragmatism: The Philosophy of F.C.S. Schiller*, ed. Reuben Abel. New York: Free Press, 1966.

Searles, Herbert L. and Shields, Allan. *A Bibliography of the Works of F.C.S. Schiller*. San Diego, CA: San Diego State College Press, 1969.

CORNELIS DE WAAL

SCHNEIDER, HERBERT WALLACE

Educated at the College of the City of New York and Columbia University, Herbert Wallace Schneider (1892–1984) wrote his doctoral dissertation, *Science and Social Progress: A Philosophical Introduction to Moral Science* (1920), under John Dewey. From 1918 until his retirement in 1957 he taught philosophy and religion at Columbia.

Schneider's publications ranged over religious studies, American intellectual history, metaphysics and political philosophy. *The Puritan Mind* (1930), in which he stressed the social context of Puritan ideas, was Schneider's most widely read work concerned with religion. In intellectual history, *A History of American Philosophy* (1946) told a more comprehensive and detailed story of American philosophy than had been told up to that time. *Sources of Contemporary Realism* (1964) was a supplement to *A History* that firmly connected the American tradition to mid-twentieth-century debates. *Ways of Being: Elements of Analytical Ontology* (1962), a work he considered his most original, presented a realistic, non-reductive metaphysics of naturalism akin to the work of several of his Columbia colleagues. Although his publications in political thought (e.g. *Three Dimensions of Public Morality* (1956)) were in many ways a development and application of the ideas of his mentor Dewey, the German scholar Peter Vogt has argued that Schneider departed from Dewey in not considering democracy fundamental to all intelligent action. This departure, Vogt claims, led Schneider in the 1920s and 1930s to lectures and publications which expressed some sympathy with Italian Fascism. Although it is widely recognized by historians that "flirtation" with Italian Fascism was common among American intellectuals of that period, in a 1976 interview Schneider denied ever being supportive of Mussolini's government.

Further reading

Schneider, Herbert Wallace. *Science and Social Progress: A Philosophical Introduction to Moral Science*. New York: Columbia University Press, 1920.

—— *Three Dimensions of Public Morality*. Bloomington, IN: Indiana University Press, 1956.

—— *Ways of Being: Elements of Analytical Ontology*. New York: Columbia University Press, 1962.

Smith, John E. "Herbert Schneider on the History of Philosophy," *Journal of the History of Philosophy* 25 (1987): 169–77.

Vogt, Peter. "Herbert Schneider and the Ideal of an Intelligent Society," *Transactions of the Charles S. Peirce Society* 38, 3 (2002): 393–411.

PETER H. HARE

SCIENTIFIC METHOD

Scientific method (SM) is a rational, originally philosophical method that has been fruitfully used by problem-solvers of all walks. It is not licensed to science alone, and never was. Still, SM refers primarily to a naturalistic account of the verifiable results of a logico-experimental method retooled specifically for the study of empirical phenomena, aided and sometimes shaped by technologically advanced measuring and observational instruments. American philosophers adopted hypothetical-deductive procedures, but revised them to explicate the collaboration, even continuity, of reason and experience, and the experimental character of human knowledge.

Scientific knowledge is a product of intention and agency under the discipline of reason and experience. It is conceived on one or more related hypotheses concerning and adjusted to what we experientially encounter. This is best achieved methodically. In Roycean terms, method is a "well-ordered system" used to propose testable responses to inquiries. Indeed, obtaining results methodically partly fulfills the classical concept of knowledge as justified, true belief. SM uses the observed to infer the unobserved, override the perspectival singularity of perception, and formulate explanations or law-determined predictions of what we encounter of our world. SM extends what we gather from experience beyond such initial limitations as its local origins, peculiar customs, or an unreflective acquiescence in common sense. By systematically classifying the contents of controlled observations, framing hypotheses and deducing observationally testable consequences, knowledge is shown to depend on more than private experience and possess an objectivity that it otherwise would not have. SM promotes reliable, reproducible results and the discovery of symmetries, asymmetries and constants needed to explain, predict and exercise some control over nature.

Thus, SM consolidates deductive and inductive inferences within three categories of procedure: observation, hypothesis formation, and testing (classification and reduction are auxiliary). These procedures are distinct but inseparable. Since conceiving is as fallible as perceiving, we must complement each with the other and revise our conceptions according to new evidence. Observation alone neither explains nor predicts, but is needed to inductively gather and classify empirical evidence, and test hypotheses. Hypotheses are logically framed generalizations that entail experimentally testable predictions. Experiments without hypotheses are impossible; re-ordering a problematic situation according to a hypothesis and observing its outcome is an experiment. Hypotheses also guide investigation: if confirmed, we attempt to modify the hypothesis by extending it over new phenomena and retest it; if not, the hypothesis either is abandoned, or is modified and retested. In either case, hypotheses guide where and where not to direct inquiry. In cases where a hypothesis entails established facts, it is explanatory; e.g. Newton's laws of motion and gravitation entail Kepler's laws of planetary motion and Galileo's time^2 law. In any case, since hypotheses are not self-testing, they must begin with and return to observation; otherwise, they would be empirically contentless or entail only what was already known.

Contributions of American philosophers to SM

American philosophers inherited a well-developed SM from their European predecessors and contemporaries, but gave it the uniquely American turn that promoted a pragmatic theory of meaning over essential definitions, the fallible experimental nature of knowledge over certainty, and warrant over absolute truth. Chauncey Wright clarified SM by correcting previously misunderstood aspects of hypotheses. He rejected the view that hypotheses are categorical generalizations, since it concealed the hypothetical–deductive structure of SM. Wright conceived scientific generalizations in terms of the testable consequences they entail instead of categorical properties, which he dismissed as mere summaries of observations. He valued experimentation as a method of discovery, but elevated its role in verifying hypotheses. Wright appreciated Mill's Methods, but denied that the content of hypotheses must originate in sensation, and insisted that the sources of hypotheses are irrelevant provided they entail testable consequences verifiable in experience. This hypothetical–deductive model, Wright argued, fits the dynamics of nature, and the explanatory and predictive interests of science reflected in the mathematical reasoning of Galileo and Newton. Obviously, many hypotheses are directly testable, but Wright recognized that others are so only indirectly and in conjunction with auxiliary hypotheses. He thus foreshadowed aspects of Carnap's later views and the Duhem–Quine thesis.

The richest analyses of the hypothetical-deductive component in SM are those of Peirce, whose pragmatism produced a rationally circumscribed experimentalism. Hypotheses, Peirce realized, that merely state "crude" enumerative generalizations or that future events resemble past events yield only repetitions, not new knowledge. This he surmounted by deploying a pragmatic theory of meaning, and distinguishing deduction as the form of necessary truth-preserving inference found in logic and mathematics, and induction as a form of probable inference characteristic of empirical science. Peirce saw SM, particularly induction, as a self-corrective endeavor that assumes, as "guiding principles," formal logic and the pragmatic principle that the meaning of a concept is all its practical consequences verifiable in experience. Peirce further distinguished crude, quantitative, and qualitative induction, and anticipated Reichenbach when he used a frequency interpretation of probability to construe quantitative induction as a statistical inference from a "fair sample" to the "whole population" from which the sample was taken. Such inferences are self-correcting in that if continued sampling undermines an earlier ratio, it does so by substituting a more accurate measure. Qualitative induction is the formation of testable hypotheses, an inference to the best explanation using abduction and retroduction. Peirce's use of these terms is not always consistent, but some passages suggest that abduction refers to forming and selecting hypotheses according to whether they explain the facts in question, while retroduction refers to experimentally testing and eliminating hypotheses that are falsified. This fits the pragmatic principle as it involves examining abductions as one would the meaning of ideas by deducing their practical consequences and experimentally testing them. This procedure also is self-correcting in that continued abductions and retroductions will guide us "in the long run" along successive approximations to the truth. Though it seems unhelpful, Peirce sometimes described abduction as "guessing" an explanation. This may fit his tychism, but guessing unhappily suggests that wildly random thoughts occupy the core of SM. However, this suggestion fades when we consider abduction together with the other procedures of SM practiced within a community of responsible inquirers. Besides, scientists like Richard Feynman have delighted in defining hypotheses as guesses without undermining SM.

In his writings on SM, Josiah Royce endorsed Peirce's views on induction but added "leading ideas" as another type of hypothesis. These are not the deductive argument forms Peirce called "guiding" or "leading principles." Rather, Royce compared them to Kant's "regulative ideas," fundamental postulates that regulate the overall structure of inquiry, but which are neither directly experimentally testable nor logically demonstrable. They are what Thomas Kuhn later called, "paradigms" within which scientists "puzzle-out" specific investigations. The "mechanical universe" is one such hypothesis. Euclid's parallel postulate, Royce held, is another, for it cannot be proved or disproved either by Euclid's other definitions and axioms or by observation. Yet, (1) affirming it entails the classical plane geometry of zero-curvature space (a paradigm of western thought for 2,000 years); (2) denying it entails either (2a) a Riemannian geometry of positive curvature, or (2b) a Lobachevskian geometry of negative curvature. Each option is logically consistent, not directly testable, but establishes a different paradigm: (1) supports a Newtonian universe, (2a) an Einsteinian universe. Thus, Royce's notion is essential to SM. Without it or something similar, Kuhn's theory of scientific revolutions might have been a nonstarter.

In Dewey's instrumental naturalism, SM as presented above was "reconstructed" in a theory of inquiry that more than repaid his debt to Peirce's pragmatism and William James' psychology. Dewey's instrumentalism uniquely reweaves the themes of pragmatism to more prominently exhibit the continuity of reasoning and experience with natural processes. There is no neutral stance where "news form nowhere" is unintrusively acquired by a quietly contemplative intellect. Rather, the procedures of SM are embedded in the activity of solving "problematic situations." Inquiry, of course, includes framing hypotheses, rendering predictions within specified conditions, and experimentally testing them by observing whether the predicted results obtain, thereby producing the object as known. Knowing, for Dewey, is an activity of coming to know something by manipulating elements of the problematic situation and exercising a measure of technological control in nature. To specify conditions and experimentally rearrange the natural and cognitive circumstances of the problem changes nature as that with which reason and experience are continuous. Thus, manipulating nature in the course of inquiry is unavoidable since inquiry consists in "transforming a problematic situation" into an object of knowledge. Since what is known by SM is an experimental product, it is tentative, incomplete, and always open to revision. It thus is rash to lay claim to certainty or absolute truth, and more appropriate to claim only "warranted assertability." This is not to banish truth, for we sometimes acquire it; rather it is a recognition of human finitude and the limitations of knowledge.

Pragmatism figures prominently in the paragraphs above because it exhibits the distinctive characteristics of American philosophy. There were and are other philosophies of science in America. The realisms of the early twentieth century were reacting to pragmatism as much as to idealism, but these were not uniquely American movements. Although the brilliant critiques by George Santayana and Arthur Lovejoy exposed problems in pragmatism, they added no new elements to SM proper. Morris Cohen's rational realism dealt squarely with SM, but mainly by defending it against a creeping subjectivism in early twentieth-century science and positivistic accounts of SM. His moderate realist ontology of logic and mathematics was a countermeasure to positivism. Nevertheless, details of his account of SM show the influence of Peirce and Royce. Pragmatism thus survived the early realist critiques and found new expression in the writings of Quine and Putnam. In all, scientific knowing remains an end of the encounter of reason and experience with nature, and SM is a means of this encounter.

Further reading

Cohen, Morris R. *Reason and Nature: An Essay on the Meaning of Scientific Method.* New York: Free Press, 1964.

Dewey, John. *Logic: the Theory of Inquiry.* New York: Irvington, 1982 (reprint).

Feynman, Richard. *The Character of Physical Law.* Cambridge, MA: MIT Press, 1985, Ch. 7.

Kuhn, Thomas S. *The Structure of Scientific Revolutions*, second edition. Chicago, IL: University of Chicago Press, 1970.

Peirce, Charles Sanders. *The Essential Peirce*, 2 vols, ed. the Peirce Edition Project. Bloomington, IN: Indiana University Press, 1998 [1992].

Royce, Josiah. *Royce's Logical Essays: Collected Logical Essays of Josiah Royce*, ed. Daniel S. Robinson. Dubuque, IA: William C. Brown, 1951.

Wright, Chauncey. *Philosophical Discussions*, ed. Charles Eliot Norton. New York: Burt Franklin, 1971.

GARY L. CESARZ

SCIENTIFIC REVOLUTIONS

Historians of science sometimes find abrupt and far-reaching changes in the course of the development of a given "science," or cumulative investigation of a given "domain." In some cases, terms such as *discovery*, *innovation*, or *advance* seem adequate. In other cases where basic techniques, assumptions, or viewpoints are or appear to be radically revised or replaced, the vague and metaphorical expression *scientific revolution* might be warranted. A paradigm case is the Copernican Revolution in astronomy. Before the revolution, astronomers described the trajectories of the planets in reference to a coordinate system centered on the earth; afterwards, they referred their observations to a system fixed in the sun.

A much earlier case is the Thalesian Revolution in geometry. Before the revolution, geometers relied almost exclusively on observation, experimentation, and intuition; afterwards, logical deduction including *reductio ad absurdum* was prominently added to the arsenal of geometric weaponry. For some centuries now, philosophers, especially epistemologists, have regarded scientific revolutions as being particularly germane to their concerns. Kant mentioned both of the above revolutions in his *Critique of Pure Reason*. While many view scientific revolutions as marks of progress, others see them as indicative of irrational elements in science.

Given that sciences are human social institutions, we should not expect precise concepts for discussing them or sharp boundaries within and between them. As a rule, the pre-revolutionary form of a science continues into and through the revolutionary period, and it coexists with the post-revolutionary form, perhaps in a diminished state, into the post-revolutionary period. In some cases, it is not clear whether a single science has been revolutionized or whether a new science has been created alongside the old one. In any given case, historians must delimit "the science" (or "sciences") in question; they must judge how abrupt and far-reaching was the change, and how extensive the penetration of revolutionary features. Given the ambiguities of crucial words and the vagueness of their various meanings, we can expect to find the appearance of wide discrepancies among accounts of the history of one "science." Where one historian sees a few long stable periods punctuated by a few major revolutions, another may find several short stable periods punctuated by several rather minor revolutions, and yet another might find a relatively smooth though sometimes bumpy evolution. Moreover, of course, we should not rule out the possibility that such differences are sometimes to be explained as much in terms of the historians' subjective tolerance or enthusiasm for excitement as in terms of substantive disagreements about objective historical facts.

The expression "scientific revolution" almost oxymoronically joins the adjective "scientific" with a noun previously referring to overthrowing a government. Accordingly, it carries conflicting connotations – which might account for some of its popularity. For years, if not centuries, the word "scientific" connoted the highest level of rigor, caution, objectivity, patient tolerance of alternative hypotheses, and courageous devotion to truth. However, the word "revolution" sometimes suggested a pre-existing establishment having an entrenched hierarchy with power, privilege, prestige, and wealth that was more concerned to perpetuate than criticize itself. Such organizations are sometimes more interested in recruiting loyal followers using increasingly intricate methods of indoctrination than in producing autonomous investigators who will critically assess received views and follow their own insights and deductions. Rigor and caution can be transformed into ritual rigidity and stubborn dogmatism.

Interest in the topic was heightened in the 1960s with the publication of Thomas Kuhn's *The Structure of Scientific Revolutions* (Chicago, 1962), one of the most influential works in historiography of science. This work not only revolutionized thinking about scientific revolutions but also revolutionized the language in which this topic is discussed. The expression *Kuhnian Revolution* is fully justified. A few years after the book was published, new editions of dictionaries added a new meaning to the word "paradigm."

In dictionaries that order meanings chronologically, the most recent meaning comes last. The 2004 *Merriam-Webster Collegiate Dictionary* entry for "revolution" ends with the sense used here:

> d: a fundamental change in the way of thinking about or visualizing something: a change of paradigm *the Copernican revolution* e: a changeover in use or preference especially in technology *the computer revolution* *the foreign car revolution* synonyms see REBELLION.

Its entry for "paradigm" reads:

> 1. EXAMPLE, PATTERN; especially: an outstandingly clear or typical example or archetype 2. an example of a conjugation or declension showing a word in all its inflectional forms 3. a philosophical and theoretical framework of a scientific school or discipline within which theories, laws, and generalizations and the experiments performed in support of them are formulated; broadly: a philosophical or theoretical framework of any kind.

Editions before 1962 lack the third meaning. Today this meaning is applied far more broadly than in the 1962 book about scientific revolutions where it originated.

To gauge the differences among these senses, notice that the first, exemplificational sense is relational; every paradigm is a paradigm *of* something. In this sense, there is no such thing as a paradigm *per se*. The third, theoretical sense is sortal. No paradigm (first sense) *of* a revolution is a revolutionary paradigm (third sense). No example *of* a revolution is a revolutionary theoretical framework. Every paradigm (first sense) of a revolution is a revolution, a historic event. Every revolutionary scientific paradigm (third sense) is a theoretical framework established through a scientific revolution. No event is a theoretical framework. These crucial observations are often overlooked.

The 1962 Kuhn book continued to use the word in the first relational exemplificational sense after initiating its use in the third sortal theoretical sense. Sometimes it is difficult to tell which is meant. Kuhn used it in the first sense to emphasize his view that in stable periods, which he called "normal science," much scientific work follows rules of "the game" and imitates "patterns" established by earlier scientists. He said on page 24 that normal science "seems an attempt to force nature into the preformed and relatively inflexible box that the paradigm supplies." Continuing on the same page, he added two of the most revealing sentences of the book:

> No part of the aim of normal science is to call forth new sorts of phenomena; indeed those that will not fit the box are often not seen at all. Nor do scientists normally aim to invent new theories, and they are often intolerant of those invented by others.

The fact that he used words having pejorative connotations has not been lost on some scientists who regard Kuhn's book as unfairly derogatory and offensive. He spoke of scientific revolutions as "paradigm shifts," which suggests unflattering comparison to figure-ground shifts in cognitive psychology, structure-ambiguity shifts in linguistics, and gestalt shifts in Gestalt psychology. In some cases, such as the Copernican Revolution, which is the subject of Kuhn's previous 1957 book, the comparison might seem somewhat justified. In others, such as the Thalesian Revolution, the comparison seems absurd.

To avoid confusion, one should note that in "paradigm shift" the word "paradigm" is being used in the third sense and the "shift" is a kind of collective mental event that takes place more or less contemporaneously in the minds of a sufficiently large or important group of scientists. As Kuhn and others have emphasized, a paradigm shift – or more generally the decision by individual scientists to persist in a pre-revolutionary paradigm or to adopt a revolutionary one – is often difficult to explain by reference to purely rational thought processes. One result of the Kuhnian Revolution was that in some circles philosophy of science became a little less like a branch of epistemology and a little more like a branch of sociology or cultural anthropology.

Further reading

Kuhn, Thomas. *The Copernican Revolution*. Cambridge, MA: Harvard University Press, 1957.

—— *The Structure of Scientific Revolutions*. Chicago, IL: University of Chicago Press, 1962.

JOHN CORCORAN

SCOTTISH COMMONSENSE SCHOOL, INFLUENCE OF

Thomas Reid, the University of Glasgow, was the leader of the Scottish Commonsense tradition which was influential in Great Britain and flourished during the nineteenth century in France and the United States. It dominated American philosophy for five decades and had a resurgence in the second half of the twentieth century.

The most significant members of the earlier tradition were Asa Mahan, James McCosh, Alexander Campbell, Henry Tappan, Francis Wayland, and Thomas Upham, all professors of philosophy and New Light opponents of the "soft" determinism of Jonathan Edwards. Roderick Chisholm, Wilfrid Sellars, and Keith Lehrer and their students were the most prominent figures of Reid's twentieth-century revival. Their defense of the adverbial view brought it center-stage in epistemology, and Lehrer, Duggan, Brody *et al.* edited fine new editions of Reid's works. The principal elements in the Scottish philosophy that influenced the Americans were Reid's metaphilosophy, presentative realism, and agency theory.

According to Reid, any philosophical claim that contradicts the truth or falsity of ordinary statements, or the grammar of ordinary language, must result from a faulty premise since drawing the deductive consequences of a set of premises can be done precisely. The most blatant false premise, which underlies the whole of British empiricism, is that illusions and hallucinations demonstrate that a person cannot be directly aware of physical objects but rather is aware of sensations or sense data.

Such claims quite consistently ended in Humean skepticism. For Reid presentative realism is the only way to avoid the total disasters of all epistemic dualisms. His own version of presentative realism is refreshingly different. Reid maintained that empiricists and positivists incorrectly assumed that a sensation is an entity when, in fact, a sensation is not something experienced but is a way of experiencing. Unfortunately Reid continued to use the word "sensation" as meaning a way of experiencing, and commentators often missed the fact that he was a presentative realist. His early American followers fortunately interpreted Reid correctly though it remained for later writers to introduce a clearer terminology. Chisholm and Sellars wrote that perceiving is an adverbial, not a nominal, locution. "Sensing" thereafter replaced "sensation" in discussing Reid's views.

Asa Mahan, first president of Oberlin, added a new dimension to the Reidian metaphilosophy. He pointed out that Berkeley was an epistemic dualist but insisted that his views did not contradict ordinary truth values of either science or daily experiences. Kepler's laws remain true whether the planets are conceived to be physical objects or a cluster of perceptions in God's mind. Mahan argued that it is not enough to keep ordinary truth values intact; it is also crucial to keep ordinary meanings intact. Propositions about my spoon and its equivalent cluster of sensations may both be true, but in ordinary language by "spoon" we mean an object that exists independently of any perception, and we do not mean "a cluster of sensations."

Reid advocated a version of agency theory designed to undercut both hard and soft determinism and thus preserve the grounds for moral accountability. The role of motives is entirely different from efficient causality. They are neither causes nor agents. A person is the efficient cause (makes something happen), not his motives. In a free act a person acts in light of motives but not as a necessary consequence of them; he is the cause of his act and nothing caused him to act the way he did. Motives are akin to guidance, advice, direction, etc., which can influence but not cause a person's decision to do *x* rather than *y*.

The early American advocates accepted most of Reid's ideas but were particularly drawn to his agency theory. Alexander Campbell, president of Bethany, was the most spectacular defender of this concept. Campbell and Robert Owen, a determinist, held a formal debate in Cincinnati in 1829. The debate, which lasted a week, attracted thousands of people who witnessed Campbell's destruction of Owen's arguments. Owen claimed that all human behavior is "necessitated" by the strongest desire or, in the case of reasoning, by the strongest motives. Campbell replied that the controversy about necessity and free will was "a mere war of words," a jargon full of sense and nonsense, of meaning and no meaning. After all, "I will," "I determine," and "I conclude" mean essentially the same thing. Given Owen's deterministic thesis, every action is blameless and non-praiseworthy; and in saying such things he transgressed the ordinary sense of moral commitments. The determinist thesis leads to the following *reductio ad absurdum*: If a ruler measured every surface as one foot long the ruler would contravene the sense of measuring concepts and be utterly useless.

James McCosh of Princeton, though he accepted most of Reid, however rejected Reid's concept of agency causality in the physical world where God is the agent of every specific event. As an alternative, McCosh devised an excellent singularist view of causality that fits scientific practice and was to become influential in twentieth-century singularist views.

The entering wedge was McCosh's denial of the familiar Humean assumption of the material equivalence of modal propositions and how they become known. McCosh had shifted the point where contingencies enter scientific inference. Scientific theories are deductive hypotheses with explanatory power. A posteriori evidence may show that this power has limitations and must be abandoned. However, any new deductive system that might replace it would again exhibit necessary relations which would be checked by a posteriori means.

Among twentieth-century Reidians, Chisholm took the lead in rejecting Humean causality because it could not account for counterfactual inferences like "This stick of dynamite would have exploded had it been properly detonated." But Chisholm never developed a singularist view that could account for counterfactual inference that McCosh had already formulated.

Further reading

Barker, S.F. and Beauchamp, T.L. (eds). *Thomas Reid: Critical Interpretation*. Philadelphia, PA: Philosophical Monographs, 1976.

Campbell, Alexander and Owen, Robert. *Debate on the Evidence of Christianity*, 2 vols, second edition. Cincinnati, OH: Robinson and Fairbank, 1829. The "Great Debate" occurs in Vol. 1.

McCosh, James. *First and Fundamental Truths*. New York: Charles Scribner's Sons, 1894.

Madden, E.H. "The Metaphilosophy of Commonsense," *American Philosophical Quarterly* 20 (1983): 23–36.

—— "McCosh on Basic Intuitions and Causality," *Transactions of the C.S. Peirce Society* 20 (1984): 119–46.

Mahan, Asa. *The Doctrine of the Will*. New York: H. Newman, 1845.

—— *Autobiography: Intellectual Moral and Spiritual*. London: T. Woolmer, 1882.

Reid, Thomas. *An Inquiry into the Human Mind*, ed. T. Duggan. Chicago, IL: University of Chicago Press, 1970.

—— *Inquiry and Essays*, ed. K. Lehrer and R.E. Beanblossom. Indianapolis, IN: Bobbs-Merrill, 1975.

—— *Essays on the Intellectual Powers of Man*, ed. B. Brody. Cambridge, MA: MIT Press, 1969

—— *Essays on the Active Powers of the Human Mind*, ed. B. Brody. Cambridge, MA: MIT Press, 1969.

EDWARD H. MADDEN

SECONDNESS

"Secondness" is a term often used generically by Charles Peirce to represent one of the three fundamental categories of his systematic philosophy: Firstness, Secondness, Thirdness. In its most general sense, secondness is expressed by that which is individual, differentiating, actual and brute, that is, as pure force (CP 1.427). It is distinguished from firstness, understood as quality and possibility, and thirdness, defined as regularity, mediation, and generality. Based on his logic of relations, the categories are claimed to be the simplest and most primitive conceptions (CP 5.177). It follows, then, that seconds are irreducible to firsts, just as thirds cannot be understood as some composition of seconds (CP 1.346). Whenever manifested, they form a relation of dependency: Thirdness must involve secondness and firstness, as secondness must involve firstness (CP 5.91). Nowhere is this clearer than in Peirce's account of signs. In order for something to be a sign it has to be the bearer of some quality or character (a first), in and through which it establishes a relation to something else (its object – a second); thus allowing it to convey to something else some information about that object (its interpretant – a third) (CP 2.274; CP 2.92). For example, a wind vane refers to its object (the wind), primarily through the brute force of the wind acting upon it, but it can only convey information about the wind, for example its direction, through the firstness or character of the wind vane – in this case, its shape and direction – and to something (its interpretant) which can correlate that information with the sign's object.

Because Peirce claims that his categories are universal, he argues that secondness is manifested in all forms of being. Formally, any dyadic relation is a second, for example "brother of" (CP 1.326). In regard to signs, indices, such as demonstrative pronouns, are paradigmatically seconds since they represent their objects by some direct connection. Quantifiers are seconds since they determine the number of things referred to in a proposition. Indeed, propositions are forms of secondness as compared to terms and inferences (CP 1.369). Among inferences, deduction is a kind of secondness since it infers with necessity and finality (CP 1.369). In sensation and perception, it is manifested as haecceity (CP 1.405), ego and non-ego (CP 1.325), and felt existence – individuals which offer resistance to our doings and happenings. It is found in acts of will and struggle (CP 1.374). Temporally, it is manifested in the past, in heredity, as that which has happened and cannot be changed, with an inertia which affects the present (CP 1.398). In the physical realm, fact and law are examples of secondness, the first in the sense of something thought to be incontrovertible, the latter thought to be something that is fixed, insistent, and necessary. Causation, in its aspect as pure force, also exemplifies secondness (CP 1.325). Cosmologically, it is the very ability of things to differentiate that exemplifies secondness in its grandest manifestation.

Further reading

Peirce, Charles Sanders. *The Collected Papers of Charles Sanders Peirce* (CP), 8 vols, edited by Charles Hartshorne, Paul Weiss, and Arthur Burks. Cambridge, MA: Harvard University Press, 1965.

JAMES JAKÓB LISZKA

SELECTIVE EMPHASIS

According to John Dewey, "selective emphasis" – roughly, the privileging of certain data of experience over others – is present in any act of thought. Whenever we think, something is emphasized and something de-emphasized: some theme, some quality, some difficulty is given our attention, while others are disregarded or relegated to the experiential background. The roots of selective emphasis lie deep, as it were, in nature. All existences evidence bias, or differential behavioral response: things react positively or negatively in the presence of other things. Such differential response is evident throughout nature, reaching all the way down to the microphysical, where sub-atomic particles are attracted to other sub-atomic particles or repelled by others. We see it in greater complexity in the animate world: photosynthetic plants are attracted to sunlight; higher animal forms pursue prey and flee predators. And we see it in its highest expression in the cognitive capacities of minded beings, in *humankind*, in our ability to *choose*. Selective emphasis, choice, is necessary to deal with any problem situation confronting us: a difficulty is felt, a problem identified, a course of action selected and acted upon in light of the particular purposes dominating the reflective act, and the problem resolved. As such, selective emphasis is central to our getting on in the world; it is, according to Dewey, the "heart-beat" of mental life. However, when choice becomes disguised, ignored, unavowed, problems arise. The "fallacy of selective emphasis" is committed when we lose sight of the fact that we *do*, relative to specific purposes, selectively emphasize certain things. The consequences of this fallacy figure prominently in the history of (western) philosophy: Mankind often faces a perilous existence, where problems, even threats to life itself, abound. To escape this peril, we have sought refuge in the simple, the permanent, the knowable. Failure properly to recognize these purpose-driven choices *as* choices has led to the conversion of such desiderata into exclusive features of reality. Much of the history of philosophy, thinks Dewey, is the playing out of the precipitate of this fallacy. Thus, for example, Plato and his eternal Forms, Locke and his completely knowable simple ideas, Hume and his sense impressions, the British neo-realists and their atomic ideas, the emphasis upon mathematical objects: the list is long, the debates endless. Dewey, however, thought that through use of the "empirical method" we may avoid the fallacy of selective emphasis. Empirical method, which reaches its most sophisticated manifestation in contemporary (natural) science, self-consciously appeals to experience and in so doing explicitly acknowledges its selective procedure. Anyone who so wishes may follow along the path of inquiry, and judge for himself the credibility of the results arrived at. Only through this methodological approach, thinks Dewey, may we set philosophy on its proper course, and avoid the problems that have plagued it because of unacknowledged selective emphasis.

Further reading

Dewey, John. *Experience and Nature* in *John Dewey: The Later Works, 1925–1953, Vol. 1, 1925*, ed. Jo Ann Boydston and Patricia R. Baysinger. Carbondale, IL: Southern Illinois University Press, 1981, pp. 3–336.

—— "Philosophies of Freedom" in *John Dewey: The Later Works, 1925–1953, Vol. 3, 1927–8*, ed. Jo Ann Boydston and David Sidorsky. Carbondale, IL: Southern Illinois University Press, 1984.

CHRISTOPHER KULP

SELF-REALIZATION

Self-realization became an explicit topic of philosophical interest to both British and American thinkers in the late nineteenth century. Self-realizationists address value questions like: What do "self" and "realization" mean? What is human welfare or well-being? What things are intrinsically good, desirable for their own sakes? What ought we to do? How does self-realization differ from selfishness and from other theories of human well-being or intrinsic goodness? Self-realizationists claim that human welfare consists in self-realization, it alone is intrinsically good, and we ought to actualize our potentialities.

"Self" can refer to many things. William James's "stream of consciousness," including its constituent experiences and activities, is the core concept of "self" in American philosophy. Most American thinkers repudiated extreme views of "self" and sought a middle ground between David Hume's moments of consciousness that have no causal connection with one another, and the Cartesian/Lockean/Kantian position that events within our stream of consciousness are connected by an underlying, enduring, unchanging, and unexperienced metaphysical substance or noumenal reality to which they belong. American idealists, pragmatists, and process philosophers heavily emphasized both the physical and social origins of the self and the temporal, social, experiential, and personal-agency aspects of self-realization.

William James greatly influenced American self-realizationists. For James, goodness consisted in satisfying the most inclusive possible set of "demands," desires, or interests. Hard experience gradually teaches us to select and fulfill those personal demands that are satisfying, that avoid dissatisfaction and destruction, that prevail at the least cost, and that harmonize best with one another. As social animals in a world containing more than one person, we must morally consider, act upon, and harmonize the claims of others with our own personal demands. Ideal goodness or self-realization requires acting both prudently and morally to fulfill as many personally and socially harmonious demands or desires as possible over many generations.

According to John Dewey's similar views, self-realization is an inherently gratifying process of "growth" that creates and acts upon good habits, exercises personal initiative, individuality, and freedom, and produces as many personal, shared, unified, harmonious, enriching, meaningful, and intrinsically satisfying consummatory experiences and activities as possible. Morally legitimate self-realization allows equal opportunities for self-realization to others and is best achieved in a democracy. Ideal social and personal selves do not pre-exist as fixed essences in isolation but must be created intelligently and experimentally in real time in interaction with a real environment. Self-realization is a practical problem to be solved within each self's concrete social and physical situation. In consummatory experiences, life's means (the journeys) exemplify and become integral parts of life's ends (the destinations); both are guides to action and ends in themselves.

Self-realizationists advocate actualizing the largest possible integrated and harmonious totality of our thoughts, feelings, desires, choices, actions, abilities, talents, and personal properties. To realize ourselves is to actualize our potentials – our capabilities, talents, desires, interests, decisions, activities, and functions; but only some, not all, of our potentials should be actualized. We cannot and should not actualize all of our potentials or satisfy all of our desires. They are so vast; many are in conflict; we lack the will, time, or opportunity; many are asinine or boring; many constitute or produce ill-being, not well-being; and many, like becoming rapists or murderers, are downright immoral. Living well inevitably involves making hard choices.

Which human potentials are relevant to the self's well-being, intrinsic goodness, and duty? With what part of ourselves do we, should we, fully identify ourselves? In answering, self-realizationists typically distinguish the "true" from the "false" self and recognize that they are often in conflict. Conflicts occur within and between selves. We should only create, affirm, and identify ourselves with our true or best self, our truly desirable capacities, talents, desires, interests, and potentials; and we should dissociate ourselves from our false self, our undesirable potentials. Various contrasts like "good/bad," "mature/immature," "deep/superficial," "higher/lower," "real/apparent," "ideal/actual," "essential/accidental," or "natural/artificial" have been used to distinguish these two selves. When people actualize only their lower selves, this leads to distress, disappointment, disapproval, disability, destruction, disaster, death, social disintegration, and the pervasive wretchedness of human existence. "Doing it my way," when this is the way of the false self, is unacceptable. Well-being consists in creating, identifying ourselves with, and actualizing our truest, best, highest, and most mature and inclusive selves. Only thereby can we live worthwhile lives, actualize intrinsic goodness, fulfill our obligations, and live in social harmony. Inferior abilities, desires, interests, and activities should be sacrificed, controlled, diminished, or extinguished. We should develop and implement long-term plans of life centered around our best selves, the richest possible integrated configuration of all the good-making properties or attributes open to us; but such plans of life can be realized only by degrees in concrete circumstances.

Self-realizationists insist that many universally beneficial desires and dispositions belong to our truest selves. By nature, everyone has much in common with everyone else. Everyone naturally has both self-beneficial and other-beneficial interests, desires, needs, and dispositions. Every human self needs the basic physical and social necessities of life, but, as complex social beings, we also have profound needs for reason, knowledge, conscience, compassion, love, identifying-with-others, self-respect, respecting others, justice, responsible decision-making, self-control, loyalty, and belonging.

Our real selves are fulfilled through both the benevolent features of universal human nature within us and our uniquely personal perspectives, activities, projects, adventures, commitments, responsibilities, and talents. Universal values exist only in, to, and for unique, concrete, conscious individuals who are largely social products. Good persons actualize their best selves and give back as they have received, and good societies have customs, practices, and educational, legal, benevolent, religious, political, and other institutions that enable and encourage the mutually compatible and supportive self-realization of their individual members. Being a good person is almost impossible without a morally supportive social environment.

Self-realization is difficult to distinguish from other ethical theories of human welfare, intrinsic goodness, and duty. Historically, self-realizationists repudiated hedonism, but if the true self were the hedonically happy self living a long-run pleasant life, then self-realizationists would just be hedonists for whom intrinsic goodness and human well-being consist in prolonged enjoyments with only minimal pains and frustrations. Ideal utilitarians affirm a plurality of intrinsic goods or ends, so if realizing the true self consists in actualizing multiple inherently worthwhile ideal goods like rationality, knowledge, autonomy, interpersonal intimacy, individuality, loyalty, fairness, virtue, compassion, conscience, creativity, freedom, adventure, enjoyment, beauty, faith, hope, and love, then self-realizationists might just be ideal utilitarians with a rich repertoire of intrinsic goods. Historical self-realizationists did not say so, but if the true self were equated with the morally conscientious good will that does things simply because they are right, then self-realization would merely affirm the "unqualified goodness" of deontological knowing and doing what is right for its own sake. Alternatively, a teleological self-realization compass would proclaim that right and self-fulfilling acts are those that have the most beneficial hedonic or ideal utilitarian consequences. Self-realization theory is profoundly challenged to specify why and how it differs from hedonistic, ideal utilitarian, deontological, or other more familiar ethical positions.

All ethical theories should ask whether unique persons or selves as such have intrinsic worth, whether they are ends in themselves, and what this means. Are unique and unrepeatable human subjects anything more than merely extrinsic receptacles for containing repeatable intrinsic goods like pleasure, knowledge, morality, enjoyable activity, compassion, virtue, and such? Or are these repeatable properties desirable mainly because they enrich the lives of unique human selves?

Self-realizationists emphasize personal self-interests, but they repudiate the selfish actualization of exclusively self-benefiting/other-exploiting capacities, desires, and interests. They recognize persisting conflicts between personal and social self-realization, but they postulate a very broad harmony between our deepest or most satisfying desires and interests and the ultimate well-being of others within the social whole. Self-regard, self-affirmation, self-preservation, and distinctive self-fulfillment are affirmed; but exclusive self-regard or selfishness belongs to undeveloped, confused, and false selfhood. Love, loyalty, empathy, compassion, benevolence, fairness, and all desires, dispositions, and deeds that intend the well-being of others are integral parts of our true selves. Our other-benefiting interests are indeed our interests. They belong to our very existence and constitution. They directly aim at the well-being of others, not at our own welfare; but, since they are essential parts of who we really are, they are also aspects of our own well-being. Their realization fulfills our desires, gives us great satisfaction, and enriches our own existence.

Further reading

Bertocci, Peter A. and Millard, Richard M. *Personality and the Good: Psychological and Ethical Perspectives.* New York: David McKay, 1963, Chs 4, 25, 26, 27.

Bradley, F.H. *Ethical Studies*, second edition. London: Oxford University Press, 1959, Chs II, V, VI, VII.

Dewey, John. "Self-Realization as the Moral Ideal" in *The Early Works of John Dewey*, Vol. 4. Carbondale, IL: Southern Illinois University Press, 1971, pp. 42–53.

Garnett, A. Campbell. "Deontology and Self-Realization," *Ethics* 51, 4 (1941): 419–38.

Gouinlock, James. *The Moral Writings of John Dewey, A Selection.* New York: Hafner Press, 1976, especially pp. 56–121.

James, William. "The Moral Philosopher and the Moral Life," in *Essays in Pragmatism.* New York: Hafner, 1954, pp. 65–87.

Maslow, Abraham. *The Farther Reaches of Human Nature.* New York: Viking Press, 1972.

Royce, Josiah. *The Philosophy of Loyalty.* New York: Macmillan, 1928.

Wright, Henry W. *Self-Realization: An Outline of Ethics.* New York: Henry Holt, 1913.

Rem B. Edwards

SELF-RELIANCE

Self-reliance is customarily taken to be the idea that there is some internal state of affairs that is a source of useful direction and correct judgment. On this reading, self-reliance is contrasted with reliance on externalities, whether they be other people (parents, friends, etc.), human institutions of any kind (schools, governments, etc.), God, or Nature. Many incarnations of the idea appear in the history of philosophy and religion – *daimon*, directing mind, conscience, inner light, genius – and deeply influence American philosophical thought about human agency, human rights, and personal identity. Ralph Waldo Emerson's use of the idea transforms the standard view, elevating it to a new degree of clarity and intensity, one that enables the term to enter American culture as a primary value, and perhaps also, a guiding myth.

In an essay of the same name (1841), Emerson accounts for the status of the self in America's new democracy. As the life of Socrates exemplifies, the crisis of self-knowledge involves the courage to act from that knowledge. Reclaiming this wisdom, Emerson transforms the ancient Delphic oracle for contemporary Americans: "Trust thyself." He admonishes his readers that the "virtue most in request is conformity," and its "aversion" is self-reliance. And yet, in order to know who you are, you must explore who you are in the midst of life with others. Personal identity – or individualness – develops through this engagement: "But do your work, and I shall know you. Do your work, and you shall reinforce yourself." Emerson claims that private discontent contributes to infirmity of will, and that only a person who "acts from himself" (as if from an aboriginal source) will find peace for himself. In this way, Emerson orients us to an inward condition (often called the self or genius, sometimes intuition and instinct), which can serve, he believes, as a better guide for human conduct than any singular appeal to an interpreted or mediated God (such as one finds in Christianity), or to the authority of other people. Emerson is convinced that we serve God and men best by summoning private power, and acting outwardly from within. His commendations in this respect, however, do not entail that we believe our life is independent of influence, or that we must live apart in order to be ourselves. Just the contrary, Emerson would support Aristotle's claim that "He who is unable to live in society, or who has no need because he is sufficient for himself, must be either a beast or a god; he is no part of a state." Trusting oneself does not require isolation, nor does it mean one is inviolable. Instead, self-trust develops only in a dynamic relation to the world of others, institutions, and myriad influences – that is, living "in the midst of the crowd."

At first glance, self-reliance appears to bar or obstruct community. Indeed the quality that enables a man to pull himself up by his bootstraps, to succeed on his own, without the support of others, to prevail against the conspiring forces of society, solely by his own resources, does complicate any real hope of interdependence – but this idea aligns more closely with the ethos of Horatio Alger or Ayn Rand than Emerson. An Emersonian understanding of the term abandons the conceit that one can really know oneself completely and thus exercise total control over oneself. Instead, Emerson takes for granted that human experience is too complicated – varied, messy, mysterious – for anyone to attempt such command. Emerson's use of the term is not just philosophical, but Romantic, in the sense that he is committed to the processes of experience: the way that the on-going, ever-expanding, evolving exchange of forces between people creates the conditions for the possibility of individuality. Problematically, self-reliance can be a compelling and easily applied archetype in storytelling – the knowing one against mindless many, the wholesome individual fighting the corrupt society – and so has been, and continues to be, appropriated in various political, rhetorical, literary, and dramatic ways. Yet as a Romantic philosophical concept in Emerson's lexicon, it is decidedly less reactionary. Where a self-reliant character in fiction is emboldened by his resistance (often to the point of righteousness), Emersonian self-reliance inspires humility, even awe. Such disorientation is precisely why a self-reliant person cannot be aloof, but must seek and subject himself to the community.

Emerson places a high value on originality, but his has also a non-standard reading of the term. As expected, he eschews the laziness that would have us delay our work, and in time force us to appropriate our own ideas from others; accepting things passively, taking them "at second hand," would then be a cause of shame. Yet, originality does not mean being originary, but honest. Original work can – and usually does – emerge from quotation. In a later essay, he says, "Original power is usually accompanied with assimilating power." It is the active manner of that adoption that makes one's work original. Being told how to be is distinguished from realizing who one is. Books, nature, and history are meant to stimulate self-development, not create a self on our behalf. Where the ancient Stoics encouraged us to change our attitude to given circumstances in order to achieve contentment, Emerson adds the need for action inspired by one's own, uniquely inspired genius. As with Montaigne's view, such action requires an acknowledgment of one's context – the state of one's government as much as the state of one's health – and a willingness to be truthful with oneself. Self-delusion precludes self-reliance. That is to say, it is dishonest to believe that one can do everything on one's own. Emerson depicts self-reliance as a faith in oneself, yet a faith that acknowledges one's connection to others, and the wider conditions of life.

Emerson's neighbor Henry David Thoreau (regarded by some as an exemplar of American self-reliance) conceived his *Walden* (1854) as an account of his experiment to live authentically. Thoreau studies the economy of living; he wishes to know what is truly necessary for life so that he can discern the boundaries of his freedom. He contrasts lives that are lived desperately with those, like his own, which are lived deliberately. Unfortunately it seems, most men are despairing: they live in deep conformity with dictates (explicit and implied) given by others, whereas Thoreau – in his self-assuredness – believes that "I should not consciously and deliberately forsake my particular calling to do the good which society demands of me." Thoreau notes that many seem to hear their inner voices, yet they lack the courage to heed them. Sure of what he hears, Thoreau's mood is not brazen or insistent, but indicative of a Bartleby: when compelled to participate in the mainstream (in popular philanthropy movements, having standard employment, raising a family, etc.), he says: "this work, which I decline." Thoreau makes much of the morning because it is a time for him to awaken himself and his fellow neighbors, and to stimulate awareness of what is truly necessary. For Thoreau, it was essential to live according to higher principles, ones he believed he already possessed.

In its more developed forms, self-reliance does not lead to, nor can it be used as a defense for, selfishness or solipsism. Rather, it orients us to a kind of knowledge that can contribute positively to the care and maintenance of virtues. It's not every man for himself, but a self for every man. The American experience has thus far suggested that a faith in the self as a liminal entity creates the conditions for tremendous innovation, inwardly and outwardly. Emerson wrote of working toward an "unattained, but attainable self," a project that reflects the transitional, revisable, experimental attributes of democracy at its best. The self, then, is not god-given, but man-made. Acknowledging the sanctity of individuals, and their claims to self-reliance, nevertheless implicates us in a divine undertaking, since working on one's self reflects the abiding connection we have to other selves.

Williams James respected what Emerson did for human – or at least, American – perceptions of what a self could become if relied upon. James believed that Emerson "electrified and emancipated his generation" by proclaiming the "sovereignty of the living individual." James himself was part of the America Emerson wrote to inspire, and James' work reflects his deep commitment to the life of the individual: the sanctity of his mind, the power of his imagination, the beguiling interplay of personality with religion and science. In his pragmatism, James reflects on the urgent need for vital interconnection between individuals, while maintaining a steadfast belief in the creative power of the individual set to his private task. In time, even solitary pursuits join up with the world in motion and reveal the ways in which individuals are connected to one another. For James, self-reliance is more of a psychological principle of sound mental health than an occult description from an ancient creed: it is the condition for finding and maintaining reliance on others, whom James, in his own troubles and traumas, so often found to be the only and abiding comfort and guide he could manage. Self-reliance is then a way to make oneself available to others, and in turn, a way of coming back to oneself with new, more refined perspectives.

John Dewey describes self-reliance in terms of individuality, which he understands to be in a period of transformation, coming up against the facts of modernity such as the pronounced influence of the mechanical, corporate, and pecuniary. Traditional, which is to say Christian, feudal, mystical, ways of understanding the self (as a sacred entity in the form of an individuated, non-perishable soul) are now over-shadowed by the continual transformation of modern society. Such changes leave individuals anxious and insecure. We can lead industries and direct commerce, but "cannot be captains of [our] own souls." We seem to live absent-mindedly, in perpetual distraction from ourselves. With basic, foundational beliefs and supports eroded, we clamor to the middle, to find comfort in the masses, conforming to widespread practices and uses. While admitting (in an Emersonian spirit) that conformity is "a name for the absence of vital interplay; the arrest and benumbing of communication," Dewey notes that we are living in the era of the machine, and that we have ourselves become parts of some aggregate collective we neither control nor understand. Dewey insists that a new self-reliance – grounded in the circumstances of the new age – will allow an individual to "reinstitute a wholeness within" himself. A fragment in the context of civilization, the individual once united within will no longer feel fragmented. At some point, Dewey hopes that social circumstances will align to liberate individuality from its stultification. When in proper relation, the community should not hamper the originality and creative expression of the individual, but save it from harmful eccentricities. While articulating the manifold ways in which contemporary society alienates man from himself, Dewey nevertheless concludes that it is the only way the true potential of individuality can be actualized. Dewey, however, does not outline a concrete plan or method for creating a society that would be the condition for the emergence of thriving individuals. Part of Dewey's omission may be traced to his belief that individuality cannot be integrated by means of a system. No one can judge how to manifest individuality in another, nor can he make for himself a comprehensive or definitive determination of what he needs to guarantee his own flourishing.

Despite a long and distinguished history of meditations on self-reliance, there are a number of contested issues to keep in mind: (1) Is there a satisfying metaphysical defense for the idea of having (or being) a self? (2) Am I self or is a self in me? (3) Do we need to prove there is a self to rely on, or should we instead emphasize reliance, in this way making self-reliance a kind of activity (instead of a quality or attribute)? Each account may yield different replies to these questions, alerting us to the possibility that self-reliance is an involuted concept undergoing continual negotiation.

Further reading

Dewey, John. *Individualism Old and New.* New York: Minton, Balch, 1929–30.

Emerson, Ralph Waldo. "Self-Reliance" in *Essays: First Series.* New York: Dover, 1993 [1841].

—— "Quotation and Originality" in *Letters and Social Aims.* New York: Macmillan, 1898 [1876].

James, William. "Address at the Emerson Centenary in Concord, 1903," *Memories and Studies* (1911): 17–34.

Thoreau, Henry David. *Walden* in *The Writings of Henry David Thoreau.* New York: Houghton Mifflin 1906 [1854].

Cavell, Stanley. *Emerson's Transcendental Etudes*, ed. David Justin Hodge. Stanford, CA: Stanford University Press, 2003.

David LaRocca

SELLARS, WILFRID

Wilfrid Stalker Sellars (1912–89), American philosopher, editor, and teacher, was the son of the distinguished Canadian-American philosopher Roy Wood Sellars, who spent most of his career at the University of Michigan. Wilfrid grew up in Ann Arbor, where the university was located, but because of his father's academic career he received some of his education in Europe. He studied at two different French lycées, and later took classes at the University of Munich. His higher education officially took place at the University of Michigan, the University of Buffalo, and Oxford University, which he attended as a Rhodes Scholar. He later spent a year doing graduate work at Harvard University.

Sellars began his teaching career in 1938 at the University of Iowa. He spent the war years as an officer in Naval Intelligence concerned with submarine warfare. When the war ended, he accepted a position at the University of Minnesota, where he became a prolific writer and an extremely popular teacher of advanced students. In fairly short order he became Professor of Philosophy, Chairman of the philosophy department, founding coeditor of the journal *Philosophical Studies*, and a member of the Minnesota Center for the Philosophy of Science. He eventually moved on to Yale University and then the University of Pittsburgh, where he became University Professor of Philosophy and Research Professor of the Philosophy of Science. He remained at Pittsburgh until the end of his life, although he accepted many guest appointments and distinguished lectureships at other institutions.

The paper most responsible for Sellars' international reputation is "Empiricism and the Philosophy of Mind" or "EPM." Like many of his writings, this paper is complicated and requires careful study. Although it covers many topics in philosophy, it is unified by a single target, which Sellars called "the myth of the given." What is directly given to the mind, according to this story, does not result from inference, past experience, or a process of learning. Two basic kinds of things are supposed to be given this way, facts and concepts. In attacking the idea that these things are directly given, Sellars developed important ideas in the two areas of philosophy associated with the words in his title: epistemology, the area to which empiricism belongs, and the philosophy of mind.

If facts are not given directly, we can grasp them only mediately, in relation to other things. If concepts are not so given, we can grasp them only in relation to other things, too. What are the "other things" Sellars considered pertinent in these cases? For facts, the other things are other facts. We can become aware of the fact that a thing is red, Sellars said, only by means of the fact that it looks a certain way to a certain sort of perceiver, a normal one, viewing it in optimal conditions. The upshot for epistemology is that no subset of individual facts can provide a foundation for knowledge in the way that empiricist philosophers have historically supposed. Sellars agreed that experience plays a fundamental role in our acquisition of knowledge, but following Kant he insisted that the organizing ability of our minds plays an equally essential role: experiential input results in knowledge only when it is organized into a unified system that relates it to observers, observational processes, and a spatio-temporal, causal system of empirical objects.

As for concepts, the other object of Sellars' critique, what "other thing" must be needed if they are grasped and adequately understood? Sellars said: "other concepts, the framework to which the given concept belongs." It is a truism that people can understand a word only if they understand how it may be joined to other words in producing meaningful sentences, and an analogous point holds for concepts, because they have combinatorial features just as words do. The consequence of this for the philosophy of mind is that an ostensibly subjective concept such as *pain* is not only applicable to the experience of any normal human being or higher animal but is so related to concepts of behavior and occasioning causes that a skeptical problem of "other minds" (as it was understood at the time) has a straightforward solution.

Another of Sellars' most important papers is "Philosophy and the Scientific Image of Man" (PASIM). The argument of this paper grows naturally out of "EPM" but it moves beyond it in an important way. If knowledge cannot be based on some special, non-revisable foundation, then the most exotic knowledge we may obtain in physics or even neurology need not be founded on the so-called common-sense knowledge that we use in everyday life. Although Sellars explicitly defended his belief in scientific realism only in a later essay, "The Language of Theories," he assumed it in "PASIM," where he distinguished a Manifest Image of humans in the world from a corresponding Scientific Image of them. Sellars argued that these images are in fact rationally incompatible. In spite of the clash between them, he viewed them both as currently indispensable, since human beings conceive of themselves in terms of the Manifest Image, and the Scientific Image is largely disjoint from certain central human concerns. Nevertheless, the Scientific Image, based as it is on the best evidence available to us, is capable of elaboration in a way that would, at least at a utopian stage of scientific knowledge, make it a suitable replacement for the Manifest Image; the normative concepts of a moral point of view could be added. Even now the Scientific Image possesses successor concepts for certain Manifest concepts; "H_2O" is an obvious example. Ideally, we could have a successor concept to *human being* or even m*oral agent*.

More than any other philosopher of his time, Sellars developed a wide-ranging philosophy that encompassed all the principal areas of the subject: metaphysics, epistemology, ethics, philosophy of language, and philosophy of science. He made important, original contributions to all these areas.

Further reading

deVries, Wilhelm. *Wilfrid Sellars*. Chesham: Acumen, 2005.
Seibt, Johanna. *Properties as Processes: A Synoptic Study of Wilfrid Sellars' Nominalism*. Atascadero, CA: Ridgeview, 1990.
Sellars, Wilfrid. *Naturalism and Ontology*. Atascadero, CA: Ridgeview, 1980.

BRUCE AUNE

SEMANTICS

Semantics is the branch of linguistics concerned with the study of the meaning of words and utterances. A traditional, and controversial, distinction is often made between semantics, syntax, and pragmatics. Syntax is the study of the structures of words and sentences in virtue of which sentences are either grammatical or ungrammatical. Pragmatics is the study not of the meaning of utterances, but, roughly, of what is implied by utterances in given contexts. This is only a rough sketch of a distinction that has been drawn in a variety of ways in the philosophical and linguistic literature.

Philosophers have a great deal of interest in the study of semantics, and it is sometimes claimed that theories of meaning are of great utility in philosophy, for philosophical disputes may be resolved through consideration of accounts of the meanings of certain words. As will be discussed below, some philosophical accounts of semantics focus primarily on mental representation – the meaning of mental representations – rather than on linguistic meaning. Influenced by H.P. Grice, many philosophers think that linguistic meaning is to be explained on the basis of mental representation. This entry focuses on two popular approaches to semantics in philosophy: referentialism and use theories of meaning.

Referentialists seek to explain the meaning of sentences or words in terms of referential relations between language and the world. These theories take a variety of forms. One popular and influential referentialist account is Donald Davidson's theory that meaning is to be explained in terms of the truth conditions of sentences. The meaning of "Snow is white" is its truth condition: "Snow is white" if and only if snow is white.

Other referentialist accounts focus on the meanings of words, rather than sentences. Direct reference accounts claim that meaning consists solely in the referential relation between words and objects, thus there is no distinction between meaning and reference. Referentialist accounts of the meaning of words such as the informational and teleological theories think that the direct reference account leaves out important facts regarding meaning – it is hard to see how. The informational theory of meaning proposed by Fred Dretske claims that the meaning of terms can be analyzed in terms of the correlation between mental representations of a certain entity and the presence of that entity. One has thoughts about cats, reliably, in the presence of cats. It is a difficult matter to specify when these correlations between thoughts and objects make for a proper account of mental representation. For instance, one would not want to claim that the concept "cat" is also about dogs given that one might believe there is a dog present when one sees a cat in a dark room at night.

The alternative to a referentialist conception of meaning is a use theory of meaning. Use theories of meaning, influenced by the work of Wittgenstein, claim that the meaning of words and sentences consists in their use. To cite a simple example, the term "and" may be used to make inferences. From "It is raining and it is snowing," I can infer "it is snowing." I can also infer from "It is raining" and "It is snowing" to "It is raining and it is snowing." The meaning of the word "and" is explained in terms of the role this term plays in making such inferences. Use theories, sometimes called inferential role or conceptual role accounts of meaning, seek to explain the meaning of words generally in terms of such regularities or rules of use.

Further reading

Davidson, Donald. *Inquiries into Truth and Interpretation*. Oxford: Clarendon Press, 1984.

Fodor, Jerry. *A Theory of Content and Other Essays*. Cambridge, MA: MIT Press, 1990.

Grice, H.P. *Studies in the Ways of Words*. Cambridge, MA: Harvard University Press, 1989.

Horwich, Paul. *Meaning*. Oxford: Oxford University Press, 1998.

FRITZ J. MCDONALD

SEMIOSIS

Semiosis is a term that C.S. Peirce coined to designate, in its broadest reach, the activity of signs. This activity might be either the formation of a sign (the process by which a sign is generated) or the interpretation of a sign (the activity by which the meaning or significance of an object or event is determined, though not necessarily in an accurate or justified manner). The formation of a fossil or the outbreak of spots all over the body are examples of semiosis in that the fossil or the spots are significant: quite apart from intention or design, they function as signs. The activity by which the biologist interprets the fossilized form of a once living organism – or by which the physician takes the spots to be indicative of measles – also illustrates semiosis. The two most important points regarding the Peircean concept of semiosis is that (1) the generation of signs does not depend on the consciousness or agency of interpreters (though the actualization of the potential significance here does depend on the work of interpreters) and (2) the emphasis falls on process and activity, not on a distinctive type of object (something called a "sign"). Whatever functions as a sign is a sign, signhood being the functional status of some objects and events. Whatever connects in a complex way what otherwise would be disparate is a sign (e.g. the eyewitness whose account links a past occurrence with people far removed in time and space from this occurrence). For Peirce, semiosis involves at least three functional components – the *object* (that which generates or perhaps only constrains the process in which meanings are formed and transformed), the *sign* (that which forges a link between one phase of experience and another, or between some facet of reality and the attention of some inquirer), and the *interpretant* (that which is generated by the sign precisely in relation to its object). While the interpretant of a sign is often mental, it need not be. For example, the music generated by inserting cylinders in a player piano would, on Peirce's account, be in this case the interpretant. In another sense, the emotions and ideas generated by listening to a piece of music would be interpretants. But, for him, consciousness does not explain the operation of signs; rather, semiosis provides an indispensable resource for understanding the workings of consciousness.

By insisting that semiosis exhibits an irreducibly triadic structure, Peirce exploits an analogy with giving. The act of giving involves a giver, gift, and recipient in such a way that any attempt to explain giving by reducing it to an act of divestiture (the giver relinquishes some item), on the one hand, and one of acquisition (an individual acquires this very same item), on the other, explains away – rather than truly explains – the phenomenon in question. The recipient acquires this item as a direct result of the giver divesting the item. The structure of object–sign–interpretant is hence analogous to that of giver–gift–recipient. So, semiosis is above all else a process, but one exhibiting an irreducibly complex form in which distinct components are functionally identified. Of course, one and the same object or event might function variously, such that it is (say) in one respect an object and in another a sign. In fact, this is typically the case. The cracks in the wall of a house can be signs of the earth shifting (the object in this case). But the shifting of the earth itself might signify an alteration in the tectonic plates of the Earth; that is, it might serve as a sign pointing us toward something more than the mere shifting of the ground underneath the house.

Further reading

Colapietro, Vincent. *Peirce's Approach to the Self.* Albany, NY: SUNY Press, 1989.

Fisch, Max H. *Peirce, Semeiotic, and Pragmatism*, ed. K.L. Ketner and C. Kloesel. Bloomington, IN: Indiana University Press, 1986.

Liszka, James J. *A General Introduction to the Semeiotic of Charles Sanders Peirce.* Bloomington, IN: Indiana University Press, 1996.

Short, T.L. *Peirce's Theory of Signs.* Cambridge: Cambridge University Press, 2007.

Vincent Colapietro

SHERBURNE, DONALD

Donald W. Sherburne spent most of his scholarly career as a professor of philosophy at Vanderbilt University. He belongs to that group of process-philosophy scholars who have paved the way for bringing Alfred North Whitehead's long feared and avoided thought into the forefront of modern philosophical scholarship. Sherburne, together with David R. Griffin, took upon themselves to edit Whitehead's magnum opus *Process and Reality.*

Sherburne took this exercise in popularizing and explicating Whitehead's thought to the next level when he published *A Key to Whitehead's Process and Reality*, in which he sheds explanatory light upon Whitehead's most famous and yet most abstruse work by rearranging and explaining Whitehead's ideas because one "will not find a linear development in PR, a beginning, a middle, and an end."

In *A Whiteheadian Aesthetics: Some Implications of Whitehead's Metaphysical Speculations*, Sherburne successfully employs Whiteheadian categories to address the fundamental issues of aesthetic theory. We know that Whitehead himself did not systematically reflect on the topics of art or aesthetic experience, but this did not stop Sherburne from utilizing process thought to give a philosophical account pertaining to the ontological status of aesthetic objects.

In Sherburne's articles "Decentering God" and "Whitehead without God" he grapples with the place of God within the Whiteheadian world. In the first article Sherburne provides arguments challenging the idea that God plays the role of the center of order, value, and meaning and proposes that the order of organization commences from "bottom up" and not "top down," whereas in the latter article Sherburne maintains that within Whiteheadian systematic thought the concept of God is unnecessary and even self-contradictory and this is why God should be "exorcized . . . from the system."

Further reading

Sherburne, Donald W. *A Key to Whitehead's Process and Reality.* New York and London: Macmillan, 1966.

Janusz Polanowski

SICK SOUL

"Sick soul" is a term made famous by William James in his book *The Varieties of Religious Experience* (1902). The sick soul or "twice-born" soul is one of two possible religious temperaments for James. It is the opposite of a "healthy-minded" approach to religion. This latter approach seems constitutionally incapable of acknowledging prolonged suffering. The healthy-minded soul is naturally disposed toward cheerfulness. It does not linger over the darker aspects of the universe, as does its counterpart, but rather conceives goodness as an essential and world-wide dimension of reality, thus deliberately excluding evil from its field of vision. By contrast, the more morbid sick soul tends to maximize evil; it is persuaded that there are evil aspects of our lives which are of its very essence. It views sin as deeply embedded in our own natural subjectivity. The sick soul suffers from religious melancholy, believing that life has lost its meaning. Tolstoy is given as an example. As opposed to a healthy-minded soul affirming that all is right with the world, the sick soul is paralyzed, overwhelmed and horrified by a principle of evil surrounding it. The most famous example James gives in *The Varieties of Religious Experience* is one from his own experience, but he masks this from the reader, presenting it rather as the report of an anonymous "sufferer":

> Whilst in this state of philosophic pessimism and general depression ... there arose in my mind the image of an epileptic patient whom I had seen in the asylum, a black-haired youth, with greenish skin, entirely idiotic, who used to sit all day on one of the benches ... like a sort of ... Peruvian mummy, moving nothing but his black eyes and looking absolutely non-human. ... *That shape am I*, I felt, potentially.
>
> (James 1902: 160–1)

The author of the story laments the fact that nothing can defend him against this fate; he awakes in the morning as a mass of quivering fear, and for months is not able to go out into the dark alone.

To the healthy-minded soul, the sick soul seems cowardly and infected by some disease. In spite of this, James cast his lot, in *The Varieties of Religious Experience* at least, with the sick soul, based on the latter's ability to provide a fuller and more adequate account of experience – it covers a wider range of experience. While we can repress evil for a time, this does not work all the time. It is better, then, to cast one's lot with the sick soul, the morbid-minded. The sick soul, if it is to be redeemed, must be "twice-born" rather than "once-born." If redemption is to take place at all, it must be through the crucible of doubt. Saintliness might be attained if one can realize that one is connected to a wider or higher life – but without being completely swallowed up in that life

Here, as elsewhere in his writings, James advocates a "thick" or "fat" contextualism, rather than a "thin" account of the issue at hand.

Further reading

James, William. *The Varieties of Religious Experience.* New York: Longmans, Green, 1902, Lectures 6 and 7.

Levinson, Henry Samuel. *The Religious Investigations of William James.* Chapel Hill, NC: University of North Carolina Press, 1981.

WILLIAM J. GAVIN

SINGER, BETH J.: AUTOBIOGRAPHY

I grew up in Brooklyn but did my undergraduate work at the University of Wisconsin in Madison, majoring in philosophy. I earned an MA in Social Psychology at Teachers College, Columbia University and a PhD in Philosophy at Columbia. Justus Buchler was my major professor and I took a course in American Philosophy with Joseph L. Blau. My dissertation was on the philosophy of George Santayana.

I taught at Manhattanville College in Purchase, New York, for several years and then went to Brooklyn College where I taught in a new interdisciplinary program for freshmen and sophomores, the New School of Liberal Arts. The School had a unique curriculum. Each semester a student chose a period in world history and took courses in four subject areas. The time periods were the Ancient World, the Medieval World, the Early Modern World, the Age of Revolutions, and the Twentieth Century. The subject areas were Social Institutions, Ideas and Philosophy, Scientific and Mathematical Developments, Literature, and the Arts. My field was Ancient Social Institutions, Ideas and Philosophy but I occasionally taught Ancient Literature as well. In 1979 the program was eliminated and those who taught in it were transferred to other departments of the college. I joined the philosophy department and remained there until I retired in 1996. I taught Ancient Philosophy, Modern Philosophy, American Philosophy, Philosophy of Art and Philosophy of Education. From 1991 to 1995 I chaired the department.

I participated in international conferences in Córdoba, Argentina, and in Utrecht, The Netherlands, and a joint Polish-American conference in Karpacz, Poland, organized by the Society for the Advancement of American Philosophy, which has a Polish branch. I also presented papers at the University of Sussex in England; in Warsaw, Kraków, Wrocław, Lublin, Lódz and Gdansk, Poland; in Szigetvár and Pécs, Hungary; and at universities in Guangzhou, Xiamen, Shanghai, and Beijing in China. I have been active in professional organizations and served as president of the Society for the Advancement of American Philosophy and Concerned Philosophers for Peace.

My publications include several books and a number of articles. Among them are *Operative Rights* and *Pragmatism, Rights and Democracy*, both of which were translated into Chinese and published in China; *Ordinal Naturalism: An Introduction to the Philosophy of Justus Buchler*; and *The Rational Society: A Critical Study of Santayana's Social Thought*. My paper "Human Nature and Community" appeared in *Open Times*, an international journal published in China. "The Democratic Solution to Ethnic Pluralism" was translated into Russian by A.B. Prozhinin and published in *Voprosy filosofii*. Several papers of mine on rights were published, including "Rights as Social Practices," "Rights of Communities and Rights of Individuals," "Rights and Norms," and "Rights and Affirmative Action." My papers on American philosophy include "Pragmatism and Pluralism" and "Dewey's Concept of Community: A Critique." I also wrote on diverse other topics and among my published papers are "Basing 'Ought' on 'Is'" and "On some Differences between Metaphysical and Scientific Discourse."

BETH J. SINGER

SINGER, IRVING

Irving Singer (1925–) is professor of philosophy at the Massachusetts Institute of Technology. He is a prolific writer, and the author of an impressive number of books on the philosophy of love, including *The Nature of Love*, a detailed and comprehensive history in three volumes of the idea of love from Plato to the present. Singer is best known for his sensitive treatment of love and sex which brings to mind a tradition of thinkers, perhaps beginning with Plato, who try to understand the fundamental drives motivating human nature. Singer prefers to avoid the controversies of professional philosophers in favor of exploring what for him are more interesting and important topics. He has also written on opera (*Mozart and Beethoven: The Concept of Love in Their Operas*), and on film (*Three Philosophical Filmmakers: Hitchcock, Welles, Renoir*).

Singer wants to build an appreciation of human values on the basis of a kind of philosophical naturalism. Following George Santayana, about whom he has written a book, and John Dewey, Singer's philosophy is organized around a worldview that stresses relations, contingency, and the overwhelming significance of human flourishing. Singer's worldview is expounded systematically in his *Meaning in Life* trilogy. He sees the world as displaying spirit, which is his name for a purposive agency of innovation and self-improvement in service to the good. Spirit works to make the world more hospitable and hence more satisfying to human beings.

At the heart of Singer's aesthetics is the distinction he draws between appraisal and bestowal. Appraising means trying to asses the utility of something we prize against the utility of other things we hold dear. But valuing has another important element. When we prize something, we impart some value to it just by virtue of prizing it. This imparting of value, "gratuitous" in the sense of being uncompelled, is what Singer calls bestowal. The distinction is important because it helps to undercut the view of writers who hold that love, and perhaps all valuing, is crassly utilitarian. Bestowal is the creating of a value for its own sake, and not at all with a view to the utility of the thing or person valued.

Further reading

Singer, Irving. *Mozart and Beethoven: The Concept of Love in Their Operas*. Baltimore, MD: Johns Hopkins University Press, 1977.

—— *The Nature of Love*, 3 vols. Chicago, IL: University of Chicago Press, 1987.

—— *Meaning in Life*, 3 vols. Baltimore, MD: Johns Hopkins University Press, 1996.

—— *George Santayana, Literary Philosopher*. New Haven, CT: Yale University Press, 2000.

—— *Three Philosophical Filmmakers: Hitchcock, Welles, Renoir*. Cambridge, MA: MIT Press, 2004.

MICHAEL BRODRICK

SITUATION

Recent work in semantics (Barwise and Perry 1983; Fenstad *et al.* 1987) cast situations as complexes of objects and relations that constitute contexts of interpretation and use of natural language utterances. As a technical device in formal semantics, situations are comparable to possible worlds except that the former are partial worlds, or *parts* of the world, rather than alternative versions of total worlds. Situations thus provide means for contextualizing information in ways that are partial rather than total.

This work in situation semantics in the 1980s revived conceptions of contextual interpretation (e.g. Ogden and Richards 1923) that pre-dated the mid-twentieth century rise of possible-worlds semantics. In American philosophy, this older notion of situations as contexts of interpretation was given a conspicuous role in John Dewey's logical theory (1938).

Logic for Dewey is a normative theory of inquiry in which inquiries are cast as transformations of situations. A situation is characterized not as a set or complex of objects or events but simply as a "contextual whole" in which objects and events are experienced. Dewey's point is that we never experience objects or events in isolation but only within some contextual whole. Thus Dewey wants to maintain a distinction between objects and events versus the contexts in which they are experienced. To characterize the latter as an instance of the former would ultimately dissolve this distinction, introducing inconsistencies that he suggests are like those that follow from a failure to distinguish sets and classes in naive set theory.

Along similar lines, a situation is characterized as "an environing experienced world," or as a "field" of experience in which observation of objects and events takes place. Likewise, a situation is cast as a "universe of experience" in which discourse takes place. Some situation will be a precondition of any coherent universe of discourse, not only in the familiar sense of quantification theory but also in the pragmatics of ordinary conversational interpretation where it is the situation as salient context which "determine[s] the relevancy, weight or coherence of any designated distinction or relation."

These characterizations of a situation are tied to Dewey's conception of *an experience* (1934) in terms of animals' active adaptive responses to instances of resistance and conflict in the course of their otherwise normal activities. It is such resistance and conflict that give situations their salience and thus their existence as fields of experience. (The astute reader will note that inquiry in this view is a particular type of experience, though limited to animals capable of rational deliberation.)

Dewey also remarked that "a situation is a whole in virtue of its immediately pervasive quality." Psychologically, one might say that a situation is sensed or felt, but mainly to emphasize that it is not an object in a discourse for which it serves as the context. Positively, the pervasively qualitative character of a situation is what gives the situation its wholeness and uniqueness. A situation in its role as a "contextual whole" is thus an indivisible and unduplicable individual situation. This is consistent with William James's radical empiricism in the sense that, on one hand, any situation is immediately experienceable as the individual that it is, though on the other hand there is no limit in principle to how complex such a contextual whole may turn out to be. This goes against the identification of empirical primitivity with empirical simplicity.

Further reading

Barwise, Jon, and Perry, John. *Situations and Attitudes*. Cambridge, MA: MIT Press, 1983.

Dewey, John. *Art as Experience*. New York: Minton, Balch, 1934. Critical edition reissued as Volume 10 of *The Later Works of John Dewey* with an introduction by Abraham Kaplan. Carbondale, IL: Southern Illinois University Press, 1987.

—— *Logic: The Theory of Inquiry*. New York: Henry Holt, 1938. Critical edition reissued as Volume 12 of *The Later Works of John Dewey* with an introduction by Ernest Nagel. Carbondale, IL: Southern Illinois University Press, 1986.

Fenstad, Jens Erik, Halvorsen, Per-Kristian, Langholm, Tore and van Benthem, Johan. *Situations, Language, and Logic*. Dordrecht: Reidel, 1987.

James, William. *Essays in Radical Empiricism*. New York: Longmans, Green, 1912. Posthumous, ed. R.B. Perry. Reprinted in the *Works of William James* series, Cambridge, MA: Harvard University Press, 1976.

Ogden, C.K., and Richards, I.A. *The Meaning of Meaning: A Study of the Influence of Language upon Thought and of the Science of Symbolism*. New York: Harcourt, Brace, 1923.

TOM BURKE

SKEPTICISM

Questions about the scope and limits of human knowledge are among the basic problems of epistemology. Philosophical skepticism answers these questions by asserting that strictly speaking, nothing can be known or it cannot be determined whether anything can be known.

Ancient Greek skepticism

The Greek word 'skeptikos' (σκεπτικός) means literally 'inquiring'; thus a person who adopts an open-minded, inquiring attitude towards questions can be called a skeptic (in a loose sense of the word). In this sense skepticism is the opposite of dogmatism, and skeptical philosophers have referred to non-skeptical philosophers as "dogmatists."

There are different varieties of skepticism. General or global skepticism is the view that knowledge is generally unattainable, whereas restricted or local skepticism holds that knowledge about a certain subject-matter is impossible. For example, moral skepticism denies or raises doubts about the possibility of moral knowledge, and skepticism about the external world is the view that our knowledge is restricted to our subjective impressions or the way things appear to us at a given moment. Another form of skepticism concerns the concept of justification rather than knowledge: according to this view, it is not even possible to be justified in believing anything (accepting anything as true), or it cannot be determined whether one is justified in accepting any proposition about a given subject-matter.

In Western philosophy, skepticism originated from two skeptical schools of ancient Greece, Academic skepticism and Pyrrhonism. Academic skepticism developed in Plato's Academy in the third century BC. as a criticism of Stoic epistemology and flourished until the first century AD. According to the Stoics, knowledge is based on sensory experience, but sense impressions can be misleading. Veridical impressions can be distinguished from misleading impressions by their clarity and force; such "cataleptic" impressions are sources of certain knowledge. Thus the Stoics thought that certain intrinsic features of cataleptic impressions, clarity and distinctness, function as the criteria of truth and knowledge. The skeptics rejected this doctrine and argued that representations carry no distinctive criterion of truth, supporting their view by examples of illusions and misperceptions (Stough 1969: 49–50). Pyrrhonism received its name from the philosopher Pyrrho of Elis (c. 360–270 BC), and remained an active philosophical movement until the third century AD. Pyrrhonists recommended the suspension of judgment (*epochē*) for all questions about external reality, and regarded this as a desirable state of mind which leads to tranquility and peace. The only skeptical philosopher whose writings have been preserved is the Pyrrhonist Sextus Empiricus (second century BC). His works, especially *Outlines of Pyrrhonism*, are the principal original sources on ancient skepticism (Mates 1996).

Skepticism in modern philosophy

Many ancient texts on skepticism, including the works of Sextus Empiricus, were discovered by Renaissance thinkers, and arguments for or against various skeptical positions have played a significant role in the development of modern epistemology from the seventeenth century to the present. The problem of skepticism is often formulated by introducing a *skeptical hypothesis* which seems to be consistent with our sensory evidence but inconsistent with some proposition whose truth is regarded as being known. This way of articulating the problem goes back (at least) to René Descartes (1596–1650), who used as the skeptical hypothesis the proposition that our ordinary beliefs might be illusions caused by an "evil demon" (*Meditations on First Philosophy*, First Meditation). The problem of skepticism can be presented schematically as the following *skeptical trilemma*:

(1) N knows that P
(2) N does not know that not-SH
(3) If N knows that P, then N knows that not-SH,

or equivalently,

(3') If N does not know that not-SH, then N does not know that P.

P is here any proposition which is regarded as being known, and SH stands for a suitable skeptical hypothesis which entails the falsity of P. The following example is due to Fred Dretske (2000). If you are in a zoo and see a striped equine animal in an area marked with the sign "Zebras," you presumably know that the animal you see is a zebra (the proposition P). A skeptic could point out that the animal might also be a mule cleverly disguised to look like a zebra (the skeptical hypothesis SH); therefore, according to the skeptic, you do not know that the animal is a zebra.

Statements (1)–(3) are jointly inconsistent: any two of them entail the negation of the third. The problem of skepticism can be solved by rejecting one of the propositions schematized by (1), (2), and (3); thus there are three possible solutions, or kinds of solutions, to the skeptical trilemma. The skeptical solution consists in the rejection of (1) and the defense of an argument from (2) and (3) to the skeptical conclusion (the negation of (1))

(4) N does not know that P.

Such an argument is called a skeptical argument against (1). A non-skeptical (commonsensical) solution requires a defense of an argument from (1) and (3) to the denial of (2), that is, the conclusion that the skeptical hypothesis is known to be false:

(5) N knows that not-SH.

The third possible solution is to accept (1) and (2) and deny (3); in this approach it is argued that one can know that P without knowing that the skeptical hypothesis is false. In recent epistemology, each of these proposals has been defended.

Skepticism and the analysis of knowledge

The concept of knowledge is often defined as justified true belief, or as true belief supported by evidence, for example, as follows:

(AK1) N knows that P if and only (i) N believes that P (accepts P), (ii) P is true, and (iii) N's evidence rules out all possibilities in which it is not the case that P.

Condition (iii) distinguishes knowledge from (mere) true belief: N's belief that P can be regarded as knowledge only if his evidence rules out all possibilities of error. If N's evidence is regarded as consisting of his entire perceptual experience and memory, it seems possible to construct for practically any proposition P accepted by N a skeptical hypothesis SH such that (2) and (3) seem to be true. In Dretske's example, the person who says that he knows that the animal he sees is a zebra could not distinguish it from a cleverly disguised mule; thus his perceptual evidence does not rule out the possibility that the animal is not a zebra, but a disguised mule.

The skeptical solution faces the problem of reconciling philosophical skepticism with our actual use of the words "know" and "knowledge," and any acceptable solution to the problem should explain the persuasive force of skeptical arguments. The skeptical solution is not as absurd as it seems at first sight if the analysis of knowledge formulated in (AK1) is regarded as an *idealized model* of knowledge and knowing. According to this view, the word "know" signifies epistemic perfection or ideal which our beliefs can approach but seldom reach. In this respect epistemological principles resemble the theoretical principles and models of other areas of inquiry: such models are regarded as models of empirical phenomena, in this case our epistemic (cognitive) states, if the latter are sufficiently similar to the former. Peter Unger has understood the concept of knowledge (or knowing) in this way. He has observed that the word "know" is an *absolute* term or a *limit* term; in this respect it resembles the expression "flat" and many other expressions used in ordinary language (1975: 54–91). To say that a surface is flat means that it has no bumps at all, but hardly any actual surface is completely flat. Even if a surface is not completely flat, we regard it as flat and call it flat when the bumps and irregularities are so insignificant that they can be ignored for practical purposes. According to Unger, the expression "know" is used in an analogous way. David Lewis has given a somewhat similar account of the concept of knowledge. He accepts the third clause of definition (AK1) in a qualified form: the statement that N knows that P is true only if N's evidence eliminates all possibilities of error – except the possibilities that can be properly ignored in the context in which the statement is made or considered (1999: 422–36). This qualification of (AK1.iii) leaves room for a commonsensical solution: N knows that P if the possibilities not ruled out by N's evidence can be ignored. What can be ignored depends on the context where the knowledge claim is considered; thus this solution to the skeptical trilemma may be called *contextualism* (DeRose 1999: 184–93).

Knowledge as reliable belief

According to (AK1), knowledge is distinguished from true belief by an *evidence condition* (condition (iii)): N knows that P only if N's evidence enables him to discriminate the possible situations in which P is true from those in which P does not hold. Some philosophers have suggested that the concept of knowledge can be defined directly in terms of an inquirer's ability to discriminate between the two kinds of possibilities, P-possibilities (those in which P holds) and not-P-possibilities (Goldman 2000: 86–7). Having this ability makes an inquirer's beliefs reliable signs of the truth of the propositions he believes: knowing something means having a belief that *tracks the truth* or depends on the truth (Nozick 1981: 178). This dependence can be expressed by the conditional

(B.Dep) If it were not the case that P, N would not believe that P.

If (B.Dep) is not satisfied, N might believe that P regardless of whether P is true; in such a case N cannot be said to know that P. N can know that P only if P is true; thus (B.Dep) may be called the *counterfactual condition* of knowledge. According to the usual interpretation of counterfactual conditionals, the dependence condition (B.Dep) can be satisfied even if the inquirer is not able to distinguish the P-possibilities from all conceivable possibilities in which P does not hold. The truth of a counterfactual conditional "if R, then S" is evaluated by considering possibilities in which the antecedent R holds, but which are otherwise as similar to the actual situation (the situation in which the conditional is being evaluated) as the truth of the antecedent permits: in other words, the evaluation is based on possibilities which would be likely to obtain if the antecedent were true. The conditional is true if and only if the consequent is true in all such "plausible" or "relevant" possibilities. Insofar as the skeptical possibilities are not counted among the relevant or plausible possibilities, N can, according to (B.Dep), know that P even if he would not be able to discriminate the P-possibilities from the skeptical possibilities. The distinction between plausible (or serious) possibilities and far-fetched possibilities can be based on objective criteria. For example, in the zebra example, if the zookeepers are in the habit of disguising the animals, a visitor may not be able to identify an animal on the basis of its appearance, and therefore does not know that the striped equine animal he is looking at is a zebra (even if it is a zebra): the animal might be a disguised mule. On the other hand, if the zookeepers do not disguise the animals and they are what they seem to be, the conditional "If the animal were not a zebra, N would not believe that the animal is a zebra" can be regarded as true (provided, of course, that N knows what zebras look like).

According to this way of responding to the skeptical challenge, an inquirer may know that P even if the skeptical possibilities are not ruled out by his evidence or by his cognitive abilities: N may know that P even if he does not know that some skeptical hypothesis inconsistent with P is false. This proposal solves the skeptical trilemma by rejecting proposition (3). This means that the concept of knowledge is not closed with respect to known logical consequence, that is, the following principle is rejected:

(K.Cons) If N knows that P, P entails Q, and N infers Q from P and accepts Q, then N knows that Q.

Even if N is able to distinguish zebras from the other species in an "honest" zoo, he might believe that he is looking at a zebra if it were a disguised mule; thus the negation of the skeptical hypothesis, "This animal is not a disguised mule," does not satisfy (B.Dep) (Nozick 1981: 204–8). The failure of (K.Cons) may be regarded as too high a price to pay for a refutation of skepticism, because our inferential knowledge depends on (K.Cons), and the very purpose of reasoning is to extend knowledge beyond what is directly evident to us. According to this objection, condition (B.Dep) holds for direct or immediate knowledge, but not necessarily for inferential knowledge.

Skepticism and pragmatism

According to Charles Peirce's (1839–1914) pragmatic epistemology, the starting-point of every inquiry is necessarily the inquirer's current belief system; it is not possible to begin epistemological inquiry by trying to doubt everything, as Descartes had suggested in the *Meditations* (Meditation II). Thus the evidence used for evaluating knowledge-claims is not restricted to the inquirer's perceptual experience and memory, but includes his beliefs, or at least the beliefs which are free from any actual doubt in the context of inquiry. The skeptical possibilities which are inconsistent with an inquirer's current beliefs do not give an inquirer any reason to revise or doubt his beliefs; they are "idle" possibilities and do not engender any genuine doubt (Peirce, "What Pragmatism Is", 1934: 5.416, p. 278). Thus such possibilities may be properly ignored in inquiry. Genuine doubt results from inconsistencies or anomalies in the inquirer's belief system, for example, from a surprising observation which makes the inquirer inclined to accept a proposition which conflicts with his earlier beliefs. (Peirce, "Issues of Pragmaticism", 1934: 5.443, p. 296). Under such circumstances an inquirer has a reason to replace some of his current beliefs by new propositions, but to be worth considering, the latter propositions or hypotheses should offer the inquirer some explanatory advantage and explain the surprising observation which created the anomaly. A skeptical hypothesis can never do this, because it is designed to be perceptually indistinguishable from its common sense counterpart (Olsson 2005: 190–3). In the zebra example, the person who sees a zebra and believes that he is looking at a zebra has no reason to doubt his belief and replace it by the assumption that the animal might be a disguised mule, unless some additional evidence makes the zebra hypothesis doubtful. The pragmatic solution to the problem of skepticism agrees with the commonsensical solution: it accepts propositions (1) and (3) and rejects (2). Merely entertaining some skeptical hypothesis does not by itself give an inquirer any reason to revise his beliefs. However, a pragmatist is sensitive to anomalies in his belief system; in this respect a pragmatist differs from a dogmatist who clings to his beliefs and disregards anomalies.

Further reading

DeRose, Keith. "Solving the Skeptical Problem" in Keith DeRose and Ted. A. Warfield (eds) *Skepticism: A Contemporary Reader*. New York: Oxford University Press, 1999, pp. 183–219. Originally published in *The Philosophical Review* 104 (1995): 1–52.

Descartes, Rene. *Meditations on First Philosophy* in *The Philosophical Works of Descartes*, Vol. I, ed. E.S. Haldane and G.R.T. Ross. Cambridge: Cambridge University Press, 1969, pp. 131–99.

Dretske, Fred. "Epistemic Operators" in S. Bernecker and F. Dretske (eds) *Knowledge: Readings in Contemporary Epistemology*. New York: Oxford University Press, 2000, pp. 42–62. Originally published in *Australasian Journal of Philosophy* 49 (1971): 1–22.

Goldman, Alvin. "Discrimination and Perceptual Knowledge" in S. Bernecker and F. Dretske (eds) *Knowledge: Readings in Contemporary Epistemology*. New York: Oxford University Press, 2000, pp. 86–102. Originally published in *The Journal of Philosophy* 73 (1976): 771–91.

Lewis, David. "Elusive Knowledge" in his *Papers in Metaphysics and Epistemology*. Cambridge: Cambridge University Press, 1999, pp. 418–45. First published in *Australasian Journal of Philosophy* 74 (1996): 549–67.

Mates, Benson. *The Skeptic Way. Sextus Empiricus's Outlines of Pyrrhonism*. New York: Oxford University Press, 1996.
Nozick, Robert. *Philosophical Explanations*. Oxford: Clarendon Press, 1981.
Olsson, Erik. *Against Coherence. Truth, Probability, and Justification*. Oxford: Clarendon Press, 2005.
Peirce, Charles S. "What Pragmatism Is" in *Collected Papers of Charles Sanders Peirce*, Vol. 5, ed. Charles Hartshorne and Paul Weiss. Cambridge, MA: Harvard University Press, 1934, Paragraphs 5.411–37 (pp. 272–92). Originally published in *Monist* 15 (1905): 161–81.
—— "Issues of Pragmaticism" in *Collected Papers of Charles Sanders Peirce*, Vol. 5, ed. Charles Hartshorne and Paul Weiss. Cambridge, MA: Harvard University Press, 1934, Paragraphs 5.438–63 (pp. 293–313). Originally published in *Monist* 15 (1905): 481–99.
Stough, Charlotte L. *Greek Skepticism. A Study in Epistemology*. Berkeley, CA: University of California Press, 1969.
Unger, Peter. *Ignorance. A Case for Skepticism*. Oxford: Clarendon Press, 1975.

Risto Hilpinen

SMITH, JOHN E.

John E. Smith (1921–) received an AB from Columbia University in 1942, a BD from Union Theological Seminary in 1945, and a PhD from Columbia in 1948. After teaching at Vassar College and then Barnard College, he joined the faculty at Yale in 1952. Smith has contributed to contemporary philosophy primarily in four distinct roles: first, as a philosopher of religion and God; second, as a defender of philosophical reflection in a sense continuous with the classical traditions of Western thought (a sense inclusive of, but not limited to, metaphysics); third, as a participant in the reconstruction of experience *and* reason so boldly undertaken by Hegel, then radically transformed by the classical American pragmatists, and significantly augmented by such authors as Josiah Royce, William Ernest Hocking, and Alfred North Whitehead (while Smith's own reconstruction of experience and reason owes much to these predecessors, it is an achievement in its own right); and, fourth, as an interpreter of philosophical thinkers, texts, and traditions (Kant, Hegel, and Nietzsche no less than Peirce James, and Dewey; German idealism as well as American; the Augustinian tradition no less than the pragmatic). His books include *Royce's Social Infinite* (1950), *The Spirit of American Philosophy* (1963; revised edition, 1983), *Experience and God* (1969; revised edition 1995), *The Analogy of Experience: An Approach to Understanding Religious Truth* (1973), *Purpose and Thought: The Meaning of Pragmatism* (1978 [1984]), and *America's Philosophical Vision* (1992).

Also noteworthy are his editorial work on such projects as that of producing a critical edition of Jonathan Edwards' voluminous writings and his practical commitment to philosophical pluralism (his efforts to institute reforms within the American Philosophical Association being an example of this commitment). In "The New Need for a Recovery of Philosophy" (1981), his presidential address to the APA, Smith called for abandoning two theses fatal to the vitality of philosophy: "first, that any single approach to philosophy is the only legitimate one, and secondly, that those pursuing philosophical inquiry other than one's own are ipso facto not engaged in philosophy at all" (242). In the context of contemporary philosophy, Smith is known as an energetic defender of a "dialectical" (or pluralistic) approach to philosophical questions flowing directly from his deepest philosophical commitments regarding such matters as the disclosive power of human experience, the integrity of persons envisioned as centers of purpose and power, also the character of the philosopher itself as a site of irreducibly distinct traditions deserving a painstaking, careful, but ultimately critical hearing.

Further reading

Colapietro, Vincent (ed.). *Reason, Experience, and God: John E. Smith in Dialogue*. New York: Fordham University Press, 1997.
Kasulis, Thomas P. and Neville, Robert Cummings (eds). *The Recovery of Philosophy in America: Essays in Honor of John Edwin Smith*. Albany, NY: SUNY Press, 1997.
Smith, John E. *Royce's Social Infinite*. New York: Liberal Arts Books, 1950.
—— *Religion and Empiricism*. Milwaukee, WI: Marquette University Press, 1967.
—— *Themes in American Philosophy*. New York: Harper and Row, 1970.
—— *Purpose and Thought: The Meaning of Pragmatism*. New Haven, CT: Yale University Press, 1983.
—— *Quasi-Religions: Humanism, Marxism, Nationalism*. New York: St Martin's Press, 1995.

Vincent Colapietro

SOCIAL CONTRACT

A social contract is a set of agreements, explicit or implicit, formed prior to the existence of a state, which delineates the normative constraints on the conduct of a state and its citizens. Each of the contract's participants agrees to the contract's terms only if doing so will maximize his or her own welfare. As a result, a contract acceptable to each participant will require compromise: specifically, relinquishing some personal freedoms to an authority. By virtue of these powers bestowed by the contract's participants, the authority is justified in compelling compliance through mandate and sanction, but only insofar as afforded by the contract Which personal freedoms are abdicated will depend on the proclivities of human nature as well as the characteristics of the participants' existence prior to the formation of the contract. As a result, different social contract theories, with different hypotheses concerning human nature, and different stipulations regarding conditions prior to the formation of the contract, will reach different conclusions vis-à-vis the content of the social contract.

Philosophers since the seventeenth century have recognized social contracts per se as apocryphal, in that the supposed cusp between pre-history and the dawn of statehood, inaugurated by an agreement, is wholly fictional. Instead, a social contract has often been regarded as a useful, fictional exemplar of a meta-ethical decision-making procedure, wherein its hypothetical outcome yields normative truths in political theory. Early American philosophers went further by altogether rejecting the classical social contract theory as too "atomistic" with respect to the relationship it posits between individuals and society.

George Herbert Mead (1863–1931) emphasized the importance of the social realm in determining individual consciousness. Individuals achieve consciousness socially by internalizing the normative standards of the society which they constitute. The society resultantly evolves as its constituents do, which, in turn, changes the normative standards internalized by its constituents. As a result of this ontological interdependence between society and the individual, the notion of individuals coming together to form a society, à la the classical social contract, is incoherent.

John Dewey (1859–1952) argued that democracy should not be seen as determined by a social contract in which the role of a uniform and static public is dovetailed with a separate and equally static role of a state. Rather, the public, composed of dynamic individuals directly participating in democracy via "neighborly communities," would themselves continually shape a society that would evolve in tandem with the individuals constituting it.

John Rawls, a contemporary theorist, was concerned with developing a decision-making procedure the outcome of which would determine normative truths in political theory. He argued that we can ascertain these truths by appealing to a thought experiment in which we extrapolate the content of a contract that is decided by participants each of whom is ideally rational, represents a member of society, and is ignorant of the morally irrelevant characteristics (e.g. personality, religion, occupation, gender, etc.) of the members they represent.

Further reading

Cook, Gary A. *G.H. Mead: The Making of a Social Pragmatist*. Bloomington, IN: University of Illinois Press, 1993.

Medina, Vicente. *Social Contract Theories*. Lanham, MD: Rowman and Littlefield, 1990.

Turner, Bryan S. (ed.). *The Blackwell Companion to Social Theory*, 2nd edition. New York: Blackwell, 2000.

Westbrook, Robert. *John Dewey and American Democracy*. Ithaca, NY: Cornell University Press, 1991.

SABA BAZARGAN

SOCIAL DARWINISM

The term *Social Darwinist* was invented in the last quarter of the nineteenth century to describe, and usually to condemn, anyone who saw in the new theory of evolution by natural selection either a rationalization for *laissez-faire* capitalism or a justification or the existing social hierarchy.

Usually cited as the prototype of a Social Darwinist is the political philosopher Herbert Spencer, a London contemporary of Charles Darwin, the evolutionary biologist. To encapsulate the main idea of Darwinian evolution, Spencer invented the phrase "survival of the fittest," which his socialist opponents interpreted as an endorsement of "dog eat dog" competition aimed at weeding out the weak and inferior. This interpretation made Social Darwinism synonymous with heartless opposition to "progressive" legislation.

Spencer, who drew laborious analogies between social and biological evolution, did indeed also believe that government should be limited to enforcing contracts, protecting property, and curtailing force and fraud; but that is a far cry from letting businessmen do as they please. Spencer also opposed "poor laws," meaning government handouts; but he did so because he preferred voluntary charity to coercive taxation, not because he was indifferent to misery, much less because he wanted the unfortunate to starve.

Spencer had many admirers in the United States, including America's leading social scientist William Graham Sumner and political writer and editor Albert Jay Nock, as well as the century's greatest industrialist and most magnanimous philanthropist Andrew Carnegie. Spencer has had no supporters among notable American philosophers; but the ubiquitous John Dewey was a vocal and influential opponent, and Supreme Court Justice Oliver Wendell Holmes once famously declaimed that the United States Constitution did not enact the "Social Statics" of Mr Herbert Spencer.

Also usually counted as a Social Darwinist is another of Spencer's English contemporaries,

Charles Darwin's more brilliant cousin Francis Galton. The polymath inventor of statistical analysis and psychometrics, Galton – a scion of distinguished families – maintained that inherited differences in intelligence explain why some groups are more successful than others. To improve the population, he advocated selective breeding.

Galton's program of eugenics enjoyed wide support among educated classes until the Nazis perverted it and misused both Galton's carefully worked out measures of intelligence and the formerly respectable concept of race. Because American philosophers had other fish in the pan and wanted no association with Nazism, they have not defended Galton; but two important twentieth-century psychologists, Arthur Jensen and Richard Herrnstein, have suffered calumny for arguing that intelligence is largely heritable and varies with race. A similar denunciation has been extended to anybody who has the temerity to suggest that ability and temperament might also vary with sex, now wrongly called gender and mistakenly thought to be a matter of choice.

As this disapproval indicates, the term "Social Darwinist" is now used to smear not just enthusiasts for free enterprise but all who doubt that human beings are blank slates on which society writes what it pleases. Critics of these doubters say that basing politics on biology is fallaciously inferring *ought* from *is,* but evolutionary psychologist Stephen Pinker replies that to deny the relevance of biology to behavior is to make the reverse mistake of inferring *is* from *ought.*

Further reading

Herrnstein, Richard J. and Murray, Charles. *The Bell Curve: Intelligence and Class Structure in American Life.* New York: Free Press, 1994.

Hofstadter, Richard. *Social Darwinism in American Thought,* revised edition. Boston, MA: Beacon Press, 1955.

Spencer, Herbert. *Man versus the State, with Six Essays on Government, Society, and Freedom.* Indianapolis, IN: Liberty Fund Classics, 1984.

MAX HOCUTT

SOCIALISM

The simplest definition of socialism is that it is the political and economic system in which the public of the nation owns the important means of production and distribution and manages them for the public good, with this being understood as the welfare of the ordinary people. But neither socialism nor the American understanding of it has been simple.

Dewey's critique of Marxian socialism

Karl Marx (1818–83) is the most well-known socialist. The important American philosopher who most eagerly adopted socialism was John Dewey (1859–1952) but he rejected most of the Marxian understanding of socialism. Dewey refused to use the name socialist or join with many other socialists because they often followed Marx or some other anti-democratic socialism. Dewey held that Marx's view of science was wrong. Marx's dialectical materialism meant that he claimed to have discovered laws determining human economic and political affairs. Dewey held that science perfects the freedom of humans to determine their own original social forms. Science is a method of projecting hypotheses to allow experimentation with alternative solutions. Dewey granted that socialism is necessary because the owners of productive property exploit the workers as Marx claimed, but Dewey denied Marx's claim that the only historically significant classes were those of owners of productive property (the bourgeoisie) and those that worked it (the proletariat). Dewey denied that class warfare was the mechanism of social advancement. Human groupings by religion, moral beliefs, ethnicity, education, geography, race, and sex often are human divisions explaining conflict better than does class. Dewey denied Marx's claim that violent revolution is the sole way of improving things for the dispossessed. Dewey warned that this doctrine of necessary violence might well result in a self-fulfilling prophecy. Dewey held that democratic means must be used if the democratic socialism he favored was to result as its end. Only if socialism had been achieved peacefully and democratically would Dewey allow force used in its defense by the proper authorities. Dewey denied that the Soviet Union was in the post-revolutionary phase which Marx called the dictatorship of the proletariat. Dewey saw much evidence that it was a dictatorship over the proletariat. Soviet communism was an autocratic sort of socialism. Dewey denied Marx's claim that religion, social forms, and the social sciences formed under feudalism or capitalism were mere covers for economic exploitation and cannot exist under socialism. Dewey opposed Marx's position that government would wither away under socialism. Dewey's government would be based in participatory democracy and is sorely needed to discover and regulate the public consequences of private acts. Dewey's democracy is not that false form of democracy which Marx claims developed under capitalism in which the majority of the rich dominate over the more numerous poor, but Dewey agrees that this sort of democracy often conjoined with capitalism must be overcome.

Dewey's own non-Marxian socialism

Rejecting Marxian socialism, Dewey would accept democratic socialism, or even better, socialistic democracy. To Dewey, socialism is the means providing for the realization of the democratic ends of liberty, equality and fraternity. He believes that democracy best liberates the powers of individual human beings. They have wonderful potentialities, capabilities that should be fully developed so that all persons flourish and become the best persons they can be. This demands much education and the guaranteed social provision of food, clothing, shelter, and medical care. More, every individual needs meaningful work and democracy. Individuals develop themselves in society with meaningful work in which they interact with natural materials and other humans. As persons act and experience the results, mind, capabilities, and human powers develop in them. The same interaction characterizes democracy. It is that system of governance in which those subject to the law may make and change the law. And Dewey's democracy is not merely political: it is the proper mode of management in every association of mature humans – the school, the club, the church, the factory, the business, the workplace.

Dewey rejects capitalism, then, because it produces for profit, not to provide individuals with what they need to develop all their potentialities. Present capitalism is based on the management/labor distinction. Dewey holds that this is the ancient philosopher's mind/body distinction now proving its baneful consequences. Managers work with their minds, laborers work with their bodies. Each is half-human. So that all may be fully human, all may develop both sides of human nature, Dewey wants worker control of their factories or businesses or workplaces, industrial autonomy. Workers would both own and manage the ideal business. Or, if they work with a natural resource like oil or coal, the state might own but workers at least must manage the workplace. Either the state or the appropriate workers would engage in long-range planning, something like the Soviet Union's five-year plans, for their businesses and for the whole economy. To Dewey, a planning economy is more important than a planned economy.

Two later academics, inspired by Dewey, and teaching something close to Dewey's sort of socialism, were his pupil, Sidney Hook (longest at New York University), and innovator in linguistics and political gadfly, Noam Chomsky (Massachusetts Institute of Technology).

Nineteenth- and early twentieth-century American socialists

Though this tension between Marx and Dewey is the most important story about socialism in American philosophy, it is not the only one. Quite apart from Marx, socialism came to the United States from other European influences. British Fabian socialism inspired the Danish-born American Laurence Gronlund to publish *The Co-Operative Commonwealth* in 1884, an exposition of democratic socialism. Edward Bellamy's 1888 novel, *Looking Backward*, created a socialist, nationalist movement here. Utopian socialism was tried in nineteenth-century New England in the Brook Farm and Fruitlands communal-living experiments.

After the American Civil War, the new great industrial enterprises experienced much labor strife. The first response of their workers was to struggle, with some success, to form labor unions. However, at about the turn of the century, American Railway Union leader Eugene V. Debs (1855–1926), who had led the workers in the 1894 Pullman strike, began to believe that more than unionization was necessary. The more for some was the Progressive movement in politics, seeking the reform of capitalism through governmental regulation. The more for Debs was founding, in 1898, the American Socialist Party, which sought the replacement of capitalism. Under Debs, the party elected many local officials but Debs never won more than 6 percent of the national vote in his five campaigns for president between 1900 and 1920. Norman Thomas (1884–1968) succeeded Debs as party leader and was its presidential candidate from 1928 to 1948. In some elections Dewey voted for both Debs and Thomas.

More contemporary socialists

Other famous Americans who were socialists include Upton Sinclair (1878–1968), the author of *The Jungle*; Helen Keller (1880–1968), the deaf and blind pupil of Anne Sullivan; Dorothy Day (1897–1980), the founder of the Catholic Worker movement; and Howard Zinn (b. 1922), the progressive historian. Michael Harrington (1928–89), was the author of *The Other America,* the book which based the Kennedy–Johnson Great Society (anti-poverty) program, and a leader of the Democratic

Socialists of America. He was a prolific author of socialistic studies and a stinging critic of capitalism. The great physicist Albert Einstein was a socialist.

Notable non-American twentieth-century philosophers who were socialists include Bertrand Russell of England and Jean-Paul Sartre of France.

Further reading

Dewey, John. *Liberalism and Social Action* in *The Later Works of John Dewey*. Carbondale, IL: Southern Illinois University Press, 1935.

Harrington, Michael. *The Other America: Poverty in the United States*. Baltimore, MD: Penguin, 1963.

McLellan, David (ed.). *Marxism: Essential Writings*. New York: Oxford University Press, 1988.

Schneider, Herbert W. *A History of American Philosophy*, second edition. New York: Columbia University Press, 1963.

Westbrook, Robert B. *John Dewey and American Democracy*. Ithaca, NY: Cornell University Press, 1991.

Zinn, Howard. *A People's History of the United States*. New York: Harper and Row, 1980.

JOSEPH BETZ

SOCIETY

Like many philosophers, those of the indigenous American philosophical tradition made human society a central theme. They did so, however, not by authoring distinctive conceptions of society, but rather by giving society a novel philosophical importance. Western philosophy has typically regarded social phenomena either as derivative from logically and causally prior subjects, that is, individual minds, or as the domain of non-philosophical, pre-scientific thought and common prejudice, in Platonic terms the realm of mere "opinion" rather than knowledge, an obstacle to truth. Where social interaction was regarded as constitutive for knowledge, it has been feared as justifying *conventionalism*, the view that the validity of moral or cognitive judgments depends upon a particular society's conventions or agreements.

In contrast, one of the most reliable generalizations about the American tradition is its *communitarianism*, meaning that it granted society a constitutive role in a range of philosophical subjects *without* endorsing conventionalism. It did this in three senses. First, the Americans typically regarded individual mind as constituted by social interaction and particularly communication. This implied that linguistic meaning is fundamentally social (a view later made famous by Ludwig Wittgenstein). Second, contrary to the misapprehensions of European thinkers hostile to American capitalism, the classic American thinkers were commonly opponents of pecuniary individualism. While they endorsed individual liberties, they saw these as only capable of actualization *in* community, making a heightened sense of community essential to moral growth. Last and perhaps most remarkably, several of the Americans argued that objective and ideal factors like truth, reality, and even logic were socially constituted, yet, again, without either accepting conventionalism or jettisoning a normative for a purely descriptive logic.

This last point can best be seen in the work of Charles Peirce, a philosopher–scientist who had no interest in developing a theory of social life *per se*. Nevertheless, in his "convergence theory" he famously defined truth and reality in terms of community.

> The real, then, is that which, sooner or later, information and reasoning would finally result in, and which is therefore independent of the vagaries of me and you. Thus, the very origin of the conception of reality shows that this conception essentially involves the notion of a COMMUNITY, without definite limits, and capable of a definite increase of knowledge. And so ... the real ... consist[s] of those [cognitions] which, at a time sufficiently future, the community will always continue to re-affirm.
>
> (CP 5.311; Peirce's emphasis)

In another striking passage, Peirce argued that logic is intrinsically social. He did not mean that it is conventional, or that its rules are the summations of social performances. He meant that to think logically we must identify with an unlimited community of inquirers, hence accept for the governance of our thinking "objective" rules that would satisfy such a community rather than the subjective ones that would satisfy only oneself.

> It seems to me that we are driven to this, that logicality inexorably requires that our interests shall not be limited. They must not stop at our own fate, but must embrace the whole community ... He who would not sacrifice his own soul to save the whole world, is, as it seems to me, illogical in all his inferences, collectively. Logic is rooted in the social principle.
>
> (CP 2.654)

Perhaps the most characteristic application of the constitutive notion of society in the American tradition lies in the philosophy of mind. Opposing both the Cartesian tradition, which made mind a non-physical substance, and the German Idealists, for whom mind became a rational spirit embodied in all things, the Americans promoted the view that mind is first of all a *function* or *activity*, rather than a substance, which *emerges* out of social interaction, particularly communication. Rather than mind causing communication, communication causes or constitutes mind. Several of the Americans took this view, but it is arguably George Herbert Mead, the founder of the field of social psychology, who gave its classic formulation. In his lectures, published later as *Mind, Self, and Society: From the Standpoint of Social Behaviorism*, Mead derived mind from "significant gesture." The more neurologically complex non-human animals are capable of communication via gesture. Humans alone make these gestures "significant" through "taking the perspective of the other" in a social interaction. Significant gesturing requires that I respond to my own sign the way my communicative partner does; that is taking her perspective. This makes the gesture a "sign." Thinking, then, is reflexive communication of the self with itself. Thought is derivative from social communication.

These ideas made it impossible for the classic American philosophers to endorse a pecuniary or "possessive" individualism, as in political libertarianism, or a radically alienated, Promethean individualism, as in the existentialism of Jean-Paul Sartre or Søren Kierkegaard. As Dewey put it, they supported individual*ity* but not individual*ism*, the view that individuality is independent and of ultimate value. For it is social institutions, communicative interaction, and education that make a functionally free individual, however much these influences are intertwined with the individual's native, genetic, or idiosyncratic components, and however important are the social changes wrought by recalcitrant individuals. The social is never absent from, nor completely antithetical to, the individual; the capitalist entrepreneur, the rebel, and the genius must satisfy a desire, speak a language or work in a symbolic medium shared with a society, able to transform a part of culture only by accepting the rest of it. Otherwise they fail to communicate at all, and become not revolutionary but merely eccentric.

These themes received their most elevated expression in the work of the American tradition's most prominent idealist, Josiah Royce. Royce accepted the social constitution of the self, and Peirce's definition of knowledge via the community of inquirers, but went farther still. In *The Problem of Christianity* his previously neo-Hegelian Absolute Mind was replaced by the "Community of Interpretation," the community of all minds in their endless quest for truth. This dovetailed with Royce's "philosophy of loyalty," his argument that it is the commitment to a shared cause which provides the meaning of human life. While there are many false causes and exclusivist communities, the "true" loyalty must harmonize with "loyalty to loyalty" itself, which presupposes that the cause, hence the community, at least prospectively includes all. Royce thereby made truth, reality, and goodness dependent upon community as an epistemic, metaphysical and ethical ideal.

Further reading

Dewey, John. *Individualism Old and New* in *The Later Works of John Dewey: 1925–53*, ed. Jo Ann Boydston. Carbondale, IL: Southern Illinois University Press, 1988.

Mead, George Herbert. *Mind, Self, and Society from the Standpoint of a Social Behaviorist*, ed. Charles W. Morris. Chicago, IL: University of Chicago Press, 1962.

Peirce, Charles S. *Collected Papers of Charles Sanders Peirce* (CP), ed. Charles Hartshorne and Paul Weiss. Cambridge, MA: Harvard University Press, 1931, Vols 2 and 5.

Royce, Josiah. *The Philosophy of Loyalty.* Nashville, TN: Vanderbilt University Press, 1995.

—— *The Problem of Christianity.* Washington, DC: Catholic University Press, 2001.

LAWRENCE CAHOONE

SOLIDARITY

"Solidarity" has been made prominent in American philosophy in the work of Richard Rorty. Rorty sometimes uses it in his dismissal of Cartesianism, and with this dismissal comes his rejection of epistemology, his disavowal of foundationalism, his critique of realism, and his discarding of objectivity. Hence, on these theoretical questions, Solidarity plays a catchall term for the anti-metaphysical, anti-spectator view of knowledge that replaces these philosophical concepts. However, its primary function comes in his social and moral philosophy. Following John Dewey, Rorty has attempted to understand social relationships in a holistic fashion. Dewey warned against two dangers in understanding the relationship between the individual and the state: over-emphasis on individualism and too much reliance on the concept of the state. On the one hand, contract theories of the state, for example, rely on an artificial notion of atomic isolated individuals and a vague notion of an original state of nature out of which the whole of social relations are meant to develop. On the other hand, theories that privilege the priority of the state over the individual, various Platonic theories, misplace an artificial and metaphysical whole as greater than its parts. Both Dewey and Rorty, rather, see the interrelationship of individual and society as mutual. The state and the individual are in a process of being formed in an active progressive movement into the future. Both, however, were liberals and saw the state existing for the good of the individual.

The problem that arises for Rorty is with his liberal theory of the state. Since for Rorty, again following Dewey, there is no natural teleology, transcendental purpose, nor intrinsic values alienation is a constant danger. As Rorty puts it, for the individual, it is socialization all the way down. But since there is no inherent good of the state, the individual is socialized in no inherently good way. And vice versa, since there is no intrinsic value to realize by any individual, there is no intrinsically good way for a citizen to participate in the formation of the state. Consequently, for Rorty, there is the need for some sort of social bond to provide legitimacy for acting decently toward those who are to be recognized as one's fellow citizens. This is where his concept of solidarity becomes central to his work. What is left once one discards the traditional theoretical understanding of the state and the individual is the on-going historical project of democratic self-government that was inherited from the Enlightenment. In private, since there is no privileged view of human nature, individuals are free to create any selves they wish. In public, however, there is an active need to share with others in the formation of a freer, more peaceful, more just democracy. This, he hopes, is to be accomplished by expanding the notion of "we": we heirs to the experiment in democracy, we heirs to bourgeois freedom, we heirs to American national pride. Whatever way it is done, what is needed is better and more interesting ways to describe the social reality in which "we" share with others. Philosophy's role for Rorty is to be poetic and help expand the moral imagination so "we" can find solidarity with those whose historical contingencies intersect with ours.

Further reading

Rorty, Richard. *Contingency, Irony, and Solidarity.* Cambridge: Cambridge University Press, 1989.

—— "Solidarity or Objectivity?" in *Objectivity, Relativism, and Truth: Philosophical Papers Volume 1.* Cambridge: Cambridge University Press, 1991, pp. 21–34.

Richard Rumana

SPACE

As point of departure for his discussion of space and time, Charles Peirce takes Kant's view that these are pure forms of intuition, and considers in some detail the problems that arise from this theory. In "Questions Concerning Certain Faculties Claimed for Man" (1868), he offers his own theory in which he describes how space is synthesized. Arguments by Berkeley have convinced him that there can be no direct intuition of space; it must be inferred. While this appears to contradict Kant, he argues that Kant himself admits that the pure intuition of space is a synthesis. Peirce sees himself as explaining how this takes place, so that his doctrine differs less from Kant's view than it might seem. Nevertheless, in "The Probability of Induction" (1878), he questions the very notion of the synthetic a priori, no doubt influenced by his logical researches, and shifts his attention to his fruitful studies of induction and scientific inquiry. Moreover, he is fully conversant with the distinctly non-Kantian notion of a non-Euclidean geometry, and frequently points to the open question whether the three angles in a triangle sum to two right angles. As he points out, this empirical question about the geometry of space can only be solved by measuring the three angles of a large, perhaps astronomically defined triangle, and might remain unsolved even then.

Space and time, says William James, are "vehicles of continuity by which the world's parts hang together." He sees the concept of space (and of time) as highly abstract in comparison with the bits of experience that lead us to formulate it. Far from being a simple Kantian intuition, it is an artificial construction. Here he is of course thinking of the concept we have of space. For George Santayana, the concept of space is one thing, and space itself is quite another. His ontology has as the most basic category the realm of matter, which constitutes a *physical space*; this is something entirely different from human representations like mathematical space and pictorial space, coming as they do from the different realms of matter and essence. He denounces theories in the empiricist tradition that fail to make the distinction and have no place for space and time as parts of the physical cosmos. For him, real space and time are neither metaphysical nor phenomenal, but simply physical; the empiricist tendency to identify them with human representations of them is muddled and erroneous. The pragmatists, however, have a different, almost opposite notion of what constitutes a faulty metaphysics; they challenge notions like absolute truth and an unknown matter that are remote from experience. The physical space that Santayana speaks of, with its radical separation from anybody's idea of space, would then be metaphysical.

James and Dewey look at space pragmatically, and are less interested in abstract arguments about its nature than in practical questions. James gives his well-known example of the squirrel. A person is walking rapidly around a tree, with a squirrel keeping out of his sight on the opposite side by scurrying around the tree at the same rate. Since the squirrel always faces the person, it might be claimed that the person does not in fact walk around the squirrel. From another point of view, however, the person certainly does go around the squirrel. In order to settle the question, what is required is merely some pragmatic account of what "go around" means. No abstract metaphysical definition will be helpful here. In like fashion, Dewey gives a caricature of traditional metaphysical treatments of space. For him, spatial distance must be understood practically; it is an obstacle separating friends and preventing discourse. To say that space is unreal and phenomenal, after the Kantian tradition, is unhelpful. No remedy for unfriendly spatial remoteness is to be found in this claim of unreality or in the noumenal world of the metaphysicians. The point for him is that whatever metaphysical notion of space is hit on, as a practical matter space is real and in a particular way objectionable. Recognition of space in this down-to-earth fashion is a prerequisite to the removal of any difficulties it presents.

W.V. Quine certainly does not deny the physical cosmos, calling it the "naïve universe of bodies." However, the ontology he seeks is to be linguistically defined, consisting of those objects referred to in a regimented discourse. This leads him to identify space with a manifold of triples of real numbers – or rather to identify space-time with similar quadruples. The relativity of space is accepted in the sense that no coordinate system is privileged. He rejects the notion of particle, and in his physics he posits a distribution of quantitative states over regions of space-time. The spatio-temporal coordinates – quadruples of reals – are represented in set theory. According to his linguistic treatment of ontology, inasmuch as the universe of discourse consists of sets, the basic existential elements of this physics will be sets. Quine's treatment of space leans toward logic and science, and is not intended to answer the practical questions about agency raised by the early pragmatists. An ontology of sets is familiar in mathematics, but it is of little assistance in understanding human action. Other recent American philosophers follow in this direction, and often appeal to modern science to deal with traditional philosophical problems. Hilary Putnam, for instance, in "Time and Physical Geometry," argues that the scientific notion of space-time offers a solution to the philosophical problem of future contingents. Appealing to assumptions from physics – special relativity and the four-dimensionality of the world – he makes the case that Aristotle was incorrect and that statements about the future already have a truth value.

Further reading

James, William. *Pragmatism*. New York: Meridian Books, 1955; see pp. 41, 93.

Peirce, Charles S. *The Essential Peirce: Selected Philosophical Writings*, Volume 1, ed. Nathan Houser and Christian Kloesel. Indianapolis, IN: Indiana University Press, 1992; see pp. 17, 167–69, 295.

Putnam, Hilary. "Time and Physical Geometry" in *Mathematics, Matter and Method: Philosophical Papers*, Volume 1. Cambridge: Cambridge University Press 1979, pp. 198–214.

Quine, W.V. "Reply to J. J. C. Smart" in *The Philosophy of W.V. Quine*, ed. Lewis E. Hahn and Paul A. Schilpp. La Salle, IL: Open Court, 1987, pp. 516–18.

Santayana, George. "Pictorial Space and Sentimental Time" in *Realm of Matter*. New York: Charles Scribner's Sons, 1930, pp. 44–74.

ANGUS KERR-LAWSON

SPECIOUS PRESENT

While there are various formulations of the doctrine of the specious present, the key idea is that the present as we experience it is not a punctate instant, but rather encompasses a brief but nonzero interval of time. The idea was introduced to philosophical and psychological audiences by William James, in his influential 1890 book *Principles of Psychology*.

The coinage stems from a quoted passage by an author James refers to as E.R. Clay. In it, Clay claims that little is understood of the relation of experience to time. He distinguishes between the Present of philosophy, a point on an abstract timeline which is the "coterminus of past and future," and the present as we experience it. The content in the world to which our experience of the now refers actually includes a small part of the immediate past, "delusively given as being a time that intervenes between the past and the future." This temporally extended experienced present is labeled "specious" because the present in a mathematical or philosophical sense by definition has no duration. Although Clay holds that the specious present of experience is a fiction insofar as the actual Present has no such duration, he also thinks it leads via this fiction to genuine knowledge about temporally extended processes in the world.

While Clay describes the specious present as including the actual present plus a short interval immediately preceding it, James goes on to argue that it also includes an element directed towards the future. The present is a saddleback, he claims, on which we sit and look both to the future and to the past. This view of the experienced present is also taken up by Edmund Husserl (see below).

The book from which James took the doctrine of the specious present, *The Alternative: A Study in Psychology*, was published anonymously in 1882, and E.R. Clay wasn't the anonymous author's real name. The author was Robert Kelly, an Irish immigrant to Boston who retired early from business to study, and wrote *The Alternative* as his sole contribution to philosophy. Another important influence on James' view of the experience of time was Shadworth Hollway Hodgson. While Hodgson's work did not have so catchy a phrase for the idea, he developed a much more sophisticated view about experience and the present, which arguably had a much greater impact on James' thinking about the experience of time than did Kelly and which presaged much of Husserl's analysis of time consciousness.

Motivation

Two standard examples are used to argue that the specious present doctrine is necessary to account for the way we perceive temporally extended events: perceiving motion and listening to a melody.

By definition, motion requires duration and cannot take place in a single punctate instant. At the very least, two such instants are required for the inference that motion has taken place. In order to perceive motion as motion, rather than infer that it has taken place, our perception thus has to encompass some duration. Consider the way we see a bird fly: it is perceived as being in motion. This contrasts with seeing the sun moving across the sky; we infer that the sun has moved by comparing its current position to a previous one. Thus this argument: it is a basic fact of experience that we perceive motion; this motion must take place over some duration, not in a punctate instant; and therefore our perception of the present must have temporal duration.

The example of motion exposes an ambiguity in interpretation of the doctrine. The specious present could be understood to mean that all events which take place within a certain short period of time are experienced as simultaneous. Because they take place so quickly, and our perceptual abilities have temporal resolution, rapid successive events may appear as simultaneous. On the other hand, even if motion is brief, rapid motion does not appear merely as a blurred line: this means we individuate successive stages, even if they seemed to occur during one present moment. This understanding of the specious present construes it as a succession perceived as a succession, contained in the present moment with temporal relations of earlier and later intact.

The example of listening to a melody highlights the difference between taking the specious present to include just the instantaneous present plus the immediate past, and to include a future-directed aspect as well. Compare the case of listening to a new song for the first time, versus listening to a well-known melody. When listening to a melody, each subsequent note is heard within the certain experiential framework of previous notes. The most recent note lingers in some fashion after it has finished and the new note is being played. This is the past-directed portion of the specious present. If the melody is not familiar, then we may not have any particular expectation of the next note, and thus not a distinct future-directed element to the experience of the present note. For well-known melodies, however, we know what note is coming next and there is an element of anticipation of that future note, while we are still listening to the current note and experiencing the lingering effects of the previous note. This is the saddle-back of the present discussed by James: both the immediate past and the immediate future are bound into our present experience.

Philosophical developments

Following its popularization by James, the specious present doctrine developed along several distinct lines in the continental tradition and in the Anglo-American analytic and theological traditions. During the first decades of the twentieth century, a number of British philosophers were engaged in debates regarding the nature of time, and utilized our experience of time as evidence; these included C.D. Broad, J. McTaggart, and Bertrand Russell. More recently, Wilfrid Sellars in *Science and Metaphysics* raises an important distinction between the temporal relations of events, and the temporal relations of conceptual representations of those events. Sellars concludes that the specious present as it is traditionally conceived "is an incoherent combination of literal simultaneity and literal successiveness." Developments in neuroscience have opened the possibility of correlating the timing of neural processes with features of our temporal experience.

A.N. Whitehead utilized the specious present to elaborate the temporal nature of God. He held that the shorter the duration encompassed by the specious present, the more fleeting is our experience; events pass more quickly out of it. The more events that can be encompassed by the specious present, the less fleeting is experience. If one took the specious present of God's awareness of the world to be equal in temporal length to all of time, then God experiences everything as always now. Charles Hartshorne has a similar position, but emphasizes that God, like humans, is limited regarding the future by the present: while the past and the present are actualized, the future is indeterminate and still merely possible for God as well as ourselves.

Josiah Royce, a theological philosopher, also thought the nature of God's temporal being could be understood in terms of the specious present. According to Royce in *The World and The Individual*, the term "present" is ambiguous between two senses: in one, we mean only the particular event in a temporal sequence that is currently taking place, for instance, a single word as it is spoken in a sentence. The second sense of present refers to the unity in consciousness of the extended temporal event, such as understanding the entire sentence even as the single word is currently spoken. This dual nature of the present is why we can understand a sentence or melody as it transpires element by element while also experiencing it as a meaningful whole. While there are upper limits to our own consciousness, and thus temporal sequences too long for us to apprehend as a unity in experience, the Absolute consciousness of God encompasses all of time. On this understanding, God has eternal knowledge of the world by experiencing it both as a single unified sequence while also experiencing the current part of the temporal sequence. This is possible by removing the arbitrary limitations of the human specious present of several seconds.

In the continental tradition, Edmund Husserl was strongly influenced by James' work, and developed a unique phenomenological approach to investigating time consciousness. In contrast to the label "specious" which indicates fictitiousness, the development of the notion in the phenomenological tradition emphasizes a nonpejorative sense of speciousness: our experience of the present does have duration, although this is not fictitious because it is not compared to an external, objective, time. Husserl divides experienced time into three parts: the primal now, which is rather like the "actual present"; retention, which is the past-directed element where just-finished sensations linger in perceptual awareness; and protention, which is the future-directed element. Protention is not perception of the future per se, but rather a kind of openness to or anticipation of it, such as the experience of anticipating the next note in a familiar melody.

Further reading

Husserl, Edmund. *The Phenomenology of Internal Time-Consciousness*, trans. James Churchill. Indianapolis, IN: Indiana University Press, 1964.

James, William. *Principles of Psychology*, Vol. I. New York: Dover, 1890.

Le Poidevin, Robin. "The Experience and Perception of Time," http://plato.stanford.edu/entries/time-experience/ (2004).

Royce, Josiah. *The World and the Individual: Nature, Man, and the Moral Order*. London: Macmillan, 1923.

HOLLY ANDERSEN

SPECTATOR THEORY OF KNOWLEDGE

A term used by John Dewey to characterize what he considered the core commitment of all non-pragmatic theories of knowledge. Roughly, Dewey held that philosophers have conceived of knowing on a visual model: as a perceiver "sees" an external object, the knower "beholds" the object known. More precisely, though he nowhere provides rigorous statement, Dewey construes the Spectator Theory as a

Defining thesis: Knowing is a relation between a subject (a mind, a person, etc.) and an object (a material object, a sense datum, etc.) that can be characterized as a passive beholding or viewing of the object by the subject;

and a

Major implication of the defining thesis: In knowing the object, the subject need not change the object.

Dewey thought that all theories of knowledge prior to his are committed to the Spectator Theory. For example, Plato was committed to the Spectator Theory when he holds, in the *Republic*, that knowing is a matter of the "soul's eye" contemplating the eternal Forms. Descartes was committed to the Spectator Theory in holding that we can attain certainty via the mind's ability to clearly and distinctly perceive certain essences or "simple natures." Locke was committed to the Theory in holding that the agreement or disagreement of ideas is "immediately" given to the mind, analogously to the visual object "given" to the eye. Many twentieth-century empiricists were committed to the Spectator Theory in the debate about sense data: proponents held that the object of direct awareness is a sense-datum; detractors held that it is, say, a material object. Both camps agree, however, that this awareness – this "passive viewing" of the object, whatever it might be – constitutes an instance of knowing.

Dewey considered the Spectator Theory indefensible; and because he thought the various special theories of knowledge essentially committed to it, he considered them indefensible as well. Four major criticisms of the Spectator Theory emerge from his writings spanning some fifty years: One criticism is based on his interpretation of the method of contemporary science. Roughly, it holds that the most effective method of knowledge acquisition yet discovered, contemporary science, requires that the inquirer engage in active manipulation of the world to acquire knowledge. This "experimentalism," however, Dewey considered incompatible with both the Spectator Theory's defining thesis – that knowing is a passive beholding relation between the knowing-subject and object known – and with the Theory's major implication – that knowing need not change the object known. But because the method of contemporary science is the best method we have for acquiring knowledge, its incompatibility with the Spectator Theory shows that it must be rejected.

A second criticism is based on Dewey's interpretation of Heisenberg's Principle of Indeterminacy, and specifically goes after the Spectator Theory's major implication. It argues that Heisenberg has shown that it is impossible to know the precise velocity and position of a micro-physical object – an electron, for example: if the value for one is fixed, the value for the other can only be specified probabilistically. This is because observation unavoidably interacts with what is to be observed: A photon of light, say, which is necessary for observation, itself has energy and so interacts with the electron. But the effects of interaction cannot be calculated away; for the calculation cannot be confirmed except by observation, which in turn introduces its own degree of displacement. From this finding Dewey draws the broader moral that the Spectator Theory is wrong in holding that knowing need not change what is (misguidedly) sought to be known – an "antecedent Reality" independent of the process of inquiry.

A third criticism is based on Dewey's notion of the instrumental nature of thought. The Spectator Theory, according to Dewey, presupposes that the (epistemic) nature and role of thought is to passively "capture" or "represent" what exists prior to, or independently of it: to "mirror" the antecedently Real. But Dewey believes that science shows that thought is not passive, but active – a type of activity that serves as an "instrument" for solving problems. What is known is, in fact, the *consequences* of this activity. The incompatibility of a proper conception of thought with the Spectator Theory should lead us to reject the latter.

A fourth criticism is based on Dewey's conviction that the Spectator Theory has given rise to intractable, global "epistemological" puzzles. Representative is the problem of the possibility of knowledge "in general" – a problem not of whether this or that particular bit of knowledge is possible, but of whether any knowledge *at all* is possible. This puzzle, thinks Dewy, grows out of the spectator theorist's failure to take proper account of knowledge as it "empirically exists," and instead conceives of knowing as a spectatorial relation between knower and known. Epistemology then finds itself confronted with the problem of how it is possible for the inner mind to know the external world. An account of knowing that produces such puzzles should be retained only if forced upon us; but of course the Spectator Theory is not forced upon us, and hence should be rejected.

Dewey, then, rejects the Spectator Theory, and seeks to replace it with a more adequate non-"epistemological," empiricist theory of knowledge – a theory of inquiry. Other contemporary philosophers, most notably Richard Rorty, have argued against the Spectator Theory as well. Whether they, or Dewey, are successful, however, remains unresolved. One important issue bearing on the success of the criticisms has to do with how one interprets the Spectator Theory. On one interpretation, it is a theory of both "coming-to-know" and of "having" knowledge – of both knowledge acquisition and knowledge possession. On another, minimalist interpretation, it is simply a theory about having knowledge. Dewey and other critics of the Spectator Theory, however, seem to have construed it in the broader fashion, and to have aimed their criticisms primarily (if not exclusively) at the acquisitional aspect of the Theory. For example, the criticism based on Heisenberg's Principle of Indeterminacy avers that the observation requisite to *come to know* the simultaneous velocity and position of a material object renders the Spectator Theory's passive beholding relation unattainable. Whether the Spectator Theory can be construed in the narrower sense remains under dispute; but if it can, most, if not all, of Dewey and company's criticisms may fall wide of the mark.

Further reading

Dewey, John. *Essays in Experimental Logic in John Dewey: The Middle Works, 1899–1924, Volume 12, 1920*, ed. Bridget A. Walsh. Carbondale, IL: Southern Illinois University Press, 1982, pp. 77–201

—— *Logic: The Theory of Inquiry* in *John Dewey: The Later Works, 1925–1953, Volume 12, 1938*, ed. Kathleen E. Poulos. Carbondale, IL: Southern Illinois University Press, 1982, pp. 3–527.

—— *The Quest for Certainty: A Study in the Relation of Knowledge and Action* in *John Dewey: The Later Works, 1925–1953, Vol. 4, 1929*, ed. Harriet Furst Simon. Carbondale, IL: Southern Illinois University Press, 1984, pp. 1–250.

Dicker, Georges. *Dewey's Theory of Knowing*. Philadelphia, PA: Philosophical Monographs, Temple University Press, 1976.

Kulp, Christopher B. *The End of Epistemology: Dewey and His Current Allies on the Spectator Theory of Knowledge.* Westport, CT: Greenwood Press, 1992.

Rorty, Richard. *Philosophy and the Mirror of Nature.* Princeton, NJ: Princeton University Press, 1979.

CHRISTOPHER KULP

SPIEGELBERG, HERBERT

An eminent phenomenologist in his own right, Herbert Spiegelberg (1904–90) is generally considered to have been one of the leading historians of phenomenology in the United States and internationally. He was born 18 May 1904 in Strasbourg in the Alsatian region of France, and came to the United States in 1937. From 1941 until 1963 he was on the faculty of Lawrence University (Appleton, Wisconsin). He joined the faculty of Washington University in 1963 and remained there until 1971 when he retired and became professor emeritus. Spiegelberg's Workshops in Phenomenology (conducted during the summers of 1965, 1966, 1967, 1969, and 1972) were centrally important in encouraging the growth of phenomenology in the United States. He died 6 September 1990.

The Phenomenological Movement: A Historical Introduction is a work of enormous scope, exacting detail, and thoughtful interpretation. In his Preface to the 1959 First Edition, Spiegelberg quotes from a 1951 article by Herbert W. Schneider of Columbia University: "No doubt, American education will gradually take account of the spread of phenomenological method and terminology, but until it does, American readers of European philosophy have a severe handicap." American philosophy did gradually take account of phenomenology, and Spiegelberg's book was an important part of the development of phenomenology in the American context.

The continuing pertinence of Spiegelberg's book to classical American philosophy is partly explained by the fact that he had a more than superficial knowledge of American philosophy, literature, and social science. Thus, at the beginning of his exposition of Heidegger, he suggestively remarks: "Coleridge, Thoreau, and T.S. Eliot are more congenial to him than the classical system builders." And again: "the phenomenological goal is closely related to that of William James in his essay 'Against a Certain Blindness in Human Beings.'" Spiegelberg's preference for the clearly and carefully stated aligns him with William James. He concludes the long book with James's characterization of metaphysics as "an unusually obstinate attempt to think clearly and consistently." Spiegelberg, having noted the many differences between phenomenologists and their procedures, suggests that their underlying unity might consist of "the unusually obstinate attempt to look at the phenomena and to remain faithful to them before even thinking about them."

Spiegelberg's article "Toward a Phenomenology of Experience" provides a compact analysis of experience that affords important comparisons with accounts of experience in Peirce, James, Dewey, Royce, Lewis, and Whitehead. Spiegelberg's analysis of the phenomenology of "context" is especially illuminating with respect to comparisons with these philosophers.

Further reading

Spiegelberg, Herbert. "Toward a Phenomenology of Experience," *American Philosophical Quarterly* I, 4 (October 1964): 325–32.

—— *The Phenomenological Movement: A Historical Introduction*, third revised and enlarged edition. Boston, MA: Martinus Nijhoff, 1982.

VICTOR KESTENBAUM

SPIRIT

Spirit in American philosophy is both historically and conceptually diverse.

Historically, the idea can be traced back to various religious and philosophical traditions from Christianity and Hinduism to idealism and empiricism. Conceptually, the idea runs the gamut from the idealistic view that Absolute Spirit is the ultimate reality in the universe, finite spirits being instantiations of the Absolute, to the naturalistic conception of spirit as an emergent property of the physical world, whose function is self-consciousness.

Although several well-known names come to mind in respect to the idea of spirit and its place in the history of American ideas, i.e. Jonathan Edwards, Amos Bronson Alcott, William Ellery Channing, Josiah Royce, *et al.*, nevertheless it is arguable that the most expressive and well-developed ideas of spirit in a philosophical sense are represented in the works of Ralph Waldo Emerson (1803–82) and George Santayana (1863–1952). It is also especially noteworthy that in the works of Emerson and Santayana the tension between spirit as a purely metaphysical entity and spirit as a consequence of natural/empirical phenomena is particularly palpable.

The idea of spirit is scattered throughout both the prose and poetic works of Emerson. However, the most sustained discussions of the idea occur in "Nature," and the essays: "Self-Reliance," "Spiritual Laws," and "The Over-Soul."

In "Nature" Emerson avoids defining spirit in a literal sense. He says it is "an ineffable essence" (40). In a well-known passage, he speaks mystically of spirit:

> Standing on the bare ground, – my head bathed by the blithe air, and uplifted into infinite space, – all mean egotism vanishes. I become a transparent eye ball; I am nothing; I see all; the currents of the Universal Being circulate through me; I am part or particle of God.
>
> (10)

If there is one idea that drives much of Emerson's thought it is the idea that spirit is implicit in the nature of things; spirit is discovered by examining one's relationship to nature. The problem that each individual faces is how to reveal that spirit, how both to see clearly and deeply into what is phenomenally given. This problem is both an intellectual and practical challenge, as suggested by some of the chapter titles of "Nature," i.e. "Beauty," "Language," "Discipline," "Idealism," and "Spirit," and suggested, too, by the essays "Self Reliance" and "The Over-Soul." Perhaps "Self Reliance" sums up the issue best. Emerson says: "Trust thyself: every heart vibrates to that iron string"(260). "Nothing is at last sacred but the integrity of your own mind" (261). Notwithstanding that "For nonconformity the world whips you with its displeasure," (264) it is our deepest impulse to seek that "aboriginal Self on which a universal reliance may be grounded" (268).

> Thus we lie in the lap of immense intelligence, which makes us receivers of its truth and organs of its activity. When we discern justice, when we discern truth, we do nothing of ourselves, but allow a passage to its beams.
>
> (269)

It should be noted that Josiah Royce developed such Emersonian ideas into his own idea of spirit, which extended to a sense of the spirit of community. Thus he held that reality is the life of an absolute mind, and that we know truth beyond ourselves because we are a part of the logos, or world-mind.

Unlike Emerson (and I might add Royce), Santayana is a metaphysical materialist, i.e. the realm of matter accounts ultimately for everything that exists and happens in the world. Among the many structures and events that develop out of the realm of matter are organisms and along with organisms "psyche." "Psyche," as Santayana says in *Realm of Spirit,* is "The self-maintaining and reproducing pattern or structure of an organism" (15). Indeed, psyche has interests in survival. However, in the case of human beings it is the matrix out of which both morality and spirit grow. Hence, for Santayana, spirit is both reducible to the material realm and ontologically a distinct realm of being itself. Santayana wishes to construe spirit as both attached to and detached from the material world. The material world is the spirit's birthplace. Therefore, it has a reverent attachment to it. The spirit also, by its very nature, is contemplative; it is "an awareness natural to animals, revealing the world and themselves in it. Other names for spirit are consciousness, attention, feeling, thought, or any word that marks the total *inner* difference between being awake or asleep, alive or dead" (18). Spirit's function is to envision the realm of essence, the infinite, although utterly inefficacious, realm of what is and what might be. The contemplative character of spirit motivates the individual to pursue a spiritual life, one that develops "intuition," one that is free from "distraction," one that pursues "liberation," and ultimately seeks "union." All these terms suggest that the spiritual life, as Santayana conceives it, is a religious life, as well as an aesthetic life. However, the spiritual life is essentially a disillusioned life, the prime virtue of which is self-knowledge.

Like Emerson's, Santayana's discussion of the spirit and spiritual life is scattered throughout his corpus. However, the main sources are *Reason in Religion*, *Platonism and the Spiritual Life*, and *Realm of Spirit*.

Further reading

Emerson, Ralph Waldo. *Essays and Poems*. New York: Library of America, 1996.

Santayana, George. *Realm of Spirit*. New York: Charles Scribner's Sons, 1940.

CHRISTOPHER PERRICONE

SPIRITUALITY

Although long used as a term to designate specific Roman Catholic practices and perspectives, "spirituality" has become commonplace as the label for a variety of attitudes and disciplines, not only those cultivated historically by Catholics and other Christians, but also by practitioners in diverse religious traditions. Indeed, the vagueness of the term has increased so dramatically in the late twentieth and early twenty-first centuries that it is no longer restricted in employment to the realm of exclusively religious phenomena. Systems of secular spirituality, organized around the purpose of achieving certain standards of physical and psychic well-being, have been developed and proliferate.

Two characteristics can be identified as distinguishing traits, important elements of what might be conceived of as a distinctively American form of spirituality. The first of these is an emphasis on the significance of aesthetic experience within the spiritual life. The second feature is a kind of pragmatism, the tendency to underscore, in any evaluation of spiritual disciplines, their long-term pragmatic effects or fruitfulness. Both characteristics can be discerned at a very early stage in the history of American thought, for example in the writings of the great Puritan philosophical theologian Jonathan Edwards. The divine revelation was communicated for Edwards, not only in the Christian scriptures but also in the "book of nature." The beauty of God's purposes was especially evident in the latter, at least to the Christian saint who was properly disposed to read the divine language embedded in the natural universe. At the same time, Edwards identified "Christian practice" as the twelfth and most important sign of the presence of divine grace in human experience. "By their fruits you will know them" is a principle that Edwards adopted from the Christian New Testament and then applied to the task of evaluating the authenticity of religious experiences reported by participants in the great Christian revivals in eighteenth-century New England.

That same principle was identified by the American philosopher Charles S. Peirce as one of the earliest formulations of the philosophy of pragmatism, and Jesus Christ was identified as one of the earliest of pragmatists. Peirce's own religious thought was a development of such insights: religious ideas and beliefs were to be evaluated in terms of their long-term effects as habits shaping human thought, feeling, and conduct. At the same time, in his longest published work devoted explicitly to a religious topic, Peirce suggested that it is the great beauty of the idea of God that makes it irresistible to anyone who contemplates it disinterestedly. Likewise, it is the beauty of the idea that accounts for its dramatic shaping influence on human thought and conduct. Both the aesthetic and pragmatic features of American spirituality were clearly manifested in Peirce's mature thought.

Not only was the idea of God distinguished for Peirce by its beauty, but the natural universe itself was to be conceived as "God's great poem," radiant with divine intentions for anyone properly disposed to interpret them. The belief that nature is a "book" of divine authorship is a perspective that linked Peirce to Edwards. More immediately, Charles's father Benjamin Peirce articulated such a perspective, as did his good friend, Ralph Waldo Emerson. It is the latter's famous essay on *Nature* that constituted what is perhaps the primary exemplar of an American aesthetic spirituality, exercising enormous influence over subsequent generations of American religious thinkers.

If the aesthetic quality of American spiritual sensibilities was best captured in Emerson's *Nature*, its pragmatic features were perhaps most perfectly embodied in William James's Gifford Lectures published at the dawn of the twentieth century as *The Varieties of Religious Experience*. Citing both Edwards and Peirce as influences, James identified "fruits for life" as a key criterion to be used in the evaluation of religious beliefs and practices. This same religious pragmatism, as well as an appreciation of beauty as a key element of religious experience, are themes that can be traced throughout the writings of such otherwise diverse American thinkers as Josiah Royce, John Dewey, George Santayana, and H. Richard Niebuhr.

In the twentieth and early twenty-first centuries American spiritual life was shaped by certain key developments. In the first place, and somewhat paradoxically, there was a revival of traditional modes of religious practice simultaneous with and alongside the proliferation of purely secular forms of spirituality. Early in the twentieth century, Santayana and Dewey had already developed thoroughly naturalized spiritual perspectives, the articulation of religious attitudes and ideals almost completely detached from any commitment to traditional Jewish or Christian beliefs. Later in that century, versions of secular spirituality, albeit less nuanced or sophisticated than the careful deliberations that these two philosophers had supplied, were commonplace. A second development was the explosion of interest among Americans in non-Christian spiritual traditions, such as Daoism, Zen Buddhism,

Hindu Yoga, Native American spirituality, Jewish Kabbalistic teachings, and Islamic Sufism.

The result of both developments was a tremendous expansion of the "menu" of alternative possibilities, in a modern pluralistic society, available for exploration by American spiritual practitioners in the twenty-first century. The revival of traditional forms of spirituality can be viewed, in part, as a reaction to such pluralism, an attempt to undermine and defeat it. Critics of this pluralistic situation have sometimes emphasized its vital connection to an American culture of consumerism. During the latter part of the twentieth century, spirituality became an important factor in the marketplace, something to be purchased and sampled, perhaps replaced by an alternative product if found to be less than satisfactory. The result of such a close linking of spiritual and economic practices was an almost inevitable superficiality, the frequent failure to develop those habits of thought and conduct considered essential to the spiritual life by all of the classical American pragmatists. Rather than the harshly negative judgment of American spiritual pluralism embodied in some modern forms of traditionalism, these same pragmatists may offer a more felicitous criterion for evaluating this plethora of possibilities, one rooted in a consideration of both the actual and potential "fruits for life" of these diverse perspectives and practices.

Further reading

Edwards, Jonathan. *A Jonathan Edwards Reader*, ed. Harry S. Stout, John E. Smith, and Kenneth P. Minkema. New Haven, CT: Yale University Press, 2003.

James, William. *The Varieties of Religious Experience*. New York: Penguin, 1982.

Levinson, Henry S. *Santayana, Pragmatism, and the Spiritual Life*. Chapel Hill, NC: University of North Carolina Press, 1992.

Peirce, Charles S. "A Neglected Argument for the Reality of God" in *The Essential Peirce: Selected Philosophical Writings*, Volume 2, ed. the Peirce Edition Project. Bloomington, IN: Indiana University Press, 1992, pp. 434–50.

Michael L. Raposa

STREAM OF CONSCIOUSNESS

It is now commonplace to invoke the "stream" metaphor when describing the felt nature of experience. In short, the "stream of consciousness" metaphor highlights the inner coherence and phenomenal unity of conscious states, such as thoughts and perceptions, as they pass one into the next. Despite its current ubiquity, this way of characterizing consciousness is not a modern convention. The "stream" or "flow" metaphor can be found in descriptions of mind and reality dating back to a number of ancient sources, including the fragments attributed to the presocratic thinker Heraclitus, the Upanishadic writings of the Hindu canon, and various Buddhist and Taoist texts and commentaries. However, it was the American psychologist and philosopher William James who gave the expression a certain technical significance and galvanized its contemporary usage.

James's article "On Some Omissions of Introspective Psychology" (1894) and his monumental *Principles of Psychology* (1890) – particularly Chapter 10 of Volume 1, "The Stream of Thought" – are the main sources of this notion, although it is an idea that is continually revisited and worked over throughout his corpus. First, it is important to note that for James the "stream of consciousness" metaphor is posited as a phenomenological descriptive. James is highly critical of standard empiricist conceptions of experience under which the content of consciousness is reducible to atomistic bits or "simple ideas" – such as bare sensations – that are then built up into composite structures that become conscious content as experienced by a subject. For James, conscious experience is a rich, highly structured affair *all the way down*. What James calls the "substantive parts" of the stream of consciousness at a given moment – "subjective states" such as thoughts, perceptions, intentions, beliefs, etc. – are always embedded in a field of experience that is phenomenally alive with felt connections and relations *between* these "substantive parts." James terms these felt connections "transitive relations." And transitive relations are as essential for consciousness as are the substantive parts themselves. Both substantive parts *and* transitive relations are constitutive elements of the stream of consciousness. James's "stream" metaphor is thus meant to capture the experiential quality of consciousness from the inside, including this holistic interrelatedness that gives consciousness its inner cohesiveness and structural integrity.

In the *Principles*, James offers five "characters" of consciousness that reinforce his stream characterization. For James, the *phenomenal* unity of consciousness – its streaming nature – emerges from the *functional* unity of its constituent "characters," as these characters are enacted within our concrete experience of the world. Since the first three characters are the most important for understanding the stream, they will be the ones here considered. The first character of the stream of consciousness James discusses is the fact that its states collectively "tend to Personal Form"; that is, they are all part of a "personal consciousness." This means two things. First, the states comprising the stream are all disclosed in a first-personal mode of givenness. In other words, they are private and privileged, part of a mind that "keeps its own thoughts to itself." Additionally, each state of the stream bears an experiential quality. The various states comprising the stream are intrinsically subjective, in that they *feel* a certain way for the subject who experiences them.

Second, James observes that the states comprising the stream of consciousness are always changing. They exhibit an inner phenomenal movement governed by "sensible intervals of time" and not sequential clock-time. For instance, the same event – such as attending a symphony – can be experienced in radically different ways by different perceivels. For one, the event is a highly pleasurable experience and seems to end almost as soon as it began. For another, the performance is a tedious affair and drags on indefinitely. Thus, the stream exhibits its own internal sensible time. But importantly, no state in the stream is numerically identical to any other state, despite the fact that multiple states can take the same object of experience. This is because "experience is remoulding us every moment," and therefore "nothing can be conceived as the same without being conceived in a novel state of mind." Novelty and flux are thus invariant features of the stream of phenomenal consciousness.

But James's third observation, that the states of the stream are "sensibly continuous," describes how this novelty and flux are organized into a cohesive stream of personal consciousness – in other words, consciousness that is *owned*. It is thus perhaps the most important feature of his characterization of the stream. For James, that states of the stream are sensibly continuous means simply that they flow one into the next "without breach, crack or division." Consciousness as lived "does not appear to itself chopped up in bits" since "it is nothing jointed." Rather, "a 'river' or 'stream' are the metaphors by which it is most naturally described." Phenomenologically, this fact refers to the felt relatedness of the states of the stream *in their flowing*. A given state is felt to be an appropriate successor to the state(s) which preceded it, both in that it follows immediately from the preceding state(s), as well as that it carries over or appropriates shared content that links it back up with the preceding state(s).

Beyond this phenomenological significance, however, the sensible continuity of the stream of consciousness has another important consequence for James. This principle is what gives rise to the feeling that each state in the stream is given to a single, enduring self. The sensible continuity of states thus underwrites the experience of selfhood. For even when there is a temporal gap between certain stream states – such as with sleep or being in a coma – the states which resume *after* the time-gap still feel as if they "belonged together with the consciousness before it, as another part of the same self." Therefore, not only does each state bear an internal reference to the state(s) which precede it, but furthermore it bears reference to a *subject* of those states who experiences them. Crucially, then, sensible continuity is responsible for subjectivity. The "stream of consciousness" is thus representative of James's life-long intellectual goal of remaining faithful to the inner dynamics and experiential realities of our conscious life.

Further reading

James, W. "On Some Omissions of Introspective Psychology," *Mind* 9, 33 (January 1884): 1–26.

—— *Principles of Psychology*, 2 vols. New York: Dover, 1890.

JOEL W. KRUEGER

SUBJECT

The range of philosophical inquiries within the tradition of classical American philosophy has in common a fundamental belief that the fruits of thought and action may be meaningfully directed towards the betterment of human life, individually and socially. From idealist thinkers Ralph Waldo Emerson (1803–82) to Josiah Royce (1855–1916), and from pragmatists William James (1842–1910) and Charles Sanders Peirce (1839–1914) to John Dewey (1859–1952), philosophy rooted in the American experience grounds the pursuit of wisdom in a world where real problems demand efficacious response. In the work of Emerson, the Socratic challenge to live the examined life becomes an injunction to live it fully through the courageous expression of self's deepest truths. Honest self-expression demands reliance on a fundamental integrity of selfhood, which will go against the grain of common opinion, alienating some and resonating in the heart of others who likewise seek a profoundly meaningful life. The self is unique and yet truth links all persons. For Emerson, the willingness to speak from the heart of self-examination means that one must bear isolation in the midst of a crowd, following no dictate but that of conscience. Yet this self is no unchanging essential entity; the very context for being a self exists as a contingent possibility of becoming one, a context historically bound and socially delimited.

From a pragmatist perspective, we are, *as* selves, both subject to and subject of the world of our experiences; that is, we are beings fundamentally grounded by the social context of our becoming. Against the Modernist construct of self as an autonomous, rational agent, the pragmatist conceptualization emphasizes the fundamentally dynamic and relational aspect of subjectivity at its core; we live as persons in a particular social milieu and the very things we think, desire, and hope for draw essentially from this originating experiential framework. Even with regard to perception and knowing, we are contextually and historically bound. Thus no static correspondence links a perceiving subject to objective facts-in-the world. The modernist theoretical divisions of subject and object, perceiver and perceived, knower and known in fact belie what James calls "a rich and active commerce between particular thoughts of ours, and the great universe of other experiences in which they play their parts and have their uses."

The links we draw between this event and that, between what we perceive and what we set out to achieve, are fundamentally social and instrumental. We make sense of experience through shared understandings – linguistic and cultural – that are organized according to what we know in view of what we want to achieve, and the ways we consider whether choices of action might lead to a greater control of circumstance and outcomes are directly related to how we frame the subject matter at hand. Neither knower nor thing known can exist absolutely separable, for this relation is a transaction. We experience the world and make sense of it *as* experiencers who formulate understandings in view of shared needs and purposes.

Much of the time, of course, everyday life is taken for granted and perspectival biases and habitual behaviors continue unexamined. Yet interruptions occur. It is in response to the unexpected or the unforeseen that questions arise and belief is disrupted; pragmatic inquiry is undertaken not merely out of hypothetical interest but is inspired by necessity, the existence of real problems, and the desire for a better outcome.

Because the relation between how we experience the world and the world of our experience is dynamical, transactional, grounded in the context of who we are and where we live, no foundation exists upon which to lay claims for certainty or reify objects of knowledge. Yet desired ends and means of action are not arbitrary enterprises. If ultimate goods and final truths are not immediately available, there are better goods and more accurate knowledge claims attained through inquiry in view of pursuing that which might well remain ever-not-quite. Commitment to truth in the long run hones thought, opinion, and allows the formulation of rules for action in present circumstance. We can aim at greater truth and more efficacious action. This is a point that resonates in the work of idealist and pragmatist American philosophers in the classical tradition.

Royce envisions reality ever at the horizon of ongoing interpretation, in view of increasingly transparent understanding. Peirce postulates inquiry in view of truth in the long run. The Jamesian rubric of truth as being "what works" also speaks to the contextually contingent commitment to do the best one can in view of immediate circumstances, while remaining open to changing opinion, even abandoning belief, or committing oneself anew not as the situation demands but as reality presses. The pragmatic commitment to fallibilism means that every claim might be re-evaluated and found wanting, but meanwhile the effort to attain the best understanding of events and issues carved out of experience allows greater breadth and depth of engagement in a shared world. What we think and how we respond to problems are themselves instantiations of social norms and cultural practices through which perceptions and judgments are made, and if we would wish to live differently, we might be more willing to engage in critical examination of present attitudes and actions in view of an imaginative reconstruction of other outcomes. Change and improvement is contextual. "Better" is a notion related to the specificities of context, and pragmatic inquiry is taken up in response to a specific circumstance – a problematic situation – that demands thoroughgoing examination from a newly critical point of view. At stake in such an inquiry is not the ascertaining of objective empirical facts, which might then be held up as universal knowledge claims – as if there were such objective facts absolutely separable from the nuances of human experience – rather, the aim of inquiry is elucidation of meanings in view of desired ends. This means that there is no dichotomy between subjective perception and objective circumstance; every situation is already meaning laden, but meanings are what we bring to experience as well. Thus pragmatic inquiry demands critical re-evaluation of those factors that render a situation problematic, but also necessitates re-examination of old attitudes and habits through which present understanding is transacted. Experience is already transactional; the goal is to make the process of inquiry experimental so that new outcomes might be envisioned as awareness shifts and broadens and our sense of a situation becomes vital and holds out the promise of growth. Dewey's view is that philosophy itself must be fundamentally critical, and from the broadest purview, since analysis of issues, interpretation and definition of problems are instrumental tools for reconstructing habits of thought and action in view of potentially more meaningful outcomes.

Further reading

Dewey, John. *John Dewey: The Later Works, 1925–1953, Vol. 4: 1929/The Quest for Certainty*, ed. Jo Ann Boydston. Carbondale, IL: Southern Illinois University Press, 1988.

Emerson, Ralph Waldo. "On Self-Reliance" (1841) in *Emerson's Essays*. New York: Harper Perennial, 1981.

James, William. "What Pragmatism Means" in *William James: Writings 1902–1910: The Varieties of Religious Experience / Pragmatism / A Pluralistic Universe / The Meaning of Truth / Some Problems of Philosophy / Essays*. New York: Library of America, 1988 [1906].

Cynthia Gayman

SUBJECT/SUPERJECT

Alfred North Whitehead (1861–1947) describes his *Process and Reality* as an essay on Speculative Philosophy, with eight Categories of Existence. Among these are "'actual entities' – also termed 'actual occasions'": "the final real things of which the world is made up … drops of experience, complex and interdependent" (Whitehead 1978: 18). The terms *actual entity* and *actual occasion* are synonymous except for God, who is the only actual entity who is not an actual occasion, the only complex and relational drop of experience that is not an event.

An actual occasion is a drop of experience or feeling that originates in feelings or prehensions of past occasions and culminates in its feeling of satisfaction, upon which it perishes to be prehended by future actual occasions. Whitehead describes this complete relation in feeling from the past to the future as *subject/superject*.

An actual occasion is a subject that prehends or feels in an act of experience that culminates in a felt satisfaction based on the entity's subjective aim. It then perishes as a subject by becoming an object available for prehension by other actual occasions, which feel or prehend its feelings and the data that compose them. In this way, each actual occasion is both subject and object. However, each is also superject – subject-superject as Whitehead typically describes it. An actual entity is both a unity of subject and object, mind and body, and also a higher unity in relation to the universe and its future. "An actual entity is to be conceived both as a subject presiding over its own immediacy of becoming, and a superject which is the atomic creature exercising its function of objective immortality" (45).

Further reading

Whitehead, Alfred North. *Adventures of Ideas*. New York: Macmillan, 1933.

—— *Modes of Thought*. New York: Capricorn, 1938.

—— *Process and Reality*, corrected edition, ed. D.R. Griffin and D.W. Sherburne. New York: Free Press, 1978.

Stephen David Ross

SUBJECTIVE AIM

"Subject aim" is a concept in Process Theology, a school of thought influenced by the metaphysical process philosophy of Alfred North Whitehead. The concept of Subjective aim refers to the capacity for self-determination possessed, at least to some degree, by everything physical, thus entailing that reality is fundamentally teleological.

According to Process Theology, the most fundamental ontological constituents are not enduring entities, but rather quantized experiences that exist ephemerally, and which serially compose processes. All of reality consists of these processes. The serially occurring quantized experiences constituting these processes have the capacity for self-determination.

Each of these experiential entities has a physical and mental component (though neither has its own *sui generis*, thus distinguishing this view from Cartesian mind–body dualism). The physical component realizes (prehends) the history of its precursors, the entities that preceded it within the process of which it is a part. It also prehends God's aim, which is, given the circumstances of the experiential entity, the best possibility for the entity, among the multitude of possible futures. The physical component of the experiential entity has the capacity, manifesting itself as a feeling or impulse, to act in accordance with God's aim. However, the mental component of each entity exerts its own influence via its capacity for self-determination. As a result, no actual entity is forced to abide by God's aim. It can make its own choice. This is the entity's subjective aim.

The more complex the process constituted by the serially ordered experiential entities, the greater the influence of the subjective aim of each of its constitutive entities. As a result, complex processes will be more attuned to the multitude of options – the possible futures – available to it. This explains why humans behave more creatively and less predictably than less complex processes, such as dogs, which, in turn, behave more creatively and less predictably than even less complex processes, such as inanimate matter. The subjective aims of the experiential, serially ordered entities constitutive of a simple process (e.g. a rock), have very little influence on the behavior of their entities, and thus, the process as a whole.

Once the experiential entity has made its choice, the entity perishes, though its decision lives on as part of a history prehended by future entities continuing the process of which the perished entity was a part. The choice of the experiential entity determines the circumstances that the subsequent entities find themselves in, and *ipso facto*, the possibilities available to them, among which is a best possibility – the aim God will suggest to the entity via its physical component. The mental component will exert its own influence, its subject aim, on the entity, after which the entity will make a choice, thus iterating the cycle.

Further reading

Kraus, Elizabeth M. *The Metaphysics of Experience: A Companion to Whitehead's Process and Reality*, second revised edition: New York: Fordham University Press, 1998.

Rescher, Nicholas. *Process Metaphysics: An Introduction to Process Philosophy*. Albany, NY: SUNY Press, 1996.

Sherburne, Donald W. (ed.). *A Key to Whitehead's Process and Reality*, reprint edition. Chicago, IL: University of Chicago Press, 1981.

Whitehead, Alfred North. *Process and Reality (Gifford Lectures Delivered in the University of Edinburgh during the Session 1927–28)*, corrected edition. New York: Free Press, 1979.

SABA BAZARGAN

SUBJECTIVISM

Objectivity seems to imply some sort of independence from the observer. This could be independence from the particular observer's beliefs, desires or attitudes. Subjectivity, in contrast, is dependent upon the observer. The truth (or justificatory ground) of a value statement, under subjectivism, is somehow derivative of the beliefs, desires or attitudes of the observer (or, according to some subjectivists, *groups* of observers).

There are two overtly linguistic conceptions of subjectivism. According to the first conception, *Simple Subjectivism*, when an agent makes a value statement that agent is directly *describing* a personal desire or attitude. For example, when the agent claims "X is good," this is equivalent to the agent asserting the proposition "I like/approve/desire X." This allows value statements to have truth conditions, but these truth conditions are purely derivative of the attitudes/desires of the observer. With this conception, if the observer endorses X, it is a necessary and sufficient condition for the "goodness" of X.

According to the second linguistic conception, *Emotivism*, when an agent makes a value statement that agent is *expressing* a personal desire or attitude. The agent is also, according to this conception, *commanding* others to feel the same way. Thus, when the agent claims "X is good," this is equivalent to the agent saying "Hurrah for X; feel the same towards X!" Unlike the other linguistic conception, emotivism denies that value statements are propositions which admit of truth or falsehood. Instead, value statements are merely a conjunction of exclamatory and imperatival sentences which cannot admit, due to their very nature, of any truth conditions whatsoever.

There are subjectivists that do not, directly, attach themselves to any particular thesis regarding the meaning of value language. These theorists are more concerned with the metaphysics of value. According to this variety of subjectivism, it is quite possible that value language implies some sort of objectivity. For example, "X is good" may actually refer to some non-natural simple property – "goodness" – that is somehow independent of the observer. Despite this tendency of our value language, the metaphysical theorist could deny that the referent actually exists. Our value language could be based upon an error. Though this language may imply objectivity, there might be nothing that exists in the universe which confers value and also happens to be independent of our desires or attitudes. Since our value language was prior to an appropriate understanding of the metaphysics of value, we should not look to such poorly constructed linguistic conventions to find out the exact nature of our values. The only things, according to these theorists, that can confer such value are the desires or attitudes of the observer. Given our better understanding of values, we may have to reconstruct our language to better reflect our advancements in metaphysics.

Further reading

Ayer, Alfred J. *Language, Truth and Logic*. New York: Dover, 1952.

Hare, Richard M. *Sorting Out Ethics*. Oxford: Clarendon Press, 1997.

MacIntyre, Alasdair. *After Virtue: a Study in Moral Theory.* Notre Dame: University of Notre Dame Press, 1981.

Mackie, John L. *Ethics: Inventing Right and Wrong*. New York: Penguin, 1990.

Stevenson, Charles L. *Ethics and Language.* New Haven: Yale University Press, 1944.

Westermarck, Edward. *Ethical Relativity.* New York: Harcourt, Brace, 1932.

Shane D. Courtland

SUBSTANCE

A philosophical tradition rooted in Aristotle's philosophy distinguishes particular things or *substances*, like persons, animals, plants, tables, chairs, stones, and planets, from their *attributes* or the ways those things are. For example, we distinguish the leaf from its length, color, and shape. The philosophy of substance is concerned with how substances and attributes are to be distinguished, and what the natures of substances are.

It is tempting to characterize substances as whatever have attributes. But the temptation is incompatible with our widespread practice of ascribing attributes to non-substances, like events (e.g. the ceremony was dull) and sometimes even other attributes (e.g. the attribute of *being non-spatial* is, presumably, non-spatial). It is unclear how best to distinguish substances from attributes. Still, substances are generally thought to possess several distinctive features which attributes lack.

One distinctive feature of substances is that they have their attributes in a way that attributes fail to have substances. The leaf has a green color. But the leaf's green color does not in the same sense have the leaf. However, philosophers have found it difficult to characterize precisely this feature of substances.

Another distinctive feature of substances is that they are capable of independent existence whereas attributes are not. A given substance could exist alone without any other substances, and without any (non-essential) particular attributes (though perhaps it must have some or other attributes, even if none are such that it must have those). The leaf is green but could exist even if it were not green, but rather brown. Attributes, however, seem incapable of independent existence. The leaf's green color cannot exist without the leaf.

A third distinctive feature of substances is that they are just those things that can survive through changes. You were once a child, now you're older. The leaf was green, now it's brown. It is unclear in what, if any, analogous sense attributes, like the color red, might undergo change.

However substances and attributes are to be distinguished, we may still ask whether there are many kinds of substances and how many instances there are of each kind. Aristotle believed that substances were hierarchically arranged by how fundamental they were. Others have rejected such a hierarchy. Some philosophers have thought that there are different kinds of substances. For example, Descartes believed that there were both mental and material substances. Others have denied that there is more than one kind of substance. Typically, whatever that one kind of substance is, they have thought that there were many instances of it. But some have even denied this: Spinoza believed that God is the one and only substance, other putative substances merely being modifications of God.

There are four dominant views within the Aristotelian tradition about the nature of substances: Aristotelianism, the Bundle Theory, the Substratum Theory, and nominalism.

According to Aristotelians, substances are unstructured, fundamental entities that have attributes. But they do not have these attributes in virtue of being made up by them. So Aristotelians cannot account for differences between particular substances by appealing to differences in the attributes that make them up. Instead, Aristotelians tend to account for these differences by conceiving of a particular substance as an individual instance of a special sort of attribute: universal kinds. Thus, two identical twins are both essentially human but are distinct particular substances because each is a separate instance of the same universal kind, *Human*. (Leibnizians would say that the two identical twins each have their own unique individual essence, or *haecceity.*) Aristotelians typically take universal kinds to be the categories that carve nature at the joints: *Human* is such a kind, but *Either-Human-or-the-Eiffel-Tower* is not. So they owe an account of what these universal kinds are. Aristotelians face the difficulty of explaining how instances of macro-level universal kinds, like *Human*, can both be unstructured and yet have micro-level material parts, like quarks. Partly in response, Aristotle and other Aristotelians have suggested that a teleological conception of substance is needed.

The remaining three views, while deriving from the Aristotelian tradition, oppose Aristotelians by taking substances to be structured entities. So substances have their attributes by somehow being made up of them.

According to the *Bundle Theory*, substances just are bundled attributes. The leaf just is its collected attributes, like leafness, greenness, and so on. The Bundle Theory appears unable to allow the possibility that there might be two bundles with the same attributes. But, to borrow Max Black's famous example, it is conceivable that nothing but two qualitatively indiscernibly different spheres had existed. Whether this objection refutes the Bundle Theory partly depends upon one's views about attributes. If attributes are taken to be universals, the objection stands. But the objection does not arise if attributes are taken to be particular property-instances or, to use D.C. Williams's influential term, *tropes.* Many Bundle Theorists take substances to be bundles of tropes. Still, it is unclear what makes some attributes compose a bundle and others not. Since bundles necessarily have the attributes that make them up, so too do substances. This makes it hard to see how substances could survive through changes of their attributes and, more generally, how they could contingently have any attributes at all.

According to the *Substratum Theory,* a view held by Locke and rejected by Hume, substances are made up of their attributes together with a *substratum,* a necessarily featureless particular. Substrata are postulated to help avoid problems that beset the Bundle Theory. Substrata account for what makes some attributes compose a substance: they do so by being had by a substratum. A substance has its attributes by being made up of a substratum which has its attributes. Attributes, then, are directly had by substrata and only indirectly by substances. The leaf, on this view, is composed of a substratum which has its attributes, like leafness, greenness, and so on. The leaf survives through changes of its attributes in virtue of its substratum having different attributes at different times. Furthermore, it is possible, on this view, for there to be two qualitatively identical substances since their respective substrata are distinct. Some have objected that we lack epistemic access to substrata since they are necessarily featureless. And it may be that the notion of substrata is incoherent. For if substrata are necessarily featureless, then they would lack the feature of being necessarily self-identical, a feature that everything must have.

Some philosophers, whom we may call *nominalists* (though the term has other uses), believe that there are only substances, no attributes. So substances are in no way made up of their attributes, nor are they merely an individual instance of some universal kind. This view has trouble accounting for the identities of and diversities between substances, manifest changes in them, and the contingency of their having the attributes they do. However, nominalists would likely reject the demands for giving such accounts.

Yet other philosophers have rejected the Aristotelian tradition's focus upon substances and attributes. D.M. Armstrong has argued that states of affairs exist and are ontologically prior to their constituent substances and attributes. Others have stressed the fundamentality of change, processes, and events. Donald Davidson has argued that events, in addition to substances and attributes, are among the fundamental constituents of reality. A more thoroughgoing focus on change, processes, and events is evident in process philosophy, most famously defended by Alfred North Whitehead, but also by American pragmatists such as C.S. Peirce, John Dewey, and William James. Whereas the Aristotelian tradition tends to explain change, processes, and events in terms of substances gaining or losing attributes, process philosophy reverses the order of explanation and conceives of change, processes, or events as being *bona fide* building blocks of reality from which substances and attributes are somehow abstracted.

Further reading

Aristotle. *Categories and De Interpretatione*, trans. J. Ackrill. Oxford: Clarendon Press, 1963.

Armstrong, D.M. *A World of States of Affairs.* Cambridge: Cambridge University Press, 1997.

Browning, Douglas and Myers, William T. (eds). *Philosophers of Process*, second edition. New York: Fordham University Press, 1998.

Descartes, Rene. *Meditations on First Philosophy*, trans. J. Cottingham. Cambridge: Cambridge University Press, 1996.

Davidson, Donald. *Essays on Actions and Events.* Oxford: Oxford University Press, 2001.

Hume, David. *A Treatise of Human Nature*, ed. P.H. Nidditch. Oxford: Clarendon Press, 1978.

Leibniz, Gottfried Wilhelm. *Philosophical Texts*, trans. and ed. R.S. Woolhouse and R. Francks. Oxford: Oxford University Press, 1998.

Locke, John. *An Essay Concerning Human Understanding*, ed. Peter H. Nidditch. Oxford: Clarendon Press: Oxford, 1975.

Loux, Michael J. *Substance and Attribute: A Study in Ontology.* Dordrecht: D. Reidel, 1978.

Spinoza, Baruch. *Ethics*, trans. Samuel Shirley. Indianapolis, IN: Hackett, 1992.

Wiggins, David. *Sameness and Substance Renewed.* Cambridge: Cambridge University Press, 2001.

MICHAEL J. RAVEN

SUMNER, WILLIAM GRAHAM

Best known as the leading advocate of "Social Darwinism" in America, William Graham Sumner (1840–1910) was born in New Jersey, graduated from Yale University in 1863, and became an ordained Episcopalian minister. Beginning in 1872, he was professor of political and social science at Yale for nearly forty years. The American counterpart of the British philosopher Herbert Spencer, Sumner embraced Spencer's view that evolution is a universal movement from simple elements to forms of increasing complexity and specialization. As the culmination of such "laws of life," humans have evolved toward self-sufficiency based on rational self-interest, and in a world of limited resources excellence in self-sufficiency epitomizes the "survival of the fittest." For Sumner, whatever inhibits unbridled personal liberty and laissez-faire commerce is both unnatural and immoral, and he equally opposed progressive efforts toward an expanded welfare state and conservative endorsements of military adventurism. Sumner's current admirers deemphasize his Social Darwinism in favor of his anticipation of contemporary libertarianism.

Further reading

Bannister, Robert C. (ed.). *On Liberty, Society, and Politics: The Essential Essays of William Graham Sumner*. Indianapolis, IN: Liberty Fund, 1992.

Davie, Maurice R. *William Graham Sumner*. New York: Crowell, 1963.

Hofstadter, Richard. *Social Darwinism in American Thought: 1860–1915*. Philadelphia, PA: University of Pennsylvania Press, 1945.

Sumner, William G. *Folkways: A Study of the Sociological Importance of Usages, Manners, Customs, Mores, and Morals*. Boston, MA: Ginn, 1906.

Sumner, William G. and Keller, Albert G. *The Science of Society*, 4 vols. New Haven, CT: Yale University Press, 1927.

FRANK X. RYAN

SYNECHISM

Synechism (from the Greek *synechismos*, derived from *synecho*, "to hold or keep together, to continue, to preserve"; EP 2.503, n. 1), the doctrine of *continuity*, is – along with tychism and agapasm – a central thesis of Charles S. Peirce's (1859–1914) speculative metaphysics and evolutionary cosmology. Associated with Peirce's category of Thirdness, synechism is the view that everything is continuous with everything else; there are no atomistic elements of reality fundamentally discontinuous from each other. According to synechism, both being as such and specific modes of being, e.g. mentality and spontaneity, are matters of degree, not something sharply separable from their opposites. Nor is there any ontological gap between reality or being, on the one hand, and appearances or phenomena, on the other (1892: EP 2.2).

Peirce describes synechism as "the tendency to regard everything as continuous," in a way that includes "the whole domain of experience in every element of it" (1893: EP 2.1). He defines it as "that tendency of philosophical thought which insists upon the idea of continuity as of prime importance in philosophy and, in particular, upon the necessity of hypotheses involving true continuity" (1902: CP 6.169; cf. 1892: EP 1.313). Synechism is, thus, both a metaphysical and methodological doctrine. One of the seminal writings in which synechism is introduced and defended is Peirce's 1892 article, "The Law of Mind" (EP 1.312–33), which argues for the "law" that ideas tend to spread continuously, affecting each other, and that they lose intensity but gain generality in this process.

Peirce thought that his logical realism, objective idealism, and tychism follow from synechism, and discussed continuity not only metaphysically but also from the perspective of mathematics. He believed that a successful proof of his pragmati(ci)sm would establish the truth of synechism (1905: EP 2.335), since continuity is essentially involved in pragmati(ci)sm. He also saw a crucial link between synechism and his scholastic realism about "generals" (1902: CP 6.172–3). Like pragmatism, synechism was, for Peirce, "a purely scientific philosophy," although he noted that it may support the reconciliation of science and religion (EP 2.3).

In his 1893 paper, "Immortality in the Light of Synechism" (EP 2.1–3), Peirce explains that the synechist must deny the Parmenidean distinction between being, which is, and not-being, which is nothing, arguing that being is "a matter of more or less, so as to merge insensibly into nothing" (EP 2.2). Thus, synechism rejects dualisms of all kinds, including the traditional dualism of the physical and the mental (psychical) as "unrelated chunks of being." Instead of being distinct categories, the physical and the psychical are "of one character," though there are differences in degree between things that are more mental and spontaneity-involving and things that are more material. Similarly, synechism rejects sharp discontinuities between the living and the non-living, offering a ground for a qualified defense of immortality, as well as discontinuities between oneself and the others: "your neighbors are, in a measure, yourself." (EP 2.2–3). Accordingly, synechism may be seen as a metaphysical basis of panpsychism, as well as of the ethical capacity for empathy.

Recent defenders of synechism and related doctrines of continuity in American philosophy include, among others, Sandra Rosenthal, whose works draw not only from Peirce but also from the other classical pragmatists. Synechism is a concept usually employed only in Peirce scholarship, however.

Further reading

Hausman, Carl R. "Evolutionary Realism and Charles Peirce's Pragmatism" in Sandra B. Rosenthal, Carl R. Hausman, and Douglas R. Anderson (eds) *Classical American Pragmatism: Its Contemporary Vitality.* Urbana, IL: University of Illinois Press, 1999.

Hookway, Christopher. *Peirce.* London: Routledge, 1985.

Parker, Kelly A. *The Continuity of Peirce's Thought.* Nashville, TN: Vanderbilt University Press, 1998.

Peirce, Charles S. *The Collected Papers of Charles Sanders Peirce*, 8 vols, ed. Charles Hartshorne and Paul Weiss (Vols 1–6), Arthur W. Burks (Vols 7–8). Cambridge, MA: Harvard University Press, 1931–58. (Cited as CP volume.paragraph.)

—— *The Writings of Charles S. Peirce*, 6 vols to date, ed. the Peirce Edition Project. Bloomington, IN: Indiana University Press, 1980–2000.

—— *The Essential Peirce: Selected Philosophical Writings*, 2 vols, ed. the Peirce Edition Project. Bloomington, IN: Indiana University Press, 1992–98. (Cited as EP volume.page.)

Reynolds, Andrew. *Peirce's Scientific Metaphysics: The Philosophy of Chance, Law, and Evolution.* Nashville, TN: Vanderbilt University Press, 2002.

Rosenthal, Sandra B. *Speculative Pragmatism.* Amherst, MA: University of Massachusetts Press, 1986.

SAMI PIHLSTRÖM

SYNTACTICS

Syntactics, semantics, and pragmatics are the three levels of investigation into semiotics, or the comprehensive study of systems of communication, as described in 1938 by the American philosopher Charles Morris (1903–79). Syntactics studies signs themselves and their interrelations in abstraction from their meanings and from their uses and users. Semantics studies signs in relation to their meanings, but still in abstraction from their uses and users. Pragmatics studies signs as meaningful entities used in various ways by humans. Taking current written English as the system of communication under investigation, it is a matter of syntactics that the two four-character strings "tact" and "tics" both occur in the ten-character string "syntactics." It is a matter of semantics that the ten-character string "syntactics" has only one sense and, in that sense, it denotes a branch of semiotics. It is a matter of pragmatics that the ten-character string "syntactics" was not used as an English word before 1937 and that it is sometimes confused with the much older six-character string "syntax." Syntactics is the simplest and most abstract branch of semiotics. At the same time, it is the most basic. Pragmatics presupposes semantics and syntactics; semantics presupposes syntactics.

The basic terms of syntactics include the following: "character" as alphabetic letters, numeric digits, and punctuation marks; "string" as sign composed of a concatenation of characters; "occur" as "t" and "c" both occur twice in "syntactics." However, perhaps the most basic terms of syntactics are "type" and "token" in the senses introduced by Charles Sanders Peirce (1839–1914), America's greatest logician, who could be considered the grandfather of syntactics, if not the father. These are explained below. The basic terms of semantics include "sense," "denotation," and "ambiguous." The strings "zero," "one minus one," and "three minus zero minus three" have different senses but the same denotation. An ambiguous string has more than one sense. For example, the string "three minus two minus one" has two senses; in one sense it has the same denotation as "three minus one," or "two," and in one sense it has the same denotation as "one minus one," or "zero." The basic terms of pragmatics include the following: "inscribe," "assert," "report," "ask," "promise," "describe," "repeat" and "imply."

Peirce's type–token distinction dates from the first few years of the 1900s. Although he made the distinction earlier, his use of the words "type" and "token" to express it dates from the 1906 *Monist* article on pragmaticism, quoted in Ogden and Richards (1923: Appendix D, section 6, esp. 280–1) and reprinted in Volume IV of *Collected Papers* (Paragraph 537). The following is from Peirce's 1906 *Monist* article (1906: 504–5).

> A common mode of estimating the amount of matter in a ... printed book is to count the number of words. There will ordinarily be about twenty "thes" on a page, and, of course, they count as twenty words. In another sense of the word "word," however, there is but one word "the" in the English language; and it is impossible that this word should lie visibly on a page, or be heard in any voice ... Such a ... Form, I propose to term a *Type*. A Single ... Object ... such as this or that word on a single line of a single page of a single copy of a book, I will venture to call a *Token* ... In order that a Type may be used, it has to be embodied in a Token, which shall be a sign of the Type, and thereby of the object the Type signifies. I propose to call such a Token of a Type an Instance of the Type. Thus, there may be twenty Instances of the Type "the" on a page.

I do not know whether Peirce ever supplemented his type–token distinction with the concept of "occurrence" as needed to make the point that, although the type "the" has only one occurrence of the type "e," the type "e" occurs twice in the type "thee" and it is instantiated, betokened, or embodied (to use Peirce's term) twice in every token of the type "thee." In order for two string occurrences in the same or different string-types to be occurrences of one and the same string-type, it is necessary and sufficient for them to be "character-by-character identical," i.e. for them to have the same length, say *L*, and for the *n*th character occurrence in one to be an occurrence of the same character-type that the *n*th character occurrence in the other is an occurrence of, for *n* between 1 and *L*.

Aside perhaps from Peirce, the most important figure in the history of syntactics was the Polish-American logician Alfred Tarski (1901–83). Tarski needed an axiomatic syntactics for his axiomatic semantics. More specifically, he needed an axiomatic theory of syntactics as a foundation for an axiomatic treatment of his 1933 semantic theory of truth. One of Tarski's theorems is that the operation of concatenation of strings is associative: given any three strings *x*, *y*, *z*, concatenating x with the result of concatenating *y* with *z* is the same as the result of concatenating *x* with *y* and then concatenating the result with *z*. For example, concatenating "syn" with "tactics" is the same as concatenating "syntac" with "tics." The mathematical theory of syntactics is called string theory. The history and philosophy of this important subject is dealt with in the article "String Theory" by J. Corcoran, W. Frank, and M. Maloney in the 1974 *Journal of Symbolic Logic*.

Further reading

Corcoran, J., Frank, W. and Maloney, M. "String Theory," *Journal of Symbolic Logic* 39 (1974): 625–37.

Morris, C. *Foundations of the Theory of Signs*. Chicago, IL: University of Chicago Press, 1938.

Ogden, C.K. and Richards, I.A. *The Meaning of Meaning*, reprint of eighth edition. Harcourt: New York, 1923.

Peirce, C.S. *Collected Papers of Charles Sanders Peirce*, ed. C. Hartshorne and P. Weiss. Cambridge: Harvard University Press, 1933.

Tarski, A. *Logic, Semantics, Metamathematics, papers from 1923 to 1938*, second edition, ed with introduction and analytic index by J. Corcoran. Indianapolis, IN: Hackett, 1983.

JOHN CORCORAN

SYNTHESIS

A synthesis is literally a bringing together of separate items into a unified whole. Synthesis is the counterpart of analysis, in which a whole is decomposed into its component parts. The distinction between analysis and synthesis as categories for philosophical methods goes back at least to the time of G.W. Leibniz and David Hume. Immanuel Kant in the late eighteenth century more prominently thematized the categories in the two editions of his *Critique of Pure Reason* (1781, 1787).

Adapting the terminology for the distinction from the difference between analytic and synthetic chemistry, Kant and much of the philosophical tradition thereafter further divided analytic from synthetic propositions. Analytic propositions are true (or false) by virtue of their predicate concepts being included in (or excluded from) their subject concepts. By analyzing or breaking down the component meanings of the subject concept it should then be possible in principle to discover the predicate concept already contained within (or excluded from) it, just as one might find two atoms of hydrogen contained within a single molecule of water. A classic example is the proposition that all bachelors are unmarried male adults, where the concept of being unmarried is already "analytically" contained within the concept of being a bachelor. Synthetic propositions in contrast are propositions that bring together a subject term with a predicate term representing a concept that is not contained analytically within the subject concept. An example is the (true or false) proposition that all bachelors in New York City are stockbrokers, where the predicate concept of being a stockbroker is not analytically contained within the concept of being a bachelor in New York City, but must rather be brought together with that concept as something external to it, so that the two can be joined into a single assertion of fact.

While there has been a major movement of analytic philosophy from the late nineteenth century to the present day, and some thinkers have promoted the terminology of philosophical synthesis, there has been no comparable intellectual trend identifying itself explicitly as synthetic philosophy. This is an unfortunate omission from the philosophical topography because much of contemporary philosophy at its best is synthetic in the sense defined. It would be valuable as a result for philosophers to become self-conscious of the synthesis or bringing together of disparate ideas into a unified whole as a way of progressing in philosophy. Synthetic philosophy, involving a deliberate joining together of compatible complementary concepts and methods, would need to become aware of its methods and develop criteria and parameters for correct or successful syntheses, at the same time that it produces fruitful new combinations of ideas like the products of synthetic chemistry.

Synthesis, self-conscious or otherwise, is widely practiced in American philosophy. Its roots go back to the post-Kantian German philosopher G.W.F. Hegel, who in turn was influential in shaping John Dewey's early thought, through the work especially of George Sylvester Morris, William

Torrey Harris, and Henry Conrad Brokmeyer. For Hegel, in his monumental *Phenomenology of Spirit* (1807), and *The Science of Logic* (1812; 1813; 1816), as well as his *Encyclopedia of the Philosophical Sciences* (1817), the dialectical unfolding of world Spirit in many different manifestations takes the form of a three-part movement of thesis, antithesis, and synthesis. Thesis comes first, antithesis then arises to oppose the thesis, and the synthesis of thesis and antithesis resolves their differences by producing something new and usually unexpected, metaphorically speaking, from the energy and tension in their opposition and the need to seek at least a momentarily stable resolution. Hegel in this way is said in his philosophy to have synthesized subject and object, matter and spirit, the human and the divine, and numerous other opposites.

Again, the American aesthetic and metaphysical thinker George Santayana develops the idea of synthesis within his own amalgam of European post-Kantian and American pragmatic and Peircean pragmaticist thought. Santayana in his four-volume work, *Realms of Being* (1927–40), regards "intuition" as key to his epistemology and ontology, in maintaining that intuition is the direct and obvious possession of the "apparent," which, he says, is always with us but "dispersed." Intuition for Santayana is accordingly a passive synthesis that presents what is successive in a detemporalized way as though its episodes were coexistent. Consciousness for Santayana thereby brings together these dispersed ingredients of the apparent in an "appropriation of essences" outside of immediate consciousness. Santayana and Josiah Royce adapt this part of the synthetic vision to differentiate a divine eternal perspective from one that is properly temporal. Santayana thereby lays the foundation for his unique metaphysics of a "realm of essence," and Royce in another way grounds an idealistic concept of God as cosmic purpose.

In recent American philosophy, in the school that has come to be known as positivistic pragmatism, W.V.O. Quine in his landmark essay, "Two Dogmas of Empiricism" mounts a celebrated attack against the analytic/synthetic distinction. The analytic/synthetic division has been held in suspicion ever since, although not all critics accept Quine's efforts to undermine the distinction. The motivation for bringing together disparate strands of philosophical thinking into a neo-pragmatic union that takes advantage of certain philosophical positions while avoiding their disadvantages remains a powerful force in contemporary philosophy.

Further reading

Dewey, John. *The Early Works, 1882–1898*, ed. J. A. Boydston. Carbondale, IL: Southern Illinois University Press, 1967.

Hahn, Lewis Edwin and Schilpp, Paul A. (eds). *The Philosophy of W. V. Quine*. Chicago, IL: Open Court, 1998.

Hegel, G.W.F. *Phenomenology of Spirit*, trans. A.V. Miller. Oxford: Oxford University Press, 1977.

Kant, Immanuel. *Prolegomena to Any Future Metaphysics That Can Come Forth as Science*, trans. L.W. Beck. Indianapolis, IN: Bobbs-Merrill, 1950.

Ortega y Gasset, José. "Hegel y América," *El Espectador* 7 (1929). Reprinted *El Espectador: Tomos VII y VIII* (El Arquero). Madrid: Revista de Occidente, 1961, pp. 3–24.

Royce, Josiah. *Lectures on Modern Idealism*, ed. J. Loewenberg. New Haven, CT: Yale University Press, 1919.

Santayana, George. *Realms of Being*, one-volume edition, with a new introduction by the author. New York: Charles Scribner's Sons, 1942. (*The Realm of Essence: Book First* (1927); *The Realm of Matter: Book Second* (1930); *The Realm of Truth: Book Third* (1937); *The Realm of Spirit: Book Fourth* (1940).)

Nelson, Lynn Hankinson and Nelson, Jack. *On Quine*. Belmont, CA: Wadsworth, 2000.

Quine, W.V.O. "Two Dogmas of Empiricism," *Philosophical Review* 60 (1951): 20–43. Reprinted in W.V.O. Quine, *From a Logical Point of View*. Cambridge, MA: Harvard University Press, 1953; second edition, revised 1961.

Dale Jacquette

T

TASTE

Taste has been an important concept in esthetics since at least the eighteenth century, and it continues to play a vital role in debate over esthetic subject matter, among both specialists and non-specialists. The very distinction between popular culture and intellectual culture is still often cast in terms of "lowbrow" versus "highbrow" tastes. On the traditional view, mass culture is characterized by the uninformed and lowest-common-denominator nature of the tastes associated with it. The tastes of the elites, on the other hand, are supposed to stand out due to the sophistication and discernment they reflect. Recent social and cultural trends have tended to somewhat confound the lowbrow–highbrow divide. The steady increase in the average level of educational attainment, for example, has meant that an ever-growing portion of the population has been exposed to high culture. In addition, many contemporary artists and authors borrow in a highly eclectic fashion from both canonical culture and popular forms of entertainment, creating works that defy easy classification. Nevertheless, the notion of taste continues to be introduced into debates about art and entertainment in order to legitimate judgments on the relative esthetic worth of artifacts and even entire genres. Is haute cuisine superior to fast food, and classical music to hard rock? To justify their responses to such questions interlocutors will often reference the idea of taste, albeit with strategies that may be radically opposed depending upon the answer given.

One common approach is to appeal to the idea of taste as a way of demonstrating the thoroughly subjective nature of esthetic preferences. Conventional wisdom has given us sayings such as "There's no accounting for taste," "To each his own," and "Beauty is in the eye of the beholder" – all of which seem to imply the relativity of taste. A popular line of reasoning asserts that since taste is radically subjective, there is no sense in which one person's taste could be better than another's. On this view, the drinking preferences of the wino and the wine connoisseur are on a par. The contradictory tack is to maintain that the very existence of recognized experts in such areas as the evaluation of wine provides evidence for the existence of good taste. According to this school of thought, although the professional critic is not necessarily infallible, his or her assessments are generally more accurate and insightful than those of the novice.

Debate between these two camps is frequently impaired by the ambiguity of the term "taste." One meaning often assigned to "taste" is that of a personal inclination that appears to be arbitrary in nature and whose origins are usually obscure (e.g. one's favorite color or food). Another meaning frequently associated with the term is that of discerning judgment in esthetic matters. When these two meanings are not clearly identified and distinguished from one another, equivocation can result. The fact that some tastes are merely personal preferences does not, of course, imply that *all* tastes have this status. As a matter of fact, we expect the professional critic to strive for impartiality and balance in rendering his or her official verdicts. The judgments of the critic are supposed to constitute useful advice for the lay public, and so they need to be shorn of the influence of purely personal factors. The movie critic who likes a particular film primarily because she happens to be infatuated with the starring actor is obviously biased, and at risk for misjudging the public value of the work. In order to fulfill her office, the critic must be aware of any idiosyncrasies that could unduly influence her judgment. Obviously, no such expectation of dispassion is present when we inquire about someone's taste in the sense of merely personal preference.

Another major source of misunderstanding about taste stems from a failure to recognize the interpersonal nature of good taste, and to situate its verdicts in the social situation in which they arise. Esthetic judgments are often treated as isolated propositions that can be adequately assessed without reference to any particular context, and whose application is universal. This contextless approach to the analysis of taste has frequently left theorists in a quandary when it comes to grounding esthetic judgments. Thinkers have either opted to squeeze taste into a faculty of mind, and so make it a wholly mental attribute of individuals, or have emphasized the objective qualities of its objects. Both approaches assume an underfunded notion of experience that leaves out the intersubjective aspect of the situations in which judgments of taste are rendered. The very idea of good taste presupposes a social context of shared meanings, since to recognize someone's judgment as "good" is to acknowledge a prima facie claim to our allegiance. Judgments of taste derive their meaning from an existential situation that constitutes a corporate *Lebenswelt* or life world, one that always exceeds the limits of the universe of discourse at hand to include non-symbolic elements of experience. After all, by definition all esthetic subject matter involves some appealing aspect of sense experience.

The life world in which good taste emerges presupposes a number of common elements in the experience of the participants (e.g. the community of film critics). The most important of these communal factors include previous acquaintance with the field in question, and common aims. Expert assessment requires familiarity with the "lay of the land," that is, a general knowledge of what has hitherto been achieved within a given domain. What counts as "good" within a particular area partially depends upon what has already been accomplished. For instance, the standard for what constitutes high-quality special effects has been continuously raised since the advent of film due to rapid technological development.

Perhaps the single greatest source of confusion about taste is the failure to recognize that apparently contradictory estimations of worth often implicitly presuppose the pursuit of different ends. Although popular culture is repeatedly chastised for failing to be genuinely artistic, the aim of those who produce it is not, generally speaking, to create works that require critical acumen in order to be appreciated. Entertainment and diversion reign supreme in the world of pop, and their associated values are convenience, immediacy, and relaxation. One can certainly decry the culture of mass entertainment, but it's only fair to recognize that its artifacts are often crafted with few artistic pretensions. If it be admitted that the value of a particular activity partially depends upon one's general aim, then fast food could at least occasionally qualify as a convenient, inexpensive, and tasty dining option, and a Hollywood thriller as a welcome form of escape from the daily grind. Furthermore, the fact that different forms and genres of art sometimes pursue different esthetic goals implies that passing comparative judgments about them is problematic, due to the incommensurable nature of what is being compared. Does it really make sense, for example, to rank classical music as superior to rock and roll, given the different characters of the musical experiences respectively achieved within the two genres? For instance, while most classical music was composed for a public of highly attentive listeners, much rock music is intended – as its name suggests – for an audience that is not only listening but also dancing. The characteristic driving, heavily accented beat of rock, which has not infrequently been denounced by critics as simplistic and primitive, makes it particularly well suited as a popular form of dance music.

Dewey on taste

Arguably the most important writer on esthetics in American philosophy was John Dewey, whose *Art as Experience* is now widely recognized as one of the classics in the field. Although the notion of taste does not play a major role in his philosophy of art, Dewey did comment briefly on taste in his *Quest for Certainty*, where he assimilates the idea into his theory of judgment. There he argues that taste comes into play in the appreciation and criticism of values, and thus represents the individual's acquired capacity for good judgment in matters that require valuation. Perhaps the most novel feature of Dewey's view is that it extends taste beyond its traditional purview of the esthetic to include all manner of values, including moral ones. Traditionally, of course, good taste was held to be distinct from moral conscience, but Dewey argues that such psychological compartmentalization was based on reifying socially established divisions and categories into mental faculties. One could add that our esthetic choices rarely affect others as significantly as do our ethical ones, and so historically society has treated esthetic dissent with less compulsion and more indulgence than it has discord in morals. Nevertheless, as concerns the process of reflection and judgment, Dewey holds that all decisions involving values are guided by our previous value commitments, which, in the case of the individual with good judgment in a particular domain, themselves often represent the outcome of careful deliberation. Because the individual confronting a moral dilemma must draw upon his or her experience in order to make an intelligent choice, conscience is just another name for good taste in morals.

Although the idea of taste only receives what amounts to an aside in Dewey's work, his philosophy prepares the way for a new understanding of taste in at least two respects. By formulating an alternative to the faculty psychology, he creates a new basis for integrating taste with deliberation and judgment. In addition, his metaphysics of experience brings out the fact that taste is not purely mental, but rather a process or phenomenon that occurs in the interaction of the individual with his or her physical and social environment.

Further reading

Adorno, Theodor and Horkheimer, Max. *Dialectic of Enlightenment*. New York: Herder and Herder, 1972.

Dewey, John. *Art as Experience*. New York: Minton, Balch, 1934.

Hume, David. "Of the Standard of Taste.," http://www.csulb.edu/~jvancamp/361r15.html

Kant, Immanuel. *Critique of Judgment*. Indianapolis, IN: Hackett, 1987.

JEFF MITCHELL

TECHNOLOGY

Philosophical discussions of tools, techniques, and technology have for the most part been dominated by European and American philosophers working in traditions such as phenomenology, existentialism, and Marxism. An earlier generation of Europeans stressed themes such as the alienating effects of tools, techniques, and systems; the alleged autonomy of technology as a reified system or world-epoch; and ends-dominated instrumental rationality *simpliciter*. For a new generation of Europeans and Americans working in these traditions, however, the prospect is more positive. Turning away from older transcendentalist models, there has been a decline of interest in the metaphysical aspects of technology and an increase of interest in phenomenological analyses of what tools and techniques do and how they function within human life.

This move was anticipated as early as the 1890s by some of the founders of American Pragmatism. Among the factors that may have contributed to this situation was the fact that tools and techniques brought from Europe to the New World by immigrants had to be adjusted to the novel circumstances of the frontier. Pragmatists emphasized active experimentation rather than metaphysical contemplation and opted for ameliorative reconstruction that employed phenomenological analysis not as an end in itself, but as an instrument for further production.

Pragmatists Charles S. Peirce, William James, and John Dewey were all at some time during their careers engaged in experimental science. Peirce was a career scientist for the US Coast and Geodetic Survey. James had a medical degree and operated an experimental laboratory at Harvard University. Dewey, who undertook experiments in perception with colleagues at the University of Chicago, was elected president of the American Psychological Association in 1898.

European critics of technology have tended to employ the term "instrumentalism" in a pejorative sense, meaning a type of thinking and action in which ends dominate means. In the versions of Pragmatism advanced by James and Dewey, however, "instrumentalism" takes on richer and more positive meanings. James emphasized the instrumental value of theories as tools for reconstructing experience and treated inquiry as a tool for "remodeling" nature. Josiah Royce wrote of true ideas as effective tools.

These themes received their fullest development in the work of Dewey. Applying the term "instrumentalism" to his own position, he argued that ideas and ideals are tools that must be tested by means of rigorous experimentation. In properly controlled inquiry ends do not dominate means: ends and means inform one another as a part of the process of intelligent production of new tools and artifacts that Dewey termed "technology."

Despite the fact that Dewey employed the term "instrumentalism" as early as 1905, his contribution to the philosophy of technology was not generally recognized until the last decade of the twentieth century. This tardy recognition may be due in part to the fact that his analysis of technology was scattered across books and essays published over more than four decades. During the formative period of philosophy of technology as a disciplinary field, moreover, Dewey's influence was temporarily eclipsed by newer philosophical and psychological movements.

Dewey distinguished technology, which he treated as an intelligent activity, from tools and techniques, which require the direction of technology. Technology is thus not a thing, a system, or a world-epoch, but instead inquiry into the nature and function of tools and techniques in the same sense in which biology is inquiry into the nature and function of life forms. Technology is neither autonomous nor reducible to what is mechanically utilitarian. Dewey characterized technology in terms that were functional rather than ontological. Technology is a way of bringing tools of all sorts – conceptual as well as tangible – to bear on raw materials – also conceptual as well as tangible – with a view to the resolution of perceived problems. Technology is not ubiquitous. Noncognitive aesthetic enjoyments, for example, lie outside the realm of technology.

Dewey's treatment of technology is deeply embedded within his wider philosophy. In his social and political philosophy he treated publics as technological artifacts; in his logic and ethics he treated abstract logical entities and moral precepts likewise – as constructed out of raw materials of prior experience in order to serve as tools for the construction of new meanings. Dewey thus avoided the charge of harboring an irreconcilable split between facts and values that has plagued some versions of Critical Theory. He also avoided two extreme views that have been a part of the literature of the philosophy of technology: (a) that the sciences are objective in the sense of "value free" and (b) that objectivity can be reduced to intersubjectivity with no remainder.

Further reading

Dewey, John. *Experience and Nature, The Collected Works of John Dewey: The Later Works, 1925–1953, Vol. 1*, ed. Jo Ann Boydston. Carbondale, IL: Southern Illinois University Press, 1981.

—— "Introduction to *Essays in Experimental Logic*," *The Collected Works of John Dewey: The Middle Works, 1899–1924, Vol. 10*, ed. Jo Ann Boydston. Carbondale, IL: Southern Illinois University Press, 1980.

Hickman, Larry A. *John Dewey's Pragmatic Technology*. Bloomington, IN: Indiana University Press, 1990.

LARRY A. HICKMAN

TEJERA, VICTORINO

Born in Caracas, Venezuela, on 2 November 1922, Victorino Tejera was educated in New York City: at Columbia College (BA in philosophy with honors) and at Columbia University where he earned his PhD in philosophy under the mentorship of Irwin Edman, J.H. Randall, Jr, and Justus Buchler. He taught at Fairleigh Dickinson University and Howard University before arriving at Stony Brook University (SUNY) in the late 1960s. He taught at Stony Brook for some thirty years where he was an important member of the doctoral program in philosophy created in the early 1970s. The program featured training in different styles of philosophy, and Tejera was a mainstay (under the leadership of Justus Buchler) of the systematic wing (style) that emphasized the history of systematic metaphysics, particularly the contributions of American philosophy. Further, Tejera was a consistent advocate for pluralism in philosophical research and teaching, and contributed regularly to the interdisciplinary focus of the PhD program.

Tejera's voluminous writings marked significant contributions in the areas of ancient Greek philosophy, aesthetics, history of philosophy, semiotics and American philosophy. In American he concentrated on such central figures as C.S. Peirce, Santayana, Randall and Buchler, publishing his findings in leading journals like *The Transactions of the C.S. Peirce Society*. His major preoccupation – to make aesthetics and concern with art central to all philosophical work – was a reflection of his lifelong love of art and was strongly influenced philosophically by his studies of Santayana, Dewey and Buchler. His early work in the history of American philosophy was extended later in his career to the fields of semiotics and communication theory. Here he made important studies of Peirce. His major books include: *American Modern: The Path Not Taken*; *Art and Human Intelligence*; *Literature, Criticism and the Theory of Signs*; and *Semiotics: From Peirce to Barthes*.

Further reading

Tejera, Victorino. *Literature, Criticism and the Theory of Signs*. Amsterdam: John Benjamins, 1995.

—— *American Modern: The Path Not Taken: Aesthetics, Metaphysics and Intellectual History in Classical American Philosophy*. Lanham, MD: Rowman and Littlefield, 1996.

—— Semiotics: From Peirce to Barthes: A Conceptual Introduction to the Study of *Communication, Interpretation and Expression*. Leiden, Boston, MA and Tokyo: Brill, 1997.

Tejera, Victorino and Hart, R.E. (eds) *Plato's Dialogues: The Dialogical Approach*. Lewiston, New York: Edwin Mellen Press, 1997.

RICHARD E. HART

TELEOLOGY

The relationship of American philosophy to the theory of teleology can as a first approximation be factored into the empiricist and psychological approach of William James, the logical and rationalist approach of Charles Peirce, the contextual and inquiry-driven approach of John Dewey, and the Platonic trope-driven naturalism of George Santayana.

William James remarked in his essay "A World of Pure Experience" that the empiricism of his time "flirts with teleology." Although the character of this flirtation shifts from figure to figure, for James and many other nineteenth-century philosophers it drew on a distinction between science and metaphysics. A mechanical and predictive point of view was appropriate to the natural sciences, but meaning and purpose became important from the broader point of view of metaphysics. In *The Principles of Psychology* he defines the subject matter of the new natural science as "[t]he Pursuance of future ends and the choice of means for their attainment," recommending this as "the mark and criterion of the presence of mentality in a phenomenon." But this is a modest teleology. It is limited to individual minds, which are assumed as postulates of scientific psychology rather than heralded as first facts about the nature of things; a "positivistic" approach is required at this empirical level, justifying the attribution of mentality by its predictive value, not its correspondence with ultimate facts. Even so, the deeper metaphysical perspective beckons. We can complete science by finding the universe ("the Kosmos," as he says) to be a realm of final purposes, or we can see in it so much mere "mechanical sprouting" from the past. James opted for the former.

James's fellow pragmatist and friend Charles Peirce also projected human purpose onto patterns in nature, but his nature was not James's neither-mental-nor-physical "pure experience" but rather a process that begins with mind and ends with matter ("effete mind"). He theorized this process through Kant and Hegel; a reduced Kantian table of three categories: "Chance is First, Law is Second, Evolution is Third;" and a process of overcoming dualities that makes the world more reasonable (the "Growth of Reasonableness," as Peirce phrased it), a neo-Lamarkian process in which things can be attracted to each other not just by chance but also through their habits and strivings (agape, or love). The beginning of the universe was a chance assemblage of chaotic feeling without personality, Firstness. This mind-stuff gradually becomes more regular through lawlike habit forming, Secondness. Eventually evolution – not mechanical Darwinian evolution, as Peirce understood it, but a process that will be marked by chance and agape – will produce an interconnected universal mind, Thirdness, in which mind will predominantly have organized itself into various forms of matter. Peirce does not apologize for the anthropomorphism of his approach, holding that every scientific explanation is a hypothesis that there is something in nature to which human reason is analogous.

One of the more visionary aspects of Peirce's teleology is his anticipation of systems theory and its study of their functional states, such as equilibria. Final causation must be understood as that mode of bringing facts about according to which a general description of result is made to come about, quite irrespective of any compulsion for it to come about in this or that particular way. Peirce's agape gets a grip on such systems, which express "attractions" that may result in an equilibrium, or instead to the "strange attractors" in chaos theory, chance-like motions of great complexity that seem to at least approximate to Peircian Firstness.

In contrast to both James's world of pure experience and Peirce's mind-like nature is John Dewey's concern that knowledge is always relative to a particular purpose, and that the intelligence of those who pursue a given purpose achieves a local unification, or little "organic unity" in a world that is otherwise untamed. Knowing always has a particular purpose, as he writes in *Essays in Experimental Logic*, to accomplish a task or overcome a difficulty, resulting in a "magnification of the work of intelligence" in the world. Dewey's contextual teleology is a myriad of purposes that aim at control of the environment, the effort at control being stimulated by "the needs, the defects, the troubles" that arise in humanity's relationship to the environment.

Dewey takes this point all the way down to the stimuli and responses that figure in the so-called "reflex arc" of human psychology, which he understands in teleological terms. As he writes in the famous 1896 essay "The Reflex Arc Concept in Psychology," stimulus and response are distinction of function with reference to reaching or maintaining an end. For this reason he prefers the term "organic circuit" to the more traditional "reflex arc," with its mechanical and atomistic connotations. Stimulus and response are always inside a "co-ordination," having their significance purely from the part played in maintaining or reconstituting the co-ordination.

Furthermore the data of inquiry are neither pure-experiential nor mind-like, but rather, as the immediate considerations from which controlled inference proceeds, they are means or instrumentalities of knowledge – things by which we know rather than things known. The reference to *we* rather than *I* is important for understanding Dewey's intention. Dewey's communities of problem-solving inquirers are far removed from the rupture between the world and the isolated knower as something outside of it, "engaged in an otiose contemplative survey of it." We strive to know the world by achieving control in response to the problems it poses for us.

Student of William James and teacher of Wallace Stevens, George Santayana's thought turn does not find purpose in James's world of pure experience, nor something mind-like in nature in Peirce's fashion. His view is naturalistic in the broad sense in which Dewey's is as well, but it replaces Dewey's Hegelian perspective by adding Platonic *tropes* to nature. In *Realms of Being* he sets up a discussion of teleology by introducing tropes, which are the order that an event enacts seen under the form of eternity. A pervasive trope can be fundamental. Such a universal trope will be realized everywhere, repeating itself uninterruptedly on its own plane. He calls such a trope *mechanical*, and to say that the world is a mechanical trope is to say that it is not fundamentally chaotic. Tropes belong to the region of Platonic Ideas. They are unitary patterns distinguishable in the movement of things, not part of the flux that executes them. Tropes are more fundamental than the "mock explanations" afforded by references to habit or law, which reduce events to their rhythms or repetitions. Another form of mock explanation is *teleology*, which fits things to their excellences, their harmonies with their surroundings, or the adaptation of their organs to their functions and of their actions to their intentions. Such correspondences exist, but they are impositions from the plane of thought on the plane of matter. One might say that functions are not intrinsic to nature but rather observer-relative, "which we impose so fatuously on the universe." These impositions do not belong to science, and this leads Santayana to deprecate the causal role of mind. Matter creates mental states and dictates the commands they issue, and even when an idea is materially fulfilled, the transition from the "personal, confused, and incomplete" to the outer world and its "comparatively foreign material" will be a "new surprise," as was the idea itself. Even this causal power of ideas comes from "their material side," which is mechanical rather than teleological. Their other side is teleological in aspiration but not reality, for this side's causal efficacy would mean "a miraculous pre-established harmony between the commands of spirit and events in the world." In this way philosophers are led to theology as a redoubt for teleology, and indeed the whole trope leads by "the crawling processes of nature" to such culminations, "but it is idle to regard the whole trope as governed by these top moments in it."

Further reading

Dewey, John. *Essays in Experimental Logic*. New York: Dover, 1916.

—— "The Reflex Arc Concept in Psychology" in Joseph Ratner (ed.) *Philosophy, Psychology and Social Practice*. New York: G.P. Putnam's Sons, 1963.

James, William. "A World of Pure Experience" in *Essays in Radical Empiricism*. Cambridge, MA: Harvard University Press, 1976.

—— *The Principles of Psychology*. Cambridge, MA: Harvard University Press, 1981.

Peirce, Charles. *Collected Papers of Charles Sanders Peirce*. Cambridge, MA: Harvard University Press, 1931–58.

Santayana, George. *Realms of Being*. New York: Charles Scribner's Sons, 1937.

WESLEY COOPER

TEMPERAMENT

In the context of American philosophy, temperament is a notion that William James popularized. In James's *Pragmatism*, temperament can be understood as the tendency of persons to feel a certain way regarding philosophical ideas (James 1975). Simply stated, people have inclinations toward certain views of the world and away from others. Some people, James claimed, emphasize principles, feelings, universals, while others lean toward hard facts, experiences and individual cases. He calls the first group "tender-minded" and the second "tough-minded." Most people fall somewhere between the extremes. These temperaments are like poles toward which we lean. We do not always follow the same tendency.

At base, temperament is a psychological feature of one's personality that plays an important role in arriving at beliefs. It is a general posture or coloring that one brings to one's experiences. Such coloring occurs in everyone's experience (not just philosophers), even if this is denied by intellectuals claiming to be free of bias. According to James, philosophy must be studied with temperaments in mind, since they are most often greater influences than are philosophical principles or argumentation. Temperament plays an important role, therefore, for understanding philosophy generally.

If James was right, then an implication must be noted: There are limits to what any philosophical position can achieve. For, if one leans at all in the direction of a particular temperament, which is unavoidable, then there will inevitably be those who differ temperamentally, and who therefore reject one's ideas. James's examples include those who believe in free will versus those who believe in determinism. Deterministic reasoning will not appeal to those who feel that free will best matches their sense of the world and of life.

James came to philosophy through the study of psychology. When he began to focus on philosophy, he noted the psychological features of philosophical exchanges, including the importance of temperament. James's work focused often on the role of feeling in philosophy. When an individual's world-views are in conflict, a feeling of discomfort arises. A person may believe that certain behaviors should be punishable by death, while believing that all killing is wrong. She may either come to believe that killing is not wrong, or she will wish to change her views about which punishment is appropriate for the behavior at issue. James would say that what guides a person in such a shift is primarily one's feelings or temperament. This natural psychological process, of altering one or the other of one's world-views, aims to end the internal conflict and leave the individual at ease until the next conflict arises.

It is important to note here the trouble with appeals to universal reason, such as Immanuel Kant's, regarding conflicts of value. While reason can be formalistic, attempting to avoid the conflicts of temperaments, it does not change the fact that persons come to their world-views on the basis of temperament. If this feature of James's Pragmatism is right, then appeals to impersonal or formalized morality are presented with a significant challenge.

Before James attended to the role of temperament, Kant offered his own perspective on its importance and on its categories. Kant defended the tradition of the temperaments from heavy criticisms. Indeed, the temperaments are described in a long-standing tradition of both philosophy and medicine. Temperament historically referred to a balance of humors. Although there have been many categorizations of different humors, the most famous include the "sanguine," the "choleric," the "melancholy," and the "phlegmatic." According to the theory, we all bear different mixtures of the temperaments, and as a consequence, we vary in character. We can see Kant's moral theory, focusing on universal maxims, as a way of dealing with the various temperaments. James found such approaches problematic because they fail to appeal to what really drives people to live and act the way they do.

J.G. Fichte also noted the importance of temperament in determining philosophical outlooks. In *The Science of Knowledge*, Fichte advances Kant's transcendental idealism, admitting that opponents of his project will not be convinced. He argues that philosophers' views about fundamental philosophical issues are "governed by *inclination* and *interest*." He states the issue more fully, explaining that "What sort of philosophy one chooses depends, therefore, on what sort of man [or woman] one is; for a philosophical system is not a dead piece of furniture that we can reject or accept as we wish; it is rather a thing animated by the soul of the person who holds it" (Fichte 1982: 15–16). More than Kant, Fichte's claims about temperament in his first and second introductions to *The Science of Knowledge* were an important influence on James. Fichte clarified the futility of attempting to prove fundamental philosophical starting points. Rather, philosophers must recognize that inquiry yields one set of results on the basis of one approach or outlook, and another set with a different approach. The consequences, furthermore, of differences in temperament for meaning and truth are important especially concerning debates in which people hold to apparently fundamental conflicting premises. In some cases, debates cannot be ended with proofs of the truth of one side or the other. Thus, a recognition of the importance of temperament must be accompanied by a recognition of the limits of the persuasive power of philosophical argument.

Given the tradition of theories of temperament, it is important to note the differences between James's views on the notion and historical ones. First, James's theory of temperament was not a full-fledged medical doctrine. James's point was primarily that the primacy philosophers generally accord to reason and to principles in the process of argument may well obfuscate the real determining factors of people's world-views. Second, the categorizations of James's discussion of temperament were simple. He distinguished primarily between two classes of philosophical tendencies. These can be classified further, and used in tests in psychology, but this was not James's purpose. For recent developments in theories of temperament, see Bordogna's article on its psychology and physiology (Bordogna 2001).

Further reading

Bordogna, Francesca. "The Psychology and Physiology of Temperament: Pragmatism in Context," *Journal of the History of the Behavioral Sciences* 37, 1 (Winter 2001): 3–25.

Fichte, J.G. *The Science of Knowledge*, ed. and trans. Peter Heath and John Lachs. New York: Cambridge University Press, 1982.

James, William. *Pragmatism* in *The Works of William James: Pragmatism*, ed. Frederick H. Burkhardt, Fredson Bowers, and Ignas K. Skrupskelis. Cambridge, MA: Harvard University Press, 1975, pp. 1–174.

Larrimore, Mark. "Substitutes for Wisdom: Kant's Practical Thought and the Tradition of the Temperaments," *Journal of the History of Philosophy* 39, 2 (April 2001): 259–88.

ERIC THOMAS WEBER

TEMPERANCE

One of the four classic virtues, temperance, according to Aristotle, is a moderate desire for the sensual pleasures. Augustine viewed temperance as a guard against "fleshy lusts." The earliest American ethical tradition, Puritanism, shared this Augustinian conception of temperance as a moral state resistant to sinful temptations. Within the context of Puritan theology, the ability to be temperate in relation to pleasure was an outward sign of inner sanctification. Even at this early stage we can note the practical attitude characteristic of so much of American philosophy. Temperance in regard to pleasure was not a form of asceticism but was a means to a more productive life, as immoderate desires distracted from the serious business of work and study. An appreciation for the benefits of temperance is also found in the *Autobiography* of Benjamin Franklin. This account of his project of moral improvement lists temperance as the first virtue to be mastered "as it tends to procure that coolness and clearness of head" required to pursue one's goals. Franklin credited his healthy constitution to temperance.

In the nineteenth century this practical attitude toward temperance was embodied by Henry David Thoreau's experiment at Walden Pond. Thoreau determined that his living conditions and diet be such as to satisfy those desires necessary to a human life in as simple and natural a way as possible, stripping away the excessive wants created by life in modern society. In contrast to the Puritans, the value of temperance was not that it kept one from the path of sin, but that it enabled one to live a more natural human life.

When we turn to pragmatism we find an emphasis on the function of temperance in the moral life. In an early treatise, *The Study of Ethics* (1894), John Dewey identifies temperance with self-control and bemoans that the negative aspect of the virtue has come to dominate. Dewey argues that temperance is the power to assert our agency: at times to say no to what we desire – because the object of that desire is not consistent with our larger ends – but more importantly the power to say yes to that which conduces to those moral ends. This identification of temperance with self-control persists in Dewey's later ethical thought. In his 1932 *Ethics*, he warns against seeing the various virtues as independent traits; instead we need to understand that the virtues interpenetrate one another in contributing to a moral character. Temperance, or self-control, treated as an independent virtue, is "a sour constraint" but understood as an aspect of moral character it is "the positive harmony characteristic of integrated interests." In other words, temperance is the power to properly organize our interests and desires so as to attain moral integrity.

In terms of impact on American history, the ideal of temperance was most significant during the Temperance movements of the nineteenth and early twentieth centuries – and here we clearly see that the negative aspects predominated. Temperance societies first appeared on American soil in the late eighteenth century. However, it was after the Civil War that the Temperance movement assumed a more prominent role in America's moral consciousness, with the Woman's Christian Temperance Union (WCTU) taking a leading role, and the strategy shifting from moderation to prohibition of alcohol use. This process culminated in the passing of the Eighteenth Amendment to the US Constitution, which banned the manufacturing, sale and transportation of alcoholic beverages.

While legislating temperance in regard to alcohol was a far cry from Dewey's approach, we can find a similarity. An instrument of the WCTU was the Department of Scientific Temperance Instruction, which agitated for mandatory instruction in the nation's schools on the dangers of alcohol use, based on supposedly scientific research. Even though this program was, in the words of one critic, "neither scientific, nor temperate, nor instructive" we see, in its use of science as a tool for moral progress and the schools as the avenue to such progress, distinctively Deweyan ideas.

As philosophy in America took a linguistic turn in the mid-twentieth century temperance, along with the virtues in general, became less a concern for American philosophers.

Further reading

Dewey, John. *The Study of Ethics: A Syllabus* in *The Early Works, Vol. 4, 1893–1894*. Carbondale, IL: Southern Illinois University Press, 1971 [1894].

—— *Ethics* in *The Later Works, Vol. 7, 1932*. Carbondale, IL: Southern Illinois University Press, 1989 [1932].

Franklin, Benjamin. *The Autobiography of Benjamin Franklin*. New York: Dover, 1996.

Stroh, Guy W. *American Ethical Thought*. Chicago, IL: Nelson Hall, 1979.

Thoreau, Henry David. *Walden and Civil Disobedience*. New York: Penguin, 1983.

John Teehan

TENDER/TOUGHMINDEDNESS

The distinction between tender-minded and tough-minded philosophical temperaments is accounted for in "Lecture I" of William James's *Pragmatism* (1907). James's background assumption is that a major hidden premise of philosophical views and doctrines is the philosopher's own personal temperament, although it is not recognized as a valid consideration within the professional philosophical community. According to James, philosophical temperaments can be classed in two opposite groups, the tender-minded and the tough-minded. Tendermindedness refers to the philosophical attitude traditionally classified as rationalistic, intellectualistic, idealistic, religious, dogmatic, monistic, freewillist, optimistic. Toughmindedness is empiricist, sensationalistic, materialistic, irreligious, pluralistic, deterministic, skeptical, pessimistic. The distinction is not intended to provide a technical detailed definition of opposing philosophical doctrines and needs to be understood as including several intermediate and mixed positions in between.

The essential feature at the bottom of the distinction, which justifies the definition as "tender" or "tough," is the ability to live up to the existential atmosphere produced by a certain "metaphysical" picture of the universe. Tendermindedness feels at loss in a world with no metaphysical foundation, order and warranty of some sort of the future. Toughmindedness can live and feel at ease in the metaphysical void of a "dangerous" and "loose" world with no transcendent stronghold and support, and committed to the power of human efforts and experience only.

The distinction echoes James's distinction between Sick and Healthy souls (*The Varieties of Religious Experience*) and has several forerunners, e.g. the distinction between Dogmatic and Academic philosophy in Sextus Empiricus (*Outlines of Pyrrhonism* I, 1), between intuitive and abstract knower in Schopenhauer (*The World as Will and Representation* §12), between Idealism and Materialism in R.W. Emerson ("The Transcendentalist"), and between Optimism and Pessimism in C. Renouvier (*Esquisse d'une classification Systématique des Doctrines Philosophiques*, 1885: 2–3).

Sergio Franzese

TERMINATING JUDGMENTS

Terminating judgments, which are epistemically basic beliefs that do not rely on other beliefs, serve an important function in understanding knowledge as justified true belief. Without terminating judgments the problem of an infinite regress may arise, for any justification itself involves knowledge which must be justified, and so forth. In the context of American philosophy this position is developed most notably in the pragmatist philosophy of C.I. Lewis, and incorporates a distinctively pragmatic appropriation of the concept of terminating judgments.

Terminating judgments are made in expressive language. The distinctive character of expressive statements, or the expressive use of language, is that such language signifies appearances or indubitable content. In referring to appearances, expressive statements neither assert nor deny any objective reality of what appears. Because expressive statements are confined to description of the immediate content of presentation, they are not subject to possible error and hence are not classified as knowledge.

Terminating judgments state the prediction of a particular passage of experience. They find their cue in what is given, but state something taken to be verifiable by some test which involves a way of acting. What such terminating judgments express is classed as knowledge, for the prediction in question calls for verification and is subject to possible error. But such judgments are capable of certitude in their verification or falsification, since initial data, act, and anticipated result are all stated in expressive language. Terminating judgments are expressed in the form, "S being given, if A then E." All of the constituents entering into the judgment ("S," "A," and "E,") require formulation in expressive language. Lewis considers this essential for knowledge, holding that if anything is to be probable, something must be certain.

In contrast, non-terminating judgments or judgments of objective fact express objective beliefs which can never be completely verified but are always further verifiable. The meaning of an objective belief or non-terminating judgment always involves possible consequences or possible terminating judgments which stretch beyond those terminating judgments actually tested. Because such beliefs can never be completely verified, they are probable, not certain.

While terminating judgments are frequently associated with the spectator theory of knowledge and foundationalism, the pragmatic understanding of terminating judgments denies both of these. The difference between terminating judgments about appearances and non-terminating judgments about objectivities reflects neither ontological, existential, nor numerical distinctions but rather the distinction between levels of interpretation. Terminating judgments withhold the normal belief in objectivities, focusing instead on what appears as it appears – usually in situations in which the existence of the believed objectivity is put into question.

The grasp of appearances is primary in the verification or justification of knowledge claims, but these appearances reflect, in the very way one grasps them, the structure of the objectivities one believes to be appearing. There are no brute uninterpreted data. Terminating judgments, expressed in the language of appearing, provide certitude in their verification or falsification in that there is no more fundamental epistemic tool by which to question them. They serve as the unquestionable basis for our fallible, probable objective beliefs. They must be taken, for all intents and purposes, as the bedrock foundation on which to build knowledge; they are in this sense pragmatically certain.

Further reading

Lewis, C.I. *An Analysis of Knowledge and Valuation*, Book II. La Salle, IL: Open Court. 1946.

—— "Replies to My Critics" in Paul A. Schilpp (ed.) *The Philosophy of C.I. Lewis* (Library of Living Philosophers). LaSalle, IL: Open Court. 1968.

—— "The Pragmatic Element in Knowledge" in *Collected Papers of Clarence Irving Lewis.* ed. John Goheen and John Mothershead, Jr. Stanford, CA: Stanford University Press. 1970.

Sandra B. Rosenthal

THAYER, HORACE STANDISH

H.S. Thayer is a pragmatist philosopher. Thayer received his PhD from Columbia University in 1949. After teaching at Columbia and elsewhere, he took a position in 1961 at City College, City University of New York, where he has remained since.

Thayer's dissertation was an examination of John Dewey's logical theory. While his subsequent research interests ranged widely to include Plato, Aristotle, Pascal, and Newton, the bulk of his work has been devoted to in-depth studies not just of Dewey but also of Peirce, James, Lewis, Mead, and the wider influence of their different "pragmatisms." Thayer's classic work on the subject, *Meaning and Action: A Critical History of Pragmatism* (1968/1980), remains to this day a recognized milestone in philosophical scholarship.

It is generally acknowledged that pragmatism had its heyday in the first couple of decades of the twentieth century, though it took thirty years before that to bubble to the surface. It also exerted declining influence on American philosophical thought for another thirty years afterwards, at least until the death of John Dewey in 1952. It went into virtual eclipse over the next couple of decades (precisely when Thayer was focusing his efforts on tracing the history of pragmatism) only to re-emerge in the 1970s as neo-positivist analytic philosophy in the United States was beginning to lose its sheen. This later revival of pragmatism was due to many factors, to the credit of many individuals working at the time, but it was greatly facilitated by Thayer's extensive and careful exegetical and critical work.

Further reading

Thayer, Horace Standish. *The Logic of Pragmatism: An Examination of John Dewey's Logic* (dissertation, Columbia University, advisor Ernest Nagel, 1949). New York: Humanities Press, 1952. Reprinted New York: Greenwood Press, 1969.

—— *Meaning and Action: A Critical History of Pragmatism*. New York: Bobbs-Merrill, 1968. Second edition, Indianapolis, IN: Hackett, 1980.

—— "Reply to Criticisms" in "Perspectives on the History of Pragmatism: A Symposium of H.S. Thayer's *Meaning and Action: A Critical History of Pragmatism,*" *Transactions of the Charles S. Peirce Society* 11 (1975): 258–87.

Tom Burke

THEISM

Theism is the rational belief in one God. Arguments and claims concerning the existence or reality of God constitute a principal point of interaction between religious beliefs, theological method, and philosophy. The philosophical desire to know the ultimate nature of things, the destiny of mankind, and the form of the good life interact and sometimes conflict with similar inquiry from theological perspectives. The early Christian theologian Tertullian spoke to the dichotomy of the goals of theology and philosophy when he posed the question "What has Athens to do with Jerusalem?" Tertullian held that the Christian story of a God incarnate in a person who was crucified and resurrected would always be an absurd idea from the standpoint of the "God of the philosophers." This uneasy relation between philosophy and religion, faith and reason, revelation and human inquiry insures that theism will remain a controversial and fecund philosophical concern.

Three major conceptions of the divine nature ground theistic argument. First is the conception of a divine Self transcending the world, interpreted in personal terms. A second conception is of a wholly immanent Order or Power to which all finite realities are subject. Third is the Monistic conception in which God is the Absolute or all-embracing totality. Judeo-Christian thought and ancient Greek philosophy reflect the first conception, Spinoza and process philosophy reflect the second conception of immanence, and the thought of Hegel and absolute idealists reflect the third. The boundaries between these conceptions are not hard and fast, and the history of Western philosophy shows the interaction and interpenetration of these philosophical conceptions. The dominant view in Western philosophy is the divine Self, and most critical approaches to God's existence presuppose the conception of a transcendent reality standing beyond both the world and human consciousness. As the ground of ultimate human respect and adoration, the supreme religious "object" is also conceived as a perfect being since only a being that manifests its perfection in perfect love is worthy of love that is unconditional. Perfection, however, conflicts with a conception of the divine as immanent in the world. God, intelligible as a delimited being, points beyond itself to the infinite order of ultimate reality that transcends finite limitations. Limitation is necessary for individuality, and so the basic conception of a divine Self, transcending the world, the ultimate object of human devotion and worship, presents a cluster of conceptual philosophical problems.

A continuum of strength of rational argument appears in the debate over the existence of God, from the position that there is rational compulsion to believe the truth about the ultimate nature of things, to the position that belief in an ultimate being rests on willful assent (or rejection) based on a judgment supported by critical examination of evidence.

Two main sources for critical rational arguments for the existence of God are Plato's orientation toward transcendent truth presupposed in the rational ordering of the material world and the immaterial world of the forms, and Aristotle's inquiry into the ultimate reason for motion, eventuating in the claim that a prime mover as pure actuality is eternal mind or thought, i.e. God. The interplay between arguments oriented toward understanding God's existence (Augustine and Anselm) and those that intend to logically demonstrate the existence of God (Aquinas) form the background of the two principal lines of critical rational argument for God, the ontological and cosmological arguments.

Ontological argument

Formulated by Anselm in his *Proslogion* this argument begins with the concept of God as "something than which nothing greater can be conceived." This something cannot be conceived not to exist, and therefore exists necessarily. This being is eternal as having no beginning or ending and exists as a whole, for the idea that eternal being has either come into existence or ceased to exist is self-contradictory, as is the idea that this being has successive phases. Anselm develops this argument from Augustine's description of God as the one "than whom there is nothing superior" in *Freedom of the Will.* Descartes includes a version of this argument in his *Meditations,* and Kant criticizes the argument on the grounds that existence cannot be a real predicate of an object. Charles Hartshorne reformulates the ontological argument to force the disjunction that God's existence is either logically necessary or logically impossible, that God's existence is not shown to be impossible, therefore God necessarily exists. Alvin Plantinga and Norman Malcolm contribute alternative versions of the argument focusing on supporting the basic logical structure of Anslem's reasoning.

Cosmological argument

This style of argument starts with the existence of the world or some particular facts within it or some feature that the world exhibits in a pervasive way. Based on the principle of causality or the principle of sufficient reason, the argument holds that an infinite regress of effects in an essentially ordered system is impossible, and therefore must originate in an unconditioned origin or first cause.

Three of Aquinas's celebrated five "Ways" to rational belief in God are versions of this argument, from motion, efficient cause, and necessary existence. Versions of the cosmological argument appear in Descartes, Locke, and Neo-scholastic philosophers. William Lane Craig's kalam argument reinforces the point that an essentially ordered series (the universe) has a definite beginning in time, and that therefore this beginning is caused by a creator that is either personal or nonpersonal.

Analysis and criticism of arguments for the existence of God developed in the early modern period as theologians sought philosophical support for their religious beliefs, and thus to some degree precipitated the phenomenon of modern atheism which claims that matter nature is "that which is to be taken as the ultimate, the active and the efficient" (Buckley 1987: 27). Within two centuries a massive shifting of cultural establishment in the West toward atheism defined human beings as constitutionally unable to believe, to know, or to be convinced in any way of the existence of the Judeo-Christian God. Theism, therefore, came to bear the burden of proof in making the positive claim of the existence of God, rather than providing rational support for a common or culturally significant habit of thought.

Theism in American philosophy

American Pragmatism is characterized by its peculiar relation to religious establishment and criticism of the Puritan tradition, typified in Edwards, the rise of experimental science, and evolution. Peirce describes a "neglected" argument for the reality of God as the *ens necessarium* that is the natural outgrowth of logic and instinctive inquiry, which he distinguishes from an "existent" being. The hypothesis of God appears in the thought of almost all inquirers and is "full of nutrition for man's highest growth," leading Peirce to suggest that skeptics of the reality of God suffer from some disorder. William James is less sympathetic to theism or the being of God, yet he considers a personal belief in the divine as an ultimate good for living with zest. In fact, James's initial description of pragmatism uses God as an example of understanding an idea by the difference it makes in practice. Royce, James's student, develops a theistic Absolute that is immanent as the explanation for the spirit of interpretant communities, most notably the Pauline church. Adopting Peirce's triadic categories and Bergsonian flux, Royce rejects the possibility of self-knowledge and hence divine foreknowledge, and focuses inquiry into God's nature on the character of divine love emerging teleologically in the consciousness of the community. Royce, James, and Peirce triangulate toward a conception of God that is independent of human thought while not completely transcendent, fully discoverable in human experience and inquiry without becoming utterly finite (except for James). John Dewey modified his early Christian idealism into vociferous anti-supernaturalism. In *A Common Faith* Dewey defines "God" as the "unity of all ideal ends arousing us to desire and action." Against the emerging dominance of Anglo/Analytic philosophy in the first half of the twentieth century that rejected theism as a vestige of discredited metaphysics, A.N. Whitehead and Hartshorne supported philosophical theism based on process rather than on the analysis of being. In recent years the mainstream analytic rejection of theism is challenged by philosophers such as Alvin Plantinga, Alasdair MacIntyre, and Nicholas Wolterstorff, in company with a minority of Continentalists such as John Caputo and Merrold Westphal, and pragmatists from divergent perspectives such as Douglas Anderson, Michael Raposa, Robert Corrington, and theologians James McClendon and Stanley Hauerwas.

Further reading

Buckley, Michael, SJ. *At the Origins of Modern Atheism*. New Haven, CT: Yale University Press, 1987.

Craig, William Lane. *The Kalam Cosmological Argument*, Eugene, OR: Wipf and Stock, 2000.

Gilson, Etienne. *God and Philosophy*. New Haven, CT: Yale University Press, 2002.

Hartshorne, Charles. *Man's Vision of God and the Logic of Theism*. Hamden, CT: Archon Books, 1964. New York: Oxford University Press, 1994.

Plantinga, Alvin, *God, Freedom, and Evil*, New York: Harper and Row, 1974.

ROGER A. WARD

THEORY-LADENNESS

The theory-ladenness of observation is the view that our observations are not independent of the theories we hold: if a micro-biologist and an untrained layperson both look at a cell through a microscope, the microbiologist may see cell-walls, a nucleus, and some specks of dust on the glass, but the untrained layperson will just see shapes and colors. Each person's observation is informed by the theory held about the object(s) in their visual field.

The theory-ladenness of observation is argued for indirectly by Willard Van Orman Quine and directly by Hilary Putnam and N.R. Hanson, Thomas Kuhn and others. The logical positivists had divided statements into observation statements and theoretical statements. Observation statements – statements containing observation terms (e.g. "green") – were taken by them to be confirmed directly by observation. Theoretical statements – statements containing theoretical terms (e.g. "electron") – however, were to be confirmed by testing their observable consequences (for example, electrons cause vapor trails in cloud chambers). If a statement has no observable consequences, then that statement is meaningless.

Willard Van Orman Quine denied the distinction between theoretical and observation statements. For Quine, statements are not confirmed individually, but as an interconnected whole. The observation that there is a vapor trail in a cloud chamber confirms not just some statements about electrons, but all of sub-atomic theory. This confirmation holism undercuts a clean distinction between theoretical and observation statements. Hilary Putnam denied a distinction between theoretical and observation terms. "Green," a purportedly observational term, could apply to an object that is too small to see. Conversely, a theoretical term like "satellite" ("satellite" is theoretical because it comes from a theory) applies to observables. Lastly, observation reports can contain theoretical terms, as in "we also observed the creation of two electron-positron pairs" (Putnam 1979: 219).

If observation is theory-laden, then what we take as evidence for our theories may not actually be independent of the theories themselves. The theory we hold infiltrates, perhaps even dictates, what counts as evidence for it. While theory-ladenness is widely accepted, it is still open to debate how much observation is infected by theory. Ian Hacking argues that making observations through a microscope requires practice with the instrument, but does not require an understanding of the underlying theory of micro-biology. A lay-person with some practice will see what the micro-biologist sees despite his ignorance of theory. More recently, Jody Azzouni has argued that some regularities, "gross regularities," are part of the foundations of our evidentiary procedures and are largely immune from infiltration by theory. Examples range from widely known regularities – that balls thrown through windows usually break the glass – to expert knowledge – that some alloys can only handle so much tension. Despite some theoretical content, these regularities are not part of any theory, and are, in fact, often established directly via observation and practice. Indeed, many of them are difficult to write down or explain (how to hold a certain tool, for instance).

Further reading

Achinstein, Peter. "The Problem of Theoretical Terms" in Baruch A. Brody (ed.) *Readings in the Philosophy of Science*. New York: Prentice Hall, 1970, pp. 234–50 [1965].

Azzouni, Jody. *Knowledge and Reference in Empirical Science*. New York: Routledge, 2000.

Hacking, Ian. *Representing and Intervening*. Cambridge, MA: Cambridge University Press, 1983.

Hanson, N.R. *Patterns of Discovery*. Cambridge, MA: Cambridge University Press, 1951.

Kuhn, Thomas. *The Structure of Scientific Revolutions*. Chicago, IL: University of Chicago Press, 1962.

Putnam, Hilary. "What Theories are Not" in H. Putnam (ed.) *Mathematics, Matter and Method: Philosophical Papers, Volume I*. Cambridge, MA: Cambridge University Press, 1979, pp. 215–27 [1962].

Quine, W.V.O. "Two Dogmas of Empiricism" in W.V.O. Quine (ed.) *From A Logical Point of View*. Cambridge, MA: Harvard University Press, 1980, pp. 20–46 [1953].

Yvonne Raley

THIRDNESS

Thirdness refers to the third of the three inseparable and comprehensive divisions or categories of experience as observed, deduced, and explicated by Charles Sanders Peirce (1839–1914), the founder of pragmatism as a philosophical doctrine. In his "One, Two, Three: Fundamental Categories of Thought and of Nature" of 1885 (CP 1.369f; W 5: 242f), Peirce referred to these categories of experience as firsts, seconds, and thirds. Those aspects of experience whose predominant trait is *immediacy* best exhibit firstness, while those aspects which exhibit *resistance* likewise show secondness. Those departments of experience that manifest *lawfulness* or systematic *habit* (broadly construed) sustain thirdness. A vigorous slap of the hand upon a table, for example, will illustrate firstness in the immediacy of a stinging, painful sensation, secondness in the resistance provided by the table, and thirdness in the background lawfulness of nature by which the pain was occasioned. Pain, then, is a *sign*. Conspicuous as examples of thirdness for Peirce are signs, and more precisely, *symbolic* signs (CP 1.372). For Peirce, such triadic logical relations in which thirdness may be observed cannot arise only from their constituent firsts and seconds, nor may such triadic logical relations, once formed, survive decomposition into their constituent firsts and seconds. The thirdness of a family (CP 1.111) or a molecule of water or a musical triad, thus, cannot be mechanically generated solely from their constituent parts. Likewise, neither the family, the molecule, the chord, nor the intangible but very Real, triadic relations that sustain them can survive fragmentation into their constituent parts. Such irreducibility demonstrates that the mechanical operations of Nominalism cannot accommodate thirdness. Such nonreduction (Burch 1991) has contemporary implications ranging from the social sciences (Samway 1995), to physics (Beil and Ketner 2004), to concert performance of classical piano literature (Stewart 2006).

Peirce's development of his categories falls into two historical stages, roughly, the first ending about 1870 (Fisch 1986: 263f) and the second proceeding from about 1885 (Esposito 1980). In his pivotal 1867 "On a New List of Categories," Peirce describes a triadic reality of Quality, Relation, and Representation (CP 1.555; W 2:49), and remarks on the influence of Kant in these respects. By "One, Two, Three" this third category is described in terms of, importantly, *mediation*. The first use of "thirdness" in print by Peirce may not have occurred until about 1890, in his "A Guess at the Riddle" (CP 1.383; W 6:166). His Harvard Lectures of 1903 include, in explicit, diagrammatic form, a summary of influences in the development of his own categories (CP 5.79). Further comments on the influences of Kant and Hegel in this regard are given in his Lowell Institute Lectures of the same year (CP 1.521f).

In the third of his summational Cambridge Conferences Lectures of 1898 (CP 6/7; see RLT, as follows), Peirce declares for firstness, secondness, and thirdness as "new scientific names," and gives as examples of thirdness laws and general rules, the workings of the "geometrical mind," and ideas as continuous systems (147f; 163). Examples from his fifth lecture include generality and continuity, the formation of mental habits or associations of ideas, and inference and learning (190f), while in his final, eighth lecture he proclaims "continuity, or Thirdness, to be … the characteristic of my doctrine" (261). As these items imply, thirds and thirdness are not static categorial classifications, but entities that evolve, develop, and *grow*. Explicitly, then, in the third of the Cambridge series, Peirce describes "every true universal, every continuum," as " … a living and conscious being" (162). The laws of nature are described in Lecture Eight as being the result of an evolutionary process "still in progress." Furthermore, Peirce notes there that the principle by which evolution thus proceeds will have the nature of a law, but it must be such a law that *it can evolve or develop itself* (240 and 241, respectively; emphasis added).

That thirds and thirdness are characterized by growth was Peirce's view no later than 1892, as given in the fifth of his lectures on the History of Science to the Lowell Institute during 1892–3. He remarks there on "the gradual coming into being and crystallization of the fundamental laws of matter and of mind," and describes how, when in the ancient world Greek ideas and those of the Phoenicians, Egyptians, and Babylonians began to react productively, "a great original life, an example of thirdness, commenced" (see CP 7.267, n. 8, and 7.270, respectively). This use of crystallization, however, by Peirce, does not imply or require a fixed terminus in the evolution or *growth* of thirdness, a world exhaustively explicated by immutable laws, a world of induration (see RLT 261). Thus, Peirce commented in his Lowell Institute Lectures of 1903 that the creation of the universe, including the laws of nature and other examples of thirdness, "is going on today and never will be done" (CP 1.615).

Historically, Peirce goes on in his article in *The Monist* (15) of 1905 titled "What Pragmatism Is" to describe thirdness as "an essential ingredient in reality" (CP 5.436). Though not mentioned specifically by name, thirdness is relied upon by Peirce, importantly, in his "Neglected Argument for the Reality of God" of 1908 (CP 6.452–93). Conclusively, definitions by Peirce of firstness, secondness, and thirdness are given in *The Century Dictionary Supplement* of 1909 (Smith 1909).

Further reading

Beil, Ralph G. and Ketner, K.L. "Quantum Switches and Circuits," US Patent 6819474, at http://patft.uspto.gov/, 2004.

Burch, Robert W. *A Peircean Reduction Thesis: The Foundations of Topological Logic*. Lubbock, TX: Texas Tech University Press, 1991.

Fisch, Max Harold. *Peirce, Semeiotic, and Pragmatism: Essays by Max H. Fisch*. K. L. Ketner and C.J.W. Kloesel, eds. Bloomington, IN: Indiana University Press, 1986.

Peirce, Charles Sanders. *The Collected Papers of Charles Sanders Peirce* (CP), 8 vols, ed. Charles Hartshorne, Paul Weiss and Arthur W. Burke. Cambridge, MA: Harvard University Press, 1958 [1931–5].

—— *Reasoning and the Logic of Things: The 1898 Cambridge Conferences Lectures by Charles Sanders Peirce* (RLT), ed. Kenneth Laine Ketner. Cambridge, MA: Harvard University Press, 1992.

—— *Writings of Charles Sanders Peirce: A Chronological Edition* (W), 6 vols to date, ed. the Peirce Edition Project. Bloomington, IN: Indiana University Press, 1982–.

Samway, Patrick H., SJ (ed.) *A Thief of Peirce – The Letters of Kenneth Laine Ketner and Walker Percy*. Jackson, MS: University Press of Mississippi, 1995.

Stewart, Arthur. "Charles Peirce, Artur Schnabel, and the Soul: Logic and Artistry on the Concert Platform," *Lamar Journal of the Humanities* 31 (2006): 1.

ARTHUR STEWART

THOREAU, HENRY DAVID

Henry David Thoreau (christened David Henry Thoreau) (12 July 1817 – 6 May 1862) was born in Concord, Massachusetts, and lived there nearly all his life. His family moved to Boston when he was four, but returned to Concord in 1823. Thoreau attended Harvard College, graduating in 1837. He worked for a time as a schoolteacher and as a self-taught land surveyor, and he participated in various ways in his family's pencil-making and graphite business. He also lectured and published during his lifetime, but he did not make a living with his writing. Although he proposed marriage to Ellen Sewall in 1840, he was rejected by her, and he never married. Befriended intellectually and personally by Ralph Waldo Emerson, Thoreau sometimes did odd jobs around the Emerson household in exchange for room and board. From May to December of 1843, when Thoreau was trying to connect with the New York publishing world, he lived with Emerson's brother's family on Staten Island, serving as a tutor to the children.

Disappointed in New York but still determined to write, Thoreau returned to Concord and constructed a small cabin on the shores of Walden Pond. He lived there from 4 July 1845 until 6 September 1847. During this period he completed a draft of *A Week on the Concord and Merrimack Rivers,* a memorial account of a canoe trip he had taken with his brother, John, in 1839. He also produced an initial version of his reflections on his life at the pond, the writing that, with revisions and expansions, was to become *Walden.* It was during this period, too, that Thoreau was arrested and spent a night in jail for refusing to pay a poll tax, an incident mentioned in *Walden* and discussed in detail in *Resistance to Civil Government* (posthumously re-titled *Civil Disobedience*).

Walden, or Life in the Woods was published in 1854 to moderate sales and measured critical success, but the book has since become a classic of American and world literature. *Walden* presents Thoreau's time at the pond as an "experiment" designed to ascertain the "necessities" of life. The form is autobiographical, but the book's reflections on the relation between the human and the natural world and on the relation of the individual to society are broadly philosophical. *Walden* contains vivid and attentive accounts of wildlife and nature – flora and fauna, the ponds, the land – but it also urges attention to questions about human beings' needs and nature. The book is sometimes taken to be a manual for a spare, simple, almost ascetic life, and Thoreau did sketch the dissatisfactions that cloud lives devoted to material possessions and conventional luxuries. In fact, Thoreau questioned convention more generally, and the book urges self-reflection, individual awakening, and confidence in the enlightenment that will follow.

The idea that each individual must hear and be obedient to his or her own inner voice also shapes the arguments of *Resistance to Civil Government.* Thoreau was deeply concerned with some specific political issues, in particular the Mexican War (1846–1848) and American slavery, and this work, as well as *Walden* and some of his short essays, make reference to his disgust with these policies and practices. (Thoreau and his family offered shelter to slaves on their way to freedom, and although Thoreau never joined an abolitionist society, he did publish essays in support of the abolitionist John Brown.) *Resistance to Civil Government* presents a fully general account of the relation between the individual and government, however, one that has had an important influence in a variety of historical circumstances.

Thoreau believed the just authority of the government to be derived solely from the consent of the governed, and he called for moral and practical attention to the nature and conditions of consent. He exhorted each individual to recognize what might be his or her implication in unsavory governmental actions and unjust institutions, and, upon recognition, to dissociate from the offending government, to withdraw support. Thoreau claimed that one does not necessarily have a duty to pursue government reform or to eradicate the evils others perpetrate. One might, he said, have "other affairs to attend to." But one must do something to effect withdrawal, so that one does not participate in or benefit from the evil. Active resistance in Thoreau's case meant not paying taxes to a government he could not wholeheartedly endorse. He saw his jailing as a point of honor, the price of conscience. Thoreau's personal example and the moral analysis contained in *Resistance to Civil Government* have been important to various political activists, most notably Mohandas Gandhi and Martin Luther King, Jr.

Thoreau became seriously ill in 1861, though he continued to write in the last year of his life. He died in Concord in 1862, of tuberculosis.

Further reading

Cavell, Stanley. *The Senses of Walden*. New York: Viking, 1972; expanded edition. Chicago, IL: University of Chicago Press, 1992.

Myerson, Joel (ed.). *The Cambridge Companion to Henry David Thoreau*. Cambridge: Cambridge University Press, 1995.

Sayre, Robert F. (ed.). *New Essays on Walden*. Cambridge: Cambridge University Press, 1992.

Thoreau, Henry David. *A Week on the Concord and Merrimack Rivers*. Boston, MA: James Munroe, 1849.

—— *Walden; or, Life in the Woods*. Boston, MA: Ticknor and Fields, 1854.

—— *The Maine Woods*. Boston, MA: Ticknor and Fields, 1864.

—— *Cape Cod*. Boston, MA: Ticknor and Fields, 1865.

KAREN HANSON

TILLICH, PAUL

Paul Johannes Tillich (1886–1965) was born in Starzeddel, near Guben, a small industrial town in the province of Brandenburg at the Silesian border. The son of a Lutheran pastor, he was raised with traditional German Orthodox-Pietistic Lutheran beliefs. After receiving his degrees, he became the *Privatdozent* of Theology at the University of Berlin from 1919 to 1924. In April of 1933, owing to his views, he was suspended from his position as Professor of Philosophy at the University of Frankfort by the Nazi government; in November of that year, he came to the United States and was finally dismissed from his Frankfort professorship the next month. Tillich wore it as a badge of honor to be the first non-Jewish professor thus dismissed by the Nazis.

Tillich's thirty-two years in the United States were spent between Union Theological Seminary, Columbia University, Harvard, and Chicago Divinity School as Nuveen Professor of Theology. He was there until his death in October of 1965.

Theology

Tillich's theology is most famously known for two elements; his definition of religion as being one's "ultimate concern" and his claim that God, as the Ground of Being, does not exist; his theology has also been criticized for using the language of orthodoxy as a guise for positions some believed to be unorthodox. That having been said, theologically and philosophically speaking, the notion of "participation," although not as well known as these two elements, is arguably the most important idea in his theology. It is in Tillich's use of this notion that we find traces of those who influenced his thought the most – Kant, Schelling and Heidegger; it is especially reminiscent of Heidegger's own discussion of "in" during the early pages of *Being and Time*. The notion of participation is also the pivotal notion of concern when we attempt to situate Tillich's thought as a whole with respect to other theological positions.

Briefly, the idea is, perhaps, best illustrated using the national flag as an example; the flag is not only a symbol of the pride each citizen feels for the nation, it is actually a part of the nation itself. The flag points beyond itself to the nation it symbolizes, while it is also a part of that very nation. Consider the following:

> Whatever we say about that which concerns us ultimately, whether or not we call it God, has a symbolic meaning. It points beyond itself while participating in that to which it points. In no other way can faith express itself adequately. The language of faith is the language of symbols.
>
> (Tillich 1957: 45)

With the notion of participation, Tillich is able to find the middle ground between transcendence and immanence; we, as existents, point beyond ourselves to that which is the Ground of our existence; but all the while we exist. Thus, as symbols, we are transcendent; but as participants we are immanent.

Since Tillich's work lies squarely within the Christian tradition, he is obliged to offer a theory of salvation, a soteriology. On Tillich's view, salvation is simply our acceptance of God's acceptance of us; that is, the *fact* of our salvation has already been established by God; it is that fact that establishes God's acceptance of us and if we are to live the life of grace, it is up to us to accept that acceptance. It is in virtue of Tillich's view of salvation and his notion of participation that his theology appears to have the most in common with the Christian tradition known as the New Thought movement. And nowhere is this similarity more evident than in his book *The Courage To Be.*

The Courage To Be

In *The Courage To Be* Tillich offers what might be termed a provisional phenomenology of participation by way of an exegetical analysis of courage. He chooses courage because he believes courage to be the locus of convergence between theological, sociological, and philosophical problems. Broadly put, Tillich understands courage as the self-affirmation of being in spite of the fact of nonbeing; where "nonbeing" is understood to embrace the threefold pairing of the following anxieties: fate and death; emptiness and meaninglessness; and guilt and condemnation.

In an express excursion through philosophical and theological thought concerning courage, Tillich introduces the reader to two distinct types of courage: the courage to be a part and the courage to be oneself. Each of these, in its own way, embraces non-being; however, if carried through radically, the former leads to the loss of the self in collectivism and the latter to the loss of the world in existentialism. Tillich's aim is to discover whether there is a species of courage that is capable of taking this threefold anxiety into itself without compromise; he notes that this can only be done if that ilk of courage is rooted in a power of being that is greater than the power of oneself and the power of one's world. That is, this particular species of courage must participate in the "power of being-itself" so as to be beyond the threat of nonbeing; to Tillich, this implies that "every courage to be has an open or hidden religious root" because religion is "the state of being grasped by the power of being-itself."

This, of course, raises two important questions: *how* is the courage to be rooted in being-itself and how must we understand being-itself in the light of the courage to be? These two questions are related to each other in that the first question deals with the ground of being as the *source* of the courage to be, while the second question intimates that the courage to be is the *key* to the ground of being; for this entry, a discussion of only the second question will suffice to give the reader a sense of Tillich's argument and what he means when he speaks of the "God above God."

Since there is something rather than nothing, this means that being-itself has already affirmed itself against nonbeing. It does this by including nonbeing within itself, using nonbeing as the means whereby it affirms itself. The self-affirmation of being-itself implies that without nonbeing, being-itself could not be the ground of life; for without nonbeing, the self-affirmation of being-itself would be nothing more than a dead tautological identity. The Divine self-affirmation is the power that makes possible the self-affirmation of the finite being, i.e. the courage to be. It is only because being-itself has the character of self-affirmation *in spite of nonbeing* that courage is possible; courage participates in the self-affirmation of being-itself. By affirming our being in courageous acts we participate in the self-affirmation of being-itself; in this sense, every act of courage is a manifestation of the ground of being, whether the actor is aware of it or not. And it is this revelatory ability of courage that makes it the key to being-itself.

The courage to take meaninglessness into itself presupposes a relation to the ground of being which Tillich terms "absolute faith"; and it is this faith that transcends the theistic ideas of God, which he claims are either irrelevant, one-sided, or just theologically wrong. Tillich argues that theistic ideas of God make God "a being beside others and as such a part of the whole of reality." However, these ideas make God *a* being and not being-*itself*. Absolute faith is the accepting of the acceptance *without* somebody or something that accepts; it is the *power of being-itself* that gives the courage to be. Tillich claims that God, understood as being-itself, although able to be affirmed through acts of courage in which we affirm the power of being, cannot be described in the same way that the God of theism can be described or in mystical terms either, since being-itself transcends both the courage to be a part and the courage to be as oneself. As thus transcendent, Tillich calls this the "God above God" that is the ultimate source of the courage to be; another way of saying this is to say that "being-itself is above any theistic idea of God."

Thus, salvation occurs for each individual when that individual accepts the fact that God has already accepted him/her; this is absolute faith and reflects the fact that the individual is in a state of having already been grasped by the God beyond God. Absolute faith is the faith that accepts the acceptance of God in spite of being unacceptable; indeed, by taking the nonbeing of unacceptability into oneself by accepting God's acceptance of oneself, one actualizes the courage to be, which is rooted in the God above the God of theism. This courage to be unites and transcends the courage to be a part and the courage to be oneself, thus avoiding the loss of self by participation and the loss of one's world by individualization. As a final note, it is the distinction between God and the God of theism that is behind Tillich's claim that God (the God above the God of theism) does not "exist" since, as being-itself, God is the very condition for the possibility of existence, hence falling outside the ambit of "existence," while the God of theism *is* an existent and falls squarely within the ambit of "existence."

Further reading

Tillich, Paul. *The Protestant Era*, trans. James Luther Adams. Chicago, IL: University of Chicago Press, 1948.
—— *Systematic Theology*, 3 vols. Chicago, IL: University of Chicago Press, 1951–63.
—— *The Courage To Be*. New Haven, CT: Yale University Press, 1952.
—— *Dynamics of Faith*. New York: Harper and Row, 1957.

JOHN M. COGAN

TIME

Much of the work on time in the twentieth-century by American philosophers has been concerned with finding a physical basis for "time's arrow." Unfortunately, the scientific technicality of their work precludes giving an account of it within the brief space allotted to this entry. Instead, the focus will be on the metaphysical theories of time of the most influential American philosophers, namely, William James, John Dewey, George Santayana, and Alfred North Whitehead. Their metaphysics were responses to the challenge of modern science's alleged bifurcation between man and nature that stripped the world of all properties that give human life meaning and value. James, Dewey, and Whitehead met this challenge by developing an anthropomorphic metaphysics that explains reality at large in terms of categories that apply to the manner in which man is engaged with the world, thereby assuring that the world will be a suitable habitat for humanity. In contrast, Santayana's strategy is to make bifurcationism look attractive, at least for those like himself who have a Platonic bent of mind. The former approach results in a humanized time containing the shifting perspectives of past, present, and future, the latter in the impersonal time of the physicist consisting in nothing but a mathematically continuous succession of durationless moments.

Humanized time

The basis of James's humanized time is his commitment to Emersonian romanticism which assumes that nature is of a piece with what we discover when we enter into our own consciousness through introspection. Accordingly, James begins his account of time with a phenomenological description of our experience of time, which then gets projected onto reality at large. In the chapter on "The Perception of Time" in *The Principles of Psychology*, James is intent on showing how our concepts of succession and the past are derived from perception, as is required by his Humean doctrine that concepts are derived by abstraction from percepts. Since a succession of perceptions is not a perception of succession, each individual pulse of perceptual experience must have a finite temporal content, called the "specious present," that encompasses successive states extending into both the near past and future. The name "specious present," which James subsequently wisely dropped, puts the shoe on the wrong foot, since, for James, it is the physicist's mathematically punctual present that is spurious, the psychological present being the true one.

Initially, James makes it appear as if the successive states of a specious present, the notes of a melody say, as well as the succession of specious presents themselves, are numerically distinct from each other, but this gets amended by his account in the chapter on "The Stream of Thought" of our consciousness being like a flowing river in which these successive states flow into each other so that sharp numerical distinctions cannot be made between them. "They melt into each other like dissolving views." (See the "Relations" entry.) This phenomenological analysis gets ontologized in his final two books, *A Pluralistic Universe* and *Some Problem of Philosophy*, by his appeal to Zeno's paradoxes to show that there cannot be a succession of numerically distinct states even if their ordering is dense, i.e. infinitely divisible, or mathematically continuous. If time is discrete, the flight of an arrow consists in a sequence of static states of the arrow, but a motion cannot be generated out of the immobile. And, if Achilles' run occurs in a dense time, there is no first distance that he is to traverse, and therefore he can't get started, his theme song being "I Can't Get Started with You."

Change can be understood only by introspecting the flow of our own consciousness, which then gets projected onto the world at large. This anthropomorphizing of reality underlies James's demand that an analysis of change must explain how a change or motion is intentionally accomplished or generated. "The continuous process to be traversed [such as running a finite distance] ... is a task – not only for our philosophical imagination, but for any real agent who might try physically to compass the entire performance." An agent could not intentionally run through a finite distance in the manner described by the physicist, since there is no initial sub-space that must be traversed and thus no initial action that must be performed; but an agent's recipe for accomplishing some task, if it is not the trivial one of "just do it," must specify an initial action.

James attempts to escape the clutches of Zeno by holding that time passes in a pulsational or atomic manner. In order to establish this, James again appeals to what goes on in our consciousness when we intentionally act. "We tell it off in pulses. We say 'now! Now! Now!' or we count 'More! More! More!' as we feel it bud." There is an apparent clash between this pulsational account and the stream of consciousness one. James gives us a hint on how to resolve this clash in his remark that "the logically distinct [elements within a specious present] are not ontologically separate." They are not ontologically separate because they melt and fuse together. The same can be said about James's successive droplets of becoming. Our intellectual distinction between immediately successive droplets is a logical abstraction, distinguishing between individuals that are not really distinct from each other.

Alfred North Whitehead, in *Process and Reality*, quotes James's droplet account of temporal passage with approval and further agrees with him that it is the only way to escape from Zeno. Each event droplet, called an "actual occasion," has a finite duration, say one of Achilles' steps, but it becomes present in a nonsuccessive manner.

> In every act of becoming there is the becoming of something with temporal extension; but that the act is not extensive, in the sense that it is divisible into earlier and later acts of becoming which correspond to the extensive divisibility of what has become.

This is succinctly captured in Whitehead's pithy remark that there is a becoming of continuity but not a continuity of becoming. After an actual occasion has become, our intellect can subdivide it to its hearts content. It is, as Aristotle had it, not an actual but only a potential infinity of successive temporal parts in the operational sense that our intellect can always further subdivide it. This is a very important point, since, given that an event is a happening and its happening is its becoming present, if it actually contained a dense ordering of temporal parts, it would become present in a dense manner, which is not possible.

Whitehead's account of temporal becoming is as romantic as it can get. For each actual occasion is unique and freely creates itself according to its subjective aim, which need not be conscious, that operates as a final cause of its actualization, and it feels satisfaction upon its completion. Furthermore, each actual occasion achieves a type of unification with every other already actualized one through a prehension of it, a feeling of its subjective state. The same sort of nineteenth-century romanticism imbues Dewey's account of time in "Time and Individuality" wherein he claims that there is an "intrinsic connection of time with individuality," in which an "individual" is honorifically defined by Dewey as a free self-cause of its own unique history, which is close to what Whitehead says about an actual occasion. It is contended that even atoms and molecules qualify as individuals in this honorific sense, thereby resulting in panpsychism. "The principle of developing career applies to all things in nature, as well as to human beings."

Impersonal time

An essential feature of humanized time is that nature itself contains the shifting perspectives of past, present, and future. The reason is that humanized time is modeled on the manner in which time enters into the life of an agent intent on bringing something about. For such an agent there is the present at which action must be taken, a past that must be made use of so as to inform the present action, and a projected future state of the completed action. Nothing could cause a greater bifurcation between man and nature than a denial of the objective reality of these temporal perspectives. And this is just what Santayana's theory of time does; for it holds that temporal relations between events are objective but that their pastness, presentness, and futurity are subjective, being illicit projections of our way of experiencing time upon nature, similar to our projecting sensible properties on to material objects. On this basis he objected to Dewey's naturalism for making these perspectives nature's own perspectives. Dewey's response was that "there is no gulf, no two spheres of existence, no 'bifurcation,'" and thus "there are in nature both foregrounds and backgrounds, heres and theres, centers and perspectives."

Santayana extols the benefits of a bifurcationist metaphysic. It is his purpose to show us how to escape from a meaningless, workaday world of biologically induced endeavorings, which is the standpoint of the moral agent intent on controlling the world, so that we can live within the eternal present, something which we do by intuiting the timeless Platonic essences and by being the spectator of all time and eternity. An important step along the way to achieving this form of platonic and Gnostic salvation is to divest ourselves of the moral agent's false, anthropomorphic view of reality, which is foisted on us by our animal nature. As Santayana put it so eloquently,

> It would seem idle from her [the workaday] point of view, and rather mad, that any spirit should ever disengage itself from that process and should come to find in it some satisfying essence, so that in discerning and possessing this essence it might transcend that remorseless flux and might look away from it to an eternal world.

Santayana did not just disagree with the humanistic view of time, he scorned it, as is evident from the incredible rhetorical invective that he directed against it. The moral agent, by abrogating a special objective ontological status to the time at which she acts, namely the present, is said to be "selfish," "egotistical," "impertinent," "stupid," "ignorant," "inept," "biased," "idolatrous," "insane," "outrageous," "fantastic," "poetical," and "superficial." Sentimental time also is called a "metaphysical illusion" that is based on "animal blindness" and "animal falsification," being a case "egregious egotism."

Further reading

James, William. *The Principles of Psychology.* Cambridge, MA: Harvard University Press, 1981.

—— *Some Problems of Philosophy.* Cambridge, MA: Harvard University Press, 1981.

Santayana, George. *The Realm of Matter.* London: Constable, 1923.

Whitehead, Alfred North. *Process and Reality.* New York: Humanities Press, 1955.

RICHARD M. GALE

TORREY, HENRY AUGUSTUS PEARSON

Clergyman and philosopher, Henry Augustus Pearson Torrey (1837–1902) was educated at the University of Vermont and Union Theological Seminary. From 1865 to 1868 he was pastor of a Congregational church. In 1868 he was appointed Marsh Professor of Intellectual and Moral Philosophy at the University of Vermont, a chair which he occupied until his death. In 1896 his university awarded him a Doctor of Laws degree. Torrey is perhaps best known as the mentor of the young John Dewey, who read the philosophical classics under his direction. Dewey's library contains an inscribed copy of Torrey's only published book, *The Philosophy of Descartes* (1892), an edition of extracts he translated. Torrey was also interested in the philosophy of Leibniz and Kant.

Further reading

Feuer, Lewis Samuel. "H.A.P. Torrey and John Dewey: Teacher and Pupil," *American Quarterly* 10, 1 (1958): 34–54.

Kurita, Osamu. "H.A.P. Torrey and John Dewey, Re-Examined." *Bulletin of the Kyoto University of Education* ser. A 58 (1981): 1–15.

Torrey, Henry A.P. "The Théodicée of Leibnitz," *Andover Review* 4, 22 (1885): 289–99; 4, 23 (1885): 407–17; 4, 24 (1885): 493–512.

—— (ed.) *The Philosophy of Descartes in Extracts from His Writings.* New York: Henry Holt, 1892.

—— "Herbert Spencer, Facts and Comments," *Philosophical Review* 12, 2 (1903): 193–9.

LARRY A. HICKMAN

TRAGEDY

Since the first quarter of the twentieth century pragmatists have been accused of not having a sense of the tragic. To have a sense of the tragic is to see inevitable moral conflict, the limits of human intelligence, and extreme emotion and suffering at the very core of the human experience. Most pragmatists, so the objection typically proceeds, focus on topics like community, democracy, science, and education with an optimism that prevents them from seeing and addressing the more tragic aspects of themselves and the world. Since these aspects are important and worthy of philosophical consideration, much of pragmatism is not as comprehensive and relevant as it should be.

Aspects of this critique have emerged from a variety of thinkers over time. For example, Randolphe Bourne's "The Collapse of the American Strategy" (1917) argued that John Dewey's philosophy didn't recognize the limits of intelligence. His article "Twilight of Idols" (1917) raised questions about whether pragmatism could adequately address and give direction to human emotions in times of crisis. Reinhold Niebuhr's *Moral Man and Immoral Society* (1932) argued that Dewey and his followers failed to see that moral conflict is inevitable and must be dealt with by power rather than intelligence. And Cornel West, in his *Keeping Faith: Philosophy and Race in America* (1993), argued that pragmatists need to recognize and confront individual and collective experiences of evil and the suffering that comes from such experiences. The ideas in this representative sample can be found in many other thinkers both past and present and are best taken together when trying to formulate a comprehensive account of tragedy.

It is true that most pragmatists have not explicitly addressed themes associated with a sense of the tragic. Of course, there have been a few exceptions, such as William James' essay "The Moral Philosopher and the Moral Life" (1891), Josiah Royce's *Sources of Religious Insight* (1912), and George Santayana's *The Life of Reason* (1905–6). But for the most part pragmatists have had other concerns. It is important, however, to draw a distinction between what a particular philosopher addresses and what that philosopher's vision and set of arguments is capable of addressing. For although many pragmatists don't address inevitable moral conflict, the limits of intelligence, and human suffering as much as some would like, it is clear that many ideas central to pragmatic thought can incorporate such themes.

Sidney Hook's 1960 essay "Pragmatism and the Tragic Sense of Life" argued for such incorporation and stated that, contrary to the prevailing opinions of the time, the pragmatic perspective on life actually gets its fundamental justification from its unique ability to recognize and address tragedy. Hook's position has two fundamental aspects. The first is that a tragic conflict is an inevitable conflict of momentous goods (values) and/or rights (obligations). This view of tragic conflict is based on a pluralistic view of morals that many pragmatists maintain. This view states that there is never *one* good in a morally problematic situation and that clinging to each possible resolution is a *cluster of goods*. Each one of these goods makes a legitimate claim on us but all of them cannot be realized at the same time and in the same degree. Thus something of importance to us must be sacrificed and this sacrifice will cause some significant degree of suffering. Hook argues that it is precisely because pragmatists have a pluralistic view of morals that they *can* embrace conflicts that are *really* tragic rather than just *apparently* tragic. Here Hook is following in the footsteps of James who, in "The Moral Philosopher and the Moral Life," argued that the moral philosopher is essentially a mediator who seeks to bring about a more inclusive moral universe by reducing the sum of dissatisfactions in moral conflict. This is by no means easy since the space-time of our world often prevents the simultaneous realization of incompatible experiences. In fact, we can hardly imagine a good that would not end up competing for the same piece of space-time with some other good. According to James, this inevitability of conflict shows our world has a tragic constitution.

The second aspect of Hook's position is that the pragmatic approach to tragic conflict is melioristic insofar as it tries to reduce the costs of, rather than totally eradicate, tragic conflict. It tries to reduce the costs of conflict by employing the method of experimental intelligence. This method entails that one forego the dogmatic preaching of solutions and explore the suggestions that emerge from the analysis of situated problems. The hope is that there will be a way to preserve as many values and/or goods as possible so that a more morally inclusive world can emerge despite necessary sacrifice and suffering. Both optimism and pessimism can discourage one from engaging in inquiry and social reform. After all, if one is optimistic one may believe things will work out no matter what; and if one is pessimistic one might not try to change anything since things will turn out bad no matter what one does. But if one is a meliorist then one might be more inclined to act and see one's actions as playing a role in reducing suffering. Of course, many argue that tragedies are best understood as situations where we have no control at all. But for pragmatists, the fact that we have a hand in how things unfold opens up the possibility for moral responsibility, regret, and remorse: things that can actually make the suffering of tragedy more intense. In fact, Hook argued that the desire to mediate as many moral conflicts as possible in a world with no guarantees allows us to see the melioristic approach as more heroic than pessimistic and optimistic approaches. And traditionally tragedies have had heroes.

Hook's introduction of pluralism and meliorism enables pragmatists to incorporate the three themes typically associated with a sense of the tragic. We have inevitable moral conflict secured by the introduction of a pluralistic view of morals; we have suffering guaranteed insofar as the sacrifice of values that are momentous to us is also guaranteed; and the limits of intelligence are admitted by adopting a melioristic view of intelligence which is not optimistic and offers no guarantees of success.

But why would our melioristic efforts fail? Here the pragmatist is also in a good position to respond in a way that draws upon ideas central to pragmatic thought. The first idea is that each individual in a pluralistic universe must respond to life's diversity from a unique perspective. In *The Principles of Psychology* (1890) James argued that such a response must be selective; indeed, our consciousness is always interested in one part of an object more than another and is constantly welcoming and rejecting things that help or hinder our interests. But this selectivity, while it helps us manage complexity and attend to things *we* feel are important, necessarily simplifies our experience and makes us inattentive to the feelings of *others.* This inevitability of inattention leads to what James referred to as a *certain blindness* in us. This blindness will influence intelligent mediation of conflict in many ways. For example, one might lack that subtle and sympathetic understanding of others necessary for successful negotiation. It may be that one's limiting habits, ideas, and feelings will lead one to maintain a bad position despite good advice. Or perhaps one will encounter others in a conflict that simply cannot *see* the importance of the pragmatic agenda and thus will not engage in compromise and negotiation.

The second idea that enables pragmatists to account for the failure of intelligent amelioration comes from Dewey's conception of experience. In his essay "The Need for a Recovery of Philosophy" Dewey asserts that the orthodox theory of experience is primarily a *knowledge* affair. What Dewey means is that philosophers – both empiricists and rationalists – have typically been concerned with experience only in relation to questions of knowledge. But Dewey's radically empirical approach led him to define experience as an affair of the intercourse of a living being with its physical and social environment. The key here is that Dewey places the act of knowing within a larger experiential context. Experience, because it is not primarily a knowledge affair, contains many things we must undergo without knowledge. As a result, there is often a radical disparity between what is experienced and what is known – a disparity that is seen again and again in tragic situations where people, despite their best intentions and well-laid plans, fail miserably in their endeavors and, in some cases, end up receiving exactly what they wanted to avoid. Pragmatists can use this vision of experience to fully embrace yet another inexorable source of blindness consistent with a sense of the tragic.

It should be clear by now that certain ideas central to pragmatism can enable pragmatists incorporate a sense of the tragic. But why *should* they incorporate such a sense? Well, one reason can be approached by understanding that pragmatism is concerned with the serious value conflicts that occur between humans and that many of these conflicts are tragic. If many serious value conflicts are tragic, and pragmatists see value conflict mediation as one of their primary functions, then tragic conflict should be recognized and addressed because it lies at the heart of normative social inquiry. Indeed, one might say that it is precisely *because* tragic conflicts involve necessary sacrifice that pragmatists should try to reduce the costs of conflict whenever possible.

Now we attempt to ameliorate conflict through negotiation and mediation. But one does not honestly negotiate and mediate if one assumes in advance that some position is the only correct one. Rather, one should assume that moral conflicts of goods and rights are not necessarily contradictions and that *all* the candidates in a morally problematic situation possess some desirable traits. Of course, many people approach moral conflicts *dogmatically,* that is, with the belief that certain values are the only *real* values. Such people will see many values in a morally problematic situation as *apparently* good or right. But if one is a pragmatist then one will be against dogmatism. For dogmatism can prevent a fair weighing of the views involved in conflict. It can prevent one from taking into account options that can lead to more inclusive resolutions. And it clearly contradicts the experimental approach to tragedy that takes each situation as a unique challenge. The interesting thing is that a sense of the tragic can help the pragmatist avoid dogmatism and enter into genuine negotiation. For if one affirms the reality of tragic conflict then one affirms the possibility that all the values involved in a conflict might be valuable and perhaps justified.

And the last reason why a pragmatist might try to incorporate a sense of the tragic is that the intelligence limitations so dramatically revealed in tragic conflict can help counter a hubris which often threatens pragmatists with their future-looking emphasis on growth. We have seen that the pragmatist's goal in a tragic situation is to give each view a voice and incorporate these voices into an inclusive whole. Of course, in a tragedy there is no hope for a totally successful incorporation devoid of sacrifice and suffering. But the chances of partial success are greater if the limitations of moral conduct revealed in tragedy are recognized. An awareness that our capacities are limited may help us detect simplifications, misunderstandings, and exclusions that we would ordinarily miss. If we forget these limits we may find it more difficult to resist the attraction of reducing the complexity of conflict to a simple harmony. Such a simplification may satisfy a simple problem-solving mentality, but it will not satisfy the demands of careful and contextualized analysis. If this is the case then pragmatists should take the limits revealed in tragic conflict seriously in order to do justice to the limits – and perhaps the possibilities – of moral inquiry.

Further reading

Bourne, Randolphe. *The Radical Will: Selected Writings, 1911–1918*, ed. Olaf Hansen. New York: Urizen, 1977.

Hook, Sidney. *Pragmatism and the Tragic Sense of Life.* New York: Basic, 1974.

McDermott, John J. (ed.) *The Writings of William James.* Chicago, IL: University of Chicago Press, 1977.

—— (ed.) *The Philosophy of John Dewey.* Chicago, IL: University of Chicago Press, 1981.

Niebuhr, Reinhold. *Moral Man and Immoral Society.* New York: Scribner's, 1960.

Royce, Josiah. *Sources of Religious Insight*. New York: Octagon Books, 1977.

Santayana, George. *The Life of Reason*. New York: Prometheus Books, 1998.

West, Cornel. *The Cornel West Reader*. New York: Basic *Civitas* Books, 1999.

DWIGHT GOODYEAR

TRANSCENDENTALISM

Transcendentalism is a term associated with an eclectic group of New England thinkers and writers, including Ralph Waldo Emerson, Elizabeth Peabody, William Ellery Channing, Margaret Fuller, and A. Bronson Alcott, among many others, who were dissatisfied with the provincialism and parochialism of American intellectual life, and who promoted their ideas in lectures, writings, and at meetings of the Transcendental Club, founded in 1836. Transcendentalism was a prominent cultural force until around 1860, helping to import and interpret European Romanticism and German Idealism into American culture; transcendentalists' ideas about religion, individualism, civic responsibility, truth, and ways of knowing influenced and shaped the pragmatism of William James and John Dewey.

The members of the Transcendental Club at first numbered hardly more than a dozen; some, like Channing, Emerson, Theodore Parker, and James Freeman Clarke, were trained as ministers; George Ripley and Orestes Brownson, both former ministers, primarily were journalists; Margaret Fuller was a literary critic and feminist; Elizabeth Peabody was an educational reformer. Many members' connection to Christian religion does not suggest that transcendentalism was primarily a religious movement; in fact, transcendentalists envisioned wide-ranging social and cultural reform. All sought to energize what they perceived as stagnant intellectual life, dominated as it was by the Unitarianism that characterized Harvard College and by a narrow view of what was worthy in literature. Philosophy and religion, they believed, rejected contemporary European thinkers and the new poetry – by Byron, Wordsworth, and Coleridge, for example – that was being published in England. The Transcendentalist Club offered its members a forum to consider such topics as mysticism, morality, education, genius, and the nature of poetry. In addition to the club, from 1840 to 1844 transcendentalists published their ideas in a journal, *The Dial*, edited by Margaret Fuller for its first two years, followed by Emerson. The journal failed for lack of subscribers, but its failure did not quash the dissemination of transcendentalist ideas in American culture. Such writers as Henry David Thoreau, Walt Whitman, and Emily Dickinson were influenced by transcendentalism.

In his lecture "The Transcendentalist," delivered on 23 December 1841, Emerson defined transcendentalism as a way of knowing more profound than experience, a concept they derived from Immanuel Kant. Countering the arguments of John Locke, Kant proposed that our knowledge of the world comes not directly from experience, but from sense impressions structured by the native concepts of the mind, through which experience is acquired and interpreted. Concerned that the growing status of scientific research would lead to a materialist perception of reality, the transcendentalists privileged intuition over empiricism, maintaining that mind creates the world. Besides Kant, Thomas Carlyle, Swedish mystic Emanuel Swedenborg, Samuel Taylor Coleridge, and other Romantic poets also served as influences in shaping transcendentalists' celebration of the individual.

Many transcendentalists had ties to Unitarianism, and they extended the emphasis on personal agency that Unitarianism promoted. Moreover, rather than envision God as existing above and apart from the world, requiring the mediation of a minister for connection with this spirit, transcendentalists believed that divinity pervaded all living things and could be perceived by all. Pantheism, then, was a central tenet of transcendentalism.

Transcendentalism's most transformative idea was the power of the self, an idea that had ethical and moral implications: self-knowledge and self-reliance would lead to an acknowledgment of civic responsibility, a recognition of one's connection to others, and a sense of self-discipline that countered selfishness or self interest. The concept of self-reliance recurs in Emerson's many lectures and essays. For Emerson, self-reliance meant both self-knowledge and empowerment to act on one's beliefs. In a democracy, each individual must take responsibility for moral and ethical decisions, not follow the dictates of the majority or of leaders, however eminent those leaders might be.

The transcendentalists' striving for community led to two utopian communal experiments: Fruitlands and Brook Farm, both established in Massachusetts in the 1840s. The communities' failure did not dampen the transcendentalists' belief that competition and materialism were antithetical to the cultivation of individualism.

Further reading

Emerson, Ralph Waldo. *Selected Essays, Lectures, and Poems*, ed. with a Foreword by Robert D. Richardson, Jr. New York: Bantam, 1990.

Gura, Philip F. and Myerson, Joel (eds). *Critical Essays on American Transcendentalism*. Boston, MA: G.K. Hall, 1982.

Myerson, Joel (ed.). *The American Transcendentalists*. Detroit, MI: Gale, 1988.

—— (ed.) *Transcendentalism: A Reader*. New York: Oxford University Press, 2000.

Rose, Anne C. *Transcendentalism as a Social Movement, 1830–1850*. New Haven, CT: Yale University Press, 1981.

LINDA SIMON

TRANSFORMATION OF AMERICAN PHILOSOPHY

With more than 11,000 practicing philosophers at work in North America, the size and scope of the academic establishment exerts a crucial formative influence on the nature of contemporary American philosophy. The recent exponential increase of people and publications has so worked out as to effect a transformation in the discipline of philosophy itself by perfectly natural and readily understandable mechanisms.

For one thing, the explosion of the discipline has constrained an increase in specialization and division of labor with the result that the field has become increasingly technical. The overall situation is one of specialists talking to other specialists. Ever heavier theoretical armaments are brought to bear on ever smaller problem-targets in ways that journal readers will occasionally wonder whether the important principle that technicalities should never be multiplied beyond necessity has been lost sight of. This increasing technicalization of philosophy has been achieved at the expense of its wider accessibility – and indeed even to its accessibility to members of the profession.

However, while philosophy nowadays makes virtually no impact on the wider culture of North America, its place in higher education is secure. To be sure, of all undergraduates in American colleges and universities, only about half of 1 percent *major* in Philosophy (compared with nearly 3 percent for English and over 15 percent for Business and Management). But owing to philosophy's role in meeting "distribution requirements" it has secured a prominent place in the curricula of post-secondary education. Unlike the United Kingdom, where post-World War II philosophers adopted a very technical and narrowly conceived idea of what the job of philosophy is – with the result of effectively assuring the discipline's declining role in the educational system – in America philosophy has managed not only to survive but to thrive in higher education.

But the explosion means expansion of the literature that, for better or for worse, we have entered into a new philosophical era where what counts is not just a dominant elite but a vast host of lesser mortals. No one among the academic philosophers of today manages to impose their agenda on more than a minimal fraction of the larger, internally diversified community. Even the most influential of contemporary American philosophers is simply yet another – somewhat larger – fish in a very populous sea where the smaller fish play an increasingly prominent role simply because there are so many more of them.

In the "heroic" era of the past, the historian of the philosophy of a place and time could safely concentrate upon the *dominant* figures and expect thereby to achieve a certain completeness with respect to "what really mattered." But such an approach is grossly unsuited to the conditions of the present era. For the reality of it is that the "dominant figures" have lost control of the agenda.

At present American philosophy is a garden where 100 flowers bloom. In recent years the source of influence has fragmented across the whole academic board. Some look for inspiration to psychology (especially to Freud), others to economics (from Marx to von Neumann), yet others to literature, or to law, or to ... The list goes on and on. In its present configuration, American philosophy indicates that the "revolt of the masses," which Ortega y Gasset thought characteristic of our era, manifests itself not only in politics and social affairs but in intellectual culture also and even in philosophy. The condition of American philosophy today is a matter of trends and fashions that go their own way without the guidance of agenda-controlling individuals. This results in a state of affairs that calls for description on a statistical rather than biographical basis. It is ironic to see the partisans of political correctness in academia condemning philosophy as an elitist discipline at the very moment when philosophy itself has abandoned elitism and succeeded in making itself over in a populist reconstruction. American philosophy has now well and truly left "the genteel tradition" behind.

And so the Great Man Theory no longer holds; a faithful picture of the work of the entire community simply cannot be conveyed by considering the work of its three (or ten or hundred) greatest members. The only way to give an accurate account of the community as a whole in its present configuration is to proceed not personalistically via individuals but holistically via statistics.

To do justice to the complexities of the current situation of American philosophy requires that a treatment by *significant trends* replace a treatment by *dominant individuals*, with individuals figuring at best in the role of exemplars. Insofar as single individuals are dealt with this must now be done against a vastly enlarged background with individuals viewed as *representative* rather than as *determinative* figures. In the context of American philosophy, quantitative developments have wrought a qualitative transformation.

Further reading

Rescher, N. *Is Philosophy Dispensable? And Other Philosophical Essays.* Frankfurt: ONTOS Verlag, 2007, pp. 99–114.

NICHOLAS RESCHER

TRUTH VALUE

Bearers of truth values – sentences, utterances, propositions, and beliefs – are generally thought to be capable of having one of two truth values: either true or false. When I utter, for example, "Grass is green," I have uttered a truth. If I were to utter "Bush was never the president of the United States," the utterance I have made is false.

It has been claimed that there are kinds of utterance that are incapable of being either true or false. For example, moral emotivists claim that utterances of sentences such as "The war is wrong" are neither true nor false – the function of such utterances is to express my attitude of disapproval to the war, not to make any kind of statement.

Among the other types of utterance that have been claimed to be incapable of being true or false are utterances of paradoxes or antinomies (such as "This sentence is not true") and utterances containing vague terms (such as "Alex Rodriguez is rich").

A distinct view from the one denying that certain sentences are capable of being true (or false) is the view that, in addition to true and false, there are other (are more) truth values. On a three-valued logic, the possible truth values are true, false, and undetermined. An application of this view is that we may attribute a truth value to the paradoxical sentence "This sentence is not true" without having to (paradoxically) claim there are true falsehoods, so long as the truth value that is attributed to this sentence is the truth value undetermined.

Further reading

Field, Hartry. "Disquotational Truth and Factually Defective Discourse," *Philosophical Review* 103 (1994): 405–52.

Horwich, Paul. *Truth*, second edition. Oxford: Oxford University Press, 1998.

Kleene, Stephen C. *Introduction to Metamathematics*. Princeton, NJ: D. Van Nostrand, 1950.

Fritz J. McDonald

TRUTH, THEORIES OF

One can find in American philosophy exponents of every kind of theory of truth. But the account of truth that is usually identified with American philosophy is the home-grown pragmatist theory of truth. It aims to be a "workaday" account, as the founder of pragmatism, Charles S. Peirce, put it – a view of truth that is firmly connected to, and works well within, our practices. The pragmatic maxim (the principle at the very heart of pragmatism) requires that we look to the consequences of a concept in order to fully understand it: "we must not begin by talking of pure ideas, – vagabond thoughts that tramp the public roads without any human habitation, – but must begin with men and their conversation" (Peirce CP 8.112). In order to get a complete grasp of a concept, we must connect the concept to that with which we have "dealings" (CP 5.416).

Peirce, along with every other classical and contemporary pragmatist, argued that "transcendental" accounts of truth, such as the correspondence theory, on which a true belief is one that corresponds to or gets right the believer-independent world, are examples of those "vagabond thoughts." They make truth "the subject of metaphysics exclusively." For the very idea of the believer-independent world, and the items within it to which beliefs or sentences might correspond, seem graspable only if we could somehow step outside of our corpus of belief. We would do better to illuminate truth by considering its linkages with inquiry, assertion, and belief. For those are the human dealings relevant to truth. All pragmatist views of truth, that is, are naturalist views; we should not add anything metaphysical to science, or to any other first-order inquiry. We have to extract the concept of truth, as it were, from our practices of inquiry, reason-giving, and deliberation.

Two very different versions of the pragmatic account of truth arise from applying the pragmatic maxim to the concept of truth – from linking the concept of truth to our practices. One version is Peirce's. He focuses on the practices of inquiry and tries to capture our cognitive aspirations to objectivity. He argues that a belief is true if it would be "indefeasible"; or would not be improved upon; or would never lead to disappointment; or would stand up to all the evidence and argument, no matter how far we were to pursue our inquiries. Although he is often held to have said that a true belief is one that is fated to be believed at the end of inquiry, he on the whole tries to stay away from unhelpful ideas such as the final end of inquiry, perfect evidence, and the like.

Anticipating recent moves in philosophical debates about truth, he was also very careful to stay away from a reductive definition of truth: he did not want to define truth as that which satisfies our aims in inquiry. A dispute about definition, he says, is usually a "profitless discussion," or a "folly" as Donald Davidson has said (CP 8.100; Davidson 1996). His pragmatist project is to try to get us to see the difference between two respectable tasks. The first is to provide an analytic or "nominal" definition of a concept like truth, which at best might be of use to someone who has never encountered the notion before. The second is to provide a pragmatic elucidation of the concept of truth on an account of the role the concept plays in practical endeavors. This is clearly the project that the pragmatist thinks is important.

The pragmatist view of truth, however, finds a very different kind of expression in the hands of Richard Rorty. When Rorty looks at the human practices which are linked to the concept of truth, he does not see our aspirations to getting things right. Rather, he argues that the concept of truth plays no role whatsoever in our practices – it can safely drop out of our vocabulary. On this second version of the pragmatist theory of truth, there is no truth (or objectivity) to be had, only solidarity, or agreement within a community, or what our peers will let us get away with saying (Rorty 1979: 176).

Rorty takes John Dewey to be the inspiration for this kind of pragmatism. Dewey argued that it is best to think of truth as warranted assertibility. There are a number of ways of interpreting Dewey here, interpretations which turn on how strong we take "warranted" to be. Some of those interpretations will have Dewey being much closer to Peirce than to Rorty.

Perhaps William James is more in line with Rorty. James argued that "True ideas are those that we can assimilate, validate, corroborate and verify" and he sometimes cashed this out by saying that truth is what "works" for us (James 1992: 100). He rather infamously suggested that if the belief in God made a positive or a good impact on someone's life, then it could reasonably be taken as true by that person (James 1992: 130).

When James first put forward this view of truth, Bertrand Russell and G.E. Moore leveled devastating criticisms of it and those criticisms continue to press what we might (very controversially) call the Rorty–Dewey–James interpretation of the pragmatist theory of truth.

As Russell pointed out, it is very difficult to know when the consequences of a belief are useful or good (Russell 1992: 201). And as Moore pointed out, usefulness is a property that may come and go (in James' own words). So is Rorty's "what our peers will let us get away with saying." Hence, on this second version of the pragmatist account of truth, "a belief, which occurs at several different times, may be true at some of the times at which it occurs, and yet untrue at others" (Moore 1992: 183). The truth of a belief, that is, seems to vary from time to time and from culture to culture. Truth, on the Rorty–Dewey–James version of pragmatism, is not a stable property of beliefs.

There is much controversy about whether any pragmatist, classical or contemporary, really intended to produce such a relativist view of truth. But the onus is on this kind of pragmatist to show how the view escapes the difficulties associated with a relativist view of truth.

One way of understanding the pragmatist theory of truth is to see it as akin to coherence theories of truth, which hold that a belief is true if it coheres with our other beliefs. The twist that Peirce gives to the coherence theory is that he insists that a subjunctive, not an indicative, conditional is required: a belief is true if it would cohere with our other well-grounded beliefs (and with experience).

Another way of interpreting Peirce's pragmatist–naturalist theory of truth is to see it as akin to contemporary deflationary views of truth. On Peirce's view, there is a point or an aim to any particular deliberation: to solve a problem, to build a better instrument, or to decide what is just or morally right in the circumstances. When we inquire, we are wondering about those things, not about whether a statement or belief has the property of truth. "Truth" is just a catch-all for the particular local aims of inquiry: empirical adequacy, predictive power, coherence with other beliefs, simplicity, explanatory power, getting a reliable guide to action, fruitfulness for other research, greater understanding of others, increased maturity, and the like. There is nothing over and above the fulfillment of those ends, nothing metaphysical, to which we aspire.

Pragmatism is thus aligned with those contemporary deflationist views of truth, on which truth is a deflated property, if it is a property at all. On one such view, the infinite string of instances of the equivalence or disquotational schema is taken to entirely capture the content of "is true." "Snow is white" is true if and only if snow is white, "Toronto is north of Buffalo" is true if and only if Toronto is north of Buffalo, and so on.

But Peirce's pragmatism breaks with deflationism in that the deflationist thinks that the only reason for holding on to the idea of truth is that it serves an important logical need. It is a useful device for infinite conjunction and disjunction and for expressing propositions which we cannot identify. Truth is a property, but there is nothing more to it than the generalizing function. It enables us to avoid cumbersome new forms of quantification (Horwich 1990: 38). Peirce argued that there were more uses of "is true" to account for than that. Truth is the aim of inquiry. It is what our beliefs aspire to. So it cannot be as trivial a property as the deflationist would have us believe. We must, on Peirce's view, examine all of the roles that truth plays in our practices of assertion, belief, and inquiry. Only then will we have a full and adequate account of it.

Further reading

Davidson, Donald. "The Folly of Trying to Define Truth," *Journal of Philosophy* 87 (1996): 263–78.

Horwich, Paul. *Truth*. Oxford: Blackwell, 1990.

James, William. *Pragmatism* in Doris Olin (ed.) *William James' Pragmatism in Focus*. London: Routledge, 1992.

Misak, Cheryl. *Truth and the End of Inquiry: A Peircean Account of Truth*, second edition. Oxford: Oxford University Press, 2004.

Moore, G.E. "Professor James's Pragmatism" in Doris Olin (ed.) *William James' Pragmatism in Focus*, London: Routledge, 1992.

Peirce, Charles Sanders. *Collected Papers of Charles Sanders Peirce* (CP), ed. C. Hartshorne and P. Weiss (Vols I–VI), A. Burks (Vols VII and VIII). Cambridge, MA: Belknap Press. 1931–5, 1958.

Rorty, Richard. *Objectivity, Relativism, and Truth: Philosophical Papers*, Vol. 1. Cambridge: Cambridge University Press, 1991.

Russell, Bertrand. "William James's Conception of Truth", in Doris Olin (ed.) *William James' Pragmatism in Focus*. London: Routledge, 1992.

CHERYL MISAK

TUCKER, GEORGE

Born in Bermuda, George Tucker (1775–1861) moved at age twenty-one to Virginia where he remained for most of his life. He began his career as an attorney and was elected to the US Congress for three terms (1819–25). At the request of Thomas Jefferson, he then became the University of Virginia's first professor of moral philosophy, a position which he retained for twenty years until his retirement. Aside from his philosophical works, Tucker authored a biography of Jefferson, a major history of the United States, a science fiction novel about the moon, a southern US novel, and several economic treatises. His philosophical writings are in the form of essays, several of which were published in two collections; others appeared separately in journals. His main philosophical influences were Scottish writers, particularly Hume, Reid and Stewart. Many of his essays express the notion of scientific and cultural progress, which, he argues, results from psychological restlessness and the desire to improve oneself. In the philosophy of mind he takes two approaches: following Reid he holds that some mental concepts and abilities are instinctively grounded in human nature; following Hume he holds that others result from the association of ideas. In aesthetics he criticizes the position that the perception of beauty is a purely subjective response; for Tucker the experience of beauty is naturally excited by an aesthetic object's external qualities, such as its light, color and form. His lengthiest philosophical essay is a critique of Hume's theory of causality. Tucker regularly wrote on the subject of slavery, first criticizing the institution but later defending it on pragmatic grounds; he projected that by around 1920 Southern slave ownership would become "a burdensome charge rather than a source of profit" and thus die out on its own. Unlike most American philosophers of his time, Tucker's philosophy is thoroughly secular with no reference to God or religion.

Further reading

McLean, Robert Colin. *George Tucker: Moral Philosopher and Man of Letters*. Chapel Hill, NC: University of North Carolina Press, 1961.

Tucker, George. *Essays on Various Subjects of Taste, Morals, and National Policy*. Georgetown, DC: J. Milligan, 1822.

—— *The Life and Philosophical Writings of George Tucker*, 4 vols, ed. James Fieser. Bristol: Thoemmes Press, 2004.

JAMES FIESER

TYCHISM

As ancient Greece entered its Golden Age (450–280 BC) its religious landscape began to shift. This shifting occurred very literally "by chance." It shifted by chance not in the sense of changing randomly, but rather in the development of novel votive practices dedicated to Chance (*Tyche*) as a deified abstraction. Citizens began to appeal to *Tyche* in the attempt to explain the spontaneous events that seemed to emerge in public and personal histories. As American pragmatism came into its own in the late 1800s, the philosophic investigation, if not the religious veneration, of *tyche* had a meaningful resurgence. Charles Sanders Peirce contributed to this resurgence, appropriating the Greek understanding of chance in his pragmaticism and expanding this understanding in his concept of tychism, his doctrine of "absolute chance." Peirce himself comments on his indebtedness to the Greeks' investigations, stating that his tychism was an elaboration on Aristotle's comment that some things are determined and others happen by chance.

The term "tychism" appears twenty-five times in Peirce's collected papers, most notably in his *Monist* series published in the early 1890s. However, the concept of chance and the epistemic and ontological indeterminacy that it implies – defines Peirce's earlier work as well. Peirce's early indeterminism appears in his 1866 Lowell Lectures and was enriched during his sustained study of quantified logic throughout the 1870s. This study led Peirce to the belief that the laws of the human mind, and the laws of nature more generally, operate in a probabilistic fashion and that these laws could not be defined in absolute terms and that variation itself defined what he would later term the "law of mind." "The Doctrine of Chances," written in the winter of 1878, stands as a succinct articulation of Peirce's position on the importance and ubiquity of probabilistic events. It presents a discussion on the chance of non-repeatable events, a discussion that Hilary Putnam would later term "Peirce's puzzle." Along these lines, Peirce's later writings do not present *tyche* as chaos or randomness, but rather identify chance as the quality of non-repeatable and novel occurrences that occur regularly but not axiomatically. In these early works, the seeds of tychism were sown.

While the seeds of tychism may have been sown in these early works, it is clear Peirce had yet to understand the ontological and epistemological import of this doctrine of chance. It was only in 1884 that he assumed a concrete position on the problem of determinism, asserting that spontaneity was a real and motivating force in the evolution of the universe and in the growth and variation of law itself. In terms of Peirce's ontological claims, many commentators point to tychism as an important wellspring of the evolutionary cosmology that defines his thought after 1886. This interpretation seems appropriate since Peirce himself indicates that his attempt to develop an account of evolution and continuity stems from his initial investigations of the nature of chance. In 1906, in a lecture to the National Academy of Science, Peirce reflected on the role that tychism played in his thinking on the nature of continuity, suggesting that synechism, his notion of evolutionary continuity, is "the synthesis of tychism and pragmatism." In regard to Peirce's epistemological claims, Carl Hausman suggests in his *Charles S. Peirce's Evolutionary Philosophy* (1993) that Peirce's acknowledgement of tychism in the world coincided with his conviction that chance must also play a vital role in any theory of human knowledge. Knowledge itself develops by hypothetical leaps and bounds rather than by the direction of pre-established axioms and laws. A closer examination of tychism provides a way of understanding these claims and situating the doctrine of chance more squarely in the history of American philosophy.

In the "Doctrine of Necessity Examined," the second article of his *Monist* series, Peirce begins to develop his mature model of tychism as a response to a train of thought that he terms "necessitarianism." According to the "necessitarian," nature operates by way of mechanistic rules that could, at least ideally, be exhaustively defined. Peirce, however, suggests that the "growth and developing complexity, which appears to be universal" cannot be understood by means of necessary laws. Similarly, he states that "variety itself, beyond comparison the most obtrusive character of the universe: no mechanism can account for this." Instead he proposes, and begins to demonstrate by his earlier studies of mathematical probability, that such phenomena can only be explained by way of chance. Here, Peirce writes that he attributes these phenomena "altogether to chance, it is true, but to chance in the form of spontaneity that is to some degree regular."

It is important to emphasize the "regularity" of *tyche*; Peirce is going to insist that chance does not imply sheer randomness, but rather gives birth to a type of order that emerges provisionally in the midst of phenomena. For Peirce, *tyche* motivates the order of nature, an order that reflects the spontaneity and adaptation that had been historically reserved for descriptions of the human mind. In this sense, the principle of tychism draws Peirce to rethink the natural world in terms of a type of idealism that he had hitherto dismissed out of hand. He admits this point in "The Law of Mind" (1892) when he writes:

> I have begun by showing that *tychism* must give birth to an evolutionary cosmology, in which all the regularities of nature and of mind are regarded as products of growth, and to a Schelling-fashioned idealism which holds matter to be mere specialized and partially deadened mind.

In this article Peirce elaborates, commenting that his interest in tychism *per se* must, at least for the time being, be put aside in order to pursue the evolutionary idealism that his investigation of chance and spontaneity has revealed. While tychism sets the stage for his later work, Peirce explicitly shifts his focus away from absolute chance toward the principle of synechism and true continuity. He justifies this move in the last article of the *Monist* series, "Evolutionary Love," (1892) when he explains that synechism in fact encompasses the principle of pure chance.

Further reading

Buchler, Justus. *Charles Peirce's Empiricism*. New York: Octagon Press, 1966.

Hausman, Carl. *Charles S. Peirce's Evolutionary Philosophy.* Cambridge: Cambridge University Press, 1993.

Parker, Kelly. *The Continuity of Peirce's Thought*. Nashville, TN: Vanderbilt University Press, 1997.

Peirce, Charles Sanders. *Collected Papers of Charles Sanders Peirce*, Vol. 6, ed. Charles Hartshorne and Paul Weiss. Cambridge, MA: Harvard University Press., 1958.

Peirce, Charles Sanders. "On the Doctrine of Necessity Examined" [1891], "Doctrine of Chances" [1878], "The Law of Mind" [1892] and "Evolutionary Love" [1893] in *The Essential Peirce*, Vol. 1, ed. the Peirce Edition Project. Bloomington, IN: Indiana University Press, 1998.

JOHN J. KAAG

TYPE–TOKEN DISTINCTION

The type–token distinction is a degenerate form of Charles Peirce's Tone–Token–Type distinction, from which it also derives. Peirce's distinction entered mainstream philosophy through Ogden and Richards's 1923 *The Meaning of Meaning.* A token is a single thing or event serving as a sign. A type is a definitely significant form; it is a sign that can be endlessly repeated while remaining the same sign in all its instantiations. The twelve instances of the word "the" in the present entry are all tokens of a single type, namely, the word "the" as it is used in the English language. A tone is an indefinite significant character. When we italicize an instance of the word "the" for emphasis, we have changed its tone. Tones are not repeatable as types are. Because each tone is unique, tones have similarities at best. Though Peirce's favorite example is a linguistic one, the distinction itself isn't. For instance, a symphony considered as to its structure is a type, an actual performance of it a token, and its aesthetic effect a tone. For Peirce, types do not exist, but they determine things that do. Tones also do not exist, but they characterize things that do. Peirce's distinction thus allows one to be a realist about types and tones, as was Peirce himself, without requiring that they must therefore exist (i.e. have the mode of being of a token).

Peirce's tone–token–type distinction conforms to his doctrine of the categories; they embody the firstness, secondness, and thirdness of a sign. Within the context of his semiotics, Peirce also refers to them as qualisign, sinsign, and legisign.

Further reading

Hardwick, Charles S. (ed.) *Semiotics and Significs: The Correspondence between Charles S. Peirce and Victoria Lady Welby.* Bloomington, IN: Indiana University Press, 1977.

Ogden, C.K. and Richards, I.A. *The Meaning of Meaning.* London: Harcourt, 1923.

Peirce, Charles S. "Prolegomena to an Apology for Pragmaticism," *Monist* 16 (1906): 492–546.

Williams, Donald C. "Tokens, Types, Words, and Terms," *Journal of Philosophy* 33, 26 (1936): 701–7.

CORNELIS DE WAAL

U

UNCONSCIOUS

The *unconscious* is used today in a variety of senses, ranging from informal, everyday uses to formally defined, elaborately theorized ones. But several meanings in particular need to be carefully distinguished, above all what Sigmund Freud identifies as the *dynamic* in contrast to the *descriptive* meaning of this term. In its dynamic sense (i.e. its strictly psychoanalytic meaning), the term continues to be the site of philosophical controversy, especially in Anglo-American philosophy (nowhere more so than among those who identify with Deweyan pragmatism, though Richard Rorty is a notable exception here). It refers to what in our own minds or psyches strenuously resists being brought to our awareness, indeed, what becomes accessible to us as conscious human actors only through an arduous process and in an indirect manner. Akin to the meanings given to the word by John Dewey in *Experience and Nature* (1925), *consciousness* designates for Freud the qualitatively immediate aspects of our mental lives and also the immediately accessible meanings so intimately associated with these aspects (Laplanche and Pontalis: 84–8; cf. LW 1.227), for example the feeling of hunger as both an immediate feeling and a somatic sign of the need for nutrition. But, for Dewey no less than Freud, there is more to mind than consciousness. Freud's understanding of the *workings* of the unconscious is, however, derived from his clinical experience with mostly neurotic individuals whose psychological obsessions, fixations, and other maladies obstructed their efforts to live meaningful, rewarding lives. In his most careful and precise formulations, then, the unconscious does not refer (as all too many of his critics allege) to a separate mental realm (see, e.g., Dewey MW 14.61) but to heterogeneous mental processes, that is, ones radically different from conscious thought (Lear 2005). The unconscious primary processes are condensation and displacement. They operate under the sway of the pleasure-principle, rather than the reality-principle. In addition, they are alogical and ahistoric in their functioning, undeterred in their course of operation by reality, reason, negation, and doubt. The ordinarily unacknowledged – indeed, typically disavowed – presence of such processes came to light in a clinical setting where resistance to certain ideas surfaced as a prominent and recurrent feature in the exchange between analyst and analysand.

Freud complained often and bitterly that his understanding of the unconscious was painstakingly derived from his clinical *experience*, but was dismissed by philosophers and others who were unacquainted with what actually transpired in psychoanalytic treatment. He insisted the human significance of the psychoanalytic unconscious is unknowable apart from the context of its derivation and application, that is, apart from the experiences from which it was derived and to which it refers. Indeed, its experiential meaning was developed from a series of experimental interventions in which both Freud and his patients were, in mostly different ways, at a loss to understand themselves and their actions. His concept of the unconscious was, accordingly, a tool crafted to assist primarily neurotic individuals in alleviating or lessening their pain by enhancing or deepening their self-understanding (Lear 2005: 563).

Although the distinction between the unconscious in its dynamic and descriptive senses is one drawn within psychoanalytic discourse, it is helpful for marking the difference between the strictly psychoanalytic use of this term and other, less technical uses. In addition, the psychoanalytic distinction between unconscious (in the dynamic sense) and *preconscious* mental processes needs to be drawn. This is also a distinction within psychoanalytic discourse. In this context it is in fact part of a threefold distinction (conscious, preconscious, and unconscious mental processes). The distinction between conscious and preconscious mental processes and states roughly corresponds to (in Jamesian terms) the distinction between what is at the center of awareness and what is either at the periphery or just beyond the periphery of consciousness: that which is at the margins of consciousness might readily become focal, just as the preconscious in Freud's sense might without difficulty become conscious. Finally, the *unconscious* must not be equated with the *subconscious.* James no less than Freud was careful in this regard, though he was animated by the opposite desire: whereas Freud rejects "the term 'subconsciousness' as incorrect and incoherent" (Gay (ed.) 576), James rejects the *unconscious* as misleading and paradoxical.

In the context of American thought, then, the distinction between the unconscious and the subconscious tends to mark the difference between psychoanalytic discourse and other discourses (most notably, pragmatist ones) in which mind is taken to encompass more than consciousness. Though certainly not always consistent in their usage, the pragmatists favor *subconscious* and its cognates over *unconscious* and its. Hence, the distinction between the unconscious and the subconscious is especially important for appreciating the differences between psychoanalytic and pragmatist approaches to mind (see, e.g., Dewey's *Experience and Nature*). Along with psychoanalysts, most pragmatists insist there is more to mind than consciousness, but their accounts of what more there is tend sharply to diverge from those offered by Freud and his progeny.

Pragmatists readily grant the *descriptive* sense but characteristically oppose the *dynamic* sense of the term. If one is knocked unconscious by a blow to the head, this means, at least, one is rendered unresponsive to environmental stimuli. In this instance, being unconscious signifies simply the lack of consciousness or awareness. In turn, consciousness signifies the capacity to respond to extra- and intra-somatic states and events, including the putative bearing of these to one another (e.g. the intense cramps one is experiencing being attributed to something which one ate). Human beings and many other species are able to respond in variable and nuanced ways, having their own distinctive "feel" (their qualitative immediacy), to somatic and environmental conditions and alterations. By virtue of especially the capacities for recollection, anticipation, and inference possessed by such species as *Homo sapiens*, objects and events are charged with meaning (clouds of this color and density signify the likelihood of rain). In particular, John Dewey identifies as one of the principal meanings of *consciousness* the grasp of the *meaning* of objects and events (such meaning often being the bearing of things on one another). He notes that this word means things in both their qualitative immediacy and immediate significance (LW 1.227, 229).

But if one is said to be unconscious of one's desire to annihilate one's father, the term carries a deeper, darker meaning (Lear 1998: 18–19, 32). This is the meaning associated with the distinctively psychoanalytic approach to human action, affectivity, and relationships. That is, it is the meaning initially elaborated by Freud and subsequently developed by a legion of theorists. Freud draws an important distinction between the purely descriptive and the dynamic sense of this term. Moreover, he explicitly contrasts, as does William James, the unconscious and the subconscious.

Like Jean-Paul Sartre and Ludwig Wittgenstein, William James articulated an influential critique of unconscious mental states (*Principles of Psychology* [New York: Dover, 1890], pp. 162–76). Though he put this forth before Freud and other psychoanalysts advanced their dynamic conception of the unconscious, his treatment of this topic is taken to be of contemporary relevance (see, e.g., Levy 1996, esp. pp. 65–82). Hence, even though William James in his *Principles of Psychology* offers one of the most succinct yet systematic and detailed critiques of the unconscious, the force of this critique (like that of Sartre's and Wittgenstein's) is variously assessed. His conclusion is in accord with what many of his and our contemporaries hold: The postulation of the unconscious "is the sovereign means for believing whatever one likes in psychology, and of turning what might become a science into a tumbling-ground for whimsies" (p. 163).

Although James in his *Principles* explicitly challenges Eduard von Hartmann's arguments, C.S. Peirce emphatically endorses them (CP 7.366; Ellenberger, pp. 208–10). Indeed, of the classical American pragmatists, C.S. Peirce was the least reluctant to use the word *unconscious* in a sense (at least) closely akin to what would become its psychoanalytic meaning. No text more finely illustrates this point than this: "Men many times fancy that they act from reason when, in point of fact, the reasons they attribute to themselves are nothing but excuses which unconscious instinct invents to satisfy the teasing 'whys' of the ego." Peirce goes on to note: "The extent of this self-delusion is such as to render philosophical rationalism a farce" (CP 1.631). In the context of his pragmatism he suggests:

> Certain obvious features of the phenomena of self-control (and especially of habit) can be expressed compactly and without any hypothetical addition, except what we distinctly rate as imagery, by saying that we have an occult nature of which and of its contents we can only judge by the conduct that it determines, and by phenomena of that conduct.

Though virtually everyone except the most extreme nominalists will admit this, "anti-synechistic thinkers wind themselves up in a factitious snarl," Peirce contends,

> by falsifying the phenomena in representing consciousness to be . . . a skin, a separate tissue, overlying an unconscious region of the occult nature, mind, soul, or physiological basis. It appears to me that in the present state of our knowledge a sound methodeutic prescribes that, in adhesion to the appearances, the difference is only relative and the demarcation not precise.
>
> (CP 5.440)

From the perspective of Jamesian pragmatism, the notion of the unconscious is unintelligible, whereas from that of Peircean pragmatism, the distinction between conscious and unconscious mental states and processes ought not to be made into a dualism.

George Santayana articulated a subtle and complex account of spirit, psyche, mind, and consciousness. While on the surface he appears to reject the notion of the unconscious in the dynamic sense, plausible arguments can be made to show he not only acknowledges unconscious mental processes but also in his own language offers a theoretical account of at least some of the phenomena which Freud and other psychoanalysts were trying to integrate into a coherent theory of the human mind (such phenomena as transference, projection, and denial). In several writings (not least of all "A Long Way Round to Nirvana"), Santayana shows himself to be a careful reader of Freud's actual texts. Insofar as he does reject Freudian notions, it is thus based (unlike the Deweyan rejection of the psychoanalytic approach) on a detailed familiarity with the central writings in the psychoanalytic tradition. But it is an open question how much Santayana agrees, under the cover of quite different language, with Freud and more generally psychoanalysis.

In any event, the deeper springs of human conduct are, for all of the American thinkers considered here, not immediately transparent even to the agents from whom actions flow. The process of coming to know our selves might be far from an untroubled series of introspective, immediate, and unproblematic determinations of our motives, desires, antipathies, and whatever else is stirring within us (cf. Dewey LW 2.229, 348; LW 15.27–33). "Everything that can be said about conscious after Freud seems . . . to be contained," Paul Ricoeur suggests, "in the formula: Consciousness is not a given but a *task*" (1974: 108). While the particular nature of this complex task remains a matter of ongoing controversy, especially in reference to psychoanalysis, the abiding appreciation *that* human consciousness defines a task, something to be wrought and won over the course of time, unites psychoanalysis and pragmatism. The pressing practical questions concern *how* self-consciousness or self-knowledge is to be obtained. There is, however, little question that, in general terms, such awareness or knowledge is to be obtained in and through some form of human dialogue or, more broadly, interaction. Nor is there much question that it involves *working through* the histories in which we are entangled, indeed, the ones by which we are defined (Laplanche and Pontalis on "Working-Through" [*Durcharbeitung*], pp. 488–9; cf. Dewey LW 3.3–10, also LW 14.98–114; Roth 1995). But whether the psychoanalytic exchange between analyst and analysand is to be counted among the fruitful forms of this dialogical process *is,* from a pragmatist viewpoint along with other divergent perspectives (e.g. Sartrean existentialism and Wittgensteinian analysis), debatable (however, see Lear; also Bollas; and Snyder).

Further reading

Archard, David. *Consciousness and the Unconscious.* La Salle, IL: Open Court, 1984.

Bettelheim, Bruno. *Freud and Man's Soul.* New York: Vintage Books, 1984.

Cavell, Marcia. *The Psychoanalytic Mind: From Freud to Philosophy.* Cambridge, MA: Harvard University Press, 1993.

Drassinower, Abraham. *Freud's Theory of Culture*. Lanham, MD: Rowman and Littlefield, 2003.
Freud, Sigmund. *New Introductory Lectures*, trans. James Strachey. New York: W.W. Norton, 1965.
Gardner, Sebastian. "The Unconscious" in Jerome Neu (ed.) *The Cambridge Companion to Freud*. Cambridge: Cambridge University Press, 1991, pp. 136–60.
Lear, Jonathan. *Freud*. New York: Routledge, 2005.
Levine, Michael P. *The Analytic Freud: Philosophy and Psychoanalysis*. London: Routledge, 2000.
Levy, Donald. *Freud among the Philosophers: The Psychoanalytic Unconscious and Its Philosophical Critics*. New Haven, CT: Yale University Press, 1996.
MacIntyre, Alasdair. *The Unconscious: A Conceptual Analysis*, revised edition. New York: Routledge, 2004.
Trilling, Lionel. *Freud and the Crisis of Culture*. Boston, MA: Beacon Press, 1995.

VINCENT COLAPIETRO

UNIVERSALS

The philosophical problem of universals is an ancient metaphysical issue, discussed by Parmenides, Plato, and Aristotle, that is still a matter of dispute among contemporary philosophers. The term "universal" is itself a matter of dispute, and is used in various technical ways in the literature. In this entry, I will follow David Armstrong's use of the term "universals" to refer to abstract entities that, unlike particulars, can be constituents of more than one object.

Philosophers have appealed to universals in order to account for properties and relations. A property is attributed to an object – for instance, a computer might have the property of being white. A relation is attributed to two or more objects – for instance, California bears the relation of being to the west of New York; and Derek Jeter, Alex Rodriguez, and Robinson Cano bear the relation of being teammates on the New York Yankees.

Consider a property, such as whiteness. My computer is white. A baseball is also white. These are two distinct objects to which we attribute a single characteristic. In virtue of what are both of these objects white? This question raises the problem of universals: the problem of universals is to explain how it is that more than one object can belong to a single type.

The realist approach (sometimes called the Platonist approach due to Plato's formulation of one version of realism) postulates an abstract entity in order to address the problem. In virtue of being suitably related to the abstract entity, the universal, the object falls under a type. If there is such an entity of universal whiteness, it is in virtue of the relation between the baseball and the computer, on the one hand, and whiteness, on the other, that both objects are white. The baseball and the computer instantiate whiteness.

A serious difficulty for the realist is to explain the relation between the universal and the object in a way that does not generate a regress. For if we need to explain the fact that the computer is white on the basis of the computer's instantiating whiteness, what explains how it is that the computer bears the relation of instantiation to whiteness? Are we not required to postulate a further relationship of instantiation to explain how it is that the computer and whiteness are related by instantiation?

In light of these difficulties, certain philosophers have rejected realism and have taken either of the alternative approaches: nominalism or the trope theory. Each approach attempts to account for properties and relations without postulating a universal.

There are many distinct forms of nominalism. On the version of nominalism that gives the theory its name, the explanation of how it is that objects fall under a certain type is given in terms of the application of predicates to objects. Attribution of whiteness to the baseball and computer amounts to nothing more than predicating the term "white" of both of these objects: the computer is white and the baseball is white. There is no need to appeal to anything beyond the objects and the predicates to explain how it is that the objects fall under a certain type. Nelson Goodman is one of the most prominent recent advocates of such a form of nominalism.

On a class nominalist theory, one appeals to the fact that objects are the members of a class in order to explain how it is they are of the same type. W.V. Quine advocates such a form of nominalism in "On What There Is." On class nominalism, it is in virtue of the computer and baseball belonging to the class of white objects that they are both white. One might think that not all classes serve as a proper basis for an account of properties, for there are more or less irrelevant classes, such as the class of dogs and cats. If there is a property of being a dog or a cat, dog-or-cathood, it is not a particularly interesting or philosophically relevant property. In light of this issue, certain class nominalists make appeal to a basic notion of naturalness, and those classes that exhibit naturalness are the ones that make for genuine properties (such as the class of dogs) whereas other, nonnatural classes (such as the class of cats and dogs) do not make for such properties. David Lewis, in "New Work for a Theory of Universals," accounts for properties and relations on the basis of class membership in all possible worlds, and uses a basic notion of naturalness to distinguish those properties and relations that are of theoretical interest from those that are not. The resemblance nominalist accounts for the type-membership of objects by appealing to a resemblance relationship: those objects that resemble each other make up a natural class. These natural classes of resembling objects make for universals.

The trope theorist, unlike the realist, does not appeal to abstract universals in order to account for properties and relations. Unlike nominalists, however, the trope theorist does appeal to an abstract object: Trope theorists hold that properties and relations are abstract particulars. There is not a single abstract object, the property of being white, that accounts for why all white objects are white. Instead, each white object contains an instance of a trope of whiteness, which is a part of that object. On an influential form of the trope theory due to D.C. Williams and Keith Campbell, falling under the same type is a matter of containing similar tropes: the white computer and white baseball contain tropes of whiteness that resemble each other. Opponents of the trope theory often object that it is quite obscure what exactly a trope is.

It may perhaps be that the entire problem of universals is misguided. Stephen Schiffer has presented the view that the term "property" is pleonastic. When one says that "The computer has the property of whiteness," this is to say nothing more than "The computer is white." If this is correct, then there would be no need to provide a philosophical analysis of properties, relations, and universals.

As Armstrong (1989) notes, the problem of universals has been a source of disputes among philosophers for centuries, and even led to violent conflicts during the Middle Ages. While the violence has ceased, the philosophical debate over universals continues.

Further reading

Armstrong, D.M. *Universals: An Opinionated Introduction*. Boulder, CO: Westview Press, 1989.

Campbell, Keith. "The Metaphysic of Abstract Particulars," *Midwest Studies in Philosophy* 6 (1981): 477–88.

Goodman, Nelson. *The Structure of Appearance*. Indianapolis, IN: Bobbs-Merrill, 1966 [1951].

Lewis, David. "New Work for a Theory of Universals," *Australasian Journal of Philosophy* 61 (1983): 343–77.

Schiffer, Stephen. *The Things We Mean*. Oxford: Clarendon Press, 2003.

Fritz J. McDonald

V

VAGUENESS

At first glance the term "vague" may seem to be an exclusively negative or unimportant one. That is, a vague situation appears to be one that needs to be cleared up or defined in a more precise fashion. The key here is to turn the vague into a "problem" to be solved. Metaphysically speaking, being or reality is viewed as possessing more defining features than mere vagueness. Epistemologically speaking, truth should be identified with objectivity or certainty, with what is immediately given or self-evident.

But the term "vague" can also be employed in a much more positive fashion – one which stresses the limitations of our knowledge. As vague, the universe is richer than any or all of our conceptual formulations of it. Language, while necessary, is not sufficient. Also, a post-Darwinian universe is constantly changing, and in that sense remains vague. Vagueness is not the opposite of certainty, and every vague situation is not necessarily a potentially problematic one. Metaphysically speaking, being or reality is broader than "being known," or "being solved." Epistemologically speaking, truth or knowledge is perspectival in nature, and essentially so. Finally, vague situations, precisely because of their indeterminacy or ambiguity, often compel commitment or choice on our part.

Both the positive and the negative connotations of vagueness can be found in the works of American philosophers. This analysis will confine itself to the views of Peirce, James, and Dewey on the vague, or vagueness. Vagueness is mentioned some 457 times in *The Collected Works of John Dewey.* It appears eight times in both Volume 5 and Volume 6 of *The Collected Papers of Charles Sanders Peirce.* "The vague" is a cardinal motif in James, and is especially strong in the "Stream of Thought" chapter of *The Principles of Psychology,* and in *A Pluralistic Universe.*

Peirce on vagueness

Sometimes Peirce seems to employ the term "vague" in the ordinary sense, wherein it has a pejorative connotation. For example, he tells us that, in mathematics, the more precise, i.e. nuanced, our position on a topic is, the less certain does it appear to be; conversely, the more certain our stance is, the more vague it is.

At other times, however, the term has a much more positive nature – being closely connected with his pragmatism, his theory of signs, and his scotistic realism, which posits the reality of generals. Peirce tells us that logicians have unfortunately not paid enough attention to vagueness, underestimating its importance for mathematics. A "sign" is deemed "vague" to the extent that it is left more or less indeterminate, so that some additional sign has the function of completing the determination. In his outlook, "the general might be defined as that to which the principle of excluded middle does not apply." For example "triangularity" in general is neither exclusively scalene nor isosceles in nature. "The *vague*," on the other hand, he tells us, "is that to which the principle of contradiction does not apply" (5.505; see also 6.496).

For example, it is false neither that a "dog," taken in the vague sense, is either large or small, male nor female. To repeat then, Peirce views a sign to be objectively indeterminate or vague to the extent that it requires further articulation to be carried out via some other conceivable sign. Most importantly for Peirce, communication between individuals cannot be entirely precise, i.e. non-vague; it is, rather, ongoing and triadic in nature.

In "Issues of Pragmaticism," Peirce reminds us that pragmatism should not be taken as a form of positivism, but rather as entailing the scholastic doctrine of realism. This outlook affirms the existence of real objects that are general. It also acknowledges that real vagues, or real possibilities, actually exist. Let us take the example of operationally defining the word "hard" in the sentence "This diamond is hard." This should be interpreted, pragmatically for Peirce, in terms of the contrary-to-fact conditional, i.e. by our saying that "if this were hard it would resist an attempt to scratch it," etc. (see 5.453). Such an articulation requires real possibilities, i.e. vagueness as real.

Finally, for Peirce, the term "god" is vague, i.e. subject to future determinations.

James on vagueness

In the chapter entitled "The Stream of Thought" in *The Principles of Psychology*, James makes a surprising statement. He tells the reader: "It is, in short, the re-instatement of the vague to its proper place in our mental life which I am so anxious to press on the attention" (PP 1: 254). And in *Psychology (Briefer Course)* he goes even further, telling the reader that it is the reinstatement of the vague "and inarticulate" to its proper place that he wants to emphasize. In *A Pluralistic Universe*, he condemns what he calls "vicious intellectualism," which assumes that everything that exists can or has been named, and that the unnamable is equivalent to the non-existent (see PU: 60). These references serve as a reminder of James's fascination with the "ineffable" in, for example, *The Varieties of Religious Experience*. They also remind us of James's love/hate relationship with language, or logic. He was later to suggest that thought can touch the surface of reality but it cannot plumb its depths, and that its inability here is permanent rather than transient in nature (see PU: 250).

Vagueness in James has several different modalities; these include the personal, the psychological, the religious, the epistemic and the metaphysical.

James's personal life saw him confront a period of depression and despair. The situation was vague in the sense that it was impossible to choose among the alternatives of freedom vs. determinism using just the conventional criteria of rational coherence and empirical data. The option was "forced, living, and momentous," as he was to put it later in "The Will to Believe." Its very vagueness compelled him to decide, one way or the other.

Second, consciousness, for James, in *The Principles of Psychology*, was an ongoing focus/continuum, a continuously changing "stream" where one was constantly forced to choose because of its very richness. It was not a substance or thing. This view of consciousness was extended to James's view of reality in *Essays in Radical Empiricism* and in *A Pluralistic Universe.* "Pure experience," for James was a many-in-one. Each and every present moment was actually a passing moment, a coming-to-be-and-a-passing away, etc. Consciousness was vague in the sense of being unfinished, and of possessing both substantive and transitive parts. Consciousness, and later, reality, went beyond the boundaries of logic; although the latter was necessary, it was not sufficient.

While both James and Peirce appreciated the vague, this topic can also be used to show their differences. As noted above, Peirce had criticized his fellow logicians for neglecting the study of vagueness, and had himself worked out a "logic" of vagueness. But to James, who viewed the universe as a "wild" rather than a "domesticated" place to be – and who believed that "ever not quite" trails along after any philosopher's view of reality, the temptation to "explain" the vague runs the danger of explaining it "away." For James, the tension between language and reality would always remain strong, and he would constantly resort to metaphors as a form of communication.

Dewey on vagueness

Dewey sometimes employed the term "vagueness" in the ordinary, rather pejorative sense of the term. In a piece entitled "The Harmful Consequences of Vagueness," he says that misunderstandings between people or about things occur due to vagueness of meaning (see LW 8.243–4; see also MW 6.281). He goes on to say that vagueness often disguises the fact that various different meanings are often unconsciously mixed together, with the result that one meaning is often substituted in place of another The implication here, and in several other places in Dewey, is that vagueness is due to a confusion which can be cleared up, or solved, much in the same way that a "problem" can be solved for Dewey. Thus, for example, he says that propositions that do not define the problem adequately are vague, resulting in confusion as to what type of solution is appropriate. Attempts at solving the problem are, as a result, wild and fumbling (see LW 14.177). From this position, then, progress is made, or development takes place "from the vague to the definite" (EW 2.46).

But there are other places in Dewey's work wherein he takes a position much closer to James in celebrating vagueness. Thus in *The Quest for Certainty* he says that "Every situation has vagueness attending it, as it shades off from a sharper focus into what is indefinite; for vagueness is added quality and not something objectionable except as it obstructs gaining an eventual object" (LW 4.188; see also MW 10.323). And in *Experience and Nature* he says:

> What is really "in" experience extends much further than that which at any time is known. From the standpoint of knowledge, objects must be distinct ... the vague and unrevealed is a limitation ... It is important for philosophic theory to be aware that the distinct and evident are prized and why they are. But it is equally important to note that the dark and the twilight abound.
> (EW 1.27–8)

In conclusion, there are two senses of the term in all three thinkers. The first sense consists in clearing up some form of ambiguity; the second is the more positive sense, and refers us, indirectly, to the richness of the universe and to its possibilities.

Further reading

Dewey, John. *The Collected Works of John Dewey*, ed. Jo Ann Boydston. Carbondale, IL: Southern Illinois University Press, 1969–91, and published as *The Early Works*: 1882–98 (EW), *The Middle Works*: 1899–1924 (MW), and *The Later Works*: 1925–53 (LW).

Gavin, William Joseph. William. *James and the Reinstatement of the Vague*. Philadelphia, PA: Temple University Press, 1992.

James, William. *The Principles of Psychology* (PP), 2 vols. New York: Henry Holt, 1890; Chapter 9: "The Stream of Thought."

—— *A Pluralistic Universe* (PU). New York: Longmans, Green, 1909; Chapter 5: "The Compounding of Consciousness"; Chapter 6: "Bergson and His Critique of Intellectualism."

Peirce, Charles S. *The Collected Papers of Charles Sanders Peirce* 8 vols, ed. Charles Hartshorne and Paul Weiss (Vols 1–6), Arthur W. Burks (Vols 7–8). Cambridge, MA: Harvard University Press, 1931–58.

WILLIAM J. GAVIN

VALIDITY

In his celebrated essay, *The Fixation of Belief* (1877), Peirce used "valid" to apply to inferences that were of a kind that would, in general, lead from true premises to true conclusions. Since then the notion has been narrowed, receiving a more or less fixed meaning among logicians by the middle of the twentieth century. Most logicians now prefer to use "valid" and "invalid" in connection with deduction and "strong" and "weak" in connection with induction. This entry restricts itself to validity in relation to deduction.

Validity is the standard of logical consequence. It is not concerned with the actual truth or falsity of the premises and conclusions of inferences or arguments, but with the relationship between them. A test of validity is whether it is possible that the premises could be true and the conclusion false at the same time. If it is not possible, the argument is valid and, if it is possible, the argument is invalid. Consider this argument,

(1) If Socrates was a philosopher then he wrote books
Socrates did not write books
Socrates was not a philosopher

Here, although the first premise and the conclusion are false, we are bound to admit the argument as valid, for we see that it is not possible for the premises to be true and the conclusion to be false. In other words, *necessarily, if the premises are true, the conclusion is true too.* Notice that this conception of validity contains the modal term "necessarily" and that the relationship between the premises and conclusion is a semantic one, involving the notions of truth and falsity.

Some philosophers (most famously Quine) object to the use of modal terms (e.g. "possible," "necessarily") and their accompanying metaphysics in logical language; they prefer to understand validity in terms of logical form. A logical form consists of variables in combination with certain terms identified as logical constants. The logical constants for propositional logic will include some of the following: "and," "or," "not," "if–then," and predicate logic will add quantifiers "all" and "some" to the list. In argument (1) we may identify two different component propositions, "Socrates was a philosopher," and "Socrates wrote books," and imagine them as substituted for the sentential variables p and q in the argument form,

(2) if p then q
not-q
not-p

An argument is said to be *formally valid just in case it is an instance of a valid argument form.* An argument form, F, is valid just in case there is no consistent substitution for the variables in F which will result in true premises and a false conclusion.

Some (e.g. Quine) take sentences rather than arguments (e.g. Haack) to be the basic locus of validity. Consider the corresponding conditional sentence of (1):

IF (*If* Socrates was a philosopher *then* he wrote books) *and* (Socrates did *not* write books)
THEN (Socrates was *not* a philosopher)

Argument (1) is valid if and only if sentence (3) is valid, i.e. logically true, and (3) is logically true just in case every consistent substitution for the component propositions in (3) results in a true sentence. It is thus possible to take either arguments or sentences as a starting point, and determine the validity of the one from the other.

Disagreement exists on whether the formal conception of validity will include all valid arguments. Those who deny it (e.g. Read) say that arguments like (3) are *materially* but not formally valid,

(3) **X is a round object**
X is not a square object

since their validity depends on the meanings of non-logical terms (e.g. "round" and "square") rather than on logical form. In reply it may be argued that the role of form is restored in (3) when the unstated assumption, "nothing is both round and square" is included as a premise.

Yet another conception of validity, prominent in formal logics, is related to showing that a conclusion can be derived as a logical consequence from its premises. A strict proof of this requires that the argument be adapted to a logical system containing one or more inference rules that license steps in derivations. *An argument is (syntactically) valid in a logical system, S, if, and only if, the conclusion of the argument can be derived from the premises of the argument using only the rules of S.*

The desire to have the syntactic and formal conceptions of validity be co-extensive has driven the development of logic. In the nineteenth century De Morgan provided an example of a valid argument that was beyond the reach of the syllogism:

(4) **All horses are animals**
Hence, all heads of horses are heads of animals

The formal logic developed in the twentieth century allowed for the analysis of relational predicates (e.g. x is a head of y) and therewith the means of showing (4) syntactically valid.

Arguments (1) and (4) are intuitively valid but more complex arguments may take us beyond what we can manage by intuition alone. Thus logic not only gives us an explanation of why we are right when we are right about the obvious cases – as a derivation in (4) would do – it also helps us decide difficult cases that go beyond our intuitions, e.g. Anselm's ontological argument.

The concept of validity is, however, beset by some unwelcome consequences. If the premises of an argument taken together cannot be true, as in

(5) 2 is even
2 is odd
Argentina is in South America

then it is not the case that the premises can be true and the conclusion false; hence, (5) passes as valid. A similar difficulty attends arguments with a logically (or necessarily) true conclusion: if a conclusion is such that it cannot be false, then, again, the argument will be valid no matter what the premises are. These outcomes undermine the relevance we think should attend valid arguments. Deductive validity, it may thus be argued, is a necessary but not a sufficient condition of logical consequence.

Further reading

Haack, Susan. *Philosophy of Logics*. Cambridge: Cambridge University Press, 1978.

Read, Stephen. *Thinking about Logic*. Oxford: Oxford University Press, 1995.

Quine, Willard Van Orman. *Philosophy of Logic*, second edition. Cambridge, MA: Harvard University Press, 1986.

Tarski, Alfred. "On the concept of logical consequence" in *Logic, Semantics, Metamathematics*, second edition, ed. John Corcoran. Indianapolis, IN: Hackett, 1983, pp. 409–20 [originally published 1936].

HANS V. HANSEN

VALUATION

In the American philosophical tradition, valuation is a term most associated with John Dewey's *Theory of Valuation*. The book was published in the second volume of the positivist Otto Neurath's *International Encyclopedia of Unified Science*, a series that later included Thomas Kuhn's *The Structure of Scientific Revolutions*. Dewey was responding critically to the ascendance of logical positivism and emotivist moral philosophy in the late 1930s. Contemporary scholarship on Dewey highlights the enduring import of his analysis of valuation. Emotivism, in contrast, waned in the 1960s and 1970s and is now almost universally rejected in philosophical ethics.

A sponge responds to environmental stimuli solely according to instincts hard-wired by natural selection. Having no desires or interests, save in a metaphorical sense that may be extended to any member of an ecosystem, the sponge has no ends (whether first or second order), and consequently it does not deliberate upon means. In contrast, on the human plane people want many things, but what is *satisfying* to a person is not ipso facto *satisfactory*. Hence, valuation is an existential feature of the human plane, and a theory of valuation is needed to clear up the muddles highlighted by this distinction between uncriticized desires and critical judgments about what should be desired.

Valuation is a neutral term that encompasses, for Dewey, both noncognitive *prizings* and critical *appraisals*. Emotivist philosophers such as A.J. Ayer reduced the latter to the former. Ayer presupposed a mentalistic psychology and, informed by a narrow interpretation of Hume's empiricism, a radical separation of value (ought) language from factual (is) language. Ayer separated private feelings from interactive social contexts, and then he identified all interests and desires with these internal and disconnected feelings. Stripped of the interwoven relations that, as an existential fact, give human behaviors moral significance, value-laden interests and desires appeared to the emotivists to be mere eruptions of morally charged yet ultimately arbitrary and subjective felt preferences. In Ayer's idiom, the only *meaning* of "You should not have stolen that" is its propositional, factual content "You stole that." That I require you to share my feelings of disapproval is as beyond the reach of substantive justification as an ejaculatory "boo!" or "hooray!" Hence, to emotivists it was a moot question whether something desired is (by reference to its interactions and connections) desirable.

Based on his theory of experience as interactive and situational, coupled with his theory of inquiry as experimental, Dewey urged that words like "good," "right," and "virtuous" have more than a strictly emotive use. Yet he simultaneously rejected the central dogma of traditional ethical theory, namely that there is a single right way to discover what is desirable and that this correct way rests on the capacity to freely set aside customs in order to discern moral laws or rules derived from one or more foundational principles.

To reject this dogma seems even to many twenty-first-century ethicists to be a prelude to the worst excesses of relativism. These ethicists tend to assume a peculiarly moral meaning of "ought" that singles out all and only moral uses. For Dewey, that an act *ought* to be done essentially means that it will meet the demands of the situation at hand. "You ought to sing the alto line rather than the soprano," "She ought to wait until after the last frost to plant tomatoes," and "He ought to be more environmentally responsible" are distinguishable in terms of their ends and subject matter, but we cannot set forth necessary and sufficient conditions to circumscribe all and only uses of "ought" that parallel the third statement. This widens the scope of moral appraisal in Dewey's ethics to include any considered evaluation of incompatible alternatives when the choice bears on the sort of character and world that is developing.

Although Dewey's dramatic widening of the moral sphere remains controversial, it does not result in an amorphous relativism: The feeling that something is good does not necessarily make it so in ethics any more than in farming or medicine. For Dewey, valuations that claim a justification transcending pragmatic fittedness are as inappropriate in ethics as in medicine. A physician is rightly regarded as a quack when she claims an *a priori* or superempirical warrant. (It is essential to Dewey's theory of valuation that means and ends are not separated, and ends emerge through situational inquiry. Hence, the end does not justify the means.) Hence, to avoid the ethical analogue of medical quackery, the judgment that a course of action is the good of this situation must be conceived as a working hypothesis qualified by ongoing inquiry.

Further reading

Ayer, A.J. *Language, Truth, and Logic*. Mineola, NY: Dover, 1952.

Dewey, John. *Theory of Valuation*, in *The Later Works*, Vol. 13, 1939, ed. Jo Ann Boydston. Carbondale, IL: Southern Illinois University Press, 1988.

STEVEN FESMIRE

VALUES

Values, conceived abstractly, are the ideas, images, and concepts that cause us to regard a thing or activity as "good," "desirable," or "worthy." Terms such as "the good," "the true," "the beautiful," and "the right" are generally designated as value terms. Significantly, values and value theory are among the most contested subjects in philosophy. American philosophers in particular have disagreed about the scope of axiology (value theory). Ralph

Barton Perry (1867–1957) maintained that axiology encompasses virtually all non-factual fields including economics, ethics, aesthetics, jurisprudence and education. In contrast, C.I. Lewis (1883–1964) claimed that values, properly understood, are but a subfield of ethics, which includes principles and virtues as well.

Values made their debut in the work of Rudolf Herman Lotze (1817–81). A German philosopher, Lotze contrasted fact and value, relegating facts to the natural sciences and values to the humanities. Subsequent to Lotze, philosophers divided into two camps, with respect to the nature and function of values. One camp insisted that values are "subjective," the property of one's inner mind, consciousness or intention. These philosophers stressed the ways in which values are profoundly emotional – the outcome of deep feelings. The other camp countered that values are "objective" in the sense that they can be observed by others. Persons manifest their values in their behaviors and through their expressions of interest. Value is that which leads to speech and action.

Somewhat related to the distinction between values as "subjective" and values as "objective" is John Dewey's (1859–1952) distinction between value as that which is empirically desired and value as that which is desirable or worth desiring. Specifically, Dewey used the term "to value" in two ways: (1) to refer to attitudes of prizing, liking, esteeming, cherishing, and (2) to designate acts of judgment such as appraising, approving, estimating, evaluating, assessing. The fact that I value my home enormously does not mean that an appraiser will assign high financial value to it or that an architect will proclaim it "beautiful."

Although philosophers tend to be interested in the topic of values, abstractly conceived, non-philosophers are generally more interested in values concretely conceived. In the everyday world, the term "values" usually refers to what human beings in general, or particular groups (Americans, Mormons, union workers, the American Medical Association and so forth), or individual persons think is good and/or desirable. Values are the thoughts, usually accompanied by strong feelings, which provide human beings with a sense of meaning and purpose in life. Understood as such, values are powerful motivators for human action and behavior. Groups and individuals who share values identify with each other and shape themselves into a "we" against which they oppose a "you."

Values tend to be implicit in homogeneous societies in which individuals share their values. In contrast, values tend to be explicit in heterogeneous societies such as the United States. Americans have moral, religious, aesthetic, political, economic, and sociocultural values that are disparate. The fact that Americans do not share their values, or more precisely, do not rank their values in the same way, largely explains why, in the realm of public policy-making, it is difficult to secure a majority vote on any matter of substance. Abortion is a case in point. Those most opposed to abortion believe that the value of life must nearly always trump the value of liberty, whereas those less opposed or unopposed to abortion claim that under certain circumstances liberty is a more important value than life.

Although it is difficult to construct a definitive list of human values, it has been suggested that this list includes life, health, freedom, loving relationships, security, literacy, numeracy, and imagination. To be sure, imagination is not nearly as important a value to most people as life or health. Yet, in circumstances where people's basic needs for food, shelter, and clothing are met, play and fantasy as well as imagination become a value for many people and groups.

Group values are those values actually held by or, more likely, idealized by particular nations, communities, institutions, societies, clubs, and so forth. When polled, most Americans, irrespective of their race or ethnicity, will list life, liberty, and the pursuit of happiness as American values. Many scholarly books and articles on the American psyche claim that values associated with individuality and autonomy such as self-discipline, self-esteem, self-reliance, self-respect, and self-awareness are quintessentially American values. Interestingly, these "self-centered" values, which presuppose that individuals are capable of controlling their destiny, are more "masculine" than "feminine" in tone. Values that stress self over others, impartiality, and rationality are associated with being a man. In contrast, values that emphasize putting others first, being sympathetic to others' problems, and emotionality are associated with being a woman. However, even if values such as independence are idealized as particularly desirable values for Americans, most Americans, be they men or women, highly value friendship, love, loyalty, cooperation, compassion and so forth in their daily interactions. Moreover, the more pluralistic the United States becomes, the more challenging it becomes to declare any specific value – with the exception of certain basic human values (for example, survival) and certain fundamental political values (for example, individual rights or freedom) – as distinctly American values. Some people whose forbears arrived from Europe to America on the *Mayflower* may still share certain Northern/Western, Anglo-Saxon, Protestant values; but chances are that even if they have been able to insulate their values from the assault of "otherness," their values will not be shared by those whose ancestors came to America on slave ships or who entered America without proper documents.

Personal values are probably the most important values in a diverse society. People who lack their own values typically lack a sense of meaning or purpose in life. For them, nothing seems to matter and life seems without urgency and significance. Because values play such an important role in people's spiritual and psychological lives, people often view others' rejection of their values as rejections of themselves. In the face of opposition to their values, many people become defensive and angry rather than self-reflective and self-critical. They regard self-interrogating their values as a sign of weakness rather than as a sign of strength. That this should be so is unfortunate, for it takes real courage to question whether what one has always viewed as good, desirable, or worthy is indeed so.

Further reading

Brentano, Franz. *The Origin of Our Knowledge of Right and Wrong*, trans. Roderick M. Chisholm and Elizabeth H. Schneewind. London: Routledge and Kegan Paul, 1968 [1889].

Findlay, J.N. *Values and Intentions: A Study in Value-Theory and Philosophy of Mind*. New York: Macmillan, 1961.

Finnis, John. *Natural Law and Natural Rights*. Oxford: Clarendon Press, 1980.

Lewis, Clarence Irving. *An Analysis of Knowledge and Valuation*. La Salle, IL: Open Court, 1946.

Nussbaum, Martha. *Women and Human Development: The Capabilities Approach*. Cambridge, MA: Cambridge University Press, 2000.

Perry, Ralph Barton. *General Theory of Value: Its Meaning and Basic Principles Construed in Terms of Interest*. New York: Longmans Green, 1926. Reprinted, Cambridge, MA: Harvard University Press, 1950.

ROSEMARIE TONG

VEBLEN, THORSTEIN

Thorstein Veblen (1857–1929) was a prominent social critic, economist, and sociologist of the early twentieth century. He is most widely known for his work concerning conspicuous consumption and status emulation, the business–industry dichotomy, and the critique of neoclassical economics. In *The Theory of the Leisure Class* (1899), his most popular work, he argues that consumption is often used as means of conveying one's pecuniary resources. Since wealth is a primary means of attaining honorific status, a prominent display of expensive goods communicates membership within the leisure class. In addition, emulation of conspicuous waste and conspicuous avoidance of labor also works to enhance social status and sense of self-worth.

In subsequent texts, Veblen broadens his critique to include analyses of the dichotomy between business and industry. He argues that the individualist values underlying the business culture, including passive acquisition of wealth and status, are antithetical to the more socially oriented industrial values that promote active participation in efficiently meeting the needs of the community. Rather than aim at the well-being of all members of society, the wasteful affluent class lives parasitically on the creative industrial community. Furthermore, the value system underlying business culture is informed by neoclassical economic theories that presuppose a hedonistic human nature that is passive and immutable. These theories portray individuals as static utilitarian creatures whose decisions are merely influenced by external stimuli. Veblen rejects these approaches as having failed to account for the insights of evolutionary thought; that is, they are pre-evolutionary insofar as they fail to perceive the ways in which the development of individual habits of thought and action are influenced by the constant adaptation of social institutions to changes in technology and economics.

Further reading

Dorfman, Joseph. *Thorstein Veblen and his America*. New York: Viking Press, 1966.

Edgell, Stephen. *Veblen in Perspective: His Life and Thought*. Armonk, NY: M. E. Sharpe, 2001.

Tilman, Rick. *Thorstein Veblen, John Dewey, C. Wright Mills and the Generic Ends of Life*. New York: Rowman and Littlefield, 2004.

Veblen, Thorstein. *The Theory of the Leisure Class*. New York: Penguin, 1994 [1899].

—— *The Theory of Business Enterprise*. New York: Cosimo Press, 2005 [1904].

—— *The Instinct of Workmanship and the State of the Industrial Arts*. New York: Augustus M. Kelly, 1964 [1914].

—— *The Engineers and the Price System*. New York: Augustus M. Kelly, 1965 [1921].

MATTHEW J. FITZSIMMONS

VERIFICATIONISM

Verificationism is the core doctrine of logical empiricism or logical positivism, which held sway over philosophy in the 1930s and 1940s. This movement was largely responsible for what is now known as "analytic" philosophy, still the dominant methodology in philosophy. Verificationism is a kind of empiricism with affinities with and foreshadows in the British empiricism of Berkeley and Hume, the early Wittgenstein, and the American pragmatism of Charles S. Peirce and William James. But the particularly strenuous brand of empiricism called verificationism was an import from Vienna and Berlin. It took itself to have a new and important resource – the formal or symbolic logic that was developed in the latter part of the nineteenth century. It recognized only sensory perception and the analytic principles of formal logic as sources of knowledge.

In the mid-1920s a group of philosophers, physicists, mathematicians, social scientists, and economists in Vienna gathered around Moritz Schlick and around the idea that all domains of inquiry, including philosophy, must be thought of as a part of science. A similar group gathered around Hans Reichenbach in Berlin. The impending war scattered the logical empiricists – Reichenbach, Rudolf Carnap, Carl Hempel, and others fled to America, where they quite literally changed the character of how philosophy was practiced in that country. Schlick was shot dead in 1936 by a deranged student. Otto Neurarth eventually ended up in England, joining A.J. Ayer, who had visited the Vienna Circle as a young man and brought the view to England – in 1936 he published the hugely influential *Language, Truth, and Logic*.

The verifiability principle was at the heart of this project. It held that all meaningful sentences are reducible, via formal deductive logic, to statements that are empirically verifiable. Thus, no meaningful question is in principle unanswerable by science. Inquiry is unified and progress is possible if all branches of inquiry are carried out in the same straightforward, logical, observational language. Domains of inquiry can achieve clarity and progress by having their theories symbolized in the language of logic and cashed out in observation. These deductive axiomatic theories, that is, are given empirical meaning by definitions which hook up the primitive terms in the formal language with observables in the world.

Philosophy was to get with the program, put its theories in scientific language and render itself clear. Most of the age-old questions and their purported answers would be shown to be fruitless and meaningless, as they will not be reducible to observation statements. They are not empirically verifiable and so they are pseudo-propositions. If science is the paradigm of rational knowledge, metaphysics is the scourge of it. At best, statements about the good, essences, the Absolute, the thing-in-itself, etc., are expressions of an attitude or feeling toward life.

Statements about what is right or wrong, for instance, are either: (1) statements about what people actually approve of, not what they ought to approve of – that is, ethics is an empirical science; or (2) they are meaningless; or (3) they express emotions or feelings. Hence the infamous "Boo–Hurrah" theory of ethics, on which to say that some act is odious is to say "Boo-hiss!" to it and to say that some act is good is to say "Hurrah!"

The verifiability principle faced some formidable objections and was revised and liberalized in light of them. One set of objections centered around the strength of the verifiability required. If a meaningful statement is one that can conclusively be shown to be true or false, then there are few, if any, candidates for meaningfulness. It turned out that all kinds of discourses were imperiled. For instance, statements about the past, about the future, and about the mental states of others are not conclusively verifiable by observation and thus are swept away as meaningless on the strong verifiability criterion. Even the statement "blue, here, now," when presented with a patch of blue, is not conclusively verifiable. Given that I might, for instance, be hallucinating or be suddenly color blind, in order for the statement to carry certainty with it, it has to be "it seems to me that blue, here, now." Hence, the statement "blue, here, now," if it is to be conclusively verified, is a statement about my mental state, not a statement about the world. And of course, the verifiability criterion was supposed to verify statements about the world, not statements about how the world seems to me.

Perhaps most worrying for the logical empiricists was the fact that much of science seemed to fail the test. For instance, hypotheses about unobservable entities, such as sub-atomic particles, seemed not to be true or false, but at best useful instruments. This instrumentalist view about the unobservable in science was held by Ernst Mach and is still held by, for instance, Bas vanFraassen. That is, the fact that these hypotheses were not verifiable by observation was not taken by all of the logical empiricists to be highly problematic.

What was more damaging was a problem about scientific laws and dispositional hypotheses. A scientific law is a universal generalization which ranges over an infinite domain and hence no finite number of positive instances will conclusively verify a law. Statements containing dispositional terms such as "soluble," "temperature," "mass," "heat" and "force" are analyzable only by counterfactual or subjunctive conditionals – "were x to be placed in water, then it would dissolve" or "were a thermometer to be in contact with *x, it would register y* degrees." First-order predicate logic is not capable of adequately characterizing counterfactual conditionals and hence a serious problem was posed here too for the verifiability criterion.

There were also important controversies about the very nature of the experience that meaningful statements were supposed to be grounded in. With the exception of Neurath, the logical empiricists agreed that there is something given to us in experience that is raw or unencumbered by the observer's language, theories, or conceptual scheme. The problem was then to say just what that was. Some of the logical empiricists (the phenomenalists) held that observation reports are about private sensations and others (the physicalists) held that they were about public physical events. The problem for the phenomenalists was that it seems impossible to communicate such private qualitative content to others – the experiencer seems to be trapped in his or her own world. The problem for the physicalists was that they seemed to be grounding knowledge in something about which we could be mistaken. That is, they seemed to abandon the aim of epistemological security.

Many moves were made to liberalize the verifiability principle: not requiring conclusive verifiability; not taking verifiability to be the entirety of meaningfulness; extending deductive logic with inductive logic, etc. But tempering the criterion in these ways amounted to abandoning some of the very ideals of clarity, rigor, and precision that drove the program. The reductionist program of analyzing terms into logic and observational predicates seemed to collapse in light of the contortions required to save scientific statements.

Indeed, it was the reaction against the reductionist program which characterized post-positivist philosophy of science in America. Thomas Kuhn, Paul Feyerabend, and Norwood Russell Hanson argued in the 1960s that science does not have the rational, deductive structure attributed to it by the logical empiricists. If we want to understand science, we must not try to rationally reconstruct it, but we must look to the historical or sociological development of theories or research programs.

So the connection between verificationism and American philosophy is both one of precedence and influence. A.J. Ayer thought that C.S. Peirce's pragmatic maxim was a direct predecessor of the verifiability criterion. He said that Peirce's position "allows no truck with metaphysics. Its standpoint is closely akin to that which was later to be adopted by the logical positivists. Peirce's pragmatic maxim is indeed identical . . . with the physicalist interpretation of the verification principle" (Ayer 1968: 45). Ayer was not quite right about that, as Peirce offered a much broader account of experience than the verificationists ever envisioned and Peirce was very clear that he was talking about an aspect of meaningfulness, not the whole of it. But Ayer is right that Peirce and James wanted to connect the legitimacy of our concepts with experience and practice – philosophical concepts that were divorced from experience and practice were spurious. Verificationism thus shares something important with American pragmatism.

In terms of influence, the logical empiricists' program set the agenda for American philosophy of science for decades and then was the received view against which American philosophy of science rebelled. Despite that rebellion, the methods of the logical empiricists continue, for the most part, to be the methods of contemporary analytic philosophy in America.

Further reading

Ayer, A.J. *Language, Truth, and Logic*. London: Victor Gollancz, 1936.

—— (ed.) *Logical Positivism*. New York: Free Press, 1959.

—— *The Origins of Pragmatism: Studies in the Philosophy of Charles Sanders Peirce and William James*. San Francisco, CA: Cooper, Freeman, 1968.

Misak, Cheryl. *Verificationism: Its History and Prospects*. London: Routledge, 1995.

Uebel, Thomas. *The Cambridge Companion to Logical Empiricism*. Cambridge: Cambridge University Press, forthcoming.

vanFraassen, Bas. *The Scientific Image*. Oxford: Clarendon Press, 1980.

CHERYL MISAK

VIRTUE

Ethics based on a conception of excellence of character, of happiness as a life lived in accordance with virtue understood as excellence, begins with Aristotle. But the conception recurs at various times in philosophic history, becoming prominent in America from the Puritans, through Jonathan Edwards, Benjamin Franklin, Samuel Johnson, and other eighteenth- and early nineteenth-century figures. For the Puritans, theology was enmeshed in a physical world understood in Aristotelian terms, thus the presence of Aristotelian tendencies in their ethical views is unsurprising. But since for the Puritan control of the world rested entirely in the hands of God, and since the natural human condition was that of the sinner, there are crucial differences. Living well is living to God, or living to the glory of God – happiness is not denied as a proper human goal, but it is a goal subordinate to humans' chief goal, which is the glory of God. We are to find out how to manage this by theology's study of nature and, primarily, of Scripture, and through this study the virtues are revealed. The standard is not Aristotle's man of practical wisdom, but rather the teachings of Scripture and the theology developed by the saints (those who have received God's grace, and are thus regenerate.) The Fall is seen as that which, in putting human will first, resulted in depravity. For the Puritans, it is piety which provides the theoretical understanding of virtue. Because the image of God remains as a trace even in fallen souls, the approval of virtue is based on the innate idea of God.

Current

Since Philippa Foot (Griffin Professor of Philosophy Emeritus at University of California Los Angeles, granddaughter of former president Grover Cleveland), virtue in American philosophy has come to be associated with "virtue ethics," usually defined as that form of ethics distinct from rule-governed or utilitarian systems. Foot sees the virtues as those character traits (developed habits of action) which are good for human beings, beneficial both to those who possess such characters and to the community. Foot claims that the virtues contribute to the well-lived life, rather than that they are constitutive of it. Michael Slote (UST Professor of Philosophy at the University of Miami) is developing what he terms "agent-based" virtue ethics, which are dependent on motives of caring or benevolence. Slote sees himself as aligned, with feminist philosophers Annette Baier (Emeritus Professor, University of Pittsburgh) and Virginia Held (Distinguished Professor of Philosophy, CUNY), in responding to the importance of motives without dependence on rules, principles, or even on the consequences of having such motives. He argues, in *Morals from Motives,* that "certain forms of overall motivation are, intuitively, morally good." Alasdair MacIntyre (Senior Research Professor of Philosophy at Notre Dame), in *After Virtue*, emphasizes the pessimistic dimension of a life lived without the recognition of virtues – excellences embedded in practices having goals, purposes and aims. He argues that the defeat of Aristotelian science should not have led, as it did, to the discarding of Aristotelian morality. MacIntyre argues,

> [t]he precepts which enjoin the various virtues and prohibit the vices instruct us how to move from potentiality to act, how to realize our true nature, and to reach our true end. To defy them will be to be frustrated and incomplete, to fail to achieve that good of rational happiness which it is peculiarly ours as a species to pursue.

Background

But long before current virtue ethics, American philosophers were considering virtue as excellence within a moral realm determined teleologically. A central commitment of the development of American moral theory and the discussion of the virtues is that theory is always engaged with practice. The virtues discussed include not only personal virtue, but the virtues engaged in public life and civic conduct. New England saw these larger settings as dependent primarily on the development of the moral individual. Later, especially in the Middle Atlantic, the South and the West, there was more direct concern with the social setting which prepares the virtues. The development of the full range of institutions, especially as these relate to education, is always connected to the development of moral virtue. This is particularly true for Thomas Jefferson (1743–1826), who saw the "moral sense," with which we are endowed by God, through which we intuit the value of actions and their relation to the rights of others, as both shaping and shaped by the condition of social institutions. Virtue, for Jefferson, consisted in utility to humanity – though what specific actions would be useful depended on the social and cultural milieu. He saw certain republican virtues (independence, self-control, self-reliance, tolerance) to be crucial for the well-working of democratic institutions.

The nineteenth century

A fuller separation of virtue from theology takes place in the nineteenth-century development of Unitarianism in America. Its humanistic form makes virtue become entirely equivalent to morality, especially in William Ellery Channing (1780–1842), who saw morality as the development of our likeness to God, which we discover and develop within ourselves. Channing influenced Ralph Waldo Emerson (1803–82), the leading Transcendentalist. Emerson stressed the relationship of virtue to the receptiveness, the readiness to receive insight and communication, through nature. "Beauty is the mark God sets upon virtue," he writes in *Nature,* and beauty is coherence with the largest whole. Thus moral virtue is coherence with the moral order of the universe, and is the condition of recognition of the spiritual whole. Moral virtue is both condition and consequence of our ability to read, to hear, to see God in the universe created through us. To see the mind of God in the universe is to see the mind of God in oneself; to develop the virtue of likeness to God is to develop the power to "build therefore your own world."

The group of thinkers known as the St Louis Hegelians, founded and led by William Torrey Harris (1835–1909) and Henry Conrad Brokmeyer (1828–1906), both learned from and departed from Hegel. Their work emphasized individual efficacy in the dynamic matrix of a teleological history, the crucial importance of the sociality of persons, and the centrality of education in producing creative individuals who could use intelligence and learning to develop their own potentialities and affect the development of the institutions which shaped them. Their emphasis was not on virtue as such, but the views they developed helped to shape the virtues of growth, of intelligence, and of creative reconstruction of social institutions in the context of a democratic society which come to be important in American Pragmatism.

Charles Sanders Peirce (1839–1914), credited with the first articulation of Pragmatism, has much to say about values but little to say about virtue, save two rather diverse claims. First, his emphasized command "Do not block the road to inquiry," makes such blockage at least the equivalent of major vice. Hence, by obversion, it is clear that openness to the continuous investigation of truth is a crucial virtue. Further, he writes that human virtue, the practical, human ideal, the achievable portion of the *summum bonum,* is identifiable as the living out of the demand to: "Sacrifice your own perfection to the perfectionment of your neighbor" (CP 6.288). The ideals of increasingly realized harmony, of increasingly encompassing and confirmed (though fallible) investigation, are the virtues to be realized by the community of actors and inquirers.

The twentieth century

William James (1842–1910) seems to contradict the notion of specific virtues of any sort when he claims, in "The Moral Philosopher and the Moral Life," "that there is no such thing possible as an ethical philosophy dogmatically made up in advance." But, in seeing the course of history as the ongoing struggle to "find the more and more inclusive order;" in urging "*[i]nvent some manner* of realizing your own ideals which will also satisfy the alien demands," James's position stresses creativity, the ability to heed the call of others, and that awareness of "the richest possible universe" in which the most ideals can be satisfied. It appears to be a consequentialist position – but does not envision any arbitrary standard of the better. James argues that we follow neither absolute rules (since ethics may demand that we break old rules and invent new ones), nor sharp principles, nor that we have a grasp of what the good consequence would be in detail. Rather, we "choose in fear and trembling," to create a richer universe. The virtue here depicted is vague, but it is the recognition of fallibility combined with ultimate responsibility for the world we make. Excellence is the ability to listen, to respond, to imagine, and to act with courage. It is a unique picture of virtue – but it is clear that James's version of ethics is more a matter of the character and habits which enable rich choices than it is of rules, principles, or calculus of utilities to be achieved.

Josiah Royce (1855–1916), although connected to the leading Pragmatists, is not best classified as a Pragmatist himself. America's leading absolute Idealist, he is unique in taking the virtue of "loyalty" as a major category. For Royce, it is loyalty to loyalty, that is the commitment and pursuit of commonality, which increases the opportunity for the self and others to *continue* the commitment and pursuit of commonality, which is the ultimate virtue. He recognizes that loyalty as such can be divisive and destructive of others' opportunity to experience and further loyalty; thus it is only the loyalty which enlarges the capacity for community in all which is the genuine virtue – capable of integrating, enriching, and fully developing personality in the individual and in communities. "My thesis is," Royce wrote, "*that all the common-place virtues, in so far as they are indeed defensible and effective, are special forms of loyalty to loyalty.*"

Examining "virtue" in the work of John Dewey (1859–1954) illuminates the narrowness of some definitions of virtue ethics. For Dewey, the differences apparent between right and wrong, good and bad, virtuous and vicious, and true and false all need to be examined in light of the processes of valuation. The gulf between fact and value is one Dewey significantly undermines. Inquiry into what he identifies as three independent variables – good, right, and virtue – is initially pursued empirically, related to what human beings actually do. In "Three Independent Factors in Morals" he claims, "Goods … have to do with deliberation upon desires and purposes; the right and obligatory with demands that are socially authorized and backed; virtues with widespread approbation." Though independent, all three factors are "intertwined in all actual moral situations." He argues that "[m]oral problems exist because we have to adapt to one another as best we can certain elements coming from each source." Conventional morality involves the goods, duties, and virtues embedded in current habits of valuation. Reflective morality is the process of reconstructing the evaluations we make in light of inquiry. In a later work, *Ethics*, Dewey claims

> the key to a correct theory of morality is recognition of the *essential unity of the self and its acts,* if the latter have any moral significance; while errors in theory arise as soon as the self and acts (and their consequences) are separated from each other, and moral worth is attributed to one more than to the other.

It is crucial to Dewey's full conception of virtue to understand the relationships of motive and consequence to the self. For Dewey, motive *is* the self acting, and consequences shape the self who acted, acts and is further disposed to act. Thus virtue, admirable character, is more than fixed disposition; it includes habit, conduct, and the habitual reconstruction of desires in light of objects, acts and consequences. As he notes in *Theory of the Moral Life,* the style of virtue is the development of interests which are wholehearted, persistent, and impartial. Growth, the growth of an integrated and responsible self in its cooperative social context, is the pattern of virtue. And the patterning of virtue as growth thus has significant bearing on the development of education and social institutions that are the matrix and condition of the flourishing of integrated and admirable selves.

One contemporary philosopher who has offered a Pragmatic version of virtue ethics is James Gouinlock (Professor of Philosophy Emeritus, Emory University), in *Rediscovering the Moral Life.* He identifies three virtues as sufficiently open and permissive to constitute a description of the dispositions requisite for leading the moral life: rationality, courage, and respect for persons. Gouinlock draws heavily on Dewey, and shows at least one strain of the possible working out of the implications of the history of American philosophy as it develops the category of virtue.

Further reading

Baier, Annette. *Moral Prejudices: Essays on Ethics.* Cambridge, MA: Harvard University Press, 1995.

Edwards, Jonathan. *The Works of Jonathan Edwards*, 2 vols. Peabody, MA: Hendrickson, 1998.

Emerson, Ralph Waldo. *The Essential Writings of Ralph Waldo Emerson* (Modern Library Classics), ed. Brooks Atkinson, introduction by Mary Oliver. New York: Random House, 2000.

Dewey, John. *John Dewey: The Later Works, 1925–1953*, 17 vols, ed. Jo Ann Boydston. Carbondale, IL: Southern Illinois University Press, 1981–90.

Foot, Philippa. *Natural Goodness.* Oxford: Oxford University Press, 2003.

Gouinlock, James. *Rediscovering the Moral Life.* Buffalo, NY: Prometheus Books, 1993.

Held, Virginia. *The Ethics of Care: Personal, Political, and Global.* New York: Oxford University Press, 2005.

James, William. *The Works of William James*, ed. Frederick Burkhardt. Cambridge, MA: Harvard University Press, 1975–88.

MacIntyre, Alasdair. *After Virtue: A Study in Moral Theory.* Notre Dame, IN: University of Notre Dame Press, 1984.

Peirce, Charles Sanders. *The Writings of Charles S. Peirce: A Chronological Edition*, Vols 1–6 currently available, ed. Nathan Houser and the Peirce Edition Project. Bloomington, IN: Indiana University Press. 1998–2000.

Slote, Michael. *Morals from Motives.* New York: Oxford University Press, 2003.

Marjorie C. Miller

WARRANTED ASSERTIBILITY

"Warranted assertibility" is a term introduced by John Dewey to avoid the implications of the word "truth" when speaking of the central desirable characteristic of a statement expressing a judgment. Independently of the technicalities of Dewey's thought, an assertion is warranted when it is adequately justified – relative to the circumstances in which it is made – in terms of its grounds (the evidence on which it is based) and its consequences (the reliability of the guidance that it provides).

The closest historical antecedents of this concept are to be found in the assessment of a statement as "credible" (*eikos*, *probabilas*) by the mild skeptics who dominated Plato's Academy in the first century BC (three centuries after its founding). Whereas no belief can be held with absolute certainty, some beliefs can be regarded as more worthy than others of acceptance and of being used to guide action. The fallibilism that is characteristic of pragmatism is close to this mild form of skepticism and an unqualified assessment of any statement as "true" is therefore not possible. The assessment of the epistemic value of any statement is subject to revision in the light of additional evidence that might come to light or because of our reassessment of its reliability when used for guidance in new situations.

It is not, however, meaningless to speak of a statement as true in the unqualified sense, although the only communicative function that would be served by doing so would be to convey the speculative suggestion that we will in fact never have reason to revise a favorable estimate of the statement's evidential basis or of its worthiness of being relied upon. As there is danger that using the word "true" for a favorable assessment will carry this implication of an unrevisable assessment – and which is one that cannot be made except from a standpoint that is not accessible to us – Dewey thought it would be wise to forestall misunderstanding by speaking of assertions expressing judgments as warranted or unwarranted rather than as true or false.

The terms "warrant" and "warranted assertibility" are now used outside the context of Dewey's philosophy; for example, the term "warrant" is sometimes used for "whatever it is that, if added to true belief, converts it into knowledge." This sort of analysis of knowledge is in Dewey's view back-to-front, inserting as it does between "warrant" and "belief" a term that involves speculation as to how the belief will fare in terms of becoming and remaining warranted. Analysis should proceed by asking what warrants a belief without the intrusion of the qualification "true," and any concept of knowledge that involves in this way the concept of truth will, like truth, have only a speculative value.

Dewey's approach to the question of what warrants a belief rests on his account of inquiry, and this should not be regarded as confined to a process of gathering and evaluating evidence (grounds) for the belief. Inquiry is initiated when on-going activity breaks down because of indeterminateness in the situation where the activity is taking place (= the problem). To render determinate the factual aspects of such a situation requires fashioning representations of the situation that allow possible courses of action to be projected. (There may be non-factual aspects to an inquiry involving the determinateness of the objective of the activity that has broken down. These need not concern us here.) Consequences that match the anticipations that are guided by a proposed representation are as important as adequate grounds for the successful conclusion of inquiry. This is because what will guide the selection of grounds (evidence) from the wealth of what a situation provides (the data) will be what best allows the situation to be made determinate and allow activity to resume unimpeded (= the resolution of the problem).

Dewey used the term "proposition" for such a representation, conceived not primarily as a linguistic entity but as an instrument for guiding experimental activity undertaken to resolve indeterminateness. A "judgment" thus is not primarily the affirmation of a linguistic entity, but a selection of that proposition, from among those considered, which resolves (makes determinate) the problematic (indeterminate) situation. (As most propositions and judgments can be expressed linguistically, it is nevertheless possible to compare Dewey's doctrines to others using the notion of "statement," as in the early paragraphs of this entry.)

Dewey's terminology has little appeal for philosophers for whom the concept of statements with permanent truth values (true or false) is the foundation of semantics both as a theory of meaning and as a theory of inference. To base semantics on the concept of warranted assertibility rather than truth would involve formal apparatus not unlike that required for intuitionist or constructivist mathematics. Constructivist mathematicians resist the principle that every meaningful statement is either true or false, because no mathematical proposition should receive a favorable assessment until it has been proven and there is no reason to think every statement or its negation can be proven.

Statements of constructivist mathematics are divided into those which have been proved, those whose negation has been proved and those for which we are still seeking a proof one way or the other. Upon finding a proof one way or the other, a statement in the third class will be moved to one of the other two, but once proved, a mathematical statement remains proved and no statements move from the first two into the third class. The concept of warranted assertibility is not in this way permanent. The justification for asserting something may be undermined through future inquiry, and statements which have been assertible with justification may be found no longer to have warrant. It may even come to be found that assertions of their negations are warranted.

Dewey would not regard it as appropriate to offer a theory of inference based on semantics – even a semantics which dispensed with "truth" and adopted "warranted assertibility" as its central concept. Inference, he believed, was fundamentally a practical activity and should be approached theoretically as a form of practice. It would likewise be inappropriate to treat linguistic meaning semantically. Significant aspects of the meaning of any representation are to be found in the guidance it offers to practice.

Further reading

Burke, Tom. *Dewey's New Logic: A Reply to Russell*. Chicago, IL: University of Chicago Press, 1994, Chapter 6.

Dewey, John. *Logic: The Theory of Inquiry*. New York, Henry Holt, 1938. In *The Later Works of John Dewey, Vol. 12*, ed. Jo Ann Boydston, Carbondale, IL: Southern Illinois University Press, 1991.

—— "Propositions, Warranted Assertibility and Truth" in *Problems of Men*. New York, The Philosophical Library, 1947, pp. 331–53. In *The Later Works of John Dewey, Vol. 14*, ed. Jo Ann Boydston. Carbondale, IL: Southern Illinois University Press, 1988, pp. 168–88.

Tiles, J.E. *Dewey (The Arguments of the Philosophers)*. London: Routledge, 1988, Chapter 5.

J.E. TILES

WASHINGTON, BOOKER T.

Booker T. Washington (1856–1915) is a figure who represents an important transformation in American history, helping to bridge the divide between the African-American slave and the civil rights movement of Martin Luther King. While many, including Lucius Outlaw, have seen fit to classify Washington as an accommodationist with regard to relations between ex-slaves and the majority white populace, this title is an over-simplification that does not acknowledge the subtlety of his thought. While Washington did famously remark in his Atlanta Cotton States and International Exposition address of 1895 that "In all things that are purely social [blacks and whites] can be as separate as the fingers, yet one as the hand in all things essential to mutual progress," the issue of where one chooses to place the emphasis in that statement may greatly alter its import (all quotes from *Up from Slavery*). A more charitable interpretation could be arrived at if one emphasizes the unity of the hand and Washington's desire for mutual progress over the possibility of separation amongst the fingers.

Washington, particularly in his autobiographical *Up from Slavery*, presents his plan for the advancement of freed slaves after the civil war. This plan, which finds its practical fulfillment in Washington's Tuskegee Normal and Industrial Institute in Tuskegee, Alabama, focused on an education centered around industrial teaching. This education went beyond the classical teachings which focused on the great books of Latin and Greek and instead provided "a practical knowledge of some one industry, together with the spirit of industry, thrift, and economy, that they would be sure of knowing how to make a living after they had left us."

The industrial teachings forwarded by Washington focused on three specific points; first, educating the student in how to live in the world as it was, particularly in terms of the racial tension present in the South during the early 1900s. Second, Washington wanted his graduates to have the skills, intelligence and moral character to provide for themselves and others. Third, Washington wanted to instill a work-ethic that saw "labor as dignified and beautiful." This position was in contrast with the educational philosophy forwarded by W.E.B. DuBois and his conception of the talented tenth, which saw the black-aristocracy lifting the political/social status of other African-Americans. Washington asserted that "It is at the bottom of life we must begin, and not at the top." Furthermore, he argued that political agitation alone would produce little positive growth for the majority of African-Americans without also possessing "property, industry, skill, economy, intelligence, and character." Still, Washington did privately contribute money to support legal attempts to gain political equality by fighting segregation.

The practical education offered at Tuskegee was designed to provide its graduates a way to make a living, to provide for themselves, and, perhaps most importantly, to help those individuals become economically indispensable in the New South. It was Washington's belief that individual self-reliance and economic prosperity were the steadiest path toward equality. It was through the improvement of economic status in the community that Washington believed that African-Americans could improve their fortunes. Emphasizing this point, he remarked that

> any man, regardless of color, will be recognized and rewarded just in proportion as he learns to do something well – learns to do it better than some one else – however humble the thing may be ... my race will succeed in proportion as it learns to do a common thing in an uncommon manner.

As was noted earlier, many saw Washington's focus shift away from an emphasis on swift political victories and the vote to more practical matters as a form of accommodation to the white majority. Washington did assert that he felt that the early attempts at altering race relations in the South during Reconstruction were based on false foundations, in that the North was manipulating the situation merely to further punish the defeated South. He further added that the federal government was in error in that it failed to "make some provision for the general education of our people ... so that the people would be the better prepared for the duties of citizenship." Washington believed that the first African-Americans selected for public office made mistakes due to their lack of preparation and that these mistakes led the whites in the South to distrust the freed slaves' ability to contribute to the political system in any constructive manner, handicapping the entire post-emancipation process of inclusion from the beginning. For Washington, winning political enfranchisement as a race could best be achieved one person at a time, through an education that emphasized the belief that prosperity comes to those individuals who strive to contribute to society.

The period stretching from Booker T. Washington's birth to death was witness to the end of slavery, but this first step of emancipation was only a single move toward converting ex-slaves into free and equal citizens of the United States. The first steps after emancipation were difficult ones that brought a fresh series of issues to be confronted and Booker T. Washington, particularly in *Up from Slavery*, presents in one text the exhilaration of freedom and the fears that come with the responsibility of forging a new road within that freedom. Washington's Tuskegee Institute, now Tuskegee University, served a vital role in this process and still works today to advance the values articulated by Washington over one hundred years ago. As the Booker T. Washington Monument at Tuskegee states, "He lifted the veil of ignorance from his people and pointed the way to progress through education and industry."

Further reading

Brundage, W. Fitzhugh (ed.). *Booker T. Washington and Black Progress: Up from Slavery 100 Years Later*. Gainesville, FL: University Press of Florida, 2003.

Carroll, Rebecca. *Uncle Tom or New Negro?: African Americans Reflect on Booker T. Washington and Up From Slavery 100 Years Later*. New York: Harlem Moon, 2006.
Harlan, Louis R. *Booker T. Washington: The Wizard of Tuskegee, 1901–1915*. New York: Oxford University Press, 1983.
Outlaw, Lucius T. *On Race and Philosophy*. New York: Routledge, 1996.
Washington, Booker T. *Up from Slavery: An Authoritative Text, Contexts, and Composition History, Criticism*. New York: Norton, 1996.
—— *My Larger Experience: Chapters from my Experience*. New York: Humanity Books, 2004.

John Scott Gray

WATSON, J.B.

Often called the father of behaviorism, John Broadus Watson (1878–1958), of rural South Carolina, was introduced to psychology at Furman University, then went to the University of Chicago for graduate work. At Chicago he was taught functionalism by the philosopher John Dewey, the psychologist James Angell, and the neurologist Jacques Loeb. As formulated by Dewey, functionalism was the proposition that "mind is not substantival but adjectival." In other words, "the mind" is not a thing but a set of functional capacities – as strength is not a thing but an ability. It followed that the best way to study "the mind" was to study the diverse ways that an animal or a human being has of responding to and coping with its world.

Taking this implication seriously, Watson declared – in 1913 at Columbia University – that such researchers as Wundt and Titchener had wasted their time trying to get their experimental subjects to "introspect" the private "contents" of otherwise inscrutable "minds." The right method of psychology was to try by means of carefully designed experiments to discover the publicly observable causes of behavior, so as to learn how to predict and control it. By then a professor at Johns Hopkins, Watson used this revolutionary method to study and alter the behavior of infants. He continued to promote his method in popular books and articles even after personal scandal forced him to leave academic life and laboratory research for a successful and remunerative career as an advertising executive.

Further reading

Buckley, Kerry W. *Mechanical Man: John Broadus Watson and the Beginnings of Behaviorism*. New York: Guilford, 1989.

Max Hocutt

WEISS, PAUL

Born of immigrant Jewish parents on the Lower East Side of New York, Paul Weiss (1901–2002) attended the City College of New York and received a PhD at Harvard under the direction of Alfred North Whitehead. While a graduate student at Harvard, he joined Charles Hartshorne in editing the first six volumes of *The Collected Papers of Charles Sanders Peirce*, the founder of pragmatism and the philosopher Weiss often called America's greatest. After a brief teaching career at Bryn Mawr College, Weiss joined the Yale University faculty where he taught for over twenty years. Retiring as Sterling Professor of Philosophy at Yale, he moved to the Catholic University of America where he continued to teach until he was ninety-two. The main part of Weiss's career took place when philosophy in America was dominated by logical positivism and analytical philosophy, with most of the opposition to that coming from Continental philosophy. Weiss was convinced that speculative philosophy in the grand tradition is essential to healthy intellectual life, however, and founded both the Metaphysical Society of America and the distinguished journal, *The Review of Metaphysics*, which he edited for many years.

One of the earliest and most decisive motifs of Weiss's thought was an aggressive rejection of authority and commitment to think things out for himself. Although he revered Whitehead as the most brilliant and challenging teacher he had ever had, his first book, *Reality* (1938), was a rejection of Whitehead's famous *Process and Reality* in favor of an alternative philosophy that emphasized Aristotelian substances over against Whitehead's Platonic philosophy of process and form. Developing his system he wrote a philosophical anthropology, *Nature and Man* (1947) and a philosophical ethics, *Man's Freedom* (1950). Although each of these books contained detailed discussions of historical philosophers, their orientation was simply to say what is true about their topics. They did not fit into any of the philosophical programs of the school that were flourishing at the time they were written, not even the American schools descended from Peirce. As a result, he had only a small audience beyond his students.

Then in 1958 he published *Modes of Being*, probably the most sophisticated systematic speculative philosophy after Whitehead's *Process and Reality* in the twentieth century. In it Weiss argued that there are four modes of being, which he named Actuality, Ideality, Existence, and God. The central problem of *Modes of Being* is the classic puzzle of the one and the many: how can many things exist that are different from one another and yet are unified in having being? Classic solutions to the problem of the one and the many, such as Plato's, Aristotle's, Neo-Platonism's, and Absolute Idealism's, emphasized the one at the expense of the many. Whitehead did not address the problem at the metaphysical level. Weiss proposed an original pluralistic solution to the problem. He said that each mode of being is a unity, of its sort, for the other modes. Each mode of being has an essence, but each is also conditioned by the other modes. For him, therefore, there are four fundamental forms of unity: Actuality is the unity of all the modes in actual things; Ideality is the unity of form and value under which all things are gathered; Existence is the unity of a dynamic space-time field in which all things exist; and God is the eternal unity that can embrace actual things in different parts and times of the dynamic field of existence and with differing forms and values. For Weiss in *Modes of Being*, there is no being of which the modes are modes, only four interconnected ways of being. Arguing that the four modes of being are the most fundamental realities, Weiss thus claimed that there are as many ones as there are many fundamental realities.

The analytical power of Weiss's four modes of being is illustrated in his analysis of how common-sense affairs are to be understood in terms of the mutual contributions of the modes. For instance, Actuality would not involve diverse actualities except for the contribution of Existence which pluralizes Actuality into different space-time locations and gives them dynamic power to occupy those locations. Actualities would not have form and value without the contribution of Ideality. Actualities would not have the depth and integrity to keep themselves together through space-time transformations and changes in form or value without the super-unity of God. The situation is the same for each of the modes: it cannot be what it is without the contributions of the other modes.

Focusing on the special conjunctions of the modes, Weiss then wrote a series of books that explore major philosophical topic fields. *Our Public Life* (1959) treats political life as a matter of human actualities conditioned by the dynamics of existence and the value-elements of ideal form. *Nine Basic Arts* (1961) and *The World of Art* (1961) are careful studies of the arts, which are treated as exemplifying the basic traits of Existence as expressed in actualities with value. *History, Written and Lived* (1962) studies the character of Ideality as punctuated by human actualities and Existence. *The God We Seek* (1964) is Weiss' philosophy of religion.

In the 1970s, after Weiss left Yale for Catholic University, he took something of a fresh start with philosophy, dropping the speculative metaphysics of which *Modes of Being* was the center and undertaking to approach philosophy as the interrogation of the surfaces of things to find the more fundamental categories beneath them, his version of phenomenology. In this, he was moving ever more explicitly in an Aristotelian direction, although the categories he eventually worked out as basic are little like Aristotle's. The crucial book reorienting his philosophy was *Beyond All Appearances* (1974) followed by a methodological study, *First Considerations* (1977). The latter book included responses to his ideas by a number of his contemporaries along with his responses to them in turn. This new project led to a social philosophy, *You, I, and the Others* (1980), an introspective study of human nature, *Privacy* (1983), and a new political philosophy, *Toward a Perfected State* (1986). *Creative Ventures* (1991) unfolded a new set of categories while it generalized from Weiss's earlier interest in art to all humanly created things, including the state. *Being and Other Realities* (1995) was his last systematic book, in which he recovered the category of being itself and related it to a number of ultimate realities that he argued lie behind what appears in the worlds of art, science, and common humanity. His last two books, *Emphatics* (2000) and *Surrogates* (2002, posthumous), study the texture of experience, the first analyzing how things stand out from experiential background, the second how things signify each other.

Whereas nearly all the other philosophers of his generation followed some philosophical school, Weiss was a genuine original, one of the most brilliant speculative and critical minds in American history. The intrinsic value of his philosophy will appear in future years when the enthusiasms for the schools have become history.

Selected works

Weiss, Paul. *Reality.* Princeton, NJ: Princeton University Press, 1938.

—— *Nature and Man*. New York: Henry Holt, 1947

—— *Man's Freedom*. New Haven, CT: Yale University Press, 1950

—— *Our Public Life*. Bloomington, IN: Indiana University Press, 1959.

—— *The God We Seek*. Carbondale, IL: Southern Illinois University Press, 1964.

—— *First Considerations.* Carbondale, IL: Southern Illinois University Press, 1977.

—— *Toward a Perfected State.* Albany, NY: SUNY Press, 1986.

—— *Being and Other Realities.* Chicago and LaSalle, IL: Open Court, 1995.
—— *Emphatics.* Nashville, TN: Vanderbilt University Press, 2000.
—— *Surrogates.* Bloomington, IN: Indiana University Press, 2002.

ROBERT CUMMINGS NEVILLE

WEISS, PAUL: AUTOBIOGRAPHY

Although it is now hard for me to believe, as far back as I can remember I have been bedeviled with a single issue. Usually vaguely, but more and more clearly as time went on, I have asked myself, "What is the answer?" I did not know what it was that I sought. I never stated the question or indicated in what direction the answer lay. But it was always there. As I looked about, spoke to my elders and even to some of my contemporaries, they seemed to be so confident in their ways, their judgments, and attitudes in almost every circumstance, while I had no good idea as to just what was needed or appropriate. I passed no judgment on them or on myself. I simply remained perplexed, in a state closer to wonder than of suspicion or trust. I now know that they had no good idea of what motivated them, or of what they took for granted. Most of those I knew had at most a tepid faith in a beneficent, caring God and, in any case, their confidence extended to areas they apparently thought eminently secular. I was not moody or unhappy; I did not brood or speculate. Instead, I was unfocused, a little bewildered, not fitting in well. My life has been a progress toward a clearer and clearer understanding that there is a primary question that all humans live in and with, and that what they do and say does not answer it properly.

Morris R. Cohen was the first great influence on my intellectual life. He was exceptionally quick-witted, widely read, critical and alert. I wanted also to be one with such great knowledge, mastery, and confidence. I admired him, but also was troubled by his desire to dominate over students, his lack of doubt and self-questioning.

More important was my encounter with both Mr and Mrs A.N. Whitehead. I had read his *Science and the Modern World* while in college. I found some things in it that perplexed me, and went to study with him as soon as I graduated. Whitehead was Cohen's antithesis in almost every way. Where Cohen was lightning-quick, Whitehead was ruminative, repetitious, and occupied with trying to get a better grip on almost every issue that came up. He was also both kind and remote, unpretentious, thoughtful, ruminative, rarely answering any question directly, but almost always carrying every topic beyond the point one might, even vaguely, have surmised might be reached. It was not clear just what path he followed, nor evident just how what he ended at was related to the beginning. He awakened and excited me. At almost every meeting my mind was set awhirl, with a jostling of many ideas that he provoked rather than suggested. Evelyn at the same time made a tremendous difference to my life. She saw to it that I had proper clothes and had needed financial help, and helped me to improve my crude social ways. I have spoken of my experience with both of them a number of times, particularly in *Philosophy in Process.* I never thought, though, that his philosophical view, though subtler and more basic than those of his contemporaries, was tenable. As time goes on, I see it to be more porous than I thought it should be if it is to be acceptable on every front. But he had the spirit of a true philosopher, the kind of detachment from himself, a concern with knowing what is so and an acute awareness of the weaknesses of the dominant views of his time.

Another great influence – I think greater than the others – was the result of a close reading of Charles S. Peirce in the course of editing *The Collected Papers.* His freshness, originality, brilliance, radical honesty of thought, his multiple insights, remarkable range, and his ceaseless effort to understand, no matter what the prevailing attitude, continues to be an inspiration and an assurance for me. There was a singular honesty and depersonalization exhibited at almost every turn by him, as he ranged over a multitude of subjects with an apparent effortless daring, backed by insight and charged with intellectual passion. I continue to be excited by his originality, admire his pertinacity, and am impressed with his range.

Viewed in terms of these illustrious predecessors, I would be inclined to say that, without attempting to do so, my works over the years exhibit some of the critical skills of Cohen, the philosophical spirit of Whitehead, and the originality of Peirce, but I do not know how or really care to assess myself in relation to them. I have, I think, without design, incorporated in my teaching and in my writings some of the sharpness of Cohen, the depersonalized interest in ideas of Whitehead, and the independence of Peirce. My views, however, have developed in quite different ways – perhaps most sharply in their emphasis on self-criticism and comprehensiveness.

A philosophy must be systematic, with each major claim not only tested but shown to support and be supported by the others. There is no field from which it is excluded, and none to which is cannot contribute. It needs to be systematic, checking each answer by the others, with presuppositions uncovered and justified. Parts must support one another, and the whole illuminate and be illuminated by the parts. It faces an endless task, to be promoted not by warring armies bent on holding on to some small unfertile territory and spending their energies in trying to destroy one another, but by those who give themselves to a radically self-critical attempt to understand what is real, what can be known, and how these interplay.

I think I have contributed to the development of a new epoch in philosophy in which a persistent self-questioning ends in a comprehensive systematic mastery of major, pivotal factors, providing a base and a test, as well as an opportunity for subsequent thought to progress in the understanding of reality in the large and the small, the near and the remote. Nothing is to be held sacrosanct, nothing to be dismissed without examination. Though I think that philosophy is not confined to descriptions, it also is not creative. Its task is to explore reality, and to understand how it could be known.

To define oneself in advance as an analyst, idealist, deconstructionist, pragmatist, and the like, is to begin as one who is self-defeated, possessing an answer that excludes all questions which are outside its power to deal with, and to, by arbitrary rejection, form a position not itself examined. In the end, there can be only one philosophy in which each part is justified and the whole can be lived. It takes more than a lifetime to enable it to advance toward a result more subtle, comprehensive, warranted, and clarifying than any one person can himself manage, or that could perhaps be achieved in any one epoch.

My greatest pleasure is one with my greatest success: an understanding of reality and knowledge that will contribute to the achievement of a complete mastery of all there is, a knowledge of the principles operative everywhere, and an understanding of how other inquiries and their results can sustain one another.

PAUL WEISS

WEISSMAN, DAVID: AUTOBIOGRAPHY

Philosophy satisfies my taste for perspective and depth. Never religious, often bored by detail and technique, I wanted a subject that addressed large issues. I don't recall my early ways of formulating questions that are plainer to me now: What are we? What is the world? What is our place within it? What would be good to do or be? How can we know that answers to the first four questions are correct?

My experience as a philosophy student was a mix of pleasure and confusion. Most of my teachers analyzed texts or disputed obscure ideas. Only a few believed that philosophy should answer questions that weren't shallow, scholastic, or antique. I looked for instructors who would tolerate me as I deciphered things for myself. Robert Browning and Paul Schilpp did that at Northwestern. John Findlay did something more at King's College, London. Findlay believed in the grandeur of philosophy. He read texts for their architecture, locating them within his own ample view. He confirmed my belief that independent, systematic reflection is appropriate and possible. But Findlay was also deeply critical. He taught me never to make a point I couldn't defend.

My thinking evolved in complementary ways, one dialectical, the other constructive. Philosophy is constructive when it describes the ambient world and our ways of engaging it. It is dialectical when this realist view opposes the idealism that pervades philosophy since Descartes and Kant.

My master's thesis on habit at the University of Chicago, then my doctoral thesis on dispositions at London – rewritten and published as *Dispositional Properties* (Southern Illinois University Press, 1965) – were early attempts to do both things.

Realism in respect to dispositions was anathema to thinkers who preferred inspectable surrogates, in this case counterfactual conditionals. Philosophers who favor such analyses have a simple formula: they ascribe to thought, language or perception anything that is not irrefutably ascribed to an extra-mental reality. Or Descartes' second *Meditation* and Kant's first *Critique* prescribe the limits of testable thought, so nothing other than percepts, words, or theories is thinkable. Error and frustration, cooperation and efficacy suggest to me that their posture is a conceit. Supposing that nature has integrity and a modal complexity of its own, I described dispositions as qualifications for relation founded in the structural properties of things diverse as minds, knives, and violins. Other realist themes were developed in successive books: *Eternal Possibilities* (Southern Illinois University Press, 1977), *Hypothesis and the Spiral of Reflection* (SUNY Press, 1989), *Truth's Debt to Value* (Yale University Press, 1993), *A Social Ontology* (Yale University Press, 2000), *The Cage* (SUNY Press, 2006), and *Styles of Thought* (forthcoming).

My dialectical concern is the idealism that reduces the existence and character of things to the thoughts or words used to think them. Idealists are skeptics who care little about the world, but much for the rigor and verifiability – the safety – of their stories about it. I resist their ideas in *Intuition and Ideality* (SUNY Press, 1987), my essays in *Descartes' Discourse on Method and Meditations on First Philosophy* (Yale University Press, 1996), *Lost Souls* (SUNY Press, 2003), and the books listed above.

Success is partial. My characterization of nature as a system of overlapping and hierarchically organized stable systems is a sketch; it needs amplification within a detailed metaphysics of nature. Supplying this more elaborate theory of nature would leave one of my five questions unanswered: what would be good to do or be? Having only scattered observations to fill the place where a moral treatise should go, I settle for the people and circumstances who determined what I would be. My mother was focused and bold. My father encouraged me to read his copy of Schopenhauer when I was ten. That inkling was the lure.

David Weissman

WEST, CORNEL

Cornel West (1953–) is a prominent American public intellectual, a humanist scholar, and Black philosopher. He is Class of 1943 University Professor of Religion at Princeton University. West received his undergraduate training at Harvard University, completing a degree in Near Eastern languages and literature in 1973, and obtained his PhD in philosophy from Princeton University in 1980. He wrote his dissertation under Richard Rorty; it was later revised and became *The Ethical Dimensions of Marxist Thought* (1991). He has taught at premier institutions such as Harvard, Yale, and Princeton, and is a frequent speaker at Black churches, community centers, synagogues, and coffee shops. He gained national recognition through his 1993 bestseller *Race Matters.* West was born to Clifton L. West, Jr, a civilian Air Force administrator, and Irene Bias West, a school teacher and principal, in Tulsa, Oklahoma, 2 June 1953. The grandson of Rev. Clifton L. West, Sr, of Metropolitan Baptist Church in Tulsa, Oklahoma, West embodies a Christian perspective as exemplified in the religious and political praxis of Dr Martin Luther King, Jr. At age ten, he participated with his family in a civil rights demonstration in Sacramento, California, and heard King speak in person. King became "*the* touchstone for personal inspiration, moral wisdom and existential insight" (West 1999: 4).

There are five major streams of thought that comprise West's philosophical world-view: Existentialist, Pragmatist, Christian, Marxist, and African-American. His existentialist position is shaped around the theme that at the heart of the human condition there is a profound sense of existential suffering, a theme which speaks to his "Kierkegaardian sensibility" (West 1999: 20). For West, this sensibility has meta-philosophical implications that require philosophizing to be "linked to existentially concrete situations" (West 1999, 20). West's understanding of philosophy as grounded within human social practices and as involving a constant, self-corrective mode of inquiry, is shaped through the pragmatist tradition – Ralph Waldo Emerson, John Dewey, William James, W.E.B. DuBois, *et al.* Not only does West share their anti-professional view of philosophical practice, but he shares their intellectual provocation, courageous efforts, moral heroism, and cultural criticism. In his own genealogical account of pragmatism, which he develops in his influential philosophical work, *The American Evasion of Philosophy*, West adds what he uniquely terms prophetic pragmatism to this autochthonous American philosophical stream of thought.

Prophetic pragmatism, according to West, is "a particular American intervention conscious and critical of its roots, and radically historical and political in its outlook" (West 1989: 237). West understands prophetic pragmatism as offering a corrective to American pragmatism in terms of providing it with greater "existential depth and political consciousness" (Putnam 2001: 35) and chiding it for its "inadequate grasp of the complex operations of power" (West 1993: 135). West's prophetic pragmatism is a form of oppositional cultural criticism; it is committed "to individuality and democracy, historical consciousness and systemic social analyses" (West 1989: 232). It is deemed "prophetic" given its link "to the Jewish and Christian tradition of prophets who brought urgent and compassionate critique to bear on the evils of their day" (West 1989: 233). It opposes "all those power structures that lack public accountability, be they headed by military generals, bureaucratic party bosses, or corporate tycoons" (West 1989: 235). For West, it is located in the Christian tradition, a tradition that offers both a narrative that provides him with sanity in the face of existential trauma and a bridge upon which to build solidarity and mutual understanding regarding "the culture of the wretched of the earth"

(West 1989: 233). Hence, West's position is that of a specifically Christian prophetic pragmatist, one who is willing to invest all in the Christian narrative, and yet "to entertain the possibility in low moments that I may be deluded" (West 1989: 233). This directly relates to West's historicist position, which has family resemblances to his pragmatist sensibilities. "The historicism I promote is one which understands transient social practices, contingent cultural descriptions, and revisable scientific theories" (West 1993: 130–1). He rejects ahistorical quests for certainty and transcendental searches for truth. His historicism is a form of fallibilism, which rejects metaphysical foundations for the justification of belief. Yet, while a contextualist and revisionist, West argues that providing good reasons for what we believe is indispensable to "any serious struggle for radical democracy and freedom" (West 1996: 132).

West's emphasis on certain social critical and indispensable tools used in the service of the struggle for freedom is linked to the Marxist tradition, the most influential secular tradition that has shaped West's philosophical project. Yet, he sees Marxism as inadequate, opting for a pluralist approach to social analysis. "My social analytical perspective is post-Marxist without being anti-Marxist or pre-Marxist; that is, it incorporates elements from Weberian, racial, feminist, gay, lesbian and ecological modes of social analysis and cultural criticism" (West 1993: 133). Working within and having influenced the Africana philosophical tradition – which brings critical reflective thought to bear specifically upon articulating and honing those cultural and philosophical resources indigenous to the African Diaspora toward the end of defending Black agency and Black critical reflective traditions and modes of being – West is aware that "American philosophy has never taken the Afro-American experience seriously" (West 1982: 11f). For West, Africana thought emphasizes the centrality of class struggle, racism, and the "political dimensions of knowledge" (West 1982: 21). Identifying two challenges, self-image and self-determination, that Blacks face in America, West stresses the importance of Black philosophical thought in re-conceptualizing Black people as agents of history, delineating a powerful hermeneutic of Black self-understanding, and the importance of praxis. "The major function of Afro-American philosophy is to reshape the contours of Afro-American history and provide a new self-understanding of the Afro-American experience which suggests desirable guidelines for action in the present" (West 2003: 11). Although West's philosophical project wrestles with the theme of evil in modernity, as a Black philosopher he is concerned with how this evil disproportionately impacts "people of African descent in particular" (West 1999: 33). Grounded within the Black homiletic tradition, West speaks in the spirit of *parrhesia* or fearless, truthful speech, grounded in *Caritas*, which is related to a form of prophetic witnessing which attends to sites of Black pain and suffering. Yet, West is attuned to the Black Blues tradition that does not allow pain and suffering to have the last word. And as a race-transcending prophet, which "is someone who never forgets about the significance of race but refuses to be confined to race" (hooks and West 1991: 49), West understands that democratic maturity cannot be achieved while the forces of sexism, free-market fundamentalism, aggressive militarism, and escalating authoritarianism continue to erode democratic pedagogy and our democratic forms of life. Through written texts, engaged conversation, music CDs (*Sketches of My Culture*) or film (*The Matrix*), West fights for the priority of democracy for those voices that reside on the underside of modernity.

Further reading

Cowan, Rosemary. *Cornel West: The Politics of Redemption*. Cambridge: Polity Press, 2003.

hooks, bell and West, Cornel. *Breaking Bread: Insurgent Black Intellectual Life*. Boston, MA: South End Press, 1991.

Johnson, Clarence Shole. *Cornel West and Philosophy*. New York: Routledge, 2003.

West, Cornel. *The American Evasion of Philosophy: A Genealogy of Pragmatism*. Madison, WI: University of Wisconsin Press, 1989.

—— *Keeping Faith: Philosophy and Race in America*. New York: Routledge, 1993.

—— *The Cornel West Reader*. New York: Basic *Civitas* Books, 1999.

Wood, Mark David. *Cornel West and the Politics of Prophetic Pragmatism*. Urbana, IL: University of Illinois Press, 2000.

Yancy, George. *Cornel West: A Critical Reader*. Malden, MA: Blackwell, 2001.

George Yancy

WHITE, MORTON GABRIEL

Educated at the College of the City of New York and Columbia University, White's (1917–) principal teachers were Emil Post, Morris Cohen and Ernest Nagel. His doctoral dissertation, *The Origins of Dewey's Instrumentalism* (1943), was directed by John Dewey. He taught at City College, Columbia and the University of Pennsylvania before moving to Harvard in 1948. In 1970 he accepted an appointment at the Institute for Advanced Study, in Princeton, New Jersey, where he is now professor emeritus.

White's chief non-historical contribution has been the development over more than a half-century of "holistic pragmatism." He has argued that many distinctions that philosophers have traditionally considered crucial must be abandoned or at least blurred. Beginning this project in the 1940s and 1950s by joining Alfred Tarski, W.V. Quine and Nelson Goodman in attacking the analytic/synthetic distinction, he went on to inveigh against the descriptive/normative distinction in *Toward Reunion in Philosophy* (1956) and later books. Although arguments for blurring such distinctions have been made by many others, White believes that none has broken down the alleged differences between the ethical, the logical and the physical as thoroughly as he has. For example, employing reasoning of the same sort that Quine uses to support the claim that ontological statements are as scientific as physical statements, White reaches a holistic conclusion that Quine flatly rejects, namely, that sensory sentences and feeling sentences are not epistemically different in kind but only (sometimes) different in degree.

Taking classical pragmatists William James and John Dewey as early proponents of holistic views similar to his own, White has published widely in American intellectual history with an emphasis on pragmatism. In the twentieth century White was arguably the most influential historian of American philosophy. Probably more than other philosophers with this specialization, his readers have included scholars in disciplines outside philosophy such as history, literature, sociology and political science.

Further reading

White, Morton G. *Social Thought in America: The Revolt Against Formalism*. New York: Viking Press, 1949.

—— *Toward Reunion in Philosophy*. Cambridge, MA: Harvard University Press, 1956.

—— *A Philosophy of Culture: The Scope of Holistic Pragmatism*. Princeton, NJ: Princeton University Press, 2002.

PETER H. HARE

WHITEHEAD, ALFRED NORTH

Alfred North Whitehead (1861–1947) was a British mathematician and philosopher, most noted for his work in logic and metaphysics. As a logician, Whitehead is most widely known for his collaboration with Bertrand Russell on *Principia Mathematica* (1913). This monumental work proposed that all mathematical truths are a subset of logical truths. While his early work advanced this still contentious claim, Whitehead later turned to questions in the philosophy of science and in scientific cosmology. During this latter portion of his career he produced the three works that define his mature metaphysical system: *Science and the Modern World* (SMW, 1925), *Process and Reality* (PR, 1929), and *Adventures of Ideas* (AI, 1933).

Science and the Modern World introduces two epistemic concepts that underlie Whitehead's cosmology: *simple location* and *misplaced concreteness.* We cannot, he argues, regard locations in time and space as *in essence* isolated from other such locations; rather, distinct times and spaces are defined through their relation to each other. Denying that latter point commits the fallacy of misplaced concreteness, wherein we falsely *abstract* one reality from the concrete context that constitutes that reality.

While SMW presents these ideas as epistemic concerns, Whitehead's preeminent philosophical work, *Process and Reality*, renders them general metaphysical principles.

For Whitehead, ultimate realities are not fixed, isolated *substances*, rather they are *actual entities* or *occasions.* Actual entities comprise pulses of subjective experience which *prehend* or unify universals or *eternal objects* into vivid units of *subjective immediacy.* These ultimate realities *prehend* each other and *eternal objects* in their processes of *becoming*, (a) securing an *initial aim* or *urge* from God's *primordial nature*, (b) *enjoying* their distinctive satisfaction in a *decisive* burst of *subjective intensity*, and (c) passing over into their *objective immortality* – as potential objects of subsequent actual entities' prehensions – in God's *consequent nature.*

Among the most distinctive elements of Whitehead's *philosophy of organism* is his claim that reality comprises not being *qua* substance or essence, but *actualities* in this teeming swarm of *becomings*, i.e. that reality comprises a pulsating *process* of transitions from actual entities' *initial aims*, through their *decisions,* to their passage into *objective immortality.* Among the most controversial elements of his cosmology are (a) his insistence that *appetition* attends all actual entities, however simple or complex, and (b) his account of God as both the *primordial* source of *initial appetitive urges*, and as the *repository* of decisions rendered by distinct *actual entities.* The former claim continues to incite debate concerning Whitehead's *subjectivism,* which ascribes *apperception* or *feeling* to all realities; the latter sustains Whitehead's enduring influence over *Process Theology*, which depicts God not as a traditional substance, but as an *enduring actual entity* essentially affected by and evolving amid *Process*, aimed at exchanges with other actual entities.

The *subjectivism* of his cosmology seemingly contrasts Whitehead's metaphysical work sharply with his *logicism*. Indeed, Whitehead describes Western philosophy as a footnote to Plato, yet proceeds to invert Plato's ontology. Whereas for Plato, reality resides in logical *Forms* or *essences*, for Whitehead reality resides in how *actual entities prehend* those *eternal objects*; whereas for Plato, such *prehensions* signal appearances that merely shadow reality, for Whitehead those prehensions are ultimate realities. Like Plato, Whitehead locates truth in the correspondence of subjective judgments to objective realities, as for example, in logical operations. But, he holds in AI that correspondence is one species of truth, a term that properly signifies all *conformal* relations of *subjective* experience to the *objective* world from which that experience emerges. Truth obtains no less, then, in the proper functioning of a biological body, or in an apt aesthetic response, which alike exemplify the conformity of *subjective* decisions to the *objects* soliciting them.

The complexity of Whitehead's description of truth underscores the challenge of locating his work within the provenance of American philosophy. While seemingly pragmatic in germ, particularly in his emphasis on vivid, felt experience, his work echoes both the spare empiricism of skeptics like Hume, and the speculative reach of idealists such as Berkeley and Hegel. While conversant with theisms such as Royce's, his work remained determinedly pluralist, refusing to reduce all realities to a singular metaphysical substance. While versed in the secular, pragmatic, and analytic trends of his time, his work was broadly theistic and metaphysical. While he aimed to develop a cosmology fully adequate to contemporary physics, his metaphysical system extended well beyond scientific boundaries. How well he accomplished that latter task remains an open question; given his emphases on *process*, *creativity* and *novelty*, any assessment of his work could scarcely be otherwise.

Further reading

Griffin, David Ray and Cobb, John B. *Founders of Constructive Postmodern Philosophy: Peirce, James, Bergson, Whitehead, and Hartshorne*. Albany, NY: SUNY Press, 1993.

Kraus, Elizabeth M. *The Metaphysics of Experience: A Companion to Whitehead's Process and Reality*. New York: Fordham University Press, 1998.

Leclerc, Ivor. *The Relevance of Alfred North Whitehead*. New York: Routledge, 2004.

Lowe, Victor (ed.). *Alfred North Whitehead: The Man and His Work*. Maryland, MD: Johns Hopkins University Press, 1990.

Nobo, Jorge. *Whitehead's Metaphysics of Extension and Solidarity*. Albany, NY: SUNY Press, 1986.

Schlipp, Paul Arthur. *The Philosophy of Alfred North Whitehead*. Chicago, IL: Open Court, 1991.

Sherburne, Donald W. and Polanowski, Janusz A. (eds). *Whitehead's Philosophy: Points of Connection*. Albany, NY: SUNY Press, 2004.

Whitehead, A.N. *Adventures of Ideas*. New York: Free Press, 1967 [1933].

—— *Function of Reason*. Boston, MA: Beacon Press, 1968 [1929].

—— *Process and Reality: An Essay in Cosmology*, corrected edition, ed. David Ray Griffin and Donald W. Sherburne. New York: Free Press, 1978 [1929].

—— *Religion in the Making*. New York: Fordham University Press, 1996 [1926].

Lisa Bellantoni

WIEMAN, HENRY NELSON

Henry Nelson Wieman (1884–1975), process philosopher and theologian, noted in his "Intellectual Autobiography" that he was the son of a Presbyterian minister and a mother "who shaped the religious development of her children not by verbal instruction but by the encompassing might of her faith" (p. 6). He attended Park College (Missouri) with the expectation of becoming a journalist. In the spring of his senior year, however, an "ecstatic experience" brought him to recognize that he "should devote my life to the problems of religious inquiry" (p. 6). After three years in seminary, he studied in Germany (with Rudolf Eucken, Wilhelm Windelband, and Ernst Troeltsch) and then served as a Presbyterian minister for four years before beginning doctoral studies at Harvard University. He had already encountered the work of Josiah Royce as an undergraduate; at Harvard, he worked with William Ernest Hocking and Ralph Barton Perry. They, along with Henri Bergson, John Dewey, and William James, were dominant influences in his 1917 doctoral dissertation "The Organization of Interests." Extended study of Alfred North Whitehead's work came later. The basis of his lifelong development of the philosophy of creativity can be discerned in the dissertation. Along with those positive contributions, his negative criticism of Karl Barth and Paul Tillich were influential in that development.

Wieman taught first at Occidental College and then, for twenty years, at the University of Chicago

Divinity School, from which he retired in 1947. He then taught at the University of Oregon, the University of Houston, and Grinnell College before coming to Southern Illinois University, Carbondale in 1956. He retired again – to Grinnell, Iowa – in 1966.

In fourteen books, many chapters in edited books, some 200 articles, and numerous sermons and addresses, Wieman developed a conception of "creative interchange," his preferred name for processes of communicative interaction, understood as a basic structure of human being, in which novelty emerges through "the creative event." As he wrote in *The Source of Human Good*, "the order or structure of the creative event is not imposed upon it but is intrinsic to the very nature of such an event"; it manifests "a creativity working antecedently to the mind, creating it along with its world" (194–5). He analyzed that event as "made up of four subevents" which, "working together," are necessary for "the creative event as it occurs in communication" (65): emergent awareness of other perspectives, via "intercommunication"; integration of those perspectives; using that awareness and integration to expand past knowledge and valuation; and, growth of community (57–65). Transformation, although not always agreement, is the outcome of creative interchange.

Echoes of Wieman's conception can be discerned in contemporary philosophy of communication that investigates communication as constitutive, rather than representational. The balance of interpersonal, social, traditional, and transcendent elements in Wieman's analysis of creativity has a broader import, however, for it informs a conception of God as "that creative good which transforms us in ways in which we cannot transform ourselves" (a phrase, William Sherman Minor reported, that Wieman often used in his classes). "We have identified God with the creative event," Wieman wrote in *The Source of Human Good*, "but this requires some qualification" (305). That "qualification" was his life's work.

Further reading

Bretall, Robert W. (ed.). *The Empirical Theology of Henry Nelson Wieman*. Carbondale, IL: Southern Illinois University Press, 1963.

Minor, William Sherman. *Creativity in Henry Nelson Wieman*. Metuchen, NJ: Scarecrow Press and American Theological Library Association, 1977.

Wieman, Henry Nelson. *Religious Experience and Scientific Method*. New York: Macmillan, 1926.

—— *The Source of Human Good*. Chicago, IL: University of Chicago Press, 1946.

—— *Man's Ultimate Commitment*. Carbondale, IL: Southern Illinois University Press, 1958.

—— "Intellectual Autobiography" in *The Empirical Theology of Henry Nelson Wieman*, ed. Robert W. Bretall. Carbondale, IL: Southern Illinois University Press, 1963, pp. 3–18.

Lenore Langsdorf

WILD, JOHN

John Wild is a bell-weather academic philosopher in the twentieth century. He was a member of the Harvard philosophy department from the 1930s up until 1961, when he was the first full professor to leave the Harvard philosophy department. Harvard was the ancestral home of American philosophy. Wild was perfectly placed to observe a vast sea-change in this philosophy.

American thought had been an integral development in the history of philosophy, and yet it had been quite distinctive as well. One cannot understand this thought – Thoreau's or Emerson's, say – without grasping that it had sprung up on this continent, this earth, under this sky, and within the pull of an ever-expanding frontier. Indigenous influences were also a part of the mix. Moreover, the American Puritans, from Cotton Mather to Jonathan Edwards, were a powerful and distinctive force in producing a diverse but home-grown world-view.

All this began to change in the 1930s, and with burning focus in the Harvard philosophy department. Logical positivism had emerged in Vienna, and the siren call of science spread far and wide. It was as if the Enlightenment were to be brightly rekindled, and the fecund nineteenth century, with its romanticism of one sort or another – and its religiously tinged thought – were to be completely eclipsed. Wild was clearly discontented with the state of the department in 1961. William Ernest Hocking (a student of William James and of Josiah Royce, early influenced by Husserl) was retired. C.I. Lewis was a link to the great past, but he had adopted positions antithetical to Wild's. For example, he held that there were immediate givens in consciousness – sense data. He had abandoned James' idea of knowledge by acquaintance, our immediate involvement with the world *as* world (whole patterns in experience, as Wild was to put it). Lewis had abandoned James' (and Dewey's) view that sense data are not primal building blocks of knowledge, but are derivative of analyses forgetful of themselves. Willard Quine, the logician, was rising to prominence, and he believed that certain issues must be decided "pragmatically"; but he assumed that only science provided knowledge worthy of the name. American philosophy was greatly narrowed.

Wild left Harvard and took up the chairmanship of the philosophy department at Northwestern. Though he was there only a short time, before returning east to Yale, it was long enough to stir the Society for Phenomenology and Existential Philosophy into being. In 1955 he had published *The Challenge of Existentialism*, which became a philosophical best-seller. His career might be described as a thinker's search for roots in history, and a rejection of the ahistorical attitude of much "analytic" philosophy. Wild concentrated on Plato, Aristotle, Spinoza, and on Heidegger, Merleau-Ponty, and William James later on. He published *Introduction to Realistic Philosophy*, and in 1953 founded the American Association for Realistic Philosophy. For Wild, the only way to stay grounded in reality is through a passionate and patient involvement in history.

It is understandable that Wild's intellectual life would culminate in his last book, *The Radical Empiricism of William James* (1969). Wild believed that James' mode of phenomenology most keenly and thoroughly discerns our immediate involvements in the world around us and through us. He prized James' discernment of the tendencies and structures that make all our other experience possible – but without the a priori transcendental apparatus, whether Kantian, Hegelian, or Husserlian. Wild followed closely James' last projects: his radical empiricism – a level of immediate experience anterior to the very distinction between subject and object; also James' vision of a pluralistic universe – endless variety, myriad forms of connectedness, the pleni-potential of our lives. James' work is unfinished, pregnant with possibilities. As Wild knew, these awaited us at the end of the twentieth century and the beginning of a new millennium.

Further reading

Wild, John. *Spinoza Selections.* New York: Charles Scribner's Sons, 1930, Introduction (50 pages).

—— *Plato's Modern Enemies and the Theory of Natural Law.* Chicago, IL: University of Chicago Press, 1953.

—— *Return to Reason: Essays in Realistic Philosophy.* Chicago, IL: University of Chicago Press, 1953.

—— *The Challenge of Existentialism.* Bloomington, IN: Indiana University Press, 1955.

—— *The Radical Empiricism of William James.* New York: Doubleday, 1969.

BRUCE WILSHIRE

WILL

It is hard to imagine a topic more important than the will and at the same time more shrouded in vagueness. As is fairly well known, Aristotle divided the soul or animating principle of the human person into three divisions: the vegetative, the volitional, and the intellectual. The first is shared most broadly with all living things; the third, he thought, is quite distinctive to human beings. The outlines of the second division, the volitional, are most problematical. One tradition, commonly construed as Aristotelian, regards any human activity as voluntary (Latin, *voluntas*, the will) which originates in the person. But this is exceedingly broad, ruling out only cases such as hurricanes, in which one's movements are often controlled by forces beyond one's will or control. Included in the broad berth of the volitional are, on the one hand, both desires and impulses – which seem simply to happen to one – and, on the other hand, deliberate actions done out of regard for some principle of reason, of prudence, of faith, whatever. These latter concern our distinctive human agency as selves or persons.

Hundreds of years after Aristotle, St Augustine took up the matter of the will and its ostensible freedom. Instead of Aristotle's detached, third-person account – what is man? – we get the piercing first-person actuality – who am I? Persons wrestle with their own conscience and with their many strong, even imperious, impulses. As valuable as are Augustine's reflections, they are limited by special interests and concerns, e.g. to free God from responsibility for evil, and also to divide soul (or the core of self) from the body. The latter, Augustine thinks, is only used by the soul, at least when the soul is at its best.

By the nineteenth century and the emergence of the "classical" American philosophers, the problematical nature of will had thickened into glaring prominence. No longer did God's will and our will with respect to that will hold center-stage. Moreover, revolutions in the sciences forced a reevaluation of the nature of will, and how that pertains to the nature of self, body, and agency. Arthur Schopenhauer, for example, maintained that the self cannot be dissociated from the body's animal lust to survive and to satisfy itself. The best for which we can strive is a brand of ascetic resignation, and also a sublimation of will in Platonic-like contemplation and in artistic creations. Immanuel Kant had taken the high ground with respect to will. In principle, we should be capable of moral behavior, that is, capable of experiencing reverence for the moral law as handed down by pure, practical reason (that is, reason pertaining to ethical practice). Any other motivation for behavior renders actions something less than moral. Subsequent thinkers, such as Friedrich Schiller and

G.W.F. Hegel, thought that Kant left us with hypostatized abstractions such as moral will, pure practical reason, etc. We must thicken up morality by connecting it with aesthetic experience, and with the bodily and cultural realities in which we are embedded.

Perhaps the most powerful attempt to span and comprehend the diverse facets of will was generated by William James in *The Principles of Psychology* (1890). He looks for a kind of continuum in levels of will. The anchor, so to speak, is the bodily self, even its simplest activity, sensory-motor behavior – instinctive reflex actions in response to stimuli raining in from all sides. For James, no gulf separates body from soul or from core self. He argues at length that there is no isolated executive function or agency that issues orders for innervations of muscles, nor is there an actual feeling of such. Given the realities of efferent and afferent neural pathways, we can be aware only of the sensory effects of what we do or have already done. This means that all levels of voluntary behavior have to be construed as awareness of certain effects *and* consenting that just these, and not others, be reproduced in our behavior. Thus the simplest level of voluntary actions presupposes some actions that are not voluntary at all. Voluntary actions increase in complexity in direct ratio to the complexity of attention involved, and to the complexity and tenor of what counts as consent to the reproduction of such effects. The fifth and final level of complexity, or of decision, is what he calls the dead heave of the will. Here there is considerable difficulty in keeping attention focused on the desired or proposed effects of actions. He even allows that this level of consent can be called *fiat* – as if we were saying to ourselves, "This shall be the case, this morally must and ought to be!" Early in his philosophical career, in his critique of Herbert Spencer's evolutionism, he had argued that we are capable on occasion of acting on this belief: "Let the law be justified though the world perish." This is reminiscent of Kant, of course, but James does not make the connection explicit, for he habitually indulged an animus against Kant. Concerning James's thought on the freedom of the will, see "Existentialism, American."

Much could be written on American philosophers' handling of will. Both H.D. Thoreau and R.W. Emerson wrote importantly of how our voluntary careers are founded in our matrix in Nature and in our kinship with the other animals. Likewise, I believe, the beliefs and practices of the Native American, Black Elk, are germane in this regard. Finally, the voluminous work of John Dewey must be recognized. His life-long concern with education should be construed as his attempts to cultivate the will by structuring learning situations so that our instinctive curiosity discovers ever more ramifying connections within environments.

The enduring vitality of American philosophy depends on maintaining a tradition in which will continues to be clarified, developed, and nourished.

BRUCE WILSHIRE

WILL TO BELIEVE

The "Will to believe" is the most famous and contentious doctrine of William James, and possibly the very core of Jamesian pragmatism. According to James's account the doctrine states that

> Our passional nature not only lawfully may, but must, decide an option between propositions, whenever it is a genuine option that cannot by its nature be decided on intellectual grounds; for to say, under such circumstances, "Do not decide, but leave the question open," is itself a passional decision, – just like deciding yes or no, – and is attended with the same risk of losing the truth.

The theoretical bases of James's notion of belief are to be found in Bain's definition of belief as "what we are ready to act on" (A. Bain, *Emotions and Will*); in Brentano's account of belief as judgment concessing existence (F. Brentano, *Psychologie vom empirischen Standpunkte*) and in Renouvier's notion of ideo-motor action (C. Renouvier, *Essais de critique générale*). James, however, rejected Bain's account of belief as a composed act and Brentano's notion of "intentional inexistence" as distinct from belief. James's doctrine of will to believe is based on his anthropological and psychological assumption of the primacy of action, as the main end of human beings, and on the leading function of emotions interest and attention in the definition of reality and as spur to action (see *Principles of Psychology* Chs XI, XXI, XXIII, XXV, XXVI). Emotions and interests constitute the *voluntary* side of the "will to believe," in the twofold meaning of deliberative and active. In this sense, in order to reject many of the criticisms which labeled his doctrine as an apology for wishful thinking, bad faith or deception, James clarifies that a voluntary belief is not a belief arbitrarily adopted or adopted by calculation. "Will" here is not to be understood as a faculty or a special act affirming any object "at will," which would lead to deception, but rather which the consistency of a certain object with the emotional and active parts of one's own nature, and the disposition or willingness to act as if that object were real. Accordingly, from the psychological point of view "belief" and "will," in their ideo-motor aspects, are partially similar and overlapping mental states, even though they involve different attitudes towards their objects. Voluntary belief means then one's conscious assumption of an object as part of "reality" and accordingly the adoption of such a conviction as a suitable reason or end for action. Such an assumption, although lacking counter-factual evidence, is legitimate since it satisfies the basic human need for keeping the stream of thought/action going.

James's doctrine of the "will to believe" was presented in 1896 as a lecture at the "Philosophical Club" of Yale and Brown Universities and its full account was published as an article in *New World* and later on as the main essay in James's book *The Will to Believe and Other Essays in Popular Philosophy* (1897).

Together with the passional and volitional basis of personal convictions and Bain's account of belief, the doctrine includes among its preliminary assumptions the notion of hypothesis as "anything that may be proposed to our belief." Hypotheses can be "living" or "dead" according to their relevance for us, that is, whether they can appeal to our psychological, cultural or practical areas of interest or not. The actual dilemma between two "living" hypotheses is an *option*. A *genuine* option is supposed to be at once *living*, *forced* and *momentous*: namely, it is a dilemma that concerns an actual field of interest, requires a *proactive answer*, has a fundamental relevance for the life of the individual and, consequently, cannot be avoided, suspended or delayed. Every time it is assumed that such an option, for metaphysical or practical reasons, in principle cannot receive a purely theoretical solution in a reasonable or appropriate span of time, or when the solution partially or totally depends on one's own choice (self-verifying belief), decision may and must be taken on an emotional and intuitive basis and despite the lack of supporting evidence, as a voluntary *belief*. Such a procedure is legitimate since according to James it is the same upon which we decide what "reality" is.

Although James introduced the "will to believe" doctrine as a justification of religious faith and a defense of the right to adopt beliefs as valid propositions in religious matters, its meaning and outcome go much beyond the religious field and reach the broader realm of the epistemological foundation of knowledge. On the basis of an emotionally grounded account of reality and rationality (*The Sentiment of Rationality*), belief appears no longer as a merely cognitive act, as in the Cartesian tradition, but entails a dispositional character; for it introduces emotional factors, subjective evaluation of consequences and action as constitutive parts of epistemological discourse.

James's doctrine is a deep attack against intellectualistic epistemology, and challenges positivist agnosticism (T.H. Huxley) and evidentialist ethics of belief according to which "it is wrong always, everywhere, and for anyone, to believe anything upon insufficient evidence" (C.K. Clifford). James's view here is that of the two basic epistemological attitudes expressed by, "we must avoid error" and "we must know the truth," is intrinsically more rational and valid than the other, since they both are expression of our passional life; the latter, however, is more likely to lead closer to truth or at least to provide more valuable advantages than the mere skeptical avoidance of error, and to this extent it appears. In fact, although it is generally true that in case of doubt the most rational attitude would be to suspend judgment and avoid error, in the case of genuine options, which require a proactive decision, the intellectual suspension of judgment, to the extent it keeps the action in check, is equivalent to a positive choice for one of the two conflicting hypotheses at stake. Consequently, in such special cases there cannot be a real neutrality and the prescription of the agnostic ethics of belief to suspend judgment works like a choice anyway. A of this situation agnosticism as the option between faith and atheism; in fact, agnosticism although intellectually different from atheism, leads at last to the same non-religious attitude and behavior.

The term "belief" is used as the equivalent of "working hypothesis" and it works in metaphysical, moral and practical matters in the same way as "hypothesis" works in the practice of science, except for the fact that scientific hypotheses for as much as they can be living and momentous, in most of the cases are not forced, since they allow suspended judgment and the wait for better evidence. Beliefs as well as hypotheses, however, are susceptible to evidence, yet they are subject to a test of a special kind, which verifies them according to their agreement with our general moral or emotional experience of the world (Ayer).

Such a criterion works in particular for what James calls "over-beliefs" (VRE 405–6): that is, all-inclusive, totalizing personal views concerning the existence and nature of absolute metaphysical, ethical, aesthetic or theological objects and values, such as God, World, Freedom, Beauty, Good, and the like. In such cases "belief" does not mean what we hold despite knowing it, not true but what we firmly and sincerely think is the case until there is better evidence. Accordingly no belief or disbelief is intrinsically better or more "true" than its opponents, and over-beliefs, while indispensable for the individual's life, are to be treated with tolerance "so long as they are not intolerant themselves." The consequence of such an assumption is James's adoption of pluralism, as a moral and political attitude.

Since its first appearance, the "will to believe" doctrine has encountered many critical receptions and reviews, starting with C.S. Peirce, D.S. Miller, B. Russell and is still one of the major targets for James's critics. Criticisms are classed in two major groups: those that hold to the evidentialist ethics of belief and those that detect one or more logical inconsistencies in James's treatment of belief. In either case the criticism assumes a theoretical standpoint (intellectualist account of knowledge, notion of rationality, propositional logic) which is completely different from the one proposed by James or exactly what James attempted to refute. Other critics followed Peirce in focusing on the extremely subjective character of the doctrine and on its potentially dangerous outcomes in terms of the defense of prejudice and fanaticism, and the undermining of scientific inquiry. James, however, always rejected such remarks as unfortunate misunderstandings of his view mostly caused by his inappropriate choice of the name of the doctrine, which more consistently should have been called "A Critique of Pure Belief." The view was not intended to stop inquiry into truth but only to legitimate decisions in those cases in which no scientific truth was available.

"The will to believe" received positive receptions from C.J. Ducasse and G. Papini, and it exerted an important influence on the development of H. Reichenbach's theory of probability and on K. Popper's fallibilism.

Further reading

Ayer, A.J. *The Origins of Pragmatism*. San Francisco, CA: Freeman Cooper, 1968, Bk II, Ch. 2.

Bird, G. *William James*. London: Routledge, 1986, Ch. 9.

Gale, R.M. *The Divided Self of William James*. Cambridge: Cambridge University Press, 1999, Ch. I, §§ 2, 3, 4.

Kauber, P. and Hare, R.M. "The Right and Duty to Will to Believe," *Canadian Journal of Philosophy*, 1974, pp. 327–43.

Perry R.B. *The Thought and Character of William James*. Boston, MA: Little, Brown, 1936, Ch. LXIII.

Seigfried C. Haddock. *William James's Radical Reconstruction of Philosophy*. Albany, NY: SUNY Press, 1990, passim.

Wernham J.C.S. *James's Will to Believe Doctrine*. McGill-Queen's University Press, 1987.

SERGIO FRANZESE

WILLIAMS, ROGER

The founder of Rhode Island, an early and vocal advocate of church–state separation, and a friend of the indigenous Native Americans whose lives and traditions would be permanently disrupted by the "new world" incursion of Europeans seeking treasure and freedom in America, Roger Williams (c. 1603–83) was an avid Separatist whose views placed him sharply at odds with the Puritan settlers of Massachusetts and their conservative religious orthodoxy.

Nearly a century before Thomas Jefferson would call for a "wall of separation" between church and state, Williams was busy founding a colonial settlement in Narragansett Bay enshrined to precisely that. His own earlier church experience, as pastor of Salem Church in Massachusetts, impressed upon him the inescapable dangers for freedom of thought and conscience of allowing civic life to be dominated by any religious agenda – even, or perhaps especially, one's own.

In October 1635 he was banished from the Massachusetts colony by its General Court. His harrowing fugitive escape to an Indian village in Narragansett Bay, after many months of harsh winter hardship, allowed him to evade deportation to England. In the spring of 1636 he established the Providence settlement on gifted land, thanks to the munificence of two Indian chieftains whose trust and respect he had gained.

Williams exploited his banishment, in heated public exchange with the noted Puritan John Cotton, as an example of intolerance resulting from the blurring of boundaries between church and state. In *The Bloudy Tenent of Persecution* (1644) he articulated his conviction that individual "liberty of conscience," or "soul-liberty," must never be sacrificed in order to appease and conform to the conventional beliefs of one's community. "Persecution for cause of conscience," he wrote, "is most evidently and lamentably contrary to the doctrine of Christ Jesus the Prince of Peace."

No mortal could credibly claim knowledge of God's own preferences in the matter of how men and women ought to worship, said Williams – or even that they should. He extended his own commitment to tolerance even to the unbelievers of his day, a lesson perhaps lost on the ardent "original intent creationists" of a later age who would loudly proclaim their insistence that freedom of religion does not signify freedom *from* religion. Williams thought otherwise, sure as he was that Christians possess a special duty to refrain from persecuting others for their various beliefs. Williams' neglected legacy to the tradition of American philosophy is thus one of proudly defiant pluralism.

Further reading

Gaustad, Edwin. *Roger Williams*. Oxford: Oxford University Press, 2005.

Gilpin, W. Clark. *The Millenarian Piety of Roger Williams*. Chicago: University of Chicago Press, 1970.

Morgan, Edmund S. *Roger Williams: The Church and the State*. New York: Harcourt, 1967.

Williams, Roger. *The Complete Writings of Roger Williams*, 7 volumes. New York: Russell and Russell, 1963.

PHILIP OLIVER

WILSHIRE, BRUCE

Bruce Wilshire is a senior professor of philosophy at Rutgers University (New Brunswick, NJ) where he presently teaches American philosophy, both Anglo and Indigenous.

In the 1960s Wilshire emerged as one of the most original interpreters of William James by highlighting the close connections between James and Continental philosophy and in particular phenomenology. In his book *William James and Phenomenology: A Study of "The Principles of Psychology"* (1969), Wilshire locates James in the phenomenological tradition revived by Franz Brentano, and it shows how James influenced Husserl. In the same work Wilshire focuses on the question of James's dualism within the *Principles* and discloses how James's stated intention to pursue a dualistic and "scientific" division of mental states from physical ones breaks down and prepares the way for his later metaphysics of radical empiricism and for his probing interpretations of religious experience.

Wilshire's lifelong interest in James marks also his study of metaphysics (*Metaphysics. An Introduction to Philosophy* 1969) and is clearly reflected in his later works, where James and other major figures of classical American philosophy are compared and related to representatives of Native American thought in the attempt to retrace a common root of American culture (*The Primal Roots of American Philosophy: Pragmatism, Phenomenology, Native American Thought*, 2000).

Since the 1970s Wilshire has become active on the national scene as a critic of the educational system (see *The Moral Collapse of the University: Professionalism, Purity, and Alienation*, 1989) and played a major role in the Pluralist rebellion in the American Philosophical Association, against the almost exclusive monopoly of analytic philosophy in the teaching of philosophy in American universities, becoming a leader of the Committee on Pluralism (see *Fashionable Nihilism: A Critique of Analytic Philosophy*, 2002). In 2001, Wilshire was awarded the Herbert Schneider Award for lifetime achievement by the Society for the Advancement of American Philosophy.

Wilshire's later production reflects his main philosophical concern, namely the role and creation of the self in its intersubjective relation with others and within the problematic antithesis between culture and nature which has troubled the modern age (*Role Playing and Identity: The Limits of Theatre as Metaphor*, 1991; *Get 'Em all, Kill 'Em! Genocide, Terrorism, Righteous Communities*, 2004).

In particular Wilshire focuses on the problem of Nature and on the loss of connection with natural roots that is at the bottom of many of the individual and social problems of western civilized human beings. Far from a romantic or new-ageist mood, Wilshire recognizes a fundamental need for individuals to recover a deep connection to the natural ground of life in order to stabilize personal identity and attain a deeper and richer meaning of life (*Wild Hunger: The Primal Roots of Modern Addiction*, 1999). In his book *The Much at Once: Music, Science, Ecstasy, the Body*, the major theme of the connection to individual natural grounds joins Wilshire's interest in theatre and contemporary music and opens an exploration of their role in the deconstruction of western culture and identity.

Further reading

Wilshire, Bruce. *William James and Phenomenology: A Study of the Principles of Psychology*. New York: AMS Press, 1977.

—— *Role Playing and Identity: The Limits of Theatre As Metaphor*. Indianapolis, IN: Indiana University Press, 1982.

—— *Wild Hunger: The Primal Roots of Modern Addiction*. New York: Rowman and Littlefield, 1999.

—— *The Primal Roots of American Philosophy: Pragmatism, Phenomenology, and Native American Thought*. Philadelphia, PA: Pennsylvania State University Press, 2000.

—— *Fashionable Nihilism: A Critique of Analytic Philosophy*. Albany, NY: SUNY Press, 2002.

SERGIO FRANZESE

WITHERSPOON, JOHN

John Witherspoon (1723–94) was born in the village of Gifford, Scotland, to Reverend James

Witherspoon and Anne Walker Witherspoon. A prodigy, he was admitted to the University of Edinburgh at the age of thirteen and in three years earned his Master of Arts degree. Upon completion of his MA, Witherspoon remained in Edinburgh to pursue theological studies. In 1743, he was licensed as a minister.

Witherspoon quickly became a preeminent figure in the Church as a skilled preacher, satirical writer, profound scholar and a leader of reform. When he entered the ministry, a movement known as Moderatism dominated the Scottish Presbyterian Church. Many Moderatist clergy dismissed church dogmas and practiced philosophical interpretations of scripture. As a staunch reformer, Witherspoon vigorously defended church dogmas and a need for scriptural interpretation to reflect orthodox principles without aid from secular works.

Witherspoon's defense of orthodoxy culminated in his famous and highly effective satire, *Ecclesiastical Characteristics* (1753). In it, he criticizes Moderatism for being more interested in rationalism than in Scripture, and hence unable to effectively uphold Presbyterian religious values and practices. Witherspoon satirically portrays the moderates as fundamentally committed to a scientific and philosophical creed, which he terms the "Athenian Creed." The "Athenian Creed" is a proclamation in which the mathematical order of Nature and Fate is glorified as the raison d'être for the universe. Witherspoon depicts this viewpoint as advocating that the world is a machine governed by absolute necessity, and hence devoid of a personal god or moral virtue. For Witherspoon, such a theological position diminished the spiritual impact of Christianity in the lives of its parishioners.

Witherspoon argues for a moral and religious philosophy based on sentiment and experience. Witherspoon's moral philosophy is well represented in his *Lectures on Moral Philosophy* (1795) in which he views Nature from a Lockean perspective as a realm to be inductively investigated. Witherspoon argues that abstract causal necessity cannot adequately sustain religious devotion or explain moral justification. If necessary laws determine humans, then religious devotion, absolutely considered, is impossible. In a deterministic universe, there is no such thing as moral choice, and a Christian life is impossible. As a result, Witherspoon argues moral justification must be empirical so that prior experiences, such as religious instruction and the revealed word of God, can structure the moral rationale and impetus of a devout Christian. In the process, particular biblical principles and church dogma are actively vindicated in the practice of an inspired and well-oriented Christian.

Perhaps his insistence on moral instruction and its experiential vindication ultimately prompted Reverend Witherspoon to travel to the American colonies in 1768, not only to accept the Presidency of Princeton University but also to unify the fractured American Presbyterian Church. True to his philosophy, Reverend Witherspoon broadened the curriculum, exposing provincial Americans to diverse disciplines, and he was known to teach students complex theories through simple examples. In his attempt to unify the American Presbyterian Church, Witherspoon traveled throughout the colonies giving sermons and lectures. He was exposed to diverse colonial life in the process. Witherspoon soon came to love his adopted homeland and by the start of the revolution was an ardent supporter of independence. Witherspoon served on the Continental Congress as a representative from New Jersey and was the only clergyman to sign the Declaration of Independence.

Further reading

Gordon, Tait L. *The Piety of John Witherspoon: Pew, Pulpit, and Public Forum*. Louisville, KY: Geneva Press, 2001.

Morrison, Jeffrey H. *John Witherspoon and the Founding of the American Republic*. Notre Dame, IN: University of Notre Dame Press, 2005.

Witherspoon, John. *Ecclesiastical Characteristics* (Early American Imprints: First Series). Worcester, MA: American Antiquarian Society, 1955–83 [1753], microfilm 10804.

—— *The Selected Writings of John Witherspoon*, ed. Thomas Miller. Carbondale, IL: Southern Illinois University Press, 1990.

NORMAN WHITMAN

WITTGENSTEIN, LUDWIG

Ludwig Wittgenstein (1889–1951) was an Austrian philosopher who has had an enormous influence on contemporary American philosophy. In his early philosophy Wittgenstein developed a logical approach to meaning with strong deflationary consequences. In the *Tractatus Logico-Philosophicus* (1961) he articulated the so-called "picture theory of meaning," according to which there is a logical isomorphism between language and reality that makes the significance of propositions possible: they can picture the world in virtue of the *logical form* they share with the facts that they depict. On this view, the domain of the non-factual – including philosophy in its entirety (and the Tractarian propositions themselves!) – lies beyond the bounds of sense. But, according to the pictorial account of meaning, our propositions *show* more than they say: they *show* their own logical form and, with that, all the logical features that language can have; and they also exhibit *normative* dimensions, that is, aspects pertaining to (ethical, aesthetic, and religious) values. Although in his later philosophy Wittgenstein became deeply critical of logical approaches to meaning (and explicitly critical of the pictorial approach), some crucial insights of the Tractarian view seem to survive, including the so-called "doctrine of showing." However, in Wittgenstein's later philosophy showing is not something accomplished by propositions but by linguistic *actions*, by the performative and practical aspects of our speech acts. In order to underscore the internal connection between language and action, Wittgenstein introduces the notion of "language-game." With this notion, Wittgenstein emphasizes that speaking is an activity, like making a move in a language game; and an activity that has a crucial *normative* dimension, that is, that it can be deemed correct or incorrect. On this practice-based view, language has an essential *holistic* dimension, for particular speech acts can only be properly understood if they are put in the context of the language-games in which they figure, that is, if they are inserted in entire linguistic practices, which in turn have to be understood in the context of "the form of life" (*Lebensform*) of a linguistic community. It is in this sense that Wittgenstein often observes that a language involves "a form of life."

The notion of "language-game" also underscores the irreducible diversity and heterogeneity of linguistic practices. On this view, language does not have an essence that can be captured in a set of necessary and sufficient conditions for what makes something linguistic; language is a family-resemblance notion, that is, a notion that binds things together without all the things that fall under the concept sharing the same properties, but exhibiting only some overlapping and criss-crossing similarities (none of which being of necessity present in all the members), just like the complex network of resemblances that appear among the members of a family. In the central work of his later philosophy, *Philosophical Investigations* (1958), Wittgenstein tries to debunk different forms of essentialism and foundationalism, articulating a new conception of philosophy as a therapeutic activity whose task is to assemble reminders that provide a perspicuous view of the multiple and heterogeneous uses of language in our practices and thus dissolve philosophical puzzles and paradoxes. In this work he also develops indeterminacy arguments about meaning and normativity in his discussions of language learning and rule-following. These arguments suggest that meaning and correctness cannot be fixed and wholly determined by intentions, rules, interpretations, behavioral regularities, or anything else. We cannot find fixers and determiners of meaning and correctness in our language-games; and, therefore, semantic and normative issues remain indefinitely open to negotiation in our practices. Given this indefinite openness to negotiation that is required of linguistic practices, Wittgenstein's rule-following discussion culminates with an argument – the so-called "Private Language Argument" – which suggests that there is no room for meaning and normativity in a language-game that is outside the realm of intersubjective negotiations and is radically private, that is, private in the sense that only one speaker can *in principle* understand it and play it. Many have argued that there are deep similarities between Wittgenstein's arguments in the *Philosophical Investigations* and the indeterminacy arguments of American philosophers writing around the same time, especially Nelson Goodman's "new riddle of induction" and Quine's "indeterminacy of translation." Other critics have emphasized the differences between these arguments and have called into question whether Wittgenstein can be considered a meaning skeptic in the same sense in which Goodman and Quine are. But beyond issues of indeterminacy, Wittgenstein's later philosophy seems to exhibit important affinities with pragmatism. This did not escape Wittgenstein's attention ("I am trying to say something that sounds like pragmatism"; 1969: 422); but he was not satisfied with this convergence. Wittgenstein was explicitly critical of some of the classic American pragmatists (especially James), while at the same time drawing from their ideas.

But however we interpret Wittgenstein's troubled relation with the pragmatist tradition, there seem to be important points of contact and shared commitments that connect his later philosophy with pragmatism: anti-essentialism and anti-foundationalism; the priority of practice and action over theory and intellect (anti-intellectualism); the emphasis on the significance of ordinary practices and their practical concerns; and the ambition to dissolve traditional philosophical problems and disputes by overcoming false dichotomies and impasses. Through the work of contemporary American pragmatists or neo-pragmatists, Wittgenstein's later philosophy has made numerous contributions to philosophical discussions of language, mind, knowledge, normativity, and culture, remaining at the center of philosophical debates in the American context and continuing to be productive to this day. Stanley Cavell has combined Wittgenstein's insights with those of Emerson and others in his discussions of skepticism, normativity, and American film and culture. Richard Rorty has exploited the convergence between Wittgenstein's and Dewey's philosophy to defend a practice-oriented linguistic relativism that presents itself as a thoroughgoing deflationism which tries to dissolve traditional philosophical debates and skeptical problems by moving the philosophical discussion to practical concerns. Drawing also on Wittgenstein and Dewey, Hilary Putnam has developed pragmatic accounts of meaning, truth, and rationality from the perspective of the engaged participant in language-games, in his internal realism and more recently in his minimal, common-sense, or naïve realism.

Further reading

Cavell, Stanley. *The Claim of Reason*. Oxford: Oxford University Press, 1979.

Crary, Alice and Read, Rupert (eds). *The New Wittgenstein*. London and New York: Routledge, 2000.

Medina, José. *The Unity of Wittgenstein's Philosophy: Necessity, Intelligibility, and Normativity*. Albany, NY: SUNY Press, 2002.

Nagl, L. and Mouffe, Chantal (eds). *The Legacy of Wittgenstein: Pragmatism or Deconstruction*. Frankfurt am Main and New York: Peter Lang, 2001.

Putnam, Hilary. *Renewing Philosophy*. Cambridge, MA: Harvard University Press, 1992.

Rorty, Richard. *Philosophy and the Mirror of Nature*. Princeton, NJ: Princeton University Press, 1979.

Wittgenstein, Ludwig. *Philosophical Investigations*. Oxford: Blackwell, 1958.

—— *On Certainty*. Oxford: Blackwell, 1969.

—— *Remarks on the Foundations of Mathematics*. Oxford: Blackwell, 1978.

—— *Culture and Value*. Chicago, IL: University of Chicago Press, 1980.

JOSÉ MEDINA

WOODBRIDGE, FREDERICK J.E.

Frederick J.E. Woodbridge (1867–1940) was born in Windsor (Ontario) in Canada. He graduated from Amherst College in 1889, and Union Theological Seminary, which he attended from 1889 to 1892. Intending a career in the ministry, he received his doctorate from the University of Berlin, which he attended from 1892 to 1894, and where he was influenced by Trendelenberg's view of Aristotle.

Woodbridge is notable for his naturalism and realism, which he encouraged in *The Journal of Philosophy,* of which he was co-founder and editor. He was sympathetic to William James, who insisted on the primacy of experience over abstract reasoning. He published James's later essays, and hosted James's lectures at Columbia, later published as *Pragmatism* (1907). Woodbridge, however, had reservations about pragmatism. Woodbridge's naturalism, which he learned from studying the Greeks, led him to deny that Plato was a Platonist. Platonism was not naturalistic.

Notably, Woodbridge spread a new Aristotelianism. For quite a while Aristotle has been understood within the context of a Thomistic interpretation, which made Aristotle distasteful to naturalists. Further inhibiting the understanding of Aristotle were English translations of Aristotle which used the Ciceronian Latin vocabulary for Greek terms, e.g. "substance" for the Greek, *ousia*, a serious mistranslation. The notion that there are four "causes" (instead of four "factors") that contributed to an outcome was unintelligible to one's ordinary notion of causation. It confused the modern reader, who would thus disregard Aristotle. Were it not for Woodbridge's lucid commentary, graduate students might have shunned Aristotle. Woodbridge published very little on Aristotle. As a consequence there is little record of his influence, except for the testimony of notable students, notably Randall and Lamprecht.

Woodbridge insisted on the primacy of the subject matter. If inquiry leads one to doubt the existence of the subject (e.g. the reality of the world), then something is wrong with the inquiry. Time is not an illusion; the world as encountered is primary. Woodbridge opposed the unbridgeable chasm between mind and nature created by British empiricism. An idea is never a copy, image, likeness, or representation. Knowledge is about the world and not about our ideas.

Woodbridge was impressed by Santayana's description of the naturalism he found in Aristotle; viz. for Aristotle, everything ideal had a natural basis and everything natural had an ideal fulfillment. He conveyed that attitude to a generation of philosophers whom he educated, including John Herman Randall, Jr, Ernest Nagel, Morris Cohen, Sidney Hook, and Sterling Lamprecht.

Although Woodbridge was opposed to dualisms of all kinds within nature, in his last work, *An Essay on Nature* (1940), he dismayed his followers. Here, he found the dualism between the natural and the supernatural important and arresting.

If there were not some kind of a need for the supernatural, there would not be a need to introduce and discuss the natural. And if this is so, there is no possibility of bridging the gap. The function that the supernatural performs arose, not in the pursuit of knowledge, but in the pursuit of happiness. He thought nature is insufficient of herself to provide security in the pursuit of happiness and, if there is to be security it must be found elsewhere. Faith in elsewhere is not to tell us about a great beyond, but to supply security in the pursuit of happiness.

The two great pursuits of mankind are so interlocked that the pursuit of knowledge without the pursuit of happiness is meaningless. Knowledge pursued for the sake of happiness, must be pursued disinterestedly if its service is to be competent. Since time immemorial, people have been seeking what knowledge cannot give them, the security and consolation of faith. Faith functioned in the pursuit of happiness. This was close to James' position.

Where Aristotle spoke of matter and form, Woodbridge spoke of structure and behavior, ultimate ideas to which the analysis of nature leads. Nature *is* structure, rather than saying that nature has structure. Woodbridge avoided the supposition of a *materia prima* which comes to be structured or of a something I-know-not-what which lies behind the structures we empirically discover. Behavior cannot be reduced to structure any more than structure can be reduced to behavior. Furthermore, behavior can only be defined in terms of the end served. These ends do not affect anything. We discover a certain structure and may be able to ascertain how its parts are related to one another; but we do not feel content that we understand it until we also note how it behaves and what end it thereby effects.

In his essay "Natural Teleology," Woodbridge argued that many different natural processes are examples of teleology, inasmuch as they tended toward certain typical outcomes, but he denied that the universe tends toward some unitary outcome.

The structure discovered in the world is not a human bias or an imposition on reluctant material. Things have relations (structures) which limit what they can do. But there is a genuinely productive activity which goes on within these limits. Relations determine what is possible and the activity determines what comes into existence. These ends do not operate; they are not efficient forces.

As our digesting occurs in a world of chemical processes, so our thinking occurs in a world that is susceptible to being thought about. And as by digesting we do not introduce chemistry into a world not already chemical, so by thinking we do not introduce the art of discussion, of logic, into a world not already capable of being discussed. There is no separate mental world.

Further reading

Woodbridge, J.F.E. *The Son of Apollo: Themes of Plato.* Boston, MA: Houghton Mifflin, 1929.

—— *Nature and Mind.* New York: Columbia University Press, 1937.

—— *An Essay on Nature.* New York: Columbia University Press, 1940.

—— *Aristotle's Vision of Nature*, posthumous edition, with introduction by John Herman Randall, Jr. New York: Columbia University Press, 1965.

ANGELO JUFFRAS

WRIGHT, CHAUNCEY

Chauncey Wright was sometimes classified by contemporaries as a British empiricist because he defended J.S. Mill's version of utilitarianism. However, his attitude toward social reform and reconstruction differed from Mill's because Wright had a pessimistic view of what reformers could achieve. Life is complex, he wrote, and in trying to untangle this complexity reformers often cause unforeseen undesirable consequences. Keep knowledge as nurse as long as possible to avoid these pitfalls, but do something before it is too late to act. If you consider the relative merit of opposing candidates too long the election will be over. According to Wright, we need to elect honest legislators to restrain the excesses of capitalism, which had degenerated into "legalized robbery."

The deepest difference between Wright and British empiricists was their different interpretations of scientific method. From Locke through Hume the empiricists interpreted scientific laws as inductions, generalizations of experience, a summary of past events. Wright, however, reintroduced the Galilean concept of a hypothetico-deductive system, that is, future oriented-predictions from theoretical concepts which can be verified by subsequent observations. This forward-empiricism was endorsed by C.S. Peirce, William James, and Wendell Holmes, younger members of the Metaphysical Club that met in Cambridge in the 1870s. The members of the club looked upon Wright as their leader, though Peirce and other pragmatists extended his emphasis on predictive hypotheses to areas where he thought it did not apply. Peirce applied Wright's prediction view to sensory statements: to say "x is hard" is to predict certain consequences, all of which constitute the meaning of "hard." In short, Peirce rejected the concept of a self-contained sensory given while Wright retained it.

Wright's cosmology, "Cosmic Weather," was at odds with the teleological systems of his time. The production of stellar systems, he held, shows on the whole no development toward a goal. Systems of worlds come and go through infinite amounts of time, and their periodic shiftings are forward and backward, never directional. This "cosmic weather" is not only impressive itself but it is also in tune with recent scientific cosmology – the Big Bang and Big Crush theories according to which stellar systems occur and decline in eternal variations. It also fits the current geological concept of the shifting of physical plates that make and un-make continents through great expanses of time.

Wright was influenced most deeply by Charles Darwin. In numerous articles in *The North American Review* and *The Nation* he clarified the logical structure of biological explanation and defended the concept of natural selection as a valid explanation of the origin of species, even though it yielded no predictions. He distinguished between physical sciences like astronomy and physics, which operate in a closed system, and the geophysical sciences, which try to apply physical and biological laws to a concrete series of events. He warned against expecting the geophysical explanations to be as precise as physical ones that do operate within a closed system. The concepts that explain a concrete series of events are far too complicated and uncontrolled to allow specific predictions. However, this does not preclude having sufficient evidence to show that the origin of species is a result of natural selection. Wright's offerings increased during the years, and Darwin was much impressed. At his own cost he had Wright's "Genesis of Species" reprinted in England, and he sent copies to his colleagues. Wright was a house guest of the Darwins in 1873, the highlight of his life.

Darwin asked Wright to clarify the concept of self-consciousness and the result was Wright's lengthy "Evolution of Self-Consciousness," his most sustained work. As perception and memory mature, a person becomes aware of the difference between signs and things signified, and this is the germ of self-consciousness, an emergent event since nothing in memory or perception anticipates it.

Further reading

Blau, Joseph L. "Chauncey Wright: Radical Empiricist," *New England Quarterly*, 19 (1946): 495–517.

Darwin, Charles. *Origin of Species*. London: John Murray, 1860.

Madden, Edward H. *Chauncey Wright and the Foundations of Pragmatism*. Seattle, WA: University of Washington Press, 1963.

—— *Chauncey Wright*. New York: Washington Square Press, 1964.

Schneider, Herbert. *A History of American Philosophy*, second edition. New York: Columbia University Press, 1963.

Wiener, Philip P. *Evolution and the Founders of Pragmatism*. Cambridge, MA: Harvard University Press, 1949.

Wright, Chauncey. *Philosophical Discussions*, ed. C.B. Norton. New York: Henry Holt, 1877.

—— *Letters of Chauncey Wright*, ed. J.R Thayer. Cambridge: John Wilson, 1878.

—— *Evolutionary Philosophy of Chauncey Wright*, ed. F.X. Ryan. Bristol: Thoemmes Press, 2000, reprint of Norton and Thayer editions and commentary by various Wright scholars.

—— *Philosophical Writings of Chauncey Wright*, ed. R.H. Madden. New York: Liberal Arts Press, 1958.

EDWARD H. MADDEN

Index

INDEX